P9-ARL-028

TESTS IN PRINT IV

Volume I

EARLIER PUBLICATIONS IN THIS SERIES

TESTS
IN PRINT IV

AN INDEX TO TESTS, TEST
REVIEWS, AND THE LITERATURE
ON SPECIFIC TESTS

Edited by

LINDA L. MURPHY

JANE CLOSE CONOLEY

JAMES C. IMPARA

Volume I

The Buros Institute of Mental Measurements
The University of Nebraska-Lincoln
Lincoln, Nebraska

1994
Distributed by The University of Nebraska Press

LC 83-18866
ISBN 0-910674-53-1

Manufactured in the United States of America

The paper used in this publication meets the minimum requirements of American National Standard of Information Sciences—Permanence of Paper for Printed Library Materials, ANSI Z39.48-1984.

Note to Users

The staff of the Buros Institute of Mental Measurements has made every effort to ensure the accuracy of the test information included in this work. However, the Buros Institute of Mental Measurements and the Editors of *Tests in Print IV* do not assume, and hereby expressly and absolutely disclaim, any liability to any party for any loss or damage caused by errors or omissions or statements of any kind in *Tests in Print IV*.

All material included in *Tests in Print IV* is intended solely for the use of our readers. None of this material may be used in advertising or for any other commercial purpose.

TABLE OF CONTENTS

INTRODUCTION

The 55-year history of the Buros Institute of Mental Measurements has witnessed an explosion of activity regarding testing/assessment approaches. In sheer numbers, diversity of method, and in importance in a variety of decision-making contexts, psychological and educational measurement is a major area of scholarship and application—-consuming the attention of tens of thousands of people.

Our efforts within this massive enterprise have had the same purpose as proposed over 50 years ago by our founder, Oscar K. Buros, that is, improve testing products by offering valid information to consumers. *Tests in Print IV (TIP IV)* is a continuation of our efforts to provide useful data to people who develop, study, and/or buy testing products.

Tests in Print consists of descriptive listings of and references to commercially published tests that are in print and available for purchase and use. It serves as a comprehensive index to the *Mental Measurements Yearbooks (MMY)* published to date.

There are key differences between the *Tests in Print* series and the *Mental Measurements Yearbook* series. The *MMY* series consists of descriptive entries, references, and critical reviews of commercially published tests in the English language. Each *MMY*, of which there are now 11, reviews tests that are new or substantially revised since the appearance of the previous *MMY*. The *MMY* series is, therefore, a hierarchical one.

Each *TIP*, of which there are now four, is a comprehensive volume describing, to the best of our ability, every test that is currently available for purchase. *TIP IV*, therefore, supersedes *TIP III*. Although it is necessary to have the entire *MMY* series to be sure of finding a review of a particular test, only the latest addition to the *TIP* series is needed for comprehensive coverage.

TIP IV can be a first strategy to locate and learn about a testing product. Because *TIP IV* indexes all 11 of the books in the *MMY* series (for tests still in print), it is an invaluable guide to both descriptive and analytical information.

TESTS IN PRINT IV

The contents of *Tests in Print IV* include: (*a*) a comprehensive bibliography of commercially available tests published as separates for use with English-speaking subjects; (*b*) bibliographies, for specific tests, of references related to the construction, validity, or use of the tests in various settings; (*c*) a test title index that includes all in-print tests, out-of-print tests (cumulative back to *TIP III*), and alternative or superseded titles for some tests; (*d*) a classified subject index which also describes the population for which each test is intended; (*e*) a publishers directory and index, including addresses and test listings by publisher; (*f*) a name index which includes the names of all authors of tests, reviews, or references; (*g*) a score index listing all scores generated by tests listed in *TIP IV*; and (*h*) a list of contributing reviewers for the entire *MMY* series.

The organization of the volume is encyclopedic in nature, with the tests being ordered alphabetically by title. Thus, if the title of a test is known, the reader can locate the test immediately without having to consult the Index of Titles. The test classifications continue to appear in the Classified Subject Index.

The page headings reflect the encyclopedic organization. The page heading of the left-hand page cites the number and title of the first test listed on that page, and the page heading of the right-hand page cites the number and title of the last test listed on that page. All numbers presented in the various indexes are test numbers, not page numbers. Page numbers, important only for the Table of Contents, are indicated at the bottom of each page.

TESTS

Tests in Print IV contains 3,009 test entries, 12.6% more than *TIP III* (1983), 22% more than *TIP II* (1974), and 43% more than *TIP I* (1961). The in-print status of these tests was confirmed by direct correspondence with publishers. Table 1 presents the number of test entries included in each major classification of the Classified Subject Index. Any classification system, of course, is to some degree dependent on human judgment. Yet broad comparisons between categories are often interesting and useful. It is interesting to note, for example, that once again the category of personality tests includes the greatest number of tests of any category in *TIP IV*.

TABLE 1
TEST ENTRIES IN *TIP IV* BY MAJOR CLASSIFICATION

Classification	Number of Test Entries
Achievement	91
Behavior Assessment	94
Developmental	145
Education	128
English	181
Fine Arts	23
Foreign Language	56
Intelligence and Scholastic Aptitude	233
Mathematics	86
Miscellaneous	257
Multi-Aptitude	20
Neuropsychological	55
Personality	669
Reading	162
Science	55
Sensory-Motor	48
Social Studies	39
Speech and Hearing	109
Vocations	568

REVIEWS AND EXCERPTS

Tests in Print IV serves as a master index of in-print tests that refers the reader to all the original test reviews and excerpted test reviews that appeared for these tests in all of the *Mental Measurements Yearbooks* to date. In addition, it refers readers to entries and reviews in earlier yearbooks for all tests which have gone out of print since *TIP III*. A total of 1,311 tests listed in *TIP III* or in the *9th*, *10th*, or *11th MMY* are now out of print. Authors of reviews and excerpts are named following the test entries in cross references to the appropriate *MMY*. Although *TIP IV* will serve a very useful function by providing a comprehensive bibliography of tests in print, the cross references to the critical reviews are also of great importance if tests are to be used wisely. Thus *TIP* and the *MMYs* are inseparable partners in the cause of promoting effective selection and use of tests.

A total of 2,415 persons have contributed reviews to one or more *MMYs*. The number of reviewers per yearbook has increased from 133 in 1938 to 660 in 1985 (with 303 in 1989 and 412 in 1992 when the *MMY* went to a more frequent publication schedule). Because of their important contributions to the *Mental Measurements Yearbooks*, a complete listing of *MMY* test reviewers is presented in the index section of *TIP IV*.

REFERENCES

This volume presents specific test bibliographies consisting of references in English on the construction, validity, and use of the tests included in the volume. There are 15,988 references listed. Because some references involved the use of more than one test, these references are multiple-listed under each of the appropriate tests. Earlier publications of the Buros Institute reported the huge growth in the amount of literature involving the use of commercially published tests, and that growth has continued unabated. It was partly to compensate for this unrestrained growth and also to keep publication costs under control that theses or dissertations in the specific test bibliographies are not included in *TIP IV*. Yet readers will continue to find specific test bibliographies of unusual completeness in this volume.

The references that are included in this volume represent a massive and continuous search effort through the professional journals by staff of the Buros Institute. Specific criteria for inclusion of a reference in an Institute publication are such that a test must have a role of some importance in the reference for it to be included. As has been traditional with Buros Institute publications, specific test bibliographies are first arranged chronologically and then alphabetically by author within year to facilitate orderly searching.

Table 2 shows the tests in *TIP IV* with the largest number of references that have been identified for specific tests since references were previously published in 1992 in *The Eleventh Mental Measurements Yearbook*. Within the table the tests are also rank-ordered according to number of references. Of the 3,009 tests in *TIP IV*, 907 have generated at least

TABLE 2

REFERENCE FREQUENCIES FOR TESTS IN *TIP IV* GENER-
ATING THE LARGEST NUMBER OF REFERENCES SINCE
THE *11TH MMY*

Test (with rank)	Number of References
1. Wechsler Adult Intelligence Scale—Revised	1131
2. Wechsler Intelligence Scale for Children, Third Edition	911
3. Beck Depression Inventory [1993 Revised]	660
4. State-Trait Anxiety Inventory	646
5. Minnesota Multiphasic Personality Inventory-2	504
6. Peabody Picture Vocabulary Test—Revised	426
7. Symptom Checklist-90-Revised	318
8. Rorschach	273
9. Raven Progressive Matrices	260
10. Present State Examination	237
11. Eysenck Personality Inventory	226
12. Bem Sex-Role Inventory	204
13. Profile of Mood States	191
14. Eysenck Personality Questionnaire [Revised]	190
15. General Health Questionnaire	183
16. College Board SAT I Reasoning Test	167
17. Halstead-Reitan Neuropsychological Test Battery	159
18. Schedule for Affective Disorders and Schizophrenia, Third Edition	152
19. Jenkins Activity Survey	146
20. Sixteen Personality Factor Questionnaire, Fifth Edition	140
21. Family Environment Scale, Second Edition	136
22. Child Behavior Checklist	135
23. Piers-Harris Children's Self-Concept Scale (The Way I Feel About Myself)	123
24. Wide Range Achievement Test 3	121
25. Stanford-Binet Intelligence Scale, Fourth Edition	120
26. Wechsler Memory Scale—Revised	117
27. Kaufman Assessment Battery for Children	114
28. Thematic Apperception Test	107
29. Assessment of Aphasia and Related Disorders, Second Edition	106
30. Coopersmith Self-Esteem Inventories	106
31. Matching Familiar Figures Test	106
32. Millon Clinical Multiaxial Inventory—II	104
33. McCarthy Scales of Children's Abilities	97
34. Multiple Affect Adjective Check List, Revised	96
35. Wisconsin Card Sorting Test	96
36. Group Embedded Figures Test	95
37. The Adjective Checklist	92
38. Kit of Factor Referenced Cognitive Tests	92
39. Woodcock-Johnson Psycho-Educational Battery—Revised	90
40. National Adult Reading Test, Second Edition	80
41. Depression Adjective Check Lists	79
42. Children's Depression Inventory	71
43. Strong Interest Inventory [fourth Edition]	64
44. Job Descriptive Index and Retirement Descriptive Index	63
45. Shipley Institute of Living Scale	63
46. Benton Visual Retention Test, Fifth Edition	62
47. Global Assessment Scale	62
48. Vineland Adaptive Behavior Scales	62
49. Brief Symptom Inventory	59

one reference and 142 have generated 20 or more references since the specific test was last listed in a Buros publication. For a comparison with earlier frequencies and for a comprehensive look at reference frequencies, Table 2 in *TIP III* and Table 4 in the *9th*, *10th*, and *11th MMY*s would be helpful. References for all in-print tests were included in *TIP III*. Tests that are new or revised are listed and

reviewed in the *MMY* and references are included. Therefore, although Table 2 provides useful information it may be misleading for comparing number of references generated for one test to those for another. For instance, the Minnesota Multiphasic Personality Inventory generated 748 references in *TIP III* and 504 references in *TIP IV*. The Wechsler Intelligence Scale for Children generated 650 references in *TIP III* and 911 references in *TIP IV*. However, the Minnesota Multiphasic Personality Inventory-2 also generated 637 additional references when it was listed and reviewed in the *11th MMY*.

The references for specific tests in *TIP IV* can be extremely helpful in assessing the relative merit of tests and suggesting their most appropriate and effective uses. They are also of unquestionable value in research.

INDEXES

As mentioned earlier, *TIP IV* includes six indexes invaluable as aids to effective use: (*a*) Index of Titles, (*b*) Index of Acronyms, (*c*) Classified Subject Index, (*d*) Publishers Directory and Index, (*e*) Index of Names, and (*f*) Score Index. Additional comment on these indexes is presented below.

Index of Titles. Because the organization of *TIP IV* is encyclopedic in nature, with the tests ordered alphabetically by title throughout the volume, the test title index does not have to be consulted to find a test for which the title is known. However, the title index has some features that make it useful beyond its function as a complete title listing. First, it includes cross-reference information useful for tests with superseded or alternative titles or tests commonly (and sometimes inaccurately) known by multiple titles. Second, it includes tests that have gone out of print since being listed in *TIP III* or the *9th*, *10th*, or *11th MMY*. To differentiate between in-print and out-of-print tests in the title index it is important to read carefully the instructions on the use of the test title index that precede the title listing. It is important to keep in mind that the numbers in this index, like those for all *TIP* and *MMY* indexes, are test numbers and not page numbers.

Index of Acronyms. Some tests seem to be better known by their acronyms than by their full titles. The Index of Acronyms can help in these instances; it refers the reader to the full title of the test and to the relevant descriptive information and reviews.

Classified Subject Index. The Classified Subject Index classifies all tests listed in *TIP IV* into 19 major categories: Achievement, Behavior Assessment, Developmental, Education, English, Fine Arts, Foreign Languages, Intelligence and Scholastic Aptitude, Mathematics, Miscellaneous, Multi-Aptitude Batteries, Neuropsychological, Personality, Reading, Science, Sensory-Motor, Social Studies, Speech and Hearing, and Vocations. Each test entry includes test title, population for which the test is intended, and test number. The Classified Subject Index is of great help to readers who seek a listing of tests in given subject areas. The Classified Subject Index represents a starting point for readers who know their area of interest but do not know how to further focus that interest in order to identify the best test(s) for their particular purposes.

Publishers Directory and Index. The Publishers Directory and Index includes the names and addresses of the publishers of all tests included in *TIP IV* plus a listing of test numbers for each individual publisher. This index can be particularly useful in obtaining addresses for specimen sets or catalogs after the test reviews have been read and evaluated. It can also be useful when a reader knows the publisher of a certain test but is uncertain about the test title, or when a reader is interested in the range of tests published by a given publisher. Several publishers are listed as "Status Unknown" because recent correspondence has been returned by the Post Office and we have been unable to obtain a current address.

Index of Names. The Index of Names provides a comprehensive list of names, indicating authorship of a test, test review, or reference.

Score Index. The Score Index is an index to all scores generated by the tests in *TIP IV.* Test titles are sometimes misleading or ambiguous, and test content may be difficult to define with precision. But test scores represent operational definitions of the variables the test author is trying to measure, and as such they often define test purpose and content more adequately than other descriptive information. A search for a particular test is most often a search for a test that measures some specific variables. Test scores and their associated labels can often be the best definitions of the variables of interest. It is, in fact, a detailed subject index based on the most critical operational features of any test— the scores and their associated labels.

HOW TO USE TIP IV

A reference work like *TIP IV* can be of far greater benefit to a reader if a little time is taken to become familiar with what it has to offer and how one might use it most effectively to obtain the information wanted. The first step in this process is to read the Introduction to *TIP IV* in its entirety. The second step is to become familiar with the six indexes and particularly with the instructions preceding each index listing. The third step is to make actual use of the book by looking up needed information. This third step is simple if one keeps in mind the following possibilities:

1. If you know the title of the test, use the alphabetical page headings to go directly to the test entry.
2. If you do not know, cannot find, or are unsure of the title of a test, consult the Index of Titles for possible variants of the title or consult the appropriate subject area of the Classified Subject Index for other possible leads or for similar or related tests in the same area. (Other uses for both of these indexes were described earlier.)
3. If you know the author of a test but not the title or publisher, consult the Index of Names and look up the author's titles until you find the test you want.
4. If you know the test publisher but not the title or author, consult the Publishers Directory and Index and look up the publisher's titles until you find the test you want.
5. If you are looking for a test that yields a particular kind of score, but have no knowledge of which test that might be, look up the score in the Score Index and locate the test or tests that include the score variable of interest.
6. Once you have found the test or tests you are looking for, read the descriptive entries for these tests carefully so that you can take advantage of the information provided. A description of the information provided in these test entries will be presented later in this section.
7. Once you have read the descriptive information, you may want to order a specimen set for a particular test so that you can examine it firsthand. The Publishers Directory and Index has the address information needed to obtain specimen sets or catalogs.

Making Effective Use of the Test Entries. The test entries include extensive information. For each test, descriptive information is presented in the following order:

a) TITLES. Test titles are printed in boldface type. Secondary or series titles are set off from main titles by a colon.

b) PURPOSE. For each test we have included a brief, clear statement describing the purpose of the test. Often these statements are quotations from the test manual.

c) POPULATION. This is a description of the groups for which the test is intended. The grade, chronological age, semester range, or employment category is usually given. "Grades 1.5—2.5, 2—3, 4—12, 13—17" means that there are four test booklets: a booklet for the middle of first grade through the middle of the second grade, a booklet for the beginning of the second grade through the end of third grade, a booklet for grades 4 through 12 inclusive, and a booklet for undergraduate and graduate students in colleges and universities.

d) PUBLICATION DATE. The inclusive range of

publication dates for the various forms, accessories, and editions of a test is reported.

e) ACRONYM. When a test is often referred to by an acronym, the acronym is given in the test entry immediately following the publication date.

f) SCORES. The number of part scores is presented along with their titles or descriptions of what they are intended to represent or measure.

g) ADMINISTRATION. Individual or group administration is indicated. A test is considered a group test unless it may be administered *only* individually.

h) FORMS, PARTS, AND LEVELS. All available forms, parts, and levels are listed.

i) MANUAL. Notation is made if no manual is available. All other manual information is included under Price Data.

j) RESTRICTED DISTRIBUTION. This is noted only for tests that are put on a special market by the publisher. Educational and psychological restrictions are not noted (unless a special training course is required for use).

k) PRICE DATA. Price information is reported for test packages (usually 20 to 35 tests), answer sheets, all other accessories, and specimen sets. The statement "$17.50 per 35 tests" means that all accessories are included unless otherwise indicated by the reporting of separate prices for accessories. The statement also means 35 tests of one level, one edition, or one part unless stated otherwise. Because test prices can change very quickly, the year that the listed test prices were obtained is also given. Foreign currency is assigned the appropriate symbol. When prices are given in foreign dollars, a qualifying symbol is added (e.g., A$16.50 refers to 16 dollars and 50 cents in Australian currency). Along with cost, the publication date and number of pages on which print occurs is reported for manuals and technical reports (e.g., '85, 102 pages). All types of machine-scorable answer sheets available for use with a specific test are also reported in the descriptive entry. Scoring and reporting services provided by publishers are reported along with information on costs. In a few cases, special computerized scoring and interpretation services are given in separate entries immediately following the test.

l) FOREIGN LANGUAGE AND OTHER SPECIAL EDITIONS. This section concerns foreign language editions published by the same publisher who sells the English edition. It also indicates special editions (e.g., Braille, large type) available from the same or a different publisher.

m) TIME. The number of minutes of actual working time allowed examinees and the approximate length of time needed for administering a test are reported whenever obtainable. The latter figure is always enclosed in parentheses. Thus, "50(60) minutes" indicates that the examinees are allowed 50

minutes of working time and that a total of 60 minutes is needed to administer the test. A time of "40—50 minutes" indicates an untimed test that takes approximately 45 minutes to administer, or—in a few instances—a test so timed that working time and administration time are very difficult to disentangle. When the time necessary to administer a test is not reported or suggested in the test materials but has been obtained through correspondence with the test publisher or author, the time is enclosed in brackets.

n) COMMENTS. Some entries contain special notations, such as: "for research use only"; "revision of the ABC Test"; "tests administered monthly at centers throughout the United States"; "subtests available as separates"; and "verbal creativity." A statement such as "verbal creativity" is intended to further describe what the test claims to measure. Some of the test entries include factual statements that imply criticism of the test, such as "1980 test identical with test copyrighted 1970."

o) AUTHOR. For most tests, all authors are reported. In the case of tests that appear in a new form each year, only authors of the most recent forms are listed. Names are reported exactly as printed on test booklets. Names of editors generally are not reported.

p) PUBLISHER. The name of the publisher or distributor is reported for each test. Foreign publishers are identified by listing the country in brackets immediately following the name of the publisher. The Publishers Directory and Index must be consulted for a publisher's address.

q) FOREIGN ADAPTATIONS. Revisions and adaptations of tests for foreign use are listed in a separate paragraph following the original edition.

r) SUBLISTINGS. Levels, editions, subtests, or parts of a test available in separate booklets are sometimes presented as sublistings with titles set in small capitals. Sub-sublistings are indented and titles are set in italic type.

s) CROSS REFERENCES. For tests that have been listed previously in a Buros Institute publication, a test entry includes—if relevant—a final paragraph containing a cross reference to the reviews, excerpts, and references for that test in those volumes. In the cross references, "T3:467" refers to test 467 in *Tests in Print III*, "8:1023" refers to test 1023 in *The Eighth Mental Measurements Yearbook*, "T2:144" refers to test 144 in *Tests in Print II*, "7:637" refers to test 637 in *The Seventh Mental Measurements Yearbook*, "P:262" refers to test 262 in *Personality Tests and Reviews I*, "2:1427" refers to test 1427 in *The 1940 Yearbook*, and "1:1110" refers to test 1110 in *The 1938 Yearbook*. In the case of batteries and programs, the paragraph also includes cross references—from the battery to the separately listed subtests and vice versa—to entries in this volume and to entries and reviews in earlier editions of *TIP* and the *MMY*.

If a reader finds something in a test description that is not understood, the descriptive material presented above can be referred to again and can often help to clarify the matter.

ACKNOWLEDGEMENTS

A volume of this kind cannot be published without the effort and cooperation of many people. The editors are grateful to all who have given of their time and expertise in the publication process.

The staff of the Buros Institute have been major contributors and vital to the success of gathering and compiling the information to be included in *TIP IV*. It has truly been a team effort. Gary Anderson, Editorial Assistant, and Rosemary Sieck, Word Processing Specialist, have worked long and hard in helping to gather and organize the thousands of bits of information included. Their careful and conscientious efforts go far beyond that required as part of normal job responsibilities. We are also grateful to Barbara Plake, Director of the Buros Institute, for her patience, interest, and support during the long publication process. The administrative and promotional support of Janice Nelsen, Institute Secretary, Jane Gustafson, Marketing Coordinator, and Ellen Weissinger, recent Associate Director, have been very important and helpful also.

The Buros Institute is part of the Department of Educational Psychology of the University of Nebraska-Lincoln and many students from the department and the university have contributed to the publication of this volume. We thank the following graduate research assistants who helped with the preparation of *TIP IV:* Janet Allison, Robert Bergman, Carol Berigan, Dennison Bhola, Molly Geil, Haeok Kim, Kwong-Liem Kwan, Maria Potenza, Michelle Schicke, Mark Shriver, Robert Spies, Richard Sonnenberg, Richard Taffe, Tracy Thorndike-Christ, Paul Turner, Lori Wennstedt, and Kris Yates. Other student assistance has come from Siew King Koay, Tina Longcor, and Heather Murphy. We are very grateful to all these students for bringing their talents and enthusiasms to the Buros Institute.

Appreciation is also extended to our past and present National and Departmental Advisory Committees for their willingness to assist in the operation of the Buros Institute. The current members of the National Advisory Committee are Richard M. Jaeger, Timothy Keith, Barbara Kerr, Frank Schmidt, and Linda Wightman. The current members of the Departmental Advisory Committee (in addition to the Buros Professional Staff) are Deborah Bandalos, Terry Gutkin, Ellen McWhirter, and Gregg Schraw.

The compilation, organization, and composition of this publication has been facilitated through the use of computer technology. We extend our thanks to several individuals at the UNL Computing Resource Center for their advice and technical support and especially to Tim Myers for the many hours he spent writing and running programs. We are also grateful for the contribution of the University of Nebraska Press, which serves as distributor of the *MMY* and *TIP* series.

Most of the publishers of the tests listed have been extremely cooperative in providing us with materials and information to make the test listings comprehensive and accurate. We appreciate their input so much. A small minority of publishers refuse to provide information and materials and we sincerely regret that we were not able to list their products. We have tried very hard to stay aware of new tests, publishers, and publisher addresses. If we have overlooked any we apologize and hope that the test authors or publishers will make us aware of omissions and discrepancies so this can be corrected in future editions.

The first two volumes of *TIP* were published by Oscar Buros and the original Buros Institute. Luella Buros continues her interest in and support of the work she and her husband began over 50 years ago. We are honored to be able to carry on the tradition.

Finally, we the editors are grateful to our friends and families for their support and patience during the years spent preparing *TIP IV*. Their encouragement has made it possible.

Linda L. Murphy
Jane Close Conoley
James C. Impara
July 1994

Tests in Print

AAMR Adaptive Behavior Scale—Residential and Community, Second Edition.
Purpose: To determine "an individual's strengths and weaknesses among adaptive domains and factors."
Population: Persons with disabilities in residential and community settings.
Publication Dates: 1969–93.
Acronym: ABS-RC:2.
Scores, 23: 18 domain scores (10 part one domain scores: Independent Functioning, Physical Development, Economic Activity, Language Development, Numbers and Time, Domestic Activity, Prevocational/Vocational Activity, Self-Direction, Responsibility, Socialization; 8 part two domain scores: Social Behavior, Conformity, Trustworthiness, Stereotyped and Hyperactive Behavior, Sexual Behavior, Self-Abusive Behavior, Social Engagement, Disturbing Interpersonal Behavior); 5 factor scores (Personal Self-Sufficiency, Community Self-Sufficiency, Personal-Social Responsibility, Social Adjustment, Personal Adjustment).
Administration: Individual.
Price Data, 1994: $89 per complete kit including examiner's manual ('93, 76 pages), 25 examination booklets, and 25 profile/summary forms; $39 per 25 examination booklets; $18 per 25 profile/summary forms; $35 per examiner's manual; software scoring and report system available ($79 for Apple or IBM; $89 for Macintosh).
Time: Administration time not reported.
Authors: Kazuo Nihira, Henry Leland, and Nadine Lambert.
Publisher: PRO-ED, Inc.

AAMR Adaptive Behavior Scale—School, Second Edition.
Purpose: "Used to assess adaptive behavior."
Population: Ages 3–21.
Publication Dates: 1981–93.
Acronym: ABS-S:2.
Scores, 21: 16 domain scores (9 part one domain scores: Independent Functioning, Physical Development, Economic Activity, Language Development, Numbers and Time, Prevocational/Vocational Activity, Self-Direction, Responsibility, Socialization; 7 part two domain scores: Social Behavior, Conformity, Trustworthiness, Stereotyped and Hyperactive Behavior, Self-Abusive Behavior, Social Engagement, Disturbing Interpersonal Behavior), 5 factor scores (Personal Self-Sufficiency, Community Self-Sufficiency, Personal-Social Responsibility, Social Adjustment, Personal Adjustment).
Administration: Individual.
Price Data, 1994: $89 per complete kit including examiner's manual ('93, 118 pages), 25 examination booklets, and 25 profile/summary forms; $39 per 25 examination booklets; $18 per 25 profile/summary forms; $35 per examiner's manual; software scoring and report system available ($79 for Apple or IBM, $89 for Macintosh).
Time: Administration time not reported.
Comments: Previously called AAMD Adaptive Behavior Scale.
Authors: Nadine Lambert, Kazuo Nihira, and Henry Leland.
Publisher: PRO-ED, Inc.
Cross References: For a review of an earlier edition

by Stephen N. Elliot, see 9:3 (9 references); see also T3:6 (55 references); for reviews of an earlier edition by Morton Bortner and C. H. Ammons and R. B. Ammons, see 8:493 (25 references); see also T2:1092 (3 references); for reviews of an earlier edition by Lovick C. Miller and Melvyn I. Semmel, see 7:37 (9 references).

TEST REFERENCES

1. Kahn, J. V. (1983). Sensorimotor period and adaptive behavior development of severely and profoundly mentally retarded children. *American Journal of Mental Deficiency, 88*, 69-75.

2. Kleinberg, J., & Galligan, B. (1983). Effects of deinstitutionalization on adaptive behavior of mentally retarded adults. *American Journal of Mental Deficiency, 88*, 21-27.

3. MacEachron, A. E. (1983). Institutional reform and adaptive functioning of mentally retarded persons: A field experiment. *American Journal of Mental Deficiency, 88*, 2-12.

4. Nihira, K., Meyers, C. E., & Mink, I. T. (1983). Reciprocal relationship between home environment and development of TMR adolescents. *American Journal of Mental Deficiency, 88*, 139-149.

5. Roszkowski, M. J., & Spreat, S. (1983). Assessment of effective intelligence: Does scatter matter? *The Journal of Special Education, 17*, 453-460.

6. Salagaras, S., & Nettelbeck, T. (1983). Adaptive behavior of mentally retarded adolescents attending school. *American Journal of Mental Deficiency, 88*, 57-68.

7. Clark, M. M., Corbisiero, J. R., Procidano, M. E., & Grossman, S. A. (1984). The effectiveness of assertive training with elderly psychiatric outpatients. *Community Mental Health Journal, 20*, 262-268.

8. Forness, S. R., & Nihira, K. (1984). Relationship between classroom behavior and adaptive behavior of institutionalized retarded children. *Education and Training of the Mentally Retarded, 19*, 222-227.

9. Heal, L. W., & Fujiura, G. T. (1984). Methodological considerations in research on residential alternatives for developmentally disabled persons. *International Review of Research in Mental Retardation, 12*, 205-244.

10. Heath, C. P., & Obrzut, J. E. (1984). Comparison of three measures of adaptive behavior. *American Journal of Mental Deficiency, 89*, 205-208.

11. Lindsey, J. D., & Armstrong, S. W. (1984). Performance of EMR and learning-disabled students on the Brigance, Peabody, and Wide Range Achievement Tests. *American Journal of Mental Deficiency, 89*, 197-201.

12. Mayfield, K. L., Forman, S. G., & Nagle, R.J. (1984). Reliability of the AAMD Adaptive Behavior Scale—Public School Version. *Journal of School Psychology, 22*, 53-61.

13. Mink, I. T., Meyers, C. E., & Nihira, K. (1984). Taxonomy of family life styles: II. Homes with slow-learning children. *American Journal of Mental Deficiency, 89*, 111-123.

14. Salagaras, S., & Nettelbeck, T. (1984). Adaptive behavior of mentally retarded adults in work-preparation settings. *American Journal of Mental Deficiency, 88*, 437-441.

15. Stack, J. G. (1984). Interrater reliabilities of the Adaptive Behavior Scale with environmental effects controlled. *American Journal of Mental Deficiency, 88*, 396-400.

16. Aman, M. G., Singh, N. N., Stewart, A. W., & Field, C. J. (1985). Psychometric characteristics of the Aberrant Behavior Checklist. *American Journal of Mental Deficiency, 89*, 492-502.

17. Felce, D., Thomas, M., Kock, U. D., & Saxby, H. (1985). An ecological comparison of small community-based houses and traditional institutions—II. Physical setting and the use of opportunities. *Behaviour Research and Therapy, 23*, 337-348.

18. Nihira, K., Mink, I. T., & Meyers, C. E. (1985). Home environment and development of slow-learning adolescents: Reciprocal relations. *Developmental Psychology, 21*, 784-794.

19. Pirodsky, D. M., Gibbs, J. W., Hesse, R. A., Hsieh, M. C., Krause, R. B., & Rodriguez, W. H. (1985). Use of the Dexamethasone Suppression Test to detect depressive disorders of mentally retarded individuals. *American Journal of Mental Deficiency, 90*, 245-252.

20. Richardson, S. A., Koller, H., & Katz, M. (1985). Appearance and mental retardation: Some first steps in the development and application of a measure. *American Journal of Mental Deficiency, 89*, 475-484.

21. Sherman, R. G., Berling, B. S., & Oppenheimer, S. (1985). Increasing community independence for adolescents with spina bifida. *Adolescence, 20*, 1-13.

22. Vallecorsa, A., & Tittle, C. K. (1985). AAMD Adaptive Behavior Scale, School Edition. *Journal of Counseling and Development, 63*, 532-534.

23. Gath, A., & Gumley, D. (1986). Family background of children with Down's Syndrome and of children with a similar degree of mental retardation. *British Journal of Psychiatry, 149*, 161-171.

24. Gersten, R., Crowell, F., & Bellamy, T. (1986). Spillover effects: Impact of vocational training on the lives of severely mentally retarded clients. *American Journal of Mental Deficiency, 90*, 501-506.

25. Huberty, T. J. (1986). Relationship of the WISC-R factors to the Adaptive Behavior Scale—School Edition in a referral sample. *Journal of School Psychology, 24*, 155-162.

26. MacDonald, L., & Barton, L. E. (1986). Measuring severity of behavior: A revision of Part II of the Adaptive Behavior Scale. *American Journal of Mental Deficiency, 90*, 418-424.

27. McCallum, R. S., Helm, H. W., Jr., & Sanderson, C. E. (1986). Local norming and validation of an adaptive behavior screening unit. *Educational and Psychological Measurement, 46*, 709-718.

28. Groden, G., Groden, J., Dondey, M., Zane, T., Pueschel, S. M., & Veliceur, W. (1987). Effects of fenfluramine on the behavior of autistic individuals. *Research in Developmental Disabilities, 8*, 203-211.

29. Huberty, T. J. (1987). Factor analysis of the WISC-R and the Adaptive Behavior Scale—School Edition for a referral sample. *Journal of School Psychology, 25*, 405-410.

30. Mink, I. T., & Nihira, K. (1987). Direction of effects: Family life styles and behavior of TMR children. *American Journal of Mental Deficiency, 92*, 57-64.

31. Vandergriff, D. V., Hester, J. R., & Mandra, D. A. (1987). Composite ratings on the AAMD Adaptive Behavior Scale. *American Journal of Mental Deficiency, 92*, 203-206.

32. Clinger, M. D., Fine, M. A., Johnson, J., Schwartzman, J., & Drude, K. P. (1988). Assessment of the psychometric properties of the Adaptive Behavior Scale with psychiatric patients. *Journal of Consulting and Clinical Psychology, 56*, 542-548.

33. Stoneman, Z., & Crapps, J. M. (1988). Correlates of stress, perceived competence, and depression among family care providers. *American Journal on Mental Retardation, 93*, 166-173.

34. Crapps, J. M., & Stoneman, Z. (1989). Friendship patterns and community integration of family care residents. *Research in Developmental Disabilities, 10*, 153-169.

35. Espie, C. A., Pashley, A. S., Bonham, K. G., Sourindhrin, I., & O'Donovan, M. (1989). The mentally handicapped person with epilepsy: A comparitive study investigating psychosocial functioning. *Journal of Mental Deficiency Research, 33*, 123-125.

36. Foster-Gaitskell, D., & Pratt, C. (1989). Comparison of parent and teacher ratings of adaptive behavior of children with mental retardation. *American Journal on Mental Retardation, 94*, 177-181.

37. Harris, V. S., & McHale, S. M. (1989). Family life problems, daily caregiving activities and the psychological well-being of mothers of mentally retarded children. *American Journal on Mental Retardation, 94*, 231-239.

38. Watkins, S. E., Thomas, D. E., Clifford, M., Tidmarsh, S. F., Sweeney, A. E., Ah-Sing, E., Dickerson, J. W. T., Cowie, V. A., & Shaw, D. M. (1989). Plasma amino acids in patients with senile dementia and in subjects with Down's syndrome at an age vulnerable to Alzheimer changes. *Journal of Mental Deficiency Research, 33*, 159-166.

39. Fine, M. A., Tangeman, P. J., & Woodard, J. (1990). Changes in adaptive behavior of older adults with mental retardation following deinstitutionalization. *American Journal on Mental Retardation, 94*, 661-668.

40. Miller, L. K., & Monroe, M. J. (1990). Musical aptitude and adaptive behavior of people with mental retardation. *American Journal on Mental Retardation, 95*, 220-227.

41. Nezu, C. M., Nezu, A. M., & Arean, P. (1991). Assertiveness and problem-solving training for mildly mentally retarded persons with dual diagnoses. *Research in Developmental Disabilities, 12*, 371-386.

42. Mathias, J. L., & Nettelbeck, T. (1992). Validity of Greenspan's models of adaptive and social intelligence. *Research in Developmental Disabilities, 13*, 113-129.

[3]

The ABC Inventory to Determine Kindergarten and School Readiness.

Purpose: Measures kindergarten and school readiness and identifies children too immature for kindergarten or first grade before enrollment.

Population: Ages 3.5–6.5.

Publication Dates: 1965–85.

Scores: Total score only.

Administration: Individual.

Price Data: Available from publisher.

Time: Administration time not reported.
Comments: An individualized computer-generated narrative report, The Learning Temperament Profile (based on child's ABC Inventory scores), available from publisher.
Authors: Normand Adair and George Blesch.
Publisher: Educational Studies & Development.
Cross References: For reviews by Carl J. Dunst and J. Jeffrey Grill, see 10:1; see also T3:7 (2 references) and T2:1691 (2 references); for a review by David P. Weikart, see 7:739 (2 references).

[4]

Aberrant Behavior Checklist.
Purpose: Constructed to rate "inappropriate and maladaptive behavior of mentally retarded individuals in residential settings."
Population: Mentally retarded adolescents and adults.
Publication Date: 1986.
Acronym: ABC.
Scores, 5: Irritability, Lethargy, Stereotypy, Hyperactivity, Inappropriate Speech.
Administration: Individual.
Price Data, 1992: $35 per complete kit including manual (32 pages); $18 per 50 checklists/score sheets.
Time: (5) minutes.
Comments: Ratings by direct care or professional staff member acquainted with individual.
Authors: Michael G. Aman and Nirbhay N. Singh.
Publisher: Slosson Educational Publications, Inc.

TEST REFERENCES

1. Aman, M. G., Teehan, C. J., White, A. J., Turbott, S. H., & Vaithianathan, C. (1989). Halperidol treatment with chronically medicated residents: Dose effects on clinical behavior and reinforcement contingencies. *American Journal on Mental Retardation, 93,* 452-460.
2. Freund, L. S., & Reiss, A. L. (1991). Rating problem behaviors in outpatients with mental retardation: Use of the Aberrant Behavior Checklist. *Research in Developmental Disabilities, 12,* 435-451.

[5]

Abortion Scale.
Purpose: To measure attitudes toward abortion.
Population: Older adolescents and adults.
Publication Dates: 1972.
Scores: Total score only.
Manual: No manual.
Price Data: Available from publisher.
Time: [10] minutes.
Comments: Supplementary article available.
Authors: Panos D. Bardis.
Publisher: Panos D. Bardis.

TEST REFERENCES

1. Iyriboz, Y., & Carter, J. A. (1986). Attitudes of a southern university human sexuality class toward sexual variance, abortion and homosexuality. *The College Student Journal, 20,* 89-93.

[6]

Abuse Risk Inventory for Women, Experimental Edition.
Purpose: To identify women who are current victims of abuse or who are at risk for abuse by their male intimate partners or ex-partners.

Population: Women seeking medical or mental health services.
Publication Date: 1989.
Acronym: ARI.
Scores: Total score only.
Administration: Group and individual.
Price Data, 1990: $8 per 25 test booklets; $2 per scoring key; $12 per manual (23 pages); $15 per specimen set (includes manual, test booklet, scoring key).
Time: (10–15) minutes.
Comments: Test booklet title is Interpersonal Relationship Survey; self-administered.
Author: Bonnie L. Yegidis.
Publisher: Consulting Psychologists Press, Inc.
Cross References: For reviews by Cynthia A. Rohrbeck and Janice G. Williams, see 11:1.

[7]

Academic Advising Inventory.
Purpose: "Designed to measure three aspects of academic advising: (1) the nature of advising relationships, seen along a developmental-prescriptive continuum, (2) the frequency of activities taking place during advising sessions, and (3) satisfaction with advising."
Population: Undergraduate students.
Publication Dates: 1984–86.
Acronym: AAI.
Scores, 3: Developmental-Prescriptive Advising, Advisor-Advisee Activity Scales, Student Satisfaction with Advising.
Administration: Group.
Price Data, 1986: $17.50 per 50 inventories; $10 per 100 answer sheets; $6 per specimen set; $5.50 per manual ('84, 87 pages); $60 per 1,000 answer sheets; $.20 per scanning/scoring.
Time: (20) minutes.
Comments: Manual entitled *Evaluating Academic Advising;* scoring service available from publisher.
Authors: Roger B. Winston, Jr. and Janet A. Sandor.
Publisher: Student Development Associates, Inc.
Cross References: For a review by Robert D. Brown, see 10:3.

TEST REFERENCES

1. Crockett, J. B., & Crawford, R. L. (1989). The relationship between Myers-Briggs Type Indicator (MBTI) scale scores and advising style preferences of college freshmen. *Journal of College Student Development, 30,* 154-161.
2. Frost, S. H. (1991). Fostering the critical thinking of college women through academic advising and faculty contact. *Journal of College Student Development, 32,* 359-366.

[8]

Academic Aptitude Test: Non-Verbal Intelligence: Acorn National Aptitude Tests.
Purpose: "Designed to evaluate that aspect of intelligence related to the aptitude for abstract academic work required in mathematical, engineering, designing and other physical sciences."
Population: Grades 7–16 and adults.
Publication Dates: 1943–57.

Scores, 4: Spatial Relations, Physical Relations, Graphic Relations, Total.
Administration: Group.
Price Data, 1985: $13.75 per 25 tests; $4 per specimen set.
Time: 26 minutes.
Authors: Andrew Kobal, J. Wayne Wrightstone, and Karl R. Kunze.
Publisher: Psychometric Affiliates.
Cross References: For a review by William B. Schrader, see 4:274.

[9]

Academic Aptitude Test: Verbal Intelligence: Acorn National Aptitude Tests.
Purpose: "Designed to evaluate mental abilities and capacities that are important in academic work."
Population: Grades 7–16 and adults.
Publication Dates: 1943–52.
Scores, 4: General Information, Mental Alertness, Comprehension of Relations, Total.
Administration: Group.
Price Data: Available from publisher.
Time: 40 minutes.
Authors: Andrew Kobal, J. Wayne Wrightstone, and Karl R. Kunze.
Publisher: Psychometric Affiliates.
Cross References: For a review by William B. Schrader, see 4:275; for a review by Marion A. Bills, see 3:215.

[10]

Academic Freedom Survey.
Purpose: "Attempted to measure academic freedom" at college level.
Population: College students and faculty.
Publication Date: 1954.
Scores, 3: Student, Faculty, Total.
Administration: Group.
Price Data, 1985: $3.50 per 25 tests; $4 per specimen set.
Time: Administration time not reported.
Authors: Paul Slivnick and Academic Freedom Committee, Illinois Division, American Civil Liberties Union.
Publisher: Psychometric Affiliates.

[11]

Academic Proficiency Battery.
Purpose: To "aid in the selection of first-year students at universities and colleges."
Population: College entrants.
Publication Date: 1969.
Acronym: APB.
Scores, 5: Social Sciences, Commercial Sciences, Natural Sciences, Mathematical Sciences, Language (Afrikaans or English).
Administration: Group.
Price Data: Available from publisher.
Time: 85(110) minutes.
Comments: All test materials are in both English or Afrikaans. Separate answer sheets (IBM 1230) must be used.
Authors: F. A. Fouche, N. F. Alberts, and C. L. J. Minnaar (test).
Publisher: Human Sciences Research Council [South Africa].

[12]

Academic-Technical Aptitude Tests.
Purpose: "To measure the abilities of boys and girls in Standards 6, 7 and 8 with the view of giving educational and vocational guidance."
Population: "Coloured pupils" in Standards 6–8 of South African school system.
Publication Dates: 1970–71.
Acronym: ATAT.
Scores, 10: Verbal Reasoning, Non-Verbal Reasoning, Computations, Spatial Perception (2-D), Mechanical Reasoning, Language Comprehension, Spatial Perception (3-D), Comparison, Co-ordination, Writing Speed.
Administration: Group.
Price Data: Available from publisher.
Time: 135(234) minutes.
Comments: The coordination and writing speed subtests are taken from the N. B. Aptitude Tests (Junior). All test materials are in both English and Afrikaans except the Technical Report which is in Afrikaans.
Authors: K. Owen (7 subtests and manual) and C.P. Celliers (language comprehension subtest).
Publisher: Human Sciences Research Council [South Africa].

[13]

Access Management Survey.
Purpose: Designed to measure the extent to which a manager provides opportunities and support for employee involvement, and the necessary resources for people to influence work-life issues.
Population: Adults.
Publication Date: 1989.
Acronym: AMS.
Scores, 5: Access to the Problem, Access to People, Access to Information and Resources, Access to Support, Access to the Solution.
Administration: Group.
Price Data, 1993: $6.95 per survey.
Time: Untimed.
Comments: Self-assessment survey.
Author: Jay Hall.
Publisher: Teleometrics International.

[14]

Accounting Aptitude Test.
Purpose: Designed to assess aptitude for an accounting career.
Population: First-year college students.
Publication Dates: 1982–92.
Scores, 3: Communication Skills, Quantitative Skills, Problem-Solving Skills.

Administration: Group or individual.
Price Data, 1994: $50 per examination kit including Form Z test booklet, Ready-Score answer document, and administrator's handbook ('92, 22 pages); $28 per 10 test booklets; $60 per 20 answer documents; $35 per administrator's handbook.
Time: 50(55) minutes.
Author: The Psychological Corporation.
Publisher: The Psychological Corporation.

[15]

Accounting Program Admission Test.

Purpose: Designed as "an objective measure of student achievement in elementary accounting."
Population: College level elementary accounting students.
Publication Date: 1988.
Acronym: APAT.
Scores, 3: Financial Accounting, Managerial Accounting, Total.
Administration: Group.
Price Data: Available from publisher.
Time: 100(110) minutes.
Comments: Formerly called the AICPA Accounting Program Admission Test; no longer affiliated with the AICPA.
Author: American Institute of Certified Public Accountants.
Publisher: The Psychological Corporation.

[16]

ACCUPLACER: Computerized Placement Tests.

Purpose: Designed to assist colleges in determining student entry skills in reading, writing, mathematics, and levels of English proficiency; scores aid in the appropriate placement of students into entry level courses.
Population: Entry level students in 2-year and 4-year institutions.
Publication Dates: 1985–93.
Acronym: CPTs.
Administration: Individual.
Price Data, 1993: Annual licensing fee and per student fee, cost available from publisher.
Time: Untimed.
Comments: Administered on computer adaptively.
Author: The College Board.
Publisher: The College Board.
a) READING COMPREHENSION.
Comments: Each student is administered a fixed number of items which are selected adaptively depending on student responses to prior items.
Price Data: $1 per test.
b) WRITING.
Scores: Total score only.
Comments: Each student is administered a fixed number of items which are adaptively delivered.
Price Data: $1 per test.
c) ARITHMETIC.
Scores: Total score only.
Comments: Each student is administered a fixed number of items which are adaptively delivered.
Price Data: $1 per test.
d) ELEMENTARY ALGEBRA.
Scores: Total score only.
Comments: Each student is administered a fixed number of items which are adaptively delivered.
Price Data: $1 per test.
e) COLLEGE LEVEL MATHEMATICS.
Comments: Each student is administered a fixed number of items covering the areas of Intermediate Algebra, College Algebra, and Precalculus.
Price Data: $2 per test.
f) LEVELS OF ENGLISH PROFICIENCY.
Scores: 3 modules: Language Usage, Sentence Meaning, Reading Skills.
Comments: Designed to identify the English proficiency levels of students; each student takes a fixed number of items; the 3 tests are administered separately.
Price Data: $2 per test.

[17]

ACER Advanced Test B40.

Purpose: "To measure general intelligence as demonstrated by the ability to see relationships and to solve problems."
Population: Ages 13 and over.
Publication Dates: 1945–83.
Acronym: B40.
Scores: Total score only.
Administration: Group.
Price Data, 1994: A$6.60 per 10 test booklets; $3.70 per scoring key; $19 per manual ('83, 7 pages); $36 per specimen set.
Time: 55(65) minutes.
Author: Australian Council for Educational Research Ltd.
Publisher: Australian Council for Educational Research Ltd. [Australia].
Cross References: For a review by Harriet C. Cobb, see 9:4; see also T2:323 (6 references) and 7:328 (4 references); for a review by C. Sanders, see 5:296 (3 references).

[18]

ACER Advanced Test B90: New Zealand Edition.

Purpose: "Designed to measure general intellectual ability."
Population: College students and adults.
Publication Date: 1991.
Scores: Total score only.
Administration: Group.
Price Data: Price information available from publisher for test materials including administrator's manual (5 pages).
Time: 50(55) minutes.
Comments: "Selected items from the ACER Advanced Test B40 and the ACER Test of Cognitive Ability."

Authors: Australian Council for Educational Research and manual by Neil Reid and Cedric Croft.
Publisher: New Zealand Council for Educational Research [New Zealand].
Cross References: For a review of ACER Advanced Test B40 by Harriet C. Cobb, see 9:4; see also T2:323 (6 references) and 7:328 (4 references); for a review of ACER Advanced Test B40 by C. Sanders, see 5:296 (3 references).

[19]
ACER Advanced Test BL-BQ, New Zealand Revision.

Purpose: Designed to "measure broad aspects of general linguistic and quantitative abilities."
Population: College and superior adults.
Publication Dates: 1953–86.
Scores, 3: Linguistic, Quantitative, Total.
Administration: Group.
Price Data: Available from publisher.
Time: 15(25) minutes for Section L (Linguistic), 20(30) minutes for Section Q (Quantitative).
Comments: Revision of ACER Advanced Test BL-BQ (9:5).
Authors: New Zealand Council for Educational Research, Neil Reid (norms supplement), Cedric Croft (norms supplement), Alison Gilmore (norms supplement), and David Philips (norms supplement).
Publisher: New Zealand Council for Educational Research [New Zealand].
Cross References: For reviews by Harriet C. Cobb and Leland K. Doebler of ACER Advanced Tests, see 9:5; see also T3:21 (1 reference) and T2:324 (3 references); for a review by Duncan Howie, see 5:295.

[20]
ACER Advanced Tests AL and AQ (Second Edition) and BL-BQ.

Purpose: "To measure general intellectual ability."
Population: College and "superior adults."
Publication Dates: 1953–82.
Acronyms: AL-AQ (2nd Edition), BL-BQ.
Administration: Group.
Price Data, 1994: A$6.60 per 10 test booklets; $3.70 per scoring key; $19 per manual ('82, 22 pages); $36 per specimen set.
Author: Australian Council for Educational Research Ltd.
Publisher: Australian Council for Educational Research Ltd. [Australia].
a) TEST AL-BL.
Scores: Linguistic.
Forms, 2: A, B.
Time: 15(25) minutes.
b) TEST AQ-BQ.
Scores: Quantitative.
Forms, 2: A, B.
Time: 20(30) minutes.
Cross References: For reviews by Harriet C. Cobb and Leland K. Doebler, see 9:5; see also T3:21 (1

reference) and T2:324 (3 references); for a review by Duncan Howie, see 5:295.

[21]
ACER Applied Reading Test.

Purpose: Designed to measure ability to read and understand technical material.
Population: Apprentices, trainees, technical and trade personnel.
Publication Dates: 1989–90.
Scores: Total score only.
Administration: Group.
Forms, 2: A, B.
Price Data, 1994: A$4.75 per test booklet; $4.50 per 10 answer sheets; $4.20 per score key; $23.50 per manual ('90, 24 pages); $42 per specimen set.
Time: 40–45 minutes.
Authors: J. M. van den Berg and I. R. Woff.
Publisher: Australian Council for Educational Research Ltd. [Australia].

[22]
ACER Higher Test PL-PQ, New Zealand Revision.

Purpose: "Designed to measure general intellectual ability."
Population: Grades 9 and over.
Publication Dates: 1944–86.
Scores, 3: Linguistic, Quantitative, Total.
Administration: Group.
Price Data: Available from publisher.
Time: 15(25) minutes for Section L (Linguistic); 20(30) minutes for Section Q (Quantitative).
Comments: Revision of ACER Higher Tests (9:11).
Authors: New Zealand Council for Educational Research, Neil Reid (norms supplement), Cedric Croft (norms supplement), Alison Gilmore (norms supplement), and David Philips (norms supplement).
Publisher: New Zealand Council for Educational Research [New Zealand].
Cross References: For reviews by Eric F. Gardner and Sharon L. Weinberg of ACER Higher Tests, see 9:11; see also T3:28 (2 references), T2:325 (1 reference), and 6:432 (1 reference); for a review by C. Sanders, see 5:297.

[23]
ACER Intermediate Test F.

Purpose: "Designed to assess the general reasoning ability of students."
Population: Ages 10–15.
Publication Dates: 1980–82.
Scores: Total score only.
Administration: Group.
Price Data, 1994: A$1.50 per test; $2.50 per scoring key; $15.50 per manual ('82, 56 pages); $18.90 per specimen set.
Time: 30(50) minutes.
Comments: Based upon a revision of ACER Intermediate Tests A and D.
Author: Marion M. deLemos (manual).

Publisher: Australian Council for Educational Research Ltd. [Australia].

[24]
ACER Intermediate Test G.
Purpose: "Designed to assess the general reasoning ability of students."
Population: Ages 10–15.
Publication Dates: 1980–82.
Scores: Total score only.
Administration: Group.
Price Data, 1994: A$1.50 per test; $2.50 per scoring key; $15.50 per manual ('82, 48 pages); $18.90 per specimen set.
Time: 30(50) minutes.
Comments: Based on a revision of the still-in-print ACER Intermediate Tests A and D.
Author: Marion M. de Lemos (manual).
Publisher: Australian Council for Educational Research Ltd. [Australia].
Cross References: For a review by Don B. Oppenheim, see 9:13.

[25]
ACER Mechanical Comprehension Test.
Purpose: "Designed to test understanding of mechanical problems."
Population: Ages 13.5 and over.
Publication Dates: 1942–56.
Scores: Total score only.
Administration: Group.
Price Data, 1994: A$3 per test booklet; $4.20 per scoring key; $4.20 per 10 answer sheets; $10.75 per manual ('56, 6 pages); $17.90 per specimen set.
Time: 30 minutes.
Author: Australian Council for Educational Research Ltd.
Publisher: Australian Council for Educational Research Ltd. [Australia].
Cross References: See T3:37 (1 reference); for reviews by John R. Jennings and Hayden S. Williams, see 5:874 (2 references); for a review by D. W. McElwain, see 4:756.

[26]
ACER Mechanical Reasoning Test.
Purpose: "Designed to assess a person's aptitude for solving problems requiring the understanding of mechanical ideas."
Population: Ages 15 and over.
Publication Dates: 1951–79.
Scores: Total score only.
Administration: Group.
Price Data, 1994: A$3 per test booklet; $4.20 per scoring key; $4.20 per 10 answer sheets; $10.75 per manual ('79, 21 pages); $17.90 per specimen set.
Time: (20)25 minutes.
Comments: Abbreviated adaptation of ACER Mechanical Comprehension Test.
Author: Australian Council for Educational Research Ltd.

Publisher: Australian Council for Educational Research Ltd. [Australia].
Cross References: See T2:2238 (3 references); for reviews by John R. Jennings and Hayden S. Williams, see 5:875.

[27]
ACER Short Clerical Test.
Purpose: Designed to measure aptitudes for routine clerical work.
Population: Age 15 and over.
Publication Dates: 1953–84.
Scores, 2: Checking, Arithmetic.
Administration: Group.
Price Data, 1994: A$8.75 per 10 test booklets; $4.40 per score key; $19 per manual; $29.50 per specimen set.
Time: 5(10) minutes per test.
Comments: Three parallel forms, Forms C and D only available for personnel selection and Form E only available to Commercial and TAFE Colleges.
Authors: Australian Council for Educational Research, J. Jenkinson (revised edition).
Publisher: The Australian Council for Education Research Limited [Australia].

[28]
ACER Speed and Accuracy Tests.
Purpose: "Designed as a test of perceptual speed."
Population: Ages 13.5 and over.
Publication Dates: 1942–63.
Scores, 2: Number Checking, Name Checking.
Administration: Group.
Forms, 2: A, B.
Price Data, 1994: A$1.75 per test booklet; $4.30 per scoring key; $3.75 per 10 answer sheets; $11.45 per manual ('63, 25 pages); $17.90 per specimen set.
Time: 20(25) minutes.
Author: Australian Council for Educational Research Ltd.
Publisher: Australian Council for Educational Research Ltd. [Australia].
Cross References: See T3:45 (2 references), T2:2118 (1 reference), and 6:1031 (2 references); for a review by D. W. McElwain of an earlier form, see 4:719.

[29]
ACER Test of Learning Ability.
Purpose: Developed as "a measure of the language and reasoning aspects of general intellectual ability that are important for academic success."
Population: Grades 4, 6.
Publication Date: 1976.
Acronym: TOLA.
Scores, 4: Verbal Comprehension, General Reasoning, Syllogistic Reasoning, Total.
Administration: Group.
Levels, 2: TOLA 4, TOLA 6.
Price Data, 1994: A$3 per test booklet; $8.50 per

10 answer sheets; $8.30 per 2 score keys; $26 per manual; $45 per specimen set.
Time: (33) minutes per level.
Author: Australian Council for Educational Research.
Publisher: Australian Council for Educational Research Ltd. [Australia].

TEST REFERENCES

1. Schofield, N. J., & Ashman, A. F. (1987). The cognitive processing of gifted, high average, and low average ability students. *British Journal of Educational Psychology, 57,* 9-20.

[30]
ACER Tests of Basic Skills—Green Series.
Purpose: Developed to assess skills in literacy and numeracy learning.
Publication Dates: 1990–92.
Administration: Group.
Price Data, 1994: A$16 per 10 literacy test booklets (specify level); $16 per 10 numeracy test booklets (specify level); $39 per specimen set (specify level).
Authors: Jan Lokan, Margaret Forster (Year 3 tests), Suzanne Jones (Year 3 tests), John Lindsey (tests), Brian Doig (tests), Susan Zammit (Year 6 tests), and Lyn Robinson (Year 6 tests).
Publisher: Australian Council for Educational Research Ltd. [Australia].

a) YEAR 3.
Population: Year 3 in Australian school system.
Scores, 2: Literacy, Numeracy.
Price Data: $10.50 per 10 "Young Aussie" magazines; $33 per teacher's manual ('92, 31 pages).
Time: 87 minutes.

b) YEAR 6.
Population: Year 6 in Australian school system.
Scores, 5: Reading, Language, Number, Measurement, Space.
Price Data: $19 per 10 "Planet" magazines; $33 per teacher's manual ('92, 32 pages).
Time: 113 minutes.

[31]
ACER Word Knowledge Test.
Purpose: Constructed to assess verbal skills and general reasoning ability.
Population: Australian years 9–11.
Publication Dates: 1984–90.
Scores: Total score only.
Administration: Group.
Editions, 2: E, F.
Restricted Distribution: Distribution of Form E restricted to personnel use.
Price Data, 1994: A$2.75 per reusable test booklet; $4.20 per 10 answer sheets; $4.10 per score key; $20.50 per manual ('90, 44 pages); $27.50 per specimen set (specify Form E or F).
Time: 10(20) minutes.
Comments: Replacement for the ACER Adult Form B.
Author: Marion M. de Lemos.

Publisher: Australian Council for Educational Research Ltd. [Australia].
Cross References: For reviews by Douglas Ayers and William R. Merz, Sr., see 11:2.

[32]
Achievement Identification Measure.
Purpose: "Determine the degree to which children exhibit the characteristics of underachievers so that preventative or curative efforts may be administered."
Population: School age children.
Publication Date: 1985.
Acronym: AIM.
Scores, 6: Competition, Responsibility, Control, Achievement, Communication, Respect.
Administration: Group.
Price Data, 1993: $95 per 30 tests, manual for administration (8 pages), manual for interpretation of scores (7 pages), and computer scoring of 30 tests; $12 per specimen set.
Time: (20) minutes.
Comments: Parent report inventory.
Author: Sylvia B. Rimm.
Publisher: Educational Assessment Service, Inc.
Cross References: For reviews by Howard M. Knoff and Sharon B. Reynolds, see 10:5.

[33]
Achievement Identification Measure—Teacher Observation.
Purpose: Identify underachievers.
Population: "Students in all grades."
Publication Date: 1988.
Acronym: AIM-TO.
Scores: 5 dimension scores: Competition, Responsibility, Achievement Communication, Independence/Dependence, Respect/Dominance.
Administration: Individual.
Price Data, 1993: $95 per set of 30 test booklets/answer sheets (scoring by publisher included); $12 per specimen set.
Time: (20) minutes.
Comments: Ratings by teacher.
Author: Sylvia B. Rimm.
Publisher: Educational Assessment Service, Inc.
Cross References: For reviews by William P. Erchul and Geoffrey F. Schultz, see 11:3.

[34]
Achievement Test for Accounting Graduates.
Purpose: Constructed to assess achievement in accounting for use in selecting applicants or placing and training of current personnel.
Population: Accounting job applicants or employees.
Publication Dates: 1989–92.
Acronym: ATAG.
Scores, 6: Financial Accounting, Auditing, Cost and Managerial Accounting, Information Systems, Taxation, Total.
Administration: Group or individual.
Forms, 2: T, V.

Restricted Distribution: Distribution restricted and test administered at licensed testing centers; details may be obtained from publisher.
Price Data, 1994: $50 per examination kit including Form V test booklet, Ready-Score answer document, and administrator's handbook ('92, 20 pages); $38 per 10 test booklets (specify Form T or V); $35 per administrator's handbook.
Time: 120(125) minutes.
Author: The Psychological Corporation.
Publisher: The Psychological Corporation.

[35]
Achievement Test in Jewish History.
Purpose: To "measure the residual knowledge of Jewish history of pupils who have completed their Jewish schooling on the elementary level."
Population: Junior high school.
Publication Date: 1962.
Scores, 4: Informational Background, Terms and Concepts, Personalities, Total.
Administration: Group.
Price Data: Not available.
Time: No time limit.
Authors: Original forms by Leon H. Spotts; revision, manual, and technical report by Gerhard Lang and National Curriculum Research Institute.
Publisher: Jewish Education Service of North America, Inc. [No reply from publisher; status unknown].

[36]
Achievement Test—Hebrew Language.
Purpose: To "measure the residual Hebrew language knowledge of pupils who have completed an elementary course of study of 5–7 years."
Population: Grades 5–7.
Publication Date: 1973.
Scores: Total score only.
Administration: Group.
Price Data: Not available.
Time: No time limit.
Authors: Testing Bureau of the National Curriculum Research Institute.
Publisher: Jewish Education Service of North America, Inc. [No reply from publisher; status unknown].

[37]
Achievement Test—Jewish Life and Observances.
Purpose: To "measure the residual knowledge of pupils in Grades 5–7 of the Jewish school, who have completed an organized course of study on the Jewish Life and Observance."
Population: Grades 5–7.
Publication Date: 1973.
Scores: Total score only.
Administration: Group.
Price Data: Not available.
Time: No time limit.

Authors: Testing Bureau of the National Curriculum Research Institute.
Publisher: Jewish Education Service of North America, Inc. [No reply from publisher; status unknown].

[38]
Achievement Test—The State of Israel.
Purpose: To "measure the residual knowledge of pupils who have completed an organized course of study on the State of Israel.
Population: Pupils who have completed an organized course of study on the State of Israel.
Publication Date: 1973.
Scores: Total score only.
Administration: Group.
Price Data: Not available.
Time: No time limit.
Author: Testing Bureau of the National Curriculum Research Institute.
Publisher: Jewish Education Service of North America, Inc. [No reply from publisher; status unknown].

[39]
Achievement Tests: Grades 1—8.
Purpose: "Designed to assess student performance in major reading objectives" for grades 2—8 of the SERIES r Macmillan reading tests.
Population: Grades 1—8.
Publication Date: 1980.
Scores, 4: Comprehension Skills, Vocabulary Skills, Decoding Skills, Study Skills.
Administration: Group.
Levels, 8: Grades 1, 2, 3, 4, 5, 6, 7, 8.
Price Data: Not available.
Time: Administration time not reported.
Comments: Criterion-referenced.
Author: Madeline A. Weinstein.
Publisher: MacMillan Publishing Co., Inc. [No reply from publisher; status unknown].

[40]
Achieving Behavioral Competencies.
Purpose: To develop a program of instruction in social/emotional skills.
Population: "Students who are seriously emotionally disturbed, close head injured, juvenile offenders, learning disabled, or at-risk for school drop-out."
Publication Date: 1992.
Acronym: ABC.
Scores, 24: Relating to Others (Building Friendships, Maintaining Friendships, Apologizing, Compromising/Negotiating, Giving/Accepting Praise or Criticism, Total), Personal Responsibility (Goal Setting, Decision Making, Assuming Responsibility, Promptness, Asking for Assistance, Total), Coping with Stress (Handling Frustration, Coping with Anger, Dealing with Stress, Accepting Authority, Resisting Peer Pressure, Total), Personal/Affective Development (Building Self-Esteem, Coping with

Authors: Testing Bureau of the National Curriculum Research Institute.
Publisher: Jewish Education Service of North America, Inc. [No reply from publisher; status unknown].

Depression, Coping with Anxiety, Controlling Impulsivity, Sensitivity to Others, Total).
Administration: Group.
Editions, 2: Individual Student Report, Class Report.
Price Data, 1994: $137.50 per set including curriculum, 25 rating forms, and computer program (IBM/Compatibles, Macintosh, and Apple).
Time: Administration time not reported.
Comments: Computer reports generated from teacher ratings.
Authors: Lawrence T. McCarron, Kathleen McConnell Fad, and Melody B. McCarron.
Publisher: McCarron-Dial Systems.

[41]

Ackerman-Schoendorf Scales for Parent Evaluation of Custody.

Purpose: "A clinical tool designed to aid mental health professionals in making child custody recommendations."
Population: Parents engaged in a dispute over custody of their children.
Publication Date: 1992.
Acronym: ASPECT.
Scores: 3 scales (Observational, Social, Cognitive-Emotional) yielding 1 score: Parental Custody Index (PCI).
Administration: Individual.
Price Data, 1993: $110 per kit including 20 parent questionnaires, 10 hand scored answer sheets, manual (77 pages), 2 prepaid mail-in WPS test report answer sheets for computer scoring and interpretation; $27.50 per 20 answer forms; $18.50 per 20 parent questionnaires; $48.50 per manual; $18.50 or less per mail-in answer sheet; $18.50 each for test report fax service.
Time: Administration time not reported.
Comments: For complete set of information to score, need results of each parent's MMPI or MMPI-2, Rorschach, WAIS-R, and WRAT-R or NEAT tests.
Authors: Marc J. Ackerman and Kathleen Schoendorf.
Publisher: Western Psychological Services.

[42]

ACS Cooperative Examination in General-Organic-Biological Chemistry.

Purpose: Designed to measure a student's achievement in general, organic, and biological chemistry.
Population: Nursing and other paramedical and home economics students.
Publication Dates: 1979–85.
Scores, 10: General (Part A, Part B, Total), Organic (Part A, Part B, Total), Biological (Part A, Part B, Total), Part A Total.
Administration: Group.
Manual: No specific manual; general directions (no date, 4 pages).
Price Data: Available from publisher.
Time: 165(180) minutes.

Comments: ACS test program is continually updated by retiring an older form of the test upon publication of a new form; separate answer sheet must be used.
Author: ACS DivCHED Examinations Institute.
Publisher: ACS DivCHED Examinations Institute.

[43]

ACS Cooperative Examination in Physical Chemistry.

Purpose: Designed to measure a student's mastery of physical chemistry.
Population: 1 year college.
Publication Dates: 1946–83.
Administration: Group.
Manual: No specific manual.
Price Data: Available from publisher.
Comments: ACS test program is continually updated by retiring an older form of the test upon publication of a new form; subtests may be administered separately or together; separate answer sheet must be used.
Author: ACS DivCHED Examinations Institute.
Publisher: ACS DivCHED Examinations Institute.
  a) THERMODYNAMICS.
  Scores, 3: Part A, Part B, Total.
  Time: 90(100) minutes.
  b) CHEMICAL DYNAMICS.
  Scores, 3: Part A, Part B, Total.
  Time: 90(100) minutes.
  c) QUANTUM CHEMISTRY.
  Scores, 3: Part A, Part B, Total.
  Time: 100(110) minutes.
Cross References: For a review by Gerald R. Van Hecke of an earlier form, see 8:842 (2 references); see also T2:1826 (2 references), 7:833 (2 references), and 6:904 (1 reference); for a review by Alfred S. Brown, see 3:559.

[44]

ACS Examination in Analytical Chemistry.

Purpose: Designed to measure a student's achievement in analytical chemistry.
Population: 1 year college.
Publication Dates: 1944–88.
Scores: Total score only.
Administration: Group.
Manual: No specific manual; general directions (no date, 4 pages).
Price Data: Available from publisher.
Time: 90(100) minutes.
Comments: ACS test program is continually updated by retiring an older form of the test upon publication of a new form; separate answer sheet must be used.
Author: ACS DivCHED Examinations Institute.
Publisher: ACS DivCHED Examinations Institute.
Cross References: See 7:836 (1 reference) and 6:907 (1 reference); for an excerpted review by H. E. Wilcox of an earlier form, see 5:735; for reviews by William B. Meldrum and William Rieman III, see 3:563.

[45]

ACS Examination in Analytical Chemistry, Graduate Level.
Purpose: Designed to measure a student's achievement in analytical chemistry.
Population: Entering college students.
Publication Dates: 1961–85.
Scores: Total score only.
Administration: Group.
Manual: No specific manual; general directions (no date, 4 pages).
Restricted Distribution: Distribution restricted to graduate schools.
Price Data: Available from publisher.
Time: 120(130) minutes.
Comments: ACS test program is continually updated by retiring an older form of the test upon publication of a new form; separate answer sheet must be used.
Author: ACS DivCHED Examinations Institute.
Publisher: ACS DivCHED Examinations Institute.
Cross References: See T2:1815 (1 reference), 7:822 (1 reference), and 6:899 (1 reference).

[46]

ACS Examination in Biochemistry.
Purpose: Designed to measure a student's achievement in biochemistry.
Population: 1 year college.
Publication Dates: 1947–82.
Scores: Total score only.
Administration: Group.
Manual: No specific manual; general directions (no date, 4 pages).
Price Data: Available from publisher.
Time: 120(130) minutes.
Comments: ACS test program is continually updated by retiring an older form of the test upon publication of a new form; separate answer sheet must be used.
Author: ACS DivCHED Examinations Institute.
Publisher: ACS DivCHED Examinations Institute.
Cross References: See 7:823 (1 reference); for an excerpted review by Wilhelm R. Frisell of an earlier form, see 6:898 (2 references).

[47]

ACS Examination in Brief Organic Chemistry.
Purpose: Designed to measure a student's achievement in organic chemistry.
Population: 1 year college.
Publication Dates: 1942–84.
Scores: Total score only.
Administration: Group.
Manual: No specific manual; general directions (no date, 4 pages).
Price Data: Available from publisher.
Time: 90(100) minutes.
Comments: ACS test program is continually updated by retiring an older form of the test upon publication of a new form; separate answer sheet must be used.

Author: ACS DivCHED Examinations Institute.
Publisher: ACS DivCHED Examinations Institute.

[48]

ACS Examination in General Chemistry.
Purpose: Designed to measure a student's achievement in general chemistry.
Population: 1 year college.
Publication Dates: 1934–89.
Scores: Total score only.
Administration: Group.
Manual: No specific manual; general directions (no date, 4 pages).
Price Data: Available from publisher.
Time: 110(120) minutes.
Comments: ACS test program is continually updated by retiring an older form of the test upon publication of a new form; separate answer sheet must be used.
Author: ACS DivCHED Examinations Institute.
Publisher: ACS DivCHED Examinations Institute.
Cross References: For a review by Frank J. Fornoff of an earlier edition, see 8:837 (3 references); see also T2:1819 (1 reference) and 7:826 (5 references); for reviews by J. A. Campbell and William Hered and an excerpted review by S. L. Burson, Jr., see 6:902 (3 references); for reviews by Frank P. Cassaretto and Palmer O. Johnson, see 5:732 (2 references); for a review by Kenneth E. Anderson, see 4:610 (1 reference); for reviews by Sidney J. French and Florence E. Hooper, see 3:557 (3 references); see also 2:1593 (5 references).

[49]

ACS Examination in General Chemistry (Brief Test).
Purpose: Designed to measure a student's achievement in general chemistry.
Population: 1 year college.
Publication Dates: 1981–89.
Scores: Total score only.
Administration: Group.
Manual: No specific manual; general directions (no date, 4 pages).
Price Data: Available from publisher.
Time: 55(60) minutes.
Comments: ACS test program is continually updated by retiring an older form of the test upon publication of a new form; separate answer sheet must be used.
Author: ACS DivCHED Examinations Institute.
Publisher: ACS DivCHED Examinations Institute.

[50]

ACS Examination in Inorganic Chemistry.
Purpose: Designed to measure a student's achievement in inorganic chemistry.
Population: 1 year college.
Publication Dates: 1961–85.
Scores: Total score only.
Administration: Group.

Manual: No specific manual; general directions (no date, 4 pages).
Price Data: Available from publisher.
Time: 120(130) minutes.
Comments: ACS test program is continually updated by retiring an older form of the test upon publication of a new form; separate answer sheet must be used.
Author: ACS DivCHED Examinations Institute.
Publisher: ACS DivCHED Examinations Institute.
Cross References: See T3:64 (1 reference), 8:838 (2 references), T2:1820 (1 reference), and 7:827 (2 references); for a review by Frank J. Fornoff and an excerpted review by George B. Kauffman of an earlier form, see 6:903 (1 reference).

[51]
ACS Examination in Instrumental Determinations.

Purpose: Designed to measure a student's achievement in instrumental determinations.
Population: 1 year college.
Publication Dates: 1966–81.
Scores: Total score only.
Administration: Group.
Manual: No specific manual; general directions (no date, 4 pages).
Price Data: Available from publisher.
Time: 110(120) minutes.
Comments: ACS test program is continually updated by retiring an older form of the test upon publication of a new form; separate answer sheet must be used.
Author: ACS DivCHED Examinations Institute.
Publisher: ACS DivCHED Examinations Institute.
Cross References: See 7:830 (1 reference).

[52]
ACS Examination in Organic Chemistry.

Purpose: Designed to measure a student's achievement in organic chemistry.
Population: 1 year college.
Publication Dates: 1942–86.
Scores: Total score only.
Administration: Group.
Manual: No specific manual; general directions (no date, 4 pages).
Price Data: Available from publisher.
Time: 115(125) minutes.
Comments: ACS test program is continually updated by retiring an older form of the test upon publication of a new form; separate answer sheet must be used.
Author: ACS DivCHED Examinations Institute.
Publisher: ACS DivCHED Examinations Institute.
Cross References: See 8:840 (3 references), 7:831 (3 references), and 6:905 (4 references); for a review by Shailer Peterson of an earlier form, see 3:558.

[53]
ACS Examination in Organic Chemistry, Graduate Level.

Purpose: Designed to measure a student's achievement in organic chemistry.

Population: Entering college students.
Publication Dates: 1961–85.
Scores, 5: Reactions and Synthesis, Mechanisms and Theory, Stereo-Chemistry, Spectroscopy and Structure Determination, Total.
Administration: Group.
Manual: No specific manual; general directions (no date, 4 pages).
Restricted Distribution: Distribution restricted to graduate schools.
Price Data: Available from publisher.
Time: 90–120(100–130) minutes.
Comments: ACS test program is continually updated by retiring an older form of the test upon publication of a new form; separate answer sheet must be used.
Author: ACS DivCHED Examinations Institute.
Publisher: ACS DivCHED Examinations Institute.
Cross References: See 8:841 (2 references), 7:832 (1 reference), and 6:900 (1 reference).

[54]
ACS Examination in Physical Chemistry for Life Sciences.

Purpose: Designed to measure a student's achievement in physical chemistry for life sciences.
Population: 1 year college.
Publication Date: 1982.
Scores: Total score only.
Administration: Group.
Manual: No specific manual; general directions (no date, 4 pages).
Price Data: Available from publisher.
Time: 100(110) minutes.
Comments: ACS test program is continually updated by retiring an older form of the test upon publication of a new form; separate answer sheet must be used.
Author: ACS DivCHED Examinations Institute.
Publisher: ACS DivCHED Examinations Institute.

[55]
ACS Examination in Physical Chemistry, Graduate Level.

Purpose: Designed to measure a student's achievement in physical chemistry.
Population: Entering college students.
Publication Dates: 1961–86.
Scores, 4: Thermodynamics, Quantum Chemistry, Dynamics, Total.
Administration: Group.
Manual: No specific manual; general directions (no date, 4 pages).
Restricted Distribution: Distribution restricted to graduate schools.
Price Data: Available from publisher.
Time: 120(130) minutes.
Comments: ACS test program is continually updated by retiring an older form of the test upon publication of a new form; separate answer sheet must be used.
Author: ACS DivCHED Examinations Institute.
Publisher: ACS DivCHED Examinations Institute.
Cross References: For a review by Gerald R. Van

Hecke of an earlier form, see 8:843 (1 reference); see also 7:834 (2 references) and 6:901 (1 reference).

[56]

ACS Examination in Polymer Chemistry.
Purpose: Designed to measure a student's achievement in polymer chemistry.
Population: 1 year college.
Publication Dates: 1978–90.
Scores: Total score only.
Administration: Group.
Manual: No specific manual; general directions (no date, 4 pages).
Price Data: Available from publisher.
Time: 75(85) minutes.
Comments: ACS test program is continually updated by retiring an older form of the test upon publication of a new form; separate answer sheet must be used.
Author: ACS DivCHED Examinations Institute.
Publisher: ACS DivCHED Examinations Institute.

[57]

ACS-NSTA Examination in High School Chemistry [Advanced Level].
Purpose: To measure achievement in high school chemistry.
Population: Advanced high school chemistry students.
Publication Dates: 1963–84.
Scores: Total score only.
Administration: Group.
Price Data: Available from publisher.
Time: 110 (120) minutes.
Comments: ACS test program is continually updated by retiring an older form of the test upon publication of a new form.
Authors: Sponsored jointly with the National Science Teachers Association.
Publisher: ACS DivCHED Examinations Institute.
Cross References: For reviews by Peter A. Dahl and John P. Penna of an earlier form, see 8:844 (1 reference); for a review by Irvin J. Lehmann, see 7:838 (3 references); for reviews by Frank J. Fornoff and William Hered, see 6:909.

TEST REFERENCES

1. Morgenstern, C. F., & Renner, J. W. (1984). Measuring thinking with standardized science tests. *Journal of Research in Science Teaching, 21,* 639-648.

[58]

ACS-NSTA Examination in High School Chemistry [Lower Level].
Purpose: To measure achievement in high school chemistry.
Population: High school first year chemistry students.
Publication Dates: 1957–83.
Scores, 3: Part I, Part II, Total.
Administration: Group.
Price Data: Available from publisher.
Time: 80 (90) minutes.

Comments: ACS test program is continually updated by retiring an older form of the test upon publication of a new form.
Authors: Sponsored jointly with the National Science Teachers Association.
Publisher: ACS DivCHED Examinations Institute.
Cross References: See 9:41 (1 reference); for a review by Edward F. DeVillafranca of an earlier form, see 8:845 (11 references); see also T2:1830 (3 references); for reviews by William R. Crawford and Irvin J. Lehmann, see 7:837 (9 references); for reviews by Frank J. Fornoff and William Hered and excerpted reviews by Christine Jansing and Joseph Schmuckler, see 6:908 (5 references); for reviews by Edward G. Rietz and Willard G. Warrington, see 5:729.

TEST REFERENCES

1. Morgenstern, C. F., & Renner, J. W. (1984). Measuring thinking with standardized science tests. *Journal of Research in Science Teaching, 21,* 639-648.

[59]

ACS Toledo Chemistry Placement Examination.
Purpose: Designed to measure a student's achievement in general chemistry.
Population: 1 year college.
Publication Dates: 1959–81.
Scores, 4: General Mathematics, General Chemical Knowledge, Specific Chemical Knowledge, Total.
Administration: Group.
Manual: No specific manual; general directions (no date, 4 pages).
Price Data: Available from publisher.
Time: 55(65) minutes.
Comments: ACS test program is continually updated by retiring an older form of the test upon publication of a new form; separate answer sheet must be used.
Author: ACS DivCHED Examinations Institute.
Publisher: ACS DivCHED Examinations Institute.
Cross References: For a review by Frank J. Fornoff of an earlier form, see 8:853 (3 references); see also T2:1847 (2 references); for reviews by Kenneth E. Anderson and William R. Crawford, see 6:920 (1 reference).

[60]

ACT Career Planning Program.
Purpose: Designed to help "counselees expand self-awareness, learn how the world of work is structured, and begin to explore personally relevant career options."
Publication Dates: 1973–86.
Administration: Group.
Price Data: Available from publisher.
Time: 111(168) minutes.
Author: American College Testing.
Publisher: American College Testing.
 a) LEVEL I.
  Population: Grades 8–10.
  Publication Dates: 1973–86.

Acronym: CPP Level I.
Scores, 18: 6 ability scores (Reading Skills, Numerical Skills, Language Usage, Clerical Skills, Mechanical Reasoning, Space Relations), 6 interest scores (Social Service, Business Contact, Business Detail, Technical, Science, Creative Arts), 6 experience scores (same as interest scores), plus items on background and career and educational plans.
b) LEVEL II.
Population: Grade 11–adults.
Publication Dates: 1976–86.
Acronym: CPP Level II.
Scores, 21: 6 ability scores (same as in *a* above), 8 interest scores (Business Contact, Business Detail, Trades, Technology, Science, Health, Creative Arts, Social Service), 7 experience scores (same as interest scores, excluding Health), plus math and English placement composites, estimated ACT composite, questions on background and plans, and 12 optional local items.
Cross References: See T3:77 (2 references); for an excerpted review by Charles C. Healy of an earlier edition, see 8:989 (16 references); see also T2:2101 (4 references).

[61]
The ACT Evaluation/Survey Service.

Purpose: A service "to assist educational institutions and agencies in the collection, interpretation, and use of student survey data" and to investigate the opinions, plans, goals, and impressions of students and/or prospective students.
Population: High school and college students and prospective adult learners/students.
Publication Dates: 1979–93.
Acronym: ESS.
Administration: Group or individual.
Comments: For measurement of groups, not individuals.
Author: American College Testing.
Publisher: American College Testing.
  a) SECONDARY SCHOOL LEVEL.
Population: High school.
Publication Dates: 1979–92.
Price Data, 1993: $7.50 per specimen set including one copy of each secondary-level instrument, sample report pages, user's guide ('92, 29 pages), sample subgroup form and ESS order form; $10 per 25 survey instruments; $5 per User's Guide; $25 per normative data reports; $6 per item catalog; $80–$100 per institutional reporting/handling fee; $45 per tape or diskette containing scoring data.
Time: (15–25) minutes.
  1) *High School Student Opinion Survey.*
Publication Dates: 1980–90.
Scores: Student's perceptions in 6 areas: High School Environment, Occupational Preparation, Educational Preparation, High School Characteristics, Additional Questions, Comments and Suggestions.

2) *Student Needs Assessment Questionnaire.*
Publication Dates: 1979–89.
Scores: Student's personal and educational needs in 4 areas: Life Goals, Individual Growth/Development/Planning, Additional Questions, Comments and Suggestions.
3) *High School Follow-Up Survey.*
Publication Date: 1990.
Scores: Student's satisfaction with high school in 5 areas: Continuing Education, Employment History, High School Experiences, Additional Questions, Comments and Suggestions.
b) POSTSECONDARY SCHOOL LEVEL.
Population: College.
Publication Dates: 1981–93.
Price Data: $8.50 per specimen set including one copy of each post-secondary instrument, sample report pages, user's guide ('92, 44 pages), sample subgrouping form, and ESS order form; $10 per 25 four-page survey instruments; $7.50 per 25 two-page survey instruments; $5 per user's guide; $6 per item catalog; $25 per normative data reports; $80–$100 per institutional reporting/handling fee; $45 per tape or diskette containing student data.
Time: (15–25) minutes.
  1) *Adult Learner Needs Assessment Survey.*
Publication Date: 1981.
Scores: Adult student's educational and personal needs in 4 areas: Personal and Educational Needs, Educational Plans and Preferences, Additional Questions, Comments and Suggestions.
  2) *Alumni Survey.*
Publication Dates: 1981–89.
Scores: Impact of college on graduates in 5 areas: Continuing Education, College Experiences, Employment History, Additional Questions, Comments and Suggestions.
  3) *Alumni Survey (2-Year College Form).*
Publication Dates: 1981–89.
Scores: Same as 2 above.
  4) *Alumni Outcomes Survey.*
Publication Date: 1993.
Scores: Alumni outcomes in 6 areas: Employment History and Experiences, Educational Outcomes, Educational Experiences, Activities and Organizations, Additional Questions, Comments and Suggestions.
  5) *College Outcomes Survey.*
Publication Date: 1992.
Scores: Student's perception of their college experience in 4 areas: College Outcomes, Satisfaction with Given Aspects of This College, Additional Questions, Comments and Suggestions.
  6) *College Student Needs Assessment Survey.*
Scores: Student's educational and personal needs in 4 areas: Career and Life Goals, Educational and Personal Needs, Additional Questions, Comments and Suggestions.
  7) *Entering Student Survey.*
Publication Dates: 1982–90.

Scores: Student's expectations for college in 4 areas: Educational Plans and Preferences, College Impressions, Additional Questions, Comments and Suggestions.

8) *Student Opinion Survey.*

Publication Dates: 1981–90.

Scores: Student's perceptions of the institution in 4 areas: College Services, College Environment, Additional Questions, Comments and Suggestions.

9) *Student Opinion Survey (2-Year College Form).*

Publication Dates: 1981–90.

Scores: Student's perceptions of the 2-year college in 5 areas: College Impressions, College Services, College Environment, Additional Items, Comments and Suggestions.

10) *Survey of Academic Advising.*

Publication Date: 1990.

Scores: Student's perception of academic advising services in 6 areas: Advising Information, Academic Advising Needs, Impressions of Your Advisor, Additional Advising Information, Additional Questions, Comments and Suggestions.

11) *Survey of Current Activities and Plans.*

Publication Date: 1988.

Scores: Student's current educational status in 5 areas: Impressions of This College, Educational Plans and Activities, Employment Plans, Additional Questions, Comments and Suggestions.

12) *Survey of Postsecondary Plans.*

Publication Dates: 1982–89.

Scores: Student's educational plans in 5 areas: Occupational Plans After High School, Educational Plans After High School, Impressions of This College, Additional Questions, Comments and Suggestions.

13) *Withdrawing/Nonreturning Student Survey.*

Publication Dates: 1979–90.

Scores: Student's reasons for leaving an institution in 4 areas: Reasons for Leaving This College, College Services and Characteristics, Optional Questions, Comments and Suggestions.

14) *Withdrawing/Nonreturning Student Survey (short form).*

Publication Dates: 1981–90.

Scores: Student's reasons for leaving an institution in 2 areas: Reasons for Leaving This College, Additional Questions.

Cross References: For a review of an earlier edition by Rodney T. Hartnett, see 9:44.

TEST REFERENCES

1. Mathiasen, R. E. (1984). Predicting college academic achievement: A research review. *College Student Journal, 18,* 380-386.
2. Smith, A. D. (1984). Discriminative analysis technique to assess selection bias in a college student attrition survey. *College Student Journal, 18,* 390-396.
3. Smith, A. D. (1984). Sex differences among community and technical college persisters and non-persisters. *College Student Journal, 18,* 60-65.
4. Cosgrove, T. J. (1986). The effects of participation in a mentoring-transcript program on freshmen. *Journal of College Student Personnel, 27,* 119-124.

5. Placier, P., Moss, G., & Blockus, L. (1992). College student personal growth in retrospect: A comparison of African American and White alumni. *Journal of College Student Development, 33,* 462-471.

[62]

ACT Proficiency Examination in Abnormal Psychology.

Purpose: Designed "to give adult learners the opportunity to earn college credit for knowledge gained outside the classroom and to provide institutions with an objective basis for awarding such credit in abnormal psychology."

Population: College and adults.

Publication Dates: 1984–94.

Scores: Total score only.

Administration: Group.

Price Data, 1993: $45 examination fee including report of score to candidate and one college.

Time: 180 minutes.

Comments: Test administered 6 times annually (February, March, May, June, October, November) at centers established by publisher.

Author: Developed by the faculty of Regents College of The University of the State of New York.

Publisher: American College Testing.

Cross References: For a review by Paul F. Zelhart, see 10:6; for information on the entire ACT Proficiency Examination Program, see 9:45 (1 reference).

[63]

ACT Proficiency Examination in Adult Nursing.

Purpose: For college accreditation of nontraditional study, advanced placement, or assessment of educational achievement.

Population: Baccalaureate level nursing students.

Publication Dates: 1976–94.

Scores: Total score only.

Administration: Group.

Price Data, 1993: $45 examination fee including report of score to candidate and one college.

Time: 180 minutes.

Comments: Test administered 6 times annually (February, March, May, June, October, November) at centers established by publisher.

Author: Developed by the faculty of Regents College of The University of the State of New York.

Publisher: American College Testing.

[64]

ACT Proficiency Examination in Anatomy and Physiology.

Purpose: For college accreditation of nontraditional study, advanced placement, or assessment of educational achievement.

Population: College and adults (associate degree).

Publication Dates: 1975–94.

Scores: Total score only.

Administration: Group.

Price Data, 1993: $45 examination fee including report of score to candidate and one college.

Time: 180 minutes.

Comments: Test administered 6 times annually (February, March, May, June, October, November) at centers established by publisher.
Author: Developed by the faculty of Regents College of The University of the State of New York.
Publisher: American College Testing.

[65]

ACT Proficiency Examination in Fundamentals of Nursing.

Purpose: For college accreditation of nontraditional study, advanced placement, or assessment of educational achievement.
Population: College and adults (associate degree).
Publication Dates: 1969–94.
Scores: Total score only.
Administration: Group.
Price Data, 1993: $45 examination fee including report of score to candidate and one college.
Time: 180 minutes.
Comments: Test administered 6 times annually (February, March, May, June, October, November) at centers established by publisher.
Author: Developed by the faculty of Regents College of The University of the State of New York.
Publisher: American College Testing.

[66]

ACT Proficiency Examination in Microbiology.

Purpose: "To give adult learners the opportunity to earn college credit for knowledge gained outside the classroom and to provide institutions with an objective basis for awarding such credit" in microbiology.
Population: College and adults.
Publication Dates: 1984–94.
Scores: Total score only.
Administration: Group.
Price Data, 1993: $45 examination fee including report of score to candidate and one college.
Time: 180 minutes.
Comments: Administered 6 times annually (February, March, May, June, October, November) at centers established by the publisher.
Authors: Developed by the faculty of Regents College of The University of the State of New York.
Publisher: American College Testing.
Cross References: For information on the entire ACT Proficiency Examination Program, see 9:45 (1 reference).

[67]

ACT Proficiency Examination in Occupational Strategy, Nursing.

Purpose: For college accreditation of nontraditional study, advanced placement, or assessment of educational achievement.
Population: College and adults (associate degree).
Publication Dates: 1973–94.
Scores: Total score only.

Administration: Group.
Price Data, 1993: $80 examination fee including report of score to candidate and one college.
Time: 180 minutes.
Comments: Test administered 6 times annually (February, March, May, June, October, November) at centers established by publisher.
Author: Developed by the faculty of Regents College of The University of the State of New York.
Publisher: American College Testing.

[68]

ACT Proficiency Examination in Professional Strategies, Nursing.

Purpose: For college accreditation of nontraditional study, advanced placement, or assessment of educational achievement.
Population: Baccalaureate level nursing students.
Publication Dates: 1979–94.
Scores: Total score only.
Administration: Group.
Price Data, 1993: $80 examination fee including report of score to candidate and one college.
Time: 180 minutes.
Comments: Test administered 6 times annually (February, March, May, June, October, November) at centers established by publisher.
Author: Developed by the faculty of Regents College of The University of the State of New York.
Publisher: American College Testing.

[69]

ACT Proficiency Examination in Psychiatric/ Mental Health Nursing.

Purpose: For college accreditation of nontraditional study, advanced placement, or assessment of educational achievement.
Population: Baccalaureate level nursing students.
Publication Dates: 1968–94.
Scores: Total score only.
Administration: Group.
Price Data, 1993: $45 examination fee including report of score to candidate and one college.
Time: 180 minutes.
Comments: Test administered 6 times annually (February, March, May, June, October, November) at centers established by publisher.
Author: Developed by the faculty of Regents College of The University of the State of New York.
Publisher: American College Testing.

[70]

ACT Proficiency Examination in Reading Instruction in the Elementary School.

Purpose: For college accreditation of nontraditional study, advanced placement, or assessment of educational achievement.
Population: College and adults.
Publication Dates: 1973–94.
Scores: Total score only.

Administration: Group.
Price Data, 1993: $45 examination fee including report of score to candidate and one college.
Time: (180) minutes.
Comments: Test administered 6 times annually (February, March, May, June, October, November) at centers established by publisher.
Author: Developed by the faculty of Regents College of The University of the State of New York.
Publisher: American College Testing.

[71]

ACT Proficiency Examination Program.
Purpose: Designed as "examinations that measure subject matter proficiency attained primarily outside typical classrooms . . . to award credit or to make other decisions concerning student proficiency."
Population: College and adults.
Publication Dates: 1964–83.
Acronym: PEP.
Scores: 2 types of scores (Standard Scores or Pass-Fail Grades) for 33 tests.
Administration: Group.
Price Data: Available from publisher.
Time: 180 minutes except as listed below.
Comments: Test administered 6 times annually (February, March, May, June, October, November) at centers established by publisher; new essay questions prepared for each testing period.
Author: Developed by the faculty of Regents College of The University of the State of New York and the New York State Education Department.
Publisher: American College Testing.

a) ADULT NURSING.
Comments: Objective; 8 credits.
b) ANATOMY AND PHYSIOLOGY.
Comments: Objective; 6 credits.
c) BUSINESS POLICY.
Comments: Essay; 3 credits.
d) COMMONALITIES IN NURSING CARE, AREAS A AND B.
Tests, 2: Area A, Area B.
Comments: Objective; 5 credits per area.
e) CORPORATION FINANCE.
Comments: Objective; 3 credits.
f) DIFFERENCES IN NURSING CARE.
Tests, 3: Area A, Area B, Area C.
Comments: Objective; 5 credits per area.
g) EDUCATIONAL PSYCHOLOGY.
Comments: Objective; 3 credits.
h) FOUNDATIONS OF GERONTOLOGY.
Comments: Objective; 3 credits.
i) FUNDAMENTALS OF NURSING.
Comments: Objective; 8 credits.
j) HEALTH RESTORATION, AREAS 1 AND 2.
Tests, 2: Area 1, Area 2.
Comments: Objective; 4 credits per area.
k) HEALTH SUPPORT, AREAS 1 AND 2.
Tests, 2: Area 1, Area 2
Comments: Objective; 4 credits per area.

l) INTRODUCTORY ACCOUNTING.
Comments: Objective; 6 credits.
m) MATERNAL AND CHILD NURSING.
   1) *Associate Degree.*
   Comments: Objective; 6 credits.
   2) *Baccalaureate Degree.*
   Comments: Objective; 8 credits.
n) MATERNITY NURSING.
Comments: Objective; 3 credits.
o) MICROBIOLOGY.
Comments: Objective; 3 credits.
p) OCCUPATIONAL STRATEGY, NURSING.
Comments: Objective; 3 credits.
q) ORGANIZATIONAL BEHAVIOR.
Comments: Essay; 3 credits.
r) PHYSICAL GEOLOGY.
Comments: Objective; 3 credits.
s) PRINCIPLES OF MANAGEMENT.
Comments: Objective; 3 credits.
t) PRINCIPLES OF MARKETING.
Comments: Objective; 3 credits.
u) PRODUCTION/OPERATIONS MANAGEMENT.
Comments: Objective; 3 credits.
v) PROFESSIONAL STRATEGIES, NURSING.
Comments: Objective; 4 credits.
w) PSYCHIATRIC/MENTAL HEALTH NURSING.
Comments: Objective; 8 credits.
x) READING INSTRUCTION IN THE ELEMENTARY SCHOOL.
Comments: Objective; 6 credits.
Cross References: See 9:45 (1 reference).

TEST REFERENCES

1. Suddick, D. E., & Collins, B. A. (1984). The use of the American College Testing Proficiency Examination for advanced upper division placement of nursing students graduated from hospital-based (diploma) nursing programs: A validation study of retention. *Educational and Psychological Measurement, 44,* 721-723.

[72]

ACT Proficiency Examinations in Commonalities in Nursing Care, Areas A and B.
Purpose: For college accreditation of nontraditional study, advanced placement, or assessment of educational achievement.
Population: College and adults (associate degree).
Publication Dates: 1973–94.
Scores: Total score only.
Administration: Group.
Price Data, 1993: $80 examination fee including report of score to candidate and one college.
Time: 180 minutes.
Comments: 2 objective tests; tests administered 6 times annually (February, March, May, June, October, November) at centers established by the publisher.
Author: Developed by the faculty of Regents College of The University of the State of New York.
Publisher: American College Testing.

[73]
ACT Proficiency Examinations in Differences in Nursing Care, Areas A, B, C.

Purpose: For college accreditation of nontraditional study, advanced placement, or assessment of educational achievement.
Population: College and adults (associate degree).
Publication Dates: 1974–94.
Scores: Total score only.
Administration: Group.
Price Data, 1993: $80 examination fee including report of score to candidate and one college.
Time: 180 minutes.
Comments: 3 objective tests; tests administered 6 times annually (February, March, May, June, October, November) at centers established by the publisher.
Author: Developed by the faculty of Regents College of The University of the State of New York.
Publisher: American College Testing.

[74]
ACT Proficiency Examinations in Health Restoration, Areas I and II.

Purpose: For college accreditation of nontraditional study, advanced placement, or assessment of educational achievement.
Population: Baccalaureate level nursing students.
Publication Dates: 1980–94.
Scores: Total score only.
Administration: Group.
Tests, 2: I, II.
Price Data, 1993: $80 examination fee including report of score to candidate and one college.
Time: 180 minutes.
Comments: Test administered 6 times annually (February, March, May, June, October, November) at centers established by publisher.
Author: Developed by the faculty of Regents College of The University of the State of New York.
Publisher: American College Testing.

[75]
ACT Proficiency Examinations in Health Support, Areas I and II.

Purpose: For college accreditation of nontraditional study, advanced placement, or assessment of educational achievement.
Population: Baccalaureate level nursing students.
Publication Dates: 1979–94.
Scores: Total score only.
Administration: Group.
Price Data, 1993: $80 examination fee including report of score to candidate and one college.
Time: 180 minutes.
Comments: Test administered 6 times annually (February, March, May, June, October, November) at centers established by publisher.
Author: Developed by the faculty of Regents College of The University of the State of New York.
Publisher: American College Testing.

[76]
ACT Proficiency Examinations in Maternal and Child Nursing.

Purpose: For college accreditation of nontraditional study, advanced placement, or assessment of educational achievement.
Population: College and adults.
Publication Dates: 1968–94.
Scores: Total score only.
Administration: Group.
Tests, 2: Associate Degree, Baccalaureate Degree.
Price Data, 1993: $45 examination fee including report of score to candidate and one college.
Time: 180 minutes.
Comments: Test administered 6 times annually (February, March, May, June, October, November) at centers established by publisher.
Author: Developed by the faculty of Regents College of The University of the State of New York.
Publisher: American College Testing.

[77]
ACT Study Power Assessment and Inventory.

Purpose: To assess students' study skills.
Population: Grades 10–12.
Publication Dates: 1987–89.
Scores, 7: Managing Time and Environment, Reading Textbooks, Taking Class Notes, Using Resources, Preparing for Tests, Taking Tests, Total.
Administration: Group or individual.
Price Data: Available from publisher for test materials including technical manual ('89, 35 pages).
Time: Administration time not reported.
Comments: Based in part on Effective Study Materials series originated and formerly published by Dr. William F. Brown.
Author: American College Testing.
Publisher: American College Testing.
a) THE STUDY POWER ASSESSMENT.
Acronym: SPA.
Comments: 100-item, self-scoring, true-false cognitive test.
b) THE STUDY POWER INVENTORY.
Acronym: SPI.
Comments: 85-item, self-scoring, multiple-choice behavioral survey.

[78]
ACT Study Skills Assessment and Inventory (College Edition).

Purpose: To assess students' study skills.
Population: College students.
Publication Dates: 1988-89.
Scores, 6: Managing Time and Environment, Reading Testbooks, Taking Class Notes, Using Information Resources, Preparing For and Taking Examinations, Total.
Administration: Group or individual.

Price Data: Available from publisher.

Time: (30–40) minutes per test.

Comments: Based in part on materials originated and formerly published by Dr. William F. Brown.

Authors: American College Testing.

Publisher: American College Testing.

a) ACT STUDY SKILLS ASSESSMENT.

Acronym: SSA.

b) ACT STUDY SKILLS INVENTORY.

Acronym: SSI.

[79]

Action Research Skill Inventory.

Purpose: Assessment of the research process skills in the practical application of scientific methodology.

Population: Adults in organizational settings.

Publication Date: 1981.

Scores, 3: (Current Skill, Desired Skill, Difference) in each of 16 areas measuring specific action research behaviors.

Administration: Group.

Price Data: Not available.

Time: Administration time not reported.

Author: Robert C. Preziosi.

Publisher: Development Publications [No reply from publisher; status unknown.]

[80]

Adaptability Test.

Purpose: "Designed to measure mental adaptability or mental alertness."

Population: Job applicants.

Publication Dates: 1942–67.

Scores: Total score only.

Administration: Group.

Forms, 2: A, B.

Price Data: Available from publisher.

Time: 15(20) minutes.

Authors: Joseph Tiffin and C. H. Lawshe.

Publisher: Science Research Associates/London House.

Cross References: See T3:111 (1 reference); see also T2:337 (3 references) and 7:333 (6 references); for a review by John M. Willits, see 5:305 (13 references); for reviews by Anne Anastasi and Marion A. Bills, see 3:216 (3 references).

TEST REFERENCES

1. Schippmann, J. S., & Prien, E. P. (1985). The Ghiselli Self-description Inventory: A psychometric appraisal. *Psychological Reports*, 57, 1171-1177.
2. Schippmann, J. S., & Prien, E. P. (1986). Individual difference correlates of two leadership styles. *Psychological Reports*, 59, 817-818.

[81]

An Adaptation of the Wechsler Preschool and Primary Scale of Intelligence for Deaf Children.

Purpose: To predict "overall academic achievement" for hearing-impaired children.

Population: Hearing-impaired children ages 4 to 6-6.

Publication Date: 1982.

Scores, 6: Animal House, Picture Completion, Mazes, Geometric Design, Block Design, Performance IQ.

Administration: Individual.

Price Data: Not available.

Time: Administration time not reported.

Comments: Adaptation of performance scales of WPPSI (2941).

Authors: Steven Ray and Stephen Mark Ulissi.

Publisher: Steven Ray Publishing (No reply from publisher; status unknown).

Cross References: For reviews by Arthur B. Silverstein and E. W. Testut, see 11:5.

[82]

Adapted Sequenced Inventory of Communication Development.

Purpose: "To assist in the identification of current communicative abilities of clients."

Population: Normal and retarded children functioning between 4 months and 4 years.

Publication Date: 1989.

Acronym: A-SICD.

Scores, 3: Receptive Scale, Expressive Scale, Skills Checklist.

Administration: Individual.

Price Data, 1989: $250 per complete kit; $40 per Interpretation Manual (88 pages) and Administration Manual (39 pages); $45 per 50 Assessment Booklets; $25 per 50 Receptive Skills Profiles and Checklists; $25 per 50 Expressive Skills Profiles and Checklists.

Time: (30–60) minutes.

Author: Sandra E. McClennen.

Publisher: University of Washington Press.

[83]

Adaptive Behavior Evaluation Scale.

Purpose: "Used as a measure of adaptive behavior in the identification of mentally retarded, behaviorally disordered, learning disabled, vision or hearing impaired, and physically handicapped students."

Population: Ages 4.5–21.

Publication Dates: 1983–88.

Acronym: ABES.

Administration: Individual.

Price Data, 1992: $81 per complete kit including technical manual ('88, 48 pages), 50 school rating forms, Parent Rating of Student Behavior technical manual ('87, 29 pages), 25 parent rating forms, and Adaptive Behavior Intervention Manual ('87, 168 pages); $20 per Adaptive Behavior Intervention Manual; $12 per computerized ABES quick score (Apple II).

Author: Stephen B. McCarney.

Publisher: Hawthorne Educational Services, Inc.

a) ADAPTIVE BEHAVIOR EVALUATION SCALE, SCHOOL VERSION.

Scores, 4: Environmental/Interpersonal, Self-Related, Task-Related, Total.

Price Data: $12 per technical manual; $30 per 50 school rating forms
Time: (15–20) minutes.
b) PARENT RATING OF STUDENT BEHAVIOR.
Acronym: PRSB.
Price Data: $19 per complete kit including technical manual ('87, 29 pages) and 25 rating forms; $6 per Parent Rating of Student Behavior technical manual; $13 per 25 rating forms.
Time: (12–15) minutes.

[84]

Adaptive Behavior Inventory.
Purpose: Helps to "evaluate a student's day-to-day ability to take care of her/himself, communicate with others, interact socially, perform academic tasks, and perform work-related or prevocational tasks."
Population: Mentally retarded students ages 6-0 through 18-11 years and normal students ages 5-0 through 18-11 years.
Publication Date: 1986.
Acronym: ABI.
Scores, 6: Self-Care Skills, Communication Skills, Social Skills, Academic Skills, Occupational Skills, Composite Quotient.
Administration: Individual.
Price Data, 1994: $59 per complete kit including 25 profile and response sheets, 25 short form response sheets, and examiner's manual (69 pages); $22 per 25 profile and response sheets; $11 per 25 short form response sheets; $28 per examiner's manual; $79 per Apple PRO-SCORE System; $79 per IBM PRO-SCORE System.
Time: (20–25) minutes.
Comments: Inventory is completed by classroom teacher or other professional having regular contact with the student; ABI-Short Form available for research and screening purposes.
Authors: Linda Brown and James E. Leigh.
Publisher: PRO-ED, Inc.
Cross References: For a review by Corinne Roth Smith, see 10:9 (2 references).

[85]

Adaptive Behavior Inventory for Children.
Purpose: Designed to "measure the child's social role performance in the family, the peer group, and the community."
Population: Ages 5–11.
Publication Dates: 1977–82.
Acronym: ABIC.
Scores, 6: Family, Community, Peer Relations, Nonacademic School Roles, Earner/Consumer, Self-Maintenance.
Administration: Individual.
Price Data, 1994: $82 per basic kit including manual ('82, 121 pages), 6 keys, and 25 record forms; $24.50 per 6 scoring keys; $22 per 25 record forms.
Time: (40–50) minutes.

Comments: A component of the System of Multicultural Pluralistic Assessment (2676); the manual includes the ABIC questions in Spanish as well as in English.
Authors: Jane R. Mercer and June F. Lewis.
Publisher: The Psychological Corporation.
Cross References: For reviews by James E. Jirsa and Benson P. Low, see 9:48 (1 reference); see T3:2387 (9 references) for ABIC and related references.

TEST REFERENCES

1. Slate, N. M. (1983). Nonbiased assessment of adaptive behavior: Comparison of three instruments. *Exceptional Children, 50,* 67-70.
2. Heath, C. P., & Obrzut, J. E. (1984). Comparison of three measures of adaptive behavior. *American Journal of Mental Deficiency, 89,* 205-208.
3. Taylor, R. L., Ziegler, E. W., & Partenio, I. (1985). An empirical investigation of the Adaptive Behavior Inventory for Children. *Psychological Reports, 57,* 640-642.
4. Honig, A. S. (1986). Stress and coping in children (Part 2): Interpersonal family relationships. *Young Children, 41*(5), 47-59.
5. Huebner, E. S., & Cummings, J. A. (1986). Influence of race and test data ambiguity upon school psychologists' decisions. *School Psychology Review, 15,* 410-417.
6. Soyster, H. D., & Ehly, S. W. (1986). Parent-rated adaptive behavior and in-school ratings of students referred for EMR evaluation. *American Journal of Mental Deficiency, 90,* 460-463.
7. Gresham, F. M., & Reschly, D. J. (1987). Dimensions of social competence: Method factors in the assessment of adaptive behavior, social skills, and peer acceptance. *Journal of School Psychology, 25,* 367-381.
8. Heflinger, C. A., Cook, V. J., & Thackrey, M. (1987). Identification of mental retardation by the System of Multicultural Pluralistic Assessment: Nondiscriminatory or nonexistent? *Journal of School Psychology, 25,* 177-183.
9. Soyster, H. D., & Ehly, S. W. (1987). Relation between parent-rated adaptive behavior and school ratings of students referred for evaluation as educable mentally retarded. *Psychological Reports, 60,* 271-277.
10. Glutting, J. J., Oakland, T., & McDermott, P. A. (1989). Observing child behavior during testing: Constructs, validity, and situational generality. *Journal of School Psychology, 27,* 155-164.

[86]

Adaptive Behavior: Street Survival Skills Questionnaire.
Purpose: "To assess fundamental community living and prevocational skills of mentally disabled adolescents and adults."
Population: Ages 9.5 and over.
Publication Dates: 1979–93.
Acronym: SSSQ.
Scores, 10: Basic Concepts, Functional Signs, Tools, Domestics, Health and Safety, Public Services, Time, Monetary, Measurements, Total.
Administration: Individual.
Price Data, 1994: $310 per complete kit including 9 picture volumes ('93, 50 pages each), 50 scoring forms, 50 planning charts, Curriculum Guide ('82, 272 pages), and manual ('83, 95 pages); $19.75 per 50 scoring forms; $13 per 50 planning charts; $42.50 per Curriculum Guide; $28.75 per manual; $225 per computer software offered by publisher.
Time: [45] minutes.
Authors: Dan Linkenhoker and Lawrence McCarron.
Publisher: McCarron-Dial Systems.

Cross References: For a review by Thomas G. Haring, see 11:6.

[87]
Adaptive Functioning Index.
Purpose: "Training and assessment tool to be used by those working with the developmentally handicapped adolescent and adult."
Population: Ages 14 and over in rehabilitation or special education settings.
Publication Dates: 1971–78.
Acronym: AFI.
Administration: Individual.
Price Data, 1983: $55 per complete kit; $4.95 per administration manual ('76, 43 pages); $4.95 per standardization manual ('77, 42 pages); $16 per program manual ('78, 198 pages); $5.20 per 10 Program Workbooks ('77, 19 pages); $5.20 per 10 Target Workbooks ('77, 12 pages).
Time: Administration time not reported.
Comments: Ratings by staff; 3 subtests: Social Education Test, Vocational Check List, Residential Check List, plus Adaptive Functioning of the Dependent Handicapped; Training Package available, includes Training Manual, Program Workbook, and Target Workbook; Program manual and workbooks not necessary for test administration; no norms.
Authors: Nancy J. Marlett and E. Anne Hughson (Program Workbook and Target Workbook).
Publisher: Vocational and Rehabilitation Research Institute [Canada].
a) SOCIAL EDUCATION TEST.
Scores, 9: Reading, Writing, Communication, Concept Attainment, Number Concepts, Time, Money Handling, Community Awareness, Motor Movements.
Price Data: $5.20 per 10 tests.
b) VOCATIONAL CHECK LIST.
Scores, 12: Basic Work Habits (Independence, Making Decisions, Use and Care of Equipment and Materials, Taking Direction), Work Skills (Speed of Movement, Ability to Follow Instructions, Competence, Skill Level), Acceptance Skills (Appearance, Attendance/Punctuality, Self-Expressions, Relation with Co-workers).
Price Data: $3.40 per 10 tests.
c) RESIDENTIAL CHECK LIST.
Scores, 15: Personal Routines (Cleanliness, Appearance and Eating, Room Management, Time Management, Health), Community Awareness (Transportation, Shopping, Leisure, Budgeting, Cooking and Home Management), Social Maturity (Communication, Consideration, Getting Friends, Keeping Friends, Handling Problems).
Price Data: $3.40 per 10 tests.
d) ADAPTIVE FUNCTIONING OF THE DEPENDENT HANDICAPPED.
Population: Profoundly handicapped of all ages.
Scores, 20: Nursing Care (Medications, Body Tone, Medical Care, Observation for Injury, Feed-

ing), Physical Development (Head, Legs, Body, Hands or Feet, Movement), Awareness (Eye Contact, Contact with His World, Contact with People, Communication, Contact with Things), Self Help (Feeding, Eating, Washing, Dressing, Toileting).
Cross References: For reviews by Nadine M. Lambert and David J. Mealor, see 9:49 (1 reference).

TEST REFERENCES

1. Berry, P., Groeneweg, G., Gibson, D., & Brown, R. I. (1984). Mental development of adults with Down syndrome. *American Journal of Mental Deficiency, 89*, 252-256.
2. Tustin, R. D., & Bond, M. J. (1991). Assessing the ability to give informed consent to medical and dental procedures. *Australia and New Zealand Journal of Developmental Disabilities, 17*, 35-47.

[88]
Adaptive Style Inventory.
Purpose: "Designed to assess individuals' ability to adapt to different learning situations."
Population: Junior high through adult.
Publication Date: 1993.
Acronym: ASI.
Scores, 16: 4 scores: Concrete Experience, Reflective Observation, Abstract Conceptualization, Active Experimentation in each of 4 situations: Acting Situation, Deciding Situation, Thinking Situation, Valuing Situation.
Administration: Group.
Price Data, 1993: $59 per complete kit including 10 questionnaires, 10 profiles and interpretive notes (14 pages), and 10 scoring booklets.
Time: Administration time not reported.
Comments: Self-scored inventory.
Authors: Richard E. Boyatzis and David A. Kolb.
Publisher: McBer & Company.

[89]
ADD-H: Comprehensive Teacher's Rating Scale, Second Edition.
Purpose: "Designed to help identify attention disorder, with or without hyperactivity."
Population: Grades K–8.
Publication Dates: 1986–91.
Acronym: ACTeRS.
Scores, 4: Attention, Hyperactivity, Social Skills, Oppositional.
Administration: Individual.
Editions, 2: Paper-and-pencil; microcomputer.
Price Data, 1994: $58 per examiner's kit including manual ('91, 26 pages) and 100 rating/profile forms; $46 per 100 rating/profile forms; $145 per microcomputer version (includes manual, IBM-PC only); $12 per introductory kit; $12 per manual.
Time: Administration time not reported.
Comments: IBM-PC necessary for administration of microcomputer edition.
Authors: Rina K. Ullmann, Esther K. Sleator, and Robert L. Sprague.
Publisher: MetriTech, Inc.
Cross References: For reviews by Ellen H. Bacon and Ayres G. D'Costa, see 11:7 (2 references).

TEST REFERENCES

1. Robins, P. M. (1992). A comparison of behavioral and attentional functioning in children diagnosed as hyperactive or learning-disabled. *Journal of Abnormal Child Psychology, 20,* 65-82.

[90]

Addiction Research Center Inventory.
Purpose: Designed to measure subjective effects of drugs and various dimensions of psychiatric disorders.
Population: Drug addicts.
Publication Dates: 1961–67.
Acronym: ARCI.
Scores: 29 scales: Carelessness, General Drug, Psychopathic Deviate, Alcohol Withdrawal, Opiate Withdrawal, 7 empirical drug scales (Alcohol, Amphetamine, Chlorpromazine, LSD, Morphine, Pentobarbital, Pyraphexyl), 7 group pattern scales (Alcohol, Amphetamine, Chlorpromazine, LSD, Morphine, Morphine-Amphetamine, Pentobarbital-Chlorpromazine-Alcohol), 10 factor scales (Reactivity, Efficiency, Patience-Impatience, Sentimental, Uncritical, Immaturity, Masculinity-Femininity, Inadequacy, Impulsivity, Neurotic Sensitivity vs. Psychopathic Toughness).
Administration: Group.
Price Data: Available from publisher.
Time: Administration time not reported.
Comments: Test booklet title is The ARC Inventory; IBM computer scoring program available.
Authors: Harris E. Hill, Charles A. Haertzen, and Richard E. Belleville.
Publisher: NIDA Addiction Research Center (Attn. Charles A. Haertzen, Ph.D.).
Cross References: See T3:113 (4 references); T2:1093 (8 references), and P:3 (15 references).

TEST REFERENCES

1. Walker, M. K. (1981). Effects of dextroamphetamine sulfate on repeated acquisition behavior and mood in humans: A preliminary report. *The Psychological Record, 31,* 29-41.

2. Griffiths, R. R., Bigelow, G. E., & Liebson, I. (1983). Differential effects of diazepam and pentobarbital on mood and behavior. *Archives of General Psychiatry, 40,* 865-873.

[91]

Additional Personality Factor Inventory—2.
Purpose: To identify personality traits using self-report.
Population: College and adults.
Publication Dates: 1975–80.
Acronym: APF2.
Scores, 10: Fear of Being Socially Unacceptable, Hope, General Activity, Anxiety-State, Existential Realization, Involvement, Unusuality, Dislikes-Annoyances, External Control, Rigidity.
Administration: Group or individual.
Price Data: Not available.
Time: (25–35) minutes.
Author: Edgar Howarth.
Publisher: Edgar Howarth [No reply from publisher; status unknown].
Cross References: For a review by Auke Tellegen, see 9:50.

[92]

Aden-Crosthwait Adolescent Psychology Achievement Test.
Purpose: "Designed to measure knowledge of adolescent psychology."
Population: College students.
Publication Dates: 1963–70.
Scores, 5: Physical, Mental, Emotional, Social, Total.
Administration: Group.
Price Data: Available from publisher.
Time: 45(50) minutes.
Authors: Robert C. Aden and Charles Crosthwait.
Publisher: Psychometric Affiliates.
Cross References: For additional information, see 7:640 (1 reference).

[93]

The Adjective Check List.
Purpose: Designed to identify personal characteristics of individuals.
Population: High school and over.
Publication Dates: 1952–80.
Acronym: ACL.
Scores, 37: Number of Adjectives Checked, Number of Favorable Adjectives, Number of Unfavorable Adjectives, Commonality, Achievement, Dominance, Endurance, Order, Intraception, Nurturance, Affiliation, Heterosexuality, Exhibition, Autonomy, Aggression, Change, Succorance, Abasement, Deference, Counseling Readiness, Self-Control, Self-Confidence, Personal Adjustment, Ideal Self, Creative Personality, Military Leadership, Masculine Attributes, Feminine Attributes, Critical Parent, Nurturing Parent, Adult, Free Child, Adapted Child, High Origence-Low Intellectence, High Origence-High Intellectence, Low Origence-Low Intellectence, Low Origence-High Intellectence.
Administration: Group.
Price Data, 1990: $8 per 25 check lists; $10 per 50 profiles; $19 per manual ('80, 113 pages); $8 per bibliography; $18 per specimen set; scoring service available from publisher; $48 per 10 prepaid profile/answer sheets.
Foreign Language Edition: Spanish edition available.
Time: [15–20] minutes.
Authors: Harrison G. Gough and Alfred B. Heilbrun, Jr. (manual and bibliography).
Publisher: Consulting Psychologists Press, Inc.
Cross References: For reviews by Phyllis Anne Teeter and John A. Zarske, see 9:52 (39 references); see also T3:116 (117 references), 8:495 (202 references), and T2:1094 (85 references); for reviews by Leonard G. Rorer and Forrest L. Vance, see 7:38 (131 references); see also P:4 (102 references).

TEST REFERENCES

1. Scarr, S. (1982). Environmental bias in twin studies. *Social Biology, 29,* 221-229.

2. Dollinger, S. J., Reader, M. J., Marnett, J. P., & Tylenda, B.

(1983). Psychological-mindedness, psychological-construing, and the judgment of deception. *Journal of General Psychology, 108*, 183-191.

3. Garrison, D. R. (1983). Psychosocial correlates of dropout and achievement in an adult high school completion program. *The Alberta Journal of Educational Research, 29*, 131-139.

4. Solano, C. H. (1983). Self-concept in mathematically gifted adolescents. *Journal of General Psychology, 108*, 33-42.

5. Alleman, E., Cochran, J., Doverspike, J., & Newman, I. (1984). Enriching mentoring relationships. *The Personnel and Guidance Journal, 62*, 329-332.

6. Alter, J. B. (1984). Creativity profile of university and conservatory dance students. *Journal of Personality Assessment, 48*, 153-158.

7. Broughton, R. (1984). A prototype stategy for construction of personality scales. *Journal of Personality and Social Psychology, 47*, 1334-1346.

8. Coche, E., Cooper, J. B., & Peterman, K. J. (1984). Differential outcomes of cognitive and interactional group therapies. *Small Group Behavior, 15*, 497-509.

9. Hedlund, B. L., & Lindquist, C. U. (1984). The development of an inventory for distinguishing among passive, aggressive, and assertive behavior. *Behavioral Assessment, 6*, 379-390.

10. Heilbrun, A. B., Jr. (1984). Cognitive defenses and life stress: An information-processing analysis. *Psychological Reports, 54*, 3-17.

11. Heilbrun, A. B., Jr. (1984). Identification with the father and peer intimacy of the daughter. *Family Relations, 33*, 597-605.

12. Heilbrun, A. B., Jr. (1984). Sex-based models of androgyny: A further cognitive elaboration of competence differences. *Journal of Personality and Social Psychology, 46*, 216-229.

13. Markert, R. J. (1984). Using discriminant analysis to identify the noncognitive characteristics of high-achieving medical students. *Psychological Reports, 55*, 331-336.

14. Megargee, E. I. (1984). A new classification system for criminal offenders, VI: Difference among the type on The Adjective Checklist. *Criminal Justice and Behavior, 11*, 349-376.

15. O'gorman, J. G., & Mallise, L. R. (1984). Extraversion and the EEG: II. A test of Gale's hypothesis. *Biological Psychology, 19*, 113-127.

16. Parkes, K. R. (1984). Locus of control, cognitive appraisal, and coping in stressful episodes. *Journal of Personality and Social Psychology, 46*, 655-668.

17. Stewart, A., & Carley, L. (1984). Personality characteristics of extreme scorers on the self-monitoring scale. *Perceptual and Motor Skills, 58*, 199-205.

18. Waltz, S. E., & Gough, H. G. (1984). External evaluation of efficacy by means of an adjective check list scale for observers. *Journal of Personality and Social Psychology, 46*, 697-704.

19. Ware, M. E., Millard, R. J., & Matthews, J. R. (1984). Strategies for evaluating field-placement programs. *Psychological Reports, 55*, 571-578.

20. Whitesel, L. S. (1984). Comparing the personality characteristics of male and female art students with those of students in English and psychology. *STUDIES in Art Education: A Journal of Issues and Research, 26*, 51-55.

21. Barnes, M. L., & Rosenthal, R. (1985). Interpersonal effects of experimenter attractiveness, attire, and gender. *Journal of Personality and Social Psychology, 48*, 435-446.

22. Baucom, D. H., Besch, P. K., & Callahan, S. (1985). Relation between testosterone concentration, sex role identity, and personality among females. *Journal of Personality and Social Psychology, 48*, 1218-1226.

23. Brown, N. W. (1985). Assessment measures that discriminate between levels of DUI clients. *Psychological Reports, 56*, 739-742.

24. Caldwell, D. F., & O'Reilly, C. A., III. (1985). Personality characteristics and self-monitoring. *Psychological Reports, 57*, 103-110.

25. Gough, H. G. (1985). A work orientation scale for the California Psychological Inventory. *Journal of Applied Psychology, 70*, 505-513.

26. Graham, J. R., & McCord, G. (1985). Interpretation of moderately elevated MMPI scores for normal subjects. *Journal of Personality Assessment, 49*, 477-484.

27. Heilbrun, A. B., Jr., & Pepe, V. (1985). Awareness of cognitive defences and stress management. *British Journal of Medical Psychology, 58*, 9-17.

28. Korten, M. J., & Ziegler, D. J. (1985). Inferred psychological needs as a function of stimulus assigned and subject-expressed political preference. *Psychological Reports, 56*, 211- 220.

29. Kotler, T. (1985). A balanced distance: Aspects of marital quality. *Human Relations, 38*, 391-407.

30. Miller, B. P., Edgington, G. P., Blake, P. S., & Fawkner, S. S. (1985). A comparison of activation measures in elite track and field athletes. *Journal of Human Movement Studies, 11*, 197-200.

31. Patnoe, S. (1985). The relationship between selected scales of the Adjective Check List and musical creativity: A validation study. *Bulletin of the Psychonomic Society, 23*, 64-66.

32. Sedge, S. K. (1985). A comparison of engineers pursuing alternate career paths. *Journal of Vocational Behavior, 27*, 56-70.

33. Solomon, R. (1985). Creativity and normal narcissism. *The Journal of Creative Behavior, 19*, 47-55.

34. White, M. S. (1985). Ego development in adult women. *Journal of Personality, 53*, 561-574.

35. Brown, R. J., & Donderi, D. C. (1986). Dream content and self-reported well-being among recurrent dreamers, past-recurrent dreamers, and noncurrent dreamers. *Journal of Personality and Social Psychology, 50*, 612-623.

36. Callahan, S. D., & Kidd, A. H. (1986). Relationship between job satisfaction and self-esteem in women. *Psychological Reports, 59*, 663-668.

37. Caracciolo, S., & Molinari, S. (1986). Convergent validity of self-reported Type A behavior pattern of patients with coronary artery disease. *Psychological Reports, 58*, 831-838.

38. De Moja, C. A. (1986). Anxiety, self-confidence, jealousy, and romantic attitudes toward love in Italian undergraduates. *Psychological Reports, 58*, 138.

39. Green, R., Mandel, J. B., Hotvedt, M. E., Gray, J., & Smith, L. (1986). Lesbian mothers and their children: A comparison with solo parent heterosexual mothers and their children. *Archives of Sexual Behavior, 15*, 167-184.

40. Gruen, R. J., & Mendelsohn, G. (1986). Emotional responses to affective displays in others: The distinction between empathy and sympathy. *Journal of Personality and Social Psychology, 51*, 609-614.

41. Heilbrun, A. B., Jr., & Han, Y. L. (1986). Sex differences in the adaptive value of androgyny. *Psychological Reports, 59*, 1023-1026.

42. Heilbrun, A. B., Jr., & Renert, D. (1986). Type A behavior, cognitive defense, and stress. *Psychological Reports, 58*, 447-456.

43. Johnson, R. C., & Nagoshi, C. T. (1986). The adjustment of offspring of within-group and interracial/intercultural marriages: A comparison of personality factor scores. *Journal of Marriage and the Family, 48*, 279-284.

44. Leder, G. C. (1986). Mathematics: Stereotyped as a male domain? *Psychological Reports, 59*, 955-958.

45. Matheson, K., & Strickland, L. (1986). The stereotype of the computer scientist. *Canadian Journal of Behavioural Science, 18*, 15-24.

46. Schuerger, J. M., & Allen, L. C. (1986). Second-order factor structure common to five personality questionnaires. *Psychological Reports, 58*, 119-126.

47. Smilansky, J., & Halberstadt, N. (1986). Inventors versus problem solvers: An empirical investigation. *The Journal of Creative Behavior, 20*, 183-201.

48. Assor, A., & Tzelgor, J. (1987). Self-ideal discrepancies as indicators of self-derogation and enhancement: Formalization of theoretical claims and a method for assessment. *Journal of Personality Assessment, 51*, 532-544.

49. Balkin, J. (1987). Psychological correlates of success in college. *Educational and Psychological Measurement, 47*(3), 795-798.

50. Heilbrun, A. B., Jr., & Friedberg, E. B. (1987). Type A behavior and stress in college males. *Journal of Personality Assessment, 51*, 555-564.

51. Helson, R., & Moane, G. (1987). Personality change in women from college to midlife. *Journal of Personality and Social Psychology, 53*, 176-186.

52. McCann, B. S., Woolfolk, R. L., Lehrer, P. M., & Schwarcz, L. (1987). Gender differences in the relationship between hostility and the Type A behavior pattern. *Journal of Personality Assessment, 51*, 355-366.

53. Peabody, D. (1987). Selecting representative trait adjectives. *Journal of Personality and Social Psychology, 52*, 59-71.

54. Thompson, R. A. (1987). Creating instructional and counseling partnerships to improve the academic performance of underachievers. *The School Counselor, 34*, 289-296.

55. Chaplin, W. F., John, O. P., & Goldberg, L. R. (1988). Conceptions of states and traits: Dimensional attributes with ideals as prototypes. *Journal of Personality and Social Psychology, 54*, 541-557.

56. Craig, R. J. (1988). Psychological functioning of cocaine freebasers derived from objective psychological tests. *Journal of Clinical Psychology, 44*, 599-606.

57. Lanning, K. (1988). Individual differences in scalability: An alternative conception of consistency for personality theory and measurement. *Journal of Personality and Social Psychology, 55*, 142-148.

58. Piedmont, R. L. (1988). The relationship between achievement motivation, anxiety, and situational characteristics on performance on a cognitive task. *Journal of Research in Personality, 22*, 177-187.

59. Raskin, R., & Terry, H. (1988). A principal-components analysis of the narcissistic personality inventory and further evidence of its construct validity. *Journal of Personality and Social Psychology, 54*, 890-902.

60. Simonton, D. K. (1988). Presidential style: Personality, biography, and performance. *Journal of Personality and Social Psychology, 55*, 928-936.

61. Siperstein, G. N., Bak, J. J., & O'Keefe, P. (1988). Relationship between children's attitudes toward and their social acceptance of mentally retarded peers. *American Journal on Mental Retardation, 93,* 24-27.

62. Udry, J. R., & Talbert, L. M. (1988). Sex hormone effects on personality at puberty. *Journal of Personality and Social Psychology, 54,* 291-295.

63. Craig, R. J., Olson, R., & Shalton, G. (1989). Differences in organization of psychological needs between inpatient and outpatient opiate addicts. *Journal of Clinical Psychology, 45,* 462-466.

64. Piedmont, R. L., DiPlacido, J., & Keller, W. (1989). Assessing gender-related differences in achievement orientation using two different achievement scales. *Journal of Personality Assessment, 53,* 229-238.

65. Suis, J., & Wan, C. K. (1989). The relation between Type A behavior and chronic emotional distress: A meta-analysis. *Journal of Personality and Social Psychology, 57,* 503-512.

66. Sutker, P. B., Thomason, B. T., Allain, A. N., Jr. (1989). Adjective self-descriptions of World War II and Korean prisoner of war and combat veterans. *Journal of Psychopathology and Behavioral Assessment, 11,* 185-192.

67. Brown, N. W., Cross, E. J., Jr., & Selby, G. (1990). Personality characteristics of black engineering students on The Adjective Checklist. *College Student Journal, 24,* 233-240.

68. Firestone, D. T. (1990). A re-examination of personality differences among allied health students. *College Student Journal, 24,* 241-248.

69. Koestner, R., Franz, C., & Weinberger, J. (1990). The family origins of empathic concern: A 26-year longitudinal study. *Journal of Personality and Social Psychology, 58,* 709-717.

70. Wink, P., & Gough, H. G. (1990). New narcissism scales for the California Psychological Inventory and MMPI. *Journal of Personality Assessment, 54,* 446-462.

71. Borman, W. C., & Hallman, G. L. (1991). Observation accuracy for assessors of work-sample performance: Consistency across task and individual-differences correlates. *Journal of Applied Psychology, 76*(1), 11-18.

72. Bridges, K., Goldberg, D., Evans, B., & Sharpe, T. (1991). Determinants of somatization in primary care. *Psychological Medicine, 21,* 473-483.

73. Cartwright, R. D., Kravitz, H. M., Eastman, C. I., & Wood, E. (1991). REM latency and the recovery from depression: Getting over divorce. *American Journal of Psychiatry, 148,* 1530-1535.

74. Koestner, R., Zuroff, D. C., & Powers, T. A. (1991). Family origins of adolescent self-criticism and its continuity into adulthood. *Journal of Abnormal Psychology, 100,* 191-197.

75. Kosmos, K. A., & Kidd, A. H. (1991). Personality characteristics of dyslexic and nondyslexic adults. *Psychological Reports, 69,* 231-234.

76. Phelps, R. E., Meara, N. M., Davis, K. L., & Patton, M. J. (1991). Blacks' and Whites' perceptions of verbal aggression. *Journal of Counseling and Development, 69,* 345-350.

77. Piedmont, R. L., McCrae, R. R., & Costa, P. T., Jr. (1991). Adjective Check List scales and the five-factor model. *Journal of Personality and Social Psychology, 60,* 630-637.

78. Raskin, R., Novacek, J., & Hogan, R. (1991). Narcissistic self-esteem management. *Journal of Personality and Social Psychology, 60,* 911-918.

79. Schmidt, C. P., & Stephans, R. (1991). Locus of control and field dependence as factors in students' evaluations of applied music instruction. *Perceptual and Motor Skills, 73,* 131-136.

80. Wink, P. (1991). Two faces of narcissism. *Journal of Personality and Social Psychology, 61,* 590-597.

81. Zrack, R. I., & Boone, D. R. (1991). Spouse attitudes toward the person with aphasia. *Journal of Speech and Hearing Research, 34,* 123-128.

82. Aubé, J., & Koestner, R. (1992). Gender characteristics and adjustment: A longitudinal study. *Journal of Personality and Social Psychology, 63,* 485-493.

83. Helson, R., & Wink, P. (1992). Personality change in women from the early 40s to the early 50s. *Psychology and Aging, 7,* 46-55.

84. Lubin, B., Cain, J., & Van Whitlock, R. (1992). Additional validity data for the Multiple Affect Adjective Check List—Revised. *Psychological Reports, 70,* 40-42.

85. Merlino Perkins, R. J., & Lynch, M. D. (1992). Student led discussion groups: An alternative for dependency. *Journal of College Student Development, 33,* 101-107.

86. Wink, P. (1992). Three narcissism scales for the California Q-Set. *Journal of Personality Assessment, 58,* 51-66.

87. York, K. L., & John, O. P. (1992). The four faces of Eve: A typological analysis of women's personality at midlife. *Journal of Personality and Social Psychology, 63,* 694-508.

88. Brown, N. W., & Cross, E. J., Jr. (1993). A comparison of personality characteristics for entering freshmen, persistors, and norm groups in engineering. *Educational and Psychological Measurement, 52,* 939-944.

89. Jones, W. H., & Kugler, K. (1993). Interpersonal correlates of the Guilt Inventory. *Journal of Personality Assessment, 61,* 246-258.

90. Piedmont, R. L., & Weinstein, H. P. (1993). A psychometric evaluation of the new NEO-PIR Facet Scales for Agreeableness and Conscientiousness. *Journal of Personality Assessment, 60,* 302-318.

91. Tetlock, P. E., Peterson, R. S., & Berry, J. M. (1993). Flattering and unflattering personality portraits of integratively simple and complex managers. *Journal of Personality and Social Psychology, 64,* 500-511.

92. Wink, P., & Helson, R. (1993). Personality change in women and their partners. *Journal of Personality and Social Psychology, 65,* 597-605.

[94]

The Adjustment Inventory.

Purpose: Developed to assess personal and social adjustment.

Publication Dates: 1934–66.

Administration: Group.

Price Data, 1990: $6 per 25 test booklets (select student or adult).

Time: (25–30) minutes.

Comments: Self-administered.

Author: Hugh M. Bell.

Publisher: Consulting Psychologists Press, Inc.

a) REVISED (1962) STUDENT FORM.

Population: High school and college.

Scores, 6: Home Adjustment, Health Adjustment, Submissiveness, Emotionality, Hostility, Masculinity-Femininity.

Price Data: $11 per 50 answer sheets/profiles; $10 per set of scoring stencils; $11 per 100 profiles; $5 per manual ('63, 26 pages); $6 per specimen set.

b) ADULT FORM,

Population: Adults.

Scores, 6: Home Adjustment, Health Adjustment, Social Adjustment, Emotional Adjustment, Occupational Adjustment, Total.

Price Data: $6.50 per 50 answer sheets; $2.50 per set of scoring keys and manual (no date, 4 pages); $3 per specimen set.

Cross References: See T3:118 (2 references), T2:1095 (77 references), and P:5 (16 references); for a review by Forrest L. Vance and an excerpted review by Laurence Siegel, see 6:59 (11 references); see also 5:30 (26 references); for reviews by Nelson G. Hanawalt and Theodore R. Sarbin, see 4:28 (104 references); for reviews by Raymond B. Cattell, John G. Darley, C. M. Louttit, and Percival M. Symonds of the original Student Form, reviews by S. J. Beck, J. P. Guilford, and Doncaster G. Humm of the Adult Form, and an excerpted review by Ruth A. Pedersen, see 2:1200 (15 references); for a review by Austin H. Turney of the Student Form, see 1:912.

TEST REFERENCES

1. Peter, B. M., & Spreen, O. (1979). Behavior rating and personal adjustment scales of neurologically and learning handicapped children during adolescence and early adulthood: Results of a follow-up study. *Journal of Clinical Neuropsychology, 1,* 75-92.

[95]

Adolescent and Adult Psychoeducational Profile.

Purpose: Assesses skills of moderately to severely retarded and autistic individuals.

Population: Adolescents and adults with moderate to severe mental retardation or autism.
Publication Date: 1988.
Acronym: AAPEP.
Scores: 3 scales (Direct Observation, Home, School/Work); 6 scores for each: Vocational Skills, Independent Functioning, Leisure Skills, Vocational Behavior, Functional Communication, Interpersonal Behavior.
Administration: Individual.
Price Data, 1994: $49 per manual (119 pages); price data for testing kit available from Residential Services, Inc., Day Program, P.O. Box 487, Carrboro, NC 27510.
Time: (60–90) minutes per scale.
Comments: Title on manual is Individualized Assessment and Treatment for Autistic and Developmentally Disabled Children, Volume IV; other materials (e.g., ball, magazines, playing cards) necessary for test administration may be supplied by examiner or purchased from Residential Services, Inc.
Authors: Gary Mesibov, Eric Schopler, Bruce Schaffer, and Rhoda Landrus.
Publisher: PRO-ED, Inc.
Cross References: For reviews by Lena R. Gaddis and J. Jeffrey Grill, see 11:8.

[96]

Adolescent Coping Scale.

Purpose: Assesses 18 possible coping strategies used by adolescents and young adults in dealing with stress.
Population: Ages 12–18.
Publication Date: 1993.
Acronym: ACS.
Scores, 18: Seek Social Support, Focus on Solving the Problem, Work Hard and Achieve, Worry, Invest in Close Friends, Seek to Belong, Wishful Thinking, Not Coping, Tension Reduction, Social Action, Ignore the Problem, Self-Blame, Keep to Self, Seek Spiritual Support, Focus on the Positive, Seek Professional Help, Seek Relaxing Diversions, Physical Recreation.
Administration: Group.
Price Data, 1993: A$90 per complete kit including manual (48 pages) and all required material in a notebook; $2.20 per questionnaire; $20 per 10 questionnaires (short form); $10 per 10 scoring sheets; $10 per 10 profile charts; $45 per manual.
Time: 10 minutes for Long Form; 3 minutes for Short Form.
Authors: Erica Frydenberg and Ramon Lewis.
Publisher: Australian Council for Educational Research Ltd. [Australia].

[97]

Adolescent Diagnostic Interview.

Purpose: "Assesses psychoactive substance use disorders."
Population: Ages 12–18.
Publication Date: 1993.
Acronym: ADI.
Scores: 8 sections to indicate presence or absence of a DSM-III-R diagnosis of psychoactive substance use disorder: Sociodemographic Factors, Psychosocial Stressors, Substance Use/Consumption History, Alcohol Use Symptoms, Cannabis Use Symptoms, Additional Drug Use Symptoms, Level of Functioning Domains, Orientation and Memory Screen; plus 8 psychiatric status screens: Depression, Mania, Eating Disorder, Delusional Thinking, Hallucinations, Attention Deficit Disorder, Anxiety Disorder, Conduct Disorder.
Administration: Individual.
Price Data, 1993: $75 per complete kit including 5 administration booklets and manual (46 pages); $32.50 per 5 administration booklets; $45 per manual.
Time: (45–55) minutes.
Comments: Structured interview for use with adolescents.
Authors: Ken C. Winters and George A. Henly.
Publisher: Western Psychological Services.

[98]

Adolescent Drinking Index.

Purpose: Constructed to screen for alcohol abuse.
Population: Ages 12–17.
Publication Dates: 1985–89.
Acronym: ADI.
Scores, 3: Self-Medicated Drinking (MED), Aggressive/Rebellious Behavior (REB), Total.
Administration: Group or individual.
Price Data, 1994: $47 per complete kit including manual ('89, 34 pages) and 25 test booklets.
Time: (5) minutes.
Comments: Test booklet title is Drinking & You.
Authors: Adele V. Harrell and Philip W. Wirtz.
Publisher: Psychological Assessment Resources, Inc.

[99]

Adolescent Language Screening Test.

Purpose: "Developed to screen for deficits in the dimensions of language use, content, and form" in adolescents.
Population: Ages 11–17.
Publication Date: 1984.
Acronym: ALST.
Scores: 7 subtests: Pragmatics, Receptive Vocabulary, Concepts, Expressive Vocabulary, Sentence Formation, Morphology, Phonology.
Administration: Individual.
Price Data, 1994: $98 per complete kit including 50 test booklets, picture book, and examiner's manual (26 pages); $23 per 25 test booklets; $49 per picture book; $24 per examiner's manual.
Time: (10–15) minutes.
Authors: Denise L. Morgan and Arthur M. Guilford.
Publisher: PRO-ED, Inc.
Cross References: For reviews by Linda Crocker, Robert T. Williams, and Amy Finch-Williams, see 10:10.

[100]

Adolescent Separation Anxiety Test.

Purpose: "Provides a measure of emotional and personality patterns which adolescents show in reaction to separation experiences."

Population: Ages 11–18.

Publication Dates: 1972–80.

Scores, 28: 18 association responses (Rejection, Impaired Concentration, Phobic Feeling, Anxiety, Loneliness, Withdrawal, Somatic, Adaptive Reaction, Anger, Projection, Empathy, Evasion, Fantasy, Well-Being, Sublimation, Intrapunitive, Identify Stress, Total), plus 10 derived response patterns (Attachment, Individuation, Hostility, Painful Tension, Reality Avoidance, Concentration Impairment and Sublimation, Self-Love, Identity Stress, Absurd Responses, Attachment-Individuation Balance).

Administration: Individual.

Forms: Separate forms for boys and girls.

Price Data: Not available.

Time: Administration time not reported.

Comments: Formerly titled Separation Anxiety Test.

Author: Henry G. Hansburg.

Publisher: Krieger Publishing Co., Inc. [No reply from publisher; status unknown].

Cross References: For reviews by Brenda Bailey-Richardson and Carolyn S. Hartsough, see 9:53.

TEST REFERENCES

1. Levitz-Jones, E. M., & Orlofsky, J. L. (1985). Separation-individuation and intimacy capacity in college women. *Journal of Personality and Social Psychology, 49,* 156-169.

[101]

Adult Attention Deficit Disorder Behavior Rating Scale.

Purpose: Designed to "identify behavior that will support a diagnosis of Attention Deficit Disorder (ADD)."

Population: Ages 16 and above.

Publication Date: 1993.

Acronym: AADDBRS.

Scores, 10: Inattention, Impulsivity, Hyperactivity, Anger Control, Academics, Anxiety, Confidence, Aggressiveness, Resistance, Social.

Administration: Individual.

Price Data, 1993: $35 per complete kit including manual (23 pages), 25 rating sheets, and 25 profile sheets; $9.50 per 25 replacement forms (rating sheets and profile sheets).

Time: (15–30) minutes.

Comments: An extension of the Attention Deficit Disorder Behavior Rating Scales (226).

Authors: Ned Owens and Betty White Owens.

Publisher: Ned Owens M.Ed. Inc.

[102]

Adult Basic Learning Examination, Second Edition.

Purpose: "Designed to measure the educational achievement of adults who may or may not have completed twelve years of schooling . . . also useful in evaluating efforts to raise the educational level of these adults."

Population: Adults with less than 12 years of formal schooling.

Publication Dates: 1986–90.

Acronym: ABLE.

Administration: Group.

Levels, 3: 1, 2, 3 and placement test (SelectABLE).

Forms, 2: E, F (equivalent forms).

Price Data, 1994: $40 per examination kit containing test booklets and directions for administration for 1 form of each of the 3 levels, hand-scorable answer sheet, Ready Score™ Answer Sheet and group record for Level 2, and SelectABLE Ready Score™ Answer Sheet; $26 per handbook of instructional techniques and materials ('86, 67 pages); $31.50 per norms booklet (specify level); $5 per Reading Supplement; ABLE Computer Scoring™ software program also available for local computer scoring. Foreign Language Edition: Spanish edition (1990) ABLE Screening Battery available for Level 2 Reading and Mathematics subtests only.

Authors: Bjorn Karlsen and Eric F. Gardner.

Publisher: The Psychological Corporation.

a) SELECTABLE.

Purpose: A screening test to determine which level of ABLE is most suitable for use with a particular individual.

Price Data: $45.50 per 25 Ready Score™ Answer Sheets; $40 per 50 hand-scorable test sheets; $23.50 per scoring key; $8 per SelectABLE Handbook ('86, 15 pages).

Time: (15) minutes.

b) LEVEL 1.

Population: Adults with 1–4 years of formal education.

Scores, 5: Vocabulary, Reading Comprehension, Spelling, Number Operations, Problem Solving.

Price Data: $56 per 25 hand-scorable test booklets and directions for administering including group record (specify Form E or F); $48.50 per scoring key (specify Form E or F); $7 per directions for administering ('86, 38 pages).

Time: (130–165) minutes.

c) LEVEL 2.

Population: Adults with 5–8 years of formal education.

Scores: Same as *b* plus Language.

Price Data: $56 per 25 hand-scorable or reusable test booklets (specify Form E or F); $48.50 per scoring key (specify Form E or F); $47.50 per 25 Ready Score™ Answer Sheets (specify Form E or F); $40 per 50 hand-scorable answer sheets and 2 group records; $7 per directions for administering Levels 2 and 3.

Time: (175–215) minutes.

d) LEVEL 3.

Population: Adults with 9–12 years of formal schooling who may or may not have completed 12 years of schooling.

Scores: Same as *c* above.
Price Data: Same as *c* above.
Time: Same as *c* above.
Cross References: For reviews by Anne R. Fitzpatrick and Robert T. Williams, see 11:9 (1 reference); see also T3:121 (6 references), 8:2 (4 references), and T2:3 (3 references); for a review by A. N. Hieronymus of the earlier edition and excerpted reviews by Edward B. Fry and James W. Hall of Levels 1 and 2 of the earlier edition, see 7:3.

[103]

Adult Career Concerns Inventory.
Purpose: "Designed to measure career planning and one's concerns with the career development tasks at various life stages."
Population: Ages 24 and over.
Publication Date: 1988.
Acronym: ACCI.
Scores, 13: 12 subscales in 4 career stages: Exploration Stage (Crystallization, Specification, Implementation), Establishment Stage (Stabilizing, Consolidating, Advancing), Maintenance Stage (Holding, Updating, Innovating), Disengagement Stage (Deceleration, Retirement Planning, Retirement Living), plus Career Change Status.
Administration: Group.
Price Data, 1992: $9 per 25 test booklets and profiles; $32 per 50 not prepaid answer sheets; $30 per manual (63 pages); $31 per specimen set.
Time: (15–30) minutes.
Comments: Self-administered and self-scored; research edition; a measure of Donald Super's hierarchy of life stages for adults; manual title is Manual for Research and Exploratory Use in Counseling.
Authors: Donald E. Super, Albert S. Thompson, and Richard H. Lindeman.
Publisher: Consulting Psychologists Press, Inc.

TEST REFERENCES

1. Slocum, J. W., Jr., & Cron, W. L. (1985). Job attitudes and performance during three career stages. *Journal of Vocational Behavior, 26*, 126-145.
2. Arbona, C. (1990). Career counseling research and Hispanics: A review of the literature. *The Counseling Psychologist, 18*, 300-323.
3. Whiston, S. C. (1990). Evaluation of the Adult Career Concerns Inventory. *Journal of Counseling and Development, 69*, 78-80.
4. Super, D. E., Osborne, L., Walsh, D. J., Brown, S. D., & Niles, S. G. (1992). Development career assessment and counseling: The C-DAC model. *Journal of Counseling and Development, 71*, 74-80.
5. Robbins, S. B., Chartrand, J. M., McFadden, K. L., & Lee, R. M. (1994). Efficacy of leader-led and self-directed career workshops for middle-aged and older adults. *Journal of Counseling Psychology, 41*, 83-90.

[104]

Adult Neuropsychological Questionnaire.
Purpose: To screen for brain dysfunction.
Population: Adults.
Publication Date: 1978.
Acronym: ANQ.
Scores: 8 content areas: General Health, Substance Abuse, Psychiatric Problems, General Neurological, Right Hemisphere, Left Hemisphere, Subcortical/Cerebellar/Spinal, Sensory/Perceptual.

Administration: Individual.
Price Data, 1994: $28 per complete kit including manual (11 pages) and 50 questionnaires.
Time: (5–10) minutes.
Comments: Can be used as adjunct to general intake interview; may be self-administered.
Author: Fernando Melendez.
Publisher: Psychological Assessment Resources, Inc.

[105]

Adult Personal Adjustment and Role Skills.
Purpose: Used to evaluate the community adjustment of adults.
Population: Adults.
Publication Date: 1981.
Acronym: PARS.
Scores, 8: Close Relations, Alienation-Depression, Anxiety, Confusion, Alcohol-Drug Use, House Activity, Child Relations, Employment.
Administration: Group.
Price Data, 1993: $13 per sampler set including manual (22 pages), answer sheet, and profile; $11 per 25 scales; $12 per manual.
Time: (20–30) minutes.
Author: Robert B. Ellsworth.
Publisher: Consulting Psychologists Press, Inc.

[106]

Adult Personality Inventory.
Purpose: Designed as "a tool for analyzing and reporting individual differences in personality, interpersonal style, and career/life-style preferences."
Population: Ages 16–Adult.
Publication Dates: 1982–88.
Acronym: API.
Scores, 25: Personality Scores (Extroverted, Adjusted, Tough-Minded, Independent, Disciplined, Creative, Enterprising); Interpersonal Style Scores (Caring, Adapting, Withdrawn, Submissive, Uncaring, Non-Conforming, Sociable, Assertive); Career/Life-Style Scores (Practical, Scientific, Aesthetic, Social, Competitive, Structured); Validity Scores (Good Impression, Bad Impression, Infrequency, Uncertainty).
Administration: Group or individual.
Time: (45–60) minutes.
Comments: Self-report; computer scored and interpreted.
Author: Samuel E. Krug.
Publisher: MetriTech, Inc.
a) API NARRATIVE REPORTS.
Purpose: "Oriented to the test taker and features an interpretive narrative that provides extensive feedback."
Price Data, 1994: $49 per Narrative Report Kit including manual ('88, 15 pages), processing of 5 reports, 2 reusable test booklets, and 5 answer sheets; $6.75–$9.75 per narrative report including processing and answer sheets; $16.50 per manual; $16 per 10 reusable test booklets.

b) API/TEST PLUS.

Purpose: Oriented to the test administrator and includes a decision model feature.

Price Data: $795 per API/Test Plus microcomputer version; $48 per occupational decision model disk; $38 per TPEXTERN program; $16 per 10 reusable test booklets; $12 per 50 answer sheets; $18.50 per 50 scannable answer sheets; $36 per 50 decision model worksheets.

Comments: Supports both on-line or off-line testing; IBM version only; optional 189-item short version requires 25–35 minutes for administration.

c) API/CAREER PROFILE.

Purpose: Oriented to the test administrator and compares individual test taker with Occupational Decision Models and user created models.

Price Data: $8.50–$11.50 per report.

Comments: Supports both on-line or off-line testing; IBM version only; optional 189-item short version requires 25–35 minutes for administration.

Cross References: For a review by Brian Bolton of an earlier edition, see 9:54.

TEST REFERENCES

1. Krug, S. E. (1986). Preliminary evidence regarding black-white differences in scores on the Adult Personality Inventory. *Psychological Reports, 58,* 203-206.
2. Bolton, B. (1991). Comments on "The Adult Personality Inventory." *Journal of Counseling and Development, 69,* 272-273.
3. Krug, S. E. (1991). Reply to Brian Bolton. *Journal of Counseling and Development, 69,* 274.
4. Krug, S. E. (1991). The Adult Personality Inventory. *Journal of Counseling and Development, 69,* 266-271.

[107]
The Adult Self Expression Scale.

Purpose: Assesses the assertiveness level of the respondent.

Population: Adults.

Publication Dates: 1974–75.

Acronym: ASES.

Scores: Total score only.

Administration: Group or individual.

Price Data: Not available.

Time: Administration time not reported.

Authors: Melvin L. Gay, James G. Hollandsworth, Jr., and John P. Galassi.

Publisher: Adult Self Expression Scale [No reply from publisher; status unknown].

Cross References: For reviews by Philip H. Dreyer and Goldine C. Gleser, see 9:55 (15 references).

TEST REFERENCES

1. Baxter, D. J., Marshall, W. L., Barbaree, H. E., Davidson, P. R., & Malcolm, P. B. (1984). Deviant sexual behavior: Differentiating sex offenders by criminal and personal history, psychometric measures, and sexual response. *Criminal Justice and Behavior, 11,* 477-501.

[108]
Adult Suicidal Ideation Questionnaire.

Purpose: "Designed to evaluate the presence and frequency of suicidal thoughts."

Population: Ages 18 and over.

Publication Dates: 1987–91.

Acronym: ASIQ.

Scores: Total score only.

Administration: Individual or group.

Price Data, 1994: $42 per complete kit including manual ('91, 62 pages) and 25 respondent forms; $20 per manual; $26 per 25 respondent forms.

Time: (5–10) minutes.

Author: William M. Reynolds.

Publisher: Psychological Assessment Resources, Inc.

[109]
Advanced Measures of Music Audiation.

Purpose: Developed to measure music aptitude.

Population: Junior high school through college.

Publication Date: 1989.

Scores, 3: Tonal, Rhythm, Total.

Administration: Group.

Price Data, 1992: $37 per complete kit including audiocassette, 100 answer sheets, and manual (54 pages); $15 per 100 answer sheets; $20 per set of scoring stencils; scoring service available from publisher at $1 per student.

Time: 16(20) minutes.

Comments: Audiocassette recorder necessary for administration; upward extension of the Intermediate Measures of Music Audiation (1249).

Author: Edwin E. Gordon.

Publisher: G.I.A. Publications, Inc.

[110]
Advanced Placement Examination in Biology.

Purpose: Designed to measure college-level achievement of students in biology.

Population: High school students desiring credit for college-level courses and admission to advanced courses.

Publication Dates: 1956–93.

Scores: Total score only.

Administration: Group.

Price Data: Available from publisher.

Time: 180(200) minutes.

Comments: Available to secondary schools for annual administration on specified days in May; inactive form and previous essay questions available; program administered by The College Board and Educational Testing Service.

Author: Educational Testing Service.

Publisher: Educational Testing Service.

Cross References: See 8:381 (1 reference); see also 7:807 (1 reference); for a review by Clarence H. Nelson of earlier forms, see 6:893 (1 reference); for a review by Clark W. Horton, see 5:724. For reviews of the APE program, see 8:471 (2 reviews) and 7:662 (2 reviews).

TEST REFERENCES

1. Stanley, J. C., & Stanley, B. S. K. (1986). High-school biology, chemistry, or physics learned well in three weeks. *Journal of Research in Science Teaching, 23,* 237-250.

[111]

Advanced Placement Examination in Chemistry.

Purpose: Designed to measure college-level achievement of students in chemistry.

Population: High school students desiring credit for college-level courses and admission to advanced courses.

Publication Dates: 1954–93.

Scores: Total score only.

Administration: Group.

Price Data: Available from publisher.

Time: 180(200) minutes.

Comments: Available to secondary schools for annual administration on specified days in May; inactive form and previous essay questions available; program administered by The College Board and Educational Testing Service.

Author: Educational Testing Service.

Publisher: Educational Testing Service.

Cross References: For a review by J. Arthur Campbell, see 8:846; see also T2:1832 (1 reference) and 6:915 (1 reference); for a review by Theo A. Ashford of an earlier form, see 5:743. For reviews of the APE program, see 8:471 (2 reviews) and 7:662 (2 reviews).

TEST REFERENCES

1. Wainer, H., & Thissen, D. (1993). Combining multiple-choice and constructed-response test scores: Toward a Marxist theory of test construction. *Applied Measurement in Education, 6*(2), 103-118.

[112]

Advanced Placement Examination in English (Composition and Literature).

Purpose: Designed to measure college-level achievement of students in English (composition and literature).

Population: High school students desiring credit for college level courses and admission to advanced courses.

Publication Dates: 1956–93.

Scores: Total score only.

Administration: Group.

Price Data: Not available.

Time: 180(200) minutes.

Comments: Available to secondary schools for annual administration on specified days in May; inactive form and previous essay questions available; program administered by The College Board and Educational Testing Service.

Author: Educational Testing Service.

Publisher: Educational Testing Service.

Cross References: For additional information and a review by Ellis Batten Page of an earlier edition, see 8:39; see also T2:51 (2 references) and 7:184 (1 reference); for a review by Robert C. Pooley of an earlier form of the English composition test, see 5:205; for a review by John S. Diekhoff of an earlier form of the literature test, see 5:211. For reviews of the APE program, see 8:471 (2 reviews) and 7:662 (2 reviews).

TEST REFERENCES

1. Rubin, D. L., & Rafoth, B. A. (1986). Social cognitive ability as a predictor of the quality of expository and persuasive writing among college freshmen. *Research in the Teaching of English, 20,* 9-21.

2. Braun, H. I. (1988). Understanding scoring reliability: Experiments in calibrating essay readers. *Journal of Educational Statistics, 13,* 1-18.

[113]

Advanced Placement Examination in English (Language and Composition).

Purpose: Designed to measure college-level achievement of students in English (language and composition).

Population: High school students desiring credit for college level courses and admission to advanced courses.

Publication Dates: 1981–93.

Scores: Total score only.

Administration: Group.

Price Data: Not available.

Time: 180(200) minutes.

Comments: Available to secondary schools for annual administration on specified days in May; inactive form and previous essay questions available; program administered by The College Board and Educational Testing Service.

Author: Educational Testing Service.

Publisher: Educational Testing Service.

Cross References: For additional information and a review by Ellis Batten Page of an earlier edition, see 8:39; see also T2:51 (2 references) and 7:184 (1 reference); for a review by Robert C. Pooley of an earlier form of the English composition test, see 5:205. For reviews of the APE program, see 8:471 (2 reviews) and 7:662 (2 reviews).

[114]

Advanced Placement Examination in European History.

Purpose: Designed to measure college-level achievement of students in European history.

Population: High school students desiring credit for college-level courses and admission to advanced courses.

Publication Dates: 1956–93.

Scores: Total score only.

Administration: Group.

Price Data: Available from publisher.

Time: 180(200) minutes.

Comments: Available to secondary schools for annual administration on specified days in May; inactive form and previous essay questions available; program administered by The College Board and Educational Testing Service.

Author: Educational Testing Service.

Publisher: Educational Testing Service.

Cross References: For additional information, see 8:908 (1 reference); see also 6:1001 (2 references). For reviews of the APE program, see 8:471 (2 reviews) and 7:662 (2 reviews).

TEST REFERENCES

1. Wainer, H., & Thissen, D. (1993). Combining multiple-choice and constructed-response test scores: Toward a Marxist theory of test construction. *Applied Measurement in Education, 6*(2), 103-118.

[115]

Advanced Placement Examination in French Language, Level 3.

Purpose: Designed to measure college-level achievement of students in the French language.
Population: High school students desiring credit for college-level courses and admission to advanced courses.
Publication Dates: 1971–93.
Scores: Total score only.
Administration: Group.
Price Data: Available from publisher.
Time: 150(170) minutes.
Comments: Available to secondary schools for annual administration on specified days in May; inactive form and previous free-response sections available; program administered by The College Board and Educational Testing Service.
Author: Educational Testing Service.
Publisher: Educational Testing Service.
Cross References: See T3:131 (1 reference); for additional information and a review by Michio Peter Hagiwara, see 8:112. For reviews of the APE program, see 8:471 (2 reviews).

[116]

Advanced Placement Examination in French Literature, Level 3.

Purpose: Designed to measure college-level achievement of students in French literature.
Population: High school students desiring credit for college-level courses and admission to advanced courses.
Publication Dates: 1954–93.
Scores: Total score only.
Administration: Group.
Price Data: Available from publisher.
Time: 180(200) minutes.
Comments: Available to secondary schools for annual administration on specified days in May; inactive form and previous free-response sections available; program administered by The College Board and Educational Testing Service.
Author: Educational Testing Service.
Publisher: Educational Testing Service.
Cross References: For additional information and reviews by Michio Peter Hagiwara and Joseph A. Murphy, see 8:113 (3 references); see also 7:268 (1 reference) and 6:368 (3 references). For a review of the APE program, see 8:471 (2 reviews) and 7:662 (2 reviews).

[117]

Advanced Placement Examination in German Language, Level 3.

Purpose: Designed to measure college-level achievement of students in German language.

Population: High school students desiring credit for college-level courses and admission to advanced courses.
Publication Dates: 1956–93.
Scores: Total score only.
Administration: Group.
Price Data: Available from publisher.
Time: 180(200) minutes.
Comments: Available to secondary schools for annual administration on specified days in May; inactive form and previous free-response sections available; program administered by The College Board and Educational Testing Service.
Author: Educational Testing Service.
Publisher: Educational Testing Service.
Cross References: For reviews of the APE program, see 8:471 (2 reviews) and 7:662 (2 reviews).

[118]

Advanced Placement Examination in History of Art.

Purpose: Designed to measure college-level achievement of students in art history.
Population: High school students desiring credit for college-level courses and admission to advanced courses.
Publication Dates: 1972–93.
Scores: Total score only.
Administration: Group.
Price Data: Available from publisher.
Time: 180(200) minutes.
Comments: Available to secondary schools for annual administration on specified days in May; inactive form and previous free-response sections available; program administered by The College Board and Educational Testing Service.
Author: Educational Testing Service.
Publisher: Educational Testing Service.
Cross References: For additional information concerning an earlier edition, see 8:83. For reviews of the APE program, see 8:471 (2 reviews) and 7:662 (2 reviews).

[119]

Advanced Placement Examination in Latin, Level 3 (Vergil).

Purpose: Designed to measure college-level achievement of students in Latin.
Population: High school students desiring credit for college-level courses and admission to advanced courses.
Publication Dates: 1972–93.
Scores: Total score only.
Administration: Group.
Price Data: Available from publisher.
Time: 120(150) minutes.
Comments: Available to secondary schools for annual administration on specified days in May; inactive form and previous essay questions available; program administered by The College Board and Educational Testing Service.

Author: Educational Testing Service.
Publisher: Educational Testing Service.
Cross References: For additional information concerning an earlier edition of the classics examination, see 8:144 (3 references). For reviews of the APE program, see 8:471 (2 reviews) and 7:662 (2 reviews).

[120]
Advanced Placement Examination in Latin Literature, Level 3.
Purpose: Designed to measure college-level achievement of students in Latin.
Population: High school students desiring credit for college-level courses and admission to advanced courses.
Publication Dates: 1980–93.
Scores: Total score only.
Administration: Group.
Price Data: Available from publisher.
Time: 120(150) minutes.
Comments: Available to secondary schools for annual administration on specified days in May; inactive form and previous essay questions available; program administered by The College Board and Educational Testing Service.
Author: Educational Testing Service.
Publisher: Educational Testing Service.
Cross References: For additional information concerning an earlier edition of the Classics examination, see 8:144 (3 references). For reviews of the APE program, see 8:471 (2 reviews) and 7:662 (2 reviews).

[121]
Advanced Placement Examination in Mathematics.
Purpose: Designed to measure college-level achievement of students in calculus.
Population: High school students desiring credit for college-level courses and admission to advanced courses.
Publication Dates: 1954–93.
Scores: Total score only.
Administration: Group.
Levels, 2: AB, BC.
Price Data: Available from publisher.
Time: 180(200) minutes.
Comments: Available to secondary schools for annual administration on specified days in May; inactive form and previous free-response sections available; program administered by The College Board and Educational Testing Service.
Author: Educational Testing Service.
Publisher: Educational Testing Service.
a) CALCULUS AB.
Comments: Equivalent of 1 year of college elementary functions and calculus.
b) CALCULUS BC.
Comments: Equivalent of 1 year of college calculus.
Cross References: See 8:309 (1 reference), T2:742 (1 reference), 7:451 (2 references), and 6:570 (4 references); for a review by Paul L. Dressel of an earlier form, see 5:419. For reviews of the APE program, see 8:471 (2 reviews) and 7:662 (2 reviews).

[122]
Advanced Placement Examination in Music Theory.
Purpose: To provide high school students with an opportunity to qualify for credit for college level courses and admission to advanced courses in music theory.
Population: High school students.
Publication Dates: 1978–93.
Administration: Group.
Price Data: Available from publisher.
Time: 150(180) minutes.
Comments: Available to secondary schools for annual administration on specified days in May; inactive form and previous free-response questions available; program administered by The College Board and Educational Testing Service.
Author: Educational Testing Service.
Publisher: Educational Testing Service.
Cross References: For additional information regarding an earlier edition of the Music Examination, see 8:90. For reviews of the APE program, see 8:471 (2 reviews).

[123]
Advanced Placement Examination in Physics.
Purpose: Designed to measure college-level achievement of students in physics.
Population: High school students desiring credit for college-level courses and admission to advanced courses.
Publication Dates: 1954–93.
Administration: Group.
Levels, 2: B, C (candidate elects only one).
Price Data: Available from publisher.
Comments: Available to secondary schools for annual administration on specified days in May; inactive forms and previous free-response sections available; program administered by The College Board and Educational Testing Service.
Author: Educational Testing Service.
Publisher: Educational Testing Service.
a) PHYSICS B.
Scores: Total score only.
Comments: Equivalent of 1-year terminal course in college physics.
Time: 180(200) minutes.
b) PHYSICS C.
Scores: 1 or 2 scores: Mechanics (Part 1), Electricity and Magnetism (Part 2).
Comments: Equivalent of 1-year nonterminal course in calculus-based college physics; 2 parts in each test booklet (candidate elects either one or both parts).
Time: 90(100) minutes for each part.
Cross References: See T3:143 (1 reference); for a review by Mario Iona, see 8:862 (3 references); see

also 6:927 (2 references); for a review by Leo Nedelsky of an earlier form, see 5:750. For reviews of the APE program, see 8:471 (2 reviews) and 7:662 (2 reviews).

[124]
Advanced Placement Examination in Spanish Language, Level 3.
Purpose: Designed to measure college-level achievement of students in Spanish language.
Population: High school students desiring credit for college-level courses and admission to advanced courses.
Publication Dates: 1976–93.
Scores: Total score only.
Administration: Group.
Price Data: Available from publisher.
Time: 165(185) minutes.
Comments: Available to secondary schools for annual administration on specified days in May; inactive form and previous free-response sections available; program administered by The College Board and Educational Testing Service.
Author: Educational Testing Service.
Publisher: Educational Testing Service.
Cross References: See T3:139 (1 reference); for a review by George W. Ayer of an earlier edition, see 8:153 (1 reference); see also 7:313 (2 references) and 6:421 (1 reference). For reviews of the APE program, see 8:471 (2 reviews) and 7:662 (2 reviews).

[125]
Advanced Placement Examination in Spanish Literature, Level 3.
Purpose: Designed to measure college-level achievement of students in Spanish literature.
Population: High school students desiring credit for college-level courses and admission to advanced courses.
Publication Dates: 1956–93.
Scores: Total score only.
Administration: Group.
Price Data: Available from publisher.
Time: 180(200) minutes.
Comments: Available to secondary schools for annual administration on specified days in May; inactive form and previous free-response sections available; program administered by The College Board and Educational Testing Service.
Author: Educational Testing Service.
Publisher: Educational Testing Service.
Cross References: For a review by George W. Ayer of an earlier edition, see 8:153 (1 reference); see also 7:313 (2 references) and 6:421 (1 reference). For reviews of the APE program, see 8:471 (2 reviews) and 7:662 (2 reviews).

[126]
Advanced Placement Examination in Studio Art.
Purpose: Designed to measure college-level achievement of students in studio art.

Population: High school students desiring credit for college-level courses and admission to advanced courses.
Publication Dates: 1972–93.
Scores: Total score only.
Administration: Group.
Price Data: Available from publisher.
Comments: Candidate submits materials (original works, written commentary, slides) for evaluation of quality, concentration, and breadth; available to secondary schools for annual administration on specified days in May; program administered by The College Board and Educational Testing Service.
Author: Educational Testing Service.
Publisher: Educational Testing Service.
Cross References: For additional information concerning an earlier edition, see 8:83. For reviews of the APE program, see 8:471 (2 reviews).

[127]
Advanced Placement Examination in United States History.
Purpose: To "measure college-level achievement of students" in United States history.
Population: High school students desiring credit for college-level courses and admission to advanced courses.
Publication Dates: 1956–93.
Scores: Total score only.
Administration: Group.
Price Data: Examination fee per student available from publisher.
Time: 180(200) minutes.
Comments: Available to secondary schools for annual administration on specified days in May; inactive form and previous essay questions available; program administered by The College Board and Educational Testing Service.
Author: Educational Testing Service.
Publisher: Educational Testing Service.
Cross References: See T2:1980 (1 reference); for a review by Harry D. Berg of an earlier form, see 6:1000 (1 reference); for reviews by James A. Field, Jr. and Christine McGuire, see 5:812. For reviews of the APE program, see 8:471 (2 reviews) and 7:662 (2 reviews).

TEST REFERENCES

1. Livingston, S. A. (1993). Small-sample equating with log-linear smoothing. *Journal of Educational Measurement, 30,* 23-39.

[128]
Advanced Placement Examinations.
Purpose: Designed to measure college-level achievement of students in various subject areas.
Population: High school students desiring credit for college level courses and admission to advanced courses.
Publication Dates: 1954–93.
Acronym: APE.
Scores: 28 tests: United States History, Biology,

Chemistry, English Composition and Literature, English Language and Composition, European History, French Language, French Literature, German Language, History of Art, Latin Literature, Latin (Vergil), Mathematics (2 tests: Calculus AB, Calculus BC), Music Theory, Physics (2 tests: Physics B, Physics C), Spanish Language, Spanish Literature, Studio Art (2 portfolios: General and Drawing), Psychology, Macroeconomics, Microeconomics, United States Government and Politics, Comparative Government and Politics, Computer Science A, Computer Science AB.

Administration: Group.
Price Data: Available from publisher.
Time: 120–180(200) minutes.
Comments: Available to secondary schools for annual administration on specified days in May; inactive forms and previous essay/free-response sections available; program administered by The College Board and Educational Testing Service.
Author: Educational Testing Service.
Publisher: Educational Testing Service.
Cross References: See T3:124 (1 reference); for additional information and reviews by Paul L. Dressel and David A. Frisbie, see 8:471 (5 references); see also T2:1045 (4 references); for reviews by Warren G. Findley and Alexander G. Wesman of an earlier program, see 7:662 (3 references); see also 6:761 (5 references). For reviews of individual tests, see 8:112 (1 review), 8:113 (2 reviews), 8:126 (1 review), 8:153 (1 review), 8:846 (1 review), 8:862 (1 review), 6:893 (1 review), 6:1000 (1 review), 5:205 (1 review), 5:211 (1 review), 5:273 (1 review), 5:419 (1 review), 5:724 (1 review), 5:743 (1 review), 5:750 (1 review), and 5:812 (2 reviews).

[129]

Advanced Test Battery.
Purpose: "Designed for use in the selection, development, or guidance of personnel at graduate level or in management positions."
Population: Personnel at graduate level or in management positions.
Publication Dates: 1979–83.
Acronym: ATB.
Administration: Group.
Levels, 2: Higher order aptitudes, Higher order aptitudes in a work setting.
Restricted Distribution: Restricted to persons who have completed the publisher's training course or members of the Division of Occupational Psychology of the British Psychological Society.
Price Data, 1989: £771 per testing kit; £96.50 per 10 Level 1 booklets; £129.50 per 10 Level 2 booklets; £5.50 per 25 score sheets; £5.50 per 25 testing logs; £19.50 per 50 profile charts ('80, 2 pages); £19.50 per 50 practice leaflets ('82, 4 pages); £29 per manual ('79, 87 pages); £110 per administration set.
Comments: Subtests available as separates; separate answer sheets must be used.

Authors: Roger Holdsworth (VA3, NA4, manual); Peter Saville (VA1, NA2, manual), Gill Nyfield (manual), Dave Hawkey (DA5, ST7, DT8), Steve Blinkhorn (VA3), and Alan Iliff (NA4).
Publisher: Saville & Holdsworth Ltd. [England].
  a) LEVEL 1. 1979–80; HIGHER ORDER APTITUDES, 3 TESTS.
    1) *Verbal Concepts.*
    Publication Date: 1980.
    Acronym: VA1.
    Price Data: £33 per 10 question booklets; £8.50 per scoring key; £41.50 per 50 answer sheets; £8.50 per administration card (no date, 2 pages).
    Time: 15(20) minutes.
    2) *Number Series.*
    Publication Date: 1980.
    Acronym: NA2.
    Price Data: £33 per 10 question booklets; £8.50 per scoring key; £41.50 per 50 answer sheets; £8.50 per administration card (no date, 2 pages).
    Time: 15(20) minutes.
    3) *Diagramming.*
    Publication Date: 1980.
    Acronym: DA5.
    Price Data: £49.50 per 10 question booklets; £8.50 per scoring key; £42.50 per 50 answer sheets; £8.50 per administration card (no date, 3 pages); £33 per 10 command cards (no date, 2 pages).
    Time: 20(25) minutes.
  b) LEVEL 2. 1979–80; HIGHER ORDER APTITUDES IN A WORK CONTEST; 4 TESTS.
    1) *Verbal Critical Reasoning.*
    Publication Date: 1983.
    Acronym: VA3.
    Price Data: £49.50 per 10 question booklets; £8.50 per scoring key; £41.50 per 50 answer sheets; £8.50 per administration card (no date, 2 pages).
    Time: 30(35) minutes.
    2) *Numerical Critical Reasoning.*
    Publication Dates: 1979–83.
    Acronym: NA4.
    Price Data: £49.50 per 10 question booklets; £8.50 per scoring key; £41.50 per 50 answer sheets; £8.50 per administration card (no date, 2 pages); £33 per 10 data cards ('79, 2 pages).
    Time: 35(40) minutes.
    3) *Spatial Reasoning.*
    Publication Dates: 1979–81.
    Acronym: ST7.
    Price Data: £22 per 10 question booklets; £6 per scoring key; £24.50 per 50 answer sheets; £6 per administration card ('81, 2 pages).
    Time: 20(25) minutes.
    4) *Diagrammatic Reasoning.*
    Publication Dates: 1979–81.
    Acronym: DT8.
    Price Data: £22 per 10 question booklets; £6

per scoring key; £24.50 per 50 answer sheets; £6 per administration card ('81, 2 pages).
Time: 15(20) minutes.

[130]

Affective Perception Inventory.
Purpose: "Designed for measuring feelings about the self relative to specific subject areas or classroom experiences."
Population: Grades 1–3, 4–8, 9–12.
Publication Dates: 1979–80.
Acronym: API.
Forms, 2: Ratings by Self, Ratings by Other.
Administration: Group.
Price Data: Available from publisher.
Foreign Language Editions: Also available in Spanish, Italian, and French.
Time: (40–60) minutes.
Comments: Ratings by self and others.
Authors: Anthony T. Soares and Louise M. Soares.
Publisher: SOARES Associates.

a) FORM P—PRIMARY LEVEL.
Population: Grades 1–9.
Scores: 9 scales: Self Concept, Student Self, Reading Perception, Arithmetic Perceptions, Science Perceptions, Social Studies Perceptions, Perceptions in the Arts, Sports and Games Perceptions, School Perceptions.

b) FORM I—INTERMEDIATE LEVEL.
Population: Grades 4–8.
Scores: 10 scales: Self Concept, Student Self, Perceptions in Language Arts, Mathematics Perceptions, Science Perceptions, Social Studies Perceptions, Perceptions in the Arts, Perceptions in Physical Education, School Perceptions, Reading Perceptions.

c) FORM A—ADVANCED LEVEL.
Population: Grades 9–12.
Scores: 12 scales: Self Concept, Student Self, English Perceptions, Mathematics Perceptions, Science Perceptions, Perceptions in the Social Sciences, Perceptions in the Arts, Perceptions in Physical Education, School Perceptions, Perceptions in Foreign Languages, Perceptions in History, Perceptions in Chemistry.
Cross References: For reviews by Rosa A. Hagin and Gerald R. Smith, see 9:59.

TEST REFERENCES

1. Handley, H. M., & Morse, L. W. (1984). Two-year study relating adolescents' self-concept and gender role perceptions to achievement and attitudes toward science. *Journal of Research in Science Teaching, 21,* 599-607.
2. Byrne, B. M., & Shavelson, R. J. (1986). On the structure of adolescent self-concept. *Journal of Educational Psychology, 78,* 474-481.
3. Byrne, B. M. (1989). Multigroup comparisons and the assumption of equivalent construct validity across groups: Methodological and substantive issues. *Multivariate Behavioral Research, 24,* 503-523.

[131]

The Affective Perception Inventory/College Level.
Purpose: Focuses on the academic dimension of self-perceptions, measuring the self as a person, a student,

against the school settings and exploring the feelings about the self relative to specific subject areas.
Population: Post-secondary school students.
Publication Dates: 1975–89.
Acronym: API.
Scores: 10 scales: Self Concept, Student Self, English Perceptions, Mathematics, Science, Social Studies, Business, Arts, Humanities, Campus Perceptions.
Administration: Group.
Price Data, 1988: $.30 per single scale; $4 per booklet of 10 scales; $8 per College Level manual ('85, 83 pages); $15 per composite test manual (information on all levels, '89, 22 pages).
Time: (45–60) minutes.
Comments: Ratings by self and others; 4th of 4 levels; highest level and most recent addition to the Affective Perception Inventory (130).
Authors: Anthony T. Soares and Louise M. Soares.
Publisher: SOARES Associates.
Cross References: For reviews by John R. Hester and Michael J. Subkoviak, see 11:11; for reviews by Rosa A. Hagin and Gerald R. Smith of the first three levels, see 9:59.

[132]

Affects Balance Scale.
Purpose: "Self-report adjective mood scale."
Population: Adults.
Publication Date: 1975.
Acronym: ABS.
Scores, 3: Positive, Negative, Total.
Administration: Group.
Manual: No manual.
Price Data, 1993: $40 per 100 tests; $25 per 100 profiles.
Time: [3–5] minutes.
Comments: Self-report; adjective check list.
Author: Leonard R. Derogatis.
Publisher: Clinical Psychometric Research, Inc.
Cross References: See 9:61 (6 references).

TEST REFERENCES

1. George, L. K., & Gwyther, L. P. (1986). Caregiver well-being: A multidimensional examination of family caregivers of demented adults. *The Gerontologist, 26,* 253-259.
2. Chuang, H. T., Devins, G. M., Hunsley, J., & Gill, M. J. (1989). Psychosocial distress and well-being among gay and bisexual men with human immunodeficiency virus infection. *American Journal of Psychiatry, 146,* 876-880.
3. Klar, Y., Mendola, R., Fisher, J. D., Silver, R. C., Chinsky, J. M., & Goff, B. (1990). Characteristics of participants in a large group awareness training. *Journal of Consulting and Clinical Psychology, 58,* 99-108.
4. Nurius, P. S., & Markus, H. (1990). Situational variability in the self-concept: Appraisals, expectancies, and asymmetries. *Journal of Social and Clinical Psychology, 9,* 316-333.
5. Aspinwall, L. G., & Taylor, S. E. (1992). Modeling cognitive adaptation: A longitudinal investigation of the impact of individual differences and coping on college adjustment and performance. *Journal of Personality and Social Psychology, 63,* 989-1003.
6. Nofzinger, E. A., Schwartz, R. M., Reynolds, C. F., III, Thase, M. E., Jennings, J. R., Frank, E., Fasiczka, A. L., Garamoni, G. L., & Kupfer, D. J. (1994). Affect intensity and phasic REM sleep in depressed men before and after treatment with cognitive-behavioral therapy. *Journal of Consulting and Clinical Psychology, 62,* 83-91.

[133]

Age Projection Test.

Purpose: Designed as "an imagery test aimed at revealing self-images at various age [and self] levels and their associated structures of imagery functioning useful toward the understanding of a presented problem or a symptom."
Population: Adults.
Publication Date: 1988.
Acronym: APT.
Scores: No scores.
Administration: Individual.
Price Data, 1992: $20 per manual (76 pages) including test.
Time: [60–120] minutes.
Author: Akhter Ahsen.
Publisher: Brandon House, Inc.

[134]

AGS Early Screening Profiles.

Purpose: Constructed to screen children for possible developmental problems or giftedness.
Population: Ages 2-0 to 6-11.
Publication Date: 1990.
Scores: 3 Profile Scores: Cognitive/Language, Motor, Self-Help/Social (Parent or Teacher), and 4 Survey Scores: Articulation, Home, Behavior (Cognitive/Language, Motor).
Administration: Individual.
Price Data, 1993: $249.95 per complete kit including test plates in easel, 25 test records, 25 Self-Help/Social Profile questionnaires, Sample Home/Health History survey, 25 score summaries, tape measure, beads and string, Motor Profile administration manual (19 pages), and manual (311 pages, including reproducible Report to Parents and blackline masters "Guide for Training Examiners"); $24.95 per 25 test records; $14.95 per 25 Self-Help/Social Profile questionnaires; $14.95 per 25 Home/Health History surveys; $8.95 per 25 score summaries; $34.95 per manual.
Time: [15–40] minutes.
Comments: Two levels of scoring: Level I scores are 6 "screening indexes" and 3 descriptive categories; Level II scores are standard scores, percentile ranks, and age equivalents; ecological assessment with ratings by parents and teachers as well as direct assessment of the child.
Authors: Patti L. Harrison (coordinating author and manual author), Alan S. Kaufman (Cognitive/Language Profile), Nadeen L. Kaufman (Cognitive/Language Profile), Robert H. Bruininks (Motor Profile), John Rynders (Motor Profile), Steven Ilmer (Motor Profile), Sara S. Sparrow (Self-Help/Social Profile), and Domenic V. Cicchetti (Self-Help/Social Profile)
Publisher: American Guidance Service.

TEST REFERENCES

1. Ittenbach, R. F., & Harrison, P. L. (1990). Race, gender, and maternal education differences on three measures of the Early Screening Profiles. *Educational and Psychological Measurement, 50*, 931-942.

2. Spiegel, A. N., Steffens, K. M., Rynders, J. E., & Bruininks, R. H. (1990). The Early Motor Profile: Correlation with the Bruininks-Oseretsky Test of Motor Proficiency. *Perceptual and Motor Skills, 71*, 645-646.

[135]

AH1 Forms X and Y.

Purpose: Designed to measure perceptual reasoning.
Population: Ages 7–11 for classroom purposes and 5–11 for research.
Publication Date: 1977.
Scores, 5: Series, Likes, Analogies, Differents, Total.
Administration: Group.
Price Data, 1993: £34.50 per 25 test booklets (specify Form X or Form Y); £9.20 per answer key; £19 per manual (28 pages); £29.90 per specimen set including booklets for Forms X and Y, manual, and scoring key.
Time: 12(40) minutes.
Comments: Downward extension of AH2/AH3 (136).
Authors: A. W. Heim, K. P. Watts, and V. Simmonds.
Publisher: NFER-Nelson Publishing Co. [England].
Cross References: For a review by Frank R. Yekovich, see 9:63.

[136]

AH2/AH3.

Purpose: Designed as parallel tests to measure general reasoning.
Population: Ages 9 and over.
Publication Dates: 1974–78.
Scores, 4: Verbal, Numerical, Perceptual, Total.
Administration: Group.
Forms, 2: AH2, AH3.
Price Data, 1989: £43.15 per 25 AH2 or AH3 tests; £9.15 per 25 answer sheets; £7.20 per marking key; £4.45 per AH 2/3 key for examples; £11.50 per AH 2/3 manual ('78, 47 pages); £34.50 per specimen set.
Time: 28(45) or 42(65) minutes.
Authors: A. H. Heim, K. P. Watts, and V. Simmonds.
Publisher: NFER-Nelson Publishing Co., Ltd. [England].
Cross References: See 9:64 (1 reference), T3:149 (14 references), and 8:175 (1 reference).

TEST REFERENCES

1. Kidd, J. M. (1984). The relationship of self and occupational concepts to the occupational preferences of adolescents. *Journal of Vocational Behavior, 24*, 48-65.
2. Helmes, E. (1987). Concurrent validity of AH2 as a brief measure of intelligence in Canadian University students. *Educational and Psychological Measurement, 47*(3), 725-730.

[137]

AH4: Group Test of General Intelligence.

Purpose: "Designed as a group test of general intelligence."
Population: Ages 10 and over.

Publication Dates: 1955–84.
Scores: Total score only.
Administration: Group.
Price Data, 1989: £22.15 per 25 tests; £6.90 per 25 answer sheets; £5.20 per marking key; £4.60 per data supplement; £9.15 per manual ('70, 17 pages); £15.55 per specimen set.
Time: 20(30–45) minutes.
Authors: A. W. Heim, K. P. Watts (test), V. Simmonds (test), and Anne Walters (data supplement).
Publisher: NFER-Nelson Publishing Co., Ltd. [England].
Cross References: See T2:331 (20 references); for a review by John Nisbet, see 7:331 (12 references); for a review by John Liggett of the original edition, see 6:506; for a review by George A. Ferguson, see 5:390 (11 references).

TEST REFERENCES

1. McDonald, R. A., & Eliot, J. (1987). The Wiggly Block work-sample and its relation to age, sex, and general intelligence. *Perceptual and Motor Skills, 65,* 675-678.
2. McDonald, R. A., & Eliot, J. (1987). Variables contributing to successful aerial photographic interpretation. *Perceptual and Motor Skills, 64,* 551-557.
3. Lim, T. K. (1988). Relationships between standardized psychometric and Piagetian measures of intelligence at the formal operations level. *Intelligence, 12,* 167-182.
4. Rabbitt, P., & McInnis, L. (1988). Do clever old people have earlier and richer first memories? *Psychology and Aging, 3,* 338-341.
5. Toh, K. A., & Woolnough, B. E. (1993). Middle school students' achievement in laboratory investigations: Explicit versus tacit knowledge. *Journal of Research in Science Teaching, 30,* 445-457.

[138]

AH5 Group Test of High Grade Intelligence.

Purpose: Designed as a test of general intelligence "for use with selected, highly intelligent subjects."
Population: "Highly intelligent pupils" ages 13 and over.
Publication Dates: 1968–84.
Scores, 3: Verbal and Numeric, Diagrammatic, Total.
Administration: Group.
Price Data, 1989: £21.85 per 25 tests; £6.35 per key; £8.65 per 25 answer sheets; £9.80 per manual ('83, 21 pages); £17.25 per specimen set including test, key, answer sheet, and manual.
Time: 40(60) minutes.
Author: A. W. Heim.
Publisher: NFER-Nelson Publishing Co., Ltd. [England].
Cross References: See 9:66 (1 reference).

TEST REFERENCES

1. Clarke, M. J., & Youngman, M. B. (1987). Dispositional associates of GCE performance in sixth form and further education college students. *British Journal of Educational Psychology, 57,* 191-204.
2. Cornish, I. M. (1989). The relationship between convergence-divergence and the free recall of discourse. *British Journal of Educational Psychology, 59,* 258-261.

[139]

AH6 Group Tests of High Level Intelligence.

Purpose: Designed as tests for general reasoning ability, effecting discrimination among selected high ability groups.

Population: "Highly intelligent" individuals age 16 through college and university.
Publication Dates: 1970–83.
Scores, 3: Verbal, Numerical Plus Diagrammatic, Total.
Administration: Group.
Price Data, 1989: £18.40 per 10 AG or SEM; £6.35 per set of 3 keys; £8.65 per 25 AG or SEM answer sheets; £11.50 per AG/SEM manual ('83, 26 pages); £20.70 per specimen set including 1 each of AG and SEM tests, answer sheets AG and SEM, key, and manual.
Authors: A. W. Heim, K. P. Watts, and V. Simmonds.
Publisher: NFER-Nelson Publishing Co., Ltd. [England].
   a) SEM.
   Purpose: Intended for potential or qualified scientists, engineers, and mathematicians.
   Time: 40(70) minutes.
   b) AG.
   Purpose: Intended for historians, linguists, economists, philosophers, and all others not included for SEM.
   Time: 35(70) minutes.
Cross References: For reviews by Thomas J. Kehle and Paul Zelhart, see 10:11.

TEST REFERENCES

1. Deary, I. J., Head, B., & Egan, V. (1989). Auditory inspection time, intelligence and pitch discrimination. *Intelligence, 13,* 135-147.

[140]

Ahr's Individual Development Survey.

Purpose: "Developed to assist school personnel in screening the entire kindergarten or first grade enrollment upon entrance to school."
Population: Grades K–1.
Publication Date: 1970.
Acronym: AIDS.
Scores, 3: The Family, The Child, The School.
Administration: Group.
Price Data: Not available.
Comments: Screening test completed by parent to identify possible learning or behavior problems.
Authors: A. Edward Ahr.
Publisher: Priority Innovations, Inc. [No reply from publisher; status unknown].
Cross References: For a review by Carol A. Gray, see 9:67.

[141]

A.I. Survey.

Purpose: "Screens for alienated attitudes that reduce performance and cause poor morale."
Population: Job applicants.
Publication Date: 1982.
Scores: Total score only.
Administration: Group or individual.
Price Data, 1990: $7.50 or less per 25 surveys; $5 per year license fee.

Time: Administration time not reported.
Comments: Also called Alienation Index Survey.
Authors: Alan L. Strand and others.
Publisher: Predictive Surveys Corporation.

[142]

Alberta Essay Scales: Models.
Purpose: Designed as "a means for checking writing skills against standards prevailing in 1964."
Population: Grade 12 English students.
Publication Date: 1977.
Scores, 2: Mechanics, Style-Content.
Administration: Group.
Price Data, 1987: $1.50 per 100 answer sheets; $1 per manual for administrator.
Time: Administration time not reported.
Authors: Verner R. Nyberg and Adell M. Nyberg.
Publisher: University of Alberta (Publication Services, Faculty of Education) [Canada].
Cross References: For reviews by Steve Graham and Pamela A. Moss, see 9:68; see also T3:151 (1 reference).

[143]

The Alcadd Test, Revised Edition.
Purpose: "Designed to: a) provide an objective measurement of alcoholic addiction that could identify individuals whose behavior and personality structure indicated that they were alcoholic addicts or had serious alcoholic problems; b) identify specific areas of maladjustment in alcoholics to facilitate therapeutic and rehabilitation activities; and c) obtain better insight into the psychodynamics of alcoholic addiction."
Population: Adults.
Publication Dates: 1949–88.
Scores, 6: Regularity of Drinking, Preference for Drinking over Other Activities, Lack of Controlled Drinking, Rationalization of Drinking, Excessive Emotionality, Total.
Administration: Individual or group.
Editions, 2: Paper-and-pencil, microcomputer.
Price Data, 1993: $55 per complete kit including 25 AutoScore test booklets ('88, 4 pages) and manual ('88, 24 pages); $29.50 per 25 AutoScore test booklets; $27.50 per manual; $125 per microcomputer edition (IBM) including diskette (tests up to 25) and user's guide; $9.50 or less per mail-in answer sheet.
Time: (5–15) minutes.
Comments: Self-administered.
Authors: Morse P. Manson, Lisa A. Melchior, and G. J. Huba.
Publisher: Western Psychological Services.
Cross References: For reviews by William L. Curlette and Paul Retzlaff, see 11:12 (1 reference); see also T3:152 (3 references), T2:1098 (1 reference), and P:7 (3 references); for a review by Dugal Campbell, see 6:60 (6 references); for reviews by Charles H. Honzik and Albert L. Hunsicker, see 4:30.

[144]

Alcohol Clinical Index.
Purpose: "To identify alcohol problems among patients."
Population: Adults at-risk for alcohol problems.
Publication Date: 1987.
Administration: Individual.
Price Data, 1990: $9.75 per user's booklet (31 pages); $9.95 per 50 questionnaires (specify test).
Time: Administration time not reported.
Authors: Harvey A. Skinner and Stephen Holt.
Publisher: Addiction Research Foundation [Canada].
a) CLINICAL SIGNS.
Scores, 6: Hand, Head, Abdomen, Body, Locomotor Function, Total.
b) MEDICAL HISTORY.
c) ALCOHOL USE.
d) RISK FACTORS.
Scores, 2: Early Indicators, Risk Factors.

[145]

Alcohol Dependence Scale.
Purpose: "Provides a brief measure of the extent to which the use of alcohol has progressed from psychological involvement to impaired control."
Population: Problem drinkers.
Publication Date: 1984.
Acronym: ADS.
Scores: Total score only.
Administration: Group.
Price Data, 1990: C$6.50 per 25 questionnaires; $14.25 per user's guide (41 pages); $15 per specimen set.
Foreign Language Edition: Questionnaire available in French.
Time: (5–10) minutes.
Comments: Test booklet title is Alcohol Use Questionnaire.
Authors: Harvey A. Skinner and John L. Horn.
Publisher: Addiction Research Foundation [Canada].
Cross References: For reviews by Robert E. Deysach and Nick J. Piazza, see 10:12 (1 reference).

TEST REFERENCES

1. Shelley-Mcintyre, B., & Lapidus, L. B. (1989). The relationship between psychological differentiation and performance expectation in alcoholics and normals. *Journal of Clinical Psychology, 45,* 454-461.
2. Solomon, K. E., & Annis, H. M. (1989). Development of a scale to measure outcome expectancy in alcoholics. *Cognitive Therapy and Research, 13,* 409-421.
3. Drake, R. E., Wallach, M. A., Teague, G. B., Freeman, D. H., Paskus, T. S., & Clark, T. A. (1991). Housing instability and homelessness among rural schizophrenic patients. *American Journal of Psychiatry, 148,* 330-336.
4. Rohsenow, D. J., Monti, P. M., Binkoff, J. A., Liepman, M. R., Nirenberg, T. D., & Abrams, D. B. (1991). Patient-treatment matching for alcoholic men in communication skills versus cognitive-behavioral mood management training. *Addictive Behaviors, 16,* 63-69.
5. Allen, J. P., & Litten, R. Z. (1993). Psychometric and laboratory measures to assist in the treatment of alcoholism. *Clinical Psychology Review, 13,* 223-239.

[146]

Alcohol Use Inventory.

Purpose: "To assess the nature of an individual's alcohol use pattern, and problems associated with that pattern."

Population: Adults and adolescents 16 years of age and over.

Publication Date: 1986–90.

Acronym: AUI.

Scores, 24: Social Improvement, Mental Improvement, Manage Moods, Marital Coping, Gregarious, Compulsive, Sustained, Loss of Control, Role Maladaptation, Delirium, Hangover, Marital Problems, Quantity, Guilt and Worry, Help Before, Receptivity, Awareness, Enhanced, Obsessed, Disruption 1, Disruption 2, Anxious Concern, Receptive Awareness, Alcohol Involvement.

Administration: Group.

Price Data, 1994: $20.75 per 10 reusable test booklets; $24 per hand-scoring key; $4.25–$5 per Profile Report; $9.20–$11.50 per Interpretive Report; $24 per 50 hand-scoring answer sheets and 50 profile forms; $70 per hand-scoring starter kit including manual, 10 test booklets, 50 answer sheets, 50 profile forms, and answer keys; $13.50 per manual ('90, 85 pages); $9.50 per Interpretive Report User's Guide.

Time: (35–60) minutes.

Comments: Reports are available via immediate on-site microcomputer scoring as well as through a mail-in scoring service or teleprocessing service.

Authors: John L. Horn, Kenneth W. Wanberg, and F. Mark Foster.

Publisher: NCS Assessments.

TEST REFERENCES

1. Hoffman, J. J., Hall, R. W., & Bartsch, T. W. (1987). On the relative importance of "psychopathic" personality and alcoholism on neuropsychological measures of frontal lobe dysfunction. *Journal of Abnormal Psychology, 96,* 158-160.

2. Nathan, P. E., & Skinstad, A. (1987). Outcomes of treatment for alcohol problems: Current methods, problems, and results. *Journal of Consulting and Clinical Psychology, 55,* 332-340.

3. Moore, R. H. (1988). The concurrent validity of the MacAndrew Alcoholism Scale among at-risk adolescent females. *Journal of Clinical Psychology, 44,* 1005-1008.

4. Thurber, S., Snow, M., & Thurber, J. (1989). Atecedents of gregarious alcoholism: An a priori model. *Journal of Clinical Psychology, 45,* 168-171.

5. Corbisiero, J. R., & Reznikoff, M. (1991). The relationship between personality type and style of alcohol use. *Journal of Clinical Psychology, 47,* 291-298.

6. Donat, D. C., Walters, J., & Hume, A. (1991). Personality characteristics of alcohol dependent inpatients: Relationship of MCMI subtypes to self-reported drinking behavior. *Journal of Personality Assessment, 57,* 335-344.

[147]

Algebra, Geometry and Trigonometry Test for Stds 9 and 10.

Purpose: "Intended for application after the Mathematics test for Seniors in order to determine in what specific section(s) of the subject pupils have problems."

Population: Standards 9 and 10 in South African schools.

Publication Date: 1973.

Scores: 3 tests: Algebra, Geometry, Trigonometry.

Administration: Group.

Levels: 2 overlapping levels (standards 9, 10) in a single booklet.

Price Data: Available from publisher.

Time: 90(100) minutes.

Comments: No specific manual for separate tests, combined manual (46 pages, English and Afrikaans) for three separate tests and another mathematics test; separate answer sheets (IBM 1230) must be used (specify separate tests).

Author: S. J. P. Kruger.

Publisher: Human Sciences Research Council [South Africa].

[148]

Algebra Test for Engineering and Science: National Achievement Tests.

Purpose: Designed to screen proficiency in trigonometry and geometry.

Population: College entrants.

Publication Dates: 1958–61.

Scores, 2: Test 1, Total.

Administration: Group.

Price Data, 1985: $17.50 per 25 test booklets; $4 per specimen set.

Time: 50(55) minutes for Test 1; 80(85) minutes for total test.

Author: A. B. Lonski.

Publisher: Psychometric Affiliates.

Cross References: For a review by Peter A. Lappan, Jr., see 6:595.

[149]

Alleman Leadership Development Questionnaire.

Purpose: "Measures the amount of mentoring activity between individuals or in an organization or work unit."

Population: Mentors and proteges.

Publication Dates: 1982–85.

Acronym: ALDQ.

Scores, 12: Teach the Job, Teach Politics, Assign Challenging Tasks, Career Counseling, General Counseling, Career Help, Demonstrated Trust, Endorse Acts/Views, Sponsor, Protect, Associate Socially, Friendship.

Administration: Group.

Restricted Distribution: Available for use only by those trained and certified by Leadership Development Consulting Co.

Price Data, 1987: $10 per manual ('85, 35 pages); $5 per questionnaire.

Time: (10–15) minutes.

Author: Elizabeth Alleman.

Publisher: Leadership Development Consulting Co.

TEST REFERENCES

1. Alleman, E., Cochran, J., Doverspike, J., & Newman, I. (1984). Enriching mentoring relationships. *The Personnel and Guidance Journal, 62,* 329-332.

[150]

Alleman Mentoring Scales Questionnaire.
Purpose: "Measures the amount, quality and impact of mentoring activity."
Population: Mentors and proteges.
Publication Date: 1987.
Acronym: AMSQ.
Scores, 10: Teach the Job, Teach Politics, Assign Challenging Tasks, Counsel, Career Help, Demonstrated Trust, Endorse Acts/Opinions, Sponsor, Protect, Friendship.
Administration: Group.
Forms, 4: Mentors, Proteges, Outside Observer, Hypothetical Mentor.
Price Data: Available from publisher.
Time: (10–15) minutes.
Author: Elizabeth Alleman.
Publisher: Leadership Development Consulting Co.

[151]

Alleman Relationship Value Questionnaire.
Purpose: "Designed to measure the quality of mentoring activity."
Population: Mentors and proteges.
Publication Date: 1985.
Acronym: ARVQ.
Scores, 10: Information, Politics, Counsel, Tough Job, Career Moves, Trust, Achievements, Protection, Friendship, Overall Relationship.
Administration: Group.
Forms, 2: Mentor, Protege.
Manual: No manual.
Price Data, 1987: $4 per questionnaire.
Time: Administration time not reported.
Author: Elizabeth Alleman.
Publisher: Leadership Development Consulting Co.

[152]

Allied Health Professions Admission Test.
Purpose: Developed to measure general academic ability and scientific knowledge.
Population: Applicants to 4-year allied health programs.
Publication Dates: 1979–93.
Scores, 5: Verbal Ability, Quantitative Ability, Biology, Chemistry, Reading Comprehension.
Administration: Group.
Restricted Distribution: Distribution restricted and test administered at licensed testing centers; details may be obtained from publisher.
Price Data: Available from publisher.
Time: 160–175 minutes.
Author: The Psychological Corporation.
Publisher: The Psychological Corporation.

[153]

Alphabet Mastery.
Purpose: Designed to measure a student's mastery of the letters of the alphabet.

Population: Second semester kindergarten to 2.5, second semester kindergarten and over.
Publication Date: 1975.
Scores: No scores; standards of mastery determined by examiner.
Administration: Group.
Manual: No manual (instructions for administration and scoring included on test).
Price Data, 1994: $5 per test (specify level).
Time: Administration time not reported.
Author: Enid L. Huelsberg.
Publisher: Academic Therapy Publications.
a) LEVEL 1: MANUSCRIPT.
Population: Second semester kindergarten to 2.5.
b) LEVEL 2: CURSIVE.
Population: Second semester kindergarten and over.
Cross References: For reviews by Michael D. Smith and Sally Anita Whiting, see 9:70.

[154]

Alternate Uses.
Purpose: "Designed to represent an expected factor of 'flexibility of thinking' in an investigation of creative thinking."
Population: Grades 6–16 and adults.
Publication Dates: 1960–78.
Scores: Total score only.
Administration: Group.
Forms, 2: Form B, C.
Price Data, 1984: $8 per 25 tests; $1 per scoring guide; $4 per manual ('78, 23 pages); $5 per specimen set.
Time: 12(20) minutes.
Authors: Paul R. Christensen, J. P. Guilford, Philip R. Merrifield, and Robert C. Wilson.
Publisher: Consulting Psychologists Press, Inc.
Cross References: For a review by Edys S. Quellmalz, see 9:71 (3 references); see also T3:157 (21 references), 8:235 (32 references), T2:542 (94 references), and 6:542 (7 references).

TEST REFERENCES

1. Schotte, D. E., & Clum, G. A. (1987). Problem-solving skills in suicidal psychiatric patients. *Journal of Consulting and Clinical Psychology, 55,* 49-54.
2. Russ, S. W. (1988). Primary process thinking, divergent thinking, and coping in children. *Journal of Personality Assessment, 52,* 539-548.
3. Zarnegar, Z., Hocevar, D., & Michael, W. B. (1988). Components of original thinking in gifted children. *Educational and Psychological Measurement, 48*(1), 5-16.
4. Cornish, I. M. (1989). The relationship between convergence- divergence and the free recall of discourse. *British Journal of Educational Psychology, 59,* 258-261.

[155]

The American Drug and Alcohol Survey.
Purpose: Designed to estimate levels of drug use in schools.
Population: Schools and school districts.
Publication Dates: 1989–90.
Scores: Item scores only.

Administration: Group.
Levels, 2: Grades 4–6, Grades 6–12 and college.
Price Data: Available from publisher.
Time: (20–30) minutes.
Comments: Results tabulated by publisher.
Authors: Eugene R. Oetting, Frederick Beauvais, and Ruth Edwards.
Publisher: Rocky Mountain Behavioral Science Institute, Inc.

TEST REFERENCES

1. Wright, D. M., & Heppner, P. P. (1993). Examining the well-being of nonclinical college students: Is knowledge of the presence of parental alcoholism useful? *Journal of Counseling Psychology, 40,* 324-334.

[156]

American High School Mathematics Examination.

Purpose: "To identify, through friendly competition, students with an interest and a talent for mathematical problem solving."
Population: High school students competing for individual and school awards.
Publication Dates: 1950–88.
Acronym: AHSME.
Scores: Total score only.
Administration: Group.
Price Data, 1989: $15 per school registration fee; $.60 per exam (specify English or Spanish); $4 per 10 solutions pamphlets; $.50 per specimen set of prior year exams (specify year and English or Spanish); price data available from publisher for additional study aids and supplementary materials.
Foreign Language and Special Editions: Spanish, Braille, and large-print editions available.
Time: 90(100) minutes.
Comments: Test administered annually in February or March at participating secondary schools.
Authors: Sponsored jointly by the Mathematical Association of America, Society of Actuaries, Mu Alpha Theta, National Council of Teachers of Mathematics, Casualty Actuarial Society, American Statistical Association, and American Mathematical Association of Two-Year Colleges.
Publisher: Mathematical Association of America; American Mathematical Society.
Cross References: For reviews by Camilla Persson Benbow and Randy W. Kamphaus, see 11:13; for a review by Thomas P. Hogan, see 8:252 (1 reference); see also T2:598 (3 references).

[157]

American History: Junior High—Objective.

Purpose: Designed to assess students' general knowledge of American history.
Population: 1, 2 semesters Grades 7–9.
Publication Dates: 1963–70.
Scores: Total score only for each test.
Administration: Group.
Scores: 12 tests: Exploration and Colonization, Revolutionary America, Foundation of a Strong Government, The Development of Democracy, Westward Expansion, First Semester Test, Division and Reunion, A Modern America, America Becomes a World Power, Post World War II, Second Semester Test, Final Test.
Manual: No manual.
Price Data, 1994: $9.95 per test book including tests and response key.
Time: Administration time not reported.
Comments: Formerly called Objective Tests in American History.
Author: John Barrett.
Publisher: Perfection Learning Corp.

[158]

American History: Senior High—Objective.

Purpose: To assess students' general knowledge of American history.
Population: 1, 2 semesters high school.
Publication Dates: 1960–70.
Scores: Total score only for each of 13 tests: The Heritage of Colonial America, Background of the Revolutionary War/the Revolutionary War and Establishing a New Government (1763–1789), The United States Constitution, Washington's Administration Through the War of 1812, Expansion Westward and the Jacksonian Era (1815 thru 1841), Expansion/War and Reconstruction (1841–1868), First Semester Examination, The Emergence of Modern America, The United States Becomes a World Power (Spanish–American War/World War I/and Settlement 1896–1921), Prosperity and Depression (1920 thru 1940), World Leadership (1940–Present), Second Semester Examination, Final Examination.
Administration: Group.
Manual: No manual.
Price Data, 1994: $12.95 per test book including tests and response key.
Time: [50] minutes per unit test; [60] minutes per test for other tests.
Comments: Formerly called Objective Tests in American History.
Author: Earl Bridgewater.
Publisher: Perfection Learning Corp.

[159]

The American Home Scale.

Purpose: "Designed to measure the socioeconomic status of individuals and groups."
Population: Grades 8–16.
Publication Date: 1942.
Scores, 5: Cultural, Aesthetic, Economic, Miscellaneous, Total.
Administration: Group.
Price Data: Available from publisher.
Time: (35–50) minutes.
Author: W. A. Kerr.
Publisher: Psychometric Affiliates.
Cross References: See T2:1039 (5 references) and 5:596 (2 references); for reviews by Henry S. Maas and Verner M. Sims, see 3:417 (7 references).

[160]
American Invitational Mathematics Examination.

Purpose: "Provides challenge and recognition to high school students in the United States and Canada who have exceptional mathematical ability."

Population: American and Canadian high school students.

Publication Dates: 1983–88.

Acronym: AIME.

Scores: Total score only.

Administration: Group.

Manual: No manual.

Price Data, 1989: $1 per practice examination set including past exam (specify year desired 1983–present) and solution pamphlet; other price data available from publisher.

Time: 180 minutes.

Comments: Administered annually, three weeks after the American High School Mathematics Examination (156), to students attaining a predetermined cutoff score on the AHSME.

Authors: Sponsored jointly by the Mathematical Association of America, Society of Actuaries, Mu Alpha Theta, National Council on Teachers of Mathematics, Casualty Actuarial Society, American Statistical Association, and American Mathematical Association of Two Year Colleges.

Publisher: Mathematics Association of America; American Mathematical Society.

Cross References: For reviews by Robert W. Lissitz and Claudia R. Wright, see 11:14.

[161]
American Junior High School Mathematics Examination.

Purpose: "To increase interest in mathematics and to develop problem solving ability through a friendly competition."

Population: American and Canadian students in grade 8 or below.

Publication Date: 1985–88.

Acronym: AJHSME.

Scores: Total score only.

Administration: Group.

Price Data, 1988: $10 per school registration fee; $10 per 25 exam booklets.

Special Edition: Braille and large-print editions available.

Time: 40 minutes.

Comments: Test administered annually in December at participating schools.

Authors: Sponsored jointly by Mathematical Association of America, Society of Actuaries, Mu Alpha Theta, National Council of Teachers of Mathematics, Casualty Actuarial Society, American Statistical Association, and American Mathematical Association of Two Year Colleges.

Publisher: Mathematics Association of America; American Mathematical Society.

Cross References: For reviews by John M. Enger and Darrell Sabers, see 11:15.

[162]
American Literacy Test.

Purpose: Constructed to assess literacy based on vocabulary.

Population: Adults.

Publication Date: 1962.

Scores: Total score only.

Administration: Group.

Price Data, 1985: $5 per 25 test booklets; $4 per specimen set.

Time: 4 minutes.

Author: John J. McCarty.

Publisher: Psychometric Affiliates.

Cross References: For a review by Victor H. Noll, see 6:328.

[163]
American Numerical Test.

Purpose: Designed to assess "numerical alertness and adaptation."

Population: Adults in "vocations which emphasize shop and white collar skills."

Publication Date: 1962.

Scores: Total score only.

Administration: Group.

Price Data, 1985: $5 per 25 test booklets; $4 per specimen set including manual (2 pages).

Time: 4 minutes.

Author: John J. McCarty.

Publisher: Psychometric Affiliates.

Cross References: For reviews by Marvin D. Glock and Richard T. Johnson, see 6:604.

[164]
The American Occupational Therapy Association, Inc. Fieldwork Evaluation for the Occupational Therapist.

Purpose: Constructed to evaluate "student competence at the completion of each Level II fieldwork experience."

Population: Occupational therapy students.

Publication Dates: 1973–87.

Scores, 3: Performance, Judgment, Attitude.

Administration: Individual.

Price Data: Available from publisher.

Time: Administration time not reported.

Comments: Ratings by supervisor; revision of the Field Work Performance Report (T3:885).

Authors: The American Occupational Therapy Association, Inc.

Publisher: The American Occupational Therapy Association, Inc.

Cross References: For information on the Field Work Performance Report, see T3:885 (2 references) and 8:1107 (1 reference).

[165]

Analysis of Readiness Skills: Reading and Mathematics.

Purpose: Developed to assess readiness in reading and mathematics.
Population: Grades K–1.
Publication Dates: 1969–72.
Scores, 5: Visual Perception of Letters, Letter Identification, Mathematics (Identification, Counting), Total.
Administration: Group.
Price Data, 1990: $25.80 per complete kit including 25 test booklets, scoring key, class record sheet, sample item chart, and manual ('72, 23 pages); $8.40 per manual including scoring key and class record sheet; $8.40 per specimen set.
Time: (30–40) minutes.
Comments: Orally administered in English or Spanish.
Authors: Mary C. Rodrigues, William H. Vogler, and James F. Wilson.
Publisher: The Riverside Publishing Co.
Cross References: See T3:178 (1 reference); for reviews by John T. Guthrie and Charles T. Myers, see 8:796.

[166]

Analytic Learning Disability Assessment.

Purpose: Designed to match student learning style with instructional strategies.
Population: Ages 8–14.
Publication Date: 1982.
Acronym: ALDA.
Scores: Fail, Weak, or Solid in 77 unit skill subtests.
Administration: Individual.
Price Data, 1992: $110 per complete kit; $35 per 20 test forms including test score formulation sheet and student worksheets.
Time: (75) minutes.
Authors: Thomas D. Gnagey and Patricia A. Gnagey.
Publisher: Slosson Educational Publications, Inc.
Cross References: For a review by Marcia B. Shaffer, see 9:72.

[167]

Analyzing the Communication Environment.

Purpose: "An inventory of ways to encourage communication in functional activities."
Population: Preschool to adolescent children with severe disabilities.
Publication Date: 1993.
Acronym: ACE.
Scores: Total score only.
Administration: Individual.
Price Data, 1994: $99 per complete kit including 90-minute VHS videotape and instructor's guide (80 pages).
Time: Administration time not reported.
Authors: Charity Rowland and Philip Schweigert.
Publisher: Communication Skill Builders.

[168]

Ann Arbor Learning Inventory.

Purpose: To evaluate competencies in visual, memory, aural, and comprehension skills.
Population: Grades K–1, 2–4, 5–8.
Publication Dates: 1977–89.
Administration: Group.
Price Data, 1991: $10 per manual (specify Level A ['82, 62 pages], Level B ['87, 58 pages], or Level C ['89, 64 pages]); $12 per 10 student booklets (specify level); $8 per Level C stimulus cards.
Time: Administration time not reported.
Authors: Barbara Meister Vitale and Waneta B. Bullock.
Publisher: Academic Therapy Publications.

a) SKILL LEVEL A.
Population: Grades K–1.
Scores, 7: Body Image, Visual Discrimination Skills, Visual Motor Coordination Skills, Visual Sequential Memory Skills, Aural Discrimination Skills, Aural Sequential Memory Skills, Aural Conceptual Skills.
b) SKILL LEVEL B.
Population: Grades 2–4.
Scores, 5: Visual Discrimination Skills, Visual Motor Coordination Skills, Sequential Memory Skills, Auditory Discrimination Skills, Comprehension Skills.
c) SKILL LEVEL C.
Population: Grades 5–8.
Scores, 6: Visual Discrimination Skills, Visual Motor Coordination Skills, Visual Sequential Memory Skills, Auditory Discrimination Skills, Auditory Sequential Memory Skills, Comprehension Skills.
Cross References: For reviews by June Ellen Shepherd and Ruth E. Tomes, see 11:16.

[169]

The Anomalous Sentences Repetition Test.

Purpose: Constructed to differentiate between dementia and depression.
Population: Ages 55 and over.
Publication Date: 1988.
Acronym: ASRT.
Scores: Total error score only.
Administration: Individual.
Price Data, 1992: £40.25 per complete kit including 25 record forms and manual (24 pages); £23 per 25 record forms.
Time: (5) minutes.
Author: David J. Weeks.
Publisher: NFER-Nelson Publishing Co., Ltd. [England].

[170]

The ANSER System Aggregate Neurobehavioral Student Health and Educational Review.

Purpose: "Assess the development, behavior, and health of children."

Population: Ages 3–12 + .
Publication Dates: 1980–85.
Acronym: The ANSER.
Scores: No scores: Parent Questionnaire covers 11 areas (Family History, Possible Pregnancy Problems, Newborn Infant Problems, Health Problems, Functional Problems, Early Development, Early Educational Experience, Skills and Interests, Activity-Attention Problems, Associated Behaviors, Associated Strengths); School Questionnaire covers Educational Setting and Program, Special Facilities Available, Results of Previous Testing, and 3 checklists (Performance Area, Activity-Attention Behavioral Observations, Associated Behavioral Observations).
Administration: Individual.
Levels, 3: Ages 3–5, 6–11, 12 + .
Price Data, 1988: $8 per Interpreter's Guide for Forms 1, 2, 3, and 4 (48 pages); $8 per specimen set (Interpreter's Guide for Forms 1, 2, 3, and 4) and sample pages from each form; $11.50 per 12 Parent Questionnaire (specify Form 1, 2, or 3); $10.50 per School Questionnaire (specify Form 1); $10 per 12 School Questionnaire (specify Form 2 or 3); $10 per 12 self-administered student profile; $11.50 per Parent Follow-Up Questionnaire, Form 5P (per 2 dozen) and Interpreter's Guide for Forms 5 and 6; $11.50 per School Follow-Up Questionnaire, Form 5S (per 2 dozen) and Interpreter's Guide for Forms 5 and 6; $11.50 per Self-Administered Follow-Up Profile, Form 6 (per 2 dozen) and Interpreter's Guide for Forms 5 and 6; $4 per specimen set (Interpreter's Guide for Forms 5 and 6 and one each of Forms 5P, 5S, and 6).
Time: Administration time not reported.
Comments: Series of questionnaires to be completed by parents, school personnel, and students; for use with children possessing learning and/or behavioral problems.
Author: Melvin D. Levine.
Publisher: Educators Publishing Service, Inc.
Cross References: For reviews by Robert G. Harrington and Kenneth W. Howell, see 9:74.

[171]

Anxiety Disorders Interview Schedule—Revised.
Purpose: To assist in diagnosing individuals with prominent anxiety symptoms.
Population: Adults.
Publication Dates: 1983–88.
Acronym: ADIS-R.
Scores, 8: DSM-III-R Diagnoses (Axis I, Axis II, Axis III, Axis IV, Axis V), Hamilton Anxiety Rating Scale, Hamilton Depression Rating Scale, Diagnostic Confidence Rating.
Administration: Individual.
Price Data, 1993: $4 per test booklet (minimum of 10); price data for specimen set including 1 manual ('88, 14 pages) and 1 test booklet available from publisher.
Time: Administration time not reported.

Authors: Peter A. DiNardo and David H. Barlow.
Publisher: Graywind Publications Incorporated.

TEST REFERENCES

1. Gross, P. R., & Eifert, G. H. (1990). Delineating generalized anxiety: A preliminary investigation. *Journal of Psychopathology and Behavioral Assessment, 12,* 345-358.
2. Turner, S. M., Beidel, D. C., & Jacob, R. G. (1994). Social phobia: A comparison of behavior therapy and atenolol. *Journal of Consulting and Clinical Psychology, 62,* 350-358.

[172]

The Anxiety Scale for the Blind.
Purpose: Designed as an "instrument for measuring manifest anxiety among blind persons."
Population: Blind and partially sighted ages 13 and over.
Publication Date: 1966–68.
Acronym: ASB.
Scores: Total score only.
Administration: Individual.
Price Data: Available from publisher.
Time: (45–50) minutes.
Author: Richard E. Hardy.
Publisher: American Foundation for the Blind.
Cross References: For an excerpted review by Barton B. Proger, see 8:498 (1 reference); see also T2:1100 (1 reference) and P:8 (3 references).

[173]

Anxiety Scales for Children and Adults.
Purpose: "To determine the presence and intensity of anxiety in adults and school-age children."
Population: Grade 2–adult.
Publication Date: 1993.
Acronym: ASCA.
Scores: Total score only.
Administration: Group.
Editions, 2: Youth, Adult.
Price Data, 1994: $84 per complete kit including examiner's manual (26 pages), 50 Forms Q, 50 Forms M, scoring acetate, and administration audiocassette; $31 per examiner's manual; $19 per 50 Form Q; $19 per 50 Form M; $6 per scoring acetate; $14 per administration audiocassette.
Time: (10–15) minutes.
Comments: Self-report; Form Q for children and Form M for adults.
Author: James Battle.
Publisher: PRO-ED, Inc.

[174]

AO Sight Screener.
Purpose: A portable vision screening instrument used "in determining if an individual requires a professional visual examination."
Population: Adults.
Publication Dates: 1945–56.
Administration: Individual.
Price Data: Not available.
Time: [3–5] minutes.
Comments: Targets are available for both readers and nonreaders of English letters and numbers.

Publisher: American Optical Corporation, Industrial Safety Division [No reply from publisher; status unknown].
Cross References: See T2:1906 (8 references) and 5:770 (8 references); for reviews by Henry A. Imus and F. Nowell Jones, see 3:460 (7 references).

[175]

Aphasia Diagnostic Profiles.

Purpose: "Provides a systematic method of assessing language and communication impairment associated with aphasia."
Population: Adults with acquired brain damage.
Publication Date: 1992.
Acronym: ADP.
Scores: Behavioral Profile Score plus 9 subtests: Personal Information, Writing, Reading, Fluency, Naming, Auditory Comprehension, Repetition, Elicited Gestures, Singing.
Administration: Individual.
Price Data, 1991: $138.99 per complete kit including 24 record forms, manual (55 pages), stimulus cards/letterboard/pointer, and carrying case; $36 per 24 record forms; $39.99 per manual; $39.99 per stimulus cards/letterboard/pointer; $24.99 per carrying case.
Time: (40–50) minutes.
Author: Nancy Helm-Estabrooks.
Publisher: The Riverside Publishing Company.

[176]

Applied Knowledge Test.

Purpose: Constructed to assess competence in utilizing math, English, science, and spatial relationship skills for the execution of tasks.
Population: Ages 14–18.
Publication Date: Test materials not dated.
Acronym: AKT.
Scores, 4: Maths, English, Science, Space.
Administration: Group.
Price Data, 1989: $10.55 per complete kit including 25 test booklets, scoring key, and manual (6 pages).
Time: 55(60) minutes.
Author: M. A. Brimer.
Publisher: Educational Evaluation Enterprises [England].
Cross References: For a review by Yong H. Sung, Hei-Ki Dong, and Steven Goldman, see 9:75.

[177]

Appraisal Interview and Card Sort.

Purpose: Designed for self and management team analysis using a card sort based on essential management qualities.
Population: Professionals and managers.
Publication Date: 1958.
Acronym: MAI.
Scores: 20 rating areas.
Administration: Individual or group.
Price Data: Available from publisher.

Time: Administration time not reported.
Comments: Workshop required; used in conjunction with Survey of Management Perception (2654).
Author: Management Research Associates.
Publisher: Management Research Associates.

[178]

Appraise Your World.

Purpose: Constructed "to measure the complexity and richness of the way individuals develop their personal worlds and make life choices."
Population: Adults.
Publication Dates: 1983–90.
Acronym: AYW.
Scores: 27 dimensions: Emphasis (Career, Economic, Community, Interpersonal, Recreation, Travel, Nature, Palate, Arts, Practical Arts, Home, Romance, Family, Intellectual, Ideological, Physical, Emotional, Spiritual), World Dynamics (Level of Experienced Security, Level of Total Satisfaction, Internal Focus of World, External Focus of World, Flexibility of Boundaries, Level of Growth, Balance of World, Level of Public Success, Level of Present Support).
Administration: Group.
Price Data: Not available.
Time: (45) minutes.
Authors: James T. Mahoney, Joan W. Chadbourne (test), and F. Carl Mahoney (manual).
Publisher: Management Research Group [No reply from publisher; status unknown].

[179]

Apraxia Battery for Adults.

Purpose: Designed "to verify the presence of apraxia in the adult patient and to gain a rough estimate of the severity of the disorder."
Population: Adult patients.
Publication Date: 1979.
Acronym: ABA.
Scores: 6 subtests: Diadochokinetic Rate, Increasing Word Length, Limb Apraxia and Oral Apraxia, Latency and Utterance Time for Polysyllabic Words, Repeated Trials Test, Inventory of Articulation Characteristics of Apraxia.
Administration: Individual.
Price Data, 1994: $69 per complete kit; $39 per 50 response forms and summary/profile sheets; $32 per manual (23 pages) and picture plates.
Time: (20) minutes.
Author: Barbara L. Dabul.
Publisher: PRO-ED, Inc.
Cross References: For a review by Norma Cooke, see 9:77 (1 reference).

TEST REFERENCES

1. Dworkin, J. P., Abkarian, G. G., & Johns, D. F. (1988). Apraxia of speech: The effectiveness of a treatment regimen. *Journal of Speech and Hearing Disorders, 53,* 280-294.
2. Odell, K., McNeil, M. R., Rosenbek, J. C., & Hunter, L. (1990). Perceptual characteristics of consonant production by apraxic speakers. *Journal of Speech and Hearing Disorders, 55,* 345-359.

3. Ordell, K., McNeil, M. R., Rosenbek, J. C., & Hunter, L. (1991). Perceptual characteristics of vowel and prosody production in apraxic, aphasic, and dysarthric speakers. *Journal of Speech and Hearing Research, 34,* 67-80.

4. Baum, S. R., & Ryan, L. (1993). Rate of speech effects in aphasia: Voice onset time. *Brain and Language, 44,* 431-445.

[180]

Aprenda: La Prueba De Logros en Español.
Purpose: Designed as a "norm-referenced achievement test for Spanish-speaking students."
Publication Dates: 1990–91.
Administration: Group.
Price Data, 1994: $19.50 each examination kit (Primary 1–Intermediate 3) including test booklet and directions for administering ('90, 47 pages), practice test and directions, and hand-scorable answer folder (Preprimer–$18.50); $12.50 for 25 practice tests and directions; $92.50 for machine-scorable test booklets and $63 for hand-scorable test booklets (Preprimer through Primary 1); $63 for reusable test booklets and $14.50 for hand- and machine-scorable answer folders (Intermediate 1–3); $25.50 per norms booklet; $19 per index of instructional objectives; $35 per technical data report; $47.50 per multilevel norms booklet ('91, 173 pages); price data for scoring services available from publisher.
Foreign Language Edition: Test booklets written in Spanish.
Author: The Psychological Corporation.
Publisher: The Psychological Corporation.

a) PREPRIMER (NIVEL PREPRIMARIO).
Population: Grades K.*5*–*1.5.*
Scores, 7: Sounds and Letters, Word Reading, Sentence Reading, Total Reading, Listening to Words and Stories, Mathematics, Total.
Time: (145) minutes.

b) PRIMARY 1 (PRIMER NIVEL PRIMARIO).
Population: Grades *1.5*–*2.5.*
Scores, 11: Word Reading, Reading Comprehension, Total Reading, Language, Spelling, Listening, Concepts of Numbers, Mathematics Computation, Mathematics Applications, Total Mathematics, Total.
Time: (235) minutes.

c) PRIMARY 2 (SEGUNDO NIVEL PRIMARIO).
Population: Grades *2.5*–*3.5.*
Scores, 11: Reading Vocabulary, Reading Comprehension, Total Reading, Language, Spelling, Listening, Concepts of Numbers, Mathematics Computations, Mathematics Applications, Total Mathematics, Total.
Time: (230) minutes.

d) PRIMARY 3 (TERCER NIVEL PRIMARIO).
Population: Grades *3.5*–*4.5.*
Scores, 14: Reading Vocabulary, Reading Comprehension, Total Reading, Language Mechanics, Language Expression, Total Language, Study Skills, Spelling, Listening, Concepts of Number, Mathematics Computation, Mathematics Applications, Total Mathematics, Total.
Time: (275) minutes.

e) INTERMEDIATE 1 (PRIMER NIVEL INTERMEDIO).
Population: Grades *4.5*–*5.5.*
Scores, 14: Reading Vocabulary, Reading Comprehension, Total Reading, Language Mechanics, Language Expression, Total Language, Study Skills, Spelling, Listening, Concepts of Numbers, Mathematics Computation, Mathematics Applications, Total Mathematics, Total.
Time: (285) minutes.

f) INTERMEDIATE 2 (SEGUNDO NIVEL INTERMEDIO).
Population: Grades *5.5*–*6.5.*
Scores: Same as *e* above.
Time: Same as *e* above.

g) INTERMEDIATE 3 (TERCER NIVEL INTERMEDIO).
Population: Grades *6.5*–*9.1.*
Scores: Same as *e* above.
Time: Same as *e* above.

[181]

The APT Inventory.
Purpose: Designed to measure an individual's relative strength on each of ten personal traits.
Population: Adults.
Publication Date: 1992.
Scores, 10: Communication, Analytical Thinking, Administrative, Relating to Others, Influencing, Achieving, Empowering, Developing, Leadership, Ethics.
Administration: Individual or group.
Manual: No manual.
Price Data, 1992: $100 per 20 sets (each set includes assessment, response sheet, and interpretation booklet).
Time: (40) minutes.
Comments: Self-administered; self-scored.
Author: Training House, Inc.
Publisher: Training House, Inc.

[182]

APT Manual Dexterity Test.
Purpose: To measure the factors of concrete visual imagery, manual dexterity including the use of tools, and finger dexterity for motor mechanics and related subordinate mechanical positions.
Population: Automobile and truck mechanics and mechanics' helpers.
Publication Dates: 1960–63.
Scores: Total time to complete task.
Administration: Group or individual.
Price Data: Not available.
Time: (10–20) minutes.
Author: Bentley Barnabas.
Publisher: Associated Personnel Technicians, Inc. [No reply from publisher; status unknown].

[183]

Aptitude Assessment Battery: Programming.
Purpose: Designed to measure programming aptitude.
Population: Programmers and trainees.
Publication Dates: 1967.

Acronym: AABP.
Scores: Total score only.
Administration: Group.
Restricted Distribution: Restricted to employers of programmers, not available to school personnel.
Price Data, 1993: $229 per candidate.
Foreign Language Edition and Other Special Editions: French, Spanish, and left-handed editions available.
Time: Untimed.
Comments: Percentile and qualitative information provided in detailed report.
Author: Jack M. Wolfe.
Publisher: Walden Personnel Testing & Training, Inc.
Cross References: See 7:1087 (1 reference).

[184]

Aptitude for and Sensitivity to Music.
Purpose: To screen for music aptitude and musical sensitivity.
Population: Standards 3–10 in South African school system and college.
Publication Date: 1982.
Forms: 2.
Administration: Group.
Price Data: Available from publisher.
Comments: Record player necessary for administration; all test materials available in English and Afrikaans.
Authors: A. W. Wegelin and K. Owen.
Publisher: Human. Sciences Research Council [South Africa].
a) JUNIOR FORM.
Acronym: ASM J.
Scores, 8: Sensitivity to Music (Fantasy, Various Endings, Mood, Total), Musical Aptitude (Interval, Rhythm, Total), Total.
Time: [90] minutes.
b) SENIOR FORM.
Acronym: ASM S.
Time: [135] minutes.
1) *High School.*
Scores, 10: Musical Aptitude (Interval, Harmony, Rhythm, Total), Sensitivity to Music (Selective Listening, Performance, Accompaniment, Mood, Total), Total.
2) *College.*
Scores, 11: Musical Aptitude (Interval, Harmony, Rhythm, Total), Sensitivity to Music (Selective Listening, Performance, Accompaniment, Mood, Degrees of Musical Enjoyment, Total), Total.

[185]

Aptitude Test Battery for Adults.
Purpose: To provide a measure of intellectual abilities especially as these abilities relate to selection and placement for training in certain fields of work.
Population: Long-term "Black" South African prisoners who have passed Standard 5.

Publication Date: 1979.
Acronym: AA.
Scores, 9: Comparison, Figure Series, Calculations, Reasoning, Mechanical Insight, Spatial Visualization/2-D, Classification, Spatial Visualization/3-D, Components.
Administration: Group.
Price Data: Available from publisher.
Time: 183(188) minutes.
Comments: Test booklet title is Aptitude Test for Adults; test booklet and manual in Afrikaans and English.
Authors: J. J. Taljaard and J. S. Gericke (test).
Publisher: Human Sciences Research Council [South Africa].

[186]

Aptitude Tests for School Beginners.
Purpose: "Obtain a differentiated picture of certain aptitudes of school beginners."
Population: Grade 1 entrants.
Publication Dates: 1974–75.
Acronym: ASB.
Scores, 8: Perception, Spatial, Reasoning, Numerical, Gestalt, Co-ordination, Memory, Verbal Comprehension (optional for Bantus, omitted for Indians).
Administration: Group.
Price Data: Available from publisher.
Time: (390–450) minutes for full battery, (180–240) minutes for abbreviated battery.
Comments: An abbreviated battery (Reasoning, Numerical, and Gestalt subtests) may be administered to obtain total score only.
Authors: D. J. Swart (manuals), T. M. Coetzee (manual for *a*), Margaretha Tredoux (manual for *b*), and N. M. Oliver (manual for *d*).
Publisher: Human Sciences Research Council [South Africa].
a) [BANTU EDITION].
Publication Dates: 1974–75.
Foreign Language Editions: Verbal Comprehension subtest in English and Afrikaans; instructions in 5 Bantu languages: N/Sotho, Tsonga, Venda, Xhosa, Zulu.
b) [COLOURED EDITION.]
Publication Date: 1974.
Foreign Language Editions: Verbal Comprehension subtest in English and Afrikaans; manual available in Afrikaans.
c) [INDIAN EDITION.]
Publication Date: 1974.
d) [WHITE EDITION.]
Publication Date: 1974.
Foreign Language Editions: Verbal Comprehension subtest available in English and Afrikaans; manual available in Afrikaans.

TEST REFERENCES

1. Oosthuizen, S. (1991). Mathematical abilities of preschool children as measured by the Aptitude Test for School Beginners. *Perceptual and Motor Skills, 73,* 1075-1080.

[187]

Aptitudes Associates Test of Sales Aptitude: A Test for Measuring Knowledge of Basic Principles of Selling.
Purpose: Designed to aid in the appraisal of one aspect of sales aptitude, understanding and appreciation of sales techniques.
Population: Applicants for sales positions and general population.
Publication Dates: 1947–84.
Scores: Total score only.
Administration: Group.
Price Data, 1987: Available from publisher.
Time: (20–30) minutes.
Author: Martin M. Bruce.
Publisher: Martin M. Bruce, Ph.D., Publishers.
Cross References: See 6:1169 (6 references); for reviews by Milton E. Hahn and Donald G. Paterson, see 4:824.

[188]

Arithmetic Reasoning Test.
Purpose: Intended to predict success in mathematical activities.
Publication Date: 1985.
Acronym: ART.
Scores: Item scores only.
Administration: Group.
Price Data: Available from publisher.
Foreign Language Edition: Test printed in both English and Afrikaans.
Authors: T. R. Taylor and M. E. Halstead.
Publisher: National Institute for Personnel Research of the Human Sciences Research Council [South Africa].
a) STANDARD LEVEL ARITHMETIC REASONING TEST.
Population: Individuals with 10–12 years of formal schooling.
Acronym: ART-SL.
Time: 35(45) minutes.
b) HIGH LEVEL ARITHMETIC REASONING TEST.
Population: Individuals with 12 years or more of formal schooling.
Acronym: ART-HL.
Time: 39(49) minutes.

[189]

Arithmetic Test (Fundamentals and Reasoning): Municipal Tests: National Achievement Tests.
Purpose: Constructed to assess arithmetic skills.
Population: Grades 3–6, 6–8.
Publication Dates: 1938–62.
Scores, 6: Computation, Number Comparisons, Comparisons, Problem Analysis, Problems, Total.
Administration: Group.
Forms, 2: A, B.
Price Data, 1985: $5 per 25 test booklets (select level); $4 per specimen set including manual.

Time: 60 minutes over 2 sessions.
Comments: Subtest of Municipal Battery.
Authors: Robert K. Speer and Samuel Smith.
Publisher: Psychometric Affiliates.
Cross References: For reviews by Foster E. Grossnickle and Charles S. Ross, see 4:406. For reviews of the complete battery, see 5:18 (1 review), 4:20 (1 review), and 2:1191 (2 reviews).

[190]

Arithmetic Test: National Achievement Tests.
Population: Grades 3–8.
Publication Dates: 1936–61.
Administration: Group.
Forms, 2: A, B.
Manual: No manual.
Price Data: Available from publisher.
Authors: Robert K. Speer and Samuel Smith.
Publisher: Psychometric Affiliates.
a) FUNDAMENTALS.
Purpose: Constructed to assess "speed, knowledge, and accuracy in computation."
Scores, 4: Fundamentals-Speed, Number Comparisons, Fundamentals-Skills, Total.
Time: (55–85) minutes.
b) REASONING.
Purpose: Designed to measure ability to compare, comprehend, analyze, and solve problems.
Scores, 5: Comparisons, Problem Analysis, Finding the Key to a Problem, Problems, Total.
Time: (40) minutes.
Cross References: For reviews by R. L. Morton and Leroy H. Schnell, see 2:1449; for reviews by William A. Brownell and W. J. Osburn, see 1:889.

[191]

Arizona Articulation Proficiency Scale, Second Edition.
Purpose: Intended as a "clinical measure of articulatory competence in children."
Population: Ages 1-6 to 13-11.
Publication Dates: 1963–86.
Acronym: AAPS.
Scores: Total score only.
Administration: Individual.
Price Data, 1993: $100 per complete kit; $57.50 per set of picture test cards; $16.50 per 25 protocol booklets; $19.50 per 100 survey forms; $27.50 per manual.
Time: (10–15) minutes.
Comments: Total score is provided in the form of severity rating, percentile, standard score, developmental age equivalent, and intelligibility description.
Authors: Janet Barker Fudala and William M. Reynolds.
Publisher: Western Psychological Services.
Cross References: For reviews by Penelope K. Hall and Charles Wm. Martin, see 11:17 (12 references); for information regarding an earlier edition, see T3:200 (8 references); for reviews by Raphael M. Haller and Ronald K. Sommers, and an excerpted

review by Barton B. Proger, see 8:954 (6 references); see also T2:2065 (2 references), 7:948 (2 references), and 6:307a (2 references).

TEST REFERENCES

1. Young, E. C., & Thompson, C. K. (1987). An experimental analysis of treatment effects on consonant clusters and ambisyllabic consonants in two adults with developmental phonological problems. *Journal of Communication Disorders, 20,* 137-149.
2. Lehman, M. E., & Sharf, D. J. (1989). Perception/production relationships in the development of the vowel duration cue to final consonant voicing. *Journal of Speech and Hearing Research, 32,* 803-815.
3. Ziegler, M., Tallal, P., & Curtiss, S. (1990). Selecting language-impaired children for research studies: Insights from the San Diego longitudinal study. *Perceptual and Motor Skills, 71,* 1079-1089.
4. Ryan, B. P. (1992). Articulation, language, rate, and fluency characteristics of stuttering and nonstuttering preschool children. *Journal of Speech and Hearing Research, 35,* 333-342.

[192]

The Arizona Battery For Communication Disorders of Dementia.

Purpose: To measure "the effects and severity of Alzheimer's Disease."
Population: Alzheimer's patients.
Publication Date: 1991.
Acronym: ABCD.
Scores, 6: Mental Status, Episodic Memory, Linguistic Expression, Linguistic Comprehension, Visuospatial Construction, Total.
Administration: Individual.
Price Data, 1994: $235 per complete kit including manual (64 pages), scoring and interpretation card, 25 response record forms, stimulus book A, stimulus book B, and nail and envelope; $40 per 25 response record forms.
Time: (45–90) minutes.
Authors: Kathryn A. Bayles and Cheryl K. Tomoeda.
Publisher: Communication Skill Builders, Inc. [distributor].

[193]

Arlin-Hills Attitude Surveys.

Purpose: Designed to measure the attitudes of a group of students "toward Teacher, Learning Processes, Language Arts, and Mathematics."
Population: Grades K–3, 4–6, 7–12.
Publication Date: 1976.
Scores: 4 subtests: Attitude Toward Language Arts, Attitude Toward Learning Processes, Attitude Toward Mathematics, Attitude Toward Teachers.
Administration: Group.
Price Data, 1987: $8.25 per 25 survey forms (specify subtest); $1.75 per administration/scoring card; $6.75 per manual (41 pages); $9 per specimen set including one survey each for 4 subtests, administration card, and manual.
Time: (10–15) minutes.
Comments: For measurement of groups, not individuals.
Author: Marshall Arlin.
Publisher: Psychologists and Educators, Inc.
Cross References: See T3:201 (2 references) and 8:499 (1 reference).

[194]

Arlin Test of Formal Reasoning.

Purpose: Designed to assess "individual's ability to use the eight specific concepts associated with (Piaget's) stages of formal operations"; profiles individual as "concrete, high concrete, transitional, low formal, or high formal."
Population: Grades 6–12 and adults.
Publication Date: 1984.
Acronym: ATFR.
Scores, 9: Volume, Probability, Correlations, Combinations, Propositions, Momentum, Mechanical Equilibrium, Frames of Reference, Total.
Administration: Group.
Price Data, 1992: $60 per complete kit; $12 per manual (28 pages).
Time: (45–50) minutes.
Author: Patricia Kennedy Arlin.
Publisher: Slosson Educational Publications, Inc.
Cross References: For a review by Toni E. Santmire, see 9:80 (5 references).

TEST REFERENCES

1. Bloland, R. M., & Michael, W. B. (1984). A comparison of the relative validity of a measure of Piagetian cognitive development and a set of conventional prognostic measures in the prediction of the future success of ninth- and tenth-grade students in algebra. *Educational and Psychological Measurement, 44,* 925-943.
2. Lim, T. K. (1988). Relationships between standardized psychometric and Piagetian measures of intelligence at the formal operations level. *Intelligence, 12,* 167-182.
3. Hagborg, W. J., & Wachman, E. M. (1992). The Arlin Test of Formal Reasoning and the identification of accelerated mathematics students. *Educational and Psychological Measurement, 52,* 437-442.

[195]

Armed Services-Civilian Vocational Interest Survey.

Purpose: Designed to assess interest in careers in the armed-services and related civilian jobs.
Population: Grades 11–12.
Publication Date: 1983.
Acronym: ASCVIS.
Scores: Ratings in 8 occupational groups: Administrative/Clerical/Personnel, Communications, Computer and Data-Processing, Construction/Engineering/Craft, Mechanical/Repairer/Machining, Service and Transportation, Health and Health Care, Scientific/Technical/Electronic.
Administration: Group.
Price Data, 1990: $16 per 35 folders.
Time: (30) minutes.
Comments: Self-administering and self-scoring; may be used in conjunction with the ASVAB (196).
Author: Robert Kauk.
Publisher: CFKR Career Materials, Inc.
Cross References: For reviews by Bruce W. Hartman and Frederick A. Schrank, see 10:13.

[196]

Armed Services Vocational Aptitude Battery [Forms 18/19].

Purpose: Intended "for use in educational and vocational counseling and to stimulate interest in job and training opportunities in the Armed Forces."

Population: High school, junior college, and young adult applicants to the Armed Forces.

Publication Dates: 1967–92.

Acronym: ASVAB.

Scores: 3 composite scores: Academic Ability, Verbal Ability, Math ability.

Subtests, 10: General Science, Arithmetic Reasoning, Word Knowledge, Paragraph Comprehension, Numerical Operations, Coding Speed, Auto-Shop Information, Math Knowledge, Mechanical Comprehension, Electronics Information.

Administration: Group.

Price Data: Administered free of charge at participating high schools by Department of Defense personnel.

Time: 144(180) minutes.

Comments: Several supplemental publications provide support for counseling: *Counselor Manual,* an interpretive guide; *Technical Manual*; *Exploring Careers: The ASVAB Workbook*; *Military Careers.*

Author: United States Military Entrance Processing Command.

Publisher: United States Military Entrance Processing Command.

Cross References: For a review by R. A. Weitzman, see 9:81 (3 references); see also T3:202 (8 references); for a review by David J. Weiss, see 8:483 (4 references); see also T2:1067 (1 reference).

TEST REFERENCES

1. Federico, P., & Landis, D. B. (1984). Cognitive styles, abilities, and aptitudes: Are they dependent or independent? *Contemporary Educational Psychology, 9,* 146-161.
2. Jensen, A. R. (1984). The Black-White difference on the K-ABC: Implications for future tests. *The Journal of Special Education, 18,* 377-408.
3. Cudeck, R. (1985). A structural comparison of conventional and adaptive versions of the ASVAB. *Multivariate Behavioral Research, 20,* 305-322.
4. Diessner, R. (1985). The criterion-related validity of the academic ability scale of the Armed Forces Vocational Aptitude Battery for a sample of American Indian students. *Educational and Psychological Measurement, 45,* 411-413.
5. Jensen, A. R. (1985). [Review of the Armed Services Vocational Aptitude Battery]. *Measurement and Evaluation in Counseling and Development, 18,* 32-37.
6. Moore, E. G. J., & Smith, A. W. (1985). Mathematics aptitude: Effects of coursework, household language, and ethnic differences. *Urban Education, 20,* 273-294.
7. Enochs, J. R., Handley, H. M., & Wollenberg, J. P. (1986). Relating learning style, reading vocabulary, reading comprehension, and aptitude for learning to achievement in the self-paced and computer-assisted instructional modes. *Journal of Experimental Education, 54,* 135-139.
8. Federico, P. (1986). Crystallized and fluid intelligence in a "new" instructional situation. *Contemporary Educational Psychology, 11,* 33-53.
9. Greaud, V. A., & Green, B. F. (1986). Equivalence of conventional and computer presentation of speed tests. *Applied Psychological Measurement, 10,* 23-34.
10. Lee, J. A., Moreno, K. E., & Sympson, J. B. (1986). The effects of mode of test administration on test performance. *Educational and Psychological Measurement, 46,* 467-474.
11. Vernon, P. A. (1986). The g-loading of intelligence tests and their relationship with reaction times: A comment on Ruchalla et al. *Intelligence, 10,* 93-100.
12. Kyllonen, P. C., & Tirre, W. C. (1988). Individual differences in associative learning and forgetting. *Intelligence, 12,* 393-421.
13. Larson, G. E., Merritt, C. R., & Williams, S. E. (1988). Infor-

mation processing and intelligence: Some implications of task complexity. *Intelligence, 12,* 131-147.
14. Kyllonen, P. C., & Christal, R. E. (1990). Reasoning ability is (little more than) working-memory capacity?! *Intelligence, 14,* 389-433.
15. Larson, G. E., & Alderton, D. L. (1990). Reaction time variability and intelligence: A "worst performance" analysis of individual differences. *Intelligence, 14,* 309-325.
16. Borman, W. C., & Hallman, G. L. (1991). Observation accuracy for assessors of work-sample performance: Consistency across task and individual-differences correlates. *Journal of Applied Psychology, 76(1),* 11-18.
17. Drasgow, F., Levine, M. V., & McLaughlin, M. E. (1991). Appropriateness measurement for some multidimensional test batteries. *Applied Psychological Measurement, 15,* 171-191.
18. Raju, N. S., Steinhaus, S. D., Edwards, J. E., & DeLessio, J. (1991). A logistic regression model for personnel selection. *Applied Psychological Measurement, 15,* 139-152.
19. Ree, M. J., & Earles, J. A. (1991). The stability of g across different methods of estimation. *Intelligence, 15,* 271-278.
20. Earles, J. A., & Ree, M. J. (1992). The predictive validity of the ASVAB for training grades. *Educational and Psychological Measurement, 52,* 721-725.
21. Hedge, J. W., & Teachout, M. S. (1992). An interview approach to work sample criterion measurement. *Journal of Applied Psychology, 77,* 453-461.
22. Tirre, W. C., & Carmen, M. P. (1992). Investigation of functional working memory in the reading span test. *Journal of Educational Psychology, 84,* 462-472.
23. Besetsny, L. K., Ree, M. J., & Earles, J. A. (1993). Special test for computer programmers? Not needed: The predictive efficiency of the Electronic Data Processing Test for a sample of Air Force recruits. *Educational and Psychological Measurement, 53,* 507-511.
24. Borman, W. C., Hanson, M. A., Oppler, S. H., Pulakos, E. D., & White, L. A. (1993). Role of early supervisory experience in supervisor performance. *Journal of Applied Psychology, 78,* 443-449.
25. Ford, J. K., Smith, E. M., Sego, D. J., & Quiñones, M. A. (1993). Impact of task experience and individual factors on training-emphasis ratings. *Journal of Applied Psychology, 78,* 583-590.
26. Nandakumar, R., & Stout, W. (1993). Refinements of Stout's procedure for assessing latent trait unidimensionality. *Journal of Educational Statistics, 18,* 41-68.
27. Woltz, D. J., & Shute, V. J. (1993). Individual difference in repetition priming and its relationship to declarative knowledge acquisition. *Intelligence, 17,* 333-359.

[197]
Arthur Point Scale of Performance Tests.

Purpose: Designed to furnish an IQ using a nonverbal format comparable to that obtained with the Binet scales.

Population: Ages 4.5 to "superior" adults.

Publication Dates: 1925–79.

Scores: Total score only.

Administration: Individual.

Price Data, 1994: $625 per complete kit; $30 per 50 Form I; $100 per carrying case; $30 per manual ('79, 43 pages).

Time: [60–90] minutes.

Author: Grace Arthur.

Publisher: Stoelting Co.

Cross References: See T2:483 (21 references); for a review by William R. Grove, see 4:335 (12 references); for an excerpted review, see 3:271 (20 references); for reviews by Andrew W. Brown and Carroll A. Whitmer and an excerpted review by Donald Snedden, see 2:1379 (17 references).

TEST REFERENCES

1. Munroe, R. H., Munroe, R. L., & Brasher, A. (1985). Precursors of spatial ability: A longitudinal study among the Logoli of Kenya. *The Journal of Social Psychology, 125,* 23-33.

[198]

ASIST: A Structured Addictions Assessment Interview for Selecting Treatment.

Purpose: To assess alcohol and drug use for the purpose of selecting treatment.
Population: Adults.
Publication Dates: 1984–90.
Acronym: ASIST.
Scores: 12 sections: Identifying Information, Basic Information, Alcohol Use, Psychoactive Drug Use, Health Screening, Other Life Areas, Previous Treatment, Client Preference for Treatment, Treatment Assessment Summary, Treatment Plan, Actual Referrals, Assessment Worker's Observation.
Administration: Individual.
Price Data, 1994: $25 per 10 questionnaires; $35 per Assessment Handbook ('90, 200 pages).
Foreign Language Edition: Questionnaire available in French.
Time: Administration time not reported.
Author: Addiction Research Foundation.
Publisher: Addiction Research Foundation [Canada].

[199]

Assessing Linguistic Behaviors: Assessing Prelinguistic and Early Linguistic Behaviors in Developmentally Young Children.

Purpose: To assess "children's performance in five areas of cognitive-social and linguistic development: cognitive antecedents to word meaning, play, communicative intentions, language comprehension and language production."
Population: Children functioning below 2 years of age.
Publication Date: 1987.
Acronym: ALB.
Scores: 5 scales: Cognitive Antecedents to Word Meaning Scale, Play Scale, Communicative Intention Scale, Language Comprehension Scale, Language Production Scale.
Administration: Individual.
Price Data, 1989: $40 per copy of Assessing Prelinguistic and Early Linguistic Behaviors in Developmentally Young Children in binder format (165 pages); $125 per copy of ½ inch VHS format of accompanying video; $250 per copy of ¾ inch U-Matic format of accompanying video.
Time: Administration time varies with scales administered.
Comments: Behavior checklist; other test materials (e.g., windup toy, doll) must be supplied by examiner.
Authors: Lesley B. Olswang, Carol Stoel-Gammon, Truman E. Coggins, and Robert L. Carpenter.
Publisher: University of Washington Press.

a) COGNITIVE ANTECEDENTS TO WORD MEANING SCALE.
Purpose: "To examine the cognitive skills for three particular early emerging semantic notions and their related pragmatic functions: Nomination, Agent, Location."
Acronym: CAWM.
Scores: 7 tasks: Nomination Task (Naming Box), Agent Tasks (Unobserved Agent, Observed Agent), Location Tasks (Doll and Cup, Containers, Block Structure and Doll, Nesting Cups).
Time: (20–30) minutes.
Authors: Lesley Olswang with contributions by Carla Brooks, Judith Cooper, and Mary Pat Daly.

b) PLAY SCALE.
Purpose: "A practical means for observing practice play and symbolic play behaviors in a clinical setting for the purpose of gleaning information about a child's understanding of objects and their functions."
Scores, 12: Single Play Episodes (Mouthing Objects, Banging Objects, Visual Regarding, Manipulating Objects, Approximating Objects, Semi-appropriate Toy Use, Nesting Objects, Grouping, Appropriate Toy Use), Multiple Play Episodes (Same-action Multiple Play Episode, Different-action Multiple Play Episode, Extended Multiple Play Episode).
Time: (35–45) minutes.
Authors: Robert L. Carpenter with contributions by Judith Cooper, Janet Ringle-Bartels, and Shelley Tinsley.

c) COMMUNICATIVE INTENTION SCALE.
Purpose: "For observing and coding several intentional behaviors in children functioning in the latter stages of sensorimotor development."
Scores: 5 categories: Commenting, Requesting, Requesting Information, Acknowledging, Answering.
Time: Administration time not reported.
Comments: "Criterion-referenced."
Authors: Truman E. Coggins with contributions by Lori Harris, Linda Pelligrini, and Susan Vethivelu.

d) LANGUAGE COMPREHENSION SCALE.
Purpose: "To obtain an accurate developmental assessment of children's comprehension during the latter stages of sensorimotor development."
Parts: 3 subsections: Action Games, Single Words, Comprehension of Word Combinations. Levels: 3 levels corresponding to 3 subsections respectively: functional level 9–15 months, 15–24 months, 18–24 months.
Time: Administration time not reported.
Authors: Truman E. Coggins with contributions by Susan E. Kellogg.

e) LANGUAGE PRODUCTION SCALE.
Purpose: "To examine the vocalizations and verbalizations of children 9 to 24 months of age."
Parts, 5: Prelinguistic Utterances, Meaningful Speech Production (Phonetic, Phonological, Syntactic, Semantic).
Time: Administration time not reported.

Authors: Carol Stoel-Gammon with contributions by Charlene Kelly, Shelly Tinsley, and Susan Kellogg.
Cross References: For reviews by Jeffrey A. Atlas and Lynn S. Bliss, see 11:18.

[200]

Assessing Reading Difficulties: A Diagnostic and Remedial Approach.

Purpose: Constructed to assess the ability to organize and categorize sounds.
Population: Ages 5 and over.
Publication Date: 1980.
Scores: 3 error scores: Last Sound Different, Middle Sound Different, First Sound Different.
Administration: Individual.
Price Data: Available from publisher.
Time: Administration time not reported.
Author: Lynette Bradley.
Publisher: Macmillan Education Ltd. [England].
Cross References: For a review by Ruth Garner, see 9:82.

[201]

Assessing Specific Competencies.

Purpose: Designed to assess examinees on skills related to employability and work maturity/job retention.
Population: Individuals seeking employment.
Publication Dates: 1984–93.
Administration: Group or individual.
Manual: No manual.
Time: (45–55) minutes.
Comments: Available on computer software.
Author: Education Associates, Inc.
Publisher: Education Associates, Inc.

a) PRE-ASSESSING SPECIFIC COMPETENCIES.
Scores: 11 skill areas: Making Career Decisions, Using Labor Market Information, Developing a Resume, Completing an Application, Interviewing for a Job, Being Consistently Punctual, Maintaining Regular Attendance, Demonstrating Positive Attitudes/Behavior, Presenting Appropriate Appearance, Exhibiting Good Interpersonal Relations, Completing Tasks Effectively.
Price Data, 1993: $2.09 per pre-test; $129 per Apple or IBM pre-test diskette; $159 per Windows version.

b) POST-ASSESSING SPECIFIC COMPETENCIES.
Scores: Same as *a* above.
Price Data: $2.09 per post-test; $129 per Apple or IBM post-test diskette; $159 per Windows version.

[202]

Assessment and Placement Services for Community Colleges.

Purpose: "Directed toward identifying the appropriate level of study for each entering student in each subject" and "to provide predictive information about performance in an entry-level course."

Population: Entering community college students.
Publication Dates: 1984–85.
Scores, 4: Reading, Writing, Mathematics (Computation, Elementary Algebra).
Administration: Group.
Forms, 2: A, B.
Price Data: Available from publisher.
Time: 70(90) minutes plus 20 minutes for optional essay.
Comments: English and mathematics tests are derived from the Comparative Guidance and Placement Program (9:253); only one mathematics test is administered depending on previous algebra experience; Student Placement Inventory and optional essay test also available.
Author: Administered for the College Entrance Examination Board by Educational Testing Service.
Publisher: The College Board.
Cross References: For reviews by Marcia J. Belcher and James B. Erdmann, see 11:19.

[203]

Assessment in Infancy: Ordinal Scales of Psychological Development.

Purpose: Designed to assess the level of psychological development in infants.
Population: Birth to age 2.
Publication Dates: 1975–82.
Scores, 6: The Development of Visual Pursuit and The Permanence of Objects, The Development of Means for Obtaining Desired Environmental Events, The Development of Imitation, The Development of Operational Causality, The Construction of Object Relations in Space, The Development of Schemes for Relating to Objects.
Administration: Individual.
Price Data, 1986: $17.50 per manual ('75, 270 pages); $10 per 5 record forms for the Uzgiris-Hunt Scales.
Time: Administration time not reported.
Authors: Ina Č. Uzgiris and J. McV. Hunt.
Publisher: University of Illinois Press.
Cross References: For a review by Arlene C. Rosenthal, see 9:83.

TEST REFERENCES

1. Sankey, C. G., Elmer, E., Halechko, A. D., & Schulberg, P. (1985). The development of abused and high-risk infants in different treatment modalities: Residential versus in-home care. *Child Abuse & Neglect, 9,* 237-243.
2. Pecyna, P. M., Feeney-Giacoma, M. E., & Neiman, G. S. (1987). Development of the object permanence concept in cleft lip and palate and noncleft and palate infants. *Journal of Communication Disorders, 20,* 233-243.
3. Dunst, C. J. (1988). Stage transitioning in the sensorimotor development of Down's syndrome infants. *Journal of Mental Deficiency Research, 32,* 405-410.
4. Macpherson, F., & Butterworth, G. (1988). Sensorimotor intelligence in severely mentally handicapped children. *Journal of Mental Deficiency Research, 32,* 465-478.
5. Seifer, R., Clark, G. N., & Sameroff, A. J. (1991). Positive effects of interaction coaching on infants with developmental disabilities and their mothers. *American Journal on Mental Retardation, 96,* 1-11.

[204]

Assessment in Mathematics.

Purpose: Developed to assess "concept development . . . acquired knowledge, skills and applications" in mathematics.

Population: Primary and lower secondary school children.

Publication Date: 1981.

Scores: 5 areas: Number, Measure, Shape, Probability and Statistics, Relations.

Administration: Individual and group.

Price Data: Available from publisher.

Time: Administration time not reported.

Comments: "Criterion-referenced."

Authors: R. W. Strong (coordinator) and Somerset Local Education Authority.

Publisher: Macmillan Education Ltd. [England].

Cross References: For reviews by Frank Broadbent and Linda Jensen Sheffield, see 9:84.

[205]

Assessment in Nursery Education.

Purpose: Designed to assess and evaluate development and performance of nursery children.

Population: Ages 3–5.

Publication Date: 1978.

Acronym: ANE.

Scores: Assessment in 5 areas: Social Skills and Social Thinking, Talking and Listening, Thinking and Doing, Manual and Tool Skills, Physical Skills.

Administration: Individual.

Price Data, 1989: £47.15 per complete kit including 1 individual record form, 1 colour selection booklet, set of shapes and patterns, and manual (174 pages); £8.05 per 30 record forms; £3.20 per colour selection booklet; £51.75 each per VHS tapes 1, 2, or 3; £3.20 per videotape notes; £33.95 per manual.

Time: Administration time not reported.

Comments: Two assessment methods: teacher's observation, children's performance tasks; accessories include video recordings.

Authors: Margaret Bate and Marjorie Smith.

Publisher: NFER-Nelson Publishing Co., Ltd. [England].

Cross References: For reviews by Robert P. Anderson and Phyllis L. Newcomer, see 9:85.

[206]

Assessment Inventory for Management.

Purpose: "For screening candidates for insurance field sales management positions."

Population: Managers.

Publication Dates: 1991–93.

Acronym: AIM.

Scores, 19: 7 Job Task Areas [Basic Task Areas (Staffing/Recruiting and Selection, Training, Performance Management—Supervision, Total); Advanced Task Areas (Business Management, Field Office Development, Total)]; 12 Job Behaviors [Interpersonal Relations (Communicating, Counseling, Supporting), Leadership (Delegating, Motivating, Rewarding, Team Building, Networking), Organization (Coordinating, Monitoring, Planning, Problem-Solving and Decision-Making)].

Administration: Group.

Price Data, 1993: $35 per complete kit including test booklet, manual ('93, 22 pages), answer booklet, 2 management questionnaires, 2 management selection interview guides, and sample feedback report; $10 per test booklet; $10 per manual; $1 per answer booklet/return envelope; $150 per scored answer booklet.

Foreign Language Edition: French Canadian edition ('92) available.

Time: (120–180) minutes.

Comments: Mail-in scoring.

Author: LIMRA International.

Publisher: Life Insurance Marketing and Research Association, Inc.

[207]

The Assessment of Aphasia and Related Disorders, Second Edition.

Purpose: Provides "insight into the patient's functioning and [serves] as a bridge to relating test scores to the common aphasic syndromes recognized by neurologists."

Population: Aphasic patients, ages 5.5–59.

Publication Dates: 1972–83.

Administration: Individual.

Price Data, 1994: $47 per complete kit including both tests, scoring booklets, and manual ('83, 140 pages).

Publisher: Lea & Febiger.

a) BOSTON DIAGNOSTIC APHASIA EXAMINATION.

Scores, 45: Severity Rating, Fluency (Articulation Rating, Phrase Length, Melodic Line, Verbal Agility), Auditory Comprehension (Word Discrimination, Body-Part Identification, Commands, Complex Ideational Material), Naming (Responsive Naming, Confrontation Naming, Animal Naming), Oral Reading (Word Reading, Oral Sentence Reading), Repetition (Repetition of Words, High-Probability, Low-Probability), Paraphasia (Neologistic, Literal, Verbal, Extended), Automatic Speech (Automatized Sequences, Reciting), Reading Comprehension (Symbol Discrimination, Word Recognition, Comprehension of Oral Spelling, Word-Picture Matching, Reading Sentences and Paragraphs), Writing (Mechanics, Serial Writing, Primer-Level Dictation, Spelling to Dictation, Written Confrontation Naming, Sentences to Dictation, Narrative Writing), Music (Singing, Rhythm), Spatial and Computational (Drawing to Command, Stick Memory, 3-D Blocks, Total Fingers, Right-Left, Map Orientation, Arithmetic, Clock Setting); plus 8 ratings: Melodic Line, Phrase Length, Articulatory Agility, Grammatical Form, Paraphasia in Running Speech, Repetition, Word Finding, Auditory Comprehension.

Price Data: $20 per 25 examination booklets ('83, 31 pages); $7.50 per set of 16 test stimulus cards.

Time: (75–100) minutes.

Authors: Harold Goodglass with the collaboration of Edith Kaplan.

b) BOSTON NAMING TEST.

Population: Ages 5.5–59.

Scores: Total score only.

Price Data: $12.50 per test ('83, 64 pages); $10 per 25 scoring booklets ('83, 8 pages).

Time: Administration time not reported.

Authors: Edith Kaplan, Harold Goodglass, and Sandra Weintraub.

Cross References: For reviews by Rita Sloan Berndt and Malcolm R. McNeil of *a* only, see 10:15 (3 references); see 9:86 (2 references); see also T3:308 (28 references) of *a* only; for reviews by Daniel R. Boone and Manfred J. Meier of *a* only, see 8:955 (1 reference).

TEST REFERENCES

1. Borod, J. C., Goodglass, H., & Kaplan, E. (1980). Normative data on the Boston Diagnostic Aphasia Examination, Parietal Lobe Battery, and the Boston Naming Test. *Journal of Clinical Neuropsychology, 2,* 209-215.
2. Grossman, M. (1980). The aphasics' identification of a superordinate's referents with basic object level and subordinate level terms. *Cortex, 16,* 459-469.
3. Hartlage, L. C., & Telzrow, C. F. (1980). The practice of clinical neuropsychology. *Clinical Neuropsychology, 2,* 200-202.
4. Baker, E., Blumstein, S. E., & Goodglass, H. (1981). Interaction between phonological and semantic factors in auditory comprehension. *Neuropsychologia, 19,* 1-15.
5. Caramazza, A., Berndt, R. S., Basili, A. G., & Koller, J. J. (1981). Syntactic processing deficits in aphasia. *Cortex, 17,* 333-348.
6. Friederici, A. D. (1981). Production and comprehension of prepositions in aphasia. *Neuropsychologia, 19,* 191-199.
7. Grossman, M., Shapiro, B. E., & Gardner, H. (1981). Dissociable musical processing strategies after localized brain damage. *Neuropsychologia, 19,* 425-433.
8. Kirshner, H. S., Webb, W. G., & Duncan, G. W. (1981). Word deafness in Wernicke's aphasia. *Journal of Neurology, Neurosurgery, and Psychiatry, 44,* 197-201.
9. Aaron, P. G., Baker, C., & Hickox, G. L. (1982). In search of the third dyslexia. *Neuropsychologia, 20,* 203-208.
10. Farver, P. F., & Farver, T. B. (1982). Performance of normal older adults on tests designed to measure parietal lobe functions. *The American Journal of Occupational Therapy, 36,* 444-449.
11. Friedman, R. B. (1982). Mechanisms of reading and spelling in a case of alexia without agraphia. *Neuropsychologia, 20,* 533-545.
12. Friedman, R. B., & Perlman, M. B. (1982). The underlying causes of semantic paralexias in a patient with deep dyslexia. *Neuropsychologia, 20,* 559-568.
13. Kirshner, H. S., & Webb, W. G. (1982). Alexia and agraphia in Wernicke's aphasia. *Journal of Neurology, Neurosurgery, and Psychiatry, 45,* 719-724.
14. Stuss, D. T., Kaplan, E. F., Benson, D. F., Weir, W. S., Chiulli, S., & Sarazin, E. F. (1982). Evidence for the involvement of orbitofrontal cortex in memory functions: An interference effect. *Journal of Comparative and Physiological Psychology, 96,* 913-925.
15. Wilson, R. S., Bacon, L. D., Kaszniak, A. W., & Fox J. H. (1982). The episodic-semantic memory distinction and paired associate learning. *Journal of Consulting and Clinical Psychology, 50,* 154-155.
16. Pieniadz, J. M., Naeser, M. A., Koff, E., & Levine, H. L. (1983). CT scan cerebral hemispheric asymmetry measurements in stroke cases with global aphasia: Atypical asymmetries associated with improved recovery. *Cortex, 19,* 371-391.
17. Behrmann, M., & Penn, C. (1984). Non-verbal communication of aphasic patients. *British Journal of Disorders of Communication, 19,* 155-168.
18. Caine, E. D., Yerevanian, B. I., & Bamford, K. A. (1984). Cognitive function and the dexamethasone suppression test in depression. *American Journal of Psychiatry, 141,* 116-118.
19. Netsu, R., & Marquardt, T. P. (1984). Pantomime in aphasia: Effects of stimulus characteristics. *Journal of Communication Disorders, 17,* 37-46.
20. Quinteros, B., Williams, D. R. R., White, C. A. M., & Pickering, M. (1984). The cost of using trained and supervised volunteers as part of a speech therapy service for dysphasic patients. *British Journal of Disorders of Communication, 19,* 205-212.
21. Risse, G. L., Rubens, A. B., & Jordan, L. S. (1984). Disturbances of long-term memory in aphasic patients: A comparison of anterior and posterior lesions. *Brain, 107,* 605-617.
22. Whelihan, W. M., Lesher, E. L., Kleban, M. H., & Granick, S. (1984). Mental status and memory assessment as predictors of dementia. *Journal of Gerontology, 39,* 572-576.
23. Williams, S. E. (1984). Influence of written form on reading comprehension in aphasia. *Journal of Communication Disorders, 17,* 165-174.
24. Baker, E. L., White, R. F., & Murawski, B. J. (1985). Clinical evaluation of neurobehavioral effects of occupational exposure to organic solvents and lead. *International Journal of Mental Health, 14*(3), 135-158.
25. Hatfield, F. M. (1985). Visual and phonological factors in acquired dysgraphia. *Neuropsychologia, 23,* 13-29.
26. Kellar, L. A., & Levick, S. E. (1985). Reversed hemispheric lateralization of cerebral function: A case study. *Cortex, 21,* 469-476.
27. Lendrem, W., & Lincoln, N. B. (1985). Spontaneous recovery of language in patients with aphasia between 4 and 34 weeks after stroke. *Journal of Neurology, Neurosurgery, and Psychiatry, 48,* 743-748.
28. Mittenberg, W., Kasprisin, A., & Farage, C. (1985). Localization and diagnosis in aphasia with the Luria-Nebraska Neuropsychological Battery. *Journal of Consulting and Clinical Psychology, 53,* 386-392.
29. Obler, L. K., Nicholas, M., Albert, M. L., & Woodward, S. (1985). On comprehension across the adult lifespan. *Cortex, 21,* 273-280.
30. Payne, M., & Cooper, W. E. (1985). Paralexic errors in Broca's and Wernicke's aphasia. *Neuropsychologia, 23,* 571-574.
31. Skenes, L. L., & McCauley, R. J. (1985). Psychometric review of nine aphasia tests. *Journal of Communication Disorders, 18,* 461-474.
32. Drummond, S. S. (1986). Characterization of irrelevant speech: A case study. *Journal of Communication Disorders, 19,* 175-183.
33. Goodglass, H., Wingfield, A., Hyde, M. R., & Theurkauf, J. C. (1986). Category specific dissociations in naming and recognition by aphasic patients. *Cortex, 22,* 87-102.
34. Leeper, H. A., Jr., Shewan, C. M., & Booth, J. C. (1986). Altered acoustic cue discrimination in Broca's and conduction aphasics. *Journal of Communication Disorders, 19,* 83-103.
35. Ludlow, C. L., Rosenberg, J., Fair, C., Buck, D., Schesselman, S., & Salazar, A. (1986). Brain lesions associated with nonfluent aphasia fifteen years following penetrating head injury. *Brain, 109,* 55-79.
36. Murdoch, B. E., Afford, R. J., Ling, A. R., & Ganguley, B. (1986). Acute computerized tomographic scans: Their value in the localization of lesions and as prognostic indicators in aphasia. *Journal of Communication Disorders, 19,* 311-345.
37. Nicholas, L. E., & Brookshire, R. H. (1986). Consistency of the effects of rate of speech on brain-damaged adults' comprehension of narrative discourse. *Journal of Speech and Hearing Research, 29,* 462-470.
38. Nicholas, L. E., MacLennan, D. L., & Brookshire, R. H. (1986). Validity of multiple-sentence reading comprehension tests for aphasic adults. *Journal of Speech and Hearing Disorders, 51,* 82-87.
39. Ober, B. A., Dronkers, N. F., Koss, E., Delis, D. C., & Friedland, R. P. (1986). Retrieval from semantic memory in Alzheimer-type dementia. *Journal of Clinical and Experimental Neuropsychology, 8,* 75-92.
40. Payne-Johnson, J. C. (1986). Evaluation of communication in patients with closed head injury. *Journal of Communication Disorders, 19,* 237-249.
41. Tarter, R. E., Hegedus, A. M., VanThiel, D. H., Gavaler, J. S., & Schade, R. R. (1986). Hepatic dysfunction and neuropsychological test performance in alcoholics with cirrhosis. *Journal of Studies on Alcohol, 47,* 74-77.
42. Thomas, C. M., & Drummond, S. S. (1986). An analysis of semantic relations between mild dysphasic and nondysphasic speakers. *Journal of Communication Disorders, 19,* 105-113.
43. Thompson, C. K., & McReynolds, L. V. (1986). Wh interrogative production in agrammatic aphasia: An experimental analysis of auditory-visual stimulation and direct-production treatment. *Journal of Speech and Hearing Research, 29,* 193-206.
44. Zaidel, D. W. (1986). Memory for scenes in stroke patients: Hemisphere processing of semantic organization in pictures. *Brain, 109,* 547-560.
45. Bates, E., Friederici, A., & Wulfeck, B. (1987). Grammatical morphology in aphasia: Evidence from three languages. *Cortex, 23,* 545-574.
46. Ernest-Baron, C. R., Brookshire, R. H., & Nicholas, L. E. (1987). Story structure and retelling of narratives by aphasic and non-brain-damaged adults. *Journal of Speech and Hearing Research, 30,* 44-49.
47. Goodman-Schulman, R., & Caramazza, A. (1987). Patterns of disgraphia and the nonlexical spelling process. *Cortex, 23,* 143-148.
48. Hart, R. P., Kwentus, J. A., Taylor, J. R., & Harkins, S. W. (1987). Rate of forgetting in dementia and depression. *Journal of Consulting and Clinical Psychology, 55,* 101-105.

49. Kimelman, M. D. Z., & McNeil, M. R. (1987). An investigation of emphatic stress comprehension in adult aphasia: A replication. *Journal of Speech and Hearing Research, 30,* 295-300.

50. Li, E. C., & Canter, G. J. (1987). An investigation of Luria's hypothesis on prompting in aphasic naming disturbances. *Journal of Communication Disorders, 20,* 469-475.

51. Marquardt, T. P., & Nicholas, J. (1987). Aerodynamic control in apraxia at three intraoral pressure levels. *Perceptual and Motor Skills, 65,* 337-338.

52. Moore, W. H., Jr. (1987). Hemispheric alpha asymmetries in fluent and dysfluent aphasics during linguistic and resting conditions. *Cortex, 23,* 123-133.

53. Naeser, M. A., Mazurski, P., Goodglass, H., Peraino, M., Laughlin, S., & Leaper, W. C. (1987). Auditory syntactic comprehension in nine aphasia groups (with CT scans) and children: Differences in degree but not order of difficulty observed. *Cortex, 23,* 359-380.

54. Niemi, J., & Koivuselkä-Sallinen, P. (1987). Temporal delay and lexical retrieval in narratives: Aphasiological observations. *Journal of Communication Disorders, 20,* 171-186.

55. Stuss, D. T., Kates, M. H., Poirier, C. A., Hylton, D., Humphreys, P., Keene, D., & Laflèche G. (1987). Evaluation of information-processing speed and neuropsychological functioning in patients with myotonic dystrophy. *Journal of Clinical and Experimental Neuropsychology, 9,* 131-146.

56. Dworkin, J. P., Abkarian, G. G., & Johns, D. F. (1988). Apraxia of speech: The effectiveness of a treatment regimen. *Journal of Speech and Hearing Disorders, 53,* 280-294.

57. Ehrlich, J. S. (1988). Selective characteristics of narrative discourse in head-injured and normal adults. *Journal of Communication Disorders, 21,* 1-9.

58. Kearns, K. P., & Simmons, N. (1988). Interobserver reliability and perceptual ratings: More than meets the ear. *Journal of Speech and Hearing Research, 31,* 131-135.

59. Li, E. C., Kitselman, K., Dusatko, D., & Spinelli, C. (1988). The efficacy of pace in the remediation of naming deficits. *Journal of Communication Disorders, 21,* 491-503.

60. O'Donnell, B. F., Drachman, D. A., Lew, R. A., & Swearer, J. M. (1988). Measuring dementia: Assessment of multiple deficit domains. *Journal of Clinical Psychology, 44,* 916-923.

61. Petiet, C. A., Townes, B. D., Brooks, R. J., & Kramer, J. H. (1988). Neurobehavioral and psychosocial functioning of women exposed to high altitude in mountaineering. *Perceptual and Motor Skills, 67,* 443-452.

62. Shalev, R. S., Weirtman, R., & Amir, N. (1988). Developmental dyscalculia. *Cortex, 24,* 555-561.

63. Wulfeck, B. B. (1988). Grammaticality judgments and sentence comprehension in agrammatic aphasia. *Journal of Speech and Hearing Research, 31,* 72-81.

64. Bolla-Wilson, K., Robinson, R. G., Starkstein, S. E., Boston, J., & Price, T. R. (1989). Lateralization of dementia of depression in stroke patients. *American Journal of Psychiatry, 146,* 627-634.

65. Dunn, N. D., Russell, S. S., & Drummond, S. S. (1989). Effect of stimulus context and response coding variables on word retrieval performances in dysphasia. *Journal of Communication Disorders, 22,* 209-223.

66. Johnstone, E. C., Owens, D. G. C., Bydder, G. M., Colter, N., Crow, T. J., & Frith, C. D. (1989). The spectrum of structural brain changes in schizophrenia: Age of onset as a predictor of cognitive and clinical impairments and their cerebral correlates. *Psychological Medicine, 19,* 91- 103.

67. Rezania, K., Hambrecht, G., & Quist, R. (1989). How do we aphasic and normal speaking subjects restate a message in response to feedback? *Journal of Communication Disorders, 22,* 13-21.

68. Shapiro, L. P., Zurf, E., Carey, S., & Grossman, M. (1989). Comprehension of lexical subcategory distinctions by aphasic patients: Proper/common and mass/count nouns. *Journal of Speech and Hearing Research, 32,* 481-488.

69. Towne, R. L., & Banick, P. L. (1989). The effect of stimulus color on naming performance of aphasic adults. *Journal of Communication Disorders, 22,* 397-405.

70. Caramazza, A., & Hillis, A. E. (1990). Where do semantic errors come from? *Cortex, 26,* 95-122.

71. Cockburn, J., Wilson, B., Baddeley, A., & Hiorns, R. (1990). Assessing everyday memory in patients with dysphasia. *British Journal of Clinical Psychology, 29,* 353-360.

72. Glosser, G., & Friedman, R. B. (1990). The continuum of deep/phonological alexia. *Cortex, 26,* 343-359.

73. Glosser, G., & Goodglass, H. (1990). Disorders in executive control functions among aphasic and other brain-damaged patients. *Journal of Clinical and Experimental Neuropsychology, 12,* 485-501.

74. Gruen, A. K., Frankle, B. C., & Schwartz, R. (1990). Word fluency generation skills of head-injured patients in an acute trauma center. *Journal of Communication Disorders, 23,* 163-170.

75. Li, E. C., & Williams, S. E. (1990). Repetition deficits in three aphasic syndromes. *Journal of Communication Disorders, 23,* 77-88.

76. Margolin, D. I., Pate, D. S., Friedrich, F. J., & Elia, E. (1990). Dysnomia in dementia and stroke patients: Different underlying cognitive deficits. *Journal of Clinical and Experimental Neuropsychology, 12,* 597-612.

77. Martin, B. J. W., & Corlew, M. M. (1990). The incidence of communication disorders in dysphagic patients. *Journal of Speech and Hearing Disorders, 55,* 28-32.

78. Odell, K., McNeil, M. R., Rosenbek, J. C., & Hunter, L. (1990). Perceptual characteristics of consonant production by apraxic speakers. *Journal of Speech and Hearing Disorders, 55,* 345-359.

79. Robin, D. A., & Schienberg, S. (1990). Subcortical lesions and aphasia. *Journal of Speech and Hearing Disorders, 55,* 90-100.

80. Damecour, C. L., & Caplan, D. (1991). The relationship of depression to symptomatology and lesion site in aphasic patients. *Cortex, 27,* 385-401.

81. Hodges, J. R. (1991). Pure apraxic agraphia with recovery after drainage of a left frontal cyst. *Cortex, 27,* 469-473.

82. Holloman, A. L., & Drummond, S. S. (1991). Perceptual and acoustical analyses of phonetic paraphasias in nonfluent and fluent dysphasia. *Journal of Communication Disorders, 24,* 301-312.

83. Jones, B. P., Duncan, C. C., Brouwers, P., & Mirsky, A. F. (1991). Cognition in eating disorders. *Journal of Clinical and Experimental Neuropsychology, 13,* 711-728.

84. Jordan, F. M., Murdoch, B. E., & Buttsworth, D. L. (1991). Closed-head-injured children's performance on narrative tasks. *Journal of Speech and Hearing Research, 34,* 572-582.

85. Katz, R. B. (1991). Limited retention of information in the graphemic buffer. *Cortex, 27,* 111-119.

86. Kohn, S. E., & Smith, K. L. (1991). The relationship between oral spelling and phonological breakdown in a conduction aphasic. *Cortex, 27,* 631-639.

87. Mattews, C. (1991). Serial processing and the "phonetic route": Lessons learned in the functional reorganization of deep dyslexia. *Journal of Communication Disorders, 24,* 21-39.

88. Mendez, M. F., & Ashla-Mendez, M. (1991). Differences between multi-infarct dementia and Alzheimer's disease on unstructured neuropsychological tasks. *Journal of Clinical and Experimental Neuropsychology, 13,* 923-932.

89. Mitrushina, M. & Satz, P. (1991). Effect of repeated administration of a neuropsychological battery in the elderly. *Journal of Clinical Psychology, 47,* 790-801.

90. Mitrushina, M., & Satz, P. (1991). Reliability and validity of the Mini-Mental State Exam in neurologically intact elderly. *Journal of Clinical Psychology, 47,* 537-543.

91. Ordell, K., McNeil, M. R., Rosenbek, J. C., & Hunter, L. (1991). Perceptual characteristics of vowel and prosody production in apraxic, aphasic, and dysarthric speakers. *Journal of Speech and Hearing Research, 34,* 67-80.

92. Reuterskiöld, C. (1991). The effects of emotionality on auditory comprehension in aphasia. *Cortex, 27,* 595-604.

93. Rubin, E. H., Kinscherf, D. A., Grant, E. A., & Storandt, M. (1991). The influence of major depression on clinical and psychometric assessment of senile dementia of the Alzheimer type. *American Journal of Psychiatry, 148,* 1164-1171.

94. Sarshad-Brenneise, R., Nicholas, L. E., & Brookshire, R. H. (1991). Effects of apparent listener knowledge and picture stimuli on aphasic and non-brain-damaged speakers' narrative discourse. *Journal of Speech and Hearing Research, 34,* 168-176.

95. Sgaramella, T. M., Ellis, A. W., & Semenza, C. (1991). Analysis of the spontaneous writing errors of normal and aphasic writers. *Cortex, 27,* 29-39.

96. Stern, R. A., & Bachman, D. L. (1991). Depressive symptoms following stroke. *American Journal of Psychiatry, 148,* 351-356.

97. Jeste, D. V., Wragg, R. E., Salmon, D. P., Harris, M. J., & Thal, L. J. (1992). Cognitive deficits of patients with Alzheimer's disease with and without delusions. *American Journal of Psychiatry, 149,* 184-189.

98. Laine, M., Kujala, P., Niemi, J., & Uusipaikka, E. (1992). On the nature of naming difficulties in aphasia. *Cortex, 28,* 537-554.

99. Lucchelli, F., & DeRenzi, E. (1992). Proper name anomia. *Cortex, 28,* 221-230.

100. Swirsky-Sacchetti, T., Field, H. L., Mitchell, D. R., Seward, J., Lublin, F. D., Knobler, R. L., & Gonzalez, C. F. (1992). The sensitivity of the Mini-Mental State Exam in the White matter dementia of multiple sclerosis. *Journal of Clinical Psychology, 48,* 779-786.

101. Baum, S. R. (1993). An acoustic analysis of rate of speech effects on vowel production in aphasia. *Brain and Language, 44,* 414-430.

102. Baum, S. R., & Ryan, L. (1993). Rate of speech effects in aphasia: Voice onset time. *Brain and Language, 44,* 431-445.

103. Blaxton, T. A., & Bookheimer, S. Y. (1993). Retrieved inhibition in anomia. *Brain and Language, 44,* 221-237.

104. Cermak, L. S., Verfaellie, M., Letourneau, L., & Jacoby, L. L. (1993). Episodic effects on picture identification for alcoholic Korsakoff patients. *Brain and Cognition, 22*, 85-97.

105. Renzi, E. D., & Lucchelli, F. (1993). The fuzzy boundaries of apperceptive agnosia. *Cortex, 29*, 187-215.

[208]

Assessment of Career Decision Making.

Purpose: Designed to "assess a student's career decision-making style and progress on three career decision-making tasks."
Population: Adolescents and adults.
Publication Date: 1985.
Acronym: ACDM.
Scores, 9: Rational, Intuitive, Dependent, School Adjustment, Satisfaction with School, Involvement with Peers, Interaction with Instructors, Occupation, Major.
Administration: Group.
Price Data, 1993: $95 per test kit including 4 test report answer sheets and manual (87 pages); $13.50 per test report and scoring service; $45 per manual.
Time: (40) minutes.
Authors: Jacqueline N. Buck and M. Harry Daniels.
Publisher: Western Psychological Services.
Cross References: For reviews by Bruce J. Eberhardt and Nicholas A. Vacc, see 10:16 (8 references).

[209]

Assessment of Chemical Health Inventory.

Purpose: "Designed to evaluate the nature and extent of adolescent and adult chemical use and associated problems."
Population: Adolescents, adults.
Publication Dates: 1988–92.
Acronym: ACHI.
Scores: 9 factors (Chemical Involvement, Alienation, Family Estrangement, Personal Consequence, Depression, Family Support, Social Impact, Self Regard, Family Chemical Use) yielding Total score.
Administration: Individual.
Price Data, 1993: $179.95 per starter set including microcomputer disk containing 25 administrations and user manual ('92, 119 pages); $9 per 10 response forms; $5.75 (sold in multiples of 50) per microcomputer disk to administer and score ACHI; $29.95 per manual.
Time: (15–25) minutes.
Comments: Requires 4th grade reading level; may be taken and scored on computer (or administered on paper); mail-in service available.
Authors: Daniel Krotz, Richard Kominowski, Barbara Berntson, and James W. Sipe.
Publisher: RENOVEX Corporation.

[210]

Assessment of Children's Language Comprehension, 1983 Revision.

Purpose: Constructed "to determine how many word classes in different combinations of length and complexity a child would be able to understand."
Population: Ages 3-0 to 6-5.

Publication Dates: 1969–83.
Acronym: ACLC.
Scores, 4: Vocabulary, Two Critical Elements, Three Critical Elements, Four Critical Elements.
Administration: Individual.
Price Data, 1990: $32 per complete kit; $20 per set of cards; $8 per 50 recording sheets; $5 per manual ('83, 32 pages).
Foreign Language Edition: Spanish language version on reverse side of recording form.
Time: (10–15) minutes.
Authors: Rochana Foster, Jane J. Giddan, and Joel Stark.
Publisher: Consulting Psychologists Press, Inc.
Cross References: For a review by Mary Ellen Pearson, see 10:17 (3 references); see also T3:212 (8 references); for a review by James A. Till of an earlier version, see 8:452 (3 references).

TEST REFERENCES

1. Coleman, R. O., & Anderson, D. E. (1978). Enhancement of language comprehension in developmentally delayed children. *Language, Speech, and Hearing Services in Schools, 9*, 241-249.

2. Abraham, S., & Stoker, R. (1988). Language assessment of hearing-impaired children and youth: Patterns of test use. *Language, Speech, and Hearing Services in Schools, 19*, 160-174.

3. Lehman, M. E., & Sharf, D. J. (1989). Perception/production relationships in the development of the vowel duration cue to final consonant voicing. *Journal of Speech and Hearing Research, 32*, 803-815.

4. Musselman, C., & Churchill, A. (1991). Conversational control in mother-child dyads. *American Annals of the Deaf, 136*, 5-16.

[211]

Assessment of Competencies for Instructor Development.

Purpose: To measure six competencies important to being an effective instructor in an industrial setting.
Population: Instructors in industrial settings.
Publication Date: 1986.
Scores, 7: Analyzing the Needs and "Entering Behavior" of the Learner, Specifying Outcomes and "Terminal Behaviors" for a Course, Designing Instructional Sequences and Learning Materials, Instructing in Both the Inductive and Deductive Modes, Maintaining Adult-to-Adult (not "Parent-Child") Relationships in Class, Staying Learner-Centered not Information-Centered, Overall Instructional Competency.
Administration: Individual or group.
Manual: No manual.
Price Data, 1993: $100 per 20 tests, 20 interpretation brochures, and 20 response sheets.
Time: (45) minutes.
Comments: Self-administered, self-scored.
Author: Training House, Inc.
Publisher: Training House, Inc.
Cross References: For a review by Stephen F. Davis, see 11:20.

[212]

Assessment of Conceptual Organization (ACO): Improving Writing, Thinking, and Reading Skills.

Purpose: Developed to assess "understanding of conceptual organization in written language."

Population: Grades 4–6, 7–12, 10–adult.
Publication Date: 1991.
Acronym: ACO.
Scores: 3 criteria: Correct Superordinate Word Chosen, Appropriateness of Topic Sentence, Relatedness of Topic Sentence and Three Other Sentences.
Administration: Group.
Price Data, 1991: $24.95 per set of 20 assessment and 20 scoring forms (select level); $29.95 per manual (57 pages).
Time: (15–20) minutes.
Comments: Optional administration and scoring procedures available for "reluctant" writers.
Author: Christian Gerhard.
Publisher: Research for Better Schools.

[213]
Assessment of Core Goals.
Purpose: Constructed to define core goals and to identify activities that will lead to satisfaction of these goals.
Population: High school and over.
Publication Dates: 1991.
Acronym: ACG.
Scores: No scores.
Administration: Group or individual.
Price Data, 1994: $40 per sampler set; $90 per on-year permission to reproduce workbook and manual (38 pages).
Time: (60–600) minutes.
Comments: Method and length of administration depends on desired depth of information.
Author: C. W. Nichols.
Publisher: Mind Garden.

[214]
Assessment of Developmental Levels by Observation.
Purpose: "To determine performance levels of students with learning and development problems."
Population: Birth–8 years.
Publication Date: 1988.
Acronym: ADLO.
Scores, 6: Relationship, Expressive Language, Receptive Language, Fine Motor Skills, Gross Motor Skills, Self-Help Skills.
Administration: Individual.
Manual: No manual.
Price Data: Available from publisher.
Time: (30–35) minutes.
Author: Enid G. Wolf-Schein.
Publisher: Psychometrics Canada Ltd. [Canada].

[215]
Assessment of Fluency in School-Age Children.
Purpose: "To determine speech, language, and physiological functioning."
Population: Ages 5–18.
Publication Date: 1983.
Acronym: AFSC.

Scores: 5 areas: Automatic Speech, Cued Speech, Spontaneous Speech, Physiological Components, Interview With Students/Assessing Attitudes.
Administration: Individual.
Price Data, 1994: $69 per complete kit including 32 Assessment forms, 32 Parent Interview forms, 32 Teacher Evaluation forms, 32 Dismissal from Therapy Program forms, and Resource Guide (220 pages); $16 per 32 Assessment of Fluency forms.
Time: (45) minutes for student evaluation; (30) minutes for parent interview; (15) minutes for classroom observation; (15) minutes for teacher evaluation.
Comments: "Criterion-referenced"; assessment includes classroom observation, parent interview, teacher evaluation of child's speech, multi-factored evaluation of child, and post therapy.
Author: Julia Thompson.
Publisher: PRO-ED, Inc.
Cross References: For reviews by Lynn S. Fuchs and E. Charles Healey, see 10:18.

[216]
Assessment of Individual Learning Style: The Perceptual Memory Task.
Purpose: "To provide measures of the individual's perception and memory for spatial relationships; visual and auditory sequential memory; intermediate term memory; and discrimination of detail."
Population: Ages 4 and over.
Publication Dates: 1984–93.
Acronym: PMT.
Scores: 7 scores, 3 alternate scores: Spatial Relations, Visual Designs Recognition, Visual Designs-Sequencing, Auditory-Visual Colors Recognition, Auditory-Visual Colors Sequencing, Discrimination Recall, Total PMT, Visual-Visual (alternate), Auditory-Auditory (alternate), Visual-Auditory (alternate).
Administration: Individual.
Price Data, 1994: $390 per complete kit including carrying case containing various subtest components, 25 scoring forms, 25 alternate forms, and manual (129 pages); $18.50 per 25 scoring forms; $11.50 per 25 alternate forms; $41.75 per manual; $350 per PMT computer report.
Time: (30–40) minutes.
Comments: PMT Computer Report (1993) is available for IBM or Macintosh and for use in profiling PMT scores for ages 14 through adult.
Author: Lawrence McCarron.
Publisher: McCarron-Dial Systems.
Cross References: For reviews by Steven Ferrara and Arlene Coopersmith Rosenthal, see 11:21 (1 reference).

[217]
Assessment of Intelligibility of Dysarthric Speech.
Purpose: Designed "to provide clinicians and researchers with a means of measuring intelligibility and speaking rate of dysarthric individuals."

Population: Adult and adolescent dysarthric speakers.
Publication Date: 1981.
Acronym: AIDS.
Scores, 6: Single Word Intelligibility (Transcription, Multiple Choice), Sentence Intelligibility (Transcription, Speaking Rate, Rate of Intelligible Speech, Communication Efficiency Ratio).
Administration: Individual.
Price Data, 1994: $89 per complete kit including examiner's manual (60 pages) and picture book of stimulus words and sentences; $149 per computerized version including clinician manual and two software disks.
Time: Administration time not reported.
Comments: Apple 48K computer with single disk drive and monochrome monitor necessary for administration of computerized version.
Authors: Kathryn M. Yorkston, David R. Beukelman, and Charles Traynor (computer program).
Publisher: PRO-ED, Inc.
Cross References: For reviews by Katharine G. Butler and C. Dale Carpenter, see 10:19.

TEST REFERENCES

1. Bellaire, K., Yorkston, K. M., & Beukelman, D. R. (1986). Modification of breath patterning to increase naturalness of a mildly dysarthric speaker. *Journal of Communication Disorders, 19,* 271-280.
2. McClean, M. D., Beukelman, D. R., & Yorkston, K. M. (1987). Speech-muscle visuomotor tracking in dysarthric and nonimpairment speakers. *Journal of Speech and Hearing Research, 30,* 276-282.
3. Kearns, K. P., & Simmons, N. (1988). Interobserver reliability and perceptual ratings: More than meets the ear. *Journal of Speech and Hearing Research, 31,* 131-135.

[218]
Assessment of Interpersonal Relations.

Purpose: "Developed to assess the quality of relationships children have with the individuals who are most important in their lives—their mothers, fathers, male peers, female peers, and teachers."
Population: Ages 9-0 to 19-11.
Publication Date: 1993.
Acronym: AIR.
Scores, 6: Mother, Father, Male Peers, Female Peers, Teachers, Total Relationship Index.
Administration: Group.
Price Data, 1994: $64 per complete kit; $39 per 50 record booklets; $27 per manual (78 pages).
Time: (20–25) minutes.
Author: Bruce A. Bracken.
Publisher: PRO-ED, Inc.

[219]
Assessment of Living Skills and Resources.

Purpose: Assesses "daily tasks that require a high level of cognitive function," or Instrumental Activities of Daily Living (IADLs), "in community-dwelling elders."
Population: Community-dwelling elders.
Publication Date: 1991.
Acronym: ALSAR.
Scores: 11 task scores (Telephoning, Reading, Lei-

sure, Medication Management, Transportation, Shopping, Meal Preparation, Laundering, Housekeeping, Home Maintenance).
Administration: Individual.
Price Data, 1994: $5 per master of the reproducible ALSAR; $55 for each of two instructional videotapes ("An Overview of IADL Assessment" and "Administration of the ALSAR"); master of the ALSAR included in the latter videotape.
Time: (15–20) minutes.
Comments: Incorporates assessment of Instrumental Activities of Daily Living (IADL); administered by health professionals from any discipline.
Authors: Theresa J. K. Drinka, Jane H. Williams, Martha Schram, Jean Farrell-Holtan, and Reenie Euhardy.
Publisher: Madison Geriatric Research, Education, and Clinical Center, VA Medical Center.

[220]
The Assessment of Phonological Processes—Revised.

Purpose: Designed to identify and evaluate the severity of phonological disorders.
Population: Preschool children, ages 9–10.
Publication Date: 1986.
Acronym: APP-R.
Scores, 13: Phonological Omissions (Syllable Reduction, Consonant Sequence Reduction, Consonant Singleton Omissions [Prevocalic, Postvocalic]), Class Deficiencies (Stridents, Velar Obstruents, Liquid-l, Liquid-r, Nasals, Glides), Total, Phonological Deviancy Score, Severity Interval Rating for Phonology; Miscellaneous Error Patterns also available.
Administration: Individual.
Levels, 2: Preschool, Multisyllabic.
Price Data, 1994: $69 per complete kit including 50 Phonological Screening Forms—Preschool, 50 Phonological Screening Forms—Multisyllabic, 50 recording forms, 50 Analysis of Phonological Processes Forms, 50 Phonological Analysis Summary Forms, and examiner's manual (92 pages); $9 per 50 screening forms; $9 per 50 recording forms; $9 per 50 analysis forms; $9 per 50 analysis summary forms; $21 per manual.
Time: (15–20) minutes.
Comments: Several additional items needed for administration must be supplied by examiner.
Author: Barbara Williams Hodson.
Publisher: PRO-ED, Inc.
Cross References: For a review by Sheldon L. Stick of an earlier version, see 9:91 (1 reference).

TEST REFERENCES

1. Kamhi, A. G., Catts, H. W., & Davis, M. K. (1984). Management of sentence production demands. *Journal of Speech and Hearing Research, 27,* 329-338.
2. Abraham, S., Stoker, R., & Allen, W. (1988). Speech assessment of hearing-impaired children and youth: Patterns of test use. *Language, Speech, and Hearing Services in Schools, 19,* 17-27.
3. Churchill, J. D., Hodson, B. W., Jones, B. W., & Novak, R. E. (1988). Phonological systems of speech-disordered clients with positive/

negative histories of otitis media. *Language, Speech, and Hearing Services in Schools, 19*, 100-107.

4. Crosley, P. A., & Dowling, S. (1989). The relationship between cluster and liquid simplification and sentence length, age, and IQ in Down's syndrome children. *Journal of Communication Disorders, 22*, 151-168.

[221]

Assessment of Qualitative and Structural Dimensions of Object Representations, Revised Edition.

Purpose: Designed to measure aspects of an individual's conceptualization of others.

Population: Adolescents and adults (patients and normals).

Publication Date: 1981–92.

Acronym: AQSDOR.

Scores: Ratings in 4 areas: Personal Qualities, Degree of Ambivalence in Description, Length of Description, Conceptual Level.

Administration: Group.

Price Data: Available from publisher.

Time: (5) minutes per description.

Comments: Subjects' descriptions of significant figures (e.g., parent) rated by judges; no reading by examinees.

Authors: Sidney J. Blatt, Eve S. Chevron, Donald M. Quinlan, Carrie E. Schaffer, and Steven Wein.

Publisher: Sidney J. Blatt.

Cross References: For a review by C. H. Swensen, see 9:92.

[222]

Assessment of School Needs for Low-Achieving Students: Staff Survey.

Purpose: Designed to measure "staff perceptions as to whether certain behaviors are occurring in their school."

Population: Teachers and administrators.

Publication Date: 1988–89.

Acronym: ASNLAS.

Scores, 9: School Programs and Policies, Classroom Management, Instruction, Teacher Expectations, Principal Leadership, Staff Development, Student Involvement in Learning, School Climate, Parent Involvement.

Administration: Group.

Price Data, 1991: $2 per survey booklet; $.25 per scoring form; $16.95 per manual ('89, 44 pages).

Time: (45–50) minutes.

Authors: Francine S. Beyer and Ronald L. Houston.

Publisher: Research for Better Schools.

Cross References: For a review by Dean H. Nafziger and Ann M. Muench, see 11:22.

[223]

A.S.S.E.T.S.—A Survey of Students' Educational Talents and Skills.

Purpose: "Helps in the identification of children's gifts and talents and in planning enrichment experiences for these students."

Population: Kindergarten–grade 3, grades 4–6.

Publication Dates: 1978–79.

Scores, 5: Interests, Talent Areas (Academic Aptitude, Motivational Characteristics, Creative Thinking Ability, Visual/Performing Arts Aptitude/Talent).

Administration: Group.

Levels, 2: Early Elementary, Later Elementary.

Price Data: Not available.

Time: Administration time not reported.

Author: Learning Publications, Inc.

Publisher: Learning Publications, Inc. [No reply from publisher; status unknown].

Cross References: For reviews by Dianna L. Newman and James O. Rust, see 10:20.

[224]

Association Adjustment Inventory.

Purpose: "Designed for use as a screening instrument for maladjustment and immaturity."

Population: Normal and institutionalized adults.

Publication Date: 1959–84.

Acronym: AAI.

Scores, 13: Juvenility, Psychotic Responses, Depressed-Optimistic, Hysteric-Non-Hysteric, Withdrawal-Sociable, Paranoid-Naive, Rigid-Flexible, Schizophrenic-Objective, Impulsive-Restrained, Sociopathic-Empathetic, Psychosomapathic-Physical Contentment, Anxious-Relaxed, Total.

Administration: Group.

Price Data, 1993: $49.50 per test package; $23.50 per IBM answer sheet package; $38 per set of IBM scoring stencils; $20 per set of fan type keys; $23.50 per profile package; $36.50 per manual (15 pages) and manuals supplement ('84, 17 pages); $58.50 per specimen set.

Time: (10) minutes.

Comments: Adaption of the Kent-Rosanoff Free Association Test.

Author: Martin M. Bruce.

Publisher: Martin M. Bruce, Ph.D., Publishers.

Cross References: For reviews by W. Grant Dahlstrom and Bertram R. Forer and an excerpted review by Edward S. Bordin, see 6:201.

[225]

Athletic Motivation Inventory.

Purpose: Constructed to measure the personality and motivation of athletes participating in competitive sports.

Population: Male and female athletes ages 13 and older and coaches.

Publication Dates: 1969–87.

Acronym: AMI.

Scores, 14: Drive, Aggressiveness, Determination, Responsibility, Leadership, Self-Confidence, Emotional Control, Mental Toughness, Coachability, Conscientiousness, Trust, Validity Scales (Accuracy, Desirability, Completion Rate).

Administration: Group or individual.

Price Data, 1991: $40 per athlete for non-profit teams (scoring and reports by publisher included in price); $85 per questionnaire for professional and recreational athletes (scoring and reports by publisher included in price).

Foreign Language Editions: French and Spanish editions available.

Time: (40–50) minutes.

Authors: Thomas A. Tutko, Leland P. Lyon, and Bruce C. Oglive.

Publisher: Institute of Athletic Motivation.

Comments: May be used for individual self-assessment.

Cross References: For a review by Andrew L. Comrey, see 8:409 (19 references).

[226]

Attention Deficit Disorder Behavior Rating Scales.

Purpose: Designed to help school personnel and psychologists make proper ADD referrals.

Population: School personnel and psychologists.

Publication Dates: 1982–93.

Acronym: ADDBRS.

Scores, 10: Inattention, Impulsivity, Hyperactivity, Anger Control, Academics, Anxiety, Confidence, Aggressiveness, Resistance, Social.

Administration: Individual.

Editions, 2: Child, Adult.

Price Data, 1993: $65 per complete kit including 25 rating sheets, 25 profile sheets, manual ('93, 14 pages), and three audiotapes (Attention Deficit Disorder, Kids on Medication, Does Your Child Have Learning Disabilities?); $30 per 25 rating scales, 25 profile sheets and manual; $9 per 25 rating sheets and 25 profile sheets; $11.50 per audiotape; $20 per set of 20 teacher information and parent information handout sheets and instructions; $35 per adult version including 25 rating sheets, 25 profile sheets, and manual.

Time: Administration time not reported.

Authors: Ned Owens and Betty White Owens.

Publisher: Ned Owens, Inc.

[227]

Attention Deficit Disorders Evaluation Scale.

Purpose: Designed to "evaluate and diagnose Attention Deficit Disorders in children and youth from input provided by teachers and parents."

Population: Ages 4.5–18.

Publication Dates: 1989–90.

Acronym: ADDES.

Scores, 4: Inattentive, Impulsive, Hyperactive, Total.

Administration: Individual.

Price Data, 1993: $159 per complete kit including 50 pre-referral checklist forms, 50 pre-referral intervention strategy documentation forms, School Version technical manual ('89, 37 pages), 50 School Version rating forms, Home Version technical manual ('89, 40 pages), 25 Home Version rating forms, intervention manual ('89, 167 pages), and intervention manual for parents ('90, 157 pages); $25 per 50 pre-referral checklist forms; $25 per 50 pre-referral intervention

strategies documentation forms; $22 per intervention manual; $149 per computerized intervention manual (IBM, Apple II, or Macintosh).

Comments: Manual titles are: The Attention Deficit Disorders Intervention Manual and The Parent's Guide to Attention Deficit Disorders.

Authors: Stephen B. McCarney and Angela Marie Bauer.

Publisher: Hawthorne Educational Services, Inc..

a) SCHOOL VERSION.

Price Data: $12 per School Version technical manual; $30 per 50 School Version rating forms; $12 per computerized School Version quick score (IBM or Apple).

Time: (15–20) minutes.

b) HOME VERSION.

Price Data: $12 per Home Version technical manual; $20 per 25 Home version rating forms; $13 per The Parent's Guide to Attention Deficit Disorders ('90, 123 pages); $12 per computerized Home Version quick score (IBM or Apple II).

Time: (12–17) minutes.

[228]

Attitudes Toward Mainstreaming Scale.

Purpose: "Developed to measure attitudes toward the integration of handicapped students into the regular classroom."

Population: Teachers.

Publication Dates: 1980–89.

Acronym: ATMS.

Scores, 4: Learning Capability, General Mainstreaming, Traditional Limiting Disabilities, Total.

Administration: Group.

Price Data: Available from publisher.

Time: Administration time not reported.

Authors: Joan D. Berryman, W. R. Neal, Jr., and Charles Berryman.

Publisher: University of Georgia.

Cross References: For reviews by Mary Elizabeth Hannah and Michael D. Orlansky, see 9:98 (1 reference); see also T3:224 (3 references).

TEST REFERENCES

1. Curtis, C. K. (1985). Are education students being prepared for mainstreaming? *Education Canada, 25,* 28-31.
2. Curtis, C. K. (1985). Education students' attitudes toward disabled persons and mainstreaming. *The Alberta Journal of Educational Research, 31,* 288-305.
3. Berryman, J. D. (1988). Attitudes Toward Mainstreaming Scale: Factorial validity for a lay population. *Educational and Psychological Measurement, 48,* 231-236.
4. Wilczenski, F. L. (1992). Reevaluating the factor structure of the Attitudes Toward Mainstreaming Scale. *Educational and Psychological Measurement, 52,* 499-504.

[229]

Attitudes Toward Working Mothers Scale.

Purpose: "Designed to assess attitudes toward the . . . dual role of mother and worker."

Population: Adults.

Publication Date: No date on test materials.

Acronym: AWM.

Scores: Total score only.

Administration: Group.
Price Data, 1983: Free of charge for inventory, scoring instructions, and mimeographed paper on construction validation of scale (23 pages).
Time: Administration time not reported.
Authors: Toby J. Tetenbaum, Jessica Lighter, and Mary Travis.
Publisher: Toby J. Tetenbaum.
Cross References: For reviews by Mark W. Roberts and Charles Wenar, see 9:99 (1 reference).

TEST REFERENCES

1. Tetenbaum, T. J., Lighter, J., & Travis, M. (1983). The construct validation of an Attitudes Toward Working Mothers Scale. *Psychology of Women Quarterly, 8,* 69-78.

[230]
The Auditory Discrimination and Attention Test.

Purpose: Designed to assess "auditory discrimination and attention for speech."
Population: Children ages 3.5–12 years referred for speech therapy.
Publication Date: 1988.
Scores: Total error score only.
Administration: Individual.
Price Data, 1990: £69 per complete set; £10.10 per 25 score sheets.
Time: (20) minutes.
Author: Rosemarie MorganBarry.
Publisher: NFER-Nelson Publishing Co., Ltd. [England].

TEST REFERENCES

1. Barr, W. B., Bilder, R. M., Goldberg, E., Kaplan, E., & Mukherjee, S. (1989). The neuropsychology of schizophrenic speech. *Journal of Communication Disorders, 22,* 327-349.

[231]
Auditory Memory Span Test.

Purpose: To measure a subject's ability to recall single syllable spoken words in progressively increasing series.
Population: Ages 5–8.
Publication Date: 1973.
Scores: Total score only.
Administration: Individual.
Price Data, 1993: $25 per 100 test booklets; $12.50 per manual (6 pages); $55 per kit including 200 tests, 100 each of Forms 1 and 2, and manual.
Time: (5–7) minutes.
Comments: 2 equivalent forms: Forms 1 and 2.
Authors: Joseph M. Wepman and Anne Morency.
Publisher: Western Psychological Services.
Cross References: For a review by J. Joseph Freilinger, see 8:933.

[232]
Auditory Selective Attention Test.

Purpose: "To measure selective attention."
Population: Adults.
Publication Date: 1993.
Acronym: ASAT.

Scores: Total Errors.
Administration: Individual.
Price Data, 1993: $100 per test (cassette tape); $5 per manual (15 pages).
Time: 30(35) minutes.
Comments: Stereo tape player and a pair of stereo headphones must be supplied by the examiner.
Authors: Winfred Arthur, Jr., Gerald V. Barrett, and Dennis Doverspike.
Publisher: Barrett and Associates, Inc.

[233]
Auditory Sequential Memory Test.

Purpose: Designed to assess ability to repeat from immediate memory an increasing series of digits.
Population: Ages 5–8.
Publication Date: 1973.
Scores: Total score only.
Administration: Individual.
Price Data, 1993: $25 per 100 test booklets; $12.50 per manual (6 pages); $55 per kit including 200 tests, 100 each of Forms 1 and 2, and manual).
Time: (5–7) minutes.
Comments: 2 equivalent forms: Forms 1 and 2.
Authors: Joseph M. Wepman and Anne Morency.
Publisher: Western Psychological Services.
Cross References: For a review by J. Joseph Freilinger, see 8:934.

TEST REFERENCES

1. Aaron, P. G., Baker, C., & Hickox, G. L. (1982). In search of the third dyslexia. *Neuropsychologia, 20,* 203-208.

[234]
Australian Second Language Proficiency Ratings.

Purpose: "Designed to measure general proficiency by matching observed language behavior against global descriptions."
Population: Adolescents and adults.
Publication Dates: 1982–84.
Acronym: ASLPR.
Scores, 4: Speaking, Listening, Reading, Writing.
Administration: Individual.
Price Data: Available from publisher.
Foreign Language Editions: French, Italian, and Japanese versions ('82) available.
Time: Administration time not reported.
Authors: D. E. Ingram and Elaine Wylie.
Publisher: Australian Department of Immigration, Local Government and Ethnic Affairs [Australia].

[235]
Autism Screening Instrument for Educational Planning, Second Edition.

Purpose: "Designed to help professionals identify individuals with autism and to provide information needed to develop appropriate educational plans."
Population: Autistic individuals ages 18 months to adult.
Publication Dates: 1978–93.
Acronym: ASIEP-2.

Administration: Individual.

Price Data, 1994: $149 per complete kit including manual ('93, 81 pages), 25 summary booklets, 25 Autism Behavior Checklist Forms, 25 Sample of Vocal Behavior Record Forms, 25 Interaction Assessment Record Forms, 25 Educational Assessment Forms, 25 Prognosis of Learning Rate Forms, toys, manipulatives, stand, and coding audiotape for Interaction Assessment; $18 per 25 summary booklets; $44 per toys, manipulatives, and stand; $9 per coding audiotape for Interaction Assessment; $32 per examiner's manual.

Time: Administration time not reported.

Comments: Subtests administered depends on results of Autism Behavior Checklist and purpose of assessment.

Authors: David A. Krug, Joel R. Arick, and Patricia J. Almond.

Publisher: PRO-ED, Inc.

a) AUTISM BEHAVIOR CHECKLIST.

Scores, 6: Sensory, Relating, Body and Object Use, Language, Social and Self Help, Total.

Price Data: $11 per 25 record forms.

b) SAMPLE OF VOCAL BEHAVIOR.

Scores, 5: Repetitive, Noncommunicative, Babbling, Unintelligible, Total.

Price Data: $11 per 25 record forms.

c) INTERACTION ASSESSMENT.

Scores, 4: Interaction, Independent Play, No Response, Negative.

Price Data: $11 per 25 record forms.

d) EDUCATIONAL ASSESSMENT.

Scores, 6: In Seat, Receptive Language, Expressive Language, Body Concept, Speech Imitation, Total.

Price Data: $11 per 25 record forms.

e) PROGNOSIS OF LEARNING RATE.

Scores, 5: Hand-Shaping, Random Position-A, Fixed Position-B, Fixed Position-C, Random Position-D.

Price Data: $11 per 25 record forms.

Cross References: For reviews by Lawrence J. Turton and Richard L. Wikoff of an earlier edition, see 9:105 (1 reference).

TEST REFERENCES

1. Atlas, J. A. (1987). Symbol use by developmentally disabled children. *Psychological Reports, 61*, 207-214.

[236]
Automated Office Battery.

Purpose: Aptitude tests designed for the selection of staff to work in offices with a high degree of automation.

Population: Student and employed clerical staff.

Publication Dates: 1985–86.

Acronym: AOB.

Scores: 3 tests: Numerical Estimation, Computer Checking, Coded Instructions.

Administration: Group.

Price Data, 1986: £108 per administration set; £110 per 10 test booklets; £55 per 50 answer sheets; £27.50 per 50 profile charts; £5.50 per administration card; £15 per 50 practice leaflets; £55 per manual and user's guide ('86, 57 pages); £500 Automated Office Battery User's Fee.

Time: 40(60) minutes for entire battery.

Comments: "Tests may be used individually or as a complete battery as particular requirements dictate."

Authors: Bill Mabey and Hazel Stevenson.

Publisher: Saville & Holdsworth Ltd. [England].

a) NUMERICAL ESTIMATION.

Purpose: A test to measure the ability to estimate the answer to a calculation.

Acronym: NE-1.

Time: 10(15) minutes.

b) COMPUTER CHECKING.

Purpose: A test to measure the ability to check machine input information with the corresponding output.

Acronym: CC-2.

Time: 12(17) minutes.

c) CODED INSTRUCTIONS.

Purpose: A test to measure the ability to comprehend and follow written instructions when a form of coded language is used.

Time: 18(23) minutes.

Cross References: For a review by Philip Ash, see 11:24.

[237]
Bader Reading and Language Inventory.

Purpose: "Designed to determine appropriate placement of students in instructional material."

Population: Children and adolescents and adults.

Publication Date: 1983.

Scores: Reading and Language Performance.

Administration: Individual.

Price Data: Not available.

Time: Administration time not reported.

Comments: A compilation of graded reading passages, word recognition lists, phonics and word analysis subtests, spelling tests, cloze tests, visual discrimination tests, auditory discrimination tests, unfinished sentences, and evaluations of language abilities.

Author: Lois A. Bader.

Publisher: Macmillan Publishing Co. [No reply from publisher; status unknown].

Cross References: For reviews by Krista J. Stewart and Dan Wright, see 10:22.

TEST REFERENCES

1. Malicky, G. V., & Norman, C. A. (1988). Reading processes in subgroups in a clinical population. *The Alberta Journal of Educational Research, 34*, 344-354.

[238]
Ball Aptitude Battery.

Purpose: For vocational guidance and employee placement decisions.

Population: High school and adults.

Publication Date: 1981.

Acronym: BAB.

Scores: Profile of 16 skill ability tests: Clerical, Idea Fluency, Inductive Reasoning, Word Association, Writing Speed, Paper Folding, Vocabulary, Ideaphoria, Finger Dexterity, Grip, Shape Assembly, Analytical Reasoning, Numerical Reasoning, Numerical Computation, Associative Memory, Auditory Memory Span.

Administration: Group.

Price Data: Price information for test materials including administration manual (40 pages), technical manual (120 pages), and counselor's manual available from publisher.

Time: (10–20) minutes for most tests; (260) minutes for battery.

Authors: Ball Foundation.

Publisher: Ball Foundation.

Cross References: For reviews by Philip G. Benson and Wilbur L. Layton, see 9:106 (5 references).

TEST REFERENCES

1. Dawis, R. V., & Sung, Y. H. (1984). The relationship of participation in school activities to abilities and interests in a high school student sample. *Journal of Vocational Behavior, 24,* 159-168.
2. Dong, H., Sung, Y. H., & Dohm, T. E. (1985). The validity of the Ball Aptitude Battery (BAB): I. Relationship to high school academic success. *Educational and Psychological Measurement, 45,* 627-637.
3. Dong, H., Sung, Y. H., & Goldman, S. H. (1985). The validity of the Ball Aptitude Battery (BAB): II. Relationship to training and occupational success. *Educational and Psychological Measurement, 45,* 951-957.
4. Hall, A. E. (1985). [Review of the Ball Aptitude Battery]. *Journal of Educational Measurement, 22,* 167-172.
5. Dong, H., Sung, Y. H., & Goldman, S. H. (1986). The validity of the Ball Aptitude Battery (BAB): III. Relationship to CAB, DAT, and GATB. *Educational and Psychological Measurement, 46,* 245-250.

[239]

The Bangs Receptive Vocabulary Checklist.

Purpose: "To provide a developmentally sequenced list of words that emerge in children's lexicons between the third birthday and entry into the first grade."

Population: Mentally retarded, hearing impaired, language/learning disabled, or autistic children ages 3-0 to 7-0.

Publication Date: 1990.

Scores: Total score only.

Administration: Individual.

Price Data, 1990: $49 per complete kit, including manual (48 pages); $15 per 25 score sheets; $12.95 per 25 achievement profiles.

Time: [60] minutes or less.

Comments: Other test materials (e.g., coins) must be supplied by examiner.

Author: Tina E. Bangs.

Publisher: Communication Skill Builders.

Cross References: For a review by Leo M. Harvill, see 11:25.

[240]

Bankson-Bernthal Test of Phonology.

Purpose: "Designed for use by speech-language clinicians to assess the phonology of preschool and school-age children."

Population: Ages 3–9.

Publication Dates: 1989–90.

Acronym: BBTOP.

Scores, 3: Word Inventory, Consonants Composite, Phonological Processes Composite.

Administration: Individual.

Price Data, 1991: $88.98 per complete kit; $34.98 per picture book; $18 per 24 record forms; $19.98 per easel and carrying case; $24.99 per manual ('90, 111 pages).

Time: (10–15) minutes.

Authors: Nicholas W. Bankson and John E. Bernthal.

Publisher: The Riverside Publishing Co.

[241]

Bankson Language Test—2.

Purpose: Constructed "to establish the presence of a language disorder and identify areas in need of further, in-depth testing."

Population: Ages 3-0 to 6-11.

Publication Dates: 1977–90.

Acronym: BLT-2.

Scores, 4: Semantic Knowledge, Morphological and Syntactic Rules, Language Quotient, Pragmatic Knowledge (optional).

Administration: Individual.

Forms, 2: BLT-2; BLT-2 Screen.

Price Data, 1994: $89 per complete kit including 25 profile/examiner's record booklets, 25 screen record forms, picture book, and manual ('90, 32 pages); $31 per picture book; $24 per 25 profile/examiner's record booklets; $11 per 25 screen record forms; $27 per manual.

Time: (30) minutes.

Comments: Revision of Bankson Language Screening Test.

Author: Nicholas W. Bankson.

Publisher: PRO-ED, Inc.

Cross References: For reviews by Ronald B. Gillam and Roger L. Towne, see 11:26 (4 references); for a review of an earlier edition by Barry W. Jones, see 9:107 (1 reference).

TEST REFERENCES

1. Beitchman, J. H., Peterson, M., & Clegg, M. (1988). Speech and language impairment and psychiatric disorder: The relevance of family demographic variables. *Child Psychiatry and Human Development, 18,* 191-207.
2. Larson, G. W., & Summers, P. A. (1988). The experimental effect of kindergarten on Bankson Language Screening Test performance. *Journal of Communication Disorders, 21,* 469-478.
3. Spence, B. H., & Whitman, T. L. (1990). Instruction and self-regulation in mentally retarded adults in a vocational setting. *Cognitive Therapy and Research, 14,* 431-445.

[242]

Bar-Ilan Picture Test for Children.

Purpose: "A semi-projective device to pinpoint the child's perception of his place in society, in his formal educational setting, and in his home, as well as his perception of his weaker points and of his potential for coping with life."

Population: Ages 4–16.

Publication Dates: 1982–89.

Scores: Guidelines for analysis in 8 areas: Emotional Makeup, Motivation, Interpersonal Behavior and Areas of Conflict, Attitudes of Teachers-Parents Toward Testee, Attitudes of Peers and Siblings Towards Testee, Degree of Mastery and Feeling of Competence, Quality of Thinking Process, Activity.
Administration: Individual.
Forms, 1: 9 drawings (6 of which have different versions for boys and girls).
Price Data, 1989: $35 per set of 15 drawings; $12 per manual ('82, 49 pages).
Time: Administration time not reported.
Comments: 1989 edition is identical to 1982 edition except Appendix II was added.
Authors: Rivkah Itskowitz and Helen Strauss.
Publisher: Dansk psykologisk Forlag [Denmark].

TEST REFERENCES

1. Zeidner, M., Klingman, A., & Itskowitz, R. (1993). Children's affective reactions and coping under threat of missile attack: A semiprojective assessment procedure. *Journal of Personality Assessment, 60,* 435-457.

[243]
The Barclay Classroom Assessment System.
Purpose: Designed for the early detection of learning-related and socio-affective problems of child functioning in the classroom.
Population: Grades 3–6.
Publication Dates: 1971–83.
Acronym: BCAS.
Scores, 47: 5 Self-Competency Scores (Artistic-Intellectual, Outdoor-Mechanical, Social-Cooperative, Enterprising, Total), 7 Group Nomination Scores (Artistic-Intellectual, Outdoor-Mechanical, Social-Cooperative, Enterprising, Reticence, Disruptiveness, Total), 9 Vocational Preference Scores (Outdoor-Mechanical, Intellectual-Scientific, Social, Conventional, Enterprising, Arts, Conservative, Status, Total), 12 Teacher Rating Scores (Personal Adjustment Positive, Personal Adjustment Negative, Social Adjustment Positive, Social Adjustment Negative, Work Habits and Attitudes Positive, Work Habits and Attitudes Negative, Total Teacher Rating Positive, Total Teacher Rating Negative, External-Predictable, External-Unpredictable, Internal-Predictable, Internal-Unpredictable), 7 Self-Rated Reinforcer Scores (Self-Stimulating, Esthetic, Intellectual or Task-Oriented, Family-Oriented, Conventional, Male Peer Group, Female Peer Group), Classroom Climate Index, and 6 Factor Scores (Task-Order Achievement, Control-Predictability, Reserved-Internal, Physical-Activity, Sociability-Affiliation, Enterprising-Dominance).
Administration: Group.
Price Data, 1993: $4.20 per evaluation booklet (price includes an individual report for each child and a classroom summary for each class); $1.50 per "Students in My Class" sheet; $30 per manual ('83, 141 pages plus test); $165 per test kit including 36 evaluation booklets, "Students in My Class" sheet, and manual.
Time: (30–40) minutes.

Comments: Formerly called The Barclay Classroom Climate Inventory (BCCI); teacher, peer, and self ratings in classes of 10 to 40 students; computer printout consists of classroom summary (lists children who may need special attention for suspected problems in classroom relationships and learning), individual reports (more detailed reports for each student), and group data tables (listing raw scores and classroom average scores).
Author: James R. Barclay.
Publisher: Western Psychological Services.
Cross References: For reviews by Norman A. Buktenica and Gale M. Morrison, see 9:108 (1 reference); see also T3:239 (5 references); for a review by Richard M. Wolf, see 8:502 (10 references).

[244]
Basic Achievement Skills Individual Screener.
Purpose: "Designed to provide norm-referenced and criterion-referenced information for reading, mathematics, and spelling."
Population: Grades 1–12 and post high school.
Publication Date: 1983.
Acronym: BASIS.
Scores, 3 or 4: Mathematics, Reading, Spelling, Writing Exercise (optional).
Administration: Individual.
Price Data, 1994: $51.50 per content booklet; $45 per 25 record forms; $51.50 per manual ('83, 232 pages); $101.50 per examiner's kit.
Time: (50–60) minutes.
Author: The Psychological Corporation.
Publisher: The Psychological Corporation.
Cross References: For reviews by Robert E. Floden and Richard E. Schutz, see 9:112.

TEST REFERENCES

1. Hambleton, R. K., & Kaplan deVries, D. (1985). Review of the Basic Achievement Skills Individual Screener (BASIS). *Journal of Counseling and Development, 63,* 383-384.
2. Radencich, M. C. (1985). Basis: Basic Achievement Skills Individual Screener. *Academic Therapy, 20,* 377-382.
3. Conley, M. W. (1986). Basic Achievement Skills Individual Screener. *The Reading Teacher, 39,* 418-420.
4. Ysseldyke, J. E. (1986). Basic Achievement Skills Individual Screener (BASIS). *Journal of Counseling Psychology, 64,* 90-91.
5. Schaughency, E. A., & Fagot, B. I. (1993). The prediction of adjustment at age 7 from activity level at age 5. *Journal of Abnormal Child Psychology, 21,* 29-50.
6. Hart, E. L., Lahey, B. B., Loeber, R., & Hanson, K. S. (1994). Criterion validity of informants in the diagnosis of disruptive behavior disorders in children: A preliminary study. *Journal of Consulting and Clinical Psychology, 62,* 410-414.

[245]
Basic Economics Test.
Purpose: "An updated economics achievement test for curriculum development, for the assessment of student understanding, and for determining the effectiveness of educational materials and teaching strategies."
Population: Grades 4–6.
Publication Dates: 1980–81.
Acronym: BET.
Scores: Total score only.

Administration: Group.
Forms, 2: A, B.
Price Data, 1987: $8 per 25 test booklets (specify Form A or B); $5 per Examiner's Manual ('81, 38 pages) which includes scoring keys and model answer sheet which may be duplicated locally.
Time: 50(55) minutes.
Comments: Substantive revision of the Test of Elementary Economics.
Authors: John F. Chizmar and Ronald S. Halinski.
Publisher: National Council on Economic Education.
Cross References: For reviews by Irvin J. Lehmann and A. Harry Passow, see 11:27; for reviews by Mary Friend Adams and James O. Hodges of an earlier edition, see 8:901 (1 reference).

[246]

Basic Educational Skills Test.
Purpose: Designed as a screening and diagnostic test to identify children who may have academic problems.
Population: Grades 1.5–5.
Publication Date: 1979.
Acronym: BEST.
Scores: 3 subtests: Reading, Writing, Mathematics.
Administration: Individual.
Price Data, 1994: $30 per test kit including manual (48 pages), test plates, and 25 recording forms; $24 per test plates; $12 per 25 recording forms; $13 per manual.
Time: (15–20) minutes per test.
Comments: Separate answer sheets must be used.
Authors: Ruth C. Segel and Sandra H. Golding.
Publisher: United Educational Services, Inc.
Cross References: For reviews by Mary Kay Corbitt and Lisa Fleisher and Charles Secolsky, see 9:114.

[247]

Basic English Skills Test.
Purpose: Designed to test listening comprehension, speaking, reading, and writing skills at a basic level when information on the attainment of basic functional language skills is needed.
Population: Limited-English-speaking adults.
Publication Dates: 1982–88.
Acronym: B.E.S.T.
Scores, 9: Oral Interview Section (Listening Comprehension, Communication, Fluency, Pronunciation, Reading/Writing, Total) and Literacy Skill Section (Reading Comprehension, Writing, Total).
Subtests, 2: Oral Interview Section, Literacy Skills Section.
Administration: Individual in part.
Parts: 4 forms (Forms B and C only in current circulation).
Price Data, 1989: $100 per complete test kit; $9 per picture cue book ('88, 15 pages); $10 per 5 interviewer's booklets ('88, 13 pages); $20 per 100 interview scoring sheets ('88, 2 pages); $40 per literacy skills testing package including 20 literacy skills test booklets ('88, 20 pages) and 20 literacy skills scoring sheets ('88, 2 pages); $15 per manual ('88, 79 pages).
Time: [75] minutes.
Comments: Orally administered in part; subtests available as separates; other test materials (e.g., 3 $1 bills, 2 dimes, etc.) must be supplied by examiner.
Authors: Center for Applied Linguistics (test), Dorry Kenyon (revised manual), and Charles W. Stansfield (revised manual) with assistance from Dora Johnson, Allene Grognet, and Dan Dreyfus.
Publisher: Center for Applied Linguistics.
Cross References: For reviews by Alan Garfinkel and Patsy Arnett Jaynes, see 11:28.

[248]

Basic Inventory of Natural Language.
Purpose: "To assess the language dominance, proficiency, and growth of students in school language arts and reading programs."
Population: Grades K–12.
Publication Dates: 1977–79.
Acronym: BINL.
Scores, 3: Fluency, Level of Complexity, Average Sentence Length.
Administration: Individual.
Levels, 2: Forms A, B (grades K–6), Forms C, D (grades 7–12).
Price Data: Not available.
Time: Administration time not reported.
Author: Charles H. Herbert.
Publisher: CHECpoint Systems, Inc. [No reply from publisher; status unknown].
Cross References: For a review by Thomas W. Guyette, see 9:115 (1 reference); see also T3:251 (1 reference).

TEST REFERENCES

1. Figueroa, R. A., Sandoval, J., & Merino, B. (1984). School psychology and limited-English-proficient (LEP) children: New competencies. *Journal of School Psychology, 22*, 131-143.
2. Sattler, J. M., & Altes, L. M. (1984). Performance of bilingual and monolingual Hispanic children on the Peabody Picture Vocabulary Test—Revised and the McCarthy Perceptual Performance Scale. *Psychology in the Schools, 21*, 313-316.

[249]

Basic Language Concepts Test.
Purpose: To screen children and identify those having serious language-concepts problems and provide diagnostic information to aid in developing effective remedies.
Population: Ages 4–6.5 and older language-deficient children in elementary schools or clinic settings.
Publication Dates: 1966–82.
Acronym: BLCT.
Scores, 5: Receptive Language Skills, Expressive Language Skills, (Sentence Repetition, Answering Questions), Analogy Skills, Total.
Administration: Individual.
Price Data, 1986: $35 per 40 test forms and manual ('82, 105 pages); $10 per 40 test forms.
Time: (10–20) minutes.

Comments: Revision of Basic Concept Inventory; "criterion-referenced."
Authors: Siegfried Engelmann, Dorothy Ross, and Virginia Bingham.
Publisher: Science Research Associates, Inc.
Cross References: For a review by Amy Finch-Williams and Robert T. Williams, see 9:23 (1 reference).

[250]

Basic Living Skills Scale.
Purpose: Determine the skill levels of pupils in seven behavioral areas.
Population: Grades 3–6.
Publication Date: 1980.
Acronym: BLSS.
Scores, 8: Self-Concept, Interpersonal Relations, Responsibility, Decision Making, Study Skills, Citizenship, Career Planning, Total.
Administration: Group.
Price Data, 1993: $35.80 per complete kit including 35 test booklets and manual (17 pages); $35.75 per 50 response booklets; $66 per 100 response booklets; $55 per 50 pupil taskbooks; $104.50 per 100 pupil taskbooks; $4.95 per teacher/counselor handbook; $4.95 per manual; $1 per pupil machine score.
Time: (15–20) minutes.
Comments: Self-administered; designed to be used as a "Criterion Reference Scale"; no data on reliability or validity.
Author: Bob Percival.
Publisher: Dallas Educational Services.
Cross References: For reviews by Bonnie W. Camp and Louis J. Heifetz, see 10:24.

[251]

Basic Mathematics Tests.
Purpose: Assesses children's understanding of basic mathematical relationships and processes.
Population: Ages 7-0 to 8-0, 8-0 to 9-0, 9-7 to 10-10, 10-0 to 12-6, 12-0 to 14-6.
Publication Dates: 1969–72.
Scores: Total score only.
Administration: Group.
Price Data, 1989: £6.45 per 10 tests (A, B, C, DE, or FG); £3.20 per manual.
Author: The National Foundation for Educational Research.
Publisher: NFER-Nelson Publishing Co., Ltd. [England].
  a) BASIC MATHEMATICS TEST A [ORAL].
  Population: Ages 7-0 to 8-0.
  Publication Date: 1971.
  Time: (45) minutes.
  b) BASIC MATHEMATICS TEST B [ORAL].
  Population: Ages 8-0 to 9-0.
  Publication Date: 1971.
  Time: (45) minutes.
  c) BASIC MATHEMATICS TEST C.
  Population: Ages 9-7 to 10-10.
  Publication Dates: 1970–72.

Time: (50) minutes.
  d) BASIC MATHEMATICS TEST DE.
  Population: Ages 10-0 to 12-6.
  Publication Dates: 1969–72.
  Time: (50) minutes.
  e) BASIC MATHEMATICS TEST FG.
  Population: Ages 12-0 to 14-6.
  Publication Date: 1969.
  Time: (50) minutes.
Cross References: See T3:252 (2 references).

TEST REFERENCES

1. Haylock, D. W. (1986). Mathematical low attainers checklist. *British Journal of Educational Psychology, 56,* 205-208.
2. Phillips, C. J. (1989). Children's learning skills: A cautionary note on ethnic differences. *British Journal of Educational Psychology, 59,* 108-112.

[252]

Basic Number Diagnostic Test.
Purpose: "Individual assessment-for-teaching in basic number skills."
Population: Ages 5–7.
Publication Date: 1980.
Scores, 13: Reciting Numbers, Naming Numbers, Copying Over, Copying Underneath, Writing Numbers in Sequence, Writing Numbers to Dictation, Counting Bricks, Selecting Bricks, Addition Sums with Objects, Addition Sums with Numerals, Subtraction Sums with Objects, Subtraction Sums with Numerals, Total.
Administration: Individual.
Price Data, 1994: £8.99 per 20 tests; £3.99 per manual (14 pages); £4.25 per specimen set.
Time: (15–25) minutes.
Comments: "Criterion-referenced."
Author: W. E. C. Gillham.
Publisher: Hodder & Stoughton Educational [England].
Cross References: For a review by Mary Montgomery Lindquist, see 9:117.

[253]

Basic Number Screening Test.
Purpose: "Quick assessment of a child's understanding of . . . number concepts and . . . number skills."
Population: Ages 7–12.
Publication Dates: 1976–80.
Scores: No scores.
Forms, 2: A, B.
Administration: Group.
Price Data, 1994: £6.45 per 20 tests (Form A); £6.45 per 20 tests (Form B); £3.99 per manual ('79, 14 pages); £4.25 per specimen set.
Time: (20–35) minutes.
Comments: May be orally administered.
Authors: W. E. C. Gillham and K. A. Hesse.
Publisher: Hodder & Stoughton Educational [England].
Cross References: For reviews by Mary Montgomery Lindquist and Marilyn N. Suydam, see 9:118.

[254]

Basic Personality Inventory.
Purpose: Constructed to be a "measure of personality and psychopathology."
Population: Ages 12 and over.
Publication Dates: 1984–89.
Acronym: BPI.
Scores, 12: Hypochondriasis, Depression, Denial, Interpersonal Problems, Alienation, Persecutory Ideas, Anxiety, Thinking Disorder, Impulse Expression, Social Introversion, Self Depreciation, Deviation.
Administration: Individual or group.
Price Data, 1991: $44 per examination kit including 10 reusable test booklets, 25 answer sheets, scoring template, 25 profile sheets, answer sheet and coupon for BPI report, and manual ('89, 87 pages); $22.75 per 25 test booklets; $5.50–$9 (depending on volume) per 25 answer sheets; $8 per scoring template; $5.50–$9 (depending on volume) per 25 profile sheets (select adult or adolescent norms); $22 per manual; scoring service offered by publisher.
Time: [35] minutes.
Author: Douglas N. Jackson.
Publisher: Sigma Assessment Systems, Inc., Research Psychologists Press Division.

TEST REFERENCES

1. Helmes, E., & Holden, R. R. (1986). Response styles and faking on the Basic Personality Inventory. *Journal of Consulting and Clinical Psychology, 54,* 853-859.
2. Jackson, D. N., Maclennan, R. N., Erdle, S. W. P., Holden, R. R., Lalonde, R. N., & Thompson, G. R. (1986). Clinical judgments of depression. *Journal of Clinical Psychology, 42,* 136-145.
3. Paunonen, S. V. (1987). Test construction and targeted factor solutions derived by multiple group and procrustes methods. *Multivariate Behavioral Research, 22,* 437- 455.
4. Helmes, E., & Barilko, O. (1988). Comparison of three multiscale inventories in identifying the presence of psychopathological symptoms. *Journal of Personality Assessment, 52,* 74-80.
5. Holden, R. R., Fekken, G. C., Reddon, J. R., Helmes, E., & Jackson, D. N. (1988). Clinical reliabilities and validities of the Basic Personality Inventory. *Journal of Consulting and Clinical Psychology, 56,* 766-768.
6. Leschied, A. W., Austin, G. W., & Jaffe, P. G. (1988). Impact of the Young Offenders Act on recidivism rates of special needs youth: Clinical and policy implications. *Canadian Journal of Behavioural Science, 20,* 322-331.
7. Holden, R. R. (1989). Disguise and the structured self-report assessment of psychopathology: II. A clinical replication. *Journal of Clinical Psychology, 45,* 583-586.
8. Reddon, J. R., & Jackson, D. N. (1989). Readability of three adult personality tests: Basic Personality Inventory, Jackson Personality Inventory, and Personality Research Form-E. *Journal of Personality Assessment, 53,* 180-183.
9. Bagby, R. M., Gillis, J. R., & Dickens, S. (1990). Detection of dissimulation with the new generation of objective personality measures. *Behavioral Sciences and the Law, 8,* 93-102.
10. Holden, R. R., & Fekken, G. C. (1990). Structured psychopathology test item characteristics and validity. *Psychological Assessment, 2,* 35-40.
11. Kroner, D. G., Reddon, J. R., & Beckett, N. (1991). Basic Personality Inventory clinical and validity scales: Stability and internal consistency. *Journal of Psychopathology and Behavioral Assessment, 13,* 147-154.
12. Retzlaff, P. D., & Bromley, S. (1991). A multi-test alcoholic taxonomy: Canonical coefficient clusters. *Journal of Clinical Psychology, 47,* 299-309.
13. Fekken, G. C., & Holden, R. R. (1992). Response latency evidence for viewing personality traits as schema indicators. *Journal of Research in Personality, 26,* 103-120.
14. Holden, R. R., Kroner, D. G., Fekken, G. C., & Popham, M. (1992). A model of personality test item response dissimulation. *Journal of Personality and Social Psychology, 63,* 272-279.
15. Schinka, J. A., & Borum, R. (1993). Readibility of adult psychopathology inventories. *Psychological Assessment, 5,* 384-386.
16. Bonynge, E. R. (1994). A cluster analysis of Basic Personality Inventory (BPI) adolescent profiles. *Journal of Clinical Psychology, 50,* 265-272.

[255]

Basic Reading Inventory, Sixth Edition.
Purpose: "To help place students in appropriate reading materials."
Population: Grades Pre-primer–10.
Publication Dates: 1978–94.
Acronym: BRI.
Scores, 12: 4 reading level scores (Independent, Instructional, Frustration, Listening) for each of 3 subtests (Word Recognition in Isolation, Word Recognition in Context, Comprehension).
Administration: Individual or group.
Forms, 5: A, B, C, LN, LE.
Time: Administration time not reported.
Author: Jerry L. Johns.
Publisher: Kendall/Hunt Publishing Company.
Cross References: For a review by Gus P. Plessas of the second edition, see 9:119.

TEST REFERENCES

1. Byrd, D. M., & Gholson, B. (1985). Reading, memory, and metacognition. *Journal of Educational Psychology, 77,* 428-436.
2. Helgren-Lempesis, V. A., & Mangrum, C. T., II. (1986). An analysis of alternate-form reliability of three commercially-prepared informal reading inventories. *Reading Research Quarterly, 21,* 209-215.
3. Kuhns, C. O., Moore, D. W., & Moore, S. A. (1986). The stability of modified miscue analysis profiles. *Reading Research and Instruction, 25,* 149-159.
4. Swindell, L. K., Peterson, S. E., & Greenway, R. (1992). Children's use of response confidence in the processing of instructional feedback. *Contemporary Educational Psychology, 17,* 379-385.

[256]

Basic School Skills Inventory—Diagnostic.
Purpose: "Designed to . . . assess the abilities of young children."
Population: Ages 4-0 to 6-11.
Publication Dates: 1975–83.
Acronym: BSSI-D.
Scores, 7: Daily Living Skills, Spoken Language, Reading, Writing, Mathematics, Classroom Behavior, Total.
Administration: Individual.
Price Data, 1994: $64 per complete kit including 50 answer sheets, picture book, and manual ('83, 70 pages); $22 per 50 answer sheets; $19 per picture book; $29 per manual.
Time: (20–30) minutes.
Comments: Basic School Skills Inventory—Screen (257) is a short form of this inventory.
Authors: Donald D. Hammill and James E. Leigh.
Publisher: PRO-ED, Inc.
Cross References: For a review by William J. Webster, see 9:120; for reviews of an earlier edition by Byron R. Egeland and Lawrence M. Kasdon, see 8:424 (2 references).

TEST REFERENCES

1. Jorgenson, C. B., Jorgenson, D. E., Gillis, M. K., & McCall, C. M. (1993). Validation of a screening instrument for young children

with teacher assessment of school performance. *School Psychology Quarterly, 8*, 125-139.

[257]

Basic School Skills Inventory—Screen.
Purpose: "Designed to select those children who may need remedial work, more comprehensive evaluation, or referral for special services."
Population: Ages 4-0 through 6-11.
Publication Date: 1983.
Acronym: BSSI-S.
Scores: Total score only.
Administration: Individual.
Price Data, 1994: $24 per complete kit including 50 answer sheets and examiner's manual (6 pages).
Time: (5–10) minutes. ·
Comments: Short form of the Basic School Skills Inventory—Diagnostic (256).
Authors: Donald D. Hammill and James E. Leigh.
Publisher: PRO-ED, Inc.
Cross References: For a review by Leland K. Doebler, see 9:121.

TEST REFERENCES

1. Jorgenson, C. B., Jorgenson, D. E., Gillis, M. K., & McCall, C. M. (1993). Validation of a screening instrument for young children with teacher assessment of school performance. *School Psychology Quarterly, 8*, 125-139.

[258]

Basic Sight Word Test.
Purpose: To assess recognition of basic "service words."
Population: Grades 1–2.
Publication Date: 1942.
Administration: Group.
Manual: No manual.
Price Data: Not available.
Time: Administration time not reported.
Author: Edward W. Dolch.
Publisher: Garrard Publishing Co. [No reply from publisher; status unknown].
Cross References: See T2:1657 (5 references).

TEST REFERENCES

1. Merritt, F. M., & McCallum, R. S. (1983). Sex-related differences in simultaneous-successive information processing? *Clinical Neuropsychology, 5*, 117-119.
2. Merritt, F. M., & McCallum, R. S. (1984). The relationship between simultaneous-successive processing and academic achievement. *The Alberta Journal of Educational Research, 30*, 126-132.

[259]

Basic Skills Inventory.
Purpose: "Designed to test common objectives or minimum competencies" for pupils in grades 1–12.
Population: Grades K–1, 1–2, 2–3, 3–4, 5–6, 7–8, 9–10, 11–12.
Publication Dates: 1980–82.
Acronym: BSI.
Administration: Group.
Price Data: Not available.
Time: (45) minutes per subtest.
Comments: Combined booklets available for grades

4–6, 7–9, and 10–12 only; answer sheets must be used for grades 4–12.
Author: Los Angeles County Office of Education.
Publisher: Los Angeles County Office of Education [No reply from publisher; status unknown].

a) READING.
1)
Population: Grades K–1.
Scores, 3: Phonetic Analysis, Vocabulary, Comprehension.
Forms, 2: Level A, Level I.
2)
Population: Grades 1–2.
Scores, 5: Phonetic Analysis, Structural Analysis, Vocabulary, Comprehension, Study Skills.
Forms, 2: Level B, Level II.
3)
Population: Grades 2–3.
Scores, 5: Same as 2 above.
Forms, 2: Level C, Level III.
4)
Population: Grades 3–4.
Scores, 5: Same as 2 above.
Form, 1: Level IV.
5)
Population: Grades 5–6.
Scores, 5: Same as 2 above.
Form, 1: Level V.
6)
Population: Grades 7–8.
Scores, 4: Structural Analysis, Vocabulary, Comprehension, Study Skills.
Form, 1: Level VI.
7)
Population: Grades 9–10.
Scores, 4: Same as 6 above.
Form, 1: Level VII.
8)
Population: Grades 11–12.
Scores, 4: Same as 6 above.
Form, 1: Level VIII.

b) LANGUAGE ARTS.
1)
Population: Grades K–1.
Scores, 3: Language Analysis, Conventions, Expression/Comprehension.
Forms, 2: Level A, Level I.
2)
Population: Grades 1–2.
Scores, 3: Same as 1 above.
Forms, 2: Level B, Level II.
3)
Population: Grades 2–3.
Scores, 3: Same as 1 above.
Forms, 2: Level C, Level III.
4)
Population: Grades 3–4.
Scores, 4: Spelling, Punctuation, Sentence Structure, Verb Usage.
Form, 1: Level IV.
5)

Population: Grades 5–6.
Scores, 4: Same as 4 above.
Form, 1: Level V.
6)
Population: Grades 7–8.
Scores, 4: Same as 4 above.
Form, 1: Level VI.
7)
Population: Grades 9–10.
Scores, 4: Same as 4 above.
Form, 1: Level VII.
8)
Population: Grades 11–12.
Scores, 4: Same as 4 above.
Form, 1: Level VIII.
c) MATHEMATICS.
1)
Population: Grades K–1.
Scores, 3: Comprehension, Computation, Application.
Forms, 2: Level A, Level I.
2)
Population: Grades 1–2.
Scores, 3: Same as 1 above.
Forms, 2: Level B, Level II.
3)
Population: Grades 2–3.
Scores, 3: Same as 1 above.
Forms, 2: Level C, Level III.
4)
Population: Grades 3–4.
Scores, 4: Basic Operations, Basic Operations with Decimals, Basic Operations with Fractions, Application.
Form, 1: Level IV.
5)
Population: Grades 5–6.
Scores, 4: Same as 4 above.
Form, 1: Level V.
6)
Population: Grades 7–8.
Scores, 4: Same as 4 above.
Form, 1: Level VI.
7)
Population: Grades 9–10.
Scores, 5: Same as 4 above plus Comprehension of Geometric Formulas.
Form, 1: Level VII.
8)
Population: Grades 11–12.
Scores, 5: Same as 4 above plus Application and Comprehension of Geometric Formulas.
Form, 1: Level VIII.
Cross References: For reviews by G. J. Robertson and V. L. Wilson, see 9:123.

[260]

Basic Tests Series.
Purpose: To assess basic skills and knowledge relevant to the world of work or postsecondary education.

Population: High school seniors and college entrants and job applicants.
Publication Dates: 1981–93.
Scores: Total scores only.
Administration: Group.
Restricted Distribution: Distribution restricted and tests administered at licensed testing centers.
Price Data, 1994: £7.25 entry fee per test (£8 Basic Tests [Special] and Basic English; £3 Proficiency Test in Arithmetic); 80p per Basic Tests booklet containing syllabus and specimen papers (specify test); price data for additional supplementary materials available from publisher.
Comments: Tests administered each May at centers established by the publisher; tests available as separates.
Author: The Associated Examining Board.
Publisher: The Associated Examining Board [England].
a) BASIC TEST IN ARITHMETIC.
Time: 10(15) minutes for Paper 1 (mental arithmetic test); 75(80) minutes for Paper 2 (written test).
1) *Proficiency Test in Arithmetic.*
Time: 90(95) minutes.
Comments: To enter this test, candidate must enter for Basic Test in Arithmetic at the same time.
b) BASIC TEST IN ENGLISH.
Time: 30(40) minutes for Paper 1 (listening); 60(65) minutes for Paper 2 (reading and writing).
Comments: Is to be renamed Basic Test in Communication Skills.
c) BASIC TEST IN LIFE SKILLS.
Time: 90(100) minutes.
d) BASIC TEST IN COMPUTER AWARENESS.
Time: 90(95) minutes.
e) BASIC TEST IN GRAPHICACY.
Time: 90(100) minutes.
f) BASIC TEST IN HEALTH, HYGIENE AND SAFETY.
Time: 75(85) minutes.
g) BASIC TEST IN GEOGRAPHY.
Time: 90(95) minutes.
h) BASIC TEST IN SCIENCE.
Time: 90(95) minutes.
Comments: Is to be renamed Basic Test in Basic Applications of Science.
i) BASIC TEST IN WORLD OF WORK.
Time: 90(100) minutes.
j) BASIC TEST (SPECIAL) IN GEOGRAPHY FOR TOURISM AND LEISURE.
Time: 90(100) minutes.
Cross References: For reviews by Steven Ferrara and Anne R. Fitzpatrick, see 11:29.

[261]

Basic Visual-Motor Association Test.
Purpose: "Test of short-term visual memory."
Population: Grades 1–9.
Publication Date: 1982.

Acronym: BVMAT.
Scores: 1 overall performance score.
Administration: Individual administration recommended for grade 1.
Forms, 2: A, B.
Price Data, 1988: $19.50 per complete battery, includes manual (45 pages), 25 tests and scoring key; $12.50 per specimen set.
Time: 3(5) minutes per form.
Author: James Battle.
Publisher: Special Child Publications.
Cross References: For reviews by Burke H. Bretzing and H. Lee Swanson, see 9:124.

[262]

BASIS-A Inventory [Basic Adlerian Scales for Interpersonal Success—Adult Form].
Purpose: Designed "to help understand how an individual's life-style, based on beliefs developed in early childhood, contributes to one's effectiveness in social, work, and intimate relationships."
Population: Adults.
Publication Date: 1993.
Acronym: BASIS.
Scores, 10: BASIS scales (Belonging-Social Interest, Taking Charge, Going Along, Wanting Recognition, Being Cautious); HELPS scales (Harshness, Entitlement, Liked By All, Perfectionism, Softness).
Administration: Group or individual.
Price Data, 1993: $70 per introductory kit including 25 test booklets, technical manual (58 pages), interpretive manual (48 pages), and 5 copies of "Interpreting Your BASIS-A Profile"; $60 per 25 test booklets; $24 per technical manual and interpretive manual; $5 per sampler kit including test booklet and "Interpreting Your BASIS-A Profile"; $20 per 25 "Interpreting Your BASIS-A Profile."
Foreign Language Edition: Test items and instructions available in Spanish.
Time: (10–15) minutes.
Comments: Self-scored.
Authors: Mary S. Wheeler, Roy M. Kern, and William L. Curlette.
Publisher: TRT Associates.

[263]

Battelle Developmental Inventory.
Purpose: To identify the developmental strengths and weaknesses of handicapped and nonhandicapped children in infant, preschool, and primary programs.
Population: Birth to 8 years.
Publication Date: 1984.
Acronym: BDI.
Scores: 30 profile scores: Adult Interaction, Expression of Feeling/Affect, Self-Concept, Peer Interaction, Coping, Social Role, Personal-Social Total, Attention, Eating, Dressing, Personal Responsibility, Toileting, Adaptive Total, Muscle Control, Body Coordination, Locomotion, Gross Motor, Fine Muscle, Perceptual Motor, Fine Motor, Motor Total, Receptive, Expres-

sive, Communication Total, Perceptual Discrimination, Memory, Reasoning and Academic Skills, Conceptual Development, Cognitive Total, Total.
Administration: Individual.
Price Data, 1989: $175 per complete kit including 15 scoring booklets, 30 screening test booklets, 5 test item books, screening test, visuals, manual (168 pages), and carrying case; $20 per 30 screening test booklets; $15 per 15 scoring booklets; $40 per VHS demonstration tape; $40 per manual.
Time: (60) minutes.
Comments: Screening test available as a separate.
Authors: Jean Newborg, John R. Stock, Linda Wnek, John Guidubaldi, and John Svinicki.
Publisher: The Riverside Publishing Co.
Cross References: For reviews by Judy Oehler-Stinnett and Kathleen D. Paget, see 10:25 (1 reference).

TEST REFERENCES

1. Malone, D. M., & Stoneman, Z. (1990). Cognitive play of mentally retarded preschoolers: Observations in the home and school. *American Journal on Mental Retardation, 94,* 475-487.
2. Rice, M. L., Buhr, J. C., & Nemeth, M. (1990). Fast mapping word-learning abilities of language-delayed preschoolers. *Journal of Speech and Hearing Disorders, 55,* 33-42.
3. Wilcox, M. J., Kouri, T. A., & Caswell, S. (1990). Partner sensitivity to communication behavior of young children with developmental disabilities. *Journal of Speech and Hearing Disorders, 55,* 679-693.
4. Matson, J. L., Fee, V. E., Coe, D. A., & Smith, D. (1991). A social skills program for developmental delayed preschoolers. *Journal of Clinical Child Psychology, 20,* 428-433.

[264]

Battelle Developmental Inventory Screening Test.
Purpose: For general screening, preliminary assessment, and/or initial identification of possible developmental strengths and weaknesses.
Population: Birth to age 8.
Publication Date: 1984.
Acronym: BDI Screening Test.
Scores, 10: Personal-Social, Adaptive, Motor (Gross Motor, Fine Motor, Total), Communication (Receptive, Expressive, Total), Cognitive, Total.
Administration: Individual.
Price Data, 1988: $70 per screening test including 30 test booklets, test item book (108 pages), and examiner's manual (52 pages); $15 per 30 screening test booklets.
Time: (10–30) minutes.
Comments: Short form of the Battelle Developmental Inventory (263); other test materials must be supplied by examiner.
Authors: Initial development by Jean Newborg, John R. Stock, and Linda Wnek; pilot norming study by John Guidubaldi; completion and standardization by John Svinicki.
Publisher: The Riverside Publishing Company.
Cross References: For reviews by David W. Barnett and Joan Ershler and Stephen N. Elliott, see 11:30.

TEST REFERENCES

1. May, D. C., & Kundert, D. K. (1992). Kindergarten screenings in New York state: Tests, purposes, and recommendations. *Psychology in the Schools, 29*(1), 35-41.

[265]
Bay Area Functional Performance Evaluation, Second Edition.

Purpose: Developed to assess "general components of functioning that are needed to perform activities of daily living."
Population: Psychiatric patients.
Publication Dates: 1978–87.
Acronym: BaFPE.
Administration: Individual.
Price Data, 1988: $135 per complete kit including 25 sorting shells rating sheets, 25 money and marketing rating sheets, 25 home drawing rating sheets, 25 block design rating sheets, 25 kinetic person drawing rating sheets, 25 marketing worksheets, 25 blank checks, seashell set, block design set, 25 SIS assessment forms, 25 TOA assessment forms, 25 SIS rating and summary score sheets, 25 TOA summary score sheets, and manual ('87, 97 pages); $63 per 25 refill sets of all 11 expendable forms; $6.50 per 25 sorting shells rating sheets, money and marketing rating sheets, home drawing rating sheets, or kinetic person drawing rating sheets; $5.75 per 25 SIS assessment forms, SIS rating and summary score sheets, or TOA assessment forms; $3.75 per 25 TOA summary score sheets, marketing worksheets, or blank checks; $20 per seashell set; $19 per block design set; $2.25 per set of reusable instruction/demonstration cards; $39.50 per manual.
Comments: Task-Oriented Assessment and Social Interaction Scale may be used separately.
Authors: Susan Lang Williams and Judith Bloomer.
Publisher: Consulting Psychologists Press, Inc.

a) TASK-ORIENTED ASSESSMENT.
Acronym: TOA.
Scores, 138: 16 Component scores: Cognitive (Memory for Written/Verbal Instruction, Organization of Time and Materials, Attention Span, Evidence of Thought Disorder, Ability to Abstract, Total), Performance (Task Completion, Errors, Efficiency, Total), Affective (Motivation/Compliance, Frustration Tolerance, Self-Confidence, General Affective Impression, Total), Total for the following 11 Parameters: Sorting Shells, Money/Marketing, Home Drawing, Block Design, Kinetic Person Drawing, Total; also 11 Qualitative Signs and Referral Indicators ratings: Language, Comprehension, Hemispatial Neglect, Memory, Abstraction, Task-Specific Observations, Total for the above parameters.
Time: (30–45) minutes.

b) SOCIAL INTERACTION SCALE.
Acronym: SIS.
Scores, 13: Parameter scores (Verbal Communication, Psychomotor Behavior, Socially Appropriate Behavior, Response to Authority Figures, Degree of Independence/Dependence, Ability to Work with Others, Participation in Group Activities), Social Situations (One-to-One, Mealtime, Unstructured Group, Structured Task or Activity Group, Structured Verbal Group), Total Interaction.
Time: [50–60] minutes.

TEST REFERENCES

1. Mathias, J. L., & Nettelbeck, T. (1992). Validity of Greenspan's models of adaptive and social intelligence. *Research in Developmental Disabilities, 13*, 113-129.

[266]
Bayley Scales of Infant Development, Second Edition.

Purpose: "Assesses the current developmental functioning of infants and children."
Population: Ages 1–42 months.
Publication Dates: 1969–93.
Acronym: BSID-II.
Scores, 2: Mental, Motor, plus 30 behavior ratings.
Administration: Individual.
Price Data, 1994: $690 per complete kit including 25 Mental Scale record forms, 25 Motor Scale record forms, 25 Behavior Rating Scale record forms, visual stimulus cards, map, manipulatives, carrying case, stimulus booklet, and manual ('93, 374 pages); $28 per 25 Mental Scale record forms, $24 per 25 Motor Scale record forms, $22 per 25 Behavior Rating Scale record forms; $55 per stimulus booklet; $55 per manual.
Time: (25–60) minutes.
Author: Nancy Bayley.
Publisher: The Psychological Corporation.
Cross References: For reviews by Michael J. Roszkowski and Jane A. Rysberg of an earlier edition, see 10:26 (80 references); see also 9:126 (42 references) and T3:270 (101 references); for a review by Fred Damarin, see 8:206 (28 references); see also T2:484 (11 references); for reviews by Roberta R. Collard and Raymond H. Holden, see 7:402 (20 references).

TEST REFERENCES

1. Wilson, R. S., & Matheny, A. P., Jr. (1983). Mental development: Family environment and genetic influences. *Intelligence, 7*, 195-215.
2. Achenbach, T. M., Edelbrock, C., & Howell, C. T. (1987). Empirically based assessment of the behavioral/emotional problems of 2- and 3-year-old children. *Journal of Abnormal Child Psychology, 15*, 629-650.
3. Bathurst, K., & Gottfried, A. W. (1987). Untestable subjects in child development research: Developmental implications. *Child Development, 58*, 1135-1144.
4. Crockenberg, S. (1987). Predictors and correlates of anger toward and punitive control of toddlers by adolescent mothers. *Child Development, 58*, 964-975.
5. Lachiewicz, A. M., Gullion, C. M., Spiridigliozzi, G. A., & Aylsworth, A. S. (1987). Declining IQs of young males with the fragile x syndrome. *American Journal on Mental Retardation, 92*, 272-278.
6. Lovaas, O. I. (1987). Behavioral treatment and normal educational and intellectual functioning in young autistic children. *Journal of Consulting and Clinical Psychology, 55*, 3-9.
7. Loveland, K. A. (1987). Behavior of young children with Down Syndrome before the mirror: Finding things reflected. *Child Development, 58*, 928-936.
8. Melby, J. N., Pease, D., & Kleckner, K. A. (1987). The Iowa Pegboard Fine-motor Task: Normative performance and research applications. *Perceptual and Motor Skills, 64*, 995-1002.
9. Morrow-Tlucak, M., Ernhart, C. B., & Liddle, C. L. (1987).

The Kent Infant Development Scale: Concurrent and predictive validity of a modified administration. *Psychological Reports, 60,* 887-894.

10. Szanjnberg, N., Ward, M. J., Krauss, A., & Kessler, D. B. (1987). Low birth-weight prematures: Preventive intervention and maternal attitude. *Child Psychiatry and Human Development, 17,* 152-165.

11. Watt, J. (1987). Temperament in small-for-dates and pre-term infants: A preliminary study. *Child Psychiatry and Human Development, 17,* 177-188.

12. Bernheimer, L. P., & Keogh, B. K. (1988). Stability of cognitive performance of children with developmental delays. *American Journal on Mental Retardation, 92,* 539-542.

13. Creighton, D. E., & Sauve, R. S. (1988). The Minnesota Infant Development Inventory in the developmental screening of high-risk infants at eight months. *Canadian Journal of Behavioural Science, 20,* 424-433.

14. Crittenden, P. M., & DiLalla, D. L. (1988). Compulsive compliance: The development of an inhibitory coping strategy in infancy. *Journal of Abnormal Child Psychology, 16,* 585-599.

15. Dunst, C. J. (1988). Stage transitioning in the sensorimotor development of Down's syndrome infants. *Journal of Mental Deficiency Research, 32,* 405-410.

16. Fisher, W., Burd, L., & Kerbeshian, J. (1988). Markers for improvement in children with pervasive developmental disorders. *Journal of Mental Deficiency Research, 32,* 357-369.

17. Goldstein, D. J., & Sheaffer, C. I. (1988). Ratio developmental quotients from the Bayley are comparable to later IQs from the Stanford-Binet. *American Journal on Mental Retardation, 92,* 379-380.

18. Humphreys, L. G., & Davey, T. C. (1988). Continuity in intellectual growth from 12 months to 9 years. *Intelligence, 12,* 183-197.

19. Macpherson, F., & Butterworth, G. (1988). Sensorimotor intelligence in severely mentally handicapped children. *Journal of Mental Deficiency Research, 32,* 465-478.

20. Mahoney, G. (1988). Maternal communication style with mentally retarded children. *American Journal on Mental Retardation, 92,* 352-359.

21. Rice, T., Fulker, D. W., DeFries, J. C., & Plomin, R. (1988). Path analysis of IQ during infancy and early childhood and an index of the home environment in the Colorado Adoption Project. *Intelligence, 12,* 27-45.

22. Sagi, A., Jaffe, M., Tirosh, E., Findler, L., & Harel, J. (1988). Maternal risk status and outcome measures: A three-stage study in Israel. *Child Psychiatry and Human Development, 19,* 145-157.

23. Wasserman, G. A., Allen, R., & Linares, L. O. (1988). Maternal interaction and language development in children with and without speech-related anomalies. *Journal of Communication Disorders, 21,* 319-331.

24. Bradley, R. H., Rock, S. L., Caldwell, B. M., & Brisby, J. A. (1989). Uses of the HOME inventory for families with handicapped children. *American Journal on Mental Retardation, 94,* 313-330.

25. Gowen, J. W., Johnson-Martin, N., Goldman, B. D., & Appelbaum, M. (1989). Feelings of depression and parenting competence of mothers of handicapped and nonhandicapped infants: A longitudinal study. *American Journal on Mental Retardation, 94,* 259-271.

26. Green, J. M., Dennis, J., & Bennets, L. A. (1989). Attention disorder in a group of young Down's syndrome children. *Journal of Mental Deficiency Research, 33,* 105-122.

27. Tirosh, E., Taub, Y., Scher, A., Jaffe, M., & Hochberg, Z. (1989). Short-term efficacy of thyroid hormone supplementation for patients with Down Syndrome and low-borderline thyroid function. *American Journal on Mental Retardation, 93,* 652-656.

28. Whiffen, V. E., & Gotlib, I. H. (1989). Infants of postpartum depressed mothers: Temperament and cognitive status. *Journal of Abnormal Psychology, 98,* 274-279.

29. DiLalla, L. F., & Thompson, L. A., Plomin, R., Phillips, K., Fagan, J. F., Haith, M. M., Cyphers, L. H., & Fulker, D. W. (1990). Infant predictors of preschool and adult IQ: A study of infant twins and their parents. *Developmental Psychology, 26,* 759-769.

30. Hill, B. P., & Singer, L. T. (1990). Speech and language development after infant tracheostomy. *Journal of Speech and Hearing Disorders, 55,* 15-20.

31. Laks, D. R., Beckwith, L., & Cohen, S. E. (1990). Mothers' use of personal pronouns when talking with toddlers. *The Journal of Genetic Psychology, 151,* 25-32.

32. Landry, S. H., & Chapieski, M. L. (1990). Joint attention of six-month-old Down Syndrome and preterm infants: I. Attention to toys and mother. *American Journal on Mental Retardation, 94,* 488-498.

33. Platt, J., & Coggins, T. E. (1990). Comprehension of social-action games in prelinguistic children: Levels of participation and effect of adult structure. *Journal of Speech and Hearing Disorders, 55,* 315-326.

34. Robinson, N. M., Dale, P. S., & Landesman, S. (1990). Validity of Stanford-Binet IV with linguistically precocious toddlers. *Intelligence, 14,* 173-186.

35. Arendt, R. E., MacLean, W. E., Jr., Halpern, L. F., Youngquist, G. A., & Baumeister, A. A. (1991). The influence of rotary vestibular stimulation upon motor development of nonhandicapped and Down syndrome infants. *Research in Developmental Disabilities, 12,* 333-348.

36. Cardon, L. R., & Fulker, D. W. (1991). Sources of continuity in infant predictors of later IQ. *Intelligence, 15,* 279-293.

37. Loveland, K. A., & Kelley, M. L. (1991). Development of adaptive behavior in preschoolers with autism or Down syndrome. *American Journal on Mental Retardation, 96,* 13-20.

38. MacLean, W. E., Jr., Ellis, D. N., Galbreath, H. N., Halpern, L. F., & Baumeister, A. A. (1991). Rhythmic motor behavior of preambulatory motor impaired Down syndrome and nondisabled children: A comparative analysis. *Journal of Abnormal Child Psychology, 19,* 319-330.

39. Nelson, L. K., & Bauer, H. R. (1991). Speech and language production at age 2: Evidence for tradeoffs between linguistic and phonetic processing. *Journal of Speech and Hearing Research, 34,* 879-892.

40. Paul, R., Looney, S. S., & Dahm, P. S. (1991). Communication and socialization skills at ages 2 and 3 in "late-talking" young children. *Journal of Speech and Hearing Research, 34,* 858-865.

41. Seifer, R., Clark, G. N., & Sameroff, A. J. (1991). Positive effects of interaction coaching on infants with developmental disabilities and their mothers. *American Journal on Mental Retardation, 96,* 1-11.

42. Thompson, L. A., Fagan, J. F., & Fulker, D. W. (1991). Longitudinal prediction of specific cognitive abilities from infant novelty preference. *Child Development, 62,* 530-538.

43. Yoder, P. J., Kaiser, A. P., & Alpert, C. L. (1991). An exploratory study of the interaction between language teaching methods and child characteristics. *Journal of Speech and Hearing Research, 34,* 155-167.

44. Braungart, J. M., & Fulker, D. W., & Plomin, R. (1992). Genetic mediation of the home environment during infancy: A sibling adoption study of the HOME. *Developmental Psychology, 28,* 1048-1055.

45. Braungart, J. M., Plomin, R., DeFries, J. C., & Fulker, D. W. (1992). Genetic influence on tester-rated infant temperament as assessed by Bayley's Infant Behavior Record: Nonadoptive and adoptive siblings and twins. *Developmental Psychology, 28,* 40-47.

46. Burt, D. B., Loveland, K. A., & Lewis, K. R. (1992). Depression and the onset of dementia in adults with mental retardation. *American Journal on Mental Retardation, 96,* 502-511.

47. Cardon, L. R., Fulker, D. W., DeFries, J. C., & Plomin, R. (1992). Continuity and change in general cognitive ability from 1 to 7 years of age. *Developmental Psychology, 28,* 64-73.

48. DiPietro, J. A., Porges, S. W., & Uhly, B. (1992). Reactivity and developmental competence in preterm and full-term infants. *Developmental Psychology, 28,* 831-841.

49. Paul, R., & Jennings, P. (1992). Phonological behavior in toddlers with slow expressive language development. *Journal of Speech and Hearing Research, 35,* 99-107.

50. Rosenblith, J. F. (1992). A singular career: Nancy Bayley. *Developmental Psychology, 28,* 747-758.

51. Ross, G., Tesman, J., Auld, P. A. M., & Nass, R. (1992). Effects of subependymal and mild intraventricular lesions on visual attention and memory in premature infants. *Developmental Psychology, 28,* 1067-1074.

52. Spitz, H. H. (1992). Does the Carolina Abecedarian Early Intervention Project prevent sociocultural mental retardation? *Intelligence, 16,* 225-237.

53. Benson, J. B., Cherny, S. S., Haith, M. M., & Fulker, D. W. (1993). Rapid assessment of infant predictors of adult IQ: Midtwin-midparent analyses. *Developmental Psychology, 29,* 434-447.

54. Diamond, K., LeFurgy, W., & Blass, S. (1993). Attitudes of preschool children toward their peers with disabilities: A year-long investigation in integrated classrooms. *Journal of Genetic Psychology, 154,* 215-221.

55. Landry, S. H., Fletcher, J. M., Denson, S. E., & Chapieski, M. L. (1993). Longitudinal outcome for low birth weight infants: Effects of intraventricular hemorrhage and bronchopulmonary dysplasia. *Journal of Clinical and Experimental Neuropsychology, 15,* 205-218.

56. Wachs, T. D., Moussa, W., Bishry, Z., Yunis, F., Sobhy, A., McCabe, G., Jerome, N., Galal, O., Harrison, G., & Kirksey, A. (1993). Relations between nutrition and cognitive performance in Egyptian toddlers. *Intelligence, 17,* 151-172.

57. Bloom, A. S., & Zelko, F. A. (1994). Variability in adaptive behavior in children with developmental delay. *Journal of Clinical Psychology, 50,* 261-265.

58. Landry, S. H., Garner, P. W., Pirie, D., & Swank, P. R. (1994). Effects of social context and mothers' requesting strategies on Down's syndrome children's social responsiveness. *Developmental Psychology, 30,* 292-302.

[267]

Beck Anxiety Inventory [1993 Edition].

Purpose: "Measures the severity of anxiety in adults and adolescents."

Population: Adults and adolescents.
Publication Dates: 1987–93.
Acronym: BAI.
Scores: Total score only.
Administration: Group or individual.
Price Data, 1994: $46 per complete kit including 25 record forms and manual ('93, 23 pages); $25.50 per 25 record forms; $22.50 per manual.
Foreign Language Edition: Also available in Spanish.
Time: (5–10) minutes.
Authors: Aaron T. Beck and Robert A. Steer.
Publisher: The Psychological Corporation.

TEST REFERENCES

1. Steer, R. A., Rissmiller, D. J., Ranieri, W. F., & Beck, A. T. (1993). Structure of the computer-assisted Beck Anxiety Inventory with psychiatric inpatients. *Journal of Personality Assessment, 60,* 532-542.
2. Trull, T. J., & Goodwin, A. H. (1993). Relation between mood changes and the report of personality disorder symptoms. *Journal of Personality Assessment, 61,* 99-111.

[268]

Beck Depression Inventory [1993 Revised].

Purpose: "Designed to assess the severity of depression in adolescents and adults."
Population: Adolescents and adults.
Publication Dates: 1961–93.
Acronym: BDI.
Scores: Total score only; item score ranges.
Administration: Group or individual.
Price Data, 1994: $46 per complete kit including 25 record forms and manual ('93, 24 pages); $25.50 per 25 record forms; $22.50 per manual.
Foreign Language Edition: Also available in Spanish.
Time: (5–15) minutes.
Authors: Aaron T. Beck and Robert A. Steer.
Publisher: The Psychological Corporation.
Cross References: For reviews by Collie W. Conoley and Norman D. Sundberg of a previous edition, see 11:31 (286 references).

TEST REFERENCES

1. Donat, D. C., & McCullough, J. P. (1983). Psychophysiological discriminants of repression at rest and in response to stress. *Journal of Clinical Psychology, 39,* 315-320.
2. Jones-Saumty, D., Hochhaus, L., Dru, R., & Zeiner, A. (1983). Psychological factors of familial alcoholism in American Indians and Caucasians. *Journal of Clinical Psychology, 39,* 783-790.
3. Livingood, A. B., Daen, P., & Smith, B. D. (1983). The depressed mother as a source of stimulation for her infant. *Journal of Clinical Psychology, 39,* 369-376.
4. Ludenia, K., & Donham, G. W. (1983). Dental outpatients: health locus of control correlates. *Journal of Clinical Psychology, 39,* 854-858.
5. Parker, J. C., Dorefler, L. A., Tatten, H. A., & Hewett, J. E. (1983). Psychological factors that influence self-reported pain. *Journal of Clinical Psychology, 39,* 22-25.
6. Schoeneman, S. Z., Reznikoff, M., & Bacon, S. J. (1983). Personality variables in coping with the stress of a spouse's chronic illness. *Journal of Clinical Psychology, 39,* 430-436.
7. Scogin, F. R., & Merbaum, M. (1983). Humorous stimuli and depression: An examination of Beck's premise. *Journal of Clinical Psychology, 39,* 165-169.
8. Steer, R. A., McElroy, M. G., & Beck, A. T. (1983). Correlates of self-reported and clinically assessed depression in outpatient alcoholics. *Journal of Clinical Psychology, 39,* 144-149.

9. Bouman, T. K., & Luteijn, F. (1986). Relations between the Pleasant Events Schedule, depression, and other aspects of psychopathology. *Journal of Abnormal Psychology, 95,* 373-377.
10. Hammen, C., Mayol, A., de Mayo, R., & Marks, T. (1986). Initial symptom levels and the life-event-depression relationship. *Journal of Abnormal Psychology, 95,* 114-122.
11. Hollon, S. D., Kendall, P. C., & Lumry, A. (1986). Specificity of depressotypic cognitions in clinical depression. *Journal of Abnormal Psychology, 95,* 52-59.
12. Kuhle, J., & Helle, P. (1986). Motivational and volitional determinants of depression: The degenerated-intention hypothesis. *Journal of Abnormal Psychology, 95,* 247-251.
13. MacLeod, C., Mathews, A., & Tata, P. (1986). Attentional bias in emotional disorders. *Journal of Abnormal Psychology, 95,* 15-20.
14. Mathews, A., & MacLeod, C. (1986). Discrimination of threat cues without awareness in anxiety states. *Journal of Abnormal Psychology, 95,* 131-138.
15. Nezu, A. M., Nezu, C. M., & Nezu, V. A. (1986). Depression, general distress, and causal attributions among university students. *Journal of Abnormal Psychology, 95,* 184-186.
16. Pignatiello, M. F., Camp, C. J., & Rasar, L. A. (1986). Musical mood induction: An alternative to the Velten technique. *Journal of Abnormal Psychology, 95,* 295-297.
17. Turner, S. M., McCann, B. S., Beidel, D. C., & Mezzich, J. E. (1986). DSM-III classification of the anxiety disorders: A psychometric study. *Journal of Abnormal Psychology, 95,* 168-172.
18. Beer, J. (1987). Depression and self-esteem of teachers. *Psychological Reports, 60,* 1097-1098.
19. Bergin, A. E., Masters, K. S., & Richards, P. S. (1987). Religiousness and mental health reconsidered: A study of an intrinsically religious sample. *Journal of Counseling Psychology, 34,* 197-204.
20. Brodbeck, C., & Michelson, L. (1987). Problem-solving skill and attributional styles of agoraphobics. *Cognitive Therapy and Research, 11,* 593-610.
21. Brown, S. D., Brady, T., Lent, R. W., Wolfert, J., & Hall, S. (1987). Perceived social support among college students: Three studies of the psychometric characteristics and counseling uses of the Social Support Inventory. *Journal of Counseling Psychology, 34,* 337-354.
22. Cole, D. A., Lazarick, D. L., & Howard, G. S. (1987). Construct validity and the relation between depression and social skills. *Journal of Counseling Psychology, 34,* 315-321.
23. Dobson, K. S., & Shaw, B. F. (1987). Specificity and stability of self-referent encoding in clinical depression. *Journal of Abnormal Psychology, 96,* 34-40.
24. Field, T. M., Sandberg, D., Goldstein, S., Garcia, R., Vega-Lahr, N., Porter, K., & Dowling, M. (1987). Play interactions and interviews of depressed and conduct disorder children and their mothers. *Child Psychiatry and Human Development, 17,* 213-234.
25. Halgin, R. P., Weaver, D. D., Edell, W. S., & Spencer, P. G. (1987). Relation of depression and help-seeking history to attitude toward seeking professional psychological help. *Journal of Counseling Psychology, 34,* 177-185.
26. Hammen, C., Gordon, D., Burge, D., Adrian, C., Jaenicke, C., & Hirohoto, D. (1987). Maternal affective disorders, illness, and stress: Risk for children's psychopathology. *American Journal of Psychiatry, 144,* 736-741.
27. Heiby, E. M., Campos, P. E., Remick, R. A., & Keller, F. D. (1987). Dexamethasone suppression and self-reinforcement correlates of clinical depression. *Journal of Abnormal Psychology, 96,* 70-72.
28. Heimberg, R. G., Vermilyea, J. A., Dodge, C. S., Becker, R. E., & Barlow, D. H. (1987). Attributional style, depression, and anxiety: An evaluation of the specificity of depressive attributions. *Cognitive Therapy and Research, 11,* 537-550.
29. Holahan, C. J., & Moos, R. H. (1987). Risk, resistance, and psychological distress: A longitudinal analysis with adults and children. *Journal of Abnormal Psychology, 96,* 3-13.
30. Hyer, L., Harkey, B., & Harrison, W. R. (1987). Use of the Harris and Lingoes depression MMPI subscales in assessing later life. *Psychological Reports, 60,* 1291-1297.
31. Jarjoura, D., & O'Hara, M. W. (1987). A structural model for postpartum responses to the somatic and cognitive items on the Beck Depression Inventory. *Journal of Psychopathology and Behavioral Assessment, 9,* 389-402.
32. Kowalik, D. L., & Gotlib, I. H. (1987). Depression and marital interaction: Concordance between intent and perception of communication. *Journal of Abnormal Psychology, 96,* 127-134.
33. Krueger, H. K., & Bornstein, P. H. (1987). Depression, sex-roles, and family variables: Comparison of bulimics, binge-eaters, and normals. *Psychological Reports, 60,* 1106.
34. Lam, D. H., Brewin, C. R., Woods, R. T., & Bebbington, P. E. (1987). Cognition and social adversity in the depressed elderly. *Journal of Abnormal Psychology, 96,* 23-26.

35. Mavissakalian, M., Perel, J., Bowler, K., & Dealy, R. (1987). Trazodone in the treatment of panic disorder and agoraphobia with panic attacks. *American Journal of Psychiatry, 144,* 785-787.

36. McMillan, M. J., & Pihl, R. O. (1987). Premenstrual depression: A distinct entity. *Journal of Abnormal Psychology, 96,* 149-154.

37. McNally, R. J., & Foa, E. B. (1987). Cognition and agoraphobia: Bias in the interpretation of threat. *Cognitive Therapy and Research, 11,* 567-581.

38. Mogg, K., Mathews, A., & Weinman, J. (1987). Memory bias in clinical anxiety. *Journal of Abnormal Psychology, 96,* 94-98.

39. Perse, T. L., Greist, J. H., Jefferson, J. W., Rosenfeld, R., & Dar, R. (1987). Fluvoxamine treatment of obsessive-compulsive disorder. *American Journal of Psychiatry, 144,* 1543-1548.

40. Rozensky, R. H., Tovian, S. M., Stiles, P. G., Fridkin, K., & Holland, M. (1987). Effects of learned helplessness on Rorschach responses. *Psychological Reports, 60,* 1011-1016.

41. Shelton, M. D., & Parsons, O. A. (1987). Alcoholics' self-assessment of their neuropsychological functioning in everyday life. *Journal of Clinical Psychology, 43,* 395-403.

42. Steer, R. A., Beck, A. T., Riskind, J. H., & Brown, G. (1987). Relationships between the Beck Depression Inventory and the Hamilton psychiatric rating scale for depression in depressed outpatients. *Journal of Psychopathology and Behavioral Assessment, 9,* 327-339.

43. Stuss, D. T., Kates, M. H., Poirier, C. A., Hylton, D., Humphreys, P., Keene, D., & Laflèche G. (1987). Evaluation of information-processing speed and neuropsychological functioning in patients with myotonic dystrophy. *Journal of Clinical and Experimental Neuropsychology, 9,* 131-146.

44. Thomas, J. R., Petry, R. A., & Goldman, J. R. (1987). Comparison of cognitive and behavioral self-control treatments of depression. *Psychological Reports, 60,* 975-982.

45. Wiener, R. L., & Merkel, W. T. (1987). Relation of depression to specific medical complaints in psychiatric inpatients. *Psychological Reports, 60,* 147-152.

46. Woody, G. E., McLellan, A. T., Luborsky, L., & O'Brien, C. P. (1987). Twelve-month follow-up of psychotherapy for opiate dependence. *American Journal of Psychiatry, 144,* 590-596.

47. Zurawski, R. M., & Smith, T. W. (1987). Assessing irrational beliefs and emotional distress: Evidence and implications of limited discriminant validity. *Journal of Counseling Psychology, 34,* 224-227.

48. Ahrens, A. H., Zeiss, A. M., & Kanfer, R. (1988). Dysphoric deficits in interpersonal standards, self-efficacy, and social comparison. *Cognitive Therapy and Research, 12,* 53-67.

49. Alden, L. E. (1988). Behavioral self-management controlled-drinking strategies in a context of secondary prevention. *Journal of Consulting and Clinical Psychology, 56,* 280-286.

50. Anderson, C. A., & Harvey, R. J. (1988). Discriminating between problems in living: An examination of measures of depression, loneliness, shyness and social anxiety. *Journal of Social and Clinical Psychology, 6,* 482-491.

51. Beach, S. R. H., Nelson, G. M., & O'Leary, K. D. (1988). Cognitive and marital factors in depression. *Journal of Psychopathology and Behavioral Assessment, 10,* 93-105.

52. Beck, A. T., Brown, G., Epstein, N., & Steer, R. A. (1988). An inventory for measuring clinical anxiety: Psychometric properties. *Journal of Consulting and Clinical Psychology, 56,* 893-897.

53. Beck, A. T., Riskind, J. H., Brown, G., & Steer, R. A. (1988). Levels of hopelessness in DSM-III disorders: A partial test of content specificity in depression. *Cognitive Therapy and Research, 12,* 459-469.

54. Bell, K. M., Plon, L., Bunney, W. E., Jr., & Potkin, S. G. (1988). S-Adenosylmethionine treatment of depression: A controlled clinical trial. *American Journal of Psychiatry, 145,* 1110-1114.

55. Bernstein, G., & Garfinkel, B. D. (1988). Pedigrees, functioning, and psychopathology in families of school phobic children. *American Journal of Psychiatry, 145,* 70-74.

56. Borkovec, T. D., & Mathews, A. M. (1988). Treatment of nonphobic anxiety disorders: A comparison of nondirective, cognitive, and coping desensitization therapy. *Journal of Consulting and Clinical Psychology, 56,* 877-884.

57. Brouwers, M. (1988). Depressive thought content among female college students with bulimia. *Journal of Counseling and Development, 66,* 425-428.

58. Colby, C. A., & Gotlib, I. H. (1988). Memory deficits in depression. *Cognitive Therapy and Research, 12,* 611-627.

59. Cole, D. A. (1988). Hopelessness, social desirability, depression, and parasuicide in two college student samples. *Journal of Consulting and Clinical Psychology, 56,* 131-136.

60. Dent, J., & Teasdale, J. D. (1988). Negative cognition and the persistence of depression. *Journal of Abnormal Psychology, 97,* 29-34.

61. Dodge, C. S., Hope, D. A., Heimberg, R. G., & Becker, R. E. (1988). Evaluation of the Social Interaction Self-Statement Test with a social phobic population. *Cognitive Therapy and Research, 12,* 211-222.

62. Fitzgerald, J. M., Slade, S., & Lawrence, R. H. (1988). Memory availability and judged frequency of affect. *Cognitive Therapy and Research, 12,* 379-390.

63. Fitzgibbon, M. L., Cella, D. F., & Sweeney, J. A. (1988). Redundancy in measures of depression. *Journal of Clinical Psychology, 44,* 372-374.

64. Forehand, R., Brady, G. H., Long, N., & Fauber, R. (1988). The interactive influence of adolescent and maternal depression on adolescent social and cognitive functioning. *Cognitive Therapy and Research, 12,* 341-350.

65. Forehand, R., Brody, G., Slotkin, J., Fauber, R., McCombs, A., & Long, N. (1988). Young adolescent and maternal depression: Assessment, interrelations, and family predictors. *Journal of Consulting and Clinical Psychology, 56,* 422-426.

66. Frank, E., Carpenter, L. L., & Kupfer, D. J. (1988). Sex differences in recurrent depression: Are there any that are significant? *American Journal of Psychiatry, 145,* 41-45.

67. Garvey, M. J., Wesner, R., & Godes, M. (1988). Comparison of seasonal and nonseasonal affective disorders. *American Journal of Psychiatry, 145,* 100-102.

68. Gaston, L., Marmar, C. R., Thompson, L. W., & Gallagher, D. (1988). Relation of patient pretreatment characteristics to the therapeutic alliance in diverse psycho therapies. *Journal of Consulting and Clinical Psychology, 56,* 483-489.

69. Griffin, P. T., & Kogut, D. (1988). Validity of orally administered Beck and Zung Depression scales in a state hospital setting. *Journal of Clinical Psychology, 44,* 756-759.

70. Hill, R. D., Gallagher, D., Thompson, L. W., & Ishida, T. (1988). Hopelessness as a measure of suicidal intent in the depressed elderly. *Psychology and Aging, 3,* 230-232.

71. Hoberman, H. M., Lewinsohn, P. M., & Tilson, M. (1988). Group treatment of depression: Individual predictors of outcome. *Journal of Consulting and Clinical Psychology, 56,* 393-398.

72. Hogg, J. A., & Deffenbacher, J. L. (1988). A comparison of cognitive and interpersonal-process group therapies in the treatment of depression among college students. *Journal of Counseling Psychology, 35,* 304-310.

73. Hollander, G. R., & Hokanson, J. E. (1988). Dysphoria and the perception of incongruent communications. *Cognitive Therapy and Research, 12,* 577-589.

74. Holroyd, K. A., Holm, J. E., Hursey, K. G., Penzien, D. B., Cordingley, G. E., Theofanous, A. G., Richardson, S. C., & Tobin, D. L. (1988). Recurrent vascular headache: Home-based behavioral treatment versus abortive pharmacological treatment. *Journal of Consulting and Clinical Psychology, 56,* 218-223.

75. Ingram, R. E., & Wisnicki, K. S. (1988). Assessment of positive automatic cognition. *Journal of Consulting and Clinical Psychology, 56,* 898-902.

76. Jacob, T., & Leonard, K. E. (1988). Alcoholic-spouse interaction as a function of alcoholism subtype and alcohol consumption interaction. *Journal of Abnormal Psychology, 97,* 231-237.

77. Jenike, M. A., & Baer, L. (1988). An open trial of buspirone in obsessive-compulsive disorder. *American Journal of Psychiatry, 145,* 1285-1286.

78. Joffe, R. T., Swinson, R. P., & Regan, J. J. (1988). Personality features of obsessive-compulsive disorder. *American Journal of Psychiatry, 145,* 1127-1129.

79. Kerns, R. D., & Haythornthwaite, J. A. (1988). Depression among chronic pain patients: Cognitive-behavioral analysis and effect on rehabilitation outcome. *Journal of Consulting and Clinical Psychology, 56,* 870-876.

80. Klein, D. N., Taylor, E. B., Harding, K., & Dickstein, S. (1988). Double depression and episodic major depression: Demographic, clinical, familial, personality, and socioenvironmental characteristics and short-term outcome. *American Journal of Psychiatry, 145,* 1226-1231.

81. Klein, E., & Uhde, T. W. (1988). Controlled study of verapamil for treatment of panic disorder. *American Journal of Psychiatry, 145,* 431-434.

82. Kleinke, C. L. (1988). The Depression Coping Questionnaire. *Journal of Clinical Psychology, 44,* 516-526.

83. Kuiper, N. A., Olinger, L. J., & Martin, R. A. (1988). Dysfunctional attitudes, stress, and negative emotions. *Cognitive Therapy and Research, 12,* 533-547.

84. Lakey, B. (1988). Self-esteem, control beliefs, and cognitive problem-solving skill as risk factors in the development of subsequent dysphoria. *Cognitive Therapy and Research, 12,* 409-420.

85. Leigh, I. W., Robins, C. J., & Welkowitz, J. (1988). Modification of the Beck Depression Inventory for use with a deaf population. *Journal of Clinical Psychology, 44,* 728-732.

86. Leitenberg, H., Rosen, J. C., Gross, J., Nudelman, S., & Vara, L. S. (1988). Exposure plus response-prevention treatment of bulimia nervosa. *Journal of Consulting and Clinical Psychology, 56,* 535-541.

87. Long, G. T. (1988). The relationship of voice stress, anxiety, and depression to life events and personal style variables. *Social Behavior and Personality, 16*, 133-145.

88. Love, A. W. (1988). Attributional style of depressed chronic low back patients. *Journal of Clinical Psychology, 44*, 317-321.

89. Mahalik, J. R., & Kivilighan, D. M., Jr. (1988). Self-help treatment for depression: Who succeeds? *Journal of Counseling Psychology, 35*, 237-242.

90. Maiuro, R. D., Cahn, T. S., Vitaliano, P. P., Wagner, B. C., & Zegree, J. B. (1988). Anger, hostility, and depression in domestically violent versus generally assaultive men and nonviolent control subjects. *Journal of Consulting and Clinical Psychology, 56*, 17-23.

91. Mallinckrodt, B., & Fretz, B. R. (1988). Social support and the impact of job loss on older professionals. *Journal of Counseling Psychology, 35*, 281-286.

92. Marcus, M. D., Wing, R. R., & Hopkins, J. (1988). Obese binge eaters: Affect, cognitions, and response to behavioral weight control. *Journal of Consulting and Clinical Psychology, 56*, 433-439.

93. Marmar, C. R., Horowitz, M. J., Weiss, D. S., Wilner, N. R., & Kaltreider, N. B. (1988). A controlled trial of brief psychotherapy and mutual-help group treatment of conjugal bereavement. *American Journal of Psychiatry, 145*, 203-209.

94. Millar, K. U., Tesser, A., & Millar, M. G. (1988). The effects of a threatening life event on behavior sequences and intrusive thought: A self-disruption explanation. *Cognitive Therapy and Research, 12*, 441-457.

95. Miranda, J., & Persons, J. B. (1988). Dysfunctional attitudes are mood-state dependent. *Journal of Abnormal Psychology, 97*, 76-79.

96. Morin, C. M., & Azrin, N. H. (1988). Behavioral and cognitive treatments of geriatric insomnia. *Journal of Consulting and Clinical Psychology, 56*, 748-753.

97. Nelson, L. D., & Stern, S. L. (1988). Mood induction in a clinically depressed population. *Journal of Psychopathology and Behavioral Assessment, 10*, 277-285.

98. Nezu, A. M., & Ronan, G. F. (1988). Social problem solving as a moderator of stress-related depressive symptoms: A prospective analysis. *Journal of Counseling Psychology, 35*, 134-138.

99. Nixon, S. J., Parsons, O. A., Schaeffer, K. W, & Hale, R. L. (1988). Subject selection biases in alcoholic samples: Effects on cognitive performance. *Journal of Clinical Psychology, 44*, 831-836.

100. Norman, W. H., Miller, I. W., & Dow, M. G. (1988). Characteristics of depressed patients with elevated levels of dysfunctional cognitions. *Cognitive Therapy and Research, 12*, 39-52.

101. Persons, J. B., Burns, D. D., & Perloff, J. M. (1988). Predictors of dropout and outcome in cognitive therapy for depression in a private practice setting. *Cognitive Therapy and Research, 12*, 557-575.

102. Peterson, C. (1988). Explanatory style as a risk factor for illness. *Cognitive Therapy and Research, 12*, 119-132.

103. Peterson, L., & Villanova, P. (1988). An Expanded Attributional Style Questionnaire. *Journal of Abnormal Psychology, 97*, 87-89.

104. Prout, H. T., & Chizik, R. (1988). Readability of child and adolescent self-report measures. *Journal of Consulting and Clinical Psychology, 56*, 152-154.

105. Rapp, S. R., Parisi, S. A., & Walsh, D. A. (1988). Psychological dysfunction and physical health among elderly medical inpatients. *Journal of Consulting and Clinical Psychology, 56*, 851-855.

106. Rapp, S. R., Walsh, D. A., Parisi, S. A., & Wallace, C. E. (1988). Detecting depression in elderly medical inpatients. *Journal of Consulting and Clinical Psychology, 56*, 509-513.

107. Robertson, M. M., Trimble, M. R., & Lees, A. J. (1988). The psychopathology of Gilles de la Tourette syndrome. *British Journal of Psychiatry, 152*, 383-390.

108. Robins, C. J. (1988). Development of experimental mood induction procedures for testing personality-event interaction models of depression. *Journal of Counseling Psychology, 44*, 958-963.

109. Rude, S. S., Krantz, S. E., & Rosenhan, D. L. (1988). Distinguishing the dimensions of valence and belief consistency in depressive and nondepressive information processing. *Cognitive Therapy and Research, 12*, 391-407.

110. Saigh, P. A. (1988). Anxiety, depression, and assertion across alternating intervals of stress. *Journal of Abnormal Psychology, 97*, 338-341.

111. Scogin, F., Beutler, L., Corbishley, A., & Hamblin, D. (1988). Reliability and validity of the short form Beck Depression Inventory with older adults. *Journal of Clinical Psychology, 44*, 853-857.

112. Segal, Z. V., Hood, J. E., Shaw, B. F., & Higgins, E. T. (1988). A structural analysis of the self-schema construct of major depression. *Cognitive Therapy and Research, 12*, 471-485.

113. Seligman, M. E. P., Castellon, C., Cacciola, J., Schulman, P., Luborsky, L., Ollove, M., & Downing, R. (1988). Explanatory style change during cognitive therapy for unipolar depression. *Journal of Abnormal Psychology, 97*, 13-18.

114. Shek, D. T. L. (1988). Reliability and factorial structure of the Chinese version of the State-Trait Anxiety Inventory. *Journal of Psychopathology and Behavioral Assessment, 10*, 303-317.

115. Smith, T. W., Peck, J. R., Milano, R. A., & Ward, J. R. (1988). Cognitive distortion in rheumatoid arthritis: Relation to depression and disability. *Journal of Consulting and Clinical Psychology, 56*, 412-416.

116. Tobin, D. L., Holroyd, K. A., Baker, A., Reynolds, R. V. C., & Holm, J. E. (1988). Development and clinical trial of a minimal contact, cognitive-behavioral treatment for tension headache. *Cognitive Therapy and Research, 12*, 325-339.

117. Vredenburg, K., O'Brien, E., & Krames, L. (1988). Depression in college students: Personality and experiential factors. *Journal of Counseling Psychology, 35*, 419-425.

118. Warren, R., McLellarn, R., & Ponzoha, L. (1988). Rationalemotive therapy vs. general cognitive-behavior therapy in the treatment of low self-esteem and related emotional disturbances. *Cognitive Therapy and Research, 12*, 21-38.

119. Webster-Stratton, C. (1988). Mothers' and fathers' perceptions of child deviance: Roles of parent and child behaviors and parent adjustment. *Journal of Consulting and Clinical Psychology, 56*, 909-915.

120. Wenzlaff, R. M., & Grozier, S. A. (1988). Depression and the magnification of failure. *Journal of Abnormal Psychology, 97*, 90-93.

121. Westermeyer, J., & Neider, J. (1988). Social networks and psychopathology among substance abusers. *American Journal of Psychiatry, 145*, 1265-1269.

122. Whiffen, V. E. (1988). Screening for postpartum depression: A methodological note. *Journal of Clinical Psychology, 44*, 367-371.

123. Wolfe, D. A., Edwards, B., Manion, I., & Koverola, C. (1988). Early intervention for parents at risk of child abuse and neglect: A preliminary investigation. *Journal of Consulting and Clinical Psychology, 56*, 40-47.

124. Abrahamson, D. J., Barlow, D. H., & Abrahamson, L. S. (1989). Differential effects of performance demand and distraction on sexually functional and dysfunctional males. *Journal of Abnormal Psychology, 98*, 241-247.

125. Ackerman, M. D., & Stevens, M. J. (1989). Acute and chronic pain: Pain dimensions and psychological status. *Journal of Clinical Psychology, 45*, 223-228.

126. Beck, J. G., Taegtmeyer, H., Berisford, M. A., & Bennett, A. (1989). Chest pain without coronary artery disease: An exploratory comparison with panic disorder. *Journal of Psychopathology and Behavioral Assessment, 11*, 209-220.

127. Beckham, E. E. (1989). Improvement after evaluation in psychotherapy of depression: Evidence of a placebo effect. *Journal of Clinical Psychology, 45*, 945-950.

128. Belk, S. S., & Snell, W. E., Jr. (1989). Stereotypic beliefs about women as moderators of stress-distress relationships. *Journal of Clinical Psychology, 45*, 665-672.

129. Bernstein, G. A., Garfinkel, B. D., & Hoberman, H. M. (1989). Self-reported anxiety in adolescents. *American Journal of Psychiatry, 146*, 384-386.

130. Biglun, A., Rothlind, J., Hops, H., & Sherman, L. (1989). Impact of distressed and aggressive behavior. *Journal of Abnormal Psychology, 98*, 218-228.

131. Brown, A., & Zeichner, A. (1989). Concurrent incidence of depression and physical symptoms among hostile young women. *Psychological Reports, 65*, 739-744.

132. Brown, J. D., & Silberschate, G. (1989). Dependency, self-criticism, and depressive attributional style. *Journal of Abnormal Psychology, 98*, 187-188.

133. Carlson, C. R., Collins, F. L., Jr., Stewart, J. F., Porzelius, J., Nitz, J. A., & Lind, C. O. (1989). The assessment of emotional reactivity: A scale development and validation study. *Journal of Psychopathology and Behavioral Assessment, 11*, 313-325.

134. Charisiou, J., Jackson, H. J., Boyle, G. J., Burgess, P., Minas, I. H., & Joshua, S. D. (1989). Are employment-interview skills a correlate of subtypes of schizophrenia? *Psychological Reports, 65*, 951-960.

135. Clark, D. A., Feldman, J., & Channon, S. (1989). Dysfunctional thinking in anorexia and bulimia nervosa. *Cognitive Therapy and Research, 13*, 377-387.

136. Cutrona, C. E. (1989). Ratings of social support by adolescents and adult informants: Degree of correspondence and prediction of depressive symptoms. *Journal of Personality and Social Psychology, 57*, 723-730.

137. Dobson, K. S. (1989). Real and perceived interpersonal responses to subclinically anxious and depressed targets. *Cognitive Therapy and Research, 13*, 37-47.

138. Dohr, K. B., Rush, A. J., & Bernstein, I. H. (1989). Cognitive biases and depression. *Journal of Abnormal Psychology, 98*, 263-267.

139. Edlund, M. J., & Swann, A. C. (1989). Continuing in treatment as a form of selection bias. *American Journal of Psychiatry, 146*, 254-256.

140. Esses, V. M. (1989). Mood as a moderator of acceptance of inter-personal feedback. *Journal of Personality and Social Psychology, 57*, 769-781.

141. Flannery, R. B., Jr., & Wieman, D. (1989). Social support, life stress, and psychological distress: An empirical assessment. *Journal of Clinical Psychology, 45*, 867-872.

142. Gartner, A. F., Marcus, R. N., Halmi, K., & Loranger, A. W. (1989). DSM-III-R personality disorders in patients with eating disorders. *American Journal of Psychiatry, 146*, 1585-1591.

143. Gatewood-Colwell, G., Kaczmarek, M., & Ames, M. H. (1989). Reliability and validity of the Beck Depression Inventory for a white and Mexican-American gerontic population. *Psychological Reports, 65*, 1163-1166.

144. Golin, S. (1989). Schema congruence and depression: Loss of objectivity in self- and other-inferences. *Journal of Abnormal Psychology, 98*, 495-498.

145. Gordon, D., Burge, D., Hammen, C., Adrian, C., Jaenicke, C., & Hiroto, D. (1989). Observations of interactions of depressed women with their children. *American Journal of Psychiatry, 146*, 50-55.

146. Gotlib, I. H., & Whiffen, V. E. (1989). Depression and marital functioning: An examination of specificity and gender differences. *Journal of Abnormal Psychology, 98*, 23-30.

147. Greenberg, M. S., & Beck, A. T. (1989). Depression versus anxiety: A test of the content-specificity hypothesis. *Journal of Abnormal Psychology, 98*, 9-13.

148. Hamburger, S. D., Swedo, S., Whitaker, A., Davies, M., & Rapoport, J. L. (1989). Growth rate in adolescents with obsessive-compulsive disorder. *American Journal of Psychiatry, 146*, 652-655.

149. Harris, V. S., & McHale, S. M. (1989). Family life problems, daily caregiving activities, and the psychological well-being of mothers of mentally retarded children. *American Journal on Mental Retardation, 94*, 231-239.

150. Harvey, P. D., Greenberg, B. R., & Serper, M. R. (1989). The Affective Lability Scale: Development, reliability, and validity. *Journal of Clinical Psychology, 45*, 786-793.

151. Heimberg, R. G., Klosko, J. S., Dodge, C. S., Shadick, R., Becker, R. E., & Barlow, D. H. (1989). Anxiety disorders, depression, and attributional style: A further test of the specificity of depressive attributions. *Cognitive Therapy and Research, 13*, 21-36.

152. Hill, C. V., Oei, T. P. S., & Hill, M. A. (1989). An empirical investigation of the specificity and sensitivity of the automatic thoughts questionnaire and dysfunctional attitudes scale. *Journal of Psychopathology and Behavioral Assessment, 11*, 291-311.

153. Hokanson, J. E., Rubert, M. P., Welker, R. A., Hollander, G. R., & Hedeen, C. (1989). Interpersonal concomitants and antecedents of depression among college students. *Journal of Abnormal Psychology, 98*, 209-217.

154. Hooley, J. M., & Teasdale, J. D. (1989). Predictors of relapse in unipolar depressives: Expressed emotion, marital distress, and perceived criticism. *Journal of Abnormal Psychology, 98*, 229-235.

155. Ingram, R. E. (1989). Affective confounds in social-cognitive research. *Journal of Personality and Social Psychology, 57*, 715-722.

156. Jenike, M. A., Buttolph, L., Baer, L., Ricciardi, J., & Holland, A. (1989). Open trial of fluoxetine in obsessive compulsive disorder. *American Journal of Psychiatry, 146*, 909-911.

157. Kendall, P. C., Howard, B. L., & Hays, R. C. (1989). Self-referent speech and psychopathology: The balance of positive and negative thinking. *Cognitive Therapy and Research, 13*, 583-598.

158. Ketelaar, T., & O'hara, M. W. (1989). Meaning of the concept "suicide" and risk for attempted suicide. *Journal of Social and Clinical Psychology, 8*, 393-399.

159. Kroll, J., & Sheehan, W. (1989). Religious beliefs and practices among 52 psychiatric inpatients in Minnesota. *American Journal of Psychiatry, 146*, 67-72.

160. Lee, C. M., & Gotlib, I. H. (1989). Clinical status and emotional adjustment of children of depressed mothers. *American Journal of Psychiatry, 146*, 478-483.

161. Lee, C. M., & Gotlib, I. H. (1989). Maternal depression and child adjustment: A longitudinal analysis. *Journal of Abnormal Psychology, 98*, 78-85.

162. Lezenwegar, M. F., & Loranger, A. W. (1989). Psychosis proneness and clinical psychopathology: Examination of the correlates of schitzotypy. *Journal of Abnormal Psychology, 98*, 3-8.

163. Maiuro, R. D., O'Sullivan, M. J., Michael, M. C., & Vitaliano, P. P. (1989). Anger, hostility, and depression in assaultive vs. suicide-attempting males. *Journal of Clinical Psychology, 45*, 531-541.

164. Malcolm, R., Ballenger, J. C., Sturgis, E. T., & Anton, R. (1989). Double-blind controlled trial comparing carbamazepine to oxazepam treatment of alcohol withdrawal. *American Journal of Psychiatry, 146*, 617-621.

165. Mathew, R. J., Wilson, W. H., & Tant, S. (1989). Responses to hypercarbia induced by acetazolamide in panic disorder patients. *American Journal of Psychiatry, 146*, 996-1000.

166. Mathews, A., Richards, A., & Eysenck, M. (1989). Interpretation of homophones related to threat in anxiety states. *Journal of Abnormal Psychology, 98*, 31-34.

167. Meyers, J. F., Lynch, P. B., & Bakal, D. A. (1989). Dysthymic and hypomanic self-referant effects associated with depressive illness and recovery. *Cognitive Therapy and Research, 13*, 195-209.

168. Miller, I. W., Norman, W. H., & Keitner, G. I. (1989). Cognitive-behavioral treatment of depressed inpatients: Six- and twelve-month follow-up. *American Journal of Psychiatry, 146*, 1274-1279.

169. Morin, C. M., & Gramling, S. E. (1989). Sleep patterns and aging: Comparison of older adults with and without insomnia complaints. *Psychology and Aging, 4*, 290-294.

170. Mueller, P., & Major, B. (1989). Self-blame, self-efficacy, and adjustment to abortion. *Journal of Personality and Social Psychology, 57*, 1059-1068.

171. Muran, J. C., Kassinove, H., Ross, S., & Muran, E. (1989). Irrational thinking and negative emotionality in college students and applications for mental health services. *Journal of Clinical Psychology, 45*, 188-194.

172. Parry, B. L., Berga, S. L., Mostofi, N., Sependa, P. A., Kripke, D. F., & Gillin, J. C. (1989). Morning versus evening bright light treatment of late luteal phase dysphoric disorder. *American Journal of Psychiatry, 146*, 1215-1217.

173. Persons, J. B., & Perloff, J. M. (1989). The relationship between attributions and depression varies across attributional dimensions and across samples. *Journal of Psychopathology and Behavioral Assessment, 11*, 47-60.

174. Ponterotto, J. G., Pace, T. M., & Kavan, M. G. (1989). A counselor's guide to the assessment of depression. *Journal of Counseling and Development, 67*, 301-309.

175. Radenhausen, R. A. (1989). Effects of mood induction on ratings of self and experimenter. *Journal of Clinical Psychology, 45*, 134-138.

176. Rholes, W. S., Michas, L., & Shroff, J. (1989). Action control as a vulnerability factor in dysphoria. *Cognitive Therapy and Research, 13*, 263-274.

177. Riskind, J. H., Castellon, C. S., & Beck, A. T. (1989). Spontaneous causal explanations in unipolar depression and generalized anxiety: Content analysis of dysfunctional-thought diaries. *Cognitive Therapy and Research, 13*, 97-108.

178. Robins, C. J., & Block, P. (1989). Cognitive theories of depression viewed from a diathesis-stress perspective: Evaluations of the models of Beck and of Abramson, Seligman, and Teasdale. *Cognitive Therapy and Research, 13*, 297-313.

179. Robins, C. J., Block, P., & Peselow, E. D. (1989). Relations of sociotropic and autonomous personality characteristics to specific symptoms in depressed patients. *Journal of Abnormal Psychology, 98*, 86-88.

180. Rokke, P. D., & Kozak, L. D. (1989). Self-control deficits in depression: A process investigation. *Cognitive Therapy and Research, 13*, 609-621.

181. Rude, S. S. (1989). Dimensions of self-control in a sample of depressed women. *Cognitive Therapy and Research, 13*, 363-375.

182. Salisbury, C. L. (1989). Construct validity on the adapted Questionnaire on Resources and Stress—Short Form. *American Journal on Mental Retardation, 94*, 74-79.

183. Scalf-McIver, L., & Thompson, K. (1989). Family correlates of bulimic characteristics in college females. *Journal of Clinical Psychology, 45*, 467-472.

184. Schenck, C. H., Milner, D. M., Hurwitz, T. D., Bundlie, S. R., & Mahowald, M. W. (1989). A polysomnographic and clinical report on sleep-related injury in 100 adult patients. *American Journal of Psychiatry, 146*, 1166-1173.

185. Schlesier-Carter, B., Hamilton, S. A., O'Neil, P. M., Lydiard, R. B., & Malcolm, R. (1989). Depression and bulimia: The link between depression and bulimic cognitions. *Journal of Abnormal Psychology, 98*, 322-325.

186. Solomon, K. E., & Annis, H. M. (1989). Development of a scale to measure outcome expectancy in alcoholics. *Cognitive Therapy and Research, 13*, 409-421.

187. Steiger, H., Fraenkel, L., & Leichner, P. P. (1989). Relationship of body-image distortion to sex-role identifications, irrational cognitions, and body weight in eating-disordered females. *Journal of Clinical Psychology, 45*, 61-65.

188. Stiles, T. C., & Götestam, K. G. (1989). The role of automatic negative thoughts in the development of dysphoric mood: An analogue experiment. *Cognitive Therapy and Research, 13*, 161-170.

189. Tashakkori, A., Barefoot, J., & Mehryar, A. H. (1989). What does the Beck Depression Inventory measure in college students?: Evidence from a non-western culture. *Journal of Clinical Psychology, 45*, 595-602.

190. Taylor, E. B., & Klein, D. N. (1989). Assessing recovery in

depression: Validity of symptom inventories. *Cognitive Therapy and Research, 13,* 1-8.

191. Watkins, P. C., Williamson, D. A., & Falkowski, C. (1989). Prospective assessment of late-luteal phase dysphoric disorder. *Journal of Psychopathology and Behavioral Assessment, 11,* 249-259.

192. Whiffen, V. E., & Gotlib, I. H. (1989). Infants of postpartum depressed mothers: Temperament and cognitive status. *Journal of Abnormal Psychology, 98,* 274-279.

193. Wierzbicki, M., & Rexford, L. (1989). Cognitive and behavioral correlates of depression in clinical and nonclinical populations. *Journal of Clinical Psychology, 45,* 872-877.

194. Zettle, R. D., & Rains, J. C. (1989). Group cognitive and contextual therapies in treatment of depression. *Journal of Clinical Psychology, 45,* 436-445.

195. Alden, L. E., & Phillips, N. (1990). An interpersonal analysis of social anxiety and depression. *Cognitive Therapy and Research, 14,* 499-513.

196. Barnett, P. A., & Gotlib, I. H. (1990). Cognitive vulnerability to depressive symptoms among men and women. *Cognitive Therapy and Research, 14,* 47-61.

197. Baron, P., & Hanna, J. (1990). Egocentrism and depressive symptomatology in young adults. *Social Behavior and Personality, 18,* 279-286.

198. Baron, R. S., Cutrona, C. E., Hicklin, D., Russell, D. W., & Lubaroff, D. M. (1990). Social support and immune function among spouses of cancer patients. *Journal of Personality and Social Psychology, 59,* 344-352.

199. Beck, A. T., Brown, G., Berchick, R. J., Stewart, B. L., & Steer, R. A. (1990). Relationship between hopelessness and ultimate suicide: A replication with psychiatric outpatients. *American Journal of Psychiatry, 147,* 190-195.

200. Blaszczynski, A., McConaghy, N., & Frankova, A. (1990). Boredom proneness in pathological gambling. *Psychological Reports, 67,* 35-42.

201. Brody, G. H., Stoneman, Z., Millar, M., & McCoy, J. K. (1990). Assessing individual differences: Effects of responding to prior questionnaires on the substantive and psychometric properties of self-esteem and depression assessments. *Journal of Personality Assessment, 54,* 401-411.

202. Catanzaro, S. J., & Mearns, J. (1990). Measuring generalized expectancies for negative mood regulation: Initial scale development and implications. *Journal of Personality Assessment, 54,* 546-563.

203. Clark, D. A., Beck, A. T., & Stewart, B. (1990). Cognitive specificity and positive-negative affectivity: Complementary or contradictory views on anxiety and depression. *Journal of Abnormal Psychology, 99,* 148-155.

204. Dahlstrom, W. G., Brooks, J. D., & Peterson, C. D. (1990). The Beck Depression Inventory: Item order and the impact of response sets. *Journal of Personality Assessment, 55,* 224-233.

205. DeJong, J. A., & Roy, A. (1990). Relationship of cognitive factors to CSF corticotropin-releasing hormone in depression. *American Journal of Psychiatry, 147,* 350-352.

206. Demitrack, M. A., Putnam, F. W., Brewerton, T. D., Brandt, H. A., & Gold, P. W. (1990). Relation of clinical variables to dissociative phenomena in eating disorders. *American Journal of Psychiatry, 147,* 1184-1188.

207. Denicoff, K. D., Joffe, R. T., Lakshmanan, M. C., Robbins, J., & Rubinow, D. R. (1990). Neuropsychiatric manifestations of altered thyroid state. *American Journal of Psychiatry, 147,* 94-99.

208. DeRubeis, R. J., & Feeley, M. (1990). Determinants of change in cognitive therapy for depression. *Cognitive Therapy and Research, 14,* 469-482.

209. Endler, N. S., & Parker, J. D. A. (1990). Multidimensional assessment of coping: A critical evaluation. *Journal of Personality and Social Psychology, 58,* 844-854.

210. Errico, A. L., Nixon, S. J., Parsons, O. A., & Tassey, J. (1990). Screening for neuropsychological impairment in alcoholics. *Psychological Assessment, 2,* 45-50.

211. Eschen, J. E., & Glenwick, D. S. (1990). An interactional approach to attributional dimensions in dysphoria. *Social Behavior and Personality, 18,* 267-278.

212. Fletcher, G. J. O., & Fitness, J. (1990). Occurrent social cognition in close relationship interaction: The role of proximal and distal variables. *Journal of Personality and Social Psychology, 58,* 464-474.

213. Fletcher, G. J. O., Fitness, J., & Blampied, N. M. (1990). The link between attributions and happiness in close relationships: The roles of depression and explanatory style. *Journal of Social and Clinical Psychology, 9,* 243-255.

214. Ford, G. G., & Procidano, M. E. (1990). The relationship of self-actualization to social support, life stress, and adjustment. *Social Behavior and Personality, 18,* 41-51.

215. Forehand, R., McCombs-Thomas, A., Wierson, M., Brody, G.,

& Fauber, R. (1990). Role of maternal functioning and parenting skills in adolescent functioning following parental divorce. *Journal of Abnormal Psychology, 99,* 278-283.

216. Frazier, P. A. (1990). Victim attributions and post-rape trauma. *Journal of Personality and Social Psychology, 59,* 298-304.

217. Frost, R. O., Benton, N., & Dowrick, P. W. (1990). Self-evaluation, videotape review, and dysphoria. *Journal of Social and Clinical Psychology, 9,* 367-374.

218. Futterman, A., Gallagher, D., Thompson, L. W., Lovett, S., & Gilewski, M. (1990). Retrospective assessment of marital adjustment and depression during the first 2 years of spousal bereavement. *Psychology and Aging, 5,* 277-283.

219. Gary, J. J., & Hoage, C. M. (1990). Bulimia nervosa: Group behavior therapy with exposure plus response revention. *Psychological Reports, 66,* 667-674.

220. Haaga, D. A. F., Stewart, B. L., Beck, A. T., & Derubeis, R. J. (1990). IQ independence of measures of dysfunctional cognition. *Journal of Psychopathology and Behavioral Assessment, 12,* 299-307.

221. Heimberg, R. G., Bruch, M. A., Hope, D. A., & Dombeck, M. (1990). Evaluating the states of mind model: Comparison to an alternative model and effects of method of cognitive assessment. *Cognitive Therapy and Research, 14,* 543-557.

222. Heimberg, R. G., Dodge, C. S., Hope, D. A., Kennedy, C. R., & Zollo, L. J. (1990). Cognitive behavioral group treatment for social phobia: Comparison with a credible placebo control. *Cognitive Therapy and Research, 14,* 1-23.

223. Hendricks, V. M. (1990). Psychiatric disorders in a Dutch addict population: Rates and correlates of DSM-III Diagnosis. *Journal of Consulting and Clinical Psychology, 58,* 158-165.

224. Henriques, J. B., & Davidson, R. J. (1990). Regional brain electrical asymmetrics discriminate between previously depressed and healthy control subjects. *Journal of Abnormal Psychology, 99,* 22-31.

225. Hewitt, P. L., & Genest, M. (1990). The ideal self: Schematic processing of perfectionistic content in dysphoric university students. *Journal of Personality and Social Psychology, 59,* 802-808.

226. Hoffart, A., & Martinsen, E. W. (1990). Agoraphobia, depression, mental health locus of control, and attributional style. *Cognitive Therapy and Research, 14,* 343-351.

227. Hummer, J. T., & Hokanson, J. E. (1990). The causal relations of attributions for interpersonal events to depression: A prospective longitudinal study. *Journal of Social and Clinical Psychology, 9,* 511-528.

228. Ingram, R. E. (1990). Attentional nonspecificity in depressive and generalized anxious affect states. *Cognitive Therapy and Research, 14,* 25-35.

229. Ingram, R. E., Slater, M. A., Atkinson, J. H., & Scott, W. (1990). Positive automatic cognition in major affective disorder. *Psychological Assessment, 2,* 209-211.

230. Johnson, J. G., & Miller, S. M. (1990). Attributional, life-event, and affective predictors of onset of depression, anxiety, and negative attributional style. *Cognitive Therapy and Research, 14,* 417-430.

231. Kathol, R. G., Mutgi, A., Williams, J., Clamon, G., & Noyes, R., Jr. (1990). Diagnosis of major depression in cancer patients according to four sets of criteria. *American Journal of Psychiatry, 147,* 1021-1024.

232. King, L. A., & Emmons, R. A. (1990). Conflict over emotional expression: Psychological and physical correlates. *Journal of Personality and Social Psychology, 58,* 864-877.

233. Klein, D. N. (1990). Depressive personality: Reliability, validity, and relation to dysthymia. *Journal of Abnormal Psychology, 99,* 412-421.

234. Krantz, S. E., & Gallagher-Thompson, D. (1990). Depression and information valence influence depressive cognition. *Cognitive Therapy and Research, 14,* 95-108.

235. Lakey, B., & Cassady, P. B. (1990). Cognitive processes in perceived social support. *Journal of Personality and Social Psychology, 59,* 337-343.

236. Lesler, D., Decker, J., Eisenberg, R. J., Ecker, C., Guerriero, J., & Mielish, G. (1990). Association between whirling responses on psychological tests and suicidal preoccupation. *Perceptual and Motor Skills, 71,* 1105.

237. Locke, K. D., & Horowitz, L. M. (1990). Satisfaction in interpersonal interactions as a function of similarity in level of dysphoria. *Journal of Personality and Social Psychology, 58,* 823-831.

238. Major, B., Cozzarelli, C., Sciacchitano, A. M., Cooper, M. L., Testa, M., & Mueller, P. M. (1990). Perceived social support, self-efficacy, and adjustment to abortion. *Journal of Personality and Social Psychology, 59,* 452-463.

239. Marcus, M. D., Wing, R. R., Ewing, L., Kern, E., McDermott, M., & Gooding, W. (1990). A double-blind, placebo-controlled trial of fluoxetine plus behavior modification in the treatment of obese binge-eaters and non-binge eaters. *American Journal of Psychiatry, 147,* 876-881.

240. McCallum, M., & Piper, W. E. (1990). The psychological mindedness assessment procedure. *Psychological Assessment, 2,* 412-418.

241. McCann, U. D., & Agras, W. W. (1990). Successful treatment of nonpurging bulimia nervosa with desipramine: A double-blind placebo-controlled study. *American Journal of Psychiatry, 147,* 1509-1513.

242. Mikulincer, M., Gerber, H., & Weisenberg, M. (1990). Judgement of control and depression: The role of self-esteem threat and self-focused attention. *Cognitive Therapy and Research, 14,* 589-608.

243. Miranda, J., Persons, J. B., & Byers, C. N. (1990). Endorsement of dysfunctional beliefs depends on current mood state. *Journal of Abnormal Psychology, 99,* 237-241.

244. Needles, D. J., & Abramson, L. V. (1990). Positive life events, attributional styles, and hopefulness: Testing a model of recovery from depression. *Journal of Abnormal Psychology, 99,* 156-165.

245. Neimeyer, G. J., Metzler, A. E., & Dongarra, T. (1990). Changing attitudes regarding the effectiveness of cognitive restructuring for treating depression. *Social Behavior and Personality, 18,* 181-188.

246. O'Boyle, M., Amadeo, M., & Self, D. (1990). Cognitive complaints in elderly depressed and pseudodemented patients. *Psychology and Aging, 5,* 467-468.

247. O'Hara, M. W., Zekoski, E. M., Phillips, L. H., & Wright, E. J. (1990). Controlled prospective study of postpartum mood disorders: Comparison of childbearing and nonchildbearing women. *Journal of Abnormal Psychology, 99,* 3-15.

248. Olin, J. T., Schneider, L. S., Eaton, E. M., Zemansky, M. F., & Pollock, V. E. (1992). The Geriatric Depression Scale and the Beck Depression Inventory as screening instruments in an older outpatient population. *Psychological Assessment, 4,* 190-192.

249. Orr, S. P., Claiborn, J. M., Altman, B., Forgue, D. F., de Jong, J. B., Pitman, R. K., & Herz, L. R. (1990). Psychometric profile of posttraumatic stress disorder, anxious, and healthy Vietnam veterans: Correlations with psychophysiologic responses. *Journal of Consulting and Clinical Psychology, 58,* 329-335.

250. Overholser, J. C. (1990). Emotional reliance and social loss: Effects on depressive symptomatology. *Journal of Personality Assessment, 55,* 618-629.

251. Park, C., Cohen, L. H., & Herb, L. (1990). Intrinsic religiousness and religious coping as life stress moderators for Catholics versus Protestants. *Journal of Personality and Social Psychology, 59,* 562-574.

252. Peselow, E. D., Robins, C., Block, P., Barouche, K., & Fieve, R. R. (1990). Dysfunctional attitudes in depressed patients before and after clinical treatment and in normal control subjects. *American Journal of Psychiatry, 147,* 439-444.

253. Rapp, S. R., Smith, S. S., & Britt, M. (1990). Identifying comorbid depression in elderly medical patients: Use of the Extracted Hamilton Depression Rating Scale. *Psychological Assessment, 2,* 243-247.

254. Riley, W. T., & McCranie, E. W. (1990). The Depressive Experiences Questionnaire: Validity and psychological correlates in a clinical sample. *Journal of Personality Assessment, 54,* 523-533.

255. Robins, C. J. (1990). Congruence of personality and life events in depression. *Journal of Abnormal Psychology, 99,* 393-397.

256. Robins, C. J., Block, P., & Peselow, E. O. (1990). Cognition and life events in major depression: A test of the mediation and interaction hypotheses. *Cognitive Therapy and Research, 14,* 299-313.

257. Salter, D., & Platt, S. (1990). Suicidal intent, hopelessness and depression in a parasuicide population: The influence of social desirability and elapsed time. *British Journal of Clinical Psychology, 29,* 361-371.

258. Schefft, B. K., & Biederman, J. J. (1990). Emotional effects of self-generated behavior and the influence of resourcefulness and depressed mood. *Journal of Social and Clinical Psychology, 9,* 354-366.

259. Schiffer, R. B., & Wineman, N. M. (1990). Antidepressant pharmacotherapy of depression associated with multiple sclerosis. *American Journal of Psychiatry, 147,* 1493-1497.

260. Schlosser, B. (1990). The assessment of subjective well-being and its relationship to the stress process. *Journal of Personality Assessment, 54,* 128-140.

261. Schmaling, K. B., & Jacobsen, N. S. (1990). Marital interaction and depression. *Journal of Abnormal Psychology, 99,* 229-236.

262. Schmidt, N. B., & Telch, M. J. (1990). Prevalence of personality disorders among bulimics, nonbulimic binge eaters, and normal controls. *Journal of Psychopathology and Behavioral Assessment, 12,* 169-185.

263. Schmidt, P. J., Grover, G. N., Hoban, M. C., & Rubinow, D. R. (1990). State-dependent alterations in the perception of life events in menstrual-related mood disorders. *American Journal of Psychiatry, 147,* 230-234.

264. Segal, Z. V., & Vella, D. D. (1990). Self-schema in major depression: Replication and extension of a priming methodology. *Cognitive Therapy and Research, 14,* 161-176.

265. Selmi, P. M., Klein, M. H., Greist, J. H., Sorrell, S. P., & Erdman, H. P. (1990). Computer-administered cognitive-behavioral therapy for depression. *American Journal of Psychiatry, 147,* 51-56.

266. Siegel, S. J., & Alloy, L. B. (1990). Interpersonal perceptions and consequences of depressive-significant other relationships: A naturalistic study of college roommates. *Journal of Abnormal Psychology, 99,* 361-373.

267. Smith, J. E., & Morgan, C. D. (1990). The neglected bulimic: The nonpurger. *Journal of Psychopathology and Behavioral Assessment, 12,* 103-118.

268. Steer, R. A., Scholl, T. O., & Beck, A. T. (1990). Revised Beck Depression Inventory scores of inner-city adolescents: Pre- and postpartum. *Psychological Reports, 66,* 315-320.

269. Stiles, W. B., Shapiro, D. A., & Firth-Cozens, J. A. (1990). Correlations of session evaluations with treatment outcome. *British Journal of Clinical Psychology, 29,* 13-21.

270. Stukenberg, K. W., Dura, J. R., & Kiecolt-Glaser, J. K. (1990). Depression screening scale validation in an elderly, community-dwelling population. *Psychological Assessment, 2,* 134-138.

271. Sullivan, M. J. L., & D'Eon, J. L. (1990). Relation between catastrophizing and depression in chronic pain patients. *Journal of Abnormal Psychology, 99,* 260-263.

272. Sutker, P. B., Winstead, D. K., Galina, Z. H., & Allain, A. N. (1990). Assessment of long-term psychosocial sequelae among POW survivors of the Korean conflict. *Journal of Personality Assessment, 54,* 170-180.

273. Taylor, G. J., Parker, J. D. A., & Bagby, R. M. (1990). A preliminary investigation of alexithymia in men with psychoactive substance dependence. *American Journal of Psychiatry, 147,* 1228-1230.

274. Tomarken, A. J., Davidson, R. J., & Henriques, J. B. (1990). Resting frontal brain asymmetry predicts affective responses to films. *Journal of Personality and Social Psychology, 59,* 791-801.

275. Troutman, B. R., & Cutrona, C. E. (1990). Nonpsychotic postpartum depression among adolescent mothers. *Journal of Abnormal Psychology, 99,* 69-78.

276. Vitaliano, P. P., DeWolfe, D. J., Maiuro, R. D., Russo, J., & Katon, W. (1990). Appraised changeability of a stressor as a modifier of the relationship between coping and depression: A test of the hypothesis of fit. *Journal of Personality and Social Psychology, 59,* 582-592.

277. Walker, E. A., Roy-Byrne, P. P., Katon, W. J., Li, L., Amos, D., & Jiranek, G. (1990). Psychiatric illness and irritable bowel syndrome: A comparison with inflammatory bowel disease. *American Journal of Psychiatry, 147,* 1656-1661.

278. Weary, G., & Williams, J. P. (1990). Depressive self-presentation: Beyond self-handicapping. *Journal of Personality and Social Psychology, 58,* 892-898.

279. Webster-Stratton, C. (1990). Long-term follow-up of families with young conduct problem children: From preschool to grade school. *Journal of Clinical Child Psychology, 19,* 144-149.

280. Wells-Parker, E., Miller, D. I., & Topping, J. S. (1990). Development of control-of-outcome scales and self-efficacy scales for women in four life roles. *Journal of Personality Assessment, 54,* 564-575.

281. Whiffen, V. E. (1990). Maternal depressed mood and perceptions of child temperament. *The Journal of Genetic Psychology, 151,* 329-339.

282. Zuroff, D. C., Igreja, I., & Mongrain, M. (1990). Dysfunctional attitudes, dependency, and self-criticism as predictors of depressive mood states: A 12-month longitudinal study. *Cognitive Therapy and Research, 14,* 315-326.

283. Acklin, M. W., Bibb, J. L., Boyer, P., & Jain, V. (1991). Early memories as expressions of relationship paradigms: A preliminary investigation. *Journal of Personality Assessment, 57,* 177-192.

284. Ahrens, A. H. (1991). Dysphoria and social comparison: Combining information regarding others' performances. *Journal of Social and Clinical Psychology, 10,* 190-205.

285. Bancroft, J., Cook, A., Davidson, D., Bennie, J., & Goodwin, G. (1991). Blunting of neuroendocrine responses to infusion of L-tryptophan in women with perimenstrual mood change. *Psychological Medicine, 21,* 305-312.

286. Bentall, R. P., Kaney, S., & Dewey, M. E. (1991). Paranoia and social reasoning: An attribution theory analysis. *British Journal of Clinical Psychology, 30,* 13-23.

287. Berger, B. D., & Adesso, V. J. (1991). Gender differences in using alcohol to cope with depression. *Addictive Behaviors, 16,* 315-327.

288. Blakely, A. A., Howard, R. C., Sosich, R. M., Murdoch, J. C., Menkes, D. B., & Spears, G. F. S. (1991). Psychiatric symptoms, personality and ways of coping in chronic fatigue syndrome. *Psychological Medicine, 21,* 347-362.

289. Block, P. (1991). Measurement and interrelations of psychiatric symptomatology in inpatients. *Psychological Reports, 68,* 1055-1056.

290. Boyce, P., Parker, G., Barnett, B., Cooney, M., & Smith, F. (1991). Personality as a vulnerability factor to depression. *British Journal of Psychiatry, 159,* 106-114.

291. Brandon, J. E., & Loftin, J. M. (1991). Relationship of fitness to depression, state and trait anxiety, internal health locus of control, and self-control. *Perceptual and Motor Skills, 73,* 563-568.

292. Bruch, M. A., Heimberg, R. G., & Hope, D. A. (1991). States of mind model and cognitive change in treated social phobics. *Cognitive Therapy and Research, 15*, 429-441.

293. Burge, D., & Hammen, C. (1991). Maternal communication: Predictors of outcome at follow-up in a sample of children at high and low risk for depression. *Journal of Abnormal Psychology, 100*, 174-180.

294. Cartwright, R. D., Kravitz, H. M., Eastman, C. I., & Wood, E. (1991). REM latency and the recovery from depression: Getting over divorce. *American Journal of Psychiatry, 148*, 1530-1535.

295. Cash, T. F., Wood, K. C., Phelps, K. D., & Boyd, K. (1991). New assessments of weight-related body image derived from extant instruments. *Perceptual and Motor Skills, 73*, 235-241.

296. Christensen, L. (1991). Issues in the design of studies investigating the behavioral concomitants of foods. *Journal of Consulting and Clinical Psychology, 59*, 874-882.

297. Christenson, G. A., Mackenzie, T. B., Mitchell, J. E., & Callies, A. L. (1991). A placebo-controlled double-blind crossover study of fluoxetine in trichtillomania. *American Journal of Psychiatry, 148*, 1566-1571.

298. Clark, D. A., & Beck, A. T. (1991). Personality factors in dysphoria: A psychometric refinement of Beck's sociotropy-autonomy scale. *Journal of Psychopathology and Behavioral Assessment, 13*, 369-388.

299. Clark, L. A., & Watson, D. (1991). Tripartite model of anxiety and depression: Psychometric evidence and taxonomic implications. *Journal of Abnormal Psychology, 100*, 316-336.

300. Cloitre, M., & Liebowitz, M. R. (1991). Memory bias in panic disorder: An investigation of the cognitive avoidance hypothesis. *Cognitive Therapy and Research, 15*, 371-386.

301. Connell, D. K., & Meyer, R. G. (1991). The Reasons for Living Inventory and a college population: Adolescent suicidal behaviors, beliefs, and coping skills. *Journal of Clinical Psychology, 47*, 485-489.

302. Conway, M., Howell, A., & Giannopoulos, C. (1991). Dysphoria and thought suppression. *Cognitive Therapy and Research, 15*, 153-166.

303. Dahlem, N. W., Zimet, G. D., & Walker, R. R. (1991). The multidimensional scale of perceived social support: A confirmation study. *Journal of Clinical Psychology, 47*, 756-761.

304. Darko, D. F., Wilson, N. W., Gillin, J. C., & Golshan, S. (1991). A critical appraisal of mitogen-induced lymphocyte proliferation in depressed patients. *American Journal of Psychiatry, 148*, 337-344.

305. Dritschel, B. H., & Teasdale, J. D. (1991). Individual differences in affect-related cognitive operations elicited by experimental stimuli. *British Journal of Clinical Psychology, 30*, 151-160.

306. Dunning, D., & Story, A. L. (1991). Depression, realism, and the overconfidence effect: Are the sadder wiser when predicting future actions and events? *Journal of Personality and Social Psychology, 61*, 521-532.

307. Dura, J. R., Stukenberg, K. W., Kiecolt-Glaser, J. K. (1991). Anxiety and depression disorders in adult children caring for demented patients. *Psychology and Aging, 6*, 467-473.

308. Dykman, B. M., Abramson, L. V., & Albright, J. S. (1991). Effects of ascending and descending patterns of success upon dysphoric and nondysphoric subjects' encoding, recall, and predictions of future success. *Cognitive Therapy and Research, 15*, 179-199.

309. Dykman, B. M., Horowitz, L. M., Abramson, L. Y., & Usher, M. (1991). Schematic and situational determinants of depressed and nondepressed students' interpretation of feedback. *Journal of Abnormal Psychology, 100*, 45-55.

310. Edelmann, R. J. (1991). Correlates of chronic blushing. *British Journal of Clinical Psychology, 30*, 177-178.

311. Ehrenberg, M. F., Cox, D. N., & Koopman, R. F. (1991). The relationship between self-efficacy and depression in adolescents. *Adolescence, 26*, 361-374.

312. Errico, A. L., King, A. C., & Parsons, O. A. (1991). The influence of depressive symptomatology on alcoholics' locus of control: A methodological note and a correction. *Journal of Clinical Psychology, 47*, 600-604.

313. Eysenck, M. W., Mogg, K., May, J., Richards, A., & Mathews, A. (1991). Bias in interpretation of ambiguous sentences related to threat in anxiety. *Journal of Abnormal Psychology, 100*, 144-150.

314. Fisher, S. (1991). The focus of pessimism in performance assessments by the depressed. *British Journal of Clinical Psychology, 30*, 271-272.

315. Fiske, V., & Peterson, C. (1991). Love and depression: The nature of depressive romantic relationships. *Journal of Social and Clinical Psychology, 10*, 75-90.

316. Fleminger, S. (1991). Left-sided Parkinson's disease is associated with greater anxiety and depression. *Psychological Medicine, 21*, 629-638.

317. Flett, G. L., Hewitt, P. L., & Mittelstaedt, W. M. (1991). Dysphoria and components of self-punitiveness: A re-analysis. *Cognitive Therapy and Research, 15*, 201-219.

318. Frazier, P. A. (1991). Self-blame as a mediator of postrape

depressive symptoms. *Journal of Social and Clinical Psychology, 10*, 47-57.

319. Gilewski, M., Farberow, N. L., Gallagher, D. E., & Thompson, L. W. (1991). Interaction of depression and bereavement on mental health in the elderly. *Psychology and Aging, 6*, 67-75.

320. Gleicher, F., & Weary, G. (1991). Effect of depression on quantity and quality of social inferences. *Journal of Personality and Social Psychology, 61*, 105-114.

321. Gotlib, I. H., Whiffen, V. E., Wallace, P. M., & Mount, J. H. (1991). Prospective investigation of postpartum depression: Factors involved in onset and recovery. *Journal of Abnormal Psychology, 100*, 122-132.

322. Heatherton, T. F., & Polivy, J. (1991). Development and validation of a scale for measuring state self-esteem. *Journal of Personality and Social Psychology, 60*, 895-910.

323. Hendryx, M. S., Haviland, M. G., & Shaw, P. G. (1991). Dimensions of alexithymia and their relationships to anxiety and depression. *Journal of Personality Assessment, 56*, 227-237.

324. Henriques, J. B., & Davidson, R. J. (1991). Left frontal hypoactivation in depression. *Journal of Abnormal Psychology, 100*, 535-545.

325. Herbert, J. D., Bellack, A. S., & Hope, P. A. (1992). Concurrent validity of the social phobia and anxiety inventory. *Journal of Psychopathology and Behavioral Assessment, 13*, 357-368.

326. Hertel, P. T., & Rude, S. S. (1991). Recalling in a state of natural or experimental depression. *Cognitive Therapy and Research, 15*, 103-127.

327. Hewitt, P. L., & Flett, G. L. (1991). Dimensions of perfectionism in unipolar depression. *Journal of Abnormal Psychology, 100*, 98-101.

328. Himmelhoch, J. M., Thase, M. E., Mallinger, A. G., & Houck, P. (1991). Tranylcypromine versus imipramine in anergic bipolar depression. *American Journal of Psychiatry, 148*, 910-916.

329. Hoffart, A., & Martinsen, E. W. (1991). Causal attributions in clinical subtypes of depression: A longitudinal study of inpatients. *Journal of Psychopathology and Behavioral Assessment, 13*, 241-256.

330. Hoffart, A., & Martinsen, E. W. (1991). Cognition and coping in agoraphobia and depression: A multivariate approach. *Journal of Clinical Psychology, 47*, 9-16.

331. Hokanson, J. E., Hummer, J. T., & Butler, A. C. (1991). Interpersonal perceptions by depressed college students. *Cognitive Therapy and Research, 15*, 443-457.

332. Holtgraves, T., & Athanassopoulou, M. (1991). Depression and processing information about others. *Journal of Research in Personality, 25*, 445-453.

333. Horowitz, L. M., Locke, K. D., Morse, M. B., Waikar, S. V., Dryer, D. C., Tarnow, E., & Ghannam, J. (1991). Self-derogations and the interpersonal theory. *Journal of Personality and Social Psychology, 61*, 68-79.

334. House, A., Dennis, M., Mogridge, L., Warlow, C., Hawton, K., & Jones, L. (1991). Mood disorders in the year after first stroke. *British Journal of Psychiatry, 158*, 83-92.

335. Hull, J. G., & Mendolia, M. (1991). Modeling the relations of attributional style, expectancies, and depression. *Journal of Personality and Social Psychology, 61*, 85-97.

336. Johnson, J. M., Petzel, T. P., & Johnson, J. E. (1991). Attributions of shy persons in affiliation and achievement situations. *The Journal of Psychology, 125*, 51-58.

337. Johnston, C. (1991). Predicting mothers' and fathers' perceptions of child behaviour problems. *Canadian Journal of Behavioural Science, 23*, 349-357.

338. Johnston, M. A., & Page, S. (1991). Subject age and gender as predictors of life stress, attributional style, and personal adjustment. *Canadian Journal of Behavioural Science, 23*, 475-478.

339. Joseph, S., Brewin, C. R., Yule, W., & Williams, R. (1991). Causal attributions and psychiatric symptoms in survivors of the Herald of Free Enterprise disaster. *British Journal of Psychiatry, 159*, 542-546.

340. Katon, W., & Roy-Byrne, P. P. (1991). Mixed anxiety and depression. *Journal of Abnormal Psychology, 100*, 337-345.

341. Kelly, B., Dunne, M., Raphael, B., Buckham, C., Zournazi, A., Smith, S., & Statham, D. (1991). Relationships between mental adjustment to HIV diagnosis, psychological morbidity and sexual behavior. *British Journal of Clinical Psychology, 30*, 370-372.

342. Laessle, R. G., Beumont, P. J. V., Butow, P., Lennarts, W., O'Connor, M., Pirke, K. M., Touyz, S. W., & Waadt, S. (1991). A comparison of nutritional management with stress management in the treatment of bulimia nervosa. *British Journal of Psychiatry, 159*, 250-261.

343. Larsson, B. S. (1991). Somatic complaints and their relationship to depressive symptoms in Swedish adolescents. *Journal of Child Psychology and Psychiatry, 32*, 821-832.

344. Lee, C. M., & Gotlib, I. H. (1991). Adjustment of children of depressed mothers: A 10-month follow-up. *Journal of Abnormal Psychology, 100*, 473-477.

345. Lenzenweger, M. F., Cornblatt, B. A., & Putnick, M. (1991). Schizotypy and sustained attention. *Journal of Abnormal Psychology, 100,* 84-89.

346. Lester, D. (1991). Alexithymia, depression, and suicidal preoccupation. *Perceptual and Motor Skills, 72,* 1058.

347. Lester, D. (1991). Depression, suicidal ideation, and autonomic reactivity. *Perceptual and Motor Skills, 73,* 294.

348. Lim, L. C. C., Lee, T., & Boey, M. (1991). Psychiatric manifestation of systemic lupus erythmatosus in Singapore: A cross-cultural comparison. *British Journal of Psychiatry, 159,* 520-523.

349. Linton, S. J. (1991). Memory for chronic pain intensity: Correlates of accuracy. *Perceptual and Motor Skills, 72,* 1091-1095.

350. Lovejoy, M. C. (1991). Maternal depression: Effects on social cognition and behavior in parent-child interactions. *Journal of Abnormal Child Psychology, 19,* 693-706.

351. Lyon, D., & Greenberg, J. (1991). Evidence of codependency in women with an alcoholic parent: Helping out Mr. Wrong. *Journal of Personality and Social Psychology, 61,* 435-439.

352. MacLeod, A. K., Williams, J. M. G., & Bekerian, D. A. (1991). Worry is reasonable: The role of explanations in pessimism about future personal events. *Journal of Abnormal Psychology, 100,* 478-486.

353. Maddocks, S. E., & Kaplan, A. S. (1991). The prediction of treatment response in bulimia nervosa: A study of patient variables. *British Journal of Psychiatry, 159,* 846-849.

354. Martin, D. J., Oren, Z., & Boone, K. (1991). Major depressives' and depthymics' performance on the Wisconsin Card Sorting Test. *Journal of Clinical Psychology, 47,* 684-690.

355. Marx, E. M., & Schulze, C. (1991). Interpersonal problem-solving in depressed students. *Journal of Clinical Psychology, 47,* 361-367.

356. Matthews, G., & Southall, A. (1991). Depression and the processing of emotional stimuli: A study of semantic priming. *Cognitive Therapy and Research, 15,* 283-302.

357. Mayer, J. D., Salovey, P., Gomberg-Kaufman, S., & Blainey, K. (1991). A broader conception of mood experience. *Journal of Personality and Social Psychology, 60,* 100-111.

358. McClusky, H. Y., Milby, J. B., Switzer, P. K., Williams, V., & Wooten, V. (1991). Efficacy of behavioral versus triazolam treatment in persistant sleep-onset insomnia. *American Journal of Psychiatry, 148,* 121-126.

359. McConaghy, N., Blaszczynski, A., & Frankova, A. (1991). Comparison of imaginal desensitization with other behavioural treatments of pathological gambling: A two- to nine-year follow-up. *British Journal of Psychiatry, 159,* 390-393.

360. McNeil, J. K., LeBlanc, E. M., & Joyner, M. (1991). The effect of exercise on depressive symptoms in the moderately depressed study. *Psychology and Aging, 6,* 487-488.

361. Mearns, J. (1991). Coping with a breakup: Negative mood regulation expectancies and depression following the end of a romantic relationship. *Journal of Personality and Social Psychology, 60,* 327-334.

362. Mebert, C. J. (1991). Dimensions of subjectivity in parents' ratings of infant temperament. *Child Development, 62,* 352-361.

363. Mehrabian, A., & Bernath, M. S. (1991). Factorial composition of commonly used self-report depression inventories: Relationships with basic dimensions of temperament. *Journal of Research in Personality, 25,* 262-275.

364. Metzger, D., Woody, G., DePhilippis, D., McLellan, T., O'Brien, C. P., & Platt, J. J. (1991). Risk factor for needle sharing among methadone-treated patients. *American Journal of Psychiatry, 148,* 636-640.

365. Mouanoutoua, V. L., Brown, L. G., Cappelletty, G. G., & Levine, R. V. (1991). A Hmong adaptation of the Beck Depression Inventory. *Journal of Personality Assessment, 57,* 309-322.

366. Nelson-Gray, R. O., Lin, K., & Torquato, R. (1991). Confidential and shared reactions of strangers and familiar observers to depressives. *Journal of Social and Clinical Psychology, 10,* 176-189.

367. Norman, R. M. G., & Malla, A. K. (1991). Dysphoric mood and symptomatology in schizophrenia. *Psychological Medicine, 21,* 897-903.

368. O'Hara, M. W., Schlechte, J. A., Lewis, D. A., & Vaner, M. W. (1991). Controlled prospective study of postpartum mood disorders: Psychological, environmental, and hormonal variables. *Journal of Abnormal Psychology, 100,* 63-73.

369. Pelham, B. W. (1991). On the benefits of misery: Self-serving biases in the depressive self-concept. *Journal of Personality and Social Psychology, 61,* 670-681.

370. Perry, W., & Viglione, D. J., Jr. (1991). The ego impairment index as a predictor of outcome in melancholic depressed patients treated with tricyclic antipressants. *Journal of Personality Assessment, 56,* 487-501.

371. Persons, J. B., Miranda, J., & Perloff, J. M. (1991). Relationships between depressive symptoms and cognitive vulnerabilities of achievement and dependency. *Cognitive Therapy and Research, 15,* 221-235.

372. Phillips, L. H. C., & O'Hara, M. W. (1991). Prospective study of postpartum depression: 4½-year follow-up of women and children. *Journal of Abnormal Psychology, 100,* 151-155.

373. Pigott, T. A., Altremus, M., Rubenstein, C. S., Hill, J. L., Bihari, K., L'Heureux, F., Bernstein, S., & Murphy, D. L. (1991). Symptoms of eating disorders in patients with obsessive-compulsive disorder. *American Journal of Psychiatry, 148,* 1552-1557.

374. Pilkonis, P. A., Heape, C. L., Ruddy, J., & Serrao, P. (1991). Validity in the diagnosis of personality disorders: The use of the LEAD standard. *Psychological Assessment, 3,* 46-54.

375. Pillow, D. R., West, S. G., & Reich, J. W. (1991). Attributional style in relation to self-esteem and depression: Mediational and interactive models. *Journal of Research in Personality, 25,* 57-69.

376. Polaino, A., & Senra, C. (1991). Measurement of depression: Comparison between self-reports and clinical assessments of depressed outpatients. *Journal of Psychopathology and Behavioral Assessment, 13,* 313-324.

377. Power, M. J., Brewin, C. R., Stuessy, A., & Mahoney, T. (1991). The emotional priming task: Results from a student population. *Cognitive Therapy and Research, 15,* 21-31.

378. Prussin, R. A., & Harvey, P. D. (1991). Depression, dietary restraint, and binge eating in female runners. *Addictive Behaviors, 16,* 295-301.

379. Rebert, W. M., Stanton, A. L., & Schwarz, R. M. (1991). Influence of personality attributes and daily moods on bulimic eating patterns. *Addictive Behaviors, 16,* 497-505.

380. Reynolds, W. M. (1991). Psychometric characteristics of the adult suicidal ideation questionnaire in college students. *Journal of Personality Assessment, 56,* 289-307.

381. Riley, W. T., Mabe, P. A., & Davis, H. C. (1991). Derivation and implications of MMPI cluster groups in clinically depressed inpatient females. *The Journal of Psychology, 125,* 723-733.

382. Rosen, A. J., Lockhart, J. J., Gants, E. S., & Westergaard, C. K. (1991). Maintenance of grip-induced muscle tension: A behavioral marker of schizophrenia. *Journal of Abnormal Psychology, 100,* 583-593.

383. Rosenblatt, A., & Greenberg, J. (1991). Examining the world of the depressed: Do depressed people prefer others who are depressed? *Journal of Personality and Social Psychology, 60,* 620-629.

384. Rubin, E. H., Kinscherf, D. A., Grant, E. A., & Storandt, M. (1991). The influence of major depression on clinical and psychometric assessment of senile dementia of the Alzheimer type. *American Journal of Psychiatry, 148,* 1164-1171.

385. Satel, S. L., Price, L. H., Palumbo, J. M., McDougle, C. J., Krystal, J. H., Gawin, F., Charney, D. S., Heninger, G. R., & Kleber, H. D. (1991). Clincial phenomenology and neurobiology of cocaine abstinence: A prospective inpatient study. *American Journal of Psychiatry, 148,* 1712-1716.

386. Schill, T., & Kramer, J. (1991). Self-defeating personality, self-reinforcement, and depression. *Psychological Reports, 69,* 137-138.

387. Shek, D. T. L. (1991). What does the Chinese version of the Beck Depression Inventory measure in Chinese students—General psychopathology or depression? *Journal of Clinical Psychology, 47,* 381-390.

388. Sotsky, S. M., Glass, D. R., Shea, M. T., Pilkonis, P. A., Collins, J. F., Elkin, I., Watkins, J. T., Imber, S. D., Leber, W. R., Moyer, J., & Oliveri, M. E. (1991). Patient predictors of response to psychotherapy and pharmacotherapy: Findings in the NIMH Treatment of Depression Collaborative Research program. *American Journal of Psychiatry, 148,* 997-1008.

389. Steer, R. A., Scholl, T. O., & Beck, A. T. (1991). Self-reported depression in younger and older pregnant inner-city adolescents. *The Journal of Genetic Psychology, 152,* 83-89.

390. Strassberg, D. S., Clutton, S., & Korboot, P. (1991). A descriptive and validity study of the Minnesota Multiphasic Personality Inventory-2 (MMPI-2) in an elderly Australian sample. *Journal of Psychopathology and Behavioral Assessment, 13,* 301-311.

391. Sullivan, M. J. L., & Conway, M. (1991). Dysphoria and valence of attributions for others' behavior. *Cognitive Therapy and Research, 15,* 273-282.

392. Sutker, P. B., Winstead, D. K., Galina, Z. H., & Allain, A. N. (1991). Cognitive deficits and psychopathology among former prisoners of war and combat veterans of the Korean conflict. *American Journal of Psychiatry, 148,* 67-72.

393. Swindell, C. S., & Hammons, J. (1991). Poststroke depression: Neurologic, physiologic, diagnostic, and treatment implications. *Journal of Speech and Hearing Research, 34,* 325-333.

394. Talbot, N. L., Duberstein, P. R., & Scott, P. (1991). Subliminal psychodynamic activation, food consumption, and self-confidence. *Journal of Clinical Psychology, 47,* 813-823.

395. Thase, M. E., Simons, A. D., Cahalane, J., McGeary, J., & Harden, T. (1991). Severity of depression and response to cognitive behavior therapy. *American Journal of Psychiatry, 148,* 784-789.

396. Thompson, L. W., Gallagher-Thompson, D., Futterman, A.,

Gilewski, M. J., & Peterson, J. (1991). The effects of late-life spousal bereavement over a 30-month interval. *Psychology and Aging, 6,* 434-441.

397. Tobin, D. L., Thonson, C., Steinberg, S., Staats, M., & Dennis, A. B. (1991). Multifactorial assessment of bulimia nervosa. *Journal of Abnormal Psychology, 100,* 14-21.

398. Turner, J., Foggo, M., Bennie, J., Carroll, S., Dick, H., & Goodwin, G. M. (1991). Psychological, hormonal and biochemical changes following carbohydrate bingeing: A placebo controlled study in bulimia nervosa and matched controls. *Psychological Medicine, 21,* 123-133.

399. Wallace, S. T., & Alden, L. E. (1991). A comparison of social standards and perceived ability in anxious and nonanxious men. *Cognitive Therapy and Research, 15,* 237-254.

400. Walsh, B. T., Hadigan, C. M., Devlin, M. J., Gladis, M., & Roose, S. P. (1991). Long-term outcome of antidepressant treatment for bulimia nervosa. *American Journal of Psychiatry, 148,* 1206-1212.

401. Watt, J. D., & Davis, F. E. (1991). The prevalence of boredom proneness and depression among profoundly deaf residential school adolescents. *American Annals of the Deaf, 136,* 409-413.

402. Welsh, M. C., Labké, E. E., & Delaney, D. (1991). Cognitive strategies and personality variables in adherence to exercise. *Psychological Reports, 68,* 1327-1335.

403. Whiffen, V. E., & Sasseville, T. M. (1991). Dependency, self-criticism, and recollections of parenting: Sex differences and the role of depressive affect. *Journal of Social and Clinical Psychology, 10,* 121-133.

404. Wilson, P. H., Henry, J., Bowen, M., & Haralambous, G. (1991). Tinnitus reaction questionnaire: Psychometric properties of a measure of distress associated with tinnitus. *Journal of Speech and Hearing Research, 34,* 197-201.

405. Agras, W. S., Rossiter, E. M., Arnow, B., Schneider, J. A., Telch, C. F., Raeburn, S. D., Bruce, B., Perl, M., & Koran, L. M. (1992). Pharmacologic and cognitive-behavioral treatment for bulimia nervosa: A controlled comparison. *American Journal of Psychiatry, 149,* 82-87.

406. Alloy, L. B., & Clements, C. M. (1992). Illusion of control: Invulnerability to negative affect and depressive symptoms after laboratory and natural stressors. *Journal of Abnormal Psychology, 101,* 234-245.

407. Alloy, L. B., Lipman, A. J., & Abramson, L. Y. (1992). Attributional style as a vulnerability factor for depression: Validation by past history of mood disorders. *Cognitive Therapy and Research, 16,* 391-407.

408. Andersen, S. M., Spielman, L. A., & Bargh, J. A. (1992). Future-event schemas and certainty about the future: Automaticity in depressives' future-event predictions. *Journal of Personality and Social Psychology, 63,* 711-723.

409. Anderson, I. M., Ware, C. J., DaRoza Davis, J. M., & Cowen, P. J. (1992). Decreased 5-HT-medicated prolactin release in major depression. *British Journal of Psychiatry, 160,* 372-378.

410. Atlas, J. A., & DiScipio, W. J. (1992). Correlations of Beck Depression Inventory and Reynolds Adolescent Depression Scale. *Psychological Reports, 70,* 621-622.

411. Barrett, D., & Loeffler, M. (1992). Comparison of dream content of depressed vs. nondepressed dreamers. *Psychological Reports, 70,* 403-406.

412. Belicki, K. (1992). Nightmare frequency versus nightmare distress: Relations to psychopathology and cognitive style. *Journal of Abnormal Psychology, 101,* 592-597.

413. Berenbaum, H., & Oltmanns, T. F. (1992). Emotional experience and expression in schizophrenia and depression. *Journal of Abnormal Psychology, 101,* 37-44.

414. Berrios, G. E., Bulbena, A., Bakshi, N., Dening, T. R., Jenaway, A., Markar, H., Martin-Santos, R., & Mitchell, S. L. (1992). Feelings of guilt in major depression. *British Journal of Psychiatry, 160,* 781-787.

415. Blankstein, K. R., Flett, G. L., & Johnston, M. E. (1992). Depression, problem-solving ability, and problem-solving appraisals. *Journal of Clinical Psychology, 48,* 749-759.

416. Braver, M., Bumberry, J., Green, K., & Rawson, R. (1992). Childhood abuse and current psychological functioning in a university counseling center population. *Journal of Counseling Psychology, 39,* 252-257.

417. Brock, G., LaClave, L., & Wyatt, A. S. (1992). The relationship of problem solving and reframing to stress and depression in female college students. *Journal of College Student Development, 33,* 124-131.

418. Burns, D. D., & Nolen-Hoeksema, S. (1992). Therapeutic empathy and recovery from depression in cognitive-behavioral therapy: A structural equation model. *Journal of Consulting and Clinical Psychology, 60,* 441-449.

419. Carey, M. P., Lubin, B., & Brewer, D. H. (1992). Measuring dysphoric mood in pre-adolescents and adolescents: A Youth Depression Adjective Checklist (Y-DACL). *Journal of Clinical Child Psychology, 21,* 331-338.

420. Cassiday, K. L., McNally, R. J., & Zeitlin, S. B. (1992). Cognitive processing of trauma cues in rape victims with post-traumatic stress disorder. *Cognitive Therapy and Research, 16,* 283-295.

421. Clark, D. A., Beck, A. T., & Brown, G. K. (1992). Sociotropy, autonomy, and life event perceptions in dysphoric and nondysphoric individuals. *Cognitive Therapy and Research, 16,* 635-652.

422. Connolly, J., Geller, S., Marton, P., & Kutcher, S. (1992). Peer responses to social interaction with depressed adolescents. *Journal of Clinical Child Psychology, 21,* 365-370.

423. Cooley, E. L. (1992). Family expressiveness and proneness to depression among college women. *Journal of Research in Personality, 26,* 281-287.

424. Cooper, M. J., Anastasiades, P., & Fairburn, C. G. (1992). Selective processing of eating-, shape-, and weight-related words in persons with bulimia nervosa. *Journal of Abnormal Psychology, 101,* 352-355.

425. Critelli, J. W., Gabriel, M. T., Ee, J. S., & Neumann, K. F. (1992). Splitting as a predictor of depression. *Perceptual and Motor Skills, 75,* 613-614.

426. Dadds, M. R., & McHugh, T. A. (1992). Social support and treatment outcome in behavioral family therapy for child conduct problems. *Journal of Consulting and Clinical Psychology, 60,* 252-259.

427. Denny, E. B., & Hunt, R. R. (1992). Affective valence and memory in depression: Dissociation of recall and fragment completion. *Journal of Abnormal Psychology, 101,* 575-580.

428. Dua, J., & Hargreaves, L. (1992). Effect of aerobic exercise on negative affect, positive affect, stress, and depression. *Perceptual and Motor Skills, 75,* 355-361.

429. Dworkin, R. H., Hartstein, G., Rosner, H. L., Walther, R. R., Sweeney, E. W., & Brand, L. (1992). A high-risk method for studying psychosocial antecedents of chronic pain: The prospective investigation of Herpes Zoster. *Journal of Abnormal Psychology, 101,* 200-205.

430. Dyck, M. J. (1992). Subscales of the dysfunctional attitude scale. *British Journal of Clinical Psychology, 31,* 333-335.

431. Egan, V., Brettle, R. P., & Goodwin, G. M. (1992). The Edinburgh cohort of HIV-Positive drug users: Pattern of cognitive impairment in relation to progression of disease. *British Journal of Psychiatry, 161,* 522-531.

432. Ehlers, A., & Breuer, P. (1992). Increased cardiac awareness in panic disorder. *Journal of Abnormal Psychology, 101,* 371-382.

433. Elliott, C. L., & Greene, R. L. (1992). Clinical depression and implicit memory. *Journal of Abnormal Psychology, 101,* 572-574.

434. Emmons, R. A. (1992). Abstract versus concrete goals: Personal striving level, physical illness and psychological well-being. *Journal of Personality and Social Psychology, 62,* 292-300.

435. Endler, N. S., Cox, B. J., Parker, J. D. A., & Bagby, R. M. (1992). Self-reports of depression and state-trait anxiety: Evidence for differential assessment. *Journal of Personality and Social Psychology, 63,* 832-838.

436. Engle-Friedman, M., Bootzin, R. R., Hazlewood, L., & Tsao, C. (1992). An evaluation of behavioral treatments for insomnia in the older adult. *Journal of Clinical Psychology, 48,* 77-90.

437. Foa, E. B., Kozak, M. J., Steketee, G. S., & McCarthy, P. R. (1992). Treatment of depressive and obsessive-compulsive symptoms in OCD by imipramine and behavior therapy. *British Journal of Clinical Psychology, 31,* 279-292.

438. Forston, M., & Stanton, A. L. (1992). Self-discrepancy theory as a framework for understanding bulimic symptomatology and associated distress. *Journal of Social and Clinical Psychology, 11,* 103-118.

439. Franche, R. L., & Dobson, K. (1992). Self-criticism and interpersonal dependency as vulnerability factors to depression. *Cognitive Therapy and Research, 16,* 419-435.

440. Frisch, M. B., Cornell, T., Villanueva, M., & Retzlaff, P. J. (1992). Clinical validation of the Quality of Life Inventory: A measure of life satisfaction for use in treatment planning and outcome assessment. *Psychological Assessment, 4,* 92-101.

441. Fuhr, S. K., & Shean, G. (1992). Subtypes of depression, efficacy, and the Depressive Experiences Questionnaire. *The Journal of Psychology, 126,* 495-506.

442. Gallagher-Thompson, D., Futterman, A., Hanley-Peterson, P., Zeiss, A., Ironson, G., & Thompson, L. W. (1992). Endogenous depression in the elderly: Prevalence and agreement among measures. *Journal of Consulting and Clinical Psychology, 60,* 300-303.

443. Garamoni, G. L., Reynolds, C. F., Thase, M. E., Frank, E., & Fasiczka, A. L. (1992). Shifts in affective balance during cognitive therapy of major depression. *Journal of Consulting and Clinical Psychology, 60,* 260-266.

444. Geiss, A. K., Hobbs, S. A., Hammersley-Maercklein, G., Kramer, J. C., & Henley, M. (1992). Psychosocial factors related to perceived compliance with cystic fibrosis treatment. *Journal of Clinical Psychology, 48,* 99-103.

445. Gelfand, D. M., Teti, D. M., & Fox, C. E. R. (1992). Sources of parenting stress for depressed and nondepressed mothers of infants. *Journal of Clinical Child Psychology, 21,* 262-272.

446. Gerlsma, C., Mosterman, I., Buwalda, S., & Emmelkamp, P. M. G. (1992). Mood and memories of parental rearing styles: A comparison of mood effects on questionnaire-cued and free recall of autobiographical memories. *Journal of Psychopathology and Behavioral Assessment, 14*, 343-361.

447. Goff, D. C., Olin, J. A., Jenike, M. A., Baer, L., & Buttolph, M. L. (1992). Disassociative symptoms in patients with obsessive-compulsive disorder. *Journal of Nervous and Mental Disease, 180*, 332-337.

448. Goldston, R. B., Gara, M. A., & Woolfolk, R. L. (1992). Emotion differentiation: A correlate of symptom severity in major depression. *Journal of Nervous and Mental Disease, 180*, 712-718.

449. Goodsmith, A. H., & Sher, K. J. (1992). Deficits in set-shifting ability in nonclinical compulsive checkers. *Journal of Psychopathology and Behavioral Assessment, 14*, 81-92.

450. Greenberg, R. P., Bornstein, R. F., Greenberg, M. D., & Fisher, S. (1992). A meta-analysis of antidepressant outcome under "blinder" conditions. *Journal of Consulting and Clinical Psychology, 60*, 664-669.

451. Hammarberg, M. (1992). Penn Inventory for Posttraumatic Stress Disorder: Psychometric properties. *Psychological Assessment, 4*, 67-76.

452. Herbert, J. D., Hope, D. A., & Bellack, A. S. (1992). Validity of the distinction between generalized social phobia and avoidant personality disorder. *Journal of Abnormal Psychology, 101*, 332-339.

453. Hewitt, P. L., Flett, G. L., & Mosher, S. W. (1992). The Perceived Stress Scale: Factor structure and relation to depression symptoms in a psychiatric sample. *Journal of Psychopathology and Behavioral Assessment, 14*, 247-257.

454. Hoffart, A., Friis, S., & Martinsen, E. W. (1992). Assessment of fear among agoraphobic patients: The agoraphobic cognition scale. *Journal of Psychopathology and Behavioral Assessment, 14*, 175-187.

455. Hokanson, J. E., & Butler, A. C. (1992). Cluster analysis of depressed college students' social behaviors. *Journal of Personality and Social Psychology, 62*, 273-280.

456. Howell, A., & Conway, M. (1992). Mood and the suppression of positive and negative self-referent thoughts. *Cognitive Therapy and Research, 16*, 535-555.

457. Hyer, L., Walker, C., Swanson, G., Sperr, S., Sperr, E., & Blount, J. (1992). Validation of PTSD measures for older combat veterans. *Journal of Clinical Psychology, 48*, 579-588.

458. Ingram, R. E., Johnson, B. R., Bernet, C. Z., & Dombeck, M. (1992). Vulnerability to distress: Cognitive and emotional reactivity in chronically self-focused individuals. *Cognitive Therapy and Research, 16*, 451-472.

459. Ivanoff, A., Smyth, N. J., Grochowski, S., Jang, S. J., & Klein, K. E. (1992). Problem solving and suicidality among prison inmates: Another look at state versus trait. *Journal of Consulting and Clinical Psychology, 60*, 970-973.

460. Johnson, K. A., Johnson, J. E., & Petzel, T. P. (1992). Social anxiety, depression, and distorted cognitions in college students. *Journal of Social and Clinical Psychology, 11*, 181-195.

461. Joiner, T. E., Alfanu, M. S., & Metalsky, G. I. (1992). When depression breeds contempt: Reassurance seeking, self-esteem, and rejection of depressed college students by their roommates. *Journal of Abnormal Psychology, 101*, 165-173.

462. Joseph, S., Andrews, B., Williams, R., & Yule, W. (1992). Crisis support and psychiatric symptomatology in adult survivors of the Jupiter cruise ship disaster. *British Journal of Clinical Psychology, 31*, 63-73.

463. Kaslow, N. J., Stark, K. D., Printz, B., Livingston, R., & Tsai, S. L. (1992). Cognitive Triad Inventory for Children: Development and relation to depression and anxiety. *Journal of Clinical Child Psychology, 21*, 339-347.

464. Kenardy, J., Fried, L., Kraemer, H. C., & Taylor, B. C. (1992). Psychological precursors of panick attacks. *British Journal of Psychiatry, 160*, 668-673.

465. Kinder, B. N., Curtis, G., & Kalichman, S. (1992). Affective differences among empirically derived subgroups of headache patients. *Journal of Personality Assessment, 58*, 516-524.

466. Kleinke, C. L. (1992). How chronic pain patients cope with pain: Relation to treatment outcome in a multidisciplinary pain clinic. *Cognitive Therapy and Research, 16*, 669-685.

467. Koenig, L. J., Clements, C. M., & Alloy, L. B. (1992). Depression and the illusion of control: The role of esteem maintenance and impression management. *Canadian Journal of Behavioral Science, 24*, 233-252.

468. Kutcher, S., Williamson, P., Marton, P., & Szalai, J. (1992). REM latency in endogenously depressed adolescents. *British Journal of Psychiatry, 161*, 399-402.

469. Kwon, S. M., & Oei, T. P. S. (1992). Different causal roles of dysfunctional attitudes and automatic thoughts in depression. *Cognitive Therapy and Research, 16*, 309-328.

470. Lakey, B., Moineau, S., & Drew, J. B. (1992). Perceived social support and individual differences in the interpretation and recall of supportive behaviors. *Journal of Social and Clinical Psychology, 11*, 336-348.

471. Leahy, J. M. (1992). Validity and reliability of the Beck Depression Inventory—short form in a group of adult bereaved females. *Journal of Clinical Psychology, 48*, 64-68.

472. Lester, D., Ferraro, T. M., & Murphy, J. A. (1992). Headache symptoms, depression, and suicidal preoccupation. *Perceptual and Motor Skills, 74*, 90.

473. Maes, M., Claes, M., Vanderwoude, M., Schotte, C., Martin, M., Blockx, P., & Cosyns, P. (1992). Adrenocorticotropin hormone, B-endorphin and cortisol responses to OCRF in melancholic patients. *Psychological Medicine, 22*, 317-329.

474. Malatesta-Magai, C., Jonas, R., Shepard, B., & Culver, L. C. (1992). Type A behavior pattern and emotion expression in younger and older adults. *Psychology and Aging, 7*, 551-561.

475. Margo, G. M., Dewan, M. J., Fisher, S., & Greenberg, R. P. (1992). Comparison of three depression rating scales. *Perceptual and Motor Skills, 75*, 144-146.

476. Marx, E. M., Williams, J. M. G., & Claridge, G. C. (1992). Depression and social problem solving. *Journal of Abnormal Psychology, 101*, 78-86.

477. Matthews, G. R., & Antes, J. R. (1992). Visual attention and depression: Cognitive biases in the eye fixations of the dysphoric and the nondepressed. *Cognitive Therapy and Research, 16*, 359-371.

478. McCranie, E. W., & Riley, W. T. (1992). Hopelessness and persistence of depression in an inpatient sample. *Cognitive Therapy and Research, 16*, 699-708.

479. Meakin, C. J. (1992). Screening for depression in the medically ill: The future of paper and pencil tests. *British Journal of Psychiatry, 160*, 212-216.

480. Metalsky, G. I., & Joiner, T. E., Jr. (1992). Vulnerability to depressive symptomatology: A prospective test of the diathesis-stress and causal mediation components of the hopelessness theory of depression. *Journal of Personality and Social Psychology, 63*, 667-675.

481. Miranda, J. (1992). Dysfunctional thinking is activated by stressful life events. *Cognitive Therapy and Research, 16*, 473-483.

482. Monroe, S. M., Kuper, D. J., & Frank, E. (1992). Life stress and treatment course of recurrent depression: 1. Response during index episode. *Journal of Consulting and Clinical Psychology, 60*, 718-724.

483. Nelson, L. D., Stern, S. L., & Cicchetti, D. V. (1992). The Dysfunctional Attitude Scale: How well can it measure depressive thinking? *Journal of Psychopathology and Behavioral Assessment, 14*, 217-223.

484. Nottingham, R. C., Rosen, D. H., & Parks, C. (1992). Psychological well-being among African American university students. *Journal of College Student Development, 33*, 356-362.

485. Nuss, W. S., & Zubenko, G. S. (1992). Correlates of persistant depressive symptoms in widows. *American Journal of Psychiatry, 149*, 346-351.

486. O'Brien, P. E., & Gaborit, M. (1992). Codependency: A disorder separate from chemical dependency. *Journal of Clinical Psychology, 48*, 129-136.

487. O'Hara, M. W., Hoffman, J. G., Philipps, L. H. C., & Wright, E. J. (1992). Adjustment in childbearing women: The Postpartum Adjustment Questionnaire. *Psychological Assessment, 4*, 160-169.

488. Peselow, E. D., Robins, C. J., Sanfilipo, M. P., Block, P., & Fieve, R. R. (1992). Sociotropy and autonomy: Relationship to antidepressant drug treatment response and endogenous-nonendogenous dichotomy. *Journal of Abnormal Psychology, 101*, 479-486.

489. Priester, M. J., & Clum, G. A. (1992). Attributional style as a diathesis in predicting depression, hopelessness, and suicide ideation in college students. *Journal of Psychopathology and Behavioral Assessment, 14*, 111-122.

490. Propst, L. R., Ostrom, R., Watkins, P., Dean, T., & Mashburn, D. (1992). Comparative efficacy of religious and nonreligious cognitive-behavioral therapy for the treatment of clinical depression in religious individuals. *Journal of Consulting and Clinical Psychology, 60*, 94-103.

491. Prud'homme, L., & Barron, P. (1992). The pattern of irrational beliefs associated with major depressive disorder. *Social Behavior and Personality, 20*, 199-212.

492. Resick, P. A., & Schnicke, M. K. (1992). Cognitive processing therapy for sexual assault victims. *Journal of Consulting and Clinical Psychology, 60*, 748-756.

493. Riskind, J. H., Kelley, K., Harman, W., Moore, R., & Gaines, H. S. (1992). The loomingness of danger: Does it discriminate focal phobia and general anxiety from depression. *Cognitive Therapy and Research, 16*, 603-622.

494. Robbins, P. R., & Tanck, R. H. (1992). Stress, coping techniques, and depressed affect: Explorations within a normal sample. *Psychological Reports, 70*, 147-152.

495. Roberts, J. E., & Monroe, S. M. (1992). Vulnerable self-esteem

and depressive symptoms: Prospective findings comparing three alternative conceptualizations. *Journal of Personality and Social Psychology, 62,* 804-812.

496. Rosenfarb, I. S., & Aron, J. (1992). The self-protective function of depressive affect and cognition. *Journal of Social and Clinical Psychology, 11,* 323-335.

497. Roy-Byrne, P. P., Vitaliano, P. P., Cowley, D. S., Luciano, G., Zheng, Y., & Dunner, D. L. (1992). Coping in panic and major depressive disorder: Relative effects of symptom severity and diagnostic comorbidity. *Journal of Nervous and Mental Disease, 180,* 179-183.

498. Ruderman, A. J., & Besbeas, M. (1992). Psychological characteristics of dieters and bulimics. *Journal of Abnormal Psychology, 101,* 383-390.

499. Sabin, N. H., & Sabin, N. (1992). Reliability and validity of the Turkish version of the Automatic Thoughts Questionnaire. *Journal of Clinical Psychology, 48,* 334-340.

500. Sanders, M. R., & Dadds, M. R. (1992). Children's and parents' cognitions about family interaction: An evaluation of video-mediated recall and thought listing procedures in the assessment of conduct-disordered children. *Journal of Clinical Child Psychology, 21,* 371-379.

501. Scott, J., Eccleston, D., & Boys, R. (1992). Can we predict the persistence of depression? *British Journal of Psychiatry, 161,* 633-637.

502. Segal, Z. V., Adams, K. E., & Shaw, B. F. (1992). Do discrepancies in interpersonal perception predict relapse? A comparison of remitted depressed patients and collaterals. *Cognitive Therapy and Research, 16,* 437-450.

503. Segal, Z. V., Shaw, B. F., Vella, D. D., & Katz, R. (1992). Cognitive and life stress predictors of relapse in remitted unipolar depressed patients: Test of the congruency hypothesis. *Journal of Abnormal Psychology, 101,* 26-36.

504. Showers, C. (1992). Compartmentalization of positive and negative self-knowledge: Keeping bad apples out of the bunch. *Journal of Personality and Social Psychology, 62,* 1063-1049.

505. Sigmon, S. T., & Nelson-Gray, R. O. (1992). Sensitivity to aversive events in depression: Antecedent, concomitant, or consequent? *Journal of Psychopathology and Behavioral Assessment, 14,* 225-246.

506. Silverstein, S. M., Raulin, M. L., Pristach, E. A., & Pomerantz, J. R. (1992). Perceptual organization and schizotypy. *Journal of Abnormal Psychology, 101,* 265-270.

507. Simons, A. D., & Thase, M. E. (1992). Biological markers, treatment outcome, and 1-year follow-up in endogenous depression: Electroencephalographic sleep studies and response to cognitive therapy. *Journal of Consulting and Clinical Psychology, 60,* 392-401.

508. Stein, P. N., & Motta, R. W. (1992). Effects of aerobic and nonaerobic exercise on depression and self-concept. *Perceptual and Motor Skills, 74,* 79-89.

509. Strauman, T. J. (1992). Self-guides, autobiographical memory, and anxiety and dysphoria: Toward a cognitive model of vulnerability to emotional distress. *Journal of Abnormal Psychology, 101,* 87-95.

510. Swann, W. B., Jr., Krull, D. S., Wenzlaff, R. M., & Pelham, B. W. (1992). Allure of negative feedback: Self-verification strivings among depressed persons. *Journal of Abnormal Psychology, 101,* 293-306.

511. Swann, W. B., Jr., Wenzlaff, R. M., & Tafarodi, R. W. (1992). Depression and the search for negative evaluations: More evidence of the role of self-verification strivings. *Journal of Abnormal Psychology, 101,* 314-317.

512. Szmukler, G. I., Andrewes, D., Kingston, K., Chen, L., Stargatt, R., & Stanky, R. (1992). Neuropsychological impairment in anorexia nervosa: Before and after refeeding. *Journal of Clinical and Experimental Neuropsychology, 14,* 347-352.

513. Taylor, C. J., & Scogin, F. (1992). Dysphoria and coping in women: The effect of threat and challenge appraisals. *Journal of Social and Clinical Psychology, 11,* 26-42.

514. Thase, M. E., Mallinger, A. G., McKnight, D., & Himmelhoch, J. M. (1992). Treatment of imipramine-resistant recurrent depression, IV: A double-blind crossover study of tranylcypromine for anergic bipolar depression. *American Journal of Psychiatry, 149,* 195-198.

515. Thurber, S., & Hollingsworth, D. K. (1992). Validity of the Achenbach and Edelbrock youth self-report with hospitalized adolescents. *Journal of Clinical Child Psychology, 21,* 249-254.

516. Turley, B., Bates, G. W., Edwards, J., & Jackson, H. J. (1992). MCMI—II personality disorders in recent-onset bipolar disorders. *Journal of Clinical Psychology, 48,* 320-329.

517. Ussery, L. W., & Prentice-Dunn, S. (1992). Personality predictors of bulimic behavior and attitudes in males. *Journal of Clinical Psychology, 48,* 722-729.

518. Watkins, P. C., Mathews, A., Williamson, D. A., & Fuller, R. D. (1992). Mood-congruent memory in depression: Emotional priming or elaboration? *Journal of Abnormal Psychology, 101,* 581-586.

519. Watson, D., & Clark, L. A. (1992). Affects separable and inseparable: On the hierarchical arrangement of the negative affects. *Journal of Personality and Social Psychology, 62,* 489-505.

520. Webster-Stratton, C. (1992). Individually administered videotape parent training: "Who benefits?" *Cognitive Therapy and Research, 16,* 31-53.

521. Wexler, B. E., & Cicchetti, D. V. (1992). The outpatient treatment of depression implications of outcome research for clinical practice. *Journal of Nervous and Mental Disease, 180,* 277-286.

522. Whisman, M. A., & Kwon, P. (1992). Parental representations, cognitive distortions, and mild depression. *Cognitive Therapy and Research, 16,* 557-568.

523. White, J., Davidson, G. C., Haaga, D. A. F., & White, K. (1992). Cognitive bias in the articulated thoughts of depressed and nondepressed psychiatric patients. *Journal of Nervous and Mental Disease, 180,* 77-81.

524. Williams, O. B., & Corrigan, P. W. (1992). The differential effects of parental alcoholism and mental illness on their adult children. *Journal of Clinical Psychology, 48,* 406-414.

525. Wilson, K. G., Sandler, L. S., Asmundson, G. J. G., Ediger, J. M., Larsen, D. K., & Walker, J. R. (1992). Panic attacks in nonclinical population: An empirical approach to case identification. *Journal of Abnormal Psychology, 101,* 460-468.

526. Workman, M., & Beer, J. (1992). Depression, suicide ideation, and aggression among high school students whose parents are divorced and use alcohol at home. *Psychological Reports, 70,* 503-511.

527. Yee, C. M., Deldin, P. J., & Miller, G. A. (1992). Early stimulus processing in dysthymia and anhedonia. *Journal of Abnormal Psychology, 101,* 230-233.

528. Zettle, R. D., Haflich, J. L., & Reynolds, R. A. (1992). Responsivity to cognitive therapy as a function of treatment format and client personality dimensions. *Journal of Clinical Psychology, 48,* 787-797.

529. Ahrens, A. H., & Haaga, D. A. F. (1993). The specificity of attributional style and expectations to positive and negative affectivity, depression, and anxiety. *Cognitive Therapy and Research, 17,* 83-98.

530. Ambrose, B., & Rholes, W. S. (1993). Automatic cognitions and the symptoms of depression and anxiety in children and adolescents: An examination of the content specificity hypothesis. *Cognitive Therapy and Research, 17,* 153-171.

531. Bagozzi, R. P. (1993). An examination of the psychometric properties of measures of negative affect in the PANAS-X scales. *Journal of Personality and Social Psychology, 65,* 836-851.

532. Barkham, M., Stiles, W. B., & Shapiro, D. A. (1993). The shape of change in psychotherapy: Longitudinal assessment of personal problems. *Journal of Consulting and Clinical Psychology, 61,* 667-677.

533. Ben-Porath, Y. S., McCully, E., & Almagor, M. (1993). Incremental validity of the MMPI-2 content scales in the assessment of personality and psychopathology by self-report. *Journal of Personality Assessment, 61,* 557-575.

534. Berenbaum, H., & Connelly, J. (1993). The effect of stress on hedonic capacity. *Journal of Abnormal Psychology, 102,* 474-481.

535. Bernbaum, M., Albert, S. G., Duckro, P. N., & Merkel, W. (1993). Personal and family stress in individuals with diabetes and vision loss. *Journal of Clinical Psychology, 49,* 670-677.

536. Borkovec, T. D., & Costello, E. (1993). Efficacy of applied relaxation and cognitive-behavioral therapy in the treatment of generalized anxiety disorder. *Journal of Consulting and Clinical Psychology, 61,* 611-619.

537. Bruch, M. A., Mattia, J. I., Heimberg, R. G., & Holt, C. S. (1993). Cognitive specificity in social anxiety and depression: Supporting evidence and qualifications due to affective confounding. *Cognitive Therapy and Research, 17,* 1-21.

538. Byrne, A., Walsh, M., Farrelly, M., & O'Driscoll, K. (1993). Depression following laryngectomy. *British Journal of Psychiatry, 163,* 173-176.

539. Cantanzaro, S. J. (1993). Mood regulation expectancies, anxiety sensitivity, and emotional distress. *Journal of Abnormal Psychology, 102,* 327-330.

540. Channon, S., Baker, J. E., & Robertson, M. M. (1993). Effects of structure and clustering on recall and recognition memory in clinical depression. *Journal of Abnormal Psychology, 102,* 323-326.

541. Conway, M., & Giannopoulos, C. (1993). Dysphoria and decision making: Limited information use for evaluations of multiattribute targets. *Journal of Personality and Social Psychology, 64,* 613-623.

542. Cooper, J. A., & Sagar, H. J. (1993). Encoding deficits in untreated Parkinson's Disease. *Cortex, 29,* 251-265.

543. Cornelius, J. R., Soloff, P. H., Perel, J. M., & Ulrich, R. F. (1993). Continuation pharmacotherapy of borderline personality disorder with haloperidol and phenelzine. *American Journal of Psychiatry, 150,* 1843-1848.

544. Cox, B. J., Swinson, R. P., Kuch, K., & Reichman, J. T. (1993). Self-report differentiation of anxiety and depression in an anxiety disorders sample. *Psychological Assessment, 5,* 484-486.

545. Creed, F., Guthrie, E., Black, D., & Tranmer, M. (1993). Psychiatric referrals within the general hospital: Comparison with re-

ferrals to general practitioners. *British Journal of Psychiatry, 162,* 204-211.

546. Digver, L., Barber, J. P., & Luborsky, L. (1993). Three concomitants: Personality disorders, psychiatric severity, and outcome of dynamic psychotherapy of major depression. *American Journal of Psychiatry, 150,* 1246-1248.

547. Dixon, W. A., Heppner, P. P., Burnett, J. W., & Lips, B. J. (1993). Hopelessness and stress: Evidence for an interactive model of depression. *Cognitive Therapy and Research, 17,* 39-52.

548. Dixon, W. A., Heppner, P. P., Burnett, J. W., Anderson, W. P., & Wood, P. K. (1993). Distinguishing among antecedents, concomitants, and consequences of problem-solving appraisal and depressive symptoms. *Journal of Counseling Psychology, 40,* 357-364.

549. Donenberg, G., & Baker, B. L. (1993). The impact of young children with externalizing behaviors on their families. *Journal of Abnormal Child Psychology, 21,* 179-198.

550. Drummond, L. M. (1993). The treatment of severe, chronic, resistant obsessive-compulsive disorder. *British Journal of Psychiatry, 163,* 223-229.

551. Ducharme, J., & Bachelor, A. (1993). Perception of social functioning in dysphoria. *Cognitive Therapy and Research, 17,* 53-70.

552. Edwards, J. A., & Weary, G. (1993). Depression and the impression-formation continuum: Piecemeal processing despite the availability of category information. *Journal of Personality and Social Psychology, 64,* 636-645.

553. Feldman, L. A. (1993). Distinguishing depression and anxiety in self-report: Evidence from confirmatory factor analysis on nonclinical and clinical samples. *Journal of Consulting and Clinical Psychology, 61,* 631-638.

554. Fell, M., Newman, S., Herns, M., Durrance, P., Manji, H., Connolly, S., McAllister, R., Weller, I., & Harrison, M. (1993). Mood and psychiatric disturbance in HIV and AIDS: Changes over time. *British Journal of Psychiatry, 162,* 604-610.

555. Fincham, F. D., & Bradbury, T. N. (1993). Marital satisfaction, depression, and attributions: A longitudinal analysis. *Journal of Personality and Social Psychology, 64,* 442-452.

556. Fischer, P. C., Smith, R. J., Leonard, E., Fuqua, D. R., Campbell, J. L., & Masters, M. A. (1993). Sex differences on affective dimensions: Continuing examination. *Journal of Counseling and Development, 71,* 440-443.

557. Flir, H., & Birbaumer, N. (1993). Comparisons of the efficacy of electromyographic biofeedback, cognitive-behavioral therapy, and conservative medical interventions in the treatment of chronic musculoskeletal pain. *Journal of Consulting and Clinical Psychology, 61,* 653-658.

558. Foa, E. B., Ilai, D., McCarthy, P. R., Shoyer, B., & Murdock, T. (1993). Information processing in obsessive-compulsive disorder. *Cognitive Therapy and Research, 17,* 173-189.

559. Furnham, A., & Li, Y. H. (1993). The psychological adjustment of the Chinese community in Britain. *British Journal of Psychiatry, 162,* 109-113.

560. Gara, M. A., Woolfolk, R. L., Cohen, B. D., Goldston, R. B., Allen, L. A., & Novalany, J. (1993). Perception of self and others in major depression. *Journal of Abnormal Psychology, 102,* 93-100.

561. Garber, J., Weiss, B., & Shanley, N. (1993). Cognitions, depressive symptoms, and development in adolescents. *Journal of Abnormal Psychology, 102,* 47-57.

562. Garner, D. M., Rockert, W., Davis, R., Garner, M. V., Olmsted, M. P., & Eagle, M. (1993). Comparison of cognitive-behavioral and supportive-expressive therapy for bulimia nervosa. *American Journal of Psychiatry, 150,* 37-46.

563. Gillis, J. S., & Bernieri, F. J. (1993). Effects of depressed mood on social perception. *Perceptual and Motor Skills, 76,* 674.

564. Glass, D. C., McKnight, J. D., & Valdimarsdottir, H. (1993). Depression, burnout, and perceptions of control in hospital nurses. *Journal of Consulting and Clinical Psychology, 61,* 147-155.

565. Gleaves, D. H., Williamson, D. A., & Barker, S. E. (1993). Confirmatory factor analysis of a multidimensional model of bulimia nervosa. *Journal of Abnormal Psychology, 102,* 173-176.

566. Guthrie, E., Creed, F., Dawson, D., & Tomenson, B. (1993). A randomized controlled trial of psychotherapy in patients with refractory irritable bowel syndrome. *British Journal of Psychiatry, 163,* 315-321.

567. Haaga, D. A. F., & Solomon, A. (1993). Impact of Kendall, Hollon, Beck, Hammen, and Ingram (1987) on treatment of the continuity issue in "depression" research. *Cognitive Therapy and Research, 17,* 313-324.

568. Haaga, D. A., McDermot, W., & Ahrens, A. H. (1993). Discriminant validity of the Inventory to Diagnose Depression. *Journal of Personality Assessment, 60,* 285-289.

569. Hart, R. P., & O'Shanick, G. J. (1993). Forgetting rates for verbal, pictorial, and figural stimuli. *Journal of Clinical and Experimental Neuropsychology, 15,* 245-265.

570. Harvey, J. M., Richards, J. C., Dziadosz, T., & Swindell, A.

(1993). Misinterpretation of ambiguous stimuli in panic disorder. *Cognitive Therapy and Research, 17,* 235-248.

571. Heimberg, R. G., Salzman, D. G., Holt, C. S., & Blendell, K. A. (1993). Cognitive-behavioral group treatment for social phobia: Effectiveness of five-year followup. *Cognitive Therapy and Research, 17,* 325-339.

572. Hewitt, P. L., & Flett, G. L. (1993). Dimensions of perfectionism, daily stress, and depression: A test of the specific vulnerability hypothesis. *Journal of Abnormal Psychology, 102,* 58-65.

573. Hewitt, P. L., & Norton, G. R. (1993). The Beck Anxiety Inventory: A psychometric analysis. *Psychological Assessment, 5,* 408-412.

574. Hillary, B. E., & Schare, M. L. (1993). Sexually and physically abused adolescents: An empirical search for PTSD. *Journal of Clinical Psychology, 49,* 161-165.

575. Hodges, K. (1993). Structured interviews for assessing children. *Journal of Child Psychology and Psychiatry, 34,* 49-68.

576. Holmbeck, G. N., & Wandrei, M. L. (1993). Individual and relational predictors of adjustment in first-year college students. *Journal of Counseling Psychology, 40,* 73-78.

577. Inch, R., & Crossley, M. (1993). Diagnostic utility of the MCMI-I and MCMI-II with psychiatric outpatients. *Journal of Clinical Psychology, 49,* 358-366.

578. Jacobson, N. S., Fruzzetti, A. E., Dobson, K., Whisman, M., & Hops, H. (1993). Couple therapy as a treatment for depression: II. The effects of relationship quality and therapy in depressive relapse. *Journal of Consulting and Clinical Psychology, 61,* 516-519.

579. Joffe, R. T., Bagby, R. M., & Levitt, A. (1993). Anxious and nonanxious depression. *American Journal of Psychiatry, 150,* 1257-1258.

580. Johnson, M. M. S. (1993). Thinking about strategies during, before, and after making a decision. *Psychology and Aging, 8,* 231-241.

581. Johnston, C., & Short, K. H. (1993). Depressive symptoms and perceptions of child behavior. *Journal of Social and Clinical Psychology, 12,* 164-181.

582. Joiner, T. E., Alfano, M. S., & Metalsky, G. I. (1993). Caught in the crossfire: Depression, self-consistency, self-enhancement, and the response of others. *Journal of Social and Clinical Psychology, 12,* 113-134.

583. Jones, E. E., & Pulos, S. M. (1993). Comparing the process in psychodynamic and cognitive-behavioral therapies. *Journal of Consulting and Clinical Psychology, 61,* 306-316.

584. Jones, E. E., Ghannam, J., Nigg, J. T., & Dyer, J. F. P. (1993). A paradigm for single-case research: The time series study of a long-term psychotherapy for depression. *Journal of Consulting and Clinical Psychology, 61,* 381-394.

585. Joseph, S., & Kuyken, W. (1993). Linking causal attributions and inhibitory processes. *Social Behavior and Personality, 21,* 1-6.

586. Kashden, J., Fremouw, W. J., Callahan, T. S., & Franzen, M. D. (1993). Impulsivity in suicidal and nonsuicidal adolescents. *Journal of Abnormal Child Psychology, 21,* 339-353.

587. Kopper, B. A. (1993). Role of gender, sex role identity, and Type A behavior in anger expression and mental health functioning. *Journal of Counseling Psychology, 40,* 232-237.

588. Lakey, B., & Edmundson, D. D. (1993). Role evaluations and stressful life events: Aggregate vs. domain-specific predictors. *Cognitive Therapy and Research, 17,* 249-267.

589. Lewinsohn, P. M., Hops, H., Roberts, R. E., Seeley, J. R., & Andrews, J. A. (1993). Adolescent psychopathology: I. Prevalence and incidence of depression and other DSM-III-R disorders in high school students. *Journal of Abnormal Psychology, 102,* 133-144.

590. Lewis, C. A. (1993). Oral pessimism and depressive symptoms. *The Journal of Psychology, 127,* 335-343.

591. Lubin, B., & Whitlock, R. V. (1993). Diagnostic efficiency of the Depression Adjective Check Lists. *Journal of Clinical Psychology, 49,* 695-701.

592. Lubin, B., Whitlock, R. V., Swearingin, S. E., & Seever, M. (1993). Self-assessment of state and trait depressive affect by college students: Reliability and validity of an adjective check list. *Journal of College Student Development, 34,* 249-255.

593. Lydiard, R. B., Brewerton, T. D., Fossey, M. D., Laraia, M. T., Stuart, G., Beinfeld, M. C., & Ballenger, J. C. (1993). CSF cholecystokinin octapeptide in patients with bulimia nervosa and in normal comparison subjects. *American Journal of Psychiatry, 150,* 1099-1101.

594. Lyubomirsky, S., & Nolen-Hoeksema, S. (1993). Self-perpetuating properties of dysphoric rumination. *Journal of Personality and Social Psychology, 65,* 339-349.

595. Marks, I. M., Swinson, R. P., Basoglu, M., Kuch, K., Noshirvani, H., O'Sullivan, G., Lelliott, P. T., Kirby, M., McNamee, G., Sengun, S., & Wickwire, K. (1993). Alprazolam and exposure alone and combined in panic disorder with agoraphobia. *British Journal of Psychiatry, 162,* 776-787.

596. Martin, E. M., Robertson, L. C., Sorensen, D. J., Jagust, W. J., Mallon, K. F., & Chirurgi, V. A. (1993). Speed of memory scan-

ning is not affected in early HIV-I infection. *Journal of Clinical and Experimental Neuropsychology, 15,* 311-320.

597. McCabe, S. B., & Gotlib, I. H. (1993). Attentional processing in clinically depressed subtests: A longitudinal investigation. *Cognitive Therapy and Research, 17,* 359-377.

598. McGrath, R. E., & Ratliff, K. G. (1993). Using self-report measures to corroborate theories of depression: The specificity problem. *Journal of Personality Assessment, 61,* 156-168.

599. McPherson, L., & Lakey, B. (1993). Content overlap inflates the relation between negative cognition and dysphoria. *Journal of Personality Assessment, 60,* 411-417.

600. Metalsky, G. I., Joiner, T. E., Jr., Hardin, T. S., & Abramson, L. Y. (1993). Depressive reactions to failure in a naturalistic setting: A test of the hopelessness and self-esteem theories of depression. *Journal of Abnormal Psychology, 102,* 101-109.

601. Mikail, S. F., DuBreuil, S., & D'Eon, J. L. (1993). A comparative analysis of measures used in the assessment of chronic pain patients. *Psychological Assessment, 5,* 117-120.

602. Mogg, K., Bradley, B. P., Williams, R., & Mathews, A. (1993). Subliminal processing of emotional information in anxiety and depression. *Journal of Abnormal Psychology, 102,* 304-311.

603. Moilanen, D. L. (1993). Depressive information processing among nonclinic, nonreferred college students. *Journal of Counseling Psychology, 40,* 340-347.

604. Moras, K., Telfer, K. A., & Barlow, D. H. (1993). Efficacy and specific effects data on New Testaments: A case study strategy with mixed anxiety-depression. *Journal of Consulting and Clinical Psychology, 61,* 412-420.

605. Moreno, J. K., Fuhriman, A., & Selby, M. J. (1993). Measurement of hostility, anger, and depression in depressed and nondepressed subjects. *Journal of Personality Assessment, 61,* 511-523.

606. Morin, C. M., Kowatch, R. A., Barry, T., & Walton, E. (1993). Cognitive-behavior therapy for late-life insomnia. *Journal of Consulting and Clinical Psychology, 61,* 137-146.

607. Morrow, L. A., Kamis, H., & Hodgson, M. J. (1993). Psychiatric symptomatology in persons with organic solvent exposure. *Journal of Consulting and Clinical Psychology, 61,* 171-174.

608. Muran, E. M., & Motta, R. W. (1993). Cognitive distortions and irrational beliefs in post-traumatic stress, anxiety, and depressive disorders. *Journal of Clinical Psychology, 49,* 166-176.

609. Nelson, L. D., Mitrushina, M., Satz, P., Sowa, M., & Cohen, S. (1993). Cross-validation of the Neuropsychology Behavior and Affect Profile in stroke patients. *Psychological Assessment, 5,* 374-376.

610. Novy, D. M., Nelson, D. V., Goodwin, J., & Rowzee, R. D. (1993). Psychometric comparability of the State-Trait Anxiety Inventory for different ethnic subpopulation. *Psychological Assessment, 5,* 343-349.

611. O'Brien, S., McKeon, P., & O'Regan, M. (1993). The efficacy and tolerability of combined antidepressant treatment in different depressive subgroups. *British Journal of Psychiatry, 162,* 363-368.

612. Orr, S. P., Pitman, R. K., Lasko, N. B., & Herz, L. R. (1993). Psychophysiological assessment of posttraumatic stress disorder imagery in World War II and Korean combat veterans. *Journal of Abnormal Psychology, 102,* 152-159.

613. Otto, M. W., Pollack, M. H., Sachs, G. S., Reiter, S. R., Meltzer-Brody, S., & Rosenbaum, J. F. (1993). Discontinuation of benzodiazepine treatment: Efficacy of cognitive-behavioral therapy for patients with panic disorder. *American Journal of Psychiatry, 150,* 1485-1490.

614. Pace, T. M., & Dixon, D. N. (1993). Changes in depressive self-schemata and depressive symptoms following cognitive therapy. *Journal of Counseling Psychology, 40,* 288-294.

615. Paradis, C. M., Friedman, S., Lazar, R. M., & Kula, R. W. (1993). Anxiety disorders in a neuromuscular clinic. *American Journal of Psychiatry, 150,* 1102-1104.

616. Parry, B. L., Mahan, A. M., Mostofi, N., Klauber, M. R., Lew, G. S., & Gillin, J. C. (1993). Light therapy of late luteal phase dysphoric disorder: An extended study. *American Journal of Psychiatry, 150,* 1417-1419.

617. Perry, S., Jacobsberg, L., Card, C. A. L., Ashman, T., Francés, A., & Fishman, B. (1993). Severity of psychiatric symptoms after HIV testing. *American Journal of Psychiatry, 150,* 775-779.

618. Persad, S. M., & Polivy, J. (1993). Differences between depressed and nondepressed individuals in the recognition of and response to facial emotional cues. *Journal of Abnormal Psychology, 102,* 358-368.

619. Priester, J. J., & Clum, G. A. (1993). Perceived problem-solving ability as a predictor of depression, hopelessness, and suicide ideation in a college population. *Journal of Counseling Psychology, 40,* 79-85.

620. Priester, M. J., & Clum, G. A. (1993). The problem-solving diathesis in depression, hopelessness, and suicide ideation: A longitudinal analysis. *Journal of Psychopathology and Behavioral Assessment, 15,* 239-254.

621. Revonsuo, A., Portin, R., Koivikko, L., Rinne, J. O., & Rinne, U. K. (1993). Slowing of information processing in Parkinson's disease. *Brain and Cognition, 21,* 87-110.

622. Robertson, M. M., Channon, S., Baker, J., & Flynn, D. (1993). The psychopathology of Gilles de la Tourette's Syndrome. *British Journal of Psychiatry, 162,* 114-117.

623. Russ, M. J., Shearin, E. N., Clarkin, J. F., Harrison, K., & Hull, J. W. (1993). Subtypes of self-injurious patients with borderline personality disorder. *American Journal of Psychiatry, 150,* 1869-1871.

624. Russo, N. F., Green, B. L., & Knight, G. (1993). The relationship of gender, self-esteem, and instrumentality to depressive symptomatology. *Journal of Social and Clinical Psychology, 12,* 218-236.

625. Safran, J. D., Segal, Z. V., Vallis, T. M., Shaw, B. F., & Wallner Samstag, L. (1993). Assessing patient suitability for short-term cognitive therapy with an interpersonal focus. *Cognitive Therapy and Research, 17,* 23-38.

626. Sahin, N., Ulusoy, M., & Sahin, N. (1993). Exploring the sociotropy-autonomy dimensions in a sample of Turkish psychiatric inpatients. *Journal of Clinical Psychology, 49,* 751-763.

627. Sayer, N. A., Sackeim, H. A., Moeller, J. R., Prudic, J., Devanand, D. P., Coleman, E. A., & Kiersky, J. E. (1993). The relations between observer-rating and self-report of depressive symptomatology. *Psychological Assessment, 5,* 350-360.

628. Segrin, C. (1993). Social skills deficits and psychosocial problems: Antecedent, concomitant, or consequence? *Journal of Social and Clinical Psychology, 12,* 336-353.

629. Shek, D. T. L. (1993). The Chinese version of the State-Trait Anxiety Inventory: Its relationship to different measures of psychological well-being. *Journal of Clinical Psychology, 49,* 349-358.

630. Spurrell, M. T., & Creed, F. H. (1993). Lymphocyte response in depressed patients and subjects anticipating bereavement. *British Journal of Psychiatry, 162,* 60-64.

631. Stacher, G., Abatzi-Wenzel, T., Wiesnagrotzki, S., Bergmann, H., Schneider, C., & Gaupman, G. (1993). Gastric emptying, body weight and symptoms in primary anorexia nervosa. *British Journal of Psychiatry, 162,* 398-402.

632. Steer, R. A., Beck, A. T., Brown, G. K., & Beck, J. S. (1993). Classification of suicidal and nonsuicidal outpatients: A cluster-analytic approach. *Journal of Clinical Psychology, 49,* 603-614.

633. Stiles, T. C., Schröder, P., & Johansen, T. (1993). The role of automatic thoughts and dysfunctional attitudes in the development and maintenance of experimentally induced dysphoric mood. *Cognitive Therapy and Research, 17,* 71-82.

634. Stiles, W. B., Barkham, M., & Shapiro, D. A. (1993). Lack of synchronized seasonal variation in the intensity of psychological problems. *Journal of Abnormal Psychology, 102,* 388-394.

635. Strauman, T. J., Lemieux, A. M., & Coe, C. L. (1993). Self-discrepancy and natural killer cell activity: Immunological consequences of negative self evaluation. *Journal of Personality and Social Psychology, 64,* 1042-1052.

636. Sutker, P. B., Allain, A. N., & Winstead, D. K. (1993). Psychopathology and psychiatric diagnoses of World War II Pacific theatre prisoner of war survivors and combat veterans. *American Journal of Psychiatry, 150,* 240-245.

637. Thackwray, D. E., Smith, M. C., Bodfish, J. W., & Meyers, A. W. (1993). A comparison of behavioral and cognitive-behavioral interventions for bulimia nervosa. *Journal of Consulting and Clinical Psychology, 61,* 639-645.

638. Torrens, M., San, L., & Cami, J. (1993). Buprenorphine versus heroin dependence: Comparison of toxicologic and psychopathologic characteristics. *American Journal of Psychiatry, 150,* 822-824.

639. Trull, T. J., & Goodwin, A. H. (1993). Relation between mood changes and the report of personality disorder symptoms. *Journal of Personality Assessment, 61,* 99-111.

640. Trull, T. J., Goodwin, A. H., Schopp, L. H., Hillenbrand, T. L., & Schuster, T. (1993). Psychometric properties of a cognitive measure of personality disorders. *Journal of Personality Assessment, 61,* 536-546.

641. Whiffen, V. E., & Gotlib, I. H. (1993). Comparison of postpartum and nonpostpartum depression: Clinical presentation, psychiatric history, and psychosocial functioning. *Journal of Consulting and Clinical Psychology, 61,* 485-494.

642. Whisman, M. A., & Kwon, P. (1993). Life stress and dysphoria: The role of self-esteem and hopelessness. *Journal of Personality and Social Psychology, 65,* 1054-1060.

643. Wilfley, D. E., Agras, W. S., Telch, C. F., Rossiter, E. M., Schneider, J. A., Cole, A. G., Sifford, L., & Raeburn, S. D. (1993). Group cognitive-behavioral therapy and group interpersonal psychotherapy for the nonpurging bulemic individual: A controlled comparison. *Journal of Consulting and Clinical Psychology, 61,* 296-305.

644. Wolkowitz, O. M., Reus, V. I., Manfredi, F., Ingbar, J., Brizendine, L., & Weingartner, H. (1993). Ketoconazole administration

in hypercortisolemic depression. *American Journal of Psychiatry, 150,* 810-812.

645. Wong, J. L., & Whitaker, D. J. (1993). Depressive mood states and their cognitive and personality correlates in college students: They improve over time. *Journal of Clinical Psychology, 49,* 615-621.

646. Ball, S. G., Otto, M. W., Pollack, M. H., & Rosenbaum, J. F. (1994). Predicting prospective episodes of depression in patients with panic disorders: A longitudinal study. *Journal of Consulting and Clinical Psychology, 62,* 359-365.

647. Brody, M. L., Walsh, B. T., & Devlin, M. J. (1994). Binge eating disorder: Reliability and validity of a new diagnostic category. *Journal of Consulting and Clinical Psychology, 62,* 381-386.

648. Butler, A. C., Hokanson, J. E., & Flynn, H. A. (1994). A comparison of self-esteem lability and low trait self-esteem as vulnerability factors for depression. *Journal of Personality and Social Psychology, 66,* 166-177.

649. Carnelley, K. B., Pietromonaco, P. R., & Jaffe, K. (1994). Depression, working models of others, and relationship functioning. *Journal of Personality and Social Psychology, 66,* 127-140.

650. Elliot, R., & Wexler, M. M. (1994). Measuring the impact of sessions in process-experiential therapy of depression: The Session Impact Scale. *Journal of Counseling Psychology, 41,* 166-174.

651. Emery, R. E., Matthews, S. G., & Kitzmann, K. M. (1994). Child custody mediation and litigation: Parents' satisfaction and functioning one year after settlement. *Journal of Consulting and Clinical Psychology, 62,* 124-129.

652. Hall, S. M., Muñoz, R. F., & Reus, V. I. (1994). Cognitive-behavioral intervention increases abstinence rates for depressive-history smokers. *Journal of Consulting and Clinical Psychology, 62,* 141-146.

653. Hatcher, S. (1994). Debt and deliberate self-poisoning. *British Journal of Psychiatry, 164,* 111-114.

654. Holmstrom, R. W., Karp, S. A., & Silber, D. E. (1994). Prediction of depression with the Apperception Personality Test. *Journal of Clinical Psychology, 50,* 234-237.

655. Jensen, M. P., Turner, J. A., & Romano, J. M. (1994). Correlates of improvement in multidisciplinary treatment of chronic pain. *Journal of Consulting and Clinical Psychology, 62,* 172-179.

656. Karney, B. R., Bradbury, T. N., Finchman, F. D., & Sullivan, K. T. (1994). The role of negative affectivity in the association between attributions and marital satisfaction. *Journal of Personality and Social Psychology, 66,* 413-424.

657. Lewinsohn, P. M., Rohde, P., & Seeley, J. R. (1994). Psychological risk factors for future adolescent suicide attempt. *Journal of Consulting and Clinical Psychology, 62,* 297-305.

658. Nofzinger, E. A., Schwartz, R. M., Reynolds, C. F., III, Thase, M. E., Jennings, J. R., Frank, E., Fasiczka, A. L., Garamoni, G. L., & Kupfer, D. J. (1994). Affect intensity and phasic REM sleep in depressed men before and after treatment with cognitive-behavioral therapy. *Journal of Consulting and Clinical Psychology, 62,* 83-91.

659. Scogin, F., & McElreath, L. (1994). Efficacy of psychosocial treatments for geriatric depression: A quantitative review. *Journal of Consulting and Clinical Psychology, 62,* 69-74.

660. Stanton, A. L., Danoff-Bung, S., Cameron, C. L., & Ellis, A. P. (1994). Coping through emotional approach: Problems of conceptualization and confounding. *Journal of Personality and Social Psychology, 66,* 350-362.

[269]

Beck Hopelessness Scale [Revised].

Purpose: Measures "the extent of negative attitudes about the future (pessimism) as perceived by adolescents and adults."

Population: Adolescents and adults.

Publication Dates: 1978–93.

Acronym: BHS.

Scores: Total score only.

Administration: Group or individual.

Price Data, 1994: $46 per complete kit including 25 record forms and manual ('93, 29 pages); $25.50 per 25 record forms; $22.50 per manual; $5.50 per scoring key.

Foreign Language Edition: Also available in Spanish.

Time: (5–10) minutes.

Authors: Aaron T. Beck and Robert A. Steer.

Publisher: The Psychological Corporation.

Cross References: For reviews by E. Thomas Dowd and Steven V. Owen of an earlier edition, see 11:32 (13 references).

TEST REFERENCES

1. Williams, J. M. G., & Broadbent, K. (1986). Autobiographical memory in suicide attempters. *Journal of Abnormal Psychology, 95,* 144-149.

2. Mazmanian, D., Mendonca, J. D., Holden, R. R., & Dufton, B. (1987). Psychopathology and response styles in the SCL-90 responses of acutely distressed persons. *Journal of Psychopathology and Behavioral Assessment, 9,* 135-148.

3. Beck, A. T., Brown, G., Epstein, N., & Steer, R. A. (1988). An inventory for measuring clinical anxiety: Psychometric properties. *Journal of Consulting and Clinical Psychology, 56,* 893-897.

4. Beck, A. T., Riskind, J. H., Brown, G., & Steer, R. A. (1988). Levels of hopelessness in DSM-III disorders: A partial test of content specificity in depression. *Cognitive Therapy and Research, 12,* 459-469.

5. Bonner, R. L., & Rich, A. (1988). Negative life stress, social problem-solving self-appraisal, and hopelessness: Implications for suicide research. *Cognitive Therapy and Research, 12,* 549-556.

6. Holden, R. R., & Fekken, G. C. (1988). Test-retest reliability of the Hopelessness Scale and its items in a university population. *Journal of Clinical Psychology, 44,* 40-46.

7. Norman, W. H., Miller, I. W., & Dow, M. G. (1988). Characteristics of depressed patients with elevated levels of dysfunctional cognitions. *Cognitive Therapy and Research, 12,* 39-52.

8. Belk, S. S., & Snell, W. E., Jr. (1989). Stereotypic beliefs about women as moderators of stress-distress relationships. *Journal of Clinical Psychology, 45,* 665-672.

9. Brown, G., & Beck, A. T. (1989). The role of imperatives in psychopathology: A reply to Ellis. *Cognitive Therapy and Research, 13,* 315-321.

10. Dohr, K. B., Rush, A. J., & Bernstein, I. H. (1989). Cognitive biases and depression. *Journal of Abnormal Psychology, 98,* 263-267.

11. Ketelaar, T., & O'hara, M. W. (1989). Meaning of the concept "suicide" and risk for attempted suicide. *Journal of Social and Clinical Psychology, 8,* 393-399.

12. Reno, R. M., & Halaris, A. E. (1989). Dimensions of depression: A comparative longitudinal study. *Cognitive Therapy and Research, 13,* 549-563.

13. Solomon, K. E., & Annis, H. M. (1989). Development of a scale to measure outcome expectancy in alcoholics. *Cognitive Therapy and Research, 13,* 409-421.

14. Beck, A. T., Brown, G., Berchick, R. J., Stewart, B. L., & Steer, R. A. (1990). Relationship between hopelessness and ultimate suicide: A replication with psychiatric outpatients. *American Journal of Psychiatry, 147,* 190-195.

15. Clark, D. A., Beck, A. T., & Stewart, B. (1990). Cognitive specificity and positive-negative affectivity: Complementary or contradictory views on anxiety and depression. *Journal of Abnormal Psychology, 99,* 148-155.

16. Needles, D. J., & Abramson, L. V. (1990). Positive life events, attributional styles, and hopefulness: Testing a model of recovery from depression. *Journal of Abnormal Psychology, 99,* 156-165.

17. Nurius, P. S., & Markus, H. (1990). Situational variability in the self-concept: Appraisals, expectancies, and asymmetries. *Journal of Social and Clinical Psychology, 9,* 316-333.

18. Rabkin, J. G., Williams, J. B. W., Neugebauer, R., Remien, R. H., & Goetz, R. (1990). Maintenance of hope in HIV-spectrum homosexual men. *American Journal of Psychiatry, 147,* 1322-1326.

19. Riley, W. T., & McCranie, E. W. (1990). The Depressive Experiences Questionnaire: Validity and psychological correlates in a clinical sample. *Journal of Personality Assessment, 54,* 523-533.

20. Beck, A. T., Steer, R. A., Sanderson, W. C., & Skeie, T. M. (1991). Panic disorder and suicidal ideation and behavior: Discrepant findings in psychiatric outpatients. *American Journal of Psychiatry, 148,* 1195-1199.

21. Page, R. M. (1991). Loneliness as a risk factor in adolescent hopelessness. *Journal of Research in Personality, 25,* 189-195.

22. Riley, W. T., Mabe, P. A., & Davis, H. C. (1991). Derivation and implications of MMPI cluster groups in clinically depressed inpatient females. *The Journal of Psychology, 125,* 723-733.

23. Catalan, J., Klimes, I., Day, A., Garrod, A., Bond, A., & Gallwey, J. (1992). The psychosocial impact of HIV infection in gay men. *British Journal of Psychiatry, 161,* 774-778.

24. Ivanoff, A., Smyth, N. J., Grochowski, S., Jang, S. J., & Klein, K. E. (1992). Problem solving and suicidality among prison inmates:

Another look at state versus trait. *Journal of Consulting and Clinical Psychology, 60,* 970-973.

25. Lennings, C. J. (1992). Suicide and time perspective: An examination of Beck and Yufit's suicide-risk indicators. *Journal of Clinical Psychology, 48,* 510-516.

26. Breslau, N. B., Kilbey, M. M., & Andreski, P. (1993). Vulnerability to psychopathology in nicotine-dependent smokers: An epidemiologic study of young adults. *American Journal of Psychiatry, 150,* 941-946.

27. Kashden, J., Fremouw, W. J., Callahan, T. S., & Franzen, M. D. (1993). Impulsivity in suicidal and nonsuicidal adolescents. *Journal of Abnormal Child Psychology, 21,* 339-353.

28. Nathawat, S. S., & Mathur, A. (1993). Marital adjustment and subjective well-being in Indian-educated housewives and working women. *The Journal of Psychology, 127,* 353-358.

29. Novy, D. M., Nelson, D. V., Goodwin, J., & Rowzee, R. D. (1993). Psychometric comparability of the State-Trait Anxiety Inventory for different ethnic subpopulation. *Psychological Assessment, 5,* 343-349.

30. Perkins, D. O., Davidson, E. J., Leserman, J., Liao, D., & Evans, D. L. (1993). Personality disorder in patients infected with HIV: A controlled study with implications for clinical care. *American Journal of Psychiatry, 150,* 309-315.

31. Priester, J. J., & Clum, G. A. (1993). Perceived problem-solving ability as a predictor of depression, hopelessness, and suicide ideation in a college population. *Journal of Counseling Psychology, 40,* 79-85.

32. Priester, M. J., & Clum, G. A. (1993). The problem-solving diathesis in depression, hopelessness, and suicide ideation: A longitudinal analysis. *Journal of Psychopathology and Behavioral Assessment, 15,* 239-254.

33. Rudd, M. D., Dahm, P. F., & Rajab, M. H. (1993). Diagnostic comorbidity in persons with suicidal ideation and behavior. *American Journal of Psychiatry, 150,* 928-934.

34. Steer, R. A., Beck, A. T., Brown, G. K., & Beck, J. S. (1993). Classification of suicidal and nonsuicidal outpatients: A cluster-analytic approach. *Journal of Clinical Psychology, 49,* 603-614.

35. Whisman, M. A., & Kwon, P. (1993). Life stress and dysphoria: The role of self-esteem and hopelessness. *Journal of Personality and Social Psychology, 65,* 1054-1060.

36. Dixon, W. A., Heppener, P. P., & Rudd, M. D. (1994). Problem-solving appraisal, hopelessness, and suicide ideation: Evidence for a mediational model. *Journal of Counseling Psychology, 41,* 91-98.

37. Hatcher, S. (1994). Debt and deliberate self-poisoning. *British Journal of Psychiatry, 164,* 111-114.

[270]

Beck Scale for Suicide Ideation.

Purpose: "To detect and measure the severity of suicidal ideation in adults and adolescents."

Population: Adults and adolescents.

Publication Dates: 1991–93.

Acronym: BSS.

Scores: Total score only; item score ranges.

Administration: Group or individual.

Price Data, 1994: $46 per complete kit including 25 record forms and manual ('93, 24 pages); $25.50 per 25 record forms; $22.50 per manual.

Foreign Language Edition: Spanish forms available.

Time: (5–10) minutes.

Comments: Computer scoring available.

Authors: Aaron T. Beck and Robert A. Steer.

Publisher: The Psychological Corporation.

[271]

Becker Work Adjustment Profile.

Purpose: Provides "information about the work habits, attitudes and skills of individuals in sheltered and competitive work."

Population: Mentally retarded, physically disabled, emotionally disturbed, learning disabled, and economically disadvantaged, ages 15 and over.

Publication Date: 1989.

Acronym: BWAP.

Scores, 5: Work Habits/Attitudes, Interpersonal Relations, Cognitive Skills, Work Performance Skills, Broad Work Adjustment.

Administration: Individual.

Price Data: Available from publisher.

Time: (10–15) minutes for Short Scale; (20–25) minutes for Full Scale.

Comments: Ratings by teachers, counselors, or other vocational professionals; 2 forms: Short Scale, Full Scale.

Authors: Ralph L. Becker.

Publisher: Elbern Publications.

Cross References: For reviews by Brian Bolton and Elliot L. Gory, see 11:33.

[272]

Bedside Evaluation and Screening Test of Aphasia.

Purpose: "To provide clinicians with a profile of a patient's language residuals in each modality on a continuum of severity ranging from no impairment to global impairment."

Population: Patients with language deficits.

Publication Date: 1987.

Acronym: BEST.

Scores, 8: Conversational Expression, Naming Objects, Describing Objects, Repeating Sentences, Pointing to Objects, Pointing to Parts of a Picture, Reading, Total.

Administration: Individual.

Levels, 4: A, B, C, D.

Price Data: Available from publisher.

Time: (15–25) minutes.

Authors: Joyce Fitch-West and Elaine S. Sands.

Publisher: PRO-ED, Inc.

Cross References: For a review by Malcolm R. McNeil, see 11:34.

[273]

Beery Picture Vocabulary Test and Beery Picture Vocabulary Screening Series.

Purpose: Designed to assess recall vocabulary.

Publication Dates: 1990–92.

Price Data, 1994: $99 per complete kit including manual ('92, 91 pages), stimulus card set, 25 Beery PVT record forms, and one each of 11 Beery PVS test booklets; $20 per manual.

Authors: Keith E. Beery and Colleen M. Taheri.

Publisher: Psychological Assessment Resources, Inc.

a) BEERY PICTURE VOCABULARY TEST.

Purpose: Designed to "measure expressive nominal vocabulary."

Population: Ages 2-6 to 39-11.

Acronym: PVT.

Administration: Individual.

Scores: Total score only.

Price Data: $18 per 25 Beery PVT record forms; $60 per Beery PVT stimulus card set.

Time: (10–15) minutes.

b) BEERY PICTURE VOCABULARY SCREENING SERIES.

Purpose: "Classroom screening and/or pretesting."

Population: Grades 2–12.
Acronym: PVS.
Administration: Individual or group.
Scores: Total score only.
Price Data: $22 per 35 Beery PVS test booklets grades 2–12.
Time: (10) minutes.

[274]

Behavioral Analysis Forms for Clinical Intervention.

Purpose: To gather client interview data in a structured manner.
Population: Behavior therapy clients.
Publication Dates: 1977–81.
Scores: Volume 1: 36 plans, questionnaires, scales, forms, schedules, and data forms in areas such as Client History, Motivation for Change, Reinforcement, and Social Performance; Volume 2: 59 questionnaires, scales, forms, schedules, and data forms in areas such as Reinforcers for Specific Populations, Survey of Phobic or Relationship Reactions, and Guidelines for Clients.
Administration: Group or individual.
Price Data: Available from publisher.
Time: Administration times vary.
Author: Joseph R. Cautela.
Publisher: Cambridge Center for Behavioral Studies.
Cross References: For reviews by Mary Lou Kelley and Francis E. Lentz, Jr., see 9:127.

[275]

Behavior Assessment System for Children.

Purpose: "To aid in the identification and differential diagnosis of emotional/behavior disorders in children and adolescents."
Population: Ages 4–18.
Publication Date: 1992.
Acronym: BASC.
Subtests: Available as separates.
Price Data, 1993: $60 per starter set including manual (350 pages), one sample each of the hand-scored forms for all levels of the Teacher Rating Scale, Parent Rating Scale, and Self-Report of Personality, the Structured Developmental History, and the Student Observation Scale; $225 per IBM BASC Enhanced Assist software (unlimited use).
Authors: Cecil R. Reynolds and Randy W. Kamphaus.
Publisher: American Guidance Service, Inc.
a) TEACHER RATING SCALES.
Price Data: $20 per 25 hand-scored forms; $12.50 per 25 computer-scored forms.
Time: (10–20) minutes.
1) *Teacher Rating Scales-Preschool.*
Population: Ages 4–5.
Scores, 14: Externalizing Problems (Aggression, Hyperactivity), Internalizing Problems (Anxiety, Depression, Somatization), Attention Problems, Atypicality, Withdrawal, Adaptive Skills (Adaptability, Social Skills), Behavioral Symptoms Index.
2) *Teacher Rating Scales-Child.*
Population: Ages 6–11.
Scores, 19: Externalizing Problems (Aggression, Hyperactivity, Conduct Problems), Internalizing Problems (Anxiety, Depression, Somatization), School Problems (Attention Problems, Learning Problems), Atypicality, Withdrawal, Adaptive Skills (Adaptability, Leadership, Social Skills, Study Skills), Behavioral Symptoms Index.
3) *Teacher Rating Scales-Adolescent.*
Population: Ages 12–18.
Scores, 18: Externalizing Problems (Aggression, Hyperactivity, Conduct Problems), Internalizing Problems (Anxiety, Depression, Somatization), School Problems (Attention Problems, Learning Problems), Atypicality, Withdrawal, Adaptive Skills (Leadership, Social Skills, Study Skills), Behavioral Symptoms Index.
b) PARENT RATING SCALES.
Price Data: $20 per 25 hand-scored forms; $12.50 per 25 computer-scored forms.
Time: (10–20) minutes.
1) *Parent Rating Scales—Preschool.*
Population: Ages 4–5.
Scores, 14: Same as *a-1* above.
2) *Parent Rating Scales-Child.*
Population: Ages 6–11.
Scores, 16: Externalizing Problems (Aggression, Hyperactivity, Conduct Problems), Internalizing Problems (Anxiety, Depression, Somatization), Attention Problems, Atypicality, Withdrawal, Adaptive Skills (Adaptability, Leadership, Social Skills), Behavioral Symptoms Index.
3) *Parent Rating Scales-Adolescent.*
Population: Ages 12–18.
Scores, 15: Externalizing Problems (Aggression, Hyperactivity, Conduct Problems), Internalizing Problems (Anxiety, Depression, Somatization), Attention Problems, Atypicality, Withdrawal, Adaptive Skills (Leadership, Social Skills), Behavioral Symptoms Index.
c) SELF-REPORT OF PERSONALITY.
Price Data: $20 per 25 hand-scored forms; $12.50 per 25 computer-scored forms.
Time: (20–30) minutes.
1) *Self-Report of Personality-Child.*
Population: Ages 8–11.
Scores, 16: Clinical Maladjustment (Anxiety, Atypicality, Locus of Control, Social Stress), School Maladjustment (Attitude to School, Attitude to Teachers), Other Problems (Depression, Sense of Inadequacy), Personal Adjustment (Relations with Parents, Interpersonal Relations, Self-Esteem, Self-Reliance), Emotional Symptoms Index.

2) *Self-Report of Personality-Adolescent*.
Population: Ages 12–18.
Scores, 18: Clinical Maladjustment (Anxiety, Atypicality, Locus of Control, Social Stress, Somatization), School Maladjustment (Attitude to School, Attitude to Teachers, Sensation Seeking), Other Problems (Depression, Sense of Inadequacy), Personal Adjustment (Relations with Parents, Interpersonal Relations, Self-Esteem, Self-Reliance), Emotional Symptoms Index.
d) STRUCTURED DEVELOPMENTAL HISTORY.
Price Data: $30 per 25 history forms.
e) STUDENT OBSERVATION SYSTEM.
Price Data: $25 per 25 observation forms.
Time: [20] minutes.

[276]

Behavior Change Inventory.
Purpose: Developed to assess the effects of a head injury on the behavior of an individual.
Population: Patients with head injury.
Publication Date: 1989.
Scores: No scores.
Administration: Individual.
Price Data, 1990: $5 per 25 test forms; $9 per manual (37 pages).
Time: (5–10) minutes.
Author: Lawrence C. Hartlage.
Publisher: Clinical Psychology Publishing Co., Inc.
Cross References: For reviews by Mark Albanese and Robert A. Reineke, see 11:36.

[277]

Behavior Dimensions Rating Scale.
Purpose: Developed to screen for emotional/behavior disorders and for monitoring behavior change.
Population: Grades K–11.
Publication Date: 1989.
Acronym: BDRS.
Scores, 5: Aggressive/Acting Out, Irresponsible/Inattentive, Socially Withdrawn, Fearful/Anxious, Total.
Administration: Individual.
Price Data, 1991: $65 per complete kit including 25 rating/profile forms and manual (77 pages); $24 per 25 rating/profile forms; $50 per manual.
Time: [5–10] minutes.
Comments: Ratings by teachers, parents, and psychologists.
Authors: Lyndal M. Bullock and Michael J. Wilson.
Publisher: The Riverside Publishing Company.
Cross References: For reviews by Martha W. Blackwell and Rosemery O. Nelson-Gray, see 11:37 (1 reference).

[278]

Behavior Disorders Identification Scale.
Purpose: "Developed to contribute to the early identification and service delivery for students with behavior disorders/emotional disturbance" through direct observations by educators and parents.
Population: Ages 4.5–21.

Publication Date: 1988.
Acronym: BDIS.
Scores, 5: Learning, Interpersonal Relations, Inappropriate Behavior Under Normal Circumstances, Unhappiness/Depression, Physical Symptoms/Fears.
Administration: Individual.
Price Data, 1993: $147 per complete kit including 50 pre-referral behavior checklist forms, 50 pre-referral intervention strategies documentations, School Version technical manual (34 pages), 50 School Version rating forms, Home Version technical manual (34 pages), 25 Home Version rating forms, and Teacher's Guide to Behavioral Interventions (291 pages); $25 per 50 pre-referral behavior checklist forms; $25 per 50 pre-referral intervention strategies documentations; $12 per School Version technical manual; $32 per 50 School Version rating forms; $12 per Home Version technical manual; $15 per 25 Home Version rating forms; $26 per Teacher's Guide to Behavioral Interventions; $12 per computerized School Version quick score (IBM or Apple II); $190 per computerized Teacher's Guide to Behavioral Interventions (IBM, Macintosh, or Apple II).
Time: [20] minutes for School Version; [15] minutes for Home Version.
Comments: "Includes both a school and home version to provide an ecological perception of student behavior problems"; "used to measure the student's improvement as a result of the intervention program developed with the intervention manual."
Authors: Fred Wright and Kathy Cummins Wunderlich (Teacher's Guide to Behavioral Interventions).
Publisher: Hawthorne Educational Services, Inc.

[279]

Behavior Evaluation Scale–2.
Purpose: To provide information about student behavior.
Population: Grades K–12.
Publication Dates: 1983–90.
Acronym: BES-2.
Scores, 6: Learning Problems, Interpersonal Difficulties, Inappropriate Behaviors, Unhappiness/Depression, Physical Symptoms/Fears, Total.
Administration: Individual.
Price Data, 1993: $111 per complete kit including 50 pre-referral behavior checklist forms, 25 data collections forms, technical manual ('90, 34 pages), 50 student record forms, and BES-2 intervention manual ('93, 244 pages); $20 per 50 pre-referral behavior checklist forms; $25 per 25 data collection forms; $12 per technical manual; $30 per student record form; $24 per intervention manual; $12 per computerized quick score (IBM or Apple II).
Time: (15–20) minutes.
Comments: "Criterion referenced"; ratings by teachers or other school personnel.
Authors: Stephen B. McCarney, Michele T. Jackson, and James E. Leigh.
Publisher: Hawthorne Educational Services, Inc.
Cross References: For reviews by J. Jeffrey Grill,

and Lester Mann and Leonard Kenowitz of the earlier edition, see 9:128.

[280]
Behavior Rating Instrument for Autistic and Other Atypical Children, 2nd Edition.
Purpose: Designed to evaluate the status of autistic, atypical, and other developmentally delayed children by assessing their present levels of functioning and measuring changes in their behavior.
Population: Autistic children.
Publication Dates: 1977–91.
Acronym: BRIAAC.
Scores, 9: Relationship to an Adult, Communication, Drive for Mastery, Vocalization and Expressive Speech, Sound and Speech Reception, Social Responsiveness, Psychobiological Development, Expressive Gesture and Sign Language, Receptive Gesture and Sign Language.
Administration: Individual.
Price Data, 1994: $124.50 per complete kit including manual ('91, 140 pages) and report form masters with permission to reproduce 50 copies; $49.50 per manual; $75 per reproducible masters and permission to make 50 copies.
Time: Untimed.
Authors: Bertram A. Ruttenberg, Enid G. Wolf-Schein, and Charles Wenar.
Publisher: Stoelting Co.
Cross References: For a review by Edward Workman of an earlier edition, see 9:129; see also T3:272 (1 reference).

TEST REFERENCES
1. Raab, M. M., Nordquist, V. W., Cunningham, J. L., & Bliem, C. D. (1986). Promoting peer regard of an autistic child in a mainstreamed preschool using pre-enrollment activities. *Child Study Journal, 16,* 265-284.

[281]
Behavior Rating Profile, Second Edition.
Purpose: "To evaluate students' behaviors at home, in school, and in interpersonal relationships."
Population: Ages 6-6 to 18-6.
Publication Dates: 1978–90.
Acronym: BRP-2.
Scores: 5 checklists: Student Rating Scales (Home, School, Peers), Teacher Rating Scale, Parent Rating Scale, plus Sociogram score.
Administration: Group.
Price Data, 1991: $114 per complete kit; $246 per 50 rating scale booklets (specify student, parent, or teacher form); $14 per 50 profile forms; $27 per manual ('90, 75 pages).
Foreign Language Edition: Spanish edition available.
Time: (15–30) minutes per scale.
Authors: Linda Brown and Donald D. Hammill.
Publisher: PRO-ED, Inc.
Cross References: For reviews by Thomas R. Kratochwill and Joseph C. Witt of an earlier edition, see 9:130 (1 reference); see also T3:273 (1 reference).

TEST REFERENCES
1. Soyster, H. D., & Ehly, S. W. (1987). Relation between parent-rated adaptive behavior and school ratings of students referred for evaluation as educable mentally retarded. *Psychological Reports, 60,* 271-277.

[282]
Behavior Rating Scale.
Purpose: Designed to sample teachers' perceptions about their pupils' behavior in the classroom.
Population: Grades K–8.
Publication Dates: 1970–75.
Scores: Total score only.
Administration: Group.
Forms, 3: Forms differ only in number of rating categories.
Manual: No manual.
Price Data: Available from publisher.
Time: Administration time not reported.
Comments: Ratings by teachers; research instrument; may be used with or separately from Characteristics Scale (419).
Authors: Patricia B. Elmore and Donald L. Beggs.
Publisher: Patricia B. Elmore.
Cross References: For a review by Jayne A. Parker, see 9:131 (2 references).

TEST REFERENCES
1. Abikoff, H., & Gittelman, R. (1985). The normalizing effects of methylphenidate on the classroom behavior of ADDH children. *Journal of Abnormal Child Psychology, 13,* 33-44.
2. Wolfe, D. A., Edwards, B., Manion, I., & Koverola, C. (1988). Early intervention for parents at risk of child abuse and neglect: A preliminary investigation. *Journal of Consulting and Clinical Psychology, 56,* 40-47.

[283]
Behavior Status Inventory.
Purpose: Developed to rate patient behaviors in a psychiatric hospital setting.
Population: Psychiatric inpatients.
Publication Dates: 1969–71.
Acronym: BSI.
Scores: Ratings in 7 areas (Personal Appearance, Manifest Behavior, Attitude, Verbal Behavior, Social Behavior, Work or School Behavior, Cognitive Behavior) and Total Patient Assets score.
Administration: Individual.
Manual: No manual.
Price Data, 1987: $15 per 25 rating forms (with instructions); $6.75 per 25 profile sheets; $5 per specimen set (with instructions).
Time: (5–10) minutes.
Author: William T. Martin.
Publisher: Psychologists and Educators, Inc.
Cross References: For a review by Alfred B. Heilbrun, Jr., see 8:505.

[284]
Behavioral Academic Self-Esteem.
Purpose: Constructed to measure "children's academic self-esteem by using direct observation of their classroom behaviors."
Population: Preschool–grade 8.
Publication Dates: 1979–82.

Acronym: BASE.
Scores, 6: Student Initiative, Social Attention, Success/Failure, Social Attraction, Self Confidence, Total.
Administration: Individual.
Price Data, 1990: $6 per 25 rating scales; $9 per manual ('82, 40 pages).
Time: (3–5) minutes.
Authors: Stanley Coopersmith and Ragnar Gilberts.
Publisher: Consulting Psychologists Press, Inc.
Cross References: For reviews by Herbert W. Marsh and Dale H. Schunk, see 9:132 (1 reference).

TEST REFERENCES

1. Chiu, L. H. (1988). Measures of self-esteem for school-age children. *Journal of Counseling and Development, 66,* 298-301.
2. Cates, J. A. (1991). Self-concept in hearing and prelingual, profoundly deaf students: A comparison of teachers' perceptions. *American Annals of the Deaf, 136,* 354-359.

[285]

Behavioral Assessment of Pain Questionnaire.
Purpose: "Used for gaining a better understanding of factors which may be maintaining the subacute and chronic noncancerous pain experience."
Population: Subacute and chronic pain patients.
Publication Dates: 1990-92.
Administration: Individual.
Price Data, 1992: $30 per sample kit including manual ('92, 44 pages); answer sheet and Mercury scoring with interpretive clinical profile, general information, scale descriptions, sample BAP clinical profile, and reprint of journal article; $10 per manual.
Foreign Language Edition: Spanish edition available.
Time: (60) minutes.
Authors: Michael J. Lewandowski and Blake H. Tearnan.
Publisher: Pendrake, Inc.
a) BEHAVIORAL ASSESSMENT OF PAIN.
Acronym: BAP.
Scores, 34: Demographic Information, Activity Interference Scale (Domestic/Household Activities, Heavy Activities, Social Activities, Personal Care Activities, Personal Hygiene Activities), Avoidance Scale, Spouse/Partner Influence Scale (Reinforcement of Pain, Discouragement/Criticism of Pain, Reinforcement of Wellness, Discouragement/Criticism of Wellness), Physician Influence Scale (Discouragement/Criticism of Pain, Reinforcement of Wellness, Discouragement/Criticism of Wellness, Reinforcement of Pain), Physician Qualities Scale, Pain Beliefs Scale (Catastrophizing, Fear of Reinjury, Expectation for Cure, Blaming Self, Entitlement, Future Despair, Social Disbelief, Lack of Medical Comprehensiveness), Perceived Consequences Scale (Social Interference, Physical Harm, Psychological Harm, Pain Exacerbation, Productivity Interference), Coping Scale, Negative Mood Scale (Depression, Anxiety, Muscular Discomfort, Change in Weight).
Price Data: $21.50 per on-site scored interpretive report; $23.50 per Mercury scored interpretive report; $5 per BAP booklet.
b) POST BEHAVIORAL ASSESSMENT OF PAIN.
Acronym: P-BAP.
Scores, 23: Avoidance, Spouse/Partner Influence Scale (Reinforcement of Pain, Discouragement/Criticism of Pain, Reinforcement of Wellness, Discouragement/Criticism of Wellness), Pain Beliefs Scale (Catastrophizing, Fear of Reinjury, Expectation for Cure, Blaming Self, Entitlement, Future Despair, Social Disbelief, Lack of Medical Comprehensiveness), Perceived Consequences Scale (Social Interference, Physical Harm, Psychological Harm, Pain Exacerbation, Productivity Interference), Coping Scale, Negative Mood Scale (Depression, Anxiety, Muscular Discomfort, Change in Weight).
Price Data: $21.50 per on-site scored P-BAP report; $23.50 per Mercury scored P-BAP report; $5 per P-BAP booklet.

[286]

Behavioral Characteristics Progression.
Purpose: Identifies specific skills exhibited during an individual's development.
Population: Physically and mentally handicapped children and adults.
Publication Date: 1973.
Acronym: BCP.
Comments: "Criterion-referenced"; manual title is BCP Observation Booklet; also available in binder format.
Scores: Item scores only.
Administration: Individual.
Price Data, 1990: $12.95 per manual ('73, 205 pages); $12.95 per binder; $125 per set of 5 method books (also available as separates).
Time: Administration time not reported.
Comments: "Criterion-referenced"; manual title is BCP Observation Booklet; also available in binder format.
Authors: The Office of the Santa Cruz Superintendent of Schools.
Publisher: VORT Corporation.
Cross References: For reviews by Rosemery O. Nelson-Gray and Harvey N. Switzky, see 11:38.

[287]

Behaviour Problems: A System of Management.
Purpose: "A systematic means of recording and analysing information on children's problem behaviour."
Population: Problem behavior children in a classroom situation.
Publication Date: 1984.
Scores: 8 areas of behavior: Classroom Conformity, Task Orientation, Emotional Control, Acceptance of Authority, Self-Worth, Peer Relationships, Self Responsibility/Problem Solving, Other.
Administration: Individual.
Price Data, 1987: £13.75 per complete set includ-

ing manual (15 pages), pad of 50 Daily Records, and pack of 10 Behaviour Checklist/Monthly Progress Charts; £4.50 per pad of 50 Daily Records; £3.50 per pack of 10 Behaviour Checklist/Monthly Progress Charts; £5.95 per manual.

Time: Administration time not reported.

Authors: Peter P. Galvin and Richard M. Singleton.

Publisher: NFER-Nelson Publishing Co., Ltd. [England].

Cross References: For reviews by Kathryn M. Benes and Terry Overton, see 11:39.

[288]

Bem Sex-Role Inventory.

Purpose: Designed to facilitate research on psychological androgyny.

Population: High school and college and adults.

Publication Dates: 1978–81.

Acronym: BSRI.

Scores, 3: Femininity, Masculinity, Femininity-minus-Masculinity Differences.

Administration: Group.

Price Data, 1991: $5 per 25 inventories; $2 per scoring key; $10 per manual ('81, 37 pages); $11 per specimen set.

Time: (10–15) minutes.

Comments: Test is titled Bem Inventory; self-administered; short and long form available (short form consists of first 30 items only).

Authors: Sandra Lipsitz Bem.

Publisher: Consulting Psychologists Press, Inc.

Cross References: For reviews by Richard Lippa and Frank D. Rayne, see 9:137 (121 references).

TEST REFERENCES

1. Holleran, P. R., Staszkiewicz, M., & Lopez, L. C. (1983). Self-reported social desirability in sex-stereotyped and androgynous individuals. *Counseling and Values, 28,* 31-41.
2. Lemkau, J. P. (1983). Women in male-dominated professions: Distinguishing personality and background characteristics. *Psychology of Women Quarterly, 8,* 144-165.
3. Lubinski, D. (1983). The Androgyny dimension: A comment on Stokes, Childs, & Fuehrer. *Journal of Counseling Psychology, 30,* 130-133.
4. Rosenwasser, S. M., Adams, V., & Tansil, K. (1983). Visual attention as a function of sex and apparel of stimulus object: Who looks at whom? *Social Behavior and Personality, 11*(2), 11-15.
5. Snow, L. J., & Parsons, J. L. (1983). Sex role orientation and female sexual functioning. *Psychology of Women Quarterly, 8,* 133-143.
6. Steward, M. S., Steward, D. S., & Dary, J. A. (1983). Women who choose a man's career: A study of women in ministry. *Psychology of Women Quarterly, 8,* 166-173.
7. Stokes, J. (1983). Androgyny as an interactive concept: A reply to Lubinski. *Journal of Counseling Psychology, 30,* 134-136.
8. Tinsley, H. E. A., Kass, R. A., Moreland, J. R., & Harren, V. A. (1983). A longitudinal study of female college students' occupational decision making. *The Vocational Guidance Quarterly, 32,* 89-102.
9. Wolff, S., & Watson, C. G. (1983). Personality adjustment differences in the Bem Masculinity and Femininity Scales. *Journal of Clinical Psychology, 39,* 543-550.
10. Al-Qataee, A. (1984). The effect of exposure to western cultures on the sex-role identity of Saudi Arabians. *Contemporary Educational Psychology, 9,* 303-312.
11. Alter, R. C. (1984). Abortion outcome as a function of sex-role identification. *Psychology of Women Quarterly, 8,* 211-233.
12. Bem, S. L. (1984). Androgyny and gender schema theory: A conceptual and empirical integration. *Nebraska Symposium on Motivation, 32,* 179-226.
13. Bennett, S. M. (1984). Family environment for sexual learning as a function of fathers' involvement in family work and discipline. *Adolescence, 19,* 609-627.
14. Borders, L. D., & Fong, M. L. (1984). Sex-role orientation research: Review and implications for counselor education. *Counselor Education and Supervision, 24,* 58-69.
15. Burda, P. C., Jr., Vaux, A., & Schill, T. (1984). Social support resources: Variation across sex and sex role. *Personality and Social Psychology Bulletin, 10,* 119-126.
16. Cunningham, J. D., & Antill, J. K. (1984). Changes in masculinity and femininity across the family life cycle: A reexamination. *Developmental Psychology, 20,* 1135-1141.
17. Diener, E., & Emmons, R. A. (1984). The independence of positive and negative affects. *Journal of Personality and Social Psychology, 47,* 1105-1117.
18. Edwards, S. W., Gordin, R. D., Jr., & Henschen, K. P. (1984). Sex-role orientations of female NCAA championship gymnasts. *Perceptual and Motor Skills, 58,* 625-626.
19. Erdwins, C. J., & Mellinger, J. C. (1984). Mid-life women: Relation of age and role to personality. *Journal of Personality and Social Psychology, 47,* 390-395.
20. Feather, N. T. (1984). Masculinity, femininity, psychological androgyny, and the structure of values. *Journal of Personality and Social Psychology, 47,* 604-620.
21. Garcia, L. T., Brennan, K., DeCarlo, M., McGlennon, R., & Tait, S. (1984). Sex differences in sexual arousal to different erotic stories. *The Journal of Sex Research, 20,* 391-402.
22. Gerson, M., & Lewis, K. L. (1984). Sex role identification and the clinical psychology student. *Professional Psychology: Research and Practice, 15,* 601-607.
23. Handley, H. M., & Morse, L. W. (1984). Two-year study relating adolescents' self-concept and gender role perceptions to achievement and attitudes toward science. *Journal of Research in Science Teaching, 21,* 599-607.
24. Hannson, R. O., Knopf, M. F., Downs, E. A., Monroe, P. R., Stegman, S. E., & Wadley, D. S. (1984). Femininity, masculinity, and adjustment to divorce among women. *Psychology of Women Quarterly, 8,* 248-260.
25. Hughes, B. C., & Warner, P. D. (1984). Sex-role perception and depression in college women. *College Student Journal, 18,* 406-415.
26. Keenan, J. M., & Brown, P. (1984). Children's reading rate and retention as a function of the number of propositions in text. *Child Development, 55,* 1556-1569.
27. Larsen, K. S., & LeRoux, J. (1984). A study of same sex touching attitudes: Scale development and personality predictors. *The Journal of Sex Research, 20,* 264-278.
28. Lemkau, J. P. (1984). Men in female-dominated professions: Distinguishing personality and background features. *Journal of Vocational Behavior, 24,* 110-122.
29. Millard, R. J., Habler, B. L., & List, J. (1984). Sex-role orientation and career indecision. *The Journal of Psychology, 117,* 217-220.
30. Nix, J., Lohr, J. M., & Mosesso, L. (1984). The relationship of sex-role characteristics to self-report and role-play measures of assertiveness in women. *Behavioral Assessment, 6,* 89-93.
31. Palkovitz, R. (1984). Parental attitudes and fathers' interactions with their 5-month-old infants. *Developmental Psychology, 20,* 1054-1060.
32. Paludi, M. A. (1984). Impact of androgynous and traditional sex-role orientations on evaluations of successful performance. *Psychology of Women Quarterly, 8,* 370-375.
33. Papiel, E. M., & DeLisi, R. (1984). An examination of spatial ability in relation to factors from the BEM Sex-Role Inventory. *Perceptual and Motor Skills, 59,* 131-136.
34. Phye, G. D., & Sola, J. L. (1984). Stability of expressive and instrumental traits in an adolescent female population. *The Journal of Genetic Psychology, 145,* 179-184.
35. Pratt, M. W., Golding, G., & Hunter, W. J. (1984). Does morality have a gender? Sex, sex role, and moral judgment relationships across the adult lifespan. *Merrill-Palmer Quarterly, 30,* 321-340.
36. Ramanaiah, N. V., & Hoffman, S. C. (1984). Effects of instructions and rating scales on item selection for the BSRI Scales. *Journal of Personality Assessment, 48,* 145-152.
37. Repetti, R. L. (1984). Determinants of children's sex stereotyping: Parental sex-role traits and television viewing. *Personality and Social Psychology Bulletin, 10,* 457-468.
38. Selva, P. C. D., & Dusek, J. B. (1984). Sex role orientation and resolution of Eriksonian crises during the late adolescent years. *Journal of Personality and Social Psychology, 47,* 204-212.
39. Spence, J. T. (1984). Gender identity and its implications for the concepts of masculinity and femininity. *Nebraska Symposium on Motivation, 32,* 59-95.
40. Stevens, M. J., Pfost, K. S., & Ackerman, M. D. (1984). The relationship between sex-role orientation and the Type A behavior pattern: A test of the main effect hypothesis. *Journal of Clinical Psychology, 40,* 1338-1341.
41. Swenson, E. V., & Ragucci, R. (1984). Effects of sex-role stereo-

types and androgynous alternatives on mental health judgments of psychotherapists. *Psychological Reports, 54*, 475-481.

42. Vance, B. K., & Green, V. (1984). Lesbian identities: An examination of sexual behavior and sex role attribution as related to age of initial same-sex sexual encounter. *Psychology of Women Quarterly, 8*, 293-307.

43. Warfel, K. A. (1984). Gender schemas and perceptions of speech style. *Communication Monographs, 51*, 253-267.

44. Weinraub, M., Clemens, L. P., Sockloff, A., Ethridge, T., Gracely, E., & Myers, B. (1984). The development of sex role stereotypes in the third year: Relationships to gender labeling, gender identity, sex-typed toy preference, and family characteristics. *Child Development, 55*, 1493-1503.

45. Winstead, B. A., Derlega, V. J., & Wong, P. T. P. (1984). Effects of sex-role orientation of behavioral self-disclosure. *Journal of Research in Personality, 18*, 541-553.

46. Yarnold, P. R. (1984). Note on the multidisciplinary scope of psychological androgyny theory. *Psychological Reports, 54*, 936-938.

47. Auten, P. D., Hull, D. B., & Hull, J. H. (1985). Sex role orientation and Type A behavior pattern. *Psychology of Women Quarterly, 9*, 288-290.

48. Baucom, D. H., Besch, P. K., & Callahan, S. (1985). Relation between testosterone concentration, sex role identity, and personality among females. *Journal of Personality and Social Psychology, 48*, 1218-1226.

49. Bernard, J. L., Bernard, S. L., & Bernard, M. L. (1985). Courtship violence and sex-typing. *Family Relations, 34*, 573-576.

50. Callan, V. J. (1985). Comparisons of mothers of one child by choice with mothers wanting a second birth. *Journal of Marriage and the Family, 47*, 155-164.

51. Capurso, R. J., & Blocher, D. H. (1985). The effects of sex-role consistent and inconsistent information on the social perceptions of complex, noncomplex, androgynous, and sex-typed women. *Journal of Vocational Behavior, 26*, 79-91.

52. Carlson, H. M., & Steuer, J. (1985). Age, sex-role categorization, and psychological health in American homosexual and heterosexual men and women. *The Journal of Social Psychology, 125*, 203-211.

53. Caron, S. L., Carter, D. B., & Brightman, L. A. (1985). Sex-role orientation and attitudes towards women: Differences among college athletes and nonathletes. *Perceptual and Motor Skills, 61*, 803-806.

54. Carter, D. B. (1985). Relationships between cognitive flexibility and sex-role orientation in young adults. *Psychological Reports, 57*, 763-766.

55. Coleman, M., & Ganong, L. H. (1985). Love and sex role stereotypes: Do macho men and feminine women make better lovers? *Journal of Personality and Social Psychology, 49*, 170-176.

56. Colley, A., Roberts, N., & Chipps, A. (1985). Sex role identity, personality and participation in team and individual sports by males and females. *International Journal of Sport Psychology, 16*, 103-112.

57. Condry, J. C., & Ross, D. F. (1985). Sex and aggression: The influence of gender label on the perception of aggression in children. *Child Development, 56*, 225-233.

58. Deaux, K., Kite, M. E., & Lewis, L. L. (1985). Clustering and gender schemata: An uncertain link. *Personality and Social Psychology Bulletin, 11*, 387-397.

59. Dillon, K. M., Wolf, E., & Katz, H. (1985). Sex roles, gender, and fear. *The Journal of Psychology, 119*, 355-359.

60. Fassinger, R. E. (1985). A causal model of college women's career choice. *Journal of Vocational Behavior, 27*, 123-153.

61. Faulkender, P. J. (1985). Relationship between Bem Sex-Role Inventory groups and attitudes of sexism. *Psychological Reports, 57*, 227-235.

62. Fong, M. L., & Borders, L. D. (1985). Effect of sex role orientation and gender on counselor skills training. *Journal of Counseling Psychology, 32*, 104-110.

63. Frable, D. E. S., & Bem, S. L. (1985). If you are gender schematic, all members of the opposite sex look alike. *Journal of Personality and Social Psychology, 49*, 459-468.

64. Ganong, L. H., & Coleman, M. (1985). Sex, sex roles, and emotional expressiveness. *The Journal of Genetic Psychology, 146*, 405-411.

65. Hackett, G. (1985). Role of mathematics self-efficacy in the choice of math-related majors of college women and men: A path analysis. *Journal of Counseling Psychology, 32*, 47-56.

66. Heerboth, J. R., & Ramanaiah, N. V. (1985). Evaluation of the BSRI Masculine and Feminine items using desirability and stereotype ratings. *Journal of Personality Assessment, 49*, 264-270.

67. Hiller, D. V., & Philliber, W. W. (1985). Internal consistency and correlates of the Bem Sex Role Inventory. *Social Psychology Quarterly, 48*, 373-380.

68. Hoffman, S. R., & Levant, R. F. (1985). A comparison of childfree and child-anticipated married couples. *Family Relations, 34*, 197-203.

69. Juni, S., Rahamim, E. L., & Brannon, R. (1985). Sex role development as a function of parent models and oedipal fixation. *The Journal of Genetic Psychology, 146*, 89-99.

70. Kabacoff, R. I., Marwit, S. J., & Orlofsky, J. L. (1985). Correlates of sex role stereotyping among mental health professionals. *Professional Psychology: Research and Practice, 16*, 98-105.

71. Koopman-Boyden, P. G., & Abbott, M. (1985). Expectations for household task allocation and actual task allocation: A New Zealand study. *Journal of Marriage and the Family, 47*, 211-219.

72. Leak, G. K., Millard, R. J., Perry, N. W., & Williams, D. E. (1985). An investigation of the nomological network of social interest. *Journal of Research in Personality, 19*, 197-207.

73. Melancon, J. G., & Thompson, B. (1985). Selected correlates of computer arcade game play. *Perceptual and Motor Skills, 61*, 1123-1129.

74. Mellinger, J. C., & Erdwins, C. J. (1985). Personality correlates of age and life roles in adult women. *Psychology of Women Quarterly, 9*, 503-514.

75. Mindingall, M. P. (1985). Characteristics of female clients that influence preference for the socially intimate and nonintimate female psychotherapists. *Journal of Clinical Psychology, 41*, 188-197.

76. Mulig, J. C., Haggerty, M. E., Carballosa, A. B., Cinnick, W. J., & Madden, J. M. (1985). Relationships among fear of success, fear of failure, and androgyny. *Psychology of Women Quarterly, 9*, 284-287.

77. Otto, M. W., & Dougher, M. J. (1985). Sex differences and personality factors in responsivity to pain. *Perceptual and Motor Skills, 61*, 383-390.

78. Pedersen, D. M., & Bond, B. L. (1985). Shifts in sex role after a decade of cultural change. *Psychological Reports, 57*, 43-48.

79. Reed-Sanders, D., Dodder, R. A., & Webster, L. (1985). The Bem Sex-Role Inventory across three cultures. *The Journal of Social Psychology, 125*, 523-525.

80. Rosenwasser, S. M., Gonzales, M. H., & Adams, V. (1985). Perceptions of a houseperson: The effects of sex, economic productivity, and subject background variables. *Psychology of Women Quarterly, 9*, 258-276.

81. Schiedel, D. G., & Marcia, J. E. (1985). Ego identity, intimacy, sex role orientation, and gender. *Developmental Psychology, 21*, 149-160.

82. Selkow, P. (1985). Male/female differences in mathematical ability: A function of biological sex or perceived gender role? *Psychological Reports, 57*, 551-557.

83. Siegel, R. G., Galassi, J. P., & Ware, W. B. (1985). A comparison of two models for predicting mathematics performance: Social learning versus math aptitude-anxiety. *Journal of Counseling Psychology, 32*, 531-538.

84. Street, S. (1985). Sex roles, feedback and self-concept. *The High School Journal, 69*, 70-80.

85. Tice, D. M., & Baumeister, R. F. (1985). Masculinity inhibits helping in emergencies: Personality does predict the bystander effect. *Journal of Personality and Social Psychology, 49*, 420-428.

86. Voelz, C. J. (1985). Effects of gender role disparity on couples' decision-making processes. *Journal of Personality and Social Psychology, 49*, 1532-1540.

87. Welkowitz, J., Lish, J. D., & Bond, R. N. (1985). The Depressive Experiences Questionnaire: Revision and validation. *Journal of Personality Assessment, 49*, 89-94.

88. Windle, M., & Sinnott, J. D. (1985). A psychometric study of the Bem Sex Role Inventory with an older adult sample. *Journal of Gerontology, 40*, 336-343.

89. Yanico, B. J. (1985). BSRI scores: Stability over four years for college women. *Psychology of Women Quarterly, 9*, 277-283.

90. Alumbaugh, R. V. (1986). Perception of an adversary as a function of masculinity, sex, and aggression/empathy. *Perceptual and Motor Skills, 62*, 427-436.

91. Anderson, K. L. (1986). Androgyny, flexibility, and individualism. *Journal of Personality Assessment, 50*, 265-278.

92. Baldwin, A. C., Critelli, J. W., Stevens, L. C., & Russell, S. (1986). Androgyny and sex role measurement: A personal construct approach. *Journal of Personality and Social Psychology, 51*, 1081-1088.

93. Burke, K. L. (1986). Comparison of psychological androgyny within a sample of female college athletes who participate in sports traditionally inappropriate for competition by females. *Perceptual and Motor Skills, 63*, 779-782.

94. Clark, M. L. (1986). Predictors of scientific majors for black and white college students. *Adolescence, 21*, 205-213.

95. Cooper, K., Chassin, L., Braver, S., Zeiss, A., & Akhtar Khavari, K. (1986). Correlates of mood and marital satisfaction among dual-worker and single-worker couples. *Social Psychology Quarterly, 49*, 322-329.

96. Costos, D. (1986). Sex role identity in young adults: Its parental antecedents and relation to ego development. *Journal of Personality and Social Psychology, 50*, 602-611.

97. Forbach, G. B., Evans, R. G., & Bodine, S. M. (1986). Gender-based schematic processing of self-descriptive information. *Journal of Research in Personality, 20,* 372-384.

98. Frank, D. I., Downard, E., & Lang, A. R. (1986). Androgyny, sexual satisfaction, and women. *Journal of Psychosocial Nursing and Mental Health Services, 24*(7), 10-15.

99. Green, R., Mandel, J. B., Hotvedt, M. E., Gray, J., & Smith, L. (1986). Lesbian mothers and their children: A comparison with solo parent heterosexual mothers and their children. *Archives of Sexual Behavior, 15,* 167-184.

100. Holloway, S. D. (1986). The relationship of mother's beliefs to children's mathematics achievement: Some effects of sex differences. *Merrill-Palmer Quarterly, 32,* 231-250.

101. Jacobson, N. S., Follette, W. C., & Pagel, M. (1986). Predicting who will benefit from behavioral marital therapy. *Journal of Consulting and Clinical Psychology, 54,* 518-522.

102. Katz, P. A., & Boswell, S. (1986). Flexibility and traditionality in children's gender roles. *Genetic, Social, and General Psychology Monographs, 112,* 105-147.

103. Kurdek, L. A., & Schmitt, J. P. (1986). Relationship quality of partners in heterosexual married, heterosexual cohabiting, and gay and lesbian relationships. *Journal of Personality and Social Psychology, 51,* 711-720.

104. Larsen, R. J., & Seidman, E. (1986). Gender schema theory and sex role inventories: Some conceptual and psychometric considerations. *Journal of Personality and Social Psychology, 50,* 205-211.

105. Liberman, D., & Gaa, J. P. (1986). The effect of response style on the validity of the BSRI. *Journal of Clinical Psychology, 42,* 905-908.

106. Long, V. O. (1986). Relationship of masculinity to self-esteem and self-acceptance in female professionals, college students, clients, and victims of domestic violence. *Journal of Consulting and Clinical Psychology, 54,* 323-327.

107. Maznah, I., & Choo, P. F. (1986). The factor structure of the Bem Sex-Role Inventory (BSRI). *International Journal of Psychology, 21,* 31-41.

108. McKeever, W. F. (1986). The influences of handedness, sex, familial sinistrality and androgyny on language laterality, verbal ability, and spatial ability. *Cortex, 22,* 521-537.

109. McNamara, K., & Hackett, G. (1986). Gender, sex-type and cognitive distortion: Self-perceptions of social competence among mild depressives. *Social Behavior and Personality, 14,* 113-121.

110. Plake, B. S., Kaplan, B. J., & Steinbrunn, J. (1986). Sex role orientation, level of cognitive development and mathematics performance in late adolescence. *Adolescence, 21,* 607-613.

111. Richardson, A. G. (1986). Sex-role orientation of Caribbean adolescents. *Perceptual and Motor Skills, 63,* 1113-1114.

112. Straub, C. A., & Rodgers, R. F. (1986). An exploration of Chickering's theory and women's development. *Journal of College Student Personnel, 27,* 216-224.

113. Teri, L., & Lewinsohn, P. M. (1986). Individual and group treatment of unipolar depression: Comparison of treatment outcome and identification of predictors of successful treatment outcome. *Behavior Therapy, 17,* 215-228.

114. Ward, C., & Sethi, R. R. (1986). Cross-cultural validation of the Bem Sex Role Inventory. Malaysian and South Indian research. *Journal of Cross-Cultural Psychology, 17,* 300-314.

115. Wehr, J. V., & Gilroy, F. D. (1986). Sex-role orientation as a predictor of preferential cognitive response style. *Journal of Clinical Psychology, 42,* 82-86.

116. White, K. M., Speisman, J. C., Jackson, D., Bartis, S., & Costos, D. (1986). Intimacy maturity and its correlates in young married couples. *Journal of Personality and Social Psychology, 50,* 152-162.

117. Windle, M. (1986). Sex role orientation, cognitive flexibility, and life satisfaction among older adults. *Psychology of Women Quarterly, 10,* 263-273.

118. Wood, D. R. (1986). Self-perceived masculinity between bearded and nonbearded males. *Perceptual and Motor Skills, 62,* 769-770.

119. Ahembaugh, R. V. (1987). Contrast of the Gender-Identity Scale with Bem's Sex-Role measures and the MF Scale of the MMPI. *Perceptual and Motor Skills, 64*(1), 136-138.

120. Bernstein, B. L., Hofmann, B., & Wade, P. (1987). Preferences for counselor gender: Students' sex role, other characteristics, and type of problem. *Journal of Counseling Psychology, 34,* 20-26.

121. Culkin, J., Tricarico, D., & Cohen, F. (1987). Sex-role orientation of nursing students at a community college. *Psychological Reports, 60,* 948-950.

122. Davidson, B., & Sollie, D. L. (1987). Sex role orientation and marital adjustment. *Social Behavior and Personality, 15,* 59-69.

123. Faulkender, P. J. (1987). Validity of using Bem Sex-Role Inventory norms on other samples: Analysis of a Southern sample. *Psychological Reports, 60,* 399-406.

124. Frable, D. E. S. (1987). Sex-typed execution and perception of

expressive movement. *Journal of Personality and Social Psychology, 53,* 391-396.

125. Hirschowitz, R. (1987). Behavioral and personality correlates of a need for power in a group of English-speaking South African women. *The Journal of Psychology, 121,* 575-590.

126. Lundy, A., & Rosenberg, J. A. (1987). Androgyny, masculinity, and self-esteem. *Social Behavior and Personality, 15,* 91-95.

127. Martin, C. L. (1987). A ratio measure of sex stereotyping. *Journal of Personality and Social Psychology, 52,* 489-499.

128. McGraw, K. M., & Bloomfield, J. (1987). Social influence on group moral decisions: The interactive effects of moral reasoning and sex role orientation. *Journal of Personality and Social Psychology, 53,* 1080-1087.

129. Moore, J. S., Graziano, W. G., & Millar, M. G. (1987). Physical attractiveness, sex role orientation, and the evaluation of adults and children. *Personality and Social Psychology Bulletin, 13,* 95-102.

130. Paulhus, D. L. (1987). Effects of group selection on correlations and factor patterns in sex role research. *Journal of Personality and Social Psychology, 53,* 314-317.

131. Rotberg, H. L., Brown, D., & Ware, W. B. (1987). Career self-efficacy expectations and perceived range of career options in community college students. *Journal of Counseling Psychology, 34,* 164-170.

132. Yarnold, P. R., & Lyons, J. S. (1987). Norms for college undergraduates for the Bem Sex-Role Inventory and the Wiggins Interpersonal Behavior Circle. *Journal of Personality Assessment, 51,* 595-599.

133. Barak, A., Golan, E., & Fisher, W. A. (1988). Effects of counselor gender and gender-role orientation on client career choice traditionality. *Journal of Counseling Psychology, 35,* 287-293.

134. Beckmann, J. C., Carbonell, J. L., & Gustafson, D. J. (1988). Are there sex differences in problem solving? An investigation of problem context and sex role type. *The Journal of Psychology, 122,* 21-32.

135. Bradbury, T. N., & Fincham, F. D. (1988). Individual difference variables in close relationships: A contextual model of marriage as an integrative framework. *Journal of Personality and Social Psychology, 54,* 713-721.

136. Brems, C., & Schlottmann, R. S. (1988). Gender-based definitions of mental health. *The Journal of Psychology, 122,* 5-14.

137. Chusmir, L. H., & Koberg, C. S. (1988). Gender identity and sex role conflict among working women and men. *The Journal of Psychology, 122,* 567-575.

138. Holmbeck, G. N., & Bale, P. (1988). Relations between instrumental and expressive personality characteristics and behaviors: A test of Spence and Helmreich's theory. *Journal of Research in Personality, 22*(1), 37-59.

139. Ingram, R. E., Cruet, D., Johnson, B. R., & Wisnicki, K. S. (1988). Self-focused attention, gender, gender role, and vulnerability to negative affect. *Journal of Personality and Social Psychology, 55,* 967-978.

140. Johnson, M. E. (1988). Influences of gender and sex role orientation on help-seeking attitudes. *The Journal of Psychology, 122,* 237-241.

141. Paulhus, D. L., & Martin, C. L. (1988). Functional flexibility: A new conception of interpersonal flexibility. *Journal of Personality and Social Psychology, 55,* 88- 101.

142. Richardson, A. G. (1988). Sex-role orientations: Differences among students and teachers. *Social Behavior and Personality, 16,* 165-168.

143. Burczyk, K., & Standing, L. (1989). Attitudes towards rape victims: Effects of victim status, sex of victim, and sex of rater. *Social Behavior and Personality, 17,* 1-8.

144. Frable, D. E. S. (1989). Sex typing and gender ideology: Two facets of the individual's gender psychology that go together. *Journal of Personality and Social Psychology, 56,* 95-108.

145. Holmbeck, G. N. (1989). Masculinity, femininity, and multiple regression: Comments on Zeldow, Daugherty, and Clark's "Masculinity, Femininity, and Psychosocial Adjustment in Medical Students: A 2-Year Follow-Up." *Journal of Personality Assessment, 53,* 583-599.

146. Hong, I., & Rust, J. (1989). Androgyny and openness to experience in a Chinese population. *Social Behavior and Personality, 17,* 215-218.

147. Jackson, L. A., & Jeffers, D. L. (1989). The Attitudes About Reality Scale: A new measure of personal epistemology. *Journal of Personality Assessment, 53,* 353-365.

148. Maupin, H. E., & Fisher, R. J. (1989). The effects of superior female performance and sex-role orientation on gender conformity. *Canadian Journal of Behavioural Science, 21,* 55-69.

149. Reynolds, A. J. (1989). Social environmental conceptions of male homosexual behavior: A university climate analysis. *Journal of College Student Development, 30,* 62-69.

150. Wilhelm, K., & Parker, G. (1989). Is sex necessarily a risk factor to depression? *Psychological Medicine, 19,* 401-413.

151. Baker, L. A., & Daniels, D. (1990). Nonshared environmental influences and personality differences in adult twins. *Journal of Personality and Social Psychology, 58,* 103-110.

152. Betz, N. E., Heesacker, R. S., & Shuttleworth, C. (1990).

Moderators of the congruence and realism of major and occupational plans in college students: A replication and extension. *Journal of Counseling Psychology, 37,* 269-276.

153. Brems, C., & Johnson, M. E. (1990). Reexamination of the Bem Sex-Role Inventory: The interpersonal BSRI. *Journal of Personality Assessment, 55,* 484-498.

154. Chusmir, L. H., & Koberg, C. S. (1990). Dual sex role identity and its relationship to sex role conflict. *The Journal of Psychology, 124,* 545-555.

155. Kaplan, M. J., Winget, C., & Free, N. (1990). Psychiatrists' beliefs about gender-appropriate behavior. *American Journal of Psychiatry, 147,* 910-912.

156. Lease, S. H., & Schmeck, R. R. (1990). The relationship of gender and gender identification to classroom participation. *College Student Journal, 24,* 392-398.

157. Leventhal, G., & Herbert, H. (1990). Effects of subjects' sex and sex-role attitudes on real and perceived performance using gender-related stimuli with traditional and nontraditional female experimenters. *Psychological Reports, 66,* 259-266.

158. Lippa, R., & Connelly, S. (1990). Gender diagnosticity: A new Bayesian approach to gender-related individual differences. *Journal of Personality and Social Psychology, 59,* 1051-1065.

159. Lohr, J. M., Nix, J., Bonge, D., & Kralik, K. (1990). Internal consistency and reliability of alternate short forms of the college women's assertion sample: Clinical and research implications. *Journal of Psychopathology and Behavioral Assessment, 12,* 129-142.

160. McCann, S. J. H., Stewin, L. L., & Short, R. H. (1990). Femininity and expected satisfaction in the stages of the family life cycle. *Psychological Reports, 66,* 1187-1194.

161. O'Heron, C. A., & Orlofsky, J. L. (1990). Stereotypic and nonstereotypic sex role trait and behavior orientations, gender identity, and psychological adjustment. *Journal of Personality and Social Psychology, 58,* 134-143.

162. Quackenbush, R. L. (1990). Sex roles and social-sexual effectiveness. *Social Behavior and Personality, 18,* 35-40.

163. Salminen, S. (1990). Sex role and participation in traditionally inappropriate sports. *Perceptual and Motor Skills, 71,* 1216-1218.

164. Yatsko, C., & Larsen, J. D. (1990). Relationship between sex-role and moral decision-making. *Psychological Reports, 66,* 59-64.

165. Cantrell, P. J., & Ellis, J. B. (1991). Gender role and risk patterns for eating disorders in men and women. *Journal of Clinical Psychology, 47,* 53-60.

166. Colvin, C. R., & Funder, D. C. (1991). Predicting personality and behavior: A boundary on the acquaintanceship effect. *Journal of Personality and Social Psychology, 60,* 884-894.

167. Faulkender, P. J. (1991). Does gender schema mediate between sex-role identity and self-actualization? *Psychological Reports, 68,* 1019-1029.

168. Gynther, M. D., Davis, A. T., & Shake, L. G. (1991). The perception of attractiveness: What about the beholders? *Journal of Clinical Psychology, 47,* 745-748.

169. Kalichman, S. C. (1991). Water levels, falling objects, and spiral tubes: An investigation of the general naivete hypothesis of physical task performance. *The Journal of Genetic Psychology, 152,* 255-262.

170. Leventhal, G., & Garcia, V. L. (1991). An examination of personal and situational factors which affect female managers and their employees. *Psychological Reports, 68,* 835-848.

171. Long, V. O. (1991). Masculinity, femininity, and women scientists' self-esteem and self-acceptance. *The Journal of Psychology, 125,* 263-270.

172. Marsh, H. W., & Byrne, B. M. (1991). Differentiated additive androgyny model: Relations between masculinity, femininity, and multiple dimensions of self-concept. *Journal of Personality and Social Psychology, 61,* 811-828.

173. McCann, S. J. H., Stewin, L. L., & Short, R. H. (1991). Sex differences, social desirability, masculinity, and the tendency to worry. *The Journal of Genetic Psychology, 152,* 295-301.

174. Russell, C. D., & Ellis, J. B. (1991). Sex-role development in single parent households. *Social Behavior and Personality, 19,* 5-9.

175. Swain, B., Shisslak, C. M., & Crago, M. (1991). Clinical features of eating disorders and individual psychological functioning. *Journal of Clinical Psychology, 47,* 702-708.

176. Turner, B. F., & Turner, C. B. (1991). Bem Sex-Role Inventory stereotypes for men and women varying in age and race among national register psychologists. *Psychological Reports, 69,* 931-944.

177. Bostwick, T. D., & Delucia, J. L. (1992). Effects of gender and specific dating behaviors on perceptions of sex willingness and date rape. *Journal of Social and Clinical Psychology, 11,* 14-25.

178. DeHeer, N. D., Wampold, B. E., & Freund, R. D. (1992). Do sex-typed and androgynous subjects prefer counselors on the basis of gender or effectiveness? They prefer the best. *Journal of Counseling Psychology, 39,* 175-184.

179. Deheer, N. D., Wampold, B. E., & Freund, R. D. (1992). Do sex-typed and androgynous subjects prefer counselors on the basis of gender or effectiveness? They prefer the best. *Journal of Counseling Psychology, 39,* 175-184.

180. Galbraith, M. (1992). Understanding career choices of men in elementary education. *Journal of Educational Research, 85,* 246-253.

181. Gurman, E. B., & Long, K. (1992). Emergent leadership and female sex role identity. *The Journal of Psychology, 126,* 309-316.

182. Hackman, M. Z., Furniss, A. H., Hills, M. J., & Paterson, T. J. (1992). Perceptions of gender-role characteristics and transformational and transactional leadership behaviours. *Perceptual and Motor Skills, 75,* 311-319.

183. Holmstrom, R. W., Karp, S. A., & Silber, D. E. (1992). Factor structure of the Apperceptive Personality Test (APT). *Journal of Clinical Psychology, 48,* 207-210.

184. Lapan, R. T., & Jingeleski, J. (1992). Circumscribing vocational aspirations in junior high school. *Journal of Counseling Psychology, 39,* 81-90.

185. Long, B. C., Kahn, S. E., & Schutz, R. W. (1992). Causal model of stress and coping: Women in management. *Journal of Counseling Psychology, 39,* 227-239.

186. Nuss, W. S., & Zubenko, G. S. (1992). Correlates of persistant depressive symptoms in widows. *American Journal of Psychiatry, 149,* 346-351.

187. Robertson, J. M., & Fitzgerald, L. F. (1992). Overcoming the masculine mystique: Preferences for alternative forms of assistance among men who avoid counseling. *Journal of Counseling Psychology, 39,* 240-246.

188. Ussery, L. W., & Prentice-Dunn, S. (1992). Personality predictors of bulimic behavior and attitudes in males. *Journal of Clinical Psychology, 48,* 722-729.

189. Ashton, W. A., & Fuehrer, A. (1993). Effects of gender and gender role identification of participant and type of social support resource on support seeking. *Sex Roles, 28,* 461-476.

190. Cantrell, P. J., & Peters, D. K. (1993). Gender roles and role conflict in feminist lesbian and heterosexual women. *Sex Roles, 28,* 379-392.

191. Carpenter, S. (1993). Organization of in-group and out-group information: The influence of gender-role orientation. *Social Cognition, 11,* 70-91.

192. Colvin, C. R. (1993). "Judgable" people: Personality, behavior, and competing explanations. *Journal of Personality and Social Psychology, 64,* 861-873.

193. Doi, S. C., & Thelen, M. H. (1993). The Fear-of-Intimacy Scale: Replication and extention. *Psychological Assessment, 5,* 377-383.

194. Keisling, B. L., & Gynther, M. D. (1993). Male perceptions of female attractiveness: The effects of targets' personal attributes and subjects' degree of masculinity. *Journal of Clinical Psychology, 49,* 190-196.

195. Kirlighan, D. M., Jr., Clements, L., Blake, C., Arnzen, A., & Brady, L. (1993). Counselor sex role orientation, flexibility, and working alliance formation. *Journal of Counseling and Development, 72,* 95-100.

196. Kolbe, R. H., & Langefeld, C. D. (1993). Appraising gender role portrayals in TV commercials. *Sex Roles, 28,* 393-417.

197. Kopper, B. A. (1993). Role of gender, sex role identity, and Type A behavior in anger expression and mental health functioning. *Journal of Counseling Psychology, 40,* 232-237.

198. Kurdek, L. A. (1993). Predicting marital dissolution: A 5-year prospective longitudinal study of newlywed couples. *Journal of Personality and Social Psychology, 64,* 221-242.

199. Long, V. O. (1993). Masculinity, femininity, and male scientists' self-esteem and self-acceptance. *The Journal of Psychology, 127,* 213-220.

200. Renn, J. A., & Calvert, S. L. (1993). The relation between gender schemas and adults' recall of stereotyped and counterstereotyped televised information. *Sex Roles, 28,* 449-459.

201. Spence, J. T. (1993). Gender-related traits and gender ideology: Evidence for a multifactorial theory. *Journal of Personality and Social Psychology, 64,* 624-635.

202. Wong, J. L., & Whitaker, D. J. (1993). Depressive mood states and their cognitive and personality correlates in college students: They improve over time. *Journal of Clinical Psychology, 49,* 615-621.

203. Howard-Hamilton, M., Lawler, A. M., Talleyrand, C., Smith, R., & Day, D. (1994). Image enhancement and career workshops for female athletes. *Journal of College Student Development, 35,* 66-68.

204. Lobel, T. E. (1994). Sex typing and the social perception of gender stereotypic and nonstereotypic behavior: The uniqueness of feminine males. *Journal of Personality and Social Psychology, 66,* 379-385.

[289]

Bench Mark Measures.

Purpose: Developed primarily to be used in conjunction with the Alphabetic Phonics Curriculum, but can also be useful as instruments to measure any student's general phonic knowledge.

Population: Ungraded.

Publication Date: 1977.

Scores: 3 levels in 4 areas: Alphabet and Dictionary Skills, Reading, Handwriting, Spelling.

Administration: Individual in part.

Price Data, 1989: $55 per complete kit, includes administrator's guide (16 pages), test booklet (26 pages), 24 summary sheets (6 pages), graph of concepts and multisensory introductions (16 pages), sheet of block capitals, set of three-dimensional letters, skeleton dictionary (Anna Gillingham and Bessie Stillman, '56, 79 pages), test cards (56), spirit duplicating master (1 page); $10 per 12 summary sheets; $1.25 per graph; $4.50 per skeleton dictionary.

Time: (30–60) minutes.

Comments: "Criterion-referenced."

Author: Aylett R. Cox.

Publisher: Educators Publishing Service, Inc.

Cross References: For a review by David J. Carroll, see 9:138.

[290]

BENCHMARKS.

Purpose: "To assess individual experiences and link learnings to developmental strategies."

Population: Managers and executives.

Publication Dates: 1990–92.

Scores, 24: Feedback in 16 Skill Areas (Resourcefulness, Doing Whatever It Takes, Being a Quick Study, Decisiveness, Leading Employees, Setting a Developmental Climate, Confronting Problem Employees, Team Orientation, Hiring Talented Staff, Building and Mending Relationships, Compassion/Sensitivity, Straightforwardness/Composure, Balance, Self-Awareness, Putting People at Ease, Flexibility); Feedback in 6 Problem Areas (Interpersonal Relationships, Difficulty in Molding Staff, Difficulty in Making Strategic Transitions, Lack of Follow-through, Overdependence, Strategic Differences with Management), Handling of Critical Jobs, Comparison Score.

Administration: Group.

Restricted Distribution: The publisher requires a 2-day certification program for those who wish to give feedback from Benchmarks in their own organization or as a consultant.

Price Data, 1993: $225 per set including 12 questionnaires, computer scoring, summary of results, and the Developmental Learning Guide ('90, 62 pages); $1,000 program fee for certification workshop.

Time: (30) minutes per survey.

Authors: Michael M. Lombardo, Cynthia D. McCauley, Russ Moxley (manual), Maxine Dalton (manual), Claire Usher (feedback report), Esther Hutchinson (Developmental Learning Guide), T. Dan Pryor (Developmental Learning Guide).

Publisher: Center for Creative Leadership.

a) BENCHMARKS GROUP PROFILE.

Purpose: "To assess the strengths and developmental needs of target groups."

Population: Upper and middle managers and executives.

Publication Date: 1990.

Price Data, 1992: $500 per report including management skills and perspectives overview, scales, importance for success, group characteristics, and overheads for class presentation; $375 per report if ordered with initial purchase.

Author: Center for Creative Leadership.

[291]

[Bender-Gestalt Test.]

Purpose: Measures perceptual-motor abilities.

Scores: Scores vary depending on adaptation used.

Administration: Individual.

Price Data, 1994: $375 per comprehensive Bender Gestalt test material set including all materials needed to administer, score, and interpret the Bender Gestalt Test for Adults and for Children; $150 per set of materials for Bender Gestalt Test: Adults including 1 set of Design Cards, 100 test score sheets, *A Visual Motor Gestalt Test and Its Clinical Use*, and *The Bender Gestalt Test: Quantification and Validity for Adults*; $230 per set of materials for Bender Gestalt Test: Children including 1 set of Design Cards, 25 children's scoring booklets, 25 children's record forms, *Bender Visual Motor Gestalt Test of Children: A Manual*, and volumes 1 and 2 of *The Bender Gestalt Test for Young Children*.

Comments: The original Bender Gestalt is listed as *a* below; the modifications listed as *b–f* consist primarily of alterations in administration procedure, new scoring systems, or expanded interpretive procedures, rather than changes in the test materials; *c* provides, in addition, for use of the materials as projective stimuli for associations.

a) BENDER VISUAL MOTOR GESTALT TEST DESIGN CARDS.

Population: Ages 4 and over.

Publication Dates: 1938–46.

Acronym: VMGT.

Price Data: $29.50 per set of cards ('46, 9 cards), directions ('46, 8 pages), and manual ('38, 187 pages).

Time: (10) minutes.

Comments: No reliability data.

Author: Lauretta Bender.

Publisher: Western Psychological Services.

b) THE BENDER GESTALT TEST.

Population: Ages 4 and over.

Publication Date: 1951.

Acronym: BGT.

Price Data: $19.50 per 100 scoring sheets (1 page); $66.50 per manual (287 pages).

Time: (10) minutes.

Comments: Utilizes same test cards as *a*.

Authors: Gerald R. Pascal and Barbara J. Suttell.

Publisher: Western Psychological Services.

c) THE BENDER VISUAL MOTOR GESTALT TEST FOR CHILDREN.

Population: Ages 4–12.

Publication Date: 1962.
Price Data: $16.50 per 25 record forms; $35 per manual ('62, 92 pages).
Time: (10) minutes without associations.
Comments: Utilizes same test cards as *a*.
Author: Aileen Clawson.
Publisher: Western Psychological Services.

d) THE BENDER GESTALT TEST FOR YOUNG CHILDREN.
Population: Ages 5–10.
Publication Dates: 1963–75.
Price Data: $140 per complete set including 2 volumes (Volume I, 195 pages; Volume II, 205 pages); $72 per Volume I; $72 per Volume II.
Time: Administration time not reported.
Comments: Includes developmental scoring system; utilizes same test cards as *a*.
Author: Elizabeth M. Koppitz.
Publisher: Western Psychological Services.

e) THE WATKINS BENDER-GESTALT SCORING SYSTEM.
Population: Ages 5–14.
Publication Date: 1976.
Acronym: WBSS.
Price Data: $26 per 100 record forms; $22.50 per manual ('76, 137 pages); $60 per complete kit including cards described in *a*.
Time: Administration time not reported.
Author: Ernest O. Watkins.
Publisher: Western Psychological Services.

f) THE CANTER BACKGROUND INTERFERENCE PROCEDURE FOR THE BENDER GESTALT TEST.
Population: Ages 12 and over.
Publication Dates: 1966–76.
Acronym: BIP; also called BIP-Bender.
Price Data: $60 per complete kit including 25 test forms ('75, 4 pages) and manual ('76, 95 pages); $32 per 25 test forms; $35 per manual.
Time: Administration time not reported.
Author: Arthur Canter.
Publisher: Western Psychological Services.

Cross References: For reviews by Jack A. Naglieri and John E. Obrzut and Carol A. Boliek, see 11:40 (92 references); for reviews by Kenneth W. Howell and Jerome M. Sattler, see 9:139 (65 references); see also T3:280 (159 references), 8:506 (253 references), and T2:1447 (144 references); for a review by Philip M. Kitay, see 7:161 (192 references); see also P:415 (170 references); for a review by C. B. Blakemore and an excerpted review by Fred Y. Billingslea, see 6:203 (99 references); see also 5:172 (118 references); for reviews by Arthur L. Benton and Howard R. White, see 4:144 (34 references); see also 3:108 (8 references).

· TEST REFERENCES

1. Black, F. W. (1983). Digit repetition in learning-disabled children. *Journal of Clinical Psychology, 39,* 263-267.
2. Faller, G. B., & Wallbrown, F. H. (1983). Comparison of the Minnesota Percepto-Diagnostic Test and Bender-Gestalt: Relationship with achievement criteria. *Journal of Clinical Psychology, 39,* 985-988.
3. Mermelstein, J. J. (1983). A process approach to the Bender-Gestalt Test and its use in differentiating schizophrenic, brain-damaged, and medical patients. *Journal of Clinical Psychology, 39,* 173-182.
4. Cobrinik, L. (1987). A process analysis of Bender Gestalt Test performance in childhood emotional disorder: A single-case study. *Child Psychiatry and Human Development, 17,* 242-256.
5. Evans, R. L., Bishop, D. S., Matlock, A. L., Stranahan, S., & Noonan, C. (1987). Predicting poststroke family function: A continuing dilemma. *Psychological Reports, 60,* 691-695.
6. Fleener, F. T. (1987). Learning disabilities and other attributes as factors in diligent activities among adolescents in a nonurban area. *Psychological Reports, 60,* 327-334.
7. Acevedo, A., Elder, I., & Harrison, A. (1988). A failure to find empirical support for Beardslee and Vaillant's prediction about alcoholism. *Journal of Clinical Psychology, 44,* 837-841.
8. Even, A., Kipper, D. A., & Yehuda, S. (1988). Recall of figure "A" of the Bender-Gestalt Test among delinquents. *Journal of Clinical Psychology, 44,* 988-994.
9. Ghassemzadeh, H. (1988). A pilot study of the Bender-Gestalt Test in a sample of Iranian normal children. *Journal of Clinical Psychology, 44,* 787-792.
10. Lewis, D. O., Pincus, J. H., Bard, B., Richardson, E., Princhep, L. S., Feldman, M., & Yeager, C. (1988). Neuropsychiatric, psychoeducational, and family characteristics of 14 juveniles condemned to death in the United States. *American Journal of Psychiatry, 145,* 584-589.
11. McIntosh, J. A., Belter, R. W., Saylor, C. F., & Finch, A. J., Jr. (1988). The Bender-Gestalt with adolescents: Comparison of two scoring systems. *Journal of Clinical Psychology, 44,* 226-230.
12. Belter, R. W., McIntosh, J. A., Finch, A. J., Jr., & Williams, L. D. (1989). The Bender-Gestalt as a method of personality assessment with adolescents. *Journal of Clinical Psychology, 45,* 414-423.
13. Goldstein, D. J., Peterson, N. C., & Sheaffer, C. I. (1989). Concurrent validity of the Gardner Test of Visual-Motor Skills. *Perceptual and Motor Skills, 69,* 605-606.
14. Hill, R. D. (1989). Residual effects of cigarette smoking on cognitive performance in normal aging. *Psychology and Aging, 4,* 251-254.
15. Lowenstein, L. F. (1989). The etiology, diagnosis, and treatment of the fire-setting behaviour of children. *Child Psychiatry and Human Development, 19,* 186-194.
16. Watkins, C. E., Jr., Campell, V. L., Hollifield, J., & Duckworth, J. (1989). Projective techniques: Do they have a place in counseling psychology training? *The Counseling Psychologist, 18,* 511-513.
17. Maloney, P., & Wagner, E. E. (1990). Predicting normal age-related changes with intelligence, projective, and perceptual-motor test variables. *Perceptual and Motor Skills, 71,* 1225-1226.
18. Schretlen, D., & Arkowitz, H. (1990). A psychological test battery to detect prison inmates who fake insanity or mental retardation. *Behavioral Sciences and the Law, 8,* 75-84.
19. Storandt, M. (1990). Bender-Gestalt Test performance in senile dementia of the Alzheimer type. *Psychology and Aging, 5,* 604-606.
20. Brannigan, G. G., & Brunner, N. A. (1991). Relationship between two scoring systems for the modified version of the Bender-Gestalt Test. *Perceptual and Motor Skills, 72,* 286.
21. Cates, J. A., & Lapham, R. F. (1991). Personality assessment of the prelingual, profoundly deaf child or adolescent. *Journal of Personality Assessment, 56,* 118-129.
22. Franzese, A., Antonini, G., Iannelli, M., Leardi, M. G., Spada, S., Vichi, R., Millefiorini, M., & Lazzari, R. (1991). Intellectual functions and personality in subjects with noncongenital myotonic muscular dystrophy. *Psychological Reports, 68,* 723-732.
23. Frey, P. D., & Pinelli, B., Jr. (1991). Visual discrimination and visuomotor integration among two classes of Brazilian children. *Perceptual and Motor Skills, 72,* 847-850.
24. Hirt, M., & Pithers, W. (1991). Selective attention and levels of coding in schizophrenia. *British Journal of Clinical Psychology, 30,* 139-149.
25. Hughes, J. R., Zagar, R., Sylvies, R. B., Arbit, J., Busch, K. G., & Bowers, N. D. (1991). Medical, family, and scholastic conditions in urban delinquents. *Journal of Clinical Psychology, 47,* 448-463.
26. Imm, P. S., Foster, K. Y., Belter, R. W., & Finch, A. J., Jr. (1991). Assessment of short-term visual memory in child and adolescent psychiatric patients. *Journal of Clinical Psychology, 47,* 440-443.
27. Margalit, M., & Almougy, K. (1991). Classroom behavior and family climate in students with learning disabilities and hyperactive behavior. *Journal of Learning Disabilities, 24,* 406-412.
28. Nielson, S., & Sapp, G. L. (1991). Bender-Gestalt developmental scores: Predicting reading and mathematics achievement. *Psychological Reports, 69,* 39-42.
29. Wagner, E. E., & Marsico, D. S. (1991). Redundancy in the Pascal-Suttell Bender-Gestalt scoring system: Discriminating organicity with only one design. *Journal of Clinical Psychology, 47,* 261-263.
30. Aikman, K. G., Belter, R. W., & Finch, A. J., Jr. (1992).

Human figure drawings: Validity in assessing intellectual level and academic achievement. *Journal of Clinical Psychology, 48*, 114-120.

31. Bolen, L. M., Hewett, B. J., Hall, C. W., & Mitchell, C. C. (1992). Expanded Koppitz scoring system of the Bender-Gestalt Visual-Motor Test for adolescents: A pilot study. *Psychology in the Schools, 29*(2), 113-115.

32. Burns, C. W. (1992). Psychoeducational decision making, test scores, and descriptive data: Selected methodological issues. *Journal of School Psychology, 30*(1), 1-16.

33. Ganschow, L., Sparks, R., & Helmick, M. (1992). Speech/language referral practices by school psychologists. *School Psychology Review, 21*(2), 313-326.

34. Lubin, B., & Sands, E. W. (1992). Bibliography of the psychometric properties of the Bender Visual-Motor Gestalt Test: 1970-1991. *Perceptual and Motor Skills, 75*, 385-386.

[292]

Bennett Mechanical Comprehension Test.

Purpose: "Measure(s) the ability to perceive and understand the relationship of physical forces and mechanical elements in practical situations."

Population: Industrial employees and high school and adult applicants for mechanical positions or engineering schools.

Publication Dates: 1940–80.

Acronym: BMCT.

Scores: Total score only.

Administration: Group.

Forms, 2: S, T (equivalent forms).

Price Data, 1994: $29 per examination kit; $99 per 25 test booklets (Form S or T); $53.50 per 50 IBM answer sheets; $25 per hand scoring key (Form S or T); $20 per manual ('69, 41 pages); $78 per cassette or reel-to-reel recording of test questions (Form S or T); scoring service offered by publisher.

Time: 30(35) minutes.

Comments: Tape recordings of test questions read aloud are available for use with examinees who have limited reading abilities.

Author: George K. Bennett.

Publisher: The Psychological Corporation.

Cross References: For a review by Hilda Wing, see 11:41 (3 references); see T3:282 (7 references); see also T2:2239 (9 references); for reviews by Harold P. Bechtoldt and A. Oscar H. Roberts, and an excerpted review by Ronald K. Hambleton, see 7:1049 (22 references); see also 6:1094 (15 references) and 5:889 (46 references); for a review by N. W. Morton of earlier forms, see 4:766 (28 references); for reviews by Charles M. Harsh, Lloyd G. Humphreys, and George A. Satter, see 3:683 (19 references).

TEST REFERENCES

1. Lowman, R. L., Williams, R. E., & Leeman, G. E. (1985). The structure and relationship of college women's primary abilities and vocational interests. *Journal of Vocational Behavior, 27*, 298-315.

2. Dagenais, F. (1992). Bennett Mechanical Comprehension Test: Normative data for a sample of Saudi Arabian technical trainees. *Perceptual and Motor Skills, 74*, 107-113.

[293]

Benton Visual Retention Test, Fifth Edition.

Purpose: "To assess visual perception, visual memory, and visuoconstructive abilities."

Population: Age 8–adults.

Publication Dates: 1946–92.

Acronym: BVRT.

Scores, 9: Omissions, Distortions, Perseverations, Rotations, Misplacements, Size Errors, Total Left, Total Right, Total.

Administration: Individual.

Forms, 3: C, D, E in a single booklet.

Price Data, 1994: $101.50 per complete set including stimulus booklet (all 30 designs), scoring template, 25 response booklets, record form, and manual ('92, 108 pages); $48 per stimulus booklet; $27 per 25 response booklets–record form; $5.50 per scoring template; $43 per manual.

Time: (5–10) minutes.

Author: Arthur L. Benton.

Publisher: The Psychological Corporation.

Cross References: See 9:140 (30 references), T3:283 (27 references), 8:236 (32 references), T2:543 (71 references), and 6:543 (22 references); for a review by Nelson G. Hanawalt, see 5:401 (5 references); for reviews by Ivan Norman Mensh, Joseph Newman, and William Schofield of the original edition, see 4:360 (3 references); for an excerpted review, see 3:297.

TEST REFERENCES

1. Hinojosa, J., Anderson, J., Goldstein, P. K., & Becker-Lewin, M. (1982). Roles and functions of the occupational therapist in the treatment of sensory integrative dysfunction. *The American Journal of Occupational Therapy, 36*, 832-834.

2. Kljajic, I., & Berry, D. (1984). Brain syndrome and WAIS PIQ VIQ difference scores corrected for test artifact. *Journal of Clinical Psychology, 40*, 271-277.

3. Tamkin, A. S., Kunce, J. T., Blount, J. B., Jr., & Magharious, W. (1984). The effectiveness of the Weigl Color-Form Sorting Test in screening for brain dysfunction. *Journal of Clinical Psychology, 40*, 1454-1459.

4. Baker, E. L., White, R. F., & Murawski, B. J. (1985). Clinical evaluation of neurobehavioral effects of occupational exposure to organic solvents and lead. *International Journal of Mental Health, 14*(3), 135-158.

5. Blanton, P. D., & Gouvier, W. D. (1985). A systematic solution to the Benton Visual Retention Test: A caveat to examiners. *Clinical Neuropsychology, 7*, 95-96.

6. Fenwick, P., Galliano, S., Coate, M. A., Rippere, V., & Brown, D. (1985). 'Psychic sensitivity,' mystical experience, head injury and brain pathology. *British Journal of Medical Psychology, 58*, 34-44.

7. Green, M., & Walker, E. (1985). Neuropsychological performance and positive and negative symptoms in schizophrenia. *Journal of Abnormal Psychology, 94*, 460-469.

8. Kellar, L. A., & Levick, S. E. (1985). Reversed hemispheric lateralization of cerebral function: A case study. *Cortex, 21*, 469-476.

9. Larrabee, G. J., Kane, R. L., Schuck, J. R., & Francis, D. J. (1985). Construct validity of various memory testing procedures. *Journal of Clinical and Experimental Neuropsychology, 7*, 239-250.

10. Lewandowski, L., Costenbader, V., & Richman, R. (1985). Neuropsychological aspects of Turner syndrome. *Clinical Neuropsychology, 7*, 144-147.

11. Lindgren, S. D., Renzi, E. D., & Richman, L. C. (1985). Cross-national comparisons of developmental dyslexia in Italy and the United States. *Child Development, 56*, 1404-1417.

12. Mayer, M., Alpert, M., Stastny, P., Perlick, D., & Empfield, M. (1985). Multiple contributions to clinical presentation of flat affect in schizophrenia. *Schizophrenia Bulletin, 11*, 420-426.

13. Scogin, F., Storandt, M., & Lott, L. (1985). Memory-skills training, memory complaints, and depression in older adults. *Journal of Gerontology, 40*, 562-568.

14. Vilkki, J. (1985). Amnesic syndromes after surgery of anterior communicating artery aneurysms. *Cortex, 21*, 431-444.

15. Acker, C. (1986). Neuropsychological deficits in alcoholics: The relative contributions of gender and drinking history. *British Journal of Addiction, 81*, 395-403.

16. Andreasen, N., Nasrallah, H. A., Dunn, V., Olson, S. C., Grove, W. M., Ehrhardt, J. C., Coffman, J. A., & Crossett, J. H. W. (1986). Structural abnormalities in the frontal system in schizophrenia. *Archives of General Psychiatry, 43*, 136-144.

17. Bird, J. M., Levy, R., & Jacoby, R. J. (1986). Computed tomog-

raphy in the elderly: Changes over time in a normal population. *British Journal of Psychiatry, 148,* 80-85.

18. Bowers, T. G., Washburn, S. E., & Livesay, J. R. (1986). Predicting neuropsychological impairment by screening instruments and intellectual evaluation indices: Implications for the meaning of Kaufman's Factor III. *Psychological Reports, 59,* 487-493.

19. Guy, J. D., Liaboe, G. P., & Wallace, C. J. (1986). Premorbid adjustment in adult male schizophrenics, as related to process vs. reactive, chronic vs. acute, age of onset, and neurologically impaired vs. non-impaired. *Journal of Clinical Psychology, 42,* 62-67.

20. Kirkcaldy, B. (1986). Intellectual and motoric correlates of Benton's Visual Retention Test. *Perceptual and Motor Skills, 63,* 154.

21. Knuckle, E. P., & Asbury, C. A. (1986). Benton Revised Visual Retention Test performance of black adolescents according to age, sex, and ethnic identity. *Perceptual and Motor Skills, 63,* 319-327.

22. Knuckle, E. P., & Asbury, C. A. (1986). WISC-R discrepancy score directions and gender as reflected in neuropsychological test performance of Black adolescents. *Journal of Research and Development in Education, 20*(1), 44-51.

23. Livesay, J. R. (1986). Clinical utility of Wechsler's deterioration index in screening for behavioral impairment. *Perceptual and Motor Skills, 63,* 619-626.

24. Miezejeski, C. M., Jenkins, E. C., Hill, A. L., Wisniewski, K., French, J. H., & Brown, W. T. (1986). A profile of cognitive deficit in females from fragile X families. *Neuropsychologia, 24,* 405-409.

25. Ney, P., Colbert, P., Newman, B., & Young, J. (1986). Aggressive behavior and learning difficulties as symptoms of depression in children. *Child Psychiatry and Human Development, 17,* 3-14.

26. Perlick, D., Stastny, P., Katz, I., Mayer, M., & Mattis, S. (1986). Memory deficits and anticholinergic levels in chronic schizophrenia. *American Journal of Psychiatry, 143,* 230-232.

27. Sanchez-Craig, M., & Lei, H. (1986). Disadvantages to imposing the goal of abstinence on problem drinkers: An empirical study. *British Journal of Addiction, 81,* 505-512.

28. Shichita, K., Hatano, S., Ohashi, Y., Shibata, H., & Matuzaki, T. (1986). Memory changes in the Benton Visual Retention Test between ages 70 and 75. *Journal of Gerontology, 41,* 385-386.

29. Steinman, D. R., & Bigler, E. D. (1986). Neuropsychological sequelae of ruptured anterior communicating artery aneurysm. *Clinical Neuropsychology, 8,* 135-140.

30. Tarbox, A. R., Connors, G. J., & McLaughlin, E. J. (1986). Effects of drinking pattern on neuropsychological performance among alcohol misusers. *Journal of Studies on Alcohol, 47,* 176-179.

31. Temple, C. M. (1986). Anomia for animals in a child. *Brain, 109,* 1225-1242.

32. Zaidel, D. W. (1986). Memory for scenes in stroke patients: Hemisphere processing of semantic organization in pictures. *Brain, 109,* 547-560.

33. Klonoff, H., Fleetham, J., Taylor, D. R., & Clark, C. (1987). Treatment outcome of obstructive sleep apnea: Physiological and neuropsychological concomitants. *The Journal of Nervous and Mental Disease, 175,* 208-212.

34. Pozzilli, C., Passafiume, D., Bastianello, S., D'Antona, R., & Lenzi, G. L. (1987). Remote effects of caudate hemorrhage: A clinical and functional study. *Cortex, 23,* 341-349.

35. Halligan, F. R., Reznikoff, M., Friedman, H. P., & LaRocca, N. G. (1988). Cognitive dysfunction and change in multiple sclerosis. *Journal of Clinical Psychology, 44,* 540-548.

36. Massman, P. J., Nussbaum, N. L., & Bigler, E. D. (1988). The mediating effect of age on the relationship between Child Behavior Checklist hyperactivity scores and neuropsychological test performance. *Journal of Abnormal Child Psychology, 16,* 89-95.

37. Mehler, M. F. (1988). Mixed transcortical aphasia in nonfamilial dysphasic dementia. *Cortex, 24,* 554-554.

38. Randall, C. M., Dickson, A. L., & Plasay, M. T. (1988). The relationship between intellectual function and adult performance on the Benton Visual Retention Test. *Cortex, 24,* 277-289.

39. Scogin, F., & Bienias, J. L. (1988). A three-year follow-up of older adult participants in a memory-skills training program. *Psychology and Aging, 3,* 334-337.

40. Katsanis, J., & Iacono, W. G. (1989). Association of left-handedness with ventricle size and neuropsychological performance in schizophrenia. *American Journal of Psychiatry, 146,* 1056-1058.

41. Krakowski, M. I., Convit, A., Jaeger, J., Lin, S., & Volarka, J. (1989). Neurological impairment in violent schizophrenic inpatients. *American Journal of Psychiatry, 146,* 849-853.

42. Robinowitz, R., Roberts, W. R., Dolan, M. P., Patterson, E. T., Charles, H. L., Atkins, H. G., & Penk, W. E. (1989). Carcinogenicity and teratogenicity vs. psychogenicity: Psychological characteristics associated with self-reported Agent Orange exposure among Vietnam combat veterans who seek treatment for substance abuse. *Journal of Clinical Psychology, 45,* 718-728.

43. Sweeney, J. A., Meisel, L., Walsh, V. L., & Castrovinci, D. (1989). Assessment of cognitive functioning in poly-substance abusers. *Journal of Clinical Psychology, 45,* 346-351.

44. Alder, A. G., Adam, J., & Arenberg, D. (1990). Individual differences assessment of the relationship between change in and initial level of adult cognitive functioning. *Psychology and Aging, 5,* 560-568.

45. Crook, T. H., III, Youngjohn, J. R., & Larrabee, G. J. (1990). The Misplaced Objects Test: A measure of everyday visual memory. *Journal of Clinical and Experimental Neuropsychology, 12,* 819-833.

46. Grant, M. L., Ilai, D., Nussbaum, N. L., & Bigler, E. D. (1990). The relationship between continuous performance tasks and neuropsychological tests in children with Attention-deficit Hyperactivity Disorder. *Perceptual and Motor Skills, 70,* 435-445.

47. DeHaan, E. H. F., & Campbell, R. (1991). A fifteen year follow-up of a case of developmental prosopagnosia. *Cortex, 27,* 489-509.

48. Hua, M., & Huang, C. (1991). Chronic occupational exposure to manganese and neurobehavioral function. *Journal of Clinical and Experimental Neuropsychology, 13,* 495-507.

49. Katsanis, J., & Iacono, W. G. (1991). Clinical, neuropsychological, and brain structural correlates of smooth-pursuit eye tracking performance in chronic schizophrenia. *Journal of Abnormal Psychology, 100,* 526-534.

50. Rubin, E. H., Kinscherf, D. A., Grant, E. A., & Storandt, M. (1991). The influence of major depression on clinical and psychometric assessment of senile dementia of the Alzheimer type. *American Journal of Psychiatry, 148,* 1164-1171.

51. Schwartz, B. S., Ford, D. P., Bolla, K. I., Agnew, J., & Bleecker, M. L. (1991). Solvent-associated olfactory dysfunction: Not a predictor of deficits in learning and memory. *American Journal of Psychiatry, 148,* 751-756.

52. Thompson, J. K., & Spana, R. E. (1991). Visuospatial ability, accuracy of size estimation, and bulimic disturbance in a noneating-disordered college sample: A neuropsychological analysis. *Perceptual and Motor Skills, 73,* 335-338.

53. Egan, V., Brettle, R. P., & Goodwin, G. M. (1992). The Edinburgh cohort of HIV-Positive drug users: Pattern of cognitive impairment in relation to progression of disease. *British Journal of Psychiatry, 161,* 522-531.

54. Faustman, W. O., Bono, M. A., Moses, J. A., & Csernansky, J. G. (1992). Season of birth and neuropsychological impairment in schizophrenia. *Journal of Nervous and Mental Disease, 180,* 644-648.

55. Ferere, H., Burns, W. J., & Roth, L. (1992). Use of the Revised Developmental Test of Visual-Motor Integration with chronic mentally ill adult population. *Perceptual and Motor Skills, 74,* 287-290.

56. Hoff, A. L., Riordan, H., O'Donnell, D. W., Morris, L., & DeLisi, L. E. (1992). Neuropsychological functioning of first episode schizophreniform patients. *American Journal of Psychiatry, 149,* 898-903.

57. Hublet, C., & Demeurisse, G. (1992). Pure topographical disorientation due to a deep-seated lesion with cortical remote effects. *Cortex, 28,* 123-128.

58. Massman, P. J., Delis, D. C., Butters, N., Dupont, R. M., & Gillin, J. C. (1992). The subcortical dysfunction hypothesis of memory deficits in depression: Neuropsychological validation in a subgroup of patients. *Journal of Clinical and Experimental Neuropsychology, 14,* 687-706.

59. Raskin, S. A., Borod, J. C., & Tweedy, J. R. (1992). Set-shifting and spatial orientation in patients with Parkinson's disease. *Journal of Clinical and Experimental Neuropsychology, 14,* 801-821.

60. Ferraro, R. F., Balota, D. A., & Connor, L. T. (1993). Implicit memory and the formation of new associations in nondemented Parkinsons disease individuals and individuals with senile dementia of the Alzheimer type: A serial reaction time investigation. *Brain and Cognition, 21,* 163-180.

61. Revonsuo, A., Portin, R., Koivikko, L., Rinne, J. O., & Rinne, U. K. (1993). Slowing of information processing in Parkinson's disease. *Brain and Cognition, 21,* 87-110.

62. Young, A. W., Flude, B. M., Hay, D. C., & Ellis, A. W. (1993). Impaired discrimination of familiar from unfamiliar faces. *Cortex, 29,* 65-75.

[294]

The Ber-Sil Spanish Test.

Purpose: Screening and evaluation of Spanish-speaking children.

Population: Ages 5–12, 13–17.

Publication Dates: 1972–87.

Administration: Individual.

Price Data, 1993: $90 per combination elementary and secondary complete kits including 50 of each test

booklet; $55 per elementary or secondary complete kit including $50 test booklets, 1 book of picture plates, 1 cassette tape; $31 per book of picture plates; $11 per cassette tape.
Author: Marjorie L. Beringer.
Publisher: The Ber-Sil Co.

a) ELEMENTARY LEVEL.
Population: Ages 5–12.
Publication Date: 1987.
Scores, 7: Vocabulary, Response to Directions, Writing, Geometric Figures, Draw a Boy or Girl, Math Skills, English Vocabulary.
Price Data: $9 per 50 test booklets; $17 per manual (83 pages); $17 per translation for available languages.
Foreign Language Editions: Cantonese, Mandarin, Ilokano, Tagalog, Korean, and Persian translations available.
Time: (45–55) minutes.

b) SECONDARY LEVEL.
Population: Ages 13–17.
Publication Date: 1984.
Scores, 4: Vocabulary, Dictation in Spanish, Draw a Person, Mathematics.
Price Data: $9 per 50 test booklets; $17 per manual (69 pages).
Foreign Language Editions: Philippine, Tagalog, and Ilokano translations available.
Time: (45) minutes.
Cross References: For reviews by J. Manuel Casas and David Strand and Giuseppe Costantino, see 10:30; for reviews by Giuseppe Costantino and Jaclyn B. Spitzer of an earlier edition, see 9:141.

[295]

Bessell Measurement of Emotional Maturity Scales.
Purpose: "To measure a child's degree of emotional maturity."
Population: Ages 5–11.
Publication Date: 1978.
Acronym: MEM.
Scores: 63 measures of behavioral functioning in 4 component areas: Awareness Traits, Relating Traits, Competence Traits, Integrity Traits.
Administration: Individual.
Price Data: Not available.
Time: (8–15) minutes for short form; (20–45) minutes for full scale.
Comments: 2 forms: Short and Full Scale.
Author: Harold Bessell.
Publisher: Psych/Graphic Publishers [No reply from publisher; status unknown].
Cross References: For reviews by Linda White Hawthorne and June M. Tuma, see 9:142.

[296]

BEST Instruments.
Purpose: A series of learning instruments designed to help managers and employees understand their behavior.

Population: Adults.
Publication Dates: 1989–94.
Acronym: BEST.
Administration: Group.
Price Data, 1994: $25 per sample pack; $15 per user's guide ('89, 16 pages); $149 per user's kit.
Comments: Subtests available as separates.
Author: James H. Brewer.
Publisher: Associated Consultants in Education.

a) MY BEST PROFILE.
Purpose: "To promote positive interpersonal relations."
Publication Date: 1989.
Scores: 4 personality types: Bold, Expressive, Sympathetic, Technical.
Price Data: $4.95 per profile; $99.95 per computer software.
Time: (15–20) minutes.

b) MY BEST COMMUNICATION STYLE.
Purpose: "To improve communication skills."
Publication Dates: 1989–90.
Scores: 4 styles: Bold, Expressive, Sympathetic, Technical.
Price Data: $2.95 per inventory.
Time: (15–20) minutes.

c) MY BEST LEADERSHIP STYLE.
Purpose: "To improve leadership skills."
Publication Dates: 1989–94.
Scores: Same as *a* above.
Price Data: $4.95 per profile; $99.95 per computer software.
Time: (15–20) minutes.

d) LEADERSHIP/PERSONALITY COMPATIBILITY INVENTORY.
Purpose: "To promote more productive leadership in organizations."
Acronym: L/PCI.
Scores: Same as *a* above plus 4 Leadership Role Characteristics: Active/Competitive, Persuasive/Interactive, Precise/Systematic, Willing/Steady.
Publication Dates: 1990–94.
Price Data: $5.95 per profile.
Time: (15–20) minutes.

e) WORKING WITH MY BOSS.
Purpose: "To improve the productive relationship between employee and supervisor."
Publication Date: 1989.
Scores: Same as *a* above.
Price Data: $4.95 per profile.
Time: (10–15) minutes.

f) PRE-EVALUATION PROFILE.
Purpose: "To prepare supervisors for performance evaluations of employees without personality type bias."
Acronym: PEP.
Publication Date: 1989.
Scores: Same as *a* above.
Price Data: $4.95 per profile.
Time: (15–20) minutes.
Comments: Supervisor completes profile for self and employee.

g) OUR BEST TEAM.
Purpose: "To build a more productive team."
Publication Date: 1989.
Scores: Same as *a* above.
Price Data: $6.95 per profile.
Time: (20–30) minutes.
Comments: Ratings of all team members are combined for a composite profile.

h) MY TIMESTYLE.
Purpose: "To develop more productive time usage."
Publication Date: 1990.
Scores: 4 timestyles: Road Runner, Race Horse, New Pup, Tom Cat.
Price Data: $2.95 per profile.
Time: (10–15) minutes.

i) MY BEST PRESENTATION STYLE.
Purpose: "To assist individuals in making more effective presentations."
Publication Date: 1989.
Scores: Same as *a* above.
Price Data: $4.95 per profile.
Time: (15–20) minutes.

j) SALES STYLE.
Purpose: "To sharpen sales skills."
Publication Date: 1990.
Scores: 4 sales styles: Quick-Sell, Persistent-Sell, Talkative-Sell, Precise-Sell.
Price Data: $2.95 per profile.
Time: (10–15) minutes.

k) MY TEACHING STYLE.
Purpose: "To help teachers understand learning style."
Publication Date: 1989.
Scores: Bold, Expressive, Sympathetic, Technical.
Price Data: $4.95 per profile.
Time: (15–20) minutes.

l) NEGOTIATING STYLE.
Purpose: "To build productive negotiating strategies."
Publication Date: 1991.
Scores: 4 negotiating styles: Pushy, Stand Pat, Buddy, Check All.
Price Data: $2.95 per profile.
Time: (10–15) minutes.

m) CAREER/PERSONALITY COMPATIBILITY INVENTORY.
Purpose: "To improve career selection."
Publication Date: No date on materials.
Acronym: C/PCI.
Scores: Bold, Expressive, Sympathetic, Technical.
Price Data: $5.95 per profile; $345 per computer software.
Time: (20–30) minutes.

[297]

Bilingual Home Inventory.
Purpose: Assesses "students with severe disabilities" within a context that is culturally and linguistically appropriate.
Population: Nonnative speakers of English.

Publication Dates: 1985–86.
Acronym: BHI.
Scores: No scores reported.
Administration: Individual.
Price Data, 1994: $10 per manual (specify edition).
Time: Administration time not reported.
Comments: Family interview assessing student skills.
Authors: Susan M. Pellegrini and Herbert Grossman.
Publisher: San Jose State University.

a) FILIPINO EDITION.
Publication Date: 1986.
Author: Ma. Luisa Villongco.

b) PORTUGUESE EDITION.
Publication Date: 1986.
Authors: Heraldo G. Da Silva and Maria A. Da Silva.

c) SPANISH EDITION.
Publication Dates: 1985–86.
Authors: Paula Hughes, Evelyn Ortiz-Stanley, and Michele Thomas.

d) VIETNAMESE EDITION.
Publication Date: 1985.
Authors: Mai Dao and Kim-Lan Nguyen.

Cross References: For reviews by Andres Barona and Dan Douglas, see 11:42.

[298]

Bilingual Syntax Measure.
Purpose: Designed to measure second-language oral proficiency with respect to syntactic structures in English and Spanish.
Population: Grades PK–2, 3–12.
Publication Dates: 1975–80.
Acronym: BSM I, BSM II.
Scores: Scores consist of assigned levels of proficiency.
Administration: Individual.
Editions, 2: English, Spanish (both of which may be administered as an indicator of language dominance).
Price Data, 1994: $282.50 per complete set including picture booklet, 35 English response booklets, 35 Spanish response booklets, class record, technical handbook, English manual, and Spanish manual (specify BSM I or BSM II); $79 per picture booklet (specify BSM I or BSM II); $69.50 per 35 BSM I response booklets (specify English or Spanish); $80.50 per 35 BSM II response booklets (specify English or Spanish); $6 per class record (specify BSM I or BSM II); $24 per BSM I technical handbook ('76, 53 pages); $24 per BSM II technical handbook ('80, 33 pages); $11 per BSM I manual ('75, 15 pages) (specify English or Spanish); $14.50 per BSM II manual ('78, 11 pages) (specify English or Spanish); $14.50 per English-Spanish reference book for educators.
Time: (10–15) minutes for each edition.
Comments: BSM II is an upward extension of the Bilingual Syntax Measure (BSM I).
Authors: Marina K. Burt, Heidi C. Dulay, and Eduardo Hernandez Ch.

Publisher: The Psychological Corporation.
Cross References: For reviews of BSM II by Eugene E. Garcia and Sylvia Shellenberger, see 9:147 (1 reference); for reviews of BSM I by Isaac I. Bejar and C. Ray Graham, and an excerpted review by John W. Oller, Jr., see 8:156 (4 references); for information on BSM I, see T3:290 (5 references).

TEST REFERENCES

1. Figueroa, R. A., Sandoval, J., & Merino, B. (1984). School psychology and limited-English-proficient (LEP) children: New competencies. *Journal of School Psychology, 22,* 131-143.
2. Saville-Trolke, M. (1984). What *really* matters in second language learning for academic achievement? *TESOL Quarterly, 18,* 199-219.

[299]

Bilingual Two Language Battery of Tests.
Purpose: To assess Native and English language proficiencies and to establish language dominance.
Population: Students and adults having any level of language proficiency.
Publication Date: 1983.
Scores, 4 or 5: Phonetics, Comprehension, Writing, Total, Oral Proficiency (optional).
Tests, 5: English-Spanish, English-Italian, English-Portuguese, English-Vietnamese, English-French.
Administration: Group.
Price Data, 1990: $12 per 25 student booklets of any one native language; $5 per 50 profiles; $10 per cassette of English-any one native language; $15 per manual (108 pages).
Time: 21(31) minutes.
Comments: Test administered by tape cassette; "criterion-referenced"; each session is a Native Language Sitting followed by an English Language Sitting.
Author: Adolph Caso.
Publisher: Branden Publishing, Inc.

[300]

Bingham Button Test.
Purpose: Assesses "knowledge and understanding of simple terms and relationships."
Population: Ages 3-6.
Publication Date: 1967.
Acronym: BBT.
Scores: Total score only.
Administration: Individual.
Price Data: Not available.
Time: [15-45] minutes.
Author: William J. Bingham.
Publisher: Bingham Button Test [No reply from publisher; status unknown].
Cross References: For a review by Alan S. Kaufman, see 8:207.

[301]

Biofeedback Certification Examination.
Purpose: A certification examination covering "the knowledge needed by providers of biofeedback services at the time they begin practice."
Population: Entry-level biofeedback service providers.

Publication Dates: 1980-84.
Scores: 11 Blueprint Areas: Introduction to Biofeedback, Preparing for Clinical Intervention, Neuromuscular Intervention: General, Neuromuscular Intervention: Specific, Central Nervous System Interventions: General, Autonomic Nervous System Interventions: General, Autonomic Nervous System Interventions: Specific, Biofeedback and Distress, Instrumentation, Adjunctive Techniques and Cognitive Interventions, and Professional Conduct.
Administration: Group.
Manual: No manual.
Price Data: Available from BCIA.
Time: (180) minutes.
Comments: Administration schedule available from BCIA.
Author: Biofeedback Certification Institute of America.
Publisher: Biofeedback Certification Institute of America.

[302]

Biographical Inventory Form U.
Purpose: "To obtain and analyze information about an individual's characteristics and background."
Population: Grades 7-12.
Publication Dates: 1976-78.
Acronym: BI.
Scores, 6: Academic Performance, Creativity, Artistic Potential, Leadership, Career Maturity, Educational Orientation.
Administration: Group.
Price Data: Available from publisher.
Time: (60-65) minutes.
Comments: Replaces earlier Alpha Biographical Inventory (7:975).
Author: Institute for Behavioral Research in Creativity.
Publisher: Institute for Behavioral Research in Creativity.
Cross References: For reviews by Christopher Borman and Courtland C. Lee, see 9:150.

[303]

Bi/Polar Inventory of Core Strengths.
Purpose: "To identify eight patterns of human strengths."
Population: Managers and adults in organizational settings.
Publication Dates: 1977-82.
Acronym: BPICS.
Scores: 8 patterns of core strengths: Administrator, Control Manager, College Professor, Inventor, Trainer, Public Relations Person, Entrepreneur, Promoter.
Administration: Group.
Forms, 2: A ('77, 2 pages, for self-ratings), B ('77, 2 pages, for ratings by up to 5 others).
Restricted Distribution: Restricted to Bi/Polar Certified Professionals, Certified Teachers, and approved researchers.

Price Data, 1994: Scoring service, $40 per analysis of core strengths ('82, 2 page computer report plus 17 pages of interpretive materials); $2.50 per sample analysis; $6 per manual ('78, 35 pages).
Time: (10) minutes.
Comments: Form C available for research purposes; ratings by self and others.
Authors: J. W. Thomas, Clyde C. Mayo (manual), and T. J. Thomas (interpretive materials).
Publisher: The Institute of Foundational Training and Development.

[304]

Birth to Three Assessment and Intervention System.

Purpose: To identify and assess developmental delays in young children and to help develop individual programs to remediate those delays.
Population: Birth to 3 years.
Publication Dates: 1979–86.
Administration: Individual.
Price Data, 1989: $130 per complete kit including 25 screening test record forms, 25 checklist record forms, screening test manual ('86, 85 pages), checklist manual ('86, 107 pages), and intervention manual ('86, 77 pages).
Time: Administration time not reported.
Comments: 2 tests: Screening Test of Learning and Language Development, Checklist of Learning and Language Behavior; tests available as separates; other test materials (e.g., small toys, bell) must be supplied by examiner.
Authors: Tina E. Bangs and Susan Dodson (coauthor of screening test).
Publisher: The Riverside Publishing Company.
a) SCREENING TEST OF LEARNING AND LANGUAGE DEVELOPMENT.
Purpose: "To serve as a screening instrument that will identify children who are at high risk for developmental delay."
Scores, 5: Language Comprehension, Language Expression, Avenues to Learning, Social/Personal Development, Motor Development.
Comments: Earlier edition called Birth to Three Developmental Scale.
b) CHECKLIST OF LEARNING AND LANGUAGE BEHAVIOR.
Purpose: "(a) To determine a child's developmental strengths and weaknesses in basic behavioral categories, (b) to provide the information necessary for writing behavioral goals and objectives for a child's Individual Developmental Plan (IDP), and (c) to provide the information needed to select activities and write lesson plans."
Scores: 5 Developmental Age scores: Language Comprehension, Language Expression, Avenues to Learning, Social/Personal Behaviors, Motor Behaviors.
Comments: "Criterion-referenced."
Cross References: For a review by Donna Spiker,

see 11:45; for a review by Bonnie W. Camp of an earlier edition, see 9:152.

[305]

The BITCH Test (Black Intelligence Test of Cultural Homogeneity).

Purpose: A vocabulary test of Afro-American expressions used as an intelligence test for blacks and, when administered to whites, as "a measure of sensitivity and responsivity" to black experience.
Population: Adolescents and adults.
Publication Date: 1972.
Acronym: BITCH.
Scores: Total score only.
Price Data, 1982: $10 per 10 tests with directions and key (8 pages); $3.75 per manual (20 pages); $5 per specimen set.
Time: [20–30] minutes.
Comments: Manual also uses the title "The BITCH-100: A Culture-Specific Test."
Author: Robert L. Williams.
Publisher: Williams (Robert L.) and Associates, Inc.
Cross References: See T3:296 (2 references). For additional information and reviews by Lee J. Cronbach and Charles J. Krauskopf, see 8:176 (8 references).

TEST REFERENCES

1. Johnson, A. B., Vickers, L., & Williams, C. (1987). School psychologists' use of techniques for nonbiased assessment. *College Student Journal, 21*, 334–339.

[306]

The Blacky Pictures: A Technique for the Exploration of Personality Dynamics.

Purpose: Designed to identify underlying psychosexual aspects of personality.
Population: Ages 5 and over.
Publication Dates: 1950–67.
Acronym: BP.
Scores, 11: Oral Eroticism, Oral Sadism, Anal Expulsiveness/Retentiveness, Oedipal Intensity, Masturbation Guilt, Castration Anxiety/Penis Envy (female only), Castration Seeking (male only), Identification Process, Sibling Rivalry, Guilt Feeling, Ego Ideal, Narcissistic Love-Object/Anaclitic Love-Object.
Price Data: Not available.
Time: (45) minutes.
Authors: Gerald S. Blum; Scoring Blanks by Earl S. Taulbee and David E. Stenmark.
Publisher: Psychodynamic Instruments [No reply from publisher; status unknown].
Cross References: See T3:298 (3 references) and P:416 (39 references); for a review by Bert R. Sappenfield, see 6:204 (34 references); for a review by Kenneth R. Newton and an excerpted review by Samuel J. Beck, see 5:125 (38 references); for a review by Albert Ellis and excerpted reviews by M. M. Genn, Ephraim Rosen, and Laurance F. Shaffer, see 4:102 (7 references).

TEST REFERENCES

1. Miller, T. W., & Veltkamp, L. J. (1989). Assessment of child sexual abuse: Clinical use of fables. *Child Psychiatry and Human Development, 20*, 123-133.

[307]

Blind Learning Aptitude Test.
Purpose: Designed to obtain a "picture of the learning potential of young blind children."
Population: Blind ages 6–20.
Publication Date: 1971.
Acronym: BLAT.
Scores: Total score only.
Administration: Individual.
Price Data: Available from publisher.
Time: [20–45] minutes.
Comments: Tactual discrimination test not employing Braille stimuli.
Author: T. Ernest Newland.
Publisher: University of Illinois Press.
Cross References: For reviews by Thomas S. Baldwin and Murray H. Tillman, see 8:320 (4 references).

[308]

The Block Survey and S.L.I.D.E.
Purpose: Designed to assess readiness for writing.
Population: Preschool and kindergarten.
Publication Date: 1990.
Scores, 5: Sequence, Language, Identicality, Directionality, Equivalence.
Administration: Individual.
Price Data, 1993: $19 per survey/manual.
Time: (15) minutes.
Comments: Manual contains both The Block Survey and S.L.I.D.E.
Authors: Donna Reid Connell and Theodore A. Callisto.
Publisher: United/DOK Publishers.

[309]

Bloom Sentence Completion Survey.
Purpose: "Designed to reveal subject's attitudes (positive, neutral, and negative) toward important factors in everyday living."
Population: Student ages 6–21, adults.
Publication Dates: 1974–75.
Acronym: BSCS.
Scores, 8: Age-Mates (students)/People (adults), Physical Self, Family, Psychological Self, Self-Directedness, Education (students)/Work (adults), Accomplishment, Irritants.
Administration: Individual.
Levels, 2: Students, Adults.
Price Data, 1994: (For all materials specify student or adult version); $44 per complete kit including 30 sentence completion forms, 30 record forms, and manual; $25 per 30 sentence completion forms and record forms; $25 per student manual ('74, 30 pages) or adult manual ('74, 62 pages).
Time: [20–30] minutes.
Author: Wallace Bloom.

Publisher: Stoelting Co.
Cross References: For reviews by Allen K. Hess and Charles A. Peterson, see 9:153.

[310]

Bloomer Learning Test.
Purpose: Identifies "academic difficulties on the basis of a pattern of strengths and weaknesses in various learning processes."
Population: Grades 1–11 and adults.
Publication Dates: 1978–81.
Acronym: BLT.
Scores: 20 subtest scores: Activity, Response Integration, Boredom, Visual Short-Term Memory, Auditory Short-Term Memory, Visual Apprehension Span, Impulse, Stimulus Complexity, Serial Learning, Recall, Relearning, Learning Set, Free Association, Emotional Ratio, Paired Associate Learning, Paired Associate Decrement, Interference, Concept Recognition, Concept Production, Problem Solving, yielding 3 IQ scores (Simple Learning, Problem Solving, Full Learning).
Administration: Group.
Price Data: Not available.
Time: (55–75) minutes in 2 sessions.
Author: Richard H. Bloomer.
Publisher: Brador Publications, Inc. [No reply from publisher; status unknown].
Cross References: For a review by Edward Earl Gotts, see 9:154.

[311]

Blox Test.
Purpose: Designed to measure the individual's perceptual ability for spatial relations.
Population: Job applicants with at least 10 years of education.
Publication Dates: 1961–63.
Scores: Total score only.
Administration: Group.
Manual: No manual.
Price Data: Available from publisher.
Time: 30(35) minutes.
Comments: Test previously known as Perceptual Battery (T3:1777).
Author: National Institute for Personnel Research of the Human Sciences Research Council.
Publisher: National Institute for Personnel Research of the Human Sciences Research Council [South Africa].

[312]

The Boder Test of Reading-Spelling Patterns.
Purpose: Designed as a diagnostic screening test for developmental dyslexia.
Population: Grades K–12 and adult.
Publication Date: 1982.
Scores, 5: Reading (Level, Age, Quotient), Spelling (Known Words/Correct, Unknown Words/Phonetic Equivalence).
Administration: Individual.

Price Data, 1994: $103.50 per complete kit including 25 reading test record forms, 25 spelling test record forms, 25 alphabet tasks record forms, 25 diagnostic summary record forms, and manual (175 pages); $32 per 25 reading test record forms; $22.50 per 25 spelling test record forms; $22.50 per 25 alphabet tasks record forms; $18 per 25 diagnostic summary forms; $47.50 per manual.

Time: (10–30) minutes.

Authors: Elena Boder and Sylvia Jarrico.

Publisher: The Psychological Corporation.

Cross References: For reviews by Frederick A. Schrank and Timothy Shanahan, see 9:155 (2 references).

TEST REFERENCES

1. Hooper, S. R., & Hynd, G. W. (1985). Differential diagnosis of subtypes of developmental dyslexia with the Kaufman Assessment Battery for Children (K-ABC). *Journal of Clinical Child Psychology, 14,* 145-152.
2. Malatesha, R. N. (1986). Visual motor ability in normal and disabled readers. *Perceptual and Motor Skills, 62,* 627-630.
3. Hooper, S. R. (1988). Relationship between the clinical components of the Boder Test of Reading-Spelling Patterns and the Stanford Achievement Test: Validity of the Boder. *Journal of School Psychology, 26,* 91-96.
4. Levy, F., & Hobbes, G. (1989). Reading, spelling, and vigilance in attention deficit and conduct disorder. *Journal of Abnormal Child Psychology, 17,* 291-298.
5. Flynn, J. M., Deering, W., Goldstein, M., & Rahbar, M. H. (1992). Electrophysiological correlates of dyslexic subtypes. *Journal of Learning Disabilities, 25,* 133-141.

[313]

Boehm Test of Basic Concepts—Preschool Version.

Purpose: To "measure a child's knowledge of twenty-six basic relational concepts considered necessary for achievement in the beginning years of school."

Population: Ages 3-0 to 5-0.

Publication Dates: 1984–86.

Scores: Total score only.

Administration: Individual.

Price Data, 1994: $84 per complete kit including picture book ('86, 112 pages), 35 individual record forms ('86, 5 pages), manual ('86, 35 pages), and class record ('86, 5 pages); $52 per picture book; $30 per 35 individual record forms; $6 per class record form; $24.50 per manual.

Time: (15) minutes.

Comments: Downward extension of the Boehm Test of Basic Concepts (314).

Author: Anne E. Boehm.

Publisher: The Psychological Corporation.

Cross References: For reviews by Judy Oehler-Stinnett and Stephanie Stein, see 11:46 (1 reference).

TEST REFERENCES

1. May, D. C., & Kundert, D. K. (1992). Kindergarten screenings in New York state: Tests, purposes, and recommendations. *Psychology in the Schools, 29*(1), 35-41.

[314]

Boehm Test of Basic Concepts—Revised.

Purpose: "Designed to assess children's mastery of the basic concepts that are both fundamental to understanding verbal instruction and essential for early school achievement."

Population: Grades K–2.

Publication Dates: 1967–86.

Acronym: Boehm-R.

Scores: Total score only.

Administration: Group.

Forms, 3: C, D, Applications (concepts used in combination).

Price Data, 1994: $34.50 per examination kit including 1 copy of each booklet (Forms C, D, and Applications), directions for each form, scoring key, class record, Parent-Teacher Conference report, and manual ('86, 69 pages); $70 per 35 sets of booklets 1 and 2, directions, class record, and scoring key (specify Form C or D); $46 per 35 sets of booklets 1 and 2, directions, class record, and scoring key (Applications); $6 per class record and scoring keys (specify Form C, D, or Applications); $6 per directions (specify Form C, D, or Applications); $32 per 35 Parent-Teacher Conference reports; $26 per manual.

Foreign Language Edition: Spanish edition (1986–88) available.

Time: (30–40) minutes for Form C or D, (15–20) minutes for Applications form.

Authors: Ann E. Boehm.

Publisher: The Psychological Corporation.

a) THE TACTILE TEST OF BASIC CONCEPTS.

Purpose: A tactile analog to the Boehm Test of Basic Concepts.

Population: Blind children grades K–2.

Publication Dates: 1976–86.

Acronym: TTBC.

Scores: Total score only.

Administration: Individual.

Price Data, 1989: $26.49 per complete test including 50 test cards, 5 practice cards, TTBC manual ('86, 22 pages), and Boehm manual ('71, 30 pages).

Time: Administration time not reported.

Author: Hilda R. Caton.

Publisher: American Printing House for the Blind, Inc.

Cross References: For reviews by Robert L. Linn, Colleen Fitzmaurice, and Joseph C. Witt, see 10:32 (16 references); see also T3:302 (18 references); for an excerpted review by Theodore A. Dahl, see 8:178 (22 references); see also T2:344 (1 reference); for reviews by Boyd R. McCandless and Charles D. Smock, and excerpted reviews by Frank S. Freeman, George Lawlor, Victor H. Noll, and Barton B. Proger, see 7:335 (1 reference).

TEST REFERENCES

1. Martin, R. P., Drew, K. D., Gaddis, L. R., & Moseley, M. (1988). Prediction of elementary school achievement from preschool temperament: Three studies. *School Psychology Review, 17,* 125-137.
2. Pilkington, C. L., Piersel, W. C., & Ponterotto, J. G. (1988). Home language as a predictor of first-grade achievement for anglo- and Mexican-American children. *Contemporary Educational Psychology, 13,* 1-14.
3. Stroebel, S. S., & Evans, J. R. (1988). Neuropsychological and environmental characteristics of early readers. *Journal of School Psychology, 26,* 243-252.
4. Glutting, J. J., Kelly, M. S., Boehm, A. E., & Burnett, T. R. (1989). Stability and predictive validity of the Boehm Test of Basic Con-

cepts—Revised among black kindergarteners. *Journal of School Psychology*, *27*, 365-371.

5. Weismer, S. E. (1991). Hypothesis-testing abilities of language-impaired children. *Journal of Speech and Hearing Research, 34*, 1329-1338.

[315]

The Booklet Category Test.
Purpose: Designed to distinguish between normal and brain damaged individuals.
Population: Ages 15 and older.
Publication Dates: 1979–81.
Acronym: BCT.
Scores: Total score only.
Administration: Individual.
Price Data, 1994: $225 per complete kit including 2-volume test, 50 scoring forms, and manual ('79, 21 pages); $22 per 50 scoring forms; $8 per manual.
Time: (30–60) minutes.
Authors: Nick A. DeFilippis and Elizabeth Mc-Campbell.
Publisher: Psychological Assessment Resources, Inc.
Cross References: For reviews by Raymond S. Dean and Thomas A. Hammeke, see 9:156.

TEST REFERENCES

1. Shelton, M. D., & Parsons, O. A. (1987). Alcoholic's self-assessment of their neuropsychological functioning in everyday life. *Journal of Clinical Psychology, 43*, 395-403.
2. Cosgrove, J., & Newell, T. G. (1991). Recovery of neuropsychological functions during reduction in use of phencyclidine. *Journal of Clinical Psychology, 47*, 159-169.
3. Sher, K. J., Walitzer, K. S., Wood, P. K., & Brent, E. E. (1991). Characteristics of children of alcoholics: Putative risk factors, substance use and abuse, and psychopathology. *Journal of Abnormal Psychology, 100*, 427-448.
4. Parsons, O. A. (1994). Neuropsychological measures and event-related potentials in alcoholics: Interrelationships, long-term reliabilities, and prediction of resumption of drinking. *Journal of Clinical Psychology, 50*, 37-46.

[316]

Borromean Family Index.
Purpose: Developed to measure "attitudes and feelings about one's family."
Population: Adolescents and adults.
Publication Date: 1975.
Scores, 2: Internal (forces that attract toward family), External (forces that pull away). 2 Subtests: For Married Persons, For Single Persons.
Administration: Group.
Price Data: Copy of test (may be locally duplicated) and manual (15 pages) available without charge.
Time: [10] minutes.
Comments: Manual is a reprint of a journal article by the author.
Author: Panos D. Bardis.
Publisher: Panos D. Bardis.
Cross References: For additional information, see 8:332 (1 reference).

[317]

Boston Assessment of Severe Aphasia.
Purpose: Developed to identify "preserved abilities that might form the beginning steps of rehabilitation programs for severely aphasic patients."

Population: Aphasic adults.
Publication Date: 1989.
Acronym: BASA.
Scores, 5: Auditory Comprehension, Praxis, Oral-Gestural Expression, Reading Comprehension, Other.
Administration: Individual.
Price Data, 1991: $178.98 per complete kit; $39.99 per package of manipulatives; $30 per set of stimulus cards; $30 per custom aluminum clipboard; $24 per 24 record forms; $30 per manual (96 pages); $30 per briefcase; $48.99 per demonstration video (not included in complete kit).
Time: (30–40) minutes.
Authors: Nancy Helm-Estabrooks, Gail Ramsberger, Alisa R. Morgan, and Marjorie Nicholas.
Publisher: The Riverside Publishing Co.

[318]

Botel Reading Inventory.
Purpose: To "determine the needed program of phonics and spelling instruction" by identifying "the word attack skills of each pupil."
Population: Grades 1–4, 1–6, 1–12.
Publication Dates: 1961–70.
Acronym: BRI.
Scores, 9: Frustration Level, Instructional Level (Placement), and Free Reading Level scores for each of tests *a* and *b*.
Administration: Group.
Price Data, 1994: $15.15 per 35 Word Recognition or Word Opposites tests (specify Form A or B); $17.33 per manual ('70, 33 pages).
Time: Administration time not reported.
Author: Morton Botel.
Publisher: Modern Curriculum Press.
a) WORD RECOGNITION TEST.
Population: Grades 1–4.
Comments: Consists of 8 "graded" 20-word lists described as samples of reading materials at 8 levels.
b) WORD OPPOSITES TEST.
Population: Grades 1–12.
Comments: Vocabulary test described as "an estimate of reading comprehension"; 10 "graded" 10-word lists at 10 levels.
Cross References: For additional information, see T3:309 (1 reference); see also T2:1658 (2 references) and 7:727 (5 references); for reviews by Ira E. Aaron and Charles M. Brown, see 6:834.

TEST REFERENCES

1. Fowler, B. F., & Ross, D. H. (1982). The comparative validities of differential placement measures for college composition courses. *Educational and Psychological Measurement, 42*, 1107-1115.

[319]

Bracken Basic Concept Scale.
Purpose: "To measure a subset of children's receptive vocabulary—basic concepts."
Population: Ages 2-6 to 7-11, 5-0 to 7-0.
Publication Dates: 1984–86.
Acronym: BBCS.

Price Data, 1994: $143.50 per complete set including examiner's manual ('84, 124 pages), Diagnostic Scale stimulus manual ('84, 243 pages), 25 Diagnostic record forms, 1 each of Screening Test Forms A and B; $21 per 25 Diagnostic record forms; $21 per 12 Screening Test booklets (specify A or B); $26.50 per examiner's manual; $95.50 per Diagnostic Scale stimulus manual.

Comments: Can be supplemented with the Bracken Concept Development Program.

Author: Bruce A. Bracken.

Publisher: The Psychological Corporation.

a) DIAGNOSTIC SCALE.

Population: Ages 2-6 to 7-11.

Scores, 8: School Readiness Composite Score, Direction/Position, Social/Emotional, Size, Texture/Material, Quantity, Time/Sequence, Total.

Administration: Individual.

Time: (20–40) minutes.

b) SCREENING TESTS.

Population: 5-0 to 7-0.

Scores: 30 concepts in 8 areas: Comparisons, Shapes, Direction/Position, Social/Emotional, Size, Texture/Material, Quantity, Time/Sequence.

Forms, 2: A, B.

Time: (5–15) minutes.

Cross References: For reviews by Timothy L. Turco and James E. Ysseldyke, see 10:33.

TEST REFERENCES

1. Rhyner, P. M. P., & Bracken, B. A. (1988). Concurrent validity of the Bracken Basic Concept Scale with language and intelligence measures. *Journal of Communication Disorders, 21,* 479-489.
2. Sterner, A. G., & McCallum, R. S. (1988). Relationship of the Gesell Developmental Exam and the Bracken Basic Concept Scale to academic achievement. *Journal of School Psychology, 26,* 297-300.
3. Bracken, B. A., Howell, K. K., Harrison, T. E., Stanford, L. D., & Zahn, B. H. (1991). Ipsative subtest pattern stability of the Bracken Basic Concept Scale and the Kaufman Assessment Battery for Children in a preschool sample. *School Psychology Review, 20,* 315-330.
4. Howell, K. K., & Bracken, B. A. (1992). Clinical utility of the Bracken Basic Concept Scale as a preschool intellectual screener: Comparison with the Stanford-Binet for African-American children. *Journal of Clinical Child Psychology, 21,* 255-261.

[320]

The BrainMap™.

Purpose: "A tool for determining the world-building (or thinking/information-processing) style of individuals and of groups."

Population: Adults.

Publication Dates: 1981–86.

Scores: 4 scales: Posterior Brain Scale, Anterior Brain Scale, Left Brain Scale, Right Brain Scale.

Administration: Group.

Price Data: Not available.

Time: [30–40] minutes.

Comments: Self-administered, self-scored.

Author: Dudley Lynch.

Publisher: Brain Technologies Corporation [No reply from publisher; status unknown].

Cross References: For a review by Manfred J. Meier, see 11:47.

[321]

Brazelton Neonatal Behavioral Assessment Scale.

Purpose: Evaluates an infant's behavioral responses to the environment.

Population: Ages 3 days to 4 weeks.

Publication Dates: 1973–84.

Acronym: BNAS.

Scores, 47: 27 Behavioral Items, 20 Elicited Responses.

Administration: Individual.

Price Data, 1990: $19.50 per manual ('84, 125 pages).

Time: (20–30) minutes.

Author: T. Berry Brazelton.

Publisher: Distributed by J. B. Lippincott Co.

Cross References: See 9:157 (9 references) and T3:311 (31 references); for a review by Anita Miller Sostek, and an excerpted review by Stephen Wolkind, see 8:208 (15 references).

TEST REFERENCES

1. McLaughlin, F. J., O'Connor, S., & Deni, R. (1981). Infant state and behavior during the first postpartum hour. *The Psychological Record, 31,* 455-458.
2. Penman, R., Meares, R., Baker, K., & Milgrom-Friedman, J. (1983). Synchrony in mother-infant interaction: A possible neurophysiological base. *British Journal of Medical Psychology, 56,* 1-7.
3. Belsky, J. (1985). Experimenting with the family in the newborn period. *Child Development, 56,* 407-414.
4. Molfese, V. J., & Thomson, B. (1985). Optimality versus complications: Assessing predictive values of perinatal scales. *Child Development, 56,* 810-823.
5. Honig, A. S. (1986). Stress and coping in children (Part 2): Interpersonal family relationships. *Young Children, 41*(5), 47-59.
6. Belsky, J., & Rovine, M. (1987). Temperament and attachment security in the strange situation: An empirical rapprochement. *Child Development, 58,* 787-795.
7. Schanberg, S. M., & Field, T. M. (1987). Sensory deprivation stress and supplemental stimulation in the rat pup and preterm human neonate. *Child Development, 58,* 1431-1447.
8. Szanjnberg, N., Ward, M. J., Krauss, A., & Kessler, D. B. (1987). Low birth-weight prematures: Preventive intervention and maternal attitude. *Child Psychiatry and Human Development, 17,* 152-165.
9. Johnson, H. L., Glassman, M. B., Fiks, K. B., & Rosen, T. S. (1990). Resilient children: Individual differences in developmental outcome of children born to drug abusers. *The Journal of Genetic Psychology, 151,* 523-539.

[322]

Bricklin Perceptual Scales.

Purpose: Yields information on a child's unconscious or nonverbal perception of his or her parents; for determining which of the parents would make the better primary caretaker for a particular child in child-custody decisions.

Population: Ages 6 and over.

Publication Dates: 1984–92.

Acronym: BPS.

Scores, 10: 5 scores each for mother and father: Perception of Competency, Perception of Supportiveness, Perception of Follow-Up Consistency, Perception of Admirable Character Traits, Total.

Administration: Individual.

Price Data, 1994: $169 per complete kit including 6 sets of 64 test cards, 6 scoring sheets, stylus-pen, foam insert and test box, manual ('92, 102 pages),

instructions, and Bricklin Updates; $69 per 6 additional sets of test cards; $79.95 per IBM computer scoring profile (specify 5.25 inch or 3.5 inch disk).
Time: (20) minutes.
Comments: IBM or compatible computer required for computer scoring profile (unlimited uses).
Author: Barry Bricklin.
Publisher: Village Publishing.
Cross References: For reviews by Rosa A. Hagin and Marcia B. Shaffer, see 11:48.

[323]

Brief Derogatis Psychiatric Rating Scale™.
Purpose: To obtain clinical observers' ratings on nine personality dimensions.
Population: Psychiatric and medical patients.
Publication Date: 1974–78.
Acronym: B-DPRS™.
Scores: 9 dimensions: Somatization, Obsessive-Compulsive, Interpersonal Sensitivity, Depression, Anxiety, Hostility, Phobic Anxiety, Paranoid Ideation, Psychoticism.
Administration: Individual.
Manual: No manual.
Price Data, 1994: $30 per 100 tests.
Time: (5) minutes.
Comments: Formerly the Brief Hopkins Psychiatric Rating Scale; short form of the Derogatis Psychiatric Rating Scale (745); self-report; can also be used with Symptom Checklist-90-Revised (2674) or Brief Symptom Inventory (324).
Author: Leonard R. Derogatis.
Publisher: NCS Assessments.

TEST REFERENCES

1. Rehm, L. P., Kaslow, N. J., & Rabin, A. S. (1987). Cognitive and behavioral targets in a self-control therapy program for depression. *Journal of Consulting and Clinical Psychology, 55,* 60-67.
2. Tracey, T. J. (1987). Stage differences in the dependencies of topic initiation and topic following behavior. *Journal of Counseling Psychology, 34,* 123-131.
3. Tracey, T. J. (1988). Relationship of responsibility attribution congruence to psychotherapy outcome. *Journal of Social and Clinical Psychology, 7,* 131-146.
4. Tracey, T. J., & Dundon, M. (1988). Role anticipations and preferences over the course of counseling. *Journal of Counseling Psychology, 35,* 3-14.
5. Duinkerke, S. J., Botter, P. A., Jansen, A. I., Van Dongen, P. A. M., Van Haaften, A. J., Boom, A. J., Van Laarhoven, J. H. M., & Busard, H. L. S. M. (1993). Ritanserin, a selective 5-HT2/1C antagonist, and negative symptoms in schizophrenia. *British Journal of Psychiatry, 163,* 451-455.

[324]

Brief Symptom Inventory™.
Purpose: "Designed to reflect the psychological symptom patterns of psychiatric and medical patients as well as non-patients."
Population: Adults and adolescents age 13 or older.
Publication Dates: 1975.
Acronym: BSI®.
Scores: 9 primary dimensions: Somatization, Obsessive-Compulsive, Interpersonal Sensitivity, Depression, Anxiety, Hostility, Phobic Anxiety, Paranoid Ideation, Psychoticism; plus 3 global indices: Global Severity Index, Positive Symptom Distress Index, Positive Symptom Total.
Administration: Group.
Price Data, 1994: $75 per hand-scoring starter kit including manual, 50 answer sheets, 50 profile forms, 2 worksheets, answer keys, and bibliography (specify Nonpatient Adult, Nonpatient Adolescent, Outpatient Psychiatric, or Inpatient Psychiatric); $32.50 per 50 hand-scoring answer sheets; $18 per answer keys; $17.50 per 50 profile forms and 2 worksheets (specify Nonpatient Adult, Nonpatient Adolescent, Outpatient Psychiatric, or Inpatient Psychiatric); $19.50 per manual; price information for Interpretive Report and Profile Report scoring and software available from publisher.
Time: (8–10) minutes.
Comments: Essentially the brief form of the Symptom Checklist-90-Revised (2674); self-report; useful in initial evaluation and measurement of patient progress during treatment to monitor change and after treatment for assessment of treatment outcome; companion clinician and observer rating forms are also available.
Authors: Leonard R. Derogatis.
Publisher: NCS Assessments.
Cross References: For reviews by Bert C. Cundick and Charles A. Peterson, see 10:35 (7 references); see also 9:160 (1 reference).

TEST REFERENCES

1. Hale, W. D., & Cochran, C. D. (1983). Sex differences in patterns of self-reported psychopathology in the married elderly. *Journal of Clinical Psychology, 39,* 647-650.
2. Pekarik, G. (1983). Improvement in clients who have given different reasons for dropping out of treatment. *Journal of Clinical Psychology, 39,* 909-913.
3. Cella, D. F., & Tross, S. (1987). Death anxiety in cancer survival: A preliminary cross-validation study. *Journal of Personality Assessment, 51,* 451-461.
4. Hirsch, B. J., & Rapkin, B. D. (1987). The transition to junior high school: A longitudinal study of self-esteem, psychological symptomatology, school life, and social support. *Child Development, 58,* 1235-1243.
5. Thompson, L. W., Gallagher, D., & Breckenridge, J. S. (1987). Comparative effectiveness of psychotherapies for depressed elders. *Journal of Consulting and Clinical Psychology, 55,* 385-390.
6. Tracey, T. J. (1987). Stage differences in the dependencies of topic initiation and topic following behavior. *Journal of Counseling Psychology, 34,* 123-131.
7. Wierzbicki, M., & Bartlett, T. S. (1987). The efficacy of group and individual cognitive therapy for mild depression. *Cognitive Therapy and Research, 11,* 337-342.
8. Cormier, L. S., & Cormier, W. H. (1988). Relation between coping strategies and distress, stress, and marital adjustment of multiple-role women. *Journal of Counseling Psychology, 35,* 187-193.
9. Emmons, R. A., & King, L. A. (1988). Conflict among personal strivings: Immediate and long-term implications for psychological and physical well-being. *Journal of Personality and Social Psychology, 54,* 1040-1048.
10. Hollander, G. R., & Hokanson, J. E. (1988). Dysphoria and the perception of incongruent communications. *Cognitive Therapy and Research, 12,* 577-589.
11. Jones, E. E., Cumming, J. D., & Horowitz, M. J. (1988). Another look at the nonspecific hypothesis of therapeutic effectiveness. *Journal of Consulting and Clinical Psychology, 56,* 48-55.
12. Lewinsohn, P. M., Hoberman, H. M., & Rosenbaum, M. (1988). A prospective study of risk factors for unipolar depression. *Journal of Abnormal Psychology, 97,* 251-264.
13. Puder, R. S. (1988). Age analysis of cognitive-behavioral group therapy for chronic pain outpatients. *Psychology and Aging, 3,* 204-207.
14. Rapp, S. R., Parisi, S. A., & Walsh, D. A. (1988). Psychological dysfunction and physical health among elderly medical inpatients. *Journal of Consulting and Clinical Psychology, 56,* 851-855.

15. Rapp, S. R., Walsh, D. A., Parisi, S. A., & Wallace, C. E. (1988). Detecting depression in elderly medical inpatients. *Journal of Consulting and Clinical Psychology, 56,* 509-513.

16. Tracey, T. J. (1988). Relationship of responsibility attribution congruence to psychotherapy outcome. *Journal of Social and Clinical Psychology, 7,* 131-146.

17. Tracey, T. J., & Dundon, M. (1988). Role anticipations and preferences over the course of counseling. *Journal of Counseling Psychology, 35,* 3-14.

18. Frey, K. S., Greenberg, M. T., & Fewell, R. R. (1989). Stress and coping among parents of handicapped children: A multidimensional approach. *American Journal on Mental Retardation, 94,* 240-249.

19. Gilbar, O. (1989). Who refuses chemotherapy? A profile. *Psychological Reports, 64,* 1291-1297.

20. Kushner, M. G., & Sher, K. J. (1989). Fear of psychological treatment and its relation to mental health service avoidance. *Professional Psychology: Research and Practice, 20,* 251-257.

21. Carscaddon, D. M. (1990). Predicting psychiatric symptoms in rural community mental health clients. *Psychological Reports, 66,* 561-562.

22. Francis, V. M., Rajan, P., & Turner, N. (1990). British community norms for The Brief Symptom Inventory. *British Journal of Clinical Psychology, 29,* 115-116.

23. Frost, R. O., Marten, P., Lahart, C., & Rosenblate, R. (1990). The dimensions of perfectionism. *Cognitive Therapy and Research, 14,* 449-468.

24. Hummer, J. T., & Hokanson, J. E. (1990). The causal relations of attributions for interpersonal events to depression: A prospective longitudinal study. *Journal of Social and Clinical Psychology, 9,* 511-528.

25. King, L. A., & Emmons, R. A. (1990). Conflict over emotional expression: Psychological and physical correlates. *Journal of Personality and Social Psychology, 58,* 864-877.

26. Klar, Y., Mendola, R., Fisher, J. D., Silver, R. C., Chinsky, J. M., & Goff, B. (1990). Characteristics of participants in a large group awareness training. *Journal of Consulting and Clinical Psychology, 58,* 99-108.

27. Palace, E. M., & Gorzalka, B. B. (1990). The enhancing effects of anxiety on arousal in sexually dysfunctional and functional women. *Journal of Abnormal Psychology, 99,* 403-411.

28. Rabkin, J. G., Williams, J. B. W., Neugebauer, R., Remien, R. H., & Goetz, R. (1990). Maintenance of hope in HIV-spectrum homosexual men. *American Journal of Psychiatry, 147,* 1322-1326.

29. Stukenberg, K. W., Dura, J. R., & Kiecolt-Glaser, J. K. (1990). Depression screening scale validation in an elderly, community-dwelling population. *Psychological Assessment, 2,* 134-138.

30. Toseland, R. W., & Smith, G. C. (1990). Effectiveness of individual counseling by professional and peer helpers for family caregivers for the elderly. *Psychology and Aging, 5,* 256-263.

31. Gilewski, M., Farberow, N. L., Gallagher, D. E., & Thompson, L. W. (1991). Interaction of depression and bereavement on mental health in the elderly. *Psychology and Aging, 6,* 67-75.

32. Hafner, R. J., & Miller, R. M. (1991). Predicting schizophrenia outcome with self-report measures of family interaction. *Journal of Clinical Psychology, 47,* 33-41.

33. Hokanson, J. E., Hummer, J. T., & Butler, A. C. (1991). Interpersonal perceptions by depressed college students. *Cognitive Therapy and Research, 15,* 443-457.

34. Norris, F. H., & Kaniasty, K. (1991). The psychological experience of crime: A test of the mediating role of beliefs in explaining the distress of victims. *Journal of Social and Clinical Psychology, 10,* 239-261.

35. Pekarik, G. (1991). Relationship of expected and actual treatment duration for adult and child clients. *Journal of Clinical Child Psychology, 20,* 121-125.

36. Perry, W., & Viglione, D. J., Jr. (1991). The ego impairment index as a predictor of outcome in melancholic depressed patients treated with tricyclic antipressants. *Journal of Personality Assessment, 56,* 487-501.

37. Schacter, D. L., Kaszniak, A. W., Kihlstrom, J. F., & Valdiserri, M. (1991). The relation between source memory and aging. *Psychology and Aging, 6,* 559-568.

38. Thompson, L. W., Gallagher-Thompson, D., Futterman, A., Gilewski, M. J., & Peterson, J. (1991). The effects of late-life spousal bereavement over a 30-month interval. *Psychology and Aging, 6,* 434-441.

39. Braver, M., Bumberry, J., Green, K., & Rawson, R. (1992). Childhood abuse and current psychological functioning in a university counseling center population. *Journal of Counseling Psychology, 39,* 252-257.

40. Donat, D. C., Geczy, B., Jr., Helmrich, J., & LeMay, M. (1992). Empirically derived personality subtypes of public psychiatric patients: Effect on self-reported symptoms, coping inclinations, and evaluation of expressed emotion in caregivers. *Journal of Personality Assessment, 58,* 36-50.

41. Emmons, R. A. (1992). Abstract versus concrete goals: Personal striving level, physical illness and psychological well-being. *Journal of Personality and Social Psychology, 62,* 292-300.

42. Hale, W. D., & Cochran, C. D. (1992). Age differences in self-reported symptoms of psychological distress. *Journal of Clinical Psychology, 48,* 633-637.

43. Hokanson, J. E., & Butler, A. C. (1992). Cluster analysis of depressed college students' social behaviors. *Journal of Personality and Social Psychology, 62,* 273-280.

44. Kashubeck, S., & Christensen, S. A. (1992). Differences in distress among adult children of alcoholics. *Journal of Counseling Psychology, 39,* 356-362.

45. Kleinke, C. L. (1992). How chronic pain patients cope with pain: Relation to treatment outcome in a multidisciplinary pain clinic. *Cognitive Therapy and Research, 16,* 669-685.

46. Kuck, J., Zisook, S., Moranville, J. T., Heaton, R. K., & Braff, D. L. (1992). Negative symptomatology in schizophrenic outpatients. *Journal of Nervous and Mental Disease, 180,* 510-515.

47. Mallinckrodt, B., & Bennett, J. (1992). Social support and the impact of job loss in dislocated blue-collar workers. *Journal of Counseling Psychology, 39,* 482-489.

48. Morgan, L., & Viglione, D. J. (1992). Sexual disturbances, Rorschach sexual responses, and mediating factors. *Psychological Assessment, 4,* 530-536.

49. Pekarik, G. (1992). Relationship of clients' reasons for dropping out of treatment to outcome and satisfaction. *Journal of Clinical Psychology, 48,* 91-98.

50. Shalev, A. Y. (1992). Posttraumatic stress disorder among injured survivors of a terrorist attack: Predictive value of early intrusion and avoidance symptoms. *Journal of Nervous and Mental Disease, 180,* 505-509.

51. Young, T. J. (1992). Locus of control and self-reported psychopathology among Native Americans. *Social Behavior and Personality, 20,* 235-236.

52. Hoyt, W. T., Strong, S. R., Corcoran, J. L., & Robbins, S. B. (1993). Interpersonal influence in a single case of brief counseling: An analytic strategy and a comparison of two indexes of influence. *Journal of Counseling Psychology, 40,* 166-181.

53. Hughes, R., Jr., Good, E. S., & Candell, K. (1993). A longitudinal study of the effects of social support on the psychological adjustment of divorced mothers. *Journal of Divorce & Remarriage, 19,* 37-56.

54. Mallinckrodt, B. (1993). Session impact, working alliance, and treatment outcome in brief counseling. *Journal of Counseling Psychology, 40,* 25-32.

55. Osman, A., Barrios, F. X., Grittmann, L. R., & Osman, J. R. (1993). The Multi-Attitude Suicide Tendency Scale: Psychometric characteristics in an American sample. *Journal of Clinical Psychology, 49,* 701-708.

56. Sexton, H. (1993). Exploring a psychotherapuetic change sequence: Relating process to intersessional and posttreatment outcome. *Journal of Consulting and Clinical Psychology, 61,* 128-136.

57. Tate, D. G., Forchheimer, M., Maynard, F., Davidoff, G., & Dijkers, M. (1993). Comparing two measures of depression in spinal cord injury. *Rehabilitation Psychology, 38,* 53-61.

58. Thompson, M. P., Norris, F. H., & Hanacek, B. (1993). Age differences in the psychological consequences of Hurricane Hugo. *Psychology and Aging, 8,* 606-616.

59. Norris, F. H., & Kaniasty, K. (1994). Psychological distress following criminal victimization in the general population: Cross-sectional, longitudinal, and prospective analyses. *Journal of Consulting and Clinical Psychology, 62,* 111-123.

[325]

Brief Test of Head Injury.

Purpose: Designed to provide information about cognitive, linguistic, and communicative abilities of patients with severe head trauma.

Population: Acute and long-term head-injured adults.

Publication Dates: 1989–91.

Acronym: BTHI.

Scores, 8: Orientation/Attention, Following Commands, Linguistic Organization, Reading Comprehension, Naming, Memory, Visual-Spatial Skills, Total.

Administration: Individual.

Price Data, 1991: $148.98 per complete kit including 24 record forms, manual ('91, 85 pages), manipu-

latives package, stimulus cards and letter board, and carrying case; $24 per 24 record forms; $9.99 per manipulatives package; $45 per stimulus cards and letter board; $24.99 per carrying case; $45 per manual.
Time: (25–30) minutes.
Authors: Nancy Helm-Estabrooks and Gillian Hotz.
Publisher: The Riverside Publishing Company.

[326]

BRIGANCE Diagnostic Assessment of Basic Skills—Spanish Edition.
Purpose: Designed to indicate language dominance and to test for English oral language proficiency.
Population: Grades kindergarten–6.
Publication Date: 1984.
Scores: 102 tests in 10 areas: Readiness, Speech, Functional Word Recognition, Oral Reading, Reading Comprehension, Word Analysis, Listening, Writing and Alphabetizing, Numbers and Computation, Measurement.
Administration: Individual.
Price Data, 1993: $99 per complete set including form (234 pages) including directions of administration and scoring; $25.90 per 10 student record books; $9.95 per optional class record book.
Time: Administration time not reported.
Comments: "Criterion-referenced"; no suggested standards of memory.
Author: Albert H. Brigance.
Publisher: Curriculum Associates, Inc.

[327]

Brigance Diagnostic Comprehensive Inventory of Basic Skills.
Purpose: Designed to assess basic skills in the areas of "readiness, reading, listening, research and study skills, spelling, language, and math."
Population: Grades K–9.
Publication Dates: 1976–83.
Scores: 198 specific-objective tests in 7 areas: Readiness, Reading, Listening, Research and Study Skills, Spelling, Language, Math, for 22 skill areas.
Administration: Individual.
Forms, 2: A, B (for 51 of the tests).
Price Data, 1993: $119 per complete set of tests; $25.95 per 10 student record books; $9.95 per class record book; $12.90 per 10 grade placement profile booklets.
Time: Specific time limits are listed on many tests; others are untimed.
Comments: "Criterion-referenced."
Author: Albert H. Brigance.
Publisher: Curriculum Associates, Inc.
Cross References: For reviews by Craig N. Mills and Mark E. Swerdlik, see 9:162.

[328]

Brigance Diagnostic Inventory of Basic Skills.
Purpose: Designed to "assess basic readiness and academic skills."
Population: Grades K–6.

Publication Date: 1976.
Acronym: IBS.
Scores: 140 specific-objective subtests in 4 areas: Readiness (24 tests), Reading (Word Recognition, 6 tests; Oral Reading, 3 tests; Word Analysis, 19 tests; Vocabulary, 5 tests), Language Arts (Handwriting, 3 tests; Grammar Mechanics, 3 tests; Spelling, 5 tests; Reference Skills, 9 tests), Mathematics (Grade Level: Numbers, 13 tests; Operations, 17 tests; Measurement, 25 tests; Geometry, 8 tests).
Administration: Individual.
Price Data, 1993: $112 per set of tests; $20 per 10 student record books; $9.95 per class record book.
Foreign Language Edition: Spanish edition available.
Time: Specific time limits are listed on many tests; others are untimed.
Comments: "Criterion-referenced"; no suggested standards of mastery for 65% of the tests; complete specimen set not available; preview excerpts free of charge.
Author: Albert Brigance.
Publisher: Curriculum Associates, Inc.
Cross References: For reviews by Corinne Roth Smith and Joseph C. Witt, see 9:163; see also T3:313 (1 reference).

TEST REFERENCES

1. Lindsey, J. D., & Armstrong, S. W. (1984). Performance of EMR and learning-disabled students on the Brigance, Peabody, and Wide Range Achievement Tests. *American Journal of Mental Deficiency, 89,* 197-201.
2. Shelton, T. L., Anastopoulos, A. D., Linden, J. D. (1985). An attribution training program with learning disabled children. *Journal of Learning Disabilities, 18,* 261-265.
3. Beden, I., Rohr, L., & Ellsworth, R. (1987). A public school validation study of the achievement sections of the Woodcock-Johnson Psycho-educational Battery with learning disabled students. *Educational and Psychological Measurement, 47*(3), 711-717.
4. Ault, M. J., Gast, D. L., & Wolery, M. (1988). Comparison of progressive and constant time-delay procedures in teaching community-sign word reading. *American Journal on Mental Retardation, 93,* 44-56.

[329]

Brigance Diagnostic Inventory of Essential Skills.
Purpose: Designed to assess skills seen as necessary for successful functioning as an adult.
Population: Grade 6–adult.
Publication Date: 1981.
Acronym: IES.
Scores: 191 tests in 26 areas: Word Recognition Grade Placement (1 test), Oral Reading (5 tests), Reading Comprehension (9 tests), Functional Word Recognition (6 tests), Word Analysis (9 tests), Reference Skills (5 tests), Schedules and Graphs (3 tests), Writing (7 tests), Forms (2 tests), Spelling (8 tests), Math Grade Placement (2 tests), Numbers (4 tests), Number Facts (4 tests), Computations of Whole Numbers (6 tests), Fractions (9 tests), Decimals (6 tests), Percents (4 tests), Measurement (15 tests), Metrics (16 tests), Math Vocabulary (3 tests), Health and Safety (6 tests), Vocational (23 tests), Money and

Finance (11 tests), Travel and Transportation (10 tests), Food and Clothing (10 tests), Oral Communication and Telephone Skills (7 tests).
Administration: Individual in part.
Price Data, 1993: $139.95 per manual (391 pages); $29.95 per 10 student record books; $9.95 per class record book.
Time: Specific time limits are listed on many tests; others are untimed.
Author: Albert Brigance.
Publisher: Curriculum Associates, Inc.
Cross References: For reviews by Paula Matuszek and Philip A. Saigh, see 9:165.

TEST REFERENCES

1. Lindsey, J. D., & Armstrong, S. W. (1984). Performance of EMR and learning-disabled students on the Brigance, Peabody, and Wide Range Achievement Tests. *American Journal of Mental Deficiency, 89,* 197-201.
2. Ault, M. J., Gast, D. L., & Wolery, M. (1988). Comparison of progressive and constant time-delay procedures in teaching community-sign word reading. *American Journal on Mental Retardation, 93,* 44-56.

[330]

BRIGANCE® Early Preschool Screen for Two-Year-Old and Two-and-a-Half-Year-Old Children.
Purpose: "Criterion-referenced" screen designed "to provide a sampling of a child's learning, development, and skills in a broad range of areas."
Population: Ages 2 to 2 ½ years.
Publication Date: 1990.
Administration: Individual.
Price Data, 1993: $49.95 per manual (69 pages with building blocks); no charge for Spanish directions.
Foreign Language Edition: Spanish component available.
Time: (15–20) minutes.
Comments: Most skills included in the assessments were excerpted from the BRIGANCE® Diagnostic Inventory of Early Development (2256).
Author: Albert H. Brigance.
Publisher: Curriculum Associates, Inc.
a) TWO-YEAR CHILD.
Scores, 9: Builds Tower with Blocks, Visual-Motor Skills, Identifies Body Parts, Picture Vocabulary, Identifies People in Picture by Pointing, Identifies Objects According to Use, Gross-Motor Skills, Verbal Fluency, Total.
Price Data: $16.95 per 30 data sheets ($49.95 per 120-pack).
b) TWO-AND-A-HALF-YEAR CHILD.
Scores, 10: Builds Tower with Blocks, Visual-Motor Skills, Identifies Body Parts, Picture Vocabulary, Identifies People in Picture by Naming, Knows Use of Objects, Quantitative Concepts, Gross-Motor Skills, Verbal Fluency, Total.
Price Data: $17 per 30 data sheets ($50 per 120-pack).
Cross References: For reviews by William M. Bart and Joseph M. Ryan, see 11:49.

[331]

BRIGANCE® K & 1 Screen for Kindergarten and First Grade Children [Revised].
Purpose: Designed to screen for readiness for kindergarten or first grade.
Population: Grades K, 1.
Publication Dates: 1982–92.
Administration: Individual.
Price Data, 1993: $59.90 per manual ('92, 88 pages).
Time: [15–20] minutes per child.
Comments: "Criterion-referenced"; 1987 edition still available.
Author: Albert H. Brigance.
Publisher: Curriculum Associates, Inc.
a) KINDERGARTEN.
Scores, 13: Personal Data Response, Color Recognition, Picture Vocabulary, Visual Discrimination-Forms and Uppercase Letters, Visual-Motor Skills, Gross-Motor Skills, Rote Counting, Identifies Body Parts, Follows Verbal Directions, Numeral Comprehension, Prints Personal Data, Syntax and Fluency, Total.
Price Data: $16.85 per 30 data sheets; $16.85 per 10 class summary folders; $49.85 per 120 3-year data sheets.
b) FIRST GRADE.
Scores, 14: Personal Data Response, Color Recognition, Picture Vocabulary, Visual Discrimination-Lowercase Letters and Words, Visual-Motor Skills, Rote Counting, Recites Alphabet, Numeral Comprehension, Recognition of Lowercase Letters, Auditory Discrimination, Draw A Person, Prints Personal Data, Numerals in Sequence, Total.
Price Data: $17.15 per 30 data sheets; $17.15 per 10 class summary folders; $50.15 per 120 4-year data sheets.
Cross References: For reviews of an earlier edition by Ann E. Boehm and Dan Wright, see 9:166.

TEST REFERENCES

1. Heifeldt, J. P. (1984). The Brigance K & 1 Screen for Kindergarten and First Grade. *The Reading Teacher, 37,* 820-824.
2. Campbell, E., Schellinger, T., & Beer, J. (1991). Relationships among the Ready or Not Parental Checklist for School Readiness, the Brigance Kindergarten and First Grade Screen, and SRA scores. *Perceptual and Motor Skills, 73,* 859-862.
3. May, D. C., & Kundert, D. K. (1992). Kindergarten screenings in New York state: Tests, purposes, and recommendations. *Psychology in the Schools, 29*(1), 35-41.

[332]

Brigance Preschool Screen.
Purpose: Screens a child's basic "skills and behavior in order to identify the child who should be referred for more comprehensive evaluation."
Population: Ages 3–4.
Publication Date: 1985.
Acronym: BPS.
Administration: Individual.
Price Data, 1993: $54 per complete kit including building blocks and manual (88 pages).

Time: (10–20) minutes.
Comments: "Criterion-referenced."
Author: Albert H. Brigance.
Publisher: Curriculum Associates, Inc.
a) AGE 3.
Scores: 11 skills: Personal Data Response, Identifies Body Parts, Gross Motor Skills, Identifies Objects, Repeats Sentences, Visual Motor Skills, Number Concepts, Builds Tower with Blocks, Matches Colors, Picture Vocabulary, Plurals.
Price Data: $17.90 per 30 3-year data sheets; $50 per 120 3-year data sheets.
b) AGE 4.
Scores: 11 skills: Personal Data Response, Identifies Body Parts, Gross Motor Skills, Tells Use of Objects, Repeats Sentences, Visual Motor Skills, Number Concepts, Builds Tower with Blocks, Identifies Colors, Picture Vocabulary, Prepositions and Irregular Plural Nouns.
Price Data: $17.50 per 30 4-year data sheets; $50.15 per 120 4-year data sheets.
Cross References: For reviews by Edith S. Heil and Timothy L. Turco, see 10:36.

[333]

Bristol Achievement Tests.
Purpose: To assess school achievement.
Population: Ages 8-0 to 11-11.
Publication Dates: 1969–82.
Administration: Group.
Levels, 3: 8-0 to 9-11, 9-0 to 10-11, 10-0 to 11-11.
Forms, 2: A, B.
Price Data, 1989: £12.10 per 25 test booklets (select level and form); £5.60 per 25 profiles; £13.80 per teacher's set (without interpretive manual) of any one level (must be purchased to obtain administrative manual); £10.10 per interpretive manual ('69, 84 pages).
Comments: Levels 4 and 5 out of print.
Publisher: NFER-Nelson Publishing Co., Ltd. [England].
a) ENGLISH LANGUAGE.
Scores, 6: Word Meaning, Paragraph Meaning, Sentence Organization, Organization of Ideas, Spelling and Punctuation, Total.
Time: 50(55) minutes.
Authors: Alan Brimer and Herbert Gross.
b) MATHEMATICS.
Scores, 6: Number, Reasoning, Space, Measurement, Arithmetic Laws and Processes, Total.
Time: 55(60) minutes.
Author: Alan Brimer.
c) STUDY SKILLS.
Scores, 6: Properties, Structures, Processes, Explanations, Interpretations, Total.
Time: 50(55) minutes.
Authors: Alan Brimer, Margaret Fidler, Wynne Harlen, and John Taylor.
Cross References: For a review by F. G. Brown of the complete battery, see 9:168; for a review by Roy A. Kress of the English test, see 9:169; for a review

by F. G. Brown of the Mathematics test, see 9:170; for a review by Kenneth J. Smith of the Study Skills test, see 9:171; for reviews by G. A. V. Morgan and A. E. F. Pillner of an earlier edition of the complete battery, see 7:4; for a review by Ralph D. Dutch of an earlier edition of the English test, see 7:185; for a review by Kenneth Lovell of an earlier edition of the Mathematics test, see 7:453; for a review by Elizabeth J. Goodacre of an earlier edition of the Study Skills test, see 7:776.

[334]

Bristol Language Development Scales.
Purpose: To provide "a comprehensive approach to the assessment of language production by children and also to the planning of appropriate therapy."
Population: Ages 1.3 to 5.0.
Publication Date: 1989.
Acronym: BLADES.
Scores, 9: Pragmatics (Function), Semantics (Sentence Meaning, Time and Aspect, Modality), Noun Phrase Elements, Syntactics (Conjunctions, Noun Phrase Structure, Sentence/Clause Structure), Total.
Administration: Individual.
Price Data, 1992: £63.25 per complete kit including 10 record forms, 10 therapy planners, and manual (126 pages); £11.25 per 10 record forms; £14.95 per 10 therapy planners; £28.75 per Language, Learning and Education manual.
Time: Administration time varies (30 minute average recording time).
Comments: The Syntax-free Scale "is intended for use with those children whose symbolic communication is not in English (or contains some non-English elements)"; samples of the child's speech must be tape recorded and transcribed; Therapy Planning Form aids in evaluating gaps in the child's performance and in planning therapy.
Authors: Mary Gutfreund, Maureen Harrison, and Gordon Wells.
Publisher: NFER-Nelson Publishing Co., Ltd. [England].

[335]

Bristol Social Adjustment Guides.
Purpose: "Offer a method for detecting and diagnosing maladjustment, unsettledness or tension in children of school age."
Population: Ages 5–15.
Publication Dates: 1956–74.
Acronym: BSAG.
Scores, 2: Adjustment, Delinquency Prediction.
Administration: Individual.
Restricted Distribution: Not for sale in the United States.
Price Data, 1994: £13.99 per The Child in School pack including 20 copies each of behavioural checklist and diagnostic form; £11.99 per Diagnostic Apparatus; £16.99 per The Child in School.
Time: (15) minutes.

Comments: Ratings by teachers and others; manual title is The Social Adjustment of Children.
Authors: D. H. Stott, E. G. Sykes, and N. C. Marston.
Publisher: Hodder & Stoughton Educational [England].
Cross References: See T3:321 (9 references), T2:1112 (17 references), and P:20 (6 references); for reviews by G. A. V. Morgan and M. L. Kellmer Pringle and excerpted reviews by R. G. Andry, Mary Engel, A. W. Heim, Read D. Tuddenham, and P. E. Vernon, see 6:68 (13 references).

TEST REFERENCES

1. McDermott, P. A. (1980). Prevalence and constituency of behavioral disturbance taxonomies in the regular school population. *Journal of Abnormal Child Psychology, 8,* 523-536.
2. Bell, B., & Cohen, R. (1981). The Bristol Social Adjustment Guide: Comparison between the offspring of alcoholic and non-alcoholic mothers. *British Journal of Clinical Psychology, 20,* 93-95.
3. McDermott, P. A. (1981). Patterns of disturbance in behaviorally maladjusted children and adolescents. *Journal of Clinical Psychology, 37,* 867-874.
4. McDermott, P. A. (1982). Generality of disordered behavior across populations of normal and deviant school children: Factorial relations analyses. *Multivariate Behavioral Research, 17,* 69-85.
5. McDermott, P. A. (1982). Syndromes of social maladaptation among elementary school boys and girls. *Psychology in the Schools, 19,* 281-286.
6. Gregory, H. M., & Beveridge, M. C. (1984). The social and educational adjustment of abused children. *Child Abuse & Neglect, 8,* 525-531.
7. Hale, R. L., & McDermott, P. A. (1984). Pattern analysis of an actuarial strategy for computerized diagnosis of childhood exceptionality. *Journal of Learning Disabilities, 17,* 30-37.
8. McDermott, P. A. (1984). Child behavior disorders by age and sex based on item factoring of the Revised Bristol Guides. *Journal of Abnormal Child Psychology, 12,* 15-36.
9. Li, A. K. F. (1985). Early rejected status and later social adjustment: A 3-year follow up. *Journal of Abnormal Child Psychology, 13,* 567-577.
10. Li, A. K. F. (1986). Low peer interaction in kindergarten children: An ecological perspective. *Journal of Clinical Child Psychology, 15,* 26-29.
11. Hale, R. L., & Dougherty, D. (1988). Differences between Ward's and UPGMA methods of cluster analysis: Implications for school psychology. *Journal of School Psychology, 26,* 121-131.
12. Hundert, J., Bruce Cassie, J. R., & Johnston, N. (1988). Characteristics of emotionally disturbed children referred to day treatment, special-class, outpatient, and assessment services. *Journal of Clinical Child Psychology, 17,* 121-130.
13. Nordick, W. S., & Li, A. K. (1992). Concurrent validity of the School Problem Screening Inventory for behavior-disordered students. *Psychology in the Schools, 29*(2), 126-131.

[336]

The British Ability Scales.
Purpose: To assess children's abilities.
Population: Ages 2.5–17.
Publication Dates: 1977–83.
Acronym: BAS.
Scores: 24 scales in 6 major areas yielding 4 IQ scores: General, Visual, Verbal, Short-Form.
Administration: Individual.
Price Data, 1983: £139 per complete set excluding Manuals 1 and 2; £76 per complete school age scales (ages 5–17); £70 per supplementary preschool and early school scales (ages 2.5–8); £45 per set of supplementary materials (to turn school age set into a complete set); £3.20 per 25 record forms (Form 1);

£16.50 per Manual 3 ('78, 194 pages); £6.50 per Manual 4 ('78, 139 pages); £3.45 per supplement to Manual 4; price data for Manual 1 ('83, 215 pages) and Manual 2 ('83, 239 pages) available from publisher.
Authors: Colin Elliott, David J. Murray (test and Manuals 3 and 4), and Lea S. Pearson (test and Manuals 3 and 4).
Publisher: NFER-Nelson Publishing Co., Ltd. [England].

a) SPEED OF INFORMATION PROCESSING.
Population: Ages 8–17.
Publication Dates: 1977–78.
Price Data: £2.20 per 25 test booklets.
Time: 6.5(10) minutes.
b) REASONING.
Population: Ages 5–17.
Publication Dates: 1977–78.
Price Data: £2.80 per 25 Form 3 record forms.
Time: Administration time not reported.
1) *Formal Operational Thinking.*
Population: Ages 8–17.
Price Data: £2.45 per set of 12 cards.
2) *Matrices.*
Population: Ages 5–17.
Price Data: £8.50 per 10 of each booklet.
3) *Similarities.*
Population: Ages 5–17.
4) *Social Reasoning.*
Population: Ages 5–17.
c) SPATIAL IMAGERY.
Population: Ages 4–17.
Publication Dates: 1977–78.
Price Data: £2.80 per 25 Form 4 record forms.
1) *Block Design.*
Population: Ages 4–17.
Scores: 2 score scales: Level (ages 4–17), Power (ages 5–17).
Price Data: £1.20 per booklet; £2.65 per set of 9 cubes.
Time: 17.5(20) minutes for Level score, 6.5(10) minutes for Power score.
2) *Rotation of Letter-Like Forms.*
Population: Ages 8–14.
Price Data: £1.95 per booklet; 60p per wooden doll.
Time: Administration time not reported.
3) *Visualization of Cubes.*
Population: Ages 8–17.
Price Data: £1.95 per booklet; £3.60 per set of 4 cubes.
Time: Administration time not reported.
d) PERCEPTUAL MATCHING.
Population: Ages 2.5–9.
Publication Dates: 1977–78.
Price Data: £2.80 per 25 Form 7 record forms.
Time: Administration time not reported.
1) *Copying.*
Population: Ages 4–8.
Price Data: £1.40 per booklet.

2) *Matching Letter-Like Forms.*
Population: Ages 5–9.
Price Data: £2.35 per booklet.
3) *Verbal-Tactile Matching.*
Population: Ages 2.5–8.
Price Data: £6.60 per white bag containing objects; £2.30 per green bag containing objects; £1.75 per demonstration bag containing objects.
e) SHORT TERM MEMORY.
Population: Ages 2.5–17.
Publication Dates: 1977–79.
Price Data: £2.80 per 25 Form 5 record forms.
1) *Recall of Designs.*
Population: Ages 5–17.
Price Data: £1 per booklet.
Time: 5 seconds exposure per item up to 19 items.
2) *Immediate Visual Recall/Delayed Visual Recall.*
Population: Ages 5–17.
Scores: 2 scale scores: Immediate, Delayed.
Price Data: 80p per card.
Time: 2 minutes per exposure.
3) *Recall of Digits.*
Population: Ages 2.5–17.
4) *Visual Recognition.*
Population: Ages 2.5–8.
Price Data: £2.65 per booklet.
f) RETRIEVAL AND APPLICATION OF KNOWLEDGE.
Population: Ages 2.5–17.
Publication Dates: 1977–82.
Price Data: £3.20 per 25 Form 6 record forms.
1) *Naming Vocabulary.*
Population: Ages 2.5–8.
Price Data: £3.75 per booklet.
Time: Administration time not reported.
2) *Word Reading.*
Population: Ages 5–14.
Price Data: £1 per card.
Time: Administration time not reported.
3) *Verbal Comprehension.*
Population: Ages 2.5–8.
Price Data: £1.30 per picture of teddy bear; £2.40 per box of toys; £6.40 per inset tray.
Time: Administration time not reported.
4) *Word Definitions.*
Population: Ages 5–17.
Time: Administration time not reported.
5) *Verbal Fluency.*
Population: Ages 3.6–17.
Price Data: £1 per booklet.
Time: Administration time not reported.
6) *Basic Arithmetic.*
Population: Ages 5–14.
Price Data: £1.45 per 25 disposable sheets.
Time: Administration time not reported.
7) *Early Number Skills.*
Population: Ages 2.5–8.
Price Data: £1.95 per booklet; £2.35 per set of 12 cubes.
Time: Administration time not reported.

Cross References: For reviews by Susan Embretson (Whitely) and Benjamin D. Wright and Mark H. Stone, see 9:172 (5 references).

TEST REFERENCES

1. Gregory, H. M., & Beveridge, M. C. (1984). The social and educational adjustment of abused children. *Child Abuse & Neglect, 8,* 525-531.
2. Wallbrown, F. H., McLoughlin, C. S., Elliott, C. D., & Blaha, J. (1984). The hierarchical factor structure of the British Ability Scales. *Journal of Clinical Psychology, 40,* 278-290.
3. Grant, D. W. (1985). Right-hemisphere function in hydrocephalic children. *Neuropsychologia, 23,* 285-289.
4. Wilsher, C., Atkins, G., & Manfield, P. (1985). Effect of Piracetam on dyslexic's reading ability. *Journal of Learning Disabilities, 18,* 19-25.
5. Nicolson, R. I., & Parrott, L. J. M. (1986). Evaluation of the CAGE authoring system for special education. *Programmed Learning & Educational Technology, 23,* 136-143.
6. Rose, D. H., Slater, A., & Perry, H. (1986). Prediction of childhood intelligence from habituation in early infancy. *Intelligence, 10,* 251-263.
7. Ward, J., & Outhred, L. (1986). The use of the British Ability Scales with a group of Australian school children—Some preliminary data. *British Journal of Educational Psychology, 56,* 84-87.
8. Cox, T. (1987). Slow starters versus long term backward readers. *British Journal of Educational Psychology, 57,* 73-86.
9. Elliott, C. D., & Tyler, S. (1987). Learning disabilities and intelligence test results: A principal components analysis of the British Ability Scales. *British Journal of Psychology, 78,* 325-333.
10. Johnston, R. S., Rugg, M. D., & Scott, T. (1987). Phonological similarity effects, memory span and developmental reading disorders: The nature of the relationship. *British Journal of Psychology, 78,* 205-211.
11. Cook, J. (1988). An investigation of the validity of the British Ability Scales with respect to the Wechsler Intelligence Scale for Children—Revised and the Wide Range Achievement Test—Revised on a group of Canadian children. *British Journal of Educational Psychology, 58,* 212-216.
12. McKay, M. F., & Neale, M. D. (1988). Patterns of performance on the British Ability Scales for a group of children with severe reading difficulties. *British Journal of Educational Psychology, 58,* 217-222.
13. Strand, S. C., & Morris, R. C. (1988). Criterion-related versus non-criterion-related prompt training with severely mentally handicapped children. *Journal of Mental Deficiency Research, 32,* 137-151.
14. Tyler, S., & Elliot, C. D. (1988). Cognitive profiles of groups of poor readers and dyslexic children on the British Ability Scales. *British Journal of Psychology, 79,* 493-508.
15. Barwick, J., Valentine, E., West, R., & Wilding, J. (1989). Relations between reading and musical abilities. *British Journal of Educational Psychology, 59,* 253-257.
16. Blatchford, P., Burke, J., Farquhar, C., Plewis, I., & Tizard, B. (1989). Teacher expectations in infant school: Associations with attainment and progress, curriculum coverage and classroom interaction. *British Journal of Educational Psychology, 59,* 19-30.
17. Buckhalt, J. A., & Jensen, A. R. (1989). The British Ability Scales Speed of Information Processing subtest: What does it measure? *British Journal of Educational Psychology, 59,* 100-107.
18. Strand, S. C. (1989). S+ versus S- fading in teaching visual discriminations to severely mentally handicapped children. *Journal of Mental Deficiency Research, 33,* 283-299.
19. Buckhalt, J. A. (1990). Criterion-related validity of The British Ability Scales short-form for black and white children. *Psychological Reports, 66,* 1059-1066.
20. Buckhalt, J. A., Reeve, T. G., & Dornier, L. A. (1990). Correlations of movement time and intelligence: Effects of simplifying response requirements. *Intelligence, 14,* 481-491.
21. Strand, S., Sturmey, P., & Newton, J. T. (1990). A classroom rating scale for use with mentally handicapped children: A replication of the ADIECAS. *British Journal of Clinical Psychology, 29,* 121-123.
22. van der Lely, H. K. J., & Harris, M. (1990). Comprehension of reversible sentences in specifically language-impaired children. *Journal of Speech and Hearing Disorders, 55,* 101-117.
23. Aldrich, F. K., & Wilson, B. (1991). Rivermead Behavioural Memory Test for Children (RBMT-C): A preliminary evaluation. *British Journal of Clinical Psychology, 30,* 161-168.
24. Newman, S., Wright, S., & Fields, H. (1991). Identification of a group of children with dyslexia by means of IQ-achievement discrepancies. *The British Journal of Educational Psychology, 61,* 139-154.
25. Beech, J. R., & Awaida, M. (1992). Lexical and nonlexical

routes: A comparison between normally achieving and poor readers. *Journal of Learning Disabilities, 25,* 196-206.

[337]

British Ability Scales: Spelling Scale.
Purpose: To provide diagnostic information about children's spelling errors.
Population: Ages 5-0 to 14-5.
Publication Date: 1992.
Acronym: BAS.
Scores: Total score only.
Subtests, 4: Four spelling lists A–D.
Administration: Individual or group.
Price Data, 1992: £46 per complete set including manual (34 pages), 50 record forms, and 50 worksheets; £13 per 50 record forms and worksheets.
Time: Administration time not reported.
Comments: Developed to supplement The British Ability Scales (336); included in Americanized version of BAS published as Differential Ability Scales (800).
Author: Colin D. Elliott.
Publisher: NFER-Nelson Publishing Co. Ltd. [England].
Cross References: For reviews by Susan Embretson (Whitely) and by Benjamin D. Wright and Mark H. Stone of The British Ability Scales, see 9:172 (5 references); for reviews by Glen P. Aylward and Robert C. Reinehr of the Differential Ability Scales, see 11:111 (1 reference).

[338]

British Picture Vocabulary Scales.
Purpose: Designed "to screen for receptive language problems, to establish a child's level of receptive vocabulary, and to provide some indication of general ability."
Population: Ages 2.5–18.
Publication Date: 1982.
Acronym: BPVS.
Scores: Total score only.
Administration: Individual.
Forms, 2: Long (156 items) for detailed assessment, short (38 items) for rapid screening.
Price Data, 1989: £55.20 per complete kit including 25 each of long and short form test records, long and short form test plates, and manual; £8.95 per 25 long form test records; £8 per 25 short form test records; £8.95 per manual (73 pages).
Time: (10–20) minutes for long form; (5–15) minutes for short form.
Authors: Lloyd M. Dunn, Leota M. Dunn, Chris Whetton, and David Pintillie.
Publisher: NFER-Nelson Publishing Co., Ltd. [England].

TEST REFERENCES

1. Griffiths, P., Boggan, J., Tutt, G., & Dickens, P. (1985). Visual discrimination learning in mentally handicapped adults: Comparative effects of two-choice and multiple-choice training methods on stimulus generalization performance. *Journal of Mental Deficiency Research, 29,* 347-357.
2. Rose, D. H., Slater, A., & Perry, H. (1986). Prediction of childhood intelligence from habituation in early infancy. *Intelligence, 10,* 251-263.
3. Snowling, M., Goulandris, N., Bowlby, M., & Howell, P. (1986). Segmentation and speech perception in relation to reading skill: A developmental analysis. *Journal of Experimental Child Psychology, 41,* 489-507.
4. Hobson, R. P., Ouston, J., & Lee, A. (1988). Emotion recognition in autism: Coordinating faces and voices. *Psychological Medicine, 18,* 911-923.
5. Hobson, R. P., Ouston, J., & Lee, A. (1988). What's in a face? The case of autism. *British Journal of Psychology, 79,* 441-453.
6. Bishop, D. V. M., & Robson, J. (1989). Accurate non-word spelling despite congenital inability to speak: Phoneme-grapheme conversation does not require subvocal articulation. *British Journal of Psychology, 80,* 1-13.
7. Espie, C. A., Pashley, A. S., Bonham, K. G., Sourindhrin, I., & O'Donovan, M. (1989). The mentally handicapped person with epilepsy: A comparative study investigating psychosocial functioning. *Journal of Mental Deficiency Research, 33,* 123-125.
8. Hobson, R. P., Ouston, J., & Lee, A. (1989). Recognition of emotion by mentally retarded adolescents and young adults. *American Journal on Mental Retardation, 93,* 434-443.
9. McPhail, C. H., & Chamove, A. S. (1989). Relaxation reduces disruption in mentally handicapped adults. *Journal of Mental Deficiency Research, 33,* 399-406.
10. Reed, J., & Clements, J. (1989). Assessing the understanding of emotional states in a population of adolescents and young adults with mental handicaps. *Journal of Mental Deficiency Research, 33,* 229-233.
11. Stansfield, J. (1990). Prevalence of stuttering and cluttering in adults with mental handicaps. *Journal of Mental Deficiency Research, 34,* 287-307.
12. van der Lely, H. K. J., & Harris, M. (1990). Comprehension of reversible sentences in specifically language-impaired children. *Journal of Speech and Hearing Disorders, 55,* 101-117.
13. Clegg, J. A., & Standen, P. J. (1991). Friendship among adults who have developmental disabilities. *American Journal on Mental Retardation, 95,* 663-671.
14. Webb, T., & Thake, A. (1991). Moderate and mild mental retardation in the Martin-Bell syndrome. *Journal of Mental Deficiency Research, 35,* 521-528.
15. Beech, J. R., & Awaida, M. (1992). Lexical and nonlexical routes: A comparison between normally achieving and poor readers. *Journal of Learning Disabilities, 25,* 196-206.
16. Gathercole, S. E., Willis, C. S., Emslie, H., & Baddeley, A. D. (1992). Phonological memory and vocabulary development during the early school years: A longitudinal study. *Developmental Psychology, 28,* 887-898.

[339]

Bruce Vocabulary Inventory.
Purpose: Constructed to measure vocabulary.
Population: Business and industry.
Publication Dates: 1959–84.
Scores: Total score only.
Administration: Group.
Price Data, 1993: $49.50 per test package; $23.50 per IBM answer sheet package; $9 per set of IBM scoring stencils; $2.50 per set of keys; $24 per manual ('59, 4 pages) and manual supplement ('84, 17 pages); $34.50 per IBM specimen set.
Time: (15–20) minutes.
Author: Martin M. Bruce.
Publisher: Martin M. Bruce, Ph.D., Publishers.
Cross References: For reviews by Fred H. Borgen and Robert Fitzpatrick, see 7:231.

[340]

Bruininks-Oseretsky Test of Motor Proficiency.
Purpose: Designed to "assess the motor functioning of children."
Population: Ages 4-5 to 14-5.
Publication Date: 1978.
Scores, 3: Gross Motor Composite, Fine Motor Composite, Battery Composite.

Administration: Individual.
Price Data, 1993: $399.95 per kit including 25 student booklets, 25 record forms for complete battery/short form, and manual (153 pages); $17.95 per 25 record forms for complete battery/short form; $9.95 per 25 record forms for short form; $18 per 25 student booklets; $59.45 per manual; $62.45 per balance beam; $5.45 per response speed stick; $4.65 per target.
Time: (45–60) minutes for long form; (15–20) minutes for short form.
Comments: Revised edition of the Oseretsky Tests of Motor Proficiency.
Author: Robert H. Bruininks.
Publisher: American Guidance Service.
Cross References: For a review by David A. Sabatino, see 9:174 (7 references); see T3:324 (3 references) and T2:1898 (15 references) for references of an earlier edition; for a review by Anna Espenschade, see 4:650 (10 references); for an excerpted review, see 3:472 (6 references).

TEST REFERENCES

1. Hinojosa, J., Anderson, J., Goldstein, P. K., & Becker-Lewin, M. (1982). Roles and functions of the occupational therapist in the treatment of sensory integrative dysfunction. *The American Journal of Occupational Therapy, 36,* 832-834.
2. Ziviani, J., Poulsen, A., & O'Brien, A. (1982). Correlation of the Bruininks-Oseretsky Test of Motor Proficiency with the Southern California Sensory Integration Tests. *The American Journal of Occupational Therapy, 36,* 519-523.
3. Lewandowski, L., Costenbader, V., & Richman, R. (1985). Neuropsychological aspects of Turner syndrome. *Clinical Neuropsychology, 7,* 144-147.
4. Butterfield, S. A., & Ersing, W. F. (1986). Influence of age, sex, etiology, and hearing loss on balance performance by deaf children. *Perceptual and Motor Skills, 62,* 659-663.
5. Church, G. E., & Broadhead, G. D. (1986). Small sample validation of discriminant analysis of motor proficiency. *Perceptual and Motor Skills, 62,* 903-909.
6. Freides, D., & Messina, C. A. (1986). Memory improvement via motor encoding in learning disabled children. *Journal of Learning Disabilities, 19,* 113-115.
7. Moore, J. B., Reeve, T. G., & Boan, T. (1986). Reliability of the short form of the Bruininks-Oseretsky Test of Motor Proficiency with five-year-old children. *Perceptual and Motor Skills, 62,* 223-226.
8. Butterfield, S. A., & Ersing, W. F. (1987). Age, sex, hearing loss, and balance in development of jumping by deaf children. *Perceptual and Motor Skills, 64,* 942.
9. Butterfield, S. A., & Ersing, W. F. (1987). Influence of age, sex, hearing loss, and balance on kicking development by deaf children. *Perceptual and Motor Skills, 65,* 312.
10. Hattie, J., & Edwards, H. (1987). A review of the Bruininks-Oseretsky Test of Motor Proficiency. *British Journal of Educational Psychology, 57,* 104-113.
11. Steffens, K. M., Semmes, R., Werder, J. K., & Bruininks, R. H. (1987). Relationship between quantitative and qualitative measures of motor development. *Perceptual and Motor Skills, 64,* 985-986.
12. Lewis, B. A., Ekelman, B. L., & Aram, D. M. (1989). A family study of severe phonological disorders. *Journal of Speech and Hearing Research, 32,* 713-724.
13. Butterfield, S. A. (1990). Influence of age, sex, hearing loss, and balance on development of sidearm striking by deaf children. *Perceptual and Motor Skills, 70,* 361-362.
14. Lewis, B. A. (1990). Familial phonological disorders: Four pedigrees. *Journal of Speech and Hearing Disorders, 55,* 160-170.
15. Spiegel, A. N., Steffens, K. M., Rynders, J. E., & Bruininks, R. H. (1990). The Early Motor Profile: Correlation with the Bruininks-Oseretsky Test of Motor Proficiency. *Perceptual and Motor Skills, 71,* 645-646.
16. Melograno, V. J., & Loovis, E. M. (1991). Effects of field-based training on teachers' knowledge and attitudes and the motor proficiency of their handicapped students. *Perceptual and Motor Skills, 72,* 1211-1214.
17. Butterfield, S. A., & Loovis, E. M. (1993). Influence of age, sex,

balance, and sport participation on development of throwing by children in grades K–8. *Perceptual and Motor Skills, 76,* 459-464.
18. DePaepe, J. L., & Ciccaglione, S. (1993). A dynamic balance measure for persons with severe and profound mental retardation. *Perceptual and Motor Skills, 76,* 619-627.

[341]
Buffalo Reading Test for Speed and Comprehension.
Purpose: "To study either the correlates of, or improvement in, speed and comprehension in reading."
Population: Grades 9–16.
Publication Dates: 1933–65.
Scores, 3: Speed, Comprehension, Total.
Administration: Group.
Forms, 2: A, B.
Price Data: Available from publisher.
Time: 30(35) minutes.
Authors: Mazie Earle Wagner and Daniel S. P. Schubert (1965 manual).
Publisher: Mazie Earle Wagner.
Cross References: See T2:1534 (1 reference); for reviews by Holland Roberts and William W. Turnbull, see 3:477.

[342]
Burks' Behavior Rating Scales.
Purpose: Identify "particular behavior problems and patterns of problems shown by children."
Population: Preschool–grade 9.
Publication Dates: 1968–77.
Acronym: BBRS.
Administration: Individual.
Price Data, 1993: $25 per 25 test booklets and profile sheets; $19.50 per 10 parents' guides; $24.50 per 10 teacher's guides; $45 per practitioner-oriented handbook.
Time: Administration time not reported.
Comments: Ratings of problem children by teachers or parents.
Author: Harold F. Burks.
Publisher: Western Psychological Services.
a) PRESCHOOL AND KINDERGARTEN.
Population: Ages 3–6.
Scores, 18: Excessive Self-Blame, Excessive Anxiety, Excessive Withdrawal, Excessive Dependency, Poor Ego Strength, Poor Physical Strength, Poor Coordination, Poor Intellectuality, Poor Attention, Poor Impulse Control, Poor Reality Contact, Poor Sense of Identity, Excessive Suffering, Poor Anger Control, Excessive Sense of Persecution, Excessive Aggressiveness, Excessive Resistance, Poor Social Conformity.
Price Data: $50 per complete kit including 25 test booklets and profile sheets and manual ('77, 41 pages); $27.50 per manual.
b) GRADES 1–9.
Population: Grades 1–9.
Scores, 19: Same scores as *a* above plus Poor Academics.
Price Data: $98.50 per complete kit including 25

test booklets and profile sheets, manual ('77, 53 pages), 2 parents' guides, 2 teacher's guides, and practitioner-oriented handbook; $30 per manual.

Cross References: For reviews by Lisa G. Bischoff and Leland C. Zlomke and Brenda R. Bush, see 11:50 (7 references); see also T3:328 (1 reference), T2:1115 (1 reference), and 7:46 (2 references).

TEST REFERENCES

1. LeVine, E., Rittenhouse, J. A., Smith, G., & Thompson, T. (1981). A cojoint, operant model for assisting profoundly behaviorally disordered adolescents. *Adolescence, 16,* 299-307.
2. Lewis, S., Horton, F. T., & Armstrong, S. (1981-82). Distress in fatally and chronically ill children: Methodological note. *OMEGA, 12,* 293-306.
3. Fontenelle, S., & Alarcon, M. (1982). Hyperlexia: Precocious word recognition in developmentally delayed children. *Perceptual and Motor Skills, 55,* 247-252.
4. LeVine, E., & Greer, M. (1984). Long-term effectiveness of the Adolescent Learning Center: A challenge to the concept of least restrictive environment. *Adolescence, 19,* 521-526.
5. Morgan, S. R. (1992). An analysis of behavioral differences of emotionally disturbed children assessed high on creativity. *Psychology in the Schools, 29,* 301-306.

[343]

Burns/Roe Informal Reading Inventory: Preprimer to Twelfth Grade, Third Edition.

Purpose: Provides information about the reading skills, abilities, and needs of individual students in order to plan an appropriate program of reading instruction.

Population: Beginning readers–grade 12.

Publication Dates: 1985–89.

Acronym: IRI.

Scores, 2: Word Recognition, Comprehension.

Administration: Individual.

Levels, 14: Preprimer, Primer, First Reader, Second Grade, Third Grade, Fourth Grade, Fifth Grade, Sixth Grade, Seventh Grade, Eighth Grade, Ninth Grade, Tenth Grade, Eleventh Grade, Twelfth Grade.

Price Data: Available from publisher.

Time: (40–50) minutes.

Comments: No time limit.

Authors: Betty D. Roe and Paul C. Burns.

Publisher: Houghton Mifflin Co.

Cross References: For reviews by Carolyn Colvin Murphy and Roger H. Bruning and by Edward S. Shapiro of an earlier edition, see 10:37.

[344]

Burt Word Reading Test, New Zealand Revision.

Purpose: Designed to provide an estimate of word recognition skills for 110 words.

Population: Ages 6-0 to 12-11 years.

Publication Date: 1981.

Scores: 1 overall performance score.

Administration: Individual.

Price Data, 1987: NZ$1.50 per 20 tests; $.40 per test card; $2.25 per manual (10 pages); $2.75 per specimen set.

Time: Untimed.

Comments: Revision and New Zealand standardization of the Burt Word Reading Test; identical to 1974 revision except for word order.

Authors: Alison Gilmore, Cedric Croft, and Neil Reid.

Publisher: New Zealand Council for Educational Research [New Zealand].

Cross References: For reviews by Mark W. Aulls and John Elkins, see 9:175 (2 references).

TEST REFERENCES

1. Silva, P. A. (1986). A comparison of the predictive validity of the Reynell Developmental Language Scales, the Peabody Picture Vocabulary Test and the Stanford-Binet Intelligence Scale. *British Journal of Educational Psychology, 56,* 201-204.
2. Thompson, G. B. (1986). When nonsense is better than sense: Non-lexical errors to word reading tests. *British Journal of Educational Psychology, 56,* 216-219.
3. Beale, I. L., Matthew, P. J., Oliver, S., & Corballis, M. C. (1987). Performance of disabled and normal readers on the continuous performance test. *Journal of Abnormal Child Psychology, 15,* 229-238.
4. Werry, J. S., Elkind, G. S., & Reeves, J. C. (1987). Attention deficit, conduct, oppositional, and anxiety disorders in children: III. Laboratory differences. *Journal of Abnormal Child Psychology, 15,* 409-428.

[345]

Bury Infant Check.

Purpose: To aid in identifying children with special needs.

Population: Children in second term of infant school.

Publication Date: 1986.

Acronym: BIC.

Administration: Individual.

Price Data, 1989: £7.20 per 10 Full Check record booklets; £5.50 per 25 Quick Check record forms; £10.30 per teacher's set including Full Check record booklet, Quick Check record form, and manual (36 pages).

Authors: Lea Pearson and John Quinn.

Publisher: NFER-Nelson Publishing Co., Ltd. [England].

a) QUICK CHECK.

Scores, 3: Language Expression, Learning Style, Total.

Time: (3–4) minutes.

Comments: Teacher-rated.

b) FULL CHECK.

Scores, 12: Language Skills (Comprehension, Expression, Total), Learning Style, Memory Skills (Visual, Auditory, Total), Number Skills, Perceptual Motor Skills (Copying Shapes, Visual Discrimination, Total), Total.

Time: (20) minutes.

Cross References: For a review by Stephan A. Henry, see 9:38.

[346]

Business Analyst Skills Evaluation.

Purpose: "Measures practical and analytical skills required for the position of Business Systems Analyst."

Population: Candidates for Business Analyst positions.

Publication Date: 1984.

Scores: 20 subtests: Logic/Flow Charting/Problem Solving, Systems Analysis, Communication Skills, Memory, Emotional Stability, People Contact Desired, Extroversion, Maturity, Dominance, Enthusiasm, Consistency, Adventurousness, Toughmindedness, Practicality, Sophistication, Self-Confidence, Self-Sufficiency, Participating, Leadership Potential, Initiative and Drive.

Administration: Group.

Price Data, 1993: $299 per person.

Time: (210) minutes.

Author: Bruce A. Winrow.

Publisher: Walden Personnel Testing & Training, Inc.

Cross References: For a review by Lenore W. Harmon, see 10:39.

[347]

Business Judgment Test, Revised.

Purpose: "Designed to be a measure of empathy or 'feel' for the generally accepted ideas and opinions on desirable courses of action in interpersonal relationships."

Population: Adults.

Publication Dates: 1953–84.

Acronym: BJT.

Scores: Total score only.

Administration: Group.

Price Data, 1993: $48.50 per test package; $2.50 per scoring key; $35 per manual ('65, 12 pages) and manual supplement ('84, 17 pages); $35.50 per specimen set.

Time: (10–20) minutes.

Author: Martin M. Bruce.

Publisher: Martin M. Bruce, Ph.D., Publishers.

Cross References: See T2:2275 (1 reference); for a review by Jerome E. Doppelt, and an excerpted review by Kenneth D. Orton, see 7:1059 (1 reference); see also 6:1101 (4 references); for a review by Edward B. Greene, see 5:893.

[348]

Buswell-John Diagnostic Test for Fundamental Processes in Arithmetic.

Purpose: Assesses how children work through arithmetic computation problems.

Population: Pupils doing unsatisfactory work in arithmetic.

Publication Dates: No date on test material.

Scores: No scores.

Administration: Individual.

Price Data: Not available.

Time: (15–20) minutes.

Authors: G. T. Buswell and Lenore John.

Publisher: Allen House [No reply from publisher; status unknown].

Cross References: For reviews by Frank A. Broadbent and Linda Jensen Sheffield, see 9:176 (4 references).

[349]

The Butler Life Science Concept Test.

Purpose: "Constructed . . . for measuring the beginning concepts . . . of living things."

Population: Grades 1–6.

Publication Dates: 1965–69.

Scores, 2: Concept, Percept.

Administration: Group.

Price Data, 1985: $13.75 per 25 test booklets; $5 per specimen set.

Time: (20–40) minutes.

Author: D. F. Butler.

Publisher: Psychometric Affiliates.

Cross References: For a review by Victor H. Noll, see 7:786.

[350]

The CAHPER Fitness Performance II Test.

Purpose: Designed "to assess fitness of men and women" and "to establish normative data . . . measured in *metric units*."

Population: Ages 7–17.

Publication Dates: 1966–80.

Scores, 6: Speed Sit Up, Standing Long Jump, Flexed Arm Hang, Shuttle Run, 50 Metre Run, Endurance Run.

Administration: Largely individual.

Price Data, 1984: $6.95 per manual ('80, 90 pages).

Foreign Language Edition: Manual written in both English and French.

Time: Administration time not reported.

Author: Canadian Association for Health, Physical Education and Recreation.

Publisher: Canadian Association for Health, Physical Education and Recreation.

Cross References: See T3:599 (1 reference), T2:919 (2 references), and 7:599 (1 reference).

[351]

CAI Study Skills Test.

Purpose: "Procedure for measuring a student's knowledge about efficient study behavior and effective scholastic motivation."

Population: College-bound high school seniors and college freshmen.

Publication Dates: 1981–83.

Acronym: SST.

Scores, 11: Time Management, Memory Improvement, Note Taking, Textbook Reading, Examination Taking, Report Writing, Oral Reporting, Scholastic Motivations, Interpersonal Relations, Concentration Improvement, Total (Study Effectiveness).

Administration: Group.

Price Data: Not available.

Time: (55) minutes.

Comments: Based upon Effective Study Test (864).

Authors: William F. Brown and Bernadette Gadzella.

Publisher: Effective Study Materials [No reply from publisher; status unknown].

TEST REFERENCES

1. Gadzella, B. M., & Williamson, J. D. (1984). Study skills, self-concept, and academic achievement. *Psychological Reports, 54,* 923-929.
2. Gadzella, B. M., Ginther, D. W., & Williamson, J. D. (1987). Study skills, learning processes and academic achievement. *Psychological Reports, 61,* 167-172.

[352]

California Achievement Tests, Forms E and F.

Purpose: "To measure achievement in the basic skills commonly found in state and district curricula."

Population: Grades K.0–K.9, K.6–2.2, 1.6–3.2, 2.6–4.2, 3.6–5.2, 4.6–6.2, 5.6–7.2, 6.6–8.2, 7.6–9.2, 8.6–11.2, 10.6–12.9.

Publication Dates: 1957–85.

Acronym: CAT/E & F.

Administration: Group.

Levels: 11 overlapping levels.

Forms, 2: E, F.

Price Data, 1993: $22.75 per 35 locator tests with answer sheets and directions (specify Grades 1–6 or Grades 6–12); $31.95 per set of 3 hand-scoring stencils for use with CompuScan answer sheets (specify Level 14, 15, 16, 17, 18, 19, or 20 and Form E or F); $23 per 50 CompuScan Complete Battery answer sheets, Levels 14–20; $13 per 50 CompuScan answer sheets, Levels 14–20 (specify Reading, Mathematics, or Listening Test/Writing Assessment/Optional Testing); $17 per 25 SCOREZE answer sheets (specify Reading and Study Skills, Mathematics, Language and Spelling, or Science and Social Studies and indicate Level 14–20); $17.50 per 50 answer sheets for Locator Tests 1 and 2; $1.18 per class record sheet for hand recording; $29 per 100 student diagnostic profile sheets for hand recording (specify Level 10–20); $6.35 per Directions, Locator Tests 1–2; $11.75 per Test Coordinator's Handbook; $11.75 per Technical Report; $19.55 per Class Management Guide; $8.35 per Multi-Level Norms book (specify Fall, Winter, or Spring); scoring service available from publisher.

Comments: Form F available in Levels 13–20 only.

Author: CTB MacMillan/McGraw-Hill.

Publisher: CTB MacMillan/McGraw-Hill.

a) LEVEL 10.

Population: Grades K.0–K.9.

Scores, 6: Reading (Visual Recognition, Sound Recognition, Vocabulary, Comprehension), Language Expression, Mathematics Concepts and Applications.

Price Data: $8.40 per 35 practice tests; $8.35 per Form E examiner's manual ('85, 45 pages).

Time: (154–169) minutes in 3 sessions.

1) *Hand-Scorable Booklet.*

Price Data: $60.20 per 35 Form E Complete Battery booklets including examiner's manual and scoring key.

2) *Machine-Scorable Booklet.*

Price Data: $101.50 per 35 Form E Complete Battery booklets including examiner's manual.

b) LEVEL 11.

Population: Grades K.6–2.2.

Scores, 6: Reading (Word Analysis, Vocabulary, Comprehension), Language Expression, Mathematics Concepts and Applications.

Price Data, 1986: $8.40 per 35 practice tests; $8.35 per Form E examiner's manual ('85, 44 pages).

Time: (175–190) minutes in 3 sessions.

1) *Hand-Scorable Booklet.*

Price Data: $60.20 per 35 Form E Complete Battery booklets including examiner's manual and scoring key.

2) *Machine-Scorable Booklet.*

Price Data: $101.70 per 35 Form E Complete Battery booklets including examiner's manual.

c) LEVEL 12.

Population: Grades 1.6–3.2.

Scores, 10: Reading (Word Analysis, Vocabulary, Comprehension), Spelling, Language (Language Mechanics, Language Expression), Mathematics (Mathematics Computation, Mathematics Concepts and Applications), Science (optional), Social Studies (optional).

Price Data: $8.35 per Form E examiner's manual ('85, 49 pages).

Time: (315–330) minutes in 3 or 4 sessions (including optional tests).

1) *Hand-Scorable Booklet.*

Price Data: $67.55 per 35 Form E Complete Battery booklets including examiner's manual and scoring key; $60.90 per 35 Form E Basic Skills Battery booklets.

2) *Machine-Scorable Booklet.*

Price Data: $105.70 per 35 Form E Complete Battery booklets.

d) LEVEL 13.

Population: Grades 2.6–4.2.

Scores, 10: Same as for *c* above.

Price Data: $8.75 per 35 practice tests; $8.35 per Form E or Form F examiner's manual ('85, 49 pages).

Time: (354–369) minutes in 3 or 4 sessions.

1) *Hand-Scorable Booklet.*

Price Data: Same as for *c* above.

Comments: Complete Battery booklet available in both Form E and Form F.

2) *Machine-Scorable Booklet.*

Price Data: Same as for *c* above.

Comments: Complete Battery booklet available in both Form E and Form F.

e) LEVEL 14.

Population: Grades 3.6–5.2.

Scores, 11: Reading (Word Analysis, Vocabulary, Comprehension), Spelling, Language (Language Mechanics, Language Expression), Mathematics

(Mathematics Computation, Mathematics Concepts and Applications), Study Skills, Science (optional), Social Studies (optional).

Price Data: $12.25 per 35 practice tests; $91 per 35 Complete Battery Form E or Form F reusable test booklets; $88.55 per 35 Form E Basic Skills Battery reusable test booklets; $8.35 per Form E and Form F examiner's manual for Levels 14–20 ('85, 51 pages).

Time: (408–423) minutes in 3 or 4 sessions.

f) LEVEL 15.

Population: Grades 4.6–6.2.

Scores, 11: Same as for *e* above.

Price Data: Same as for *e* above.

Time: (408–423) minutes.

g) LEVEL 16.

Population: Grades 5.6–7.2.

Scores, 11: Same as for *e* above.

Price Data: Same as for *e* above.

Time: (408–423) minutes.

h) LEVEL 17.

Population: Grades 6.6–8.2.

Scores, 10: Same as for *e* above but without Word Analysis.

Price Data: Same as for *e* above.

Time: (393–408) minutes.

i) LEVEL 18.

Population: Grades 7.6–9.2.

Scores, 10: Same as for *h* above.

Price Data: Same as for *e* above.

Time: (393–408) minutes.

j) LEVEL 19.

Population: Grades 8.6–11.2.

Scores, 10: Same as for *h* above.

Price Data: Same as for *e* above.

Time: (393–408) minutes.

k) LEVEL 20.

Population: Grades 10.6–12.9.

Scores, 10: Same as for *h* above.

Price Data: Same as for *e* above.

Cross References: For reviews by Peter W. Airasian and James L. Wardrop, see 10:41 (68 references); for reviews by Bruce G. Rogers and Victor L. Willson of the 1978 edition, see 9:180 (19 references); see also T3:344 (68 references); for reviews by Miriam M. Bryan and Frank Womer of the 1970 edition, see 8:10 (33 references); for reviews by Jack C. Merwin and Robert D. North of the 1957 edition, see 6:3 (19 references); for a review by Charles O. Neidt, see 5:2 (10 references); for reviews by Warren G. Findley, Alvin W. Schindler, and J. Harlan Shores of the 1950 edition, see 4:2 (8 references); for a review by Paul A. Witty of the 1943 edition, see 3:15 (3 references); for reviews by C. W. Odell and Hugh B. Wood of an earlier edition, see 2:1193 (1 reference); for a review by D. Welty Lefever and an excerpted review by E. L. Abell, see 1:876. For reviews of subtests, see 8:45 (2 reviews), 8:257 (1 review), 8:719 (2 reviews), 6:251 (1 review), 5:177 (2 reviews), 5:468 (1 review), 4:151 (2 reviews), 4:411 (1 review), 4:530 (2 reviews, 1 excerpt), 2:1292 (2 reviews), 2:1459 (2 reviews), 2:1563 (1 review), 1:893 (1 review), and 1:1110 (2 reviews).

TEST REFERENCES

1. Faller, G. B., & Wallbrown, F. H. (1983). Comparison of the Minnesota Percepto-Diagnostic Test and Bender-Gestalt: Relationship with achievement criteria. *Journal of Clinical Psychology, 39*, 985-988.
2. White, M., & Miller, S. R. (1983). Dyslexia: A term in search of a definition. *The Journal of Special Education, 17*, 5-10.
3. Bryant-Tuckett, R., & Silverman, L. H. (1984). Effects of the subliminal stimulation of symbiotic fantasies on the academic performance of emotionally handicapped students. *Journal of Counseling Psychology, 31*, 295-305.
4. Carswell, L., & White, W. F. (1984). Problems of reporting socioeconomic bias among reading scores and standardized reading tests. *Perceptual and Motor Skills, 58*, 181-182.
5. Tepper, M. E., & Powers, S. (1984). Prediction of high school algebra achievement with attributional, motivational, and achievement measures. *Perceptual and Motor Skills, 59*, 120-122.
6. Lloyd, C. V. (1985). The effect of a priming activity of schema acquisition of low prior knowledge subjects. *National Reading Conference Yearbook, 34*, 84-88.
7. Lorsbach, T. C., & Gray, J. W. (1986). Item identification speed and memory span performance in learning disabled children. *Contemporary Educational Psychology, 11*, 68-78.
8. Boger, D., Boger, C. C., & Huarng, Y. (1987). The relationship between teacher performance, standardized test and other admissions requirements. *College Student Journal, 21*, 306-311.
9. Curry, J. F., Anderson, D. R., Zitlin, M., & Guise, G. (1987). Validity of academic achievement measures with emotionally handicapped children. *Journal of Clinical Child Psychology, 16*, 51-56.
10. Entwisle, D. R., Alexander, K. L., Pallas, A. M., & Cadigan, D. (1987). The emergent academic self-image of first graders: Its response to social structure. *Child Development, 58*, 1190-1206.
11. Ganschow, L., & Weber, D. B. (1987). Effects of mode of presentation on comprehension of below average, average and above average readers. *Perceptual and Motor Skills, 64*, 899-905.
12. Harper, L. V., & Huie, K. S. (1987). Relations among preschool children's adult and peer contacts and later academic achievement. *Child Development, 58*, 1051- 1065.
13. Kapinus, B. A., Gambrell, L. B., & Koskinen, D. S. (1987). Effects of practice in retelling upon the reading comprehension of proficient and less proficient readers. *Yearbook of the National Reading Conference, 36*, 135-141.
14. Kippel, G. M., & Weiner, M. (1987). National percentiles for California Achievement Test and comparable scores on Degrees of Reading Power test. *Perceptual and Motor Skills, 64*, 860-862.
15. Patti, P., Kose, G., & Duncan, J. (1987). Effects of discrimination training on reading improvement among adults. *Perceptual and Motor Skills, 65*, 723-728.
16. Scott, R. (1987). Gender and race achievement profiles of black and white third-grade students. *The Journal of Psychology, 121*, 629-634.
17. Stevens, R., & White, W. (1987). Impact of teachers' morale on the classroom. *Perceptual and Motor Skills, 65*, 767-770.
18. Tolan, P. H. (1987). Implications of age of onset for delinquency risk. *Journal of Abnormal Child Psychology, 15*, 47-65.
19. Vacc, N. A., Vacc, N. N., & Fogelman, M. S. (1987). Preschool screening: Using the DIAL as a predictor of first-grade performance. *Journal of School Psychology, 25*, 45-51.
20. Vincenzi, H. (1987). Depression and reading ability in sixth-grade children. *Journal of School Psychology, 25*, 155-160.
21. Good, R. H., III, & Salvia, J. (1988). Curriculum bias in published, norm-referenced reading tests: Demonstrable effects. *School Psychology Review, 17*, 51-60.
22. Lorsbach, T. C., & Worman, L. J. (1988). Negative transfer effects in learning disabled children: Evidence for cognitive rigidity? *Contemporary Educational Psychology, 13*, 116-125.
23. McGrew, K. S., & Pehl, J. (1988). Prediction of future achievement by the Woodcock-Johnson Psycho-Educational Battery and the WISC-R. *Journal of School Psychology, 26*, 275-281.
24. Nadson, J. S., Michael, W. B., & Michael, J. J. (1988). The factorial and concurrent validity of a revised form of the Study Attitudes and Methods Survey (SAMS). *Educational and Psychological Measurement, 48*, 969-977.
25. Poteat, G. M., Wuensch, K. L., & Gregg, N. B. (1988). An investigation of differential prediction with the WISC-R. *Journal of School Psychology, 26*, 59-68.
26. Webster, R. E. (1988). Variability in reading achievement test scores as related to reading curriculum. *Educational and Psychological Measurement, 48*, 815-825.
27. Glutting, J. J., Oakland, T., & McDermott, P. A. (1989).

Observing child behavior during testing: Constructs, validity, and situational generality. *Journal of School Psychology, 27,* 155-164.

28. Jussim, L. (1989). Teacher expectations: Self-fulfilling prophecies, perceptual biases, and accuracy. *Journal of Personality and Social Psychology, 57,* 469-480.

29. Kelly, D. B., & Greene, R. L. (1989). Detection of faking good on the MMPI in a psychiatric inpatient population. *Psychological Reports, 65,* 747-750.

30. Koskinen, P. S., Gambrell, L. B., & Kapinus, B. (1989). The effects of rereading and retelling upon young children's reading comprehension. *Yearbook of the National Reading Conference, 38,* 233-239.

31. Lorsbach, T. C., & Worman, L. J. (1989). The development of explicit and implicit forms of memory in learning disabled children. *Contemporary Educational Psychology, 14,* 67-76.

32. Mantzicopoulous, P., Morrison, D. C., Hinshaw, S. P., & Carte, E. T. (1989). Nonpromotion in kindergarten: The role of cognitive, perceptual, visual-motor, behavioral, achievement, socioeconomic, and demographic characteristics. *American Educational Research Journal, 26,* 107-121.

33. Midkiff, R. M., Jr., Burke, J. P., & Helmstadte, G. C. (1989). A causal model of mathematics performance in early adolescence: The role of sex. *Psychological Reports, 64,* 167-176.

34. Oakland, T., & Stern, W. (1989). Variables associated with reading and math achievement among a heterogeneous group of students. *Journal of School Psychology, 27,* 127-140.

35. Clements, D. H., & Nastasi, B. K. (1990). Dynamic approach to measurement of children's metacomponential functioning. *Intelligence, 14,* 109-125.

36. Davaliby, F. J. (1990). Adjunct questions in prose: A question position-by-reading ability interaction. *American Annals of the Deaf, 135,* 50-53.

37. Heyman, W. B. (1990). The self-perception of a learning disability and its relationship to academic self-concept and self-esteem. *Journal of Learning Disabilities, 23,* 472-475.

38. Krinsky, S. G. (1990). The feeling of knowing in deaf adolescents. *American Annals of the Deaf, 135,* 389-395.

39. Lorsbach, T. C., & Worman, L. J. (1990). Episodic priming in children with learning disabilities. *Contemporary Educational Psychology, 15,* 93-102.

40. McAfee, M. C., Kelly, J. F., & Samar, V. J. (1990). Spoken and written English errors of postsecondary students with severe hearing impairment. *Journal of Speech and Hearing Disorders, 55,* 628-634.

41. Russell, R. L., Greenwald, S., & Shirk, S. R. (1991). Language change in child psychotherapy: A meta-analytic review. *Journal of Consulting and Clinical Psychology, 59,* 916-919.

42. Arcia, E., Ornstein, P. A., & Otto, D. A. (1991). Neurobehavioral Evaluation System (NES) and school performance. *Journal of School Psychology, 29,* 337-352.

43. Clements, D. H. (1991). Enhancement of creativity in computer environments. *American Educational Research Journal, 28,* 173-187.

44. Cobb, P., Wood, T., Yackel, E., Nicholls, J., Wheatley, G., Trigatti, B., & Perlwitz, M. (1991). Assessment of a problem-centered second-grade mathematics project. *Journal for Research in Mathematics Education, 22,* 3-29.

45. Haas, N. S., & Sullivan, H. (1991). Use of ethnically matched role models in career materials for Hispanic students. *Contemporary Educational Psychology, 16,* 272-278.

46. LoMaglio, L. J. (1991). Using the TOEFL to measure the reading proficiency levels of deaf college applicants. *American Annals of the Deaf, 136,* 261-264.

47. Rosenbach, J. H., & Rusch, R. R. (1991). IQ and achievement: 1930s to 1980s. *Psychology in the Schools, 28,* 304-309.

48. Silver, R., & Carrion, E. (1991). Using the Silver Drawing Test in school and hospital. *The American Journal of Art Therapy, 30,* 36-43.

49. Cowen, E. I., Wyman, P. A., & Work, W. C. (1992). The relationship between retrospective reports of early child temperament and adjustment at ages 10-12. *Journal of Abnormal Child Psychology, 20,* 39-50.

50. Morvitz, E., & Motta, R. W. (1992). Predictors of self-esteem: The roles of parent-child perceptions, achievement, and class placement. *Journal of Learning Disabilities, 25,* 72-80.

51. Caldas, S. J. (1993). Reexamination of input and process factor effects on public school achievement. *Journal of Educational Research, 86,* 206-214.

52. Miller, S. A., Davis, T. L., Wilde, C. A., & Brown, J. (1993). Parents' knowledge of their children's preferences. *International Journal of Behavioral Development, 16,* 35-60.

[353]

California Brief Life History Inventory.

Purpose: Designed to describe a client's background and present circumstances.

Population: Clients of mental health professionals, guidance counselors, psychologists.

Publication Date: 1984.

Acronym: CBLHI.

Scores: No scores; 7 areas: General Information, Present Problems, History, Childhood and Relatives, Education, Occupation, Miscellaneous.

Administration: Individual.

Editions, 2: Student, Adult.

Price Data: Available from publisher.

Time: (30) minutes.

Authors: Donald I. Templer and David M. Veleber.

Publisher: United Educational Services, Inc.

[354]

The California Child Q-Set.

Purpose: "Designed to describe a child's behavior and personality."

Population: Children.

Publication Date: 1980.

Acronym: CCQ.

Scores: Q-sort rating of children by teachers and counselors in 9 categories ranging from extremely uncharacteristic to extremely characteristic.

Administration: Group.

Price Data, 1990: $9 per Q-set deck including instructions (5 pages).

Time: (35–60) minutes.

Comments: For an upward extension see The California Q-Set (362).

Authors: Jeanne Block and Jack Block.

Publisher: Consulting Psychologists Press, Inc.

Cross References: For a review by Alfred B. Heilbrun, Jr., see 9:181; see also T3:348 (2 references).

TEST REFERENCES

1. Block, J., & Funder, D. C. (1986). Social roles and social perception: Individual differences in attribution and error. *Journal of Personality and Social Psychology, 51,* 1200-1207.

2. Gjerde, P. F., Block, J., & Block, J. H. (1986). Egocentrism and ego resiliency: Personality characteristics associated with perspective-taking from early childhood to adolescence. *Journal of Personality and Social Psychology, 51,* 423-434.

3. Harrington, D. M., Block, J. H., & Block, J. (1987). Testing aspects of Carl Rogers' theory of creative environments: Child-rearing antecedents of creative potential in young adolescents. *Journal of Personality and Social Psychology, 52,* 851-856.

4. Ozer, D. J. (1987). Personality, intelligence, and spatial visualization: Correlates of mental rotations test performance. *Journal of Personality and Social Psychology, 53,* 129-134.

5. Mischel, W., Shada, Y., & Peake, P. K. (1988). The nature of adolescent competencies predicted by preschool delay of gratification. *Journal of Personality and Social Psychology, 54,* 687-696.

6. Gilleseen, A. H. N., van Ijzendoorn, H. W., & van Lieshout, C. F. M. (1992). Heterogeneity among peer-rejected boys: Subtypes and stabilities. *Child Development, 63,* 893-905.

[355]

The California Critical Thinking Dispositions Inventory.

Purpose: "Measures one's disposition or inclination toward critical thinking."

Population: High school, college, and adult.

Publication Date: 1992.

Acronym: CCTDI.

Scores, 8: Truth-Seeking, Inquisitiveness, Open-Mindedness, Confidence, Analyticity, Systematicity, Cognitive Maturity, Total.
Administration: Group or individual.
Price Data, 1993: $75 per specimen kit including inventory, scoring templates, and manual (27 pages); $30 per 20 copies of inventory ($60 per 50 copies, $110 per 100 copies, and $205 per 225 copies).
Time: (15–20) minutes.
Authors: Peter A. Facione and Noreen C. Facione.
Publisher: The California Academic Press.

[356]

California Critical Thinking Skills Test.
Purpose: Designed to be "a standardized assessment instrument targeting core critical thinking skills at the post-secondary level."
Population: College and adult.
Publication Dates: 1990-92.
Acronym: CCTST.
Scores, 6: Analysis, Evaluation, Inference, Inductive Reasoning, Deductive Reasoning, Total.
Administration: Group.
Forms, 2: A, B (alternate).
Price Data, 1992: $60 per specimen kit including Form A, Form B, and manual ('92, 20 pages); $35 per 20 copies of test (volume discounts available); $10 per Delphi Report (22 pages).
Time: 45 minutes.
Author: Peter A. Facione.
Publisher: The California Academic Press.

[357]

California Diagnostic Mathematics Tests.
Purpose: Developed to assess mathematics achievement for use in instructional planning and program evaluation.
Publication Date: 1988.
Acronym: CDMT.
Administration: Group.
Price Data, 1993: $11.90 per 35 practice tests (select Levels A, B–C, D–F); $19.60 per 35 locator tests (select Levels A–C, D–F); $18.50 per 50 locator test answer sheets (Levels D–F); $10.65 per set of hand scoring stencils (select Levels D, E, F); $29 per 100 student diagnostic profiles; $1.20 per class report form; $6.40 per locator test directions; $8.35 per examiner's manual and answer keys (select level); $11.75 per teacher's guide (select Levels A–B, C–D, or E–F); $8.35 per norms book (31 pages); $8.35 per technical report; $40.15 per specimen set; TestMate software available for local scanning and scoring; scoring service available from publisher.
Time: Administration time not reported.
Author: CTB/McGraw-Hill.
Publisher: CTB Macmillan/McGraw-Hill.
a) LEVEL A.
Population: Grades 1.1–2.9.
Scores, 3: Number Concepts, Computation, Applications.

Price Data: $50.05 per 35 hand-scorable test books; $81.55 per 35 machine-scorable (NCS) test books.
b) LEVEL B.
Population: Grades 2.6–3.9.
Scores, 3: Same as *a* above.
Price Data: Same as *a* above.
c) LEVEL C.
Population: Grades 3.6–4.9.
Scores, 3: Same as *a* above.
Price Data: Same as *a* above.
d) LEVEL D.
Population: Grades 4.6–6.9.
Scores, 3: Same as *a* above.
Price Data: $37.45 per 35 reusable tests; $17 per 25 SCOREZE answer sheets for hand scoring; $13 per 50 CompuScan machine-scorable answer sheets; $13 per 50 SCANTRON machine-scorable answer sheets for use with computer-linked scanners.
e) LEVEL E.
Population: Grades 6.6–8.9.
Scores, 3: Same as *a* above.
Price Data: Same as *d* above.
f) LEVEL F.
Population: Grades 8.6–12.
Scores, 3: Same as *a* above plus Life Skills.
Price Data: Same as *d* above.
Cross References: For reviews by Michael B. Bunch and Jerry Johnson, see 11:52.

[358]

California Diagnostic Reading Tests.
Purpose: Developed to assess reading achievement for use in instructional planning and program evaluation.
Publication Date: 1989.
Acronym: CDRT.
Administration: Group.
Price Data, 1994: $11.90 per 35 practice books (select Levels A, B–C, D–F); $19.60 per 35 locator tests (select Levels A–C, D–F); $18.50 per 50 locator test answer sheets (Levels D–F only); $31.45 per set of scoring stencils (Levels D–F only); $29 per 100 student diagnostic profiles; $1.20 per class record sheet for hand scoring (select level); $6.40 per locator test directions; $8.35 per examiner's manual including answer keys (select level); $11.75 per teacher's guide (select Levels A–B, C–D, E–F); $8.35 per norms book (32 pages); $8.35 per technical report; $40.15 per specimen set; TestMate software available for local scanning and scoring; scoring service available from publisher.
Time: Tests are untimed.
Author: CTB/McGraw-Hill.
Publisher: CTB Macmillan/McGraw-Hill.
a) LEVEL A.
Population: Grades 1.1–2.9.
Scores, 3: Word Analysis, Vocabulary, Comprehension.
Price Data: $50.45 per 35 hand-scorable test books; $81.55 per 35 machine-scorable test books.

b) LEVEL B.
Population: Grades 2.6–3.9.
Scores, 3: Same as *a* above.
Price Data: Same as *a* above.
c) LEVEL C.
Population: Grades 3.6–4.9.
Scores, 3: Same as *a* above.
Price Data: Same as *a* above.
d) LEVEL D.
Population: Grades 4.6–6.9.
Scores, 4: Same as *a* above plus Applications.
Price Data: $37.45 per 35 reusable test books; $34.25 per 25 SCOREZE answer sheets; $23 per 50 machine-scorable answer sheets (select Compu-Scan or SCANTRON).
e) LEVEL E.
Population: Grades 6.6–8.9.
Scores, 4: Same as *d* above.
Price Data: Same as *d* above.
f) LEVEL F. .
Population: Grades 8.6–12.
Scores, 3: Vocabulary, Comprehension, Applications.
Price Data: Same as *d* above.
Cross References: For a review by T. Steuart Watson, see 11:53.

[359]
The California Life Goals Evaluation Schedules.
Purpose: Designed to measure "future direction."
Population: Ages 15 and over.
Publication Dates: 1966–69.
Acronym: CLGES.
Scores, 10: Esteem, Profit, Fame, Power, Leadership, Security, Social Service, Interesting Experiences, Self-Expression, Independence.
Administration: Group.
Price Data, 1993: $120 per complete kit; $22.50 per 25 tests; $22 per scoring key; $19.50 per 100 answer sheets; $19.50 per 100 profiles; $40 per manual ('69, 32 pages plus tests and profile).
Time: (30–45) minutes.
Author: Milton E. Hahn.
Publisher: Western Psychological Services.
Cross References: See T3:349 (2 references) and T2:1118 (2 references); for a review by Robert W. Lundin, see 7:47 (3 references).

TEST REFERENCES

1. Kobasa, S. C. (1979). Personality and resistance to illness. *American Journal of Community Psychology, 7,* 413-423.
2. Smith, N. M. (1981). The relationship between the Rorschach whole response and level of cognitive functioning. *Journal of Personality Assessment, 45,* 13-19.
3. Friedman, H. S., & Booth-Kewley, S. (1987). Personality, Type A behavior, and coronary heart disease: The role of emotional expression. *Journal of Personality and Social Psychology, 53,* 783-792.
4. Hull, J. G., Van Treuren, R. R., & Virnelli, S. (1987). Hardiness and health: A critique and alternative approach. *Journal of Personality and Social Psychology, 53,* 518-530.
5. Contrada, R. J. (1989). Type A behavior, personality hardiness, and cardiovascular responses to stress. *Journal of Personality and Social Psychology, 57,* 895-903.
6. Roth, D. L., Wiebe, D. J., Fillingim, R. B., & Shay, K. A. (1989). Life events, fitness, hardiness, and health: A simultaneous analysis of proposed stress-resistance effects. *Journal of Personality and Social Psychology, 56,* 136-142.
7. Wiebe, D. J. (1991). Hardiness and stress moderation: A test of proposed mechanisms. *Journal of Personality and Social Psychology, 60,* 89-99.

[360]
California Preschool Social Competency Scale.
Purpose: "Designed to measure the adequacy of preschool children's interpersonal behavior and the degree to which they assume social responsibility."
Population: Ages 2.5–5.5.
Publication Date: 1969.
Acronym: CPSCS.
Scores: Total score only.
Administration: Individual.
Price Data, 1991: $10.50 per 25 scales; $4 per manual (16 pages); $5 per specimen.
Time: Administration time not reported.
Comments: Ratings by teachers.
Authors: Samuel Levine, Freeman F. Elzey, and Mary Lewis.
Publisher: Consulting Psychologists Press, Inc.
Cross References: See T3:353 (1 reference); for reviews by Hugh Lytton and Robert C. Calfee, and an excerpted review by Barton B. Proger, see 8:513 (2 references).

TEST REFERENCES

1. Camras, L. A., Grow, J. G., & Ribordy, S. C. (1983). Recognition of emotional expression by abused children. *Journal of Clinical Child Psychology, 12,* 325-328.
2. Larsen, J. M., Hite, S. J., & Hart, C. H. (1983). The effects of preschool on educationally advantaged children: First phases of a longitudinal study. *Intelligence, 7,* 345-352.
3. Odom, S. L., Deklyen, M., & Jenkins, J. R. (1984). Integrating handicapped and nonhandicapped preschoolers: Developmental impact on nonhandicapped children. *Exceptional Children, 51,* 41-48.
4. Telzrow, C. F. (1984). Practical applications of the K-ABC in the identification of handicapped preschoolers. *The Journal of Special Education, 18,* 311-324.
5. Eno, L., & Woehlke, P. (1987). Comparison of achievement in half-day, every-day and all-day, alternate-day early childhood programs for handicapped children. *Psychological Reports, 60,* 923-927.
6. Ladd, G. W., & Price, J. M. (1987). Predicting children's social and school adjustment following the transition from preschool to kindergarten. *Child Development, 58,* 1168-1189.

[361]
California Psychological Inventory, Revised Edition.
Purpose: To assess personality characteristics and to predict what people will say and do in specified contexts.
Population: Ages 13 and over.
Publication Dates: 1956–87.
Acronym: CPI.
Scores, 20: Dominance (Do), Capacity for Status (Cs), Sociability (Sy), Social Presence (Sp), Self-Acceptance (Sa), Independence (In), Empathy (Em), Responsibility (Re), Socialization (So), Self-Control (Sc), Good Impression (Gi), Communality (Cm), Well-Being (Wb), Tolerance (To), Achievement via Conformance (Ac), Achievement via Independence (Ai), Intellectual Efficiency (Ie), Psychological-Mind-

edness (Py), Flexibility (Fx), Femininity/Masculinity (Fm).

Administration: Group.

Price Data, 1987: $18.75 per 25 tests; $6 per 50 hand-scored answer sheets; price data for 100 profiles (specify male or female) available from publisher; $39 or less per 10 prepaid CPI answer sheets; price data for 10 prepaid answer sheets producing Gough Interpretive Report or McAllister Interpretive Report available from publisher; price data for computer-administered version and computer scoring available from publisher; price data for scoring stencils available from publisher; $13.50 per Administrator's Guide ('87, 134 pages); $17 per specimen set.

Foreign Language Editions: French, German, Italian, and Spanish editions available in previous edition.

Time: (45–60) minutes.

Comments: Previous edition (9:182) still available; 1 form.

Author: Harrison G. Gough.

Publisher: Consulting Psychologists Press, Inc.

Cross References: For reviews by Brian Bolton and George Engelhard, Jr., see 11:54 (108 references); for reviews by Donald H. Baucom and H. J. Eysenck, see 9:182 (61 references); see also T3:354 (195 references); for a review by Malcolm D. Gynther, see 8:514 (452 references); see also T2:1121 (166 references); for reviews by Lewis R. Goldberg and James A. Walsh and an excerpted review by John O. Crites, see 7:49 (370 references); see also P:27 (249 references); for a review by E. Lowell Kelly, see 6:71 (116 references); for reviews by Lee J. Cronbach and Robert L. Thorndike and an excerpted review by Laurance F. Shaffer, see 5:37 (33 references).

TEST REFERENCES

1. Schut, B. H., Hutzell, R. R., Whiddon, M., & Hartman, J. (1983). Further evaluation of the CPI Repeated Item Short Form. *Journal of Clinical Psychology, 39*, 67-70.
2. Bergin, A. E., Masters, K. S., & Richards, P. S. (1987). Religiousness and mental health reconsidered: A study of an intrinsically religious sample. *Journal of Counseling Psychology, 34*, 197-204.
3. Brown, N. W., & Hunter, J. (1987). Empathy scores of nurses, psychiatrists and hospital administrators on the California Psychological Inventory. *Psychological Reports, 60*, 295-300.
4. Dyer, E. D. (1987). Ten-year differences in level of entering students' profile on the California Psychological Inventory. *Psychological Reports, 60*, 822.
5. Beach, D. A. (1988). Health Care Providers Inventory: A method for evaluating nursing aides. *The Journal of Psychology, 122*, 89-94.
6. Creamer, M., & Campbell, I. M. (1988). The role of interpersonal perception in dyadic adjustment. *Journal of Clinical Psychology, 44*, 424-430.
7. Haemmerlie, F. M., Montgomery, R. L., & Melchers, J. (1988). Social support, perceptions of attractiveness, weight, and the CPI in socially anxious males and females. *Journal of Clinical Psychology, 44*, 435-441.
8. Montross, J. F., Neas, F., Smith, C. L., & Hensley, J. H. (1988). The effects of role-playing high gender identification on the California Psychological Inventory. *Journal of Clinical Psychology, 44*, 160-164.
9. Moore, R. H. (1988). The concurrent validity of the MacAndrew Alcoholism Scale among at-risk adolescent females. *Journal of Clinical Psychology, 44*, 1005-1008.
10. Pierce, N. F. S., & Faulkender, P. J. (1988). Manifest need patterns for four psychological competence status groups differing on interpersonal/intrapersonal competencies. *The Journal of Psychology, 122*, 249-257.
11. Holliman, N. B., & Guthrie, P. C. (1989). A comparison of the Millon Clinical Multiaxial Inventory and the California Psychological Inventory in assessment of a nonclinical population. *Journal of Clinical Psychology, 45*, 373-382.
12. Thurber, S., Snow, M., & Thurber, J. (1989). Atecedents of gregarious alcoholism: An a priori model. *Journal of Clinical Psychology, 45*, 168-171.
13. Brems, C., & Johnson, M. E. (1990). Reexamination of the Bem Sex-Role Inventory: The interpersonal BSRI. *Journal of Personality Assessment, 55*, 484-498.
14. Crowley, C., Koch, R., Fishler, K., Wenz, E., & Ireland, J. (1990). Clinical trial of "off diet" older phenylketonurics with a new phenylalanine-free product. *Journal of Mental Deficiency Research, 34*, 361-369.
15. Davis, G. L., Hoffman, R. G., & Nelson, K. S. (1990). Differences between Native-Americans and Whites on the California Psychological Inventory. *Psychological Assessment, 2*, 238-242.
16. Gibson, D. R. (1990). Personality correlates of logical and sociomoral judgment. *Journal of Personality and Social Psychology, 59*, 1296-1300.
17. Heilbrun, A. B., Jr. (1990). The measurement of criminal dangerousness as a personality construct: Further validation of a research index. *Journal of Personality Assessment, 54*, 141-148.
18. Helson, R., & Picano, J. (1990). Is the traditional role bad for women? *Journal of Personality and Social Psychology, 59*, 311-320.
19. Hough, L. M., Eaton, N. K., Dunnette, M. D., Kamp, J. D., & McCloy, R. A. (1990). Criterion-related validities of personality constructs and the effect of response distortion on those validities. *Journal of Applied Psychology, 75*(5), 581-595.
20. Ittenbach, R. F., & Harrison, P. L. (1990). Predicting ego-strength from problem-solving ability of college students. *Measurement and Evaluation in Counseling and Development, 23*, 128-136.
21. Kosson, D. S., Smith, S. S., & Newman, J. P. (1990). Evaluating the construct validity of psychopathy in Black and White male inmates: Three preliminary studies. *Journal of Abnormal Psychology, 99*, 250-259.
22. Loehlin, J. C., & Gough, H. G. (1990). Genetic and environmental variation on the California Psychological Inventory vector scales. *Journal of Personality Assessment, 54*, 463-468.
23. McCallum, M., & Piper, W. E. (1990). The psychological mindedness assessment procedure. *Psychological Assessment, 2*, 412-418.
24. Sundberg, N. D., Latkin, C. A., Littman, R. A., & Hagan, R. A. (1990). Personality in a religious commune: CPIs in Rajneeshpuram. *Journal of Personality Assessment, 55*, 7-17.
25. Van Hutton, V. (1990). Test review: The California Psychological Inventory. *Journal of Counseling and Development, 69*, 75-77.
26. Wink, P., & Gough, H. G. (1990). New narcissism scales for the California Psychological Inventory and MMPI. *Journal of Personality Assessment, 54*, 446-462.
27. Earleywine, M., & Finn, P. R. (1991). Sensation seeking explains the relation between behavioral disinhibition and alcohol consumption. *Addictive Behaviors, 16*, 123-128.
28. Gipe, J. P., Richards, J. C., Levitov, J., & Speaker, R. (1991). Psychological and personal dimensions of prospective teachers' reflective abilities. *Educational and Psychological Measurement, 51*, 913-921.
29. Gough, H. G., Bradley, P., & McDonald, J. S. (1991). Performance of residents in anesthesiology as related to measures of personality and interests. *Psychological Reports, 68*, 979-994.
30. Haemmerlie, F. M., & Merz, C. J. (1991). Concurrent validity between the California Psychological Inventory—Revised and the Student Adaptation to College Questionnaire. *Journal of Clinical Psychology, 47*, 664-668.
31. Lanning, K., & Gough, H. G. (1991). Shared variance in the California Psychological Inventory and the California Q-Set. *Journal of Personality and Social Psychology, 60*, 596-606.
32. Raskin, R., Novacek, J., & Hogan, R. (1991). Narcissistic self-esteem management. *Journal of Personality and Social Psychology, 60*, 911-918.
33. Richards, L., Rollerson, B., & Phillips, J. (1991). Perceptions of submissiveness: Implications for victimization. *The Journal of Psychology, 125*, 407-411.
34. Wink, P. (1991). Two faces of narcissism. *Journal of Personality and Social Psychology, 61*, 590-597.
35. Aubé, J., & Koestner, R. (1992). Gender characteristics and adjustment: A longitudinal study. *Journal of Personality and Social Psychology, 63*, 485-493.
36. Gough, H. G., & Bradley, P. (1992). Delinquent and criminal behavior as assessed by the revised California Psychological Inventory. *Journal of Clinical Psychology, 48*, 298-308.
37. Helson, R., & Wink, P. (1992). Personality change in women from the early 40s to the early 50s. *Psychology and Aging, 7*, 46-55.
38. Holmstrom, R. W., Karp, S. A., & Silber, D. E. (1992). Factor

structure of the Apperceptive Personality Test (APT). *Journal of Clinical Psychology, 48,* 207-210.

39. King, L. A., Emmons, R. A., & Woodley, S. (1992). The structure of inhibition. *Journal of Research in Personality, 26,* 85-102.

40. Levenson, R. W., & Reuf, A. M. (1992). Empathy: A physiological substrate. *Journal of Personality and Social Psychology, 63,* 234-246.

41. Naugle, R. I., & Rodgers, D. A. (1992). Personality inventory responses of males with medically intractable seizures. *Journal of Personality Assessment, 59,* 500-514.

42. Schmit, M. J., & Ryan, A. M. (1992). Test-taking dispositions: A missing link? *Journal of Applied Psychology, 77,* 629-637.

43. Sieber, K. O., & Meyers, L. S. (1992). Validation of the MMPI-2 social introversion subscales. *Psychological Assessment, 4,* 185-189.

44. Strack, S. (1992). Profile clusters for men and women on the Personality Adjective Check List. *Journal of Personality Assessment, 59,* 204-217.

45. Thurber, S., & Hollingsworth, D. K. (1992). Validity of the Achenbach and Edelbrock youth self-report with hospitalized adolescents. *Journal of Clinical Child Psychology, 21,* 249-254.

46. Wallbrown, F. H., & Jones, J. A. (1992). Reevaluating the factor structure of the Revised California Psychological Inventory. *Educational and Psychological Measurement, 52,* 379-386.

47. Wink, P. (1992). Three narcissism scales for the California Q-Set. *Journal of Personality Assessment, 58,* 51-66.

48. York, K. L., & John, O. P. (1992). The four faces of Eve: A typological analysis of women's personality at midlife. *Journal of Personality and Social Psychology, 63,* 694-508.

49. Baron, L., Reznikoff, M., & Glenwick, D. S. (1993). Narcissism, interpersonal adjustment, and coping in children of Holocaust survivors. *The Journal of Psychology, 127,* 257-269.

50. DeFrancesco, J. J., & Taylor, J. (1993). A validation note on the revised socialization scale of the California Psychological Inventory. *Journal of Psychopathology and Behavioral Assessment, 15,* 53-56.

51. Giancola, P. R., Peterson, J. B., & Pihl, R. O. (1993). Risk for alcoholism, antisocial behavior, and response preservation. *Journal of Clinical Psychology, 49,* 423-428.

52. McGue, M., Bacon, S., & Lykken, D. T. (1993). Personality stability and changes in early adulthood: A behavioral genetic analysis. *Developmental Psychology, 29,* 96-109.

53. Steele, C. M., Spencer, S. J., & Lynch, M. (1993). Self-image resilience and dissonance: The role of affirmational resources. *Journal of Personality and Social Psychology, 64,* 885-896.

54. Tetlock, P. E., Peterson, R. S., & Berry, J. M. (1993). Flattering and unflattering personality portraits of integratively simple and complex managers. *Journal of Personality and Social Psychology, 64,* 500-511.

55. Zebb, B. J., & Meyers, L. S. (1993). Reliability and validity of the revised California Psychological Inventory Vector 1 Scale. *Educational and Psychological Measurement, 53,* 271-280.

56. John, O. P., & Robins, R. W. (1994). Accuracy and bias in self-perception: Individual differences in self-enhancement and the role of narcissism. *Journal of Personality and Social Psychology, 66,* 206-219.

57. Schinka, J. A., & Borum, R. (1994). Readability of normal personality inventories. *Journal of Personality Assessment, 62,* 95-101.

[362]

The California Q-Set.

Purpose: Designed as an objective measure of personality.

Population: Adults.

Publication Dates: 1961–78.

Acronym: CQ-Set.

Scores: Ratings in 9 categories ranging from extremely uncharacteristic to extremely characteristic.

Administration: Individual.

Price Data, 1990: $10 per Q-sort deck; $10 per 50 sorting guide and recording forms; $15 per manual ('78, 166 pages) entitled *The Q-Set Method in Personality Assessment and Psychiatric Research*; $6 per Predicting More of the People More of the Time.

Time: (35–45) minutes.

Comments: For a downward extension see The California Child Q-Set (354).

Author: Jack Block.

Publisher: Consulting Psychologists Press, Inc.

Cross References: See T3:356 (1 reference); for reviews by Allen L. Edwards and David T. Lykken and excerpted reviews by Samuel J. Beck and John E. Exner, Jr., see 6:72 (2 references); see also P:28 (1 reference).

TEST REFERENCES

1. LaRussa, G. W. (1977). Portia's decision: Women's motives for studying law and their later career satisfaction as attorneys. *Psychology of Women Quarterly, 1,* 350-364.

2. Lifton, P. D. (1983). Measures of autonomy. *Journal of Personality Assessment, 47,* 514-523.

3. Elder, G. H., Jr., Nguyen, T. V., & Caspi, A. C. (1985). Linking family hardship to children's lives. *Child Development, 56,* 361-375.

4. Epting, F. R., Rigdon, M. A., Oliver, A. M., & West, C. A. (1986). Theoretical orientation and therapists' view of the healthy client. *Social Behavior and Personality, 14*(1), 45-49.

5. McCrae, R. R., Costa, P. T., Jr., & Busch, C. M. (1986). Evaluating comprehensiveness in personality systems: The California Q-Set and the five-factor model. *Journal of Personality, 54,* 430-446.

6. Funder, D. C., & Dobroth, K. M. (1987). Differences between traits: Properties associated with interjudge agreement. *Journal of Personality and Social Psychology, 52,* 409-418.

7. Harrington, D. M., Block, J. H., & Block, J. (1987). Testing aspects of Carl Rogers's theory of creative environments: Child-rearing antecedents of creative potential in young adolescents. *Journal of Personality and Social Psychology, 52,* 851-856.

8. Ozer, D. J. (1987). Personality, intelligence, and spatial visualization: Correlates of mental rotations test performance. *Journal of Personality and Social Psychology, 53,* 129-134.

9. Funder, D. C., & Colvin, C. R. (1988). Friends and strangers: Acquaintanceship, agreement, and the accuracy of personality judgment. *Journal of Personality and Social Psychology, 55,* 149-158.

10. Block, J. H., Gjerde, P. F., & Block, J. H. (1991). Personality antecedents of depressive tendencies in 18-year-olds: A prospective study. *Journal of Personality and Social Psychology, 60,* 726-738.

11. Lanning, K., & Gough, H. G. (1991). Shared variance in the California Psychological Inventory and the California Q-Set. *Journal of Personality and Social Psychology, 60,* 596-606.

12. Wink, P. (1991). Two faces of narcissism. *Journal of Personality and Social Psychology, 61,* 590-597.

13. Caspi, A., Block, J., Block, J. H., Klopp, B., Lynam, D., Moffitt, T. E., & Stouthamer-Loeber, M. (1992). A "common language" version of the California Child Q-Set for personality assessment. *Psychological Assessment, 4,* 512-523.

14. Wink, P. (1992). Three narcissism scales for the California Q-Set. *Journal of Personality Assessment, 58,* 51-66.

15. York, K. L., & John, O. P. (1992). The four faces of Eve: A typological analysis of women's personality at midlife. *Journal of Personality and Social Psychology, 63,* 494-508.

16. Rosenberg, B. G., & Hyde, J. S. (1993). The only child: Is there only one kind of only? *Journal of Genetic Psychology, 154,* 269-282.

17. Tetlock, P. E., Peterson, R. S., & Berry, J. M. (1993). Flattering and unflattering personality portraits of integratively simple and complex managers. *Journal of Personality and Social Psychology, 64,* 500-511.

18. Westenberg, P. M., & Black, J. (1993). Ego development and individual differences in personality. *Journal of Personality and Social Psychology, 65,* 792-800.

19. John, O. P., & Robins, R. W. (1994). Accuracy and bias in self-perception: Individual differences in self-enhancement and the role of narcissism. *Journal of Personality and Social Psychology, 66,* 206-219.

20. Reise, S. P., & Oliver, C. J. (1994). Development of a California Q-Set indicator of primary psychopathy. *Journal of Personality Assessment, 62,* 130-144.

[363]

California Test of Personality.

Purpose: Designed to identify and reveal the status of certain factors in personality and social adjustment.

Population: Grades K–3, 4–8, 7–10, 9–14, adults.

Publication Dates: 1939–53.

Acronym: CTP.

Scores, 15: Self-Reliance, Sense of Personal Worth, Sense of Personal Freedom, Feeling of Belonging,

Withdrawing Tendencies, Nervous Symptoms, Total Personal Adjustment, Social Standards, Social Skills, Anti-Social Tendencies, Family Relations, School Relations or Occupational Relations (adult level), Community Relations, Total Social Adjustment, Total Adjustment.

Administration: Group.

Price Data: Available from publisher.

Time: (45–60) minutes.

Authors: Ernest W. Tiegs, Willis W. Clark, and Louis P. Thorpe.

Publisher: CTB MacMillan/McGraw-Hill.

a) PRIMARY.

Population: Grades K–3.

Publication Dates: 1940–53.

b) ELEMENTARY.

Population: Grades 4–8.

Publication Dates: 1939–53.

c) INTERMEDIATE.

Population: Grades 7–10.

Publication Dates: 1939–53.

d) SECONDARY.

Population: Grades 9–14.

Publication Dates: 1942–53.

e) ADULT.

Population: Adults.

Publication Dates: 1942–53.

Cross References: For a review by Rosa A. Hagin, see 9:183 (2 references); see also T3:357 (22 references), 8:516 (67 references), T2:1123 (196 references), P:29 (73 references), and 6:73 (49 references); for a review by Verner M. Sims, see 5:38 (93 references); for reviews by Laurance F. Shaffer and Douglas Spencer and an excerpted review by Earl R. Gabler of the original edition, see 3:26 (27 references); for reviews by Raymond B. Cattell, Percival M. Symonds, and P. E. Vernon and an excerpted review by Marion M. Lamb of the elementary and secondary levels, see 2:1213.

TEST REFERENCES

1. Maitland, J. G., Cruise, R. J., & Blitchington, P. (1983). A factor analysis of the California Test of Personality—Secondary Level. *Journal of Clinical Psychology, 39,* 75-80.
2. Sexton, M. E. (1983). Alienation, dogmatism, and related personality characteristics. *Journal of Clinical Psychology, 39,* 80-86.
3. DelRosario, M. W., Brines, J. L., & Coleman, W. R. (1984). Emotional response patterns to body weight-related cues: Influence of body weight image. *Personality and Social Psychology Bulletin, 10,* 369-375.
4. Niklason, L. B. (1984). Nonpromotion: A pseudoscientific solution. *Psychology in the Schools, 21,* 485-499.
5. Ottensbacher, K., & Cooper, H. M. (1984). The effect of social class placement on the social adjustment of mentally retarded children. *Journal of Research and Development in Education, 17*(2), 1-14.
6. Shorkey, C. T., & Armendariz, J. (1985). Personal worth, self-esteem, anomia, hostility and irrational thinking of abusing mothers: A multivariate approach. *Journal of Clinical Psychology, 41,* 414-421.
7. Ternay, M. R., Wilborn, B., & Day, H. D. (1985). Perceived child-parent relationships and child adjustment in families with both adopted and natural children. *The Journal of Genetic Psychology, 146,* 261-272.
8. Glancy, M., Willits, F. K., & Farrell, P. (1986). Adolescent activities and adult success and happiness: Twenty-four years later. *Sociology and Social Research, 70,* 242-250.
9. Mutchler, T. E., Jr., Hunt, E. J., Koopman, E. J., & Mutchler, R. D. (1991). Single-parent mother/daughter empathy, relationship

adjustment, and functioning of the adolescent child of divorce. *Journal of Divorce & Remarriage, 17,* 115-129.

[364]

California Verbal Learning Test, Research Edition, Adult Version.

Purpose: Assesses "multiple strategies and processes involved in learning and remembering verbal material."

Population: Adolescents and adults.

Publication Dates: 1983–87.

Acronym: CVLT.

Scores, 5: Semantic Clustering, Serial Clustering, Correct, Perseverations, Intrusions.

Administration: Individual.

Price Data, 1994: $32 per 25 record forms; $98.50 per set including 25 record forms and manual (91 pages); $73 per manual.

Time: (15) minutes plus a 20-minute delay when nonverbal testing may occur.

Comments: 2 lists (A and B) administered in various combinations using Immediate Free Recall, Short-Delay Free Recall, Cued Recall, and Long Delay Testing.

Authors: Dean C. Delis, Joel H. Kramer, Edith Kaplan, and Beth A. Ober.

Publisher: The Psychological Corporation.

TEST REFERENCES

1. Kramer, J. H., & Delis, D. C. (1987). Interference effects on the California Verbal Learning Test: A construct validation study. *Psychological Assessment, 3,* 299-302.
2. Crosson, B., Novack, T. A., Trenerry, M. R., & Craig, P. L. (1988). California Verbal Learning Test (CVLT) performance in severely head-injured and neurologically normal adult males. *Journal of Clinical and Experimental Neuropsychology, 10,* 754-768.
3. Hermann, B. P., Wyler, A. R., Steenman, H., & Richey, E. T. (1988). The interrelationship between language function and verbal learning/memory performance in patients with complex-partial seizures. *Cortex, 24,* 245-253.
4. Dywan, J., & Jacoby, L. (1990). Effects of aging on source monitoring: Differences in susceptibility to false fame. *Psychology and Aging, 5,* 379-387.
5. Massman, P. J., Delis, D. C., Butters, N., Levin, B. E., & Salmon, D. P. (1990). Are all subcortical dementias alike? Verbal learning and memory in Parkinson's and Huntington's disease patients. *Journal of Clinical and Experimental Neuropsychology, 12,* 729-744.
6. Delias, D. C., Massman, P. J., Butters, N., Salmon, D. P., Cermak, L. S., & Kramer, J. H. (1991). Profiles of demented and amnesic patients on the California Verbal Learning Test: Implications for the assessment of memory disorders. *Psychological Assessment, 3,* 19-26.
7. Smith, D. E., & McCrady, B. S. (1991). Cognitive impairment among alcoholics: Impact on drunk refusal skill acquisition and treatment outcome. *Addictive Behaviors, 16,* 265-274.
8. Massman, P. J., Delis, D. C., Butters, N., Dupont, R. M., & Gillin, J. C. (1992). The subcortical dysfunction hypothesis of memory deficits in depression: Neuropsychological validation in a subgroup of patients. *Journal of Clinical and Experimental Neuropsychology, 14,* 687-706.
9. Swirsky-Sacchetti, T., Field, H. L., Mitchell, D. R., Seward, J., Lublin, F. D., Knobler, R. L., & Gonzalez, C. F. (1992). The sensitivity of the Mini-Mental State Exam in the white matter dementia of multiple sclerosis. *Journal of Clinical Psychology, 48,* 779-786.
10. Cullum, C. M., Thompson, L. L., & Smernoff, E. N. (1993). Three-word recall as a measure of memory. *Journal of Clinical and Experimental Neuropsychology, 15,* 321-329.
11. Reed, B. R., Jagust, W. J., & Coulter, L. (1993). Anosognosia in Alzheimer's disease: Relationships to depression, cognitive function, and cerebral perfusion. *Journal of Clinical and Experimental Neuropsychology, 15,* 231-244.
12. Seidenberg, M., Hermann, B., Haltiner, A., & Wyler, A. (1993). Verbal recognition memory performance in unilateral temporal lobe epilepsy. *Brain and Language, 44,* 191-200.

[365]
Callahan Anxiety Pictures.
Purpose: Measures anxiety in children by means of projective "experimental and clinical evaluation."
Population: Ages 5–13.
Publication Date: 1978.
Acronym: CAP.
Scores: Total score only.
Administration: Group.
Price Data: Not available.
Time: Administration time not reported.
Author: Roger J. Callahan.
Publisher: Sunset Distributors [No reply from publisher; status unknown].
Cross References: For a review by Julien Worland, see 9:184 (2 references).

[366]
The Callier-Azusa Scale: G Edition.
Purpose: A developmental scale "designed to aid in the assessment of deaf-blind and severely and profoundly handicapped children."
Population: Deaf-blind and severely/profoundly handicapped children.
Publication Date: 1978.
Scores: 18 subscales in 5 areas: Motor Development (Postural Control, Locomotion, Fine Motor, Visual Motor), Perceptual Development (Vision, Auditory, Tactile), Daily Living Skills (Dressing, Personal Hygiene, Feeding, Toileting), Cognition, Communication and Language (Cognition, Receptive, Expressive, Speech), Social Development (Adults, Peers, Environment).
Administration: Individual.
Price Data: Available from publisher.
Time: Administration time not reported.
Comments: Criterion-referenced.
Author: Robert Stillman (Editor).
Publisher: Callier Center for Communication Disorders.

[367]
Camelot Behavioral Checklist.
Purpose: Assesses adaptive behavior of mentally retarded individuals.
Population: Mentally retarded.
Publication Dates: 1974–77.
Acronym: CBC.
Scores, 11: Self Help, Physical Development, Home Duties, Vocational Behaviors, Economic Behaviors, Independent Travel, Numerical Skills, Communication Skills, Social Behaviors, Responsibility, Total.
Administration: Individual.
Price Data: Not available.
Time: 25–35 minutes.
Comments: Ratings by parents, ward attendants, and teachers.
Author: Ray W. Foster.
Publisher: Camelot Behavioral Systems [No reply from publisher; status unknown].

Cross References: For a review by Elliott L. Gory, see 9:186.

TEST REFERENCES
1. Orr, D. P., Weller, S. C., Satterwhite, B., & Pless, I. B. (1984). Psychosocial implications of chronic illness in adolescence. *The Journal of Pediatrics, 104*, 152-157.
2. Garris, R. P., & Hazinski, L. (1988). The effect of social skills training procedures on the acquisition of appropriate interpersonal skills for mentally retarded adults. *Journal of Psychopathology and Behavioral Assessment, 10*, 225-240.

[368]
Campbell Interest and Skill Survey.
Purpose: "Measures self-reported interests and skills."
Population: Ages 15 years to adult.
Publication Dates: 1989–92.
Acronym: CISS.
Scores, 99: 7 Orientation Scales (Influencing, Organizing, Helping, Creating, Analyzing, Producing, Adventuring), 29 Basic Scales (Leadership, Law/Politics, Public Speaking, Sales, Advertising/Marketing, Supervision, Financial Services, Office Practices, Adult Development, Child Development, Counseling, Religious Activities, Medical Practice, Art/Design, Performing Arts, Writing, International Activities, Fashion, Culinary Arts, Mathematics, Science, Mechanical Crafts, Woodworking, Farming/Forestry, Plants/Gardens, Animal Care, Athletics/Physical Fitness, Military/Law Enforcement, Risks/Adventure), 58 Occupational Scales (Attorney, Financial Planner, Hotel Manager, Manufacturer's Representative, Marketing Director, Realtor, CEO/President, Human Resources Director, School Superintendent, Advertising Account Executive, Media Executive, Public Relations Director, Corporate Trainer, Secretary, Bank Manager, Insurance Agent, Retail Store Manager, Hospital Administrator, Accountant/CPA, Bookkeeper, Child Care Worker, Guidance Counselor, Religious Leader, Teacher K–12, Social Worker, Psychologist, Nursing Administrator, Commercial Artist, Fashion Designer, Liberal Arts Professor, Librarian, Musician, Translator/Interpreter, Writer/Editor, Restaurant Manager, Chef, Physician, Chemist, Medical Researcher, Math/Science Teacher, Computer Programmer, Statistician, Systems Analyst, Carpenter, Electrician, Veterinarian, Airline Mechanic, Agribusiness Manager, Landscape Architect, Architect, Police Officer, Military Officer, Ski Instructor, Test Pilot, Athletic Coach, Athletic Trainer, Emergency Medical Technician, Fitness Instructor), 2 Special Scales (Academic Focus, Extraversion), 3 Procedural Checks (Response Percentage Check, Inconsistency Check, Omitted Items Check).
Administration: Individual or group.
Price Data, 1994: $31 per hardcover manual ('92, 332 pages); $20 per softcover manual; $6 per 50 interest/skill pattern worksheets; $12 per 25 Microtest Q System answer sheets; $4.60 per Microtest Q System report; $20.50 per 100 report cover sheets; $35 per preview package including soft cover manual and

25 answer sheets; $5.40 per mail-in answer sheet/report.
Time: (35) minutes.
Comments: Each scale contains both an interest and a skill score; combined gender scales allow for broadest interpretation of survey results; workshops available.
Author: David Campbell.
Publisher: NCS Assessments.

TEST REFERENCES

1. Campbell, D. P. (1993). A new integrated battery of psychological surveys. *Journal of Counseling and Development, 71, 575-587.*

[369]
Campbell Leadership Index.
Purpose: "An adjective checklist designed to be used in the assessment of leadership characteristics."
Population: Leaders.
Publication Date: 1991.
Acronym: CLI.
Scores, 22: Ambitious, Daring, Dynamic, Enterprising, Experienced, Farsighted, Original, Persuasive, Energy, Affectionate, Considerate, Empowering, Entertaining, Friendly, Credible, Organized, Productive, Thrifty, Calm, Flexible, Optimistic, Trusting.
Administration: Group or individual.
Price Data: Available from publisher.
Time: (25-30) minutes.
Comments: Self-ratings plus 3-5 observer ratings.
Author: David Campbell.
Publisher: NCS Assessments.

TEST REFERENCES

1. Campbell, D. P. (1993). A new integrated battery of psychological surveys. *Journal of Counseling and Development, 71, 575-587.*

[370]
Campbell Organizational Survey.
Purpose: Designed to measure attitudes of employees regarding the organization.
Population: Working adults.
Publication Dates: 1988-90.
Acronym: COS.
Scores, 14: The Work Itself, Working Conditions, Freedom from Stress, Co-Workers, Supervision, Top Leadership, Pay, Benefits, Job Security, Promotional Opportunities, Feedback/Communications, Organizational Planning, Support for Innovation, Overall Satisfaction Index.
Administration: Group.
Price Data, 1990: $50 per administration kit including manual ('90, 175 pages), booklet, roster sheet, and group/subgroup coding worksheet; $17 per individual for scoring and reporting; $35 per group and subgroup report; $75 per demographic subgroup report.
Time: (15-25) minutes.
Comments: A component of Campbell Development Surveys (CDS); scoring and reporting discounts for 50, 250, 1,000, or 2,500+ examinees.

Author: David Campbell.
Publisher: NCS Assessments.

TEST REFERENCES

1. Campbell, D. P. (1993). A new integrated battery of psychological surveys. *Journal of Counseling and Development, 71, 575-587.*

[371]
Canadian Achievement Tests, Form A.
Purpose: "Designed to measure achievement of students in the areas of reading, spelling, language, and mathematics."
Population: Grades 1.6-2.9, 2.6-3.9, 3.6-4.9, 4.6-5.9, 5.6-6.9, 6.6-7.9, 7.6-9.9, 9.6-12.9.
Publication Dates: 1981-83.
Acronym: CAT, Form A.
Administration: Group.
Price Data: Not available.
Comments: Criterion-referenced; subtests available as separates; 8 overlapping levels.
Author: Canadian Test Centre/McGraw-Hill Ryerson Ltd.
Publisher: Canadian Test Centre/McGraw-Hill Ryerson Ltd. [No reply from publisher; status unknown].
a) LOCATOR TESTS.
Population: Grades 2-6, 6-12.
Scores, 2: Reading Vocabulary, Mathematics.
Time: (22) minutes.
b) LEVEL 12.
Population: Grades 1.6-2.9.
Scores, 9: Reading (Phonic Analysis, Structural Analysis, Reading Vocabulary, Reading Comprehension), Spelling, Language (Mechanics, Expression), Mathematics (Computation, Concepts and Applications).
Time: (190) minutes per complete battery.
c) LEVEL 13.
Population: Grades 2.6-3.9.
Scores, 9: Same as for *b* above.
Time: (198) minutes for complete battery.
d) LEVEL 14.
Population: Grades 3.6-4.9.
Scores, 8: Reading (Vocabulary, Comprehension), Spelling, Language (Mechanics, Expression), Mathematics (Computation, Concepts and Applications), Reference Skills.
Time: (202) minutes for complete battery.
e) LEVEL 15.
Population: Grades 4.6-5.9.
Scores, 8: Same as for *d* above.
f) LEVEL 16.
Population: Grades 5.6-6.9.
Scores, 8: Same as for *d* above.
g) LEVEL 17.
Population: Grades 6.6-7.9.
Scores, 8: Same as for *d* above.
h) LEVEL 18.
Population: Grades 7.6-9.9.
Scores, 8: Same as for *d* above.

i) LEVEL 19.
Population: Grades 9.6–12.9.
Scores, 8: Same as for *d* above.
Cross References: For a review by L. A. Whyte, see 9:187.

TEST REFERENCES

1. Anderson, R. N., Greene, M. L., & Loewen, P. S. (1988). Relationship among teacher's and student's thinking skills, sense of efficacy, and student achievement. *The Alberta Journal of Educational Research, 34,* 148-165.
2. Meyer, N. E., Dyck, D. G., & Petrinack, R. J. (1989). Cognitive appraisal and attributional correlates of depressive symptoms in children. *Journal of Abnormal Child Psychology, 17,* 325-336.
3. Kowaz, A. M., & Marcia, J. E. (1991). Development and validation of a measure of Eriksonian industry. *Journal of Personality and Social Psychology, 60,* 390-397.

[372]
Canadian Cognitive Abilities Test, Form 7.
Purpose: "Designed to assess the development of cognitive abilities related to verbal, quantitative, and non-verbal reasoning and problem solving."
Population: Grades K–2, 3–12.
Publication Dates: 1970–90.
Acronym: CCAT.
Scores, 3: Verbal, Quantitative, Non-Verbal.
Administration: Group.
Price Data, 1994: $7.95 per 10 class record sheets; $21.95 per technical notes ('90, 34 pages).
Comments: Canadian version of Cognitive Abilities Test, Form 7.
Authors: Original edition by Robert L. Thorndike and Elizabeth P. Hagen; Canadian revision by Edgar N. Wright.
Publisher: Nelson Canada [Canada].
  a) PRIMARY BATTERIES.
  Population: Grades K–1, 2–3.
  Levels, 2: Primary 1, 2.
  Price Data: $43.95 per 35 test booklets; $5.45 per scoring key; $16.45 per examiner's manual ('89, 85 pages); $27.45 per examination kit.
  Time: (90) minutes (untimed).
  b) MULTILEVEL EDITION.
  Population: Grades 3–12.
  Price Data: $9.45 per test booklet (Levels A–H); $3.95 per Level A test booklet; $20.45 per 35 hand/machine scorable answer sheets; $17.45 per examiner's manual ('89, 101 pages); $6.95 per supplemental manual Level A with key; $13.45 per scoring mask; $29 per examination kit.
  Time: (90) minutes.
Cross References: For reviews by Giuseppe Costantino and Jack A. Cummings, see 10:42 (3 references); see also T3:361 (5 references) and 8:180 (2 references).

[373]
Canadian Dental Aptitude Test.
Purpose: "Designed to measure general academic achievement, comprehension of scientific information, and perceptual ability."
Population: Dental school applicants.

Publication Dates: 1946–93.
Scores, 7: Reading Comprehension, Natural Sciences (Biology, General Chemistry, Total), Perceptual Ability Test, Chalk Carving Test, Academic Average.
Administration: Group.
Price Data: Available from publisher.
Time: 235(330) minutes in 2 sessions.
Comments: Based on the Dental Admission Testing program (733).
Author: Department of Testing Services.
Publisher: American Dental Association.

[374]
Canadian Occupational Interest Inventory.
Purpose: Developed to help identify types of employment from which clients may derive the most satisfaction.
Population: High school or college students.
Publication Dates: 1981–82.
Acronym: COII.
Scores, 5: Things/People, Business Contact/Scientific, Routine/Creative, Social/Solitary, Prestige/Production.
Administration: Group.
Price Data, 1994: $59.95 per 25 test booklets; $16.95 per 35 answer sheets; $7.95 per set of scoring stencils; $16.65 per 35 profile sheets; $16.65 per 35 profile and charts; $31.95 per administrator's manual ('82, 50 pages); $25.45 per technical manual ('82, 30 pages); $47.95 per glossary of interests ('82, 118 pages); $30.45 per specimen set.
Foreign Language Edition: French edition available.
Time: [40] minutes.
Authors: Luc Bégin, Luc Lavallée (test and technical manual), and J. A. Gordon Booth (manuals).
Publisher: Nelson Canada [Canada].
Cross References: For a review by Richard W. Johnson, see 9:188.

[375]
Canadian Tests of Basic Skills, Forms 7 and 8.
Purpose: Constructed to measure growth in the fundamental skills crucial to day-to-day learning.
Publication Dates: 1955–90.
Acronym: CTBS.
Administration: Group.
Price Data, 1993: $9.45 per multilevel test booklet (select Levels 9–14 or 15–18); $9.95 per 35 pupil profile charts (select Levels 5–14 or 15–18); $5 per 10 profile sheets for averages (select Levels 5–14 or 15–18); $5.95 per 10 class record sheets (select Levels 5–14 or 15–18); $9.50 per 35 reports to parents (Levels 5–8); $10.40 per 35 How are Your Basic Skills? (Levels 9–14); $17.95 per teacher's guide (select Levels 5–6 or 7–8); $16.45 per teacher's guide (select Levels 9–14 or 15–18); $42.45 per manual ('90, 138 pages); $15 per Level 5–8 examination kit; $29 per examination kit (select Levels 9–14 or 15–18); scoring service available from publisher.

Comments: 2 forms: 7, 8; Form 8 not available for Levels 5–8 and 15–18.
Authors: A. N. Hieronymus, H. D. Hoover, E. F. Lindquist, and others (original Level 5–14 tests); Dale P. Scannell and others (original Level 15–18 tests); Ethel King-Shaw and others (Canadian adaptation).
Publisher: Nelson Canada [Canada].
a) LEVEL 5.
Population: Grades K.1–1.5.
Scores, 6: Listening, Word Analysis, Vocabulary, Language, Mathematics, Total.
Price Data: $39.95 per 25 test booklets; $24.95 per set of scoring masks.
Time: (150) minutes over 5 days.
b) LEVEL 6.
Population: Grades K.8–1.9.
Scores, 7: Listening, Word Analysis, Vocabulary, Reading, Language, Mathematics, Total.
Price Data: Same as *a* above.
Time: (205) minutes over 5 days.
c) LEVEL 7.
Population: Grades 1.7–2.6.
Scores, 17: Listening, Word Analysis, Vocabulary, Reading, Language (Spelling, Capitalization, Punctuation, Usage and Expression, Total), Work-Study Skills (Visual Materials, Reference Materials, Total), Mathematics (Concepts, Problems, Computation, Total), Total.
Price Data: Same as *a* above.
Time: (227) minutes over 5 days.
d) LEVEL 8.
Population: Grades 2.7–3.5.
Scores, 17: Same as *c* above.
Price Data: Same as *a* above.
Time: Same as *c* above.
e) LEVEL 9.
Population: Grade 3.
Scores, 15: Vocabulary, Reading Comprehension, Language (Spelling, Capitalization, Punctuation, Usage and Expression, Total), Work-Study (Visual Materials, Reference Materials, Total), Mathematics (Concepts, Problem Solving, Computation, Total), Total.
Price Data: $18.95 per 35 answer sheets; $12.95 per set of scoring masks.
Time: (256) minutes in 4–8 sessions.
f) LEVEL 10.
Population: Grade 4.
Scores, 15: Same as *e* above.
Price Data: Same as *e* above.
Time: Same as *e* above.
g) LEVEL 11.
Population: Grade 5.
Scores, 15: Same as *e* above.
Price Data: Same as *e* above.
Time: Same as *e* above.
h) LEVEL 12.
Population: Grade 6.
Scores, 15: Same as *e* above.
Price Data: Same as *e* above.

Time: Same as *e* above.
i) LEVEL 13.
Population: Grade 7.
Scores, 15: Same as *e* above.
Price Data: Same as *e* above.
Time: Same as *e* above.
j) LEVEL 14.
Population: Grades 8–9.
Scores, 15: Same as *e* above.
Price Data: Same as *e* above.
Time: Same as *e* above.
k) LEVEL 15.
Population: Grade 9.
Scores, 6: Reading Comprehension, Mathematics, Written Expression, Using Sources of Information, Total, Applied Proficiency Skills.
Price Data: $20.45 per 35 answer sheets; $12.45 per scoring masks.
Time: 160(190) minutes in 2 sessions.
l) LEVEL 16.
Population: Grade 10.
Scores, 6: Same as *k* above.
Price Data: Same as *e* above.
Time: Same as *k* above.
m) LEVEL 17.
Population: Grade 11.
Scores, 6: Same as *k* above.
Price Data: Same as *e* above.
Time: Same as *k* above.
n) LEVEL 18.
Population: Grade 12.
Scores, 6: Same as *k* above.
Price Data: Same as *e* above.
Time: Same as *k* above.
Cross References: For reviews by John O. Anderson and Jean-Jacques Bernier and Martine Hebert, see 11:55 (9 references); see also T3:363 (15 references) and 8:11 (1 reference); for a review by L. B. Birch of an earlier edition, see 7:6.

TEST REFERENCES

1. Bowers, P. (1989). Naming speed and phonological awareness: Independent contributors to reading disabilities. *Yearbook of the National Reading Conference, 38,* 165-172.
2. Bulcock, J. W., Whitt, M. E., & Beebe, M. J. (1991). Gender differences, student well-being, and high school achievement. *Alberta Journal of Educational Research, 37,* 209-224.
3. Kowaz, A. M., & Marcia, J. E. (1991). Development and validation of a measure of Eriksonian industry. *Journal of Personality and Social Psychology, 60,* 390-397.
4. Randhawa, B. S. (1991). Gender differences in academic achievement: A closer look at mathematics. *Alberta Journal of Educational Research, 37,* 241-257.
5. Bisanz, G. L., Das, J. P., Varnhagen, C. K., & Henderson, H. R. (1992). Structural components of reading time and recall for sentences in narratives: Exploring changes with age and reading ability. *Journal of Educational Psychology, 84,* 103-114.

[376]

The Candidate Profile Record.

Purpose: Constructed to predict successful performance in clerical positions.
Population: Applicants for clerical positions.
Publication Dates: 1982–89.
Scores: Total score only.

Administration: Group.
Price Data: Available from publisher.
Time: (30–45) minutes.
Authors: Richardson, Bellows, Henry & Co., Inc.
Publisher: Richardson, Bellows, Henry & Co., Inc.

[377]

Canfield Instructional Styles Inventory.
Purpose: Constructed to identify instructional preferences.
Population: Instructors.
Publication Dates: 1976–88.
Acronym: ISI.
Scores, 21: Conditions for Instruction (Peer, Organization, Goal Setting, Competition, Instructor, Detail, Independence, Authority), Areas of Interest (Numeric, Qualitative, Inanimate, People), Modes of Instruction (Lecturing, Readings, Iconic, Direct Experience), Influence (A-influence, B-influence, C-influence, D-influence, Total Influence).
Administration: Group or individual.
Price Data, 1993: $60 per complete kit including 5 inventory booklets and manual ('88, 55 pages); $40 per 10 inventory booklets; $42.50 per manual.
Time: (30–40) minutes for individual administration; (35–40) minutes for group administration.
Comments: May be self-administered.
Authors: Albert A. Canfield and Judith S. Canfield.
Publisher: Western Psychological Services.
Cross References: For reviews by Nancy L. Allen and Jerrilyn V. Andrews, see 11:56; for reviews of an earlier edition by Thomas B. Bradley and C. Dean Miller, see 9:514.

TEST REFERENCES

1. Pettigrew, F. E., Bayless, M. A., Zakrajsek, D. B., & Goc-Karp, G. (1985). Compatibility of students' learning and teaching styles of their ratings of college teaching. *Perceptual and Motor Skills, 61*, 1215-1220.

[378]

Canfield Learning Styles Inventory.
Purpose: Designed to assess learning preferences.
Population: Junior High School, High School, College, Adults in business settings.
Publication Dates: 1976–88.
Acronym: LSI.
Scores, 21: Conditions for Learning (Peer, Organization, Goal Setting, Competition, Instructor, Detail, Independence, Authority), Area of Interest (Numeric, Qualitative, Inanimate, People), Mode of Learning (Listening, Reading, Iconic, Direct Experience), Expectation for Course Grade (A-expectation, B-expectation, C-expectation, D-expectation, Total expectation).
Administration: Group.
Forms, 4: A (College), B (High School), C (Junior High School), E (College-Easy).
Price Data, 1993: $100 per complete kit including 2 each of Forms A, B, C, and E inventory booklets, 1 Form ABC computer-scorable booklet, 1 Form E computer-scorable booklet, and manual ('88, 76 pages); $45 per 10 inventory booklets (specify form); $10.50–$12.50 per computer-scorable booklet (price depends on quantity ordered and includes scoring service by publisher); $45 per manual; $210 per IBM microcomputer disk.
Time: (30–40) minutes.
Author: Albert A. Canfield.
Publisher: Western Psychological Services.
Cross References: For a review by Stephen L. Benton, see 11:57 (2 references); for reviews of an earlier edition by John Biggs and C. Dean Miller, see 9:609 (1 reference).

TEST REFERENCES

1. Heikkinen, M., Pettigrew, F., & Kakrajsek, D. (1985). Learning styles vs. teaching styles—studying the relationship. *NASSP Bulletin, 69*(478), 80-85.
2. Pettigrew, F. E., Bayless, M. A., Zakrajsek, D. B., & Goc-Karp, G. (1985). Compatibility of students' learning and teaching styles of their ratings of college teaching. *Perceptual and Motor Skills, 61*, 1215-1220.
3. Blustein, D. L., Judd, T. P., Krom, J., Viniar, B., Padilla, E., Wedemeyer, R., & Williams, D. (1986). Identifying predictors of academic performance of community college students. *Journal of College Student Personnel, 27*, 242-249.
4. Enochs, J. R., Handley, H. M., & Wollenberg, J. P. (1986). Relating learning style, reading vocabulary, reading comprehension, and aptitude for learning to achievement in the self-paced and computer-assisted instructional modes. *Journal of Experimental Education, 54*, 135-139.
5. Gruber, C. P., & Carriuolo, N. (1991). Construction and preliminary validation of a learner typology for the Canfield Learning Styles Inventory. *Educational and Psychological Measurement, 51*, 839-855.

[379]

CAP Assessment of Writing.
Purpose: Designed to measure "students' writing abilities through the writing and assessment of actual student essays."
Population: Grades 3–4, 5–6, 7–8, 9–10, 11–12.
Publication Date: 1988–91.
Scores, 5: 6-point rating scale used for holistic scoring (Total) and for diagnostic scoring (Content, Organization, Usage and Sentence Structure, Mechanics).
Administration: Group.
Levels, 5: Elementary 1, Elementary 2, Secondary 1, Secondary 2, Secondary 3.
Price Data, 1993: $44 per 35 test booklets (specify level) and manual (7 pages); $5.25 per student for holistic scoring; $7.90 per student for holistic and diagnostic scoring.
Time: 40 minutes.
Comments: Part of Comprehensive Assessment Program; customized (unnormed) test available for Elementary and Adult levels.
Authors: John W. Wick, Louis A. Gatta, and Thomas Valentin.
Publisher: American College Testing Program.

[380]

Capitalization and Punctuation Tests.
Purpose: Measures skills in capitalization and punctuation before and after direct instruction.
Population: Students of English.
Publication Date: 1985.
Scores: Item scores only.
Administration: Group.

Forms, 2: Diagnostic, Achievement.
Manual: No manual.
Price Data, 1989: $15.95 per complete kit including 25 Diagnostic tests, 25 Achievement tests, and answer keys; $8.95 per 25 tests (Diagnostic or Achievement) with answer key; $.36 per additional copy.
Time: Administration time not reported.
Comments: For use as pre- and post-tests.
Authors: Kenneth Stratton and George Christian.
Publisher: Stratton-Christian Press, Inc.

[381]

Cardall Test of Practical Judgement.
Purpose: To measure problem-solving ability in everyday life.
Population: Adults in business and industry.
Publication Dates: 1942–80.
Scores: 3: Factual, Empathetic, Total.
Administration: Group.
Price Data, 1990: $12 per review set including manual ('61, 4 pages); $30 per 25 test booklets.
Foreign Language Edition: French edition available.
Time: (30) minutes.
Author: Alfred J. Cardall.
Publisher: Institute of Psychological Research, Inc. [Canada].
Cross References: See 6:1102 (4 references) and 4:784 (6 references). For reviews by Glen U. Cleeton and Howard R. Taylor of an earlier edition, see 3:694.

[382]

Career Ability Placement Survey.
Purpose: Designed to measure abilities as they relate to careers.
Population: Junior high, high school, college, and adults.
Publication Dates: 1976–92.
Acronym: CAPS.
Scores: Scores in 14 COPSystem Career Clusters: Science-Professional, Science-Skilled, Technology-Professional, Technology-Skilled, Consumer Economics, Outdoor, Business-Professional, Business-Skilled, Clerical, Communication, Arts-Professional, Arts-Skilled, Service-Professional, Service-Skilled.
Administration: Group.
Price Data, 1993: $61.75 per 25 self-scoring test booklets [$228.50 per 100, $770 per 500]; $10.25 per 25 Self-Interpretation Profile and Guides [$36.25 per 100, $168.50 per 500]; $36.25 per 25 machine-scoring test booklets [$122.50 per 100, $578.75 per 500]; $5.75 per 25 CAPS tests (by each test) [$78.75 per 500]; $1.30 each scoring by publisher; $12 per hand-scoring keys; $2 per examiner's manual ('92, 22 pages); $6.75 per technical manual ('92, 59 pages); $8.50 per administration tape; $18.50 per CAPS Visuals; $8 per specimen set.
Time: (5) minutes per test; (50) minutes for entire battery.

Authors: Lila F. Knapp and Robert R. Knapp.
Publisher: EdITS/Educational and Industrial Testing Service.

TEST REFERENCES

1. Ellis, B. B. (1990). Assessing intelligence cross-nationally: A case for differential item functioning detection. *Intelligence, 14*, 61-78.

[383]

Career Anchors: Discovering Your Real Values, Revised Edition.
Purpose: Designed to help a person identify their career anchor, uncover their real values, and use them to make better career choices.
Population: Adults.
Publication Date: 1990.
Scores, 8: Technical/Functional Competence, General Managerial Competence, Autonomy/Independence, Security/Stability, Entrepreneurial Creativity, Service/Dedication to a Cause, Pure Challenge, Lifestyle.
Administration: Group.
Price Data, 1993: $24.95 per complete kit including instrument (67 pages) and trainer's manual (20 pages); $9.95 per instrument.
Time: (180–240) minutes.
Comments: Self-rating plus interview with a partner.
Author: Edgar H. Schein.
Publisher: Pfeiffer and Company, International Publishers.

[384]

Career Assessment Inventories for the Learning Disabled.
Purpose: "Developed to facilitate career exploration, choice, and preparation for the learning disabled individual."
Population: Ages 6–adult.
Publication Date: 1983.
Acronym: CILD.
Administration: Individual.
Price Data, 1993: $45 per complete kit including manual (64 pages) and 50 inventories; $18 per 50 Attributes/Ability Inventories; $9 per 50 Interest Inventories; $15 per manual; $15 per specimen set including manual and sample forms.
Time: (10–15) minutes per test.
Authors: Carol Weller and Mary Buchanan.
Publisher: Academic Therapy Publications.
a) ATTRIBUTES INVENTORY.
Scores, 6: Realistic, Investigative, Artistic, Social, Enterprising, Conventional.
b) ABILITY INVENTORY.
Scores, 6: Verbal Understanding, Conversation, Visual, Spatial, Fine Motor, Gross Motor.
c) INTEREST INVENTORY.
Scores, 6: Same as *b* above.
Comments: May be orally administered.
Cross References: For a review by Courtland C. Lee, see 9:193.

[385]
Career Assessment Inventory, Second Edition (Vocational Version).

Purpose: "A vocational interest assessment tool for individuals planning to enter occupations requiring 0–2 years of post-secondary training."
Population: Grade 9 through adult.
Publication Dates: 1973–94.
Scores, 125: 2 Administrative Indices (Total Responses, Response Patterning), 4 Nonoccupational (Fine Arts-Mechanical, Occupational Extroversion-Introversion, Educational Orientation, Variability of Interests), 6 General Themes (Realistic, Investigative, Artistic, Social, Enterprising, Conventional), 22 Basic Interest Area Scales (Mechanical/Fixing, Electronics, Carpentry, Manual/Skilled Trades, Agriculture, Nature/Outdoors, Animal Service, Science, Numbers, Writing, Performing/Entertaining, Arts/Crafts, Social Service, Teaching, Child Care, Medical Service, Religious Activities, Business, Sales, Office Practices, Clerical/Clerking, Food Service), 91 Occupational Scales (Aircraft Mechanic, Auto Mechanic, Bus Driver, Camera Repair Technician, Carpenter, Conservation Officer, Dental Laboratory Technician, Drafter, Electrician, Emergency Medical Technician, Farmer/Rancher, Firefighter, Forest Ranger, Hardware Store Manager, Janitor/Janitress, Machinist, Mail Carrier, Musical Instrument Repair, Navy Enlisted, Orthodontist/Prosthetist, Painter, Park Ranger, Pipefitter/Plumber, Police Officer, Printer, Radio/TV Repair, Security Guard, Sheet Metal Worker, Telephone Repair, Tool/Die Maker, Truck Driver, Veterinary Technician, Chiropractor, Computer Programmer, Dental Hygienist, Electronic Technician, Math-Science Teacher, Medical Laboratory Technician, Radiological Technician, Respiratory Therapeutic Technician, Surveyor, Advertising Artist/Writer, Advertising Executive, Author/Writer, Counselor-Chemical Dependency, Interior Designer, Legal Assistant, Librarian, Musician, Newspaper Reporter, Photographer, Piano Technician, Athletic Trainer, Child Care Assistant, Cosmetologist, Elementary School Teacher, Licensed Practical Nurse, Nurse Aide, Occupational Therapist Assistant, Operating Room Technician, Physical Therapist Assistant, Registered Nurse, Barber/Hairstylist, Buyer/Merchandiser, Card/Gift Shop Manager, Caterer, Florist, Food Service Manager, Hotel/Motel Manager, Insurance Agent, Manufacturing Representative, Personnel Manager, Private Investigator, Purchasing Agent, Real Estate Agent, Reservation Agent, Restaurant Manager, Travel Agent, Accountant, Bank Teller, Bookkeeper, Cafeteria Worker, Court Reporter, Data Entry Operator, Dental Assistant, Executive Housekeeper, Medical Assistant, Pharmacy Technician, Secretary, Teacher Aide, Waiter/Waitress).
Administration: Group.
Price Data, 1994: $18 per manual ('84, 152 pages); $37.50 each per preview package for Mictotest

Q, Microtest, and mail-in reports including 3 interpretive reports and a manual; $12 per 25 interpretive report answer sheets (specify Microtest Q/Microtest or Arion teleprocessing); $5.70–$7.10 per Microtest Q and Microtest interpretive report; $6.70–$8.10 per Arion or mail-in interpretive report; $12 per 25 profile report answer sheets (specify Microtest Q/Microtest or Arion teleprocessing); $3.55–$4.20 per Microtest Q and Microtest profile report; $4.55–$5.20 per Arion or mail-in profile report.
Foreign Language Editions: Spanish and French editions available.
Time: (30–45) minutes.
Author: Charles B. Johansson.
Publisher: NCS Assessments.
Cross References: For reviews by Jerard F. Kehoe and Nicholas A. Vacc, see 11:59 (1 reference); see also T3:367 (1 reference); for additional information and reviews of an earlier edition by Jack L. Bodden and Paul R. Lohnes, see 8:993.

TEST REFERENCES

1. Wood, J. M., & Bootzin, R. R. (1990). The prevalence of nightmares and their independence from anxiety. *Journal of Abnormal Psychology, 99,* 64-68.
2. Zarrella, K. L., & Schuerger, J. M. (1990). Temporal stability of occupational interest inventories. *Psychological Reports, 66,* 1067-1074.
3. Chartrand, J. M., Camp, C. C., & McFadden, K. L. (1992). Predicting academic adjustment and career indecision: A comparison of self-efficacy, interest congruence, and commitment. *Journal of College Student Development, 33,* 293-300.
4. Reed, J. R., Patton, M. J., & Gold, P. B. (1993). Effects of turn-taking sequences in vocational test interpretation interviews. *Journal of Counseling Psychology, 40,* 144-155.

[386]
Career Assessment Inventory—The Enhanced Version.

Purpose: A vocational interest assessment tool focusing on careers requiring "various amounts of post-secondary education."
Population: Grade 9 through adult.
Publication Dates: 1975–94.
Scores, 142: 6 themes (Realistic, Investigative, Artistic, Social, Enterprising, Conventional), 25 basic interest (Mechanical/Fixing, Electronics, Carpentry, Manual/Skilled Trades, Protective Service, Athletics/Sports, Nature/Outdoors, Animal Service, Mathematics, Scientific Research/Development, Medical Science, Writing, Creative Arts, Performing/Entertaining, Educating, Community Service, Medical Service, Religious Activities, Public Speaking, Law/Politics, Management/Supervision, Sales, Office Practices, Clerical/Clerking, Food Service), 111 occupational (Accountant, Advertising Artist/Writer, Advertising Executive, Aircraft Mechanic, Architect, Athletic Trainer, Author/Writer, Auto Mechanic, Bank Manager, Bank Teller, Barber/Hairstylist, Biologist, Bookkeeper, Bus Driver, Buyer/Merchandiser, Cafeteria Worker, Camera Repair Technician, Card/Gift Shop Manager, Carpenter, Caterer, Chef, Chemist, Child Care Assistant, Chiropractor, Computer Programmer, Computer Scientist, Conservation Officer, Cosmetologist, Counselor-Chemical Dependency,

Court Reporter, Data Input Operator, Dental Assistant, Dental Hygienist, Dental Lab Technician, Dentist, Dietitian, Drafter, Economist, Elected Public Official, Electrician, Electronic Technician, Elementary School Teacher, Emergency Medical Technician, Engineer, Executive Housekeeper, Farmer/Rancher, Firefighter, Florist, Food Service Manager, Forest Ranger, Guidance Counselor, Hardware Store Manager, Hospital Administrator, Hotel/Motel Manager, Insurance Agent, Interior Designer, Janitor/Janitress, Lawyer, Legal Assistant, Librarian, Machinist, Mail Carrier, Manufacturing Representative, Mathematician, Math-Science Teacher, Medical Assistant, Medical Lab Technician, Military Enlisted, Military Officer, Musical Instrument Repair, Musician, Newspaper Reporter, Nurse Aide, Nurse/LPN, Nurse/RN, Occupational Therapist, Operating Room Technician, Orthotist/Prosthetist, Painter, Park Ranger, Personnel Manager, Pharmacist, Pharmacy Technician, Photographer, Physical Therapist, Physician, Piano Technician, Pipefitter/Plumber, Police Officer, Printer, Private Investigator, Psychologist, Purchasing Agent, Radio/TV Repair, Radiologic Technician, Real Estate Agent, Religious Leader, Reservation Agent, Respiratory Therapy Technician, Restaurant Manager, Secretary, Security Guard, Sheet Metal Worker, Surveyor, Teacher Aide, Telephone Repair Technician, Tool and Die Maker, Travel Agent, Truck Driver, Veterinarian, Waiter/Waitress.
Administration: Group or individual.
Price Data, 1994: $37.50 each per preview packages for Microtest Q, Microtest, or mail-in reports including 3 interpretive reports and manual; $12 per 25 answer sheets including test items to be used with Microtest Q, Microtest, or Arion II scoring; $18 per manual ('86, 218 pages); $5.70–$7.10 per Microtest Q and Microtest interpretive report; $6.70–$8.10 per Arion teleprocessing or mail-in interpretive report; $3.55–$4.20 per Microtest Q and Microtest profile report; $4.55–$5.20 per Arion or mail-in profile report.
Time: (35–40) minutes.
Author: Charles B. Johansson.
Publisher: NCS Assessments.
Cross References: For a review by James B. Rounds, see 10:43 (2 references); see also T3:367 (1 reference); for reviews by Jack L. Bodden and Paul R. Lohnes of an earlier edition, see 8:993.

[387]
Career Assessment Program.
Purpose: To develop a plan for career exploration.
Population: High school to adult.
Publication Date: 1993.
Acronym: CAP.
Administration: Group.
Restricted Distribution: Distribution restricted to licensed sites.
Price Data: Available from publisher.
Comments: Tests may be computer administered and scored.

Author: Educational Technologies, Inc.
Publisher: Educational Technologies, Inc.
   a) APTITUDE BASED CAREER DECISION TEST.
Purpose: "Used to assist individuals in selecting a career based on their aptitudes."
Acronym: ABCD.
Scores, 7: Clerical Perception, Vocabulary, Numerical Computation, Numerical Reasoning, Spatial Visualization, Inductive Reasoning, Analytical Reasoning.
Time: (100) minutes.
   b) INTEREST BASED CAREER DECISION TEST.
Purpose: "Used to assist individuals select a career based on their interests."
Acronym: IBCD.
Scores: Ratings grouped into 3 areas: Data, People, Things.
Time: (30–45) minutes.
Comments: Self-report survey.

[388]
Career Beliefs Inventory.
Purpose: Designed to assist people to identify career beliefs that may prevent them from reaching their career goals.
Population: Grade 8 and older.
Publication Date: 1991.
Acronym: CBI.
Scores, 26: Administrative Index, Employment Status, Career Plans, Acceptance of Uncertainty, Openness, Achievement, College Education, Intrinsic Satisfaction, Peer Equality, Structured Work Environment, Control, Responsibility, Approval of Others, Self-Other Comparisons, Occupation/College Variation, Career Path Flexibility, Post-Training Transition, Job Experimentation, Relocation, Improving Self, Persisting While Uncertain, Taking Risks, Learning Job Skills, Negotiating/Searching, Overcoming Obstacles, Working Hard.
Administration: Individual or group.
Price Data, 1993: $30 per 25 test booklets; $40 per 10 prepaid answer sheets (price includes scoring by publisher); $30 per manual (48 pages); $14 per 25 hand-scorable answer sheets; $20 per 10 report booklets; $30 per scoring key; $32 per sampler set.
Time: Administration time not reported.
Author: John D. Krumboltz.
Publisher: Consulting Psychologists Press, Inc.

[389]
Career Counseling Personal Data Form.
Purpose: "Designed to provide [background] information useful in career counseling."
Population: Vocational counselees.
Publication Date: 1962.
Scores: No scores.
Administration: Group.
Manual: No manual.
Price Data, 1993: $47 per package of forms; $25 per specimen set.

Time: (30–40) minutes.
Author: John B. Ahrens.
Publisher: Martin M. Bruce, Ph.D., Publishers.

[390]

Career Decision Scale.

Purpose: Developed to provide "an estimate of career indecision."
Population: Grades 9–12 and college.
Publication Dates: 1976–87.
Scores, 2: Certainty, Career Decision.
Administration: Group or individual.
Price Data, 1994: $33 per complete kit including 50 test booklets and manual ('87, 28 pages); $25 per 50 test booklets; $10 per manual.
Time: (10–15) minutes.
Authors: Samuel H. Osipow, Clarke G. Carney (test), Jane Winer (test), Barbara Yanico (test), and Maryanne Koschier (test).
Publisher: Psychological Assessment Resources, Inc.
Cross References: For reviews by Lenore W. Harmon and David O. Herman, see 9:194 (4 references).

TEST REFERENCES

1. Hartman, B. W., & Fuqua, D. R. (1982). The construct validity of The Career Decision Scale adapted for graduate students. *The Vocational Guidance Quarterly, 31,* 69-77.
2. Hartman, B. W., Fuqua, D. R., & Hartman, P. T. (1983). The predictive potential of the Career Decision Scale in identifying chronic career indecision. *The Vocational Guidance Quarterly, 32,* 103-108.
3. Utz, P. W. (1983). A comparison of three groups of vocationally indecisive students. *Journal of Counseling Psychology, 30,* 262-266.
4. Allis, M. R. (1984). [Review of the Career Decision Scale]. *Measurement and Evaluation in Counseling, 17,* 98-100.
5. Bacorn, C. N., & Dixon, D. N. (1984). The effects of touch on depressed and vocationally undecided clients. *Journal of Counseling Psychology, 31,* 488-496.
6. Cesari, J. P., Winer, J. L., & Piper, K. R. (1984). Vocational decision status and the effect of four types of occupational information on cognitive complexity. *Journal of Vocational Behavior, 25,* 215-224.
7. Glaize, D. L., & Myrick, R. D. (1984). Interpersonal groups or computers? A study of career maturity and career decidedness. *The Vocational Guidance Quarterly, 32,* 168-176.
8. Millard, R. J., Habler, B. L., & List, J. (1984). Sex-role orientation and career indecision. *The Journal of Psychology, 117,* 217-220.
9. Pinder, F. A., & Fitzgerald, P. W. (1984). The effectiveness of a computerized guidance system in promoting career decision making. *Journal of Vocational Behavior, 24,* 123-131.
10. Slaney, R. B. (1984). Relation of career indecision to changes in expressed vocational interests. *Journal of Counseling Psychology, 31,* 349-355.
11. Waas, G. A. (1984). Cognitive differentiation as a function of information type and its relation to career choice. *Journal of Vocational Behavior, 24,* 66-72.
12. Carver, D. S., & Smart, D. W. (1985). The effects of a career and self-exploration course for undecided freshmen. *Journal of College Student Personnel, 26,* 37-43.
13. Graef, M. I., Wells, D. L., Hyland, A. M., & Muchinsky, P. M. (1985). Life history antecedents of vocational indecision. *Journal of Vocational Behavior, 27,* 276-297.
14. Hartman, B. W., Fuqua, D. R., & Blum, C. R. (1985). A path-analytic model of career indecision. *Vocational Guidance Quarterly, 33,* 231-240.
15. Hartman, B. W., Fuqua, D. R., Blum, C. R., & Hartman, P. T. (1985). A study of the predictive validity of the career decision scale in identifying longitudinal patterns of career indecision. *Journal of Vocational Behavior, 27,* 202-209.
16. Larson, L. M., & Heppner, P. P. (1985). The relationship of problem-solving appraisal to career decision and indecision. *Journal of Vocational Behavior, 26,* 55-65.
17. Neimeyer, G. J., Nevill, D. D., Probert, B., & Fukuyama, M. (1985). Cognitive structures in vocational development. *Journal of Vocational Behavior, 27,* 191-201.
18. Osipow, S. H., & Reed, R. (1985). Decision making style and career indecision in college students. *Journal of Vocational Behavior, 27,* 368-373.
19. Robbins, S. B., & Patton, M. J. (1985). Self-psychology and career development: Construction of the superiority and goal instability scales. *Journal of Counseling Psychology, 32,* 221-231.
20. Blustein, D. L., Judd, T. P., Krom, J., Viniar, B., Padilla, E., Wedemeyer, R., & Williams, D. (1986). Identifying predictors of academic performance of community college students. *Journal of College Student Personnel, 27,* 242-249.
21. Cooper, S. E. (1986). The effects of group and individual vocational counseling on career indecision and personal indecisiveness. *Journal of College Student Personnel, 27,* 39-42.
22. Davis, R. C., & Horne, A. M. (1986). The effect of small group counseling and a career course on career decidedness and maturity. *Vocational Guidance Quarterly, 34,* 255-262.
23. Hartman, B. W., Fuqua, D. R., & Jenkins, S. J. (1986). The reliability/generalizability of the construct of career indecision. *Journal of Vocational Behavior, 28,* 142-148.
24. Krieshok, T. S., Arnold, J. J., Kuperman, B. D., & Schmitz, N. K. (1986). Articulation of career values: Comparison of three measures. *Journal of Counseling Psychology, 33,* 475-478.
25. Lent, R. W., Brown, S. D., & Larkin, K. C. (1986). Self-efficacy in the prediction of academic performance and perceived career options. *Journal of Counseling Psychology, 33,* 265-269.
26. Lent, R. W., Larkin, K. C., & Hasegawa, C. S. (1986). Effects of a "focused interest" career course approach for college students. *Vocational Guidance Quarterly, 34,* 151-159.
27. Schroer, A. C. P., & Dorn, F. J. (1986). Enhancing the career and personal development of gifted college students. *Journal of Counseling and Development, 64,* 567-571.
28. Erwin, T. D. (1987). The construct validity of Holland's differentiation concept. *Measurement and Evaluation in Counseling and Development, 20,* 106-112.
29. Hartman, B. W., Jenkins, S. J., Fuqua, D. R., & Sutherland, V. E. (1987). An analysis of gender differences in the factor structure of the Career Decision Scale. *Educational and Psychological Measurement, 47*(4), 1099-1106.
30. Lent, R. W., Brown, S. D., & Larkin, K. C. (1987). Comparison of three theoretically derived variables in predicting career and academic behavior: Self-efficacy, interest congruence, and consequence thinking. *Journal of Counseling Psychology, 34,* 293-298.
31. Blustein, D. L. (1988). A canonical analysis of career choice crystallization and vocational maturity. *Journal of Counseling Psychology, 35,* 294-297.
32. Erwin, T. D. (1988). Some evidence for the construct validity of the Map of College Majors. *Measurement and Evaluation in Counseling and Development, 20,* 158-161.
33. Fuqua, D. R., Newman, J. L., & Seaworth, T. B. (1988). Relation of state and trait anxiety to different components of career indecision. *Journal of Counseling Psychology, 35,* 154-158.
34. Hartman, B. W., Fuqua, D. R., & Jenkins, S. J. (1988). Multivariate generalizability analysis of three measures of career indecision. *Educational and Psychological Measurement, 48,* 61-68.
35. Larson, L. M., Heppner, P. P., Ham, T., & Dugan, K. (1988). Investigating multiple subtypes of career indecision through cluster analysis. *Journal of Counseling Psychology, 35,* 439-446.
36. Lazarick, D. L., Fishbein, S. S., Loiello, M. A., & Howard, G. S. (1988). Practical investigations of volition. *Journal of Counseling Psychology, 35,* 15-26.
37. Dorn, F. J. (1989). An examination of client motivation and career certainty. *Journal of College Student Development, 30,* 237-241.
38. Arbona, C. (1990). Career counseling research and Hispanics: A review of the literature. *The Counseling Psychologist, 18,* 300-323.
39. Osipow, S. H. (1991). Developing instruments for use in counseling. *Journal of Counseling and Development, 70,* 322-326.
40. Osipow, S. H. (1991). Response to Vondracek, Dorn, and Hackett. *Journal of Counseling and Development, 70,* 332-333.
41. Vondracek, F. W. (1991). Osipow on the Career Decision Scale: Some comments. *Journal of Counseling and Development, 70,* 327.
42. Wanberg, C. R., & Muchinsky, P. M. (1992). A typology of career decision status: Validity extension status model. *Journal of Counseling Psychology, 39,* 71-80.
43. Chartrand, J. M., Camp, C. C., & McFadden, K. L. (1992). Predicting academic adjustment and career indecision: A comparison of self-efficacy, interest congruence, and commitment. *Journal of College Student Development, 33,* 293-300.
44. Mau, W. C., & Jepsen, D. A. (1992). Effects of computer-assisted instruction in using formal decision-making strategies to choose a college major. *Journal of Counseling Psychology, 39,* 185-192.
45. Mau, W., & Jepsen, D. A. (1992). Effects of computer-assisted instruction in using formal decision-making strategies to choose a college major. *Journal of Counseling Psychology, 39,* 185-192.

46. Savickas, M. L., Carden, A. D., Toman, S., & Jarjourg, D. (1992). Dimensions of career decidedness. *Measurement and Evaluation in Counseling and Development, 25,* 102-112.

47. Wanberg, C. R., & Muchinsky, P. M. (1992). A typology of career decision status: Validity extension of the vocational decision status model. *Journal of Counseling Psychology, 39,* 71-80.

48. Kush, K., & Cochran, L. (1993). Enhancing a sense of agency through career planning. *Journal of Counseling Psychology, 40,* 434-439.

49. Stead, G. B., & Watson, M. B. (1993). How similar are the factor structures of the Career Decision Scale, the Career Decision Profile, and the Career Factors Inventory? *Educational and Psychological Measurement, 53,* 281-290.

[391]

Career Development Inventory [Consulting Psychologists Press, Inc.]

Purpose: "Measures several affective and cognitive aspects of the earlier stages of career development."

Population: Grades 8–12, college.

Publication Dates: 1979–84.

Acronym: CDI.

Scores, 8: Career Planning, Career Exploration, Decision Making, World-of-Work Information, Knowledge of Preferred Occupational Group, Career Development Attitudes, Career Development Knowledge and Skills, Total.

Administration: Group.

Levels, 2: School Form, College and University Form.

Price Data, 1993: $30 per sampler set including user's manual, test booklet, and prepaid answer sheets for both high school and college and university inventories; $23 per 25 reusable high school test booklets; $48 per 10 prepaid high school answer sheets; $45 per 25 reusable college and university test booklets; $48 per 10 prepaid college and university answer sheets; $19 per user's manual; $22 per technical manual; $35 per complete manual set.

Time: (55–65) minutes.

Authors: Donald E. Super, Albert S. Thompson, Richard H. Lindeman, Jean P. Jordaan, and Roger A. Myers.

Publisher: Consulting Psychologists Press, Inc.

Cross References: For a review by James W. Pinkney, see 9:195 (4 references).

TEST REFERENCES

1. Phillips, S. D., & Strohmer, D. C. (1983). Vocationally mature coping strategies and progress in the decision-making process: A canonical analysis. *Journal of Counseling Psychology, 30,* 395-402.

2. Healy, C. C., & Mourton, D. L. (1984). The effects of an abbreviated Self-Directed Search on the career decision competencies of community college students. *Vocational Guidance Quarterly, 33,* 55-62.

3. Healy, C. C., Mourton, D. L., Anderson, E. C., & Robinson, E. (1984). Career maturity and the achievement of community college students and disadvantaged university students. *Journal of College Student Personnel, 25,* 347-352.

4. Savickas, M. L. (1984). Construction and validation of a physician career development inventory. *Journal of Vocational Behavior, 25,* 106-123.

5. Savickas, M. L., Silling, S. M., & Schwartz, S. (1984). Time perspective in vocational maturity and career decision making. *Journal of Vocational Behavior, 25,* 258-269.

6. Super, D. E., & Nevill, D. D. (1984). Work role salience as a determinant of career maturity in high school students. *Journal of Vocational Behavior, 25,* 30-44.

7. Trebilco, G. R. (1984). Career education and career maturity. *Journal of Vocational Behavior, 25,* 191-202.

8. Graef, M. I., Wells, D. L., Hyland, A. M., & Muchinsky, P. M. (1985). Life history antecedents of vocational indecision. *Journal of Vocational Behavior, 27,* 276-297.

9. Hansen, J. C. (1985). [Test review of the Career Development Inventory]. *Measurement and Evaluation in Counseling and Development, 17,* 220-224.

10. Healy, C. C., & Mourton, D. L. (1985). Congruence and vocational identity: Outcomes of career counseling with persuasive power. *Journal of Counseling Psychology, 32,* 441-444.

11. MacCulloch, W., & Cochran, L. (1985). The career development of peer counsellors in a vocational counselling program. *Canadian Counsellor, 19,* 128-134.

12. Neimeyer, G. J., Nevill, D. D., Probert, B., & Fukuyama, M. (1985). Cognitive structures in vocational development. *Journal of Vocational Behavior, 27,* 191-201.

13. Punch, K. F., & Sheridan, B. E. (1985). Some measurement characteristics of the Career Development Inventory. *Measurement and Evaluation in Counseling and Development, 17,* 196-202.

14. Healy, C. C., & Mourton, D. L. (1987). The relationship of career exploration, college jobs, and grade point average. *Journal of College Student Personnel, 28,* 28-34.

15. Blustein, D. L. (1988). A canonical analysis of career choice crystallization and vocational maturity. *Journal of Counseling Psychology, 35,* 294-297.

16. Palmer, Sylvia, & Cochran, L. (1988). Parents as agents of career development. *Journal of Counseling Psychology, 35,* 71-76.

17. Rodriguez, M., & Blocher, D. (1988). A comparison of two approaches to enhancing career maturity in Puerto Rican college women. *Journal of Counseling Psychology, 35,* 275-280.

18. Arbona, C. (1990). Career counseling research and Hispanics: A review of the literature. *The Counseling Psychologist, 18,* 300-323.

19. King, S. (1990). Comparing two causal models of career maturity for hearing-impaired adolescents. *American Annals of the Deaf, 135,* 43-49.

20. Super, D. E., Osborne, L., Walsh, D. J., Brown, S. D., & Niles, S. G. (1992). Development career assessment and counseling: The C-DAC model. *Journal of Counseling and Development, 71,* 74-80.

[392]

Career Directions Inventory.

Purpose: "Designed to identify areas of greater or lesser interest from among a wide variety of occupations" to assist in educational and career planning.

Population: High school and college and adults.

Publication Dates: 1982–86.

Acronym: CDI.

Scores: 15 Basic Interest scales: Administration, Art, Clerical, Food Service, Industrial Arts, Health Service, Outdoors, Personal Service, Sales, Science & Technology, Teaching/Social Service, Writing, Assertive, Persuasive, Systematic.

Administration: Group.

Price Data, 1990: $15 per examination kit including machine-scorable question/answer document and manual ('86, 61 pages); $3.50 per Basic Report including machine-scorable answer sheet and 4-page report; $7 per Extended Report including machine-scorable question/answer sheet and 12-page report; $10.50 per manual; $150 per CDI SigmaSoft software package.

Foreign Language Editions: Question/answer documents and Extended Reports available in French.

Time: (30–50) minutes.

Comments: Must be computer scored through mail-in scoring service or on-site CDI software.

Author: Douglas N. Jackson.

Publisher: Sigma Assessment Systems, Inc., Research Psychologists Press Division.

Cross References: For reviews by Darrell L. Sabers and Fredrick A. Schrank, see 9:44.

[393]

The Career Exploration Inventory.
Purpose: Designed to measure both work and leisure interests.
Population: Adults.
Publication Date: 1992.
Acronym: CEI.
Scores, 15: Mechanical, Animal Care, Plants, Physical Sciences, Life Sciences, Artistic, Literary Arts, Social Service, Physical Performing, Personal Service, Persuading/Influencing, Protecting, Leading, Clerical, Financial Detail.
Administration: Group.
Manual: No manual.
Price Data: Available from publisher.
Time: Administration time not reported.
Comments: Self-administered and self-scored.
Author: John J. Liptak.
Publisher: JIST Works, Inc.

[394]

Career Exploration Series, 1992 Revision.
Purpose: Designed for career guidance using "a series of six job interest inventories that focus on specific occupational fields."
Population: Grades 7–12 and college and adults.
Publication Dates: 1979–92.
Acronym: CES.
Scores: 6 areas: Agriculture-Forestry-Conservation, Science-Mathematics-Health, Business, Industrial, Consumer Economics, Design-Art-Communications.
Administration: Group.
Price Data, 1993: $45 per class set of 30 inventories (5 of each title); $249 per complete CES software set (6 programs); $40 per 25 reusable booklets (specify title); $8.75 per 25 answer folders (specify title); $49.95 per software package (specify title, computer type, and disk size).
Time: (50–60) minutes.
Comments: Self-administered and self-scored interest inventories.
Authors: Arthur Cutler, Francis Ferry, Robert Kauk, and Robert Robinett.
Publisher: CFKR Career Materials, Inc.
Cross References: For reviews by Mark Pope and William I. Sauser, Jr., see 11:60; for reviews by Bruce R. Fretz and Robert B. Slaney of the original edition, see 9:196.

[395]

Career Guidance Inventory.
Purpose: "Designed to provide measures of relative interest in postsecondary instructional programs."
Population: Students and prospective students at trade, vocational, or technical school, or at community college.
Publication Dates: 1972–89.
Acronym: CGI.
Scores, 47: Agribusiness and Agricultural Production, Renewable Natural Resources, Business

(Accounting and Finance, Data Processing, Clerical/Typing/Word Processing, Office Supervision and Management, Secretarial), Marketing and Distribution (General Marketing, Financial Services, Hospitality/Recreation/Tourism, Real Estate), Communications and Communications Technologies, Computer and Information Sciences, Cosmetology and Barbering, Engineering and Related Technologies (Architectural, Civil, Electrical and Electronic, Environmental Control, Industrial Production, Mechanical Engineering, Mining and Petroleum), Allied Health (Dental Services, Diagnostic and Treatment Services, Miscellaneous Services, Medical Laboratory Technologies, Mental Health/Human Services, Nursing and Related Services, Rehabilitation Services), Vocational Home Economics (Child Care and Guidance, Clothing/Apparel/Textiles, Food Production/Management/Services, Institutional/Home Management/Supporting Services), Protective Services, Construction Trades (Brickmason/Stonemason/Tile Setting, Carpentry, Electrical and Power Transmission Installation, Plumbing/Pipefitting/Steamfitting), Mechanics and Repairers (Electrical and Electronic Equipment Repair, Heating/Air Conditioning/Refrigeration Mechanics, Industrial Equipment Maintenance and Repair, Vehicle and Mobile Equipment), Precision Production (Drafting, Graphic and Printing Communications, Precision Metal Work, Woodworking), Transportation and Material Moving, Visual Arts (Fine Arts).
Administration: Group.
Price Data, 1991: $3 per reusable test booklet; $35 per 25 answer sheet/interpretation guides; $6 per administrator's manual ('89, 43 pages); $10 per specimen set of all Career Guidance Inventory and Educational Interest Inventory (859) components.
Time: [45–60] minutes.
Comments: Self-administered, self-scored.
Author: James E. Oliver.
Publisher: Wintergreen/Orchard House, Inc.
Cross References: For reviews by E. Jack Asher, Jr., and Michael B. Bunch, see 11:61; for a review by James B. Rounds, Jr., of an earlier edition, see 9:197; for a review by Bert W. Westbrook, see 8:996.

[396]

Career Interest Inventory.
Purpose: "Designed to assist students in making decisions concerning their educational and vocational plans."
Publication Dates: 1989–91.
Administration: Group.
Price Data, 1994: $11.50 per examination kit including Level 1 machine-scorable answer document, Level 2 hand-scorable booklet, directions for administering, and student profile; $32.50 per counselor's manual ('91, 120 pages); $11.50 per 25 Exploring Interests: An Introduction to the Career Interests Inventory; $4.50 per directions for administering ('90, 29 pages); $1.62 scoring charge per Level 1

answer document; $.59 for first copy and $.17 per each additional copy of individual report; $.56 for first copy and $.05 per each additional copy of counselor's report (by Teacher/Counselor or School); $.53 for first copy and $.18 per each additional copy of student record label; $.42 for first copy and $.10 per each additional copy of occupational interest report (by School); $.27 for first copy and $15.58 per set of career planning summary (by Teacher/Counselor); $.20 for first copy and $15.58 per set of career planning summary (by School); $.15 for first copy and $13.35 per set of career planning summary (by District); $70 (not refundable) plus $.28 per pupil for student data tape; $.35 per pupil for student data diskette; $12.50 for first 1,000 and $3.20 per each additional 1,000 for return of test booklets; $6.39 for first 1,000 plus $1.74 per each additional 1,000 for return of answer documents; $10.47 for first 1,000 plus $3.20 per each additional 1,000 for return of mixed documents.

Time: (30–40) minutes.
Authors: The Psychological Corporation.
Publisher: The Psychological Corporation.

a) LEVEL 1.
Population: Grades 7–9.
Scores, 47: 15 Occupational Interests (Social Sciences, Clerical Services, Health Services, Agriculture, Customer Services, Fine Arts, Mathematics and Science, Building Trades, Educational Services, Legal Services, Transportation, Sales, Management, Benchwork, Machine Operation), 16 High School Subject Interests (Speech or Drama, Metal Shop or Woodworking, Mathematics, Auto Repair, Science, Cooking or Sewing, Art or Music, Farming or Livestock Care, Newspaper Writing, Typing or Office Machines, Social Studies, Health Care, Creative Writing, Computers, English or Literature, Bookkeeping or Office Practices), 16 High School Activity Interests (Mathematics Club, Farming Club, Speech or Debate Team, School Library Aide, School Play, Automobile Club, Science Fair, Teacher's Aide, Student Government, Office Helper or Assistant, School Literary Magazine, School Officer, Photography Club, Business Club, School Newspaper, Computer Club).
Price Data: $37.50 per 25 hand-scorable booklets; $37.50 per 25 Type 1 machine-scorable answer documents; $37.50 per 25 Type 2 machine-scorable answer documents.

b) LEVEL 2.
Population: Grades 10–12 and adults.
Scores, 35: 15 Occupational Interests (same as Level 1), 20 Post-High School Course Interests (Marketing or Sales, Computer Programming, Electronics or Electrical Trades, Plumbing or Welding, Automotive Repair, Carpentry or Home Building, Word Processing or Typing, Haircutting or Styling, Bookkeeping or Office Practices, Cooking or Sewing, Music or Art, Farming or Livestock Care, Mathematics or Science, English or Foreign Language, Business Law or Management,

Creative Writing, Speech or Drama, Photography, Health Care, Newspaper Writing).
Price Data: $40.50 per 25 hand-scorable booklets; $40.50 per 25 Type 1 machine-scorable answer documents; $40.50 per 25 Type 2 machine-scorable answer documents.

[397]

Career Interests Test.
Purpose: To determine "the relative career interests of young persons and adults."
Population: Young persons and adults.
Publication Dates: 1971–83.
Scores, 6: Outdoor-Physical, Scientific-Theoretical, Social Service, Aesthetic-Literary, Commerical-Clerical, Practical-Technical.
Administration: Group.
Price Data: Available from publisher.
Time: (30–35) minutes.
Author: Educational & Industrial Test Services Ltd.
Publisher: Educational & Industrial Test Services Ltd. [England].
Cross References: For reviews by Christopher Borman and Dan Zakay, see 9:198.

[398]

Career Maturity Inventory.
Purpose: "Constructed to measure the maturity of attitudes and competencies that are critical in realistic career decision making."
Population: Grades 6–12.
Publication Dates: 1973–78.
Acronym: CMI.
Administration: Group.
Price Data, 1993: $19.50 per 50 hand-scorable answer sheets; $37.40 per set of hand-scoring stencils; $1 per hand-scoring stencil; $30 per 100 profile sheets; $7.15 per administration manual ('78, 52 pages); $10.05 per theory and research handbook ('78, 44 pages); $17.98 per specimen set; $30.38 or less per 10 Compuscan answer sheets (includes prepaid computer scoring).
Comments: Formerly entitled Vocational Development Inventory (VDI).
Author: John O. Crites.
Publisher: Chronicle Guidance Publications, Inc.

a) ATTITUDE SCALE, SCREENING FORM A-2.
Price Data: $46.90 per 35 tests ('78, 7 pages).
Time: (30) minutes.

b) ATTITUDE SCALE, COUNSELING FORM B-1.
Scores, 5: Decisiveness, Involvement, Independence, Orientation, Compromise.
Price Data: $46.90 per 35 tests ('78, 7 pages).
Time: (40) minutes.

c) COMPETENCE TEST.
Scores, 5: Self-Appraisal, Occupational Information, Goal Selection, Planning, Problem Solving.
Price Data: $77.35 per 35 tests ('78, 38 pages).
Time: (120) minutes.
Cross References: See 9:199 (12 references) and T3:374 (48 references); for reviews by Martin R.

Katz and Donald G. Zytowski, and an excerpted review by Garth Sorenson, see 8:997 (152 references); see also T2:2103 (35 references).

TEST REFERENCES

1. Pelhan, J. P., & Fretz, B. R. (1982). Racial differences and attributes of career choice unrealism. *The Vocational Guidance Quarterly, 31,* 36-42.
2. Bernardelli, A., Stefano, J. D., & Dumont, F. (1983). Occupational information-seeking as a function of perception of locus of control and other personality variables. *Canadian Counsellor, 17,* 75-81.
3. Chodzinski, R. T. (1983). Validity concerns for counsellors using the 1978 edition of the Career Maturity Inventory. *Canadian Counsellor, 18,* 5-12.
4. Amatea, E. S., Clark, J. E., & Cross, E. G. (1984). Life-styles: Evaluating a life role planning program for high school students. *The Vocational Guidance Quarterly, 32,* 249-259.
5. Crook, R. H., Healy, C. C., & O'Shea, D. W. (1984). The linkage of work achievement to self-esteem, career maturity, and college achievement. *Journal of Vocational Behavior, 25,* 70-79.
6. Glaize, D. L., & Myrick, R. D. (1984). Interpersonal groups or computers? A study of career maturity and career decidedness. *The Vocational Guidance Quarterly, 32,* 168-176.
7. Lee, C. C. (1984). Predicting the career choice attitudes of rural Black, White, and Native American high school students. *The Vocational Guidance Quarterly, 32,* 177-184.
8. Savickas, M. L. (1984). Career maturity: The construct and its measurement. *The Vocational Guidance Quarterly, 32,* 222-231.
9. Sherry, P., & Staley, K. (1984). Career exploration groups: An outcome study. *Journal of College Student Personnel, 25,* 155-159.
10. Ware, M. E., Millard, R. J., & Matthews, J. R. (1984). Strategies for evaluating field-placement programs. *Psychological Reports, 55,* 571-574.
11. Carver, D. S., & Smart, D. W. (1985). The effects of a career and self-exploration course for undecided freshmen. *Journal of College Student Personnel, 26,* 37-43.
12. Crites, J. O., Wallbrown, F. H., & Blaha, J. (1985). The Career Maturity Inventory: Myths and realities—A rejoinder to Westbrook, Cutts, Madison, and Arcia (1980). *Journal of Vocational Behavior, 26,* 221-238.
13. Fassinger, R. E. (1985). A causal model of college women's career choice. *Journal of Vocational Behavior, 27,* 123-153.
14. Healy, C. C., O'Shea, D., & Crook, R. H. (1985). Relation of career attitudes to age and career progress during college. *Journal of Counseling Psychology, 32,* 239-244.
15. Khan, S. B., & Alvi, S. A. (1985). Career maturity in relation to differences in school curriculum. *Canadian Counsellor, 12,* 144-151.
16. Pavlak, M. F., & Kammer, P. P. (1985). The effects of a career guidance program on the career maturity and self-concept of delinquent youth. *Journal of Vocational Behavior, 26,* 41-54.
17. Stowe, R. W. (1985). Convergent and discriminant validity of Crite's Career Maturity Inventory Attitude Scale, Counseling Form B-1. *Educational and Psychological Measurement, 45,* 763-770.
18. Ware, M. E. (1985). Assessing a career development course for upper-level college students. *Journal of College Student Personnel, 26,* 152-155.
19. Westbrook, B. W. (1985). What research says about career maturity...: A response to Crites, Wallbrown, and Blaha (1985). *Journal of Vocational Behavior, 26,* 239-250.
20. Davis, R. C., & Horne, A. M. (1986). The effect of small group counseling and a career course on career decidedness and maturity. *Vocational Guidance Quarterly, 34,* 255-262.
21. Robbins, S. B., & Tucker, K. R., Jr. (1986). Relation to goal instability to self-directed and interactional career counseling workshops. *Journal of Counseling Psychology, 33,* 418-424.
22. Wallbrown, F. H., Silling, S. M., & Crites, J. O. (1986). Testing Crite's model of career maturity: A hierarchical strategy. *Journal of Vocational Behavior, 28,* 183-190.
23. Kennedy, S. R., & Dimick, K. M. (1987). Career maturity and professional sports expectations of college football and basketball players. *Journal of College Student Personnel, 28,* 293-297.
24. Windish, K. C., & Lester, D. (1987). Scores on the Career Maturity Inventory and self-confidence. *Psychological Reports, 60,* 690.
25. McNeill, B. W., & Stoltenberg, C. D. (1988). A test of the elaboration likelihood mode for therapy. *Cognitive Therapy and Research, 12,* 69-80.
26. Arbona, C. (1990). Career counseling research and Hispanics: A review of the literature. *The Counseling Psychologist, 18,* 300-323.
27. Westbrook, B. W., & Sanford, E. E. (1992). The relationship between career choice attitudes and career choice competencies of Black 9th-grade pupils. *Educational and Psychological Measurement, 52,* 347-351.
28. Luzzo, D. A. (1993). Predicting the career maturity of undergraduates: A comparison of personal, educational, and psychological factors. *Journal of College Student Development, 34,* 271-275.
29. Luzzo, D. A. (1993). The relationship between undergraduates' locus of control and career development. *Journal of College Student Development, 34,* 227-228.
30. Westbrook, B. W., & Sanford, E. E. (1993). Relation between self-appraisal and appropriateness of career choices of male and female adolescents. *Educational and Psychological Measurement, 53,* 291-299.

[399]

Career Occupational Preference System, Interest Inventory, Form R.

Purpose: Designed to measure interests as they relate to careers using simplified language.

Population: Grade 6 through high school.

Publication Dates: 1984–89.

Acronym: COPS-R.

Scores: Scores in the 14 COPSystem Career Clusters: Science-Professional, Science-Skilled, Technology-Professional, Technology-Skilled, Consumer Economics, Outdoor, Business-Professional, Business-Skilled, Clerical, Communication, Arts-Professional, Arts-Skilled, Service-Professional, Service-Skilled.

Administration: Group.

Price Data, 1993: $20.50 per 25 self-scoring forms [$74 per 100, $348.25 per 500]; $11 per 25 machine-scoring forms [$38.75 per 100, $182.25 per 500]; $1.30 each scoring by publisher; $4.25 per technical manual ('89, 34 pages); $2 per examiner's manual ('89, 14 pages); $5.75 per specimen set; $28.50 per 25 COPS-R Comprehensive Career Guides [$95.25 per 100, $447.50 per 500]; $4.50 per 25 COPS-R Summary Guides [$17 per 100, $74.25 per 500]; $18.50 per COPS-R Visuals.

Time: (20) minutes.

Authors: Lila F. Knapp and Robert R. Knapp.

Publisher: EdITS/Educational and Industrial Testing Service.

TEST REFERENCES

1. Knapp, R. R., & Knapp, L. (1979). Relationship of work values to occupational activity interests. *Measurement and Evaluation in Guidance, 12,* 71-76.
2. Stewart, W. W., Davis, P. D., Wilson, R. C., & Porter, T. (1981). Expressed versus tested vocational interests of incarcerated and non-incarcerated adolescents. *Journal of Applied Rehabilitation Counseling, 12,* 126-129.
3. Christian, J. K., & Bringmann, W. G. (1982). Comparison of computerized versus standardized feedback and accurate versus inaccurate feedback. *Psychological Reports, 50,* 1067-1070.
4. Knapp, L., & Knapp, R. R. (1982). Clustered occupational interest measurement based on sex-balanced inventory items. *Journal of Educational Measurement, 19,* 75-81.
5. Knapp-Lee, L., & Michael, W. B. (1983). The construct validity of a career interest inventory representing eight major clusters of professional level occupational activities. *Educational and Psychological Measurement, 43,* 211-222.
6. Omizo, M. M., & Michael, W. B. (1983). Relationship of COPSystem interest inventory scales to Vocational Preference Inventory (VPI) scales in a college sample: Construct validity of scales based on professed occupational interest. *Educational and Psychological Measurement, 43,* 595-601.
7. Knapp-Lee, L., Michael, W. B., & Grutter, J. (1984). Relationship of the COPSystem, Form P Interest Inventory (COPS-P) scales to Vocational Preference Inventory scales (VPI): Construct validity of scales based on professed occupational interest in a college sample. *Educational and Psychological Measurement, 44,* 455-461.
8. Knapp-Lee, L., Michael, W. B., & Grutter, J. (1984). Relation-

ship of interest measurement from the COPSystem Interest Inventory (Form P) and the Strong-Campbell Interest Inventory (SCII): Construct validation of two measures of interest at the college level. *Educational and Psychological Measurement, 44,* 743-751.

9. Knapp, R. R., Knapp, L., & Knapp-Lee, L. (1985). Occupational interest measurement and subsequent career decisions: A predictive follow-up study of the COPSystem Interest Inventory. *Journal of Counseling Psychology, 32,* 348-354.

10. Knapp-Lee, L. J., & Michael, W. B. (1985). The construct validity of a career interest inventory representing sixteen subclusters within eight major career clusters of professional level occupational activities. *Educational and Psychological Measurement, 45,* 881-888.

11. Kane, S. T. (1989). A review of the COPS Interest Inventory. *Journal of Counseling and Development, 67,* 361-363.

12. Zarrella, K. L., & Schuerger, J. M. (1990). Temporal stability of occupational interest inventories. *Psychological Reports, 66,* 1067-1074.

[400]

Career Occupational Preference System, Intermediate Inventory.

Purpose: To measure career interests and provide a rating of interests based on knowledge of school subjects and activities familiar to elementary and intermediate grade students.

Population: Elementary through high school with 4th grade reading level.

Publication Dates: 1981–92.

Acronym: COPS-II.

Scores: Scores in 14 COPSystem Career Clusters: Science-Professional, Science-Skilled, Technology-Professional, Technology-Skilled, Consumer Economics, Outdoor, Business-Professional, Business-Skilled, Clerical, Communication, Arts-Professional, Arts-Skilled, Service-Professional, Service-Skilled.

Administration: Group.

Price Data, 1993: $21.75 per 25 self-scoring test booklets [$78.75 per 100, $370.75 per 500]; $2 per examiner's manual ('92, 23 pages); $3.25 per specimen set; $4.50 per 25 COPS-II Summary Guide [$17 per 100, $74.25 per 500]; $18.50 per COPS-II Visuals.

Time: (15–20) minutes.

Authors: Robert R. Knapp and Lila F. Knapp.

Publisher: EdITS/Educational and Industrial Testing Service.

[401]

Career Occupational Preference System— Professional Level Interest Inventory.

Purpose: Designed to measure career interest for those wanting to focus on the professional level careers.

Population: College and adult professionals, college-bound senior high school students.

Publication Dates: 1982–89.

Acronym: COPS-P.

Scores: Scores in the 14 COPSystem Career Clusters: Business-Professional, Business-Skilled, Science-Professional, Science-Skilled, Technology-Professional, Technology-Skilled, Consumer Economics, Outdoor, Clerical, Communication, Arts-Professional; Arts-Skilled, Service-Professional, Service-Skilled.

Administration: Group.

Price Data, 1993: $10.50 per 25 self-scoring forms [$38.25 per 100, $179.75 per 500]; $10.25 per 25 Self-Interpretation Profiles and Guide [$36.25 per 100, $168.50 per 500]; $11 per 25 machine-scoring forms [$38.75 per 100, $182.25 per 500]; $1.30 each scoring by publisher; $18 per hand-scoring keys; $4.25 per technical manual ('89, 37 pages); $2 per examiner's manual ('89, 15 pages); $18.50 per set of COPS-P Visuals; $7.50 per specimen set.

Time: (15–20) minutes.

Authors: Lisa Knapp-Lee, Lila F. Knapp, and Robert R. Knapp.

Publisher: EdITS/Educational and Industrial Testing Service.

[402]

Career Orientation Placement and Evaluation Survey.

Purpose: Designed to measure values having a demonstrated effect on vocational motivation.

Population: Grade 7 through high school, college, and adult.

Publication Dates: 1981–92.

Acronym: COPES.

Scores: Scores in 14 COPSystem Career Clusters: Science-Professional, Science-Skilled, Technology-Professional, Technology-Skilled, Consumer Economics, Outdoor, Business-Professional, Business-Skilled, Clerical, Communication, Arts-Professional, Arts-Skilled, Service-Professional, Service-Skilled.

Administration: Group.

Price Data, 1993: $10.50 per 25 self-scoring test booklets [$38.25 per 100, $179.75 per 500]; $3.75 per 25 Self-interpretation Profiles and scoring test booklets [$10.25 per 100, $48.50 per 500]; $11 per 25 machine-scoring test booklets [$38.75 per 100, $182.50 per 500]; $1.30 each scoring by publisher; $5.50 per specimen set including manual ('90, 13 pages); $4.25 per technical manual ('92, 36 pages); $2 per examiner's manual; $7.50 per COPES visuals.

Time: (15–20) minutes.

Authors: Robert R. Knapp and Lila F. Knapp.

Publisher: EdITS/Educational and Industrial Testing Service.

[403]

Career Problem Check List.

Purpose: "Developed to help career teachers, career officers, and counsellors . . . identify the problems secondary school or college students may be experiencing in making career plans."

Population: Ages 14–17.

Publication Date: 1983.

Acronym: CPCL.

Scores: 7 areas: Problems at School or College, Problems in Making Decisions, Problems at Home, Problems in Obtaining Specific Occupational Information, Problems in Applying for a Job or for a Course, Problems in Starting Work, Problems Outside Work.

Administration: Group.

Price Data, 1987: £8.65 per 25 checklists; £6.90 per manual (16 pages).

Time: (10–15) minutes.
Author: A. D. Crowley.
Publisher: NFER-Nelson Publishing Co., Ltd. [England].
Cross References: For a review by Nicholas A. Vacc and James Pickering, see 9:200.

[404]

The Career Profile System, Second Edition.
Purpose: "Predicts an individual's probability of success in an insurance sales career."
Population: Insurance sales representatives and candidates for insurance.
Publication Dates: 1983–92.
Administration: Individual.
Price Data: Available from publisher.
Foreign Language Editions: English-speaking Canada and French-speaking Canada editions available; U.S. Spanish edition of Initial Career Profile available in 1994.
Time: (55–65) minutes.
Comments: Profiles processed by publisher.
Author: Life Insurance Marketing and Research Association, Inc.
Publisher: Life Insurance Marketing and Research Association, Inc.
a) STUDENT CAREER PROFILE.
Population: High school–college.
Scores: Total score and ratings in 3 areas: Industry Contacts, Achievement Orientation, Economic Maturity.
   1) *Candidate Self-Assessment.*
   Scores: 11 areas: Motivating Goals (External Goals, Internal Goals, Nonwork Goals), Knowledge and Expectations of the Career (Knowledge of the Career, Expectations of the Commitment Required, Expectations of Sales Process, Income Expectations), The Candidate's Concerns (Acceptance as a Sales Representative, Potential Drawbacks of Career, Impact on Social Relationships, Income).
b) INITIAL CAREER PROFILE.
Population: Inexperienced candidates.
Scores: Total score and ratings in 6 areas: Commitment to Present Situation, Belief in the Value of Insurance, Financial Situation, Income Expectations, Career Expectations, Work History.
   1) Same as *a*-1 above.
c) ADVANCED CAREER PROFILE.
Population: Experienced candidates.
Scores: Total score and ratings in 5 areas: Position Familiarity, Professional Involvement, Belief in the Value of Insurance, Insurance Earnings, Income Needs and Expectations.
   1) *Candidate Self-Assessment.*
   Scores: 11 areas: Satisfaction with Present Insurance Sales Career (Training and Support, Compensation, Evaluation of Products, Evaluation of Current Agency, Administrative Issues), Sales Results (Number of Sales, Total Annualized Premiums, Persistency), Insurance Income

(Income History, Income Needs, Income Expectations).

[405]

Career Survey.
Purpose: "To provide students, clients, and their counselors with information which may stimulate the counseling process . . . to encourage students and clients to explore career areas which they may not have previously considered . . . to provide a means for self-reflection and clarification of long-range plans in order to make short-range educational decisions which are consistent with those plans."
Population: Grade 7 through adults.
Publication Date: 1984.
Scores, 14: 12 interest scales (Accommodating/Entertaining, Humanitarian/Caretaking, Plant/Animal Caretaking, Mechanical, Business Detail, Sales, Numerical, Communications/Promotion, Science/Technology, Artistic Expression, Educational/Social, Medical) and 2 ability scales (Verbal, Nonverbal).
Administration: Group.
Price Data, 1993: $37.50 per 35 career survey booklets, 35 career orientation booklets, and directions for administration (16 pages); $34 per 35 interest survey booklets including interests only, 35 orientation booklets, and directions for administration; $19 per review kit; scoring service and additional packages available from publisher.
Time: (60–70) minutes.
Author: American College Testing.
Publisher: American College Testing Program.
Cross References: For reviews by Christopher Borman and George Domino, see 10:46.

[406]

Career Values Card Sort.
Purpose: Defines factors that affect career satisfaction, the intensity of feelings about these factors, determines areas of value conflict and congruence, helps make career decisions.
Population: Adults.
Publication Date: 1993–94.
Scores: No scores.
Administration: Group or individual.
Price Data, 1994: $8 per complete kit including manual ('93, 19 pages) and set of cards; $4 per set of cards; $5 per manual.
Time: (20–30) minutes.
Comments: Self-administered.
Authors: Richard L. Knowdell.
Publisher: Career Research & Testing, Inc.

[407]

Caregiver's School Readiness Inventory.
Purpose: Constructed to predict a preschool child's success in school.
Population: Ages 3-11 to 5-10.
Publication Date: 1989.
Acronym: CSRI.
Scores: Total score only.

Administration: Individual.
Price Data, 1990: $12.50 per 200 rating forms;
$6.50 per manual (36 pages); $10.50 per specimen
set.
Time: [2–3] minutes.
Comments: Ratings by parents.
Author: Marvin L. Simner.
Publisher: Phylmar Associates.

[408]
Caring Relationship Inventory.

Purpose: Designed to "measure the . . . elements of
love or caring in human relationships."
Population: Premarital and marital counselees.
Publication Dates: 1966–75.
Acronym: CRI.
Scores, 7: Affection, Friendship, Eros, Empathy,
Self-Love, Being Love, Deficiency Love.
Administration: Individual.
Price Data, 1993: $15 per 25 tests (specify male or
female form); $9.50 per 50 profile sheets; $16.50 per
7 hand-scoring keys; $2.90 per manual ('75, 15
pages); $6.20 per specimen set including manual and
1 copy of all forms.
Time: (40) minutes.
Author: Everett L. Shostrom.
Publisher: EdITS/Educational and Industrial Test-
ing Service.
Cross References: For reviews by Donald L.
Mosher and Robert F. Stahmann, see 8:333 (5 refer-
ences); for a review by Albert Ellis, see 7:561; see also
P:31 (1 reference).

TEST REFERENCES

1. Dailey, D. M. (1979). Adjustment of heterosexual and homosexual
couples in pairing relationships: An exploratory study. *The Journal of Sex
Research, 15*, 143-157.
2. Silverman, M. S., & Urbaniak, L. (1983). Marriage encounter:
Characteristics of participants. *Counseling and Values, 28*, 42-51.
3. Zuckerman, M., Neeb, M., Ficher, M., Fishkin, R. E., Goldman, A., Fink, P. J., Cohen, S. N., Jacobs, J. A., & Weisberg, M.
(1985). Nocturnal penile tumescence and penile responses in the waking
state in diabetic and non-diabetic sexual dysfunctionals. *Archives of Sexual
Behavior, 14*, 109-129.

[409]
Carlson Psychological Survey.

Purpose: Developed as "a psychometric instrument
intended primarily for individuals accused or convicted of crimes."
Population: Criminal offenders.
Publication Dates: 1981–82.
Acronym: CPS.
Scores: 5 scale scores: Chemical Abuse, Thought
Disturbance, Anti-Social Tendencies, Self-Deprecia-
tion, Validity.
Administration: Group.
Price Data, 1990: $22 per examination kit includ-
ing 10 question and answer booklets, 10 scoring
sheets, 10 profiles, and manual ('82, 32 pages);
$15.25 per 25 question and answer booklets; $4.75
per 25 scoring sheets; $4.75 per 25 profiles; $10.50
per manual.
Foreign Language Editions: *Psicologico Texto*

(PT) designed specifically for use with Spanish-literate
offenders; question and answer booklets available in
French.
Time: [10–20] minutes.
Author: Kenneth A. Carlson.
Publisher: Sigma Assessment Systems, Inc.,
Research Psychologists Press Division.
Cross References: For a review by H. C. Ganguli,
see 9:203.

TEST REFERENCES

1. Friesen, W. J., & Wright, P. G. (1985). The validity of the Carlson Psychological Survey with adolescents. *Journal of Personality Assessment, 49*, 422-426.
2. Wright, P. G., & Friesen, W. J. (1985). The Carlson Psychological Survey with adolescents: Norms and scales reliabilities. *Canadian Journal of Behavioural Science, 17*, 389-399.

[410]
Carolina Picture Vocabulary Test (for Deaf and Hearing Impaired).

Purpose: "To measure the receptive sign vocabulary
in individuals where manual signing [is] the primary
mode of communication."
Population: Deaf and hearing-impaired children
ages 2.5–16.
Publication Date: 1985.
Acronym: CPVT.
Scores: Total score only.
Administration: Individual.
Price Data, 1994: $94 per complete program; $57
per picture book; $19 per 50 record forms; $21 per
manual (38 pages).
Time: (10–30) minutes.
Authors: Thomas L. Layton and David W. Holmes.
Publisher: PRO-ED, Inc.
Cross References: For additional information, see
11:62 (1 reference).

[411]
Carrow Auditory-Visual Abilities Test.

Purpose: Designed to facilitate "identification and
analysis of children's language and/or learning dis-
orders."
Population: Ages 4–10.
Publication Date: 1981.
Acronym: CAVAT.
Administration: Individual.
Price Data, 1989: $135 per complete kit including
3 tests, 15 copies of 3 response/scoring booklets, cas-
sette tape, manual, and carrying case; $32 per 45
response/scoring booklets.
Time: (90) minutes for entire battery; (5) minutes
per subtest.
Author: Elizabeth Carrow-Woolfolk.
Publisher: The Riverside Publishing Co.
a) VISUAL ABILITIES BATTERY.
Scores: 5 subtests: Visual Discrimination Match-
ing, Visual Discrimination Memory, Visual-Motor
Copying, Visual-Motor Memory, Motor Speed.
b) AUDITORY ABILITIES BATTERY.
Scores: 9 subtests: Picture Memory, Picture
Sequence Selection, Digits Forward, Digits Back-

ward, Sentence Repetition, Word Repetition, Auditory Blending, Auditory Discrimination in Quiet, Auditory Discrimination in Noise.

Cross References: For reviews by Curtis Dudley-Marling and John Salvia, see 9:204.

TEST REFERENCES

1. Cole, K. N., & Dale, P. S. (1986). Direct language instruction and interactive language instruction with language delayed preschool children: A comparison study. *Journal of Speech and Hearing Research, 29,* 206-217.

2. Watson, M. M., Rastatter, M. P., & Colcord, R. (1986). Time compression and spectral characteristics of phonemes. *Perceptual and Motor Skills, 62,* 9-10.

3. Watson, M., Stewart, M., & Krause, K. (1990). Identification of time-compressed sentential stimuli by good vs. poor readers. *Perceptual and Motor Skills, 71,* 107-114.

[412]

Carrow Elicited Language Inventory.

Purpose: To diagnose "specific expressive language deficits by eliciting data on a child's productive use of imitated grammatical structures."

Population: Ages 3–7.

Publication Date: 1974.

Acronym: CELI.

Scores, 18: Grammar (Articles, Adjectives, Nouns, Noun Plurals, Pronouns, Verbs, Negatives, Contradictions, Adverbs, Prepositions, Demonstratives, Conjunctions), Type (Substitutions, Omissions, Additions, Transpositions, Reversals), Total.

Administration: Individual.

Price Data, 1989: $69 per complete kit including manual (49 pages), guide, cassette tape, 25 scoring/analysis forms, 10 verb protocol forms, and vinyl folder; $28 per 50 scoring/analysis forms; $28 per 50 verb protocol forms.

Time: [10–15] minutes.

Comments: No reading by examinees; audio tape necessary for administration.

Author: Elizabeth Carrow.

Publisher: The Riverside Publishing Co.

Cross References: See T3:378 (17 references); for a review by Courtney B. Cazden, see 8:957 (3 references).

TEST REFERENCES

1. Dailey, K., & Boxx, J. R. (1979). A comparison of three imitative tests of expressive language and a spontaneous language sample. *Language, Speech, and Hearing Services in Schools, 10,* 6-13.

2. Hemingway, B. L., Montague, J. C., Jr., & Bradley, R. H. (1981). Preliminary data on revision of a sentence repetition test for language screening with black first grade children. *Language, Speech, and Hearing Services in Schools, 12,* 153-159.

3. Werner, E. O., & Kresheck, J. D. (1981). Variability in scores, structures, and error on three measures of expressive language. *Language, Speech, and Hearing Services in Schools, 12,* 82-89.

4. Fujiki, M., & Willbrand, M. L. (1982). A comparison of four informal methods of language evaluation. *Language, Speech, and Hearing Services in Schools, 13,* 42-52.

5. Mattes, L. J. (1982). The Elicited Language Analysis Procedure: A method for scoring sentence imitation tasks. *Language, Speech, and Hearing Services in Schools, 13,* 37-41.

6. McDade, H. L., Simpson, M. A., & Lamb, D. E. (1982). The use of elicited imitation as a measure of expressive grammar: A question of validity. *Journal of Speech and Hearing Disorders, 47,* 19-24.

7. Bountress, N. G. (1983). Effect of segregated and integrated educational settings upon selected dialectal features. *Perceptual and Motor Skills, 57,* 71-78.

8. Fujiki, M., & Brinton, B. (1983). Sampling reliability in elicited imitation. *Journal of Speech and Hearing Disorders, 48,* 85-89.

9. Isaacs, L. D., & Haynes, W. O. (1984). Linguistic processing and performance in articulation-disordered subgroups of language-impaired children. *Journal of Communication Disorders, 17,* 109-120.

10. Hoskins, C. (1985). Relationship between expressive language ability and rhythm perception, pitch perception, vocal range, and vocal midpoint among mentally retarded adults. *Perceptual and Motor Skills, 60,* 644-646.

11. Brinton, B., Fujiki, M., Winkler, E., & Loeb, D. F. (1986). Responses to requests for clarification in linguistically normal and language-impaired children. *Journal of Speech and Hearing Disorders, 51,* 370-378.

12. Lieberman, R. J., & Michael, A. (1986). Content relevance and content coverage in tests of grammatical ability. *Journal of Speech and Hearing Disorders, 51,* 71-81.

13. Fujiki, M., & Brinton, B. (1987). Elicited imitation revisited: A comparison with spontaneous language production. *Language, Speech, and Hearing Services in Schools, 18,* 301-311.

14. Gross, C., & Leder, S. B. (1987). Effect of a programatic context on elicited imitation. *Perceptual and Motor Skills, 65,* 455-459.

15. Liles, B. Z. (1987). Episode organization and cohesive conjunctives in narratives of children with and without language disorder. *Journal of Speech and Hearing Research, 30,* 185-196.

16. Abraham, S., & Stoker, R. (1988). Language assessment of hearing-impaired children and youth: Patterns of test use. *Language, Speech, and Hearing Services in Schools, 19,* 160-174.

17. Edmonds, P., & Haynes, W. O. (1988). Topic manipulation and conversational participation as a function of familiarity in school-age languaged-impaired and normal language peers. *Journal of Communication Disorders, 21,* 209-228.

18. Bliss, L. S. (1989). Selected syntactic usage of language-impaired children. *Journal of Communication Disorders, 22,* 277-289.

19. Lehman, M. E., & Sharf, D. J. (1989). Perception/production relationships in the development of the vowel duration cue to final consonant voicing. *Journal of Speech and Hearing Research, 32,* 803-815.

20. Skarakis-Doyle, E., & Mullin, K. (1990). Comprehension monitoring in language-disordered children: A preliminary investigation of cognitive and linguistic factors. *Journal of Speech and Hearing Disorders, 55,* 700-705.

21. Skarakis-Doyle, E., MacLellan, N., & Mullin, K. (1990). Nonverbal indicants of comprehension monitoring in language-disordered children. *Journal of Speech and Hearing Disorders, 55,* 461-467.

22. Ziegler, M., Tallal, P., & Curtiss, S. (1990). Selecting language-impaired children for research studies: Insights from the San Diego longitudinal study. *Perceptual and Motor Skills, 71,* 1079-1089.

[413]

Cattell Infant Intelligence Scale.

Purpose: Designed to measure the infant's developmental progress.

Population: Ages 3–30 months.

Publication Dates: 1940–60.

Acronym: CIIS.

Scores: Ratings in 4 areas: Willingness, Self-Confidence, Social-Confidence, Attention.

Administration: Individual.

Price Data, 1994: $529 per basic set including all necessary equipment, 25 record forms, and carrying case (manual not included); $73 per manual entitled *The Measurement of Intelligence of Infants and Young Children* ('60, 274 pages); $25 per 25 record forms.

Time: (20–30) minutes.

Comments: Downward extension of Stanford-Binet Intelligence Scale, Second Revision.

Author: Psyche Cattell.

Publisher: The Psychological Corporation.

Cross References: See T3:381 (19 references); for a review by Fred Damarin, see 8:209 (7 references); see also T2:487 (27 references) and 6:515 (22 references); for reviews by Florence M. Teagarden and Beth L. Wellmann and excerpted reviews by Rachel Stutsman Ball, C. M. Louttit, T. L. McCulloch,

Norma V. Schneidmann, and Helen Speyer, see 3:281.

TEST REFERENCES

1. Deckner, C. W., Soraci, S. A., Jr., Deckner, P. O., & Blanton, R. L. (1981). Consistency among commonly used procedures for assessment of abnormal children. *Journal of Clinical Psychology, 37,* 856-862.
2. Deckner, C. W., Deckner, P. O., & Blanton, R. L. (1982). Sustained responding under intermittent reinforcement in psychotic children. *Journal of Abnormal Child Psychology, 10,* 203-213.
3. Deckner, C. W., Soraci, S. A., Jr., Blanton, R. L., & Deckner, P. O. (1984). The relationships among two experimental and four psychometric assessments of abnormal children. *Journal of Clinical and Child Psychology, 13,* 157-164.
4. Ritvo, E. R., Freeman, B. J., Yuwiler, A., Geller, E., Yokota, A., Schroth, P., & Novak, P. (1984). Study of fenfluramine in outpatients with the syndrome of autism. *The Journal of Pediatrics, 105,* 823-828.
5. Mundy, P., Sigman, M., Ungerer, J., & Sherman, T. (1986). Defining the social deficits of autism: The contribution of non-verbal communication measures. *Journal of Child Psychology and Psychiatry and Allied Disciplines, 27,* 657-669.
6. O'Connor, L., & Schery, T. K. (1986). A comparison of microcomputer-aided and traditional language therapy for developing communication skills in nonoral toddlers. *Journal of Speech and Hearing Disorders, 51,* 356-361.
7. Rantakallio, P., & von Wendt, L. (1986). Mental retardation and subnormality in a birth cohort of 12,000 children in Northern Finland. *American Journal of Mental Deficiency, 90,* 380-387.
8. Werner, E. E. (1986). Resilient offspring of alcoholics: A longitudinal study from birth to age 18. *Journal of Studies on Alcohol, 47,* 34-40.
9. Lovaas, O. I. (1987). Behavioral treatment and normal educational and intellectual functioning in young autistic children. *Journal of Consulting and Clinical Psychology, 55,* 3-9.
10. Mundy, P., Sigman, M., Kasari, C., & Yirmiya, N. (1988). Nonverbal communication skills in Down syndrome child. *Child Development, 59,* 235-249.
11. Drash, P. W., Raver, S. A., Murrin, M. R., & Tudor, R. M. (1989). Three procedures for increasing vocal response to therapist prompt in infants and children with Down Syndrome. *American Journal on Mental Retardation, 94,* 64-73.
12. Atkinson, L. (1990). Reliability and validity of ratio developmental quotients from the Cattell Infant Intelligence Scale. *American Journal on Mental Retardation, 95,* 215-219.
13. Kasari, C., Mundy, P., Yirmiya, N., & Sigman, M. (1990). Affect and attention in children with Down Syndrome. *American Journal on Mental Retardation, 95,* 55-67.

[414]

CERAD (Consortium to Establish a Registry for Alzheimer's Disease) Assessment Battery.

Purpose: "To develop brief, standardized instruments for the assessment of patients with probable Alzheimer's disease."

Population: Patients with mild to moderate dementia.

Publication Date: 1987.

Acronym: CERAD.

Scores: Information gathered in 19 areas: Demographic, Drug Inventory, Informant History (Clinical, Blessed Dementia Rating Scale), Subject History (Assessment of Insight, Short Blessed Test, Depression and Calculation and Language), Examinations (Physical, Neurological), Laboratory Studies, Diagnostic Impression, Neuropsychological Battery (Neuropsychology Battery Status, Verbal Fluency Categories, Boston Naming Test, Mini-Mental State Exam, Word List Memory, Constructional Praxis, Word List Recall, Word List Recognition).

Administration: Individual.

Restricted Distribution: Current use only with permission of CERAD Steering Committee.

Price Data: Price information available from publisher.

Foreign Language Editions: Forms available in French and Spanish.

Time: [50-70] minutes.

Comments: Manual title is *Instruction Manual for Assessment of Patient and Control Subjects Entered into the CERAD Study.*

Author: Consortium to Establish a Registry for Alzheimer's Disease, Albert Heyman (Principal Investigator).

Publisher: CERAD Administrative CORE.

[415]

Certified Picture Framer Examination.

Purpose: "To provide professional recognition to competent individuals who are engaged in the business of picture framing."

Population: Individuals actively involved in the business of picture framing for one year.

Publication Date: 1986-93.

Acronym: CPF.

Scores: Total score only.

Administration: Group.

Price Data, 1994: Registration fee $200 for members of PPFA or $300 for nonmembers.

Time: (210) minutes.

Comments: Test administered on specific dates at centers established by the publisher.

Author: Certification Board of the Professional Picture Framers Association.

Publisher: Professional Picture Framers Association.

[416]

CGP Self-Scoring Placement Tests in English and Mathematics (Drawn from the CGP).

Purpose: Designed to give faculty and administrators information about the characteristics of entering students for counseling and placing students.

Population: Students entering postsecondary institutions with open-door policies.

Publication Dates: 1972-79.

Administration: Group or individual.

Price Data: Available from publisher.

Time: 90(105) minutes.

Comments: Also called Self-Scoring Placement Tests in English and Mathematics; self-scoring edition of the achievement/placement tests (Form UPG) in the Comparative Guidance and Placement Program (CGP; 9:253); student usually takes 4 tests (Reading, Written English Expression, and 2 Mathematics tests in prescribed combinations depending on amount of algebra studied) but single tests may be administered; NOTE: The full and modified CGP program is no longer offered.

Author: The College Board by Educational Testing Service.

Publisher: Educational Testing Service.

a) SELF-SCORING ENGLISH PLACEMENT TESTS.
   Time: 25(30) minutes per test.

1) *Written English Expression Placement Test.*
Comments: Same as Sentences test of out-of-print CGP.

2) *Reading Placement Test.*
Comments: Same as Reading test of out-of-print CGP.

b) SELF-SCORING MATHEMATICS PLACEMENT TESTS.
Comments: 4 tests usually administered in following pairs: Computation and Applied Arithmetic for students with less than 1 year of high school algebra, Computation and Elementary Algebra for students with 1 year, Elementary and Intermediate Algebra for students with more than 1 year.
Time: 20(25) minutes per test.

1) *Computation Placement Test.*
Comments: Same as Mathematics Test C, Part 1, of out-of-print CGP.

2) *Applied Arithmetic Placement Test.*
Comments: Same as Mathematics Test C, Part 2, of out-of-print CGP.

3) *Elementary Algebra Placement Test.*
Comments: Same as Mathematics Test D, Part 2, of out-of-print CGP.

4) *Intermediate Algebra Placement Test.*
Comments: Same as Mathematics Test E, Part 2, of out-of-print CGP.

Cross References: For reviews by Ronald K. Hambleton and J. Thomas Hastings, see 8:7; for reviews of subtests, see 8:61 (1 review) and 8:289 (1 review); for reference to reviews of the CGP Program, see 8:475.

[417]

Change Agent Questionnaire.
Purpose: Assesses "the underlying assumptions and practical strategies employed by agents of change as they seek to influence others."
Population: Adults.
Publication Dates: 1969–73.
Acronym: CAQ.
Scores, 20: Client-Centered Change (Philosophy, Strategy, Evaluation, Total), Charismatic Change (Philosophy, Strategy, Evaluation, Total), Custodial Change (Philosophy, Strategy, Evaluation, Total), Compliance Change (Philosophy, Strategy, Evaluation, Total), Credibility Change (Philosophy, Strategy, Evaluation, Total).
Administration: Group.
Manual: No manual.
Price Data, 1992: $49.95 per 10-pack of test instruments.
Time: Administration time not reported.
Authors: Jay Hall and Martha S. Williams.
Publisher: Teleometrics International.

[418]

Character Assessment Scale.
Purpose: Measurement of character strengths and weaknesses "founded on biblical principles."
Population: Adults.

Publication Dates: 1980–83.
Acronym: CAS.
Scores, 25: 8 moral resource scales (Truth, Respect, Concern, Anger, Money, Time/Energy, Sexuality, Body/Health), 8 character strength scales (Honesty, Humility, Peacemaking, Resourcefulness, Enthusiasm, Sexual Integrity, Physical Fitness, Compassion), 8 character weakness scales (Denial, Envy, Vanity, Resentment, Greed, Laziness, Lust, Gluttony), Total Morality Index.
Administration: Group or individual.
Price Data, 1992: $15 per 25 test booklets; $5 per 25 answer sheets; $25 per 25 feedback booklets; $20 per manual ('83, 34 pages).
Time: (45) minutes.
Comments: Self report.
Author: Paul F. Schmidt.
Publisher: Institute for Character Development.

[419]

Characteristics Scale.
Purpose: To determine teachers' views of important pupil characteristics and behaviors.
Population: Grades K–8.
Publication Dates: 1970–75.
Scores: Total score only.
Administration: Group.
Manual: No manual.
Price Data: Available from publisher.
Time: Administration time not reported.
Comments: Ratings by teachers; research instrument; may be used with or separately from Behavior Rating Scale (282).
Authors: Patricia B. Elmore and Donald L. Beggs.
Publisher: Patricia B. Elmore.

[420]

Chart of Initiative and Independence.
Purpose: Designed as "an assessment of environmental opportunities available to clients and . . . of their current and potential use of those resources."
Population: Mentally handicapped adults.
Publication Date: 1980.
Acronym: CII.
Scores: No scores.
Administration: Individual.
Price Data, 1985: £3.45 per 25 individual assessment forms; £3.45 per 25 Development Programme forms; £.85 per Residential Policy form; £3.95 per 25 Preliminary Assessment forms; £1.25 per manual of activities (10 pages); £1.05 per preliminary assessment manual (9 pages); £5.45 per complete manual (67 pages).
Time: Administration time not reported.
Comments: 4 formats: Individual Assessment Format (assesses present behavior), Development Programme Format (assesses future behavior), Residential Policy Format (assesses residential policy), Preliminary Assessment Format (short form of individual assessment to be used by social workers).
Authors: I. Macdonald and T. Couchman.

Publisher: NFER-Nelson Publishing Co., Ltd. [England].
Cross References: For reviews by Morton Bortner and Wayne C. Piersel, see 9:209.

[421]

Charteris Reading Test.
Purpose: Measures reading achievement.
Population: Ages 10–13.
Publication Date: 1985.
Scores: Total score only.
Administration: Group.
Price Data, 1994: £9.99 per 20 test booklets; £5.50 per manual (15 pages); £5.99 per specimen set.
Time: (60) minutes.
Author: Moray House Institute of Education, Edinburgh.
Publisher: Hodder & Stoughton Educational [England].

[422]

Chatterji's Non-Language Preference Record.
Purpose: Helps in identifying interests in broad interest areas to determine suitable educational or vocational field of training.
Population: Ages 11–16.
Publication Date: 1962.
Scores, 10: Fine Arts, Literary, Scientific, Medical, Agricultural, Mechanical, Crafts, Outdoor, Sports, Household Work.
Administration: Group.
Price Data: Not available.
Time: (45) minutes.
Author: S. Chatterji.
Publisher: Manasayan [India] [No reply from publisher; status unknown].
Cross References: See T2:2173 (6 references).

[423]

Checklist for Child Abuse Evaluation.
Purpose: "Provides a standard format for evaluating abuse in children and adolescents."
Population: Children and adolescents.
Publication Dates: 1988–90.
Acronym: CCAE.
Scores: 24 sections: Identification and Case Description, The Child's Status, Accuracy of Allegations by the Reporter, Interview with the Child (Physical/Behavioral Observations, Disclosure, Emotional Abuse, Sexual Abuse, Physical Abuse, Neglect), Events Witnessed or Reported by Others (Neglect, Emotional Abuse, Sexual Abuse, Physical Abuse), The Child's Psychological Status, History and Observed/Reported Characteristics of the Accused, Credibility of the Child—Observed/Reported, Competence of the Child—Observed/Reported, Conclusions (Consistency of Other Information, Allegation Motives, Substantiation of Allegations, Competence of the Child as a Witness, Level of Stress Experienced by the Child, Protection of the Child), Treatment Recommendations.

Administration: Individual.
Price Data, 1994: $43 per complete kit including manual ('90, 19 pages), and 10 checklists; $11 per manual; $36 per 10 checklists; $75 per 25 checklists.
Time: Untimed.
Author: Joseph Petty.
Publisher: Psychological Assessment Resources, Inc.

[424]

Checklist of Adaptive Living Skills.
Purpose: "A criterion-referenced measure of adaptive living skills and a tool for program planning."
Population: Infants to adults.
Publication Date: 1991.
Acronym: CALS.
Scores: 4 areas: Personality Living Skills, Home Living Skills, Community Living Skills, Employment Skills; and 24 subscales: Socialization, Eating, Grooming, Toileting, Dressing, Health Care, Sexuality, Clothing Care, Meal Planning and Preparation, Home Cleaning and Organization, Home Maintenance, Home Safety, Home Leisure, Social Interaction, Mobility and Travel, Time Management, Money Management and Shopping, Community Safety, Community Leisure, Community Participation, Job Search, Job Performance and Attitudes, Employee Relations, Job Safety.
Administration: Individual.
Price Data, 1991: $65 per examiner's manual (63 pages) and 25 checklists; $45 per 25 checklists.
Time: [60] minutes.
Comments: "Designed to be completed by a respondent who has had the opportunity to observe the learner in natural environments for a period of three or more months"; conceptually and statistically linked to two normative measures of adaptive behavior: Scales of Independent Behavior (SIB; 2335) and Inventory for Client and Agency Planning (ICAP; 1260); companion publication is the Adaptive Living Skills Curriculum.
Authors: Lanny E. Morreau and Robert H. Bruininks.
Publisher: The Riverside Publishing Company.

[425]

Checklist/Guide to Selecting a Small Computer.
Purpose: To help a business avoid costly and time-consuming mistakes when selecting a computer.
Population: Individuals selecting a small computer for a business.
Publication Date: 1980.
Scores: Ratings of "essentials" or "nice-to-have" characteristics in 10 areas: Display Features, Keyboard Features, Printer Features, Controller Features, Software, Word Processing, Service, Training, Miscellaneous, Costs.
Administration: Group.
Price Data, 1990: $5 per manual (33 pages including all materials for administration).

Time: Administration time not reported.
Author: Wilma E. Bennett.
Publisher: Pilot Books.
Cross References: For reviews by Douglas B. Eamon and C. Michael Levy, see 9:210.

[426]
Chelsea Diagnostic Mathematics Tests.

Purpose: "Designed as diagnostic instruments to be used both for ascertaining a child's level of understanding and to identify the incidence of errors."
Population: Ages 10–15.
Publication Dates: 1984–85.
Scores: 10 tests: Algebra, Fractions 1, Fractions 2, Graphs, Measurement, Number Operations, Place-Value and Decimals, Ratio and Proportion, Reflection and Rotation, Vectors.
Administration: Group.
Price Data, 1989: £97.75 per complete kit including 10 each of the test booklets, set of marking overlays, and teacher's guide ('85, 154 pages); £7.20 per 10 tests (Algebra, Fractions 1, Fractions 2, Number Operations, or Ratio and Proportion); £8.35 per 10 tests (Graphs, Place-Value and Decimals, Reflection and Rotation, or Vectors); £9.20 per 10 tests (Measurement); £6.35 per 10 Reflection and Rotation marking overlays; £17.25 per teacher's guide; £25.30 per specimen set including 1 each of tests and teacher's guide).
Time: (30–70) minutes per test.
Authors: Kathleen Hart, Margaret Brown, Daphne Kerslake, Dietmar Kuchemann, and Graham Ruddock.
Publisher: NFER-Nelson Publishing Co., Ltd. [England].

[427]
The Chessington O. T. Neurological Assessment Battery.

Purpose: "Developed for Occupational Therapists to assess the functional ability of neurological patients on a standardised battery of tests."
Population: Ages 16–65 +.
Publication Date: 1986–93.
Acronym: COTNAB.
Scores, 36: Ability, Time, and Overall Performance scores for 12 tests: Visual Perception (Overlapping Figures, Hidden Figures, Sequencing), Constructional Ability (2D Construction, 3D Construction, Block Printing), Sensory-Motor Ability (Stereognosis and Tactile Discrimination, Dexterity, Coordination), Ability to Follow Instructions (Written Instructions, Visual Instructions, Spoken Instructions).
Administration: Individual.
Price Data: Available from publisher.
Time: Administration time not reported.
Authors: Ruth Tyerman, Andy Tyerman, Prue Howard, and Caroline Hadfield.
Publisher: Nottingham Rehab Limited [England].

[428]
Chicago Early Assessment and Remediation LaboratorY.

Purpose: To assess individual abilities and provide remedial instructional activities in weak areas of functioning.
Population: Ages 3–6.
Publication Dates: 1981–84.
Acronym: Chicago EARLY.
Scores, 5: Gross Motor, Fine Motor, Language, Visual Discrimination, Memory.
Administration: Individual.
Price Data, 1989: $129 per complete kit including Assessment Pictures, Puzzles, Drawing Worksheets, Score Sheets, Social/Emotional Checklist, Individual Progress Record Sheets, Class Summary Sheets, 3 jars of blocks, bean bag, bag with zipper, small cardboard box, box of crayons, Assessment Manual ('84, 58 pages), Instructional Activities Guide ('84, 264 pages); $3.95 per 25 Drawing Worksheets; $3.95 per 25 score sheets; $4.95 per 50 Social/Emotional Checklists; $3.95 per 25 Individual Progress Record Sheets; $2.95 per 15 Class Summary Sheets; $9.95 per Assessment Manual; $17.95 per Instructional Activities Guide.
Foreign Language Edition: Spanish edition available.
Time: (15–30) minutes.
Comments: Screening instrument.
Author: Board of Education of the City of Chicago.
Publisher: Educational Teaching Aids.
Cross References: For reviews by Norman A. Constantine and Margaret Rogers Wiese, see 11:63.

TEST REFERENCES

1. Mason, J. M., Kerr, B. M., Sinha, S., & McCormick, C. (1990). Shared book reading in an early start program for at-risk children. *Yearbook of the National Reading Conference, 39,* 189-198.

[429]
The Child Abuse Potential Inventory, Form VI.

Purpose: "To assist in the screening of suspected physical child abuse cases."
Population: Male and female parents or primary caregivers who are suspected of physical child abuse.
Publication Dates: 1980-93.
Acronym: CAP Inventory.
Scores: 12 scale scores: Abuse scale (Distress, Rigidity, Unhappiness, Problems With Child and Self, Problems With Family, Problems With Others, Total Physical Child Abuse), Validity scales (Lie Scale, Random Response Scale, Inconsistency Scale), Loneliness, Ego-Strength, and 3 Response Distortion Indexes (Faking-Good, Faking-Bad, Random Response).
Administration: Individual administration recommended.
Price Data: Available from publisher.
Time: (12–20) minutes.
Author: Joel S. Milner.

Publisher: Psytec Inc.
Cross References: For reviews by Stuart N. Hart and Gary B. Melton, see 10:50 (5 references).

TEST REFERENCES

1. Ayoub, C., Jacewitz, M. M., Gold, R. G., & Milner, J. S. (1983). Assessment of a program's effectiveness in selecting individuals "at risk" for problems in parenting. *Journal of Clinical Psychology, 39,* 334-339.
2. Haddock, M. D., & McQueen, W. M. (1983). Assessing employee potentials for abuse. *Journal of Clinical Psychology, 39,* 1021-1029.
3. Robertson, K. R., & Milner, J. S. (1983). Construct validity of the Child Abuse Potential Inventory. *Journal of Clinical Psychology, 39,* 426-429.
4. Robertson, K. R., & Milner, J. S. (1987). An inconsistency scale for the Child Abuse Potential Inventory. *Psychological Reports, 60,* 699-703.
5. Milner, J. S., Charlesworth, J. R., Gold, R. G., & Gold, S. R. (1988). Convergent validity of the Child Abuse Potential Inventory. *Journal of Clinical Psychology, 44,* 281-285.
6. Wolfe, D. A., Edwards, B., Manion, I., & Koverola, C. (1988). Early intervention for parents at risk of child abuse and neglect: A preliminary investigation. *Journal of Consulting and Clinical Psychology, 56,* 40-47.
7. Milner, J. S. (1989). Applications of the Child Abuse Potential Inventory. *Journal of Clinical Psychology, 20,* 132-139.
8. Poteat, G. M., Cope, J. G., Choate, C., & Grossnickle, W. F. (1989). Wife abuse as it affects work behavior in a center for mentally retarded persons. *Journal of Clinical Psychology, 45,* 324-330.
9. During, S. M., & McMahon, R. J. (1991). Recognition of emotional facial expressions by abusive mothers and their children. *Journal of Clinical Child Psychology, 20,* 132-139.
10. Mollerstrom, W. W., Patchner, M. A., & Milner, T. S. (1992). Family functioning and child abuse potential. *Journal of Clinical Psychology, 48,* 445-454.

[430]

Child and Adolescent Adjustment Profile.

Purpose: Designed to "measure five factor-analyzed areas of adjustment."
Population: Children and adolescents seen in mental health centers.
Publication Dates: 1977–81.
Acronym: CAAP Scale.
Scores, 5: Peer Relations, Dependency, Hostility, Productivity, Withdrawal.
Administration: Group.
Price Data, 1990: $8 per 25 scales, profile included; $9.50 per manual ('81, 17 pages); $10 per specimen set.
Time: (10) minutes.
Comments: Pre- and Post-treatment ratings by significant other.
Authors: Robert B. Ellsworth and Shanae L. Ellsworth.
Publisher: Consulting Psychologists Press, Inc.
Cross References: For reviews by Robert H. Deluty and David R. Wilson, see 9:211.

TEST REFERENCES

1. Hundert, J., Bruce Cassie, J. R., & Johnston, N. (1988). Characteristics of emotionally disturbed children referred to day treatment, special-class, outpatient, and assessment services. *Journal of Clinical Child Psychology, 17,* 121-130.

[431]

Child Anxiety Scale.

Purpose: Designed to detect "anxiety-based disturbances in young children."

Population: Grades K–5.
Publication Date: 1980.
Acronym: CAS.
Scores: Total score only.
Administration: Group.
Price Data, 1994: $43.25 per introductory kit including cassette tape, scoring key, 50 answer sheets, and manual (27 pages); $15 per cassette tape; $10.75 per 50 answer sheets; $11.50 per manual (30 pages).
Time: (15) minutes.
Comments: Cassette tape includes questionnaire items and instructions.
Author: John S. Gillis.
Publisher: Institute for Personality and Ability Testing, Inc.
Cross References: For reviews by Susanna Maxwell and F. E. Sterling, see 9:212.

TEST REFERENCES

1. Argulewicz, E. N., & Miller, D. C. (1984). Self-report measures of anxiety: A cross-cultural investigation of bias. *Hispanic Journal of Behavioral Sciences, 6,* 397-406.
2. Cooley, E. J., & Ayres, R. (1985). Convergent and discriminant validity of the mental processing scales of the Kaufman Assessment Battery for Children. *Psychology in the Schools, 22,* 373-377.
3. Margalit, M., & Heiman, T. (1986). Learning-disabled boys' anxiety, parental anxiety, and family climate. *Journal of Clinical Child Psychology, 15,* 248-253.
4. Omizo, M. M., Omizo, S. A., & D'Andrea, M. J. (1992). Promoting wellness among elementary school children. *Journal of Counseling and Development, 71,* 194-198.

[432]

The Child "At Risk" for Drug Abuse Rating Scale.

Purpose: "Seeks to assess risk factors for later drug abuse."
Population: Preschool–grade 6.
Publication Date: 1990.
Acronym: DARS.
Scores, 4: Developmental History, Family Relations, Child Behavior Pattern, Total.
Administration: Individual.
Price Data, 1990: $11 per manual (20 pages); $25 per program with diskette.
Time: (15) minutes.
Comments: Program designed to run on PC XT like computer with a minimum of 256K of memory.
Author: Russell N. Cassel.
Publisher: Psychologists and Educators, Inc.

[433]

Child Behavior Checklist.

Purpose: To assess the competencies and problems of children and adolescents through the use of ratings and reports by different informants.
Population: Ages 2–18.
Publication Dates: 1980–94.
Price Data, 1994: $10 per 25 Child Behavior Checklists (specify Ages 2–3 or Ages 4–18); $10 per 25 CBCL profiles (specify age and sex); $7 per CBCL scoring templates (specify level); $10 per 25 Teacher's

Report Forms; $10 per 25 TRF profiles; $7 per TRF templates; $10 per 25 Youth Self-Report Forms; $7 per YSR templates; $10 per 25 YSR profiles; $10 per 25 Direct Observation Forms; $10 per 25 SCICA protocol forms; $10 per 25 combined SCICA observation and self-report scoring forms; $10 per 25 profiles for handscoring SCICA; $25 per CBCL/2–3 manual ('92, 210 pages); $25 per CBCL/4–18 manual ('91, 288 pages); $25 per TRF manual ('92, 214 pages); $25 per YSR manual ('91, 221 pages); $25 per SCICA manual ('94, 210 pages); $95 per SCICA videotape; computer programs available for computer scoring and profiling; $25 per Empirically Based Taxonomy ('93, 212 pages).

Comments: Behavior checklists; forms available as separates.

Author: Thomas M. Achenbach.

Publisher: Thomas M. Achenbach, Ph.D.

a) CHILD BEHAVIOR CHECKLIST.

Purpose: "To record in a standardized format the behavioral problems and competencies of children . . . as reported by their parents or others who know the child well."

Comments: Ratings by parents.

1) *Ages 2–3.*

Population: Ages 2–3.

Publication Dates: 1986–92.

Acronym: CBCL/2–3.

Scores: 6 scales: Withdrawn, Anxious/Depressed, Sleep Problems, Somatic Problems, Aggressive, Destructive.

Time: (15) minutes.

2) *Ages 4–18.*

Population: Ages 4–18.

Publication Dates: 1980–91.

Acronym: CBCL/4–18.

Parts: 2 profiles: Boys Aged 4–18, Girls Aged 4–18.

Scores: 15 scales: Syndrome Scales (Withdrawn, Somatic Complaints, Anxious/Depressed, Social Problems, Thought Problems, Attention Problems, Aggressive Behavior, Delinquent Behavior), plus Internalizing, Externalizing, Total Problems, Competence Scales (Activities, Social, School, Total Competence).

Time: (15) minutes.

b) TEACHER'S REPORT FORM.

Purpose: "To obtain teachers' reports of their pupils' problems and adaptive functioning in a standardized format."

Population: Ages 5–18.

Publication Dates: 1982–91.

Acronym: TRF.

Forms: 2 profiles: Boys Aged 5–18; Girls Aged 5–18.

Scores, 13: Same as CBCL/4–18 above plus Academic Performance, Adaptive Functioning.

Time: (15) minutes.

Comments: Ratings by teachers.

c) YOUTH SELF-REPORT.

Purpose: "To obtain 11- to 18-year-olds' reports of their own competencies and problems in a standardized format."

Population: Ages 11–18.

Publication Dates: 1983–91.

Acronym: YSR.

Scores, 14: Same as CBCL/4–18 above without School Scale.

Time: (15) minutes.

Comments: Ratings by self.

d) DIRECT OBSERVATION FORM.

Purpose: "To obtain direct observational data in situations such as school classrooms, lunchrooms, recess, and group activities."

Population: Ages 5–14.

Publication Date: 1981–86.

Acronym: DOF.

Scores, 10: Behavior Problems, Internalizing, Externalizing, Withdrawn-Inattentive, Nervous-Obsessive, Depressed, Hyperactive, Attention-Demanding, Aggressive, On-Task Behavior.

Time: (10) minutes for each observation period.

Comments: Ratings by trained observer.

e) SEMISTRUCTURED CLINICAL INTERVIEW FOR CHILDREN AND ADOLESCENTS.

Purpose: "To advance the application of empirically based assessment to clinical interviews."

Population: Ages 6–12.

Publication Date: 1994.

Acronym: SCICA.

Scores: 8 syndrome scales: Aggressive Behavior, Anxious, Anxious/Depressed, Attention Problems, Family Problems, Resistant, Strange, Withdrawn.

Time: (60–90) minutes.

Comments: Videotape and IBM computer scoring program available.

Cross References: For reviews by Sandra L. Christenson and Stephen N. Elliott and R. T. Busse of the Teacher's Report Form and the Youth Self-Report, see 11:64 (216 references); for additional information and reviews by B. J. Freeman and Mary Lou Kelley, see 9:213 (5 references).

TEST REFERENCES

1. Gordon, A. H., Lee, P. A., Dulcan, M. K., & Finegold, D. N. (1986). Behavioral problems, social competency, and self perception among girls with congenital adrenal hyperplasia. *Child Psychiatry and Human Development, 17,* 129-138.

2. Jaffe, P., Wolfe, D., Wilson, S. K., & Zaki, L. (1986). Family violence and child adjustment: A comparative analysis of girls' and boys' behavior symptoms. *American Journal of Psychiatry, 143,* 74-76.

3. Achenbach, T. M., Edelbrock, C., & Howell, C. T. (1987). Empirically based assessment of the behavioral/emotional problems of 2- and 3-year-old children. *Journal of Abnormal Child Psychology, 15,* 629-650.

4. Hammen, C., Gordon, D., Burge, D., Adrian, C., Jaenicke, C., & Hirohoto, D. (1987). Maternal affective disorders, illness, and stress: Risk for children's psychopathology. *American Journal of Psychiatry, 144,* 736-741.

5. Weisz, J. R., Weiss, B., Wasserman, A. A., & Rintoul, B. (1987). Control-related beliefs and depression among clinic-referred children and adolescents. *Journal of Abnormal Psychology, 96,* 58-63.

6. Beitchman, J. H., Peterson, M., & Clegg, M. (1988). Speech and language impairment and psychiatric disorder: The relevance of family demographic variables. *Child Psychiatry and Human Development, 18,* 191-207.

7. Bornstein, M. T., Bornstein, P. H., & Walters, H. A. (1988).

Children of divorce: Empirical evaluation of a group-treatment program. *Journal of Clinical Child Psychology, 17*, 248-254.

8. Capelli, M., McGrath, P. J., MacDonald, N. E., Boland, M., Fried, P., & Katsanis, J. (1988). Parent, family, and disease factors as predictors of psychosocial functioning in children with cystic fibrosis. *Canadian Journal of Behavioural Science, 20*, 413-423.

9. Cohen, N. J., Kershner, J., & Wehrspann, W. (1988). Correlates of competence in a child psychiatric population. *Journal of Consulting and Clinical Psychology, 56*, 97-103.

10. Compas, B. E., Malcarne, V. L., & Fondacaro, K. M. (1988). Coping with stressful events in older children and young adolescents. *Journal of Consulting and Clinical Psychology, 56*, 405-411.

11. Costello, E. J., Costello, A. J., Edelbrock, C., Burns, B. J., Dulcan, M. K., Brent, D., & Janiszewski, S. (1988). Psychiatric disorders in pediatric primary care. *Archives of General Psychiatry, 45*, 1107-1116.

12. Friedrich, W. N., & Luecke, W. J. (1988). Young school-age sexually aggressive children. *Professional Psychology: Research and Practice, 19*, 155-164.

13. Matson, J. L., Barrett, R. P., & Helsel, W. J. (1988). Depression in mentally retarded children. *Research in Developmental Disabilities, 9*, 39-46.

14. Webster-Stratton, C. (1988). Mothers' and fathers' perceptions of child deviance: Roles of parent and child behaviors and parent adjustment. *Journal of Consulting and Clinical Psychology, 56*, 909-915.

15. Webster-Stratton, C., Kolpacoff, M., & Hollinsworth, T. (1988). Self-administered videotape therapy for families with conduct-problem children: Comparison with two cost-effective treatments and a control group. *Journal of Consulting and Clinical Psychology, 56*, 558-566.

16. Cohen, N. J. (1989). Sex differences in child psychiatric outpatients: Cognitive, personality, and behavioral characteristics. *Child Psychiatry and Human Development, 20*, 113-122.

17. Dyson, L., Edgar, E., & Crnic, K. (1989). Psychological predictors of adjustment by siblings of developmentally disabled children. *American Journal on Mental Retardation, 94*, 292-302.

18. Kendall, P. C., Cantwell, D. P., & Kazdin, A. E. (1989). Depression in children and adolescents: Assessment issues and recommendations. *Cognitive Therapy and Research, 13*, 109-146.

19. Lee, C. M., & Gotlib, I. H. (1989). Clinical status and emotional adjustment of children of depressed mothers. *American Journal of Psychiatry, 146*, 478-483.

20. Lee, C. M., & Gotlib, I. H. (1989). Maternal depression and child adjustment: A longitudinal analysis. *Journal of Abnormal Psychology, 98*, 78-85.

21. Mabe, P. A., & Treiber, F. A. (1989). Social desirability response tendencies in psychiatric inpatient children. *Journal of Clinical Psychology, 45*, 194-201.

22. Ballard, M., & Cummings, E. M. (1990). Response to adults' angry behavior in children of alcoholic and nonalcoholic parents. *The Journal of Genetic Psychology, 151*, 195-209.

23. Boggs, S. R., Eyberg, S., & Reynolds, L. A. (1990). Construct validity of the Eyberg Child Behavior Inventory. *Journal of Clinical Child Psychology, 19*, 75-78.

24. Dawson, P. M., Griffith, K., & Boeke, K. M. (1990). Combined medical and psychological treatment of hospitalized children with encopresis. *Child Psychiatry and Human Development, 20*, 181-190.

25. Dickson, J. M., Saylor, C. F., & Finch, A. J., Jr. (1990). Personality factors, family structure, and sex of drawn figure on The Draw-A-Person Test. *Journal of Personality Assessment, 55*, 362-366.

26. Frankel, F., & Weiner, H. (1990). The child conflict index: Factor analysis, reliability, and validity for clinic-referred and nonreferred children. *Journal of Clinical Child Psychology, 19*, 239-248.

27. Horn, W. F., Ialongo, N., Greenberg, G., Packard, T., & Smith-Unberry, C. (1990). Additive effects of behavioral parent training and self-control therapy with attention deficit hyperactivity disordered children. *Journal of Clinical Child Psychology, 19*, 98-110.

28. Horwitz, W. A., & Kazak, A. E. (1990). Family adaptation to childhood cancer: Sibling and family systems variables. *Journal of Clinical Child Psychology, 19*, 221-228.

29. Marcus, R. F., & Mirle, J. (1990). Validity of a child interview measure of attachment as used in child custody evaluations. *Perceptual and Motor Skills, 70*, 1043-1054.

30. Mattison, R. E., Handford, H. A., Kales, H. C., Goodman, A. L., & McLaughlin, R. E. (1990). Four-year predictive value of the Children's Depression Inventory. *Psychological Assessment, 2*, 169-174.

31. Noam, G. G., & Recklitis, C. J. (1990). The relationship between defenses and symptoms in adolescent psychopathology. *Journal of Personality Assessment, 54*, 311-327.

32. Rotheram-Borus, M. J. (1990). Adolescents' reference-group choices, self-esteem, and adjustment. *Journal of Personality and Social Psychology, 59*, 1075-1081.

33. Shapiro, J. P., Leifer, M., Martone, M. W., & Kassem, L.

(1990). Multimethod assessment of depression in sexually abused girls. *Journal of Personality Assessment, 55*, 234-248.

34. Sullivan, A., Kelso, J., & Stewart, M. (1990). Mothers' views on the ages of onset for four childhood disorders. *Child Psychiatry and Human Development, 20*, 269-278.

35. Thurber, S., & Snow, M. (1990). Assessment of adolescent psychopathology: Comparison of mother and daughter perspectives. *Journal of Clinical Child Psychology, 19*, 249-253.

36. Webster-Stratton, C. (1990). Long-term follow-up of families with young conduct problem children: From preschool to grade school. *Journal of Clinical Child Psychology, 19*, 144-149.

37. Williams, C. L., Ben-Porath, Y. S., Uchiyama, C., Weed, N. C., & Archer, R. P. (1990). External validity of the new Devereux Adolescent Behavior Rating Scales. *Journal of Personality Assessment, 55*, 73-85.

38. Auerbach, J. G., & Lerner, Y. (1991). Syndromes derived from the Child Behavior Checklist for clinically referred Israeli boys aged 6-11: A research note. *Journal of Child Psychology and Psychiatry, 32*, 1017-1024.

39. Bloomquist, M. L., August, G. J., & Ostrander, R. (1991). Effects of a school-based cognitive-behavioral intervention for ADHD children. *Journal of Abnormal Child Psychology, 19*, 591-605.

40. Bornstein, R. A., & Yang, V. (1991). Neuropsychological performance in medicated and unmedicated patients with Tourette's disorder. *American Journal of Psychiatry, 148*, 468-471.

41. Brown, J. H., Eichenberger, S. A., Portes, P. R., & Christensen, D. N. (1991). Family functioning factors associated with the adjustment of children of divorce. *Journal of Divorce & Remarriage, 17*, 81-95.

42. Burge, D., & Hammen, C. (1991). Maternal communication: Predictors of outcome at follow-up in a sample of children at high and low risk for depression. *Journal of Abnormal Psychology, 100*, 174-180.

43. Campbell, S. B., March, C. L., Pierce, E. W., Ewing, L. J., & Szumowski, E. K. (1991). Hard-to-manage preschool boys: Family context and the stability of externalizing behavior. *Journal of Abnormal Child Psychology, 19*, 301-318.

44. Chassin, L., Rogosch, F., & Barrera, M. (1991). Substance use and symptomology among adolescent children of alcoholics. *Journal of Abnormal Psychology, 100*, 449-463.

45. Cohen, N. J., & Lipsett, L. (1991). Recognized and unrecognized language impairment in psychologically disturbed children: Child symptomatology, maternal depression, and family dysfunction. Preliminary report. *Canadian Journal of Behavioural Science, 23*, 376-389.

46. Compas, B. E., Phares, V., Banez, G. A., & Howell, D. C. (1991). Correlates of internalizing and externalizing behavior problems: Perceived competence, causal attributions, and parental symptoms. *Journal of Abnormal Child Psychology, 19*, 197-218.

47. During, S. M., & McMahon, R. J. (1991). Recognition of emotional facial expressions by abusive mothers and their children. *Journal of Clinical Child Psychology, 20*, 132-139.

48. Evans, S. W., & Short, E. J. (1991). A qualitative and serial analysis of social problem solving in aggressive boys. *Journal of Abnormal Child Psychology, 19*, 331-340.

49. Fischer, M., & Newby, R. F. (1991). Assessment of stimulant response in ADHD children using a refined multimethod clinical protocol. *Journal of Clinical Child Psychology, 20*, 232-244.

50. Forehand, R., Frame, C. L., Wierson, M., Armistead, L., & Kempton, T. (1991). Assessment of incarcerated juvenile delinquents: Agreement across raters and approaches to psychopathology. *Journal of Psychopathology and Behavioral Assessment, 13*, 17-25.

51. Holden, G. W., & Ritchie, K. L. (1991). Linking extreme marital discord, child rearing, and child behavior problems: Evidence from battered women. *Child Development, 62*, 311-327.

52. Johnston, C. (1991). Predicting mothers' and fathers' perceptions of child behaviour problems. *Canadian Journal of Behavioural Science, 23*, 349-357.

53. Kolko, D. J., & Kazdin, A. E. (1991). Aggression and psychopathology in matchplaying and firesetting children: A replication and extension. *Journal of Clinical Child Psychology, 20*, 191-201.

54. Lee, C. M., & Gotlib, I. H. (1991). Adjustment of children of depressed mothers: A 10-month follow-up. *Journal of Abnormal Psychology, 100*, 473-477.

55. Massey, O. T., & Murphy, S. E. (1991). A study of the utility of The Child Behavior Checklist with residentially placed children. *Evaluation and Program Planning, 14*, 319-324.

56. Pekarik, G. (1991). Relationship of expected and actual treatment duration for adult and child clients. *Journal of Clinical Child Psychology, 20*, 121-125.

57. Phillips, L. H. C., & O'Hara, M. W. (1991). Prospective study of postpartum depression: 4 ½-year follow-up of women and children. *Journal of Abnormal Psychology, 100*, 151-155.

58. Rey, J. M., & Bird, K. D. (1991). Sex differences in suicidal

behavior in referred adolescents. *British Journal of Psychiatry, 158*, 776-781.

59. Rojas, E. B., & Tuber, S. (1991). The animal preference test and its relationship to behavioral problems in young children. *Journal of Personality Assessment, 57*, 141-148.

60. Simonian, S. J., Tarnowski, K. J., Stancin, T., Friman, P. C., & Atkins, M. S. (1991). Disadvantaged children and families in pediatric primary care settings: II: Screening for behavior disturbance. *Journal of Clinical Child Psychology, 20*, 360-371.

61. Skelton, D. L., Glynn, M. A., & Berta, S. M. (1991). Aggressive behavior as a function of taekwondo ranking. *Perceptual and Motor Skills, 72*, 179-182.

62. Walker, L. S., Garber, J., & Greene, J. W. (1991). Somatization symptoms in pediatric abdominal pain patients: Relation to chronicity of abdominal pain and parent somatization. *Journal of Abnormal Child Psychology, 19*, 379-394.

63. Barkley, R. A., Geuvremont, D. C., Anastopoulos, A. D., & Fletcher, K. E. (1992). A comparison of three family therapy programs for treating family conflicts in adolescents with attention-deficit hyperactivity disorder. *Journal of Consulting and Clinical Psychology, 60*, 450-462.

64. Barkley, R. A., Grodzinsky, G., & Dupaul, G. J. (1992). Frontal lobe functions in attention deficit disorder with and without hyperactivity: A review and research report. *Journal of Abnormal Child Psychology, 20*, 163-188.

65. Beckwith, L., Rodning, C., & Cohen, S. (1992). Preterm children at early adolescence and continuity and discontinuity in maternal responsiveness from infancy. *Child Development, 63*, 1198-1208.

66. Blatt, S. J., Hart, B., Quinlan, D. M., Leadbeater, B., & Auerbach, J. (1992). Interpersonal and self-critical dysphoria and behavioral problems in adolescents. *Journal of Youth and Adolescence, 22*, 253-269.

67. Capuano, F., & Dubeau, D. (1992). Development and validation of the Preschool Socioaffective Profile. *Psychological Assessment, 4*, 442-450.

68. Christensen, A., Margolin, G., & Sullaway, M. (1992). Interparental agreement on child behavior problems. *Psychological Assessment, 4*, 419-425.

69. Coie, J. D., Lochman, J. E., Terry, R., & Hyman, C. (1992). Predicting early adolescent disorder from childhood aggression and peer rejection. *Journal of Consulting and Clinical Psychology, 60*, 783-792.

70. Crowley, S. L., Worchel, F. F., & Ash, M. J. (1992). Self-report, peer-report, and teacher-report measures of childhood depression: An analysis by item. *Journal of Personality Assessment, 59*, 189-203.

71. D'Angelo, E., Woolf, A., Bessette, J., Rappaport, L., & Ciborowski, J. (1992). Correlates of medical compliance among hemophilic boys. *Journal of Clinical Psychology, 48*, 672-680.

72. Damon, L., Hewitt, S. K., Koverola, C., Lang, R. A., Wolfe, V., & Broughton, D. (1992). Child Sexual Behvior Inventory: Normative and clinical comparisons. *Psychological Assessment, 4*, 303-311.

73. Day, D. M., Bream, L. A., & Pal, A. (1992). Proactive and reactive aggregation: An analysis of subtypes based on teacher perceptions. *Journal of Clinical Child Psychology, 21*, 210-217.

74. Delaney, D. C., Olson, K., & Labbe, E. E. (1992). Skin temperature biofeedback: Evaluation of non-clinical children's responses. *Journal of Behavior Therapy and Experimental Psychiatry, 23*, 37-42.

75. DuPaul, G. J. (1992). How to assess attention-deficit hyperactivity disorder within school settings. *School Psychology Quarterly, 7*(1), 60-74.

76. DuPaul, G. J., Anastopoulos, A. D., Shelton, T. L., Guevremount, D. C., & Metevia, L. (1992). Multimethod assessment of attention-deficit hyperactivity disorder: The diagnostic utility of clinic-based tests. *Journal of Clinical Child Psychology, 21*, 394-402.

77. Evenson, R. C., Binner, P. R., & Adams, C. J. (1992). Predicting risk for hospitalization with the Child Behavior Checklist. *Journal of Clinical Child Psychology, 21*, 388-393.

78. Hanson, C. L., Henggeler, S. W., Harris, M. A., Cigrang, J. A., Schinkel, A. M., Rodrigue, J. R., & Klesges, R. C. (1992). Contributions of sibling relations to the adaptation of youths with insulin-dependent diabetes mellitus. *Journal of Consulting and Clinical Psychology, 60*, 104-112.

79. Henggeler, S. W., Melton, G. B., & Smith, L. A. (1992). Family preservation using multisystemic therapy: An effective alternative to incarcerating serious juvenile offenders. *Journal of Consulting and Clinical Psychology, 60*, 953-961.

80. Hinshaw, S. P., Han, S. S., Erhardt, D., & Huber, A. (1992). Internalizing and externalizing behavior problems in preschool children: Correspondence among parent and teacher ratings and behavior observations. *Journal of Clinical Child Psychology, 21*, 143-150.

81. Hinshaw, S. P., Heller, T., & McHale, J. P. (1992). Covert antisocial behavior in boys with attention-deficit hyperactivity disorder: External validation and effects of methylphenidate. *Journal of Consulting and Clinical Psychology, 60*, 274-281.

82. Inderbitzen-Pisaruk, H., Shawchuck, C. R., & Hoiser, T. S.

(1992). Behavioral characteristics of child victims of sexual abuse: A comparison study. *Journal of Clinical Child Psychology, 21*, 14-19.

83. Jordan, B. K., Marmar, C. R., Fairbank, J. A., Schlenger, W. E., Kulka, R. A., Hough, R. L., & Weiss, D. S. (1992). Problems in families of male Vietnam veterans with posttraumatic stress disorder. *Journal of Consulting and Clinical Psychology, 60*, 916-926.

84. Kazdin, A. E., Siegel, T. C., & Bass, D. (1992). Cognitive problem-solving skills training and parent management training in the treatment of antisocial behavior in children. *Journal of Consulting and Clinical Psychology, 60*, 733-747.

85. Kolko, D. J., & Kazdin, A. E. (1992). The emergence and recurrence of child firesetting: A one-year prospective study. *Journal of Abnormal Child Psychology, 20*, 17-37.

86. Lucas, C. P. (1992). The order effect: Reflections on the validity of multiple test presentations. *Psychological Medicine, 22*, 197-202.

87. Macmann, G. M., Barnett, D. W., Burd, S. A., Jones, T., LeBuffe, P. A., O'Malley, D., Shade, D. B., & Wright, A. (1992). Construct validity of the Child Behavior Checklist: Effects of item overlap on second-order factor structure. *Psychological Assessment, 4*, 113-116.

88. Miller, K. E., King, C. A., Shain, B. N., & Naylor, M. W. (1992). Suicidal adolescents' perceptions of their family environment. *Suicide and Life-Threatening Behavior, 22*, 226-239.

89. O'Donohue, W. T., & Elliott, A. N. (1992). Treatment of the sexually abused child: A review. *Journal of Clinical Child Psychology, 21*, 218-228.

90. Pekarik, G. (1992). Posttreatment adjustment of clients who drop out early vs. late in treatment. *Journal of Clinical Psychology, 48*, 379-387.

91. Pekarik, G. (1992). Relationship of clients' reasons for dropping out of treatment to outcome and satisfaction. *Journal of Clinical Psychology, 48*, 91-98.

92. Prange, M. E., Greenbaum, P. E., Silver, S. E., Friedman, R. M., Kutash, K., & Duchnowski, A. J. (1992). Family functioning and psychopathology among adolescents with severe emotional disturbances. *Journal of Abnormal Child Psychology, 20*, 83-102.

93. Robins, P. M. (1992). A comparison of behavioral and attentional functioning in children diagnosed as hyperactive or learning-disabled. *Journal of Abnormal Child Psychology, 20*, 65-82.

94. Schoenherr, S. J., Brown, R. T., Baldwin, K., & Kaslow, N. J. (1992). Attributional styles and psychopathology in pediatric chronic-illness groups. *Journal of Clinical Child Psychology, 21*, 380-387.

95. Snow, J. H. (1992). Mental flexibility and planning skills in children and adolescents with learning disabilities. *Journal of Learning Disabilities, 25*, 265-270.

96. Sternberg, K. J., Lamb, M. E., Greenbaum, C., Cicchetti, D., Dawud, S., Cortes, R. M., Krispin, O., & Lorey, F. (1992). Effects of domestic violence on children's behavior problems and depression. *Developmental Psychology, 29*, 44-52.

97. Thurber, S., & Hollingsworth, D. K. (1992). Validity of the Achenbach and Edelbrock youth self-report with hospitalized adolescents. *Journal of Clinical Child Psychology, 21*, 249-254.

98. Trovato, J., Harris, J., Pryor, C. W., & Wilkinson, C. (1992). Teachers in regular classrooms: An applied setting for successful behavior programming. *Psychology in the Schools, 29*(1), 52-61.

99. Verhulst, F. C., & van der Ende, J. (1992). Agreement between parents' reports and adolescents' self-reports of problem behavior. *Journal of Child Psychology and Psychiatry*, 1011-1023.

100. Webster-Stratton, C. (1992). Individually administered videotape parent training: "Who benefits?" *Cognitive Therapy and Research, 16*, 31-53.

101. Weiss, B., Polintano, M., Nelson, W. M., Weisz, J. R., Carey, M., & Finch, A. J. (1992). Relations among self-reported depressive symptoms in clinic-referred children versus adolescents. *Journal of Abnormal Psychology, 101*, 391-397.

102. Worchel, F. F., Rae, W. A., Olson, T. K., & Crowley, S. L. (1992). Selective responsiveness of chronically ill children to assessments of depression. *Journal of Personality Assessment, 59*, 605-615.

103. Anastopoulos, A. D., Shelton, T. L., DuPaul, G. J., & Guevremont, D. C. (1993). Parent training for attention-deficit hyperactivity disorder: Its impact on parent functioning. *Journal of Abnormal Child Psychology, 21*, 581-596.

104. Anderson, C. A., & Hammen, C. L. (1993). Psychosocial outcomes of children of unipolar depressed, bipolar, medically ill, and normal women: A longitudinal study. *Journal of Consulting and Clinical Psychology, 61*, 448-454.

105. Atkins, M. S., & Stoff, D. M. (1993). Instrumental and hostile aggression in childhood disruptive behavior disorders. *Journal of Abnormal Child Psychology, 21*, 165-178.

106. Atkins, M. S., Stoff, D. M., Osborne, M. L., & Brown, K. (1993). Distinguishing instrumental and hostile aggression: Does it make a difference? *Journal of Abnormal Child Psychology, 21*, 355-365.

107. Barling, J., MacEwen, K. E., & Nolte, M. (1993). Home-maker role experiences affect toddler behaviors via maternal well-being and parenting behavior. *Journal of Abnormal Child Psychology, 21*, 213-229.

108. Charlebois, P., LeBlanc, M., Gagnon, C., Larivée, S., & Tremblay, R. (1993). Age trends in early behavioral predictors of serious antisocial behaviors. *Journal of Psychopathology and Behavioral Assessment, 15*, 23-41.

109. Donenberg, G., & Baker, B. L. (1993). The impact of young children with externalizing behaviors on their families. *Journal of Abnormal Child Psychology, 21*, 179-198.

110. DuPaul, G. J., & Henningson, P. N. (1993). Peer tutoring effects on the classroom performance of children with attention deficit hyperactivity disorder. *School Psychology Review, 22*, 134-142.

111. Gold, N. (1993). Depression and social adjustment in siblings of boys with autism. *Journal of Autism and Developmental Disorders, 23*, 147-163.

112. Gould, M. S., Bird, H., & Jaramillo, B. S. (1993). Correspondence between statistically derived behavior problem syndromes and child psychiatric diagnoses in a community sample. *Journal of Abnormal Child Psychology, 21*, 287-313.

113. Guevremont, D. C., & Foster, S. L. (1993). Impact of social problem-solving training on aggressive boys: Skill acquisition behavior, change, and generalization. *Journal of Abnormal Child Psychology, 21*, 13-27.

114. Henggeler, S. W., Melton, G. B., Smith, L. A., Foster, S. L., Hanley, J. H., & Hutchinson, C. M. (1993). Assessing violent offending in serious juvenile offenders. *Journal of Abnormal Child Psychology, 21*, 233-243.

115. Hodges, K. (1993). Structured interviews for assessing children. *Journal of Child Psychology and Psychiatry, 34*, 49-68.

116. Jensen, P. S., Shervette, R. E., Xenakis, S. N., & Richters, J. (1993). Anxiety and depressive disorders in attention deficit disorder with hyperactivity: New findings. *American Journal of Psychiatry, 150*, 1203-1209.

117. Johnston, C., & Short, K. H. (1993). Depressive symptoms and perceptions of child behavior. *Journal of Social and Clinical Psychology, 12*, 164-181.

118. Loeber, R., Keenan, K., Lahey, B. B., Green, S. M., & Thomas, C. (1993). Evidence for developmentally based diagnoses of oppositional defiant disorder and conduct disorder. *Journal of Abnormal Child Psychology, 21*, 377-410.

119. Lynam, D., Moffitt, T., & Stouthamer-Loeber, M. (1993). Explaining the relation between IQ and delinquency: Class, race, test motivation, school failure, or self-control? *Journal of Abnormal Psychology, 102*, 187-196.

120. Masten, A. S., Miliotis, D., Graham-Bermann, S. A., Ramirez, M., & Neeman, J. (1993). Children in homeless families: Risks to mental health and development. *Journal of Consulting and Clinical Psychology, 61*, 335-343.

121. Merrell, K. W. (1993). Using behavior rating scales to assess social skills and antisocial behavior in school settings: Development of the School Social Behavior Scales. *School Psychology Review, 22*, 115-133.

122. Pennington, B. F., Groisser, D., & Welsh, M. C. (1993). Contrasting cognitive deficits in attention deficit hyperactivity disorder versus reading disability. *Developmental Psychology, 29*, 511-523.

123. Sadowski, C., & Kelley, M. L. (1993). Social problem solving in suicidal adolescents. *Journal of Consulting and Clinical Psychology, 61*, 121-127.

124. Schaughency, E. A., & Fagot, B. I. (1993). The prediction of adjustment at age 7 from activity level at age 5. *Journal of Abnormal Child Psychology, 21*, 29-50.

125. Thurber, S., & Osborn, R. A. (1993). Comparison of parent and adolescent perspectives on deviance. *Journal of Genetic Psychology, 154*, 25-31.

126. Walker, L. S., Garber, J., & Greene, J. W. (1993). Psychosocial correlates of recurrent childhood pain: A comparison of pediatric patients with recurrent abdominal pain, organic illness, and psychiatric disorders. *Journal of Abnormal Psychology, 102*, 248-258.

127. Weist, M. D., Finney, J. W., Barnard, M. J., Davis, C. D., & Ollendick, T. H. (1993). Empirical selection of psychosocial treatment targets for children and adolescents with diabetes. *Journal of Pediatric Psychology, 18*, 11-28.

128. Weisz, J. R., Suwanlert, S., Chaiyasit, W., Weiss, B., Achenbach, T. M., & Eastman, K. L. (1993). Behavioral and emotional problems among Thai and American adolescents: Parent reports for ages 12-16. *Journal of Abnormal Psychology, 102*, 395-403.

129. Wolchik, S. A., Ramierez, R., Sandler, I. N., Fisher, J. L., Organista, P. B., & Brown, C. (1993). Inner-city, poor children of divorce: Negative divorce-related events, problematic beliefs and adjustment problems. *Journal of Divorce & Remarriage, 19*, 1-20.

130. Epkins, C. C., & Meyers, A. W. (1994). Assessment of childhood depression, anxiety, and aggression: Convergent and discriminant validity of self-, parent-, teacher-, and peer-report measures. *Journal of Personality Assessment, 62*, 364-381.

131. Fombonne, E. (1994). The Chatres study: I. Prevalence of psychiatric disorders among French school-aged children. *British Journal of Psychiatry, 164*, 69-79.

132. Kendall, P. C. (1994). Treating anxiety disorders in children: Results of a randomized clinical trial. *Journal of Consulting and Clinical Psychology, 62*, 100-110.

133. Sanders, M. R., Shepherd, R. W., Cleghorn, G., & Woolford, H. (1994). The treatment of recurrent abdominal pain in children: A controlled comparison of cognitive-behavioral family intervention and standard pediatric care. *Journal of Consulting and Clinical Psychology, 62*, 306-314.

134. Stolberg, A. L., & Mahler, J. (1994). Enhancing treatment gains in a school-based intervention for children of divorce through skill training, parental involvement, and transfer procedures. *Journal of Consulting and Clinical Psychology, 62*, 147-156.

135. Weisz, J. R., McCabe, M. A., & Dennig, M. D. (1994). Primary and secondary control among children undergoing medical procedures: Adjustment as a function of coping style. *Journal of Consulting and Clinical Psychology, 62*, 324-332.

[434]

Child Care Inventory.

Purpose: Developed to evaluate child care programs in order to improve program effectiveness or to determine the level of program implementation.

Population: Child care programs.

Publication Date: 1986.

Scores: 11 performance areas: Classroom Arrangement, Safety, Curriculum, Interacting, Scheduling, Child Assessment, Health, Special Needs, Parent Involvement, Outdoor Play, Infant Programs.

Administration: Individual.

Price Data, 1992: $19.95 per complete kit including test booklet and manual (32 pages); $9.95 per test booklet; $10.95 per manual.

Time: Administration time not reported.

Authors: Martha S. Abbott-Shim and Annette M. Sibley.

Publisher: Humanics Publishing Group.

[435]

CHILD Center Operational Assessment Tool.

Purpose: Identifies prereading skills of children preparatory to teaching reading and spelling.

Population: Regular or special education students.

Publication Dates: 1971–77.

Acronym: OAT.

Administration: Group.

Price Data: Not available.

Time: Administration time not reported.

Comments: Criterion-referenced.

Author: The Child Center.

Publisher: The Child Center [No reply from publisher; status unknown].

a) READING/SPELLING TEST.

Publication Dates: 1971–77.

Scores: 3 areas: Primary Learning Abilities, Phonic Encoding-Decoding, Structural Analysis Encoding-Decoding.

Comments: Both forms are to be used together.

b) MATH TEST.
Publication Date: 1971.

1) *Basic Concepts*.
Scores: 4 areas: Numeration, Basic Operations, Place Value, Fractions.

2) *Operational Skills*.
Scores: 6 areas: Addition and Subtraction, Multiplication, Division, Fractions, Decimals, Percents.

c) LANGUAGE TEST.
Publication Date: 1971.
Scores: 3 areas: Memory and Sequencing, Auditory Discrimination, Similarities.

d) BEHAVIORAL QUESTIONNAIRE.
Publication Date: 1971.
Scores, 8: Learning, Lability, Coordination, Self-Esteem, Concentration, Inappropriate Involuntary Behavior, Motor Expression, School Attitude.
Comments: Ratings by teachers.

[436]

Child Development Inventory.
Purpose: "Designed to provide systematic ways of obtaining in-depth developmental information from parents."
Population: Ages 1-3 to 6-3.
Publication Dates: 1968–92.
Acronym: CDI.
Scores, 9: Social, Self Help, Gross Motor, Fine Motor, Expressive Language, Language Comprehension, Letters, Numbers, General Development.
Administration: Individual.
Price Data, 1993: $55 per complete set including 10 test booklets, 25 answer sheets, 25 CDI profiles, and manual ('92, 44 pages) with scoring template; $13 per 10 test booklets; $9 per 25 answer sheets; $9 per 25 CDI profiles; $25 per manual with scoring template; $27 per specimen set.
Time: [30–50] minutes.
Comments: Formerly called the Minnesota Child Development Inventory.
Author: Harold Ireton.
Publisher: Behavior Science Systems, Inc.
Cross References: For a review of an earlier edition by Jane A. Rysberg, see 9:712; see also T3:1492 (6 references); for a review by William L. Goodwin, see 8:220 (3 references).

TEST REFERENCES

1. Labeck, L. J., Ireton, H., & Leeper, S. D. (1983). On-line computerized assessment of young children using the Minnesota Child Development Inventory. *Child Psychiatry and Human Development, 14*, 49-54.
2. Achenbach, T. M., & Edelbrock, C. S. (1984). Psychopathology of childhood. *Annual Review of Psychology, 35*, 227-256.
3. Bates, J. E., & Bayles, K. (1984). Objective and subjective components in mothers' perceptions of their children from age 6 months to 3 years. *Merrill-Palmer Quarterly, 30*, 111-130.
4. Bickett, L., Reuter, J., & Stancin, T. (1984). The use of the McCarthy Scales of Children's Abilities to assess moderately mentally retarded children. *Psychology in the Schools, 21*, 305-312.
5. Telzrow, C. F. (1984). Practical applications of the K-ABC in the identification of handicapped preschoolers. *The Journal of Special Education, 18*, 311-324.
6. Achenbach, T. M., Edelbrock, C., & Howell, C. T. (1987).

Empirically based assessment of the behavioral/emotional problems of 2- and 3-year-old children. *Journal of Abnormal Child Psychology, 15*, 629-650.
7. Bathurst, K., & Gottfried, A. W. (1987). Untestable subjects in child development research: Developmental implications. *Child Development, 58*, 1135-1144.
8. Byrne, J. M., Smith, D. J., & Backman, J. E. (1987). Cognitive impairment in preschoolers: Identification using the Personality Inventory for Children—Revised. *Journal of Abnormal Child Psychology, 15*, 239-246.
9. White, S., Halpin, B. M., Strom, G. A., & Santilli, G. (1988). Behavioral comparisons of young sexually abused, neglected, and nonreferred children. *Journal of Clinical Child Psychology, 17*, 53-61.
10. Chaffe, C. A., Cunningham, C. E., Secord-Gilbert, M., Elbard, H., & Richards, J. (1990). Screening effectiveness of the Minnesota Child Development Inventory Expressive and Receptive Language scales: Sensitivity, specificity, and predictive value. *Psychological Assessment, 2*, 80-85.
11. Hill, B. P., & Singer, L. T. (1990). Speech and language development after infant tracheostomy. *Journal of Speech and Hearing Disorders, 55*, 15-20.
12. Chaffee, C. A., Cunningham, C. E., Secord-Gilbert, M., Elbard, H., & Richards, J. (1991). The influence of parenting stress and child behavior problems on parental estimates of expressive and receptive language development. *Journal of Abnormal Child Psychology, 19*, 65-74.
13. Hadadian, A., & Rose, S. (1991). An investigation of parents' attitudes and the communication skills of their deaf children. *American Annals of the Deaf, 136*, 273-277.
14. May, D. C., & Kundert, D. K. (1992). Kindergarten screenings in New York state: Tests, purposes, and recommendations. *Psychology in the Schools, 29*(1), 35-41.

[437]

Child Language Ability Measures.
Purpose: "Designed to measure language development."
Population: Ages 2–8.
Publication Dates: 1979.
Acronym: CLAM.
Scores: 6 tests: Vocabulary Comprehension, Grammar Comprehension, Inflection Production, Grammar Imitation, Grammar Formedness Judgment, Grammar Equivalence Judgment.
Administration: Individual.
Price Data: Available from publisher.
Time: (15) minutes per test.
Comments: Tests may be administered separately or in any of 11 combinations.
Authors: Christy Moynihan and Albert Mehrabian.
Publisher: Albert Mehrabian.
Cross References: For a review by Allen Jack Edwards, see 10:51.

[438]

Child Neuropsychological Questionnaire.
Purpose: Developed to evaluate children suspected of having brain dysfunctions.
Population: Children.
Publication Date: 1978.
Acronym: CNQ.
Scores: Overall evaluation of neuropsychological impairment.
Administration: Individual.
Price Data, 1994: $28 per complete kit including manual (6 pages) and 50 questionnaires.
Time: Administration time not reported.
Author: Fernando Melendez.
Publisher: Psychological Assessment Resources, Inc.

[439]
The Childhood Autism Rating Scale.
Purpose: "To identify children with autism, and to distinguish them from developmentally handicapped children without the autism syndrome."
Population: Ages 2 and over.
Publication Dates: 1986–88.
Acronym: CARS.
Scores: 16 rating scores: Relating to People, Imitation, Emotional Response, Body Use, Object Use, Adaptation to Change, Visual Response, Listening Response, Taste/Smell/Touch Response and Use, Fear or Nervousness, Verbal Communication, Nonverbal Communication, Activity Level, Level and Consistency of Intellectual Response, General Impressions, Total.
Administration: Individual.
Price Data, 1993: $50 per complete kit including 25 rating scales and manual ('88, 20 pages); $16.50 per 25 rating scales; $35 per manual.
Time: Administration time not reported.
Comments: Revision of the Childhood Psychosis Rating Scale; ratings by professionals trained to administer the CARS.
Authors: Eric Schopler, Robert J. Reichler, and Barbara Rochen Renner.
Publisher: Western Psychological Services.
Cross References: For reviews by Barry M. Prizant and J. Steven Welsh, see 11:65 (4 references).

TEST REFERENCES

1. Donovan, A. M. (1988). Family stress and ways of coping with adolescents who have handicaps: Maternal perceptions. *American Journal on Mental Retardation, 92,* 502-509.
2. Layton, T. L. (1988). Language training with autistic children using four different modes of presentation. *Journal of Communication Disorders, 21,* 333-350.
3. Freeman, N. L., Perry, A., & Factor, D. C. (1991). Child behaviours as stressors: Replicating and extending the use of the CARS as a measure of stress: A research note. *Journal of Child Psychology and Psychiatry, 32,* 1025-1030.
4. Matson, J. L., Compton, L. S., & Sevin, J. A. (1991). Comparison and item analysis of the MESSY for autistic and normal children. *Research in Developmental Disabilities, 12,* 361-369.
5. Ozonoff, S., Pennington, B. F., & Rogers, S. J. (1991). Executive function deficits in high-functioning autistic individuals: Relationships to theory of mind. *Journal of Child Psychology and Psychiatry, 32,* 1081-1105.
6. Eaves, R. C., & Milner, B. (1993). The criterion-related validity of the Childhood Autism Rating Scale and the Autism Behavior Checklist. *Journal of Abnormal Child Psychology, 21,* 481-491.

[440]
Children of Alcoholics Screening Test.
Purpose: Measures children's and adults' attitudes, feelings, perceptions, and experiences related to their parents' drinking behavior; also identifies probable children of alcoholics (CoAs) and adult children of alcoholics (ACoAs).
Population: School-age children through adults.
Publication Dates: 1981–93.
Acronym: CAST.
Scores: Total score only.
Administration: Group or individual.
Price Data, 1993: $30 per Clinician/Researcher set including manual ('93, 106 pages), research abstracts, and 50 test forms.

Time: (5–10) minutes.
Comments: Reduced rate is available for additional forms used in research or mass testing.
Author: John W. Jones.
Publisher: Camelot Unlimited.
Cross References: For reviews by Stuart N. Hart and Steven P. Schinke, see 10:52; for reviews by Susanna Maxwell and Barrie G. Stacey, see 9:217.

TEST REFERENCES

1. Dinning, W. D., & Berk, L. A. (1989). The Children of Alcoholics Screening Test: Relationship to sex, family environment, and social adjustment in adolescents. *Journal of Clinical Psychology, 45,* 335-339.
2. Harman, M. J., & Arbona, C. (1991). Psychological adjustment among adult children of alcoholics: A cross-cultural study. *The Journal of Psychology, 125,* 641-648.
3. Clair, D. J., & Genest, M. (1992). The Children of Alcoholics Screening Test: Reliability and relationship to family environment, adjustment, and alcohol-related stressors of adolescent offspring of alcoholics. *Journal of Clinical Psychology, 48,* 414-420.
4. Kashubeck, S., & Christensen, S. A. (1992). Differences in distress among adult children of alcoholics. *Journal of Counseling Psychology, 39,* 356-362.
5. Williams, O. B., & Corrigan, P. W. (1992). The differential effects of parental alcoholism and mental illness on their adult children. *Journal of Clinical Psychology, 48,* 406-414.
6. Workman, M., & Beer, J. (1992). Depression, suicide ideation, and aggression among high school students whose parents are divorced and use alcohol at home. *Psychological Reports, 70,* 503-511.
7. Garbarino, C., & Strange, C. (1993). College adjustment and family environments of students reporting parental alcohol problems. *Journal of College Student Development, 34,* 261-266.
8. Wright, D. M., & Heppner, P. P. (1993). Examining the well-being of nonclinical college students: Is knowledge of the presence of parental alcoholism useful? *Journal of Counseling Psychology, 40,* 324-334.

[441]
Children's Abilities Scales.
Purpose: Designed as a broad assessment of a pupil's abilities as the pupil enters a secondary school.
Population: Ages 11-0 to 12-6.
Publication Dates: 1982–84.
Acronym: CAS.
Scores, 10: Verbal (Word Pairs, Word Overlap, Total), Spatial (Flags [Part 1], Flags [Parts 1 and 2], Dice, Total), Non-Verbal (Symbols, Shapes, Total).
Administration: Group.
Price Data, 1989: £132.25 per introductory pack including class set of 30 pupil's books, 3 answer sheet packs, and manual ('84, 39 pages); £3.40 per reusable pupil's book; £6.85 per 2 scoring keys; £10.30 per answer sheet pack; £9.50 per manual; £23.30 per specimen set (pupil's book, 10 answer sheets, and manual).
Time: (140) minutes for the battery, (15–35) minutes for any one test.
Authors: Chris Whetton and Roy Childs.
Publisher: NFER-Nelson Publishing Co., Ltd. [England].
Cross References: For reviews by Stephen N. Elliott and Stephan A. Henry, see 10:53.

[442]
Childrens Adaptive Behavior Scale, Revised.
Purpose: Provides a means to gather information on the relevant knowledge and concepts requisite to adaptive functioning.
Population: Ages 5–11.

Publication Dates: 1980–83.
Acronym: CABS.
Scores, 6: Language Development, Independent Functioning, Family Role Performance, Economic-Vocational Activity, Socialization, Total.
Administration: Individual.
Price Data, 1987: $1 per student booklet; $14.95 per manual ('83, 42 pages); $19.95 per specimen set including 5 student booklets, picture book, and manual.
Time: (45–50) minutes.
Comments: Other test materials (e.g., coins, blocks, scissors, paper) must be supplied by examiner.
Authors: Richard H. Kicklighter and Bert O. Richmond.
Publisher: Humanics Publishing Group.
Cross References: For reviews by Kenneth A. Kavale and Esther Sinclair, see 10:55 (1 reference); for reviews by Thomas R. Kratochwill and Corinne R. Smith of the original edition, see 9:218; see also T3:395 (1 reference).

TEST REFERENCES

1. Gresham, F. M., & Reschly, D. J. (1987). Dimensions of social competence: Method factors in the assessment of adaptive behavior, social skills, and peer acceptance. *Journal of School Psychology, 25,* 367-381.

[443]
Children's Academic Intrinsic Motivation Inventory.

Purpose: "To measure academic intrinsic motivation . . . defined as enjoyment of school learning characterized by an orientation toward mastery, curiosity, persistence, and the learning of challenging, difficult, and novel tasks."
Population: Grades 4–8.
Publication Date: 1986.
Acronym: CAIMI.
Scores: 5 scales: Reading, Math, Social Studies, Science, General.
Administration: Individual or group.
Price Data, 1994: $44 per complete kit including 25 test booklets, 25 profile forms, and manual (24 pages); $30 per 25 test booklets; $8 per 25 profile forms; $8 per manual.
Time: (20) minutes for individual administration; (60) minutes for group administration.
Comments: Self-report inventory.
Author: Adele Eskeles Gottfried.
Publisher: Psychological Assessment Resources, Inc.
Cross References: For a review by C. Dale Posey, see 10:54.

[444]
Children's Apperception Test [1991 Revision].

Purpose: A projective "method of investigating personality by studying the dynamic meaningfulness of the individual differences in perception of standard stimuli."
Population: Ages 3–10.
Publication Dates: 1949–92.

Acronym: C.A.T.
Scores: No scores.
Administration: Individual.
Editions, 3: Animal, Human, Supplement, plus Short Form.
Price Data, 1993: $85 per C.A.T.-A, C.A.T.-S, C.A.T.-H, manual ('91, 24 pages), 30 recording and analysis blanks, and 10 copies of Haworth's Schedule of Adaptive Mechanisms in C.A.T. Responses; $23.50 per C.A.T.-A or C.A.T.-H; $27.50 per C.A.T.-S; $9.30 per 25 recording and analysis blanks (short form); $9.30 per 30 Haworth's Schedules.
Time: (15–20) minutes.
Authors: Leopold Bellak and Sonya Sorel Bellak.
Publisher: C.P.S., Inc.
Cross References: For reviews by Clifford V. Hatt and Marcia B. Shaffer of an earlier edition, see 9:219 (1 reference); see also T3:396 (1 reference), T2:1451 (23 references), and P:419 (18 references); for reviews by Bernard L. Murstein and Robert D. Wirt, see 6:206 (19 references); for reviews by Douglas T. Keeny and Albert I. Rabin, see 5:126 (15 references); for reviews by John E. Bell and L. Joseph Stone and excerpted reviews by M. M., Genn, Herbert Herman, Robert R. Holt, Laurance F. Shaffer, and Adolf G. Woltmann, see 4:103 (2 references).

TEST REFERENCES

1. Champion, L., Doughtie, E. B., Johnson, P. J., & McCreary, J. H. (1984). Preliminary investigation into the Rorschach response patterns of children with documented learning disabilities. *Journal of Clinical Psychology, 40,* 329-333.
2. Kalliopuska, M., & Karila, I. (1987). Association of motor performance and cognitive, linguistic, and socioemotional factors. *Perceptual and Motor Skills, 65,* 399-405.
3. Miller, T. W., & Veltkamp, L. J. (1989). Assessment of child sexual abuse: Clinical use of fables. *Child Psychiatry and Human Development, 20,* 123-133.
4. Ganschow, L., Sparks, R., & Helmick, M. (1992). Speech/language referral practices by school psychologists. *School Psychology Review, 21*(2), 313-326.

[445]
Children's Apperceptive Story-Telling Test.

Purpose: "Identification of social, emotional, and/or behavioral problems in children."
Population: Ages 6–13.
Publication Date: 1989.
Acronym: CAST.
Scores: 19 scores and 9 indicators: Adaptive Thematic (Instrumentality, Interpersonal Cooperation, Affiliation, Positive Affect), Nonadaptive Thematic (Inadequacy, Alienation, Interpersonal Conflict, Limits, Negative Affect), Adaptive Problem-Solving (Positive Preoperational, Positive Operational), Nonadaptive Problem-Solving (Refusal, Unresolved, Negative Preoperational, Negative Operational), Factor Profile (Adaptive, Nonadaptive, Immature, Uninvested), Thematic Indicators (Sexual Abuse, Substance Abuse, Divorce, Hypothetical Thought, Emotionality, Self-Validation), Life Tasks (Family, Peer, School).
Administration: Individual.
Price Data, 1994: $109 per complete kit including 31 picture cards; 50 record/scoring forms, and manual

('89, 290 pages); $49 per set of 31 picture cards; $29 per 50 record/scoring forms; $34 per manual.
Time: (20–40) minutes.
Comments: Orally administered.
Author: Mary F. Schneider.
Publisher: PRO-ED, Inc.

[446]

Children's Articulation Test.
Purpose: Designed to "assess child's ability to produce consonants, vowels and diphthongs in an in-depth relationship to other consonants and vowels."
Population: Ages 3–11.
Publication Date: 1989.
Acronym: CAT.
Scores, 7: Medial Vowels/Diphthongs, Final Consonants, Initiating Consonants, Abutting Consonants, Abutting Consonants and Vowels/Diphthongs, Connected Speech, Language Concepts.
Administration: Individual.
Price Data, 1994: $32.95 per test; $6.75 per 25 scoring sheets.
Time: [15] minutes.
Author: George S. Haspiel.
Publisher: Dragon Press.

[447]

Children's Attention and Adjustment Survey.
Purpose: "Designed to measure the diagnostic criteria of inattention, impulsivity, hyperactivity, and aggressiveness or conduct problems."
Population: Ages 5–13.
Publication Date: 1990.
Acronym: CAAS.
Scores, 7: Inattention, Impulsivity, ADD, Hyperactivity, ADHD, Conduct Problems, DSM III-R ADHD.
Administration: Individual.
Editions, 2: School, Home.
Price Data, 1993: $31.95 per 25 self-scorable booklets (select School or Home form); $15.90 per 25 scoring profiles; $26.50 per manual (75 pages); $95.45 per starter set including manual and 25 each of Home Form, School Form, and Scoring Profile.
Time: (2–5) minutes per form.
Comments: Ratings by teacher or parent.
Authors: Nadine Lambert, Carolyn Hartsough, and Jonathan Sandoval.
Publisher: American Guidance Service, Inc.

[448]

Children's Auditory Verbal Learning Test-2.
Purpose: Constructed to assess the presence and severity of learning and memory impairment in children.
Population: Ages 6-6 to 17-11.
Publication Dates: 1988–93.
Acronym: CAVLT-2.
Scores, 6: Immediate Memory Span, Level of Learning, Immediate Recall, Delayed Recall, Recognition Accuracy, Total Intrusions.

Administration: Individual.
Price Data, 1994: $65 per complete kit including 25 test booklets and manual ('93, 68 pages); $28 per 25 test booklets; $40 per manual.
Time: (25–30) minutes.
Comments: Orally administered.
Author: Jack L. Talley.
Publisher: Psychological Assessment Resources, Inc.

[449]

Children's Category Test.
Purpose: "Designed to assess non-verbal learning and memory, concept formation, and problem-solving abilities."
Population: Ages 5-0 to 16-11.
Publication Date: 1993.
Acronym: CCT.
Scores, 6: Subtest I, Subtest II, Subtest III, Subtest IV, Subtest V, Total.
Administration: Individual.
Levels, 2: Level 1 (Ages 5 to 8), Level 2 (Ages 9 to 16).
Price Data, 1994: $280 per complete kit including manual (72 pages), 25 Level 1 record forms, 25 Level 2 record forms, stimulus booklet, and color response cards (1 for each level); $17.50 per 25 record forms; $35 per manual; $120 per Level 1 stimulus booklet; $95 per Level 2 stimulus booklet; $9 per 2 response cards.
Time: (15–20) minutes.
Author: Thomas Boll.
Publisher: The Psychological Corporation.

[450]

Children's Depression Inventory.
Purpose: A self-rating assessment of children's depression.
Population: Ages 8–17.
Publication Dates: 1977–82.
Acronym: CDI.
Scores: Total score only.
Administration: Individual and small groups.
Price Data: Available from publisher for test, instructions for administration, scoring template, reference list, and manuscripts.
Foreign Language Editions: Translations available in Arabic, Bulgarian, Italian, Hungarian, Hebrew, Spanish, German, French, and Portuguese.
Time: [10–15] minutes.
Comments: For research use only.
Author: Maria Kovacs.
Publisher: Western Psychiatric Institute and Clinic.
Cross References: For reviews by Michael G. Kavan and Howard M. Knoff, see 11:66 (63 references).

TEST REFERENCES

1. Fauber, R., Forehand, R., Long, N., Burke, M., & Faust, J. (1987). The relationship of young adolescent Children's Depression Inventory (CDI) scores to their social and cognitive functioning. *Journal of Psychopathology and Behavioral Assessment, 9,* 161-172.
2. Field, T. M., Sandberg, D., Goldstein, S., Garcia, R., Vega-Lahr, N., Porter, K., & Dowling, M. (1987). Play interactions and interviews

of depressed and conduct disorder children and their mothers. *Child Psychiatry and Human Development, 17,* 213-234.

3. Hammen, C., Gordon, D., Burge, D., Adrian, C., Jaenicke, C., & Hirohoto, D. (1987). Maternal affective disorders, illness, and stress: Risk for children's psychopathology. *American Journal of Psychiatry, 144,* 736-741.

4. Weisz, J. R., Weiss, B., Wasserman, A. A., & Rintoul, B. (1987). Control-related beliefs and depression among clinic-referred children and adolescents. *Journal of Abnormal Psychology, 96,* 58-63.

5. Brown, R. T., Borden, K. A., Clingerman, S. R., & Jenkins, P. (1988). Depression in attention deficit-disordered and normal children and their parents. *Child Psychiatry and Human Development, 18,* 119-132.

6. Capelli, M., McGrath, P. J., MacDonald, N. E., Boland, M., Fried, P., & Katsanis, J. (1988). Parent, family, and disease factors as predictors of psychosocial functioning in children with cystic fibrosis. *Canadian Journal of Behavioural Science, 20,* 413-423.

7. Doerfler, L. A., Felner, R. D., Rowlison, R. T., Raley, P. A., & Evans, E. (1988). Depression in children and adolescents: A comparative analysis of the utility and construct validity of two assessment measures. *Journal of Consulting and Clinical Psychology, 56,* 769-772.

8. Forehand, R., Brady, G. H., Long, N., & Fauber, R. (1988). The interactive influence of adolescent and maternal depression on adolescent social and cognitive functioning. *Cognitive Therapy and Research, 12,* 341-350.

9. Forehand, R., Brody, G., Slotkin, J., Fauber, R., McCombs, A., & Long, N. (1988). Young adolescent and maternal depression: Assessment, interrelations, and family predictors. *Journal of Consulting and Clinical Psychology, 56,* 422-426.

10. McCauley, E., Mitchell, J. R., Burke, P., & Moss, S. (1988). Cognitive attributes of depression in children and adolescents. *Journal of Consulting and Clinical Psychology, 56,* 903-908.

11. Prout, H. T., & Chizik, R. (1988). Readability of child and adolescent self-report measures. *Journal of Consulting and Clinical Psychology, 56,* 152-154.

12. Saylor, C. F., Finch, A. J., & McIntosh, J. A. (1988). Self-reported depression in psychiatric, pediatric, and normal populations. *Child Psychiatry and Human Development, 18,* 250-254.

13. Wendel, N. H., Nelson, W. M., III, Politano, P. M., Mayhall, C. A., & Finch, A. J., Jr. (1988). Differentiating inpatient clinically-diagnosed and normal children using the Children's Depression Inventory. *Child Psychiatry and Human Development, 19,* 98-108.

14. Adelman, H. S., Taylor, L., & Nelson, P. (1989). Minors' dissatisfaction with their life circumstances. *Child Psychiatry and Human Development, 20,* 135-147.

15. Berr, J. (1989). Relationship of divorce to self-concept, self-esteem, and grade point average of fifth and sixth grade school children. *Psychological Reports, 65,* 1379-1383.

16. Cole, D. A. (1989). Psychopathology of adolescent suicide: Hopelessness, coping beliefs, and depression. *Journal of Abnormal Psychology, 98,* 248-255.

17. Kendall, P. C., Cantwell, D. P., & Kazdin, A. E. (1989). Depression in children and adolescents: Assessment issues and recommendations. *Cognitive Therapy and Research, 13,* 109-146.

18. Ponterotto, J. G., Pace, T. M., & Kavan, M. G. (1989). A counselor's guide to the assessment of depression. *Journal of Counseling and Development, 67,* 301-309.

19. Saigh, P. A. (1989). The validity of the DSM-III posttraumatic stress disorder classification as applied to children. *Journal of Abnormal Psychology, 98,* 189-192.

20. Tesser, A., Forehand, R., Brody, G., & Long, N. (1989). Conflict: The role of calm and angry parent-child discussion in adolescent adjustment. *Journal of Social and Clinical Psychology, 8,* 317-330.

21. Armistead, L., McCombs, A., Forehand, R., Wierson, M., Long, N., & Fauber, R. (1990). Coping with divorce: A study of young adolescents. *Journal of Clinical Child Psychology, 19,* 79-84.

22. Cole, D. A. (1990). Relation of social and academic competence to depressive symptoms in childhood. *Journal of Abnormal Psychology, 99,* 422-429.

23. Finch, A. J., Jr., Imm, P. S., & Belter, R. W. (1990). Brief Rorschach records with children and adolescents. *Journal of Personality Assessment, 55,* 640-646.

24. Hodges, K. (1990). Depression and anxiety in children: A comparison of self-report questionnaires to clinical interview. *Psychological Assessment, 2,* 376-381.

25. Hodges, K., & Craighead, W. E. (1990). Relationship of Children's Depression Inventory factors to diagnosed depression. *Psychological Assessment, 2,* 489-492.

26. Kazdin, A. E. (1990). Evaluation of the Automatic Thoughts Questionnaire: Negative cognitive processes and depression among children. *Psychological Assessment, 2,* 73-79.

27. Larson, R. W., Rafaelli, M., Richards, M. H., Ham, M., & Jewell, L. (1990). Ecology of depression in late childhood and early ado-lescence: A profile of daily states and activities. *Journal of Abnormal Psychology, 99,* 92-102.

28. Mattison, R. E., Handford, H. A., Kales, H. C., Goodman, A. L., & McLaughlin, R. E. (1990). Four-year predictive value of the Children's Depression Inventory. *Psychological Assessment, 2,* 169-174.

29. Tharinger, D. J., & Stark, K. (1990). A qualitative versus quantitative approach to evaluating The Draw-A-Person and Kinetic Family Drawing: A study of mood- and anxiety-disorder children. *Psychological Assessment, 2,* 365-375.

30. Cole, D. A. (1991). Preliminary support for a competency-based model of depression in children. *Journal of Abnormal Psychology, 100,* 181-190.

31. Kempton, T., Armistead, L., Wierson, M., & Forehand, R. (1991). Presence of a sibling as a potential buffer following parental divorce: An examination of young adolescents. *Journal of Clinical Child Psychology, 20,* 434-438.

32. Luthar, S. S. (1991). Vulnerability and resilience: A study of high-risk adolescents. *Child Development, 62,* 600-616.

33. Moss, N. D., & Dadds, M. R. (1991). Body weight attributions and eating self-efficacy in adolescence. *Addictive Behaviors, 16,* 71-78.

34. Pliszka, S. R. (1991). Antidepressants in the treatment of child and adolescent psychopathology. *Journal of Clinical Child Psychology, 20,* 313-320.

35. Walker, L. S., Garber, J., & Greene, J. W. (1991). Somatization symptoms in pediatric abdominal pain patients: Relation to chronicity of abdominal pain and parent somatization. *Journal of Abnormal Child Psychology, 19,* 379-394.

36. Wierzbicki, M., & Sayler, M. K. (1991). Depression and engagement in pleasant and unpleasant activities in normal children. *Journal of Clinical Psychology, 47,* 499-505.

37. Brady, E. U., & Kendall, P. C. (1992). Comorbidity of anxiety and depression in children and adolescents. *Psychological Bulletin, 111,* 244-255.

38. Crowley, S. L., Worchel, F. F., & Ash, M. J. (1992). Self-report, peer-report, and teacher-report measures of childhood depression: An analysis by item. *Journal of Personality Assessment, 59,* 189-203.

39. Dixon, J. F., & Ahrens, A. H. (1992). Stress and attributional styles as predictors of self-reported depression in children. *Cognitive Therapy and Research, 16,* 623-634.

40. Inderbitzen-Pisaruk, H., Shawchuck, C. R., & Hoiser, T. S. (1992). Behavioral characteristics of child victims of sexual abuse: A comparison study. *Journal of Clinical Child Psychology, 21,* 14-19.

41. Ines, T. M., & Sacco, W. P. (1992). Factors related to correspondence between teacher ratings of elementary student depression and student self-ratings. *Journal of Consulting and Clinical Psychology, 60,* 140-142.

42. Kaslow, N. J., Stark, K. D., Printz, B., Livingston, R., & Tsai, S. L. (1992). Cognitive Triad Inventory for Children: Development and relation to depression and anxiety. *Journal of Clinical Child Psychology, 21,* 339-347.

43. McGough, J., & Curry, J. F. (1992). Utility of the SCL-90-R with depressed and conduct-disordered adolescent inpatients. *Journal of Personality Assessment, 59,* 552-563.

44. Nolen-Hoeksema, S., Girgus, J. S., & Seligman, M. E. P. (1992). Predictors and consequences of childhood depressive symptoms: A 5-year longitudinal study. *Journal of Abnormal Psychology, 101,* 405-422.

45. O'Donohue, W. T., & Elliott, A. N. (1992). Treatment of the sexually abused child: A review. *Journal of Clinical Child Psychology, 21,* 218-228.

46. Saigh, P. A. (1992). Verbal mediated childhood post-traumatic stress disorder. *British Journal of Psychiatry, 161,* 704-706.

47. Sanders, M. R., Dodds, M. R., Johnston, B. M., & Cash, R. (1992). Childhood depression and conduct disorder: I. Behavioral, affective, and cognitive aspects of family problem-solving interactions. *Journal of Abnormal Psychology, 101,* 495-504.

48. Schoenherr, S. J., Brown, R. T., Baldwin, K., & Kaslow, N. J. (1992). Attributional styles and psychopathology in pediatric chronic-illness groups. *Journal of Clinical Child Psychology, 21,* 380-387.

49. Weiss, B., Politano, M., Nelson, W. M., Weisz, J. R., Carey, M., & Finch, A. J. (1992). Relations among self-reported depressive symptoms in clinic-referred children versus adolescents. *Journal of Abnormal Psychology, 101,* 391-397.

50. Worchel, F. F., Rae, W. A., Olson, T. K., & Crowley, S. L. (1992). Selective responsiveness of chronically ill children to assessments of depression. *Journal of Personality Assessment, 59,* 605-615.

51. Ambrose, B., & Rholes, W. S. (1993). Automatic cognitions and the symptoms of depression and anxiety in children and adolescents: An examination of the content specificity hypothesis. *Cognitive Therapy and Research, 17,* 153-171.

52. Cole, D. A., & Turner, J. E., Jr. (1993). Models of cognitive mediation and moderation in child depression. *Journal of Abnormal Psychology, 102,* 271-281.

53. Cole, D. A., & White, K. (1993). Structure of peer impressions

of children's competence: Validation of the peer nomination of multiple competencies. *Psychological Assessment, 5,* 449-456.

54. DeMoss, K., Milich, R., & DeMers, S. (1993). Gender, creativity, depression and attributional style in adolescents with high academic ability. *Journal of Abnormal Child Psychology, 21,* 455-467.

55. Fitzpatrick, K. M. (1993). Exposure to violence and presence of depression among low-income, African-American youth. *Journal of Consulting and Clinical Psychology, 61,* 528-531.

56. Fristad, M. A., Jedel, R., Weller, R. A., & Weller, E. B. (1993). Psychosocial functioning in children after the death of a parent. *American Journal of Psychiatry, 150,* 511-513.

57. Garber, J., Weiss, B., & Shanley, N. (1993). Cognitions, depressive symptoms, and development in adolescents. *Journal of Abnormal Psychology, 102,* 47-57.

58. Gold, N. (1993). Depression and social adjustment in siblings of boys with autism. *Journal of Autism and Developmental Disorders, 23,* 147-163.

59. Hoza, B., Pelham, W. E., Milich, R., Pillow, D., & McBride, K. (1993). The self-perceptions and attributions of attention deficit hyperactivity disordered and nonreferred boys. *Journal of Abnormal Child Psychology, 21,* 271-286.

60. Jeney-Gammon, P. J., Daugherty, T. K., Finch, A. J., Belter, R. W., & Foster, K. Y. (1993). Children's coping styles and report of depressive symptoms following a natural disaster. *Journal of Genetic Psychology, 154,* 259-267.

61. Jensen, P. S., Shervette, R. E., Xenakis, S. N., & Richters, J. (1993). Anxiety and depressive disorders in attention deficit disorder with hyperactivity: New findings. *American Journal of Psychiatry, 150,* 1203-1209.

62. Last, C. G., & Perrin, S. (1993). Anxiety disorders in African-American and White children. *Journal of Abnormal Child Psychology, 21,* 153-164.

63. Laurent, J., & Stark, K. D. (1993). Testing the cognitive content-specificity hypothesis with anxious and depressed youngsters. *Journal of Abnormal Psychology, 102,* 226-237.

64. Laurent, J., Landau, S., & Stark, K. D. (1993). Conditional probabilities in the diagnosis of depressive and anxiety disorders in children. *School Psychology Review, 22,* 98-114.

65. Masten, A. S., Miliotis, D., Graham-Bermann, S. A., Ramirez, M., & Neeman, J. (1993). Children in homeless families: Risks to mental health and development. *Journal of Consulting and Clinical Psychology, 61,* 335-343.

66. Wagner, W. G., Kilcrease-Fleming, D., Fowler, W. E., & Kazelskis, R. (1993). Brief-term counseling with sexually-abused girls: The impact of sex of counselor on client's therapeutic involvement, self-concept, and depression. *Journal of Counseling Psychology, 40,* 490-500.

67. Walker, L. S., Garber, J., & Greene, J. W. (1993). Psychosocial correlates of recurrent childhood pain: A comparison of pediatric patients with recurrent abdominal pain, organic illness, and psychiatric disorders. *Journal of Abnormal Psychology, 102,* 248-258.

68. Weisz, J. R., Sweeney, L., Proffitt, V., & Carr, T. (1993). Control-related beliefs and self-reported depressive symptoms in late childhood. *Journal of Abnormal Psychology, 102,* 411-418.

69. Epkins, C. C., & Meyers, A. W. (1994). Assessment of childhood depression, anxiety, and aggression: Convergent and discriminant validity of self-, parent-, teacher-, and peer-report measures. *Journal of Personality Assessment, 62,* 364-381.

70. Kendall, P. C. (1994). Treating anxiety disorders in children: Results of a randomized clinical trial. *Journal of Consulting and Clinical Psychology, 62,* 100-110.

71. Stolberg, A. L., & Mahler, J. (1994). Enhancing treatment gains in a school-based intervention for children of divorce through skill training, parental involvement, and transfer procedures. *Journal of Consulting and Clinical Psychology, 62,* 147-156.

[451]

Childrens Depression Scale [Second Research Edition].

Purpose: Constructed to assess childhood depression.
Population: Ages 9–16.
Publication Dates: 1978–87.
Acronym: CDS.
Scores, 10: Depressive (Affective Response, Social Problems, Self Esteem, Preoccupation with Sickness, Guilt, Miscellaneous, Total), Positive (Pleasure and Enjoyment, Miscellaneous, Total).
Administration: Individual.
Forms, 3: Child, Parent (Boys, Girls).

Price Data, 1994: $155 per complete kit including set of cards, 25 questionnaires for each sex, 50 record forms, and manual ('87, 55 pages); $26 per set of cards; $10 per 10 questionnaires (select Boys or Girls); $10 per 10 record forms; $32 per manual.
Foreign Language Edition: Australian Edition available from Australian Council for Educational Research, Ltd.
Time: Administration time not reported.
Comments: Questionnaire titles are Parent's Questionnaire [Parents of Boys, Parents of Girls].
Authors: Moshe Lang and Miriam Tisher.
Publisher: Consulting Psychologists Press, Inc.
Cross References: For reviews by Howard M. Knoff and F. E. Sterling of an earlier Australian Edition, see 9:220; see also T3:397 (1 reference).

TEST REFERENCES

1. Fine, S., Moretti, M., Haley, G., & Marriage, K. (1984). Depressive disorder in children and adolescents: Dysthymic disorder and the use of self-rating scales in assessment. *Child Psychiatry and Human Development, 14,* 223-229.

2. Haley, G. M. T., Fine, S., Marriage, K., Moretti, M. M., & Freeman, R. J. (1985). Cognitive bias and depression in psychiatrically disturbed children and adolescents. *Journal of Consulting and Clinical Psychology, 53,* 535-537.

3. Reynolds, W. M., Anderson, G., & Bartell, N. (1985). Measuring depression in children: A multimethod assessment investigation. *Journal of Abnormal Child Psychology, 13,* 513-526.

4. Rotundo, N., & Hensley, V. R. (1985). The children's depression scale. A study of its validity. *The Journal of Child Psychology and Psychiatry and Allied Disciplines, 26,* 917-927.

5. Kazdin, A. E., Colbus, D., & Rodgers, A. (1986). Assessment of depression and diagnosis of depressive disorder among psychiatrically disturbed children. *Journal of Abnormal Child Psychology, 14,* 499-515.

6. Matson, J. L., Barrett, R. P., & Helsel, W. J. (1988). Depression in mentally retarded children. *Research in Developmental Disabilities, 9,* 39-46.

7. Wendel, N. H., Nelson, W. M., III, Politano, P. M., Mayhall, C. A., & Finch, A. J., Jr. (1988). Differentiating inpatient clinically-diagnosed and normal children using the Children's Depression Inventory. *Child Psychiatry and Human Development, 19,* 98-108.

8. Comunion, A. L. (1989). Some characteristics of relations among depression, anxiety, and self-efficacy. *Perceptual and Motor Skills, 69,* 755-764.

9. Kazdin, A. E. (1989). Identifying depression in children: A comparison of alternative selection criteria. *Journal of Abnormal Child Psychology, 17,* 437-454.

10. Kendall, P. C., Cantwell, D. P., & Kazdin, A. E. (1989). Depression in children and adolescents: Assessment issues and recommendations. *Cognitive Therapy and Research, 13,* 109-146.

11. Mabe, P. A., & Treiber, F. A. (1989). Social desirability response tendencies in psychiatric inpatient children. *Journal of Clinical Psychology, 45,* 194-201.

12. Patton, W. (1991). Relationship between self-image and depression in adolescents. *Psychological Reports, 68,* 867-870.

13. Miller, K. E., King, C. A., Shain, B. N., & Naylor, M. W. (1992). Suicidal adolescents' perceptions of their family environment. *Suicide and Life-Threatening Behavior, 22,* 226-239.

[452]

Children's Embedded Figures Test.

Purpose: Designed as a measure of personality based on perceptual functioning.
Population: Ages 5–12.
Publication Dates: 1963–71.
Acronym: CEFT.
Scores: Total score only.
Administration: Individual.
Price Data, 1990: $26 per test kit including simple cardboard forms, 38 color plates, clear plastic envelopes, star rubber stamp, and pad of recording sheets;

$8 per 50 recording sheets; $7.50 per EPT manual ('71, 32 pages).

Time: (15–30) minutes.

Comments: Revision of the Goodenough-Eagle modification of the Embedded Figures Test; combined manual for this test, Embedded Figures Test (882), and Group Embedded Figures Test (1094).

Authors: Stephen A. Karp, Norma Konstadt (test), and manual coauthors Herman A. Witkin, Phillip K. Oltman, and Evelyn Raskin.

Publisher: Consulting Psychologists Press, Inc.

Cross References: See 9:221 (8 references), T3:398 (34 references), 8:519 (53 references), and T2:1127 (14 references); for a review by Sheldon A. Weintraub, see 7:53 (15 references); see also P:36 (7 references) and 6:746 (2 references).

TEST REFERENCES

1. Brown, R. T., & Wynne, M. E. (1984). An analysis of attentional components in hyperactive and normal boys. *Journal of Learning Disabilities, 17,* 162-166.
2. Brown, R. T., Wynne, M. E., & Slimmer, L. W. (1984). Attention deficit disorder and the effect of methylphenidate on attention, behavioral, and cardiovascular functioning. *Journal of Clinical Psychiatry, 45,* 473-476.
3. Burlingame, K., Eliot, J., & Hardy, R. C. (1984). Revision of the Tent Series of the Children's Embedded Figures Test: A possible predictor of early reading achievement. *Perceptual and Motor Skills, 59,* 757-758.
4. Burton, E., & Sinatra, R. (1984). Relationship of cognitive style and word type for beginning readers. *Reading World, 24*(1), 65-75.
5. Daly, E. B. (1984). Relationship of stress and ego energy to field-dependent perception in older adults. *Perceptual and Motor Skills, 59,* 919-926.
6. Fogliani-Messina, T. M., & Fogliani, A. M. (1984). Perceptual experience in learning to read. *Perceptual and Motor Skills, 59,* 479-482.
7. Halperin, J. M., Gittelman, R., Klein, D. F., & Rudel, R. B. (1984). Reading disabled hyperactive children: A distinct subgroup of Attention Deficit Disorder with hyperactivity? *Journal of Abnormal Child Psychology, 12,* 1-14.
8. Hardy, R. C., Eliot, J., & Burlingame, K. (1984). Children's Embedded Figures Test: An examination of item difficulty in grades K-4. *Perceptual and Motor Skills, 59,* 21-22.
9. Saracho, O. N. (1984). The Goodenough-Harris Drawing Test as a measure of field-dependence/independence. *Perceptual and Motor Skills, 59,* 887-892.
10. Saracho, O. N. (1984). Young children's academic achievement as a function of their cognitive styles. *Journal of Research and Development in Education, 18*(1), 44-50.
11. Talbot, S., Godin, G., Drouin, D., & Goulet, C. (1984). Cognitive styles of young ice hockey players. *Perceptual and Motor Skills, 59,* 692-694.
12. Brown, R. T., Wynne, M. E., & Medenis, R. (1985). Methylphenidate and cognitive therapy: A comparison of treatment approaches with hyperactive boys. *Journal of Abnormal Child Psychology, 13,* 69-87.
13. Foorman, B. R., Sadowski, B. R., & Basen, J. A. (1985). Children's solutions for figural matrices: Developmental differences in strategies and effects of matrix characteristics. *Journal of Experimental Child Psychology, 39,* 107-130.
14. Ismail, M., & Kong, N. W. (1985). Relationship of locus of control, cognitive style, anxiety, and academic achievement of a group of Malaysian primary school children. *Psychological Reports, 57,* 1127-1134.
15. Lonner, W. J., Thorndike, R. M., Forbes, N. E., & Ashworth, C. (1985). The influence of television on measured cognitive abilities. *Journal of Cross-Cultural Psychology, 16,* 355-380.
16. Campbell, S. B., Ewing, L. J., Breaux, A. M., & Szumowski, E. K. (1986). Parent-referred problem three-year-olds: Follow-up at school entry. *Journal of Child Psychology and Psychiatry and Allied Disciplines, 27,* 473-488.
17. Hardy, R. C., Eliot, J., & Burlingame, K. (1986). Factor structure of shortened Children's Embedded Figures Test for different age groups. *Perceptual and Motor Skills, 63,* 479-486.
18. Saracho, O. N. (1986). Validation of two cognitive measures to assess field-dependence/independence. *Perceptual and Motor Skills, 63,* 255-263.
19. Hardy, R. C., Eliot, J., & Burlingame, K. (1987). Stability over age and sex of children's responses to Embedded Figures Test. *Perceptual and Motor Skills, 64,* 399-406.
20. Ozer, D. J. (1987). Personality, intelligence, and spatial visualization: Correlates of mental rotations test performance. *Journal of Personality and Social Psychology, 53,* 129-134.
21. Stoner, S. B., & Glynn, M. A. (1987). Cognitive styles of school-age children showing attention deficit disorders with hyperactivity. *Psychological Reports, 61,* 119-125.
22. Wagner, D. A., & Spratt, J. E. (1987). Cognitive consequences of contrasting pedagogies: The effects of Quranic preschooling in Morocco. *Child Development, 58,* 1207-1219.
23. Pennings, A. H. (1991). Altering the strategies in embedded-figure and water-level tasks via instruction: A neo-Piagetian learning study. *Perceptual and Motor Skills, 72,* 639-660.
24. Young, E. R., & Fouts, J. T. (1993). Field dependence/independence and the identification of gifted students. *Journal for the Education of the Gifted, 16,* 299-310.

[453]

Children's Inventory of Self-Esteem.

Purpose: Constructed to measure self-esteem.

Population: Ages 5–12.

Publication Date: 1987–90.

Acronym: CISE.

Scores, 15: Passive, Aggressive, and Total scores for each of the following scales: Belonging, Exceptionality, Control, Ideals, Total.

Administration: Group or individual.

Price Data, 1994: $40 per complete kit including 10 reusable inventories, 50 answer sheets, 25 profile/strategy booklets, and manual ('90, 25 pages).

Time: (10) minutes.

Comments: Ratings by parents and teachers.

Author: Richard A. Campbell.

Publisher: Brougham Press.

[454]

Children's Personality Questionnaire, 1985 Edition.

Purpose: Designed to measure personality traits to predict and evaluate the course of personal, social, and academic development.

Population: Ages 8–12.

Publication Dates: 1959–85.

Acronym: CPQ.

Scores, 14 to 18: 14 primary factors [Cool vs. Warm (A), Concrete Thinking vs. Abstract Thinking (B), Affected by Feelings vs. Emotionally Stable (C), Phlegmatic vs. Excitable (D), Obedient vs. Dominant (E), Sober vs. Enthusiastic (F), Expedient vs. Conscientious (G), Shy vs. Bold (H), Tough-Minded vs. Tender-Minded (I), Vigorous vs. Guarded (J), Forthright vs. Shrewd (N), Self-Assured vs. Apprehensive (O), Undisciplined Self-Conflict vs. Controlled (Q3), Relaxed vs. Tense (Q4)]; 4 optional secondary factors (Extraversion, Anxiety, Tough Poise, Independence).

Administration: Group.

Forms, 4: A, B, C, D.

Price Data, 1994: $29.25 per handscoring introductory kit including test booklet (Form A) and technical handbook with scoring keys ('85, 79 pages); $14 per technical handbook; $18 per 25 reusable test booklets (Form A or B); $24.25 per 25 reusable test booklets (Form C or D); $10.75 per 50 answer sheets; $15 per 50 answer-profile sheets; $10.75 per 50 profile sheets; $13.50 per scoring key (separate scoring keys required for Forms A/C and B/D); $20.25 per 25 machine-scorable answer sheets; $23.75 per computer interpretation introductory kit including test booklet (Form A), technical handbook, and machine-scorable answer sheet; $20 or less per computer interpretation.

Foreign Language Editions: German and Spanish editions available (Forms A and B, 1963); South African edition available from Human Sciences Research Council in Pretoria, South Africa.

Time: (30–60) minutes per form.

Comments: Test booklet is entitled "What You Do and What You Think."

Authors: Rutherford B. Porter and Raymond B. Cattell.

Publisher: Institute for Personality and Ability Testing, Inc.

Cross References: For reviews by Steven Klee and Howard M. Knoff, see 9:222 (11 references); for a review by Harrison G. Gough, see 8:520 (46 references); see also T3:1129 (60 references) and P:38 (14 references); for reviews by Anne Anastasi, Wilbur L. Layton, and Robert D. Wirt of the 1963 edition, see 6:122 (2 references).

TEST REFERENCES

1. Carpenter, P. (1984). 'Green Stamp Therapy' revisited: The evolution of 12 years of behavior modification and psychoeducational techniques with young delinquent boys. *Psychological Reports, 54*, 99-111.

2. Oates, R. K. (1984). Personality development after physical abuse. *Archives of Disease in Childhood, 59*, 147-150.

3. Stevenson, D. T., & Romney, D. M. (1984). Depression in learning disabled children. *Journal of Learning Disabilities, 17*, 579-582.

4. Karnes, F. A., McCallum, R. S., & Oehler, J. J. (1985). The relationship between learning style preference and personality variables: An exploratory investigation with gifted students. *Gifted Child Quarterly, 29*, 172-174.

5. Karnes, F. A., Oehler, J. J., & Jones, G. E. (1985). The relationship between electromyogram level and the Children's Personality Questionnaire as measures of tension in upper elementary gifted students. *Journal of Clinical Psychology, 41*, 169-172.

6. Cattell, R. B., & Krug, S. E. (1986). The number of factors in the 16PF: A review of the evidence with special emphasis on methodological problems. *Educational and Psychological Measurement, 46*, 509-522.

7. Handford, H. A., Mayes, S. D., Bagnato, S. J., & Bixler, E. O. (1986). Relationships between variations in parents' attitudes and personality traits of hemophilic boys. *American Journal of Orthopsychiatry, 56*, 424-434.

8. Marjoribanks, K. (1986). Ability and environment correlates of attitudes and aspirations: Personality group differences. *British Journal of Educational Psychology, 56*, 322-331.

9. Loehlin, J. C., Willerman, L., & Horn, J. M. (1987). Personality resemblance in adoptive families: A 10-year follow-up. *Journal of Personality and Social Psychology, 53*, 961-969.

[455]

Children's Problems Checklist.

Purpose: "To identify relevant problems, establish rapport, and provide written documentation of presenting problems consistent with community standards of care."

Population: Ages 5–12.

Publication Date: 1985.

Acronym: CPC.

Scores: 11 areas: Emotions, Self-Concept, Peers and Play, School, Language and Thinking, Concentration

and Organization, Activity Level and Motor Control, Behavior, Values, Habits, Health.

Administration: Group.

Manual: No manual.

Price Data, 1994: $26 per 50 checklists.

Time: (10–20) minutes.

Comments: Ratings by parent or guardian.

Author: John A. Schinka.

Publisher: Psychological Assessment Resources, Inc.

Cross References: For a review by Wayne C. Piersel, see 10:56.

[456]

Children's Role Inventory.

Purpose: "A measure assessing the roles played by children in their alcoholic families."

Population: Adult children of alcoholics.

Publication Date: 1988.

Acronym: CRI.

Scores: 4 role categories: Hero, Mascot, Lost Child, Scapegoat.

Administration: Group.

Manual: No manual.

Price Data: Available from publisher.

Time: Administration time not reported.

Authors: Ann E. Potter and Dale E. Williams.

Publisher: Dale E. Williams (the author)

[457]

Children's Version of the Family Environment Scale.

Purpose: "Provides a measure of young children's subjective appraisal of their family environment."

Population: Ages 5–12.

Publication Date: 1984.

Acronym: CV/FES.

Scores, 10: Cohesion, Expressiveness, Conflict, Independence, Achievement Orientation, Intellectual-Cultural Orientation, Active-Recreational Orientation, Moral-Religious Emphasis, Organization, Control.

Administration: Group.

Price Data, 1992: $48 per complete kit; $9 per manual (15 pages); $21 per 10 (reusable) test answer booklets; $8 per 50 profiles; $7 per 50 examiner's worksheets; $8 per 50 individual student answer sheets.

Time: Administration time not reported.

Comments: Downward extension of the Family Environment Scale (9:408).

Authors: Christopher J. Pino, Nancy Simons, and Mary Jane Slawinowski.

Publisher: Slosson Educational Publications, Inc.

Cross References: For a review by Nancy A. Busch-Rossnagel, see 10:57.

[458]

Chinese Proficiency Test.

Purpose: "Designed to evaluate the proficiency in Chinese listening and reading comprehension attained by Americans and other English-speaking learners of Chinese."

Population: Adults.
Publication Date: 1988.
Acronym: CPT.
Scores, 4: Listening Comprehension, Structure, Reading, Total.
Administration: Group.
Price Data: Available from publisher.
Time: 120(180) minutes.
Comments: Mail-in scoring.
Author: Center for Applied Linguistics.
Publisher: Center for Applied Linguistics.

[459]

Chinese Speaking Test.
Purpose: "To evaluate the level of oral proficiency in Chinese attained by American and other English-speaking learners of Chinese."
Population: Adults.
Publication Dates: 1988–89.
Acronym: CST.
Scores: Total score only.
Administration: Individual or group.
Price Data: Available from publisher.
Time: (43) minutes.
Comments: Examinee responses recorded on test tape scored by publisher.
Author: Staff of the Division of Foreign Language Education and Testing.
Publisher: Center for Applied Linguistics.

[460]

Christensen Dietary Distress Inventory.
Purpose: Designed to provide an objective assessment of the probability of diet contributing to emotional distress.
Population: Ages 18 and above.
Publication Date: 1990.
Acronym: CDDI.
Scores: Total score only.
Administration: Group.
Price Data: Available from publisher.
Time: (10–15) minutes.
Comments: Self-report inventory.
Author: Larry Christensen.
Publisher: Pro-Health Publications.

TEST REFERENCES

1. Christensen, L. (1991). Issues in the design of studies investigating the behavioral concomitants of foods. *Journal of Consulting and Clinical Psychology, 59,* 874-882.

[461]

Christensen-Guilford Fluency Tests.
Purpose: Measure for verbalized creative thinking abilities.
Population: Junior high school through college and adult.
Publication Dates: 1957–73.
Scores: 4 tests: Word Fluency, Ideational Fluency, Associational Fluency, Expressional Fluency.
Administration: Group.

Price Data: Available from publisher.
Authors: Paul P. Christensen and J. P. Guilford.
Publisher: Consulting Psychologists Press, Inc.
a) WORD FLUENCY.
Publication Date: 1958.
Time: 4(10) minutes.
b) IDEATIONAL FLUENCY 1.
Publication Date: 1957.
Time: 12(20) minutes.
c) ASSOCIATIONAL FLUENCY 1.
Forms, 2: A, B.
Time: 4(10) minutes.
d) EXPRESSIONAL FLUENCY.
Time: 8(15) minutes.

TEST REFERENCES

1. Judd, L. L. (1979). Effect of lithium on mood, cognition, and personality function in normal subjects. *Archives of General Psychiatry, 36,* 860-865.

[462]

Chronic Pain Battery.
Purpose: Constructed to assess chronic pain by collecting "medical, psychological, behavioral, social, demographic and pain data."
Population: Patients ages 18 and over.
Publication Dates: 1983–86.
Acronym: CPB.
Scores: 10 topics: Demographic and Social History, Past and Present Pain History, Past Treatment, Medications, Medical History, Personality-Pain Coping Style, Patient Expectations and Goals, Behavioral-Learning Factors, Psychosocial Factors, Patient Problem Ratings.
Administration: Group or individual.
Manual: No manual.
Price Data, 1994: $20 per specimen set including question book, answer sheet, and sample report.
Time: (30–60) minutes.
Comments: Comprises the Pain Assessment Questionnaire—Revised and the Symptom Checklist 90—Revised (2674); self-administered; self-report; symptom inventory questionnaire.
Authors: Stephen R. Levitt.
Publisher: Pain Resource Center, Inc.

[463]

Chronicle Career Quest®.
Purpose: Designed to "help individuals identify careers related to personal interests and preferences."
Publication Dates: 1989–93.
Acronym: CCQ.
Scores: 12 G.O.E. clusters: Artistic, Scientific, Plants and Animals, Protective, Mechanical, Industrial, Business Detail, Selling, Accommodating, Humanitarian, Leading Influencing, Physical Performing.
Administration: Group or individual.
Forms, 2: S and L.
Price Data, 1994: $3.50 per specimen set including 1 each Form S and L, Interest Inventory, Interpretation Guide ('93, 20 pages), Administrator's Guide

('92, 20 pages), and Career Paths; $8 per 100 Occupational Profiles; $5.50 per 50 summary sheets; $4 per 50 Career Paths Chart; $10 per Technical Manual ('92, 30 pages); $12 per Career Crosswalk.
Time: (10–15) minutes for Interest Inventory (Form S and Form L); (10–15) minutes for Interpretation Guide (Form S and Form L); (20–45) minutes for Career Paths (Form S); (180–240) minutes for Career Paths (Form L).
Author: Chronicle Guidance Publications, Inc.
Publisher: Chronicle Guidance Publications, Inc.

a) FORM S.
Population: Grades 7–10.
Price Data: $40.50 per kit including 25 Interest Inventories, 25 Interpretation Guides, and Administrator's Guide; $18.75 per 25 reusable Career Paths (Form S).

b) FORM L.
Population: Grades 9–16 and adult.
Price Data: $49.50 per kit of 25 Interest Inventories, 25 Interpretation Guides, and Administrator's Guide; $20.75 per 25 reusable Career Paths (Form L).

[464]
CID Phonetic Inventory.
Purpose: To evaluate the hearing-impaired "child's speech ability at the phonetic level."
Population: Hearing-impaired children.
Publication Date: 1988.
Scores, 7: Suprasegmental Aspects, Vowels and Diphthongs, Initial Consonants, Consonants with Alternating Vowels, Final Consonants, Alternating Consonants, Average.
Administration: Individual.
Price Data, 1989: $24 per complete kit including manual (24 pages), 25 rating forms, and 166 stimulus cards; $5 per 25 rating forms.
Time: (30–35) minutes.
Author: Jean S. Moog.
Publisher: Central Institute for the Deaf.
Cross Reference: For a review by Vincent J. Samar, see 11:67.

[465]
CID Picture SPINE.
Purpose: To "provide a measure of speech intelligibility for severely and profoundly hearing-impaired children and adolescents."
Population: Hearing-impaired children ages 6–13.
Publication Date: 1988.
Scores: Total score only.
Administration: Individual.
Price Data, 1989: $100 per complete kit including 300 picture cards, 25 response forms (4 pages), and test manual (31 pages); $5 per 25 response forms.
Time: (20–30) minutes.
Authors: Randall Monsen, Jean S. Moog, and Ann E. Geers.
Publisher: Central Institute for the Deaf.
Cross Reference: For a review by Vincent J. Samar, see 11:68.

TEST REFERENCES
1. Dagenais, P. A., & Critz-Crosby, P. (1992). Comparing tongue positioning by normal-hearing and hearing-impaired children during vowel production. *Journal of Speech and Hearing Research, 35*, 35-44.

[466]
CID Preschool Performance Scale.
Purpose: Designed to measure the intelligence of hearing-impaired and language-impaired children.
Population: Hearing- and language-impaired and normal children ages 2 to 5-5.
Publication Date: 1984.
Scores, 7: Manual Planning, Manual Dexterity, Form Perception, Perceptual-Motor Skills, Preschool Skills, Part/Whole Relations, Total.
Administration: Individual.
Price Data, 1994: $750 per complete kit including manipulatives for subtests, manual (29 pages), and 30 recording booklets; $25 per manual; $30 per 30 recording booklets.
Time: (40) minutes.
Comments: Adaptation of the Randall's Island Performance Series.
Authors: Ann E. Geers, Helen S. Lane, and Central Institute for the Deaf.
Publisher: Stoelting Co.

[467]
The City University Colour Vision Test, Second Edition 1980.
Purpose: To assess defects of color vision.
Population: Adults and children.
Publication Date: 1980.
Scores, 3: Chroma Four, Chroma Two, Overall.
Administration: Individual.
Manual: No manual (introductory notes and instructions included in binder of test plates).
Price Data, 1992: $163 per complete kit including profile sheets, 10 test pages, and instructions.
Time: Administration time not reported.
Author: Robert Fletcher.
Publisher: Keeler Instruments, Inc.

[468]
Clark-Madison Test of Oral Language.
Purpose: "To evaluate children's expressive capacity with various grammatical and syntactical components of language."
Population: Ages 4-0 to 8-11.
Publication Dates: 1981–84.
Scores: Total score only.
Administration: Individual.
Price Data, 1994: $84 per complete kit including 50 response forms, 50 analysis forms, stimulus materials, picture book, and examiner's manual ('84, 236 pages); $24 per 50 response and analysis forms; $62 per examiner's manual.
Time: (10–20) minutes.
Authors: John B. Clark and Charles L. Madison.
Publisher: PRO-ED, Inc.
Cross References: For a review by Barry W. Jones, see 10:58.

[469]

The Clark Wilson Group Multi-Level Feedback Instruments and Development Programs.

Purpose: Designed to identify group or individual training needs, assess the effects of training, support interactive and participatory management, and to be used in organizational and management studies.

Population: Organizations, executives, managers, and employees.

Publication Dates: 1973–93.

Administration: Group.

Price Data: Available from publisher.

Time: Administration time not reported.

Comments: Publisher suggests allowing 6 weeks to administer surveys and give feedback.

Authors: Clark L. Wilson and others noted below.

Publisher: The Clark Wilson Group.

a) QUALITY SERIES.

1) *Quality Values in Practice.*

Purpose: Assesses organizational readiness for "TQM" initiatives.

Population: All levels in organization.

Publication Date: 1991.

Acronym: QVIP.

Scores, 19: Strength of Leadership, Resistance to Change, Information Quality, Strategic Planning, Marketing Planning, Organizational Stretch, Teamwork Development, Internal Quality Standards, Satisficing, Operational Results, Customer Satisfaction, Readiness to Compete, Managing Diversity, Information Filtering, Reward Sharing, Employee Commitment, Tension/Pressure, Positive Program Support, Negative Program Response.

Authors: Paul M. Connolly and Clark L. Wilson.

b) LEADERSHIP SERIES.

1) *Executive Leadership.*

Purpose: Assesses executive competencies such as strategic foresight and oversight.

Population: Executives.

Publication Date: 1988.

Acronym: EXEC.

Scores, 17: Leadership Vision, Risk-Taking/Venturesomeness, Marketplace Awareness, Organization Awareness, Managing Complexities, Information/Data Support, Organization Stretch, Team Development, Information/Data Support, Standards of Performance, Push/Pressure, Coping with Stress, Sharing Credit, Effectiveness/Outcomes, Cultural Appreciation, Temporary Sources of Power, Lasting Sources of Power.

Authors: Paul M. Connolly and Clark L. Wilson.

2) *Leadership Practices.*

Purpose: Designed to provide feedback on an individual's vision, influence, and drive for change.

Population: Managers and executives.

Publication Date: 1986.

Acronym: SLP.

Scores, 23: Vision/Imagination, Risk-Taking/Venturesomeness, Organizational Sensitivity, Personal Awareness, Persuasiveness, Teaming, Standards of Performance, Perseverance, Push/Pressure, Recognition/Reinforcement, Effectiveness/Outcomes, Personal Standards, Consistency, Coping with Stress, Charisma, Control of Incentives/Pay, Personal Connections, Job Title/Position, Pressure, Technical Competence, Managerial Competence, Teamwork, Compatible Values.

Authors: Donal O'Hare and Clark L. Wilson.

c) MANAGEMENT SERIES.

1) *Management Practices.*

Purpose: Assesses basic managerial competencies.

Population: Managers.

Publication Date: 1973.

Acronym: SMP.

Scores, 23: Clarification of Goals and Objectives, Upward Communication, Orderly Work Planning, Expertise, Work Facilitation, Feedback, Time Emphasis, Control of Details, Goal Pressure, Delegation (Permissiveness), Recognition for Good Performance, Approachability, Teambuilding, Interest in Subordinate Growth, Building Trust, Work Involvement, Coworker Competence, Team Atmosphere, Opportunity for Growth, Tension Level, Organization Climate, General Morale, Commitment.

Author: Clark L. Wilson.

2) *Peer Relations.*

Purpose: Assesses organizational skills for specialists.

Population: Managers and individual contributors.

Publication Date: 1974.

Acronym: SPR.

Scores, 22: Clarity of Your Own Goals, Clarity of Communications, Encouraging Peer Participation, Orderly Work Planning, Problem Solving, Expertise, Teamwork/Cooperation, Feedback to Peers, Time Emphasis, Attention to Details, Pressure on Peers, Acknowledging Peer Contributions, Approachability, Dependability, Work Involvement, Coworker Competence, Team Atmosphere, Opportunity for Growth, Tension Level, Organization Climate, General Morale, Commitment.

Author: Clark L. Wilson.

3) *Working with Others.*

Purpose: Assesses supervisory skills for the first-time or prospective manager.

Publication Date: 1991.

Acronym: WWO.

Scores, 12: Clarity of Own Goals, Assertiveness, Problem Solving/Resourcefulness, Teamwork, Willingness to Listen, Attention to Details, Push/Pressure, Recognition, Effective-

ness/Productivity, Approachability, Dependability, Tolerance of Diversity.
Author: Clark L. Wilson.
4) Coaching Practices.
Purpose: Assesses coaching and appraising skills for performance management.
Population: Managers and executives.
Publication Date: 1993.
Acronym: SCP.
Scores, 14: Commitment to Coaching, Planning for Personal Growth, Coaching Skills, Coaching for Teamwork, Technical/Functional Expertise, Organization Awareness, Assessment Skills, Responding to Defensiveness, Control of Details, Delegation (Permissiveness), Recognizing Good Performance, Approachability, Trust, Overall Effectiveness.
Authors: Richard L. Dowall and Clark L. Wilson.
d) SALES SERIES.
1) Sales Management Practices.
Purpose: Assesses managerial competencies for field sales managers.
Population: Sales managers.
Publication Date: 1975.
Acronym: SSMP.
Scores, 23: Clarification of Goals and Objectives, Upward Communication, Orderly Work Planning, Expertise, Work Facilitation, Feedback, Time Emphasis, Control of Details, Goal Pressure, Delegation (Permissiveness), Recognition of Good Performance, Approachability, Teambuilding, Interest in Subordinate Growth, Building Trust, Work Involvement, Coworker Competence, Team Atmosphere, Opportunity for Growth, Tension Level, Organization Climate, General Morale, Commitment.
Author: Clark L. Wilson.
2) Sales Relations.
Purpose: Provides feedback on skills of sales representatives from customers and prospects.
Population: Sales representatives.
Publication Date: 1975.
Acronym: SSR.
Scores, 11: Understanding Us, Communicating Effectively, Account Service, Analyzing Needs, Presenting Benefits, Asking for the Order, Answering Objections, Selling Pressure, Professionalism, Approachability, Overall Satisfaction.
Author: Clark L. Wilson.
e) TEAM SERIES.
1) Executive Team.
Purpose: Coordinates efforts of top management groups.
Population: Executive teams.
Publication Date: 1993.
Acronym: XT.
Scores, 16: Clarity of Mission/Strategic Goals, Leadership for Growth/Productivity, Resistance to Change, Marketing Focus, Organization

Awareness, Consensus Planning, Team Atmosphere, Information/Data Support, Human Resource Development, Organization Stretch, Monitoring Executive Plans, Satisficing, Internal Problems, Sharing Credit, Coping with Stress, Effectiveness/Outcomes.
Authors: Paul M. Connolly and Clark L. Wilson.
2) Our Team.
Purpose: Provides feedback from team members on team negotiating skills and conflict resolution.
Population: Teams (Work Groups, Task Forces, Quality Circles, Project Teams, Design Teams, Teams with or without Leaders).
Publication Date: 1989.
Acronym: OT.
Scores, 14: Clarity of Goals and Priorities, Coworker Competence, Consensus Planning, Team Atmosphere, Newcomer Support, Conflict Resolution, Management Support, Management Feedback, Monitoring the Team's Work, Tension/Stress Level, Domination, Satisficing, Recognition/Satisfaction, Effectiveness/Outcomes.
Author: Clark L. Wilson.
3) My Team Mates.
Purpose: Provides feedback from team mates on a member's teaming skills.
Population: Team members.
Publication Date: 1989.
Acronym: MTM.
Scores, 14: Clarity of Personal Goals, Innovativeness, Functional Expertise, Teamwork, Leadership for Consensus, Negotiating Skills, Personal Awareness, Monitoring Personal Output, Coping with Stress and Ambiguity, Pressure on Team Mates, Risk Avoidance, Acknowledging Others' Efforts, Personal Values, Personal Effectiveness.
Author: Clark L. Wilson.

TEST REFERENCES

1. Whaley, K. W., & Hegstrom, T. G. (1992). Perceptions of school principal communication effectiveness and teacher satisfaction on the job. *Journal of Research and Development in Education, 25,* 224-231.

[470]
Class Achievement Test in Mathematics.
Purpose: "To survey the extent to which individual students and class groups have mastered aspects of primary mathematics."
Population: Years 4–5, 6–7 in Australian schools.
Publication Dates: 1979–86.
Acronym: CATIM.
Scores, 6: Counting and Place Value, Whole Numbers and Money, Fractions, Measurement I, Measurement II, Total.
Administration: Group.
Levels, 2: Years 4/5, Years 6/7.
Price Data, 1994: A$2 per test and answer strip sheet; $2 per class analysis sheet; $7.50 per teacher's

manual ('86, 31 pages) (specify Year 4/5 or Year 6/7); $12 per specimen set.
Time: 45(55) minutes.
Comments: Levels available as separates.
Authors: Greg Cornish, John Foyster, Peter Jeffery, David Sewell, Robin Wines, John Izard, and Graham Ward.
Publisher: Australian Council for Educational Research Ltd. [Australia].
Cross References: For reviews by Gary J. Stainback and Richard M. Wolf, see 11:69.

TEST REFERENCES

1. Marjoribanks, K. (1992). Family capital, children's individual attributes, and academic achievement. *The Journal of Psychology, 126,* 529-538.

[471]

The Class Activities Questionnaire.
Purpose: Developed to provide "a measure of the instructional climate."
Population: Students and teachers grades 6–12.
Publication Date: 1982.
Acronym: CAQ.
Scores: 5 dimensions: Lower Thought Processes, Higher Thought Processes, Classroom Focus, Classroom Climate, Student Opinions.
Administration: Group.
Price Data, 1987: $20.95 per class set including 30 student forms, 2 teacher forms, and computer analysis; $7.95 per manual (52 pages); $8.50 per specimen set.
Time: (20–30) minutes.
Author: Joe M. Steele.
Publisher: Creative Learning Press, Inc.
Cross References: For a review by Robert W. Hiltonsmith, see 9:226 (1 reference).

[472]

Classroom Atmosphere Questionnaire.
Purpose: Assesses classroom atmosphere through ratings of teacher by students.
Population: Grades 4–9.
Publication Date: 1971.
Acronym: CAQ.
Scores, 2: Acceptance-Understanding, Problem Solving Skills.
Administration: Group.
Manual: No manual.
Price Data: Not available.
Time: Administration time not reported.
Comments: Ratings of teacher by students.
Author: James K. Hoffmeister.
Publisher: Test Analysis & Development Corporation [No reply from publisher; status unknown].
Cross References: For a review by Edward F. Iwanicki, see 8:366.

[473]

The Classroom Communication Skills Inventory: A Listening and Speaking Checklist.
Purpose: Evaluates "oral communication skills that have been determined to be important for listening and speaking in the school setting and are essential for classroom learning."
Population: Students.
Publication Date: 1993.
Acronym: CCSI.
Scores: 10 ratings: Basic Speech and Hearing Processes (Auditory Perception, Speech), Classroom Communication (Attention, Class Participation), Language Content and Structure (Vocabulary, Grammar, Organization of Language), Interpersonal Classroom Communication (Using Language for a Variety of Purposes, Conversing Effectively, Using Appropriate Nonverbal Communication Skills).
Administration: Individual.
Price Data, 1993: $25 per teacher manual (51 pages) and 25 record forms.
Time: (10–15) minutes.
Author: The Psychological Corporation.
Publisher: The Psychological Corporation.

[474]

Classroom Environment Index.
Purpose: "Designed to measure the psychological environment of the classroom."
Population: Grades 5–12 and college.
Publication Date: 1971.
Acronym: CEI.
Scores, 38: 30 press scores (Abasement-Assurance, Achievement, Adaptability-Defensiveness, Affiliation, Aggression-Blame Avoidance, Change-Sameness, Conjunctivity-Disjunctivity, Counteraction, Deference-Restiveness, Dominance-Tolerance, Ego Achievement, Emotionality-Placidity, Energy-Passivity, Exhibitionism-Inferiority Avoidance, Fantasied Achievement, Harm Avoidance-Risk Taking, Humanities and Social Science, Impulsiveness-Deliberation, Narcissism, Nurturance, Objectivity-Projectivity, Order-Disorder, Play-Work, Practicalness-Impracticalness, Reflectiveness, Science, Sensuality-Puritanism, Sexuality-Prudishness, Supplication-Autonomy, Understanding), 6 factor scores (Humanistic Intellectual Climate, Group Intellectual Life, Achievement Standards, Personal Dignity, Orderliness, Science) based on combinations of the press scores, 2 second-order factor scores (Development Press, Control Press).
Administration: Group.
Price Data: Not available.
Time: Administration time not reported.
Comments: Previously listed under Stern Environment Indexes; self-administered.
Authors: George G. Stern and William J. Walker.
Publisher: FAAX Corporation [No reply from publisher; status unknown].
Cross References: See also T3:408 (1 reference), T2:1395 (38 references), 7:143 (59 references), P:256 (65 references), and 6:92 (19 references).

TEST REFERENCES

1. Dow, I. I. (1983). The effect of school management patterns on organizational effectiveness. *The Alberta Journal of Educational Research, 29,* 31-45.

2. Walker, W. J., & Richman, J. (1984). Dimensions of classroom environmental press. *Psychological Reports, 55,* 555-562.

[475]

Classroom Environment Scale, Second Edition.

Purpose: Designed to "assess the social climate of junior high and high school classrooms. It focuses on teacher-student and student-student relationships and on the organizational structure of a classroom."

Population: Junior high and senior high teachers and students.

Publication Dates: 1974–87.

Acronym: CES.

Scores, 9: Relationship dimensions (Involvement, Affiliation, Teacher Support), Personal Growth/Goal Orientation dimensions (Task Orientation, Competition), System Maintenance and Change dimensions (Order and Organization, Rule Clarity, Teacher Control, Innovation).

Administration: Group.

Forms, 3: Real Form (Form R), Ideal Form (Form I), Expectations Form (Form E), and a Short Form (Form S) by administering and scoring the first 36 items of Form R.

Price Data, 1990: $10 per 25 test booklets; $7 per 50 answer sheets; $5 per 50 profiles; $65 per 10 prepaid narratives; $3 per scoring key; $11.50 per manual ('87, 61 pages); $18 per specimen set including manual, user's guide, scoring key, test booklet, answer sheet, and profile.

Time: [15–20] minutes.

Comments: One of ten Social Climate Scales (2495).

Authors: Rudolf H. Moos and Edison J. Trickett.

Publisher: Consulting Psychologists Press, Inc.

Cross References: For reviews by Richard A. Saudargas and Corinne Roth Smith, see 10:60 (16 references); see also T3:409 (9 references); for reviews by Maurice J. Eash and C. Robert Pace of an earlier edition, see 8:521 (3 references). For a review of the Social Climate Scales, see 8:681.

TEST REFERENCES

1. Hadley, T., & Graham, J. W. (1987). The influence of cognitive development on perceptions of environmental press. *Journal of College Student Personnel, 28,* 388-394.
2. Hattie, J., & Watkins, D. (1988). Preferred classroom environment and approach to learning. *British Journal of Educational Psychology, 58,* 345-349.
3. Madonna, S., Jr., Bailey, G. K., & Wesley, A. L. (1990). Classroom environment and locus of control in identifying high and low self-concept in fourth- and fifth-graders. *Psychological Reports, 66,* 1152-1154.
4. Scantlebury, K., & Kahle, J. B. (1993). The implementation of equitable teaching strategies by high school biology student teachers. *Journal of Research in Science Teaching, 30,* 537-545.
5. Robbins, S. B., Chartrand, J. M., McFadden, K. L., & Lee, R. M. (1994). Efficacy of leader-led and self-directed career workshops for middle-aged and older adults. *Journal of Counseling Psychology, 41,* 83-90.

[476]

Classroom Reading Inventory, Seventh Edition.

Purpose: To identify the student's reading skills and/ or abilities.

Population: Grades 2–8, high school and adults.

Publication Dates: 1965–94.

Acronym: CRI.

Scores, 6: Word Recognition, Comprehension, Independent Reading Level, Instructional Reading Level, Frustration Reading Level, Hearing Capacity Level.

Administration: Individual in part.

Forms: Form A (elementary, subskills format); Form B (elementary, literature format); Form C (junior high or middle school students); Form D (for use with high school and adults).

Price Data: Available from publisher.

Time: (24) minutes.

Author: Nicholas J. Silvaroli.

Publisher: Brown and Benchmark Publishers, a Division of Wm. C. Brown Communications.

Cross References: For reviews by Ira E. Aaron and Sylvia M. Hutchinson and Janet A. Norris, see 10:61 (4 references); for a review of an earlier edition by Marjorie S. Johnson, see 8:749; see also T2:1618 (1 reference); for an excerpted review by Donald L. Cleland, see 7:715.

TEST REFERENCES

1. Carrick, D. A., & Kinzer, C. K. (1985). Oral reading miscues and dialect variation: A study across black and standard English IRI passages. *National Reading Conference Yearbook, 34,* 344-349.
2. Malicky, G. V., & Norman, C. A. (1988). Reading processes in subgroups in a clinical population. *The Alberta Journal of Educational Research, 34,* 344-354.
3. Webster, R. E. (1988). Variability in reading achievement test scores as related to reading curriculum. *Educational and Psychological Measurement, 48,* 815-825.
4. Flynn, J. M., Deering, W., Goldstein, M., & Rahbar, M. H. (1992). Electrophysiological correlates of dyslexic subtypes. *Journal of Learning Disabilities, 25,* 133-141.

[477]

CLEP General Examinations.

Purpose: For college accreditation of nontraditional study, advanced placement, or assessment of educational attainment.

Population: Persons entering college or already in college.

Publication Dates: 1964–94.

Administration: Group.

Price Data: Available from publisher.

Time: (90) minutes per test.

Comments: Forms available to colleges for local administration and scoring; program administered by The College Board and Educational Testing Service.

Author: Educational Testing Service.

Publisher: Educational Testing Service.

a) ENGLISH COMPOSITION AND ENGLISH COMPOSITION WITH ESSAY.

b) HUMANITIES.

c) MATHEMATICS.

d) NATURAL SCIENCES.

e) SOCIAL SCIENCES AND HISTORY.

Cross References: See T3:411 (1 reference); for more information and a review by Lawrence M. Aleamoni and John E. Milholland, see 8:8 (20 references); see also T2:10 (7 references).

TEST REFERENCES

1. Johnson, J. J., & Knight, K. H. (1987). College Level Examination Program scores as predictors of grade point average. *Educational and Psychological Measurement, 47*(4), 1031-1036.

[478]

CLEP General Examinations: English Composition and English Composition Test with Essay.

Purpose: For college accreditation of nontraditional study, advanced placement, or assessment of educational attainment.
Population: Persons entering college or already in college.
Publication Dates: 1964–94.
Scores: Total score only.
Administration: Group.
Price Data: Available from publisher.
Time: (45) minutes per composition test; (45) minutes per essay.
Comments: English Composition Test with Essay administered in January, April, June, and October only; English Composition test administered monthly at centers throughout the United States; program administered by The College Board and Educational Testing Service.
Author: Educational Testing Service.
Publisher: Educational Testing Service.
Cross References: See T3:412 (1 reference); for additional information, see 8:42 (4 references) and T2:58 (1 reference); for reviews of the CLEP program, see 8:473 (3 reviews) and 7:664 (3 reviews).

[479]

CLEP General Examinations: Humanities.

Purpose: For college accreditation of nontraditional study, advanced placement, or assessment of educational attainment.
Population: Persons entering college or already in college.
Publication Dates: 1964–94.
Scores: Total score only.
Administration: Group.
Price Data: Available from publisher.
Time: (90) minutes.
Comments: Tests administered monthly at centers throughout the United States; program administered by The College Board and Educational Testing Service.
Author: Educational Testing Service.
Publisher: Educational Testing Service.
Cross References: For additional information and a review by William E. Kline, see 8:254 (1 reference); for reviews of the CLEP program, see 8:473 (3 reviews) and 7:664 (3 reviews).

[480]

CLEP General Examinations: Mathematics.

Purpose: For college accreditation of nontraditional study, advanced placement, or assessment of educational attainment. .

Population: Persons entering college or already in college.
Publication Dates: 1964–94.
Scores: Total score only.
Administration: Group.
Price Data: Available from publisher.
Time: (90) minutes.
Comments: Tests administered monthly at centers throughout the United States; program administered by The College Board and Educational Testing Service.
Author: Educational Testing Service.
Publisher: Educational Testing Service.
Cross References: For a review by William E. Kline, see 8:254 (1 reference).

[481]

CLEP General Examinations: Natural Sciences.

Purpose: For college accreditation of nontraditional study, advanced placement, or assessment of educational attainment.
Population: Persons entering college or already in college.
Publication Dates: 1964–94.
Scores: Total score only.
Administration: Group.
Price Data: Available from publisher.
Time: (90) minutes.
Comments: Tests administered monthly at centers throughout the United States; program administered by The College Board and Educational Testing Service.
Author: Educational Testing Service.
Publisher: Educational Testing Service.
Cross References: For additional information by George G. Mallinson, see 8:824 (2 references); for reviews of the CLEP program, see 8:473 (3 reviews) and 7:664 (3 reviews).

[482]

CLEP General Examinations: Social Sciences and History.

Purpose: For college accreditation of nontraditional study, advanced placement, or assessment of educational attainment.
Population: Persons entering college or already in college.
Publication Dates: 1964–94.
Scores: Total score only.
Administration: Group.
Price Data: Available from publisher.
Time: (90) minutes.
Comments: Tests administered monthly at centers throughout the United States; program administered by The College Board and Educational Testing Service.
Author: Educational Testing Service.
Publisher: Educational Testing Service.
Cross References: For additional information and a review by Richard E. Gross, see 8:886 (1 reference);

for reviews of the CLEP program, see 8:473 (3 reviews) and 7:664 (3 reviews).

[483]
CLEP Subject Examination in American Government.
Purpose: For college accreditation of nontraditional study, advanced placement, or assessment of educational attainment.
Population: Persons entering college or already in college.
Publication Dates: 1965–94.
Scores: Total score only.
Administration: Group.
Price Data: Available from publisher.
Time: (90) minutes.
Comments: Tests administered monthly at centers throughout the United States; program administered by The College Board and Educational Testing Service.
Author: Educational Testing Service.
Publisher: Educational Testing Service.
Cross References: For additional information and a review by Howard D. Mehlinger, see 8:919. For reviews of the CLEP program, see 8:473 (3 reviews) and 7:664 (3 reviews).

[484]
CLEP Subject Examination in American History I: Early Colonizations to 1877.
Purpose: For college accreditation of nontraditional study, advanced placement, or assessment of educational attainment.
Population: Persons entering college or already in college.
Publication Dates: 1980–94.
Scores: Total score only.
Administration: Group.
Price Data: Available from publisher.
Time: (90) minutes.
Comments: Tests administered monthly at centers throughout the United States; program administered by The College Board and Educational Testing Service.
Author: Educational Testing Service.
Publisher: Educational Testing Service.

[485]
CLEP Subject Examination in American History II: 1865 to the Present.
Purpose: For college accreditation of nontraditional study, advanced placement, or assessment of educational attainment.
Population: Persons entering college or already in college.
Publication Dates: 1980–94.
Scores: Total score only.
Administration: Group.
Price Data: Available from publisher.
Time: (90) minutes.
Comments: Tests administered monthly at centers

throughout the United States; program administered by The College Board and Educational Testing Service.
Author: Educational Testing Service.
Publisher: Educational Testing Service.

[486]
CLEP Subject Examination in American Literature.
Purpose: For college accreditation of nontraditional study, advanced placement, or assessment of educational attainment.
Population: Persons entering college or already in college.
Publication Dates: 1971–94.
Scores: Total score only; optional essay, locally scored.
Administration: Group.
Price Data: Available from publisher.
Time: (90) minutes.
Comments: Tests administered monthly at centers throughout the United States; program administered by The College Board and Educational Testing Service.
Author: Educational Testing Service.
Publisher: Educational Testing Service.
Cross References: For additional information and a review by Leo P. Ruth, see 8:64. For reviews of the CLEP program, see 8:473 (3 reviews).

[487]
CLEP Subject Examination in Analysis and Interpretation of Literature.
Purpose: For college accreditation of nontraditional study, advanced placement, or assessment of educational attainment.
Population: Persons entering college or already in college.
Publication Dates: 1964–94.
Scores: Total score only; optional essay, locally scored.
Administration: Group.
Price Data: Available from publisher.
Time: (90) minutes.
Comments: Tests administered monthly at centers throughout the United States; program administered by The College Board and Educational Testing Service.
Author: Educational Testing Service.
Publisher: Educational Testing Service.
Cross References: For additional information and a review by John C. Sherwood, see 8:65 (1 reference). For reviews of the CLEP program, see 8:473 (3 reviews) and 7:664 (3 reviews).

[488]
CLEP Subject Examination in Calculus with Elementary Functions.
Purpose: For college accreditation of nontraditional study, advanced placement, or assessment of educational attainment.

Population: Persons entering college or already in college.
Publication Dates: 1974–94.
Scores: Total score only.
Administration: Group.
Price Data: Available from publisher.
Time: (90) minutes.
Comments: Tests administered monthly at centers throughout the United States; program administered by The College Board and Educational Testing Service.
Author: Educational Testing Service.
Publisher: Educational Testing Service.
Cross References: For a review by J. Phillip Smith, see 8:255. For reviews of the CLEP program, see 8:473 (3 reviews).

[489]

CLEP Subject Examination in College Algebra.

Purpose: For college accreditation of nontraditional study, advanced placement, or assessment of educational attainment.
Population: Persons entering college or already in college.
Publication Dates: 1968–94.
Scores: Total score only.
Administration: Group.
Price Data: Available from publisher.
Time: (90) minutes.
Comments: Tests administered monthly at centers throughout the United States; program administered by The College Board and Educational Testing Service.
Author: Educational Testing Service.
Publisher: Educational Testing Service.
Cross References: For additional information and a review by J. Philip Smith, see 8:297. For reviews of the CLEP program, see 8:473 (3 reviews) and 7:664 (3 reviews).

[490]

CLEP Subject Examination in College Algebra-Trigonometry.

Purpose: For college accreditation of nontraditional study, advanced placement, or assessment of educational attainment.
Population: Persons entering college or already in college.
Publication Dates: 1968–94.
Scores: Total score only.
Administration: Group.
Price Data: Available from publisher.
Time: 90 minutes.
Comments: Tests administered monthly at centers throughout the United States; program administered by The College Board and Educational Testing Service.
Author: Educational Testing Service.
Publisher: Educational Testing Service.
Cross References: For a review by Peter A. Lap-

pan, Jr., see 8:256 (1 reference); for a review by Carl G. Willis, see 7:454. For reviews of the CLEP program, see 8:473 (3 reviews) and 7:664 (3 reviews).

[491]

CLEP Subject Examination in College Composition.

Purpose: For college accreditation of nontraditional study, advanced placement, or assessment of educational attainment.
Population: Persons entering college or already in college.
Publication Dates: 1965–94.
Scores: Total score only; optional essay, locally scored.
Administration: Group.
Price Data: Available from publisher.
Time: (90) minutes.
Comments: Tests administered monthly at centers throughout the United States; program administered by The College Board and Educational Testing Service.
Author: Educational Testing Service.
Publisher: Educational Testing Service.
Cross References: For a review by Charlotte Croon Davis, see 8:43 (2 references); for reviews of the CLEP program, see 8:473 (3 reviews) and 7:664 (3 reviews).

[492]

CLEP Subject Examination in College French, Levels 1 and 2.

Purpose: For college accreditation of nontraditional study, advanced placement, or assessment of educational attainment.
Population: Persons entering college or already in college.
Publication Dates: 1975–94.
Scores, 3: Reading Comprehension, Listening Comprehension, Total.
Administration: Group.
Price Data: Available from publisher.
Time: (90) minutes.
Comments: Tests administered monthly at centers throughout the United States; program administered by The College Board and Educational Testing Service.
Author: Educational Testing Service.
Publisher: Educational Testing Service.
Cross References: For a review by Michio Peter Hagiwara, see 8:115. For reviews of the CLEP program, see 8:473 (3 reviews).

[493]

CLEP Subject Examination in College Level German, Levels 1 and 2.

Purpose: For college accreditation of nontraditional study, advanced placement, or assessment of educational attainment.
Population: Persons entering college or already in college.

Publication Dates: 1975–94.
Scores, 3: Reading Comprehension, Listening Comprehension, Total.
Administration: Group.
Price Data: Available from publisher.
Time: (90) minutes.
Comments: Tests administered monthly at centers throughout the United States; program administered by The College Board and Educational Testing Service.
Author: Educational Testing Service.
Publisher: Educational Testing Service.
Cross References: For reviews by Stefan R. Fink and Herbert Lederer, see 8:127. For reviews of the CLEP program, see 8:473 (3 reviews).

[494]
CLEP Subject Examination in College Spanish, Levels 1 and 2.
Purpose: For college accreditation of nontraditional study, advanced placement, or assessment of educational attainment.
Population: Persons entering college or already in college.
Publication Dates: 1975–94.
Scores, 3: Reading Comprehension, Listening Comprehension, Total.
Administration: Group.
Price Data: Available from publisher.
Time: 90 minutes.
Comments: Tests administered monthly at centers throughout the United States; program administered by The College Board and Educational Testing Service.
Author: Educational Testing Service.
Publisher: Educational Testing Service.
Cross References: For reviews of the CLEP program, see 8:473 (3 reviews).

[495]
CLEP Subject Examination in Educational Psychology.
Purpose: For college accreditation of nontraditional study, advanced placement, or assessment of educational attainment.
Population: Persons entering college or already in college.
Publication Dates: 1967–94.
Scores: Total score only.
Administration: Group.
Price Data: Available from publisher.
Time: (90) minutes.
Comments: Tests administered monthly at centers throughout the United States; program administered by The College Board and Educational Testing Service.
Author: Educational Testing Service.
Publisher: Educational Testing Service.
Cross References: For reviews of the CLEP program, see 8:473 (3 reviews) and 7:664 (3 reviews).

[496]
CLEP Subject Examination in English Literature.
Purpose: For college accreditation of nontraditional study, advanced placement, or assessment of educational attainment.
Population: Persons entering college or already in college.
Publication Dates: 1970–94.
Scores: Total score only; optional essay, locally scored.
Administration: Group.
Price Data: Available from publisher.
Time: (90) minutes.
Comments: Tests administered monthly at centers throughout the United States; program administered by The College Board and Educational Testing Service.
Author: Educational Testing Service.
Publisher: Educational Testing Service.
Cross References: For additional information and a review by Edward M. White, see 8:66. For reviews of the CLEP program, see 8:473 (3 reviews).

[497]
CLEP Subject Examination in Freshman College Composition.
Purpose: For college accreditation of nontraditional study, advanced placement, or assessment of educational attainment.
Population: Persons entering college or already in college.
Publication Date: 1994.
Scores: Total score only; optional essay, scored locally.
Administration: Group.
Price Data: Available from publisher.
Time: (90) minutes.
Comments: Tests administered monthly at centers throughout the United States; program administered by The College Board and Educational Testing Service; will replace College Composition (491) and Freshman English (498) examinations.
Author: Educational Testing Service.
Publisher: Educational Testing Service.

[498]
CLEP Subject Examination in Freshman English.
Purpose: For college accreditation of nontraditional study, advanced placement, or assessment of educational attainment.
Population: Persons entering college or already in college.
Publication Dates: 1973–94.
Scores: Total score only; optional essay, locally scored.
Administration: Group.
Price Data: Available from publisher.
Time: 90 minutes.
Comments: Tests administered monthly at centers

throughout the United States; program administered by The College Board and Educational Testing Service.
Author: Educational Testing Service.
Publisher: Educational Testing Service.
Cross References: For a review by Leonard S. Feldt of an earlier edition, see 8:44 (1 reference). For reviews of the CLEP program, see 8:473 (3 reviews).

[499]

CLEP Subject Examination in General Biology.
Purpose: For college accreditation of nontraditional study, advanced placement, or assessment of educational attainment.
Population: Persons entering college or already in college.
Publication Dates: 1970–94.
Scores: Total score only.
Administration: Group.
Price Data: Available from publisher.
Time: (90) minutes.
Comments: Tests administered monthly at centers throughout the United States; program administered by The College Board and Educational Testing Service.
Author: Educational Testing Service.
Publisher: Educational Testing Service.
Cross References: For additional information and a review by Clarence H. Nelson, see 8:832. For reviews of the CLEP program, see 8:473 (3 reviews) and 7:664 (3 reviews).

[500]

CLEP Subject Examination in General Chemistry.
Purpose: For college accreditation of nontraditional study, advanced placement, or assessment of educational attainment.
Population: Persons entering college or already in college.
Publication Dates: 1964–94.
Scores: Total score only.
Administration: Group.
Price Data: Available from publisher.
Time: (90) minutes.
Comments: Tests administered monthly at centers throughout the United States; program administered by The College Board and Educational Testing Service.
Author: Educational Testing Service.
Publisher: Educational Testing Service.
Cross References: For additional information and a review by J. Arthur Campbell, see 8:847. For reviews of the CLEP program, see 8:473 (3 reviews) and 7:664 (3 reviews).

[501]

CLEP Subject Examination in Human Growth and Development.
Purpose: For college accreditation of nontraditional

study, advanced placement, or assessment of educational attainment.
Population: Persons entering college or already in college.
Publication Dates: 1969–94.
Scores: Total score only.
Administration: Group.
Price Data: Available from publisher.
Time: 90 minutes.
Comments: Tests administered monthly at centers throughout the United States; program administered by The College Board and Educational Testing Service.
Author: Educational Testing Service.
Publisher: Educational Testing Service.
Cross References: For reviews of the CLEP program, see 8:473 (3 reviews) and 7:664 (3 reviews).

[502]

CLEP Subject Examination in Information Systems and Computer Applications.
Purpose: For college accreditation of nontraditional study, advanced placement, or assessment of educational attainment.
Population: Persons entering college or already in college.
Publication Dates: 1968–90.
Scores: Total score only.
Administration: Group.
Price Data: Available from publisher.
Time: (90) minutes.
Comments: Tests administered monthly at centers throughout the United States; program administered by The College Board and Educational Testing Service; previously entitled CLEP Subject Examination in Computers and Data Processing.
Author: Educational Testing Service.
Publisher: Educational Testing Service.
Cross References: For reviews of the CLEP program, see 8:473 (3 reviews) and 7:664 (3 reviews).

[503]

CLEP Subject Examination in Introduction to Management.
Purpose: For college accreditation of nontraditional study, advanced placement, or assessment of educational attainment.
Population: Persons entering college or already in college.
Publication Dates: 1969–94.
Scores: Total score only.
Administration: Group.
Price Data: Available from publisher.
Time: (90) minutes.
Comments: Tests administered monthly at centers throughout the United States; program administered by The College Board and Educational Testing Service.
Author: Educational Testing Service.
Publisher: Educational Testing Service.

Cross References: For reviews of the CLEP program, see 8:473 (3 reviews) and 7:664 (3 reviews).

[504]

CLEP Subject Examination in Introductory Accounting.

Purpose: For college accreditation of nontraditional study, advanced placement, or assessment of educational attainment.
Population: Persons entering college or already in college.
Publication Dates: 1970–94.
Scores: Total score only.
Administration: Group.
Price Data: Available from publisher.
Time: 90 minutes.
Comments: Tests administered monthly at centers throughout the United States; program administered by The College Board and Educational Testing Service.
Author: Educational Testing Service.
Publisher: Educational Testing Service.
Cross References: For reviews of the CLEP program, see 8:473 (3 reviews).

[505]

CLEP Subject Examination in Introductory Business Law.

Purpose: For college accreditation of nontraditional study, advanced placement, or assessment of educational attainment.
Population: Persons entering college or already in college.
Publication Dates: 1970–94.
Scores: Total score only.
Administration: Group.
Price Data: Available from publisher.
Time: (90) minutes.
Comments: Tests administered monthly at centers throughout the United States; program administered by The College Board and Educational Testing Service.
Author: Educational Testing Service.
Publisher: Educational Testing Service.
Cross References: For reviews of the CLEP program, see 8:473 (3 reviews) and 7:664 (3 reviews).

[506]

CLEP Subject Examination in Introductory Macroeconomics.

Purpose: For college accreditation of nontraditional study, advanced placement, or assessment of educational attainment.
Population: Persons entering college or already in college.
Publication Dates: 1974–94.
Scores: Total score only.
Administration: Group.
Price Data: Available from publisher.
Time: (90) minutes.
Comments: Tests administered monthly at centers throughout the United States; program administered by The College Board and Educational Testing Service.
Author: Educational Testing Service.
Publisher: Educational Testing Service.
Cross References: For reviews of the CLEP program, see 8:473 (3 reviews).

[507]

CLEP Subject Examination in Introductory Microeconomics.

Purpose: For college accreditation of nontraditional study, advanced placement, or assessment of educational attainment.
Population: Persons entering college or already in college.
Publication Dates: 1974–94.
Scores: Total score only.
Administration: Group.
Price Data: Available from publisher.
Time: (90) minutes.
Comments: Tests administered monthly at centers throughout the United States; program administered by The College Board and Educational Testing Service.
Author: Educational Testing Service.
Publisher: Educational Testing Service.
Cross References: For reviews of the CLEP program, see 8:473 (3 reviews).

[508]

CLEP Subject Examination in Introductory Psychology.

Purpose: For college accreditation of nontraditional study, advanced placement, or assessment of educational attainment.
Population: Persons entering college or already in college.
Publication Dates: 1967–94.
Scores: Total score only.
Administration: Group.
Price Data: Available from publisher.
Time: (90) minutes.
Comments: Tests administered monthly at centers throughout the United States; program administered by The College Board and Educational Testing Service; previously entitled CLEP Subject Examination in General Psychology.
Author: Educational Testing Service.
Publisher: Educational Testing Service.
Cross References: See T3:442 (2 references); for additional information and a review by Alfred E. Hall of an earlier edition, see 8:460. For reviews of the CLEP program, see 8:473 (3 reviews) and 7:664 (3 reviews).

[509]

CLEP Subject Examination in Introductory Sociology.

Purpose: For college accreditation of nontraditional study, advanced placement, or assessment of educational attainment.

Population: Persons entering college or already in college.
Publication Dates: 1965–94.
Scores: Total score only.
Administration: Group.
Price Data: Available from publisher.
Time: (90) minutes.
Comments: Tests administered monthly at centers throughout the United States; program administered by The College Board and Educational Testing Service.
Author: Educational Testing Service.
Publisher: Educational Testing Service.
Cross References: For reviews of the CLEP program, see 8:473 (3 reviews) and 7:664 (3 reviews).

[510]

CLEP Subject Examination in Principles of Marketing.
Purpose: For college accreditation of nontraditional study, advanced placement, or assessment of educational attainment.
Population: Persons entering college or already in college.
Publication Dates: 1968–94.
Scores: Total score only.
Administration: Group.
Price Data: Available from publisher.
Time: 90 minutes.
Comments: Tests administered monthly at centers throughout the United States; program administered by The College Board and Educational Testing Service.
Author: Educational Testing Service.
Publisher: Educational Testing Service.
Cross References: For reviews of the CLEP program, see 8:473 (3 reviews) and 7:664 (3 reviews).

[511]

CLEP Subject Examination in Trigonometry.
Purpose: For college accreditation of nontraditional study, advanced placement, or assessment of educational attainment.
Population: Persons entering college or already in college.
Publication Dates: 1968–94.
Scores: Total score only.
Administration: Group.
Price Data: Available from publisher.
Time: (90) minutes.
Comments: Tests administered monthly at centers throughout the United States; program administered by The College Board and Educational Testing Service.
Author: Educational Testing Service.
Publisher: Educational Testing Service.
Cross References: For reviews of the CLEP program, see 8:473 (3 reviews) and 7:664 (3 reviews).

[512]

CLEP Subject Examination in Western Civilization I: Ancient Near East to 1648.
Purpose: For college accreditation of nontraditional study, advanced placement, or assessment of educational attainment.
Population: Persons entering college or already in college.
Publication Dates: 1964–94.
Scores: Total score only.
Administration: Group.
Price Data: Available from publisher.
Time: (90) minutes.
Comments: Tests administered monthly at centers throughout the United States; program administered by The College Board and Educational Testing Service.
Author: Educational Testing Service.
Publisher: Educational Testing Service.
Cross References: For reviews of the CLEP program, see 8:473 (3 reviews) and 7:664 (3 reviews).

[513]

CLEP Subject Examination in Western Civilization II: 1648 to Present.
Purpose: For college accreditation of nontraditional study, advanced placement, or assessment of educational attainment.
Population: Persons entering college or already in college.
Publication Dates: 1964–94.
Scores: Total score only.
Administration: Group.
Price Data: Available from publisher.
Time: (90) minutes.
Comments: Tests administered monthly at centers throughout the United States; program administered by The College Board and Educational Testing Service.
Author: Educational Testing Service.
Publisher: Educational Testing Service.
Cross References: For reviews of the CLEP program, see 8:473 (3 reviews) and 7:664 (3 reviews).

[514]

Clerical Abilities Battery.
Purpose: Assesses clerical abilities "for use in hiring and promoting clerical personnel."
Population: Clerical applicants and employees and business school students.
Publication Dates: 1985–87.
Acronym: CAB.
Scores: 7 tests: Filing, Comparing Information, Copying Information, Using Tables, Proofreading, Addition and Subtraction, Reasoning with Numbers.
Administration: Group.
Forms, 2: A, B.
Restricted Distribution: Distribution of Form A restricted to personnel departments in business and industry.

Price Data, 1994: $110 per complete kit including 5 test booklets of each test, 7 keys, and manual ('87, 22 pages); $35 per 25 test booklets (Filing ['87, 7 pages], Copying Information ['87, 6 pages], Comparing Information ['87, 5 pages], Using Tables ['87, 6 pages], Proofreading ['87, 6 pages], Addition and Subtraction ['87, 7 pages], Reasoning with Numbers ['87, 7 pages]); $52 per set of scoring stencils; $24 per manual.
Time: 70(105) minutes for the battery; 5(10) minutes each for first four tests, 15(20) minutes each for next two tests, 20(25) minutes for last test.
Comments: Tests available as separates.
Author: The Psychological Corporation.
Publisher: The Psychological Corporation.
Cross References: For reviews by Joseph C. Ciechalski and Bikkar S. Randhawa, see 11:71.

[515]

Clerical Aptitude Test: Acorn National Aptitude Tests.
Purpose: Designed to measure qualities associated with good clerical performance.
Population: Grades 7–12 and adult clerks.
Publication Dates: 1943–50.
Scores, 4: Business Practice, Number Checking, Date and Name and Address Checking, Total.
Administration: Group.
Price Data, 1985: $8.75 per 25 test booklets; $4 per specimen set.
Time: 40(50) minutes.
Authors: Andrew Kobal, J. Wayne Wrightstone, and Karl R. Kunze.
Publisher: Psychometric Affiliates.
Cross References: See T3:464 (2 references); see also 5:847 (1 reference); for reviews by Marion A. Bills, Donald G. Paterson, Henry Weitz, and E. F. Wonderlic, see 3:623.

[516]

Clerical Skills Series.
Purpose: "Designed to measure proficiency in paper work tasks typical of . . . clerical occupations."
Population: Clerical workers.
Publication Dates: 1966–86.
Administration: Group.
Price Data, 1993: $49.50 per complete kit; $23.50 per profile sheet package; $36 per manual ('66, 20 pages) and manuals supplement ('84, 17 pages).
Author: Martin M. Bruce.
Publisher: Martin M. Bruce, Ph.D., Publishers.
  a) ALPHABETIZING-FILING.
  Time: 8(13) minutes.
  b) ARITHMETIC.
  Time: 8(13) minutes.
  c) CLERICAL SPEED AND ACCURACY.
  Time: 3(5) minutes.
  d) CODING.
  Time: 2(7) minutes.

  e) EYE-HAND ACCURACY.
  Time: 5(10) minutes.
  f) GRAMMAR AND PUNCTUATION.
  Time: (5–10) minutes.
  g) SPELLING.
  Time: (15–20) minutes.
  h) SPELLING-VOCABULARY.
  Time: (15–20) minutes.
  i) VOCABULARY.
  Time: (10–15) minutes.
  j) WORD FLUENCY.
  Time: 5(10) minutes.
Cross References: For a review by Robert Fitzpatrick, see 7:988.

[517]

Clerical Staff Selector.
Purpose: "Evaluates the suitability of candidates for all levels of experience for the position of clerk."
Population: Candidates for clerks.
Publication Dates: 1954–84.
Scores: 4 tests: Problem Solving Ability, Numerical Skills, Attention to Detail, N.P.F. (emotional stability).
Administration: Group.
Price Data, 1993: $99 per person.
Foreign Language Edition: French edition available.
Time: (60) minutes.
Authors: Tests from various publishers compiled, distributed, and scored (optional) by Walden Personnel Testing & Training, Inc.
Publisher: Walden Personnel Testing & Training, Inc.
Cross References: For a review by Ruth G. Thomas, see 10:62.

[518]

Clifton Assessment Procedures for the Elderly.
Purpose: Designed to assess cognitive and behavioral competence of the elderly.
Population: Ages 60 and over.
Publication Dates: 1979–81.
Acronym: CAPE.
Administration: Group.
Price Data, 1994: £4.99 per 20 report forms; £6.99 per manual ('79, 34 pages); £7.99 per specimen set.
Time: Administration time not reported.
Comments: Distributed in the U.S.A. by The Psychological Corporation; 2 tests plus combination short version; authors recommend administering both tests concurrently, however, they can be use separately.
Authors: A. H. Pattie and C. J. Gilleard.
Publisher: Hodder & Stoughton Educational [England].
  a) COGNITIVE ASSESSMENT SCALE.
  Acronym: CAS.
  Scores, 4: Information/Orientation, Mental Abil-

ity, Psychomotor (adaptation of Gibson Spiral Maze), Total.

Price Data: £4.99 per 20 tests (CAS); £7.99 per 20 mazes.

b) BEHAVIOUR RATING SCALE.

Acronym: BRS.

Scores, 5: Physical Disability, Apathy, Communication Difficulties, Social Disturbance, Total.

Price Data: £4.99 per 20 tests.

Comments: Shortened version of Stockton Geriatric Rating Scale.

c) SURVEY VERSION.

Price Data: £4.99 per survey pack including instruction sheet and 20 survey forms.

Comments: Short version of CAPE for quick assessment; consists of Information/Orientation scale of the CAS and the Physical Disability scale of the BRS.

Cross References: For reviews by Alicia Skinner Cook and K. Warner Schaie, see 9:231 (2 references); see also T3:471 (1 reference).

TEST REFERENCES

1. Chanfreau-Rona, D., Bellwood, S., & Wylie, B. (1984). Assessment of a behavioural programme to treat incontinent patients in psychogeriatric wards. *British Journal of Clinical Psychology, 23,* 273-279.
2. Gilleard, C. J., Belford, H., Gilleard, E., Whittick, J. E., & Gledhill, K. (1984). Emotional distress amongst the supporters of the elderly mentally infirm. *British Journal of Psychiatry, 145,* 172-177.
3. Katona, C. L. E., & Aldridge, C. R. (1985). The Dexamethasone Suppression Test and depressive signs in dementia. *Journal of Affective Disorders, 8,* 83-89.
4. McPherson, F. M., & Tregaskis, D. (1985). The short-term stability of the survey version of CAPE. *British Journal of Clinical Psychology, 24,* 205-206.
5. McPherson, F. M., Gamsu, C. V., Kiemle, G., Ritchie, S. M., Stanley, A. M., & Tregaskis, D. (1985). The concurrent validity of the survey version of the Clifton Assessment Procedures for the Elderly (CAPE). *British Journal of Clinical Psychology, 24,* 83-91.
6. Bell, J. S., & Gilleard, C. J. (1986). Psychometric prediction of psychogeriatric day care outcome. *British Journal of Clinical Psychology, 25,* 195-200.
7. McLaren, S. M., Barry, F., & McPherson, F. M. (1986). Prediction of survival by three psychological measures. *British Journal of Clinical Psychology, 25,* 223-224.
8. McPherson, F. M., Gamsu, C. V., Cockram, L. L., & Cooke, D. (1986). Use of the CAPE Pm test with disabled patients. *British Journal of Clinical Psychology, 25,* 145-146.
9. McPherson, F. M., Gamsu, C. V., Cockram, L. L., & Gormley, A. J. (1986). Inter-scorer agreement in scoring errors on the Pm (Maze) test of the CAPE. *British Journal of Clinical Psychology, 25,* 225-226.
10. Oyebode, J. R., Barker, W. A., Blessed, G., Dick, D. J., & Britton, P. G. (1986). Cognitive functioning in Parkinson's disease: In relation to prevalence of dementia and psychiatric diagnosis. *British Journal of Psychiatry, 149,* 720-725.
11. Hills, A. A. (1987). Adjustment to relocation of long-stay patients with a psychiatric hospital setting. *Psychological Reports, 60,* 123-128.
12. Lam, D. H., Brewin, C. R., Woods, R. T., & Bebbington, P. E. (1987). Cognition and social adversity in the depressed elderly. *Journal of Abnormal Psychology, 96,* 23-26.
13. Morgan, K., Dallosso, H. M., Arie, T., Byrne, E. J., Jones, R., & Waite, J. (1987). Mental health and psychological well-being among the old and the very old living at home. *The British Journal of Psychiatry, 150,* 801-807.
14. O'Carroll, R. E., Baike, E. M., & Whittick, J. E. (1987). Does the National Adult Reading Test hold in dementia? *British Journal of Clinical Psychology, 26,* 315-316.
15. Burns, A., Marsh, A., & Bender, D. A. (1989). Dietary intake and clinical, anthropometric and biochemical indices of malnutrition in elderly demented patients and non-demented subjects. *Psychological Medicine, 19,* 383-391.
16. Chanfreau, D., Deadman, J. M., George, H., & Taylor, K. E. (1990). Transfer of long-stay psychiatric patients: A preliminary report of inter-institutional relocation. *British Journal of Clinical Psychology, 29,* 59-69.
17. Ebmeier, K. P., Calder, S. A., Crawford, J. R., Stewart, L., Cochrane, R. H. B., & Besson, J. A. O. (1991). Dementia in idiopathic Parkinson's disease: Prevalence and relationship with symptoms and signs of Parkinsonism. *Psychological Medicine, 21,* 69-76.
18. O'Carroll, R., Whittick, J., & Baikie, E. (1991). Parietal signs and sinister prognosis in dementia: A four-year follow-up study. *British Journal of Psychiatry, 158,* 358-361.
19. Morgan, K., Lilley, J. M., Arie, T., Byrne, E. J., Jones, R., & Waite, J. (1993). Incidence of dementia in a representative British sample. *British Journal of Psychiatry, 163,* 467-470.

[519]

Clinical Analysis Questionnaire.

Purpose: Designed to assess both deviant behavior and normal coping skills.

Population: Ages 16 and over.

Publication Dates: 1970–80.

Acronym: CAQ.

Administration: Group.

Price Data, 1994: $52 per hand-scoring introductory kit including test booklet, scoring keys, answer sheet, individual record folder, and manual ('80, 86 pages); $38.75 per computer interpreted introductory kit including test booklet, answer sheet, prepaid processing form, and manual; $34.25 per 25 reusable test booklets (specify standard or short form); $23 per 2 short form scoring keys or 4 standard form scoring keys; $10.75 per 25 hand-scorable or 25 machine-scorable answer sheets (specify short or standard form); $13.20 per 25 individual record folders; $17.50 per machine-scorable convenience pack; $23 or less per report for scoring and interpretive services.

Foreign Language Edition: Spanish edition available.

Time: (120) minutes for both parts of standard form; (100) minutes for both parts of short form.

Author: Samuel E. Krug.

Publisher: Institute for Personality and Ability Testing, Inc.

a) PART I (NORMAL PERSONALITY TRAITS).

Scores, 21: 16 primary factor scores: Warmth (A), Intelligence (B), Emotional Stability (C), Dominance (E), Impulsivity (F), Conformity (G), Boldness (H), Sensitivity (I), Suspiciousness (L), Imagination (M), Shrewdness (N), Insecurity (O), Radicalism (Q), Self-Sufficiency (Q2), Self-Discipline (Q3), Tension (Q4), plus 5 second-order factor scores: Extraversion (Ex), Anxiety (Ax), Tough Poise (Ct), Independence (In), Superego Strength (Se).

Comments: Normal personality traits from the 16PF.

b) PART II (THE CLINICAL FACTORS).

Scores, 16: 12 primary factor scores: Hypochondriasis (D1), Suicidal Depression (D2), Agitation (D3), Anxious Depression (D4), Low Energy Depression (D5), Guilt and Resentment (D6), Boredom and Withdrawal (D7), Paranoia (Pa), Psychopathic Deviation (Pp), Schizophrenia (Sc), Psychasthenia (As), Psychological Inadequacy (Ps), plus 4 second-order factor scores: Socialization (So),

Depression (D), Psychoticism (P), Neuroticism (Ne).

Cross References: For a review by George Guthrie, see 9:232 (4 references); see also T3:472 (11 references); for a review by Douglas McNair, see 8:522 (7 references); see also T2:1131 (1 reference) and 7:54 (1 reference).

TEST REFERENCES

1. Cugley, J. A. M., & Savage, R. D. (1984). Cognitive impairment and personality adjustment in Vietnam veterans. *Australian Psychologist, 19,* 205-216.
2. Hadiyono, J. E. P., & Kahn, M. W. (1985). Personality differences and sex similarities in American and Indonesian college students. *The Journal of Social Psychology, 125,* 703-708.
3. Kameoka, V. A. (1986). The structure of the Clinical Analysis Questionnaire and depression symptomology. *Multivariate Behavioral Research, 21,* 105-122.
4. McMillan, C. L., & Lynn, R. (1986). Differential assessment and the treatment of alcoholism. *British Journal of Clinical Psychology, 25,* 261-273.
5. Vélez-Díaz, A., & González-Reigosa, F. (1987). The Spanish version of the Clinical Analysis Questionnaire: A precautionary note. *Journal of Personality Assessment, 51,* 414-416.
6. Myers, R., Boughner, S., & Wallbrown, F. (1992). Personality profiles for administrators and staff in a private correctional facility. *Psychological Reports, 70,* 195-198.
7. Lorr, M., & Strack, S. (1994). Personality profiles of police candidates. *Journal of Clinical Psychology, 50,* 200-208.

[520]

Clinical Evaluation of Language Fundamentals—Preschool.

Purpose: "Measures a broad range of expressive and receptive language skill in preschool-aged children."
Population: Ages 3-0 to 6-11.
Publication Dates: 1991–92.
Acronym: CELF-Preschool.
Scores, 9: Receptive Language (Linguistic Concepts, Sentence Structure, Basic Concepts, Total), Expressive Language (Recalling Sentences in Context, Formulating Labels, Word Structure, Total), Total.
Administration: Individual.
Price Data, 1994: $157.50 per complete kit including examiner's manual ('92, 120 pages), 25 record forms, and 3 stimulus manuals; $31.50 per examiner's manual; $26.25 per 25 record forms; $84 per stimulus manual 1; $21 per stimulus manual 2 or stimulus manual 3.
Time: (30–45) minutes.
Comments: A downward extension of the Clinical Evaluation of Language Fundamentals—Revised (521).
Authors: Elisabeth H. Wiig, Wayne Secord, and Eleanor Semel.
Publisher: The Psychological Corporation.

[521]

Clinical Evaluation of Language Fundamentals—Revised.

Purpose: "For the identification, diagnosis, and follow-up evaluation of language skill deficits in school-age children."
Population: Ages 5-0 to 16-11.
Publication Dates: 1980–87.

Acronym: CELF-R.
Scores, 14: Linguistic Concepts, Word Structure, Sentence Structure, Oral Directions, Formulated Sentences, Recalling Sentences, Word Classes, Sentence Assembly, Semantic Relationships, Word Associations, Listening to Paragraphs, Receptive Language Score, Expressive Language Score, Total Language Score.
Administration: Individual.
Levels: 2 overlapping levels: Ages 5–7, Ages 8 and over.
Price Data, 1993: $265 per total battery; $127 per 2 stimulus manuals; $50.50 per examiner's manual ('87, 219 pages); $35 per technical manual ('87, 95 pages); $23 per package of 12 record forms.
Time: (45–60) minutes for administration of all subtests.
Comments: Revised edition of Clinical Evaluation of Language Functions; 11 subtests; CELF-R Clinical Assistant, a software package that provides interpretive reports, is also available.
Authors: Eleanor Semel, Elisabeth H. Wiig, and Wayne Secord.
Publisher: The Psychological Corporation.
Cross References: For reviews by Linda Crocker and David A. Shapiro, see 11:72; for a review by Dixie D. Sanger of the earlier edition, see 9:233 (2 references); see also T3:474.

TEST REFERENCES

1. Spector, C. C. (1990). Linguistic humor comprehension of normal and language-impaired adolescents. *Journal of Speech and Hearing Disorders, 55,* 533-541.
2. Evans, J. L., & Craig, H. K. (1992). Language sample collection and analysis: Interview compared to freeplay assessment contexts. *Journal of Speech and Hearing Research, 35,* 343-353.
3. Coon, H., Carey, G., Fulker, D. W., & DeFries, J. C. (1993). Influences of school environment on the academic achievement scores of adopted and nonadopted children. *Intelligence, 17,* 79-104.
4. Lincoln, A. J., Courchesne, E., Harms, L., & Allen, M. (1993). Contextual probability evaluation in autistic, receptive developmental language disorder, and control children: Event-related brain potential evidence. *Journal of Autism and Developmental Disorders, 23,* 37-58.
5. Powell, T. W. (1993). Critical values for evaluating CELF-R receptive and expressive language score discrepancies. *Perceptual and Motor Skills, 76,* 367-370.

[522]

Clinical Evaluation of Language Fundamentals—Revised Screening Test.

Purpose: "Identifies children with possible language disorders."
Population: Ages 5–16.
Publication Date: 1989.
Acronym: CELF-R Screening Test.
Administration: Individual.
Price Data, 1994: $119.50 per complete kit including examiner's manual (128 pages), stimulus manual, and 25 record forms; $33.50 per examiner's manual; $61.50 per stimulus manual; $29 per 25 record forms; $50 per briefcase.
Authors: Eleanor Semel, Elisabeth H. Wiig, and Wayne Secord.
Publisher: The Psychological Corporation.

a) CELF-R SCREENING TEST, SECTIONS 1—3.
Population: Ages 5–7.
Scores: Section Scores for Sections 1–3, Total, Oral Expression [optional] (Story Organization, Story Details, Sentence Structure and Meaning, Storytelling Mechanics).
Time: (3.5–8) minutes.
b) CELF-R SCREENING TEST, SECTIONS 2—6.
Population: Ages 8–12.
Scores: Section Scores for Sections 2–6, Total, Written Expression [optional] (Story Organization, Story Details and Elaboration, Sentence Structure and Meaning, Writing Mechanics).
Time: (4.5–13) minutes.
c) CELF-R SCREENING TEST, SECTIONS 3—6.
Population: Ages 13–16.
Scores: Section Scores for Sections 3–6, Total, Written Expression [optional] (Story Organization, Story Details and Elaboration, Sentence Structure and Meaning, Writing Mechanics).
Time: (4–12.5) minutes.

[523]

Clinical Experience Record for Nursing Students.

Purpose: Evaluates the "performance and progress of nursing students."
Population: Nursing students and nurses.
Publication Dates: 1960–75.
Acronym: CERNS.
Scores: No scores.
Administration: Individual.
Price Data: Not available.
Time: Administration time not reported.
Comments: Two assessment areas: Clinical Performance Record, Performance/Progress Record.
Authors: John C. Flanagan, Angeline C. Marchese, Grace Fivars, and Shirley A. Tuska (manual).
Publisher: Psychometric Techniques Associates [No reply from publisher; status unknown].
Cross References: For additional information, see 8:1120 (1 reference).

[524]

Clinical Language Intervention Program.

Purpose: "An intervention program for children with problems in semantics, morphology, syntax, memory, and pragmatics."
Population: Grades K–8.
Publication Dates: 1982–92.
Acronym: CLIP.
Scores: Item scores in 4 areas: Syntax, Semantics, Memory, Pragmatics.
Administration: Group or individual.
Price Data, 1994: $273 per complete kit including professional's guide ('82, 329 pages), picture manual ('82, 181 pages), language intervention activities manual ('82, 124 pages), and 12 progress checklists; $51.50 per professional's guide; $196.50 per picture manual; $36.50 per language intervention activities manual; $7 per 12 progress checklists; $29 per work-

sheet booklet (specify semantics, syntax, morphology, or pragmatics).
Comments: Matches language skills assessed in Clinical Evaluation of Language Fundamentals—Revised (521) and Wiig Criterion Referenced Inventory of Language (2961).
Authors: Eleanor Semel and Elisabeth H. Wiig.
Publisher: The Psychological Corporation.

[525]

Clinical Observations of Motor and Postural Skills.

Purpose: Designed to assist occupational therapists in performing assessments of children with suspected developmental and coordination disorders.
Population: Ages 5–9.
Publication Date: 1994.
Acronym: COMPS.
Scores: 6 items: Slow Movements, Finger-Nose Touching, Rapid Forearm Rotation, Prone Extension Posture, Asymmetrical Tonic Neck Reflex, Supine Flexion Posture.
Administration: Individual.
Price Data: Available from publisher.
Time: (15–20) minutes.
Comments: Ratings by therapist.
Authors: Brenda N. Wilson, Nancy Pollock, Bonnie J. Kaplan, and Mary Law.
Publisher: Therapy Skill Builders.

[526]

Clinical Rating Scale.

Purpose: Designed to type marital and family systems and identify intervention targets.
Population: Couples and families.
Publication Dates: 1980–1990.
Acronym: CRS.
Scores: 3 ratings (Cohesion, Change, Communication) yielding Family System Type.
Administration: Group.
Price Data, 1990: $5 per manual (includes unlimited copying privileges).
Time: Administration time not reported.
Author: David H. Olson.
Publisher: Family Social Science.

[527]

Clinical Record Keeping System.

Purpose: A set of record keeping systems to enhance the quality of mental health services.
Population: Adults and children.
Publication Date: 1980–83.
Scores: A collection of 25 record keeping forms: Clinical Interview Technique (Adults/Children, Marriage/Family), Mental Health Check Up, Neuropsychological Screening Exam, Relationship Satisfaction Survey, Health History, Progress Note Method (Adults/Children, Marriage/Family), Treatment Plan and Review (Adults/Children, Marriage/Family), Crisis Intervention Record, Clinical Notes, Thermal

Biofeedback, Quit Smoking Now, Weight Control, Awards For Kids, Children's Mental Health Record, Consent and Request for Release of Information, QSN Progress Chart, Career Path Strategy, Learning Opportunity Method, Psychological Consultation in Hospital, Professional Service Survey, Discharge Summary and Aftercare, Health Insurance Claim Form.
Manual: Various instructional material available.
Price Data: Not available.
Authors: Various authors.
Publisher: The Wilmington Institute [No reply from publisher; status unknown].

[528]

Clinical Support System Battery.
Purpose: "Designed for use with the potential school dropout student, and/or with chemical dependency rehabilitation programs."
Population: High school–adult.
Publication Dates: 1990–91.
Administration: Individual.
Time: Administration time not reported.
Comments: May be used with or without biofeedback equipment. Programs designed as a companion piece to the initial Life Style Analysis Test.
Author: Russell N. Cassel.
Publisher: Psychologists and Educators, Inc.

a) LIFE STYLE ANALYSIS TEST.
Purpose: To assess one's degree of wellness in relation to one's emotional stress.
Acronym: LFSTYLE.
Scores, 10: Positive Life Style (Self-Esteem, Satisfaction, Assertiveness, Involvement, Total Ego Strength), Negative Life Style (Loneliness, Anxiety, Health Worry, Depression, Total Stress Load).
Price Data, 1990: $11 per manual ('90, 38 pages); $25 per program diskette; $11 per added diskette.

b) NEURAL FUNCTIONING ASSESSMENT.
Purpose: To assess anxiety level.
Scores, 5: Relax, Disprof [guided imagery dissonance profile], Neural [neural personality cluster], Emote [unconscious need presence], Riskage [estimated coronary age].
Price Data: $11 per manual ('91, 36 pages); $25 per program diskette; $11 per added diskette.
Comments: Requires TRI-BI-SENSOR with 4 biofeedback units. Price data available from publisher.

c) THE NEED GRATIFICATION ASSESSMENT TEST.
Purpose: "To assess level of need status."
Scores, 12: Home and Family, Religion and Inner Development, Affiliation and Social, Law and Security, School and Learning, Romance and Psychosexual, Sports and Risk Taking, Health and Safety, Travel and Relaxation, Aesthetic and Beauty, Money and Productivity, Survival and Pollution.
Price Data: $11 per manual ('90, 11 pages); $25 per program diskette; $11 per added diskette.

d) THE IDENTITY STATUS TEST.
Purpose: Assesses perception of "to love and to be loved."
Scores, 7: Intimate and Private, Heart and Soul, Committed Fully, Personal Acceptance, Compassion and Forgiveness, Romanticism, Total.
Price Data: $11 per manual ('91, 16 pages); $25 per program diskette; $11 per added diskette.

e) THE INDEPENDENCE VERSUS REGRESSION TEST.
Purpose: Assesses perception of unlicensed freedom in relation to perception of exaggerated constraints.
Scores, 8: Freedoms (Coping Style, Conforming, Sympathetic, Locus of Control), Constraints (Rationalization, Regression, Repression, Escapist).
Price Data: $11 per manual ('91, 14 pages); $25 per program diskette; $11 per added diskette.

f) THE COSMIC CONSCIOUSNESS TEST.
Purpose: Measures freedom to "escape earthly bounds and achieve cosmic consciousness."
Scores, 7: Mutuality and Synergy, Spirituality and Love, Loyalty and Pride, Caring and Commitment, Depersonalization and Reward, Parent/Child Role, Total.
Price Data: $11 per manual ('90, 7 pages); $15 per program diskette; $11 per added diskette.

[529]

Closure Flexibility (Concealed Figures).
Purpose: "To measure the ability to hold a configuration in mind despite distracting irrelevancies."
Population: Industrial employees.
Publication Dates: 1956–65.
Scores: Total score only.
Administration: Group.
Price Data, 1992: $30 per 25 booklets; $5 per score key; $10 per interpretation and research manual ('65, 20 pages).
Time: (10) minutes.
Authors: L. L. Thurstone and T. E. Jeffrey.
Publisher: SRA/London House.
Cross References: See T3:477 (5 references), T2:547 (9 references), and 7:435 (9 references); for a review by Leona E. Tyler, see 6:545 (4 references).

[530]

Closure Speed (Gestalt Completion).
Purpose: "To measure the ability to see apparently disorganized or unrelated parts as a meaningful whole."
Population: Industrial employees.
Publication Dates: 1956–66.
Scores: Total score only.
Administration: Group.
Price Data, 1992: $30 per 25 booklets; $5 per score key; $10 per interpretation and research manual ('66, 18 pages).
Time: 3(8) minutes.
Authors: L. L. Thurstone and T. E. Jeffrey.
Publisher: SRA/London House.
Cross References: See T3:478 (2 references),

T2:548 (1 reference), and 7:436 (2 references); for a review by Leona E. Tyler, see 6:546 (3 references).

TEST REFERENCES

1. Bouma, A., & Ippel, M. J. (1983). Individual differences in mode of processing in visual asymmetry tasks. *Cortex, 19, 51-67.*
2. Swinnen, S., Vandenberghe, J., & VanAssche, E. (1986). Role of cognitive style constructs field dependence-independence and reflection-impulsivity in skill acquisition. *Journal of Sport Psychology, 8, 51-69.*

[531]
Cloze Reading Tests 1–3, Second Edition.

Purpose: Designed to provide a method of testing reading skills.
Population: Ages 8-0 to 10-6, 8-5 to 11-10, 9-5 to 12-6.
Publication Date: 1982–92.
Scores: Overall performance score.
Administration: Individual or group.
Levels, 3: Level 1 (Ages 8-0 to 10-6), Level 2 (Ages 8-5 to 11-10), Level 3 (Ages 9-5 to 12-6).
Price Data, 1994: £5.99 per 20 tests (specify Test 1, 2, or 3); £5.50 per manual (16 pages); £5.99 per specimen set.
Time: 35(45) minutes.
Author: D. Young.
Publisher: Hodder & Stoughton Educational [England].
Cross References: For a review by Esther Geva, see 9:237.

TEST REFERENCES

1. Carey, S. T., & Cummins, J. (1983). Achievement, behavioral correlates and teachers' perceptions of francophone and anglophone immersion students. *The Alberta Journal of Education Research, 29,* 159-167.
2. Searls, E. F., & Neville, D. D. (1988). An exploratory review of sentence-combining research related to reading. *Journal of Research and Development in Education, 21*(3) 1-15.
3. Haarmann, H. J., & Kolk, H. H. J. (1992). The production of grammatical morphology in Broca's and Wernicke's aphasics: Speed and accuracy factors. *Cortex, 28,* 97-112.

[532]
Clyde Mood Scale.

Purpose: To measure human emotions and behavior, which are influenced by stress or drugs.
Population: Normals and schizophrenics.
Publication Dates: 1963–83.
Acronym: CMS.
Scores, 6: Friendly, Aggressive, Clear Thinking, Sleepy, Depressed, Jittery.
Administration: Individual.
Price Data: Not available.
Time: (5–15) minutes.
Author: Dean J. Clyde.
Publisher: Clyde Computing Service [No reply from publisher; status unknown].
Cross References: For a review by Cynthia M. Sheehan, see 9:238; for a review by David T. Lykken of the original edition, see 7:55.

TEST REFERENCES

1. Henauer, S. A., Gillespie, H. K., & Hollister, L. E. (1984). Yohimbine and the model anxiety state. *Journal of Clinical Psychiatry, 45,* 512-515.

[533]
Clymer-Barrett Readiness Test, Revised Edition.

Purpose: "Measures the important skills and general background necessary for success in beginning instruction—especially reading."
Population: Grades K–1.
Publication Dates: 1966–83.
Acronym: CBRT.
Scores, 4: Visual Discrimination, Auditory Discrimination, Visual-Motor Coordination, Total.
Administration: Group.
Forms, 2: A, B.
Price Data: Available from publisher.
Time: (90) minutes in 3 sessions; (30) minutes for short form.
Comments: Formerly called Clymer-Barrett Prereading Battery; short screening form consisting of 2 of the 6 subtests yields a single score.
Authors: Theodore Clymer and Thomas C. Barrett.
Publisher: Chapman, Brook & Kent.
Cross References: For reviews by James McCarthy and Barton B. Proger, see 9:239; see also T3:482 (5 references) and T2:1699 (2 references); for reviews by Roger Farr and Kenneth J. Smith of an earlier edition, see 7:744 (2 references).

TEST REFERENCES

1. Spaanenburg, L. B. W. (1984). Clymer-Barrett Readiness Test. *The Reading Teacher, 38,* 56-57.

[534]
C.O.A.C.H.: Cayuga-Onondaga Assessment for Children with Handicaps, Version 7.0.

Purpose: A tool to assist in educational planning.
Population: Preschool and school-aged learners with moderate, severe, or profound handicap.
Publication Dates: 1985–90.
Acronym: COACH.
Scores: Item scores only.
Administration: Individual.
Price Data: Available from publisher.
Time: (60) minutes (part 1 of 3 parts).
Comments: "Criterion-referenced"; ratings by a team including a parent, student (where appropriate), educators, related service personnel, and family advocate; previous versions available on microfiche from ERIC.
Authors: Michael F. Giangreco, Chigee J. Cloninger, and Virginia S. Iverson.
Publisher: Brookes Publishing Co., Inc.
Cross References: For a review by Jay Kuder and David E. Kapel, see 11:73.

[535]
Coaching Process Questionnaire.

Purpose: "Provides managers with an assessment of their coaching ability."
Population: Managers and employees.
Publication Date: 1992.

Acronym: CPQ.
Administration: Group.
Time: Administration time not reported.
Comments: Self-scored instrument.
Author: McBer & Company.
Publisher: McBer & Company.

a) PARTICIPANT VERSION.
Population: Managers.
Scores, 5: Diagnostic Skills, Coaching Techniques, Coaching Qualities, Coaching Model, Overall CPQ score.
Price Data, 1993: $60 per complete kit including 10 questionnaires, and 10 profiles and interpretive notes.

b) EMPLOYEE VERSION.
Population: Employees.
Scores, 5: Diagnostic Skills, Coaching Techniques, Coaching Qualities, Coaching Model, Overall Employee score.
Price Data: $25 per 10 questionnaires.

[536]

Cognitive Abilities Scale.
Purpose: Allows a comprehensive assessment of cognitive development relevant to later school success.
Population: Ages 2-0 to 3-11.
Publication Date: 1987.
Acronym: CAS.
Scores, 6: Language, Reading, Mathematics, Handwriting, Enabling Behaviors, Cognitive Quotient.
Administration: Individual.
Price Data, 1994: $114 per complete kit including 25 examiner record books, child's book, picture cards, toys, and examiner's manual (87 pages); $34 per 25 examiner record books; $7 per child's book; $10 per set of picture cards; $44 per set of toys; $24 per manual.
Time: (30–45) minutes.
Author: Sharon Bradley-Johnson.
Publisher: PRO-ED, Inc.
Cross References: For reviews by A. Dirk Hightower and Gary J. Robertson, see 10:65.

[537]

Cognitive Abilities Test, Form 4.
Purpose: Designed "to assess the development of cognitive abilities related to verbal, quantitative and nonverbal reasoning and problem solving."
Population: Grades K–1, 2–3, 3–12.
Publication Dates: 1954–86.
Acronym: CogAT.
Administration: Group.
Price Data, 1989: $13.50 per technical and administrative manuals; $75 per VHS videotape.
Comments: Third component of the Riverside Basic Skills Assessment Program; Form 3 still available.
Authors: Robert L. Thorndike and Elizabeth Hagen.
Publisher: The Riverside Publishing Co.

a) PRIMARY BATTERY.
Population: Grades K–1, 2–3.

Publication Dates: 1979–86.
Scores, 3: Verbal, Quantitative, Nonverbal.
Levels, 2: Primary Battery, Level 1 and Primary Battery, Level 2.
Price Data, 1989: $57 per 35 MRC machine-scorable tests (specify level); $46.20 per 35 hand-scorable tests (specify level); $8.40 per manual for Levels 1 & 2 ('86, 42 pages); $2.40 per scoring key (specify level); $66.45 per 35 NCS directions for administration (specify level); $11.25 per 35 practice tests for Levels 1 & 2; $2.10 per directions for Levels 1 & 2 practice tests.
Time: 90(110) minutes in at least 3 sessions.
Comments: Scoring service available from publisher.

b) MULTILEVEL EDITION.
Population: Grades 3–12.
Publication Dates: 1978–86.
Scores, 3: Verbal, Quantitative, Nonverbal.
Levels: 8 overlapping levels: Level A through Level H.
Price Data, 1989: $4.50 per multilevel battery test, Levels A–H; $49.20 per 35 tests (specify level); $4.05 per directions for administration for separate level booklets; $4.30 per 35 MRC answer sheets including 1 examiner's manual and materials needed for machine scoring (specify level); $36.30 per 100 MRC answer sheets and materials for machine scoring (specify level); $16.35 per 2 MRC scoring masks (specify level); $3 per scoring key; $129 per 250 NCS 7010 answer sheets; $33 per 100 practice tests for Levels A–H; $8.40 per examiner's manual for Levels A–H ('86, 36 pages); $9 per 35 class record folders for Levels 1 & 2 and A–H.
Time: 90(140) minutes in 3 sessions.
Comments: Scoring service available from publishers.
Cross References: For reviews by Anne Anastasi and Douglas Fuchs, see 10:66 (13 references); for a review by Charles J. Ansorge of an earlier edition, see 9:240 (5 references); see also T3:483 (32 references); for reviews by Kenneth D. Hopkins and Robert C. Nichols, see 8:181 (12 references); for reviews by Marcel L. Goldschmid and Carol K. Tittle and an excerpted review by Richard C. Cox of the primary batteries, see 7:343.

TEST REFERENCES

1. Bachman, E. E., Sines, J. O., Watson, J. A., Lauer, R. M., & Clarke, W. R. (1986). The relations between Type A behavior, clinically relevant behavior, academic achievement, and IQ in children. *Journal of Personality Assessment, 50,* 186-192.
2. Kapinus, B. A., Gambrell, L. B., & Koskinen, D. S. (1987). Effects of practice in retelling upon the reading comprehension of proficient and less proficient readers. *Yearbook of the National Reading Conference, 36,* 135-141.
3. Marx, R. W., Howard, D. C., & Winne, P. H. (1987). Student's perception of instruction, cognitive style, and achievement. *Perceptual and Motor Skills, 65,* 123-134.
4. Kleinman, M. J., & Russ, S. W. (1988). Primary process thinking and anxiety in children. *Journal of Personality Assessment, 52,* 254-262.
5. Koskinen, P. S., Gambrell, L. B., & Kapinus, B. (1989). The effects of rereading and retelling upon young children's reading comprehension. *Yearbook of the National Reading Conference, 38,* 233-239.

6. Carlisle, J. F., & Felbinger, L. (1991). Profiles of listening and reading comprehension. *Journal of Educational Research, 84,* 345-354.

7. Crosser, S. L. (1991). Summer birth date children: Kindergarten entrance age and academic achievement. *Journal of Educational Research, 84,* 140-146.

8. Dobbins, D. A., & Tafa, E. (1991). The "stability" of identification of underachieving readers over different measures of intelligence and reading. *The British Journal of Educational Psychology, 61,* 155-163.

9. Gambrell, L. B., Koskinen, P. S., & Kapinus, B. A. (1991). Retelling and the reading comprehension of proficient and less-proficient readers. *Journal of Educational Research, 84,* 356-362.

10. Mathinos, D. A. (1991). Conversational engagement of children with learning disabilities. *Journal of Learning Disabilities, 24,* 439-446.

11. Rosenbach, J. H., & Rusch, R. R. (1991). IQ and achievement: 1930s to 1980s. *Psychology in the Schools, 28,* 304-309.

12. Swanson, H. L., O'Connor, J. E., & Carter, K. R. (1991). Problem-solving subgroups as a measure of intellectual giftedness. *The British Journal of Educational Psychology, 61,* 55-72.

13. Swanson, H. L., Reffel, J., & Trahan, M. (1991). Naturalistic memory in learning-disabled and skilled readers. *Journal of Abnormal Child Psychology, 19,* 117-147.

14. Bisanz, G. L., Das, J. P., Varnhagen, C. K., & Henderson, H. R. (1992). Structural components of reading time and recall for sentences in narratives: Exploring changes with age and reading ability. *Journal of Educational Psychology, 84,* 103-114.

15. Hagborg, W. J., & Wachman, E. M. (1992). The Arlin Test of Formal Reasoning and the identification of accelerated mathematics students. *Educational and Psychological Measurement, 52,* 437-442.

16. Meyer, M. J., Day, S. L., & Lee, Y. B. (1992). Symmetry in building block design for learning disabled and nonlearning disabled boys. *Perceptual and Motor Skills, 74,* 1031-1039.

17. Lochman, J. E., Wayland, K. K., & White, K. J. (1993). Social goals: Relationship to adolescent adjustment and to social problem solving. *Journal of Abnormal Child Psychology, 21,* 135-151.

18. Mason, D. A., & Good, T. L. (1993). Effects of two-group and whole-class teaching on regrouped elementary students' mathematics achievement. *American Educational Research Journal, 30,* 328-360.

19. Young, E. R., & Fouts, J. T. (1993). Field dependence/independence and the identification of gifted students. *Journal for the Education of the Gifted, 16,* 299-310.

[538]

Cognitive Abilities Test, Second Edition [British Edition].

Purpose: Measures "the individual's ability to use and manipulate abstract and symbolic relationships."

Population: Ages 7–15.

Publication Dates: 1973–86.

Acronym: CAT.

Scores, 3: Verbal, Quantitative, Nonverbal.

Administration: Group.

Levels, 6: 6 overlapping levels (A–F) in a single booklet.

Price Data, 1989: £5.50 per pupil's booklet; £6.85 per 25 practice tests; £6.30 per 25 answer sheets (specify level); £7.35 per 25 handscoring overlays; £5.50 per 25 circular profiles; £13.75 per administration manual ('86, 96 pages); £20.15 per specimen set; scoring service offered by publisher.

Time: 20(40) minutes for practice test; 32(60) minutes per battery.

Authors: Robert L. Thorndike, Elizabeth Hagen, and Norman France (manual).

Publisher: NFER-Nelson Publishing Co., Ltd. [England].

Cross References: For reviews by Anne Anastasi and Douglas Fuchs of the U.S. edition, see 10:66 (13 references); for a review by Charles J. Ansorge of an earlier edition, see 9:240 (5 references); see also T3:483 (32 references); for reviews by Kenneth D. Hopkins and Robert C. Nichols, see 8:181 (12 references); for reviews by Marcel L. Goldschmid and Carol K. Tittle and an excerpted review by Richard C. Cox of the primary batteries, see 7:343.

[539]

Cognitive Behavior Rating Scales.

Purpose: "To allow a family member, or other reliable observer, to rate the presence and severity of cognitive impairment, behavioral deficits, and observable neurological signs."

Population: Patients with possible neurological impairment.

Publication Date: 1987.

Acronym: CBRS.

Scores: 9 scales: Language Deficit, Apraxia, Disorientation, Agitation, Need for Routine, Depression, Higher Cognitive Deficits, Memory Disorder, Dementia.

Administration: Individual.

Price Data, 1994: $45 per complete kit including manual, 25 reusable item booklets, and 50 rating booklets.

Time: (15–20) minutes.

Author: J. Michael Williams.

Publisher: Psychological Assessment Resources, Inc.

Cross References: For reviews by Ron Edwards and David J. Mealor, see 11:74.

[540]

Cognitive Control Battery.

Purpose: Helps "to predict, diagnose, and treat learning disabilities."

Population: Ages 4–12.

Publication Dates: 1987–88.

Acronym: CCB.

Scores: Scattered Scanning Test, 6 scores: Motor Tempo, Number Correct Shapes Marked, Ratio I, Total Distance, Ratio II, Mean Distance; Fruit Distraction Test, Time and Errors scores for each of the following: Card 2, Card 3/Card 2, Card 4/Card 2; Leveling-Sharpening House Test, 3 scores: First Stop, Number Correct Changes, Ratio.

Administration: Individual.

Parts, 3: Scattered Scanning Test, Fruit Distraction Test, Leveling-Sharpening House Test.

Price Data, 1993: $325 per complete set including picture book ('88, 132 pages), stimulus materials, 25 Form 1 Test Sheets, 25 Form 2 Test Sheets, Line Measure, 25 Motor Tempo Sheets, 25 Training Forms, 25 Record Booklets, and manual ('88, 213 pages); $19.50 per 100 Form 1 Test Sheets; $24.50 per 25 Form 2 Test Sheets; $19.50 per 100 Motor Tempo Sheets; $19.50 per 100 Training Forms; $16.50 per 25 Record Booklets; $80 per manual.

Time: (28–33) minutes.

Author: Sebastiano Santostefano.

Publisher: Western Psychological Services.

Cross References: For reviews by Scott W. Brown and Hope J. Hartman, see 11:75 (2 references).

[541]
Cognitive Diagnostic Battery.
Purpose: Designed "as a method for assessing and differentiating among aspects of cognitive dysfunction."
Population: Psychiatric and retarded patients.
Publication Date: 1982.
Acronym: CDB.
Administration: Individual or group.
Price Data, 1994: $63 per complete kit including 5 tests, 50 Span of Attention forms, 50 record forms, and manual (120 pages); $16 per 50 record forms; $8 per 50 Span of Attention forms; $14 per manual.
Author: Stanley R. Kay.
Publisher: Psychological Assessment Resources, Inc.
a) COLOR-FORM PREFERENCE TEST.
Acronym: CFP.
Scores: 2 scale scores: Color-Form Scale, Identity Scale.
Time: (3–5) minutes.
b) COLOR-FORM REPRESENTATION TEST.
Acronym: CFR.
Time: (3–5) minutes.
c) EGOCENTRICITY OF THOUGHT TEST.
Acronym: EOT.
Time: (1–3) minutes.
d) PROGRESSIVE FIGURE DRAWING TEST.
Acronym: PFDT.
Scores, 8: 7 drawing scores (Vertical Line, Circle, Cross, Square, Triangle, Tree, Diamond) and derived mental age score.
Time: (1–3) minutes.
e) SPAN OF ATTENTION TEST.
Acronym: SOA.
Time: (1–7) minutes.
Cross References: For reviews by John L. Fisk and Arthur B. Silverstein, see 9:241.

TEST REFERENCES
1. Kay, S. R., Opler, L. A., & Fiszbein, A. (1986). Significance of positive and negative syndromes in chronic schizophrenia. *British Journal of Psychiatry, 149*, 439-448.

[542]
Cognitive Skills Assessment Battery, Second Edition.
Purpose: "To provide teachers with information regarding children's progress relative to teaching goals in the cognitive and physical-motor areas."
Population: PreK–K.
Publication Dates: 1974–81.
Acronym: CSAB.
Scores: 98 item scores (49 consist of plus or minus) in 18 areas: Basic Information (4 scores), Identification of Body Parts (4 scores), Color Identification (4 scores), Shape Identification (4 scores), Symbol Discrimination (10 scores), Visual-Auditory Discrimination (5 scores), Auditory Discrimination (6 scores), Number Knowledge (10 scores), Letter Naming (2 scores), Vocabulary (6 scores), Information from Pictures (4 scores), Picture Comprehension (4 scores), Story Comprehension (4 scores), Multiple Directions (4 scores), Large Muscle Coordination (4 scores), Visual-Motor Coordination (6 scores), Memory (8 scores), Response During Assessment (8 scores).
Administration: Individual.
Price Data, 1994: $51.95 per testing materials including 30 response sheets ('81, 4 pages); $8.95 per refill (1 class record, 30 pupil response sheets); $3.50 per assessors manual ('81, 61 pages); $3.95 per specimen set (including 1 sample easel page).
Time: (20–25) minutes.
Comments: "Criterion-referenced."
Authors: Ann E. Boehm and Barbara R. Slater.
Publisher: Teachers College Press.
Cross References: For reviews by Esther E. Diamond and Susan Embretson (Whitely), see 9:242; see also T3:484 (2 references); for reviews by Kathryn Hoover Calfee and Barbara K. Keogh, see 8:797.

TEST REFERENCES
1. Brown, J. O., Grubb, S. B., Wicker, T. E., & O'Tuel, F. S. (1985). Health variables and school achievement. *Journal of School Health, 55*, 21-23.
2. Lidz, C. S., & Ballester, L. E. (1986). Diagnostic implications of McCarthy Scale General Cognitive Index/Binet IQ discrepancies for low-socioeconomic-status preschool children. *Journal of School Psychology, 24*, 381-385.
3. Glutting, J. J., Kelly, M. S., Boehm, A. E., & Burnett, T. R. (1989). Stability and predictive validity of the Boehm Test of Basic Concepts—Revised among black kindergarteners. *Journal of School Psychology, 27*, 365-371.

[543]
Coitometer.
Purpose: Designed to "measure knowledge of the physical aspects of human coitus."
Population: Adults.
Publication Date: 1974.
Scores: Total score only.
Administration: Group.
Manual: No manual.
Price Data: Instrument is available without charge from author.
Time: [10] minutes.
Author: Panos D. Bardis.
Publisher: Panos D. Bardis.

[544]
College Adjustment Scales.
Purpose: Identifies developmental and psychological problems experienced by college students.
Population: College and university students.
Publication Date: 1991.
Acronym: CAS.
Scores, 9: Anxiety, Depression, Suicidal Ideation, Substance Abuse, Self-Esteem Problems, Interpersonal Problems, Family Problems, Academic Problems, Career Problems.
Administration: Individual or group.
Price Data, 1994: $57 per complete kit including manual (25 pages), 25 reusable item booklets, and 25 answer sheets; $20 per 25 reusable item booklets; $20 per 25 answer sheets; $20 per manual.

Time: (15–20) minutes.
Authors: William D. Anton and James R. Reed.
Publisher: Psychological Assessment Resources, Inc.

TEST REFERENCES

1. Pinkney, J. W. (1992). Inventory of College Adjustment Scales. *Measurement and Evaluation in Counseling and Development, 25,* 42-45.

[545]

College Basic Academic Subjects Examination.

Purpose: Designed to assess skills and competencies typically achieved through the general education component of a college curriculum.
Population: College students having completed the general education component of a college curriculum (i.e., late sophomores or early juniors).
Publication Dates: 1989–90.
Acronym: College BASE.
Administration: Group.
Price Data, 1991: $27.45 per registration form per group or partial group of 50 students (48 for the Institutional Matrix Form).
Comments: "Criterion-referenced."
Author: Steven J. Osterlind.
Publisher: The Riverside Publishing Co.

a) LONG FORM.
Scores, 40: Competency (Interpretive Reasoning, Strategic Reasoning, Adaptive Reasoning), Skill (Social Science Procedures, Political/Economic Structures, Geography, Significance of U.S. Events, Significance of World Events, Physical Sciences, Life Sciences, Interpreting Results, Laboratory/Field Techniques, Observation/Experimental Design, Geometrical Calculations, 2- & 3-Dimensional Figures, Equations & Inequalities, Evaluating Expressions, Using Statistics, Properties and Notations, Practical Applications, Expository Writing Sample, Conventions of Written English, Writing as a Process, Understanding Literature, Reading Analytically, Reading Critically), Cluster (Social Sciences, History, Fundamental Concepts, Laboratory & Field Work, Geometry, Algebra, General Mathematics, Writing, Reading & Literature), Subject (Social Studies, Science, Mathematics, English), Composite.
Price Data, 1991: $17.10 per student with writing exercise, $10.80 per student without writing exercise (includes all test materials, scoring, and delivery of score reports); materials package consists of 50 test books ('90, 44 pages), 50 answer books ('90, 8 pages), Manual for Examiners and Test Coordinators ('90, 27 pages), Guide to Test Content ('90, 27 pages), Coordinator's Data Sheet, and Examiner's Data Sheet.
Time: 210(240) minutes with writing exercise; 160(180) minutes without writing exercise.
Comments: Writing exercise is optional.
b) SHORT FORM.
Scores, 24: Same as Long Form without Social Studies and Science sections.

Price Data, 1991: $14.85 per student with writing exercise, $8.55 per student without writing exercise (includes all test materials, scoring, and delivery of score reports); materials package same as *a* above.
Time: 110(120) minutes with writing exercise; 60(80) minutes without writing exercise.
Comments: Writing exercise is optional.
c) INSTITUTIONAL MATRIX FORM.
Scores, 5: Composite Score, Subject Scores, Cluster Scores, Skill Scores, Competency Scores.
Price Data, 1991: $6.30 per student; materials package includes 4 matrix test books each for Forms 1–12, 48 matrix answer sheets, Coordinator's Data Sheet, Examiner's Data Sheet, Manual for Examiners and Test Coordinators ('90, 26 pages), and Guide to Test Content.
Cross References: For reviews by William E. Coffman and Delwyn L. Harnisch, see 11:76.

[546]

College Board One-Hour Achievement Test in American History and Social Studies (Drawn from the SAT II: Subject Tests).

Purpose: "To place students at the appropriate level of study in college."
Population: Entering college freshmen.
Publication Dates: 1962–94.
Scores: Total score only.
Administration: Group or individual.
Price Data: Rental fee per student available from publisher.
Time: (60) minutes.
Comments: Active forms of College Board SAT II: Subject Tests in American History and Social Studies available for local administration and scoring by colleges, universities, and other appropriate organizations; form change/update done in 3-year cycles; previously known as College Placement Test.
Author: Educational Testing Service.
Publisher: Educational Testing Service.
Cross References: For a review by Howard R. Anderson of an earlier form, see 6:966; for a review by Ralph W. Tyler, see 5:786; for a review by Robert L. Thorndike, see 4:662. For a review of an earlier form of the program, see 7:665.

[547]

College Board One-Hour Achievement Test in Biology (Drawn from the SAT II: Subject Tests).

Purpose: "To place students at the appropriate level of study in college."
Population: Entering college freshmen.
Publication Dates: 1962–94.
Scores: Total score only.
Administration: Group or individual.
Price Data: Rental fee per student available from publisher.
Time: (60) minutes.

Comments: Active forms of College Board SAT II: Subject Tests in Biology available for local administration and scoring by colleges, universities, and other appropriate organizations; previously known as College Placement Test.
Author: Educational Testing Service.
Publisher: Educational Testing Service.
Cross References: See 8:834 (1 reference); for a review by Elizabeth Hagen of an earlier form, see 5:723; for a review by Clark W. Horton, see 4:600. For a review of an earlier form of the program, see 7:665.

[548]

College Board One-Hour Achievement Test in Chemistry (Drawn from the SAT II: Subject Tests).
Purpose: "To place students at the appropriate level of study in college."
Population: Entering college freshmen.
Publication Dates: 1962–94.
Scores: Total score only.
Administration: Group or individual.
Price Data: Rental fee per student available from publisher.
Time: (60) minutes.
Comments: Active forms of College Board SAT II: Subject Tests in Chemistry available for local administration and scoring by colleges, universities, and other appropriate organizations; previously known as College Placement Test.
Author: Educational Testing Service.
Publisher: Educational Testing Service.
Cross References: For a review by William Hered of earlier forms, see 6:914; for a review by Max D. Engelhart, see 5:742; for a review by Evelyn Raskin, see 4:617. For a review of an earlier form of the program, see 7:665.

[549]

College Board One-Hour Achievement Test in French Reading (Drawn from the SAT II: Subject Tests)
Purpose: "To place students at the appropriate level of study in college."
Population: Entering college freshmen.
Publication Dates: 1962–94.
Scores: Total score only.
Administration: Group or individual.
Price Data: Rental fee per student available from publisher.
Time: (60) minutes.
Comments: Active forms of College Board SAT II: Subject Tests in French Reading available for local administration and scoring by colleges, universities, and other appropriate organizations; previously known as College Placement Test.
Author: Educational Testing Service.
Publisher: Educational Testing Service.
Cross References: See 8:119 (1 reference) and 7:271 (1 reference); for a review by Walter V. Kaul-

fers of earlier forms, see 4:237. For a review of an earlier form of the program, see 7:665.

[550]

College Board One-Hour Achievement Test in French with Listening (Drawn from the SAT II: Subject Tests).
Purpose: "To place students at the appropriate level of study in college."
Population: Entering college freshmen.
Publication Dates: 1971–94.
Scores, 3: Listening, Reading, Total.
Administration: Group or individual.
Price Data: Rental fee per student available from publisher.
Time: (60) minutes.
Comments: Active forms of College Board SAT II: Subject Test in French with Listening available for local administration and scoring by colleges, universities, and other appropriate organizations; cassette required; previously known as College Placement Test.
Author: Educational Testing Service.
Publisher: Educational Testing Service.
Cross References: For a review of an earlier form of the program, see 7:665.

[551]

College Board One-Hour Achievement Test in German Reading (Drawn from the SAT II: Subject Tests).
Purpose: "To place students at the appropriate level of study in college."
Population: Entering college freshmen.
Publication Dates: 1962–94.
Scores: Total score only.
Administration: Group or individual.
Price Data: Rental fee per student available from publisher.
Time: (60) minutes.
Comments: Active forms of College Board SAT II: Subject Tests in German Reading available for local administration and scoring by colleges, universities, and other appropriate organizations; previously known as College Placement Test.
Author: Educational Testing Service.
Publisher: Educational Testing Service.
Cross References: See 7:285 (2 references); for a review by Gilbert C. Kettelkamp of earlier forms, see 6:383; for a review by Harold B. Dunkel, see 5:272; for a review by Herbert Schueler, see 4:244. For a review of an earlier form of the program, see 7:665.

[552]

College Board One-Hour Achievement Test in German with Listening (Drawn from the SAT II: Subject Tests).
Purpose: "To place students at the appropriate level of study in college."
Population: Entering college freshmen.
Publication Dates: 1971–94.

Scores, 3: Listening, Reading, Total.
Administration: Group or individual.
Price Data: Rental fee per student available from publisher.
Time: (60) minutes.
Comments: Active forms of College Board SAT II: Subject Test in German with Listening available for local administration and scoring by colleges, universities, and other appropriate organizations; cassette required; previously known as College Placement Test.
Author: Educational Testing Service.
Publisher: Educational Testing Service.
Cross References: See 8:130 (1 reference). For a review of an earlier form of the program, see 7:665.

[553]

College Board One-Hour Achievement Test in Italian (Drawn from the SAT II: Subject Tests).
Purpose: "To place students at the appropriate level of study in college."
Population: Entering college freshmen.
Publication Dates: 1962–94.
Scores: Total score only.
Administration: Group or individual.
Price Data: Rental fee per student available from publisher.
Time: (60) minutes.
Comments: Active forms of College Board SAT II: Subject Tests in Italian Reading available for local administration and scoring by colleges, universities, and other appropriate organizations; previously known as College Placement Test.
Author: Educational Testing Service.
Publisher: Educational Testing Service.
Cross References: For a review by Paolo Valesio of earlier forms, see 7:300. For a review of an earlier form of the program, see 7:665.

[554]

College Board One-Hour Achievement Test in Latin Reading (Drawn from the SAT II: Subject Tests).
Purpose: "To place students at the appropriate level of study in college."
Population: Entering college freshmen.
Publication Dates: 1962–94.
Scores: Total score only.
Administration: Group or individual.
Price Data: Rental fee per student available from publisher.
Time: (60) minutes.
Comments: Active forms of College Board SAT II: Subject Tests in Latin Reading available for local administration and scoring by colleges, universities, and other appropriate organizations; previously known as College Placement Test.
Author: Educational Testing Service.
Publisher: Educational Testing Service.
Cross References: For a review by Konrad Gries

of an earlier form, see 5:280; for a review by Harold B. Dunkel, see 4:250. For a review of an earlier form of the program, see 7:665.

[555]

College Board One-Hour Achievement Test in Literature (Drawn from the SAT II: Subject Tests).
Purpose: "To place students at the appropriate level of study in college."
Population: Entering college freshmen.
Publication Dates: 1968–94.
Scores: Total score only.
Administration: Group or individual.
Price Data: Rental fee per student available from publisher.
Time: (60) minutes.
Comments: Active forms of College Board SAT II: Subject Tests in Literature available for local administration and scoring by colleges, universities, and other appropriate organizations; previously known as College Placement Test.
Author: Educational Testing Service.
Publisher: Educational Testing Service.
Cross References: For a review of an earlier form of the program, see 7:665.

[556]

College Board One-Hour Achievement Test in Mathematics (Drawn from the SAT II: Subject Tests).
Purpose: "To place students at the appropriate level of study in college."
Population: Entering college freshmen.
Publication Dates: 1964–94.
Scores: Total score only.
Administration: Group or individual.
Levels, 2: Level 1, Level 2.
Price Data: Rental fee per student available from publisher.
Time: (60) minutes for each level.
Comments: Active forms of College Board SAT II: Subject Tests in Mathematics available for local administration and scoring by colleges, universities, and other appropriate organizations; these forms do not allow use of calculators; newer Mathematics Level I and II tests permitting calculators are scheduled for introduction in 1996–97; previously known as College Placement Test.
Author: Educational Testing Service.
Publisher: Educational Testing Service.
Cross References: For a review of an earlier form of the program, see 7:665.

[557]

College Board One-Hour Achievement Test in Modern Hebrew (Drawn from the SAT II: Subject Tests).
Purpose: "To place students at the appropriate level of study in college."
Population: Entering college freshmen.

Publication Dates: 1962–94.
Scores: Total score only.
Administration: Group or individual.
Price Data: Rental fee per student available from publisher.
Time: (60) minutes.
Comments: Active forms of College Board SAT II: Subject Tests in Hebrew available for local administration and scoring by colleges, universities, and other appropriate organizations; previously known as College Placement Test.
Author: Educational Testing Service.
Publisher: Educational Testing Service.
Cross References: For a review of an earlier form of the program, see 7:665.

[558]
College Board One-Hour Achievement Test in Physics (Drawn from the SAT II: Subject Tests).
Purpose: "To place students at the appropriate level of study in college."
Population: Entering college freshmen.
Publication Dates: 1962–94.
Scores: Total score only.
Administration: Group or individual.
Price Data: Rental fee per student available from publisher.
Time: (60) minutes.
Comments: Active forms of College Board SAT II: Subject Tests in Physics available for local administration and scoring by colleges, universities, and other appropriate organizations; previously known as College Placement Test.
Author: Educational Testing Service.
Publisher: Educational Testing Service.
Cross References: For a review by Theodore G. Phillips of an earlier form, see 5:749; for a review by Palmer O. Johnson, see 4:633. For a review of an earlier form of the program, see 7:665.

[559]
College Board One-Hour Achievement Test in Spanish Reading (Drawn from the SAT II: Subject Tests).
Purpose: "To place students at the appropriate level of study in college."
Population: Entering college freshmen.
Publication Dates: 1962–94.
Scores: Total score only.
Administration: Group or individual.
Price Data: Rental fee per student available from publisher.
Time: (60) minutes.
Comments: Active forms of College Board SAT II: Subject Tests in Spanish Reading available for local administration and scoring by colleges, universities, and other appropriate organizations; previously known as College Placement Test.
Author: Educational Testing Service.
Publisher: Educational Testing Service.

Cross References: See 8:161 (1 reference) and 7:316 (1 reference). For a review of an earlier form of the program, see 7:665.

[560]
College Board One-Hour Achievement Test in Spanish with Listening (Drawn from the SAT II: Subject Tests).
Purpose: "To place students at the appropriate level of study in college."
Population: Entering college freshmen.
Publication Dates: 1971–94.
Scores: Total score only.
Administration: Group or individual.
Price Data: Rental fee per student available from publisher.
Time: (60) minutes.
Comments: Active forms of College Board SAT II: Subject Test in Spanish with Listening available for local administration and scoring by colleges, universities, and other appropriate organizations; cassette required; previously known as College Placement Test.
Author: Educational Testing Service.
Publisher: Educational Testing Service.
Cross References: For a review of an earlier form of the program, see 7:665.

[561]
College Board One-Hour Achievement Test in World History (Drawn from the SAT II: Subject Tests).
Purpose: "To place students at the appropriate level of study in college."
Population: Entering college freshmen.
Publication Dates: 1963–94.
Scores: Total score only.
Administration: Group or individual.
Price Data: Rental fee per student available from publisher.
Time: (60) minutes.
Comments: Active forms of College Board SAT II: Subject Tests in World History available for local administration and scoring by colleges, universities, and other appropriate organizations; previously known as College Placement Test.
Author: Educational Testing Service.
Publisher: Educational Testing Service.
Cross References: For a review by David K. Heenan, see 6:967. For a review of an earlier form of the program, see 7:665.

[562]
College Board One-Hour Achievement Test in Writing (Drawn from the SAT II: Subject Tests).
Purpose: "To place students at the appropriate level of study in college."
Population: Entering college freshmen.
Publication Dates: 1962–94.
Scores: Total score only.

Administration: Group or individual.
Price Data: Rental fee per student available from publisher.
Time: (60) minutes.
Comments: Active forms of College Board SAT II: Subject Tests in Writing available for local administration and scoring by colleges, universities, and other appropriate organizations; previously known as College Placement Test.
Author: Educational Testing Service.
Publisher: Educational Testing Service.
Cross References: See 8:48 (20 references); for a review by John C. Sherwood of an earlier form, see 7:190 (3 references); for reviews by Charlotte Croon Davis, Robert C. Pooley, and Holland Roberts of earlier forms, see 6:287; for a review by Charlotte Croon Davis with Frederick B. Davis, see 4:178. For a review of an earlier form of the program, see 7:665.

[563]

College Board One-Hour Achievement Tests (Drawn from the SAT II: Subject Tests).

Purpose: "To place students at the appropriate level of study in college."
Population: Entering college freshmen.
Publication Dates: 1962–94.
Scores: 3 (Listening, Reading, Total) for Listening-Reading tests; total score only for other tests.
Administration: Group or individual.
Tests: American History and Social Studies, Biology, Chemistry, Writing (Multiple Choice with Direct Writing Sample), English Composition, World History, French Reading, German Reading, Hebrew Reading, Latin Reading, Literature, Mathematics (2 levels), Physics, Spanish Reading, French with Listening, Chinese with Listening, Spanish with Listening, German with Listening, Math Levels I and II permitting use of calculators.
Time: (60) minutes.
Comments: Active forms of College Board SAT II: Subject Tests available for local administration and scoring by colleges, universities, and other appropriate organizations; previously known as College Placement Tests.
Author: Educational Testing Service.
Publisher: Educational Testing Service.
Cross References: See T3:507 (2 references); for a review by John R. Hills of the College Placement Tests, see 7:665.

[564]

College Board SAT I Reasoning Test.

Purpose: To measure "the developed verbal and mathematical reasoning abilities related to successful performance in college."
Population: Candidates for college entrance.
Publication Dates: 1926–94.
Acronym: SAT I.
Scores, 2: Verbal Reasoning, Mathematical Reasoning.
Administration: Group.

Forms: 7–9 forms issued annually.
Price Data: Examination fees per candidate available from publisher. Price data for guidelines on the uses of College Board test scores and related data, guide to the College Board Validity Study Service, technical handbook, SAT Program guide, student bulletins, Taking the SAT I, test and technical data, SAT I Question and Answer Service, SAT I Student Answer Service, SAT Score Verification Service, and Clerical Scoring Service are all available from the publisher.
Time: (180) minutes.
Comments: The SAT I is administered 7 times annually (January, March or April, May, June, October, November, and December) at centers established by the publisher. The Test of Standard Written English is no longer available at SAT I national administrations. The SAT I: Reasoning Test replaced the College Board Scholastic Aptitude Test and Test of Standard Written English in 1994. Scores from Verbal Reasoning and Math Reasoning sections of the SAT I vocabulary and reading subscores have been discontinued in the SAT I. Score analysis data by item type/content available for Verbal and Math beginning in 1994. The SAT I scale will be recentered in 1995; equivalence tables will be available for converting scores from one scale to another. SAT forms are available for local administration and scoring through the College Entry-Level Assessment (CELA) Program. SAT I forms will be offered through CELA in the near future. Special administration arrangements available for students with disabilities, including Braille, cassette tape, regular type, and large-type editions available with extra time.
Authors: The College Board and Educational Testing Service.
Publisher: Educational Testing Service.
Cross References: For reviews by Sanford J. Cohn and Lee J. Cronbach of an earlier edition, see 9:244 (31 references); see T3:501 (152 references), 8:182 (217 references), and T2:357 (148 references); for reviews by Philip H. Dubois and Wimburn L. Wallace of an earlier form, see 7:344 (298 references); for reviews by John E. Bowers and Wayne S. Zimmerman, see 6:449 (79 references); for a review by John T. Dailey, see 5:318 (20 references); for a review by Frederick B. Davis, see 4:285 (22 references). For reviews of the testing program, see 6:760 (2 reviews).

TEST REFERENCES

1. Alexander, K. L., & Pallas, A. M. (1983). Reply to Benbow and Stanley. *American Educational Research Journal, 20,* 475-477.
2. Ayres, Q. W. (1983). Student achievement at predominantly white and predominantly black universities. *American Educational Research Journal, 20,* 291-304.
3. Barnes, V., Potter, E. H., & Fiedler, F. E. (1983). Effect of interpersonal stress on the prediction of academic performance. *Journal of Applied Psychology, 68,* 686-697.
4. Benbow, C. P., & Stanley, J. C. (1983). Differential course-taking hypothesis revisited. *American Educational Research Journal, 20,* 469-473.
5. Benbow, C. P., Stanley, J. C., Kirk, M. K., & Zonderman, A. B. (1983). Structure of intelligence in intellectually precocious children and in their parents. *Intelligence, 7,* 129-152.
6. O'Tuel, F. S., Ward, M., & Rawl, R. K. (1983). The SOI as an identification tool for the gifted: Windfall or washout? *Gifted Child Quarterly, 27,* 126-134.

7. Pallas, A. M., & Alexander, K. L. (1983). Sex differences in quantitative SAT performance: New evidence on the differential coursework hypothesis. *American Educational Research Journal, 20,* 165-182.

8. Powers, D. E., & Alderman, D. L. (1983). Effects of test familiarization on SAT performance. *Journal of Educational Measurement, 20,* 71-79.

9. Raz, N., Willerman, L., Ingmundson, P., & Hanlon, M. (1983). Aptitude-related differences in auditory recognition masking. *Intelligence, 7,* 71-90.

10. Renninger, K. A., & Snyder, S. S. (1983). Effects of cognitive style on perceived satisfaction and performance among students and teachers. *Journal of Educational Psychology, 75,* 668-676.

11. Stanley, J. C., & Benbow, C. P. (1983). SMPY's first decade: Ten years of posing problems and solving them. *The Journal of Special Education, 17,* 11-25.

12. Abrams, H. G., & Jernigan, L. P. (1984). Academic support services and the success of high-risk college students. *American Educational Research Journal, 21,* 261-274.

13. Angoff, W. H., & Schrader, W. B. (1984). A study of hypotheses basic to the use of rights and formula scores. *Journal of Educational Measurement, 21,* 1-17.

14. Badgett, J. L., Hunkler, R. F., & Porter, C. M. (1984). Authoritarianism and academic achievement of men and women: A canonical profile. *Counseling and Values, 28,* 76-81.

15. Belz, H. F., & Geary, D. C. (1984). Father's occupation and social background: Relation to SAT scores. *American Educational Research Journal, 21,* 473-478.

16. Blosser, P. E. (1984). What research says: Achievement in science. *School Science and Mathematics, 84,* 514-521.

17. Deboer, G. E. (1984). A study of gender effects in the science and mathematics course-taking behavior of a group of students who graduated from college in the late 1970s. *Journal of Research in Science Teaching, 21,* 95-103.

18. Deboer, G. E. (1984). Factors related to the decision of men and women to continue taking science courses in college. *Journal of Research in Science Teaching, 21,* 325-329.

19. Dew, K. M. H., Galassi, J. P., & Galassi, M. D. (1984). Math anxiety: Relation with situational test anxiety, performance, physiological arousal, and math avoidance behavior. *Journal of Counseling Psychology, 31,* 580-583.

20. Doverspike, D., Cellar, D., Barrett, G. V., & Alexander, R. (1984). Sex differences in short-term memory processing. *Perceptual and Motor Skills, 58,* 135-139.

21. Farr, R., Courtland, M. C., & Beck, M. D. (1984). Scholastic aptitude test performance and reading ability. *Journal of Reading, 28,* 208-214.

22. Jackson, W. K., & Williamson, M. L. (1984). Academic scholarship and freshman statistics: A case study. *College Student Journal, 18,* 177-179.

23. Karmos, A. H., & Karmos, J. S. (1984). Attitudes toward standardization achievement tests and their relation to achievement test performance. *Measurement and Evaluation in Counseling and Development, 17,* 56-66.

24. Kohlberg, L., Ricks, D., & Snarey, J. (1984). Childhood development as a predictor of adaptation in adulthood. *Genetic Psychology Monographs, 110,* 91-172.

25. Mathiasen, R. E. (1984). Predicting college academic achievement: A research review. *College Student Journal, 18,* 380-386.

26. McDaniel, M. A., & Pressley, M. (1984). Putting the keyword method in context. *Journal of Educational Psychology, 76,* 598-609.

27. Pascarella, E. T. (1984). College environmental influences on students' educational aspirations. *Journal of Higher Education, 55,* 751-771.

28. Powell, B., & Steelman, L. C. (1984). Variations in state SAT performance: Meaningful or misleading? *Harvard Educational Review, 54,* 389-412.

29. Searleman, A., Herrmann, D. J., & Coventry, A. K. (1984). Cognitive abilities and left-handedness: An interaction between familial sinistrality and strength of handedness. *Intelligence, 8,* 295-304.

30. Smith, A. D. (1984). Discriminative analysis technique to assess selection bias in a college student attrition survey. *College Student Journal, 18,* 390-396.

31. Sternberg, R. J. (1984). The Kaufman Assessment Battery for Children: An information-processing analysis and critique. *The Journal of Special Education, 18,* 269-279.

32. Terenzini, P. T., Theophilides, C., & Lorang, W. G. (1984). Influences on students' perceptions of their academic skill development during college. *Journal of Higher Education, 55,* 621-636.

33. Wainer, H. (1984). An exploratory analysis of performance on the SAT. *Journal of Educational Measurement, 21,* 81-91.

34. Wainer, H., Wadkins, J. R. J., & Rogers, A. (1984). Was there one distractor too many? *Journal of Educational Statistics, 9,* 5-24.

35. Wollman, W., & Lawrenz, F. (1984). Identifying potential 'dropouts' from college physics classes. *Journal of Research in Science Teaching, 21,* 385-390.

36. Alexander, V. D., & Thoits, P. A. (1985). Token achievement: An examination of proportional representation and performance outcomes. *Social Forces, 64,* 332-340.

37. Anderson, R. E. (1985). Does money matter? *Journal of Higher Education, 56,* 623-639.

38. Boli, J., Allen, M. L., & Payne, A. (1985). High-ability women and men in undergraduate mathematics and chemistry courses. *American Educational Research Journal, 22,* 605-626.

39. Caporael, L. R. (1985). College students' computer use. *Journal of Higher Education, 56,* 172-188.

40. Conklin, R. C. (1985). Teacher competency testing: The present situation and some concerns on how teachers are tested. *Education Canada, 25,* 12-15.

41. Crouse, J. (1985). Does the SAT help colleges make better selection decisions? *Harvard Educational Review, 55, 55,* 195-219.

42. Crouse, J. (1985). This time the college board is wrong. *Harvard Educational Review, 55,* 478-486.

43. Deboer, G. E. (1985). Characteristics of male and female students who experienced success or failure in their first college science course. *Journal of Research in Science Teaching, 22,* 153-162.

44. Deroyer, R., Baker, D., & White, M. (1985). Test score junkies. *The High School Journal, 69,* 1-5.

45. Dreher, M. J., & Singer, H. (1985). Predicting college success: Learning from text, background knowledge attitude toward school, and the SAT as predictors. *National Reading Conference Yearbook, 34,* 362-368.

46. Fischer, F. W., Shankweiler, D., & Liberman, I. Y. (1985). Spelling proficiency and sensitivity to word structure. *Journal of Memory and Language, 24,* 423-441.

47. Hanford, G. H. (1985). Yes, the SAT does help colleges. *Harvard Educational Review, 55,* 324-331.

48. Henry, T., Creswell, J., & Humphrey, E. (1985). Nebraska study looks at indicators of excellence, says centers of quality exist. *NASSP Bulletin, 69,* 87-93.

49. Hogrebe, M. C., Dwinell, P. L., & Ervin, L. (1985). Student perceptions as predictors of academic performance in college developmental studies. *Educational and Psychological Measurement, 45,* 639-646.

50. Malak, J. F., & Hegeman, J. N. (1985). Using Verbal SAT scores to predict Nelson-Denny scores for reading placements. *Journal of Reading, 28,* 301-309.

51. Markel, G., Bizer, L., & Wilhelm, R. M. (1985). The LD adolescent and the SAT. *Academic Therapy, 20,* 397-409.

52. Nelson, F. H. (1985). New perspectives on the teacher quality debate: Empirical evidence from the National Longitudinal Survey. *Journal of Educational Research, 78,* 133-140.

53. Nettles, M. T., Thoeny, A. R., & Gosman, E. J. (1986). Comparative and predictive analyses of black and white students' college achievement and experiences. *Journal of Higher Education, 57,* 289-318.

54. Noether, G. E. (1985). Elementary estimates: An introduction to nonparametrics. *Journal of Educational Statistics, 10,* 211-221.

55. Nowack, K. M., & Hanson, A. L. (1985). Academic achievement of freshmen as a function of residence hall housing. *NASPA Journal, 22*(3), 22-27.

56. Olivas, M. A. (1985). Financial and packaging policies: Access and ideology. *Journal of Higher Education, 56,* 462-475.

57. Pascarella, E. T. (1985). Students' affective development within the college environment. *Journal of Higher Education, 56,* 640-663.

58. Payne, D. A., & Evans, K. A. (1985). The relationship of laterality to academic aptitude. *Educational and Psychological Measurement, 45,* 971-976.

59. Rosenbaum, P. R., & Rubin, D. B. (1985). Discussion of "on state education statistics": A difficulty with regression analyses of regional test score averages. *Journal of Educational Statistics, 10,* 326-333.

60. Rosenstein, L. D. (1985). Effect of color of the environment on task performance and mood of males and females with high or low scores on the Scholastic Aptitude Test. *Perceptual and Motor Skills, 60,* 550.

61. Rounds, J., & Andersen, D. (1985). Assessment for entrance to community college: Research studies of three major standardized tests. *Journal of Research and Development in Education, 18*(2), 54-57.

62. Schaffner, P. E. (1985). Competitive admission practices when the SAT is optional. *Journal of Higher Education, 56,* 55-72.

63. Schuman, H., Walsh, E., Olson, C., & Etheridge, B. (1985). Effort and reward: The assumption that college grades are affected by quantity of study. *Social Forces, 63,* 945-966.

64. Siegel, R. G., Galassi, J. P., & Ware, W. B. (1985). A comparison of two models for predicting mathematics performance: Social learning versus math aptitude-anxiety. *Journal of Counseling Psychology, 32,* 531-538.

65. VanTassel-Baska, J. (1985). The talent search model: Implications for secondary school reform. *NAASP Bulletin, 69*(482), 39-47.

66. Wainer, H., Holland, P. W., Swinton, S., & Wang, M. H. (1985). On "state education statistics." *Journal of Educational Statistics, 10,* 293-325.

67. Ware, N. C., Steckler, N. A., & Leserman, J. (1985). Undergraduate women: Who chooses a science major? *Journal of Higher Education, 56,* 73-84.

68. White, W. F., Nylin, W. C., & Esser, P. R. (1985). Academic course grades as better predictors of graduation from a commuter-type college than SAT scores. *Psychological Reports, 56,* 375-378.

69. Benbow, C. P. (1986). Physiological correlates of extreme intellectual precocity. *Neuropsychologia, 24,* 719-725.

70. Benbow, C. P., & Minor, L. L. (1986). Mathematically talented males and females and achievement in the high school sciences. *American Educational Research Journal, 23,* 425-436.

71. Bickel, R., & Chang, M. (1986). Public schools, private schools, and high school achievement: A review and response with College Board Achievement Test data. *The High School Journal, 69,* 91-106.

72. Bron, G. D., & Gordon, M. P. (1986). Impact of an orientation center on grade point average and attrition. *The College Student Journal, 20,* 242-246.

73. Bunce, D. M., & Heikkinen, H. (1986). The effects of an explicit problem-solving approach on mathematical chemistry achievement. *Journal of Research in Science Teaching, 23,* 11-20.

74. Centra, J. A. (1986). Handicapped student performance on the Scholastic Aptitude Test. *Journal of Learning Disabilities, 19,* 324-327.

75. Deboer, G. E. (1986). Perceived science ability as a factor in the course selections of men and women in college. *Journal of Research in Science Teaching, 23,* 343-352.

76. Hellman, D. A., & Beaton, S. (1986). The pattern of violence in urban public schools: The influence of school and community. *Journal of Research in Crime and Delinquency, 23,* 102-127.

77. Mannan, G., Charleston, L., & Saghafi, B. (1986). A comparison of the academic performance of black and white freshman students on an urban commuter campus. *Journal of Negro Education, 55,* 155-161.

78. Page, E. B., & Feifs, H. (1986). SAT scores and American states: Seeking for useful meaning. *Journal of Educational Measurement, 22,* 305-312.

79. Pollins, L. D. (1986). Quality of in-school special services and the school/university program relationships for extremely gifted students. *Journal of Special Education, 19,* 103-110.

80. Raymond, C. L., & Benbow, C. P. (1986). Gender differences in mathematics: A function of parental support and student sex typing? *Developmental Psychology, 22,* 808-819.

81. Rubin, D. L., & Rafoth, B. A. (1986). Social cognitive ability as a predictor of the quality of expository and persuasive writing among college freshmen. *Research in the Teaching of English, 20,* 9-21.

82. Singer, J. M., & Stake, J. E. (1986). Mathematics and self-esteem: Implications for women's career choice. *Psychology of Women Quarterly, 10,* 339-352.

83. Solmon, L. C., & LaPorte, M. A. (1986). The crisis of student quality in higher education. *Journal of Higher Education, 57,* 370-392.

84. Spring, C., Sassenrath, J., & Ketellapper, H. (1986). Ecological validity of adjunct questions in a college biology course. *Contemporary Educational Psychology, 11,* 79- 89.

85. Stanley, J. C., & Stanley, B. S. K. (1986). High-school biology, chemistry, or physics learned well in three weeks. *Journal of Research in Science Teaching, 23,* 237-250.

86. Wainer, H. (1986). Five pitfalls encountered while trying to compare states on their SAT scores. *Journal of Educational Measurement, 23,* 69-81.

87. Weiner, N. C., & Robinson, S. E. (1986). Cognitive abilities, personality and gender differences in math achievement of gifted adolescents. *Gifted Child Quarterly, 30,* 83-87.

88. Weiss, A. S., Mangrum, C. T., II, & Llabre, M. M. (1986). Differential effects of differing vocabulary presentation. *Reading Research and Instruction, 25,* 265-276.

89. Williams, R. A., Lusk, S. L., & Kline, N. W. (1986). Knowledge of aging and cognitive styles in baccalaureate nursing students. *The Gerontologist, 26,* 545-550.

90. Dyer, H. S. (1987). The effects of coaching for scholastic aptitude. *NASSP Bulletin, 71*(496), 46-53.

91. Houston, L. N. (1987). The predictive validity of a study habits inventory for first semester undergraduates. *Educational and Psychological Measurement, 47*(4), 1025-1030.

92. Hull, J. G., Van Treuren, R. R., & Virnelli, S. (1987). Hardiness and health: A critique and alternative approach. *Journal of Personality and Social Psychology, 53,* 518-530.

93. Jones, L. K. (1987). Adapting to the first semester of college: A test of Heath's model of maturing. *Journal of College Student Personnel, 28,* 205-211.

94. Peterson, C., & Barrett, L. C. (1987). Explanatory style and academic performance among university freshmen. *Journal of Personality and Social Psychology, 53,* 603-607.

95. Rock, D. A., Bennett, R. E., & Kaplan, B. A. (1987). Internal construct validity of a college admissions test across handicapped and nonhandicapped groups. *Educational and Psychological Measurement, 47*(1), 193-205.

96. Schurr, K. T., Ellen, A. S., & Ruble, V. E. (1987). Actual course difficulty as a factor in accounting for the achievement and attrition of college students. *Educational and Psychological Measurement, 47*(4), 1049-1054.

97. Beckham, J. C., Carbonell, J. L., & Gustafson, D. J. (1988). Are there sex differences in problem solving? An investigation of problem context and sex role type. *The Journal of Psychology, 122,* 21-32.

98. Benton, S. L., Kiewra, K. A., & Beans, R. O. (1988). Attributes of organizational ability related to writing ability. *Contemporary Educational Psychology, 13,* 87-89.

99. Cook, L. L., Dorans, N. J., & Eignor, D. R. (1988). An assessment of the dimensionality of three SAT-verbal test editions. *Journal of Educational Statistics, 13,* 19-43.

100. Glass, C. R., & Knight, L. A. (1988). Cognitive factors in computer anxiety. *Cognitive Therapy and Research, 12,* 351-366.

101. Humphreys, L. G. (1988). Trends in levels of academic achievement of blacks and other minorities. *Intelligence, 12,* 231-260.

102. Marchant, H. G., III, Royer, J. M., & Greene, B. A. (1988). Superior reliability and validity for a new form of sentence verification technique for measuring comprehension. *Educational and Psychological Measurement, 48,* 827-834.

103. McCauley, D. P. (1988). Effects of specific factors on blacks' persistence at a predominantly white university. *Journal of College Student Development, 29,* 48-51.

104. Payne, D. A. (1988). Brain dominance cognitive style and the Graduate Record Examination Aptitude Test. *Educational and Psychological Measurement, 48*(1), 175-179.

105. Pollio, H. R., Eison, J. A., & Milton, O. (1988). College grades as an adaptation level phenomenon. *Contemporary Educational Psychology, 13,* 146-156.

106. Schurr, K. T., Ruble, V. E., & Henriksen, L. W. (1988). Relationships of Myers-Briggs Type Indicator personality characteristics and self-reported academic problems and skill ratings with Scholastic Aptitude Test scores. *Educational and Psychological Measurement, 48,* 187-196.

107. Dorans, N. J. (1989). Two new approaches to assessing differential item functioning: Standardization and the Mantel-Haenzel method. *Applied Measurement in Education, 2,* 217-233.

108. Epstein, S., & Meier, P. (1989). Constructive thinking: A broad coping variable with specific components. *Journal of Personality and Social Psychology, 57,* 332-350.

109. Galicki, S. J., & McEwen, M. K. (1989). The relationship of residence to retention of black and white undergraduate students at a predominantly white university. *Journal of College Student Development, 30,* 389-394.

110. Larson, G. E., & Saccuzzo, D. P. (1989). Cognitive correlates of general intelligence: Toward a process theory of g. *Intelligence, 13,* 5-31.

111. Schurr, K. T., Ruble, V. E., Henriksen, L. W., & Alcorn, B. K. (1989). Relationships of National Teacher Examination Communication Skills and General Knowledge scores with high school and college grades, Myers-Briggs Type Indicator characteristics, and self-reported skill ratings and academic problems. *Educational and Psychological Measurement, 49,* 243-252.

112. Trippi, J. F., & Baker, S. B. (1989). Student and residential correlates of black student grade performance and persistence at a predominantly white university campus. *Journal of College Student Development, 30,* 136-143.

113. Trippi, J., & Stewart, J. B. (1989). The relationship between self-appraisal variables and the college grade performance and persistence of Black freshmen. *Journal of College Student Development, 30,* 484-491.

114. Wainer, H. (1989). Eelworms, bullet holes, and Geraldine Ferraro: Some problems with statistical adjustment and some solutions. *Journal of Educational Statistics, 14,* 121-140.

115. Dwinell, P. L., & Ginter, E. J. (1990). Developmental factors and performance in remedial courses. *Psychological Reports, 66,* 35-38.

116. Eignor, D. R., Stocking, M. L., & Cook, L. L. (1990). Simulation results of effects on linear and curvilinear observed- and true-score equating procedures of matching on a falliable criterion. *Applied Measurement in Education, 3*(1), 37-52.

117. Gregg, N., & Hoy, C. (1990). Referencing: The cohesive use of pronouns in the written narrative of college underprepared writers, nondisabled writers, and writers with learning disabilities. *Journal of Learning Disabilities, 23,* 557-563.

118. Holland, P. W., & Wainer, H. (1990). Sources of uncertainty often ignored in adjusting state mean SAT scores for differential participa-

tion rates: The rules of the game. *Applied Measurement in Education, 3*(2), 167-184.

119. Lawrence, I. M., & Dorans, N. J. (1990). Effect on equating results of matching samples on an anchor test. *Applied Measurement in Education, 3*(1), 19-36.

120. Linn, R. L. (1990). Admissions Testing: Recommended uses, validity, differential prediction, and coaching. *Applied Measurement in Education, 3*(4), 297-318.

121. Livingston, S. A., Dorans, N. J., & Wright, N. K. (1990). What combination of sampling and equating methods works best? *Applied Measurement in Education, 3*(1), 93-95.

122. Nist, S. L., & Simpson, M. L. (1990). The effects of PLAE upon students' test performance and metacognitive awareness. *Yearbook of the National Reading Conference, 39,* 321-327.

123. Pace, A. J., Walters, K., & Sherk, J. K. (1990). What determines course achievement? An investigation of several possible influences on academic outcomes. *Yearbook of the National Reading Conference, 39,* 374-351.

124. Pennebaker, J. W., Colder, M., & Sharp, L. K. (1990). Accelerating the coping process. *Journal of Personality and Social Psychology, 58,* 528-537.

125. Pressley, M., Ghatala, E., Pirie, J., & Woloshyn, V. E. (1990). Being really, really certain you know the main idea doesn't mean you do. *Yearbook of the National Reading Conference, 39,* 249-256.

126. Arbona, C., & Novy, D. M. (1991). Hispanic college students: Are there within-group differences? *Journal of College Student Development, 32,* 335-341.

127. Britton, B. K., & Gülgöz, S. (1991). Using Kintsch's computational model to improve instructional text: Effects of repairing inference calls on recall and cognitive structures. *Journal of Educational Psychology, 83,* 329-345.

128. Britton, B. K., & Tesser, A. (1991). Effects of time-management practices on college grades. *Journal of Educational Psychology, 83,* 405-510.

129. Cantor, J., Engle, R. W., & Hamilton, G. (1991). Short-term memory, working memory, and verbal abilities: How do they relate? *Intelligence, 15,* 229-246.

130. Dark, V. J., & Benbow, C. P. (1991). Differential enhancement of working memory with mathematical versus verbal precocity. *Journal of Educational Psychology, 83,* 48-60.

131. Frost, S. H. (1991). Fostering the critical thinking of college women through academic advising and faculty contact. *Journal of College Student Development, 32,* 359-366.

132. Hatcher, L., Prus, J. S., Englehard, B., & Farmer, T. M. (1991). A measure of academic situational constraints: Out-of-class circumstances that inhibit college student development. *Educational and Psychological Measurement, 51,* 953-962.

133. Hertel, P. T., & Rude, S. S. (1991). Recalling in a state of natural or experimental depression. *Cognitive Therapy and Research, 15,* 103-127.

134. Kalichman, S. C. (1991). Water levels, falling objects, and spiral tubes: An investigation of the general naivete hypothesis of physical task performance. *The Journal of Genetic Psychology, 152,* 255-262.

135. Katz, S., Blackburn, A. B., & Lautenschlager, G. J. (1991). Answering reading comprehension items without passages on the SAT when items are quasi-randomized. *Educational and Psychological Measurement, 51,* 747-754.

136. Mislevy, R. J., Beaton, A. E., Kaplan, B., & Sheehan, K. M. (1991). Estimating population characteristics from sparse matrix samples of item responses. *Journal of Educational Measurement, 29,* 133-161.

137. Robbins, A. S., Spence, J. T., & Clark, H. (1991). Psychological determinants of health and performance: The tangled web of desirable and undesirable characteristics. *Journal of Personality and Social Psychology, 61,* 755-765.

138. Sher, K. J., Walitzer, K. S., Wood, P. K., & Brent, E. E. (1991). Characteristics of children of alcoholics: Putative risk factors, substance use and abuse, and psychopathology. *Journal of Abnormal Psychology, 100,* 427-448.

139. Sireci, S. G., Thissen, D., & Wainer, H. (1991). On the reliability of testlet-based tests. *Journal of Educational Measurement, 28,* 237-247.

140. Trippi, J., & Cheatham, H. E. (1991). Counseling effects on African American college student graduation. *Journal of College Student Development, 32,* 342-349.

141. Wainer, H., Sireci, S. G., & Thissen, D. (1991). Differential testlet functioning: Definitions and detection. *Journal of Educational Measurement, 28,* 197-219.

142. Watson, B. U. (1991). Some relationships between intelligence and auditory discrimination. *Journal of Speech and Hearing Research, 34,* 621-627.

143. Willerman, L., Schultz, R., Rutledge, J. N., & Bigler, E. D. (1991). In vivo brain size and intelligence. *Intelligence, 15,* 223-228.

144. Young, J. W. (1991). Improving the prediction of college performance of ethnic minorities using the IRT-based GPA. *Applied Measurement in Education, 4*(3), 229-239.

145. Aspinwall, L. G., & Taylor, S. E. (1992). Modeling cognitive adaptation: A longitudinal investigation of the impact of individual differences and coping on college adjustment and performance. *Journal of Personality and Social Psychology, 63,* 989-1003.

146. Becker, B. J. (1992). Using results from replicated studies to estimate linear models. *Journal of Educational Statistics, 17,* 341-362.

147. Chartrand, J. M., Camp, C. C., & McFadden, K. L. (1992). Predicting academic adjustment and career indecision: A comparison of self-efficacy, interest congruence, and commitment. *Journal of College Student Development, 33,* 293-300.

148. D'zurilla, T. J., & Sheedy, C. F. (1992). The relation between social problem-solving ability and subsequent level of academic competence in college students. *Cognitive Therapy and Research, 16,* 589-599.

149. Dorans, N. J., Schmitt, A. P., & Bleistein, C. A. (1992). The standardization approach to assessing comprehensive differential item functioning. *Journal of Educational Measurement, 29,* 309-319.

150. Goldman, S. R., & Murray, J. D. (1992). Knowledge of connectors and cohesion devices in text: A comparative study of Native-English and English-as-a-second-language speakers. *Journal of Educational Psychology, 84,* 504-519.

151. Hall, V. C., & Edmondson, B. (1992). Relative importance of aptitude and prior domain knowledge on immediate and delayed posttests. *Journal of Educational Psychology, 84,* 219-223.

152. King, J. (1992). Comparison of self-questioning, summarizing, and notetaking-review as strategies for learning from lectures. *American Educational Research Journal, 29,* 303-323.

153. King-Johnson, D. A. (1992). Using analogies to form conceptual models to facilitate transfer. *Contemporary Educational Psychology, 17,* 1-7.

154. Mills, C. J., Ablard, K. E., & Lynch, S. J. (1992). Academically talented students' preparation for advanced-level coursework after individually-paced precalculus class. *Journal for the Education of the Gifted, 16,* 3-17.

155. Roznowski, M., & Bassett, J. (1992). Training test-wiseness and flawed item types. *Applied Measurement in Education, 5*(1), 35-48.

156. Watson, B. U. (1992). Auditory temporal acuity in normally achieving and learning-disabled college students. *Journal of Speech and Hearing Research, 35,* 148-156.

157. Wilczenski, F. L., & Gillespie-Silver, P. (1992). Challenging the norm: Academic performance of university students with learning disabilities. *Journal of College Student Development, 33,* 197-202.

158. Young, B. D., & Sowa, C. J. (1992). Predictors of academic success for Black student athletes. *Journal of College Student Development, 33,* 318-324.

159. Baron, J., & Norman, M. F. (1993). SATs, achievement tests, and high-school class rank as predictors of college performance. *Educational and Psychological Measurement, 52,* 1047-1055.

160. Carson, C. C., Huelskamp, R. M., & Woodall, T. D. (1993). Perspectives on education in America: An annotated briefing, April 1992. *Journal of Educational Research, 86,* 267-278.

161. Frary, R. B. (1993). Statistical detection of multiple-choice answer copying: Review and commentary. *Applied Measurement in Education, 6*(2), 153-165.

162. Nandakumar, R., & Stout, W. (1993). Refinements of Stout's procedure for assessing latent trait unidimensionality. *Journal of Educational Statistics, 18,* 41-68.

163. Peutony, J. F. (1993). Cultural literacy: A concurrent validation. *Educational and Psychological Measurement, 52,* 967-972.

164. Redmond, M. R., Mumford, M. D., & Teach, R. (1993). Putting creativity to work: Effects of leader behavior on subordinate creativity. *Organizational Behavior and Human Decision Processes, 55,* 120-151.

165. Schnurr, P. P., Rosenberg, S. D., & Friedman, M. J. (1993). Change in MMPI scores from college to adulthood as a function of military service. *Journal of Abnormal Psychology, 102,* 288-296.

166. Shepperd, J. A. (1993). Developing a prediction model to reduce a growing number of psychology majors. *Teaching of Psychology, 20,* 97-101.

167. Williams, V. S. L., & Wakeford, M. E. (1993). The predictive validity of the National Teachers Examinations used for admission to teacher education programs. *Educational and Psychological Measurement, 53,* 533-539.

[565]

College Board SAT II: Subject Test in American History and Social Studies.

Purpose: To measure achievement in American history and social studies.

Population: Candidates for college entrance.
Publication Dates: 1937–94.
Administration: Group.
Price Data: Available from publisher.
Comments: Test administered 5 times annually (January, May, June, November, December) at centers established by publisher; active form, entitled College Board One-Hour Achievement Test in American History and Social Studies, is available for local administration and scoring by colleges, universities, and other appropriate organizations; replaces College Board Achievement Test in American History and Social Studies.
Authors: Program administered by The College Board and Educational Testing Service.
Publisher: Educational Testing Service.
Cross References: See T2:1939 (1 reference); for a review by Howard R. Anderson of earlier forms, see 6:966; for a review by Ralph W. Tyler, see 5:786 (3 references); for a review by Robert L. Thorndike, see 4:662 (6 references). For reviews of an earlier form of the testing program, see 6:760 (2 reviews).

TEST REFERENCES

1. Bickel, R., & Chang, M. (1986). Public schools, private schools, and high school achievement: A review and response with College Board Achievement Test data. *The High School Journal, 69,* 91-106.

[566]

College Board SAT II: Test in Biology.

Purpose: To measure achievement in biology.
Population: Candidates for college entrance.
Publication Dates: 1915–94.
Administration: Group.
Price Data: Available from publisher.
Comments: Test administered 5 times annually (January, May, June, November, December) at centers established by publisher; active form, entitled College Board One-Hour Achievement Test in Biology, is available for local administration and scoring by colleges, universities, and other appropriate organizations; replaces College Board Achievement Test in Biology.
Authors: Program administered by The College Board and Educational Testing Service.
Publisher: Educational Testing Service.
Cross References: See 8:833 (1 reference), 7:813 (2 references), and 6:892 (3 references); for a review by Elizabeth Hagen of an earlier form, see 5:723; for a review by Clark W. Horton, see 4:600. For reviews of an earlier form of the testing program, see 6:760 (2 reviews).

[567]

College Board SAT II: Subject Test in Chemistry.

Purpose: To measure achievement in chemistry.
Population: Candidates for college entrance.
Publication Dates: 1937–94.
Administration: Group.
Price Data: Available from publisher.

Comments: Test administered 5 times annually (January, May, June, November, December) at centers established by the publisher; active form, entitled College Board One-Hour Achievement Test in Chemistry, is available for local administration and scoring by colleges, universities, and other appropriate organizations.
Authors: Program administered by The College Board and Educational Testing Service.
Publisher: Educational Testing Service.
Cross References: See 7:844 (3 references); for a review by William Hered of earlier forms, see 6:914 (4 references); for a review by Max D. Engehart, see 5:742 (2 references); for a review by Evelyn Raskin, see 4:617 (4 references). For reviews of an earlier form of the testing program, see 6:760 (2 reviews).

TEST REFERENCES

1. Angoff, W. H., & Schrader, W. B. (1984). A study of hypotheses basic to the use of rights and formula scores. *Journal of Educational Measurement, 21,* 1-17.

[568]

College Board SAT II: Subject Test in Chinese with Listening.

Purpose: To measure achievement in Chinese.
Population: Candidates for college entrance with 2–4 years high school Chinese.
Publication Date: 1994.
Scores, 4: Usage, Listening, Reading, Total.
Administration: Group.
Price Data: Available from publisher.
Comments: Test administered once annually (November) in high schools.
Author: Program administered by The College Board and Educational Testing Service.
Publisher: Educational Testing Service.

[569]

College Board SAT II: Subject Test in Italian.

Purpose: To measure achievement in Italian.
Population: Candidates for college entrance with 2–4 years high school Italian.
Publication Dates: 1990–94.
Scores, 4: Usage, Listening, Reading, Total.
Administration: Group.
Price Data: Available from publisher.
Comments: Test administered once annually (December) at centers established by publisher.
Author: Program administered by The College Board and Educational Testing Service.
Publisher: Educational Testing Service.

[570]

College Board SAT II: Subject Test in Japanese with Listening.

Purpose: To measure achievement in Japanese.
Population: Candidates for college entrance with 2–4 years high school Japanese.
Publication Dates: 1993–94.
Scores, 4: Usage, Listening, Reading, Total.

Administration: Group.
Price Data: Available from publisher.
Comments: Test administered once annually (November) in high schools.
Author: Program administered by The College Board and Educational Testing Service.
Publisher: Educational Testing Service.

[571]

College Board SAT II: Subject Test in Latin.
Purpose: To measure achievement in Latin.
Population: Candidates for college entrance with 2–4 years high school Latin.
Publication Dates: 1937–94.
Administration: Group.
Price Data: Available from publisher.
Comments: Test administered 2 times annually (June, December) at centers established by the publisher; active forms, entitled College Board One-Hour Achievement Test in Latin, are available for local administration and scoring by colleges, universities, and other appropriate organizations; replaces College Board Achievement Test in Latin.
Authors: Program administered by The College Board and Educational Testing Service.
Publisher: Educational Testing Service.
Cross References: For a review by Konrad Gries of an earlier form, see 5:280 (1 reference); for a review by Harold B. Dunkel, see 4:250 (2 references). For reviews of an earlier form of the testing program, see 6:760 (2 reviews).

[572]

College Board SAT II: Subject Test in Literature.
Purpose: To measure achievement in literature.
Population: Candidates for college entrance.
Publication Dates: 1968–94.
Administration: Group.
Price Data: Available from publisher.
Comments: Test administered 5 times annually (January, May, June, November, December) at centers established by the publisher; an active form, entitled College Board One-Hour Achievement Test in Literature, is available for local administration and scoring by colleges, universities, and other appropriate organizations; replaces College Board Achievement Test in Literature.
Authors: Program administered by The College Board and Educational Testing Service.
Publisher: Educational Testing Service.
Cross References: See 7:217 (2 references). For reviews of an earlier form of the testing program, see 6:760 (2 reviews).

[573]

College Board SAT II: Subject Test in Modern Hebrew.
Purpose: To measure achievement in Hebrew.
Population: Candidates for college entrance with 2–4 years high school Hebrew.

Publication Dates: 1989–94.
Administration: Group.
Price Data: Available from publisher.
Comments: Test administered once annually (June) at centers established by the publisher; an active form, entitled College Board One-Hour Achievement Test in Modern Hebrew, is available for local administration and scoring by colleges, universities, and other appropriate organizations.
Authors: Program administered by The College Board and Educational Testing Service.
Publisher: Educational Testing Service.
Cross References: For reviews of an earlier form of the testing program, see 6:760 (2 reviews).

[574]

College Board SAT II: Subject Test in Physics.
Purpose: To measure achievement in physics.
Population: Candidates for college entrance.
Publication Dates: 1937–94.
Administration: Group.
Price Data: Available from publisher.
Comments: Test administered 5 times annually (January, May, June, November, December) at centers established by the publisher; active forms, entitled College Board One-Hour Achievement Test in Physics, are available for local administration and scoring by colleges, universities, and other appropriate organizations; replaces College Board Achievement Test in Physics.
Authors: Program administered by The College Board and Educational Testing Service.
Publisher: Educational Testing Service.
Cross References: See 8:863 (1 reference), 7:855 (2 references), and 6:926 (4 references); for a review by Theodore G. Phillips of an earlier form, see 5:749 (2 references); for a review by Palmer O. Johnson, see 4:633 (3 references). For reviews of an earlier form of the testing program, see 6:760 (2 reviews).

TEST REFERENCES

1. Kopp, C. B., & Vaughn, B. E. (1982). Sustained attention during exploratory manipulation as a predictor of cognitive competence in pre-term infants. *Child Development, 53,* 174-182.

[575]

College Board SAT II: Subject Test in World History.
Purpose: To measure achievement in world history.
Population: Candidates for college entrance.
Publication Dates: 1937–94.
Administration: Group.
Price Data: Available from publisher.
Comments: Test administered 2 times annually (June, December) at centers established by the publisher; active form, entitled College Board One-Hour Achievement Test in World History, is available for local administration and scoring by colleges, universities, and other appropriate organizations; replaces College Board Achievement Test in European History and World Cultures.

Authors: Program administered by The College Board and Educational Testing Service.
Publisher: Educational Testing Service.
Cross References: For a review by David K. Heenan of earlier forms, see 6:967. For reviews of an earlier form of the testing program, see 6:760 (2 reviews).

[576]
College Board SAT II: Subject Tests in French.

Purpose: To measure achievement in French.
Population: Candidates for college entrance with 2–4 years high school French.
Publication Dates: 1937–94.
Scores, 3: Reading, Listening, Total.
Administration: Group.
Price Data: Available from publisher.
Comments: The French Reading Test is administered 4 times annually (January, May, June, December) at centers established by the publisher; active form, entitled College Board One-Hour Achievement Test in French Reading, is available for local administration and scoring by colleges, universities, and other appropriate organizations; the French Subject Test with Listening is administered once annually (November) in high schools and is not yet available for local scoring and administration.
Authors: Program administered by The College Board and Educational Testing Service.
Publisher: Educational Testing Service.
Cross References: For a review by Helen L. Jorstad, see 8:116; see also 6:366 (4 references) and 5:263 (2 references); for a review by Walter V. Kaulfers of earlier forms, see 4:237 (7 references). For reviews of an earlier form of the testing program, see 6:760 (2 reviews).

[577]
College Board SAT II: Subject Tests in German.

Purpose: To measure achievement in German.
Population: Candidates for college entrance with 2–4 years high school German.
Publication Dates: 1937–94.
Scores, 3: Reading, Listening, Total.
Administration: Group.
Price Data: Available from publisher.
Comments: The German Reading test is administered 2 times annually (June, December) at centers established by the publisher; active forms, entitled College Board One-Hour Achievement Test in German Reading, are available for local administration and scoring by colleges, universities, and other appropriate organizations; the German Subject Tests with Listening is administered once annually (November) in high schools and is not yet available for local scoring and administration.
Authors: Program administered by The College Board and Educational Testing Service.
Publisher: Educational Testing Service.

Cross References: For a review by Randall L. Jones of an earlier form, see 8:128; for a review by Gilbert C. Kettelkamp of earlier forms, see 6:383; for a review by Harold B. Dunkel, see 5:272 (3 references); for a review by Herbert Shueler, see 4:244 (3 references). For reviews of an earlier form of the testing program, see 6:760 (2 reviews).

[578]
College Board SAT II: Subject Tests in Mathematics.

Purpose: To measure achievement in mathematics.
Population: Candidates for college entrance.
Publication Dates: 1937–94.
Administration: Group.
Price Data: Available from publisher.
Comments: Administered 5 times annually (January, May, June, November, December) at centers established by publisher; active forms entitled College Board One-Hour Achievement Tests in Mathematics, Level 1 and Level 2 are available for local administration and scoring by colleges, universities, and other appropriate organizations; replaces College Board Achievement Tests in Mathematics; the final administration of the Level 2 test was January 1994; it will be replaced by the Mathematics Level IIC Subject Test (requires use of a scientific calculator) at all administrations beginning May 1994; the Level 2C Test will be available for local administration and scoring by colleges, universities, and other appropriate organizations beginning fall 1994..
Authors: Program administered by The College Board and Educational Testing Service.
Publisher: Educational Testing Service.
Cross References: For reviews by Jeremy Kilpatrick and Peter A. Lappan, Jr. of Level 1, see 8:258 (4 references); see also 7:456 (4 references). For additional information concerning Level 2, see 8:259 (1 reference); see also 7:457 (1 reference). For reviews of earlier forms of the testing program, see 6:760 (2 reviews).

TEST REFERENCES

1. Bickel, R., & Chang, M. (1986). Public schools, private schools, and high school achievement: A review and response with College Board Achievement Test data. *The High School Journal, 69,* 91-106.
2. Harris, A. M., & Carlton, S. T. (1993). Patterns of gender differences on mathematics items on the Scholastic Aptitude Test. *Applied Measurement in Education, 6*(2), 137-151.

[579]
College Board SAT II: Subject Tests in Spanish.

Purpose: To measure achievement in Spanish.
Population: Candidates for college entrance with 2–4 years high school Spanish.
Publication Dates: 1937–94.
Administration: Group.
Price Data: Available from publisher.
Comments: The Spanish Reading Test is administered 4 times annually (January, May, June, December) at centers established by the publisher; active

forms, entitled College Board One-Hour Achievement Test in Spanish Reading, are available for local administration and scoring by colleges, universities, and other appropriate organizations; the Spanish Subject Test with Listening is administered once annually (November) in high schools and is not yet available for local administration and scoring.
Authors: Program administered by The College Board and Educational Testing Service.
Publisher: Educational Testing Service.
Cross References: See 6:419 (1 reference), 5:287 (1 reference), and 4:259 (3 references). For reviews of an earlier form of the testing program, see 6:760 (2 reviews).

[580]

College Board SAT II: Writing Subject Test.
Purpose: To measure students' writing skills.
Population: Candidates for college entrance.
Publication Dates: 1943–93.
Scores, 3: Writing Sample, Multiple-Choice, Total.
Administration: Group.
Manual: No manual.
Price Data: Available from publisher.
Time: (60) minutes.
Comments: Test administered 5 times annually (January, May, June, November, December) at centers established by publisher; available for local administration and scoring by colleges, universities, and other appropriate organizations beginning fall 1994; replaces College Board English Composition Test.
Author: Educational Testing Service.
Publisher: Educational Testing Service.
Cross References: For reviews by Dale P. Scannell and John C. Sherwood of an earlier form, see 9:243. For reviews on the College Board Achievement Test in English Composition (without essay) by David P. Harris and Leo P. Ruth, see 8:46 (2 references); see also T2:64 (1 reference) and 7:188 (10 references); for reviews by Charlotte Croon Davis, Robert C. Pooley, and Holland Roberts of earlier forms, see 6:287 (6 references); see also 5:204 (14 references); for a review by Charlotte Croon Davis (with Frederick B. Davis), see 4:178 (6 references). For reviews of an earlier form of the testing program, see 6:760 (2 reviews).

TEST REFERENCES

1. Breland, H. M., & Duran, R. P. (1985). Assessing English composition skills in Spanish-speaking populations. *Educational and Psychological Measurement, 45,* 309-318.
2. Bickel, R., & Chang, M. (1986). Public schools, private schools, and high school achievement: A review and response with College Board Achievement Test data. *The High School Journal, 69,* 91-106.

[581]

College Board SAT Program.
Purpose: To provide "tests and related educational services for students who plan to continue their education beyond high school."
Population: Candidates for college entrance.
Publication Dates: 1901–94.
Acronym: SAT Program.

Administration: Group.
Price Data: Price data is available from the publisher for priced and free materials including technical report ('84, 225 pages), supervisor's manual ('94, 48 pages), student bulletins, test familiarization material for students, score use and interpretation booklets for counselors and admissions officers, summary report guides for high schools and for colleges, state and national reports on college-bound seniors, guide to the College Board Validity Study Service, SAT Program Guide, and test and technical data; examination fees include reporting of scores to the candidate's secondary school and 1–4 colleges and/or scholarship services.
Comments: Formerly called the College Board Admissions Testing Program; the SAT I is administered 7 times annually (January, March or April, May, June, October, November, December) at centers established by the publisher; the SAT II: Subject Tests are administered 5 times annually (January, May, June, November, December) at centers established by the publisher, though not all tests are available at each administration; several SAT II Tests are only available in participating secondary schools one time per year; Student Descriptive Questionnaire provides background information to colleges and scholarship services; special administration arrangements available for students with disabilities, including Braille, cassette tape, regular type, and large-type editions available with extra time.
Author: Educational Testing Service.
Publisher: Educational Testing Service.
a) COLLEGE BOARD SAT I: REASONING TEST.
Publication Dates: 1926–94.
Acronym: SAT I.
Price Data: Examination fee per candidate available from publisher.
Time: (180) minutes.
Comments: The SAT I: Reasoning Test replaced the College Board Scholastic Aptitude Test and the Test of Standard Written English in 1994. Scores from Verbal Reasoning and Math Reasoning sections of the SAT I are on the same scale and comparable to those of the earlier SAT. The vocabulary and reading subscores have been discontinued in the SAT I. Score analysis data by item type/content available for Verbal and Math beginning in 1994. The Test of Standard Written English, administered with the SAT, has been discontinued with the advent of the SAT I. The SAT I scale will be recentered in 1995; equivalence tables will be available for converting scores from one scale to another. SAT forms are available for local administration and scoring through the College Entry-Level Assessment (CELA) Program. SAT I forms will be offered through CELA in the near future.
b) COLLEGE BOARD SAT II: SUBJECT TESTS.
Publication Dates: 1901–94.
Scores: 21 tests in 17 subjects: Writing (including an essay at every national administration), Literature, American History & Social Studies, World History, Math Level I, Math Level IIC (Calcula-

tor), Biology, Chemistry, Physics, French (reading only), French (reading and listening), German (reading only), German (reading and listening), Spanish (reading only), Spanish (reading and listening), Modern Hebrew, Italian, Latin, Japanese (reading and listening), Chinese (reading and listening), and English Language Proficiency (to be introduced in 1995, reading and listening).

Price Data: Examination fees per candidate available from publisher. Price data for guidelines on the uses of College Board test scores and related data, guide to the College Board Validity Study Service, Writing Sample Copy Service, technical handbook, SAT Program guide, student bulletins, Taking the SAT II, test and technical data, and Clerical Scoring Service are all available from the publisher.

Time: (60) minutes.

Comments: Formerly called the College Board Achievement Tests; candidate elects 1 to 3 tests as specified by individual college or scholarship program requirements; language tests having a listening component are only administered in participating high schools; candidates have the option of reviewing their SAT II scores prior to deciding whether or not to have these scores reported to colleges or scholarship services; some Subject Tests are available for local administration and scoring through the College Entry-Level Assessment Program. Large-type and Braille versions of some tests are available for students with disabilities. The administration schedule of each Subject Test is available from the publisher.

Cross References: See T3:500 (3 references), 8:472 (6 references), T2:1048 (9 references), and 7:663 (16 references); for reviews by Benno G. Fricke and Dean K. Whitla of an earlier program, see 6:760 (12 references); see also 5:599 (3 references) and 4:526 (9 references). For reviews of individual tests, see 8:46 (2 reviews), 8:128 (1 review), 8:147 (1 review), 8:258 (2 reviews), 7:344 (2 reviews), 6:287 (3 reviews, 6:289 (1 review), 6:383 (1 review), 6:384 (2 reviews), 6:449 (2 reviews), 6:568 (1 review), 6:569 (1 review), 6:914 (1 review), 6:966 (1 review), 6:967 (1 review), 5:272 (1 review), 5:277 (1 review), 5:280 (1 review), 5:318 (1 review), 5:723 (1 review), 5:742 (1 review), 5:749 (1 review), 5:786 (1 review), 4:178 (1 review), 4:237 (1 review), 4:244 (1 review), 4:250 (1 review), 4:285 (1 review), 4:367 (1 review), 4:368 (1 review), 4:600 (1 review), 4:617 (1 review), 4:633 (1 review), and 4:662 (1 review).

[582]

College Characteristics Index.

Purpose: "A measure of college climate."

Population: College.

Publication Dates: 1957–70.

Acronym: CCI.

Scores, 49: 30 press scores (Abasement-Assurance, Achievement, Adaptability-Defensiveness, Affiliation, Aggression-Blame Avoidance, Change-Sameness, Conjunctivity-Disjunctivity, Counteraction, Deference-Restiveness, Dominance-Tolerance, Ego Achievement, Emotionality-Placidity, Energy-Passivity, Exhibitionism-Inferiority Avoidance, Fantasied Achievement, Harm Avoidance-Risk Taking, Humanities and Social Science, Impulsiveness-Deliberation, Narcissism, Nurturance, Objectivity-Projectivity, Order-Disorder, Play-Work, Practicalness-Impracticalness, Reflectiveness, Science, Sensuality-Puritanism, Sexuality-Prudishness, Supplication-Autonomy, Understanding), 11 factor scores (Aspiration Level, Intellectual Climate, Student Dignity, Academic Climate, Academic Achievement, Self Expression, Group Life, Academic Organization, Social Form, Play-Work, Vocational Climate) based on combinations of the press scores, 3 second-order factor scores (Intellectual Climate, Non-Intellectual Climate, Impulse Control), 5 composite culture factor scores (Expressive, Intellectual, Protective, Vocational, Collegiate) based on combinations of need scores with press scores.

Administration: Group.

Forms, 2: Long, Short.

Price Data: Not available.

Time: (20–25) minutes for short form; (40–45) minutes for long form.

Comments: Previously listed under Stern Environment Indexes; press scores obtained using long form only; self-administered.

Authors: George G. Stern and C. Robert Pace (long form).

Publisher: FAAX Corporation [No reply from publisher; status unknown].

Cross References: See T3:502 (1 reference) and T2:1395 (38 references); for reviews by Wilbur L. Layton and Rodney W. Skager, see 7:143 (59 references); see also P:256 (65 references) and 6:92 (19 references).

TEST REFERENCES

1. Gem, J. M. (1984). Research into the climates of Australian schools, colleges, and universities: Contributions and potential of need-press theory. *The Australian Journal of Education, 28,* 227-248.

[583]

College English Placement Test.

Purpose: Designed to "measure students' understanding of the basic structure of English and their ability to manipulate the language effectively."

Population: College entrants.

Publication Date: 1969.

Acronym: CEPT.

Scores: Total score only.

Administration: Group.

Parts, 2: Part 1 (Objective Test), Part 2 (Essay I, Essay II).

Price Data, 1989: $49.50 per 50 tests; $37.50 per self-marking answer sheets; $4.80 per manual (16 pages); $6 per examiner's kit.

Time: 45(50) minutes for Part 1; 25(30) minutes for Essay I; 35(40) minutes for Essay II.

Authors: Oscar M. Haugh and James I. Brown.

Publisher: The Riverside Publishing Co.
Cross References: See T3:503 (1 reference); for excerpted reviews by Ramon Veal (with W. Geiger Ellis), see 8:47 (2 references); see also T2:65 (2 references); for reviews by Clarence Derrick and Osmond E. Palmer, see 7:189.

[584]

College English Test: National Achievement Tests.

Purpose: Designed to measure the student's mastery of elements of the English language.
Population: High school and college freshmen.
Publication Dates: 1937–43.
Scores, 7: Punctuation, Capitalization, Language Usage, Sentence Structure, Modifiers, Miscellaneous Principles, Total.
Administration: Group.
Forms, 2: A, B.
Price Data: Available from publisher.
Time: 45(50) minutes.
Author: A. C. Jordan.
Publisher: Psychometric Affiliates.
Cross References: For a review by Osmond E. Palmer, see 5:178; for reviews by Constance M. McCullough and Robert W. Howard, see 2:1269.1.

[585]

College Level Examination Program.

Purpose: Designed as a way for college accreditation of nontraditional study, advanced placement, or assessment of educational attainment.
Population: 1–2 years of college or equivalent.
Publication Dates: 1964–94.
Acronym: CLEP.
Price Data: Available from publisher.
Comments: Tests administered monthly at centers throughout the United States; 2 series of examinations; program administered by The College Board and Educational Testing Service.
Author: Educational Testing Service.
Publisher: Educational Testing Service.

a) CLEP GENERAL EXAMINATIONS.
Scores: 5 tests: English Composition, Humanities, Mathematics, Natural Sciences, Social Sciences and History.
Time: (90) minutes per test.
Comments: Separate answer sheets must be used.
b) CLEP SUBJECT EXAMINATIONS.
Scores: 29 tests: See listings below.
Time: (90) minutes per test.
Comments: Composition and Literature tests have optional essay supplement that is scored by the college; separate answer sheets must be used.
1) *Business.*
   (a) Information Systems and Computer Applications.
   (b) Introduction to Management.
   (c) Introductory Accounting.
   (d) Introductory Business Law.
   (e) Principles of Marketing.

2) *Composition and Literature.*
   (a) American Literature.
   (b) Analysis and Interpretation of Literature.
   (c) Freshman College Composition.
   (d) English Literature.
3) *Foreign Languages.*
   (a) College French, Levels 1 and 2.
   (b) College German, Levels 1 and 2.
   (c) College Spanish, Levels 1 and 2.
4) *History and Social Sciences.*
   (a) American Government.
   (b) American History I: Early Colonization to 1877.
   (c) American History II: 1865 to the Present.
   (d) Educational Psychology.
   (e) Introductory Psychology.
   (f) Human Growth and Development.
   (g) Introductory Macroeconomics.
   (h) Introductory Microeconomics.
   (i) Introductory Sociology.
   (j) Western Civilization I: Ancient Near East to 1648.
   (k) Western Civilization II: 1648 to the Present.
5) *Science and Mathematics.*
   (a) Calculus with Elementary Functions.
   (b) College Algebra.
   (c) College Algebra—Trigonometry.
   (d) General Biology.
   (e) General Chemistry.
   (f) Trigonometry.
Cross References: See 9:245 (1 reference) and T3:506 (7 references); for reviews by Paul L. Dressel, David A. Frisbie, and Wimburn L. Wallace of an earlier program, see 8:473 (15 references); for reviews of the General Examinations, see 8:8 (2 reviews); for reviews of the separate Subject Examinations, see 8:43 (1 review), 8:44 (1 review), 8:64 (1 review), 8:65 (1 review), 8:66 (1 review), 8:255 (1 review), 8:256 (1 review), 8:297 (1 review), 8:365 (1 review), 8:460 (1 review), 8:832 (1 review), 8:847 (1 review), 8:911 (1 review), , 8:919 (1 review), 8:1119 (1 review), and 8:1120 (1 review); see also T2:1050 (4 references); for reviews by Alexander W. Astin, Benjamin S. Bloom, and Warren G. Findley, see 7:664 (7 references).

[586]

College Major Interest Inventory.

Purpose: Designed "to identify the academic majors that best match a student's pattern of interests."
Population: High school and college students.
Publication Date: 1990.
Acronym: CMII.
Scores: 135 scale scores: 6 Educational Area Interest Scales (Mechanical-Technical, Rational-Scientific, Aesthetic-Cultural, Social-Personal, Business-Management, Clerical-Data), 33 Educational Cluster Scales (Accounting, Administration, Agriculture, Art, Athletics, Biological Science, Clerical, Creative Writing, Dramatics, Engineering, Finance, Journalism, Labo-

ratory Work, Language-Literature, Mathematics, Mechanical Activities, Medical Service, Military Activities, Music, Outdoors, Philosophy, Physical Science, Political Science, Public Speaking, Recreation, Religious Activities, Sales, Science Writing, Social Science, Social Service, Teaching, Technical Design, Technical Skills), 12 Personal Characteristics Scales (Accurate, Analytical, Coordinated, Creative, Helpful, Industrious, Organized, Outdoors-Oriented, Practical, Risk-Taker, Scholarly, Theoretical), 13 School and College Scales (Agriculture, Architecture, Arts & Sciences, Business, Education, Engineering, Journalism, Law, Medicine, Music, Nursing, Pharmacy, Vocational-Technical), 65 Academic Major Scales (Anthropology, Applied Math, Architecture, Biology-Environmental/Population/Organismic, Biology-Molecular/Cellular/Developmental, Business-Accounting, Business-Administration, Business-Finance, Business-General [Female Only], Business-International, Business-Management, Business-Marketing, Business-Real Estate, Chemistry, Communications, Computer Science, Conservation Education, Counseling, Distributive Studies, Economics, Education-Elementary, Education-Secondary, Engineering [Female only], Engineering-Aerospace, Engineering-Architectural, Engineering-Chemical, Engineering-Civil, Engineering-Design Economics, Engineering-Electrical, Engineering-Mechanical, Engineering-Physics, English Literature, Environmental Design, Fine Arts-B.A. Degree, Fine Arts-B.F.A. Degree, French, Geography, Geology, History, Individually Structured, International Affairs, Journalism-Advertising, Journalism-General, Journalism-News Editing, Law, Law Enforcement, Mathematics, Medical Technician, Medicine, Music, Nursing, Pharmacy, Philosophy, Physical Education, Physical Therapy, Physics, Political Science, Psychology, Public Administration, Recreation, Religious Studies, Sociology, Spanish, Speech Disorders, Theater), 5 Academic Achievement Interest Scales (Business, Social Science, Humanities, Natural Science, Engineering), Educational Level Interest Scale.

Administration: Group.

Price Data, 1992: $48 per 10 prepaid test booklets/answer sheets; $28 per manual (75 pages); $29 per specimen set.

Time: (35–45) minutes.

Comments: Formerly the Colorado Educational Interest Inventory; separate reports created for men and women students.

Authors: Robert D. Whetstone and Ronald G. Taylor.

Publisher: Consulting Psychologists Press, Inc.

[587]

College Outcome Measures Program.

Purpose: To help "colleges define and assess general education outcomes of college."

Population: College students.

Publication Dates: 1976–91.

Acronym: COMP.

Administration: Group.

Restricted Distribution: Distribution restricted to colleges.

Price Data, 1993: $50 per complete package including specimen copies of all tests, support materials package, and technical materials package including report ('92, 180 pages); $15 per specimen copies of all instruments (1 each); $20 per support materials package including college assessment planning book, COMPguide 1 (directions) ('91, 31 pages), COMPguide 2 (support) ('91, 60 pages), guide for matching COMP outcomes to program outcomes, good practices in general education, increasing student competence and persistence, and relevant articles; $15 per 1982–92 technical report ('92, 180 pages); $15 per Appendices A–E; $10 per 1976–81 technical report ('82, 96 pages); $4 per increasing student competence and persistence.

Comments: "Developed to assist in program evaluation"; 6 tests available as separates.

Authors: American College Testing Program, Aubrey Forrest (1976–81 technical manual), and Joe M. Steele (1982–91 technical manual).

Publisher: American College Testing Program.

a) THE OBJECTIVE TEST.

Scores, 7: Process Areas (Communicating, Solving Problems, Clarifying Values), Content Areas (Functioning within Social Institutions, Using Science and Technology, Using the Arts), Total.

Price Data: $7.50–$19 per student (depending on number tested per year).

Time: (150–160) minutes.

b) THE COMPOSITE EXAMINATION.

Scores, 9: Process Areas (Communicating, Solving Problems, Clarifying Values), Content Areas (Functioning within Social Institutions, Using Science and Technology, Using the Arts), Performance Areas (Writing, Speaking), Total.

Price Data: $11–$25 per student (depending on number tested per year).

Time: (390–400) minutes.

c) SPEAKING SKILLS ASSESSMENT.

Scores, 4: Audience, Discourse, Delivery, Total.

Price Data: $3–$6 per student (depending on number tested per year).

Time: (15–20) minutes.

d) WRITING SKILLS ASSESSMENT.

Scores, 4: Audience, Organization, Language, Total.

Price Data: Same as *c* above.

Time: (80–90) minutes.

e) ASSESSMENT OF REASONING AND COMMUNICATING.

Scores, 4: Reasoning, Writing, Speaking, Total.

Price Data: Same as *a* above.

Time: (120–130) minutes.

f) THE ACTIVITY INVENTORY.

Scores, 7: Same as *a* above.

Price Data: $2–$5 per student (depending on number tested per year).

Time: (90–100) minutes.

TEST REFERENCES

1. Hendel, D. D. (1991). Evidence of convergent and discriminant validity in three measures of college outcomes. *Educational and Psychological Measurement, 51*, 351-358.

[588]

College Student Experiences Questionnaire.

Purpose: Designed to measure the quality of effort college students invest in using the college resources provided for their learning and development and to relate this to their estimate of progress toward educational goals.
Population: College students.
Publication Dates: 1979–92.
Acronym: CSEQ.
Scores, 8: Background Information, College Activities, Conversations, Reading/Writing, Opinions About College, The College Environment, Estimate of Gains, Additional Questions.
Administration: Group.
Price Data, 1993: $.75 per questionnaire; $1.50 per questionnaire processing; $70 disk fee (including student responses, scores, and a summary report of the results); $11 per Norms for the Third Edition and Psychometric Supplement ('92, 117 pages).
Time: (30–40) minutes.
Author: C. Robert Pace.
Publisher: UCLA Center for the Study of Evaluation.
Cross References: For reviews by David A. Decoster and Susan McCammon, see 10:67; for reviews by Robert D. Brown and John K. Miller, see 9:246 (1 reference).

TEST REFERENCES

1. Van Kuren, N. E., & Creamer, D. G. (1989). The conceptualization and testing of a causal model of college student disciplinary status. *Journal of College Student Development, 30*, 257-265.
2. Bauer, K. W. (1992). Self-reported gains in academic and social skills. *Journal of College Student Development, 33*, 492-498.
3. DeSousa, D. J., & King, P. M. (1992). Are White students really more involved in collegiate experiences than Black students. *Journal of College Student Development, 33*, 363-369.
4. Arnold, J. C., Kuh, G. D., Vesper, N., & Schuh, J. H. (1993). Student age and enrollment status as determinants of learning and personal development at metropolitan institutions. *Journal of College Student Development, 34*, 11-16.

[589]

Collegiate Assessment of Academic Proficiency.

Purpose: Designed to assess general education skills typically attained by the end of the first two years of college.
Population: Students in the first 2 years of college.
Publication Dates: 1989–92.
Acronym: CAAP.
Administration: Group.
Restricted Distribution: Available to institutions signing a participation agreement and paying a participation fee.
Price Data, 1993: $175 per year institutional participation fee; test module prices (including scoring and reporting) available from publisher.
Time: 40(50) minutes per test.

Author: American College Testing.
Publisher: American College Testing.
a) WRITING SKILLS.
Publication Date: 1990.
Scores, 3: Usage/Mechanics, Rhetorical Skills, Total.
b) MATHEMATICS.
Publication Date: 1989.
Scores, 2: Algebra, Total.
c) READING.
Publication Date: 1989.
Scores, 3: Arts/Literature, Social Studies/Sciences, Total.
d) CRITICAL THINKING.
Publication Date: 1989.
Scores: Total score only.
e) SCIENCE REASONING.
Publication Date: 1989.
Scores: Total score only.
f) WRITING (ESSAY).
Publication Date: 1990.
Scores: Total score only.
Comments: Total of 3 individual essays.

TEST REFERENCES

1. Pascarella, E., Bohr, L., Nora, A., Zusman, B., Inman, P., & Desler, M. (1993). Cognitive impacts of living on campus versus commuting to college. *Journal of College Student Development, 34*, 216-219.

[590]

Collis-Romberg Mathematical Problem Solving Profiles.

Purpose: Assesses student progress through a variety of mathematical problem-solving skills.
Population: Ages 9–13, 13–17.
Publication Date: 1992.
Scores, 6: Number, Algebra, Space, Measurement, Chance and Data, Total.
Administration: Group.
Levels, 2: Junior, Senior.
Price Data, 1994: $99 per complete set including profiles A and B, and manual (72 pages); $35 per manual.
Time: (40–50) minutes.
Comments: Junior version (Ages 9–13) uses Parts A to C of each question; Senior version (Ages 13–17) uses Parts A to D of each question.
Authors: K. F. Collis and T. A. Romberg.
Publisher: The Australian Council for Educational Research Limited [Australia].

[591]

Columbia Mental Maturity Scale, Third Edition.

Purpose: Designed to provide "an estimate of the general reasoning ability of children."
Population: Ages 3-6 to 9-11.
Publication Dates: 1954–72.
Acronym: CMMS.
Scores: Total score only.
Administration: Individual.
Price Data, 1994: $394 per complete kit including

95 item cards, Guide for Administering and Interpreting ('72, 61 pages); $41 per 35 individual record forms; $17.50 per English-Spanish Reference Handbook for Educators; $42.50 per Guide for Administering and Interpreting including Spanish Directions.

Time: (15–20) minutes.

Comments: Requires no verbal response and a minimal motor response.

Authors: Bessie B. Burgemeister, Lucille Hollander Blum, and Irving Lorge.

Publisher: The Psychological Corporation.

Cross References: See T3:534 (15 references); for reviews by Byron R. Egeland and Alan S. Kaufman, and an excerpted review by Joseph M. Petrosko, see 8:210 (18 references); see also T2:489 (43 references); for reviews by Marshall S. Hiskey and T. Earnest Newland of the 1959 edition, see 6:517 (22 references); see also 5:402 (13 references).

TEST REFERENCES

1. Anwar, F., & Hermelin, B. (1981). Movement after-effects in normal development. *Psychological Research, 43*, 307-315.
2. Jorm, A. F., Share, D. L., Maclean, R., & Matthews, R. (1984). Phonological confusability in short-term memory for sentences as a predictor of reading ability. *British Journal of Psychology, 74*, 393-400.
3. Kamhi, A. G., Catts, H. W., Koenig, L. A., & Lewis B. A. (1984). Hypothesis-testing and nonlinguistic symbolic abilities in language-impaired children. *Journal of Speech and Hearing Disorders, 49*, 169-176.
4. Kamphaus, R. W., & Reynolds, C. R. (1984). Development and structure of the Kaufman Assessment Battery for Children. *The Journal of Special Education, 18*, 213-228.
5. Kamhi, A. G., Lee, R. F., & Nelson, L. K. (1985). Word, syllable, and sound awareness in language-disordered children. *Journal of Speech and Hearing Disorders, 50*, 207-212.
6. Weismer, S. E. (1985). Constructive comprehension abilities exhibited by language-disordered children. *Journal of Speech and Hearing Research, 28*, 175-184.
7. Cole, K. N., & Dale, P. S. (1986). Direct language instruction and interactive language instruction with language delayed preschool children: A comparison study. *Journal of Speech and Hearing Research, 29*, 206-217.
8. Jorm, A. F., Share, D. L., Maclean, R., & Matthews, R. (1986). Cognitive factors at school entry predictive of specific reading retardation and general reading backwardness: A research note. *Journal of Child Psychology and Psychiatry and Allied Disciplines, 27*, 45-54.
9. Jorm, A. F., Share, D. L., Matthews, R., & Maclean, R. (1986). Behaviour problems in specific reading retarded and general reading backward children: A longitudinal study. *Journal of Child Psychology and Psychiatry and Allied Disciplines, 27*, 33-43.
10. Rantakallio, P., & von Wendt, L. (1986). Mental retardation and subnormality in a birth cohort of 12,000 children in Northern Finland. *American Journal of Mental Deficiency, 90*, 380-387.
11. O'Connor, N., & Hermelin, B. (1987). Visual and graphic abilities of the idiot savant artist. *Psychological Medicine, 17*, 79-90.
12. O'Connor, N., & Hermelin, B. (1987). Visual memory and motor programmes: Their use by idiot-savant artists and controls. *British Journal of Psychology, 78*, 307- 323.
13. Fisher, W., Burd, L., & Kerbeshian, J. (1988). Markers for improvement in children with pervasive developmental disorders. *Journal of Mental Deficiency Research, 32*, 357-369.
14. Kamhi, A. G., Catts, H. W., Mauer, D., Apel, K., & Gentry, B. (1988). Phonological and spatial processing abilities in language- and reading-impaired children. *Journal of Speech and Hearing Disorders, 53*, 316-327.
15. Meline, T. J. (1988). The encoding of novel referents by language-impaired children. *Language, Speech, and Hearing Services in Schools, 19*, 119-127.
16. Nippold, M. A., Erskine, B. J., & Freed, D. B. (1988). Proportional and functional analogical reasoning in normal and language-impaired children. *Journal of Speech and Hearing Disorders, 53*, 440-448.
17. Byrne, K., Abbeduto, L., & Brooks, P. (1990). The language of children with spina bifida and hydrocephalus: Meeting task demands and mastering syntax. *Journal of Speech and Hearing Disorders, 55*, 118-123.
18. Johnston, J. R., & Bowman, S. (1990). Gardner Picture Vocabulary Tests: Relationship between performance in expression and reception. *International Journal of Clinical Neuropsychology, 12*, 103-106.
19. Kamhi, A. G., Minor, J. S., & Mauer, D. (1990). Content analysis and intratest performance profiles on the Columbia and TONI. *Journal of Speech and Hearing Research, 33*, 375-379.
20. Weismer, S. E. (1991). Hypothesis-testing abilities of language-impaired children. *Journal of Speech and Hearing Research, 34*, 1329-1338.

[592]
The Columbus: Picture Analysis of Growth Towards Maturity.

Purpose: Designed "as an aid in exploring and analyzing developmental processes in children."

Population: Ages 5–18.

Publication Dates: 1969–81.

Scores: No scores.

Administration: Individual.

Price Data, 1990: $69 per complete kit including manual ('69, 76 pages) and 24 picture cards.

Time: [30–60] minutes.

Author: M. J. Langeveld.

Publisher: S. Karger, AG [Switzerland].

Cross References: For excerpted reviews by C. H. Ammons (with R. B. Ammons) and Steven G. Vandenberg, see 7:164 (1 reference).

[593]
Combined Cognitive Preference Inventory.

Purpose: Designed to measure how a student processes information intellectually.

Population: Students.

Publication Date: [no date on materials].

Acronym: CCPI.

Scores: 4 cognitive preference areas: Recall, Principles, Questioning, Application.

Administration: Group.

Manual: No manual.

Price Data: Available from publisher.

Time: (20) minutes.

Author: Pinchas Tamir.

Publisher: Israel Science Teaching Center [Israel].

[594]
Communication Abilities Diagnostic Test.

Purpose: Constructed to assess language development.

Population: Ages 3-0 to 9-11.

Publication Date: 1990.

Acronym: CADeT.

Scores: 6 subscores: Words, Structure, Grammar, Meaning, Pragmatics, Comprehension, plus 4 composite scores: Semantics, Syntax, Language Expression, Total Language.

Administration: Individual.

Price Data, 1991: $148.98 per complete kit; $49.98 per set of 2 story books; $34.98 per game board/cards/pieces; $15.99 per 12 record forms; $24.99 per examiner's manual (155 pages); $15 per technical manual (36 pages).

Time: (30–45) minutes.

Authors: Elizabeth B. Johnston and Andrew V. Johnston.

Publisher: The Riverside Publishing Co.

[595]
Communication and Symbolic Behavior Scales.
Purpose: "A standardized method of examining communicative and symbolic behaviors of children."
Population: 9 months to 6 years.
Publication Date: 1993.
Acronym: CSBS.
Scores, 7: Communicative Functions, Gestural Communicative Means, Vocal Communicative Means, Verbal Communicative Means, Reciprocity, Social-Affective Signaling, Symbolic Behavior.
Administration: Individual.
Price Data: Available from publisher.
Time: (60–70) minutes.
Comments: Assessments videotaped for analysis.
Authors: Amy M. Wetherby and Barry M. Prizant.
Publisher: The Riverside Publishing Company.

[596]
Communication Knowledge Inventory.
Purpose: To measure knowledge about person to person communication practices.
Population: High school through adult.
Publication Dates: 1970–78.
Acronym: RCK.
Scores: Total score only.
Administration: Group.
Manual: No manual; fact sheet available.
Price Data: Available from publisher.
Time: (10–20) minutes.
Comments: Self-administered.
Authors: W. J. Reddin and Ken Rowell.
Publisher: Organizational Tests Ltd. [Canada].
Cross References: For a review by Gregory J. Boyle, see 11:77.

[597]
Communication Response Style: Assessment.
Purpose: To assess an individual's communication response style.
Population: Adults.
Publication Dates: 1981–87.
Scores, 4: Empathic Response Score, Critical Response Score, Searching Response Score, Advising Response Score.
Administration: Group or individual.
Manual: No manual.
Price Data, 1993: $60 per set of 20 including test, answer sheets, and interpretation sheets.
Time: (20) minutes.
Comments: Self-administered, self-scored.
Author: Madelyn Burley-Allen.
Publisher: Training House, Inc.
Cross References: For reviews by Janet Norris and Gargi Roysircar Sodowsky, see 11:78.

[598]
Communication Sensitivity Inventory.
Purpose: Constructed "to discover the characteristic response of the manager to others who come to him with problems."
Population: Managers.
Publication Dates: 1970–78.
Scores, 4: Feeling Response, Challenge Response, More Information Response, Recommendation Response.
Administration: Group.
Price Data, 1989: $40 per complete kit including 10 test inventories, fact sheet (no date, 2 pages), and administration guide ('78, 4 pages).
Time: (10–20) minutes.
Comments: Self-administered.
Authors: K. R. Rowell and W. J. Reddin.
Publisher: Organizational Tests Ltd. [Canada].

[599]
Communications Profile Questionnaire.
Purpose: To teach the "Johari Window" communications model, identify one's communication style, learn techniques to give feedback and get information effectively, and to develop a plan to modify one's communication style as appropriate.
Population: Managers and employees.
Publication Dates: 1974–83.
Acronym: CPQ.
Scores: Communication Style.
Administration: Group.
Forms, 2: Participant, Companion.
Price Data, 1987: $6 per set including 1 participant form, 2 companion forms, and scoring and interpretation booklet ('83, 15 pages); $15 per leader's guide (no date, 16 pages).
Foreign Language Edition: Spanish version of Generic Management available.
Time: 195(225) minutes.
Comments: 4 versions: Generic Management, Sales Management, Health Care Management, Non-Manager.
Author: Don Michalak.
Publisher: Michalak Training Associates, Inc.
Cross References: For reviews by Daniel J. Mueller and Lyle F. Schoenfeldt, see 10:68.

[600]
Communicative Abilities in Daily Living.
Purpose: "To assess the functional communication skills of aphasic adults."
Population: Aphasic adults.
Publication Date: 1980.
Acronym: CADL.
Scores: Total score only.
Administration: Individual.
Price Data, 1994: $119 per complete kit including scoring kit, picture book, audiotape cassette, and administration manual (125 pages); $32 per scoring kit; $43 per picture book; $19 per audiotape cassette; $29 per administration manual.
Time: (40–50) minutes.
Comments: Intended as a supplemental test; other test materials (e.g., shoelace, watches, white jacket) must be supplied by examiner.
Author: Audrey L. Holland.

Publisher: PRO-ED, Inc.
Cross References: For a review by Rita Sloan Berndt, see 10:69 (2 references).

[601]

Communicative Evaluation Chart From Infancy to Five Years.
Purpose: "Early detection of childhood communicative disabilities."
Population: Ages 3 months to 5 years.
Publication Dates: 1963–64.
Acronym: CEC.
Scores, 2: Language, Performances.
Administration: Individual.
Manual: No manual.
Price Data, 1989: $1 per chart ('64, 4 pages); $37.50 per 50 charts.
Time: Administration time not reported.
Authors: Ruth M. Anderson, Madeline Miles, and Patricia A. Matheny.
Publisher: Educators Publishing Service, Inc.
Cross References: For additional information, see 7:949.

[602]

Community College Goals Inventory.
Purpose: "To help colleges delineate their goals and establish priorities among them."
Population: Community colleges.
Publication Dates: 1979–81.
Acronym: CCGI.
Scores, 20: General Education, Intellectual Orientation, Lifelong Learning, Cultural/Aesthetic Awareness, Personal Development, Humanism/Altruism, Vocational/Technical Preparation, Developmental/Remedial Preparation, Community Services, Social Criticism, Counseling and Advising, Student Services, Faculty/Staff Development, Intellectual Environment, Innovation, College Community, Freedom, Accessibility, Effective Management, Accountability.
Administration: Group.
Price Data: Available from publisher.
Time: (45–50) minutes.
Comments: Ratings by faculty, administrators, trustees.
Author: ETS Community and Junior College Programs.
Publisher: Educational Testing Service.
Cross References: For a review by Hazel M. Crain, see 9:250.

[603]

Community College Student Experiences Questionnaire.
Purpose: To measure the quality of effort community college students invest in using the college resources provided for their learning and development and to relate this to their estimate of progress toward educational goals.
Population: Community college students.
Publication Date: 1990–92.
Acronym: CCSEQ.

Scores: Responses noted in 9 areas: Background, Work, Family, College Program, College Courses, College Activities, Estimate of Gains, College Environment, Additional Questions.
Administration: Group.
Price Data, 1993: $.75 per questionnaire; $1.50 per questionnaire processing; $70 tape/disk fee (including student responses, scores, and a summary report of the results); $11 per test manual and comparative data ('92, 95 pages).
Time: 20(30) minutes.
Authors: Jack Friedlander, C. Robert Pace, and Penny W. Lehman.
Publisher: UCLA Center for the Study of Evaluation.

[604]

Community Opinion Inventory.
Purpose: "To identify areas the public sees as being done well, and areas seen as not done well" in the local school.
Population: Adults who do not have children enrolled in school.
Publication Date: 1990.
Scores: 5 subscales: General Support Climate, Program Awareness, Responsiveness to the Community, Equality of Opportunity, Resource Stewardship.
Administration: Group.
Parts, 2: A (Likert-scale items), B (open-ended items).
Price Data, 1993: $7 per 25 inventories (Part A); $5.25 per 25 inventories (Part B); $5.25 per 25 machine-scored answer sheets; $6.50 per Administrator's Manual (12 pages).
Time: Untimed.
Author: National Study of School Evaluation.
Publisher: National Study of School Evaluation.

[605]

Community Oriented Programs Environment Scale.
Purpose: Designed to "assess the social environments of community-based psychiatric treatment programs, day programs, sheltered workshops, rehabilitation centers and community care homes."
Population: Patients and staff of community oriented psychiatric facilities.
Publication Date: 1974.
Acronym: COPES.
Scores, 10: Involvement, Support, Spontaneity, Autonomy, Practical Orientation, Personal Problem Orientation, Anger and Aggression, Order and Organization, Program Clarity, Staff Control.
Administration: Group.
Price Data, 1990: $10 per 25 test booklets; $7 per 50 answer sheets; $5 per 50 profiles; $3 per scoring key; $17 per manual ('74, 29 pages); $21 per specimen set.
Time: Administration time not reported.
Comments: A part of the Social Climate Scales (2495).

Author: Rudolf H. Moos.
Publisher: Consulting Psychologists Press, Inc.
Cross References: See T3:542 (6 references); for a review by Richard I. Lanyon, see 8:525 (17 references); for a review of the Social Climate Scales, see 8:681.

TEST REFERENCES

1. Kohn, M., Jeger, A. M., & Koretzky, M. B. (1979). Social-ecological assessment of environments: Toward a two-factor model. *American Journal of Community Psychology, 7,* 481-495.
2. Nevid, J. S., Capurso, R., & Morrison, J. K. (1980). Patient's adjustment to family-care as related to their perceptions of real-ideal differences in treatment environments. *American Journal of Community Psychology, 8,* 117-120.
3. Shadish, W. R., Jr., Straw, R. B., McSweeny, A. J., Koller, D. L., & Bootzin, R. R. (1981). Nursing home care for mental patients: Descriptive data and some propositions. *American Journal of Community Psychology, 9,* 617-633.
4. Bell, M. D., & Ryan, E. R. (1984). Integrating psychosocial rehabilitation into the hospital psychiatric service. *Hospital and Community Psychiatry, 35,* 1017-1023.
5. Fairchild, H. H., & Wright, C. (1984). A social-ecological assessment and feedback-intervention of an adolescent treatment agency. *Adolescence, 19,* 263-275.
6. Novak, A. R. (1984). A systems theory approach to deinstitutionalization policies and research. *International Review of Research in Mental Retardation, 12,* 245-283.
7. Bell, M. D., & Ryan, E. R. (1985). Where can therapeutic community ideals be realized? An examination of three treatment environments. *Hospital and Community Psychiatry, 36,* 1286-1290.
8. Coulton, C. J., Fitch, V., & Holland, T. P. (1985). A typology of social environments in community care homes. *Hospital and Community Psychiatry, 36,* 373-377.
9. Hellman, I. D., Greene, L. R., Morrison, T. L., & Abramowitz, S. I. (1985). Organizational size and perceptions in a residential treatment program. *American Journal of Community Psychology, 13,* 99-109.
10. Friedman, A. S., & Glickman, N. W. (1986). Program characteristics for successful treatment of adolescent drug abuse. *The Journal of Nervous and Mental Disease, 174,* 669-679.
11. Mosher, L. R., Kresky-Wolff, M., Matthews, S., & Menn, A. (1986). Milieu therapy in the 1980s: A comparison of two residential alternatives to hospitalization. *Bulletin of the Menninger Clinic, 50,* 257-268.

[606]

Complex Figure Test.

Purpose: To serve as an index of brain damage.
Population: Ages 16 and over.
Publication Dates: 1970–73.
Acronym: CFT.
Scores, 4: Interruption, Omission, Sequence, Total.
Administration: Individual.
Price Data: Available from publisher.
Time: Administration time not reported.
Comments: Originally published in Dutch in 1970 as a revision of *Test de Copie d'une Figure Complexe* (1959) by Andre Rey.
Author: R. S. H. Visser.
Publisher: Swets Test Service [Netherlands].
Cross References: For an excerpted review by C. H. Ammons and R. B. Ammons, see 8:528 (1 reference).

TEST REFERENCES

1. Huhtaniemi, P., Haier, R. J., Fedio, P., & Buchsbaum, M. S. (1983). Neuropsychological characteristics of college males who show attention dysfunction. *Perceptual and Motor Skills, 57,* 399-406.
2. Solms, M., Kaplan-Solms, K., Saling, M., & Miller, P. (1988). Inverted vision after frontal lobe disease. *Cortex, 24,* 499-509.
3. Bernard, L. C. (1990). Prospects for faking believable memory deficits on neuropsychological tests and the use of incentives in simulation research. *Journal of Clinical and Experimental Neuropsychology, 12,* 715-728.
4. Dywan, J., & Jacoby, L. (1990). Effects of aging on source monitoring: Differences in susceptibility to false fame. *Psychology and Aging, 5,* 379-387.
5. Shay, K. A., & Roth, D. L. (1992). Association between aerobic fitness and visuospatial performance in healthy older adults. *Psychology and Aging, 7,* 15-24.
6. Tombaugh, T. N., & Schmidt, J. P. (1992). The Learning and Memory Battery (LAMB): Development and standardization. *Psychological Assessment, 4,* 193-206.
7. Hamby, S. L., Wilkins, J. W., & Barry, N. S. (1993). Organizational quality on the Rey-Osterrieth and Taylor Complex Figure Tests: A new scoring system. *Psychological Assessment, 5,* 27-33.
8. Uddo, M., Vasterling, J. J., Brailey, K., & Sutker, P. B. (1993). Memory and attention in combat-related post-traumatic stress disorder (PTSD). *Journal of Psychopathology and Behavioral Assessment, 15,* 43-52.

[607]

Composite International Diagnostic Interview.

Purpose: "For use in epidemiological studies of mental disorders."
Population: Adults.
Publication Date: 1993.
Acronym: CIDI.
Scores, 18: Demographics, Tobacco Use Disorder, Somatoform Disorders, Panic Disorder, Generalized Anxiety, Phobic Disorders, Major Depressive Episode and Dysthymia, Manic Episode, Schizophrenic and Schizophreniform Disorders, Eating Disorders, Alcohol Abuse and Dependence, Obsessive Compulsive Disorder, Drug Abuse and Dependence, Organic Brain Syndrome, Psychosexual Dysfunctions, Comments by the Respondent and the Interviewer, Interviewer Observations, Interviewer Rating.
Administration: Individual.
Price Data: Available from publisher.
Time: (75–95) minutes.
Author: World Health Organization.
Publisher: American Psychiatric Press, Inc.

[608]

Comprehension of Oral Language.

Purpose: To assess receptive skills for spoken Spanish and English; can be used to identify dominant language.
Population: Grades K–1.
Publication Dates: 1962–73.
Scores: Total score only.
Administration: Group.
Price Data: Not available.
Foreign Language Editions: Parallel editions in English and Spanish.
Time: (30–35) minutes.
Comments: 2 forms: A, B; administered orally.
Author: Guidance Testing Associates.
Publisher: Guidance Testing Associates [No reply from publisher; status unknown].
Cross References: For reviews by Richard R. Duran and Robert Rueda, see 9:254.

[609]

Comprehensive Ability Battery.

Purpose: "Features 20 tests, each designed to measure a single primary ability factor . . . important in industrial settings and career and vocational counseling."

Population: Ages 15 and over.
Publication Dates: 1975–82.
Acronym: CAB.
Administration: Group.
Price Data, 1994: $19 per 10 test booklets (CAB-1, CAB-2, CAB-3/4 are reusable); $13 per 50 answer sheets (CAB-1/2, CAB-3/4); $10.50 per 50 profile sheets; $14 per audio cassette tape (required for AA and Ms tests); $13.75 per scoring key and instructions (specify Level CAB-1/2/3/4); $27.50 per 2 scoring keys and instructions (CAB-5).
Authors: A. Ralph Hakstian and Raymond B. Cattell.
Publisher: Institute for Personality and Ability Testing, Inc.

a) CAB-1.
Scores: 4 test scores: Verbal Ability (V), Numerical Ability (N), Spatial Ability (S), Speed of Closure (Cs).
Time: 21.75(30) minutes.

b) CAB-2.
Scores: 5 test scores: Perceptual Speed and Accuracy (P), Inductive Reasoning (I), Flexibility of Closure (Cf), Associative Memory (Ma), Mechanical Ability (Mk).
Time: 28(35) minutes.

c) CAB-3/4.
Scores: 5 test scores: Memory Span (Ms), Meaningful Memory (Mm), Spelling (Sp), Auditory Ability (AA), Esthetic Judgment (E).
Time: (25–30) minutes.
Comments: MS and AA administered by audio cassette tape.

d) CAB-5.
Scores: 6 test scores: Spontaneous Flexibility (Fs), Ideational Fluency (Fi), Word Fluency (W), Originality (O), Aiming (A), Representational Drawing (RD).
Time: 32(40) minutes.
Comments: Test booklets not reusable; nonmachine scorable tests.
Cross References: For reviews by Robert C. Nichols and Karl R. White, see 9:255; see also T3:547 (5 references); for reviews by John B. Carroll and Robert M. Thorndike, see 8:484 (3 references).

TEST REFERENCES

1. Kline, P., & Cooper, C. (1984). The factor structure of the Comprehensive Ability Battery. *British Journal of Educational Psychology, 54,* 106-110.
2. Hakstian, A. R., & Woolsey, L. K. (1985). Validity studies using the Comprehensive Ability Battery (CAB): IV. Predicting achievement at the university level. *Educational and Psychological Measurement, 45,* 329-341.
3. Cooper, C., Kline, P., & Maclaurin-Jones, L. (1986). Inspection time and primary abilities. *British Journal of Educational Psychology, 56,* 304-308.
4. Dong, H., Sung, Y. H., & Goldman, S. H. (1986). The validity of the Ball Aptitude Battery (BAB): III. Relationship to CAB, DAT, and GATB. *Educational and Psychological Measurement, 46,* 245-250.
5. Kline, P., & Cooper, C. (1986). Psychoticism and creativity. *The Journal of Genetic Psychology, 147,* 183-188.
6. Hakstain, A. R., Woolsey, L. K., & Schroeder, M. L. (1987).
Validity of a large-scale assessment battery in an industrial setting. *Educational and Psychological Measurement, 47*(1), 165-178.
7. Kline, P., Auld, K., & Cooper, C. (1987). Five new personality scales: Their location in the factor space of personality measures. *Journal of Clinical Psychology, 43,* 328-336.
8. Mohr, E. (1987). Cognitive style and order of recall effects in dichotic listening. *Cortex, 23,* 223-236.
9. Kagan, D. M., & Berg, K. E. (1988). The relationship between aerobic activity and cognitive performance under stress. *The Journal of Psychology, 122,* 451-462.
10. Brookings, J. B. (1990). A confirmatory factor analytic study of time-sharing performance and cognitive abilities. *Intelligence, 14,* 43-59.
11. McNamara, T. P., Sternberg, R. J., & Hardy, J. K. (1991). Processing verbal relations. *Intelligence, 15,* 193-221.

[610]

Comprehensive Adult Student Assessment System.
Purpose: Used for "assessing adult basic skills within a functional context" to "place learnees into appropriate instructional levels, diagnose learners' needs, monitor progress, and certify mastery of functional basic skills."
Population: Adults.
Publication Dates: 1980–93.
Acronym: CASAS.
Administration: Group.
Restricted Distribution: Agency training is required before tests can be provided.
Price Data: Available from publisher.
Time: (60) minutes per test.
Comments: The CASAS system "currently offers more than 80 standardized assessment instruments including multiple choice, written response, and performance-based assessment . . . . has the capacity to customize assessment to measure specific competencies and learner outcomes."
Author: CASAS.
Publisher: CASAS.

a) APPRAISAL TESTS.
1) *Life Skills Appraisal.*
Scores: 2 tests: Reading, Math.
2) *ESL Appraisal (English as a Second Language).*
Scores: 4 tests: Reading, Listening, Writing, Oral.
Comments: Places students into a Level A, B, or C pretest of the CASAS Listening Series.
3) *GAIN Appraisal (Greater Avenues for Independence).*
Scores: 3 tests: Reading, Math, Listening.
4) *ECS Appraisal (Employability Competency System).*
Scores: 2 tests: Reading, Math.
Comments: Places students into Levels A, B, or C of the CASAS Basic Skills for Employability pretests.
5) *Workplace Appraisal.*
Scores: 2 tests: Reading, Reading/Math.
Comments: Not a pre-employment test; designed to be used at worksite to provide an initial assessment of workers' functional reading skills of materials encountered at the worksite.
6) *IRCA Pre-Enrollment Appraisal.*
Scores: 4 tests: Reading, Listening, Writing, Oral.

Comments: "Designed for use with the amnesty population, it may also be used with non-amnesty ESL students.

b) CASAS TESTS FOR MONITORING PROGRESS.

Comments: All tests serve as pre/post-tests.

1) *Life Skills Survey Achievement Tests.*

(a) Reading.

Levels: 4 levels (A, B, C, D), each with 2 forms.

(b) Math.

Levels: 4 levels (A, B, C, D), each with 2 forms.

(c) Listening Comprehension (for ESL students).

Levels: 3 levels (A, B, C), each with 2 forms.

2) *Basic Skills for Employability Tests.*

(a) Reading.

Levels: 3 levels (A, B, C), each with 2 forms.

(b) Math.

Levels: 3 levels (A, B, C), each with 2 forms.

(c) Listening Comprehension (for ESL students).

Levels: 3 levels (A, B, C), each with 2 forms.

c) CASAS TESTS FOR SPECIAL POPULATIONS.

Population: Developmentally disabled students.

Levels: 3 levels (AA, AAA, AAAA), each with 2 forms.

Comments: Pretests and corresponding posttests are available.

d) CASAS CERTIFICATION TESTS.

Comments: "Designed to determine if a student is ready to move to a higher level of instruction or to be certified as completing a program of instruction."

1) *Life Skills Certification (Exit) Tests.*

Scores: 1 test: Reading/Math.

Levels: 3 levels (A, B, C), each with 1 form.

2) *Employability Certification (Exit) Tests.*

Scores: 2 tests: Reading, Math.

Levels: 2 levels (B, C), each with 1 form for each test.

3) *GAIN Certification (Exit) Tests.*

Scores: 3 tests: Basic Skills Certification Reading/Math, ESL Certification Listening/Reading, ESL Certification Applied Performance Test.

Comments: Available only to California County Welfare Departments for use with GAIN participants.

e) CASAS TEST FOR WRITING ASSESSMENT.

Purpose: "Measures a student's functional writing skill abilities within a life skills context."

Comments: Pretest and posttest are available.

f) OCCUPATION SPECIFIC TESTS.

Purpose: "Assess whether a person is ready to enter an occupational training program."

Scores: 5 areas: Auto Mechanic, Clerical, Food Service, Health Occupations Level B, Health Occupations Level C.

g) CASAS SECONDARY DIPLOMA TESTS.

Scores: 8 areas: Math, Economics, American Government, United States History, English/Language Arts, World History, Biological Science, Physical Science.

Comments: Tests are available for pretesting and posttesting.

[611]

Comprehensive Assessment of School Environments.

Purpose: Developed to assess perceptions of the school climate and student, teacher, and parent satisfaction with each individual's personal environment in order "to foster data-based decision making for school improvement."

Population: Junior and senior high schools.

Publication Dates: 1986–89.

Acronym: CASE.

Administration: Group.

Price Data, 1994: $6 per 35 surveys (specify form) and manual ('87, 36 pages); $5 per 35 machine-scorable answer sheets; $5 per examiner's manual; $95 per microcomputer scoring package (Apple IIe, IBM-PC); $5 per specimen set; scoring service available from Western Michigan University.

Time: Administration time not reported.

Comments: Test booklet titles are School Climate Survey, Parent Satisfaction Survey, Teacher Satisfaction Survey, and Student Satisfaction Survey.

Authors: Cynthia Halderson (manuals and climate survey), Edgar A. Kelley (manuals and climate survey), James W. Keefe (manuals and climate survey), Paul S. Berge (technical manual), John A. Glover (climate survey), Carrie Sorenson (climate survey), Carol Speth (climate survey), Neal Schmitt (satisfaction surveys), and Brian Loher (satisfaction surveys).

Publisher: National Association of Secondary School Principals.

a) SCHOOL CLIMATE SURVEY.

Scores: Student, Teacher, and Parent scores for the following 10 subscales: Teacher-Student Relationships, Security and Maintenance, Administration, Student Academic Orientation, Student Behavioral Values, Guidance, Student-Peer Relationships, Parent & Community-School Relationships, Instructional Management, Student Activities.

b) PARENT SATISFACTION SURVEY.

SCORES, 9: Parent Involvement, Curriculum, Student Activities, Teachers, Support Services, School Building/Supplies/Maintenance, Student Discipline, School Administrators, School Information Services.

c) TEACHER SATISFACTION SURVEY.

Scores, 9: Administration, Compensation, Opportunities for Advancement, Student Responsibility & Discipline, Curriculum and Job Tasks, Co-workers, Parents and Community, School Building/Supplies/Maintenance, Communication.

d) STUDENT SATISFACTION SURVEY.
Scores, 8: Teachers, Fellow Students, School-work, Student Activities, Student Discipline, Decision-Making Opportunities, School Building/Supplies/Upkeep, Communication.
Cross References: For reviews by Nancy L. Allen and Frederick T. L. Leong, see 11:80.

[612]
Comprehensive Assessment of Symptoms and History.
Purpose: "Designed as a structured interview and recording instrument for documenting the signs, symptoms, and history of subjects evaluated in research studies of the major psychoses and affective disorders."
Population: Psychiatric patients.
Publication Date: 1987.
Acronym: CASH.
Scores: Interview divided into 3 major sections: Present State (Sociodemographic Data, Evaluation of Current Condition, Psychotic Syndrome, Manic Syndrome, Major Depressive Syndrome, Treatment, Cognitive Assessment, Global Assessment Scale, Diagnosis for Current Episode), Past History (History of Onset and Hospitalization, Past Symptoms of Psychosis, Characterization of Course, Past Symptoms of Affective Disorder), Lifetime History (History of Somatic Therapy, Alcoholism, Drug Use and Abuse and Dependence, Modified Premorbid Adjustment Scale, Premorbid or Intermorbid Personality, Functioning During Past Five Years, Global Assessment Scale, Diagnosis for Lifetime).
Administration: Individual.
Price Data: Available from publisher.
Time: [60–180] minutes.
Comments: The CASH is one component of a modular assessment battery available from the publisher.
Author: Nancy C. Andreasen.
Publisher: Nancy C. Andreasen.

TEST REFERENCES

1. Liddle, P. F. (1987). Schizophrenic syndromes, cognitive performance and neurological dysfunction. *Psychological Medicine, 17*, 49-57.
2. Andreasen, N. C., Swayze, V., II, Flaum, M., Alliger, R., & Cohen, G. (1990). Ventricular abnormalities in affective disorder: Clinical and demographic correlates. *American Journal of Psychiatry, 147*, 893-900.
3. Perry, P. J., Miller, D. D., Arndt, S. V., & Cadoret, R. J. (1991). Clozapine and norclozapine plasma concentrations and clinical response of treatment-refractory schizophrenic patients. *American Journal of Psychiatry, 148*, 231-235.
4. Arndt, S., Tyrrell, G., Flaum, M., & Andreasen, N. C. (1992). Comorbidity of substance abuse and schizophrenia: The role of pre-morbid adjustment. *Psychological Medicine, 22*, 379-388.

[613]
Comprehensive Behavior Rating Scale for Children.
Purpose: A teacher rating scale designed to measure various dimensions of a child's school functioning.
Population: Ages 6–14.
Publication Date: 1990.
Acronym: CBRSC.

Scores: 9 scales: Inattention-Disorganization, Reading Problems, Cognitive Deficits, Oppositional-Conduct Disorders, Motor Hyperactivity, Anxiety, Sluggish Tempo, Daydreaming, Social Competence.
Administration: Individual.
Price Data, 1994: $69.50 per complete kit including manual (10 pages), 25 profile and questionnaire forms, and scoring key; $14.50 per 25 profile and questionnaire forms; $37.50 per manual; $22.50 per scoring key.
Time: (10–15) minutes.
Authors: Ronald Neeper, Benjamin B. Lahey, and Paul J. Frick.
Publisher: The Psychological Corporation.

[614]
Comprehensive Drinker Profile.
Purpose: To provide "an intensive and comprehensive history and status of the individual client with regard to his or her use and abuse of alcohol."
Population: Problem drinkers and alcoholics.
Publication Dates: 1984–87.
Acronym: CDP.
Scores: Problem drinking indices.
Administration: Individual.
Price Data, 1994: $63 per complete kit including 25 interview forms, 8 card sets, and manual ('84, 81 pages); $42 per 25 forms; $14 per set of cards; $14 per manual.
Comments: 3 adjunct instruments available as separates.
Authors: G. Alan Marlatt and William R. Miller.
Publisher: Psychological Assessment Resources, Inc.
a) BRIEF DRINKER PROFILE.
Publication Date: 1987.
Acronym: BDP.
Price Data: $38 per 25 forms; $11 per CDP manual supplement (54 pages).
Time: 50 minutes.
Comments: Abbreviated version of the Comprehensive Drinker Profile; CDP manual and card sets required for administration and interpretation.
b) FOLLOW-UP DRINKER PROFILE.
Publication Date: 1987.
Acronym: FDP.
Price Data: $22 per 15 forms; $11 per CDP manual supplement.
Time: (30–50) minutes.
Comments: To be used in conjunction with the CDP or BDP; CDP manual and card sets required for administration and interpretation.
c) COLLATERAL INTERVIEW FORM.
Purpose: To provide information not available from the client.
Population: Friends and family of the client.
Publication Date: 1987.
Acronym: CIF.
Price Data: $22 per 15 forms; $11 per CDP manual supplement.
Time: Administration time not reported.
Comments: CDP manual required.

Cross References: For reviews by Robert R. Mowrer and Nick J. Piazza, see 10:70 (1 reference).

TEST REFERENCES

1. Williams, J. G., & Morrice, A. (1992). Measuring drinking patterns among college students. *Psychological Reports, 70,* 231-238.

[615]

A Comprehensive English Language Test for Speakers of English as a Second Language.

Purpose: To measure English language ability of nonnative speakers.
Population: Nonnative speakers of English.
Publication Date: 1970.
Acronym: CELT.
Administration: Group.
Price Data: Not available.
Authors: David P. Harris and Leslie A. Palmer.
Publisher: Webster Division, McGraw-Hill Book Co., Inc. [No reply from publisher; status unknown].
a) LISTENING (L-A).
Time: 40 minutes.
b) STRUCTURE (S-A).
Time: 45 minutes.
c) VOCABULARY (V-A).
Time: 35 minutes.
Cross References: See T3:549 (4 references); for a review by John B. Carroll, see 7:260.

TEST REFERENCES

1. Politzer, R. L., & McGroarty, M. (1985). An exploratory study of learning behaviors and their relationship to gains in linguistic and communicative competence. *TESOL Quarterly, 19,* 103-123.
2. Spurling, S., & Ilyin, D. (1985). The impact of learner variables on language test performance. *TESOL Quarterly, 19,* 283-301.

[616]

Comprehensive Identification Process.

Purpose: Screening program "to identify every child in a community who is eligible for a special preschool program or needs some kind of medical attention or therapy to function at full potential when he or she enters school."
Population: Ages 2.5–5.5.
Publication Date: 1975.
Acronym: CIP.
Scores, 25: 24 scores listed below plus final recommendations (scores consist of classification into 1 of 3 categories: pass, rescreen or refer to agency or program, complete evaluation recommended).
Administration: Individual.
Price Data, 1993: $145 per complete kit including the following materials: $18.25 per screening booklet; $27.85 per symbol booklet; $16.10 per 35 parent interview forms; $12.90 per 35 observation of behavior forms; $16.10 per 35 speech and expressive language record forms; $26.50 per 35 record folders; $42 per training filmstrip (English edition only); $24.10 per technical report (English edition only); $17.10 per interviewer's manual (30 pages); $18.25 per screening administrator's manual (48 pages).

Foreign Language Edition: Spanish edition available.
Time: (25–35) minutes.
Author: R. Reid Zehrbach.
Publisher: Scholastic Testing Service, Inc.
a) CIP CHILD INTERVIEWER'S RECORD FORM.
Scores, 5: Hearing Screening, Vision Screening, Developmental (Fine Motor, Cognitive-Verbal, Gross Motor).
Comments: Testing materials and equipment for hearing and vision screening must be obtained locally.
b) CIP SPEECH AND EXPRESSIVE LANGUAGE RECORD FORM.
Scores, 5: Articulation, Voice, Fluency, Expressive Language, Total.
Time: 10 minutes.
Author: Joan Good Erickson.
c) CIP OBSERVATION OF BEHAVIOR FORM.
Scores, 7: Hearing and Receptive Language, Vision, Physical/Motor, Speech and Expressive Language, Social Behavior (Response, Interaction), Affective Behavior.
d) CIP PARENT INTERVIEW FORM.
Scores, 7: Pregnancy/Birth/Hospitalization, Walking/Toilet Training, Hearing, Vision, Speech and Expressive Language, Medical, Social Affect.
Comments: History and ratings by parent.
Cross References: For reviews by Robert P. Anderson and Phyllis L. Newcomer, see 8:425 (1 reference).

TEST REFERENCES

1. Miller, L. J., & Sprong, T. A. (1986). Psychometric and qualitative comparison of four preschool screening instruments. *Journal of Learning Disabilities, 19,* 480-484.

[617]

Comprehensive Personality Profile.

Purpose: "To identify individuals with personality traits that are compatible with both occupational and organizational demands."
Population: Adults.
Publication Dates: 1985–93.
Acronym: CPP.
Scores, 17: Primary Scales (Emotional Intensity, Intuition, Recognition Motivation, Sensitivity, Assertiveness, Trust, Exaggeration), Secondary Traits (Ego Drive, Interpersonal Warmth, Stability, Empathy, Objectivity, Independence, Aggressiveness, Decisiveness, Tolerance, Efficiency).
Administration: Group.
Price Data, 1993: $125 per 5 kits including manual ('93, 48 pages), 5 questionnaires, and IBM compatible scoring software.
Time: (15–25) minutes.
Comments: Also available in French and Spanish; title on questionnaire is CPP Compatibility Questionnaire.
Authors: Wonderlic Personnel Test, Inc. and Larry L. Craft (questionnaire).
Publisher: Wonderlic Personnel Test, Inc.

TEST REFERENCES

1. Guastello, S. J., Guastello, D. D., & Craft, L. L. (1989). Assessment of the Barnum effect in computer-based test interpretations. *The Journal of Psychology, 123*, 477-484.

[618]

Comprehensive Receptive and Expressive Vocabulary Test.

Purpose: "Measures both receptive and expressive oral vocabulary."
Population: Ages 5-0 to 17-11.
Publication Date: 1994.
Acronym: CREVT.
Scores, 3: Receptive Vocabulary, Expressive Vocabulary, Total.
Administration: Individual.
Price Data, 1994: $114 per complete kit; $29 per 25 profile record forms (specify Form A or B); $34 per photo album picture book; $26 per manual.
Time: (20–30) minutes.
Authors: Gerald Wallace and Donald D. Hammill.
Publisher: PRO-ED, Inc.

[619]

Comprehensive Scales of Student Abilities: Quantifying Academic Skills and School-Related Behavior Through the Use of Teacher Judgments.

Purpose: To provide "a quick teacher rating scale of student ability."
Population: Ages 6-0 to 17-0.
Publication Date: 1994.
Acronym: CSSA.
Scores, 9: Verbal Thinking, Speech, Reading, Writing, Handwriting, Mathematics, General Facts, Basic Motor Generalizations, Social Behavior.
Administration: Individual.
Price Data, 1994: $64 per complete kit including 100 profile/record forms and manual (52 pages); $39 per 100 profile/record forms; $27 per manual.
Time: (5–10) minutes.
Authors: Donald D. Hammill and Wayne P. Hresko.
Publisher: PRO-ED, Inc.

[620]

Comprehensive Screening Test for Determining Optimal Communication Mode.

Purpose: "To evaluate the clients' performative skills in the areas of vocal production (Oral Skills Battery), gestural and motor production (Manual Skills Battery), and response to symbols and pictorial content (Pictographic Skills Battery)."
Population: Low functioning non-speaking persons.
Publication Date: 1984.
Acronym: CST.
Scores: 9 subtests: Manual Training Prerequisites, Movement Patterning, Cognitive Correlates for Manual Communication, Prerequisites Visual Training, Attending Behaviors and Accuracy Movement, Cognitive Correlates, Pre-Speech and Oral Awareness, Pre-Articulatory and Articulatory Skills, Auditory Awareness.
Administration: Individual.
Price Data, 1994: $45 per manual (50 pages) and reproducible forms for 9 subtests.
Time: (45) minutes.
Authors: Linda Infante House and Brenda S. Rogerson.
Publisher: United Educational Services, Inc.
Cross References: For reviews by Marilyn E. Demorest and Kenneth L. Sheldon, see 10:71.

[621]

Comprehensive Test of Adaptive Behavior.

Purpose: "Evaluates how well a retarded student is functioning independently in the environment."
Population: Birth–age 60.
Publication Date: 1984.
Acronym: CTAB.
Scores: 31 scores in 6 skill areas: 5 self-help skills (Toileting, Grooming, Dressing, Eating, Subtotal), 7 home living skills (Living Room, Kitchen-Cooking, Kitchen-Cleaning, Bedroom, Bath and Utility, Yard Care, Subtotal), 7 independent living skills (Health, Telephone, Travel, Time-Telling, Economic, Vocational, Subtotal), 4 social skills (Self-Awareness, Interaction, Leisure Skills, Subtotal), 3 sensory and motor skills (Sensory Awareness, Motor, Subtotal), 4 language and academic skills (Language Concepts, Math Skills, Reading and Writing, Subtotal), Total.
Administration: Individual.
Price Data: Available from publisher.
Time: Administration time not reported.
Comments: More comprehensive version of the Normative Adaptive Behavior Checklist (1819).
Authors: Gary L. Adams and Jean Hartleben (Parent/Guardian Survey).
Publisher: The Psychological Corporation.

TEST REFERENCES

1. Thackrey, M. (1991). A principal components analysis of the Comprehensive Test of Adaptive Behavior. *American Journal on Mental Retardation, 96*, 213-215.

[622]

Comprehensive Test of Visual Functioning.

Purpose: Designed to identify and differentiate type of visual perceptual dysfunction.
Population: Ages 8 and over.
Publication Date: 1990.
Acronym: CTVF.
Scores, 9: Visual/Letter Integration, Visual/Writing Integration, Nonverbal Visual Closure, Nonverbal Visual Reasoning/Memory, Spatial Orientation/Memory/Motor, Spatial Orientation/Motor, Visual Design/Motor, Visual Design/Memory/Motor, Total.
Administration: Individual.
Price Data, 1992: $79 per complete kit including manual (64 pages), stimulus cards/easel, and stimulus items; $18 per manual; $35 per examiner's directions and scoring protocol (18 pages); $22.50 per 25 examinee test booklets; $22.50 per stimulus cards/easel.
Time: (25) minutes.

Comments: "Norm-referenced"; includes 4 additional subtests (Visual Acuity, Visual Processing/Figure-Ground, Visual Tracking, Reading Word Analysis) which do not contribute to the overall visual performance quotient.
Authors: Sue L. Larson, Evelyn Buethe, and Gary J. Vitali.
Publisher: Slosson Educational Publications, Inc.

[623]

Comprehensive Tests of Basic Skills, Fourth Edition.
Purpose: "Designed to measure achievement in . . . reading, language, spelling, mathematics, study skills, science, and social studies."
Publication Dates: 1968–90.
Acronym: CTBS/4.
Administration: Group.
Price Data, 1994: $29 per 100 basic/complete battery profile sheets (specify level); $1.15 per class record sheet; $8.35 per examiner's manual (specify level and edition); $8.35 per multi-level norms book ('89, 125 pages); $19.55 per class management guide ('90, 192 pages); $11.75 per test coordinator's handbook ('90, 146 pages); $5.90 per technical report; $2.05 per preview materials book; scoring service available from publisher.
Author: CTB/McGraw-Hill.
Publisher: CTB Macmillan/McGraw-Hill.

a) LEVEL K.
Population: Grades K.0–K.9.
Scores, 7: Reading (Visual Recognition, Sound Recognition, Vocabulary, Comprehension, Total), Mathematics Concepts and Applications, Total.
Editions, 3: Complete, Survey, Benchmark.
Price Data: $70.70 per 35 complete battery machine-scorable test books; $46.90 per 35 complete battery hand-scorable test books; $59.85 per 35 survey machine-scorable test books; $39.90 per 35 survey hand-scorable test books; $8.40 per 35 practice tests.
Time: (117) minutes.
b) LEVEL 10.
Population: Grades K.6–1.6.
Scores, 6: Reading (Word Analysis, Vocabulary, Comprehension, Total), Mathematics Concepts and Applications, Total.
Editions, 3: Same as *a* above.
Price Data: Same as *a* above.
Time: (113) minutes.
c) LEVEL 11.
Population: Grades 1.0–2.2.
Scores, 13: Reading (Word Analysis, Vocabulary, Comprehension, Total), Language (Mechanics, Expression, Total), Mathematics (Computation, Concepts and Applications, Total), Science, Social Studies, Total.
Editions, 6: Same as *a* above plus Basic, Reading, and Mathematics.
Price Data: $95.55 per 35 basic machine-scorable test books; $67.90 per 35 basic hand-scorable test

books; $66.15 per 35 reading or mathematics machine-scorable test books; $43.75 per 35 reading or mathematics hand-scorable test books; $104.65 per 35 complete battery machine-scorable test books; $67.90 per 35 complete battery hand-scorable test books; $89.95 per 35 survey machine-scorable test books; $54.50 per 35 survey hand-scorable test books; $22.75 per 35 locator tests; $8.40 per 35 practice tests; $22.75 per 50 locator test answer sheets; $6.35 per locator test directions.
Time: (242) minutes.
d) LEVEL 12.
Population: Grades 1.6–3.2.
Scores, 14: Scores same as *c* above plus Spelling.
Editions, 6: Same as *c* above.
Price Data: Same as *c* above.
Time: (287) minutes.
e) LEVEL 13.
Population: Grades 2.6–4.2.
Scores, 14: Same as *d* above.
Editions, 6: Same as *c* above.
Price Data: Same as *c* above.
Time: (325) minutes.
f) LEVEL 14.
Population: Grades 3.6–5.2.
Scores, 15: Same as *d* above plus Study Skills.
Editions, 6: Same as *c* above.
Price Data: $85.75 per 35 basic reusable test books; $48.05 per 35 reading or mathematics reusable test books; $88.90 per 35 complete battery reusable test books; $75.95 per 35 survey reusable test books; $11.20 per 35 practice tests; $22.75 per 35 locator tests; $23.40 per 50 basic, complete, CompuScan answer sheets; $13 per 50 reading or mathematics CompuScan answer sheets; $17 per 25 basic or complete battery SCOREZE answer sheets (specify subject area); $17 per 25 survey SCOREZE answer sheets (specify subject area); $17.50 per 50 locator answer sheets; $31.95 per basic, complete, battery, hand-scoring stencils; $21.80 per survey hand-scoring stencils; $6.35 per locator test directions.
Time: (341) minutes.
g) LEVEL 15.
Population: Grades 4.6–6.2.
Scores, 15: Same as *f* above.
Editions, 6: Same as *c* above.
Price Data: Same as *f* above.
Time: Same as *f* above.
h) LEVEL 16.
Population: Grades 5.6–7.2.
Scores, 15: Same as *f* above.
Editions, 6: Same as *c* above.
Price Data: Same as *f* above.
Time: Same as *f* above.
i) LEVEL 17/18.
Population: Grades 6.6–9.2.
Scores, 15: Same as *f* above.
Editions, 6: Same as *c* above.
Price Data: Same as *f* above.
Time: Same as *f* above.

j) LEVEL 19/20.
Population: Grades 8.6–11.2.
Scores, 15: Same as *f* above.
Editions, 6: Same as *c* above.
Price Data: Same as *f* above.
Time: Same as *f* above.
k) LEVEL 21/22.
Population: Grades 10.6–12.9.
Scores, 15: Same as *f* above.
Editions, 6: Same as *c* above.
Price Data: Same as *f* above.
Time: Same as *f* above.

Cross References: For reviews by Kenneth D. Hopkins and M. David Miller, see 11:81 (70 references); for reviews by Robert L. Linn and Lorrie A. Shepard of an earlier form, see 9:258 (29 references); see also T3:551 (59 references); for reviews by Warren G. Findley and Anthony J. Nitko of an earlier edition, see 8:12 (13 references); see also T2:11 (1 reference); for reviews by J. Stanley Ahmann and Frederick G. Brown and excerpted reviews by Brooke B. Collison and Peter A. Taylor (rejoinder by Verna White) of Forms Q and R, see 7:9. For reviews of subtests of earlier editions, see 8:721 (1 review), 8:825 (1 review), 7:685 (1 review), 7:514 (2 reviews), and 7:778 (1 review).

TEST REFERENCES

1. Lomax, R. G. (1983). Applying structural modeling to some component processes of reading comprehension development. *The Journal of Experimental Education, 52*, 33-40.
2. Gagne, E. D., Yarbrough, D. B., Weidemann, C., & Bell, M. S. (1984). The effects of text familiarity and cohesion on retrieval of information learned from text. *The Journal of Experimental Education, 52*, 207-213.
3. Gunderson, L. (1984). One last word list. *The Alberta Journal of Educational Research, 30*, 259-269.
4. Carrick, D. A., & Kinzer, C. K. (1985). Oral reading miscues and dialect variation: A study across black and standard English IRI passages. *National Reading Conference Yearbook, 34*, 344-349.
5. Neville, D. D., & Searls, E. F. (1985). The effect of sentence-combining and kernel-identification training on the syntactic componet of reading comprehension. *Research in the Teaching of English, 19*, 37-61.
6. Schwartz, R. M., & Raphael, T. E. (1985). Instruction in the concept of definition as a basis for vocabulary acquisition. *National Reading Conference Yearbook, 34*, 116-123.
7. Martin, M. A., & Konopak, B. C. (1987). An instructional investigation of students' ideas generated during content area writing. *Yearbook of the National Reading Conference, 36*, 265-271.
8. Mantzicopoulous, P., Morrison, D. C., Hinshaw, S. P., & Carte, E. T. (1989). Nonpromotion in kindergarten: The role of cognitive, perceptual, visual-motor, behavioral, achievement, socioeconomic, and demographic characteristics. *American Educational Research Journal, 26*, 107-121.
9. DuPaul, G. J. (1991). Parent and teacher ratings of ADHD symptoms: Psychometric properties in a community-based sample. *Journal of Clinical Child Psychology, 20*, 245-253.
10. DuPaul, G. J., Rapport, M. D., & Perriello, L. M. (1991). Teacher ratings of academic skills: The development of the Academic Performance Rating Scale. *School Psychology Review, 20*, 284-300.
11. Hagborg, W. J., Masella, G., Palladino, P., & Shepardson, J. (1991). A follow-up study of high school students with a history of grade retention. *Psychology in the Schools, 28*, 310-317.
12. Silver, R., & Carrion, F. (1991). Using the Silver Drawing Test in school and hospital. *The American Journal of Art Therapy, 30*, 36-43.
13. Swanson, H. L., O'Connor, J. E., & Carter, K. R. (1991). Problem-solving subgroups as a measure of intellectual giftedness. *The British Journal of Educational Psychology, 61*, 55-72.
14. Swanson, H. L., Reffel, J., & Trahan, M. (1991). Naturalistic memory in learning-disabled and skilled readers. *Journal of Abnormal Child Psychology, 19*, 117-147.
15. Yen, W. M., & Candell, G. L. (1991). Increasing score reliability with item-pattern scoring: An empirical study in five score metrics. *Applied Measurement in Education, 4*(3), 209-228.
16. Baxter, G. P., Shavelson, R. J., Goldman, S. R., & Pine, J. (1992). Evaluation of procedure-based scoring for hands-on science assessment. *Journal of Educational Measurement, 29*, 1-17.
17. Hagborg, W. J., & Wachman, E. M. (1992). The Arlin Test of Formal Reasoning and the identification of accelerated mathematics students. *Educational and Psychological Measurement, 52*, 437-442.
18. Juvonen, J., & Bear, G. (1992). Social adjustment of children with and without learning disabilities in integrated classrooms. *Journal of Educational Psychology, 84*, 322-330.
19. Lapan, R. T., & Jingeleski, J. (1992). Circumscribing vocational aspirations in junior high school. *Journal of Counseling Psychology, 39*, 81-90.
20. Matzicopoulos, P., & Morrison, D. (1992). Kindergarten retention: Academic and behavioral outcomes through the end of second grade. *American Educational Research Journal, 29*, 182-198.
21. Widaman, K. F., MacMillan, D. L., Hemsley, R. E., Little, T. D., & Balow, I. H. (1992). Differences in adolescents' self-concept as a function of academic level, ethnicity, and gender. *American Journal on Mental Retardation, 96*, 387-404.
22. Ford, D. V. (1993). Support for the achievement ideology and determinants of underachievement as perceived by gifted, above-average, and average Black students. *Journal for the Education of the Gifted, 16*, 280-298.
23. Hiebert, J., & Wearne, D. (1993). Instructional tasks, classroom discourse, and students' learning in second-grade arithmetic. *American Educational Research Journal, 30*, 393-425.

[624]

Computer Literacy and Computer Science Tests.

Purpose: "The tests of Computer Literacy measure concepts related to understanding the capabilities, applications, and implications of computer technology." The Computer Science test assesses "skills related to software development, the design and operation of hardware, and specific problem solving applications."
Publication Date: 1984.
Administration: Group.
Price Data: Not available.
Time: 45(60) minutes per test.
Comments: Examiner's manual title is Computer Literacy and Science Tests.
Author: Roy M. Gabriel.
Publisher: Northwest Regional Educational Laboratory [No reply from publisher; status unknown].
a) COMPUTER LITERACY TEST.
Population: Grades 4, 7, and 11.
Scores, 5: Interacting with Computers, Functions and Uses of Computers, Problem Solving, Computers' Impact on Society, Total.
Levels, 3: Grade 4, Grade 7, Grade 11.
b) COMPUTER SCIENCE TEST.
Population: Grades 9–12.
Scores, 4: Writing Programs, Hardware Operations, Problem Solving with Computers, Total.
Cross References: For a review by Gary L. Marco, see 11:82 (1 reference).

[625]

Computer Operator Aptitude Battery.

Purpose: Predict "ability to perform computer operator job and potential for learning computer programming."
Population: Experienced computer operators and trainees.

Publication Dates: 1973–74.
Acronym: COAB.
Scores, 4: Sequence Recognition, Format Checking, Logical Thinking, Total.
Administration: Group.
Price Data, 1985: $85 per test booklets (set of five); $52 per answer sheets (set of five); $10 per examiner's manual ('74, 19 pages).
Time: 45(55) minutes.
Comments: Tape cassette available for administration.
Author: A. Holloway.
Publisher: Science Research Associates/London House.

[626]

Computer Programmer Aptitude Battery.
Purpose: To "measure abilities related to success in computer programmer and systems analysis fields."
Population: Applicants for training or employment as computer programmers or systems analysts.
Publication Dates: 1964–85.
Acronym: CPAB.
Scores, 6: Verbal Meaning, Reasoning, Letter Series, Number Ability, Diagramming, Total.
Administration: Group.
Price Data, 1987: $85 per 5 reusable test booklets; $52 per 25 hand-scorable answer sheets; $10 per examiner's manual ('85, 32 pages).
Time: 79(89) minutes.
Authors: Jean Maier Palormo and Bruce M. Fisher (manual revision).
Publisher: Science Research Associates/London House.
Foreign Adaptations: British edition; 1964–71; standardization supplement by Peter Saville; NFER-Nelson Publishing Co., Ltd. [England].
Cross References: For reviews by Roderick K. Mahurin and William D. Schafer, see 11:85; see also T3:557 (1 reference); for additional information and a review by Nick L. Smith, see 8:1079 (3 references); see also T2:2334 (2 references); for reviews by Richard T. Johnson and Donald J. Veldman, see 7:1089 (2 references).

[627]

[Computer Programmer Test Package].
Purpose: "To assist in the screening and selection of applicants most likely to succeed in the programming area" and to assist a supervisor in quantifying an "objective evaluation of a programmer's work performance."
Administration: Group.
Parts, 2: Aptitude Profile Test, Performance Rating Scale.
Price Data, 1987: $30 per complete set including all materials below plus research summary ('84, 9 pages).
Author: Industrial Psychology International, Inc.
Publisher: Industrial Psychology International, Inc.

a) APTITUDE PROFILE TEST.
Population: Applicants for computer programming jobs.
Publication Dates: 1981–84.
Scores: 5 subtests: Office Terms, Numbers, Judgment, Parts, Perception.
Price Data: $16 per instruction kit including manual ('84, 4 pages) and all aptitude profile material; $10 per set of subtests and profile sheet.
Time: 30(40) minutes.
b) PERFORMANCE RATING SCALE.
Population: Computer programmers.
Publication Date: 1984.
Scores: Item scores only.
Price Data: $16 per instruction kit including 3 performance rating scales, manual ('84, 4 pages), and norms sheet; $21 per 20 performance rating scales.
Time: Administration time not reported.
Comments: Ratings by supervisor.
Cross References: For reviews by David O. Herman and Kevin L. Moreland, see 11:86.

[628]

Comrey Personality Scales.
Purpose: Developed to measure major personality characteristics.
Population: Ages 16 and over.
Publication Date: 1970.
Acronym: CPS.
Scores, 10: Trust vs. Defensiveness (T), Orderliness vs. Lack of Compulsion (O), Social Conformity vs. Rebelliousness (C), Activity vs. Lack of Energy (A), Emotional Stability vs. Neuroticism (S), Extraversion vs. Introversion (E), Mental Toughness vs. Sensitivity (M), Empathy vs. Egocentrism (P), Validity Check (V), Response Bias (R).
Administration: Group.
Price Data, 1993: $17 per 25 tests; $11.50 per 50 answer sheets; $102 per 500 answer sheets; $12.50 per 50 machine-scoring answer sheets; $107.25 per 500 machine-scoring answer sheets; $12.50 per 50 profile sheets; $78.75 per 500 profile sheets; $3.25 per manual (40 pages); $20 per Handbook of Interpretations; $6.25 per specimen set; $3.35 per hand-scoring instructions.
Time: (35–50) minutes.
Comments: Comrey Personality Scales, Short Form is also available with same scales and prices.
Author: Andrew L. Comrey.
Publisher: EdITS/Educational and Industrial Testing Service.
Cross References: See 9:261 (8 references) and T3:558 (22 references); for a review by Edgar Howarth, see 8:527 (27 references); for reviews by R. G. Demaree and M. Y. Quereshi, see 7:59 (20 references).

TEST REFERENCES

1. Berry, D. T. R., & Wilse, B. W. (1984). Interrelations of trait personality and sleep structure variables: Further negative results. *Perceptual and Motor Skills, 59*, 611-614.

2. Comrey, A. L. (1984). Comparison of two methods to identify major personality factors. *Applied Psychological Measurement, 8,* 397-408.
3. Meier, S. T. (1984). The construct validity of burnout. *Journal of Occupational Psychology, 57,* 211-219.
4. O'Malley, M. N., & Gillette, C. S. (1984). Exploring the relations between traits and emotions. *Journal of Personality, 52,* 274-284.
5. Thomas, D. A., & Reznikoff, M. (1984). Sex role orientation, personality structure, and adjustment in women. *Journal of Personality Assessment, 48,* 28-36.
6. Comrey, A. L., & Schiebel, D. (1985). Personality factor structure in psychiatric outpatients and normals. *Multivariate Behavioral Research, 20,* 419-426.
7. Comrey, A. L., & Schiebel, D. (1985). Personality test correlates of psychiatric case history data. *Journal of Consulting and Clinical Psychology, 53,* 470-479.
8. Johnson, R. C., Ahern, F. M., Nagoshi, C. T., McClearn, G. E., Vandenberg, S. G., & Wilson, J. R. (1985). Age and group-specific cohort effects on personality test scores: A study of three Hawaiian populations. *Journal of Cross-Cultural Psychology, 16,* 467-481.
9. Marsh, H. W. (1985). The structure of masculinity/femininity: An application of confirmatory factor analysis to higher-order factor structures and factorial invariance. *Multivariate Behavioral Research, 20,* 427-449.
10. Stoner, S. B., & Panek, P. E. (1985). Age and sex differences with the Comrey Personality Scales. *The Journal of Psychology, 119,* 137-142.
11. Swimmer, G. I., & Ramanaiah, N. V. (1985). Convergent and discriminate validity of selected assertiveness measures. *Journal of Personality and Social Psychology, 49,* 243-249.
12. Friedland, D. L., & Michael, W. B. (1987). The reliability of a promotion job knowledge examination scored by number of items right and by four confidence weighting procedures and its corresponding concurrent validity estimates relative to performance criterion ratings. *Educational and Psychological Measurement, 47(1),* 179-188.
13. Montag, I., & Comrey, A. L. (1987). Millon MCMI scales factor analyzed and correlated with MMPI and CPS scales. *Multivariate Behavioral Research, 22,* 401-413.
14. Noller, P., Law, H. & Comrey, A. L. (1987). Cattell, Comrey, and Eysenck personality factors compared: More evidence for the five robust factors? *Journal of Personality and Social Psychology, 53,* 775-782.
15. Weiss, A. S. (1987). Psychological distress and well-being in Hare Krishnas. *Psychological Reports, 61,* 23-25.
16. Weiss, A. S., & Comrey, A. L. (1987). Personality characteristics of Hare Krishnas. *Journal of Personality Assessment, 51,* 399-413.
17. Weiss, A. S., & Comrey, A. L. (1987). Personality factor structure among Hare Krishnas. *Educational and Psychological Measurement, 47(2),* 317-328.
18. Noller, P., Law, H., & Comrey, A. L. (1988). Factor analysis of the Comrey Personality Scales in an Australian sample. *Multivariate Behavioral Research, 23,* 397-411.
19. Hough, L. M., Eaton, N. K., Dunnette, M. D., Kamp, J. D., & McCloy, R. A. (1990). Criterion-related validities of personality constructs and the effect of response distortion on those validities. *Journal of Applied Psychology, 75(5),* 581-595.
20. Caprara, G. V., Barbaranelli, C., & Comrey, A. L. (1992). Validation of the Comrey Personality Scales on an Italian sample. *Journal of Research in Personality, 26,* 21-31.
21. Brief, D. E., & Comrey, A. L. (1993). A profile of personality for a Russian sample: As indicated by the Comrey Personality Scales. *Journal of Personality Assessment, 60,* 267-284.

[629]

Comrey Personality Scales—Short Form.

Purpose: To provide a comprehensive, multidimensional assessment instrument for measuring eight personality dimensions.
Population: High school, college, and adults.
Publication Date: 1993.
Acronym: CPS Short Form.
Scores, 10: Trust vs. Defensiveness, Orderliness vs. Lack of Compulsion, Social Conformity vs. Rebelliousness, Activity vs. Lack of Energy, Emotional Stability vs. Neuroticism, Extraversion vs. Introversion, Mental Toughness vs. Sensitivity, Empathy vs. Egocentrism, Validity Check, Response Bias.
Administration: Group.
Price Data, 1993: $50 per 50 test booklets and

answer sheets combined [$70 per 100, $250 per 500]; $4.35 per hand-scoring instructions; $11.50 per 50 profile sheets [$21 per 100, $95.25 per 500].
Time: Administration time not reported.
Comments: Includes same scales as the Comrey Personality Scales (628) but has fewer items per scale.
Author: Andrew L. Comrey.
Publisher: EdITS/Educational and Industrial Testing Service.

[630]

Concept Assessment Kit—Conservation.

Purpose: To "determine child's level of conservation by his conservation behavior and his comprehension of the principle involved."
Population: Ages 4–7.
Publication Date: 1968.
Acronym: CAK.
Administration: Individual.
Price Data, 1993: $46.50 per complete kit including Forms A, B, and C, and manual (29 pages); $9 per 25 tests [$31 per 100 tests, $117 per 500 tests] (specify Form A or B); $9 per 25 Form C tests [$27.50 per 100, $112 per 500]; $2.90 per manual.
Authors: Marcel L. Goldschmid and Peter M. Bentler.
Publisher: EdITS/Educational and Industrial Testing Service.
a) FORMS A AND B.
Scores, 13: 2 scores (Behavior, Explanation) in each of 6 areas (2-Dimensional Space, Number, Substance, Continuous Quantity, Weight, Discontinuous Quantity), Total.
Time: (15) minutes per form.
b) FORM C.
Scores, 13: 2 scores (Behavior, Explanation) in each of 3 Areas and 3 Lengths, Total.
Cross References: See T3:559 (17 references), 8:238 (32 references), and T2:549 (5 references); for a review by J. Douglas Ayers, and excerpted reviews by Rheta DeVries (with Lawrence Kohlberg), Vernon C. Hall (with Michael Mery), and Charles D. Smock, see 7:437 (5 references).

TEST REFERENCES

1. Bernard, R. M. (1982). Young children's perception of implied motion portrayal in still photographs. *Perceptual and Motor Skills, 55,* 1267-1276.
2. Krebs, D., & Gillmore, J. (1982). The relationship among the first stages of cognitive development, role-taking abilities, and moral development. *Child Development, 53,* 877-886.
3. Frankel, M. T., & Moye, E. R. (1984). The effects of cognitive level on clustering in free recall. *The Journal of Psychology, 117,* 239-243.
4. Lehnert, L. (1984). Relation of ability to conserve and use of specific syntactic features. *Perceptual and Motor Skills, 59,* 839-846.
5. Kahn, J. V. (1985). Evidence of the similar-structure hypothesis controlling for organicity. *American Journal of Mental Deficiency, 89,* 372-378.
6. Konstantareas, M. M., & Homatidis, S. (1985). Cognitive, perspective-taking skills and quality of play in behaviorally disturbed children. *Child Psychiatry and Human Development, 16,* 97-112.
7. Speece, D. L., McKinney, J. D., & Appelbaum, M. I. (1986). Longitudinal development of conservation skills in learning disabled children. *Journal of Learning Disabilities, 19,* 302-307.

8. Goh, D. S., & Wood, J. M. H. (1987). Development of conservation and academic achievement in learning disabled children. *Psychological Reports, 60,* 71-77.

9. Sigman, M., & Erdynast, A. (1988). Interpersonal understanding and moral judgement in adolescents with emotional and cognitive disorders. *Child Psychiatry and Human Development, 19,* 36-44.

10. Campbell, F. A., & Ramey, C. T. (1990). The relationship between Piagetian cognitive development, mental test performance, and academic achievement in high-risk students with and without early educational experience. *Intelligence, 14,* 293-308.

11. Kinney, A. (1990). Disturbed children's and adolescents' comprehension of psychological mechanisms of defense. *The Journal of Genetic Psychology, 151,* 419-428.

[631]
Concept Attainment Test.
Purpose: To measure the "ability to develop a system of reasoning."
Population: College and adults.
Publication Date: 1959.
Acronym: CAT.
Scores: Total score only.
Administration: Group.
Manual: No manual.
Price Data: Available from publisher.
Time: 50(60) minutes.
Author: J. M. Schepers.
Publisher: National Institute for Personnel Research of the Human Sciences Research Council [South Africa].

TEST REFERENCES
1. Platt, J. E., Campbell, M., Green, W. H., & Grega, D. M. (1984). Cognitive effects of lithium carbonate and haloperidol in treatment-resistant aggressive children. *Archives of General Psychiatry, 41,* 657-662.

[632]
Conceptual Systems Test.
Purpose: Measures an individual's level of abstractness-concreteness.
Population: Grades 7 and over.
Publication Date: 1971.
Acronym: CST.
Scores, 6: Divine Fate Control, Need for Structure Order, Need to Help People, Need for People, Interpersonal Aggression, Anomie.
Administration: Group.
Manual: No manual.
Price Data: Not available.
Time: (25–30) minutes.
Authors: O. J. Harvey and James K. Hoffmeister.
Publisher: Test Analysis and Development Corporation [No reply from publisher; status unknown].
Cross References: See T3:563 (2 references); for a review by Andrew L. Comrey, see 8:529 (24 references); see also T2:1142 (5 references).

TEST REFERENCES
1. Koballa, T. R., Jr., & Shrigley, R. L. (1983). Credibility and persuasion: A sociopsychological approach to changing the attitudes toward energy conservation of preservice elementary school science teachers. *Journal of Research in Science Teaching, 20,* 683-696.
2. Isaacson, D. K., & Williams, J. D. (1984). The relationship of conceptual systems theory and Piagetian theory. *The Journal of Psychology, 117,* 3-6.

3. Kagan, D. M. (1987). Cognitive level of student teachers and their perceptions of cooperating teachers. *The Alberta Journal of Educational Research, 33,* 180-190.

[633]
Concise Word Reading Test.
Purpose: Assesses "word reading skill."
Population: Ages 7–12.
Publication Date: 1969.
Scores: Total score only.
Administration: Individual.
Price Data: Not available.
Time: (3–4) minutes.
Author: R. J. Andrews.
Publisher: Teaching and Testing Resources [No reply from publisher; status unknown].

[634]
Conflict Management Appraisal.
Purpose: "Designed to provide information about the various ways people react to and try to manage the differences between themselves and others."
Population: Adults.
Publication Date: 1986.
Acronym: CMA.
Scores, 20: 5 conflict management styles (9/1 Win-Lose, 1/9 Yield-Lose, 1/1 Lose-Leave, 5/5 Compromise, 9/9 Synergistic) for each of 4 contexts (Personal Orientation, Interpersonal Relationships, Small Group Relationships, Intergroup Relationships).
Administration: Individual.
Price Data, 1992: $6.95 per instrument.
Time: (30) minutes.
Comments: Adaptation of the Conflict Management Survey (635); to be used in conjunction with the Conflict Management Survey; ratings by person well acquainted with subject.
Author: Jay Hall.
Publisher: Teleometrics International.

[635]
Conflict Management Survey.
Purpose: "Designed to provide information about the various ways people react to and try to manage the differences between themselves and others."
Population: Adults.
Publication Dates: 1969–86.
Acronym: CMS.
Scores, 20: 5 conflict management styles (9/1 Win-Lose, 1/9 Yield-Lose, 1/1 Lose-Leave, 5/5 Compromise, 9/9 Synergistic) for each of 4 contexts (Personal Orientation, Interpersonal Relationships, Small Group Relationships, Intergroup Relationships).
Administration: Group.
Price Data, 1990: $6.95 per instrument.
Time: Administration time not reported.
Comments: Self-ratings.
Author: Jay Hall.
Publisher: Teleometrics International.
Cross References: For a review by Frank J. Landy, see 8:1173 (2 references).

[636]

Conners' Rating Scales.

Purpose: Designed to "evaluate the reported problem behavior of the child."

Population: Ages 3–17.

Publication Date: 1989.

Administration: Individual.

Price Data, 1993: $99 per complete user package including 25 CPRS-48, CPRS-93, CTRS-28, and CTRS-39 QuikScore™ forms and manual; $20 per 25 QuikScore™ forms (select form); $27 per manual; $145 per IBM microcomputer software (50 uses).

Author: C. Keith Conners.

Publisher: Multi-Health Systems, Inc.

   a) CONNERS' PARENT RATING SCALES.

   Comments: Ratings by parents.

   1) *Conners' Parent Rating Scales-93.*

   Acronym: CPRS-93.

   Scores, 8: Conduct Disorder, Fearful-Anxious, Restless-Disorganized, Learning Problem, Psychosomatic, Obsessional, Antisocial, Hyperactive-Immature.

   Time: (30) minutes.

   2) *Conners' Parent Rating Scales-48.*

   Acronym: CPRS-48.

   Scores, 6: Conduct Problem, Learning Problem, Psychosomatic, Impulsive-Hyperactive, Anxiety, Hyperactivity Index.

   Time: (20) minutes.

   b) CONNERS' TEACHER RATING SCALES.

   Time: (15) minutes.

   Comments: Ratings by teachers.

   1) *Conners' Teacher Rating Scales-39.*

   Acronym: CTRS-39.

   Scores, 7: Hyperactivity, Conduct Problem, Emotional Overindulgent, Anxious-Passive, Asocial, Daydream-Attention Problem, Hyperactivity Index.

   2) *Conners' Teacher Rating Scales-28.*

   Acronym: CTRS-28.

   Scores, 4: Conduct Problem, Hyperactivity, Inattentive-Passive, Hyperactivity Index.

Cross References: For reviews by Brian K. Martens and Judy Oehler-Stinnett, see 11:87 (83 references).

TEST REFERENCES

1. Tarnowski, K. J., Holden, E. W., & Prinz, R. J. (1986). Children's evaluations of their own peer relations. *Child Psychiatry and Human Development, 17,* 28-37.
2. Glow, R. A., Glow, P. H., & White, M. (1987). Parent-perceived child behavior problems: Comparison of normative and clinical factors of the Adelaide-Conners Parent Rating Scale. *Journal of Psychopathology and Behavioral Assessment, 9,* 255-280.
3. Lahey, B. B., McBurnett, K., Piacentini, J. C., Hartdagen, S., Walker, J., Frick, P. J., & Hynd, G. W. (1987). Agreement of parent and teacher rating scales with comprehensive clinical assessments of attention deficit disorder with hyperactivity. *Journal of Psychopathology and Behavioral Assessment, 9,* 429-439.
4. Beitchman, J. H., Peterson, M., & Clegg, M. (1988). Speech and language impairment and psychiatric disorder: The relevance of family demographic variables. *Child Psychiatry and Human Development, 18,* 191-207.
5. Doerfler, L. A., Felner, R. D., Rowlison, R. T., Raley, P. A., & Evans, E. (1988). Depression in children and adolescents: A comparative

analysis of the utility and construct validity of two assessment measures. *Journal of Consulting and Clinical Psychology, 56,* 769-772.
6. Rosén, L. A., Bender, M. E., Sorrell, S., Booth, S. R., McGrath, M. L., & Drabman, R. S. (1988). Effects of sugar (sucrose) on children's behavior. *Journal of Consulting and Clinical Psychology, 56,* 583-589.
7. Strauss, C. C., Lahey, B. B., Frick, P., Frame, C. L., & Hynd, G. W. (1988). Peer social status of children with anxiety disorders. *Journal of Consulting and Clinical Psychology, 56,* 137-141.
8. Cohen, N. J. (1989). Sex differences in child psychiatric outpatients: Cognitive, personality, and behavioral characteristics. *Child Psychiatry and Human Development, 20,* 113-122.
9. Conte, R., & Humphreys, R. (1989). Repeated reading using audiotaped material enhances oral reading in children with reading difficulties. *Journal of Communication Disorders, 22,* 65-79.
10. Band, E. B., & Weisz, J. R. (1990). Developmental differences in primary and secondary control coping and adjustment to juvenile diabetes. *Journal of Clinical Child Psychology, 19,* 150-158.
11. Diamond, J. M., & Deane, F. P. (1990). Conners Teacher Questionnaire: Effects and implications of frequent administration. *Journal of Clinical Child Psychology, 19,* 202-204.
12. Fisher, M., Barkley, R. A., Edelbrock, C. S., & Smallish, L. (1990). The adolescent outcome of hyperactive children diagnosed by research criteria: II. Academic, attentional, and neuropsychological status. *Journal of Consulting and Clinical Psychology, 58,* 580-588.
13. Horn, W. F., Ialongo, N., Greenberg, G., Packard, T., & Smith-Unberry, C. (1990). Additive effects of behavioral parent training and self-control therapy with attention deficit hyperactivity disordered children. *Journal of Clinical Child Psychology, 19,* 98-110.
14. Arcia, E., Ornstein, P. A., & Otto, D. A. (1991). Neurobehavioral Evaluation System (NES) and school performance. *Journal of School Psychology, 29,* 337-352.
15. Berk, L. E., & Potts, M. K. (1991). Development and functional significance of private speech among attention-deficit hyperactivity disordered and normal boys. *Journal of Abnormal Child Psychology, 19,* 357-377.
16. Bloomquist, M. L., August, G. J., & Ostrander, R. (1991). Effects of a school-based cognitive-behavioral intervention for ADHD children. *Journal of Abnormal Child Psychology, 19,* 591-605.
17. Brown, R. T., Jaffe, S. L., Silverstein, J., & Magee, H. (1991). Methylphenidate and adolescents hospitalized with conduct disorder: Dose effects on classroom behavior, academic performance, and impulsivity. *Journal of Clinical Child Psychology, 20,* 282-292.
18. Conte, R., & Regehr, S. M. (1991). Learning and transfer of inductive reasoning rules in overactive children. *Cognitive Therapy and Research, 15,* 129-139.
19. DuPaul, G. J. (1991). Parent and teacher ratings of ADHD symptoms: Psychometric properties in a community-based sample. *Journal of Clinical Child Psychology, 20,* 245-253.
20. DuPaul, G. J., Rapport, M. D., & Perriello, L. M. (1991). Teacher ratings of academic skills: The development of the Academic Performance Rating Scale. *School Psychology Review, 20,* 284-300.
21. Evans, S. W., & Pelham, W. E. (1991). Psychostimulant effects on academic and behavioral measures for ADHD junior high school students in a lecture format classroom. *Journal of Abnormal Child Psychology, 19,* 537-552.
22. Fischer, M., & Newby, R. F. (1991). Assessment of stimulant response in ADHD children using a refined multimethod clinical protocol. *Journal of Clinical Child Psychology, 20,* 232-244.
23. Gadow, K. D., Nolan, E. E., Paolicelli, L. M., & Sprafkin, J. (1991). A procedure for assessing the effects of methylphenidate in hyperactive children in public school settings. *Journal of Clinical Child Psychology, 20,* 268-276.
24. Hubbard, J. A., & Newcomb, A. F. (1991). Initial dyadic peer interaction of attention deficit-hyperactivity disorder and normal boys. *Journal of Abnormal Child Psychology, 19,* 179-195.
25. Johnston, C. (1991). Predicting mothers' and fathers' perceptions of child behaviour problems. *Canadian Journal of Behavioural Science, 23,* 349-357.
26. Klorman, R., Brumaghim, J. T., Fitzpatrick, P. A., & Borgstedt, A. D. (1991). Methylphenidate speeds evaluation processes of attention deficit disorder adolescents during a continuous performance test. *Journal of Abnormal Child Psychology, 19,* 263-283.
27. Milich, R., & Okazaki, M. (1991). An examination of learned helplessness among attention-deficit hyperactivity disordered boys. *Journal of Abnormal Child Psychology, 19,* 607-623.
28. Milich, R., Carlson, C. L., Pelham, W. E., Jr., & Licht, B. G. (1991). Effects of methylphenidate on the persistence of ADHD boys following failure experiences. *Journal of Abnormal Child Psychology, 19,* 519-536.
29. O'Neill, M. E., & Douglas, V. I. (1991). Study strategies and story recall in attention deficit disorder and reading disability. *Journal of Abnormal Child Psychology, 19,* 671-692.

30. Olson, S. L., & Brodfeld, P. L. (1991). Assessment of peer rejection and externalizing behavior problems in preschool boys: A short-term longitudinal study. *Journal of Abnormal Child Psychology, 19,* 493-503.

31. Pearson, D. A., Lane, D. M., & Swanson, J. M. (1991). Auditory attention switching in hyperactive children. *Journal of Abnormal Child Psychology, 19,* 479-492.

32. Pelham, W. E., Milich, R., Cummings, E. M., Murphy, D. A., Schaughency, E. A., & Greiner, A. R. (1991). Effects of background anger, provocation and methylphenidate on emotional arousal and aggressive responding in attention-deficit hyperactivity disordered boys with and without concurrent aggressiveness. *Journal of Abnormal Child Psychology, 19,* 407-426.

33. Schachar, R. J., & Wachsmith, R. (1991). Family dysfunction and psychosocial adversity: Comparison of attention deficit disorder, conduct disorder, normal and clinical controls. *Canadian Journal of Behavioural Science, 23,* 332-348.

34. Sharma, V., Halperin, J. H., Newcorn, J. N., & Wolf, L. E. (1991). The dimension of focussed attention: Relationship to behavior and cognitive functioning in children. *Perceptual and Motor Skills, 72,* 787-793.

35. Tryon, W. W., Pinto, L. P., & Morrison, D. F. (1991). Reliability assessment of pedometer activity measurements. *Journal of Psychopathology and Behavioral Assessment, 13,* 27-44.

36. Aman, M. G., Werry, J. S., & Turbott, S. H. (1992). Behavior of children with seizures: Comparison with norming and effect of seizure type. *Journal of Nervous and Mental Disease, 180,* 124-129.

37. Cohen, S., & Bromet, E. (1992). Maternal predictors of behavioral disturbance in preschool children: A research note. *Journal of Child Psychology and Psychiatry, 33,* 941-946.

38. Pelham, W. E., Murphy, D. A., Vannatta, K., Milich, R., Licht, B. G., Gnagy, E. M., Greenslade, K. E., Greiner, A. R., & Vodde-Hamilton, M. (1992). Methylphenidate and attributions in boys with attention-deficit hyperactivity disorder. *Journal of Consulting and Clinical Psychology, 60,* 282-292.

39. Saigh, P. A. (1992). Verbal mediated childhood post-traumatic stress disorder. *British Journal of Psychiatry, 161,* 704-706.

40. Abikoff, H., Courtney, M., Pelham, W. E., & Koplewicz, H. S. (1993). Teachers' ratings of disruptive behaviors: The influence of halo effects. *Journal of Abnormal Child Psychology, 21,* 519-533.

41. Fee, V. E., Matson, J. L., Moore, L. A., & Benavidez, D. A. (1993). The differential validity of hyperactivity/attention deficits and conduct problems among mentally retarded children. *Journal of Abnormal Child Psychology, 21,* 1-11.

42. Fergusson, D. M., Lynskey, M. T., & Horwood, L. J. (1993). The effect of maternal depression on maternal ratings of child behavior. *Journal of Abnormal Child Psychology, 21,* 245-269.

43. Fischer, M., Barkley, R. A., Fletcher, K. E., & Smallish, L. (1993). The stability of dimensions of behavior in ADHD and normal children over an 8-year followup. *Journal of Abnormal Child Psychology, 21,* 315-337.

44. Granger, D. A., Whalen, C. K., & Henker, B. (1993). Perceptions of methylphenidate effects on hyperactive children's peer interactions. *Journal of Abnormal Child Psychology, 21,* 535-549.

45. Healey, J. M., Newcorn, J. H., Halperin, J. M., Wolf, J. E., Pascualvaca, D. M., Schmeidler, J., & O'Brien, J. D. (1993). The factor structure of ADHD items in DSM-III-R: Internal consistency and external validation. *Journal of Abnormal Child Psychology, 21,* 441-453.

46. Hoza, B., Pelham, W. E., Milich, R., Pillow, D., & McBride, K. (1993). The self-perceptions and attributions of attention deficit hyperactivity disordered and nonreferred boys. *Journal of Abnormal Child Psychology, 21,* 271-286.

47. Jenkins, J. M., & Smith, M. A. (1993). A prospective study of behavioural disturbance in children who subsequently experience parental divorce: A research note. *Journal of Divorce & Remarriage, 19,* 143-160.

48. Merrell, K. W. (1993). Using behavior rating scales to assess social skills and antisocial behavior in school settings: Development of the School Social Behavior Scales. *School Psychology Review, 22,* 115-133.

49. Pliszka, S. R., Hatch, J. P., Borcherding, S. H., & Rogeness, G. A. (1993). Classical conditioning in children with attention deficit hyperactivity disorder (ADHD) and anxiety disorders: A test of Quay's model. *Journal of Abnormal Child Psychology, 21,* 411-423.

50. Schaughency, E. A., & Fagot, B. I. (1993). The prediction of adjustment at age 7 from activity level at age 5. *Journal of Abnormal Child Psychology, 21,* 29-50.

[637]

Consequences.

Purpose: Measure ideational fluency and originality.
Population: Grades 9–16.
Publication Date: 1958.

Scores, 2: Originality, Ideational Fluency.
Administration: Group.
Forms, 2: A1, A2.
Price Data, 1987: $12 per lot of 25 tests; $6 per manual ('74, 8 pages for third edition); $1.75 per scoring guide, $7 per review set.
Time: 10(13) minutes.
Comments: Mimeographed manual, third edition (8 pages); Form A1 consists of first 5 items and Form A2 consists of last 5 items of the original 1958 (single-form) 10-item test.
Authors: Paul R. Christensen, P. R. Merrifield, and J. P. Guilford.
Publisher: Consulting Psychologists Press, Inc.
Cross References: See T2:551 (71 references); for a review by Goldine C. Gleser of the 10-item test, see 6:547 (13 references).

TEST REFERENCES

1. McCrae, R. R. (1987). Creativity, divergent thinking, and openness to experience. *Journal of Personality and Social Psychology, 52,* 1258-1265.

2. Zarnegar, Z., Hocevar, D., & Michael, W. B. (1988). Components of original thinking in gifted children. *Educational and Psychological Measurement, 48*(1), 5-16.

[638]

Content Inventories: English, Social Studies, Science.

Purpose: Screen reading and study skills.
Population: Grades 4–12.
Publication Date: 1979.
Acronym: CI.
Scores: 3 reading levels: Independent, Instructional, Frustration.
Price Data, 1984: $7.95 per test materials.
Time: (30–50) minutes for each part.
Authors: Lana McWilliams and Thomas A. Rakes.
Publisher: Kendall/Hunt Publishing Co.
Cross References: For a review by Kathryn H. Au, see 9:264.

[639]

Content Mastery Examination for Educators.

Purpose: "Designed for use in licensing teachers, counselors, administrators, and reading and media specialists. Basic Skills also designed for use at entrance to college of education."
Population: Teachers, school administrators, and other educational specialists; Basic Skills also for entrants to colleges of education.
Publication Date: 1991.
Acronym: CMEE.
Administration: Group.
Parts: 24 tests.
Restricted Distribution: Distribution restricted; details may be obtained from publisher.
Price Data: Available from publisher.
Time: (120–180) minutes per test.
Comments: "Criterion-referenced."
Authors: IOX Assessment Associates.
Publisher: National Computer Systems [Iowa City, IA].

a) ADMINISTRATION AND SUPERVISION.
Scores: 10 content areas: School Law, Educational Finance, Collective Bargaining, Personnel Practices for Professional Staff, Student Personnel Services, Student Assessment and Program Evaluation, Curriculum, Public School Governance and School Community Relations, Leadership, Operational Management and Computer Technology.

b) ART EDUCATION.
Scores: 5 content areas: Art History, Art Community, Technical Aspects of Production, Visual Elements and Principles, Aesthetic Issues.

c) BASIC SKILLS.
Scores: 9 content areas: Reading (Vocabulary/Word Recognition, Reading Comprehension, Reference Selection and Usage), Writing (Writing Assignment, Standard American English Conventions), Math (Number Concepts and Operations, Measurement, Geometry, Statistics).

d) BIOLOGY.
Scores: 10 content areas: Introduction to Biology, The Basis of Life, Cell Structure and Functions, Microscopic and Submicroscopic Forms of Life, Plants, Animals, Developmental Biology, Genetics, Evolution, Ecology and Conservation.

e) BUSINESS EDUCATION.
Scores: 8 content areas: Equipment Operation, Business Communications, Economics, Basic Finance, Business and Consumer Law, Business Management, Career Development and Planning, Marketing Education.

f) CHEMISTRY.
Scores: 14 content areas: Fundamental Chemical Concepts and Basic Laboratory Tools and Techniques, Atomic Theory, The Periodic Table, States of Matter, Solutions, Bonding, Stoichiometry, Thermochemistry, Reaction Rates, Equilibrium, Oxidation Reduction and Electrochemistry, Nuclear Chemistry, Organic Chemistry, Current Chemical/Societal Problems.

g) EARLY CHILDHOOD EDUCATION.
Scores: 10 content areas: Early Childhood Development, Early Childhood Programs, Children with Special Needs, Language Arts, Reading, Visual and Performing Arts, Social Studies, Mathematics, Science, Physical Education and Health.

h) EARTH AND SPACE SCIENCE.
Scores: 11 content areas: Basic Earth Materials, Agents of Change, Earth Structure and Geological Processes, Geologic History, Ocean Structure, Ocean Shores and Floors, The Atmosphere, Weather, The Universe, The Solar System, Stars.

i) ELEMENTARY EDUCATION.
Scores: 8 content areas: Language Arts, Reading, Visual and Performing Arts, Social Studies, Mathematics, Science, Physical Education and Health, Special Education.

j) ENGLISH.
Scores: 3 content areas: Language Knowledge and Skills, Composition Knowledge and Skills, Literary Knowledge and Skills.

k) FRENCH.
Scores: 5 content areas: Grammar, Vocabulary, Reading Comprehension, Aural/Oral Communication, Culture.

l) HEALTH EDUCATION.
Scores: 10 content areas: Health in the United States, Physical Growth and Development, Mental and Emotional Health, Sexuality, Fitness, Substance Use and Abuse, Nutrition, Community and Environmental Health, Wellness and Disease, Consumer Health and Safety.

m) HOME ECONOMICS.
Scores: 7 content areas: Management, Child Development/Care/Guidance, Clothing and Textiles, Consumer Education, Food and Nutrition, Family Relationships, Housing and Home Furnishings.

n) MATHEMATICS.
Scores: 8 content areas: Algebra, Functions, Geometry from a Synthetic Perspective, Geometry from an Algebraic Perspective, Trigonometry, Statistics and Probability, Discrete Mathematics, Calculus.

o) MUSIC.
Scores: 7 content areas: Style Characteristics, Representative Composers, Representative Musical Forms, Music Notation, Elements of Music, Rehearsal Preparations and Procedures, Listening.

p) PEDAGOGY.
Scores: 7 content areas: Student Characteristics, Learning Theories, Planning, Classroom Management, Instructional Methods, Principles of Effective Instruction, Assessment/Evaluation/Working with Parents.

q) PHYSICAL EDUCATION.
Scores: 8 content areas: Physical Development, Motor Learning, Biomechanics and Kinesiology, Exercise Physiology, Psychosocial Development, Humanities, Legal Issues, Components of a Balanced Physical Education Program.

r) PHYSICS.
Scores: 5 content areas: Mechanics, Heat, Wave Motion, Electricity and Magnetism, Modern Physics.

s) READING SPECIALIST.
Scores: 8 content areas: Foundations of Reading and Basic Instructional Approaches, Word Recognition, Comprehension, Reading Across the Curriculum, Affective Aspects of Reading Instruction, Teaching Students with Special Needs, Assessment, Classroom Organization/Program Administration/Resources.

t) SCHOOL GUIDANCE AND COUNSELING.
Scores: 8 content areas: Human Growth and Development, Technical Aspects of Counseling, Individual and Group Assessment, Legal and Ethical Issues in Counseling, Referral and Community Resources, Life-Style and Career Planning, The Counselor as Consultant, The Counselor as Psychological Helper.

u) SCHOOL LIBRARY MEDIA SPECIALIST.
Scores: 5 content areas: Professionalism, Collection Management, Organization of the Library, Administration, Roles of the Library Media Specialist.

v) SOCIAL STUDIES.
Scores: 5 content areas: World History, United States History, Government, Geography, Social Science Theory.

w) SPANISH.
Scores: 5 content areas: Grammar, Vocabulary, Reading Comprehension, Culture, Aural/Oral Communication.

x) SPECIAL EDUCATION.
Scores: 9 content areas: Legal Requirements of PL 94-142, Classification and Characteristics of Disorders, Assessment, Individual Behavior Management, Instruction, Working with the Community, Class Behavior Management, Consultation/Collaboration, Paraprofessional Management.

[640]

Continuing Education Assessment Inventory.
Purpose: Designed "to assess the development of maximum independence for teenagers and adults whose disability is identified as mental retardation."
Population: Mentally retarded adolescents and adults.
Publication Date: 1975.
Acronym: CEAI.
Scores: Ratings in 7 areas: Independence, Leisure Time, Prevocational, Self-Care, Mobility, Communication, Personal and Social Development.
Administration: Individual.
Price Data, 1990: $3.50 per circular progress program chart; $6 per manual (37 pages).
Time: Administration time not reported.
Authors: Gertrude A. Barber, Beth Lane, Shirley Johnson, and Alfred R. Riccomini.
Publisher: The Barber Center Press, Inc.
Cross References: For a review by Rodney T. Hartnett, see 9:265.

[641]

Continuous Symbol Checking Test.
Purpose: Designed to predict job performance for work which can, largely, be autonomously performed.
Population: Job applicants.
Publication Date: 1989.
Acronym: CSC.
Scores, 5: Accuracy, Consistency, Rate of Learning, Rate of Work, Quality of Work.
Administration: Group.
Price Data: Available from publisher.
Foreign Language Edition: Test printed in both English and Afrikaans.
Time: 60(80) minutes.
Authors: H. Reuning and R. B. Lombard (manual revision).

Publisher: National Institute for Personnel Research of the Human Sciences Research Council [South Africa].

[642]

Continuous Visual Memory Test.
Purpose: Assesses Visual Memory.
Population: Ages 18–70 + .
Publication Dates: 1983–88.
Acronym: CVMT.
Scores, 6: Acquisition (Hits, False Alarms, d-Prime, Total), Delayed Recognition, Visual Discrimination.
Administration: Individual.
Price Data, 1994: $73 per complete kit including manual ('88, 19 pages), stimulus cards, and 50 scoring forms; $11 per manual; $21 per 50 scoring forms; $44 per stimulus cards.
Time: (45–50) minutes.
Authors: Donald E. Trahan and Glenn J. Larrabee.
Publisher: Psychological Assessment Resources, Inc.

TEST REFERENCES

1. Trahan, D. E., Larrabee, G. J., & Quintana, J. W. (1990). Visual recognition memory in normal adults and patients with unilateral vascular lesions. *Journal of Clinical and Experimental Neuropsychology, 12,* 857-872.
2. Berry, L. H., & Jesky-Smith, R. (1991). Validation of a pictorial recall test in three visual formats. *Perceptual and Motor Skills, 73,* 689-690.
3. Drake, A. I., & Hannay, H. J. (1992). Continuous recognition memory tests: Are the assumptions of the theory of signal detection met? *Journal of Clinical and Experimental Neuropsychology, 14,* 539-544.
4. Trahan, D. E., & Larrabee, G. J. (1993). Clinical and methodological issues in measuring rate of forgetting with the Verbal Selective Reminding Test. *Psychological Assessment, 5,* 67-71.

[643]

Cooper-Farran Behavioral Rating Scales.
Purpose: Designed to assess social and cognitive skills.
Population: Kindergartners.
Publication Date: 1991.
Acronym: CFBRS.
Scores, 2: Interpersonal Skills, Work-Related Skills.
Administration: Individual.
Price Data, 1991: $7 per 25 test forms; $5 per 25 scoring sheets; $17 per manual (44 pages); $18 per specimen set.
Time: (10–20) minutes.
Comments: Ratings by teacher.
Authors: David H. Cooper and Dale C. Farran.
Publisher: Clinical Psychology Publishing Co., Inc.

TEST REFERENCES

1. Speece, D. L., & Cooper, D. H. (1990). Ontogeny of school failure: Classification of first-grade children. *American Educational Research Journal, 27,* 119-140.

[644]

The Cooper-McGuire Diagnostic Word-Analysis Test.
Purpose: "Identifies the degree to which pupils have acquired" reading skills.

Population: Grades 1–5 and over.
Publication Dates: 1970–72.
Scores: 3 readiness-for-word-analysis goals (Letter Names and Shapes, Auditory Discrimination of Letter Sounds and Blending Ability, Visual Discrimination of Word Forms), 2 phonic analysis goals (Consonant Sounds, Vowel Sounds), 4 structural analysis goals (Root Words and Endings, Compound Words and Contractions, Prefixes and Suffixes, Syllables); 32 overlapping tests with 1 to 13 tests administered at a given reader level.
Administration: Individual and group.
Price Data: Not available.
Comments: Criterion-referenced.
Authors: J. Louis Cooper and Marion L. McGuire.
Publisher: Croft, Inc. [No reply from publisher; status unknown].
Cross References: For a review by John McLeod, see 8:750.

[645]
The Cooperative Institutional Research Program.
Purpose: "A national longitudinal study of the American higher educational system" based on freshman survey data.
Population: First-time, full-time entering college freshmen.
Publication Dates: 1966–94.
Acronym: CIRP.
Scores: No scores.
Administration: Group.
Price Data, 1993: $275 participation fee; $1 per returned survey.
Time: (40) minutes.
Comments: Test entitled Student Information Form (T3:2333); national norms reported annually.
Authors: Alexander W. Astin, William S. Korn, and Ellyne R. Riggs.
Publisher: Higher Education Research Institute, University of California-Los Angeles.
Cross References: For a review by Harvey Resnick, see 9:266. For a review by Albert B. Hood of the Student Information Form, see 8:397 (15 references).

TEST REFERENCES
1. Leslie, L. L. (1984). Changing patterns in student financing of higher education. *Journal of Higher Education, 55,* 313-346.
2. Pascarella, E. T. (1985). Students' affective development within the college environment. *Journal of Higher Education, 56,* 640-663.
3. Jacobs, J. A. (1986). The sex-segregation of fields of study: Trends during the college years. *Journal of Higher Education, 57,* 134-154.
4. Smart, J. C., & Pascarella, E. T. (1986). Socioeconomic achievements of former college students. *Journal of Higher Education, 57,* 529-549.
5. Solmon, L. C., & LaPorte, M. A. (1986). The crisis of student quality in higher education. *Journal of Higher Education, 57,* 370-392.
6. Blai, B. (1987). College and university freshmen shift values, attitudes and goals. *College Student Journal, 21,* 194-200.
7. Smart, J. C. (1987). Student satisfaction with graduate education. *Journal of College Student Personnel, 28,* 218-222.
8. Ryan, F. J. (1989). Participation in intercollegiate athletics: Affective outcomes. *Journal of College Student Development, 30,* 122-128.

[646]
Cooperative Preschool Inventory, Revised Edition.
Purpose: Indicates "achievement in areas necessary for success in school."
Population: Ages 3–6.
Publication Dates: 1965–74.
Acronym: CPI.
Scores: Total score only.
Administration: Individual.
Price Data, 1992: $17.40 per specimen set including directions for administering and scoring ('70, 12 pages), answer recording leaflet, and handbook ('70, 34 pages); $11.40 per 20 answer recording leaflets; $2.05 per directions for administering and scoring; $8.15 per handbook.
Foreign Language Edition: Also available in Spanish (1974).
Time: (15) minutes.
Comments: Handbook title is Preschool Inventory.
Authors: Bettye M. Caldwell and Judith H. Freund.
Publisher: CTB Macmillan/McGraw-Hill.
Cross References: See T3:581 (6 references) and T2:490 (4 references); for a review by Joseph L. French and an excerpted review by Dale Carlson, see 7:404 (5 references).

TEST REFERENCES
1. Ernhart, C. B., Spaner, S. D., & Jordan, T. E. (1977). Validity of selected preschool screening tests. *Contemporary Educational Psychology, 2,* 78-89.
2. Rickel, A. U., & Smith, R. L. (1979). Maladapting preschool children: Identification, diagnosis, and remediation. *American Journal of Community Psychology, 7,* 197-208.
3. Rickel, A. U., & Lampi, L. (1981). A two-year follow-up study of a preventive mental health program for preschoolers. *Journal of Abnormal Child Psychology, 9,* 455-464.
4. Travers, J. R., (1981). Federal regulations and the lives of children in day care. *Prevention in Human Services, 1*(1/2), 59-86.
5. George, N. M., Braun, B. A., & Walker, J. M. (1982). A prevention and early intervention mental health program for disadvantaged pre-school children. *The American Journal of Occupational Therapy, 36,* 99-106.
6. Miller, L. B., & Bizzell, R. P. (1983). Long-term effects of four preschool programs: Sixth, seventh, and eighth grades. *Child Development, 54,* 727-741.
7. Powers, S., & Medina, M., Jr. (1984). Reliability and validity of the Cooperative Preschool Inventory for English- and Spanish-speaking Hispanic children. *Educational and Psychological Measurement, 44,* 963-966.
8. Powers, S., & Lopez, R. L., Jr. (1985). Perceptual, motor, and verbal skills of monolingual and bilingual Hispanic children: A discriminant analysis. *Perceptual and Motor Skills, 60,* 999-1002.
9. Powers, S., & Medina, M., Jr. (1985). Factorial validity of the Cooperative Preschool Inventory for English- and Spanish-speaking Hispanic children. *The Journal of Psychology, 119,* 277- 280.
10. Powers, S., Wagner, M. J., Lopez, R. L., Jr., & Jones, P. B. (1986). Comparison of item responses of English- and Spanish-speaking children using minimum loglt chi-squared regression. *Psychological Reports, 59,* 235-239.
11. Glutting, J. J., & McDermott, P. A. (1988). Generality of test-session observations to kindergarteners' classroom behavior. *Journal of Abnormal Child Psychology, 16,* 527-537.
12. Duax, T. (1992). Attrition at a nonselective magnet school: A case study of a Milwaukee public school. *Journal of Research and Development in Education, 25,* 172-181.

[647]
Coopersmith Self-Esteem Inventories.
Purpose: "Designed to measure evaluative attitudes

toward the self in social, academic, family, and personal areas of experience."
Population: Ages 8–15, 16 and above.
Publication Date: 1981.
Acronym: SEI.
Administration: Group.
Price Data, 1991: $6 per 25 School Form test booklets; $3 School Form scoring key; $4.50 per 25 Adult Form test booklets; $3 per Adult Form scoring key; $7.50 per manual (22 pages); $8 per specimen set.
Time: (10–15) minutes.
Author: Stanley Coopersmith.
Publisher: Consulting Psychologists Press, Inc.
a) SCHOOL FORM.
Population: Ages 8–15.
Scores, 6: General Self, Social Self-Peers, Home-Parents, School-Academic, Total Self Score, Lie.
Comments: Separate answer sheets may be used.
b) ADULT FORM.
Population: Ages 16 and above.
Cross References: For reviews by Christopher Peterson and James T. Austin and Trevor E. Sewell, see 9:267 (32 references).

TEST REFERENCES

1. Scruggs, T. E., & Mastropieri, M. A. (1983). Self-esteem differences by sex and ethnicity: Native American, handicapped Native American, and Anglo children. *Journal of Instructional Psychology, 10,* 177-179.
2. Allen, W. H., & VanSickle, R. (1984). Learning teams and low achievers. *Social Education, 48,* 60-64.
3. Byrne, B. M. (1984). The general/academic self-concept nomological network: A review of construct validation research. *Review of Educational Research, 54,* 427-456.
4. Dembo, M. H., Sweitzer, M., & Lauritzen, P. (1984). An evaluation of group parent education: Behavioral, PET, and Adlerian programs. *Review of Educational Research, 55,* 155-200.
5. Hesketh, B. (1984). Attribution theory and unemployment: Kelly's covariation model, self-esteem, and locus of control. *Journal of Vocational Behavior, 24,* 94-109.
6. Hoge, D. R., & McCarthy, J. D. (1984). Influence of individual and group identity salience in the global self-esteem of youth. *Journal of Personality and Social Psychology, 47,* 403-414.
7. Kaslow, N., Rehm, L. P., & Siegel, A. W. (1984). Social-cognitive and cognitive correlates of depression in children. *Journal of Abnormal Child Psychology, 12,* 605-620.
8. Lochman, J. E., Burch, P. R., Curry, J. F., & Lampron, L. B. (1984). Treatment and generalization effects of cognitive-behavioral and goal-setting interventions with aggressive boys. *Journal of Consulting and Clinical Psychology, 52,* 915-916.
9. Marron, J. A., & Kayson, W. A. (1984). Effects of living status, gender, and year in college on college students' self-esteem and life-change experiences. *Psychological Reports, 55,* 811-814.
10. Martin, J. D., & Coley, L. A. (1984). Intercorrelations of some measures of self-concept. *Educational and Psychological Measurement, 44,* 517-521.
11. McCarthy, J. D., & Hoge, D. R. (1984). The dynamics of self-esteem and delinquency. *American Journal of Sociology, 90,* 396-410.
12. Miller, L. B., & Bizzell, R. P. (1984). Long-term effects of four preschool programs: Ninth- and tenth-grade results. *Child Development, 55,* 1570-1587.
13. Mink, I. T., Meyers, C. E., & Nihira, K. (1984). Taxonomy of family life styles: II. Homes with slow-learning children. *American Journal of Mental Deficiency, 89,* 111-123.
14. Nadler, A., Mayseless, O., Peri, N., & Chemerinski, A. (1984). Effects of opportunity to reciprocate and self-esteem on help-seeking behavior. *Journal of Personality, 53,* 23-35.
15. Phillips, R. H. (1984). Increasing positive self-referent statements to improve self-esteem in low-income elementary school children. *Journal of School Psychology, 22,* 155-163.
16. Savin-Williams, R. C., & Demo, D. H. (1984). Developmental change and stability in adolescent self-concept. *Developmental Psychology, 20,* 1100-1110.

17. Stasinos, D. P. (1984). Enhancing the creative potential and self-esteem of mentally handicapped Greek children. *Journal of Creative Behavior, 18,* 117-132.
18. Stevenson, D. T., & Romney, D. M. (1984). Depression in learning disabled children. *Journal of Learning Disabilities, 17,* 579-582.
19. Yates, A. J., & Sambrailo, F. (1984). Bulimia nervosa: A descriptive and therapeutic study. *Behaviour Research and Therapy, 22,* 503-517.
20. Abadzi, H. (1985). Ability grouping effects on academic achievement and self-esteem: Who performs in the long run as expected. *Journal of Educational Research, 79,* 36-40.
21. Ahmed, S. M. S., Valliant, P. M., & Swindle, D. (1985). Psychometric properties of Coopersmith Self-Esteem Inventory. *Perceptual and Motor Skills, 61,* 1235-1241.
22. Andersen, S. M., & Williams, M. (1985). Cognitive/effective reactions in the improvement of self-esteem: When thoughts and feelings make a difference. *Journal of Personality and Social Psychology, 49,* 1086-1097.
23. Chiu, L. (1985). The reliability and validity of the Coopersmith Self-Esteem Inventory—Form B. *Educational and Psychological Measurement, 45,* 945-949.
24. DeFranceso, J. J., & Taylor, J. (1985). Dimensions of self-concept in primary and middle school learning disabled and nondisabled students. *Child Study Journal, 15,* 99-105.
25. Dorr, D., Pozner, R., & Stephens, J. (1985). Relationship of trait anxiety to self-esteem of children in grades 4, 5, and 6. *Psychological Reports, 57,* 467-473.
26. Elawar, M. C., & Corno, L. (1985). A factorial experiment in teachers' written feedback on student homework: Changing teacher behavior a little rather than a lot. *Journal of Educational Psychology, 77,* 162-173.
27. Gibbs, J., & Norwich, B. (1985). The validity of a short form of the Coopersmith Self Esteem Inventory. *British Journal of Educational Psychology, 55,* 76-80.
28. Grace, P. S., Jacobson, R. S., & Fullager, C. J. (1985). A pilot comparison of purging and non-purging bulimics. *Journal of Clinical Psychology, 41,* 173-180.
29. Halpin, G., Halpin, G., & Whiddon, T. (1985). Factors related to adolescents' level of aspiration. *Psychological Reports, 56,* 203-209.
30. Hart, J. G. (1985). LAWSEQ: Its relation to other measures of self-esteem and academic ability. *British Journal of Educational Psychology, 55,* 167-169.
31. Holliday, B. G. (1985). Differential effects of children's self-perceptions and teachers' perceptions on black children's academic achievement. *Journal of Negro Education, 54,* 71-81.
32. Kawash, G. F., Kerr, E. N., & Clewes, J. L. (1985). Self-esteem in children as a function of perceived parental behavior. *The Journal of Psychology, 119,* 235-242.
33. Meier, S. T., & Schmeck, R. R. (1985). The burned-out college student: A descriptive profile. *Journal of College Student Personnel, 26,* 63-69.
34. Mendelson, B. K., & White, D. R. (1985). Development of self-body-esteem in overweight youngsters. *Developmental Psychology, 21,* 90-96.
35. Omizo, M. M., Amerikaner, M. J., & Michael, W. B. (1985). The Coopersmith Self-Esteem Inventory as a predictor of feelings and communication satisfaction toward parents among learning disabled, emotionally disturbed, and normal adolescents. *Educational and Psychological Measurement, 45,* 389-395.
36. Poole, M. E., & Low, B. C. (1985). Career and marriage: Orientations of adolescent girls. *The Australian Journal of Education, 29,* 36-46.
37. Rodman, H., Pratto, D. J., & Nelson, R. S. (1985). Child care arrangements and children's functioning: A comparison of self-care and adult-care children. *Developmental Psychology, 21,* 413-418.
38. Shelton, T. L., Anastopoulos, A. D., & Linden, J. D. (1985). An attribution training program with learning disabled children. *Journal of Learning Disabilities, 18,* 261-265.
39. Simon, M. J. (1985). The Egocentricity Index and self-esteem in court ordered psychiatric evaluations. *Journal of Personality Assessment, 49,* 437-439.
40. Valliant, P. M., Bezzubyk, I., Daley, L., & Asu, M. E. (1985). Psychological impact of sport on disabled athletes. *Psychological Reports, 56,* 923-929.
41. Goldberg, S., Marcovitch, S., MacGregor, D., & Lojkasek, M. (1986). Family responses to developmentally delayed preschoolers: Etiology and the father's role. *American Journal of Mental Deficiency, 90,* 610-617.
42. Henkin, B., & Fish, J. M. (1986). Gender and personality differences in the appreciation of cartoon humor. *The Journal of Psychology, 120,* 157-175.
43. Hofmann, R., & Zippco, D. (1986). Effects of divorce upon

school self-esteem and achievement of 10-, 11-, and 12-year-old children. *Perceptual and Motor Skills, 62,* 397-398.

44. Kazdin, A. E., Rodgers, A., & Colbus, D. (1986). The Hopelessness Scale for Children: Psychometric characteristics and concurrent validity. *Journal of Consulting and Clinical Psychology, 54,* 241-245.

45. Mboya, M. M. (1986). Black adolescents: A descriptive study of their self-concepts and academic achievement. *Adolescence, 21,* 689-696.

46. Richardson, A. G., & Lee, J. (1986). Self-concept and attitude to school as predictors of academic achievement by West Indian adolescents. *Perceptual and Motor Skills, 62,* 577-578.

47. Robison-Awana, P., Kehle, T. J., & Jenson, W. R. (1986). But what about smart girls? Adolescent self-esteem and sex role perceptions as a function of academic achievement. *Journal of Educational Psychology, 78,* 179-183.

48. Sholomskas, D., & Axelrod, R. (1986). The influence of mother-daughter relationships on women's sense of self and current role choices. *Psychology of Women Quarterly, 10,* 171-182.

49. Stiffman, A. R., Jung, K. G., & Feldman, R. A. (1986). A multivariate risk model for childhood behavior problems. *American Journal of Orthopsychiatry, 56,* 204-211.

50. Valliant, P. M., & Leith, B. (1986). Impact of relaxation training and cognitive therapy on coronary patients post surgery. *Psychological Reports, 59,* 1271-1278.

51. Verleur, D., Hughes, R. E., & deRios, M. D. (1986). Enhancement of self-esteem among female adolescent incest victims: A controlled comparision. *Adolescence, 21,* 843-854.

52. Beer, J. (1987). Depression and self-esteem of teachers. *Psychological Reports, 60,* 1097-1098.

53. Chiu, L. H. (1987). Development of the Self-Esteem Rating Scale for Children (Revised). *Measurement and Evaluation in Counseling and Development, 20,* 36-41.

54. Chiu, L. H. (1987). Sociometric status and self-esteem of American and Chinese school children. *The Journal of Psychology, 121,* 547-552.

55. de Man, A., & Devisse, T. (1987). Locus of control, mental ability, self-esteem and alienation. *Social Behavior and Personality, 15*(2), 233-236.

56. Fichten, C. S., Bourdon, C. V., Amsel, R., & Fox, L. (1987). Validation of the College Interaction Self-Efficacy Questionnaire: Students with and without disabilities. *Journal of College Student Personnel, 28,* 449-458.

57. Gurney, P. W. (1987). The use of operant techniques to raise self-esteem in maladjusted children. *British Journal of Educational Psychology, 57,* 87-94.

58. Lundy, A., & Rosenberg, J. A. (1987). Androgyny, masculinity, and self-esteem. *Social Behavior and Personality, 15,* 91-95.

59. Omizo, M. M., & Omizo, S. A. (1987). The effects of eliminating self-defeating behavior of learning-disabled children through group counseling. *The School Counselor, 34,* 282-288.

60. Pats, B. F. (1987). Variables affecting college seniors' expectations about returning home. *Journal of College Student Personnel, 28,* 246-252.

61. Richardson, A. G. (1987). Differences in adolescents' self-esteem across cultures. *Psychological Reports, 61,* 19-22.

62. Stark, K. D., Reynolds, W. M., & Kaslow, N. J. (1987). A comparison of the relative efficacy of self-control therapy and a behavioral problem-solving therapy for depression in children. *Journal of Abnormal Child Psychology, 15,* 91-113.

63. Chiu, L. H. (1988). Measures of self-esteem for school-age children. *Journal of Counseling and Development, 66,* 298-301.

64. Craske, M. L. (1988). Learned helplessness, self-worth motivation and attribution retraining for primary school children. *British Journal of Educational Psychology, 58,* 152-164.

65. Dubow, E. F., & Cappas, C. L. (1988). Peer social status and reports of children's adjustment by their teachers, by their peers, and by their self-ratings. *Journal of School Psychology, 26,* 69-75.

66. Hogg, J. A., & Deffenbacher, J. L. (1988). A comparison of cognitive and interpersonal-process group therapies in the treatment of depression among college students. *Journal of Counseling Psychology, 35,* 304-310.

67. Kawash, G. F., & Clewes, J. L. (1988). A factor analysis of a short form of the CRPBI: Are children's perceptions of control and discipline multidimensional? *The Journal of Psychology, 122,* 57-67.

68. Kinney, P., & Miller, M. J. (1988). The relationship between self-esteem and academic achievement. *College Student Journal, 22,* 358-362.

69. Meyers, L. S., & Wong, D. T. (1988). Validation of a new test of locus of control: The Internal Control Index. *Educational and Psychological Measurement, 48,* 753- 761.

70. Berr, J. (1989). Relationship of divorce to self-concept, self-esteem, and grade point average of fifth and sixth grade school children. *Psychological Reports, 65,* 1379-1383.

71. Connolly, J. (1989). Social self-efficacy in adolescence: Relations with self-concept, social adjustment, and mental health. *Canadian Journal of Behavioural Science, 21,* 258-269.

72. Enright, K. M., & Ruzicka, M. F. (1989). Relationship between perceived parental behaviors and the self-esteem of gifted children. *Psychological Reports, 65,* 931-937.

73. Hennessey, B. A., Amabile, T. M., & Martinage, M. (1989). Immunizing children against the negative effects of reward. *Contemporary Educational Psychology, 14,* 212-227.

74. Konstantareas, M. M., & Homatidis, S. (1989). Parental perception of learning-disabled children's adjustment problems and related stress. *Journal of Abnormal Child Psychology, 17,* 177-186.

75. Lawton, J. M., Fergusson, D. M., & Horwood, L. J. (1989). Self-esteem and defensiveness: An analysis of the self-esteem inventory. *Psychological Reports, 64,* 1307-1320.

76. Towbes, L. C., Cohen, L. H., & Glyshaw, K. (1989). Instrumentality as a life-stress moderator for early versus middle adolescents. *Journal of Personality and Social Psychology, 57,* 109-119.

77. Calhoun, G., Jr., & Sethi, R. (1987). The self-esteem of pupils from India, the United States, and the Philippines. *The Journal of Psychology, 121,* 199-202.

78. Fisher, D., & Beer, J. (1990). Codependency and self-esteem among high school students. *Psychological Reports, 66,* 1101-1102.

79. Heyman, W. B. (1990). The self-perception of a learning disability and its relationship to academic self-concept and self-esteem. *Journal of Learning Disabilities, 23,* 472-475.

80. Holtzen, D. W., & Agresti, A. A. (1990). Parental responses to gay and lesbian children: Differences in homophobia, self-esteem, and sex-role stereotyping. *Journal of Social and Clinical Psychology, 9,* 390-399.

81. Kawash, G., & Kozeluk, L. (1990). Self-esteem in early adolescence as a function of position within Olson's Circumplex Model of Marital and Family Systems. *Social Behavior and Personality, 18,* 189-196.

82. Kozeluk, L., & Kawash, G. (1990). Comparison of the Coopersmith Self-Esteem Inventory and the Battle Culture-Free Self-Esteem Inventory. *Perceptual and Motor Skills, 70,* 1162.

83. Stark, L. J., Spirito, A., Lewis, A. V., & Hart, K. J. (1990). Encopresis: Behavioral parameters associated with children who fail medical management. *Child Psychiatry and Human Development, 20,* 169-179.

84. Tharinger, D. J., & Stark, K. (1990). A qualitative versus quantitative approach to evaluating The Draw-A-Person and Kinetic Family Drawing: A study of mood- and anxiety-disorder children. *Psychological Assessment, 2,* 365-375.

85. Drummond, R. J., & Hansford, S. G. (1991). Dimensions of self-concept of pregnant unwed teens. *The Journal of Psychology, 125,* 65-59.

86. Joubert, C. E. (1991). Self-esteem and social desirability in relation to college students' retrospective perceptions of parental fairness and disciplinary practices. *Psychological Reports, 69,* 115-120.

87. Miller, M. J., Wadsworth, E. R., & Springer, T. P. (1991). Chance receptivity as a function of self concept: An exploratory study. *Perceptual and Motor Skills, 72,* 291-295.

88. Miller, W. R., Hedrick, K. E., & Orlofsky, D. R. (1991). The Helpful Responses Questionnaire: A procedure for measuring therapeutic empathy. *Journal of Clinical Psychology, 47,* 444-448.

89. Mooney, S. P., Sherman, M. F., & Lo Presto, C. T. (1991). Academic locus of control, self-esteem, and perceived distance from home as predictors of college adjustment. *Journal of Counseling and Development, 69,* 445-448.

90. Persinger, M. A., & Makarec, K. (1991). Greater right hemisphericity is associated with lower self-esteem in adults. *Perceptual and Motor Skills, 73,* 1244-1246.

91. Raskin, R., Novacek, J., & Hogan, R. (1991). Narcissistic self-esteem management. *Journal of Personality and Social Psychology, 60,* 911-918.

92. Strassberg, D. S., Clutton, S., & Korboot, P. (1991). A descriptive and validity study of the Minnesota Multiphasic Personality Inventory-2 (MMPI-2) in an elderly Australian sample. *Journal of Psychopathology and Behavioral Assessment, 13,* 301-311.

93. Wolman, R., & Taylor, K. (1991). Psychological effects of custody disputes on children. *Behavioral Sciences and the Law, 9,* 399-417.

94. Wright, R. A., Caldwell, J. A., Evans, M. T., & Riter, M. (1991). Effort, energy, and appraisals of an aversive incentive: Effects of self-esteem and avoidant task difficulty. *Journal of Research in Personality, 25,* 45-56.

95. Fling, S., Smith, L., Rodriguez, T., Thornton, D., Atkins, E., & Nixon, K. (1992). Video games, aggression, and self esteem: A survey! *Social Behavior and Personality, 20,* 39-46.

96. Grossi, V., & Violato, C. (1992). Attempted suicide among adolescents: A stepwise discriminant analysis. *Canadian Journal of Behavioral Science, 24,* 410-413.

97. Guastello, S. J., Rieke, M. L., Guastello, D. D., & Billings,

S. W. (1992). A study of cynicism, personality, and work values. *The Journal of Psychology, 126*, 37-48.

98. Lavallée, M. R., & Persinger, M. A. (1992). Left ear (right temporal lobe) suppressions during dichotic listening, ego-alien intrusion experiences and spiritualistic beliefs in normal women. *Perceptual and Motor Skills, 75*, 547-551.

99. Lochman, J. E. (1992). Cognitive-behavioral intervention with aggressive boys: Three-year follow-up and preventive effects. *Journal of Consulting and Clinical Psychology, 60*, 426-432.

100. Morvitz, E., & Motta, R. W. (1992). Predictors of self-esteem: The roles of parent-child perceptions, achievement, and class placement. *Journal of Learning Disabilities, 25*, 72-80.

101. Petrie, K., & Brook, R. (1992). Sense of coherence, self-esteem, depression and hopeless as correlates of reattempting suicide. *British Journal of Clinical Psychology, 31*, 293-300.

102. Schmidt, L. A., & Robinson, T. N., Jr. (1992). Low self-esteem in differentiating fearful and self-conscious forms of shyness. *Psychological Reports, 70*, 255-257.

103. Gatten, C. W., Brookings, J. B., & Bolton, B. (1993). Mood fluctuations in female multiple sclerosis patients. *Social Behavior and Personality, 21*, 103-106.

104. Lochman, J. E., Wayland, K. K., & White, K. J. (1993). Social goals: Relationship to adolescent adjustment and to social problem solving. *Journal of Abnormal Child Psychology, 21*, 135-151.

105. Nelson, C., & Valliant, P. M. (1993). Personality dynamics of adolescent boys where the father was absent. *Perceptual and Motor Skills, 76*, 435-443.

106. Smoll, F. L., Smith, R. E., Barnett, N. P., & Everett, J. J. (1993). Enhancement or children's self-esteem through social support training for youth sport coaches. *Journal of Applied Psychology, 78*, 602-610.

[648]

Coping Inventory.

Purpose: "Assess the behavior patterns and skills that are the resources a person uses to meet personal needs and to adapt to the demands of the environment."
Population: Ages 3–16, adults.
Publication Date: 1985.
Scores, 9: 3 scores (Productive, Active, Flexible) for Coping with Self, Coping with Environment, plus Adaptive Behavior Index.
Administration: Individual.
Levels: 2.
Time: Administration time not reported.
Author: Shirley Zeitlin.
Publisher: Scholastic Testing Service, Inc.
a) SELF-RATED FORM.
Population: Adult.
Price Data, 1993: $25.50 per starter set including manual (6 pages) and 10 forms; $13.50 per 10 inventories; $11.95 per manual; $19 per specimen set.
Comments: Self-report ratings of adaptive behavior.
b) OBSERVATION FORM.
Population: Ages 3–16.
Price Data: $41.50 per starter set including manual (75 pages) and 20 forms; $26.60 per 20 inventories; $22.60 per manual; $24.50 per specimen set.
Comments: Ratings of adaptive behavior by adult informant.

TEST REFERENCES

1. Leon, G. R., Ben-Porath, Y. S., & Hjemboe, S. (1990). Coping patterns and current functioning in a group of Vietnam and Vietnam-era nurses. *Journal of Social and Clinical Psychology, 9*, 334-353.

[649]

Coping Resources Inventory.

Purpose: Developed to assess a person's resources for coping with stress.
Population: High school and over.
Publication Dates: 1987–88.
Acronym: CRI.
Scores, 6: Cognitive, Social, Emotional, Spiritual/Philosophical, Physical, Total.
Administration: Group.
Price Data, 1992: $10 per 25 test booklets; $49 per 10 prepaid answer sheets; $28 per 50 not prepaid answer sheets; $36 per set of scoring stencils; $16 per 50 profiles; $12 per manual ('88, 30 pages); $13 per specimen set.
Time: (10) minutes.
Comments: For research use only.
Authors: Allen L. Hammer and M. Susan Marting.
Publisher: Consulting Psychologists Press, Inc.

TEST REFERENCES

1. Armistead, L., McCombs, A., Forehand, R., Wierson, M., Long, N., & Fauber, R. (1990). Coping with divorce: A study of young adolescents. *Journal of Clinical Child Psychology, 19*, 79-84.
2. Brack, G., Gay, M. F., & Matheney, K. B. (1993). Relationships between attachment and coping resources among late adolescents. *Journal of College Student Development, 34*, 212-215.

[650]

Coping Resources Inventory for Stress.

Purpose: "Designed to measure coping resources which are believed to help lessen the negative effects of stress."
Population: Adults.
Publication Dates: 1988–93.
Acronym: CRIS.
Scores, 16: Self-Disclosure, Self-Directedness, Confidence, Acceptance, Social Support, Financial Freedom, Physical Health, Physical Fitness, Stress Monitoring, Tension Control, Structuring, Problem Solving, Cognitive Restructuring, Functional Beliefs, Social Ease, Coping Resource Effectiveness.
Administration: Group.
Price Data, 1993: $2.95 per test booklet; $16.95 per manual ('93, 65 pages); $19.95 per interpretive report; $8.95 per profile report; $29.95 per specimen set including test booklet, manual, pre-paid answer sheet, and interpretive report; $399 per PC-CRIS test administration and scoring program (with PC-CRIS manual); $11.95 per PC-CRIS Interpretive or Profile report; $9.95 per PC-CRIS test administration program.
Foreign Language Edition: Spanish edition available.
Time: (45–90) minutes.
Comments: Computer (PC-CRIS) administration and software package available.
Authors: William L. Curlette, David W. Aycock, Kenneth B. Matheny, James L. Pugh, and Harry F. Taylor.
Publisher: Health Prisms, Inc.

TEST REFERENCES

1. Brack, G., Gay, M. F., & Matheney, K. B. (1993). Relationships between attachment and coping resources among late adolescents. *Journal of College Student Development, 34*, 212-215.
2. Matheny, K. B., Aycock, D. W., Curlette, W. L., & Junker, G. N. (1993). The Coping Resources Inventory for stress: A measure of perceived resourcefulness. *Journal of Clinical Psychology, 49*, 815-830.
3. Ryland, E. B., Riordan, R. J., & Brack, G. (1994). Selected characteristics of high-risk students and their enrollment persistence. *Journal of College Student Development, 34*, 54-58.

[651]

Coping With Stress.

Purpose: Constructed as a self-assessment tool to identify sources of stress and responses to stress.

Population: Adults.

Publication Date: 1989.

Scores, 9: Reaction to Stress (Obsessive, Hysteria, Anxiety, Phobia, Total, Normal), Adjustment to Stress (Healthy, Unhealthy), Sources of Stress.

Administration: Group.

Price Data, 1994: $60 per complete kit including 20 test folders, 20 response sheets, and 20 interpretation sheets.

Time: [20] minutes administration; [10] minutes scoring; [30] minutes interpretation.

Comments: Self-administered, self-scored.

Author: Training House, Inc.

Publisher: Training House, Inc.

[652]

COPSystem Picture Inventory of Careers.

Purpose: To measure career interest for persons with reading or language difficulties.

Population: Elementary through adult-non-verbal.

Publication Date: 1993.

Acronym: COPS-PIC.

Scores: Interest scores in 14 COPSystem Career Clusters: Science-Professional, Science-Skilled, Technology-Professional, Technology-Skilled, Consumer Economics, Outdoor, Business-Professional, Business-Skilled, Clerical, Communication, Arts-Professional, Arts-Skilled, Service-Professional, Service-Skilled.

Administration: Group.

Price Data, 1993: $24.25 per 25 booklets and answer sheets combined including profile and guide [$86.25 per 100, $401 per 500]; $18 per set of hand-scoring keys; $1.30 each scoring by publisher; $2 per manual ('93, 6 pages); $2.50 per specimen set.

Time: (30) minutes.

Author: Lisa Knapp-Lee.

Publisher: EdITS/Educational and Industrial Testing Service.

[653]

The Cornell Class-Reasoning Test, Form X.

Purpose: "A multiple-choice deductive logic class-reasoning test."

Population: Grades 4–12.

Publication Date: 1964.

Scores: Deductive Logic.

Administration: Group.

Manual: No manual.

Price Data: Available from publisher.

Time: Untimed.

Comments: Subtitle on test booklet is Cornell Critical Thinking Test Series.

Authors: Robert H. Ennis, William L. Gardiner, Richard Morrow, Dieter Paulus, and Lucille Ringel.

Publisher: Illinois Critical Thinking Project.

Cross References: See T2:1753 (1 reference).

[654]

The Cornell Conditional-Reasoning Test.

Purpose: Designed as "a multiple-choice deductive logic conditional-reasoning test."

Population: Grades 4–12.

Publication Date: 1964.

Scores: Deductive Logic.

Administration: Group.

Manual: No manual.

Price Data: Available from publisher.

Time: Untimed.

Comments: Subtitle on test booklet is Cornell Critical Thinking Test Series.

Authors: Robert H. Ennis, William L. Gardiner, John Gazzetta, Richard Morrow, Dieter Paulus, and Lucille Ringel.

Publisher: Illinois Critical Thinking Project.

Cross References: See T2:1754 (1 reference).

[655]

Cornell Critical Thinking Tests.

Purpose: Assesses general critical thinking ability including "induction, deduction, evaluation, observation, credibility (of statements made by others), assumption identification, and meaning."

Publication Dates: 1961–85.

Acronym: CCTT.

Scores: Total score only for each level.

Administration: Group.

Levels, 2: X, Z.

Price Data, 1993: $16.95 per 10 test booklets (specify level); $7.95 per 10 machine-gradable answer sheets; $6.95 per manual ('85, 32 pages); $10 per specimen set including both tests, answer sheet, and manual.

Time: (50) minutes.

Comments: Identical to 1971 edition except for minor format and wording changes; 1 form.

Authors: Robert H. Ennis, Jason Millman, and Thomas N. Tomko (manual).

Publisher: Critical Thinking Press & Software.

a) LEVEL X.

Population: Grades 4–14.

b) LEVEL Z.

Population: Advanced and gifted high school students and college students and adults.

Cross References: For reviews by Jan N. Hughes and Koressa Kutsick Malcolm, see 11:88 (3 references); see also 9:269 (1 reference), T3:606 (7 references), T2:1755 (2 references), and 7:779 (10 references).

TEST REFERENCES

1. Farley, M. J., & Elmore, P. B. (1993). The relationship of reading comprehension to critical thinking skills, cognitive ability, and vocabulary for a sample of underachieving college freshmen. *Educational and Psychological Measurement, 52*, 921-931.

[656]
The Cornell Inventory for Student Appraisal of Teaching and Courses.

Purpose: "Provides teachers with feedback of student opinion."
Population: College teachers.
Publication Dates: 1972–73.
Scores: Item norms only.
Administration: Group.
Price Data: Not available.
Time: (15–20) minutes.
Authors: James B. Maas and Thomas R. Owen (manual).
Publisher: James B. Maas [No reply from publisher; status unknown].
Cross References: For a review by Wilbert J. McKeachie, see 8:367.

[657]
The Cornell Learning and Study Skills Inventory.

Purpose: To identify "specific competencies that are requisite for effective learning at the secondary school and college levels of instruction."
Population: Grades 7–13, 13–16.
Publication Date: 1970.
Acronym: CLASSIC.
Scores, 9: Goal Orientation, Activity Structure, Scholarly Skills, Lecture Mastery, Textbook Mastery, Examination Mastery, Self Mastery, Total, Reading Validity Index.
Administration: Group.
Price Data, 1987: $20 per 25 Secondary Form test booklets; $27.50 per 25 College Form test booklets; $6.75 per scoring key; $6.75 per 25 answer sheets; $5 per hand scoring stencils (College Form); $6.75 per 25 profiles (junior high, senior high, junior college, and senior college, graduate level); $6.75 per manual (31 pages); $9 per specimen set including manual and forms; specify Secondary Form or College Form for all test materials.
Time: (30–50) minutes.
Comments: Self-administered.
Authors: Walter Pauk and Russell Cassel.
Publisher: Psychologists and Educators, Inc.
a) SECONDARY SCHOOL FORM.
Population: Grades 7–13.
b) COLLEGE FORM.
Population: Grades 13–16.
Cross References: For reviews by Allen Berger and Richard D. Robinson, see 8:815 (1 reference); see also T2:1756 (2 references).

TEST REFERENCES

1. Crittenden, M. R., Kaplan, M. H., & Heim, J. K. (1984). Developing effective study skills and self-confidence in academically able young adolescents. *Gifted Child Quarterly, 28*, 25-30.

[658]
Cornell Medical Index—Health Questionnaire.

Purpose: For collecting pertinent medical and psychiatric data from patients.
Population: Ages 14 and over.
Publication Dates: 1949–56.
Scores: Total score only.
Administration: Group or individual.
Price Data: Not available.
Foreign Language Edition: French Canadian and Spanish editions available.
Time: (10–30) minutes.
Comments: Self-administered.
Authors: Keeve Brodman, Albert J. Erdmann, Jr., and Harold G. Wolff.
Publisher: Cornell University Medical College [No reply from publisher; status unknown].
Cross References: See 9:270 (15 references), T3:609 (33 references), 8:530 (46 references), and T2:1145 (42 references); for reviews by Eugene E. Levitt and David T. Lykken, see 7:61 (32 references); see also P:49 (77 references).

TEST REFERENCES

1. Baum, S. K., & Boxley, R. L. (1983). Depression and old age identification. *Journal of Clinical Psychology, 39*, 584-590.
2. Conger, R. D., McCarty, J. A., Yang, R. K., Lahey, B. B., & Kropp, J. P. (1984). Perception of child, child-rearing values, and emotional distress as mediating links between environmental stressors and observed maternal behavior. *Child Development, 55*, 2234-2247.
3. Iwata, O. (1984). The relationship of noise sensitivity to health and personality. *Japanese Psychological Research, 26*, 75-81.
4. Lahey, B. B., Conger, R. D., Atkeson, B. M., & Treiber, F. A. (1984). Parenting behavior and emotional status of physically abusive mothers. *Journal of Consulting and Clinical Psychology, 52*, 1062-1071.
5. Scoles, P., Fine, E. W., & Steer, R. A. (1984). Personality characteristics and drinking patterns of high risk drivers never apprehended for driving while intoxicated. *Journal of Studies on Alcohol, 45*, 411-416.
6. Borins, E. F. M., & Forsythe, P. J. (1985). Past trauma and present functioning of patients attending a women's psychiatric clinic. *American Journal of Psychiatry, 142*, 460-463.
7. Klein, M. H., Greist, J. H., Gurman, A. S., Neimeyer, R. A., Lesser, D. P., Bushnell, N. J., & Smith, R. E. (1985). A comparative outcome study of group psychotherapy vs. exercise treatments for depression. *International Journal of Mental Health, 13*(3/4), 148-177.
8. Heppner, P. P., Kampa, M., & Brunning, L. (1987). The relationship between problem-solving self-appraisal and indices of physical and psychological health. *Cognitive Therapy and Research, 11*(2), 155-168.
9. Rounsaville, B. J., Dolinsky, Z. S., Babor, T. F., & Meyer, R. E. (1987). Psychopathology as a predictor of treatment outcome in alcoholics. *Archives of General Psychiatry, 44*, 505-513.
10. Vázquez-Barquero, J. L., Díez-Manrique, J. F., Peña, C., Aldama, J., Rodríguez, C. S., Arango, J. M., & Mirapeix, C. (1987). A community mental health survey in Cantabria: A general description of morbidity. *Psychological Medicine, 17*, 227-241.
11. Wiener, R. L., & Merkel, W. T. (1987). Relation of depression to specific medical complaints in psychiatric inpatients. *Psychological Reports, 60*, 147-152.
12. Aldwin, C. M., Levenson, M. R., Spiro, A., III, & Bossé, R. (1989). Does emotionality predict stress? Findings from the normative aging study. *Journal of Personality and Social Psychology, 56*, 618-624.
13. Aldwin, C. M., Spiro, A., III, Levenson, M. R., & Bossé, R. (1989). Longitudinal findings from the normative aging study: I. Does mental health change with age? *Psychology and Aging, 4*, 295-306.
14. Carmody, T. P., Crossen, J. R., & Wiens, A. N. (1989). Hostility as a health risk factor: Relationships with neuroticism, type A behavior, attentional focus, and interpersonal style. *Journal of Clinical Psychology, 45*, 754-762.
15. Norton, N. C. (1989). Three scales of alexithymia: Do they measure the same thing? *Journal of Personality Assessment, 53*, 621-637.
16. Levenson, R. W., Carstensen, L. L., & Gottman, J. M. (1993). .

Long-term marriage: Age, gender, and satisfaction. *Psychology and Aging*, *8*, 303-313.

[659]

Cornell Word Form 2.
Purpose: "To assess mental health adjustment using a forced choice word association technique."
Population: Adults.
Publication Dates: 1946–55.
Acronym: C.W.F.-2.
Scores: Total score only.
Administration: Individual.
Price Data: Not available.
Time: [5–15] minutes.
Comments: Title on test is C.W.F.
Authors: Arthur Weider, Bela Mittlemann, David Wechsler, and Harold G. Wolff.
Publisher: Cornell University Medical College [No reply from publisher; status unknown].
Cross References: See T2:1146 (1 reference), P:50 (2 references), and 5:44 (11 references); for a review by S. B. Sells, see 6:80 (1 reference).

[660]

Correctional Institutions Environment Scale.
Purpose: "Measures the social environments of both juvenile and adult correctional programs."
Population: Residents and staff of juvenile and adult correctional facilities.
Publication Date: 1974.
Acronym: CIES.
Scores, 9: Involvement, Support, Expressiveness, Autonomy, Practical Orientation, Personal Problem Orientation, Order and Organization, Clarity, Staff Control.
Administration: Group.
Price Data, 1993: $13 per 25 reusable test booklets; $10 per 25 answer sheets; $8 per 25 profiles; $8 per scoring key; $35 per manual (39 pages); $36 per sampler set.
Time: (15–20) minutes.
Comments: A part of The Social Climate Scales (2495).
Author: Rudolf H. Moos.
Publisher: Consulting Psychologists Press, Inc.
Cross References: See T3:612 (1 reference); for a review by Kenneth A. Carlson, see 8:531 (16 references). For a review of The Social Climate Scales, see 8:681.

TEST REFERENCES

1. Wright, K. N., & Boudouris, J. (1982). An assessment of the Moos Correctional Institutions Environment Scale. *Journal of Research in Crime and Delinquency, 19,* 255-276.
2. Novak, A. R. (1984). A systems theory approach to deinstitutionalization policies and research. *International Review of Research in Mental Retardation, 12,* 245-283.
3. Palumbo, D. J., & Hallett, M. A. (1993). Conflict versus consensus models in policy evaluation and implementation. *Evaluation and Program Planning, 16,* 11-23.

[661]

Correctional Officer's Interest Blank.
Purpose: Designed to predict performance of correctional officers.

Population: Applicants for jobs in penal institutions and correctional agencies.
Publication Dates: 1953–82.
Acronym: COIB.
Scores: Total score only.
Administration: Group.
Restricted Distribution: Restricted to state and federal correctional agencies and penal institutions.
Price Data, 1991: $10 per 25 test booklets; $8.75 per manual ('82, 24 pages); $16.75 per scoring keys; $9 per specimen set.
Time: (10) minutes.
Authors: Harrison G. Gough and F. L. Aumack (test).
Publisher: Consulting Psychologists Press, Inc.
Cross References: For reviews by Robert J. Howell and R. Lynn Richards and Samuel Roll, see 10:75.

[662]

Correctional Policy Inventory: A Survey of Correctional Philosophy and Characteristic Methods of Dealing with Offenders.
Purpose: Developed to identify the correctional philosophies utilized in particular situations.
Population: Correctional managers.
Publication Date: 1970.
Scores, 4: Reintegration, Rehabilitation, Reform, Restraint.
Administration: Group.
Price Data: Available from publisher.
Time: [20] minutes.
Author: Vincent O'Leary.
Publisher: National Council on Crime and Delinquency.
Cross References: See 8:1092 (2 references).

[663]

Corrective Reading Mastery Tests.
Purpose: To posttest sections of the SRA decoding or comprehension programs.
Population: Grades 4–12 and adults in the Corrective Reading Program.
Publication Dates: 1980–81.
Administration: Group.
Comments: "Criterion-referenced"; 6 tests.
Authors: Siegfried Engleman and Linda Garcia Olen.
Publisher: Science Research Associates, Inc.
a) COMPREHENSION A: THINKING BASICS.
Publication Date: 1980.
Scores, 19: Deductions, Classification, True-False, Description (I, II), Same (I, II), Analogies (I, II), Inductions (I, II), Statement Inference, Definitions, Basic Evidence, Opposites, Animal Facts (I, II), Calendar Facts, Poems.
Price Data, 1987: $21.90 per set, includes manual (11 pages) and 20 tests.
Time: (25–40) minutes.
b) COMPREHENSION B: COMPREHENSION SKILLS.
Publication Date: 1980.

Price Data, 1987: $42.50 per set, includes manual (13 pages) and 20 tests.
Time: (20–40) minutes per subtest.
1) *Test 1.*
Scores, 17: Deductions (I, II), Basic Evidence, Analogies, Contradictions (I, II), Body Systems, Body Rules, Sentence Combinations (I, II), Parts of Speech, Subject-Predicate, Definitions (I, II), Statement Inference, Writing Directions, Following Directions.
Comments: To be completed after Lesson 70 of Comprehension B.
2) *Test 2.*
Scores, 16: Basic Evidence (I, II), Contradictions, Similies, Body Rules, Economic Rules, Statement Inference (I, II), Following Directions, Definitions, Sentence Combinations, Subject-Predicate, Sentence Analysis, Writing Directions, Editing, Writing Paragraphs.
Comments: To be completed at the end of Comprehension B.

c) COMPREHENSION C: CONCEPT APPLICATIONS.
Publication Date: 1981.
Price Data, 1987: Same as for *b* above, includes manual (15 pages) and 20 tests.
Time: (20–30) minutes per subtest.
1) *Test 1.*
Scores, 17: Deductions (I, II), Basic Evidence, Argument Rules, Contradictions (I, II), Maps/Pictures/Graphs, Basic Comprehension Passages, Supporting Evidence, Definitions, Editing (I, II), Combining Sentences, Writing Directions, Filling Out Forms, Identifying Contradictory Directions, Information.
Comments: To be completed after Lesson 70 of Comprehension C.
2) *Test 2.*
Scores, 19: Main Ideas, Morals, Specific-General, Visual-Spatial Organization, Outlining, Deductions, Argument Rules (I, II), Ought Statements, Contradictions, Words or Deductions, Maps/Pictures/Graphs, Supporting Evidence, Editing, Combining Sentences, Definitions, Meaning From Context (I, II), Information.
Comments: To be completed at end of Comprehension C.

d) DECODING A: WORD-ATTACK BASICS.
Publication Date: 1980.
Scores, 14: Word Identification (Short and Long Vowels, Sound Combinations, Final Blends, Initial Blends, Consonant Digraphs, Irregular Words), Sentence Reading (Time, Errors), Dictation (Sound Dictation, Spelling From Dictation), Word Completion (Rhyming Dictation, Word Completion), Workbook Skills (Matching Completion, Circle Games).
Price Data, 1987: Same as for *a* above, includes manual (11 pages) and 20 tests.
Time: (35–40) minutes.
e) DECODING B: DECODING STRATEGIES.

Publication Date: 1980.
Price Data, 1987: Same as for *b* above.
Time: (10–15) minutes per subtest.
1) *Test 1.*
Scores, 12: Word Identification (Short-Vowel Words, Consonant Digraphs, ed Endings in Short-Vowel Words, Word Endings s and ing, Word Endings er and est, Sound Combinations ea/ar/ai, Sound Combinations ol/or/oa/ow, Irregular Words, Vowel-Conversion Words), Story Reading (Rate, Accuracy, Comprehension).
Comments: To be completed after Lesson 60 of Decoding B.
2) *Test 2.*
Scores, 13: Word Identification (Short-Vowel Words, ed Endings and Contractions, s and es Endings, Other Endings, Irregular Words and Difficult Discriminations, Vowel-Conversion Words, Difficult Multisyllabic Words, Sound Combinations ou/al/ar/igh/tch, Sound Combinations ir/ur/er/io/wa, Combinations orel/soft c/g/tion/ure, Story Reading (Rate, Accuracy, Comprehension).
Comments: To be completed at end of Decoding B.

f) DECODING C: SKILL APPLICATIONS.
Publication Date: 1980.
Price Data, 1987: Same as for *b* above.
Time: (10–15) minutes per subtest.
1) *Test 1.*
Scores, 13: Word Identification (Sound Combinations ou/ai/ur, Sound Combinations ir/er/or/al, Sound Combinations oi/ee/ea/au/aw, Sound Combinations ure/tion, Soft c and Soft g, Affixes un/dis/ex/ly, Affixes pre/ly/re/ex, Difficult Words, Words with Endings), Vocabulary (Vocabulary Words), Story Reading (Rate, Accuracy, Comprehension).
Comments: To be completed after Lesson 69 of Decoding C.
2) *Test 2.*
Scores, 11: Word Identification (Sound Combinations, Prefixes, Suffixes ible/able/by/less/ness, Suffixes ial/tion/ure, Affixes, Endings, Difficult Words), Vocabulary (Vocabulary Words), Story Reading (Rate, Accuracy, Comprehension).
Comments: To be completed at end of Decoding C.

Cross References: For a review by Esther Geva, see 9:272.

[664]
Cosmetology Student Admissions Evaluation.

Purpose: To "determine the aptitude and dexterity of an applicant to the cosmetology field."
Population: Cosmetology school applicants.
Publication Dates: 1977–85.
Scores, 5: Interest Inventory, Word Analogies, Comprehension and Reasoning, Manual Dexterity, Total.
Administration: Individual in part.

Price Data, 1989: $18.37 List, $13 School price per examination kit including 12 examination booklets ('85, 23 pages) and 12 evaluation sheets; $9.93 List, $6.95 School price per manual ('85, 40 pages); $7.07 List, $4.95 School price per 50 remedial work guide cards; $17.14 List, $12 School price per examination plus audio cassette tape.

Foreign Language Edition: Spanish edition available.

Time: (34) minutes.

Comments: Examiner must be trained to score Manual Dexterity; other test materials (e.g., mannequin, professional comb, etc.) must be supplied by examiner.

Authors: Anthony B. Colletti and Robert M. Denmark (manual).

Publisher: Keystone Publications.

Cross References: For reviews by Craig N. Mills and Steven J. Osterlind, see 11:89.

[665]
Cotswold Junior Ability Tests.

Purpose: Measures intelligence, understanding of numbers, mastery of the vocabulary, arithmetic processes, and the comprehension and use of English.

Population: Ages 8.5–9.5, 9.5–10.5.

Publication Dates: 1949–69.

Administration: Group.

Price Data: Not available.

Comments: Tests A, B, C, and E are out of print.

Author: C. M. Fleming.

Publisher: Gibson (Robert) & Sons, Glasgow, Ltd. [Scotland] [No reply from publisher; status unknown].

a) JUNIOR MENTAL ABILITY, D.

Population: Ages 8.5–9.5.

Publication Dates: 1967–69.

Scores: Total score only.

Time: 30(40) minutes.

b) JUNIOR MENTAL ABILITY, F.

Population: Ages 9.5–10.5.

Publication Dates: 1967–69.

Scores: Total score only.

Time: 30(40) minutes.

[666]
Cotswold Personality Assessment P.A. 1.

Purpose: "Devised as an aid to the assessment of the personal characteristics of boys and girls."

Population: Ages 11–16.

Publication Date: 1960.

Scores, 6: 3 Preferences (Things, People, Ideas), and 3 Attitudes (Using One's Hands, Being with Other People, Talking About School).

Administration: Group.

Price Data: Not available.

Time: Administration time not reported.

Comments: Manual (6 pages) subtitle is A Study of Preferences and Values for Use in School and Clubs.

Author: C. M. Fleming.

Publisher: Gibson (Robert) & Sons, Glasgow, Ltd.

[Scotland] [No reply from publisher; status unknown].

Cross References: For reviews by Ralph D. Dutch and G. A. V. Morgan, see 6:81 (1 reference).

[667]
Counselor and Client Verbal Response Category Systems.

Purpose: To "provide a standardized method for analyzing counselor and client verbal behavior."

Population: Counselors in training.

Publication Date: 1981.

Scores: 23 categories: Counselor (Minimal Encourager, Silence, Approval/Reassurance, Information, Direct Guidance, Closed Question, Open Question, Restatement, Reflection, Interpretation, Confrontation, Verbal Referent, Self Disclosure, Other) Client (Simple Responses, Requests, Description, Experiencing, Exploration of Counselor-Client Relationship, Insight, Discussion of Plans, Silence, Other).

Administration: Group.

Price Data, 1994: $15 per manual (62 pages).

Time: Administration time not reported.

Comments: 2 systems: Counselor, Client; interaction must be taped and transcribed.

Authors: Clara E. Hill, Carole Greenwald, Kathryn G. Reed, Darlene Charles, Mary K. O'Farrell, and Jean A. Carter.

Publisher: Marathon Consulting and Press.

TEST REFERENCES

1. Hill, C. E., Corbett, M. M., Kanitz, B., Rios, P., Lightsey, R., & Gomes, M. (1992). Client behavior in counseling and therapy sessions: Development of a pantheoretical measure. *Journal of Counseling Psychology, 39,* 539-549.

[668]
Couple's Pre-Counseling Inventory, Revised Edition, 1987.

Purpose: "Provides a comprehensive portrait of couples' strengths and concerns—the basis for planning specific treatment strategies."

Population: Married or cohabiting couples beginning counseling.

Publication Dates: 1972–87.

Acronym: CPCI.

Scores: 13 areas: Demographic Data, General and Specific Happiness with the Relationship, Caring Behaviors, Conflict Management, Communication Assessment, Sexual Interaction, Moods and Management of Personal Life, Decision Making, Division of Home/Child Care/Work Responsibilities, Child Management, Goals of Counseling, Previous Marriages and/or Relationships, Additional Information.

Administration: Group.

Price Data, 1994: $21.95 per set including 25 forms and counselor's guide ('87, 38 pages); $25 per couple computer scoring service available from COMPUSCORE, Inc.

Time: Administration time not reported.

Comments: Revision of the Marital Pre-Counseling Inventory; may be scored by hand or by computer.

Authors: Richard B. Stuart and Barbara Jacobson.
Publisher: Research Press.
Cross References: For reviews by David N. Dixon and Gerald L. Stone, see 11:92; for reviews by Lee N. June and Marlene W. Winell of an earlier edition, see 9:277; see also T3:1373 (1 reference).

TEST REFERENCES

1. Boen, D. L. (1988). A practitioner looks at assessment in marital counseling. *Journal of Counseling and Development, 66,* 484–486.

[669]

The Couples BrainMap™.
Purpose: "To help partners gain new perspective of, and value for, their relationship."
Population: Couples.
Publication Dates: 1981–86.
Scores, 4: I-Organize, I-Explore, I-Pursue, I-Preserve.
Administration: Group.
Price Data: Not available.
Time: 40(50) minutes.
Comments: Self-administered, self-scored.
Authors: Sherry Lynch, Dudley Lynch, Phyllis Miller, and Sherod Miller.
Publisher: Brain Technologies Corporation [No reply from publisher; status unknown].
Cross References: For a review by Alicia Skinner Cook and Richard E. Guest, see 11:91.

[670]

Course Evaluation Questionnaire.
Purpose: Designed to provide information about how students regard some of their educational experiences.
Population: High school and college.
Publication Dates: 1971–72.
Acronym: CEQ.
Scores, 5: Openness to Students and Ideas, Contextual Approach to Learning, Dynamism Enthusiasm, Organization Clarity, Quality Meaningfulness.
Administration: Group.
Manual: No manual.
Price Data: Not available.
Time: Administration time not reported.
Comments: Ratings by students.
Author: James K. Hoffmeister.
Publisher: Test Analysis & Development Corporation [No reply from publisher; status unknown].
Cross References: For reviews by J. Stanley Ahmann and William C. McGahie, see 8:368 (1 reference).

[671]

Course Finder 2000.
Purpose: Assesses "students' interests and preferences, and identifies suitable higher education courses at appropriate universities/colleges in Great Britain."
Population: Students entering higher education.
Publication Date: 1992–93.
Acronym: CF2000.
Administration: Group.
Price Data: Available from publisher.

Time: (45–60) minutes.
Comments: For use in Great Britian.
Authors: Malcolm Morrisby, Glen Fox, and Mark Parkinson.
Publisher: The Morrisby Organisation [England].

[672]

Course-Faculty Instrument.
Purpose: Student evaluation of business courses and instructors.
Population: Business faculty and courses.
Publication Date: 1976.
Acronym: CFI.
Administration: Group.
Manual: No manual.
Price Data: Not available.
Time: Administration time not reported.
Comments: Reprints containing information regarding development, validation, attributes, and correlates are available.
Authors: Richard D. Freedman and Stephen A. Stumpf.
Publisher: New York University [No reply from publisher; status unknown].
Cross References: For reviews by Rabindra N. Kanungo and Charles K. Parsons, see 9:278 (1 reference); see also T3:621 (7 references).

[673]

A Courtship Analysis.
Purpose: Designed to "help dating or engaged couples know and understand each other."
Population: Dating or engaged couples.
Publication Dates: 1961–79.
Scores: No scores.
Administration: Group.
Price Data: Not available.
Time: Administration time not reported.
Author: Gelolo McHugh.
Publisher: Family Life Publications, Inc. [No reply from publisher; status unknown].
Cross References: For a review by Andrew Christensen, see 9:279 (1 reference); for a review by William R. Reevy of the original edition, see 6:675.

[674]

CPF [Second Edition].
Purpose: "To assess extroversion and preference for social contact."
Population: Ages 16–adult.
Publication Dates: 1954–92.
Acronym: CPF.
Scores, 3: Validity Scores (Uncertainty, Good Impression), Total Extroversion.
Administration: Group or individual.
Price Data, 1994: $14 per specimen set including manual ('92, 10 pages), 3 test booklets, and scoring key; $21 per 20 test booklets; $10 per manual.
Time: (5–10) minutes.
Comments: Previously listed as a subtest of the

Employee Attitude Series of the Job-Tests Program (T3:1219).
Author: Samuel E. Krug.
Publisher: Industrial Psychology International Ltd.

[675]

CPH Patient Attitude Scale.
Purpose: Measures attitude of mental patients about the nature, cause, and treatment of mental illness, and attitudes about mental hospital activities and personnel.
Population: Mental patients.
Publication Dates: 1972–74.
Scores, 5: Authoritarian Control, Negative Hospital Orientation, External Control, Mental Illness and Treatment as Physical, Letdown of Control for Therapeutic Gain.
Administration: Group.
Price Data: Not available.
Time: Administration time not reported.
Comments: For research use only; test booklet title is CPH Factor Scale.
Authors: Marvin W. Kahn and F. Jones Nelson.
Publisher: Marvin W. Kahn [No reply from publisher; status unknown].
Cross References: For additional information, see 8:511 (6 references).

[676]

C-R Opinionaire.
Purpose: Measures degree of "conservatism" and "radicalism" on a number of issues.
Population: Grades 11–16 and adults.
Publication Dates: 1935–50.
Scores: Conservatism-Radicalism.
Administration: Group.
Forms, 2: J, K.
Price Data: Available from publisher.
Time: Administration time not reported.
Author: Theodore F. Lentz.
Publisher: Lentz Peace Research Laboratory.
Cross References: See T2:1116 (7 references) and P:21 (3 references); for a review by George W. Hartmann, see 4:39 (5 references); for a review by Goodwin Watson, see 2:1212 (5 references); for a review by H. H. Remmers, see 1:899.

TEST REFERENCES

1. Holzman, T. G., Pellegrino, J. W., & Glaser, R. (1982). Cognitive dimensions of numerical rule induction. *Journal of Educational Psychology, 74,* 360-373.

[677]

Crane Oral Dominance Test: Spanish/English.
Purpose: "To determine if the student has a dominant language, if the student is bilingual . . . , or if the student needs concentrated language, concept, and memory development to function adequately in either language."
Population: Ages 4–8.
Publication Date: 1976.
Acronym: CODT.

Scores, 4: Spanish Dominant, English Dominant, Bilingual, Indeterminable.
Administration: Individual.
Price Data, 1987: $34.64 per 30 test booklets and manual (11 pages).
Time: (20) minutes.
Comments: Both English and Spanish used in administration and in pupil responses.
Author: Barbara J. Crane.
Publisher: Bilingual Educational Services.
Cross References: For excerpted reviews by Protase E. Woodford and Porfirio Sanchez, see 8:162 (1 reference).

[678]

Crawford Psychological Adjustment Scale.
Purpose: Assessment of behaviors related to psychological adjustment.
Population: Psychiatric inpatients.
Publication Date: 1968.
Acronym: CPAS.
Scores: 7 scores based upon 25 behavior ratings: Socio-Economic-Environmental Competence, Derangement of Thought Processes and Peculiar Behavior, Physical Behavior, Communications, Social Acceptability and Moderation of Behavior, Management of Hostility, Total.
Administration: Group.
Price Data: Available from publisher.
Time: [15–30] minutes.
Author: Paul L. Crawford.
Publisher: Paul L. Crawford.
Cross References: See T2:1148 (1 reference).

[679]

Crawford Small Parts Dexterity Test.
Purpose: "A performance test designed to measure fine eye-hand coordination."
Population: High school and adults.
Publication Dates: 1946–81.
Acronym: CSPDT.
Scores, 2: Pins and Collars, Screws.
Administration: Individual.
Price Data, 1994: $430 per complete set including manual ('81, 22 pages) and spare parts; $28 per manual.
Time: (10–15) minutes.
Authors: John E. Crawford and Dorothea M. Crawford.
Publisher: The Psychological Corporation.
Cross References: See T3:627 (4 references) and T2:2223 (12 references); for a review by Neil D. Warren, see 5:871 (8 references); for a review by Raymond A. Katzell, see 4:752; for a review by Joseph E. Moore, see 3:667.

TEST REFERENCES

1. Berger, Y. (1985). Does the Crawford Small Parts Dexterity Test require new norms. *Perceptual and Motor Skills, 60,* 948-950.
2. Riggio, R. E., & Sotoodeh, Y. (1987). Screening tests for use in hiring microassemblers. *Perceptual and Motor Skills, 65,* 167-172.

[680]
Creative Behavior Inventory.

Purpose: Designed to measure "behavioral characteristics associated with creativity."
Population: Grades 1–6, 7–12.
Publication Date: 1989.
Acronyms: CBI1, CBI2.
Scores, 5: Contact, Consciousness, Interest, Fantasy, Total.
Administration: Individual.
Levels, 2: I (elementary), II (secondary).
Price Data: Price data for materials including manual (70 pages) available from publisher.
Time: Administration time not reported.
Comments: Ratings by teachers; manual title is Understanding the Creative Activity of Students.
Author: Robert J. Kirschenbaum.
Publisher: Creative Learning Press, Inc.
Cross References: For a review by Richard M. Clark, see 11:93.

[681]
Creative Styles Inventory.

Purpose: "Identifies an individual's preference for assimilating information using either an intuitive or a logical style."
Population: High school (advanced).
Publication Date: 1986.
Acronym: CSI.
Scores: Total score only.
Administration: Group.
Price Data, 1993: $49 per complete kit including 10 inventories and 10 interpretive booklets (4 pages).
Time: (10–15) minutes.
Comments: Self-scored inventory.
Author: Bernice McCarthy and Excel, Inc.
Publisher: McBer & Company.

[682]
Creativity Assessment Packet.

Purpose: To assess creative potential.
Population: Grades 3–12.
Publication Dates: 1980–86.
Acronym: CAP.
Administration: Group.
Price Data, 1994: $84 per complete kit including 25 of each test and manual ('80, 24 pages); $17 per manual.
Author: Frank Williams.
Publisher: PRO-ED, Inc.
a) TEST OF DIVERGENT THINKING.
Scores, 6: Fluency, Flexibility, Originality, Elaboration, Titles, Total.
Forms, 2: A, B.
Price Data: $17 per 25 tests (specify Form A or Form B).
Time: 20(25) minutes for grades 6–12; 25(30) minutes for grades 3–5.
b) TEST OF DIVERGENT FEELING.
Scores, 5: Curiosity, Imagination, Complexity, Risk-Taking, Total.

Price Data: $19 per 25 tests.
Time: 10(20) minutes.
c) THE WILLIAMS SCALE.
Scores, 9: Fluency, Flexibility, Originality, Elaboration, Curiosity, Imagination, Complexity, Risk-Taking, Total.
Price Data: $17 per 25 tests.
Time: Administration time not reported.
Comments: Ratings by parents and teachers.
Cross References: For reviews by Fred Damarin and Carl L. Rosen, see 9:280.

TEST REFERENCES

1. Long, S., & Hiebert, E. H. (1985). Effects of awareness and practice in mental imagery on creative writing of gifted children. *National Reading Conference Yearbook, 34,* 381-385.
2. Kagan, D. M. (1988). Measurements of divergent and complex thinking. *Educational and Psychological Measurement, 48,* 873-884.
3. Cameron, B. A., Brown, D. M., Carson, D. K., Meyer, S. S., & Bittner, M. T. (1993). Children's creative thinking and color discrimination. *Perceptual and Motor Skills, 76,* 595-598.

[683]
Creativity Attitude Survey.

Purpose: Designed to assess attitudes toward creative behaviors and oneself as a creative thinker.
Population: Grades 4–6.
Publication Date: 1971.
Acronym: CAS.
Scores: Total score only.
Administration: Group.
Price Data, 1987: $15 per 25 tests; $4.50 per manual (8 pages); $5 per specimen set.
Time: (10) minutes.
Author: Charles E. Schaefer.
Publisher: Psychologists and Educators, Inc.
Cross References: For reviews by Philip V. Vernon and Kaoru Yamamoto, see 8:240 (1 reference); see also T2:553 (1 reference).

[684]
Creativity Tests for Children.

Purpose: To measure different aspects of divergent production ability.
Population: Grades 4–6.
Publication Dates: 1971–76.
Administration: Group.
Price Data: Available from publisher.
Authors: J. P. Guilford and others listed.
Publisher: SOI Systems.
a) ADDING DECORATIONS.
Time: 6(10) minutes.
Authors: Arthur Gershon, Sheldon Gardner, and Philip R. Merrifield.
b) DIFFERENT LETTER GROUPS.
Time: 8(12) minutes.
Author: Arthur Gershon.
c) HIDDEN LETTERS.
Time: 5(8) minutes.
d) KINDS OF PEOPLE.
Time: 6(10) minutes.
Author: Arthur Gershon.

e) MAKE SOMETHING OUT OF IT.
Time: 5(8) minutes.
f) MAKING OBJECTS.
Time: 5(8) minutes.
Authors: Sheldon Gardner, Arthur Gershon, and Philip K. Merrifield.
g) NAMES FOR STORIES.
Time: 8(12) minutes.
h) SIMILAR MEANINGS.
Time: 6(10) minutes.
Authors: Philip R. Merrifield.
i) WHAT TO DO WITH IT.
Time: 7(11) minutes.
Authors: Philip R. Merrifield (Form A), Robert C. Wilson (Form B), and Paul R. Christensen (Form B).
j) WRITING SENTENCES.
Time: 7(11) minutes.
Cross References: See T3:630 (1 reference); for reviews by John W. French and Kaoru Yamamoto, see 8:241 (1 reference).

[685]

The Creatrix Inventory.
Purpose: "To help people identify their levels of creativity as well as their orientations toward risk taking."
Population: Members of organizations.
Publication Dates: 1971–86.
Acronym: C&RT.
Scores, 2: Creativity, Risk Taking; plotted on matrix to determine 1 of 8 styles: Reproducer, Modifier, Challenger, Practicalizer, Innovator, Synthesizer, Dreamer, Planner.
Administration: Group.
Price Data, 1987: $5.95 per manual ('86, 26 pages) including inventory and scoring instructions plus administrator's guide (2 pages).
Time: Administration time not reported.
Comments: Catalog uses the title Creativity and Risk-Taking.
Author: Richard E. Byrd.
Publisher: Pfeiffer & Company International Publishers.
Cross References: For reviews by Harrison G. Gough and John F. Wakefield, see 11:95.

[686]

Cree Questionnaire.
Purpose: "To measure an individual's overall creative potential."
Population: Adults.
Publication Dates: 1957–81.
Acronym: CQ.
Scores, 14: Overall Creative Potential, plus 13 technical dimension scores grouped under 4 broad headings: Social Orientation, Work Orientation, Internal Functioning, Interests and Skills.
Administration: Group.
Forms, 2: A, B.
Price Data, 1992: $30 per 25 booklets (specify

Form A or B); $5 per score sheet (specify Form A or B); $10 per interpretation and research manual ('80, 51 pages).
Time: (20) minutes.
Authors: T. G. Thurstone and J. Melinger.
Publisher: SRA/London House.
Cross References: For a review by Janet M. Stoppard, see 9:282; see also T2:1149 (1 reference) and P:53 (3 references); for reviews of an earlier edition by Allyn Miles Munger and Theodor F. Naumann, see 6:84.

[687]

Crichton Vocabulary Scale.
Purpose: Designed to provide an index of a child's "acquired fund of verbal information."
Population: Ages 4.5–11.
Publication Date: 1950.
Scores, 3: Definitions of Set One, Definitions of Set Two, Total.
Administration: Individual.
Price Data: Available from publisher.
Time: Administration time not reported.
Comments: Designed for use with the Coloured Progressive Matrices.
Author: J. C. Raven.
Publisher: H. K. Lewis & Co., Ltd. [England].
Cross References: See T3:632 (2 references) and T2:491 (3 references); for a review by Morton Bortner, see 6:518 (1 reference); for reviews by Charlotte Banks and W. D. Wall, see 4:337.

TEST REFERENCES

1. Berg, I., Casswell, G., Goodwin, A., Hullin, R., McGuire, R., & Tagg, G. (1985). Classification of severe school attendance problems. *Psychological Medicine, 15,* 157-165.
2. Lytton, H., Maunula, S. R., & Watts, D. (1987). Moral judgements and reported moral acts: A tenuous relationship. *The Alberta Journal of Educational Research, 33,* 150-162.
3. Lytton, H., Watts, D., & Dunn, B. E. (1987). Twin-singleton differences in verbal ability: Where do they stem from? *Intelligence, 11,* 359-369.

[688]

Criterion Test of Basic Skills.
Purpose: "Developed to assess the basic reading and arithmetic skills of individual students."
Population: Grades K–8.
Publication Date: 1976.
Administration: Individual.
Price Data, 1994: $55 per test kit including manual (96 pages), 25 arithmetic recording forms, 25 reading recording forms, 25 math problem sheets, and stimulus cards booklet; $10 per 25 arithmetic recording forms; $10 per 25 reading recording forms; $4 per math problem sheets; $8 per stimulus cards booklet; $17 per manual; $17 per specimen set.
Time: (10–15) minutes.
Comments: "Criterion-referenced"; mastery level defined as 90–100% correct; instructional level defined as 50–89% correct; frustration level defined as 0–49% correct; no information presented in support of increasing difficulty levels (student takes only subtests

beginning with 2 mastery scores and ending with 2 frustration scores) or relevancy to grade levels.

Authors: Keith Lundell, William Brown, and James Evans.

Publisher: Academic Therapy Publications.

a) READING.

Scores: 19 specific-objective subtests in 6 areas: Letter Recognition (3 subtests), Letter Sounding (4 subtests), Blending and Sequencing (3 subtests), Special Sounds (6 subtests), Sight Words, Letter Writing (2 subtests).

b) ARITHMETIC.

Scores: 26 specific-objective subtests in 11 areas: Counting, Numbers and Numerals (4 subtests), Addition (3 subtests), Subtraction (3 subtests), Multiplication (2 subtests), Division (2 subtests), Money Measurement (2 subtests), Telling Time (2 subtests), Symbols, Fractions (3 subtests), Decimals and Percents (3 subtests).

Cross References: See T3:635 (1 reference).

[689]

Criterion Validated Written Tests for Clerical Worker.

Purpose: For selection of clerical employees.

Population: Candidates for clerical positions.

Publication Dates: 1984–94.

Scores: 9 scores for 2 equivalent forms: Memorization, Information Ordering, Number Facility, Time-Sharing, Problem Sensitivity, Dealing with People, Deductive Reasoning, Verbal Comprehension, Total.

Administration: Group.

Manual: No manual.

Restricted Distribution: Restricted to Civil Service Commissions, Personnel Directors, City Managers, and other "responsible officials."

Price Data, 1993: Rental and scoring service, $245 for the first 5 candidates; $10–$16 for each additional candidate ($245 minimum).

Time: 210(230) minutes.

Author: McCann Associates, Inc.

Publisher: McCann Associates, Inc.

[690]

Criterion Validated Written Tests for Firefighter.

Purpose: For the selection of firefighter candidates.

Population: Prospective firefighters.

Publication Dates: 1976–92.

Scores: 7 subtests and total: Interest in Firefighting, Compatibility, Map Reading, Spatial Visualization, Visual Pursuit, Understanding and Interpreting Table and Text Material About Firefighting, Mechanical Aptitude, Total.

Administration: Group.

Form, 1: Form ESV-100 (100 items).

Restricted Distribution: Distribution restricted to civil service commissions, city managers, and "other responsible officials."

Price Data, 1993: Rental and scoring service: $245

for first 5 candidates; $10–$16 for each additional candidate.

Time: 131(141) minutes.

Comments: Practice test and candidate study guide available; formerly called Statistically Validated Written Tests for Firefighter.

Author: McCann Associates, Inc.

Publisher: McCann Associates, Inc.

[691]

Criterion Validated Written Tests for Police Officer.

Purpose: Designed as a "police officer entrance test."

Population: Prospective police officers.

Publication Dates: 1980–93.

Time: 170(180) minutes.

Administration: Group.

Restricted Distribution: Distribution restricted to qualified municipal officials.

Forms, 2: Form 100, Form N-100.

Price Data, 1993: Rental and scoring service, $245 for the first 5 candidates; $10–$16 for each additional candidate.

Scores: 7 subtests and total: Observational Ability, Ability to Exercise Judgment and Common Sense, Interest in Police Work, Ability to Exercise Judgment-Map Reading, Ability to Exercise Judgment-Dealing With People, Ability to Read and Comprehend Police Test Material, Reasoning Ability, Total.

Comments: Candidate study guide available.

Author: McCann Associates, Inc.

Publisher: McCann Associates, Inc.

[692]

Critical Reasoning Test Battery.

Purpose: To assist students in subject and career choices and employers with the selection of job candidates.

Population: Students and employees ages 15 and over.

Publication Dates: 1981–83.

Acronym: CRTB.

Administration: Group.

Restricted Distribution: Distribution restricted to persons who have completed the publisher's training course or members of the Division of Occupational Psychology of the British Psychological Society.

Price Data, 1989: £370 per complete kit; £99 per 10 test booklets (reusable) including 3 tests; £44 per 10 reusable test booklets; £6 per scoring key; £5.50 per 25 score sheets; £33 per 50 answer sheets; £11 per 50 profile charts; £19.50 per 50 practice leaflets; £5.50 per 25 testing logs; £6 per administration card; £20 per manual ('83, 71 pages); £55 per administration set.

Comments: 3 subtests available as separates.

Authors: Peter Saville, Roger Holdsworth, Gill Nyfield, David Hawkey, Susan Bawtree, and Ruth Holdsworth.

Publisher: Saville & Holdsworth Ltd. [England].

a) VERBAL EVALUATION.
Publication Dates: 1982–83.
Acronym: VC1.
Time: 30(35) minutes.
b) INTERPRETING DATA.
Publication Dates: 1982–83.
Acronym: NC2.
Price Data: £19.50 per 10 data cards for NC2 only (reusable).
Time: 30(35) minutes.
c) DIAGRAMMATIC SERIES.
Publication Dates: 1982–83.
Acronym: DC3.
Time: 20(25) minutes.

[693]

Critical Reasoning Tests.
Purpose: Assesses intellectual skills needed for a managerial level post.
Population: Prospective managers.
Publication Date: 1992.
Acronym: CRT.
Administration: Group.
Price Data: Available from publisher.
Authors: Pauline Smith and Chris Whetton.
Publisher: NFER-Nelson Publishing Co., Ltd. [England].
a) VERBAL TEST.
Purpose: "Assesses how well a candidate can cope with different reasoning tasks."
Scores: Total score only.
Time: (28–33) minutes.
b) NUMERICAL TEST.
Purpose: "Assesses how well the candidate interprets numerical information."
Scores: Total score only.
Time: (30–35) minutes.

[694]

Croft Readiness Assessment in Comprehension Kit.
Purpose: "Measures performance on oral and written language readiness" and pattern readiness.
Population: Children for whom diagnostic information in reading is needed.
Publication Date: 1978.
Acronym: CRAC-Kit.
Scores: 3 subtests: Oral Language Readiness, Comprehensive Readiness, Pattern Readiness, with 3 scores each: Concrete, Semi-Abstract, Abstract.
Administration: Individual.
Levels: 2 levels.
Price Data: Not available.
Time: Administration time not reported.
Authors: Marion L. McGuire and Marguerite J. Bumpus.
Publisher: Croft, Inc. [No reply from publisher; status unknonwn].
Cross References: For reviews by Jerry D. Harris and Annette B. Weinshank, see 9:286 (1 reference).

[695]

Cross Reference Test.
Purpose: Constructed to assess "skill in routine checking tasks."
Population: Clerical job applicants.
Publication Date: 1959.
Scores: Total score only.
Administration: Group.
Price Data: Available from publisher.
Time: 5(10) minutes.
Author: James W. Curtis.
Publisher: Psychometric Affiliates.
Cross References: For a review by Philip H. Kriedt, see 6:1039.

[696]

Crown-Crisp Experiential Index.
Purpose: To obtain diagnostic information typically gained in a formal clinical psychiatric examination.
Population: Normal and psychoneurotic adults.
Publication Date: 1979.
Acronym: CCEI.
Scores, 7: Free-Floating Anxiety, Depression, Hysteria, Phobic Anxiety, Obsessionality, Somatic Anxiety, Total.
Administration: Group.
Price Data, 1994: £6.99 per 20 tests; £5.99 per scoring template; £6.99 per manual (32 pages); £7.50 per specimen set.
Time: (5–10) minutes.
Comments: Formerly published under the title Middlesex Hospital Questionnaire; distribution restricted to qualified persons.
Authors: Sidney Crown and A. H. Crisp.
Publisher: Hodder & Stoughton Educational [England].
Cross References: For reviews by A. J. Devito and D. S. Payne, see 9:287 (13 references); see also T3:369 (22 references); for reviews by H. J. Eysenck and Lester M. Libo, see 8:615 (26 references); see also T2:1279 (8 references); for a review by D. F. Clark, see 7:103 (5 references).

TEST REFERENCES

1. Abou-Saleh, M. T., & Coppen, A. (1983). Classification of depressive illnesses: Clinico-psychological correlates. *Journal of Affective Disorders, 6,* 53-66.
2. Alderman, K. J., Mackay, C. J., Lucas, E. G., Spry, W. B., & Bell, B. (1983). Factor analysis and reliability studies of the Crown-Crisp Experiential Index (CCEI). *British Journal of Medical Psychology, 56,* 329-345.
3. Birtchnell, J., & Kennard, J. (1983). What does the MMPI Dependency scale really measure? *Journal of Clinical Psychology, 39,* 532-543.
4. Clarke, M. G., & Palmer, R. L. (1983). Eating attitudes and neurotic symptoms in university students. *British Journal of Psychiatry, 142,* 299-304.
5. Hafner, R. J. (1984). Predicting the effects on husbands of behaviour therapy for wives agoraphobia. *Behaviour Research and Therapy, 22,* 217-226.
6. Holland, A. J., Hall, A., Murray, R., Russell, G. F. M., & Crisp, A. H. (1984). Anorexia nervosa: A study of 34 twin pairs and one set of triplets. *British Journal of Psychiatry, 145,* 414-419.
7. Moore, N. C., Summer, K. R., & Bloor, R. N. (1984). Do patients like psychometric testing by computer? *Journal of Clinical Psychology, 40,* 875-877.
8. Abou-Saleh, M. T., Oleesky, D. A., & Crisp, A. H. (1985).

Dexamethasone suppression and energy balance: A study of anorexic patients. *Journal of Psychiatric Research, 19,* 203-206.

9. Hallam, R. S., & Jakes, S. C. (1985). Tinnitus: Differential effects of therapy in a single case. *Behaviour Research and Therapy, 23,* 691-694.

10. Norton, K. R. W., Crisp, A. H., & Bhat, A. V. (1985). Why do some anorexics steal? Personal, social and illness factors. *Journal of Psychiatric Research, 19,* 385-390.

11. Szmukler, G. I., Eisler, I., Russell, G. F. M., & Dare, C. (1985). Anorexia nervosa, parental 'expressed emotion' and dropping out of treatment. *British Journal of Psychiatry, 147,* 265-271.

12. Adam, K., Tomeny, M., & Oswald, I. (1986). Physiological and psychological differences between good and poor sleepers. *Journal of Psychiatric Research, 20,* 301-316.

13. Falkowski, J., Hatcher, S., Sondhi, R., Fong, K., & Young, K. (1986). Personality and drinking behavior in medical students. *British Journal of Addiction, 81,* 573-575.

14. Jakes, S. C., Hallam, R. S., Rachman, S., & Hinchcliffe, R. (1986). The effects of reassurance, relaxation training and distraction on chronic tinnitus sufferers. *Behaviour Research and Therapy, 24,* 497-507.

15. Meadows, G. N., Palmer, R. L., Newball, E. U. M., & Kenrick, J. M. T. (1986). Eating attitudes and disorder in young women: A general practice based survey. *Psychological Medicine, 16,* 351-357.

16. Macaulay, A. J., Stern, R. S., Holmes, D. M., & Stanton, S. L. (1987). Micturition and the mind: Psychological factors in the aetiology and treatment of urinary symptoms in women. *British Medical Journal, 294,* 540-543.

17. Shaw, G. K., Majumdar, S. K., Wallers, S., MacGarvie, J., & Dunn, G. (1987). Tiapride in the long-term management of alcoholics of anxious or depressive temperament. *The British Journal of Psychiatry, 150,* 164-168.

18. Hafner, R. J., & Spence, N. S. (1988). Marriage duration, marital adjustment and psychological symptoms: A cross-sectional study. *Journal of Clinical Psychology, 44,* 309-316.

19. Lewis, S. N. C., & Cooper, C. L. (1988). The transition to parenthood in dual-earner couples. *Psychological Medicine, 18,* 477-486.

20. Robertson, M. M., Trimble, M. R., & Lees, A. J. (1988). The psychopathology of Gilles de la Tourette syndrome. *British Journal of Psychiatry, 152,* 383-390.

21. Robertson, M. M., Trimble, M. R., & Lees, A. J. (1989). Self-injurious behaviour and the Gilles de la Tourette syndrome: A clinical study and review of the literature. *Psychological Medicine, 19,* 611-625.

22. Edwards, J. R., & Baglioni, A. J. (1991). Relationship between Type A behavior pattern and mental and physical symptoms: A comparison of global and component measures. *Journal of Applied Psychology, 76(2),* 276-290.

23. Jakes, S. C., Hallam, R. S., McKenna, L., & Hinchcliffe, R. (1992). Group cognitive therapy for medical patients: An application to tinnitus. *Cognitive Therapy and Research, 16,* 67-82.

[697]

CRS Placement/Diagnostic Test.

Purpose: Designed to diagnose and locate the student's CRS (Crane Reading System) level.

Population: Grades Preprimer–2.

Publication Dates: 1977–78.

Scores: Total score only.

Administration: Group.

Price Data: Price information for test materials including general directions ('77, 7 pages) available from publisher.

Foreign Language Edition: Spanish version available.

Time: Administration time not reported.

Author: Barbara J. Crane.

Publisher: Bilingual Educational Services.

a) ENGLISH VERSION.

1) *Level A.*

Population: Grade Preprimer.

Subtests, 4: Rhyming, Words That Begin Alike, Long Vowel Recognition, Consonant Sounds.

2) *Levels B, C, and D (Beginning Consonant Sounds).*

Population: Preprimer–primer.

Comments: Levels determined by number of errors.

3) *Level E (Blends).*

Population: Grade 1.

4) *Level F (Vowel Recognition).*

Population: Grade 1.

5) *Level G (Digraphs).*

Population: Grade 1.

6) *Levels H, I, and J (Special Vowel Patterns).*

Population: Grades 1–2.

Comments: Levels determined by number of errors.

b) SPANISH VERSION.

1) *Level A.*

Subtests, 2: Rhyming, Words That Begin Alike.

2) *Level B (Beginning Consonant Sounds—S, M, F, R, N, L, Z).*

3) *Level C (Beginning Consonant Sounds—B, P, T, D, V, CH).*

4) *Level D (Beginning Consonant Sounds—C, G, LL, Q, J, Y).*

5) *Level E (Special Patterns).*

[698]

Cultural Literacy Test.

Purpose: Designed to assess "general knowledge in the humanities, social sciences, and sciences."

Population: Grades 11–12.

Publication Date: 1989.

Scores, 4: Humanities, Social Sciences, Sciences, Composite; plus "criterion-referenced" scores for 23 objective areas.

Administration: Group.

Editions, 3: Machine-scorable (A, B), hand-scorable (Survey Edition B).

Price Data, 1991: $135 per complete machine-scorable test kit including 35 test booklets, 35 student report folders, administration and interpretation manual (30 pages), and materials needed for machine scoring; $42.30 per 35 Survey Edition reusable test booklets including administration and interpretation manual; $42.30 per 35 Survey Edition answer sheets including directions for administration and 35 student report folders; $6.90 per 35 student report folders; $6 per Guide to Cultural Literacy; $2.10 per administrator's summary (21 pages).

Time: 50 minutes.

Author: Cultural Literacy Foundation.

Publisher: The Riverside Publishing Co.

TEST REFERENCES

1. Peutony, J. F. (1993). Cultural literacy: A concurrent validation. *Educational and Psychological Measurement, 52,* 967-972.

2. Stanovich, K. E., & Cunningham, A. E. (1993). Where does knowledge come from? Specific associations between print exposure and information acquisition. *Journal of Educational Psychology, 85,* 211-229.

[699]

Culture Fair Intelligence Test.

Purpose: Designed to measure individual intelligence with minimal influence from verbal fluency, educational level, and ethnic/racial group membership.

Publication Dates: 1933–73.
Acronym: CFIT.
Scores: Total scores only.
Administration: Group or individual.
Foreign Language Edition: Spanish edition of Scales 2 and 3 available.
Comments: Formerly called Culture Free Intelligence Test; test booklet title is Test of *g: Culture Fair.*
Authors: Raymond B. Cattell and A. K. S. Cattell (Scales 2 and 3).
Publisher: Institute for Personality and Ability Testing, Inc.
a) SCALE 1.
Population: Ages 4–8 and mentally retarded adults.
Publication Dates: 1933–69.
Administration: Individual in part.
Price Data, 1994: $48.25 per introductory kit including 25 test booklets, scoring key, reusable classification cards, and handbook ('69, 15 pages); $19 per 25 test booklets; $3.50 per scoring key; $21 per reusable classification test cards; $4.75 per handbook; $9 per specimen set including test booklet, scoring key, and handbook.
Time: (22–60) minutes.
Comments: Identical to Cattell Intelligence Tests, Scale O: Dartington Scale; materials for Following Directions test must be assembled locally.
b) SCALE 1.
Population: Ages 8–14 and average adults.
Publication Dates: 1949–73.
Forms, 2: A, B.
Price Data: $26.50 per introductory kit including test booklet, scoring keys, answer sheets, manual ('73, 26 pages), and technical supplement ('73, 31 pages); $20.25 per 25 test booklets (specify Form A or B); $3.50 per scoring keys for answer sheets; $3.50 per scoring keys for test booklets; $10.75 per 50 answer sheets (specify Form A or B); $33 per cassette tape recording of Scale 2 instructions; $6.95 per manual; $7.75 per technical supplement; $9.25 per specimen set including test booklets (Forms A and B), answer sheets, and manual.
Time: 12.5(30) minutes.
Comments: Cassette recording available for individual untimed administration of Form A.
c) SCALE 3.
Population: Grades 9–16 and adults of superior intelligence.
Publication Dates: 1950–73.
Forms, 2: A, B.
Price Data: $12.50 per 25 test booklets (specify Form A or B); all other price data identical to *b* above.
Time: (30) minutes.
Cross References: See 9:290 (13 references), T3:643 (51 references), 8:184 (38 references), and T2:364 (61 references); for reviews by John E. Milholland and Abraham J. Tannenbaum, see 6:453 (15 references); for a review by I. MacFarlane Smith of *a*, see 5:343 (11 references); for reviews by Raleigh M. Drake and Gladys C. Schwesinger, see 4:300 (2 references).

TEST REFERENCES

1. Raz, N., Willerman, L., Ingmundson, P., & Hanlon, M. (1983). Aptitude-related differences in auditory recognition masking. *Intelligence,* 7, 71-90.
2. Smith, G. A., & Stanley, G. (1983). Clocking g: Relating intelligence and measures of timed performance. *Intelligence,* 7, 353-368.
3. Kingma, J. (1984). Traditional intelligence, Piagetian tasks, and initial arithmetic in kindergarten and primary school grade one. *The Journal of Genetic Psychology,* 145, 49-60.
4. Murray, A. M., & Mishra, S. P. (1984). Interactive effects of item content and ethnic group membership on performance on the McCarthy Scales. *Journal of School Psychology,* 21, 263-270.
5. Turnage, J. J., & Muchinsky, P. M. (1984). A comparison of the predictive validity of assessment center evaluations versus traditional measures in forecasting supervisory job performance: Interpretive implications of criterion distortion for the assessment paradigm. *Journal of Applied Psychology,* 69, 595-602.
6. Gonzales, R. R., & Roll, S. (1985). Relationship between acculturation, cognitive style, and intelligence. *Journal of Cross-Cultural Psychology,* 16, 190-205.
7. Hayslip, B., Jr., & Brookshire, R. G. (1985). Relationships among abilities in elderly adults: A time lag analysis. *Journal of Gerontology,* 40, 748-750.
8. LaBuda, M. C., Vogler, G. P., DeFries, J. C., & Fulker, D. W. (1985). Multivariate familial analysis of cognitive measures in the Colorado Family Reading Study. *Multivariate Behavioral Research,* 20, 357-368.
9. Dillbeck, M. C., Assimakis, P. D., Raimondi, D., Orme-Johnson, D. W., & Rowe, R. (1986). Longitudinal effects of the Transcendental Meditation and TM-Sidhi program on cognitive ability and cognitive style. *Perceptual and Motor Skills,* 62, 731-738.
10. Harris, R. N., & Snyder, C. R. (1986). The role of uncertain self-esteem in self-handicapping. *Journal of Personality and Social Psychology,* 51, 451-458.
11. Kingma, J. (1986). The range of seriation training effects in young kindergarten children. *Contemporary Educational Psychology,* 11, 276-289.
12. Ramos, N., & Die, A. H. (1986). The WAIS-R Picture Arrangement subtest: What do scores indicate? *The Journal of General Psychology,* 113, 251-261.
13. Schneider, W., Borkowski, J. G., Kurtz, B. E., & Kerwin, K. (1986). Metamemory and motivation. A comparison of strategy use and performance in German and American children. *Journal of Cross-Cultural Psychology,* 17, 315-336.
14. Stankov, L. (1986). Kvashchev's experiment: Can we boost intelligence? *Intelligence,* 10, 209-230.
15. Blomquist, K. B., & Danner, F. (1987). Effects of physical conditioning on information-processing efficiency. *Perceptual and Motor Skills,* 65, 175-186.
16. Fogarty, G. (1987). Timesharing in relation to broad ability domains. *Intelligence,* 11, 207-231.
17. Hakstain, A. R., Woolsey, L. K., & Schroeder, M. L. (1987). Validity of a large-scale assessment battery in an industrial setting. *Educational and Psychological Measurement,* 47(1), 165-178.
18. Karnes, F. A., & D'Ilio, V. R. (1987). Correlations of scores on verbal and non-verbal measures of intelligence for intellectually gifted students. *Perceptual and Motor Skills,* 64(1), 101-102.
19. Smith, G. A., & Stanley, G. (1987). Comparing subtest profiles of g loadings and correlations with RT measures. *Intelligence,* 11, 291-298.
20. Ward, R., & Eliot, J. (1987). A study of migrant children. *Psychological Reports,* 60, 120-122.
21. Rindskopf, D., & Rose, T. (1988). Some theory and applications of confirmatory second-order factor analysis. *Multivariate Behavioral Research,* 23, 51-67.
22. Stankov, L., & Chen, K. (1988). Training and changes in fluid and crystallized intelligence. *Contemporary Educational Psychology,* 13, 382-397.
23. Hayslip, B., Jr. (1989). Alternative mechanisms for improvements in fluid ability performance among older adults. *Psychology and Aging,* 4, 122-124.
24. Schneider, W., & Korkel, J. (1989). The knowledge base and text recall: Evidence from a short-term longitudinal study. *Contemporary Educational Psychology,* 14, 382-393.
25. Sternberg, R. J., & Gastel, J. (1989). Coping with novelty in human intelligence: An empirical investigation. *Intelligence,* 13, 187-197.
26. Brookings, J. B. (1990). A confirmatory factor analytic study of time-sharing performance and cognitive abilities. *Intelligence,* 14, 43-59.
27. Nurmi, J-E., & Lainekiri, J. (1991). Verbal fluency and the mea-

surement of future-oriented goals and hopes: Comparison of questionnaire and interview data. *Perceptual and Motor Skills, 73,* 137-138.

28. Taimela, S. (1991). Factors affecting reaction-time testing and the interpretation of results. *Perceptual and Motor Skills, 73,* 1195-1202.

29. Egan, V., & Deary, I. J. (1992). Are specific inspection time strategies prevented by concurrent tasks? *Intelligence, 16,* 151-167.

30. Hunt, H. T., Gervais, A., Shearing-Johns, S., & Travis, F. (1992). Transpersonal experiences in childhood: An exploratory empirical study of selected adult groups. *Perceptual and Motor Skills, 75,* 1135-1153.

31. Maylor, E. A., & Valentine, T. (1992). Linear and nonlinear effects of aging on categorizing and naming faces. *Psychology and Aging, 7,* 317-323.

32. Chaiken, S. R. (1993). Two models for an inspection time paradigm: Processing distraction and processing speed versus processing speed and asymptotic strength. *Intelligence, 17,* 257-283.

33. Maylor, E. A. (1993). Aging and forgetting in prospective and retrospective memory tasks. *Psychology and Aging, 8,* 420-428.

34. Spencer, W. D., & Raz, N. (1994). Memory for facts, source, and context: Can frontal lobe dysfunction explain age-related differences? *Psychology and Aging, 9,* 149-159.

[700]

Culture-Free Self-Esteem Inventories, Second Edition.

Purpose: Provides a measure of self-esteem and a monitoring of treatment progress.
Population: Grades 2–9, ages 16–65.
Publication Dates: 1981–92.
Acronym: CFSEI-2.
Administration: Group.
Forms, 2: Forms A and B for children grades 2–9, and Form AD for adults ages 16 to 65.
Price Data, 1994: $104 per complete kit including examiner's manual ('92, 84 pages), 50 Form A, 50 Form B, 50 Form AD, scoring acetate, and administration audiocassette; $33 per examiner's manual; $6 per scoring acetate; $14 per administration audiocassette.
Foreign Language Editions: All CFSEI-2 forms and the administration audiocassette are available in French and Spanish.
Comments: Previous edition entitled Culture-Free Self-Esteem Inventories for Children and Adults; derivative entitled North American Depression Inventories for Children and Adults.
Author: James Battle.
Publisher: PRO-ED, Inc.

a) FORM A.
Population: Grades 2–9.
Scores, 6: General Self-Esteem, Social/Peer-Related Self-Esteem, Academic/School-Related Self-Esteem, Parental/Home-Related Self-Esteem, Lie Subtest, Total.
Price Data: $19 per 50 Form A.
Time: (15–20) minutes.
b) FORM B.
Population: Grades 2–9.
Scores, 6: Same as for *a* above.
Price Data: $19 per 50 Form B.
Time: (5–10) minutes.
c) FORM AD.
Population: Ages 16–65.
Scores, 5: General Self-Esteem, Social/Peer-Related Self-Esteem, Personal Self-Esteem, Lie Subtest, Total.

Price Data: $19 per 50 Form AD.
Time: (15–20) minutes.
Cross References: For reviews by Gerald R. Adams and Janet Morgan Riggs of the original edition, see 9:291 (1 reference); see also T3: 644 (1 reference). For reviews by Patricia A. Bachelor and Michael G. Kavan of the North American Depression Inventories for Children and Adults, see 11:265 (1 reference).

TEST REFERENCES

1. Stevenson, D. T., & Romney, D. M. (1984). Depression in learning disabled children. *Journal of Learning Disabilities, 17,* 579-582.
2. Battle, J., Carson, N. G., Ord, L. C., Hawkins, W. L., Precht, D., & Labercane, G. (1986). Standardization of the lie scale of the Culture-Free Self-Esteem Inventory for Children. *Psychological Reports, 59,* 231-234.
3. Battle, J., Hawkins, W. L., Carson, N. G., Ord, L. C., & Precht, D. (1986). Standardization of the lie scale of the Culture-Free Self-Esteem Inventory for Adults. *Psychological Reports, 59,* 892-894.
4. Broad, J., Burke, J., Byford, S. R., & Sims, P. (1986). Clinical application of the Children's Action Tendency Scale. *Psychological Reports, 59,* 71-74.
5. Battle, J. (1987). Relationship between self-esteem and depression among children. *Psychological Reports, 60,* 1187-1190.
6. Kalliopuska, M. (1987). Relation of empathy and self-esteem to active participation in Finnish baseball. *Perceptual and Motor Skills, 65,* 107-113.
7. Hietolahti-Ansten, M., & Kalliopuska, M. (1990). Self-esteem and empathy among children actively involved in music. *Perceptual and Motor Skills, 71,* 1364-1366.
8. Kozeluk, L., & Kawash, G. (1990). Comparison of the Coopersmith Self-Esteem Inventory and the Battle Culture-Free Self-Esteem Inventory. *Perceptual and Motor Skills, 70,* 1162.
9. Drummond, R. J., & Hansford, S. G. (1991). Dimensions of self-concept of pregnant unwed teens. *The Journal of Psychology, 125,* 65-59.

[701]

Culture Shock Inventory.

Purpose: Developed "to acquaint those who expect to work outside their own culture with some of the factors that may cause them to be less effective."
Population: Managers.
Publication Dates: 1970–78.
Scores, 8: Lack of Western Ethnocentrism, Experience, Cognitive Flex, Behavioral Flex, Cultural Knowledge (Specific, General), Cultural Behavior—General, Interpersonal Sensitivity.
Administration: Group.
Price Data, 1989: $40 per complete kit including 10 test inventories, fact sheet ('77, 2 pages), and administration guide ('78, 4 pages).
Time: (10–20) minutes.
Comments: Self-administered.
Authors: W. J. Reddin and Ken Rowell.
Publisher: Organizational Tests Ltd. [Canada].

TEST REFERENCES

1. Steward, R. J. (1993). Cross-cultural training for professional staff. *Journal of College Student Development, 34,* 441.

[702]

Current and Past Psychopathology Scales.

Purpose: To evaluate both current and past psychopathology and social functioning.
Population: Ages 15–84.
Publication Dates: 1968–72.
Acronym: CAPPS.

Scores, 26: Current Scales (Reality Testing-Social Disturbance, Depression-Anxiety, Impulse Control, Somatic Concern-Functioning, Disorganization, Obsessive-Guilt-Phobic, Elation-Grandiosity, Summary Role), Past Scales (Depression-Anxiety, Impulse Control, Social-Sexual Relations, Reality Testing, Dependency, Somatic Concern-Functioning, Obsessive-Compulsive, Anger-Excitability, Manic, Sexual Disturbance, Memory-Orientation, Disorganized, Organicity, Neurotic Childhood, Phobia, Retardation-Stubborn, Hysterical Symptoms, Intellectual Performance).
Administration: Individual.
Price Data, 1993: $1 per booklet ('72, 10 pages); $.20 per score sheet; $1 per training procedures and instruction sheet; $.25 per summary scoring sheet; $.25 per editing and coding instructions.
Time: (15–30) minutes.
Authors: Jean Endicott and Robert L. Spitzer.
Publisher: Department of Research Assessment and Training, New York State Psychiatric Institute.

TEST REFERENCES

1. Jeremy, R. J., & Bernstein, V. J. (1984). Dyads at risk: Methadone-maintained women and their four-month-old infants. *Child Development, 55,* 1141-1154.
2. Schulsinger, F., Parnas, J., Petersen, E. T., Schulsinger, H., Teasdale, T. W., Mednick, S. A., Moller, L., & Silverton, L. (1984). Cerebral ventricular size in the offspring of schizophrenic mothers. *Archives of General Psychiatry, 41,* 602-606.
3. Wallace, C. J. (1986). Functional assessment in rehabilitation. *Schizophrenia Bulletin: National Institute of Mental Health, 12,* 604-630.
4. Hooley, J. M., Richters, J. E., Weintraub, S., & Neale, J. M. (1987). Psychopathology and marital distress: The positive side of positive symptoms. *Journal of Abnormal Psychology, 96,* 27-33.

[703]
Current News Test.
Purpose: To assess knowledge of current events.
Population: Grades 9–12.
Publication Dates: 1948–90.
Scores, 7: National Affairs, International, Business, Society, The Arts, Lifestyle, Essays.
Administration: Group.
Price Data: Available from publisher.
Time: Administration time not reported.
Comments: Two new tests issued annually: spring term review (covering mid-December to mid-April) issued in May, fall term review (covering September to mid-December) issued in December.
Author: Phyllis Hersh Keaton.
Publisher: Newsweek Education Department.

[704]
Curtis Completion Form.
Purpose: Intended as a "sentence completion test designed to evaluate emotional maturity and adjustment."
Population: Grades 11–16 and adults.
Publication Dates: 1950–68.
Acronym: CCF.
Scores: Total score only.
Administration: Group.

Price Data, 1993: $35 per complete kit; $16.50 per 25 forms; $22 per manual ('68, 9 pages plus one sample each of English, French, and Spanish forms).
Foreign Language Editions: French and Spanish editions available.
Time: (30–35) minutes.
Author: James W. Curtis.
Publisher: Western Psychological Services.
Cross References: See T2:1454 (1 reference) and P:421 (3 references); for reviews by Irwin G. Sarason and Laurance F. Shaffer, see 6:208 (2 references); for a review by Alfred B. Heilbrun, Jr., see 5:128.

[705]
Curtis Interest Scale.
Purpose: Developed to identify vocational interest patterns.
Population: Grades 9–16 and adults.
Publication Date: 1959.
Scores, 10: Business, Mechanics, Applied Arts, Direct Sales, Production, Science, Entertainment, Interpersonal, Computation, Farming; 1 rating: Desire for Responsibility.
Administration: Group.
Price Data, 1985: $5 per 25 test booklets; $5 per 50 profiles; $4 per specimen set.
Time: (6–12) minutes.
Comments: Self-administered.
Author: James W. Curtis.
Publisher: Psychometric Affiliates.
Cross References: See T2:2177 (1 reference); for reviews by Warren T. Norman and Leona E. Tyler, see 6:1052.

[706]
[Curtis Object Completion and Space Form Tests].
Purpose: "Devised to provide estimates of individual competence in two basic areas of mechanical aptitude and pattern visualization."
Population: Applicants for mechanical and technical jobs.
Publication Dates: 1960–61.
Scores: Total scores only.
Administration: Group.
Price Data: Available from publisher.
Time: 1(6) minutes per test.
Author: James W. Curtis.
Publisher: Psychometric Affiliates.
    a) OBJECT-COMPLETION TEST.
    b) SPACE FORM TEST.
Cross References: For reviews by Richard S. Melton and I. Macfarlane Smith, see 6:1085.

[707]
Curtis Verbal-Clerical Skills Tests.
Purpose: "Devised to provide estimates of individual competence in . . . verbal skill usually identified with office and clerical work."
Population: Applicants for clerical positions.
Publication Dates: 1963–65.

Acronym: CVCST.
Scores: 4 tests: Computation, Checking, Comprehension, Capacity.
Administration: Group.
Price Data, 1985: $5 per specimen set including manual ('64, 4 pages), 4 tests, and key; $2.75 per 25 tests.
Time: 8(10) minutes.
Author: James W. Curtis.
Publisher: Psychometric Affiliates.

[708]
The Custody Quotient.
Purpose: Provides relevant information about the knowledge, attributes, and skills of adults involved in custody disputes.
Population: Parents or other adults seeking access or custody.
Publication Dates: 1987–88.
Acronym: CQ.
Scores, 13: Emotional Needs, Physical Needs, No Dangers, Good Parenting, Parent Assistance, Planning, Home Stability, Prior Caring, Acts/Omissions, Values, Custody Quotient, Joint Custody Quotient, Frankness.
Administration: Individual.
Price Data: Not available.
Time: Administration time not reported.
Comments: Research edition; ratings by trained examiner based on an interview and observations; orally administered.
Authors: Robert Gordon and Leon A. Peek.
Publisher: The Wilmington Institute [No reply from publisher; status unknown].
Cross References: For a review by Lisa G. Bischoff, see 11:98.

[709]
Customer Reaction Survey.
Purpose: Assesses customers' perceptions of salespeople's interpersonal skills.
Population: Salespeople.
Publication Date: 1972–79.
Acronym: CRS.
Scores, 4: Observed Exposure, Observed Feedback, Preferred Exposure, Preferred Feedback.
Administration: Group.
Price Data, 1990: $5.95 per test, including score interpretation guide ('79, 4 pages).
Time: Administration time not reported.
Comments: Ratings by customers; also called Customer Reaction Index; based on the Johari Window Model of interpersonal relations.
Authors: Jay Hall and C. Leo Griffith.
Publisher: Teleometrics International.

[710]
Customer Service Representative.
Purpose: To evaluate technical and interpersonal skills of persons for the customer service position; available also to measure computer use skills.

Population: Candidates for customer service positions.
Publication Date: 1992.
Acronym: CUSTSERV.
Scores: Total score only.
Administration: Group.
Price Data, 1994: $299 per person.
Time: (180) minutes.
Comments: Detailed evaluation report provided on each candidate; scored by publisher.
Author: Bruce A. Winrow.
Publisher: Walden Personnel Testing & Training, Inc. [Canada].

[711]
Cutrona Child Study Profile of Psycho-Educational Abilities.
Purpose: A diagnostic tool to help teachers focus an awareness on psychoeducational ability areas and to provide an appropriate program for the child.
Population: K–3.
Publication Dates: 1970–75.
Scores: Ratings in 10 areas: General Behavior, Gross-Motor Development, Fine-Motor Development, Body Image and Awareness, Tactile-Kinesthetic Development, Visual-Motor Perception, Auditory Perception, Time Orientation, Non-Verbal Conceptualization, Numerical Conceptualization.
Price Data: Available from publisher.
Time: (90) minutes.
Author: Michael P. Cutrona.
Publisher: Cutronics Educational Institute.

[712]
Cutrona Reading Inventory.
Purpose: To determine reading grade level.
Population: Grades K–6, 7–12, and adult.
Publication Date: 1975.
Scores, 3: Independent, Instructional, or Frustration Reading Grade Level.
Administration: Individual.
Levels, 2: K–6; 7–12 and adult.
Price Data: Available from publisher.
Time: [10] minutes.
Author: M. P. Cutrona.
Publisher: Cutronics Educational Institute.

[713]
DABERON-2: Screening for School Readiness.
Purpose: Developed to "identify . . . students who may not be ready to enter formal academic instruction."
Population: Ages 3-0 to 7-11.
Publication Dates: 1972–91.
Scores: Total score only.
Administration: Individual.
Price Data, 1994: $89 per complete kit including 24 presentation cards, 25 screen forms, 25 readiness reports, 5 classroom summary forms, object kit of manipulatives, and manual ('91, 38 pages); $5 per set

of presentation cards; $18 per 25 screen forms; $18 per 25 readiness reports; $6 per 5 classroom summary forms; $24 per object kit of manipulatives; $24 per manual.

Time: (20–40) minutes.

Authors: Virginia A. Danzer, Mary Frances Gerber, Theresa M. Lyons, and Judith K. Voress.

Publisher: PRO-ED, Inc.

Cross References: For reviews by Stephen N. Axford and Selma Hughes, see 11:100 (1 reference).

[714]

Daily Stress Inventory.

Purpose: Constructed to measure "the number and relative impact of common minor stressors frequently experienced in everyday life."

Population: Ages 18 and over.

Publication Dates: 1988-89.

Acronym: DSI.

Scores, 3: Event, Impact, I/E Ratio.

Administration: Group or individual.

Price Data, 1994: $46 per introductory kit including 50 rating booklets, 50 stress tracking charts, and manual; $25 per 50 rating booklets; $13 per 50 stress tracking charts; $11 per manual.

Time: (5) minutes each day.

Authors: Phillip J. Brantley and Glenn N. Jones (manual).

Publisher: Psychological Assessment Resources, Inc.

Cross References: For reviews by Steven C. Hayes and Bert W. Westbrook and Thomas E. Powell, see 11:101.

[715]

Dallas Pre-School Screening Test.

Purpose: "Designed to screen the primary learning areas for children from three to six years of age."

Population: Ages 3–6.

Publication Date: 1972.

Scores, 6: Psychological, Auditory, Visual, Language, Motor, Articulation Development (optional).

Administration: Individual.

Price Data, 1993: $30.50 per 25 pupil record forms, stimuli book, and manual (42 pages).

Time: (15–20) minutes.

Authors: Robert R. Percival and Suzanne C. Poxon (stimuli book).

Publisher: Dallas Educational Services.

Cross References: For a review by James E. Ysseldyke, see 11:102.

[716]

DANTES Subject Standardized Tests.

Purpose: Gives "colleges and universities the opportunity . . . to offer civilian students credit for education acquired in nontraditional environments."

Population: College students wishing to earn credit by examination.

Publication Dates: 1983–93.

Acronym: DANTES.

Administration: Group.

Parts: 50 tests in 7 areas.

Price Data, 1987: $25 for each test administered by the institution which may set its own fee to students; scoring by publisher included in price.

Time: Untimed, requiring approximately (90) minutes per test.

Comments: Originally available only to military personnel through Defense Activity for Non-Traditional Education Support (an agency of the U.S. Department of Defense), but since 1983 available to institutions of higher education for all their students; "testing-on-demand" program administered by individual institutions under agreement with publisher.

Author: Defense Activity for Non-Traditional Education Support.

Publisher: Educational Testing Service.

a) MATHEMATICS.

Scores: Total score for each of 2 tests:
1) *Introductory College Algebra.*
2) *Principles of Statistics.*

b) SOCIAL SCIENCE.

Scores: Total score for each of 11 tests:
1) *Contemporary Western Europe: 1946–1990.*
2) *Introduction to the Modern Middle East.*
3) *A History of the Vietnam War.*
4) *Geography.*
5) *War and Peace in the Nuclear Age.*
6) *Lifespan Developmental Psychology.*
7) *General Anthropology.*
8) *Introduction to Law Enforcement.*
9) *Criminal Justice.*
10) *Fundamentals of Counseling.*
11) *Art of the Western World.*

c) PHYSICAL SCIENCE.

Scores: Total score for each of 5 tests:
1) *Astronomy.*
2) *Here's to Your Health.*
3) *Environment and Humanity: The Race to Save the Planet.*
4) *Principles of Physical Science I.*
5) *Physical Geology.*

d) BUSINESS.

Scores: Total score for each of 15 tests:
1) *Principles of Finance.*
2) *Principles of Financial Accounting.*
3) *Personnel/Human Resource Management.*
4) *Organizational Behavior.*
5) *Introduction to Computers with BASIC Programming.*
6) *Introduction to Business.*
7) *Risk and Insurance.*
8) *Principles of Real Estate.*
9) *Money and Banking (Revised).*
10) *Basic Marketing (Revised).*
11) *Business Mathematics.*
12) *Business Law II.*
13) *Introductory Cost Accounting.*
14) *Auditing I.*
15) *Principles of Supervision.*

e) FOREIGN LANGUAGE.

Scores: Total score for each of 5 tests:

1) *Beginning German I.*
2) *Beginning German II.*
3) *Beginning Spanish I.*
4) *Beginning Spanish II.*
5) *Beginning Italian I.*
Comments: Cassettes available for all tests.
f) APPLIED TECHNOLOGY.
Scores: Total score for each of 9 tests:
   1) *Basic Automotive Service.*
   2) *Introduction to Carpentry.*
   3) *Basic Technical Drafting.*
   4) *Fundamentals of Electronics (Revised).*
   5) *Electric Circuits.*
   6) *Electronic Devices.*
   7) *Technical Writing (Revised).*
   8) *Principles of Electronic Communication Systems.*
   9) *Principles of Refrigeration Technology.*
f) HUMANITIES.
Scores: Total score for each of 3 tests:
   1) *Ethics in America.*
   2) *Principles of Public Speaking.*
   3) *Introduction to World Religions.*
Cross References: For reviews by Laura L. B. Barnes and William A. Mehrens, see 11:103.

[717]

Database Professional Staff Selector.
Purpose: To measure essential skills needed by the database professional.
Population: Candidates for database positions.
Publication Date: 1992.
Acronym: DBASEPR.
Scores: Total score only.
Administration: Group.
Price Data, 1994: $299 per person.
Time: (180) minutes.
Comments: Detailed evaluation report provided on each candidate; scored by publisher.
Author: Stephen Silver.
Publisher: Walden Personnel Testing & Training, Inc. [Canada].

[718]

Dating Problems Checklist.
Purpose: Assesses relationship concerns that occur during courtship and marriage.
Population: High school and college.
Publication Dates: 1961–79.
Acronym: DPCL.
Scores: No scores.
Administration: Group.
Price Data: Not available.
Time: Administration time not reported.
Comments: Checklist of frequently described dating problems.
Author: Gelolo McHugh.
Publisher: Family Life Publications, Inc. [No reply from publisher; status unknown].
Cross References: For a review by Andrew Christensen, see 9:297; for reviews by Clifford R. Adams and Robert A. Harper, see 6:676.

[719]

A Dating Scale.
Purpose: To measure "liberalism of attitudes toward dating."
Population: Adolescents and adults.
Publication Date: 1962.
Scores: Total score only.
Administration: Group.
Price Data: Scale is available without charge from author.
Time: [10] minutes.
Comments: The manual is a reprint of a journal article by the author.
Author: Panos D. Bardis.
Publisher: Panos D. Bardis.
Cross References: For additional information and a review by Charles F. Warnath, see 8:335 (3 references).

[720]

Decision Making Inventory.
Purpose: "Designed to assess an individual's preferred style of decision making."
Population: High school and college, working adults.
Publication Dates: 1983–86.
Acronym: DMI.
Scores, 4: Information Gathering Style (Spontaneous, Systematic), Information Processing Style (Internal, External).
Administration: Group.
Forms, 2: H, I.
Price Data, 1994: $35 per complete kit including 25 inventories, 2 scoring grids, manual ('83, 68 pages), and scoring supplement ('86, 18 pages); $28 per 50 scales.
Time: (10) minutes.
Authors: William C. Coscarelli, Richard Johnson (test), and JaDean Johnson (test).
Publisher: Marathon Consulting and Press.
Cross References: For reviews by George Domino and Barbara A. Kerr, see 10:77 (3 references).

[721]

Decoding Skills Test.
Purpose: Measures the reading levels and decoding skills of elementary school readers and identifies reading disabled children and provides a diagnostic profile of their decoding skill development.
Population: Grades 1.0–5.8 +.
Publication Date: 1985.
Acronym: DST.
Scores: 3 subtests yielding 12 Scores: Basal Vocabulary (Instructional Level, Frustration Level), Phonic Patterns (Monosyllabic, Polysyllabic), Contextual Decoding (Instructional Level [Reading Rate, Error Rate, Phonic Words, Comprehension], Frustration Level [Reading Rate, Error Rate, Phonic Words, Comprehension]).
Administration: Individual.
Price Data, 1985: $56.50 per complete kit includ-

ing 24 scoring booklets (15 pages), presentation book (22 pages), and manual (57 pages); $3 per 12 scoring booklets.
Time: (30–45) minutes.
Comments: "Criterion-referenced."
Authors: Ellis Richardson and Barbara DiBenedetto.
Publisher: York Press, Inc.
Cross References: For reviews by Stephen N. Elliott and Timothy S. Hartshorne, see 10:78.

[722]

Deductive Reasoning Test.
Purpose: "Intended as a selection instrument for scientific, entrepreneurial and other high level professional and occupational personnel."
Population: Candidates for graduate scientists and higher level professional occupations.
Publication Dates: 1972–73.
Acronym: DRT.
Scores: Total score only.
Administration: Group.
Price Data: Price information available from publisher for test materials including manual ('73, 19 pages).
Time: (40–50) minutes.
Author: J. M. Verster.
Publisher: National Institute for Personnel Research of the Human Sciences Research Council [South Africa].
Cross References: For reviews by Lloyd G. Humphreys and Robert P. Markley, see 9:302.

[723]

Defense Mechanisms Inventory [Revised].
Purpose: To "measure and predict responses to conflict and threat."
Population: Adults and college students.
Publication Dates: 1968–93.
Acronym: DMI.
Scores, 5: Turning Against Object, Projection, Principalization, Turning Against Self, Reversal.
Administration: Individual.
Forms: 2 forms (Male, Female) for each of 3 versions (Adolescent, Adult, Elderly).
Price Data, 1994: $109 per DMI Introductory Kit including administration manual ('93, 147 pages), clinical manual ('93, 126 pages), 20 reusable adult test booklets (10 male and 10 female), 25 answer sheets, set of 5 scoring keys, 25 adult profile forms, and the supplementary bibliography; $27 per 10 male and 10 female reusable test booklets (specify Adult [A], Elderly [E], or Adolescent [Y]); $8 per 25 answer sheets; $10 per 25 profile forms (specify Adult or College); $12 per 5 scoring templates; $10 per supplemental bibliography.
Time: (30–45) minutes.
Comments: Title of administration manual is Defense Mechanisms: Their Classification, Correlates, and Measurement with the Defense Mechanisms Inventory; title of clinical manual is Defenses in Psy-

chotherapy: The Clinical Application of the Defense Mechanisms Inventory.
Authors: David Ihilevich and Goldine C. Gleser.
Publisher: Psychological Assessment Resources, Inc.
Cross References: For a review by James J. Hennessy of the earlier edition, see 10:79 (8 references); see also T3:665 (14 references), 8:534 (30 references), and T2:1152 (5 references); for a review by James A. Walsh, see 7:63 (4 references).

TEST REFERENCES

1. Vickers, R. R., Jr., & Hervig, L. K. (1981). Comparison of three psychological defense mechanism questionnaires. *Journal of Personality Assessment, 45,* 630-638.
2. Evans, R. G. (1982). Defense mechanisms in females as a function of sex-role orientation. *Journal of Clinical Psychology, 38,* 816-817.
3. Juni, S. (1982). The composite measure of the Defense Mechanism Inventory. *Journal of Research in Personality, 16,* 193-200.
4. Juni, S. (1982). Use of the defense orientation construct as a predictor of acceptance of feedback. *Psychological Reports, 50,* 1215-1218.
5. Massong, S. R., Dickson, A. L., Ritzler, B. A., & Layne, C. C. (1982). A correlational comparison of defense mechanism measures: The Defense Mechanism Inventory and the Blacky Defense Preference Inventory. *Journal of Personality Assessment, 46,* 477-480.
6. Massong, S. R., Dickson, A. L., Ritzler, B. A., & Layne, C. C. (1982). Assertion and defense mechanism preference. *Journal of Counseling Psychology, 29,* 591-596.
7. Thompson, M., Greenberg, R. P., & Fisher, S. (1982). Defense mechanisms, somatic symptoms and lateral eye movements in females. *Perceptual and Motor Skills, 55,* 939-942.
8. Wilson, J. F. (1982). Recovery from surgery and scores on the Defense Mechanisms Inventory. *Journal of Personality Assessment, 46,* 312-319.
9. Cramer, P. (1988). The Defense Mechanism Inventory: A review of research and discussion of the scales. *Journal of Personality Assessment, 52,* 142-164.
10. Labouvie-Vief, G., DeVoe, M., & Bulka, D. (1989). Speaking about feelings: Conceptions of emotion across the life span. *Psychology and Aging, 4,* 425-437.
11. Nestor, P. G., & Safer, M. A. (1990). A multi-method investigation of individual differences in hemisphericity. *Cortex, 26,* 409-421.
12. Noam, G. G., & Recklitis, C. J. (1990). The relationship between defenses and symptoms in adolescent psychopathology. *Journal of Personality Assessment, 54,* 311-327.
13. Banks, H. C., & Juni, S. (1991). Defense mechanisms in minority African-American and Hispanic youths: Standardization and scale reliabilities. *Journal of Personality Assessment, 56*(2), 327-334.
14. Mittelstaedt, W. H., & Wollert, R. (1991). Blame and the development of depressed mood. *Canadian Journal of Behavioural Science, 23,* 1-11.
15. Recklitis, C. J., Noam, G. G., & Borst, S. R. (1992). Adolescent suicide and defensive style. *Suicide and Life-Threatening Behavior, 22,* 374-387.

[724]

Defining Issues Test.
Purpose: "Gives information about the process by which people judge what ought to be done in moral dilemmas."
Population: Grades 9–12 and college and adults.
Publication Dates: 1979–87.
Acronym: DIT.
Scores, 12: Consistency Check, M (meaningless items) score, P (principled moral thinking) score, U (utilizer) score, D (composite) score, A (antiestablishment) score, and stage scores (2, 3, 4, 5A, 5B, and 6).
Administration: Group.
Forms, 2: Short form, long form.
Price Data, 1987: $25 per manual including both forms and scoring information ('86, 96 pages); scoring service available from publisher; $1.90 or less per

prepaid scoring sheet including all reports, handling costs, etc.

Time: (30–40) minutes for short form; (40–50) minutes for long form.

Comments: 2 optional companion booklets available: *Development in Judging Moral Issues* from the Center for the Study of Ethical Development, and *Moral Development: Advances in Theory and Research* from Praeger Press.

Authors: James R. Rest, with model computer scoring programs by Steve Thoma, Mark Davison, Stephen Robbins, and David Swanson.

Publisher: Center for the Study of Ethical Development.

Cross References: For reviews by Rosemary E. Sutton and Bert W. Westbrook and K. Denise Bane, see 11:104 (34 references); for reviews by Robert R. McCrae and Kevin L. Moreland, see 9:304 (22 references); see also T3:666 (8 references).

TEST REFERENCES

1. Okatahi, A., & Parish, T. S. (1987). Do moral dilemma discussions enhance individuals across areas of development. *College Student Journal, 21,* 357-359.
2. Little, G. L., & Robinson, K. D. (1989). Relationship of DUI recidivism to moral reasoning, sensation seeking, and MacAndrew alcoholism scores. *Psychological Reports, 65,* 1171-1174.
3. Ryan, R. M., & Connell, J. P. (1989). Perceived locus of causality and internalization: Examining reasons for acting in two domains. *Journal of Personality and Social Psychology, 57,* 749-761.
4. Levenson, M. R. (1990). Risk taking and personality. *Journal of Personality and Social Psychology, 58,* 1073-1080.
5. Tevino, L. K., & Youngblood, S. A. (1990). Bad apples in bad barrels: A causal analysis of ethical decision-making behavior. *Journal of Applied Psychology, 75*(4), 378-385.
6. Thoma, S. J., Rest, J. R., & Davison, M. L. (1991). Describing and testing a moderator of the moral judgment and action relationship. *Journal of Personality and Social Psychology, 61,* 659-669.
7. Kilgannon, S. M., & Erwin, T. D. (1992). A longitudinal study about the identity and moral development of Greek students. *Journal of College Student Development, 33,* 253-259.
8. Murk, D. A., & Addleman, J. A. (1992). Relations among moral reasoning, locus of control, and demographic variables among college students. *Psychological Reports, 70,* 467-476.
9. Narváez, D. (1993). High achieving students and moral judgment. *Journal for the Education of the Gifted, 16,* 268-279.
10. Reiman, A. J., & Thies-Sprinthall, L. (1993). Promoting the development of mentor teachers: Theory and research programs using guided reflection. *Journal of Research and Development in Education, 26,* 177-185.

[725]

DeGangi-Berk Test of Sensory Integration.

Purpose: "Designed to overcome problems in detecting sensory integrative dysfunction in the early years."

Population: Ages 3–5.

Publication Date: 1983.

Acronym: TSI.

Scores, 4: Postural Control, Bilateral Motor Integration, Reflex Integration, Total.

Administration: Individual.

Price Data, 1993: $150 per complete kit; $19.50 per 100 star designs; $16.50 per 25 record booklets; $35 per manual (48 pages).

Time: (30) minutes.

Comments: Other test materials (e.g., stopwatch, carpeted scooter board, hula hoop) must be supplied by examiner.

Authors: Ronald A. Berk and Georgia A. DeGangi.

Publisher: Western Psychological Services.

Cross References: For a review by R. A. Bornstein, see 10:80.

[726]

Degrees of Reading Power.

Publication Dates: 1979–91.

Acronym: DRP.

Scores: Total score only.

Administration: Group.

Price Data, 1994: $13.35 per 30 NCS answer sheets; $12.25 per set of scoring keys (select level and form); $24.75 per Primary/Standard teacher's manual ('89, 112 pages); $31.25 per Advanced teacher's manual ('90, 98 pages); $15.75 per 5 test administration manuals (select Primary, Standard, or Advanced); $21 per Primary/Standard norms booklet ('88, 45 pages); $27 per *DRP: An Effectiveness Measure in Reading* ('87, 200 pages); $13 per norms update technical report ('89, 23 pages); $22.50 per validity and reliability technical report (select Primary or Advanced).

Time: (45–50) minutes (untimed).

Comments: Practice tests may be used to select appropriate test form for student; also provides readability analysis of instructional material in print.

Author: Touchstone Applied Science Associates (TASA), Inc..

Publisher: Touchstone Applied Science Associates (TASA), Inc.

a) PRIMARY.

Purpose: Constructed to measure "how well students are able to construct meaning from prose material."

Population: Grades 1–3.

Forms, 2: E, F.

Price Data: $75 per 30 machine-scorable test booklets (select form); $8.25 per 30 practice booklets.

b) STANDARD.

Purpose: Same as *a* above.

Population: Grades 3–5, 5–8, 8–12 and over.

Forms, 2: E, F.

Levels, 3: 3, 5, 7.

Price Data: $53.50 per 30 test booklets (select level and form); $10.50 per 30 practice booklets (select Level 5 or 7); $13.25 per 30 NCS answer sheets.

c) ADVANCED.

Purpose: Constructed to measure "how well students are able to reason with text."

Population: Grades 6–9, 9–12 and over.

Forms, 2: R, S.

Levels, 2: 2, 4.

Price Data: $64 per 30 test booklets (select level and form); $13.75 per 30 practice booklets; $13.25 per 30 NCS answer sheets.

Cross References: For reviews of an earlier form by Roger Bruning and Gerald S. Hanna, see 9:305 (1 reference).

TEST REFERENCES

1. Carswell, L., & White, W. F. (1984). Problems of reporting socioeconomic bias among reading scores and standardized reading tests. *Perceptual and Motor Skills, 58,* 181-182.
2. Farr, R., Courtland, M. C., & Beck, M. D. (1984). Scholastic aptitude test performance and reading ability. *Journal of Reading, 28,* 208-214.
3. Weiner, M., & Kippel, G. (1984). The relationship of the California Achievement Test to the Degrees of Reading Power Test. *Educational and Psychological Measurement, 44,* 497-500.
4. Carver, R. P. (1985). Measuring readability using DRP units. *Journal of Reading Behavior, 17,* 303-316.
5. Carver, R. P. (1985). Why is the Degrees of Reading Power Test invalid? *National Reading Conference Yearbook, 34,* 350-354.
6. Wood, P. H., Nemeth, J. S., & Brooks, C. C. (1985). Criterion-related validity of the Degrees of Reading Power test (Form CP-1A). *Educational and Psychological Measurement, 45,* 965-969.
7. Duffelmeyer, F. A., & Adamson, S. (1986). Matching students with instructional level materials using the Degrees of Reading Power system. *Reading Research and Instruction, 25,* 192-200.
8. Kippel, G. M., Weiner, M., & Sontag, M. (1986). A longitudinal study of the Degrees of Reading Power test. *Perceptual and Motor Skills, 62,* 424-426.
9. White, W. F., Karlin, A., & Burke, C. (1986). Perception of home environment and school abilities as predictors of reading power and school achievements. *Perceptual and Motor Skills, 62,* 819-822.
10. Henderson, J. G., Jr. (1987). Effects of depression upon reading: A case study for distinguishing effortful from automatic processes. *Perceptual and Motor Skills, 64*(1), 191-200.
11. Hildebrand, M., & Hoover, H. D. (1987). A comparative study of the reliability and validity of the Degrees of Reading Power and the Iowa Tests of Basic Skills. *Educational and Psychological Measurement, 47*(4), 1091-1098.
12. Kippel, G. M., & Weiner, M. (1987). National percentiles for California Achievement Test and comparable scores on Degrees of Reading Power test. *Perceptual and Motor Skills, 64,* 860-862.
13. Maria, K., & Mons Johnson, J. (1990). Correcting misconceptions: Effect of type of test. *Yearbook of the National Reading Conference, 39,* 329-337.
14. Nist, S. L., Simpson, M. L., Olejnik, S., & Mealey, D. L. (1991). The relationship between self-selected study processes and test performance. *American Educational Research Journal, 28,* 849-874.

[727]

Degrees of Word Meaning.

Purpose: Developed to "assess the size of students' reading vocabularies by measuring their understanding of the meaning of words in naturally occurring contexts."

Population: Grades 3–8.

Publication Date: 1993.

Acronym: DWM.

Scores: Total score only.

Administration: Group.

Levels: 6 overlapping levels.

Price Data, 1994: $31.25 per user's manual (96 pages); $15.75 per 5 test administration procedures; $41 per 30 test booklets (select level); $10.50 per 30 practice booklets; $13.25 per 30 NCS answer sheets; $12.25 per scoring key (select level).

Time: Untimed.

Author: Touchstone Applied Science Associates (TASA), Inc.

Publisher: Touchstone Applied Science Associates (TASA), Inc.

[728]

Delaware County Silent Reading Test, Second Edition.

Purpose: "Designed to measure pupil achievement in typical . . . reading materials."

Population: Grades 1.5, 2, 2.5, 3, 3.5, 4, 5, 6, 7, 8.

Publication Date: 1965.

Scores, 5: Interpretation, Organization, Vocabulary, Structural Analysis, Total.

Administration: Group.

Levels, 10: Grades 1.5, 2, 2.5, 3, 3.5, 4, 5, 6, 7, 8.

Manual: No manual.

Price Data: Available from publisher.

Time: Administration time not reported.

Comments: Teacher's guide for each level.

Authors: Judson E. Newburg and Nicholas A. Spennato.

Publisher: Delaware County Intermediate Unit.

Cross References: For a review by Allen Berger, see 7:686.

[729]

Dementia Rating Scale.

Purpose: Measures the cognitive status of individuals with known cortical impairment.

Population: Individuals suffering from brain dysfunction.

Publication Dates: 1973–88.

Acronym: DRS.

Scores, 6: Attention, Initiation/Perseveration, Construction, Conceptualization, Memory, Total.

Administration: Individual.

Price Data, 1994: $59 per complete kit including 25 scoring/recording forms, stimulus cards, and manual ('88, 28 pages); $32 per 25 scoring/recording forms; $16 per set of stimulus cards; $15 per manual.

Time: (15–45) minutes.

Author: Steven Mattis.

Publisher: Psychological Assessment Resources, Inc.

Cross References: For a review by R. A. Bornstein, see 11:107 (2 references).

TEST REFERENCES

1. Jacobs, D., Ancoli-Israel, S., Parker, L., & Kripke, D. F. (1989). Twenty-four-hour-sleep-wake patterns in a nursing home population. *Psychology and Aging, 4,* 352-356.
2. Nebes, R. D., & Brady, C. B. (1990). Preserved organization of semantic attributes in Alzheimer's disease. *Psychology and Aging, 5,* 574-579.
3. Nebes, R. D., & Brady, C. B. (1991). The effect of contextual constraint on semantic judgements by Alzheimer patients. *Cortex, 27,* 237-246.
4. Janowsky, J. S., & Thomas-Thrapp, L. J. (1993). Complex figure recall in the elderly: A deficit in memory or constructional strategy? *Journal of Clinical and Experimental Neuropsychology, 15,* 159-169.

[730]

The Demos D Scale: An Attitude Scale for the Identification of Dropouts.

Purpose: "Designed to determine verbalized opinions which reflect attitudes presumably related to dropping out of school."

Population: Grades 7–12.

Publication Dates: 1965–70.

Acronym: DDS.

Scores: 5 attitude Scores: Teachers, Education, Peers and Parents, School Behavior, Total.
Administration: Group.
Price Data, 1993: $30 per kit including 25 forms and manual ('70, 11 pages); $16.50 per 25 forms; $16.50 per manual.
Time: Administration time not reported.
Comments: Also called Demos Dropout Scale.
Author: George D. Demos.
Publisher: Western Psychological Services.
Cross References: See T2:1153 (1 reference); for reviews by John R. Braun and Leonard V. Gordon, see 7:64.

[731]
The Dennis Test of Child Development.
Purpose: Assess developmental status of children at kindergarten or first grade in "five major areas of child growth."
Population: Kgn–grade 1.
Publication Dates: 1966–74.
Acronym: DCD.
Scores, 7: Gross Motor, Fine Motor, Visual Perception, Attention (Auditory), Language, Mental Age Development, Developmental Quotient.
Administration: Group.
Price Data: Not available.
Time: (22) minutes.
Author: William H. Dennis.
Publisher: William H. Dennis [No reply from publisher; status unknown].

[732]
Dennis Test of Scholastic Aptitude.
Purpose: Measures scholastic aptitude.
Population: Grades 4–8, 5–8.
Publication Dates: 1961–63.
Acronym: DTSA.
Scores: 5 subtests: Arithmetic Reasoning, Verbal Concepts, Memory, Abstract Reasoning, General Information.
Administration: Group.
Levels, 2: Form 2, Form 3.
Price Data: Not available.
Time: (40) minutes.
Author: William H. Dennis.
Publisher: William H. Dennis [No reply from publisher; status unknown].

[733]
Dental Admission Test.
Purpose: "Designed to measure general academic achievement, comprehension of scientific information, and perceptual ability."
Population: Dental school applicants.
Publication Dates: 1946–93.
Acronym: DAT.
Scores, 8: Natural Sciences (Biology, General Chemistry, Organic Chemistry, Total), Reading Comprehension, Quantitative Reasoning, Perceptual Ability, Academic Average.

Administration: Group.
Price Data: Available from publisher.
Time: 235(330) minutes in 2 sessions.
Comments: Formerly called Dental Aptitude Testing Program; test administered 2 times annually (April, October) at centers established by publisher.
Author: Department of Testing Services.
Publisher: American Dental Association.
Cross References: For reviews by Henry M. Cherrick and Linda M. DuBois, see 9:308; see also T3:673 (2 references); for reviews by Robert L. Linn and Christine H. McGuire of an earlier edition, see 8:1085 (7 references); see also T2:2337 (8 references), 7:1091 (28 references), 5:916 (6 references), and 4:788 (2 references).

[734]
Dental Assistant Test.
Purpose: Developed to help screen for dental assistant positions.
Population: Dental assistant applicants.
Publication Date: 1975.
Scores: 8 tests: Attention to Details, Organization Skills, Perception of Objects in Space, Perception of Spatial Perspective, Following Directions, Detail Judgments, Dexterity, Logic and Reasoning.
Administration: Group.
Price Data: Available from publisher.
Time: (40–45) minutes.
Comments: Self-administered.
Authors: Mary Meeker and Robert Meeker.
Publisher: SOI Systems.

[735]
Dental Receptionist Test.
Purpose: Developed to help screen for dental receptionist positions.
Population: Dental receptionist applicants.
Publication Date: 1975.
Scores: 8 tests: Attention to Details, Vocabulary, Verbal Reasoning, Following Directions, Management of Details, Management of Numerical Information, Dexterity, Logic and Reasoning.
Administration: Group.
Price Data: Available from publisher.
Time: (45–50) minutes.
Comments: Self-administered.
Authors: Mary Meeker and Robert Meeker.
Publisher: SOI Institute.

[736]
The Denver Articulation Screening Exam.
Purpose: Designed to identify significant developmental delay in the acquisition of speech sounds.
Population: Ages 2.5 to 6.0.
Publication Dates: 1971–73.
Acronym: DASE.
Scores, 2: DASE Word Score, Intelligibility Rating.
Administration: Individual.
Price Data, 1994: $4.50 per 25 test forms; $4.75 per set of picture cards for use with "shy or immature"

children; $200 per training videotape; $12 per manual/workbook ('73, 43 pages).
Time: (10–15) minutes.
Comments: Orally administered.
Authors: Amelia F. Drumwright and William K. Frankenburg (manual).
Publisher: Denver Developmental Materials, Inc.
Cross References: See T3:675 (1 reference); for a review by Harold A. Peterson, see 8:958.

[737]

Denver Audiometric Screening Test.
Purpose: Constructed to identify children who have a serious hearing loss.
Population: Ages 3–6.
Publication Date: 1973.
Acronym: DAST.
Scores: 3 ratings for each ear: Pass, Fail, Uncertain.
Administration: Individual.
Price Data, 1994: $4 per 25 test forms; $200 per training videotape; $10.25 per manual/workbook (33 pages); $10 per reference manual.
Time: [5–10] minutes.
Authors: William K. Frankenburg, Marion Downs, and Elynor Kazuk.
Publisher: Denver Developmental Materials, Inc.
Cross References: For a review by Lear Ashmore, see 9:309.

[738]

Denver Community Mental Health Questionnaire—Revised.
Purpose: Assesses client social history by means of a 79-item questionnaire.
Population: Mental health clients.
Publication Date: 1978.
Acronym: DCMHQ-R.
Scores: 13 scales covering 4 areas: Personal Distress, Alcohol and Drug Abuse, Social and Community Functioning, Client Satisfaction.
Administration: Individual.
Price Data: Not available.
Time: (20–30) minutes.
Author: James A. Ciarlo.
Publisher: James A. Ciarlo [No reply from publisher; status unknown].
Cross References: For a review by R. W. Payne, see 9:310 (3 references); see also T3:677 (2 references).

TEST REFERENCES

1. Wallace, C. J. (1986). Functional assessment in rehabilitation. *Schizophrenia Bulletin: National Institute of Mental Health, 12,* 604-630.

[739]

Denver Eye Screening Test.
Purpose: Developed to detect problems in visual acuity and screen for eye diseases.
Population: Ages 6 months and over.
Publication Date: 1973.
Acronym: DEST.

Scores: 3 ratings for each eye: Normal, Abnormal, Untestable.
Administration: Individual.
Price Data, 1994: $4 per 25 test forms; $15 per set of test materials including picture cards, occluder, cord, and spinning toy; $6.75 per set of picture cards; $4.25 per occluder; $1.75 per cord; $3.50 per spinning toy; $150 per training videotape; $11 per manual/workbook (40 pages); $9 per reference manual.
Time: (5–10) minutes.
Comments: "Criterion-referenced."
Authors: William K. Frankenburg, Arnold D. Goldstein, and John Barker.
Publisher: Denver Developmental Materials.
  a) VISION TESTS.
    1) *Fixation.*
    Population: Ages 6 months to 2.5 years.
    2) *Picture Card.*
    Population: Ages 2.5 to 3.
    3) *"E."*
    Population: Ages 3 and over.
  b) TESTS FOR NON-STRAIGHT EYES.
  Population: Ages 6 months and over.

[740]

Denver II.
Purpose: Designed to screen for developmental delays.
Population: Birth to age 6.
Publication Dates: 1967–90.
Scores: Item scores in 4 areas (Personal-Social, Fine Motor-Adaptive, Language, Gross Motor) and 5 test behavior ratings (Typical, Compliance, Interest in Surroundings, Fearfulness, Attention Span).
Administration: Individual.
Price Data, 1994: $58 per complete package; $33 per test kit; $15 per 100 test forms; $210 per training videotape (rental price $90); $17 per training manual ('90, 50 pages); $19 per technical manual ('90, 91 pages).
Time: (10–15) minutes for abbreviated version; (20–25) minutes for entire test.
Comments: Revision of the Denver Developmental Screening Test.
Authors: W. K. Frankenburg, Josiah Dodds, Phillip Archer, Beverly Bresnick, Patrick Maschka, Norma Edelman, and Howard Shapiro.
Publisher: Denver Developmental Materials, Inc.

TEST REFERENCES

1. Hohlstein, R. R. (1982). The development of prehension in normal infants. *The American Journal of Occupational Therapy, 36,* 170-176.
2. Call, J. D. (1984). Child abuse and neglect in infancy: Sources of hostility within the parent-infant dyad and disorders of attachment in infancy. *Child Abuse & Neglect, 8,* 185-202.
3. Howard, D. P., & DeSalazar, M. N. (1984). Language and cultural differences in the administration of the Denver Development Screening Test. *Child Study Journal, 14,* 1-9.
4. Klecan-Aker, J. S., & Lopez, B. (1984). A clinical taxonomy for the categorization of pragmatic language functions in normal preschool children. *Journal of Communication Disorders, 17,* 121-131.
5. Shaheen, S. J. (1984). Neuromaturation and behavior development: The case of childhood lead poisoning. *Developmental Psychology, 20,* 542-550.

6. Mayfield, M. I. (1985). Parents, children and reading: Helping Canadian Native Indian parents of preschoolers. *The Reading Teacher, 39,* 301-305.

7. Padget, S. Y. (1985). Miller Assessment for Preschoolers (MAP). *The Reading Teacher, 39,* 184-188.

8. Sankey, C. G., Elmer, E., Halechko, A. D., & Schulberg, P. (1985). The development of abused and high-risk infants in different treatment modalities: Residential versus in-home care. *Child Abuse & Neglect, 9,* 237-243.

9. Shaner, J. M., Peterson, K. L., & Roscoe, B. (1985). Older adolescent females' knowledge of child development norms. *Adolescence, 20,* 53-59.

10. Funk, S. G., Sturner, R. A., & Green, J. A. (1986). Preschool prediction of early school performance: Relationship of McCarthy Scales of Children's Abilities prior to school entry to achievement in kindergarten, first, and second grades. *Journal of School Psychology, 24,* 181-194.

11. Miller, L. J., & Sprong, T. A. (1986). Psychometric and qualitative comparison of four preschool screening instruments. *Journal of Learning Disabilities, 19,* 480-484.

12. Raab, M. M., Nordquist, V. W., Cunningham, J. L., & Bliem, C. D. (1986). Promoting peer regard of an autistic child in a mainstreamed preschool using pre-enrollment activities. *Child Study Journal, 16,* 265-284.

13. Preisser, D. A., Hodson, B. W., & Paden, E. P. (1988). Developmental phonology: 18–29 months. *Journal of Speech and Hearing Disorders, 53,* 125-130.

14. Wolfe, D. A., Edwards, B., Manion, I., & Koverola, C. (1988). Early intervention for parents at risk of child abuse and neglect: A preliminary investigation. *Journal of Consulting and Clinical Psychology, 56,* 40-47.

15. Espie, C. A., Pashley, A. S., Bonham, K. G., Sourindhrin, I., & O'Donovan, M. (1989). The mentally handicapped person with epilepsy: A comparative study investigating psychosocial functioning. *Journal of Mental Deficiency Research, 33,* 123-125.

16. Hodges, W. F., Landis, T., Day, E., & Oderberg, N. (1991). Infant and toddlers and post divorce parental access: An initial exploration. *Journal of Divorce & Remarriage, 16,* 239-252.

17. Stein, A., Gath, D. H., Bucher, J., Bond, A., Day, A., & Cooper, P. J. (1991). The relationship between post-natal depression and mother-child interaction. *British Journal of Psychiatry, 158,* 46-52.

18. Valdez-Menchaca, M. C., & Whitehurst, G. J. (1992). Accelerating language development through picture book reading: A systematic extension to Mexican day care. *Developmental Psychology, 28,* 1106-1114.

[741]
Departmental Evaluation of Chairperson Activities for Development.

Purpose: To diagnose administrative performance and discover ways to effectively improve it.

Population: College and university department chairpersons.

Publication Dates: 1977–82.

Acronym: DECAD.

Scores, 5: Responsibilities, Evaluation Summary, Administrative Methods, Characterization of Department, Diagnostic Summary.

Administration: Group.

Price Data: Available from publisher.

Time: (15–30) minutes.

Comments: Ratings of departmental chairperson by chairperson and faculty for evaluation and development.

Authors: Center for Faculty Evaluation and Deveopment; Donald D. Hoyt (interpretive guide).

Publisher: Center for Faculty Evaluation and Development.

TEST REFERENCES

1. Knight, W. H., & Holen, M. C. (1985). Leadership and the perceived effectiveness of department chairpersons. *Journal of Higher Education, 56,* 677-690.

[742]
Depression Adjective Check Lists.

Purpose: Developed to "measure self-reported depressive mood."

Population: Grades 9–16 and adults.

Publication Dates: 1967–88.

Acronym: DACL.

Forms, 7: A, B, C, D, E, F, G.

Scores: Total score only.

Administration: Group.

Price Data, 1990: $7 per 25 tests (specify form); $5 per scoring key; $6 per manual ('81, 34 pages); $10 per specimen set including 1 each of 7 test booklets, scoring key, and manual.

Time: (5) minutes.

Author: Bernard Lubin.

Publisher: Consulting Psychologists Press.

Cross References: See 9:315 (21 references); T3:681 (46 references), 8:536 (20 references), and T2:1154 (2 references); for reviews by Leonard D. Goodstein and Douglas M. McNair, see 7:65 (3 references); see also P:57 (4 references).

TEST REFERENCES

1. Sutker, P. B., Allain, A. N., Brantley, P. J., & Randall, C. L. (1982). Acute alcohol intoxication, negative affect, and autonomic arousal in women and men. *Addictive Behaviors, 7,* 17-25.

2. Fordyce, M. W. (1983). A program to increase happiness: Further studies. *Journal of Counseling Psychology, 30,* 483-498.

3. Thase, M. E., Hersen, M., Bellack, A. S., Himmelhoch, J. M., & Kupfer, D. J. (1983). Validation of a Hamilton subscale for endogenomorphic depression. *Journal of Affective Disorders, 5,* 267-278.

4. Baucom, D. H., & Danker-Brown, P. (1984). Sex role identity and sex-stereotyped tasks in the development of learned helplessness in women. *Journal of Personality and Social Psychology, 46,* 422-430.

5. Chu, C. R. L., Lubin, B., & Sue, S. (1984). Reliability and validity of the Chinese Depression Adjective Check Lists. *Journal of Clinical Psychology, 40,* 1409-1413.

6. Dauber, R. B. (1984). Subliminal psychodynamic activation in depression: On the role of autonomy issues in depressed college women. *Journal of Abnormal Psychology, 93,* 9-18.

7. Davis, G. R., Armstrong, H. E., Jr., Donovan, D. M., & Temkin, N. R. (1984). Cognitive-behavioral treatment of depressed affect among epileptics: Preliminary findings. *Journal of Clinical Psychology, 40,* 930-935.

8. Ellis, H. C., Thomas, R. L., & Rodriguez, I. A. (1984). Emotional mood states and memory: Elaborative encoding, semantic processing, and cognitive effort. *Journal of Experimental Psychology: Learning, Memory, and Cognition, 10,* 470-482.

9. Farakhan, A., Lubin, B., & O'Connor, W. A. (1984). Life satisfaction and depression among retired black persons. *Psychological Reports, 55,* 452-454.

10. Feksi, A., Harris, B., Walker, R. F., Riad-Fahmy, D., & Newcombe, R. G. (1984). 'Maternity blues' and hormone levels in saliva. *Journal of Affective Disorders, 6,* 351-355.

11. Godfrey, H. P. D., & Knight, R. G. (1984). The validity of actometer and speech activity measures in the assessment of depressed patients. *British Journal of Psychiatry, 145,* 159-163.

12. McKnight, D. L., Nelson, R. O., Hayes, S. C., & Jarrett, R. B. (1984). Importance of treating individually assessed response classes in the amelioration of depression. *Behavior Therapy, 15,* 315-335.

13. Ranieri, D., & Zeiss, A. M. (1984). Induction of depressed mood: A test of opponent-process theory. *Journal of Personality and Social Psychology, 47,* 1413-1422.

14. Richman, C. L., Brown, K. P., & Clark, M. L. (1984). The relationship between self-esteem and maladaptive behaviors in high school students. *Social Behavior and Personality, 12,* 177-185.

15. Salovey, P., & Rodin, J. (1984). Some antecedents and consequences of social-comparison jealousy. *Journal of Personality and Social Psychology, 47,* 780-792.

16. Strohmer, D. C., Biggs, D. A., & McIntyre, W. F. (1984). Social comparison information and judgments about depression and seeking counseling. *Journal of Counseling Psychology, 31,* 591-594.

17. Vestre, N. D. (1984). Irrational beliefs and self-reported depressed mood. *Journal of Abnormal Psychology, 93,* 239-241.

18. Brown, N. W. (1985). Assessment measures that discriminate between levels of DUI clients. *Psychological Reports, 56,* 739-742.

19. Ellis, H. C., Thomas, R. L., McFarland, A. D., & Lane, J. W. (1985). Emotional mood states and retrieval in episodic memory. *Journal of Experimental Psychology: Learning, Memory, and Cognition, 11,* 363-370.

20. Flor, H., Turk, D. C., & Birbaumer, N. (1985). Assessment of stress-related psychophysiological reactions in chronic back pain patients. *Journal of Consulting and Clinical Psychology, 53,* 354-364.

21. Garcia, K. A. M., & Beck, R. C. (1985). Mood and recognition memory: A comparison of two procedures. *Bulletin of the Psychonomic Society, 23,* 450-452.

22. Green, M., & Wisner, W. (1985). Evaluation of a multimodal structured group approach in treatment of depression. *Psychological Reports, 56,* 984-986.

23. Hundleby, J. D., & Loucks, A. D. (1985). Personality characteristics of young adult migraineurs. *Journal of Personality Assessment, 49,* 497-500.

24. Kerns, R. D., & Turk, D. C. (1985). Depression and chronic pain: The mediating role of the spouse. *Journal of Marriage and the Family, 46,* 845-852.

25. Lefkowitz, M. M., & Tesiny, E. P. (1985). Depression in children: Prevalence and correlates. *Journal of Consulting and Clinical Psychology, 53,* 647-656.

26. Lubin, B., & Collins, J. F. (1985). Depression Adjective Check Lists: Spanish, Hebrew, Chinese and English versions. *Journal of Clinical Psychology, 41,* 213-217.

27. Lubin, B., Natalicio, L., & Seever, M. (1985). Performance of bilingual subjects on Spanish and English versions of the Depression Adjective Check Lists. *Journal of Clinical Psychology, 41,* 218-219.

28. Monroe, S. M., Thase, M. E., Hersen, M., Himmelhoch, J. M., & Bellack, A. S. (1985). Life events and the endogenous-nonendogenous distinction in the treatment and posttreatment course of depression. *Comprehensive Psychiatry, 26,* 175-186.

29. Parker, G., Tennant, C., & Blignault, I. (1985). Predicting improvement in patients with non-endogenous depression. *British Journal of Psychiatry, 146,* 132-139.

30. Prout, H. T., & Schaefer, B. M. (1985). Self-reports of depression by community-based mildly mentally retarded adults. *American Journal of Mental Deficiency, 90,* 220-222.

31. Tietjen, A. M., & Bradley, C. F. (1985). Social support and maternal psychosocial adjustment during the transition to parenthood. *Canadian Journal of Behavioural Science, 17,* 109-121.

32. Wetzler, S. (1985). Mood state-dependent retrieval: A failure to replicate. *Psychological Reports, 56,* 759-765.

33. Cutrona, C. E. (1986). Behavioral manifestations of social support: A microanalytic investigation. *Journal of Personality and Social Psychology, 51,* 201-208.

34. Dobson, K. S., & Joffe, R. (1986). The role of activity level and cognition in depressed mood in a university sample. *Journal of Clinical Psychology, 42,* 264-271.

35. Graff, R. W., Whitehead, G. I., III, & LeCompte, M. (1986). Group treatment with divorced women using cognitive-behavioral and supportive-insight methods. *Journal of Counseling Psychology, 33,* 276-281.

36. Mable, H. M., Balance, W. D. G., & Galgan, R. J. (1986). Body-image distortion and dissatisfaction in university students. *Perceptual and Motor Skills, 63,* 907-911.

37. McNamara, K., & Hackett, G. (1986). Gender, sex-type and cognitive distortion: Self-perceptions of social competence among mild depressives. *Social Behavior and Personality, 14,* 113-121.

38. Pignatiello, M. F., Camp, C. J., & Rasar, L. A. (1986). Musical mood induction: An alternative to the Velten technique. *Journal of Abnormal Psychology, 95,* 295-297.

39. Rubio, C. T., & Lubin, B. (1986). College student mental health: A person-environment interactional analysis. *Journal of Clinical Psychology, 42,* 205-212.

40. Shamir, B. (1986). Self-esteem and the psychological impact of unemployment. *Social Psychology Quarterly, 49,* 61-72.

41. Shamir, B. (1986). Unemployment and household division of labor. *Journal of Marriage and the Family, 48,* 195-206.

42. Tanaka-Matsumi, J., & Kameoka, V. A. (1986). Reliabilities and concurrent validities of popular self-report measures of depression, anxiety, and social desirability. *Journal of Consulting and Clinical Psychology, 54,* 328-333.

43. Townsend, D. W., & Fontaine, G. (1986). Cross-cultural validity of the Depression Adjective Check List with a sample of black and white juvenile offenders. *Psychological Reports, 59,* 671-674.

44. Wierzbicki, M. (1986). Similarity of monozygotic and dizygotic twins in level and lability of subclinically depressed mood. *Journal of Clinical Psychology, 42,* 577-585.

45. Brannon, S. E., & Nelson, R. O. (1987). Contingency management treatment of outpatient unipolar depression: A comparison of reinforcement and extinction. *Journal of Consulting and Clinical Psychology, 55,* 117-119.

46. Shoskes, J. E., & Glenwick, D. S. (1987). The relationship of the Depression Adjective Check List to positive affect and activity level in older adults. *Journal of Personality Assessment, 51,* 565-571.

47. Zekoski, E. M., O'Hara, M. W., & Wills, K. E. (1987). The effects of maternal mood on mother-infant interaction. *Journal of Abnormal Child Psychology, 15,* 361-378.

48. Eddy, B. A., & Lubin, B. (1988). The Children's Depression Adjective Check Lists (C-DACL) with emotionally disturbed adolescent boys. *Journal of Abnormal Child Psychology, 16,* 83-88.

49. Fitzgibbon, M. L., Cella, D. F., & Sweeney, J. A. (1988). Redundancy in measures of depression. *Journal of Clinical Psychology, 44,* 372-374.

50. McAdams, D. P., Lensky, D. B., Daple, S. A., & Allen, J. (1988). Depression and the organization of autobiographical memory. *Journal of Social and Clinical Psychology, 7,* 332-349.

51. Robins, C. J. (1988). Development of experimental mood induction procedures for testing personality-event interaction models of depression. *Journal of Clinical Psychology, 44,* 958-963.

52. Strohmer, D. C., Moilanen, D. L., & Barry, L. J. (1988). Personal hypothesis testing: The role of consistency and self-schema. *Journal of Counseling Psychology, 35,* 56-65.

53. Beckham, E. E. (1989). Improvement after evaluation in psychotherapy of depression: Evidence of a placebo effect. *Journal of Clinical Psychology, 45,* 945-950.

54. Chartier, G. M., & Ranieri, D. J. (1989). Comparison of two mood induction procedures. *Cognitive Therapy and Research, 13,* 275-282.

55. Hobfoll, S. E., Bridges, A., Lomranz, J., Eyal, N., & Tzemach, M. (1989). Pulse of a nation: Depressive mood reactions of Israelis to the Israel-Lebanon war. *Journal of Personality and Social Psychology, 56,* 1002-1012.

56. Newmann, J. P. (1989). Aging and depression. *Psychology and Aging, 4,* 150-165.

57. Ponterotto, J. G., Pace, T. M., & Kavan, M. G. (1989). A counselor's guide to the assessment of depression. *Journal of Counseling and Development, 67,* 301-309.

58. Stiles, T. C., & Götestam, K. G. (1989). The role of automatic negative thoughts in the development of dysphoric mood: An analogue experiment. *Cognitive Therapy and Research, 13,* 161-170.

59. Zemore, R., & Rinholm, J. (1989). Vulnerability to depression as a function of parental rejection and control. *Canadian Journal of Behavioural Science, 21,* 364-376.

60. Davis-Berman, J. (1990). Physical self-efficacy, perceived physical status, and depressive symptomatology in older adults. *The Journal of Psychology, 124,* 207-215.

61. Hops, H., Lewinsohn, P. M., Andrews, J. A., & Roberts, R. E. (1990). Psychosocial correlates of depressive symptomatology among high school students. *Journal of Clinical Child Psychology, 19,* 211-220.

62. Lubin, B., Collins, J. F., Seever, M., Whitlock, R. V., & Dennis, A. J. (1990). Relationships among readability, reliability, and validity in a self-report Adjective Check List. *Psychological Assessment, 2,* 256-261.

63. Beckingham, A. C., & Lubin, B. (1991). Reliability and validity of the trait form of set 2 of the Depression Adjective Check Lists with Canadian elderly. *Journal of Clinical Psychology, 47,* 407-414.

64. Hertel, P. T., & Rude, S. S. (1991). Recalling in a state of natural or experimental depression. *Cognitive Therapy and Research, 15,* 103-127.

65. Lomranz, J., Lubin, B., Eyal, N., & Joffe, A. (1991). Measuring depressive mood in elderly Israeli: Reliability and validity of the Depression Adjective Check Lists. *Psychological Reports, 68,* 1311-1316.

66. Lubin, B., Collins, J. F., Seever, M., & Whitlock, R. V. (1991). Readability of the Depression Adjective Check Lists (DACL) and the Multiple Affect Adjective Check List—Revised (MAACL-R). *Journal of Clinical Psychology, 47,* 91-93.

67. Martin, R. B., & Labott, S. M. (1991). Mood following emotional crying: Effects of the situation. *Journal of Research in Personality, 25,* 218-244.

68. Mittelstaedt, W. H., & Wollert, R. (1991). Blame and the development of depressed mood. *Canadian Journal of Behavioural Science, 23,* 1-11.

69. Souza, E. R. D., Lubin, B., & Whitlock, R. V. (1991). Preliminary report on reliability and validity of the trait form of the Depression Adjective Check List in a representative community sample. *Journal of Clinical Psychology, 47,* 418-420.

70. Rosenfarb, I. S., & Aron, J. (1992). The self-protective function of depressive affect and cognition. *Journal of Social and Clinical Psychology, 11,* 323-335.

71. Sigmon, S. T., & Nelson-Gray, R. O. (1992). Sensitivity to aversive events in depression: Antecedent, concomitant, or consequent? *Journal of Psychopathology and Behavioral Assessment, 14,* 225-246.

72. Stein, P. N., & Motta, R. W. (1992). Effects of aerobic and nonaerobic exercise on depression and self-concept. *Perceptual and Motor Skills, 74,* 79-89.

73. Baker, R. C., & Guttfreund, D. G. (1993). The effects of written autobiographical recollection induction procedures on mood. *Journal of Clinical Psychology, 49,* 563-568.

74. Beckingham, A. C., Coutu-Wakulczyk, G., & Lubin, B. (1993). French-language validation of the DACL and MAACL-R. *Journal of Clinical Psychology, 49,* 685-695.

75. Feldman, L. A. (1993). Distinguishing depression and anxiety in self-report: Evidence from confirmatory factory analysis on nonclinical and clinical samples. *Journal of Consulting and Clinical Psychology, 61,* 631-638.

76. Lubin, B., & Whitlock, R. V. (1993). Diagnostic efficiency of the Depression Adjective Check Lists. *Journal of Clinical Psychology, 49,* 695-701.

77. Lubin, B., Whitlock, R. V., Swearingin, S. E., & Seever, M. (1993). Self-assessment of state and trait depressive affect by college students: Reliability and validity of an adjective check list. *Journal of College Student Development, 34,* 249-255.

78. Stiles, T. C., Schröder, P., & Johansen, T. (1993). The role of automatic thoughts and dysfunctional attitudes in the development and maintenance of experimentally induced dysphoric mood. *Cognitive Therapy and Research, 17,* 71-82.

79. DeSouza, E. R., Lubin, B., & Zanelli, J. (1994). Norms, reliability, and concurrent validity measures of the Portuguese version of the Depression Adjective Check Lists. *Journal of Clinical Psychology, 50,* 208-215.

[743]

Depression and Anxiety in Youth Scale.

Purpose: Designed to help professionals identify depression and anxiety in children and youth.

Population: Ages 6-0 to 19-0.

Publication Date: 1994.

Acronym: DAYS.

Administration: Group.

Price Data, 1994: $89 per complete kit including 50 student rating scales, 50 teacher rating scales, 50 parent rating scales, 50 profile/record forms, scoring keys, and manual (39 pages); $17 per 50 record forms; $17 per 50 profile/record forms; $26 per manual.

Authors: Phyllis L. Newcomer, Edna M. Barenbaum, and Brian R. Bryant.

Publisher: PRO-ED, Inc.

a) STUDENT SELF-REPORT SCALE (SCALE S).

Scores, 2: Depression, Anxiety.

Time: (15–20) minutes.

b) TEACHER RATING SCALE (SCALE T).

Scores, 2: Depression, Anxiety.

Time: (5–10) minutes.

c) PARENT RATING SCALE (SCALE P).

Scores, 3: Depression, Anxiety, Social Maladjustment.

Time: (6–10) minutes.

[744]

Depressive Experiences Questionnaire.

Purpose: Designed to assess an individual's depressive experience.

Population: Adolescents and adults (patients and normals).

Publication Dates: 1979–89.

Acronym: DEQ.

Scores, 3: Dependency, Self-Criticism, Efficacy.

Administration: Group.

Manual: No manual.

Price Data: Available from publisher.

Time: Administration time not reported.

Authors: Sidney J. Blatt, Carrie E. Schaffer, Susan A. Bers, and Donald M. Quinlan.

Publisher: Sidney J. Blatt.

Cross References: See 9:316 (2 references) and T3:682 (1 reference).

TEST REFERENCES

1. Stein, N., Fruchter, H. J., & Trief, P. (1983). Experiences of depression and illness behavior in patients with intractable chronic pain. *Journal of Clinical Psychology, 39,* 31-33.

2. Blatt, S. J., Rounsaville, B., Eyre, S., & Wilber, C. (1984). The psychodynamics of opiate addiction. *The Journal of Nervous and Mental Disease, 172,* 342-352.

3. Welkowitz, J., Lish, J. D., & Bond, R. N. (1985). The Depressive Experiences Questionnaire: Revision and validation. *Journal of Personality Assessment, 49,* 89-94.

4. Brewin, C. R., & Furnham, A. (1987). Dependency, self-criticism and depressive attributional style. *British Journal of Clinical Psychology, 26,* 225-226.

5. Zuroff, D. C., & Mongrain, M. (1987). Dependency and self-criticism: Vulnerability factors for depressive affective states. *Journal of Abnormal Psychology, 96,* 14-22.

6. Klein, D. N., Taylor, E. B., Harding, K., & Dickstein, S. (1988). Double depression and episodic major depression: Demographic, clinical, familial, personality, and socioenvironmental characteristics and short-term outcome. *American Journal of Psychiatry, 145,* 1226-1231.

7. Shapiro, J. P. (1988). Relationships between dimensions of depressive experience and perceptions of the lives of people in general. *Journal of Personality Assessment, 52,* 297-308.

8. Brewin, C. R., Furnham, A., & Howes, M. (1989). Demographic and psychological determinants of homesickness and confiding among students. *British Journal of Psychology, 80,* 467-477.

9. Brown, J. D., & Silberschate, G. (1989). Dependency, self-criticism, and depressive attributional style. *Journal of Abnormal Psychology, 98,* 187-188.

10. Klein, D. N. (1989). The Depressive Experiences Questionnaire: A further evaluation. *Journal of Personality Assessment, 53,* 703-715.

11. Wilhelm, K., & Parker, G. (1989). Is sex necessarily a risk factor to depression? *Psychological Medicine, 19,* 401-413.

12. Frost, R. O., Marten, P., Lahart, C., & Rosenblate, R. (1990). The dimensions of perfectionism. *Cognitive Therapy and Research, 14,* 449-468.

13. Klein, D. N. (1990). Depressive personality: Reliability, validity, and relation to dysthymia. *Journal of Abnormal Psychology, 99,* 412-421.

14. Riley, W. T., & McCranie, E. W. (1990). The Depressive Experiences Questionnaire: Validity and psychological correlates in a clinical sample. *Journal of Personality Assessment, 54,* 523-533.

15. Viglione, D. J., Jr., Clemmey, P. A., & Camenzuli, L. (1990). The Depressive Experiences Questionnaire: A critical review. *Journal of Personality Assessment, 55,* 52-64.

16. Zuroff, D. C., Igreja, I., & Mongrain, M. (1990). Dysfunctional attitudes, dependency, and self-criticism as predictors of depressive mood states: A 12-month longitudinal study. *Cognitive Therapy and Research, 14,* 315-326.

17. Zuroff, D. C., Quinlan, D. M., & Blatt, S. J. (1990). Psychometric properties of the Depressive Experiences Questionnaire in a college population. *Journal of Personality Assessment, 55,* 65-72.

18. Blaney, P. H., & Kutcher, G. S. (1991). Measures of depressive dimensions: Are they interchangeable? *Journal of Personality Assessment, 56,* 502-512.

19. Flett, G. L., Hewitt, P. L., & Mittelstaedt, W. M. (1991). Dysphoria and components of self-punitiveness: A re-analysis. *Cognitive Therapy and Research, 15,* 201-219.

20. Luthar, S. S. (1991). Vulnerability and resilience: A study of high-risk adolescents. *Child Development, 62,* 600-616.

21. Talbot, N. L., Duberstein, P. R., & Scott, P. (1991). Subliminal psychodynamic activation, food consumption, and self-confidence. *Journal of Clinical Psychology, 47,* 813-823.

22. Whiffen, V. E., & Sasseville, T. M. (1991). Dependency, self-criticism, and recollections of parenting: Sex differences and the role of depressive affect. *Journal of Social and Clinical Psychology, 10,* 121-133.

23. Bers, S. A., & Quinlan, D. M. (1992). Perceived-competence deficit in anorexia nervosa. *Journal of Abnormal Psychology, 101,* 423-431.

24. Blatt, S. J., Shaffer, C. E., Bers, S. A., & Quinlan, D. M. (1992). Psychometric properties of the depressive experiences questionnaire for adolescents. *Journal of Personality Assessment, 59,* 82-88.

25. Franche, R. L., & Dobson, K. (1992). Self-criticism and interpersonal dependency as vulnerability factors to depression. *Cognitive Therapy and Research, 16*, 419-435.

26. Fuhr, S. K., & Shean, G. (1992). Subtypes of depression, efficacy, and the Depressive Experiences Questionnaire. *The Journal of Psychology, 126*, 495-506.

27. Quinlan, D. M., Blatt, S. J., Chevron, E. S., & Wein, S. J. (1992). The analysis of descriptions of parents: Identification of a more differentiated factor structure. *Journal of Personality Assessment, 59*, 340-351.

28. Sincoff, J. B. (1992). Ambivalence and defense: Effects of a repressive style on normal adolescents' and young adults' mixed feelings. *Journal of Abnormal Psychology, 101*, 251-256.

29. Sadeh, A., Rubin, S. S., & Berman, E. (1993). Parental and relationship representations and experiences of depression in college students. *Journal of Personality Assessment, 60*, 192-204.

30. Sanfilipo, M. P. (1993). Depression, gender, gender role traits, and the wish to be held. *Sex Roles, 28*, 583-605.

[745]

Derogatis Psychiatric Rating Scale.
Purpose: Multidimensional psychiatric rating scale for use by clinician to assist in validating patient-reported results.
Population: Adults and adolescents.
Publication Dates: 1974-92.
Acronym: DPRS.
Administration: Individual.
Comments: Formerly called Hopkins Psychiatric Rating Scale (9:483).
Author: Leonard R. Derogatis.
Publisher: NCS Assessments.

a) BRIEF DEROGATIS PSYCHIATRIC RATING SCALE.
Acronym: B-DPRS.
Scores, 10: Primary Dimensions (Somatization, Obsessive-Compulsive, Interpersonal Sensitivity, Depression, Anxiety, Hostility, Phobic Anxiety, Paranoid Ideation, Psychoticism) and Global Pathology Index.
Price Data, 1994: $30 per 100 forms; $50 per 50 scannable forms.
Time: (1-2) minutes.

b) DEROGATIS PSYCHIATRIC RATING SCALE.
Acronym: DPRS.
Scores, 18: Same as brief edition plus Sleep Disturbance, Psychomotor Retardation, Hysterical Behavior, Abjection-Disinterest, Conceptual Dysfunction, Disorientation, Excitement, Euphoria.
Price Data: $32 per 100 forms.
Time: (2-5) minutes.
Cross References: See 9:483 (1 reference).

TEST REFERENCES

1. Horowitz, M. J., Marmar, C., Weiss, D. S., DeWitt, K. N., & Rosenbaum, R. (1984). Brief psychotherapy of bereavement reactions. *Archives of General Psychiatry, 41*, 438-448.

2. Pilkonis, P. A., Imber, S. D., Lewis, P., Rubinsky, P. (1984). A comparative outcome study of individual, group, and conjoint psychotherapy. *Archives of General Psychiatry, 41*, 431-437.

3. Casper, R. C., Redmond, D. E., Jr., Katz, M. M., Schaffer, C. B., Davis, J. M., & Koslow, S. H. (1985). Somatic symptoms in primary affective disorder: Presence and relationship to the classification of depression. *Archives of General Psychiatry, 42*, 1098-1104.

4. Horne, R. L., Pettinati, H. M., Sugerman, A., & Varga, E. (1985). Comparing bilateral to unilateral electroconvulsive therapy in a randomized study with EEG monitoring. *Archives of General Psychiatry, 42*, 1087-1092.

5. Wood, W. D., & Swanson, D. A. (1985). Development and application of criteria for classes of psychotherapy based on patients' requests for service. *British Journal of Medical Psychology, 58*, 45-54.

6. Sokol, S. M., & Ruzecki, V. L. (1991). Number impairments following hypokalemia: A case study. *Cortex, 27*, 447-452.

[746]

Derogatis Sexual Functioning Inventory.
Purpose: Multidimensional assessment of sexual functioning.
Population: Adults.
Publication Dates: 1975-79.
Acronym: DSFI.
Scores, 12: Information, Experience, Drive, Attitudes, Psychological Symptoms, Affects, Gender Role, Definition, Fantasy, Body Image, Sexual Satisfaction, Total, Patient's Evaluation of Current Functioning.
Administration: Group.
Price Data, 1993: $2 per nonreusable test ('78, 8 pages); $8 per manual ('79, 36 pages); $.35 per profile form (specify male or female).
Time: (45-60) minutes.
Author: Leonard R. Derogatis.
Publisher: Clinical Psychometric Research, Inc.
Cross References: For reviews by Edward S. Herold and David L. Weis, see 9:317 (3 references); see also T3:683 (6 references).

TEST REFERENCES

1. Andersen, B. L., & Jochimsen, P. R. (1985). Sexual functioning among breast cancer, gynecologic cancer, and healthy women. *Journal of Consulting and Clinical Psychology, 53*, 25-32.

2. Sakheim, D. K., Barlow, D. H., Beck, J. G., & Abrahamson, D. J. (1985). A comparison of male heterosexual and male homosexual patterns of sexual arousal. *The Journal of Sex Research, 21*, 183-198.

3. Zuckerman, M., Neeb, M., Ficher, M., Fishkin, R. E., Goldman, A., Fink, P. J., Cohen, S. N., Jacobs, J. A., & Weisberg, M. (1985). Nocturnal penile tumescence and penile responses in the waking state in diabetic and non-diabetic sexual dysfunctionals. *Archives of Sexual Behavior, 14*, 109-129.

4. Cella, D. F., & Tross, S. (1986). Psychological adjustment to survival from Hodgkin's disease. *Journal of Consulting and Clinical Psychology, 54*, 616-622.

5. Conte, H. R. (1986). Multivariate assessment of sexual dysfunction. *Journal of Consulting and Clinical Psychology, 54*, 149-157.

6. McEwan, K. L., Costello, C. G., & Taylor, P. J. (1987). Adjustment to infertility. *Journal of Abnormal Psychology, 96*, 108-116.

7. Malec, J., Wolberg, W., Romsaas, E., Trump, D., & Tanner, M. (1988). Millon Clinical Multiaxial Inventory (MCMI) findings among breast clinic patients after initial evaluation and at 4- or 8-month follow-up. *Journal of Clinical Psychology, 44*, 175-181.

8. Palace, E. M., & Gorzalka, B. B. (1990). The enhancing effects of anxiety on arousal in sexually dysfunctional and functional women. *Journal of Abnormal Psychology, 99*, 403-411.

9. Reed, L. A., & Meyers, L. S. (1991). A structural analysis of religious orientation and its relation to sexual attitudes. *Educational and Psychological Measurement, 51*, 943-952.

10. Kalichman, S. C., Dwyer, M., Henderson, M. C., & Hoffman, L. (1992). Psychological and sexual functioning among outpatient sexual offenders against children: A Minnesota Multiphasic Personality Inventory (MMPI) cluster analytic study. *Journal of Psychopathology and Behavioral Assessment, 14*, 259-276.

[747]

Derogatis Stress Profile.
Purpose: "Designed to assess and represent stress at three distinct but related levels of measurement."
Population: Adults.
Publication Dates: 1984-86.
Acronym: DSP.
Scores: 3 domains: Environmental Events, Emotional Response, Personality Mediators; 11 dimensions: Time Pressure, Driven Behavior, Attitude

Posture, Relaxation Potential, Role Definition, Vocational Satisfaction, Domestic Satisfaction, Health Posture, Hostility, Anxiety, Depression; 2 global scores: Subjective Stress, Total Stress.
Administration: Group.
Price Data, 1993: $50 per 50 tests; $17.50 per 50 score profile forms; $8 per summary report and scoring instructions ('86, 14 pages); $75 per 50 uses of computer scoring program.
Time: 10(15) minutes.
Author: Leonard R. Derogatis.
Publisher: Clinical Psychometric Research, Inc.

TEST REFERENCES

1. D'Zurilla, T. J., & Nezu, A. M. (1990). Developmental and preliminary evaluation on the Social Problem-Solving Inventory. *Psychological Assessment, 2*, 156-163.

[748]
Description of Body Scale.
Purpose: Designed to assess conscious views of self and of others concerning aspects of body structure, voice quality and movement.
Population: Adolescents and adults.
Publication Date: 1980.
Acronym: DOBS.
Scores, 5: Masculinity-Femininity of Body, Consistency of Present Body Description, Ideal Body Description, Self-Ideal Body Description Difference Score, Incongruence Between Present and Ideal Body Description.
Administration: Group or individual.
Price Data, 1993: $25 per 50 tests; $12 per specimen set; $2 per test for scoring service ($50 minimum).
Time: Administration time not reported.
Comments: May be rated by an observer.
Author: Richard E. Carney.
Publisher: Timao Foundation for Research and Development.
Cross References: For a review by James J. Jupp, see 9:318.

[749]
Descriptive Tests of Language Skills.
Purpose: "To help college teachers assign entering students to appropriate English courses, identify students who may need special assistance in particular aspects of reading and language use before undertaking college-level work, tailor instruction in reading and composition to individual student needs, and plan instruction for classes or groups of students."
Population: Beginning students in two- and four-year institutions.
Publication Dates: 1978–88.
Acronym: DTLS.
Administration: Group.
Price Data: Available from publisher.
Author: The College Board.
Publisher: The College Board.
a) READING COMPREHENSION.
Scores, 4: Identifying Word and/or Phrase Meaning Through Context, Understanding Literal and Interpretive Meaning, Understanding Writers' Assumptions/Opinions and Tone, Total.
Time: 45 minutes; 50 minutes for optional essay section.
b) CRITICAL REASONING.
Scores, 4: Interpreting Information, Using Information Appropriately, Evaluating Information, Total.
Time: 45 minutes; 30 minutes for optional essay section.
c) CONVENTIONS OF WRITTEN ENGLISH.
Scores, 4: Maintaining Consistency, Using Standard Forms, Connecting Ideas Appropriately, Total.
Time: 35 minutes; 25 minutes for essay section.
d) SENTENCE STRUCTURE.
Scores, 4: Using Complete Sentences, Relating Ideas in Sentences Logically, Making Meaning Clear, Total.
Time: 30 minutes.
Cross References: For a review by Francis X. Archambault, Jr., see 11:108 (4 references); see also T3:685 (1 reference).

TEST REFERENCES

1. Prola, M. (1984). Irrational beliefs and reading comprehension. *Perceptual and Motor Skills, 59*, 777-778.
2. Smith, E. R. (1985). Community college reading tests: A statewide survey. *Journal of Reading, 28*, 52-55.
3. Blustein, D. L., Judd, T. P., Krom, J., Viniar, B., Padilla, E., Wedemeyer, R., & Williams, D. (1986). Identifying predictors of academic performance of community college students. *Journal of College Student Personnel, 27*, 242-249.
4. Sabban, Y., & Kay, P. M. (1987). Distinction between essay and objective tests in assessing writing skills of underprepared college students. *Journal of Research and Development in Education, 21*(1), 61-68.

[750]
Descriptive Tests of Mathematics Skills.
Purpose: Designed to help colleges place students in appropriate entry-level courses in mathematics, assess students' skills in particular areas of mathematics, and measure student performance upon completion of a program of instruction in mathematics.
Population: Beginning students in two- and four-year institutions.
Publication Dates: 1978–88.
Acronym: DTMS.
Administration: Group.
Price Data: Available from publisher.
Time: (30) minutes per test.
Comments: Revised edition; 4 tests; tests may be used independently or in combination with other tests in the series.
Author: The College Board.
Publisher: The College Board.
a) ARITHMETIC SKILLS.
Scores, 6: Operations with Whole Numbers, Operations with Fractions, Operations with Decimals, Ratio/Proportion and Percent, Applications, Total.
b) ELEMENTARY ALGEBRA SKILLS.
Scores, 5: Operations with Real Numbers, Opera-

tions with Algebraic Expressions, Solutions of Equations and Inequalities, Applications, Total.

c) INTERMEDIATE ALGEBRA SKILLS.

Scores, 5: Algebraic Operations, Solutions of Equations and Inequalities, Geometry, Applications, Total.

d) FUNCTIONS AND GRAPHS (CALCULUS READINESS).

Scores, 4: Algebraic Functions, Exponential and Logarithmic Functions, Trigonometric Functions, Total.

Cross References: For reviews by Stephen B. Dunbar and John R. Hester, see 11:109.

TEST REFERENCES

1. Suddick, D. E., & Collins, B. A. (1984). Descriptive tests of mathematics skills: A follow-up of performance of older master's level students. *Perceptual and Motor Skills, 58,* 465-466.
2. Kostka, M. P., & Wilson, C. K. (1986). Reducing mathematics anxiety in nontraditional-age female students. *Journal of College Student Personnel, 27,* 530-534.

[751]

Detention Promotion Tests—Complete Service.

Purpose: Specifically prepared and tailor-made test for promotion of detention workers.

Population: Detention workers under consideration for promotion.

Publication Dates: 1990–93.

Scores: 6 subtests: Detention-Related Technical Knowledges, Knowledge of the Behavioral Sciences and Human Relations, Supervisory and Managerial Knowledges, Administrative Knowledges, Knowledge of Inmate Legal Rights, Ability to Understand and Interpret Table and Text Material, and Total.

Administration: Group.

Price Data, 1993: Rental and scoring services, $700 per first 5 candidates; $16.50–$41 for each additional candidate ($700 minimum).

Time: [210] minutes.

Comments: Candidate Study Guide available; formerly called Deluxe Detention Promotion Tests.

Author: McCann Associates, Inc.

Publisher: McCann Associates, Inc.

[752]

Detroit Tests of Learning Aptitude, Third Edition.

Purpose: Designed to measure "general intelligence and discrete ability areas."

Population: Ages 6-0 to 17-11.

Publication Dates: 1935–91.

Acronym: DTLA-3.

Scores: 11 subtest Scores: Word Opposites, Design Sequences, Sentence Imitation, Reversed Letters, Story Construction, Design Reproduction, Basic Information, Symbolic Relations, Word Sequences, Story Sequences, Picture Fragments; and 16 composite Scores: General Mental Ability Composite, Optimal Level Composite, Domain Composites (Verbal, Nonverbal, Attention-Enhanced, Attention-Reduced,

Motor-Enhanced, Motor-Reduced), Theoretical Composites (Fluid Intelligence, Crystallized Intelligence, Associative Level, Cognitive Level, Simultaneous Processing, Successive Processing, Verbal Scale, Performance Scale).

Administration: Individual.

Price Data, 1994: $198 per complete kit; $34 per 25 examiner record booklets; $18 per 25 response forms; $18 per 25 Profile/Summary forms; $44 per Picture Book 1 (for Design Sequences, Story Construction, Design Reproduction, Symbolic Relations); $16 per Picture Book 2 (for Story Sequences); $14 per Picture Fragments Flipbook; $32 per examiner's manual ('91, 151 pages); $98 per software scoring and report system (specify Apple or IBM).

Time: (50–120) minutes.

Author: Donald D. Hammill.

Publisher: PRO-ED, Inc.

Cross References: For reviews by Arthur B. Silverstein and Joan Silverstein of an earlier edition, see 10:85 (15 references); see also 9:320 (11 references) and T3:691 (20 references); for a review by Arthur B. Silverstein of an earlier edition, see 8:213 (14 references); see also T2:493 (3 references) and 7:406 (10 references); for a review by F. L. Wells, see 3:275 (1 reference); for reviews by Anne Anastasi and Henry Feinburg and an excerpted review by D. A. Worcester (with S. M. Corey), see 1:1058.

TEST REFERENCES

1. Gold, P. C., & Horn, P. L. (1983). Intelligence and achievement of adult illiterates in a tutorial project: A preliminary analysis. *Journal of Clinical Psychology, 39,* 107-113.
2. Ney, P., Colbert, P., Newman, B., & Young, J. (1986). Aggressive behavior and learning difficulties as symptoms of depression in children. *Child Psychiatry and Human Development, 17,* 3-14.
3. Gross, C., & Leder, S. B. (1987). Effect of a programatic context on elicited imitation. *Perceptual and Motor Skills, 65,* 455-459.
4. Liles, B. Z. (1987). Episode organization and cohesive conjunctives in narratives of children with and without language disorder. *Journal of Speech and Hearing Research, 30,* 185-196.
5. John, K. R., & Rattan, G. (1991). A comparison of short-term memory tests as predictors of reading achievement for learning-disabled and educable mentally retarded students. *Journal of School Psychology, 29,* 309-318.
6. Ganschow, L., Sparks, R., & Helmick, M. (1992). Speech/language referral practices by school psychologists. *School Psychology Review, 21*(2), 313-326.
7. Swanson, H. L. (1992). Generality and modifiability of working memory among skilled and less skilled readers. *Journal of Educational Psychology, 84,* 473-488.

[753]

Detroit Tests of Learning Aptitude—Adult.

Purpose: Designed to identify strengths and weaknesses in mental abilities and to identify examinees who are markedly deficient in general mental ability.

Population: Ages 16-0 and over.

Publication Date: 1991.

Acronym: DTLA-A.

Scores, 20: 12 subtest scores: Word Opposites, Story Sequences, Sentence Imitation, Reversed Letters, Mathematical Problems, Design Sequences, Basic Information, Quantitative Relations, Word Sequences, Design Reproduction, Symbolic Relations, Form Assembly and 8 composite scores (Linguistic Verbal,

Linguistic Nonverbal, Attention-Enhanced, Attention-Reduced, Motor-Enhanced, Motor-Reduced, General Mental Ability, Optimal).
Administration: Individual.
Price Data, 1994: $209 per complete kit including picture book 1, picture book 2, 25 response forms, 25 examiner record booklets, 25 profile/summary forms, and manual (120 pages); $44 per picture book 1; $19 per picture book 2; $18 per 25 response forms; $39 per 25 examiner record booklets; $18 per 25 profile/summary forms; $32 per manual; $98 per microcomputer scoring and report system software (Apple or IBM).
Time: (90–150) minutes.
Comments: Upward extension of the Detroit Tests of Learning Aptitude (Second Edition) (10:85) and (Third Edition) (752).
Authors: Donald D. Hammill and Bryan R. Bryant.
Publisher: PRO-ED, Inc.

[754]

Detroit Tests of Learning Aptitude—Primary, Second Edition.
Purpose: Constructed to identify strengths and weaknesses in mental abilities and to identify "children who are markedly deficient in general mental ability."
Population: Ages 3–9.
Publication Dates: 1986–91.
Acronym: DTLA-P:2.
Scores, 7: Linguistic (Verbal, Nonverbal), Attentional (Enhanced, Reduced), Motoric (Enhanced, Reduced), General Mental Ability.
Administration: Individual.
Price Data, 1994: $119 per complete kit including picture book, 25 response forms, 25 profile/examiner record forms, and manual ('91, 106 pages); $39 per picture book; $23 per 25 response forms; $29 per 25 profile/examiner record forms; $32 per manual; $98 per microcomputer scoring and report system software (Apple or IBM).
Time: (15–45) minutes.
Comments: Downward extension of the Detroit Tests of Learning Aptitude (Second Edition) (10:85) and (Third Edition) (752).
Authors: Donald D. Hammill and Bryan R. Bryant.
Publisher: PRO-ED, Inc.
Cross References: For reviews of an earlier edition by Cathy F. Telzrow and Stanley F. Vasa, see 10:84 (1 reference).

[755]

Developing Cognitive Abilities Test [Second Edition].
Purpose: "Measures learning characteristics and abilities that contribute to academic performance."
Population: Grades 1–2, 3, 4, 5, 6, 7–8, 9–10, 11–12.
Publication Dates: 1980–89.
Acronym: DCAT.
Scores, 7: Verbal, Quantitative, Spatial, Basic Abilities, Application Abilities, Critical Thinking Abilities, Total.
Administration: Group.
Levels, 8: C/D, E, F, G, H, I/J, K, L.
Price Data, 1993: $49.50 per 25 machine-scorable test booklets (specify Level C/D or Level E only) with 1 Directions for Administration; $38.50 per 25 reusable test booklets (specify Level E–L) with 1 Directions for Administration; $16.50 per 35 answer sheets; $39.50 per 100 answer sheets; $4.30 per Directions for Administration (specify Level C/D ['89, 43 pages], Level E [machine-scorable] ['89, 19 pages], or Levels E-L ['89, 19 pages]); $23.50 per Norms Book ('91, 44 pages); $17 per Technical Manual; scoring service available from publisher.
Authors: John W. Wick, Donald L. Beggs, and John T. Mouw.
Publisher: American College Testing.
a) LEVEL C/D.
Population: Grades 1–2.
Time: (83–90) minutes.
Comments: Examiner-paced.
b) LEVEL E.
Population: Grade 3.
Time: 60(70) minutes.
c) LEVEL F.
Population: Grade 4.
Time: 60(70) minutes.
d) LEVEL G.
Population: Grade 5.
Time: 60(70) minutes.
e) LEVEL H.
Population: Grade 6.
Time: 60(70) minutes.
f) LEVEL I/J.
Population: Grades 7–8.
Time: 60(70) minutes.
g) LEVEL K.
Population: Grades 9–10.
Time: 60(70) minutes.
h) LEVEL L.
Population: Grades 11–12.
Time: 60(70) minutes.
Cross References: For a review by Glen P. Aylward, see 11:110 (5 references); for a review by Lynn H. Fox of the original edtion, see 9:321.

TEST REFERENCES

1. Farley, M. J., & Elmore, P. B. (1993). The relationship of reading comprehension to critical thinking skills, cognitive ability, and vocabulary for a sample of underachieving college freshmen. *Educational and Psychological Measurement, 52,* 921-931.

[756]

Developing Skills Checklist.
Purpose: Designed to measure skills and behaviors that children typically develop between prekindergarten and the end of kindergarten.
Population: Ages 4–6.8.
Publication Date: 1990.
Acronym: DSC.

Scores: 9 scales: Mathematical Concepts and Operations, Language, Memory, Auditory, Print Concepts, Motor, Visual, Writing and Drawing Concepts, Social-Emotional.
Administration: Individual.
Price Data: Price information available from publisher for test materials including Norms Book and Technical Bulletin (90 pages).
Time: Administration time not reported.
Authors: CTB Macmillan/McGraw-Hill.
Publisher: CTB Macmillan/McGraw-Hill.

[757]

Developmental Activities Screening Inventory—II.
Purpose: "Designed to provide early detection of developmental difficulties."
Population:: Ages birth to 60 months.
Publication Dates: 1977–84.
Acronym: DASI-II.
Scores: Total score only.
Administration: Individual.
Price Data, 1994: $59 per complete kit including 50 record forms, 37 Picture Cards, 5 Set-Configuration Cards, 2 pairs of Numeral Cards, 3 pairs of Word Cards, 4 Shape Cards, and examiner's manual ('84, 103 pages); $17 per 50 record forms; $19 per 56 Picture Cards; $26 per examiner's manual.
Time: (25–30) minutes.
Comments: Behavior checklist; same test materials (form board, bell) must be supplied by examiner.
Authors: Rebecca R. Fewell and Mary Beth Langley.
Publisher: PRO-ED, Inc.
Cross References: For reviews by Dennis C. Harper and William B. Michael, see 10:87; see also 9:323 (1 reference).

[758]

Developmental Assessment for the Severely Handicapped.
Purpose: To provide a discrete profile of functioning levels of skills across social-emotional, language, sensory-motor, activities of daily living, and preacademic areas.
Population: Individuals functioning within the 0–6 year developmental range.
Publication Date: 1980.
Acronym: DASH.
Scores: 5 developmental areas: Language, Sensory-Motor, Social-Emotional, Activities of Daily Living, Preacademic.
Administration: Individual.
Levels: 1 form in 5 booklets: Language (38 pages), Sensory-Motor (31 pages), Social-Emotional (23 pages), Activities of Daily Living (28 pages), Preacademic (47 pages).
Price Data, 1994: $98 per complete kit including manual (84 pages), 5 of each scale, and 25 each of other forms; $39 per 10 copies of any 1 scale; $17 per 50 Individualized Educational Plans; $11 per 50 Daily Plan Sheets; $11 per 50 Comprehensive Program Records.
Time: (120–180) minutes.
Comments: "Criterion-referenced"; criterion performance levels 1–7.
Author: Mary Kay Dykes.
Publisher: PRO-ED, Inc.
Cross References: For reviews by Harvey N. Switzky and David P. Wacker, see 9:324.

[759]

Developmental Assessment of Life Experiences [1986 Edition].
Purpose: Developed to assess motor, intellectual, and adaptive skills of disabled persons.
Population: Individuals in developmental settings.
Publication Dates: 1974–86.
Acronym: D.A.L.E. System.
Administration: Individual.
Price Data, 1990: $10.50 per complete set; $3.50 per Level I inventory; $3.50 per Level II inventory; $5 per manual ('86, 54 pages).
Time: Administration time not reported.
Authors: Gertrude A. Barber, John P. Mannino, and Robert J. Will.
Publisher: The Barber Center Press, Inc.
a) LEVEL I.
Scores: 5 categories: Sensory Motor, Language, Self-Help, Cognition Skills, Socialization.
b) LEVEL II.
Scores: 5 categories: Personal Hygiene, Personal Management, Communications, Residence/Home Management, Community Access.
Cross References: For a review by Frank M. Gresham of an earlier edition, see 9:295.

[760]

Developmental Challenge Profile: Learning from Job Experiences.
Purpose: "Designed to encourage managers and executives to think about their jobs from a developmental perspective."
Population: Managers.
Publication Date: 1993.
Scores: 16 developmental components: Transitions (Unfamiliar Responsibilities, Proving Yourself), Creating Change (Developing New Directions, Inherited Problems, Reduction Decisions, Problems with Employees), High Level of Responsibility (High Stakes, Managing Business Diversity, Job Overload, Handling External Pressure), Non-authority Relationships (Influencing Without Authority), Obstacles (Adverse Business Conditions, Lack of Top Management Support, Lack of Personal Support, Difficult Boss), Support (Supportive Boss).
Administration: Individual or group.
Price Data, 1993: $20 per profile.
Time: Administration time not reported.
Comments: Used in conjunction with BENCH-MARKS (290) which assesses managerial strengths and weaknesses.

Authors: Patricia J. Ohlott, Cynthia D. McCauley, and Marian N. Ruderman.
Publisher: Center for Creative Leadership.

[761]
Developmental History Checklist for Children.

Purpose: To document the developmental history of children.
Population: Ages 5–12.
Publication Date: 1989.
Scores: 7 Content Areas: Presenting Information, Personal Information/Family Background, Early Developmental History, Educational History, Medical History/Health Status, Family History, Current Behavior/Relationships.
Administration: Individual.
Manual: No manual.
Price Data, 1994: $30 per 25 checklists.
Time: Administration time not reported.
Comments: Designed to be completed by a parent, guardian, or clinician.
Authors: Edward H. Dougherty and John A. Schinka.
Publisher: Psychological Assessment Resources, Inc.

[762]
Developmental Indicators for the Assessment of Learning—Revised/AGS Edition.

Purpose: Constructed as a screening instrument to identify children with potential developmental problems and children who appear to be developing in an advanced manner.
Population: Ages 2-0 to 5-11.
Publication Dates: 1983–90.
Acronym: DIAL-R.
Scores, 4: Motor, Concepts, Language, Total.
Subtests, 3: Motor, Concepts, Language.
Administration: Individual.
Price Data, 1993: $249.95 per complete kit including area subtests for motor, concepts, and language areas, set of administrative forms (100 cutting cards, 50 record booklets), 50 parent information forms, training packet, and manual ('90, 148 pages); $119.95 per upgrade packet including set of administrative forms, 50 parent information forms, training packet, and manual; $34.40 per set of administrative forms; $17.45 per 50 Parent-Child Activity forms; $8.95 per set of 3 operator's handbooks.
Time: (20–30) minutes.
Comments: Revision of the 1983 revision of the Developmental Indicators for the Assessment of Learning.
Authors: Carol Mardell-Czudnowski and Dorothea S. Goldenberg.
Publisher: American Guidance Service.
Cross References: For reviews by David W. Barnett and G. Michael Poteat of an earlier version, see 10:89 (6 references); see also 9:326 (1 reference) and T3:696 (2 references); for reviews by J. Jeffrey Grill

and James J. McCarthy of an earlier edition, see 8:428 (3 references).

TEST REFERENCES

1. Vacc, N. A., Vacc, N. N., & Fogelman, M. S. (1987). Preschool screening: Using the DIAL as a predictor of first-grade performance. *Journal of School Psychology, 25,* 45-51.
2. Barnett, D. W., Faust, J., & Sarmir, M. A. (1988). A validity study of two preschool screening instruments: The LAP-D and DIAL-R. *Contemporary Educational Psychology, 13,* 26-32.
3. Gridley, B. E., Miller, G., Barke, C., Fischer, W., & Smith, D. (1990). Construct validity of the K-ABC with an at-risk preschool population. *Journal of School Psychology, 28,* 39-49.
4. May, D. C., & Kundert, D. K. (1992). Kindergarten screenings in New York state: Tests, purposes, and recommendations. *Psychology in the Schools, 29*(1), 35-41.
5. Schellinger, T., Beer, J., & Beer, J. (1992). Relationships between scores on the DIAL-R Concepts Scale and SRA scores. *Psychological Reports, 70,* 271-274.
6. Chew, A. L., & Lang, W. S. (1993). Concurrent validation and regression line comparisons on the Spanish edition of The Lollipop Test (La Prueba Lollipop) on a bilingual population. *Educational and Psychological Measurement, 53,* 173-182.

[763]
Developmental Observation Checklist System.

Purpose: "For the assessment of very young children with respect to general development (DC), adjustment behavior (ABC), and parent stress and support (PSSC)."
Population: Birth to age 6.
Publication Date: 1994.
Acronym: DOCS.
Scores, 12: Developmental Checklist (Cognition, Language, Social, Motor, Total); Adjustment Behavior Checklist (Mother, Father, Both Parents, Teacher); Parental Stress and Support Checklist (Mother, Father, Both Parents).
Administration: Individual.
Parts, 3: Developmental Checklist, Adjustment Behavior Checklist, Parental Stress and Support Checklist.
Price Data, 1994: $84 per complete kit including manual (91 pages), 25 profile/record forms, 25 DC profile/record forms, 25 ABC profile/record forms, and 25 PSSC profile/record forms; $28 per manual; $9 per 25 profile/record forms; $34 per 25 DC profile/record forms; $9 per ABC or PSSC profile/record forms; $89 per Macintosh PRO-SCORE system; $79 per IBM PRO-SCORE system.
Time: Administration time not reported.
Authors: Wayne P. Hresko, Shirley A. Miguel, Rita J. Sherbenou, and Steve D. Burton.
Publisher: PRO-ED, Inc.

[764]
Developmental Profile II.

Purpose: "Designed to assess a child's functional, developmental age level."
Population: Birth to age 9.5.
Publication Dates: 1972–86.
Acronym: DP-II.
Scores: Ratings in 5 areas: Physical Age, Self-Help Age, Social Age, Academic Age, Communication Age.

Administration: Group.
Price Data, 1993: $110 per kit including 25 scoring/profile forms, manual ('86, 95 pages), and 2 test report answer sheets; $42.50 per 25 scoring/profile forms; $50 per manual; $11 per test report answer sheet; $195 per microcomputer diskette for administration, scoring, and interpretation (25 uses per diskette).
Time: (20–40) minutes.
Comments: May be administered and scored by hand or using computer program; IBM PC, XT, AT, or compatibles needed for administration or in-house scoring by computer.
Authors: Gerald Alpern, Thomas Boll, and Marsha Shearer.
Publisher: Western Psychological Services.
Cross References: For reviews by A. Dirk Hightower and E. Scott Huebner, see 10:90 (3 references); for reviews by Dennis C. Harper and Sue White, see 9:327; see also T3:698 (5 references); for a review by Jane V. Hunt of the original edition, see 8:215 (1 reference).

TEST REFERENCES

1. Bloom, A. S., & Zelko, F. A. (1994). Variability in adaptive behavior in children with developmental delay. *Journal of Clinical Psychology, 50,* 261-265.

[765]
Developmental Task Analysis.

Purpose: To rate a child's accomplishment of behavioral tasks that are basic to success in learning.
Population: Grades K–6.
Publication Date: 1969.
Scores: 5 ratings: Social and Personal, Motor, Perceptual, Language, Thinking.
Administration: Individual.
Manual: No manual.
Price Data, 1989: $5 per 10 forms.
Time: (20–30) minutes.
Comments: Ratings by parent or other observer.
Author: Robert E. Valett.
Publisher: Fearon Education, David S. Lake Publishers.

[766]
Developmental Tasks for Kindergarten Readiness.

Purpose: Provide "school personnel with knowledge about a child's skills as or before (s)he enters school."
Population: Children prior to kindergarten entrance.
Publication Date: 1978.
Acronym: DTKR.
Scores: 12 subtest scores: Social Interaction, Name Printing, Body Concepts, Auditory Sequencing, Auditory Association, Visual Discrimination, Visual Memory, Visual Motor, Color Naming, Relational Concepts, Number Knowledge, Alphabet Knowledge.
Administration: Individual.
Price Data, 1989: $40 per complete kit; $22.50 per 25 record booklets; $9.75 per set of stimulus cards; $10 per manual (54 pages).

Time: (20–30) minutes.
Author: Walter J. Lesiak, Jr.
Publisher: Clinical Psychology Publishing Co., Inc.
Cross References: For reviews by Carol A. Gray and Sue White, see 9:328.

TEST REFERENCES

1. Lidz, C. S., & Ballester, L. E. (1986). Diagnostic implications of McCarthy Scale General Cognitive Index/Binet IQ discrepancies for low-socioeconomic-status preschool children. *Journal of School Psychology, 24,* 381-385.

[767]
Developmental Test of Visual Perception, Second Edition.

Purpose: Measures visual-perceptual and visual-motor abilities.
Population: Ages 4-0 to 10-11.
Publication Dates: 1961–93.
Acronym: DTVP-2.
Scores, 9: Motor-Reduced Visual Perception (Position in Space, Figure Ground, Visual Closure, Form Constancy), Visual-Motor Integration (Eye-Hand Coordination, Copying, Spatial Relations, Visual-Motor Speed), General Visual Perception.
Administration: Group.
Price Data, 1994: $124 per complete kit including examiner's manual ('93, 73 pages), picture book, 25 profile examiner record forms, and 25 response booklets; $29 per examiner's manual; $32 per picture book; $18 per 25 profile examiner record forms; $49 per 25 response booklets; $79 per IBM score system; $89 per Macintosh score system.
Time: (35–45) minutes.
Comments: 1993 revision of the Marianne Frostig Developmental Test of Visual Perception (DTVP).
Authors: Donald D. Hammill, Nils A. Pearson, and Judith K. Voress.
Publisher: PRO-ED, Inc.
Cross References: For reviews by Richard E. Darnell and David A. Sabatino of the earlier edition, see 9:650 (4 references); see also T3:1371 (25 references), 8:882 (72 references), and T2:1921 (43 references); for reviews by Brad S. Chissom, Newell C. Kephart, and Lester Mann, see 7:871 (117 references); for reviews by James M. Anderson and Mary C. Austin, see 6:553 (7 references).

TEST REFERENCES

1. Woo, E. Y. C., & Hoosain, R. (1984). Visual and auditory functions of Chinese dyslexics. *Psychologia, 27,* 164-170.
2. Ramseyer, G. C., & Cashen, V. M. (1985). The relationship of level of eye-hand coordination and answer marking format to the test performance of first-and second-grade pupils; implications for test validity. *Educational and Psychological Measurement, 45,* 369-375.

[768]
Developmental Test of Visual-Motor Integration [Third Revision].

Purpose: Constructed to screen for visual-motor problems.
Publication Dates: 1967–89.
Acronym: VMI.

Scores: Total score only.
Administration: Group.
Price Data, 1994: $20.42 per manual ('89, 112 pages).
Time: Administration time not reported.
Authors: Keith E. Beery and Norman A. Buktenica (tests).
Publisher: Modern Curriculum Press.

a) SHORT FORM.
Population: Ages 3–8.
Price Data: $41.12 per 25 test booklets.
b) SHORT FORM.
Population: Ages 3–18.
Price Data: $57.13 per 25 test booklets.

Cross References: See 9:329 (15 references) and T3:701 (57 references); for reviews of an earlier version by Donald A. Leton and James A. Rice, see 8:870 (24 references); see also T2:1875 (6 references); for a review by Brad S. Chissom, see 7:867 (5 references).

TEST REFERENCES

1. Hartlage, L. C., Telzrow, C. F., DeFilippis, N. A., Shaw, J. B., & Noonan, M. (1983). Personality correlates of functional cerebral asymmetry in preschool children. *Clinical Neuropsychology, 5,* 14-15.
2. Merritt, F. M., & McCallum, R. S. (1983). Sex-related differences in simultaneous-successive information processing? *Clinical Neuropsychology, 5,* 117-119.
3. Halperin, J. M., Gittelman, R., Klein, D. F., & Rudel, R. B. (1984). Reading disabled hyperactive children: A distinct subgroup of Attention Deficit Disorder with hyperactivity? *Journal of Abnormal Child Psychology, 12,* 1-14.
4. Merritt, F. M., & McCallum, R. S. (1984). The relationship between simultaneous-successive processing and academic achievement. *The Alberta Journal of Educational Research, 30,* 126-132.
5. Obrzut, A., Nelson, R. B., & Obrzut, J. E. (1984). Early school entrance for intellectually superior children: An analysis. *Psychology in the Schools, 21,* 71-77.
6. Perlmutter, B. F., & Bryan, J. H. (1984). First impressions, ingratiation, and the learning disabled child. *Journal of Learning Disabilities, 17,* 157-161.
7. Sandoval, J. (1984). Repeating the first grade: How the decision is made. *Psychology in the Schools, 21,* 457-462.
8. Shaheen, S. J. (1984). Neuromaturation and behavior development: The case of childhood lead poisoning. *Developmental Psychology, 20,* 542-550.
9. Webb, J., & Abe, K. (1984). Cross-cultural validity of the Developmental Test of Visual-Motor Integration. *Perceptual and Motor Skills, 58,* 183-188.
10. Breen, M. J., Carlson, M., & Lehman, J. (1985). The Revised Developmental Test of Visual Motor Integration: Its relation to the VMI, WISC-R, and Bender Gestalt for a group of elementary aged learning disabled students. *Journal of Learning Disabilities, 18,* 136-138.
11. Connelly, J. B. (1985). Published tests—which ones do special education teachers perceive as useful? *Journal of Special Education, 19,* 149-155.
12. Cunningham, C. E., Siegel, L. S., & Offord, D. R. (1985). A developmental dose-response analysis of the effects of methylphenidate on the peer interactions of attention deficit disordered boys. *Journal of Child Psychology and Psychiatry, 26,* 955-971.
13. Latorre, R. A. (1985). Kindergarten screening: A cross-validation of the Florida Kindergarten Screening Battery. *The Alberta Journal of Educational Research, 31,* 174-190.
14. Marozas, D. S., & May, D. C. (1985). Effects of figure-ground reversal on the visual-perceptual and visuo-motor performances of cerebral palsied and normal children. *Perceptual and Motor Skills, 60,* 591-598.
15. Rose, S. A., & Wallace, I. F. (1985). Cross-modal and intramodal transfer as predictors of mental development in full-term and preterm infants. *Developmental Psychology, 21,* 949-962.
16. Strawser, S., & Weller, C. (1985). Use of adaptive behavior and discrepancy criteria to determine learning disabilities severity subtypes. *Journal of Learning Disabilities, 18,* 205-211.
17. Webster, R. E. (1985). The criterion-related validity of psycho-

educational tests for actual reading ability of learning disabled students. *Psychology in the Schools, 22,* 152-159.
18. Aylward, E. H., & Schmidt, S. (1986). An examination of three tests of visual-motor integration. *Journal of Learning Disabilities, 19,* 328-330.
19. Goldstein, D. J., Smith, K. B., & Waldrep, E. E. (1986). Factor analytic study of the Kaufman Assessment Battery for Children. *Journal of Clinical Psychology, 42,* 890-894.
20. Hinshaw, S. P., Carte, E. T., & Morrison, D. C. (1986). Concurrent prediction of academic achievement in reading disabled children: The role of neuropsychological and intellectual measures at different ages. *Clinical Neuropsychology, 8,* 3-8.
21. Knoff, H. M., Cotter, V., & Coyle, W. (1986). Differential effectiveness of receptive language and visual-motor assessments in identifying academically gifted elementary school students. *Perceptual and Motor Skills, 63,* 719-725.
22. Morris, R., Blashfield, R., & Satz, P. (1986). Developmental classification of reading-disabled children. *Journal of Clinical and Experimental Neuropsychology, 8,* 371-392.
23. Shinn-Strieker, T. (1986). Patterns of cognitive style in normal and handicapped children. *Journal of Learning Disabilities, 19,* 572-576.
24. Cunningham, C. E., & Siegel, L. S. (1987). Peer interactions of normal and attention-deficit-disordered boys during free-play, cooperative task, and simulated classroom situations. *Journal of Abnormal Child Psychology, 15,* 247-268.
25. McCauley, E., Kay, T., Ito, J., & Treder, R. (1987). The turner syndrome: Cognitive deficits, affective discrimination, and behavior problems. *Child Development, 58,* 464-473.
26. Strein, W. (1987). Effects of age and visual-motor skills on preschool children's computer-game performance. *Journal of Research and Development in Education, 20*(2), 70-72.
27. Massman, P. J., Nussbaum, N. L., & Bigler, E. D. (1988). The mediating effect of age on the relationship between Child Behavior Checklist hyperactivity scores and neuropsychological test performance. *Journal of Abnormal Child Psychology, 16,* 89-95.
28. Stroebel, S. S., & Evans, J. R. (1988). Neuropsychological and environmental characteristics of early readers. *Journal of School Psychology, 26,* 243-252.
29. Goldstein, D. J., Peterson, N. C., & Sheaffer, C. I. (1989). Concurrent validity of the Gardner Test of Visual-Motor Skills. *Perceptual and Motor Skills, 69,* 605-606.
30. Mantzicopoulous, P., Morrison, D. C., Hinshaw, S. P., & Carte, E. T. (1989). Nonpromotion in kindergarten: The role of cognitive, perceptual, visual-motor, behavioral, achievement, socioeconomic, and demographic characteristics. *American Educational Research Journal, 26,* 107-121.
31. Glutting, J. J., & McDermott, P. A. (1990). Childhood learning potential as an alternative to traditional ability measure. *Psychological Assessment, 2,* 398-403.
32. Grant, M. L., Ilai, D., Nussbaum, N. L., & Bigler, E. D. (1990). The relationship between continuous performance tasks and neuropsychological tests in children with Attention-deficit Hyperactivity Disorder. *Perceptual and Motor Skills, 70,* 435-445.
33. Brand, H. J. (1991). Correlation for scores on Revised Test of Visual-Motor Integration and Copying Test for a South African sample. *Perceptual and Motor Skills, 73,* 225-226.
34. Frey, P. D., & Pinelli, B., Jr. (1991). Visual discrimination and visuomotor integration among two classes of Brazilian children. *Perceptual and Motor Skills, 72,* 847-850.
35. Stone, B. J., & Gridley, B. E. (1991). Test bias of a kindergarten screening battery: Predicting achievement for White and Native American elementary students. *School Psychology Review, 20,* 132-139.
36. Thompson, N. M., Fletcher, J. M., Chapieski, L., Landry, S. H., Miner, M. E., & Bixby, J. (1991). Cognitive and motor abilities in preschool hydrocephalics. *Journal of Clinical and Experimental Neuropsychology, 13,* 245-258.
37. Watson, J. M., & Wagner, E. E. (1991). Redundancy in perceptual-motor testing: Confirmation and generalization. *Perceptual and Motor Skills, 72,* 585-586.
38. Ferere, H., Burns, W. J., & Roth, L. (1992). Use of the Revised Developmental Test of Visual-Motor Integration with chronic mentally ill adult population. *Perceptual and Motor Skills, 74,* 287-290.
39. Ganschow, L., Sparks, R., & Helmick, M. (1992). Speech/language referral practices by school psychologists. *School Psychology Review, 21*(2), 313-326.
40. Robins, P. M. (1992). A comparison of behavioral and attentional functioning in children diagnosed as hyperactive or learning-disabled. *Journal of Abnormal Child Psychology, 20,* 65-82.
41. Jorgenson, C. B., Jorgenson, D. E., Gillis, M. K., & McCall, C. M. (1993). Validation of a screening instrument for young children with teacher assessment of school performance. *School Psychology Quarterly, 8,* 125-139.

42. Lincoln, A. J., Courchesne, E., Harms, L., & Allen, M. (1993). Contextual probability evaluation in autistic, receptive developmental language disorder, and control children: Event-related brain potential evidence. *Journal of Autism and Developmental Disorders, 23*, 37-58.

[769]

Devereux Behavior Rating Scale—School Form.

Purpose: To evaluate "behaviors typical of children and adolescents with moderate to severe emotional disturbance."

Population: Ages 5–18.

Publication Dates: 1990–93.

Acronym: BRSS.

Scores, 4: Interpersonal Problems, Inappropriate Behaviors/Feelings, Depression, Physical Symptoms/Fears.

Administration: Individual.

Forms, 2: Children, Adolescents.

Price Data, 1994: $95 per complete kit including manual ('93, 42 pages), 25 answer documents 5–12, and 25 ready score answer documents 13–18; $50 per manual; $22.50 per 25 ready score answer documents 5–12; $22.50 per 25 ready score answer documents 13–18.

Time: (5–10) minutes.

Comments: Ratings by parents and teachers.

Authors: Jack A. Naglieri, Paul A. LeBuffe, and Steven I. Pfeiffer.

Publisher: The Psychological Corporation.

[770]

The Devine Inventory.

Purpose: Designed to assist "in the selection, deployment and development of individuals" in job settings.

Population: Employees and prospective employees.

Publication Date: 1989.

Scores, 3: Problem Solving, Self Description, Personal Choices.

Administration: Group or individual.

Price Data, 1991: $1.75 per reusable booklet; $12.50 per 25 response forms.

Time: Administration time not reported.

Author: Donald W. Devine.

Publisher: Donald W. Devine & Associates.

[771]

DF Opinion Survey.

Purpose: Measurement of motivational factors related to personality and interest research, personnel selection, and vocational assessment.

Population: Grades 12–16 and adults.

Publication Dates: 1954–56.

Acronym: DFOS.

Scores, 10: Need for Attention, Liking for Thinking, Adventure vs. Security, Self-Reliance vs. Dependence, Aesthetic Appreciation, Cultural Conformity, Need for Freedom, Realistic Thinking, Need for Precision, Need for Diversion.

Administration: Group.

Price Data, 1989: $4 per review set (includes manual, test booklet, answer sheet, and profile); $2.50 per manual ('56, 3 pages); $11 per scoring key; $19 per 25 tests; $12 per 50 answer sheets; $9.50 per 50 profile sheets.

Time: (45) minutes.

Authors: J. P. Guilford, Paul R. Christensen, and Nicholas A. Bond, Jr.

Publisher: Consulting Psychologists Press, Inc.

Cross References: See T2:1151 (7 references) and P:54 (12 references); for reviews by Andrew R. Baggaley, John W. French, and Arthur W. Meadows, see 5:45.

[772]

Diagnosing Organizational Culture.

Purpose: "Designed to help consultants and organizational members identify the shared values and beliefs that constitute an organization's culture."

Population: Adults.

Publication Dates: 1992–93.

Scores: 5 scores (Power, Role, Achievement, Support, Total) in each of two areas: Existing Culture, Preferred Culture.

Administration: Group.

Price Data, 1993: $24.95 per complete kit including trainer's manual ('93, 58 pages) and instrument ('92, 30 pages); $8.95 per instrument.

Time: (45–60) minutes.

Authors: Roger Harrison and Herb Stokes (instrument only).

Publisher: Pfeiffer & Company International Publishers.

[773]

Diagnosis and Remediation of Handwriting Problems.

Purpose: "To provide the teacher with a systematic means of identifying faults of handwriting . . . as remedial materials . . . for clinical assessment and empirical research . . . teacher education."

Population: Children with at least 2 years of instruction in writing.

Publication Date: 1985.

Acronym: DRHP.

Scores, 2: Faults of Concept and Style, Faults Suggestive of Motor or Perceptual Problems.

Administration: Group.

Price Data, 1985: $39.50 per complete kit including 20 student writing sheets, 20 diagnostic record forms, 6 student's specimens of writing sheets, 1 group score sheet, 1 diagnostic template, and manual (64 pages); $1.92 per 20 student writing sheets; $4.02 per 20 diagnostic record forms; $2.43 per 10 student's specimens of writing sheets; $3 per 10 group score sheets; $19.50 per 10 diagnostic templates; $15 per manual.

Time: (20) minutes.

Authors: Denis H. Stott, Fred A. Moyes, and Shelia E. Henderson.

Publisher: Durkin Hayes Publishing Ltd. [Canada].

Cross References: For a review by Edward A. Polloway, see 10:91.

[774]
Diagnostic Achievement Battery, Second Edition.

Purpose: "To assess children's abilities in listening, speaking, reading, writing, and mathematics."
Population: Ages 6-0 to 14-11.
Publication Dates: 1984–90.
Acronym: DAB-2.
Scores, 20: Spoken Language (Listening [Sentence Completion, Characteristics], Speaking [Synonyms, Grammatic Completion]), Written Language (Reading [Reading Comprehension, Alphabet/Word Knowledge], Writing [Punctuation, Spelling, Capitalization, Writing Composition]), Mathematics (Math Calculation, Math Reasoning), Total Achievement.
Administration: Individual.
Price Data, 1994: $119 per complete kit; $29 per student booklet; $34 per 25 profile/answer sheets; $29 per 25 student worksheets; $31 per manual ('90, 99 pages); $79 per computer scoring system (specify IBM or Apple).
Time: (60–120) minutes.
Authors: Phyllis L. Newcomer and Dolores Curtis (student booklet).
Publisher: PRO-ED, Inc.
Cross References: For a review by William J. Webster of the original edition, see 9:333.

TEST REFERENCES

1. Lewandowski, L. J. (1985). Diagnostic Achievement Battery. *The Reading Teacher, 39,* 306–309.

[775]
Diagnostic Achievement Test for Adolescents, Second Edition.

Purpose: To provide "examiners with an estimate of students' listening and speaking skills and their knowledge of information commonly taught in schools."
Population: Ages 12-0 to 18-11.
Publication Dates: 1986–93.
Acronym: DATA-2.
Scores, 22: 13 subtest scores (Receptive Vocabulary, Receptive Grammar, Expressive Grammar, Expressive Vocabulary, Word Identification, Reading Comprehension, Spelling, Writing Composition, Math Calculation, Math Problem Solving, Science, Social Studies, Reference Skills) and 9 composite scores (Listening, Speaking, Reading, Writing, Math, Spoken Language, Written Language, Achievement Screener, Total Achievement).
Administration: Individual.
Price Data, 1994: $104 per complete kit including examiner's manual ('93, 73 pages), 25 student response forms, 25 profile/examiner record forms, and a student booklet; $29 per examiner's manual; $18 per 25 student response forms; $39 per 25 profile/examiner record forms; $22 per student booklet; $89 per

Macintosh PRO-SCORE; $79 per IBM PRO-SCORE.
Time: (60–120) minutes.
Authors: Phyllis L. Newcomer and Brian R. Bryant.
Publisher: PRO-ED, Inc.
Cross References: For reviews of an earlier edition by Randy W. Kamphaus and James E. Ysseldyke, see 10:92.

[776]
A Diagnostic Achievement Test in Spelling.

Purpose: Measures spelling ability and diagnoses specific spelling deficiencies.
Population: Grades 2–10.
Publication Date: 1980.
Scores: Total score determining grade placement.
Administration: Group.
Price Data: Not available.
Time: [20–25] minutes.
Comments: Administered to determine pupil's proper placement in the Prescriptive Spelling Program.
Authors: William Wittenberg, William J. McKeough, and Patricia P. Ramsey.
Publisher: Barnell Loft, Ltd. [No reply from publisher; status unknown].
Cross References: For reviews by C. Dale Carpenter and Jeffrey K. Smith, see 10:93.

[777]
Diagnostic Assessments of Reading.

Purpose: Constructed to assess skills in reading and language.
Population: Grades 1–12.
Publication Date: 1992.
Acronym: DAR.
Scores: Mastery level scores in 6 areas: Word Recognition, Word Analysis, Oral Reading, Silent Reading Comprehension, Spelling, Word Meaning.
Administration: Individual.
Price Data, 1992: $150 per complete kit including testing materials listed below plus teaching strategies materials; $12 per student book; $15 per 15 student record booklets; $30 per response record with directions for administration; $6 per manual (33 pages).
Time: (20–30) minutes.
Authors: Florence G. Roswell and Jeanne S. Chall.
Publisher: The Riverside Publishing Co.

[778]
Diagnostic Guide to DSM III.

Purpose: Checklist for "clinician generated diagnoses" according to DSM III (does not include child, sexual, or adjustment disorders).
Population: Adults.
Publication Date: 1983.
Scores: 8 axis I scores (Organic Disorders, Substance Abuse, Psychosis, Paranoid, Affective, Anxiety, Somatoform, Dissociative), 1 axis II score (Personality Disorder), and 3 ratings (Presence of Medical His-

tory, Severity of Psychosocial Stressor, Highest Level of Adaptive Functioning Last Year).
Administration: Individual.
Price Data: Not available.
Time: 10(20) minutes.
Authors: Joel Butler, Frank Lawlis, and Myrna Niccolette.
Publisher: The Wilmington Press [No reply from publisher; status unknown].

TEST REFERENCES

1. Nelson-Gray, R. O., Lin, K., & Torquato, R. (1991). Confidential and shared reactions of strangers and familiar observers to depressives. *Journal of Social and Clinical Psychology, 10,* 176-189.
2. Brown, G. W., Lemyre, L., & Bifulco, A. (1992). Social factors and recovery from anxiety and depressive disorders. *British Journal of Psychiatry, 161,* 44-54.
3. D'Amato, T., Campion, D., Gorwood, Ph., Jay, M., Sabate, O., Petit, C., Abbar, M., Malafosse, A., Leboyer, M., Hillaire, D., Clerget-Darpoux, F., Feingold, J., Waksman, G., & Mallet, J. (1992). Evidence for a pseudoautosomal locus for schizophrenia II. *British Journal of Psychiatry, 161,* 59-62.
4. Chadda, R. K., Bhatia, M. S., Shome, S., & Thakur, K. N. (1993). Psychosocial dysfunction in somatising patients. *British Journal of Psychiatry, 163,* 510-513.
5. Craig, T. K. J., Boardman, A. P., Mills, K., Daly-Jones, O., & Drake, H. (1993). The south London somatisation study I: Longitudinal course and the influence of early life experiences. *British Journal of Psychiatry, 163,* 579-588.
6. Dilsaver, S. C., Del Medico, V. J., & Qamar, A. B. (1993). State-dependent pain in winter depression. *British Journal of Psychiatry, 163,* 672-674.
7. Duinkerke, S. J., Botter, P. A., Jansen, A. I., Van Dongen, P. A. M., Van Haaften, A. J., Boom, A. J., Van Laarhoven, J. H. M., & Busard, H. L. S. M. (1993). Ritanserin, a selective 5-HT2/1C antagonist, and negative symptoms in schizophrenia. *British Journal of Psychiatry, 163,* 451-455.
8. Fiordelli, E., Beghi, E., Bogiun, G., & Crespi, V. (1993). Epilepsy and psychiatric disturbance: A cross-sectional study. *British Journal of Psychiatry, 163,* 446-450.
9. Gala, C., Pergami, A., Catalan, J., Durbano, F., Musicco, M., Riccio, M., Baldeweg, T., & Invernizzi, G. (1993). The psychosocial impact of HIV infection in gay men, drug users and heterosexuals. *British Journal of Psychiatry, 163,* 651-659.
10. McKeith, I. G., Bartholomew, P. H., Irvine, E. M., Cook, J., Adams, R., & Simpson, A. E. S. (1993). Single photon emission computerised tomography in elderly patients with Alzheimer's disease and multi-infarct dementia. *British Journal of Psychiatry, 163,* 597-603.
11. Morgan, K., Lilley, J. M., Arie, T., Byrne, E. J., Jones, R., & Waite, J. (1993). Incidence of dementia in a representative British sample. *British Journal of Psychiatry, 163,* 467-470.
12. Patel, P., Goldberg, D., & Moss, S. (1993). Psychiatric morbidity in older people with moderate and severe learning disability: II. *British Journal of Psychiatry, 163,* 481-491.
13. Rubin, P., Karle, A., Moller-Madsen, S., Hertel, C., Povlsen, U. J., Noring, U., & Hemmingsen, R. (1993). Computerized tomography in newly diagnosed schizophrenia and schizophreniform disorder. *British Journal of Psychiatry, 163,* 604-612.
14. Soni, S. D., Tench, D., & Routledge, R. C. (1993). Serum iron abnormalities in neuroleptic-induced akathisia in schizophrenic patients. *British Journal of Psychiatry, 163,* 669-672.
15. Stallard, P., & Law, F. (1993). Screening and psychological debriefing of adolescent survivors of life-threatening events. *British Journal of Psychiatry, 163,* 660-665.
16. Trimble, M. R., & Pugh, C. (1993). Psychiatric injury after Hillsborough. *British Journal of Psychiatry, 163,* 425-429.
17. Warner, R., & Huxley, P. (1993). Psychopathology and quality of life among mentally ill patients in the community: British and U.S. samples compared. *British Journal of Psychiatry, 163,* 505-509.

[779]

Diagnostic Interview for Borderline Patients.

Purpose: Designed to discriminate borderline patients from patients with schizophrenia, neurotic depression, and mixed diagnoses.

Population: Patients.
Publication Dates: [1982–83].
Scores, 6: Social Adaptation, Impulse Action Patterns, Affects, Psychosis, Interpersonal Relations, Total.
Administration: Individual.
Price Data: Available from publisher.
Time: (50–90) minutes.
Authors: John G. Gunderson (interview), Pamela S. Ludolph (manual), Kenneth R. Silk (manual), Naomi E. Lohr (manual), and Dewey G. Cornell (manual).
Publisher: Interview distributed by Pfizer (no reply from publisher; status unknown); manual distributed by Pamela S. Ludolph.
Cross References: For reviews by Robert E. Deysach and Charles A. Peterson, see 10:95 (12 references).

TEST REFERENCES

1. Zubenko, G. S., George, A. W., Soloff, P. H., & Schulz, P. (1987). Sexual practices among patients with borderline personality disorder. *American Journal of Psychiatry, 144,* 748-752.
2. Angus, L. E., & Marziali, E. (1988). A comparison of three measures for the diagnosis of borderline personality disorder. *American Journal of Psychiatry, 145,* 1453-1454.
3. Joffe, R. T., Swinson, R. P., & Regan, J. J. (1988). Personality features of obsessive-compulsive disorder. *American Journal of Psychiatry, 145,* 1127-1129.
4. Nurnberg, H. G., Hurt, S. W., Feldman, A., & Suh, R. (1988). Evaluation of diagnostic criteria for borderline personality disorder. *American Journal of Psychiatry, 145,* 1280-1284.
5. Paris, J., & Frank, H. (1989). Perceptions of parental bonding in borderline patients. *American Journal of Psychiatry, 146,* 1498-1499.
6. Sansone, R. A., Fine, M. A., Seuferer, S., & Bovenzi, J. (1989). The prevalence of borderline personality symptomatology among women with eating disorders. *Journal of Clinical Psychology, 45,* 603-610.
7. Swartz, M. S., Blazer, D. G., George, L. K., Winfield, I., Zakris, J., & Dye, E. (1989). Identification of borderline personality disorder with the NIMH Diagnostic Interview Schedule. *American Journal of Psychiatry, 146,* 200-205.
8. Kavoussi, R. J., Coccaro, E. F., Klar, H. M., Bernstein, D., & Siever, L. J. (1990). Structured interviews for borderline personality disorder. *American Journal of Psychiatry, 147,* 1522-1525.
9. Ludolph, P. S., Westen, D., Misle, B., Jackson, A., Wixom, J., & Wiss, F. C. (1990). The borderline diagnosis in adolescents: Symptoms and developmental history. *American Journal of Psychiatry, 147,* 470-476.
10. Marziali, E., & Oleniuk, J. (1990). Object representations in descriptions of significant others: A methodological study. *Journal of Personality Assessment, 54,* 105-115.
11. Ogata, S. N., Silk, K. R., Goodrich, S., Lohr, N. E., Westen, D., & Hill, E. M. (1990). Childhood sexual and physical abuse in adult patients with borderline personality disorder. *American Journal of Psychiatry, 147,* 1008-1013.
12. Ronningstam, E., & Gunderson, J. (1990). Identifying criteria for narcissistic personality disorders. *American Journal of Psychiatry, 147,* 918-922.
13. Westen, D., Lohr, N., Silk, K. R., Gold, L., & Kerber, K. (1990). Object relations and social cognition in borderlines, major depressives, and normals: A Thematic Apperception Test analysis. *Psychological Assessment, 2,* 355-364.
14. Zanarini, M. C., Gunderson, J. G., Frankenburg, F. R., & Chauncey, D. L. (1990). Discriminating borderline personality disorder from other Axis II disorders. *American Journal of Psychiatry, 147,* 161-167.
15. Nigg, J. T., Silk, K. R., Westen, D., Lohr, N. E., Gold, L. J., Goodrich, S., & Ogata, S. (1991). Object representation in the early memories of sexually abused borderline patients. *American Journal of Psychiatry, 148,* 864-869.
16. O'Leary, K. M., Brouwers, P., Gardner, D. L., & Cowdry, R. W. (1991). Neuropsychological testing of patients with borderline personality disorder. *American Journal of Psychiatry, 148,* 106-111.
17. Zweig-Frank, H., & Paris, J. (1991). Parents' emotional neglect and overprotection according to the recollections of patients with borderline personality disorder. *American Journal of Psychiatry, 148,* 648-651.
18. Baker, L., Silk, K. R., Westen, D., Nigg, J. T., & Lohr,

N. E. (1992). Malevolence, splitting, and parental ratings by border-lines. *Journal of Nervous and Mental Disease, 180*, 258-264.

19. Nigg, J. T., Lohr, N. E., Westen, D., Gold, L. J., & Silk, K. R. (1992). Malevolent object representations in borderline personality disorder and major depression. *Journal of Abnormal Psychology, 101*, 61-67.

[780]

Diagnostic Inventory for Screening Children.

Purpose: A diagnostic screening tool used to identify developmental delays in preschool children.
Population: Birth–5 years.
Publication Dates: 1984–88.
Acronym: DISC.
Scores, 8: Fine Motor, Receptive Language, Expressive Language, Gross Motor, Auditory Attention and Memory, Visual Attention and Memory, Self-Help, Social.
Administration: Individual.
Price Data, 1994: $563 per complete kit; $29 per manual ('88, 163 pages); $86 per 40 record forms; $13 per 40 summary Sheet A; $12 per 40 summary Sheet B; $12 per 40 item performance summary sheets; $14.50 per training videotape manual; $13 per age equivalents profile.
Time: (15–45) minutes.
Authors: Jeanette Amdur, Marian Mainland, and Kevin Parker.
Publisher: The Psychological Corporation.

TEST REFERENCES

1. Parker, K. C. H., Mainland, M. K., & Amdur, J. R. (1990). The Diagnostic Inventory for Screening Children: Psychometric, factor, and validity analyses. *Canadian Journal of Behavioural Science, 22*, 361-376.

2. Cooper, P. J., & Goodyer, I. (1993). A community study of depression in adolescent girls. I: Estimates of symptom and syndrome prevalence. *British Journal of Psychiatry, 163*, 369-374.

3. Goodyer, I., & Cooper, P. J. (1993). A community study of depression in adolescent girls. II: The clinical features of identified disorder. *British Journal of Psychiatry, 163*, 374-380.

[781]

Diagnostic Mathematics Profiles.

Purpose: Constructed to diagnose problems in addition, subtraction, multiplication, and division.
Population: Australian school years 3–6.
Publication Date: 1990.
Scores: Item scores only.
Administration: Group or individual.
Parts, 4: Addition, Subtraction, Multiplication, Division.
Price Data, 1994: A$37.50 per test package including 30 copies of each part; $14.50 per manual (23 pages).
Time: Administration time not reported.
Author: Brian Doig.
Publisher: Australian Council for Educational Research Ltd. [Australia].

[782]

Diagnostic Reading Scales.

Purpose: Designed to "identify strengths and weaknesses that affect reading proficiency at the grade levels in which reading is normally taught."

Population: Grades 1–7 and poor readers in Grades 8–12.
Publication Dates: 1963–81.
Acronym: DRS-81.
Scores, 15: 3 derived Scores: Instructional Level, Independent Level, Potential Level, plus 12 raw Scores: Initial Consonants, Final Consonants, Consonant Digraphs, Consonant Blends, Initial Consonant Substitution, Initial Consonant Sounds Recognized Auditorily, Auditory Discrimination, Short and Long Vowel Sounds, Vowels with R, Vowel Diphthongs and Digraphs, Common Syllables or Phonograms, Blending.
Administration: Individual.
Price Data, 1994: $36.15 per specimen set including student reading book, examiner's record booklet, examiner's manual ('81, 59 pages), and test reviewer's guide; $10.25 per student reading book; $82.25 per 35 examiner's record booklets; $12.20 per examiner's manual; $7.15 per examiner's cassette; $12.25 per technical report; $12.60 per CTB test organizer.
Time: (60) minutes for entire battery.
Author: George D. Spache.
Publisher: CTB MacMillan/McGraw-Hill.
Cross References: For reviews by Ray R. Buss and Steve Wise, see 9:338 (4 references); see also T3:719 (13 references); for reviews by Nancy L. Roser and Robert L. Schreiner, and an excerpted review by Jerry Stafford of an earlier edition, see 8:753 (15 references); see also T2:1624 (4 references); for a review by Rebecca C. Barr, see 7:717 (7 references); for a review by N. Dale Bryant, see 6:821.

TEST REFERENCES

1. Gold, P. C., & Horn, P. L. (1983). Intelligence and achievement of adult illiterates in a tutorial project: A preliminary analysis. *Journal of Clinical Psychology, 39*, 107-113.

2. Lomax, R. G. (1983). Applying structural modeling to some component processes of reading comprehension development. *The Journal of Experimental Education, 52*, 33-40.

3. Koskinen, P. S., & Blum, I. H. (1984). Repeated oral reading and the acquisition of fluency. *National Reading Conference Yearbook, 33*, 183-187.

4. Lewis, H. W. (1984). A structured group counseling program for reading disabled elementary students. *The School Counselor, 31*, 454-459.

5. Lomax, R. G. (1984). A component processes model of reading comprehension development: A comparison of normal and learning disabled children. *National Reading Conference Yearbook, 33*, 308-316.

6. Paris, S. G., & Jacobs, J. E. (1984). The benefits of informed instruction for children's reading awareness and comprehension skills. *Child Development, 55*, 2083-2093.

7. Connelly, J. B. (1985). Published tests—which ones do special education teachers perceive as useful? *Journal of Special Education, 19*, 149-155.

8. Lipa, S. (1985). Diagnostic Reading Scales. *The Reading Teacher, 38*, 664-667.

9. Webster, R. E. (1988). Variability in reading achievement test scores as related to reading curriculum. *Educational and Psychological Measurement, 48*, 815-825.

[783]

Diagnostic Reading Tests.

Purpose: Assesses reading skills "in four areas: auditory discrimination and word attack, vocabulary, comprehension, and rates of reading."
Population: Grades K–4, 4–8, 7–13.

Publication Dates: 1947–52.
Acronym: DRT.
Administration: Group.
Price Data: Not available.
Time: Administration time not reported.
Author: Committee on Diagnostic Reading Tests, Inc.
Publisher: Committee on Diagnostic Reading Tests, Inc. [No reply from publisher; status unknown].

   a) DIAGNOSTIC READING TESTS: KINDERGARTEN THROUGH FOURTH GRADES.
   b) DIAGNOSTIC READING TESTS: LOWER LEVEL.
   c) DIAGNOSTIC READING TESTS: UPPER LEVEL.

Cross References: See T3:720 (5 references), 8:754 (4 references), T2:1626 (21 references); for reviews by Albert J. Kingston and B. H. VanRoekel, see 6:823 (21 references); for reviews by Frederick B. Davis, William W. Turnbull, and Henry Weitz, see 4:531 (19 references).

TEST REFERENCES

1. Butter, E. J., & Jeffcott, R. E. (1982). Prediction of adults' reading performance as a function of auditory and visual cognitive styles and intelligence. *Perceptual and Motor Skills, 54,* 359-362.
2. Jacobowitz, T., & Haupt, E. J. (1984). Retrieval speed in reading comprehension: Failure to generalize. *National Reading Conference Yearbook, 33,* 241-246.
3. Searls, E. F., & Neville, D. D. (1988). An exploratory review of sentence-combining research related to reading. *Journal of Research and Development in Education, 21*(3) 1-15.

[784]

The Diagnostic Screening Batteries.
Purpose: Designed to provide clinicians with a structured intake interview procedure that samples a broad range of clinical possibilities in a systematic fashion.
Population: Ages 2 to adults.
Publication Dates: 1984–89..
Scores: No scores.
Administration: Individual.
Editions, 3: Child, Adolescent, Adult.
Price Data: Available from publisher.
Time: Administration time not reported.
Comments: Computer administration; IBM and Apple versions available.
Authors: James J. Smith, Joseph M. Eisenberg, and Joseph M. Ferraro.
Publisher: Reason House, Ltd.

[785]

Diagnostic Screening Test: Achievement.
Purpose: Designed "for estimating practical data about student's overall school achievement level in general, and achievement in Science, Social Studies, and Literature and the Arts more specifically."
Population: Grades K–12.
Publication Date: 1977.
Acronym: DSTA.
Scores, 5: Science, Social Studies, Literature and the Arts, Practical Knowledge, Total Achievement.
Administration: Group.

Price Data, 1992: $40 per complete kit including manual (12 pages) and 50 test forms; $26 per 50 test forms.
Time: (5–10) minutes.
Authors: Thomas D. Gnagey and Patricia A. Gnagey.
Publisher: Slosson Educational Publications, Inc.
Cross References: For a review by Edward F. Iwanicki, see 9:339.

[786]

Diagnostic Screening Test: Language, Second Edition.
Purpose: Designed "for estimating over-all achievement level in written language."
Population: Grades 1–12.
Publication Date: 1977.
Acronym: DSTL.
Scores, 8: Punctuation, Grammar, Spelling Rules, Sentence Structure, Capitalization, Formal Knowledge of Language, Applied Knowledge of Language, Total Language.
Administration: Group.
Price Data, 1992: $40 per complete kit including manual (12 pages) and 50 test forms; $26 per 50 test forms.
Time: (5–10) minutes.
Authors: Thomas D. Gnagey and Patricia A. Gnagey.
Publisher: Slosson Educational Publications, Inc.
Cross References: For reviews by Janice Arnold Dole and Edward J. Iwanicki, see 9:340.

[787]

Diagnostic Screening Test: Math, Third Edition.
Purpose: Designed for estimating practical data about students' mathematical skills.
Population: Grades 1–11.
Publication Date: 1980.
Acronym: DSTM.
Scores, 31: Basic Process Scores (Addition, Subtraction, Multiplication, Division, Total), Specialized Process Scores (Money, Time, Percent, U.S. Measurement, Metric Measurement, Total), Concept Scores (Process, Sequencing, Simple Computation, Complex Computation, Special Manipulations, Use of Zero, Decimals, Simple Fractions, Manipulation in Fractions), 11 consolidation index scores.
Administration: Group.
Price Data, 1992: $38 per complete kit including manual (17 pages), 25 test Form A, and 25 test Form B; $19 per 50 test Form A; $19 per 50 test Form B.
Time: (5–20) minutes.
Author: Thomas D. Gnagey.
Publisher: Slosson Educational Publications, Inc.
Cross References: For reviews by Edward F. Iwanicki and Stanley F. Vasa, see 9:341.

[788]

Diagnostic Screening Test: Reading, Third Edition.

Purpose: Designed "for estimating practical data about students' reading skills."
Population: Grades 1–12.
Publication Date: 1979.
Acronym: DSTR.
Scores, 16: Comfort Reading Level, Instructional Reading Level, Frustration Reading Level, Comprehension Reading Level, Listening Level, Phonics/Sight Ratio, Word Attack Skill Analysis (c-v/c, v-r, v-l, v-v, c-v-c, Silent e, Mix, Site, Total), Consolidation Index.
Administration: Individual.
Price Data, 1992: $38 per complete kit including manual (13 pages), 25 test Form A, and 25 test Form B; $19 per 50 test Form A; $19 per 50 test Form B.
Time: (5–10) minutes.
Authors: Thomas D. Gnagey and Patricia A. Gnagey.
Publisher: Slosson Educational Publications, Inc.
Cross References: For a review by Edward F. Inwanick, see 9:342; for a review by P. David Pearson of an earlier edition, see 8:755.

[789]

Diagnostic Screening Test: Spelling, Third Edition.

Purpose: Designed to gather diagnostic information regarding spelling skills.
Population: Grades 1–12.
Publication Date: 1979.
Acronym: DSTS.
Scores, 12: 3 scores (Verbal, Written, Total) for each of 3 categories (Phonics, Sight, Total); 3 Consolidation Index scores (Phonics Written, Sight Written, Total Spelling Written).
Administration: Group.
Price Data, 1992: $38 per complete kit including manual (13 pages), 25 test Form A, and 25 test Form B; $19 per 50 test Form A; $19 per 50 test Form B.
Time: (5–10) minutes.
Author: Thomas D. Gnagey.
Publisher: Slosson Educational Publications, Inc.
Cross References: For reviews by Edward F. Iwanicki and Robert E. Schafer, see 9:343 (4 references).

[790]

Diagnostic Spelling Potential Test.

Purpose: Constructed to assess "present level of spelling performance and . . . potential for spelling improvement."
Population: Ages 7 and over.
Publication Date: 1982.
Acronym: DSPT.
Scores, 5: Spelling, Word Recognition (Sight, Phonetic), Visual Recognition, Auditory-Visual Recognition.

Administration: Individual.
Forms, 2: A, B.
Price Data, 1994: $45 per complete kit including 25 tests (Form A), 25 profile sheets, and manual (160 pages); $10 per 25 tests (specify form and subtest); $4 per 25 profile sheets; $18 per manual; $18 per specimen kit.
Time: (25–40) minutes.
Author: John Arena.
Publisher: Academic Therapy Publications.
Cross References: For reviews by Marcee J. Meyers and Ruth Noyce, see 9:345 (1 reference).

TEST REFERENCES

1. Ormrod, J. E., & Lounge, J. P. (1990). Automaticity in spelling competence. *Perceptual and Motor Skills, 71,* 384-386.

[791]

Diagnostic Spelling Test.

Purpose: "Designed for the identification and diagnosis of spelling difficulty."
Population: Ages 8–12.
Publication Dates: 1981–82.
Acronym: DST.
Scores, 9: Homophones, Common Words, Proof-Reading, Letter Strings, Nonsense Words, Dictionary Use, Dictation, Total, Self-Concept.
Administration: Group.
Forms, 2: A, B.
Price Data, 1989: £9.80 per 25 pupil's booklets (Form A or Form B); £7.20 per teacher's manual ('82, 18 pages) and specimen set.
Time: (50–60) minutes.
Authors: Denis Vincent and Jenny Claydon.
Publisher: NFER-Nelson Publishing Co., Ltd. [England].
Cross References: For reviews by Gwyneth M. Boodoo and Philip L. Smith, see 9:346.

[792]

Diagnostic Teacher-Rating Scale.

Purpose: Ratings by pupils of qualities liked and disliked in their teachers.
Population: Grades 4–12.
Publication Dates: 1938–52.
Scores: 8 ratings: Liking for Teacher, Ability to Explain, Kindness-Friendliness-Understanding, Fairness in Grading, Discipline, Work Required, Liking for Lessons, Total.
Administration: Group and individual.
Price Data, 1994: $20 per kit; $10 per specimen set.
Time: Administration time not reported.
Comments: Ratings by pupils; originally published in 1938 for use in grades 4–8.
Author: Mary Amatora.
Publisher: Educators'/Employers' Tests and Services Associates.
Cross References: For additional information, see 6:696; for a review by Dorothy M. Clendenen, see 5:534 (5 references); see also 4:795 (2 references).

[793]

Diagnostic Test for Students of English as a Second Language.

Purpose: To assess language skills.
Population: Applicants from non-English countries for admission into American colleges.
Publication Date: 1953.
Scores: Total score only.
Administration: Group.
Price Data: Not available.
Time: 60(65) minutes.
Author: A. L. Davis.
Publisher: Webster Division, McGraw-Hill Book Co., Inc. [No reply from publisher; status unknown].
Cross References: See T2:227 (1 reference); for review by N. Brooks and H. T. Manuel, see 5:255.

[794]

Diagnostic Test of Arithmetic Strategies.

Purpose: "Designed to measure the procedures elementary school children use to perform arithmetic calculations."
Population: Grades 1–6.
Publication Date: 1984.
Acronym: DTAS.
Scores: No scores; 4 areas: Setting Up the Problem, Number Facts, Written Calculations, Informal Skills.
Administration: Individual.
Forms, 4: Addition, Subtraction, Multiplication, Division.
Price Data, 1994: $89 per complete kit including 25 answer sheets and work sheets for each form plus manual (63 pages); $16 per 25 answer sheets and worksheets (specify addition, subtraction, multiplication, or division); $29 per manual.
Time: (70–90) minutes.
Authors: Herbert P. Ginsberg and Steven C. Mathews.
Publisher: PRO-ED, Inc.
Cross References: For a review by Lawrence M. Aleamoni, see 9:348.

[795]

Diagnostic Test of Library Skills.

Purpose: To evaluate students' current knowledge of library skills.
Population: Grades 5–9.
Publication Date: 1981.
Acronym: DTLS.
Scores: Total score only.
Administration: Group.
Forms, 2: A, B.
Price Data, 1986: $26.95 per complete kit including 50 test booklets, 100 answer sheets, 1 scoring key, teacher's guide (2 pages); reorder form for individual components.
Time: (30) minutes.
Authors: Barbara Feldstein and Janet Rawdon.
Publisher: Learnco, Inc.

[796]

Diagnostic Test of Library Skills—Advanced.

Purpose: To evaluate students' current knowledge of library skills.
Population: Grades 9–12.
Publication Date: 1993.
Acronym: DTLS-A.
Scores: Total score only.
Administration: Group.
Price Data, 1993: $29.95 per complete kit including 50 test booklets, 100 answer sheets, scoring key, teacher's guide, and reorder form for individual components.
Time: (30) minutes.
Comments: Upward extension of Diagnostic Test of Library Skills (795).
Author: Susan E. Bailey.
Publisher: Learnco Inc.

[797]

Diagnostic Tests for Minimal Math Competencies.

Purpose: Designed to identify areas of student strength and weakness in general mathematics competencies.
Population: High school students.
Publication Date: 1980.
Scores: Diagnostic tests for 28 competencies: One Digit/One Step/Addition and Subtraction, One Digit/One Step/Multiplication and Division, One or More Digits/One or More Steps/Addition/Subtraction/Multiplication or Division, Elapsed Time/Clocks, Elapsed Time/Calendar, Equivalent Amounts of Money and Operations on Money Amounts, Fractions/Addition and Subtraction, Fractions/Multiplication and Division, Mixed Numbers/All Operations, Determining Percents and Decimal Equivalents from Whole Numbers and Fractions, Decimals and Percents/Addition and Subtraction, Decimals and Percents/Multiplication and Division, U.S. Measures of Length, U.S. Measures of Capacity, U.S. Measures of Weight, Metric Measures of Length, Metric Measures of Capacity, Metric Measures of Weight, Temperature Scales, Ratios and Proportions, Areas and Perimeters of Rectangles, Areas and Perimeters of Plane Figures Other than Rectangles, Angles and Lines, Statistics: Averages and the Range, Line Graphs, Bar Graphs, Circle Graphs, Tables.
Administration: Group.
Price Data, 1993: $18.95 per set of tests.
Time: Administration time not reported.
Authors: Fred Pyrczak and John Longmire.
Publisher: J. Weston Walch, Publisher.

[798]

Diagnostic Tests in Mathematics.

Purpose: "To determine the nature and extent of the problems encountered by a pupil" in mathematics.
Population: Standards 1–5 in South African schools.
Publication Dates: 1977–79.

Scores: 24 error scores: Basic Addition and Subtraction Facts (Addition, Subtraction), Multiplication and Division Tables (Multiplication, Division), Addition, Subtraction, Multiplication, Division scores for Basic Operations <100, Basic Operations <1000, Basic Operations <100,000, Vulgar Fractions (Concept of Vulgar Fractions, Addition, Subtraction, Multiplication, Division), Decimal Fractions (Concept of Decimal Fractions, Addition, Subtraction).
Administration: Group.
Price Data: Available from publisher.
Foreign Language Edition: Tsonga and Afrikaans editions also available.
Time: (570–615) minutes.
Authors: R. C. Roos.
Publisher: Human Sciences Research Council [South Africa].

[799]
Diagnostic Word Patterns Tests.
Purpose: Designed to assess students' knowledge of sound-symbol relationships, word patterns, and spelling generalizations.
Population: Grades 3 and over.
Publication Dates: 1969–78.
Administration: Group.
Price Data, 1989: $3.80 per 50 Individual Student Charts (Specify Test 1, 2, or 3); $4.40 per 9 Cards for Word Recognition Tests; $3.85 per teacher's manual ('78, 21 pages).
Time: Administration time not reported.
Comments: "Criterion-referenced"; may be administered orally as a spelling test or visually as a word recognition test.
Author: Evelyn Buckley.
Publisher: Educators Publishing Service, Inc.
a) TEST 1.
Scores: 10 response areas: Vowel-Consonant Pattern, Vowel-Consonant-Consonant Pattern, Consonant-Consonant-Vowel-Consonant Pattern, Consonant-Consonant-Vowel-Consonant-Consonant Pattern, Generalization for k and ck, Common Consonant Digraphs, Adding -ed, Generalization for ch and tch, Common Letter Combination Patterns, Nonphonetic Words.
b) TEST 2.
Scores: 10 response areas: Vowel-Consonant-Silent e Pattern, ai and ay, oa and ow, ea and ee, ie and igh, ou and ow, au and aw, Vowel Controlled by r Pattern, oo, Nonphonetic Words.
c) TEST 3.
Scores: 10 response areas: ea and e, oi and oy, Suffixes, 1-1-1 Generalization, Vowel Controlled by r Pattern, Suffixes, Silent-e Words with Suffixes, Two Syllable Words with Short Vowels, Two-Syllable Words with Short and Long Vowels, Nonphonetic Words.
Cross References: For reviews by Priscilla A. Drum, and Patricia Herman and P. David Pearson, see 9:351.

[800]
Differential Ability Scales.
Purpose: Designed to measure cognitive abilities and achievement.
Population: Ages 2-6 to 17-11.
Publication Dates: 1990.
Acronym: DAS.
Administration: Individual.
Price Data, 1994: $495 per complete kit with briefcase; $28 per 20 preschool forms; $28 per 20 school-age record forms; $9.50 per 20 basic number skills and spelling worksheets; $9.50 per 10 speed of information processing booklets (select A, B, C); $9.50 per 10 sequential and quantitative reasoning booklets; $58.50 per administration manual ('90, 445 pages); $24 per technical handbook ('90, 379 pages).
Author: Colin D. Elliott.
Comments: Based on the British Ability Scales (336).
Publisher: The Psychological Corporation.
a) COGNITIVE BATTERY.
  1) *Preschool.*
  Population: Ages 2-6 to 7-11.
  Time: (25–65) minutes.
    (a) Ages 2-6 to 3-5.
    Scores, 7: Block Building, Verbal Comprehension, Picture Similarities, Naming Vocabulary, Total General Conceptual Ability, Recall of Digits, Recognition of Pictures.
    (b) Ages 3-6 to 5-11.
    Scores, 14: Verbal Ability (Verbal Comprehension, Naming Vocabulary, Total), Nonverbal Ability (Picture Similarities, Pattern Construction, Copying, Total), Early Number Concepts, Total General Conceptual Ability, Block Building, Matching Letter-Like Forms, Recall of Digits, Recall of Objects, Recognition of Pictures.
  2) *School-Age.*
  Population: Ages 5-0 to 17-11.
  Scores, 13: Verbal Ability (Word Definitions, Similarities, Total), Nonverbal Reasoning Ability (Matrices, Sequential and Quantitative Reasoning, Total), Spatial Ability (Recall of Designs, Pattern Construction, Total), Total General Conceptual Ability, Recall of Digits, Recall of Objects, Speed of Information Processing.
  Time: (40–65) minutes.
b) SCHOOL ACHIEVEMENT.
Population: Ages 6-0 to 17-11.
Scores, 3: Basic Number Skills, Spelling, Word Reading.
Time: (15–25) minutes.
Cross References: For reviews by Glen P. Aylward and Robert C. Reinehr, see 11:111 (1 reference).

TEST REFERENCES

1. Kercher, A. C., & Sandoval, J. (1991). Reading disability and the Differential Ability Scales. *Journal of School Psychology, 29,* 293-307.

2. Stone, B. J. (1992). Joint confirmatory factor analyses of the DAS and WISC-R. *Journal of School Psychology, 30*(2), 185-195.

3. Stone, B. J. (1992). Prediction of achievement by Asian-American and white children. *Journal of School Psychology, 30*(1), 91-99.

[801]

Differential Aptitude Tests—Computerized Adaptive Edition.

Purpose: A system of computer programs that measures the "abilities of examinees for the purpose of educational and vocational guidance."
Population: Grades 8–12.
Publication Date: 1987.
Acronym: DAT Adaptive.
Scores, 9: Verbal Reasoning, Numerical Ability, Total, Abstract Reasoning, Clerical Speed and Accuracy, Mechanical Reasoning, Space Relations, Spelling, and Language Usage.
Administration: Individual.
Price Data, 1994: FOR APPLE COMPUTERS: $54.50 per examination kit including user's manual (103 pages), demonstration diskettes A and C, orientation booklet, score report folder, sample individual report, and product summary; $145.50 per start-up package including diskette A, reusable diskette B/C, reusable user's manual, diskette jacket/waiting list form, 10 orientation booklets, and 10 score report folders, $75 per replenishment package including diskette A, diskette jacket/waiting list form, 10 orientation booklets, and 10 score report folders; FOR IBM COMPUTERS: $54.50 per examination kit including demonstration disks 1 and 2, guide to the demonstration software, orientation booklet, score report folder, orientation booklet score report folder, sample individual report, and product summary; $145.50 per 10-use start-up package available in 5.25-inch or 3.5-inch diskettes including user's manual, disks 1, 2, and 3, disk jacket/waiting list form, 10 orientation booklets, and 10 score report folders; $303.50 per 35-use start-up package in 5.25-inch or 3.5-inch diskettes including same accessories as 10-use start-up package with 35 orientation booklets and 35 score report folders; $75 per 10-use replenishment package in 5.25-inch or 3.5-inch diskettes including disk 1, disk jacket/waiting list form, 10 orientation booklets, and 10 score report folders; $30.50 each for disk 2 and disk 3; $25.50 per administrator handbook; $20.50 per counselor's manual.
Time: (90) minutes.
Comments: Computer requirements: Apple (IIc, IIe, and II+, Franklin Ace 1000, and Laser 128; 64K memory, two drives; monochrome or color monitor); IBM (PC, XT, AT, PS/1, and compatibles; 256K memory; two disk drives; two 5.25-inch or 3.5-inch floppy, or one 5.25-inch and one 3.5-inch floppy; monitor with graphic capability, a Hercules or color graphics [CGA, EGA] card); contains the Differential Aptitude Tests (DAT) and the optional Career Planning Questionnaire; adaptive selection of test items from the traditional DAT (802).
Author: The Psychological Corporation.
Publisher: The Psychological Corporation.

[802]

Differential Aptitude Tests, Fifth Edition.

Purpose: "Designed to measure students' ability to learn or to succeed in a number of different areas."
Population: Grades 7–9, grades 10–12 and adults.
Publication Date: 1947–92.
Acronym: DAT.
Scores: 9 tests (Verbal Reasoning, Numerical Reasoning, Abstract Reasoning, Perceptual Speed and Accuracy [Part 1, Part 2], Mechanical Reasoning, Space Relations, Spelling, Language Usage) and Total Scholastic Aptitude.
Administration: Group.
Levels, 2: 1, 2.
Price Data, 1994: $37.50 per 25 Form C partial battery test booklets (Levels 1 or 2) including Directions for Administering ('90, 47 pages); $81.50 per 25 Form C complete battery test booklets (Levels 1 or 2) including Directions for Administering; $63.50 per 100 Type 1 machine-scorable answer documents with DAT (Levels 1 or 2, Form C), $96 per 100 Type 1 machine-scorable answer documents with DAT (Levels 1 or 2, Form C) and Level 1 or Level 2 Career Interest Inventory; $82 per Type 2 machine-scorable answer documents with 100 Perceptual Speed and Accuracy—Part 1 answer sheets and DAT (Levels 1 and 2, Form C); $43 per Ready-Score answer documents with 25 Perceptual Speed and Accuracy—Part 1 answer sheets, Profile Your DAT scores pamphlet, and Levels 1 or 2 of Form C; $21.50 per norms booklet (Fall or Spring); $21.50 per Using the DAT with Adults; $17.50 per 25 Practice Tests including a practice test for the Career Interest Inventory and Directions; $74.50 per Guide to Career Student Workbook; $12 per 25 Exploring Aptitudes: An Introduction to the Differential Aptitude Tests; $12 per 25 Using Test Results for Decision-Making; $21.50 per Technical Manual ('92, 192 pages); $3 per Directions for Practice Test; $4.50 per Directions for Administering; price information for scoring and reporting services available from publisher.
Time: 156(206) minutes.
Comments: 2 forms (C, D) per level; partial battery includes only 2 subtests (Verbal Reasoning and Numerical Reasoning); can be used in conjunction with Career Interest Inventory (396).
Authors: G. K. Bennett, H. G. Seashore, and A. G. Wesman.
Publisher: The Psychological Corporation.
Cross References: For reviews of Forms V and W by Ronald K. Hambleton and Daryl Sander, see 9:352 (19 references); see also T3:732 (26 references); for reviews by Thomas J. Bouchard, Jr., and Robert L. Linn and an excerpted review by Gerald S. Hanna of earlier forms, see 8:485 (56 references); see also T2:1069 (64 references); for a review by M. Y. Qureshi and an excerpted review by Jack C. Merwin of earlier forms, see 7:673 (139 references); for reviews by J. A. Keats and Richard E. Schutz, see 6:767 (52 references); for reviews by John B. Carroll

and Norman Frederiksen, see 5:605 (49 references); for reviews by Harold Bechtoldt, Ralph F. Berdie, and Lloyd G. Humphreys, see 4:711 (27 references); for an excerpted review, see 3:620.

TEST REFERENCES

1. Brown, D., Fulkerson, K. F., Vedder, M., & Ware, W. B. (1983). Self-estimate ability in black and white 8th-, 10th-, and 12th-grade males and females. *The Vocational Guidance Quarterly, 32,* 21-28.
2. Ford, M. E., & Tisak, M. S. (1983). A further search for social intelligence. *Journal of Educational Psychology, 75,* 196-206.
3. Garrison, D. R. (1983). Psychosocial correlates of dropout and achievement in an adult high school completion program. *The Alberta Journal of Educational Research, 29,* 131-139.
4. Sternberg, R. J., & Gardner, M. K. (1983). Unities in inductive reasoning. *Journal of Experimental Psychology: General, 112,* 80-116.
5. Housner, L. D. (1984). The role of imaginal processing in the retention of visually-presented sequential motoric stimuli. *Research Quarterly for Exercise and Sport, 55,* 24-31.
6. Samar, V. J., & Sims, D. G. (1984). Visual evoked-response components related to speechreading and spatial skills in hearing and hearing-impaired adults. *Journal of Speech and Hearing Research, 27,* 162-172.
7. Wittig, M. A., Sasse, S. H., & Giacomi, J. (1984). Predictive validity of five cognitive skills tests among women receiving engineering training. *Journal of Research in Science Teaching, 21,* 537-546.
8. Aaron, P. G. (1985). The paradoxical relationship between intelligence and reading disability. *Perceptual and Motor Skills, 61,* 1251-1261.
9. Fennema, E., & Tartre, L. A. (1985). The use of spatial visualization in mathematics by girls and boys. *Journal for Research in Mathematics Education, 16,* 184-206.
10. Merriman, W. E., Keating, D. P., & List, J. A. (1985). Mental rotation of facial profiles: Age-, sex-, and ability related differences. *Developmental Psychology, 21,* 888-900.
11. Pedersen, K., Bleyer, D. R., & Elmore, P. B. (1985). Attitudes and career interests of junior high school mathematics students: Implications for the classroom. *Arithmetic Teacher, 32*(7), 45-49.
12. Ackerman, P. L. (1986). Individual differences in information processing: An investigation of intellectual abilities and task performance during practice. *Intelligence, 10,* 101-139.
13. Campos, A., & Cofán, E. (1986). Rotation of images and primary mental abilities: Influence on information and sex. *Perceptual and Motor Skills, 63,* 644-646.
14. Dong, H., Sung, Y. H., & Goldman, S. H. (1986). The validity of the Ball Aptitude Battery (BAB): III. Relationship to CAB, DAT, and GATB. *Educational and Psychological Measurement, 46,* 245-250.
15. Hult, R. E., Jr., & Brous, C. W. (1986). Spatial visualization: Athletic skills and sex differences. *Perceptual and Motor Skills, 63,* 163-168.
16. Vallis, T. M., & Bucher, B. (1986). Individual difference factors in the efficacy of covert modeling and self-instructional training for fear reduction. *Canadian Journal of Behavioural Science, 18,* 146-158.
17. Weiner, N. C., & Robinson, S. E. (1986). Cognitive abilities, personality and gender differences in math achievement of gifted adolescents. *Gifted Child Quarterly, 30,* 83-87.
18. Embretson, S. E. (1987). Improving the measurement of spatial aptitude by dynamic testing. *Intelligence, 11,* 333-358.
19. French, C. C., & Beaumont, J. G. (1987). The reaction of psychiatric patients to computerized assessment. *British Journal of Clinical Psychology, 26,* 267-278.
20. Johnson, E. S., & Meade, A. C. (1987). Developmental patterns of spatial ability: An early sex difference. *Child Development, 58,* 725-740.
21. Kinnear, P. R., & Wood, M. (1987). Memory for topographic contour maps. *British Journal of Psychology, 78,* 395-402.
22. Hunt, E., Pellegrino, J. W., Frick, R. W., Farr, S. A., & Alderton, D. (1988). The ability to reason about movement in the visual field. *Intelligence, 12,* 77-100.
23. Subtelny, J., & Snell, K. B. (1988). Efficacy of a distinctive feature model of therapy for hearing-impaired adolescents. *Journal of Speech and Hearing Disorders, 53,* 194-201.
24. Cassidy, T., & Lynn, R. (1991). Achievement motivation, educational attainment, cycles of disadvantage and social competence: Some longitudinal data. *The British Journal of Educational Psychology, 61,* 1-12.
25. Dura, J. R., Stukenberg, K. W., & Kiecolt-Glaser, J. K. (1991). Anxiety and depression disorders in adult children caring for demented patients. *Psychology and Aging, 6,* 467-473.
26. McNamara, T. P., Sternberg, R. J., & Hardy, J. K. (1991). Processing verbal relations. *Intelligence, 15,* 193-221.
27. Thompson, J. K., & Spana, R. E. (1991). Visuospatial ability, accuracy of size estimation, and bulimic disturbance in a noneating-disordered college sample: A neuropsychological analysis. *Perceptual and Motor Skills, 73,* 335-338.
28. Hattrup, K., Schmitt, N., & Landis, R. S. (1992). Equivalence of constructs measured by job-specific and commercially available aptitude tests. *Journal of Applied Psychology, 77,* 298-308.
29. Schneider, W. J., & Nevid, J. S. (1993). Overcoming math anxiety: A comparison of stress inoculation training and systematic desensitization. *Journal of College Student Development, 34,* 283-288.
30. Westbrook, B. W., & Sanford, E. E. (1993). Relation between self-appraisal and appropriateness of career choices of male and female adolescents. *Educational and Psychological Measurement, 53,* 291-299.
31. Wilson, J., & Wright, C. R. (1993). The predictive validity of student self-evaluations, teachers' assessments, and grades for performance on the Verbal Reasoning and Numerical Ability Scales of the Differential Aptitude Test for a sample of secondary school students attending rural Appalachia schools. *Educational and Psychological Measurement, 53,* 259-270.

[803]

Differential Aptitude Tests for Personnel and Career Assessment.

Purpose: Designed to measure ability to learn in eight aptitude areas.

Population: Adult.

Publication Dates: 1972–91.

Acronym: DAT for PCA.

Scores, 9: General Cognitive Abilities Tests (Verbal Reasoning, Numerical Ability, Total), Perceptual Abilities Tests (Abstract Reasoning, Mechanical Reasoning, Space Relations), Clerical and Language Tests (Spelling, Language Usage, Clerical Speed and Accuracy).

Administration: Group.

Price Data, 1994: $78 per 25 General Cognitive Abilities Battery tests; $98 per 25 Perceptual Abilities Battery tests; $78 per 25 Clerical/Language Battery tests; $48 per 25 tests (select Verbal Reasoning, Numerical Reasoning, Abstract Reasoning, Spelling, Language Usage, or Clerical Speed and Accuracy); $74 per 25 tests (select Mechanical Reasoning or Space Relations); $38 per 25 ready-score answer sheets (select battery); $25 per 50 General Cognitive Abilities Battery hand-scorable answer sheets; $25 per 50 Perceptual Abilities Battery or Clerical/Language Battery hand-scorable answer sheets; $25 per 50 specific test hand-scorable answer sheets (select test); $21 per set of General Cognitive Abilities Battery scoring keys; $21 per set of Perceptual Abilities Battery or Clerical/Language Battery scoring keys; $15 per set of scoring keys for specific tests (select test); $28 per directions for administering (includes norms) ('89, 32 pages); $28 per technical manual ('91, 43 pages); $40 per examination kit.

Time: 114(144) minutes.

Comments: Abbreviated form of the Differential Aptitude Tests, Form V/W (9:352).

Authors: George K. Bennett, Harold G. Seashore, and Alexander G. Wesman.

Publisher: The Psychological Corporation.

[804]

Differential Test of Conduct and Emotional Problems.

Purpose: "Designed to effect differentiations between conduct problem, emotionally disturbed and noninvolved populations."

Population: Grades K–12.
Publication Dates: 1990–91.
Acronym: DT/CEP.
Scores, 2: Emotional Disturbance Scale, Conduct Problem Scale.
Administration: Group.
Price Data, 1991: $50 per complete set including manual ('90, 58 pages), score forms, and scoring template; $16 per 50 score forms.
Time: (15–20) minutes.
Comments: Ratings by teachers.
Author: Edward J. Kelly.
Publisher: Slosson Educational Publications, Inc.

TEST REFERENCES

1. Kelly, E. J., & Vactor, J. C. V. (1991). Distinguishing between conduct problem and emotionally disturbed students in secondary school: A five-instrument discriminant analysis. *Psychological Reports, 69,* 303-311.

[805]

Dimensions of Excellence Scales.
Purpose: To assess the quality and effectiveness of a school or district.
Population: Schools or districts.
Publication Date: 1988.
Acronym: DOES.
Administration: Group.
Price Data: Available from publisher.
Comments: Ratings by students, parents, and school staff.
Authors: Russell A. Dusewicz and Francine S. Beyer.
Publisher: Research for Better Schools.
a) STUDENT SCALE.
Scores: 4 dimensions: School Climate, Teacher Behavior, Monitoring and Assessment, Student Discipline and Behavior.
Time: (30) minutes.
b) PARENT SCALE.
Scores, 8: Same as *a* above plus Leadership, Curriculum, Staff Development, Parent Involvement.
Time: (20–30) minutes.
c) SCHOOL STAFF SCALE.
Scores, 8: Same as *b* above.
Time: (45) minutes.
Cross References: For reviews by Janet F. Carlson and William P. Erchul, see 11:112.

[806]

Dimensions of Self-Concept.
Purpose: Designed to "measure non-cognitive factors associated with self-esteem or self-concept in a school setting."
Publication Dates: 1976–89.
Acronym: DOSC.
Scores, 5: Level of Aspiration, Anxiety, Academic Interest and Satisfaction, Leadership and Initiative, Identification vs. Alienation.
Administration: Group.
Price Data, 1993: $8.75 per 25 tests (specify form) [$31.25 per 100 tests, $117 per 500 tests]; $3.25 per

technical manual ('89, 23 pages); $6.25 per specimen set.
Comments: Self-report instrument.
Authors: William B. Michael, Robert A. Smith, and Joan J. Michael.
Publisher: EdITS/Educational and Industrial Testing Service.
a) FORM E.
Population: Grades 4–6.
Time: (20–40) minutes.
b) FORM S.
Population: Grades 7–12.
Time: (15–35) minutes.
c) FORM H.
Population: College.
Time: (15–35) minutes.
Cross References: For a review by Sharon Johnson-Lewis, see 11:113 (10 references); for reviews by Herbert G. W. Bischoff and Alfred B. Heilbrun, Jr., see 9:353 (4 references); see also T3:734 (5 references).

TEST REFERENCES

1. Al-Samarrai, N., Michael, W. B., & Hocevar, D. (1993). The development and validation of an Arabic version of an academic self-concept scale. *Educational and Psychological Measurement, 53,* 249-257.

[807]

The Diplomacy Test of Empathy.
Purpose: Constructed to measure empathic ability.
Population: Business and industrial personnel.
Publication Dates: 1960–62.
Scores: Total score only.
Administration: Group.
Price Data, 1985: $5 per 25 test booklets; $5 per specimen set.
Time: (20–25) minutes.
Comments: Revision of Primary Empathic Abilities; title on test is Diplomacy Test of Empathic Ability.
Author: Willard A. Kerr.
Publisher: Psychometric Affiliates.
Cross References: See T2:1160 (1 reference) and P:64 (2 references); for reviews by Arthur H. Brayfield and Richard S. Hatch, see 6:85 (1 reference); for a review by Robert L. Thorndike of the earlier test, see 5:99.

[808]

Discourse Comprehension Test.
Purpose: To assess "comprehension and retention of stated and implied main ideas and details in a set of stories."
Population: Aphasic or head injured adults.
Publication Date: 1993.
Acronym: DCT.
Scores, 9: Number of Words, Number of Unfamiliar Words, Number of Sentences, Mean Sentence Length, Number of Minimal Terminal Units, Ratio of Clauses to Terminal Units, Listening Difficulty, Number of Unfamiliar Words, Reading Difficulty.
Administration: Individual.
Price Data, 1994: $65 per complete kit including

manual (108 pages), audio tape, 12 story cards, and vinyl carrying case.
Time: Administration time not reported.
Comments: Stories can be read aloud, heard on tape, or read silently.
Authors: Robert H. Brookshire and Linda E. Nicholas.
Publisher: Communication Skill Builders.

[809]

Dissociative Experiences Scale.
Purpose: "Developed to serve as a clinical tool to help identify patients with dissociative psychopathology and as a research tool to provide a means of quantifying dissociative experiences."
Population: Late adolescent–adult.
Publication Dates: 1986.
Acronym: DES.
Scores: Total score only.
Administration: Group or individual.
Price Data, 1992: $2 per DES manual (24 pages); $1 per DES.
Foreign Language Editions: Available in French, Spanish, Italian, Dutch, Hindi, Cambodian, Czech, Swedish, Norwegian, Japanese, and Hebrew.
Time: [10] minutes.
Comments: Self-report inventory; translation also in progress for version of the DES in German.
Authors: Eve Bernstein Carlson and Frank W. Putnam.
Publisher: Eve Bernstein Carlson (the author).

TEST REFERENCES

1. Goff, D. C., Olin, J. A., Jenike, M. A., Baer, L., & Buttolph, M. L. (1992). Disassociative symptoms in patients with obsessive-compulsive disorder. *Journal of Nervous and Mental Disease, 180*, 332-337.

[810]

Distar Mastery Tests.
Purpose: "Assess individual student achievement in terms of specific learning objectives."
Population: Preschool–Grade 3.
Publication Date: 1978.
Acronym: DMT.
Administration: Group.
Price Data, 1984: $36.65 per kit including 25 tests, 25 practice sheets, and examiner's manual (with answer key) for any one test.
Time: (30–60) minutes per test.
Comments: "Criterion-referenced"; determines mastery for the Distar reading, language, and arithmetic programs.
Author: Science Research Associates, Inc.
Publisher: Science Research Associates, Inc.
a) READING I.
Publication Date: 1977.
Scores: 3 areas: Sound Recognition, Vocabulary, Comprehension.
b) READING II.
Publication Date: 1978.
Scores: 5 areas: Letter Recognition, Sound Recog-

nition, Vocabulary, Deductive Thinking Rules, Comprehension.
c) LANGUAGE I.
Publication Date: 1978.
Scores: 7 to 8 areas: Description of Objects and Actions, Actions, Instructional Words, Classification, Information, Applications, Shapes, Statement Production (optional).
d) LANGUAGE II.
Publication Date: 1978.
Scores: 7 to 8 areas: Word Skills, Sentence Skills, Reasoning Skills, Directional Skills, Information, Applications, Take-Homes, Statement Production (optional).
e) ARITHMETIC I.
Publication Date: 1978.
Scores: 9 areas: Symbol Identification, Groups, Horizontal Addition and Algebra Addition, Horizontal and Vertical Subtraction, Vertical Addition, Oral Story Problems, Ordinal Counting, More-Less, Written Story Problems.
f) ARITHMETIC II.
Publication Date: 1978.
Scores: 7 areas: Column Addition, Column Subtraction, Telling Time, Multiplying and Reducing Fractions, Measurement, Coins, Written Story Problems.
Cross References: For reviews by Jason Millman and Craig N. Mills, see 9:354.

[811]

Diversity Awareness Profile.
Purpose: "Designed to assist people in becoming aware of ways in which they discriminate against, judge, or isolate others."
Population: Employees or managers.
Publication Date: 1991.
Acronym: DAP.
Scores: Total score only.
Administration: Group.
Forms, 2: Employee, Manager.
Price Data, 1991: $3.95 each for (1–50 copies); $3.75 each for (51–100) copies; $3.55 each for (101–300) copies; $3.35 each for (301 or more) copies.
Time: (90) minutes.
Author: Karen Grote.
Publisher: Pfeiffer & Company International Publishers.

[812]

Dos Amigos Verbal Language Scales.
Purpose: Designed to assess the level of language development in both English and Spanish.
Population: Ages 5-0 to 13-5.
Publication Dates: 1973–74.
Scores, 3: English, Spanish, Dominant Language.
Administration: Individual.
Price Data, 1994: $25 per complete kit; $15 per 25 recording forms; $15 per manual ('74, 45 pages).
Time: (20) minutes.

Comments: No reading by examinees; examiner must speak Spanish.
Author: Donald E. Critchlow.
Publisher: United Educational Services, Inc.
Cross References: For an excerpted review by Richard V. Teschner, see 8:163 (2 references).

TEST REFERENCES

1. Gerken, K. C. (1978). Language dominance: A comparison of measures. *Language, Speech, and Hearing Services in Schools, 9,* 187-196.

[813]
The Draw-A-Person.
Purpose: To provide clinical interpretations of the DAP.
Population: Ages 5 and over.
Publication Date: 1963.
Acronym: DAP.
Scores: Total score only.
Administration: Group.
Price Data, 1993: $37.50 per manual (74 pages, catalogue for interpretative analysis).
Time: [5–10] minutes.
Author: William H. Urban.
Publisher: Western Psychological Services.
Cross References: See 9:358 (23 references) and T3:751 (44 references); for reviews by Dale B. Harris and Phillip M. Kitay, see 7:165.

TEST REFERENCES

1. Scarr, S. (1982). Effects of birth weight on later intelligence. *Social Biology, 29,* 230-237.
2. Elliott, S. N., Piersel, W. C., & Galvin, G. A. (1983). Psychological re-evaluations: A survey of practices and perceptions of school psychologists. *Journal of School Psychology, 21,* 99-105.
3. Handler, L. (1984). Anxiety as measured by the Draw-A-Person test: A response to Sims, Dana, and Bolton. *Journal of Personality Assessment, 48,* 82-84.
4. Hardman, P. K. (1984). The training of psycho-educational technicians (para-professionals) to administer a screening battery which delineates dyslexia and hyperkinesis. *Journal of Learning Disabilities, 17,* 453-456.
5. Holmes, C. B., & Stephens, C. L. (1984). Consistency of edging on the Bender-Gestalt, Memory-For-Designs, and Draw-A-Person tests. *The Journal of Psychology, 117,* 269-271.
6. Houston, L. N. (1984). Self-esteem, locus of control, and conservatism. *Psychological Reports, 55,* 851-854.
7. Lothstein, L. M., & Roback, H. (1984). Black female transsexuals and schizophrenia: A serendipitous finding? *Archives of Sexual Behavior, 13,* 371-386.
8. Oas, P. (1984). Validity of the Draw-A-Person and Bender Gestalt Tests as measures of impulsivity with adolescents. *Journal of Consulting and Clinical Psychology, 52,* 1011-1019.
9. Pfeffer, K. (1984). Interpretation of studies of ethnic identity: Draw-A-Person as a measure of ethnic identity. *Perceptual and Motor Skills, 59,* 835-838.
10. Posey, C. D., & Hess, A. K. (1984). The fakability of subtle and obvious measures of aggression by male prisoners. *Journal of Personality Assessment, 48,* 137-144.
11. Farylo, B., & Paludi, M. A. (1985). Research with the Draw-A-Person Test: Conceptual and methodological issues. *The Journal of Psychology, 119,* 575-580.
12. Jensen, K. W. (1985). Sex of the administrator as a variable affecting drawing a person. *Perceptual and Motor Skills, 60,* 72-74.
13. Johnson, S. T., Starnes, W. T., Gregory, D. & Blaylock, A. (1985). Program of assessment, diagnosis, and instruction (PADI): Identifying and nurturing potentially gifted and talented minority students. *Journal of Negro Education, 54,* 416-430.
14. McCabe, D., & Hilmo, J. (1985). Pictures speak louder than test scores. *Academic Therapy, 20,* 333-345.

15. Oas, P. (1985). Clinical utility of an index of impulsivity on the Draw-A-Person test. *Perceptual and Motor Skills, 60,* 310.
16. Oas, P. (1985). Impulsivity and delinquent behavior among incarcerated adolescents. *Journal of Clinical Psychology, 41,* 422-424.
17. Pfeffer, K. (1985). Sex-identification and sex-typing in some Nigerian children's drawings. *Social Behavior and Personality, 13,* 69-72.
18. Spillman, C. V., & Lutz, J. P. (1985). Focus on research: Criteria for successful experiences in kindergarten. *Contemporary Education, 56,* 109-113.
19. Stingle, S. F., & Cook, H. (1985). Age and sex differences in the cooperative and noncooperative behavior of pairs of American children. *The Journal of Psychology, 119,* 335-345.
20. Rantakallio, P., & von Wendt, L. (1986). Mental retardation and subnormality in a birth cohort of 12,000 children in Northern Finland. *American Journal of Mental Deficiency, 90,* 380-387.
21. Stevenson, H. W., & Newman, R. S. (1986). Long-term prediction of achievement and attitudes in mathematics and reading. *Child Development, 57,* 646-659.
22. Keltikangas-Jarvinen, L. (1987). Body-image disturbances ensuing from juvenile rheumatoid arthritis, a preliminary study. *Perceptual and Motor Skills, 64,* 984.
23. Pfeffer, K. (1987). Effects of instructions to subjects on Draw-A-Person as a measure of ethnic identity. *Perceptual and Motor Skills, 64,* 780-782.
24. Scribner, C. M., & Handler, L. (1987). The interpreter's personality in Draw-A-Person interpretation: A study of interpersonal style. *Journal of Personality Assessment, 51,* 112-122.
25. Strommen, E. F., & Smith, J. K. (1987). Internal consistency and bias considerations of the Goodenough-Harris Draw-A-Person Test. *Educational and Psychological Measurement, 47(3),* 731-736.
26. Willis, W. G. (1987). Retention/promotion decisions: Selective use of data? *Perceptual and Motor Skills, 64(1),* 287-290.
27. Babad, E., Bernieri, F., & Rosenthal, R. (1989). When less information is more informative: Diagnosing teacher expectations from brief samples of behaviour. *British Journal of Educational Psychology, 59,* 281-295.
28. Tuber, S., & Coates, S. (1989). Indices of psychopathology in Rorschachs of boys with severe gender identity disorder: A comparison with normal control subjects. *Journal of Personality Assessment, 53,* 100-112.
29. Dickson, J. M., Saylor, C. F., & Finch, A. J., Jr. (1990). Personality factors, family structure, and sex of drawn figure on The Draw-A-Person Test. *Journal of Personality Assessment, 55,* 362-366.
30. Pontius, A. A. (1990). Phases in the representation of intraobject spatial relations of the face as precursors to literacy: A testable hypothesis engendered by neolithic art. *Perceptual and Motor Skills, 71,* 323-333.
31. Rekers, G. A., & Morey, S. M. (1990). The relationship of measures of sex-typed play with clinician ratings on degree of gender disturbance. *Journal of Clinical Psychology, 46,* 28-34.
32. Rekers, G. A., Rosen, A. C., & Morey, S. M. (1990). Projective test findings for boys with gender disturbance: Draw-A-Person test, It Scale, and Make-A-Picture Story test. *Perceptual and Motor Skills, 71,* 771-779.
33. Tharinger, D. J., & Stark, K. (1990). A qualitative versus quantitative approach to evaluating The Draw-A-Person and Kinetic Family Drawing: A study of mood- and anxiety-disorder children. *Psychological Assessment, 2,* 365-375.
34. Cates, J. A., & Lapham, R. F. (1991). Personality assessment of the prelingual, profoundly deaf child or adolescent. *Journal of Personality Assessment, 56,* 118-129.
35. Missaghi-Lakshman, M., & Whissell, C. (1991). Children's understanding of facial expression of emotion: II. Drawing of emotion-faces. *Perceptual and Motor Skills, 72,* 1228-1230.
36. Paul, R., Looney, S. S., & Dahm, P. S. (1991). Communication and socialization skills at ages 2 and 3 in "late-talking" young children. *Journal of Speech and Hearing Research, 34,* 858-865.
37. Gustafson, J. L., & Waehler, C. A. (1992). Assessing concrete and abstract thinking with the Draw-A-Person technique. *Journal of Personality Assessment, 59,* 439-447.
38. Naglieri, J. A., & Pfeiffer, S. I. (1992). Performance of disruptive behavior disordered and normal samples on The Draw-A-Person: Screening procedure for emotional disturbance. *Psychological Assessment, 4,* 156-159.
39. Rubenzer, S. (1992). A comparison of traditional and computer-generated psychological reports in an adolescent inpatient setting. *Journal of Clinical Psychology, 48,* 817-827.
40. Skillman, G., Dabbs, P., Mitchell, M., McGrath, M., Lewis, J., & Brems, C. (1992). Appropriateness of the Draw-A-Person Test with Alaskan native populations. *Journal of Clinical Psychology, 48,* 561-564.

[814]

Draw A Person: A Quantitative Scoring System.

Purpose: "To meet the need for a modernized, recently normed, and objective scoring system to be applied to human figure drawings produced by children and adolescents."
Population: Ages 5–17.
Publication Date: 1988.
Acronym: DAP.
Scores, 4: Man, Woman, Self, Total.
Administration: Group.
Price Data, 1994: $89 per complete kit including 25 student record/response forms, scoring chart, and manual ('88, 100 pages); $61 per scoring chart and manual; $28.50 per 25 student record/response forms.
Time: 15(25) minutes.
Author: Jack A. Naglieri.
Publisher: The Psychological Corporation.
Cross References: For reviews by Merith Cosden and W. Grant Willis, see 11:114 (1 reference).

TEST REFERENCES

1. Haddad, F. A., & Juliano, J. M. (1991). Relations among scores on Matrix Analogies Test, Draw-A-Person, and the Iowa Tests of Basic Skills for low socioeconomic children. *Psychological Reports, 69,* 299-302.
2. Jones, E., & Badger, T. (1991). Deaf children's knowledge of internal human anatomy. *The Journal of Special Education, 25*(2), 252-260.
3. Kamphaus, R. W., & Pleiss, K. L. (1991). Draw-A-Person techniques: Tests in search of a construct. *Journal of School Psychology, 29,* 395-401.

[815]

Draw-A-Person Quality Scale.

Purpose: Designed as a projective measure of intellectual functioning.
Population: Ages 16–25.
Publication Dates: 1955–65.
Acronym: DPQS.
Scores: 7 ratings of drawing quality.
Administration: Group.
Price Data: Available from publisher.
Foreign Language Edition: Spanish edition available.
Time: [10–20] minutes.
Authors: Mazie Earle Wagner and Herman J. P. Schubert.
Publisher: Herman J. P. Schubert.
Cross References: See P:423 (3 references); for a review by Philip L. Harriman, see 5:129 (3 references).

[816]

Draw A Person: Screening Procedure for Emotional Disturbance.

Purpose: Designed to screen for children who may have emotional disorders.
Population: Ages 6–17.
Publication Date: 1991.
Acronym: DAP:SPED.
Scores: Total score only.
Administration: Group.
Price Data, 1994: $64 per complete kit including 25 record forms and manual (77 pages); $29 per 25 record forms; $29 per manual.
Time: 15(20) minutes.
Author: Jack A. Naglieri, Timothy J. McNeish, and Achilles N. Bardos.
Publisher: PRO-ED, Inc.

TEST REFERENCES

1. McNeish, T. J., & Naglieri, J. A. (1993). Identification of individuals with serious emotional disturbance using the Draw a Person: Screening Procedure for Emotional Disturbance. *The Journal of Special Education, 27,* 115-121.

[817]

Draw-a-Story: Screening for Depression and Age or Gender Differences.

Purpose: Designed to identify depression.
Population: Ages 5 and over.
Publication Dates: 1987–93.
Acronym: DAS.
Scores: 2 task scores: Draw-A-Story, Stimulus Drawing Task.
Administration: Group or individual.
Forms, 2: A, B.
Price Data, 1993: $25 per test including manual ('93, 111 pages).
Time: (5–15) minutes.
Comments: Previous edition titled Draw-a-Story: Screening for Depression and Emotional Needs.
Author: Rawley Silver.
Publisher: Ablin Press Distributors.
Cross References: For reviews of the earlier edition by Walter Katkovsky and David Lachar, see 11:115.

TEST REFERENCES

1. Silver, R., & Carrion, F. (1991). Using the Silver Drawing Test in school and hospital. *The American Journal of Art Therapy, 30,* 36-43.

[818]

Driver Risk Inventory.

Purpose: "Designed for DUI/DWI offender risk assessment."
Population: Convicted DUI and DWI offenders.
Publication Dates: 1986–92.
Acronym: DRI.
Scores: Behaviors/characteristics relevant to DUI offenders in 5 areas: Validity, Alcohol, Drugs, Driver Risk, Stress Coping Abilities.
Administration: Individual or group.
Price Data, 1992: $5 to $6 per test; other price data available from publisher.
Time: (30–35) minutes.
Comments: Self-administered, computer-scored test.
Author: Behavior Data Systems, Ltd.
Publisher: Behavior Data Systems, Ltd.

[819]

[Driver Selection Forms and Tests].

Purpose: To improve hiring decisions for truck drivers through a structured assessment system involving

telephone checks, patterned interview, and assessment of basic character traits.
Population: Truck drivers.
Publication Date: 1943–73.
Administration: Individual.
Manual: No manual.
Price Data: Not available.
Comments: All revised forms essentially the same as or identical with earlier forms.
Publisher: Dartnell [No reply from publisher; status unknown].

a) EMPLOYMENT APPLICATION.
Publication Dates: 1946–64.
b) TELEPHONE CHECK.
Publication Dates: 1946–73.
Author: Robert N. McMurry.
c) DRIVER INTERVIEW.
Publication Dates: 1946–64.
d) PHYSICAL EXAMINATION RECORD.
Publication Dates: 1946–54.
e) SELECTION AND EVALUATION SUMMARY.
Publication Dates: 1950–72.
Author: Robert N. McMurry.
f) STANDARDIZED TEST: TRAFFIC AND DRIVING KNOWLEDGE FOR DRIVERS OF MOTOR TRUCKS.
Publication Dates: 1946–64.
Authors: Amos E. Neyhart and Helen L. Neyhart.
g) ROAD TEST IN TRAFFIC FOR TESTING, SELECTING, RATING, AND TRAINING TRUCK DRIVERS.
Publication Dates: 1943–64.
Scores, 3: Specific Driving Skill, General Driving Habits and Attitudes, Total.
Author: Amos E. Neyhart.
Cross References: For additional information and a review by Joseph E. Moore, see 6:1197; for a review by S. Rains Wallace, Jr., see 4:789.

[820]

Dropout Prediction & Prevention.
Purpose: Developed to identify students at risk for dropping out of school.
Population: Grades 9–12.
Publication Date: 1990.
Acronym: DPP.
Scores: Total score only.
Administration: Individual.
Price Data, 1991: $4 per 25 scales (select High School Form or Experimental Form for 8th Grade); $15 per manual (93 pages); $15.50 per specimen set.
Time: [5] minutes.
Comments: Scale information obtained from student cumulative records.
Authors: Clarence E. Nichols and Rochelle E. Nichols.
Publisher: Clinical Psychology Publishing Co., Inc.

[821]

Drug Use Questionnaire.
Purpose: To assess "potential involvement with drugs."

Population: Clients of addiction treatment.
Publication Date: 1982.
Acronym: DAST-20.
Scores: Total score only.
Administration: Group.
Price Data: Available from publisher.
Foreign Language Edition: Available in French.
Time: (5–10) minutes.
Comments: Self-report inventory; manual is entitled "Director of Client Outcome Measures for Addiction Treatment Programs"; previously entitled Drug Abuse Screening Test.
Author: Harvey A. Skinner.
Publisher: Addiction Research Foundation [Canada].

[822]

Durrell Analysis of Reading Difficulty, Third Edition.
Purpose: Designed to screen for reading problems.
Population: Grades 1–6.
Publication Dates: 1937–80.
Acronym: DARD.
Scores, 16 to 21: Oral Reading, Silent Reading, Listening Comprehension, Word Recognition, Word Analysis, Listening Vocabulary, Sounds in Isolation (Letters, Blends and Digraphs, Phonograms, Initial Affixes, Final Affixes), Spelling, Phonic Spelling of Words, Visual Memory of Words (Primary, Secondary), Identifying Sounds in Words, Prereading Phonics Abilities Inventories (Optional, Including Syntax Matching, Letter Names in Spoken Words, Phonemes in Spoken Words, Naming Lower Case Letters, Writing Letters from Dictation).
Administration: Individual.
Price Data, 1994: $83 per examiner's kit including tachistoscope, reading booklet, 5 record booklets, and manual ('80, 63 pages); $27.50 per reading booklet; $26 per tachistoscope; $49.50 per 35 record booklets; $14.50 per manual.
Time: (35–50) minutes.
Authors: Donald D. Durrell and Jane H. Catterson.
Publisher: The Psychological Corporation.
Cross References: For reviews by Nancy L. Roser and Byron H. Van Roekel, see 9:360 (3 references); see also T3:766 (14 references) and T2:1628 (18 references); for reviews by James Maxwell and George D. Spache of an earlier edition, see 5:660; for a review by Helen M. Robinson of the original edition, see 4:561 (2 references); for reviews by Guy L. Bond and Miles A. Tinker, see 2:1533; for a review by Marion Monroe, see 1:1098.

TEST REFERENCES

1. White, M., & Miller, S. R. (1983). Dyslexia: A term in search of a definition. *The Journal of Special Education, 17*, 5-10.
2. Ballinger, C. T., Varley, C. K., & Nolen, P. A. (1984). Effects of methylphenidate on reading in children with attention deficit disorder. *American Journal of Psychiatry, 141*, 1590-1593.
3. Aaron, P. G. (1985). The paradoxical relationship between intelligence and reading disability. *Perceptual and Motor Skills, 61*, 1251-1261.
4. Brown, R. T., Wynne, M. E., & Medenis, R. (1985). Methylphenidate and cognitive therapy: A comparison of treatment approaches with hyperactive boys. *Journal of Abnormal Child Psychology, 13*, 69-87.

5. Brown, R. T., Borden, K. A., Wynne, M. E., Schleser, R., & Clingerman, S. R. (1986). Methylphenidate and cognitive therapy with ADD children: A methodological reconsideration. *Journal of Abnormal Child Psychology, 14,* 481-497.

6. Grant, J., & Brown, C. (1986). Precocious readers: A comparative study of early reading and nonearly reading kindergarten entrants. *The Alberta Journal of Educational Research, 32,* 222-233.

7. Ney, P., Colbert, P., Newman, B., & Young, J. (1986). Aggressive behavior and learning difficulties as symptoms of depression in children. *Child Psychiatry and Human Development, 17,* 3-14.

8. Roth, F. P., & Spekman, N. J. (1986). Narrative discourse: Spontaneously generated stories of learning-disabled and normally achieving students. *Journal of Speech and Hearing Disorders, 51,* 8-23.

9. Wharry, R. E., & Kirkpatrick, S. W. (1986). Vision and academic performance of learning disabled children. *Perceptual and Motor Skills, 62,* 323-336.

10. Willows, D. M., & Ryan, E. B. (1986). The development of grammatical sensitivity and its relationship to early reading achievement. *Reading Research Quarterly, 21,* 253-266.

11. Lovett, M. W. (1987). A developmental approach to reading disability: Accuracy and speed criteria of normal and deficient reading skill. *Child Development, 58,* 234-260.

12. Benezra, E., & Douglas, V. I. (1988). Short-term serial recall in ADDH, normal, and reading-disabled boys. *Journal of Abnormal Child Psychology, 16,* 511-525.

13. Roth, F. P., & Spekman, N. J. (1989). The oral syntactic proficiency of learning disabled students: A spontaneous story sampling analysis. *Journal of Speech and Hearing Research, 32,* 67-77.

14. Madden, N. A., Slavin, R. E., Karweit, N. L., Dolan, L. J., & Wasik, B. A. (1993). Success for all: Longitudinal effects of a restructuring program for inner-city elementary schools. *American Educational Research Journal, 30,* 123-148.

[823]

Dvorine Color Vision Test.

Purpose: Designed as a "method of identifying individuals with defective color vision."

Population: Ages 3 and over.

Publication Dates: 1944–58.

Scores, 2: Nomenclature, Color Perception.

Administration: Individual.

Price Data, 1994: $260 per booklet of color plates ('53, 33 pages, manual and 24 color plates); $25 per 35 record forms.

Time: [3–5] minutes.

Comments: Revision of Dvorine Color Perception Testing Charts; also called Dvorine Pseudo-Isochromatic Plates.

Author: Israel Dvorine.

Publisher: The Psychological Corporation.

Cross References: See T3:767 (1 reference), T2:1911 (13 references), and 6:955 (12 references); for excerpted reviews by Elsie Murray, Laurance F. Shaffer, and Miles A. Tinker, see 5:773 (13 references); for excerpted reviews by Knight Dunlap, Carel C. Koch, Elsie Murray (reply by Israel Dvorine), and Miles A. Tinker, see 3:462 (4 references).

TEST REFERENCES

1. Fine, B. J., & Kobrick, J. L. (1983). Individual differences in distance estimation: Comparison of judgments in the field with those from projected slides of the same scenes. *Perceptual and Motor Skills, 57,* 3-14.

[824]

Dyadic Adjustment Scale.

Purpose: Designed to measure the quality of adjustment in marriage and similar dyadic relationships.

Population: People who have any committed couple relationship including unmarried cohabitation.

Publication Date: 1989.

Acronym: DAS.

Scores, 5: Dyadic Consensus, Dyadic Satisfaction, Affectional Expression, Dyadic Cohesion, Total.

Administration: Group or individual.

Price Data, 1993: $40 per complete kit including test manual (55 pages) and 20 QuikScore™ forms; $25 per 20 QuikScore™ forms; $19 per manual; $125 per disk for computer administration (specify IBM 5.25 inch, IBM 3.5 inch, or Apple).

Time: (5–10) minutes.

Comments: Computer program allows for 50 administrations.

Author: Graham B. Spanier.

Publisher: Multi-Health Systems, Inc.

Cross References: For reviews by Karen S. Budd and Nancy Heilman and Richard B. Stuart, see 11:117 (17 references).

TEST REFERENCES

1. Cooper, A., & Stoltenberg, C. D. (1987). Comparison of a sexual enhancement and a communication training program on sexual and marital satisfaction. *Journal of Counseling Psychology, 34,* 309-314.

2. Boen, D. L. (1988). A practitioner looks at assessment in marital counseling. *Journal of Counseling and Development, 66,* 484-486.

3. Camper, P. M., Jacobson, N. S., Holtzworth-Munroe, A., & Schmaling, K. B. (1988). Causal attributions for interactional behaviors in married couples. *Cognitive Therapy and Research, 12,* 195-209.

4. Creamer, M., & Campbell, I. M. (1988). The role of interpersonal perception in dyadic adjustment. *Journal of Clinical Psychology, 44,* 424-430.

5. Jacob, T., & Leonard, K. E. (1988). Alcoholic-spouse interaction as a function of alcoholism subtype and alcohol consumption interaction. *Journal of Abnormal Psychology, 97,* 231-237.

6. Margolin, G., John, R. S., & Lleberman, L. (1988). Affective responses to conflictual discussions in violent and nonviolent couples. *Journal of Consulting and Clinical Psychology, 56,* 24-33.

7. Wilson, G. L., Bornstein, P. H., & Wilson, L. J. (1988). Treatment of relationship dysfunction: An empirical evaluation of group and conjoint behavioral marital therapy. *Journal of Consulting and Clinical Psychology, 56,* 929-931.

8. Biglun, A., Rothlind, J., Hops, H., & Sherman, L. (1989). Impact of distressed and aggressive behavior. *Journal of Abnormal Psychology, 98,* 218-228.

9. Hooley, J. M., & Teasdale, J. D. (1989). Predictors of relapse in unipolar depressives: Expressed emotion, marital distress, and perceived criticism. *Journal of Abnormal Psychology, 98,* 229-235.

10. Christensen, A., & Heavey, C. L. (1990). Gender and social structure in the demand/withdraw pattern of marital conflict. *Journal of Personality and Social Psychology, 59,* 73-81.

11. Kolko, D. J., & Kazdin, A. E. (1990). Matchplay and firesetting in children: Relationship to parent, marital, and family dysfunction. *Journal of Clinical Child Psychology, 19,* 229-238.

12. O'Hara, M. W., Zekoski, E. M., Phillips, L. H., & Wright, E. J. (1990). Controlled prospective study of postpartum mood disorders: Comparison of childbearing and nonchildbearing women. *Journal of Abnormal Psychology, 99,* 3-15.

13. Schmaling, K. B., & Jacobsen, N. S. (1990). Marital interaction and depression. *Journal of Abnormal Psychology, 99,* 229-236.

14. Campbell, S. B., March, C. L., Pierce, E. W., Ewing, L. J., & Szumowski, E. K. (1991). Hard-to-manage preschool boys: Family context and the stability of externalizing behavior. *Journal of Abnormal Child Psychology, 19,* 301-318.

15. Dadds, M. R., & Powell, M. B. (1991). The relationship of interpersonal conflict and global marital adjustment to aggression, anxiety, and immaturity in aggressive and nonclinic children. *Journal of Abnormal Child Psychology, 19,* 553-567.

16. Ginsberg, D., Hall, S. M., & Rosinski, M. (1991). Partner interactions and smoking cessation: A pilot study. *Addictive Behaviors, 16,* 195-202.

17. Hickie, I., Parker, G., Wilhelm, K., & Tennant, C. (1991). Perceived interpersonal risk factors of non-endogenous depression. *Psychological Medicine, 21,* 399-412.

18. Hjemboe, S., & Butcher, J. N. (1991). Couples in marital distress: A study of personality factors as measured by the MMPI-2. *Journal of Personality Assessment, 57,* 216-237.

19. Phillips, L. H. C., & O'Hara, M. W. (1991). Prospective study

of postpartum depression: 4 ½-year follow-up of women and children. *Journal of Abnormal Psychology, 100,* 151-155.

20. Richmond, L. D., Craig, S. S., & Ruzicka, M. F. (1991). Self-monitoring and marital adjustment. *Journal of Research in Personality, 25,* 177-188.

21. Sayers, S. L., & Baucom, D. H. (1991). Role of femininity and masculinity in distressed couples' communication. *Journal of Personality and Social Psychology, 61,* 641-647.

22. Abidin, R. R., Jenkins, C. L., & McGoughey, M. C. (1992). The relationships of early family variables to children's subsequent behavioral adjustment. *Journal of Clinical Child Psychology, 21,* 60-69.

23. Christensen, A., Margolin, G., & Sullaway, M. (1992). Interparental agreement on child behavior problems. *Psychological Assessment, 4,* 419-425.

24. Goldman, A., & Greenberg, L. (1992). Comparison of integrated systemic and emotionally focused approaches to couples therapy. *Journal of Consulting and Clinical Psychology, 60,* 962-969.

25. O'Hara, M. W., Hoffman, J. G., Philipps, L. H. C., & Wright, E. J. (1992). Adjustment in childbearing women: The Postpartum Adjustment Questionnaire. *Psychological Assessment, 4,* 160-169.

26. Sanders, M. R., & Dadds, M. R. (1992). Children's and parents' cognitions about family interaction: An evaluation of video-mediated recall and thought listing procedures in the assessment of conduct-disordered children. *Journal of Clinical Child Psychology, 21,* 371-379.

27. Schwebel, A. I., Dunn, R. L., Moss, B. F., & Renner, M. A. (1992). Factors associated with relationship stability in geographically separated couples. *Journal of College Student Development, 33,* 222-230.

28. Stein, J. A., Newcomb, M. D., & Beutler, P. M. (1992). Differential effects of parent and grandparent drug use on behavior problems of male and female children. *Developmental Psychology, 29,* 31-43.

29. Suitor, J. J., & Pillemer, K. (1992). Status transitions and marital satisfaction: The case of adult children caring for elderly parents suffering from dementia. *Journal of Social and Personal Relationships, 9*(4), 549-562.

30. Whisman, M. A., & Jacobson, N. S. (1992). Change in marital adjustment following marital therapy: A comparison of two outcome measures. *Psychological Assessment, 4,* 219-223.

31. Donenberg, G., & Baker, B. L. (1993). The impact of young children with externalizing behaviors on their families. *Journal of Abnormal Child Psychology, 21,* 179-198.

32. Greenberg, L. S., Ford, C. L., Alden, L. S., & Johnson, S. M. (1993). In-session change in emotionally focused therapy. *Journal of Consulting and Clinical Psychology, 61,* 78-84.

33. Greenberger, E., & O'Neil, R. (1993). Spouse, parent, worker: Role, commitments and role-related experiences in the construction of adults' well-being. *Developmental Psychology, 29,* 181-197.

34. Halford, W. K., Sanders, M. R., & Behrens, B. C. (1993). A comparison of the generalization of behavioral marital therapy and enhanced behavioral marital therapy. *Journal of Consulting and Clinical Psychology, 61,* 51-60.

35. Libell, M. B., Marder, S. R., Mintz, J., Mintz, L. I., Tompson, M., Wirshing, W., Johnston-Cronk, K., & McKenzie, J. (1993). Parents' perceptions of family emotional climate and outcome in schizophrenia. *British Journal of Psychiatry, 162,* 751-754.

36. Reissman, C., Aron, A., & Bergen, M. R. (1993). Shared activities and marital satisfaction: Causal direction and self-expansion versus boredom. *Journal of Social and Personal Relationships, 10*(2), 243-254.

37. Snyder, D. K., Mangrum, L. F., & Wills, R. M. (1993). Predicting couples' response to marital therapy: A comparison of short- and long-term predictors. *Journal of Consulting and Clinical Psychology, 61,* 61-69.

[825]

Dyadic Parent-Child Interaction Coding System: A Manual.

Purpose: "For use in assessing the quality of parent-child social interaction."

Population: Children ages 2–10 and their parents.

Publication Date: 1981.

Acronym: DPICS.

Scores: 24 behavioral frequency scores in 4 general areas: Parent Behaviors, Child Behaviors, Child Responses to Commands, Parent Responses to Deviant Child Behaviors.

Administration: Individual.

Price Data: Price data including manual (87 pages) available from publisher.

Time: 15(20) minutes.

Comments: Behavioral ratings by clinician in 3 standard situations.

Authors: Sheila M. Eyberg and Elizabeth A. Robinson.

Publisher: Sheila M. Eyberg, Ph.D.

Cross References: For reviews by Robert J. McMahon and Phillip S. Strain, see 9:361 (1 reference); see also T3:768 (1 reference).

TEST REFERENCES

1. Kniskern, J. R., Robinson, E. A., & Mitchell, S. K. (1983). Mother-child interaction in home and laboratory settings. *Child Study Journal, 13,* 23-39.

2. Kazak, A. E., & Marvin, R. S. (1984). Differences, difficulties and adaptation: Stress and social networks in families with a handicapped child. *Family Relations, 33,* 67-77.

3. Webster-Stratton, C. (1984). Predictors of treatment outcome in parent training for conduct disordered children. *Behavior Therapy, 16,* 223-243.

4. Webster-Stratton, C. (1984). Randomized trial of two parent-training programs for families with conduct disordered children. *Journal of Consulting and Clinical Psychology, 52,* 666-678.

5. Webster-Stratton, C. (1985). Comparison of abusive and nonabusive families with conduct-disordered children. *American Journal of Orthopsychiatry, 55,* 59-69.

6. Webster-Stratton, C. (1985). Comparisons of behavior transactions between conduct-disordered children and their mothers in the clinic and at home. *Journal of Abnormal Child Psychology, 13,* 169-183.

7. Webster-Stratton, C. (1988). Mothers' and fathers' perceptions of child deviance: Roles of parent and child behaviors and parent adjustment. *Journal of Consulting and Clinical Psychology, 56,* 909-915.

8. Webster-Stratton, C., & Hammond, M. (1988). Maternal depression and its relationship to life stress, perceptions of child behavior problems, parenting behaviors, and child conduct problems. *Journal of Abnormal Child Psychology, 16,* 299-315.

9. Webster-Stratton, C., Kolpacoff, M., & Hollinsworth, T. (1988). Self-administered videotape therapy for families with conduct-problem children: Comparison with two cost-effective treatments and a control group. *Journal of Consulting and Clinical Psychology, 56,* 558-566.

10. McNeil, C. B., Eyberg, S., Eisenstadt, T. H., Newcomb, K., & Funderburk, B. (1991). Parent-child interaction therapy with behavior problem children: Generalization of treatment effects to the school setting. *Journal of Clinical Child Psychology, 20,* 140-151.

11. Webster-Stratton, C. (1992). Individually administered videotape parent training: "Who benefits?" *Cognitive Therapy and Research, 16,* 31-53.

[826]

Dysarthria Examination Batttery.

Purpose: Designed to "assess motor speech disorders."

Population: Children and adults.

Publication Date: 1993.

Scores, 5: Respiration, Phonation, Resonation, Articulation, Prosody.

Administration: Individual.

Price Data, 1994: $55 per complete kit including test booklet, 3 stimulus cards, 20 scoring forms, and manual (48 pages); $15 per 20 scoring forms.

Time: (60) minutes.

Author: Sakina S. Drummond.

Publisher: Communication Skill Builders.

[827]

Dyslexia Determination Test.

Purpose: To identify individuals who exhibit dyslexic patterns of responding in the areas of reading, writing, and spelling.

Population: Preschool–college.
Publication Dates: 1980–81.
Acronym: DDT.
Scores: 6 subtests: Dysnemkinesia (Writing of Numbers, Writing of Letters), Dysphonesia (Decoding, Encoding), Dyseidesia (Decoding, Encoding).
Administration: Individual.
Price Data: Not available.
Time: Administration time not reported.
Authors: John R. Griffin and Howard N. Walton.
Publisher: I-MED, Instructional Materials & Equipment Distributors [No reply from publisher; status unknown].
Cross References: For a review by Fred M. Grossman, see 9:362.

[828]
Dyslexia Schedule.
Purpose: Collect social information about children who have been referred for reading difficulties.
Population: Children having reading difficulties and first grade entrants.
Publication Dates: 1968–69.
Acronym: DS.
Scores: Total score only.
Administration: Group.
Price Data, 1988: $1.80 per 12 Dyslexia Schedules; $.90 per 12 School Entrance Check List; $3.25 per manual ('69, 32 pages); $5.95 per specimen set.
Time: (10–15) minutes for checklist.
Comments: An 89-item questionnaire to be filled out by the child's parents with score based on 24 discriminating items; 21 of these 24 items are published separately under the title School Entrance Check List (SECL) for screening use.
Author: John McLeod.
Publisher: Educators Publishing Service, Inc.
Cross References: For a review by Martin Kling, see 7:729 (3 references).

[829]
The Dyslexia Screening Survey.
Purpose: "Screening primary phonetic-auditory, visual, and multisensory processing skills in children who may be dyslexic."
Population: Children in primary grades.
Publication Date: 1980.
Scores: Checklist of basic developmental skills or criterion tasks divided into 7 steps: Functional Reading Level, Reading Potential, Significant Reading Discrepancy, Specific Processing Skill Deficiencies, Neuropsychological Dysfunctions, Associated Factors, Developmental-Remedial Strategies.
Administration: Individual.
Manual: No manual.
Price Data, 1988: $7.95 per 10 forms.
Time: Administration time not reported.
Author: Robert E. Valett.
Publisher: Fearon Education.

Cross References: For reviews by Fred M. Grossman and Deborah King Kundert, see 10:98.

[830]
E. S. Survey.
Purpose: "Screens applicants and employees for emotional stability and control."
Population: Job applicants and employees.
Publication Date: 1970.
Scores: Overall score, "Fake Good" Index.
Administration: Group.
Price Data, 1990: $7.50 or less per 25 surveys; $5 per year license fee.
Time: (5–10) minutes.
Authors: Alan L. Strand and others.
Publisher: Predictive Surveys Corporation.
Cross References: For reviews by Jeanette N. Cleveland and James W. Pinkney, see 9:364.

[831]
Early Child Development Inventory.
Purpose: "A brief screening inventory . . . designed to help identify children with developmental and other problems that may interfere with the child's ability to learn."
Population: Ages 1-3 to 3-0.
Publication Date: 1988.
Acronym: ECDI.
Scores: General Development Score, Possible Problems List (24); 4 ratings: Child Description, Major Problem, Parent's Questions Regarding Child, Parent's Functioning.
Administration: Individual or group.
Price Data, 1994: $9 per 25 Question-Answer sheets; $7 per manual (15 pages).
Time: (15) minutes.
Comments: Parent-completed questionnaire.
Authors: Harold Ireton.
Publisher: Behavior Science Systems, Inc.
Cross References: For a review by Robert W. Hiltonsmith, see 11:119.

[832]
The Early Childhood Behavior Scale.
Purpose: Designed to assess behaviors related to early childhood emotional disturbance and behavior disorder.
Population: 36–72 months.
Publication Dates: 1991–92.
Acronym: ECBS.
Scores, 4: Academic Progress, Social Relationships, Personal Adjustment, Total.
Administration: Individual.
Price Data, 1993: $55 per complete kit including technical manual ('92, 36 pages), intervention manual ('91, 130 pages), and 50 rating forms; $10 per technical manual; $20 per intervention manual; $25 per 50 rating forms.
Time: (15–20) minutes.
Comments: Ratings by teachers or parents.
Author: Stephen B. McCarney.
Publisher: Hawthorne Educational Services, Inc.

[833]

Early Childhood Environment Rating Scale.
Purpose: Provides rating scales for the assessment of various environmental characteristics of early childhood facilities.
Population: Early childhood settings.
Publication Date: 1980.
Scores: Ratings in 7 areas: Personal Care Routines of Children, Furnishings and Display for Children, Language-Reasoning Experiences, Fine and Gross Motor Activities, Creative Activities, Social Development, Adult Needs.
Administration: Group.
Price Data, 1994: $8.95 per rating scale, includes administration instructions (44 pages); $7.95 per 30 scoring sheets.
Time: (120) minutes.
Authors: Thelma Harms and Richard M. Clifford.
Publisher: Teachers College Press.
Cross References: For reviews by Richard Elardo and Cathy Fultz Telzrow, see 9:365.

TEST REFERENCES

1. McCartney, K. (1984). Effect of quality of day care environment on children's language development. *Developmental Psychology, 20,* 244-260.
2. Kontos, S., & Stevens, R. (1985). High quality child care: Does your center measure up? *Young Children, 40*(2), 5-9.
3. Bjorkman, S., Poteat, M., & Snow, C. W. (1986). Environmental ratings and children's social behavior: Implications for the assessment of day care quality. *American Journal of Orthopsychiatry, 56,* 271-277.
4. Bryant, D. M., Clifford, R. M., & Peisner, E. S. (1991). Best practices for beginners: Developmental appropriateness in kindergarten. *American Educational Research Journal, 28,* 783-803.
5. Schliecker, E., White, D. R., & Jacobs, E. (1991). The role of day care quality in the prediction of children's vocabulary. *Canadian Journal of Behavioural Science, 23,* 12-24.
6. Howes, C., & Hamilton, C. E. (1992). Children's relationships with child care teachers: Stability and concordance with parental attachments. *Child Development, 63,* 867-878.
7. Howes, C., & Matheson, C. C. (1992). Sequences in the development of competent play with peers: Social and social pretend play. *Developmental Psychology, 28,* 961-974.

[834]

Early Coping Inventory.
Purpose: Measures adaptive behavior.
Population: Ages 4–36 months.
Publication Date: 1988.
Scores, 4: Sensorimotor Organization, Reactive Behavior, Self-Initiated Behavior, Total.
Administration: Individual.
Price Data, 1993: $41.50 per complete kit including manual (62 pages) and 20 inventories (9 pages); $26.50 per 20 inventories; $22.60 per manual; $24.50 per specimen set.
Time: Administration time varies.
Comments: Downward extension of the Coping Inventory (648); ratings of adaptive behavior by an adult.
Authors: Shirley Zeitlin and G. Gordon Williamson with Margery Szczepanski.
Publisher: Scholastic Testing Service, Inc.
Cross References: For reviews by Harlan J. Stientjes and Logan Wright and Wade L. Hamil, see 11:120.

[835]

Early Intervention Developmental Profile.
Purpose: Designed to yield information for planning comprehensive developmental programs for children with all types of handicaps.
Population: Children with handicaps who function at the 0–35 month age level.
Publication Dates: 1977–91.
Scores, 8: Perceptual/Fine Motor, Cognition, Language, Social/Emotional, Self-Care (Feeding, Toileting, Dressing), Gross Motor.
Administration: Individual.
Price Data: Available from publisher.
Time: (50–60) minutes.
Comments: Stimulation activities manual included; also available in Spanish; see Preschool Developmental Profile (2080) for extended ages.
Authors: D. Sue Schafer, Martha S. Moersch, Sally J. Rogers, Diane B. D'Eugenio, Sara L. Brown, Carol M. Donovan, and Eleanor Whiteside Lynch.
Publisher: The University of Michigan Press.

TEST REFERENCES

1. Bagnato, S. J. (1984). Team congruence in developmental diagnosis and intervention: Comparing clinical judgment and child performance measures. *School Psychology Review, 13,* 7-16.

[836]

Early Language Milestone Scale, Second Edition.
Purpose: To assess speech and language development during infancy and early childhood.
Population: Birth to 36 months.
Publication Dates: 1983–93.
Acronym: ELM Scale-2.
Scores, 4: Auditory Expressive, Auditory Receptive, Visual, Global Language.
Administration: Individual.
Price Data, 1994: $89 per complete kit including manual ('93, 95 pages), object kit, and 100 records; $29 per manual; $29 per 100 record forms; $34 per object kit.
Time: (1–10) minutes.
Author: James Coplan.
Publisher: PRO-ED, Inc.
Cross References: For a review of an earlier edition by Ruth M. Noyce, see 10:99 (2 references).

[837]

Early Learning: Assessment and Development.
Purpose: Early identification of children's areas of strengths and weaknesses.
Population: Ages 5-3 and 5-6 through the first year of school and older children with specific learning disabilities.
Publication Date: 1981.
Scores: 5 areas: Movement Skills—Fine and Gross Motor, Perceptual Skills, Communication—Language and Listening Skills, Learning and Memory, Emotional and Social Development.

Administration: Individual.
Price Data: Available from publisher.
Time: Administration time not reported.
Comments: Test materials (e.g., balls, bean bag) must be supplied by examiner.
Authors: Audrey Curtis and Mary Wignall.
Publisher: Macmillan Education Ltd. [England].
Cross References: For reviews by Dennis Deloria and William B. Michael, see 9:367.

[838]
Early Mathematical Language.
Purpose: Constructed to assess mathematical language.
Population: Children in their first year at school.
Publication Date: 1982.
Scores: 6 booklets: Position in Space, Number, Length, Weight and Shape, Volume and Capacity, Time.
Administration: Individual.
Price Data: Available from publisher.
Time: Administration time not reported.
Authors: Margaret Williams and Heather Somerwill.
Publisher: Macmillan Education Ltd. [England].

[839]
Early Mathematics Diagnostic Kit.
Purpose: "To provide the teacher with an effective means of diagnosing early difficulties in the learning of mathematics."
Population: Ages 4–8.
Publication Dates: 1977–87.
Acronym: EMDK.
Scores: 10 areas: Number, Shape, Representation, Length, Weight, Capacity, Memory, Money, Time, Foundation.
Administration: Individual.
Price Data, 1989: £63.25 per complete kit including 25 record booklets, book of test items, set of coloured cubes, set of 3 small boxes, manual ('87, 32 pages); £6.35 per 10 record forms; £8.05 per manual.
Time: 30(35) minutes.
Comments: Item checklist.
Authors: David Lumb and Margaret Lumb.
Publisher: NFER-Nelson Publishing Co., Ltd. [England].
Cross References: For reviews by John M. Enger and G. Michael Poteat, see 11:121.

[840]
Early Memories Procedure.
Purpose: "Method of exploring personality organization, especially current life concerns, based on an individual's memory of the past."
Population: Ages 10 and over with at least a fourth-grade reading level.
Publication Dates: 1989–92.
Scores: No scores.
Administration: Group.
Price Data, 1994: $63 per 10 test booklets; $4 per manual.

Time: (90–240) minutes.
Comments: Instrument may be interpreted according to a Freudian, Adlerian, Ego-Psychological or Cognitive-Perceptual model.
Author: Arnold R. Bruhn.
Publisher: Arnold R. Bruhn and Associates.

TEST REFERENCES
1. Bruhn, A. R. (1992). The Early Memories Procedure: A projective test of autobiographical memory, Part I. *Journal of Personality Assessment*, 58, 1-15.

[841]
Early School Assessment.
Purpose: Designed to measure prereading and mathematics skills.
Population: End of prekindergarten to middle of kindergarten, middle of kindergarten to beginning of grade 1.
Publication Date: 1990.
Acronym: ESA.
Scores, 7: Prereading (Language, Visual [also used in Mathematics total], Auditory, Memory, Total), Mathematics Concepts and Operations (Visual [also used in Prereading total], Total).
Administration: Group.
Levels, 2: 1, 2.
Price Data: Price Data available from publisher for test materials including: complete testing kit including 35 machine- or hand-scorable test booklets (select level), 35 practice books, scoring key, class record sheet for hand scoring, and examiner's manual (81 pages, select level); 35 parent conference forms (select level); teacher's guide (51 pages, select level); preliminary norms book; preliminary technical bulletin; test organizer; scoring service available from publisher.
Time: 229 (Level 2) to 239 (Level 1) minutes over 8 sessions.
Authors: CTB MacMillan/McGraw-Hill.
Publisher: CTB MacMillan/McGraw-Hill.

[842]
Early School Inventory.
Population: Ages 5–7.
Publication Dates: 1986–87.
Acronym: ESI.
Price Data, 1994: $46 per ESI manual for interpretation and use ('87, 222 pages) including normative information, 1 ESI-D, and 1 ESI-P skill record.
Time: Administration time not reported.
Authors: Joanne R. Nurss and Mary E. McGauvran.
Publisher: The Psychological Corporation.
  a) EARLY SCHOOL INVENTORY—DEVELOPMENTAL.
  Purpose: "Provides a systematic method for gathering information about a child's development for use in planning effective instruction."
  Acronym: ESI-D.
  Scores, 4: Physical Development, Language Development, Cognitive Development, Social-Emotional Development.
  Price Data: $36.50 per 35 self-scoring checklists

273

and directions for administering; $3 per ESI-D skill record.

Administration: Group.

b) EARLY SCHOOL INVENTORY—PRELITERACY.

Purpose: Provides information about "a child's progress in acquiring the preliteracy skills needed when learning to read and write."

Acronym: ESI-P.

Scores, 3: Print Concepts, Writing Concepts, Story Structure.

Price Data: $44.50 per 35 self-scoring sheets, directions, and one set of 4 cards; $32 per 35 self-scoring sheets; $3.50 per directions; $15 per cards; $3 per ESI-P skill record.

Administration: Individual.

[843]

Early School Personality Questionnaire.

Purpose: Measures personality dimensions.

Population: Ages 6–8.

Publication Dates: 1966–76.

Acronym: ESPQ.

Scores: 13 primary factors (Reserved vs. Warm-hearted, Dull vs. Bright, Affected by Feelings vs. Emotionally Stable, Undemonstrative vs. Excitable, Obedient vs. Dominant, Sober vs. Enthusiastic, Disregards Rules vs. Conscientious, Shy vs. Venturesome, Tough-Minded vs. Tender-Minded, Vigorous vs. Circumspect Individualism, Forthright vs. Shrewd, Self-Assured vs. Guilt-Prone, Relaxed vs. Tense), and 4 second-order factors (Extraversion, Anxiety, Tough Poise, Independence).

Administration: Group.

Price Data, 1994: $23 per introductory kit including manual, 2 answer booklets, profile sheet, and scoring keys; $10 per manual; $10 per 25 child's answer booklets; $15 per 50 profile sheets/second-order worksheets; $13.65 per tape recording of items; $12 per scoring keys.

Time: Untimed.

Authors: Richard W. Coan and Raymond B. Cattell.

Publisher: Institute for Personality and Ability Testing, Inc.

Cross References: See T3:772 (4 references); for additional information and reviews by Jacob O. Sines and Robert L. Thorndike, see 8:540 (8 references); see also T2:1163 (3 references); for a review by Lovick C. Miller, see 7:71 (8 references); see also P:66 (7 references).

TEST REFERENCES

1. Harris, W. J., Drummond, R. J., & Schultz, E. W. (1977). An investigation of relationships between teachers' ratings of behavior and children's personality traits. *Journal of Abnormal Child Psychology, 5,* 43-52.

2. Handford, H. A., Mayes, S. D., Bagnato, S. J., & Bixler, E. O. (1986). Relationships between variations in parents' attitudes and personality traits of hemophilic boys. *American Journal of Orthopsychiatry, 56,* 424-434.

3. Dudek, S. Z., Strobel, M., & Thomas, A. D. (1987). Chronic learning problems and maturation. *Perceptual and Motor Skills, 64,* 407-429.

[844]

Early Screening Inventory.

Purpose: "A brief developmental screening instrument . . . designed to identify children who may need special educational services in order to perform adequately in school."

Population: Ages 3–6.

Publication Dates: 1976–87.

Acronym: ESI.

Administration: Individual.

Levels, 2: Three Year Olds, Four to Six Year Olds.

Price Data, 1994: $43.95 per complete kit including test and manual ('83, 64 pages), score sheets, screening materials, and parent questionnaires; $11.50 per test and manual; $11.50 per 30 score sheets; $11.95 per screening materials; $9.95 per 30 parent questionnaires.

Foreign Language Edition: Spanish version ('87) available.

Time: (15–20) minutes.

Comments: Originally introduced as the Eliot-Pearson Screening Inventory; test also includes a parent questionnaire; Spanish version ('87) available; manual for Revision for Three Year Olds and Spanish version available directly from S. J. Meisels.

Authors: Samuel J. Meisels and Martha Stone Wiske.

Publisher: Teachers College Press.

a) THREE YEAR OLDS.

Scores: 4 areas: Draw-a-Person, Visual-Motor/Adaptive, Language and Cognition, Gross Motor/Body Awareness.

b) FOUR TO SIX YEAR OLDS.

Scores: Same as *a*.

c) PARENT QUESTIONNAIRE.

Cross References: For reviews by Denise M. Dezolt and Kevin Menefee, see 11:122 (1 reference).

[845]

Early Speech Perception Test.

Purpose: "Developed to obtain increasingly more accurate information about speech discrimination skills as the profoundly hearing-impaired child's verbal abilities develop."

Publication Date: 1990.

Acronym: ESP.

Administration: Individual.

Price Data, 1992: $150 per ESP kit including manual (32 pages), scoring forms, box of toys, full-color picture cards, and audio cassette tape; $50 per Macintosh computer diskette; $25 per randomization audiotape.

Time: (15–20) minutes.

Comments: Information available from publisher regarding specialized hardware and software equipment necessary for administering the computerized version of the ESP test battery.

Authors: Jean S. Moog and Anne E. Geers.

Publisher: Central Institute for the Deaf.

a) ESP STANDARD VERSION.

Population:: Ages 6–15.

Scores, 4: Pattern Perception, Spondee Identification, Monosyllable Identification, Total.
Price Data: $3 per 25 standard version scoring forms.
b) ESP LOW-VERBAL VERSION.
Population: Ages 3–6.
Scores, 4: Pattern Perception Test, Word Identification Test (Spondee Identification, Monosyllable Identification), Total.
Price Data: $3 per 25 low-verbal version scoring forms.

[846]

Early Years Easy Screen.
Purpose: Constructed to screen for strengths and weaknesses in the areas of physical and cognitive development.
Population: Ages 4–5.
Publication Date: 1991.
Acronym: EYES.
Scores, 6: Level of Performance in 6 areas: Pencil Coordination, Active Body, Number, Oral Language, Visual Reading, Auditory Reading.
Administration: Group.
Price Data: Available from publisher.
Time: (160–194) minutes over several sessions.
Comments: Other test materials (e.g., bean bag, beads) must be supplied by examiner.
Authors: Joan Clerehugh, Kim Hart, Rosalind Pither, Kay Rider, and Kate Turner.
Publisher: NFER-Nelson Publishing Co., Ltd. [England].

[847]

Eating Disorder Inventory-2.
Purpose: Constructed as a self-report measure of psychological features commonly associated with anorexia nervosa and bulimia nervosa.
Population: Ages 12 and over.
Publication Dates: 1984–91.
Acronym: EDI.
Scores, 11: Drive for Thinness, Bulimia, Body Dissatisfaction, Ineffectiveness, Perfectionism, Interpersonal Distrust, Interoceptive Awareness, Maturity Fears, Asceticism (provisional), Impulse Regulation (provisional), Social Insecurity (provisional).
Administration: Group or individual.
Price Data, 1994: $73 per complete kit including 25 item booklets, 25 symptom checklists, 25 answer sheets, 25 profile forms, and manual ('91, 74 pages); $16 per 25 item booklets; $16 per 25 symptom checklists; $16 per 25 answer sheets; $10 per 25 profile forms; $20 per manual.
Time: (20) minutes.
Comments: Computer version available.
Author: David M. Garner.
Publisher: Psychological Assessment Resources, Inc.
Cross References: For a review of an earlier edition by Cabrini S. Swassing, see 10:100 (16 references).

TEST REFERENCES

1. Yager, J., Landsverk, J., & Edelstein, C. K. (1987). A 20-month follow-up study of 628 women with eating disorders, I: Course and severity. *American Journal of Psychiatry, 144,* 1172-1177.
2. Rosen, J. C., Silberg, N. T., & Gross, J. (1988). Eating Attitudes Test and Eating Disorders Inventory: Norms for adolescent girls and boys. *Journal of Consulting and Clinical Psychology, 56,* 305-308.
3. Welch, G., Hall, A., & Walkey, F. (1988). The factor structure of the Eating Disorder Inventory. *Journal of Clinical Psychology, 44,* 51-56.
4. Heilbrun, A. B., Jr., & Flodin, A. (1989). Food cues and perceptual distortion of the female body: Implications for food avoidance in the early dynamics of anorexia nervosa. *Journal of Clinical Psychology, 45,* 843-851.
5. Laessle, R. G., Tuschl, R. J., Kotthaus, B. C., & Pirke, K. M. (1989). A comparison of the validity of three scales for the assessment of dietary restraint. *Journal of Abnormal Psychology, 98,* 504-507.
6. Szekely, B. C., Raffeld, P. C., & Snodgrass, G. (1989). Anonymity, sex, and weight-preoccupation as variables on the Eating Disorders Inventory with normal college students. *Psychological Reports, 65,* 795-800.
7. Cash, T. F., Counts, B., & Huffine, C. E. (1990). Current and vestigial effects of overweight among women: Fear of fat, attitudinal body image, and eating behaviors. *Journal of Psychopathology and Behavioral Assessment, 12,* 157-167.
8. Dacey, C. M., Nelson, W. M., III, & Aikman, K. G. (1990). Prevalence rate and personality comparisons of bulimic and normal adolescents. *Child Psychiatry and Human Development, 20,* 243-251.
9. Heilbrun, A. B., Jr., & Witt, N. (1990). Distorted body image as a risk factor in anorexia nervosa: Replication and clarification. *Psychological Reports, 66,* 407-416.
10. Smith, J. E., & Morgan, C. D. (1990). The neglected bulimic: The nonpurger. *Journal of Psychopathology and Behavioral Assessment, 12,* 103-118.
11. Thomas, C. D., & Freeman, R. J. (1990). The Body Esteem Scale: Construct validity of the female subscales. *Journal of Personality Assessment, 54,* 204-212.
12. Cantrell, P. J., & Ellis, J. B. (1991). Gender role and risk patterns for eating disorders in men and women. *Journal of Clinical Psychology, 47,* 53-60.
13. Gibson, S. G., & Thomas, C. D. (1991). Self-rated competence, current weight, and body-image among college women. *Psychological Reports, 69,* 336-338.
14. Heatherton, T. F., Polivy, J., & Herman, C. P. (1991). Restraint, weight loss, and variability of body weight. *Journal of Abnormal Psychology, 100,* 78-83.
15. Heilbrun, A. B., Jr., & Worobow, A. L. (1991). Attention and disordered eating behavior: I. Disattention to satiety cues as a risk factor in the development of bulimia. *Journal of Clinical Psychology, 47,* 3-9.
16. Pike, K. M., & Rodin, J. (1991). Mothers, daughters, and disordered eating. *Journal of Abnormal Psychology, 100,* 198-204.
17. Rebert, W. M., Stanton, A. L., & Schwarz, R. M. (1991). Influence of personality attributes and daily moods on bulimic eating patterns. *Addictive Behaviors, 16,* 497-505.
18. Simmons, D. D. (1991). Dietary restraint as values-related motivation: A psychometric clarification. *The Journal of Psychology, 125,* 189-194.
19. Smith, J. E., Hillard, M. C., & Roll, S. (1991). Rorschach evaluation of adolescent bulimics. *Adolescence, 26,* 687-696.
20. Smith, J. E., Hillard, M. C., Walsh, R. A., Kubacki, S. R., & Morgan, C. D. (1991). Rorschach assessment of purging and nonpurging bulimics. *Journal of Personality Assessment, 56,* 277-288.
21. Thompson, J. K., Fabian, L. J., Moulton, D. O., Dunn, M. E., & Altabe, M. N. (1991). Development and validation of the physical appearance related teasing scale. *Journal of Personality Assessment, 56,* 513-521.
22. Baell, W. K., & Wertheim, E. H. (1992). Predictors of outcome in the treatment of bulimia nervosa. *British Journal of Clinical Psychology, 31,* 330-332.
23. Kenny, M. E., & Hart, K. (1992). Relationship between parental attachment and eating disorders in an inpatient and a college sample. *Journal of Counseling Psychology, 39,* 521-526.
24. Kent, J. S., & Clopton, J. R. (1992). Bulimic women's perceptions of their family relationships. *Journal of Clinical Psychology, 48,* 281-292.
25. Patton, C. J. (1992). Fear of abandonment and binge eating: A subliminal psychodynamic activation investigation. *Journal of Nervous and Mental Disease, 180,* 484-490.
26. Reeves, P. C., & Johnson, M. E. (1992). Relationship between family-of-origin functioning and self-perceived correlates of eating disorders among female college students. *Journal of College Student Development, 33,* 44-49.
27. Ussery, L. W., & Prentice-Dunn, S. (1992). Personality pre-

dictors of bulimic behavior and attitudes in males. *Journal of Clinical Psychology, 48*, 722-729.

28. Williamson, D. A., Gleaves, D. H., & Sowin, S. S. (1992). Empirical classification of eating disorder not otherwise specified: Support for DSM-IV changes. *Journal of Psychopathology and Behavioral Assessment, 14*, 201-216.

29. Gleaves, D. H., & Eberenz, K. (1993). The psychopathology of anorexia nervosa: A factor analytic investigation. *Journal of Psychopathology and Behavioral Assessment, 15*, 141-152.

30. Gleaves, D. H., Williamson, D. A., & Barker, S. E. (1993). Confirmatory factor analysis of a multidimensional model of bulimia nervosa. *Journal of Abnormal Psychology, 102*, 173-176.

31. Goldbloom, D. S., & Olmsted, M. P. (1993). Pharmacotherapy of bulimia nervosa with fluoxetine: Assessment of clinically significant attitudinal change. *American Journal of Psychiatry, 150*, 770-774.

32. Leon, G. R., Fulkerson, J. A., Perry, C. L., & Cudeck, R. (1993). Personality and behavioral vulnerabilities associated with risk status for eating disorders in adolescent girls. *Journal of Abnormal Psychology, 102*, 438-444.

33. Lydiard, R. B., Brewerton, T. D., Fossey, M. D., Laraia, M. T., Stuart, G., Beinfeld, M. C., & Ballenger, J. C. (1993). CSF cholecystokinin octapeptide in patients with bulimia nervosa and in normal comparison subjects. *American Journal of Psychiatry, 150*, 1099-1101.

34. Phelps, L., & Wilczenski, F. (1993). Eating Disorder Inventory-2: Cognitive-behavioral dimensions with nonclinical adolescents. *Journal of Clinical Psychology, 49*, 508-515.

35. Silverstein, B., Perlick, D., Clauson, J., & McKoy, E. (1993). Depression combined with somatic symptomatology among adolescent females who report concerns regarding maternal achievement. *Sex Roles, 28*, 637-653.

36. Stacher, G., Abatzi-Wenzel, T., Wiesnagrotzki, S., Bergmann, H., Schneider, C., & Gaupman, G. (1993). Gastric emptying, body weight and symptoms in primary anorexia nervosa. *British Journal of Psychiatry, 162*, 398-402.

37. Thackwray, D. E., Smith, M. C., Bodfish, J. W., & Meyers, A. W. (1993). A comparison of behavioral and cognitive-behavioral interventions for bulimia nervosa. *Journal of Consulting and Clinical Psychology, 61*, 639-645.

38. Williamson, D. A., Gleaves, D. H., Watkins, P. C., & Schlundt, D. G. (1993). Validation of self-ideal body size discrepancy as a measure of body dissatisfaction. *Journal of Psychopathology and Behavioral Assessment, 15*, 57-68.

[848]

Eating Inventory.
Purpose: To assess "three dimensions of eating behavior found to be important in recognizing and treating eating-related disorders: cognitive control of eating, disinhibition, and hunger."
Population: Ages 17 and older.
Publication Dates: 1983–88.
Scores, 3: Cognitive Restraint of Eating, Disinhibition, Hunger.
Administration: Group.
Price Data, 1994: $83 per complete kit including 25 questionnaires, 25 answer sheets, and manual ('88, 37 pages); $24 per 25 questionnaires; $34.50 per 25 answer sheets; $34.50 per manual.
Time: (15–20) minutes.
Authors: Albert J. Stunkard and Samuel Messick.
Publisher: The Psychological Corporation.

TEST REFERENCES

1. Simmons, D. D. (1991). Dietary restraint as values-related motivation: A psychometric clarification. *The Journal of Psychology, 125*, 189-194.

[849]

Eby Gifted Behavior Index.
Purpose: Designed to identify students for gifted programming based on the use of gifted behaviors.
Population: Elementary and high school and college students.
Publication Date: 1989.

Scores, 8: General, Verbal, Math/Science/Problem-Solving, Musical, Visual/Spatial, Social/Leadership, Mechanical/Technical/Inventiveness, Product Rating.
Administration: Individual.
Price Data, 1991: $24.95 per complete kit including manual (16 pages).
Time: Administration time not reported.
Comments: Ratings by teachers; checklists may be used separately.
Author: Judy W. Eby.
Publisher: United/DOK Publishers.

[850]

Eckstein Audiometers.
Purpose: For the measurement and evaluation of hearing losses.
Population: Grades K and over.
Publication Dates: 1961–73.
Subtests: 7 models (solid state).
Administration: Individual.
Price Data: Available from publisher.
Time: Administration time not reported.
Author: Eckstein Bros., Inc.
Publisher: Eckstein Bros., Inc.
a) TETRA-TONE SCREENING AUDIOMETER MODEL 46.
Publication Dates: 1968–69.
Comments: For screening in schools and medical offices; 4 frequencies; 4 hearing classifications.
b) MINIATURE AUDIOMETER MODEL 60.
Publication Date: 1961.
Comments: For air conduction screening and threshold testing in schools and medical offices; 7 frequencies.
c) AUDIOMETER MODEL 350-I.
Publication Dates: 1964–72.
Comments: Air conduction threshold testing in industry.
d) FULL RANGE PORTABLE AUDIOMETERS.
Publication Date: 1970–72.
Comments: 2 models (may be AC operated).
1) *Model 390.*
Comments: For pure tone air conducting testing.
2) *Model 390 MB.*
Comments: Diagnostic Model for pure tone air and bone conducting testing.
e) DIAGNOSTIC AUDIOMETER, MODEL 400.
Publication Date: 1969.
Comments: Air and bone conduction; calibrated speech and pure tone.
f) CLINICAL AUDIOMETER, MODEL 500-A.
Publication Date: 1970.
Comments: Calibrated speech and pure tone.

[851]

[Economics/Objective Tests].
Purpose: To assess students' general knowledge of high school economics.
Population: 1 semester high school.
Publication Date: 1970.

Scores: Total score only for each test.
Administration: Group.
Tests, 5: Concepts in Economics, Price/Income and Personal Growth, Money/Banking and Insurance, International Trade, Final Test.
Manual: No manual.
Price Data, 1994: $7.95 per test book including tests and response key.
Time: Administration time not reported.
Comments: Formerly called Economics Tests.
Author: Perfection Learning Corp.
Publisher: Perfection Learning Corp.

[852]

ECOScales.
Purpose: Designed "for assessing the interactive and communicative skills of preconversational children and their adult caregivers."
Population: Delayed child-significant adult dyads.
Publication Date: 1989.
Scores: Ratings on behaviors in 5 areas of competencies: Becoming Play Partners, Becoming Turntaking Partners, Becoming Communicating Partners, Becoming Language Partners, Becoming Conversation Partners.
Administration: Individual.
Price Data, 1991: $48.99 per complete kit including 24 ECOScales forms, 24 practice plans and records, and manual (141 pages); $15.93 per 24 ECOScales forms; $14.94 per 24 practice plans and records; $19.95 per manual.
Time: [10–30] minutes.
Comments: Ratings by professional based on observations and interview.
Authors: James D. MacDonald, Yvonne Gillette, and Thomas A. Hutchinson (manual).
Publisher: The Riverside Publishing Co.

[853]

Edinburgh Picture Test.
Purpose: To assess reasoning ability in young children.
Population: Ages 6-6 to 8-3.
Publication Dates: 1985–91.
Scores, 6: Doesn't Belong, Classification, Reversed Similarities, Analogies, Sequences, Total.
Administration: Group.
Price Data, 1994: £5.25 per specimen set; £8.99 per 20 test booklets; £4.99 per manual (1988, 15 pages).
Time: (30–60) minutes.
Authors: Godfrey Thomson Unit, University of Edinburgh.
Publisher: Hodder & Stoughton Educational [England].

[854]

The Edinburgh Questionnaires (1982 Edition).
Purpose: Constructed to measure "personal interests and organisational climate."

Population: Adults.
Publication Date: 1982.
Scores: 3 sections: Quality of Working Life (Working Conditions, Type of Work Wanted, Relationships, General), Important Activities, Consequences (Compatibility, Perceptions of Task and Personal Reactions, Reactions of Superiors, Reactions of Colleagues and Workmates, Benefits and Disbenefits to Others, Competencies Engaged).
Administration: Group.
Price Data: Available from publisher.
Time: Administration time not reported.
Comments: Research use only.
Author: John Raven.
Publisher: NFER-Nelson Publishing Co., Ltd. [England].
Cross References: For a review by Bruce Shertzer, see 10:102.

[855]

Edinburgh Reading Tests.
Purpose: To assess pupil progress in reading.
Population: Ages 7-0 to 9-0, 8-6 to 10-6, 10-0 to 12-6, 12-0 to 16-0.
Publication Dates: 1972–93.
Administration: Group.
Levels, 4: Stages 1, 2, 3, 4.
Comments: Upward and downward extension plus second editions.
Publisher: Hodder & Stoughton Educational [England].
a) STAGE 1.
Population: Ages 7-0 to 9-0.
Publication Dates: 1977–93.
Scores, 5: Vocabulary, Syntax, Sequences, Comprehension, Total.
Forms, 2: A, B.
Price Data, 1994: £10.99 per 20 copies of test (specify Form A or Form B); £4.50 per manual (31 pages); £5.25 per specimen set.
Time: (30–55) minutes.
Authors: Test by The Godfrey Thomson Unit, University of Edinburgh, in association with The Scottish Education Department and The Educational Institute of Scotland; manual by D. J. Carroll.
b) STAGE 2 [THIRD EDITION].
Population: Ages 8-6 to 10-6.
Publication Dates: 1972–92.
Scores, 7: Vocabulary, Comprehension of Sequences, Retention of Significant Details, Use of Context, Reading Rate, Comprehension of Essential Ideas, Total.
Price Data: £13.50 per 20 copies of test booklet; £7.25 per manual ('92, 39 pages); £7.99 per specimen set.
Time: (30–35) minutes for practice test; (40) minutes for part I; (35) minutes for part II.
Comments: Includes 2 parts plus a practice test.
Authors: Test by The Godfrey Thomson Unit, University of Edinburgh, in association with The

Scottish Education Department and The Educational Institute of Scotland; manual by M. J. Hutchings and E. M. J. Hutchings.

c) STAGE 3 [THIRD EDITION].
Population: Ages 10-0 to 12-6.
Publication Dates: 1973–92.
Scores, 6: Reading for Facts; Comprehension of Sequences, Retention of Main Ideas, Comprehension of Points of View, Vocabulary, Total.
Price Data: £15.99 per 20 test booklets; £7.25 per manual ('92, 39 pages); £7.99 per specimen set.
Time: (30–35) minutes for practice test; (40) minutes for part I; (35) minutes for part II.
Authors: Test by Moray House Institute of Education, in association with The Scottish Education Department and The Educational Institute of Scotland; manual by Ron Mackenzie.

d) STAGE 4.
Population: Ages 12-0 to 16-0.
Publication Date: 1977.
Scores, 6: Skimming, Vocabulary, Reading for Facts, Points of View, Comprehension, Total.
Price Data: £15.99 per 20 test booklets; £6.99 per manual (34 pages); £7.99 per specimen set.
Time: 60(70) minutes.
Authors: Test by The Godfrey Thomson Unit, University of Edinburgh, in association with The Scottish Education Department and The Educational Institute of Scotland; manual by D. J. Carroll.

e) SHORTENED EDINBURGH READING TEST.
Purpose: Designed as a survey and screening instrument of written language attainment.
Population: Ages 10-0 to 11-6.
Scores, 3: Vocabulary, Syntax and Sequence, Comprehension.
Time: (40) minutes.
Comments: Questions selected from items in the full Edinburgh Reading Tests.
Authors: Godfrey Thomson Unit for Educational Research, Moray House Institute of Education, and the Child Health and Education Study, University of Bristol.
Cross References: For reviews by Nancy L. Roser and Byron H. Van Roekel, see 9:374 (1 reference); see T3:775 (2 references); for reviews by Douglas A. Pidgeon and Earl F. Rankin of the first editions of Stages 2 and 3, see 8:724.

TEST REFERENCES
1. Dobbins, D. A., & Tafa, E. (1991). The "stability" of identification of underachieving readers over different measures of intelligence and reading. *The British Journal of Educational Psychology, 61,* 155-163.

[856]
Educational Abilities Scales.
Purpose: "Designed to yield additional information to assist with the selection of options subjects in the final two years of compulsory schooling."
Population: Ages 13–15.
Publication Dates: 1982–83.

Acronym: EAS.
Scores: 10 tests yielding 5 scales: Clerical Aptitude, Mechanical Comprehension, Symbolic Reasoning, Spatial Reasoning, Science Reasoning.
Administration: Group.
Price Data, 1985: £2.45 per reusable student book; £4.45 per 10 answer booklets; £2.45 per 25 profiles; £4 per 10 developer pens; £5.95 per manual ('83, 45 pages) and scoring stencil; £8.95 per specimen set.
Time: 150(200) minutes in 2 sessions.
Authors: Andy Stillman and Chris Whetton.
Publisher: NFER-Nelson Publishing Co., Ltd. [England].

TEST REFERENCES
1. Zenke, L., & Alexander, L. (1984). Teaching thinking in Tulsa. *Educational Leadership, 42,* 81-84.

[857]
Educational Administrator Effectiveness Profile.
Purpose: Assesses school administrators' on-the-job skills and behavior.
Population: Public school administrators.
Publication Date: 1984.
Acronym: EAEP.
Scores: 11 ratings: Setting Goals and Objectives, Planning, Making Decisions and Solving Problems, Managing Business and Fiscal Affairs, Assessing Progress, Delegating Responsibilities, Communicating, Building and Maintaining Relationships, Demonstrating Professional Commitment, Improving Instruction, Developing Staff.
Administration: Group.
Price Data: Available from publisher.
Comments: Ratings by self and five co-workers.
Authors: Human Synergistics, Inc. and Tom Webber (leader's manual).
Publisher: Human Synergistics, Inc.
Cross References: For reviews by Jan N. Hughes and Leslie T. Raskind, see 10:103.

[858]
Educational Development Series (1992 Edition).
Purpose: A battery of ability and achievement tests and questions on interests and plans.
Population: Grades K–12.
Publication Dates: 1963–92.
Acronym: EDS.
Administration: Group.
Levels: 13.
Price Data, 1993: $34.50 per 10 test booklets (Levels 13C–16D) and manual ('92, 15–30 pages); $39.75 per 10 test booklets (Levels 17C–18D) and manual; $23.80 per 50 answer sheets (Levels 13C–18D); $2.45 per student for complete battery standard scoring; $28 per specimen set of specified grades (K–2, 3–5, 6–8, 9–12).
Authors: O. F. Anderhalter, R. H. Bauernfeind, V. M. Cashew, Mary E. Greig, Walter M. Lifton,

George Mallinson, Jacqueline Mallinson, Joseph F. Papenfuss, and Neil Vail.
Publisher: Scholastic Testing Service, Inc.

a) LEVEL 10D.
Population: Grade K.
Publication Date: 1992.
Scores, 8: Cognitive Skills (Verbal, Nonverbal, Total), Basic Skills (Reading, Language, Mathematics, Total), Battery Average.
Price Data: $4.36 per student for rental and scoring service.
Time: (160–180) minutes in 5 sessions.

b) LEVEL 11C.
Population: Grade 1.
Publication Date: 1992.
Scores, 11: Cognitive Skills (Verbal, Nonverbal, Total), Basic Skills (Reading, Language, Mathematics, Total), Reference Skills, Science, Social Studies, Battery Average.
Price Data: $4.57 per student for rental and scoring service.
Time: (280–300) minutes in 5 sessions.

c) LEVEL 12C.
Population: Grade 2.
Publication Date: 1992.
Scores, 12: Cognitive Skills (Verbal, Nonverbal, Total), Basic Skills (Reading, Language Arts, Mathematics, Total), Reference Skills, Science, Social Studies, Battery Average, School Interests.
Price Data: $4.57 per student for rental and scoring service.
Time: (295–315) minutes in 5 sessions.

d) LEVEL 13C.
Population: Grade 3.
Publication Date: 1992.
Scores, 12: Same as for *c* above.
Price Data: $3.55 per student for rental and scoring service.
Time: (320–340) minutes in 5 sessions.
Comments: Separate answer sheets must be used in Levels 13C–18D.

e) LEVEL 14C.
Population: Grade 4.
Publication Date: 1992.
Scores, 14: Cognitive Skills (Verbal, Nonverbal, Total), Basic Skills (Reading, Language Arts, Mathematics, Total), Reference Skills, Science, Social Studies, Battery Average, Career Interests, School Plans, School Interests.
Price Data: Same as for *d* above.
Time: (345–365) minutes in 3 sessions.

f) LEVEL 15C.
Population: Grade 5.
Publication Date: 1992.
Scores, 14: Same as for *e* above.
Price Data: Same as for *d* above.
Time: (345–365) minutes in 3 sessions.

g) LEVEL 15D.
Population: Grade 6.
Publication Date: 1992.
Scores, 14: Same as for *e* above.

Price Data: Same as for *d* above.
Time: (345–365) minutes in 3 sessions.

h) LEVEL 16C.
Population: Grade 7.
Publication Date: 1992.
Scores, 14: Same as for *e* above.
Price Data: Same as for *d* above.
Time: (345–365) minutes in 3 sessions.

i) LEVEL 16D.
Population: Grade 8.
Publication Date: 1992.
Scores, 14: Same as for *e* above.
Price Data: Same as for *d* above.
Time: (345–365) minutes in 3 sessions.

j) LEVEL 17C.
Population: Grade 9.
Publication Date: 1992.
Scores, 14: Same as for *e* above.
Price Data: Same as for *d* above.
Time: (350–370) minutes in 3 sessions.

k) LEVEL 17D.
Population: Grade 10.
Publication Date: 1992.
Details: Same as for *j* above.

l) LEVEL 18C.
Population: Grade 11.
Publication Date: 1992.
Details: Same as for *j* above.

m) LEVEL 18D.
Population: Grade 11.
Publication Date: 1992.
Details: Same as for *j* above.

Cross References: For a review by Esther E. Diamond of an earlier edition, see 9:376; see also T3:2325 (1 reference); for reviews by Samuel T. Mayo and William A. Mehrens of forms copyrighted 1976 and earlier see 8:27; see also T2:33 (1 reference); for a review by Robert D. North of forms copyrighted 1968 and earlier see 7:22.

TEST REFERENCES

1. Freebody, P., & Tirre, W. C. (1985). Achievement outcomes of two reading programmes: An instance of aptitude-treatment interaction. *British Journal of Educational Psychology, 55,* 53-60.
2. Kennedy, E. (1992). A multilevel study of elementary male Black students and White students. *Journal of Educational Research, 86,* 105-110.

[859]
Educational Interest Inventory.
Purpose: Designed to identify personal preference for different college educational programs.
Population: Prospective college students.
Publication Date: 1989.
Acronym: EII.
Scores: 47 scales: Agriculture (Agribusiness/Agricultural Production, Agricultural Sciences, Renewable Natural Resources), Architecture and Environmental Design, Area/Ethnic Studies, Business/Management (Accounting and Finance, Administration and Management, Human Resources Management, Marketing/Distribution), Communications, Computer and

Information Sciences, Education (Pre-Elementary and Elementary, Secondary and Post-Secondary, Special Education, Physical Education, Industrial Arts), Engineering (Chemical, Civil, Electrical/Electronic, Mechanical), Foreign Languages, Health Sciences (General Medicine, Dentistry, Nursing, Pharmacy, Medical Laboratory), Home Economics, Law, Letters, Library and Archival Sciences, Life Sciences/ General Biology, Mathematics, Philosophy and Religion, Theology, Physical Sciences (Chemistry, Geological Sciences, Physics), Psychology, Protective Services, Public Affairs/Social Work, Social Sciences (Economics, History, Political Sciences/Government, Sociology), Visual and Performing Arts (Fine Arts, Drama, Music).
Administration: Group.
Price Data, 1991: $3 per reusable test booklet; $35 per 25 answer sheets and profile guides; $6 per manual (43 pages); $10 per specimen set of all Educational Interest Inventory and Career Guidance Inventory components.
Time: [45–60] minutes.
Comments: Self-administered; self-scored; manual is for the EII and the Career Guidance Inventory (395).
Author: James E. Oliver.
Publisher: Wintergreen/Orchard House, Inc.
Cross References: For reviews by Lois T. Strauss and David E. Kapel and Jim Fortune and Javaid Kaiser, see 11:123.

[860]

Educational Leadership Practices Inventory.
Purpose: Reflects Ideal versus Actual attitudes for individual and group teaching style patterns.
Population: Teachers and administrators.
Publication Dates: 1955–79.
Acronym: ELPI.
Scores, 2: Ideal, Actual.
Administration: Group.
Price Data, 1988: $12.75 per specimen set including reusable test booklet, 25 self-scoring answer sheets, and manual ('67, 14 pages).
Time: (30–45) minutes.
Comments: Computer form available.
Authors: Charles W. Nelson and Jasper J. Valenti (inventory).
Publisher: Management Research Associates.
Cross References: For reviews by Ernest J. Kozma and Darrell Sabers, see 11:125.

[861]

Educational Process Questionnaire.
Purpose: "To aid teachers in their own self-development by providing objective information about the processes used in the teacher's own actual classroom."
Population: Grades 4–12.
Publication Dates: 1973–87.
Acronym: EPQ.
Scores: 5 scale scores: Reinforcement of Self-Concept, Academic Learning Time, Feedback, Expectations, Development of Multiple Talents.

Administration: Group.
Price Data, 1988: $20 per 35 reusable booklets; $3 per 35 answer sheets; $5 per specimen set including booklet, answer sheet, and administration manual ('87, 22 pages); $30 per 35-pupil classroom scoring services (scoring performed during first week of November, February, and May); $.75 per student (above 35 in classroom) scoring services.
Time: 35(45) minutes.
Comments: Ratings by students.
Author: The Institute for Behavioral Research in Creativity.
Publisher: The Institute for Behavioral Research in Creativity.
Cross References: For a review by William L. Curlette, see 11:125.

[862]

Edwards Personal Preference Schedule.
Purpose: Developed to measure "a number of relatively independent *normal* personality variables."
Population: College and adults.
Publication Dates: 1953–59.
Acronym: EPPS.
Scores, 16: Achievement, Deference, Order, Exhibition, Autonomy, Affiliation, Intraception, Succorance, Dominance, Abasement, Nurturance, Change, Endurance, Heterosexuality, Aggression, Consistency.
Administration: Group.
Price Data, 1994: $50 per 25 schedule booklets; $27.50 per 50 hand-scorable answer documents; $35.50 per 50 NCS machine-scorable answer documents; $35.50 per 50 IBM answer documents; $25.50 per scoring template for hand-scorable answer documents including manual ('59, 27 pages); $61.50 per keys for IBM answer documents including manual; $23 per manual; $30.50 per examination kit.
Time: (40–50) minutes.
Author: Allen L. Edwards.
Publisher: The Psychological Corporation.
Cross References: See 9:378 (16 references), see also T3:780 (70 references), 8:542 (334 references), and T2:1164 (226 references); for reviews by Alfred B. Heilbrun, Jr., and Michael G. McKee, see 7:72 (391 references); see also P:67 (363 references); for reviews by John A. Radcliffe and Lawrence J. Stricker and an excerpted review by Edward S. Bordin, see 6:87 (284 references); for reviews by Frank Barron, Ake Bjerstedt, and Donald W. Fiske and excerpted reviews by John W. Gustad and Laurance F. Shaffer, see 5:47 (50 references).

TEST REFERENCES

1. Care, E., & Naylor, F. (1984). The factor structure of expressed preferences for school subjects. *The Australian Journal of Education, 28,* 145-153.
2. Emmons, R. A. (1984). Factor analysis and construct validity of the Narcissistic Personality Inventory. *Journal of Personality Assessment, 48,* 291-300.
3. Erdwins, C. J., & Mellinger, J. C. (1984). Mid-life women: Relation of age and role to personality. *Journal of Personality and Social Psychology, 47,* 390-395.
4. Johnson, W. A. (1984). Non-intellectual factors useful for pre-

dicting career selection between regular class and special class pre-service teachers. *College Student Journal, 18,* 273-279.

5. Johnson, W., Johnson, S. T., & Asbury, C. A. (1984). Multivariate methods useful for distinguishing attitudinal and personality characteristics of special education and regular elementary pre-service trainees. *Journal of Research and Development in Education, 17*(2), 43-50.

6. Lloyd, J., & Barenblatt, L. (1984). Intrinsic intellectuality: Its relations to social class, intelligence, and achievement. *Journal of Personality and Social Psychology, 46,* 646-654.

7. Peretti, P. O., & Statum, J. A. (1984). Father-son inter-generational transmission of authoritarian paternal attitudes. *Social Behavior and Personality, 12*(1), 85-90.

8. Spittle, B. J., & Sears, M. R. (1984). Bronchial asthma: Lack of relationships between allergic factors, illness severity and psychosocial variables in adult patients attending an asthma clinic. *Psychological Medicine, 14,* 847-852.

9. Sternberg, R. J., & Soriano, L. J. (1984). Styles of conflict resolution. *Journal of Personality and Social Psychology, 47,* 115-126.

10. Valliant, P. M., Asu, M. E., Cooper, D., & Mammola, D. (1984). Profile of dangerous and non-dangerous offenders referred for pre-trial psychiatric assessment. *Psychological Reports, 54,* 411-418.

11. Wilson, M. L. (1984). Female homosexuals' need for dominance and endurance. *Psychological Reports, 55,* 79-82.

12. Callaway, M. R., Marriott, R. G., & Esser, J. K. (1985). Effects of dominance on group decision making: Toward a stress-reduction explanation of groupthink. *Journal of Personality and Social Psychology, 49,* 949-952.

13. Kahans, D., & Crafti, N. (1985). Dynamics of interpersonal and intrapersonal perception. *Social Behavior and Personality, 13*(1), 15-25.

14. Mathiasen, R. E. (1985). Characteristics of the college honors student. *Journal of College Student Personnel, 26,* 171-173.

15. Mellinger, J. C., & Erdwins, C. J. (1985). Personality correlates of age and life roles in adult women. *Psychology of Women Quarterly, 9,* 503-514.

16. Robitaille, J., Jones, E., Gold, R. G., Robertson, K. R., & Milner, J. S. (1985). Child abuse potential and authoritarianism. *Journal of Clinical Psychology, 41,* 839-844.

17. Schippmann, J. S., & Prien, E. P. (1985). The Ghiselli Self-description Inventory: A psychometric appraisal. *Psychological Reports, 57,* 1171-1177.

18. Schroth, M. L. (1985). The effect of differing measuring methods on the relationship of motives. *The Journal of Psychology, 119,* 213-218.

19. Stevens, D. P., & Truss, C. V. (1985). Stability and change in adult personality over 12 and 20 years. *Developmental Psychology, 21,* 568-584.

20. Abbott, D. A., & Meredith, W. H. (1986). Strengths of parents with retarded children. *Family Relations, 35,* 371-375.

21. Assor, A., Aronoff, J., & Messé, L. A. (1986). An experimental test of defensive processes in impression formation. *Journal of Personality and Social Psychology, 50,* 644-650.

22. Jacobson, N. S., Follette, W. C., & Pagel, M. (1986). Predicting who will benefit from behavioral marital therapy. *Journal of Consulting and Clinical Psychology, 54,* 518-522.

23. Kerr, B. A. (1986). Career counseling for the gifted: Assessments and interventions. *Journal of Counseling and Development, 64,* 602-604.

24. Raskin, P. M. (1986). The relationship between identity and intimacy in early adulthood. *The Journal of Genetic Psychology, 147,* 167-181.

25. Schippmann, J. S., & Prien, E. P. (1986). Individual difference correlates of two leadership styles. *Psychological Reports, 59,* 817-818.

26. Schuerger, J. M., & Allen, L. C. (1986). Second-order factor structure common to five personality questionnaires. *Psychological Reports, 58,* 119-126.

27. Singer, M. S., & Singer, A. E. (1986). Relation between transformational vs transactional leadership preference and subordinates' personality: An exploratory study. *Perceptual and Motor Skills, 62,* 775-780.

28. Kassera, W., & Russo, T. (1987). Factor analysis of personality preferences and vocational interests. *Psychological Reports, 60,* 63-66.

29. Roger, D., & Nesshoever, W. (1987). Individual differences in dyadic conversational strategies: A further study. *British Journal of Social Psychology, 26,* 247-255.

30. Sternberg, R. J., & Dobson, D. M. (1987). Resolving interpersonal conflicts: An analysis of stylistic consistency. *Journal of Personality and Social Psychology, 52,* 794-812.

31. Bennett, J. B. (1988). Power and influence as distinct personality traits: Development and validation of a psychometric measure. *Journal of Research in Personality, 22,* 361-394.

32. Johnson, J. A., Germer, C. K., Efran, J. S., & Overton, W. F. (1988). Personality as the basis for theoretical predilections. *Journal of Personality and Social Psychology, 55,* 824-835.

33. Kerr, B. A., & Ghrist-Priebe, S. L. (1988). Intervention for multipotentiality: Effects of a career counseling laboratory for gifted high school students. *Journal of Counseling and Development, 66,* 366-369.

34. Piedmont, R. L. (1988). The relationship between achievement motivation, anxiety, and situational characteristics on performance on a cognitive task. *Journal of Research in Personality, 22,* 177-187.

35. Pierce, N. F. S., & Faulkender, P. J. (1988). Manifest need patterns for four psychological competence status groups differing on interpersonal/intrapersonal competencies. *The Journal of Psychology, 122,* 249-257.

36. Bailey, K. G., & Nava, G. (1989). Psychological kinship, love, and liking: Preliminary validity data. *Journal of Clinical Psychology, 45,* 587-594.

37. Piedmont, R. L., DiPlacido, J., & Keller, W. (1989). Assessing gender-related differences in achievement orientation using two different achievement scales. *Journal of Personality Assessment, 53,* 229-238.

38. Schuerger, J. M., Zarrella, K. L., & Hotz, A. S. (1989). Factors that influence the temporal stability of personality by questionnaire. *Journal of Personality and Social Psychology, 56,* 777-783.

39. Hough, L. M., Eaton, N. K., Dunnette, M. D., Kamp, J. D., & McCloy, R. A. (1990). Criterion-related validities of personality constructs and the effect of response distortion on those validities. *Journal of Applied Psychology, 75*(5), 581-595.

40. Cantwell, Z. M. (1991). Manifest needs of prospective counselors: A comparative study. *The Journal of Psychology, 125,* 101-108.

41. Fuhr, S. K., & Shean, G. (1992). Subtypes of depression, efficacy, and the Depressive Experiences Questionnaire. *The Journal of Psychology, 126,* 495-506.

42. Piedmont, R. L., McCrae, R. R., & Costa, P. T., Jr. (1992). An assessment of the Edwards Personal Preference Schedule from the perspective of the five-factor model. *Journal of Personality Assessment, 58,* 67-78.

43. Steward, R. J. (1993). Two faces of academic success: Case studies of American Indians on a predominantly Anglo university campus. *Journal of College Student Development, 34,* 191-196.

44. Thorson, J. A., & Powell, F. C. (1993). Sense of humor and dimensions of personality. *Journal of Clinical Psychology, 49,* 799-809.

[863]

The Effective School Battery.

Purpose: "To identify a school's strengths and weaknesses, to develop improvement plans, and to evaluate improvement projects."

Population: Grades 7–12, teachers.

Publication Date: 1984.

Acronym: ESB.

Administration: Individual or group.

Price Data, 1994: $29 per introductory kit including user's manual (105 pages), coordinator's manual (14 pages), survey administrator's instructions (3 pages), 1 each of the student and teacher survey booklets and answer sheets; $20 per extra user's manual; $5 per coordinator's manual; $7 per 10 administrator's instructions; $65 report fee per school; $42 per district-wide summary report.

Author: Gary G. Gottfredson.

Publisher: Psychological Assessment Resources, Inc.

a) STUDENT SURVEY.

Population: Grades 7–12.

Scores: 19 scales: Parental Education, Positive Peer Associations, Educational Expectation, Social Integration, Attachment to School, Belief in Rules, Interpersonal Competency, Involvement, Positive Self-Concept, School Effort, Avoidance of Punishment, School Rewards, Invalidity, Safety, Respect for Students, Planning and Action, Fairness of Rules, Clarity of Rules, Student Influence.

Price Data: $42 per 50 survey booklets; $13 per 50 answer sheets.

Time: (25–50) minutes.

b) TEACHER SURVEY.

Population: Teachers.

Scores: 16 scales: Pro-Integration Attitude, Job

Satisfaction, Interaction with Students, Personal Security, Classroom Orderliness, Professional Development, Nonauthoritarian Attitude, Safety, Morale, Planning and Action, Smooth Administration, Resources, Race Relations, Parent/Community Involvement, Student Influence, Avoidance of Use of Grades as a Sanction.

Price Data: $20 per 25 survey booklets; $9 per 25 answer sheets.

Time: Students: (50) minutes; Teachers: (30) minutes.

Cross References: For a review by James R. Barclay, see 10:104.

TEST REFERENCES

1. Gottfredson, D. C., & Gottfredson, G. D., & Hybl, L. G. (1993). Managing adolescent behavior: A multiyear, multischool study. *American Educational Research Journal, 30,* 179-215.

[864]

Effective Study Test.

Purpose: "Measures a student's knowledge about effective study methods and factors influencing their development."

Population: Grades 8–12, 11–13.

Publication Dates: 1964–72.

Acronym: EST.

Scores, 6: Reality Orientation, Study Organization, Writing Behavior, Reading Behavior, Examination Behavior, Total.

Administration: Group.

Price Data: Not available.

Foreign Language Edition: Spanish edition.

Time: (35–45) minutes.

Author: William F. Brown.

Publisher: Effective Study Materials [No reply from publisher; status unknown].

Cross References: For a review by A. Garr Cranney, see 8:816 (2 references).

TEST REFERENCES

1. Nisbet, J., Ruble, V. E., & Schurr, K. T. (1982). Predictors of academic success with high risk college students. *Journal of College Student Personnel, 23,* 227-235.
2. Brown, S. D., & Nelson, T. L. (1983). Beyond the uniformity myth: A comparison of academically successful and unsuccessful text-anxious college students. *Journal of Counseling Psychology, 30,* 367-374.

[865]

Effectiveness Motivation Scale.

Purpose: To assess levels of motivation in specific environments.

Population:: Ages 3–5.

Publication Dates: 1973–76.

Scores, 3: E (Strength of Effectiveness Motivation), W (Withdrawal), Q (Inconsequence).

Administration: Individual.

Price Data: Available from publisher.

Time: Administration time not reported.

Comments: Manual title is Stott-Sharp Effectiveness Motivation Scale; test booklet title is Scale of Effectiveness Motivation; ratings by teachers.

Authors: John D. Sharp, D. H. Stott, J. B. Albin (manual), and H. L. Williams (manual).

Publisher: NFER-Nelson Publishing Co., Ltd. [England].

[866]

The Egan Bus Puzzle Test.

Purpose: "Designed to assess language development and some performance skills of young children."

Population: 20 months to 4 years.

Publication Date: No date on test materials.

Scores, 6: Expressive Verbal Labels, Comprehension (Verbal Labels, Recognition of Shape, Orientation of Piece to Recess), Comprehension of Sentences, Expressive Language.

Administration: Individual.

Price Data, 1993: £62 per complete set including manual (no date, 36 pages), board, and 25 forms; £56 per board and manual; £12.50 per 25 forms.

Time: (7–8) minutes.

Authors: Dorothy F. Egan and Rosemary Brown.

Publisher: The Test Agency Ltd. [England].

Cross References: For a review by Sheldon L. Stick, see 10:105.

[867]

Ego Function Assessment.

Purpose: Designed as a "mental status examination" to assess ego function.

Population: Adults.

Publication Date: 1989.

Acronym: EFA.

Scores, 12: Reality Testing, Judgment, Sense of Reality, Regulation and Control of Drives, Object Relations, Thought Processes, Adaptive Regression in the Service of the Ego, Defensive Functions, Stimulus Barrier, Autonomous Functions, Synthetic Functions, Mastery-Competence.

Administration: Individual.

Price Data, 1983: $12 per manual (64 pages); $9.50 per 10 blanks.

Time: Administration time not reported.

Author: Leopold Bellak.

Publisher: C.P.S., Inc.

[868]

The Ego Strength Q-Sort Test.

Purpose: Designed to "assess the general strength of one's ego."

Population: Grades 9–16 and adults.

Publication Dates: 1956–58.

Acronym: ESQST.

Scores, 6: Ego-Status, Social Status, Goal Setting and Striving, Good Mental Health, Physical Status, Total.

Administration: Individual or group.

Price Data: Available from publisher.

Time: (50–90) minutes.

Author: Russell N. Cassel.

Publisher: Psychometric Affiliates.

Cross References: See T2:1167 (1 reference); for

reviews by Allen L. Edwards and Harrison G. Gough, see 6:88 (3 references).

[869]

Eidetic Parents Test.
Purpose: To provide stimuli meant to arouse eidetic images of parents to aid in exploring emotional attachments that affect current functioning.
Population: Clinical patients and marriage and family counselees.
Publication Date: 1972.
Acronym: EPT.
Scores: No scores; verbal reporting by individuals of subjective visual images (called eidetics) of increasingly surrealistic situations.
Administration: Individual.
Price Data: Available from publisher.
Time: (60) minutes for brief report; "many hours" for comprehensive report.
Author: Akhter Ahsen.
Publisher: Brandon House, Inc.
Cross References: For additional information and a review by Charles Warnath and excerpted reviews by Gregory Sarmousakis, Barry Bricklin, and Manas Raychaudhuri, see 8:546 (8 references).

[870]

Eight State Questionnaire.
Purpose: To assess eight specific emotional states and moods.
Population: Ages 17 and over.
Publication Dates: 1971–76.
Acronym: 8SQ.
Scores, 8: Anxiety, Stress, Depression, Regression, Fatigue, Guilt, Extraversion, Arousal.
Administration: Group.
Forms, 2: A, B.
Price Data, 1994: $13.25 per 10 reusable test booklets; $11 per scoring key; $10.75 per 25 answer sheets; $10.75 per 25 profile sheets; $7.75 per manual ('76, 36 pages); $10.75 per specimen set including 1 test booklet (both Form A and Form B), manual, and answer sheet.
Time: (25–35) minutes.
Authors: James P. Curran and Raymond B. Cattell.
Publisher: Institute for Personality and Ability Testing, Inc.
Cross References: See T3:787 (1 reference); for a review by Benjamin Kleinmuntz, see 8:547 (5 references).

TEST REFERENCES

1. Boyle, G. J. (1983). Effects on academic learning of manipulating emotional states and motivational dynamics. *British Journal of Educational Psychology, 53,* 347-357.
2. Sirignano, S. W., & Lachman, M. E. (1985). Personality change during the transition to parenthood: The role of perceived infant temperament. *Developmental Psychology, 21,* 558-567.
3. Boyle, G. J. (1986). Analysis of typological factors across the Eight State Questionnaire and the Differential Emotions Scale. *Psychological Reports, 59,* 503-510.
4. Boyle, G. J. (1987). Content similarities and differences in Cattell's Sixteen Personality Factor Questionnaire, Eight State Questionnaire, and Motivation Analysis Test. *Psychological Reports, 60,* 179-186.

5. Boyle, G. J. (1987). Quantitative and qualitative intersections between the Eight State Questionnaire and the Profile of Mood States. *Educational and Psychological Measurement, 47*(2), 437-443.
6. Hertzog, C., & Nesselroade, J. R. (1987). Beyond autoregressive models: Some implications of the trait-state distinction for the structural modeling of developmental change. *Child Development, 58,* 93-109.
7. Boyle, G. J. (1988). Central clinical states: An examination of the Profile of Mood States and the Eight State Questionnaire. *Journal of Psychopathology and Behavioral Assessment, 10,* 205-215.
8. Usala, P. D., & Hertzog, C. (1991). Evidence of differential stability of state and trait anxiety in adults. *Journal of Personality and Social Psychology, 60,* 471-479.
9. Ainsworth, R. A., Simpson, L., & Cassell, D. (1993). Effects of three colors in an office interior on mood and performance. *Perceptual and Motor Skills, 76,* 235-241.

[871]

Einstein Assessment of School-Related Skills.
Purpose: "To identify children who are at risk for, or are experiencing, learning difficulties; and who therefore should be referred for a comprehensive evaluation."
Population: Grades K–5.
Publication Date: 1988.
Administration: Individual.
Levels, 6: Kindergarten, First Grade, Second Grade, Third Grade, Fourth Grade, Fifth Grade.
Price Data: Available from publisher.
Time: (10) minutes.
Authors: Ruth L. Gottesman and Frances M. Cerullo.
Publisher: Modern Curriculum Press.
a) KINDERGARTEN LEVEL.
Scores, 5: Language/Cognition, Letter Recognition, Auditory Memory, Arithmetic, Visual-Motor Integration.
b) FIRST GRADE LEVEL.
Scores, 7: Language/Cognition, Word Recognition, Oral Reading, Reading Comprehension, Auditory Memory, Arithmetic, Visual-Motor Integration.
c) SECOND GRADE LEVEL.
Scores: Same as *b* above.
d) THIRD GRADE LEVEL.
Scores: Same as *b* above.
e) FOURTH GRADE LEVEL.
Scores: Same as *b* above.
f) FIFTH GRADE LEVEL.
Scores: Same as *b* above.
Cross References: For a review by Gloria A. Galvin, see 11:126 (1 reference).

TEST REFERENCES

1. Bennett, R. E., Gottesman, R. L., Rock, D. A., & Cerullo, F. (1993). Influence of behavior perceptions and gender on teacher's judgements of students' academic skills. *Journal of Educational Psychology, 85,* 347-356.

[872]

Ekwall/Shanker Reading Inventory—Third Edition.
Purpose: "Designed to assess the full range of students' reading abilities."
Population: Grades 1–9.
Publication Dates: 1979–93.
Acronym: ESRI.

Administration: Individual.
Price Data: Available from publisher.
Authors: Eldon E. Ekwall and James L. Shanker.
Publisher: Allyn and Bacon.

a) GRADED WORD LIST.
Purpose: "To obtain a quick estimate of the student's independent, instructional, and frustration reading levels."
Acronym: GWL.
Scores, 3: Independent Reading Level, Instructional Reading Level, Frustration Level.
Time: (5–10) minutes

b) ORAL AND SILENT READING.
Purpose: To obtain an assessment of the student's independent, instructional, and frustration reading levels in oral and silent reading.
Scores, 3: 3 scores (Independent Reading Level, Instructional Reading Level, Frustration Level) in each of two areas (Oral, Silent Reading).
Time: (10–30) minutes.

c) LISTENING COMPREHENSION.
Purpose: "To obtain the level at which a student can understand material when it is read to him or her."
Scores: Listening Comprehension Level.
Time: (5–10) minutes.

d) THE BASIC SIGHT WORDS AND PHRASES TEST.
Purpose: To determine basic sight words and basic sight word phrases that can be recognized and pronounced instantly by the student.
Scores, 2: Basic Sight Words, Basic Sight Phrases.
Time: (5–12) minutes.

e) LETTER KNOWLEDGE.
Purpose: "To determine if the student can associate the letter symbols with the letter names."
Scores, 2: Letters (Auditory), Letters (Visual).
Time: Administration time not reported.

f) PHONICS.
Purpose: "To determine if the student has mastered letter-sound (phonics)."
Scores, 9: Initial Consonants, Initial Blends and Digraphs, Ending Sounds, Vowels, Phonograms, Blending, Substitution, Vowel Pronunciation, Application in Context.
Time: Administration time not reported.

g) STRUCTURAL ANALYSIS.
Purpose: "To determine if the student can use structural analysis skills to aid in decoding unknown words."
Scores, 10: Hearing Word Parts, Inflectional Endings, Prefixes, Suffixes, Compound Words, Affixes, Syllabication, Application in Context (Part I, Part II, Total).
Time: Administration time not reported.

h) KNOWLEDGE OF CONTRACTIONS TEST.
Purpose: "To determine if the student has knowledge of contractions."
Scores, 3: Number of Words Pronounced, Number of Words Known, Total.
Time: Administration time not reported.

i) EL PASO PHONICS SURVEY.
Purpose: "To determine if the student has the ability to pronounce and blend 90 phonic elements."
Scores, 4: Initial Consonant Sounds; Ending Consonant; Initial Consonant Clusters; Vowels, Vowel Teams, and Special Letter Combinations.
Time: Administration time not reported.

j) QUICK SURVEY WORD LIST.
Purpose: "To determine quickly if the student has mastered phonics and structural analysis."
Scores: Comments.
Time: Administration time not reported.

k) READING INTEREST SURVEY.
Purpose: "To assess the student's attitude toward reading and school, areas of reading interest, reading experiences, and conditions affecting reading in the home."
Scores: Comments.
Time: Administration time not reported.

Cross References: For reviews by Lynn S. Fuchs and Mary Beth Marr of an earlier edition, see 9:380.

TEST REFERENCES

1. Helgren-Lempesis, V. A., & Mangrum, C. T., II. (1986). An analysis of alternate-form reliability of three commercially-prepared informal reading inventories. *Reading Research Quarterly, 21,* 209-215.
2. Padrón, Y. N., Knight, S. L., & Waxman, H. C. (1986). Analyzing bilingual and monolingual students' perceptions of their reading strategies. *The Reading Teacher, 39,* 430-433.
3. Conte, R., & Humphreys, R. (1989). Repeated reading using audiotaped material enhances oral reading in children with reading difficulties. *Journal of Communication Disorders, 22,* 65-79.

[873]

El Circo.
Purpose: Constructed to assess Spanish-speaking children's comprehension of simple mathematical concepts and basic linguistic structures in both Spanish and English.
Population: Ages 3-11 to 7-7.
Publication Date: 1980.
Price Data: Available from publisher.
Author: Educational Testing Service.
Publisher: CTB MacMillan/McGraw-Hill.

a) LANGUAGE CHECK.
Purpose: Developed to assess whether a child's Spanish skills are sufficient to take the other measures in Spanish.
Scores: Item scores and mode of response scores (Spanish, English, Mixture Spanish-English, Nonverbal).
Administration: Individual.
Time: (5–10) minutes.
Comments: Administered entirely in Spanish.

b) PRACTICE MATERIALS.
Scores: Item scores.
Administration: Group.
Time: (5–10) minutes.
Comments: Administered in Spanish.

c) WHAT WORDS ARE FOR.
Scores: Item scores in 4 areas: Verb Tense, Prepositions, Possessives, Other Linguistic Structures.

Administration: Individual for preschool; group for grades K–1.
Time: (15–20) minutes.
Comments: Administered mainly in English.
d) PARA QUE SIRVEN LAS PALABRAS.
Scores: Item scores in 4 areas: Verb Tense, Prepositions, Word Order, Other Linguistic Structures.
Administration: Same as *c* above.
Time: Same as *c* above.
Comments: Administered entirely in Spanish.
e) CUANTO Y CUANTOS.
Scores: Item scores in 3 areas: Counting, Relational Terms, Numerical Terms.
Administration: Same as *c* above.
Time: Same as *c* above.
Comments: Administered entirely in Spanish.
Cross References: For reviews by Edward N. Argulewicz and J. Manuel Casas, see 9:381 (1 reference).

[874]
Electrical and Electronics Test.
Purpose: "Examines knowledge of fundamental laws, symbols and definitions and requires the application of them to familiar equipment."
Population: Students in electrical or electronics programs ages 15 and over.
Publication Date: No date on test materials.
Scores: Total score only.
Administration: Group.
Price Data, 1994: £6.50 per test booklet; £2.50 per answer key; £12.50 per manual; £27 per specimen set.
Time: (15–30) minutes.
Author: The Test Agency Ltd.
Publisher: The Test Agency Ltd. [England].

[875]
Electrical Maintenance Trainee.
Purpose: "To measure the knowledge and skills required for electrical maintenance."
Population: Applicants for jobs requiring electrical knowledge and skills.
Publication Date: 1991.
Scores: Total score only.
Administration: Group.
Price Data, 1993: $498 per complete kit including 10 reusable test booklets, 100 answer sheets, manual (14 pages), and scoring key.
Time: (150–210) minutes.
Authors: Roland T. Ramsay.
Publisher: Ramsay Corporation.

[876]
Electrical Sophistication Test.
Purpose: "Intended to discriminate between persons with substantial knowledges of electricity and those with no, little, and merely chance knowledge."
Population: Job applicants.
Publication Dates: 1963–65.
Scores: Total score only.
Administration: Group.

Price Data: Available from publisher.
Time: (5–10) minutes.
Author: Stanley G. Ciesla.
Publisher: Psychometric Affiliates.
Cross References: For a review by Charles F. Ward, see 7:1125.

[877]
Electromechanical Vocational Assessment Manuals.
Purpose: Designed to evaluate a variety of work abilities (tasks) of blind or visually impaired persons.
Population: Blind or visually impaired adults.
Publication Date: 1983.
Scores, 6: Fine Finger Dexterity Work Task Unit, Foot Operated Hinged Box Work Task Unit, Hinged Box Work Task Unit, Index Card Work Task Unit, Multifunctional Work Task Unit, Revolving Assembly Table Work Task Unit.
Administration: Individual.
Price Data: Available from publisher.
Time: 50(60) minutes for any one task unit.
Comments: Special administration equipment required.
Author: Rehabilitation Research and Training Center in Blindness and Low Vision.
Publisher: Rehabilitation Research and Training Center in Blindness and Low Vision.

[878]
Electronic and Instrumentation Technician Test.
Purpose: "To evaluate the knowledge of electronics and instrumentation workers in specific subject areas."
Population: Applicants or incumbents for jobs where electronics and instrumentation knowledge is a necessary part of training or job activities.
Publication Date: 1985.
Acronym: E&ITT.
Scores, 8: Motor Control, Digital Electronics/Computers, Analog/Radio, Schematics/Test Instruments, Power Supplies/Power Distribution, AC & DC Theory, Mechanical Maintenance, Total.
Administration: Group.
Price Data, 1993: $498 per complete kit including 10 reusable test booklets, 100 answer sheets, manual (16 pages), and scoring key.
Time: 180(190) minutes.
Author: Roland T. Ramsay.
Publisher: Ramsay Corporation.
Cross References: For a review by Alan R. Suess, see 10:106.

[879]
Electronics Test—Form G2.
Purpose: "To measure the knowledge and skills required for electronics jobs."
Population: Electronics employees and applicants for electronics jobs.
Publication Dates: 1987–94.
Scores: Total score only.

Administration: Group.
Price Data, 1993: $498 per 10 reusable test booklets, manual ('94, 13 pages), scoring key, and 100 blank answer sheets.
Time: (120) minutes.
Author: Roland T. Ramsay.
Publisher: Ramsay Corporation.

[880]

Eliot-Price Perspective Test.
Purpose: "Designed to measure the ability to perceive and to imagine object arrangments from different viewpoints."
Population: Grades 2 and over.
Publication Dates: 1974–75.
Scores: Total score only.
Administration: Group.
Price Data: Available from publisher.
Time: (20) minutes.
Comments: For research use only.
Authors: John Eliot and Lewis Price.
Publisher: John Eliot (the author).
Cross References: See T3:792 (1 reference).

[881]

Elizur Test of Psycho-Organicity: Children and Adults.
Purpose: Designed to "diagnose brain conditions," such as organic from nonorganic problems.
Population: Ages 6 and over, 10 and over.
Publication Dates: 1959–69.
Acronym: ETPO.
Scores, 3: Drawings, Digits, Blocks.
Administration: Individual.
Levels, 2: Children, Adults.
Price Data, 1993: $135 per kit including 10 protocol booklets, test materials, and manual ('69, 55 pages); $19.50 per 25 protocol booklets; $38 per manual.
Time: (10–15) minutes.
Author: Abraham Elizur.
Publisher: Western Psychological Services.
Cross References: See 3:793 (1 reference); for reviews by Joseph M. Wepman and Aubrey J. Yates, and an excerpted review by Muriel D. Lezak, see 7:75 (5 references).

[882]

Embedded Figures Test.
Purpose: A perceptual test designed to reflect competence at perceptual disembedding.
Population: Ages 10 and over.
Publication Dates: 1950–71.
Acronym: EFT.
Scores: Total score only.
Administration: Individual.
Forms, 2: A, B.
Price Data, 1990: $27 per kit including card sets, stylus, and 50 recording sheets; $20 per card sets: Forms A and B with simple figures and practice items;

$2.50 per stylus; $8 per 50 recording sheets; $7.50 per manual ('71, 32 pages).
Time: (10–45) minutes.
Comments: 3 minutes-per-figure Forms A and B estimated from the original 24-figure, 5 minutes-per-figure test; no specific manual, combined manual for this and Children's Embedded Figures Test (452) and Group Embedded Figures Test (1094); colored versions of the original black-and-white figures by K. Gottschaldt ('26).
Authors: Herman A. Witkin, Philip K. Oltman (manual), Evelyn Raskin (manual), and Stephen A. Karp (manual).
Publisher: Consulting Psychologists Press, Inc.
Cross References: See 9:382 (23 references), T3:794 (88 references), 8:548 (134 references), T2:1169 (149 references), and P:71 (47 references); for reviews by Harrison G. Gough and Leona E. Tyler, see 6:89 (24 references); see also 5:49 (9 references).

TEST REFERENCES

1. Bick, P. A. (1983). Physiological and psychological correlates of motion sickness. *British Journal of Medical Psychology, 56*, 189-196.
2. Query, W. T. (1983). Field dependency, n power and locus of control variables in alcohol aversion. *Journal of Clinical Psychology, 39*, 279-283.
3. Bartram, D., & Bayliss, R. (1984). Automated testing: Past, present and future. *Journal of Occupational Psychology, 57*, 221-237.
4. Binnie-Dawson, J. L. M. (1984). Bio-social and endocrine bases of spatial ability. *Psychologia, 27*, 129-151.
5. Blackburn, J. A. (1984). The influence of personality, curriculum, and memory correlates on formal reasoning in young adults and elderly persons. *Journal of Gerontology, 39*, 207-209.
6. Brown, M. S. (1984). Do confusing information and egocentric instructions influence perception? *Perceptual and Motor Skills, 59*, 15-20.
7. Davies, M. F. (1984). Conceptual and empirical comparisons between self-consciousness and field dependence-independence. *Perceptual and Motor Skills, 58*, 543-549.
8. Gilbertson, A. D. (1984). Perceptual differentiation among drug addicts: Correlations with intelligence and MMPI scores. *Journal of Clinical Psychology, 40*, 334-339.
9. Grasha, A. F. (1984). Learning styles: The journey from Greenwich Observatory (1796) to the college classroom (1984). *Improving College & University Teaching, 32*, 46-53.
10. Guyot, G. W., Fairchild, L., & Johnson, B. (1984). Embedded Figures Test performance and self-concept of elementary school children. *Perceptual and Motor Skills, 58*, 61-62.
11. Hennecke, L. (1984). Stimulus augmenting and field dependence in children of alcoholic fathers. *Journal of Studies on Alcohol, 45*, 486-492.
12. Killian, G. A., Holzman, P. S., Davis, J. M., & Gibbons, R. (1984). Effects of psychotropic medication on selected cognitive and perceptual measures. *Journal of Abnormal Psychology, 93*, 58-70.
13. Kingsland, R. C., & Greene, L. R. (1984). Psychological differentiation and clinical depression. *Cognitive Therapy and Research, 8*, 599-605.
14. Lesnik-Oberstein, M., & Cohen, L. (1984). Cognitive style, sensation seeking, and assortative mating. *Journal of Personality and Social Psychology, 46*, 112-117.
15. Loranger, M., Gosselin, D., & Kaley, R. (1984). The effects of cognitive style and course content on classroom social behavior. *Psychology in the Schools, 21*, 92-96.
16. Paradise, L. V., & Block, C. (1984Z). The relationship of teacher-student cognitive style to academic achievement. *Journal of Research and Development in Education, 17*(4), 57-61.
17. Ronning, R. R., McCurdy, D., & Ballinger, R. (1984). Individual differences: A third component in problem-solving instruction. *Journal of Research in Science Teaching, 21*, 71-82.
18. Spellacy, F. J., & Brown, W. G. (1984). Prediction of recidivism in young offenders after brief institutionalization. *Journal of Clinical Psychology, 40*, 1070-1074.
19. Welkowitz, L. A., & Calkins, R. P. (1984). Effects of cognitive and exemplar modeling on field dependence-independence. *Perceptual and Motor Skills, 58*, 439-442.

20. Aboud, F. E. (1985). Children's application of attribution principles to social comparisons. *Child Development, 56,* 682-688.

21. Blake, M. E. (1985). The relationship between field dependence-independence and the comprehension of expository and literary text types. *Reading World, 24*(4), 53-62.

22. Falcone, D. J. (1985). Laterality and field dependence. *Perceptual and Motor Skills, 61,* 651-657.

23. Hentschel, U., & Kiessling, M. (1985). Season of birth and personality: Another instance of noncorrespondence. *The Journal of Social Psychology, 125,* 577-585.

24. Hooper, F. H., Hooper, J. O., & Colbert, K. K. (1985). Personality and memory correlates of intellectual functioning in adulthood: Piagetian and psychometric assessments. *Human Development, 28,* 101-107.

25. Huss, E. T., & Kayson, W. A. (1985). Effects of age and sex on speed of finding embedded figures. *Perceptual and Motor Skills, 61,* 591-594.

26. Jenkins, F., & Davies, G. (1985). Contamination of facial memory through exposure to misleading composite pictures. *Journal of Applied Psychology, 70,* 164-176.

27. Manning-Melean, L., & Fernández-Ballesteros, R. (1985). Tactile perceptual task and field dependence-independence. *Perceptual and Motor Skills, 61,* 503-506.

28. Steiger, H., Negrete, J. C., & Marcil, G. (1985). Field dependence in alcoholics: Relation to years of drinking, severity of alcohol dependence and emotional distress. *Journal of Studies on Alcohol, 46,* 486-489.

29. Waber, D. P., Mann, M. B., Merola, J., & Moylan, P. M. (1985). Physical maturation rate and cognitive performance in early adolescence: A longitudinal examination. *Developmental Psychology, 21,* 666-681.

30. Brown, R. T., Borden, K. A., Wynne, M. E., Schleser, R., & Clingerman, S. R. (1986). Methylphenidate and cognitive therapy with ADD children: A methodological reconsideration. *Journal of Abnormal Child Psychology, 14,* 481-497.

31. MacLeod, C. M., Jackson, R. A., & Palmer, J. (1986). On the relation between spatial ability and field dependence. *Intelligence, 10,* 141-151.

32. Rhodewalt, F., & O'Keefe, J. (1986). Type A behavior, field dependence, and hypervigilance: Toward increased Type A specificity. *Motivation and Emotion, 10,* 105-114.

33. Smilansky, J., & Halberstadt, N. (1986). Inventors versus problem solvers: An empirical investigation. *The Journal of Creative Behavior, 20,* 183-201.

34. Taylor, A. E., Saint-Cyr, J. A., & Lang, A. E. (1986). Frontal lobe dysfunction in Parkinson's disease: The cortical focus of neostriatal outflow. *Brain, 109,* 845-883.

35. Goodenough, D. R., Oltman, P. K., & Cox, P. W. (1987). The nature of individual differences in field dependence. *Journal of Research in Personality, 21,* 81-99.

36. McCauley, E., Kay, T., Ito, J., & Treder, R. (1987). The turner syndrome: Cognitive deficits, affective discrimination, and behavior problems. *Child Development, 58,* 464-473.

37. Ozer, D. J. (1987). Personality, intelligence, and spatial visualization: Correlates of mental rotations test performance. *Journal of Personality and Social Psychology, 53,* 129-134.

38. Thompson, G., & Knox, A. B. (1987). Designing for diversity: Are field-dependent learners less suited to distance education programs of instruction? *Contemporary Educational Psychology, 12,* 17-29.

39. Van Blerkom, M. L. (1987). Haptic lateralization, field dependence, and sex. *Perceptual and Motor Skills, 64,* 907-914.

40. Van Blerkom, M. L. (1988). Field dependence, sex role self-perceptions, and mathematics achievement in college students: A closer examination. *Contemporary Educational Psychology, 13,* 339-347.

41. Burton, A., Morton, N., & Abbess, S. (1989). Mode of processing and hemisphere differences in the judgement of musical stimuli. *British Journal of Psychology, 80,* 169-180.

42. Coursey, R. D., Lees, R. W., & Siever, L. J. (1989). The relationship between smooth pursuit eye movement impairment and psychological measures of psychopathology. *Psychological Medicine, 19,* 343-358.

43. DeHaan, E. H. F., & Campbell, R. (1991). A fifteen year follow-up of a case of developmental prosopagnosia. *Cortex, 27,* 489-509.

44. O'Leary, K. M., Brouwers, P., Gardner, D. L., & Cowdry, R. W. (1991). Neuropsychological testing of patients with borderline personality disorder. *American Journal of Psychiatry, 148,* 106-111.

45. Pennings, A. H. (1991). Altering the strategies in embedded-figure and water-level tasks via instruction: A neo-Piagetian learning study. *Perceptual and Motor Skills, 72,* 639-660.

46. Fergusson, L. C. (1992). Field independence and art achievement in mediating and nonmediating college students. *Perceptual and Motor Skills, 75,* 1171-1175.

47. Hunt, H. T., Gervais, A., Sheraing-Johns, S., & Travis, F.

(1992). Transpersonal experiences in childhood: An exploratory empirical study of selected adult groups. *Perceptual and Motor Skills, 75,* 1135-1153.

48. Parkin, A. J., & Walter, B. M. (1992). Recollective experience, normal aging, and frontal dysfunction. *Psychology and Aging, 7,* 290-298.

[883]

EMO Questionnaire.

Purpose: "Designed to assess an individual's personal-emotional adjustment."

Population: Adults.

Publication Dates: 1958-78.

Scores: 10 diagnostic dimensions: Rationalization, Inferiority Feelings, Hostility, Depression, Fear and Anxiety, Organic Reaction, Projection, Unreality, Sex, Withdrawal, plus Buffer Score and 4 second-order adjustment factors: Internal, External, Somatic, General.

Administration: Group.

Forms, 2: A, B.

Price Data, 1992: $30 per 25 booklets (specify Form A or Form B); $5 per 25 score sheets; $20 per interpretation and research manual ('77, 126 pages).

Time: (30) minutes.

Authors: George O. Baehr and Melany E. Baehr.

Publisher: SRA/London House.

Cross References: For reviews by Allan L. Lavoie and Paul McReynolds, see 9:383; see also T2:1170 (1 reference); for reviews by Bertram D. Cohen and W. Grant Dahlstrom, see 6:90 (1 reference).

TEST REFERENCES

1. Jones, J. W., Joy, D. S., & Martin, S. L. (1990). A multidimensional approach for selecting child care workers. *Psychological Reports, 67,* 543-553.

[884]

Emotional and Behavior Problem Scale.

Purpose: "Developed to contribute to the early identification and service delivery for students with behavior disorders/emotional disturbance."

Population: Ages 4.5-21.

Publication Date: 1989.

Acronym: EBPS.

Scores, 12: Theoretical (Learning, Interpersonal Relations, Inappropriate Behavior Under Normal Circumstances, Unhappiness/Depression, Physical Symptoms/Fears, Total); Empirical (Social Aggression/Conduct Disorder, Social-Emotional Withdrawal/Depression, Learning/Comprehension Disorder, Avoidance/Unresponsiveness, Aggressive/Self-Destructive, Total).

Administration: Individual.

Price Data, 1993: $57 per complete kit including technical manual (47 pages), 50 rating forms, and IEP and intervention manual (205 pages); $10 per technical manual; $25 per 50 rating forms; $22 per IEP and intervention manual; $12 per computerized quick score (IBM or Apple II); $149 per computerized IEP and intervention manual (IBM or Apple II).

Time: (15) minutes.

Comments: Ratings by teachers.

Author: Frederick Wright.
Publisher: Hawthorne Educational Services, Inc.

[885]
Emotional Behavioral Checklist.
Purpose: To assess an individual's overt emotional behavior.
Population: Ages 16 and over.
Publication Date: 1986.
Acronym: EBC.
Scores, 8: Impulsivity-Frustration, Anxiety, Depression-Withdrawal, Socialization, Self-Concept, Aggression, Reality Disorientation, Total EBC.
Administration: Individual.
Manual: No manual.
Price Data, 1994: $16.75 per 25 checklists.
Time: Administration time not reported.
Comments: Included in the Auxiliary Component of the McCarron-Dial System (1569).
Authors: Jack G. Dial, Carolyn Mezger, Theresa Massey, and Lawrence T. McCarron.
Publisher: McCarron-Dial Systems.
Cross References: For reviews by William A. Stock and Hoi K. Suen, see 11:130.

[886]
The Emotional Empathic Tendency Scale.
Purpose: To measure an individual's vicarious emotional response to perceived emotional experiences of others.
Population: Ages 15 and older.
Publication Dates: 1972–94.
Acronym: EETS.
Scores: Total score only.
Administration: Group or individual.
Price Data: Price data available from publisher for test kit including scale, scoring directions, norms, manual ('94, 7 pages), and literature review.
Time: (10–15) minutes.
Authors: Albert Mehrabian and Norm Epstein.
Publisher: Albert Mehrabian.

[887]
Emotional or Behavior Disorder Scale.
Purpose: Designed to identify behavior problems of students in the home or school environment.
Population: Ages 4.5 to 21.
Publication Dates: 1991–92.
Acronym: EBDS.
Scores, 4: Academic, Social Relationships, Personal Adjustment, Total.
Administration: Individual.
Price Data, 1993: $86 per complete kit including School Version technical manual ('92, 33 pages) and 50 rating forms, Home Version technical manual ('92, 31 pages) and 25 rating forms, and intervention manual ('91, 202 pages); $22 per intervention manual.
Time: (15–20) minutes.
Author: Stephen B. McCarney.
Publisher: Hawthorne Educational Services, Inc.

a) SCHOOL VERSION.
Price Data: $10 per technical manual; $30 per 50 rating forms.
b) HOME VERSION.
Price Data: $10 per technical manual; $14 per 25 rating forms.

[888]
Emotional Problems Scales.
Purpose: "To assess emotional and behavioral problems in individuals with mild mental retardation or borderline intelligence."
Population: Ages 14 and over.
Publication Dates: 1984–91.
Acronym: EPS.
Price Data, 1994: $75 per complete kit including manual ('91, 31 pages), 25 BRS test booklets, 25 SRI test booklets, SRI scoring keys, and 25 profile forms; $20 per manual; $14 per 25 profile forms; $345 per IBM computer report.
Comments: Previous editions titled Prout-Strohmer Personality Inventory and Strohmer-Prout Behavior Rating Scale.
Authors: H. Thompson Prout and Douglas C. Strohmer.
Publisher: Psychological Assessment Resources, Inc.
a) BEHAVIOR RATING SCALES.
Acronym: BRS.
Scores, 12: Thought/Behavior Disorder, Verbal Aggression, Physical Aggression, Sexual Maladjustment, Distractibility, Hyperactivity, Somatic Concerns, Depression, Withdrawal, Low Self-Esteem, Externalizing Behavior Problems, Internalizing Behavior Problems.
Administration: Individual.
Price Data, 1993: $16 per 25 test booklets.
Time: (20–25) minutes.
b) SELF-REPORT INVENTORY.
Acronym: SRI.
Scores, 7: Positive Impression, Thought/Behavior Disorder, Impulse Control, Anxiety, Depression, Low Self-Esteem, Total Pathology.
Administration: Individual.
Price Data, 1993: $16 per 25 test booklets; $15 per scoring keys.
Time: (30–35) minutes.
Cross References: For reviews by Richard Brozovich and Ernest A. Bauer and by Peter F. Merenda of the Prout-Strohmer Personality Inventory, see 11:311.

[889]
Emotions Profile Index.
Purpose: Designed as a measure of personality traits.
Population: College and adults.
Publication Date: 1974.
Acronym: EPI.
Scores, 9: Timid, Aggressive, Trustful, Distrustful, Controlled, Dyscontrolled, Gregarious, Depressed, Bias.
Administration: Group or individual.

Price Data, 1993: $40 per kit including 25 tests, profile sheets, and manual (13 pages plus test and profile); $21.50 per 25 tests and profile sheets; $22.50 per manual.
Time: (10–15) minutes.
Authors: Robert Plutchik and Henry Kellerman.
Publisher: Western Psychological Services.
Cross References: See T3:796 (2 references); for a review by Douglas N. Jackson, see 8:549 (33 references).

[890]

The Empathy Test.
Purpose: Constructed to assess empathy.
Population: Junior high school and over.
Publication Dates: 1947–62.
Scores: Total score only.
Administration: Group.
Forms, 3: A, B, C.
Price Data: Available from publisher.
Time: (6–15) minutes.
Authors: W. A. Kerr and B. J. Speroff.
Publisher: Psychometric Affiliates.
Cross References: See T2:1171 (10 references) and P:73 (1 reference); for a review by Wallace B. Hall, see 6:91 (9 references); for a review by Robert L. Thorndike, see 5:50 (20 references).

TEST REFERENCES

1. Kirschenbaum, D. S., De Voge, J. B., Marsh, M. E., & Steffen, J. J. (1980). Multimodal evaluation of therapy versus consultation components in a large inner-city early intervention program. *American Journal of Community Psychology, 8,* 587-601.
2. Radin, N., & Sagi, A. (1982). Childrearing fathers in intact families, II: Israel and the USA. *Merrill-Palmer Quarterly, 28,* 111-136.

[891]

Employability Development Plan.
Purpose: Assist staff in employment and training organizations in recording and analyzing needs of participants.
Population: Employees.
Publication Date: 1985.
Scores: No scores.
Administration: Individual.
Price Data: Available from publisher.
Time: Administration time not reported.
Authors: LaVerne Ludden, Bonnie Maitlen, and Michael Farr.
Publisher: JIST Works, Inc.

[892]

The Employability Inventory.
Purpose: A self-assessment instrument to assess job seeking and job keeping skils.
Population: Prospective employees.
Publication Date: 1987.
Scores: Item scores only.
Administration: Group.
Forms, 2: Card deck; computer software.
Price Data, 1993: $12.75 per card deck version; $79.99 per software package (specify IBM 5.25,

IBM 3.5, or Apple 5.25); $99 per Windows software package.
Time: Administration time not reported.
Authors: John D. Hartz, Merle Stephey, Donald Steel, and Susan Kosmo.
Publisher: Education Associates, Inc.

[893]

Employability Maturity Interview.
Purpose: "Developed to assess readiness for the vocational rehabilitation planning process."
Population: Rehabilitation clients.
Publication Date: 1987.
Acronym: EMI.
Scores: Total score only.
Administration: Individual.
Price Data, 1994: $10 per complete kit; $7.50 per 50 test forms; $10 per 100 test forms; $5 per manual (29 pages).
Time: (15–20) minutes.
Comments: Based upon the Adult Vocational Maturity Assessment Interview.
Authors: Richard Roessler and Brian Bolton.
Publisher: Arkansas Research & Training Center in Vocational Rehabilitation.
Cross References: For a review by William R. Koch, see 11:132.

[894]

Employee Aptitude Survey.
Purpose: Designed to predict future job performance.
Population: Ages 16–adult.
Publication Dates: 1952–85.
Acronym: EAS.
Administration: Group.
Price Data: Available from publisher.
Time: (50) minutes.
Authors: G. Grimsley (*a–h*), F. L. Ruch (*a–g, i, j*), N. D. Warren (*a–g*), and J. S. Ford (*a, c, e–g*).
Publisher: Psychological Services Inc.
a) TEST 1, VERBAL COMPREHENSION.
Publication Dates: 1956–84.
Scores: Total score only.
b) TEST 2, NUMERICAL ABILITY.
Publication Dates: 1952–63.
Scores: Total score only.
c) TEST 3, VISUAL PURSUIT.
Publication Date: 1956.
Scores: Total score only.
d) TEST 4, VISUAL SPEED AND ACCURACY.
Publication Dates: 1952–80.
Scores: Total score only.
e) TEST 5, SPACE VISUALIZATION.
Publication Dates: 1957–85.
Scores: Total score only.
f) TEST 6, NUMERICAL REASONING.
Publication Dates: 1957–85.
Scores: Total score only.
g) TEST 7, VERBAL REASONING.
Publication Dates: 1952–63.
Scores: Total score only.

h) TEST 8, WORD FLUENCY.
Publication Dates: 1953–63.
Scores: Total score only.
i) TEST 9, MANUAL SPEED AND ACCURACY.
Publication Dates: 1953–63.
Scores: Total score only.
j) TEST 10, SYMBOLIC REASONING.
Publication Dates: 1957–85.
Scores: Total score only.
Cross References: See T3:799 (4 references) and T2:1071 (14 references); for reviews by Paul F. Ross and Erwin K. Taylor, and an excerpted review by John O. Crites, see 6:769 (4 references); for reviews by Dorothy C. Adkins and S. Rains Wallace, see 5:607.

TEST REFERENCES

1. Hattrup, K., Schmitt, N., & Landis, R. S. (1992). Equivalence of constructs measured by job-specific and commercially available aptitude tests. *Journal of Applied Psychology, 77,* 298-308.

[895]

Employee Effectiveness Profile.
Purpose: "Designed to assist managers in identifying the overall effectiveness of individual employees."
Population: Managers.
Publication Date: 1986.
Scores: Total score only.
Administration: Individual.
Price Data, 1992: $7.95 each (1–25 profiles) (24 pages); $3.95 each (1–50 short forms); quantity discounts available.
Time: No time limit.
Author: J. William Pfeiffer.
Publisher: Pfeiffer & Company International Publishers.

[896]

Employee Involvement Survey.
Purpose: Assesses employees' actual and desired opportunities for personal involvement and influence in the workplace.
Population: Business and industry employees.
Publication Date: 1988.
Acronym: EIS.
Scores, 5: Basic Creature Comfort, Safety and Order, Belonging and Affiliation, Ego-Status, Actualization and Self-Expression.
Administration: Group.
Price Data, 1990: $6.95 per test booklet (14 pages).
Time: Administration time not reported.
Comments: Self-administered, self-scored.
Authors: Jay Hall.
Publisher: Teleometrics International.

[897]

Employee Performance Appraisal.
Purpose: "Designed as a tool to aid in performance appraisal and merit review."
Population: Business and industry.

Publication Dates: 1962–84.
Acronym: EPA.
Scores: 7 merit ratings: Quantity of Work, Quality of Work, Job Knowledge, Initiative, Interpersonal Relationships, Dependability, Potential.
Administration: Group.
Manual: No manual; included in Manuals Supplement ('84) along with 13 tests from this publisher.
Price Data, 1993: $26 per package of forms; $14.50 per specimen set.
Time: [10–20] minutes.
Comments: Ratings by supervisors.
Author: Martin M. Bruce.
Publisher: Martin M. Bruce, Ph.D., Publishers.
Cross References: For a review by Jean Maier Palormo, see 6:1116.

[898]

[Employee Rating and Development Forms].
Purpose: To improve personnel evaluation of employees through a structured assessment system involving patterned merit review, patterned exit review, and personal history review.
Population: Executive, industrial, office, and sales personnel.
Publication Dates: 1950–64.
Administration: Individual.
Price Data: Not available.
Author: Robert N. McMurry.
Publisher: Dartnell [No reply from publisher; status unknown].
a) [PATTERNED MERIT REVIEW FORMS].
   1) *Patterned Merit Review Form—Executive.*
Publication Dates: 1955–59.
   2) *Patterned Merit Review Form—Plant and Office.*
Publication Dates: 1955–64.
   3) *Patterned Merit Review Form—Sales.*
Publication Dates: 1955–59.
   4) *Patterned Merit Review Form—Technical, Office, Special Skills.*
Publication Dates: 1956–64.
   5) *Statement of Supervisory Expectancies.*
Publication Dates: 1958–64.
b) PATTERNED EXIT INTERVIEW.
Publication Dates: 1953–65.
c) PERSONAL HISTORY REVIEW FORM.
Publication Date: 1957.
Cross References: For additional information and a review by Richard S. Barrett, see 6:1117; for reviews by Harry W. Karn and Floyd L. Ruch, see 4:781.

[899]

Employee Reliability Inventory.
Purpose: Designed to be used as a preemployment instrument assessing a number of different dimensions of reliable and productive work behavior."
Population: Prospective employees.
Publication Dates: 1986–93.
Acronym: ERI.

Scores, 7: Freedom from Disruptive Alcohol and Substance Use, Emotional Maturity, Conscientiousness, Trustworthiness, Long Term Job Commitment, Safe Job Performance, Courtesy.
Administration: Group.
Price Data, 1992: $14 or less (volume discounts available) per questionnaire including User's Manual ('93, 52 pages), Addendum for Courtesy Scale ('93, 7 pages), all documentation, training, toll-free (or in-house computer) scoring, technical support, and consultation; $55 per Americans With Disabilities Act Kit including User's Manual Addendum ('92, 19 pages), Audio version, Braille version, and Large Print version.
Special Editions: Braille, Large Print, and Audio versions available.
Time: (12–15) minutes.
Author: Gerald L. Borofsky.
Publisher: Bay State Psychological Associates, Inc.; distributed by Wonderlic Personnel Test, Inc.

TEST REFERENCES

1. Borofsky, G. L. (1992). Assessing the likelihood of reliable workplace behavior: Further contributions to the validation of the Employee Reliability Inventory. *Psychological Reports, 70,* 563-592.
2. Borofsky, G. L., & Smith, M. (1993). Reductions in turnover, accidents, and absenteeism: The contribution of a pre-employment screening inventory. *Journal of Clinical Psychology, 49,* 109-116.

[900]

The Employment Barrier Identification Scale.
Purpose: Identifies and assesses "barriers to a JPTA participant's getting and holding a suitable job."
Population: JPTA participants age 15 and over.
Publication Date: 1982.
Acronym: EBIS.
Scores: Total score only.
Administration: Individual or group.
Price Data: Not available.
Time: [30] minutes.
Comments: May be orally administered.
Authors: John M. McKee, Bettye B. Burkhalter, and Susan P. McKee.
Publisher: PACE Learning Systems, Inc. [No reply from publisher; status unknown].

[901]

Employment Values Inventory.
Purpose: "A measure of personal values associated with work and the working environment."
Population: Adults.
Publication Dates: 1988–92.
Scores, 14: Work Ethic, Social Outgoingness, Risk-Taking, Stability, Responsibility, Need For Achievement, Task Orientation, Leadership, Training and Development, Innovation, Intellectual Demands, Status, Structure, Inclusion.
Administration: Individual or group.
Price Data: Available from publisher.
Time: (30–40) minutes.
Comments: Computer administration and scoring available.

Author: Selby MillSmith Limited.
Publisher: Selby MillSmith Limited [England].

[902]

Empowerment Inventory.
Purpose: To identify actions that individuals, managers, and work teams can take to raise one's level of empowerment.
Population: Work team members/employees.
Publication Date: 1993.
Acronym: EI.
Scores, 4: Choice, Competence, Meaningfulness, Progress.
Administration: Group or individual.
Price Data, 1994: $6.25 per inventory.
Time: (20) minutes.
Comments: Self-scored.
Authors: Kenneth W. Thomas and Walter G. Tymon.
Publisher: XICOM, Inc.

[903]

End-of-Course Tests.
Purpose: "To measure the subject matter taught in a selected number of junior and senior high school courses."
Population: Secondary school students.
Publication Date: 1986.
Scores, 9: Algebra, Geometry, Physics, Chemistry, Biology, World History, American History, Consumer Economics, Computer Literacy.
Subtests: Available as separates.
Administration: Group.
Price Data: Available from publisher.
Time: 405(410) minutes for the battery; 45(50) minutes for any one test.
Author: CTB MacMillan/McGraw-Hill.
Publisher: CTB Macmillan/McGraw-Hill.
Cross References: For reviews by Ernest W. Kimmel and Bikkar S. Randhawa, see 11:135.

[904]

Endeavor Instructional Rating System.
Purpose: Student ratings of courses and instructors.
Population: College.
Publication Dates: 1973–79.
Acronym: EIRS.
Scores, 9: 7 item scores (Hard Work, Advanced Planning, Class Discussion, Personal Help, Presentation Clarity, Grade Accuracy, Increased Knowledge), and 2 composite scores (Student Perception of Achievement, Student-Instructor Rapport).
Administration: Group.
Price Data: Not available.
Time: (5–10) minutes.
Author: Peter W. Frey.
Publisher: Endeavor Information Systems, Inc. [No reply from publisher; status unknown].
Cross References: See 9:386 (1 reference), and T3:818 (2 references); for a review by Kenneth O. Doyle, Jr., see 8:370 (5 references).

[905]

Endler Multidimensional Anxiety Scales.

Purpose: Developed to assess state and trait anxiety and the respondent's perception of threat in the immediate situation.
Population: Ages 15 and over.
Publication Date: 1991.
Acronym: EMAS.
Administration: Group.
Price Data, 1993: $90 per complete kit including 10 EMAS-S AutoScore test forms, 10 EMAS-T/EMAS-P AutoScore test forms, 2 EMAS-S prepaid answer sheets, 2 EMAS-T/EMAS-P prepaid answer sheets, and manual; $26.50 per 25 test forms (select EMAS-S or EMAS-T/EMAS-P); $12.50 per prepaid test report answer sheets (select EMAS-S or EMAS-T/EMAS-P); $45 per manual; $150 per IBM microcomputer edition.
Time: (25) minutes.
Comments: Tests may be used separately.
Authors: Norman S. Endler, Jean M. Edwards, and Romeo Vitelli.
Publisher: Western Psychological Services.
a) EMAS-STATE.
Acronym: EMAS-S.
Scores, 3: Cognitive-Worry, Autonomic-Emotional, Total.
b) EMAS-TRAIT.
Acronym: EMAS-T.
Scores, 4: Social Evaluation, Physical Danger, Ambiguous, Daily Routines.
c) EMAS-PERCEPTION.
Acronym: EMAS-P.
Scores: Item scores only.

TEST REFERENCES

1. Davis, C., & Cowles, M. (1989). Automated psychological testing: Method of administration, need for approval, and measures of anxiety. *Educational and Psychological Measurement, 49,* 311-320.
2. Endler, N. S., & Parker, J. D. A. (1990). Multidimensional assessment of coping: A critical evaluation. *Journal of Personality and Social Psychology, 58,* 844-854.
3. Endler, N. S., & Parlar, J. D. A. (1990). The analysis of a construct that does not exist: Misunderstanding the multidimensional nature of trait anxiety. *Educational and Psychological Measurement, 50,* 265-271.
4. King, P. R., & Endler, N. S. (1990). The trait anxiety-perception score: A composite predictor for state anxiety. *Journal of Personality and Social Psychology, 58,* 679-684.
5. Endler, N. S., Parker, J. D. A., Bagby, R. M., & Cox, B. J. (1991). Multidimensionality of state and trait anxiety: Factor structure of the Endler Multidimensional Anxiety Scales. *Journal of Personality and Social Psychology, 60,* 919-926.
6. Endler, N. S., Cox, B. J., Parker, J. D. A., & Bagby, R. M. (1992). Self-reports of depression and state-trait anxiety: Evidence for differential assessment. *Journal of Personality and Social Psychology, 63,* 832-838.
7. Davis, C., Brewer, H., & Weinstein, M. (1993). A study of appearance anxiety in young men. *Social Behavior and Personality, 21,* 63-74.

[906]

English as a Second Language Oral Assessment, Revised.

Purpose: Measures "students' ability to speak and understand English."
Population: Adult nonnative speakers of English.
Publication Dates: 1978-80.
Acronym: ESLOA.
Scores, 4: Auditory Comprehension, Basic Survival Vocabulary, Information Questions, Past/Future/Conditional Tenses.
Administration: Individual.
Price Data, 1989: $7.25 per manual ('80, 75 pages) including test; $2 per 50 answer sheets.
Time: Administration time not reported.
Authors: Joye Jenkins Coy, David R. Gonzalez, and Kathy Santopietro.
Publisher: Literacy Volunteers of America, Inc.
Cross References: For reviews by James D. Brown and Charlene Rivera, see 11:136.

[907]

English Picture Vocabulary Test.

Purpose: "Designed to assess levels of listening vocabulary."
Publication Dates: 1962–68.
Scores: Total score only.
Time: Administration time not reported.
Authors: M. A. Brimer and Lloyd M. Dunn.
Publisher: Educational Evaluation Enterprises [England].
a) FULL RANGE VERSION.
Population: Ages 3-0 and over.
Administration: Individual.
Price Data, 1989: $16.90 per complete kit including test book, 50 record sheets, and manual; $10.15 per test book; $3.70 per 50 record sheets; $3.70 per manual.
b) TEST 1.
Population: Ages 5-0 to 8-11.
Administration: Individual.
Price Data, 1989: $10.95 per complete kit including same materials as *a* above; $4.30 per test book; $3.70 per 50 record sheets.
c) TEST 2.
Population: Ages 7-0 to 11-11.
   1) *Individual.*
   Price Data, 1989: Same as *b* above.
   2) *Group.*
   Price Data, 1989: $8.15 per administration set including 50 test booklets, scoring keys, and manual ('63, 45 pages); $7.40 per 50 test booklets; $1.60 per manual and key.
d) TEST 3.
Population: Ages 11-0 and over.
Administration: Group.
Price Data, 1989: Same as *c-2* above.
Cross References: See T3:823 (15 references); see also T2:495 (3 references); for a review by Kenneth Lovell of Tests 1-2, see 7:408 (5 references); for reviews by L. B. Birch and Philip M. Levy, see 6:520.

TEST REFERENCES

1. Johnston, R. S. (1982). Phonological coding in dyslexic readers. *The British Journal of Psychology, 73,* 455-460.
2. Cox, T. (1983). Cumulative deficit in culturally disadvantaged children. *British Journal of Educational Psychology, 53,* 317-326.
3. McWhirter, L., Young, V., & Majury, J. (1983). Belfast chil-

dren's awareness of violent death. *The British Journal of Social Psychology, 22*, 81-92.

4. Albery, L., & Enderby, P. (1984). Intensive speech therapy for cleft palate children. *British Journal of Disorders of Communication, 19*, 115-124.

5. Taylor, B., & Wadsworth, J. (1984). Breast feeding and child development at five years. *Developmental Medicine and Child Neurology, 26*, 73-80.

6. Wadsworth, J., Taylor, B., Osborn, A., & Butler, N. (1984). Teenage mothering: Child development at five years. *Journal of Child Psychology and Psychiatry, 25*, 305-313.

7. Stevenson, J., Richman, N., & Graham, P. (1985). Behaviour problems and language abilities at three years and behavioural deviance at eight years. *The Journal of Child Psychology and Psychiatry and Allied Disciplines, 26*, 215-230.

8. Wadsworth, J., Burnell, I., Taylor, B., & Butler, N. (1985). The influence of family type on children's behaviour and development at five years. *Journal of Child Psychology and Psychiatry, 26*, 245-254.

9. Coltheart, V., Laxon, V. J., Keating, G. C., & Pool, M. M. (1986). Direct access and phonological encoding processes in children's reading: Effects of word characteristics. *British Journal of Educational Psychology, 56*, 255-270.

10. Raine, A., Hulme, C., Chadderton, H., & Bailey, P. (1991). Verbal short-term memory span in speech-disordered children: Implications for articulatory coding in short-term memory. *Child Development, 62*, 415-423.

[908]

English Placement Test.

Purpose: Place students into homogeneous ability levels as they enter an intensive English course.
Population: Entrants to courses in English as a second language.
Publication Dates: 1972–78.
Acronym: EPT.
Scores, 5: Listening, Grammar, Vocabulary, Reading, Total.
Administration: Group.
Price Data: Available from publisher.
Time: (75) minutes.
Comments: Tape recording available for administration.
Authors: Mary Spaan and Laura Strowe.
Publisher: English Language Institute, University of Michigan.
Cross References: For a review by John L. D. Clark, see 8:102.

TEST REFERENCES

1. Breland, H. M., & Griswold, P. A. (1982). Use of a performance test as a criterion in a differential validity study. *Journal of Educational Psychology, 74*, 713-721.
2. Bachman, L. F. (1985). Performance on cloze tests with fixed-ratio and rational deletions. *TESOL Quarterly, 19*, 535-556.
3. Mannan, G., Charleston, L., & Saghafi, B. (1986). A comparison of the academic performance of black and white freshman students on an urban commuter campus. *Journal of Negro Education, 55*, 155-161.

[909]

English Progress Test.

Purpose: "Designed to provide a continuous assessment of English skill."
Population: Ages 7-3 to 15-6.
Publication Dates: 1952–72.
Scores: Total score only for each of 13 subtests.
Administration: Group.
Price Data, 1989: £5.50 per 10 tests (specify level); £3.20 per manual (specify level); £6.05 per primary specimen set; £5.20 per secondary specimen set.
Time: (40–50) minutes per test.
Comments: Tests B, C, D, and F are out of print.
Publisher: NFER-Nelson Publishing Co., Ltd. [England].

a) ENGLISH PROGRESS TEST A.
Population: Ages 8-0 to 9-0.
Publication Dates: 1952–60.
Author: A. F. Watts.

b) ENGLISH PROGRESS TEST E.
Population: Ages 12-0 to 13-0.
Publication Date: 1956.
Authors: M. A. Brimer and A. F. Watts.

c) ENGLISH PROGRESS TEST G.
Population: Ages 13-0 to 15-6.
Publication Date: 1962.
Author: Test by S. M. Unwin.

d) ENGLISH PROGRESS TEST A2.
Population: Ages 7-3 to 8-11.
Publication Dates: 1962–66.
Authors: M. A. Brimer and A. F. Watts.

e) ENGLISH PROGRESS TEST B2.
Population: Ages 8-6 to 10-0.
Publication Dates: 1959–60.
Authors: Manuals by Valerie C. Land.

f) ENGLISH PROGRESS TEST C2.
Population: Ages 9-6 to 11-0.
Publication Date: 1961.
Author: Valerie Land.

g) ENGLISH PROGRESS TEST D2.
Population: Ages 10-6 to 12-0.
Publication Dates: 1963–64.
Author: Jennifer Henchman.

h) ENGLISH PROGRESS TEST E2.
Population: Ages 11-0 to 13-0.
Publication Dates: 1962–72.
Author: Test by S. M. Unwin.

i) ENGLISH PROGRESS TEST F2.
Population: Ages 12-0 to 13-6.
Publication Dates: 1963–72.
Authors: Test by Jennifer Henchman and Elsa Hendry.

j) ENGLISH PROGRESS TEST B3.
Population: Ages 8-0 to 9-6.
Publication Dates: 1970–72.

k) ENGLISH PROGRESS TEST C3.
Population: Ages 9-0 to 10-9.
Publication Dates: 1970–72.

l) ENGLISH PROGRESS TEST D3.
Population: Ages 10-0 to 11-8.
Publication Dates: 1970–72.

m) ENGLISH PROGRESS TEST F3.
Population: Ages 12-0 to 13-6.
Publication Date: 1969.
Cross References: For reviews by Neil Gourlay and Stanley Nisket of Tests A–F, see 5:187.

TEST REFERENCES

1. Potter, F. (1982). The use of the linguistic context: Do good and poor readers use different strategies? *The British Journal of Educational Psychology, 52*, 16-23.
2. Hermelin, B., & O'Conner, N. (1986). Spatial representations in

mathematically and in artistically gifted children. *British Journal of Educational Psychology, 56,* 150-157.

   3. O'Connor, N., & Hermelin, B. (1987). Visual memory and motor programmes: Their use by idiot-savant artists and controls. *British Journal of Psychology, 78,* 307- 323.

   4. Annett, M., & Manning, M. (1989). The disadvantages of dextrality for intelligence. *British Journal of Psychology, 80,* 213-226.

[910]

English Skills Assessment.

Purpose: ACER adaptation of STEP Series and DTLS by Educational Testing Service and The College Board.

Population: Grades 11–12 and first year of post-secondary education.

Publication Dates: 1969–82.

Acronym: ESA.

Scores, 11: Part I (Spelling, Punctuation and Capitalization, Comprehension I, Total), Part II (Comprehension II, Usage, Vocabulary, Sentence Structure, Logical Relationships [optional], Total), Total.

Administration: Group.

Price Data, 1994: A$3 per test booklet; $17.70 per 10 answer sheets; $17.70 per manual; $27 per specimen set.

Time: 50(70) minutes for Part I; 60(70) minutes for Part II.

Author: Australian Council for Educational Research (adaptation).

Publisher: Australian Council for Educational Research Ltd. [Australia].

Cross References: For a review by John C. Sherwood, see 9:389.

TEST REFERENCES

1. Boyle, G. J., Start, B., & Hall, E. J. (1989). Prediction of academic achievement using the School Motivation Analysis Test. *British Journal of Educational Psychology, 59,* 92-99.

[911]

English Test: Municipal Tests: National Achievement Tests.

Purpose: "To test . . . mastery in language usage (words and sentences), punctuation and capitalization, and expression of ideas."

Population: Grades 3–8.

Publication Dates: 1938–56.

Scores, 5: Language Usage-Words, Language Usage-Sentences, Punctuation and Capitalization, Expressing Ideas, Total.

Administration: Group.

Forms, 2: A, B; **Levels, 2:** Grades 3–6, Grades 6–8.

Price Data, 1985: $5 per 25 test booklets; $4 per specimen set.

Time: 30(35) minutes.

Comments: Subtest of the formerly published Municipal Battery (see 4:20).

Authors: Robert K. Speer and Samuel Smith.

Publisher: Psychometric Affiliates.

Cross References: See T2:77 (1 reference) and 5:190. For reviews of the complete battery, see 5:18 (1 review), 4:20 (1 review), and 2:1191 (2 reviews).

[912]

English Test: National Achievement Tests.

Purpose: To test skills in English language usage.

Population: Grades 3–12.

Publication Dates: 1936–57.

Administration: Group.

Levels, 2: Grades 3–8, Grades 7–12; Forms, 2: A, B.

Price Data, 1985: $4 per specimen set; $7 per 25 test booklets (A or B).

Time: (40) minutes.

Authors: Robert K. Speer and Samuel Smith.

Publisher: Psychometric Affiliates.

  a) GRADES 3—8.

Publication Dates: 1936–38.

Scores, 7: Capitalization, Punctuation, Language Usage (Sentences), Language Usage (Words), Expressing Ideas, Letter Writing, Total.

  b) GRADES 7—12.

Publication Dates: 1936–57.

Scores, 7: Word Usage, Punctuation, Vocabulary, Language Usage (Sentences), Expressing Ideas, Expressing Feeling, Total.

Cross References: See T2:78 (1 reference) and 5:191; for a review by Winifred L. Post, see 4:162; for a review by Harry A. Greene, see 3:126.

[913]

Enhanced ACT Assessment.

Purpose: "To help students develop postsecondary plans."

Population: Grades 10–12.

Publication Dates: 1959–92.

Administration: Group.

Price Data: Available from publisher.

Time: 175 (190) minutes.

Comments: Tests administered 5 times per year (February, April, June, October, December) at centers established by the publisher; previous version entitled ACT Assessment Program (9:43).

Author: American College Testing.

Publisher: American College Testing.

  a) ACT ENGLISH TEST.

Purpose: "Measures the student's understanding of the conventions of standard written English."

Scores, 3: Usage/Mechanics, Rhetorical Skills, Total.

Time: 45 minutes.

  b) ACT MATHEMATICS TEST.

Purpose: Measures reasoning and mathematical skills.

Scores, 4: Pre-Algebra/Elementary Algebra, Algebra/Coordinate Geometry, Plane Geometry/Trigonometry, Total.

Time: 60 minutes.

  c) ACT READING TEST.

Purpose: "Measures reading comprehension as a product of skill in referring and reasoning."

Scores, 3: Social Studies/Sciences, Arts/Literature, Total.

Time: 35 minutes.

d) ACT SCIENCE REASONING TEST.

Purpose: "Measures the interpretation, analysis evaluation, reasoning, and problem solving skills required in the natural sciences."

Scores: Total score only.

Time: 35 minutes.

Cross References: For reviews by Lewis R. Aiken and Edward Kifer of the ACT Assessment Program, see 9:42 (27 references); see also T3:76 (76 references); for a review by John R. Hills, see 8:469 (208 references); see also T2:1044 (97 references); for a review by Wimburn L. Wallace of an earlier program, see 7:330 (265 references); for reviews by Max D. Engelhart and Warren G. Findley and an excerpted review by David V. Tiedeman, see 6:1 (14 references).

TEST REFERENCES

1. Gottfredson, L. S. (1982). The sex fairness of unnormed interest inventories. *The Vocational Guidance Quarterly, 31,* 128-132.
2. Galbraith, R. C. (1983). Individual differences in intelligence: A reappraisal of the confluence model. *Intelligence, 7,* 185-194.
3. Abrams, H. G., & Jernigan, L. P. (1984). Academic support services and the success of high-risk college students. *American Educational Research Journal, 21,* 261-274.
4. Blosser, P. E. (1984). What research says: Achievement in science. *School Science and Mathematics, 84,* 514-521.
5. Edge, O. P., & Friedberg, S. H. (1984). Factors affecting achievement in the first course in calculus. *The Journal of Experimental Education, 52,* 136-140.
6. Feltz, D. L., & Weiss, M. R. (1984). The impact of girls' interscholastic sport participation on academic orientation. *Research Quarterly for Exercise and Sport, 55,* 332-339.
7. Kolen, M. J. (1984). Effectiveness of analytic smoothing in equipercentile equating. *Journal of Educational Statistics, 9,* 25-44.
8. Merritt, F. M., & McCallum, R. S. (1984). The relationship between simultaneous-successive processing and academic achievement. *The Alberta Journal of Educational Research, 30,* 126-132.
9. Mosely, J. N., Mickler, J. E., & Stegall, H. H. (1984). Focus on research: A candid look at accreditation. *Contemporary Education, 55,* 242-245.
10. Pascarella, E. T. (1984). College environmental influences on students' educational aspirations. *Journal of Higher Education, 55,* 751-771.
11. Pedrini, D. T., Tritchler, D. L., & Pedrini, B. C. (1984). Prediction of college freshman grade point average and attrition/persistence: ANOVA, MANOVA, MULREG, LANCOR. *College Student Journal, 18,* 18-27.
12. Wollman, W., & Lawrenz, F. (1984). Identifying potential 'dropouts' from college physics classes. *Journal of Research in Science Teaching, 21,* 385-390.
13. Conklin, R. C. (1985). Teacher competency testing: The present situation and some concerns on how teachers are tested. *Education Canada, 25,* 12-15.
14. Dong, H., Sung, Y. H., & Dohm, T. E. (1985). The validity of the Ball Aptitude Battery (BAB): I. Relationship to high school academic success. *Educational and Psychological Measurement, 45,* 627-637.
15. Glennen, R. E., & Baxley, D. M. (1985). Reduction of attrition through intrusive advising. *NASPA Journal, 22*(3), 10-14.
16. Henry, T., Creswell, J., & Humphrey, E. (1985). Nebraska study looks at indicators of excellence, says centers of quality exist. *NASSP Bulletin, 69,* 87-93.
17. Jeffries, S. (1985). English grammar terminology as an obstacle to second language learning. *The Modern Language Journal, 69,* 385-390.
18. Johnston, K. L., & Aldridge, B. G. (1985). Examining a mathematical model of mastery learning in a classroom setting. *Journal of Research in Science Teaching, 22,* 543-554.
19. McPhee, S. A., & Kerr, M. E. (1985). Scholastic aptitude and achievement as predictors of performance on competency tests. *Journal of Educational Research, 78,* 186-190.
20. Osigweh, C. A. B. (1985). Measuring performance in a business school. *Delta Pi Epsilon Journal, 27,* 130-141.
21. Pascarella, E. T. (1985). Students' affective development within the college environment. *Journal of Higher Education, 56,* 640-663.
22. Rounds, J., & Andersen, D. (1985). Assessment for entrance to community college: Research studies of three major standardized tests. *Journal of Research and Development in Education, 18*(2), 54-57.
23. Wainer, H., Holland, P. W., Swinton, S., & Wang, M. H. (1985). On "state education statistics." *Journal of Educational Statistics, 10,* 293-325.
24. Wood, P. H., Nemeth, J. S., & Brooks, C. C. (1985). Criterion-related validity of the Degrees of Reading Power test (Form CP-1A). *Educational and Psychological Measurement, 45,* 965-969.
25. Bee, R. H., & Beronja, T. A. (1986). Modeling the academic performance of the undetermined major. *The College Student Journal, 20,* 23-33.
26. Bee, R. H., & Beronja, T. A. (1986). Ridge regression: An analysis of the undetermined major. *The College Student Journal, 20,* 348-354.
27. Keeley, S. M., & Browne, M. N. (1986). How college seniors operationalize critical thinking behavior. *The College Student Journal, 20,* 389-395.
28. Ormrod, J. E. (1986). Learning to spell: Three studies at the university level. *Research in the Teaching of English, 20,* 160-173.
29. Phelps, L., Schmitz, C. D., & Boatright, B. (1986). The effects of halo and leniency on cooperating teacher reports using Likert-type rating scales. *The Journal of Educational Research, 79,* 151-154.
30. Taylor, J. B., & Worden, T. W. (1986). Knowledge-based competence as a predictor of effective classroom practice. *The College Student Journal, 20,* 15-20.
31. Yunker, P. J., Yunker, J. A., & Sterner, J. (1986). On the relationship between test anxiety and grades in accounting courses. *The College Student Journal, 20,* 275-282.
32. Erwin, T. D. (1987). The construct validity of Holland's differentiation concept. *Measurement and Evaluation in Counseling and Development, 20,* 106-112.
33. Lewis, M. W., Lewis, A. C., & Smith, T. E. C. (1987). Intellectual characteristics of university students in remedial programs. *Measurement and Evaluation in Counseling and Development, 20,* 127-133.
34. Miller, C. D., Alway, M., & McKinley, D. L. (1987). Effects of learning styles and strategies on academic success. *Journal of College Student Personnel, 28,* 399-404.
35. Bartling, C. A. (1988). Longitudinal changes in the study habits of successful college students. *Educational and Psychological Measurement, 48,* 527-535.
36. Benton, S. L., Kiewra, K. A., & Beans, R. O. (1988). Attributes of organizational ability related to writing ability. *Contemporary Educational Psychology, 13,* 87-89.
37. Harris, D. J., & Kolen, M. J. (1988). Bootstrap and traditional standard errors of the point-biserial. *Educational and Psychological Measurement, 48,* 43-51.
38. Heard, S. A., & Ayers, J. B. (1988). Validity of the American College Test in predicting success on the Pre-Professional Skills Test. *Educational and Psychological Measurement, 48*(1), 197-200.
39. Humphreys, L. G. (1988). Trends in levels of academic achievement of blacks and other minorities. *Intelligence, 12,* 231-260.
40. Kerr, B. A., & Colangelo, N. (1988). The college plans of academically talented students. *Journal of Counseling and Development, 67,* 42-48.
41. Kiewra, K. A., & Benton, S. L. (1988). The relationship between information-processing ability and notetaking. *Contemporary Educational Psychology, 13,* 33-44.
42. Pollio, H. R., Eison, J. A., & Milton, O. (1988). College grades as an adaptation level phenomenon. *Contemporary Educational Psychology, 13,* 146-156.
43. Cooper, S. E., & Robinson, D. A. G. (1989). The influence of gender and anxiety on mathematics performance. *Journal of College Student Development, 30,* 459-461.
44. Lichtman, C. M., Bass, A. R., & Ager, J. W., Jr. (1989). Differences between black and white students in attribution patterns from an urban commuter university. *Journal of College Student Development, 30,* 4-10.
45. Noble, J. P., & Sawyer, R. L. (1989). Predicting grades in college freshman English and mathematics courses. *Journal of College Student Development, 30,* 345-353.
46. Pascarella, E. T. (1989). The development of critical thinking: Does college make a difference? *Journal of College Student Development, 30,* 19-26.
47. Roberts, G. H., & White, W. G., Jr. (1989). Health and stress in developmental college students. *Journal of College Student Development, 30,* 515-521.
48. Betz, N. E., Heesacker, R. S., & Shuttleworth, C. (1990). Moderators of the congruence and realism of major and occupational plans in college students: A replication and extension. *Journal of Counseling Psychology, 37,* 269-276.
49. Linn, R. L. (1990). Admissions Testing: Recommended uses, validity, differential prediction, and coaching. *Applied Measurement in Education, 3*(4), 297-318.
50. Pace, A. J., Walters, K., & Sherk, J. K. (1990). What determines course achievement? An investigation of several possible influences on aca-

demic outcomes. *Yearbook of the National Reading Conference, 39,* 374-351.

51. Zarrella, K. L., & Schuerger, J. M. (1990). Temporal stability of occupational interest inventories. *Psychological Reports, 66,* 1067-1074.

52. Ackerman, T. A. (1991). The use of unidimensional parameter estimates of multidimensional items in adaptive testing. *Applied Psychological Measurement, 15,* 13-24.

53. Cone, A. L. (1991). Sophomore academic retention associated with a freshman study skills and college adjustment course. *Psychological Reports, 69,* 312-314.

54. Harris, D. J. (1991). A comparison of Angoff's design I and design II for vertical equating using traditional and IRT methodology. *Journal of Educational Measurement, 28,* 221-235.

55. Harris, D. J. (1991). Effects of passage and item scrambling on equating relationships. *Applied Psychological Measurement, 15,* 247-256.

56. Kolen, M. J. (1991). Smoothing methods for estimating test score distributions. *Journal of Educational Measurement, 28,* 257-282.

57. Sher, K. J., Walitzer, K. S., Wood, P. K., & Brent, E. E. (1991). Characteristics of children of alcoholics: Putative risk factors, substance use and abuse, and psychopathology. *Journal of Abnormal Psychology, 100,* 427-448.

58. Williams, J. E. (1991). Modeling test anxiety, self concept and high school students' academic achievement. *Journal of Research and Development in Education, 25*(1), 51-57.

59. Young, R. B., & Rogers, G. (1991). The impact of an early advising program on the success of Black freshmen and White freshmen. *Journal of College Student Development, 32,* 375-376.

60. Brasfield, D., McCoy, J., & Milkman, M. (1992). The effect of university math on student performance in principles of economics. *Journal of Research and Development in Education, 25,* 240-247.

61. Dickinson, D. D. (1992). Effects of the student-teaching experience. *Journal of Research and Development in Education, 25,* 218-223.

62. Gehlert, K., Timberlake, D., & Wagner, B. (1992). The relationship between vocational identity and academic achievement. *Journal of College Student Development, 33,* 143-148.

63. Giddan, N. S., & Whitner, P. A. (1992). Personal essay: A qualitative evaluation technique. *Journal of College Student Development, 33,* 277-279.

64. Goff, M., & Ackerman, P. L. (1992). Personality-intelligence relations: Assessment of typical intellectual engagement. *Journal of Educational Psychology, 84,* 537-552.

65. Hood, A. B., Craig, A. F., & Ferguson, B. W. (1992). The impact of athletics, part-time employment, and other activities on academic achievement. *Journal of College Student Development, 33,* 447-453.

66. Kolen, M. J., Hanson, B. A., & Brennan, R. L. (1992). Conditional standard errors of measurement for scale scores. *Journal of Educational Measurement, 29,* 285-307.

67. Mehrens, W. A., & Popham, J. W. (1992). How to evaluate the legal defensibility of high-stakes tests. *Applied Measurement in Education, 5,* 265-283.

68. Mitchell, J. V. (1992). Interrelationships and predictive efficacy for indices of intrinsic, extrinsic: Self-assessed motivation for learning. *Journal of Research and Development in Education, 25,* 148-155.

69. Nandakumar, R., & Stout, W. (1993). Refinements of Stout's procedure for assessing latent trait unidimensionality. *Journal of Educational Statistics, 18,* 41-68.

70. Roznowski, M. (1993). Measures of cognitive processes: Their stability and other psychometric and measurement properties. *Intelligence, 17,* 361-388.

71. Semb, G. B., Ellis, J. A., & Araujo, J. (1993). Long-term memory for knowledge learned in school. *Journal of Educational Psychology, 85,* 305-316.

[914]

The Ennis-Weir Critical Thinking Essay Test.

Purpose: "To help evaluate a person's ability to appraise an argument and to formulate in writing an argument in response, thus recognizing a creative dimension in critical thinking ability."

Population: High school and college.

Publication Dates: 1983–85.

Scores: Critical Thinking Ability.

Administration: Group.

Price Data, 1993: $9.95 per set including 1 reproducible test, scoring sheet, scoring directions, and manual ('85, 16 pages).

Time: (40) minutes.

Authors: Robert H. Ennis and Eric Weir.

Publisher: Critical Thinking Press and Software.

Cross References: For reviews by James A. Poteet and Gail E. Tompkins, see 10:107.

[915]

ENRIGHT Diagnostic Inventory of Basic Arithmetic Skills.

Purpose: Developed to assess arithmetic computational skills and to analyze error patterns.

Population: Grade 4 to adult.

Publication Date: 1983.

Scores: 3-step hierarchical testing system (Wide-Range Placement Test, Skill Placement Tests, Skill Tests, plus Basic Facts Tests) for error analysis of 144 arithmetic skills in 13 sections: Addition of Whole Numbers, Subtraction of Whole Numbers, Multiplication of Whole Numbers, Division of Whole Numbers, Conversion of Fractions, Addition of Fractions, Subtraction of Fractions, Multiplication of Fractions, Division of Fractions, Addition of Decimals, Subtraction of Decimals, Multiplication of Decimals, Division of Decimals.

Administration: Group.

Forms, 2: A, B.

Price Data, 1993: $99 per complete kit including 10 student tests and record books and manual (326 pages); $4.65 per student tests and record books.

Time: Administration time not reported.

Comments: "Criterion-referenced."

Author: Brian E. Enright.

Publisher: Curriculum Associates, Inc.

Cross References: For reviews by Douglas K. Smith and Jeffrey K. Smith, see 10:108.

[916]

Entrance Examination for Schools of Nursing [RN Entrance Examination].

Purpose: Constructed to assess academic achievement for use in selection and placement of students.

Population: Applicants to schools of registered nursing.

Publication Dates: 1938–91.

Acronym: RNEE.

Scores, 6: Verbal Ability, Numerical Ability, Life Sciences, Physical Sciences, Reading Skill, Total.

Administration: Group.

Restricted Distribution: Distribution restricted and test administered at licensed testing centers; details may be obtained from publisher.

Price Data: Available from publisher.

Time: 160(175) minutes.

Comments: Title on test is RN Entrance Examination for Schools of Nursing.

Author: The Psychological Corporation.

Publisher: The Psychological Corporation.

Cross References: For reviews by Carolyn Dawson and Christine H. McGuire, see 8:1121; see also T2:2379 (1 reference), 7:1115 (3 references), and 6:1156 (2 references).

[917]

Entrance Examination for Schools of Practical/Vocational Nursing.
Purpose: "Designed to measure achievement in areas critical for success in the basic practical/vocational nursing curriculum."
Population: Applicants to practical/vocational nursing schools.
Publication Dates: 1942–91.
Acronym: PNEE.
Scores, 5: Verbal Ability, Numerical Ability, Science, Reading Skill, Total.
Administration: Group.
Restricted Distribution: Distribution restricted and test administered at licensed testing centers; details may be obtained from publisher.
Price Data: Available from publisher.
Time: 180(195) minutes.
Author: The Psychological Corporation.
Publisher: The Psychological Corporation.
Cross References: See 7:1116 (2 references).

[918]

Entrepreneurial Style and Success Indicator.
Purpose: Assesses variables thought to be related to entrepreneurial success and increase understanding of entrepreneurial style.
Population: Adults.
Publication Dates: 1988–89.
Acronym: ESSI.
Scores, 4: Behavioral Action, Cognitive Analysis, Interpersonal Harmony, Affective Expression, plus 28 Success Factors.
Administration: Group.
Price Data, 1993: $15 per test booklet; $10 per interpretations booklet ('88, 42 pages); $15 per audiotape (Business With Style); $35 per professional's guide ('89, 73 pages).
Time: (120–180) minutes for Basic; (360–720) minutes for Advanced.
Comments: May be self-administered.
Authors: Howard L. Shenson, Terry D. Anderson (test and audiotape), Jonathan Clark (audiotape), and Susan Clark (audiotape).
Publisher: Consulting Resource Group International, Inc.

[919]

Environmental Response Inventory.
Purpose: "Created to measure environmental dispositions—individual differences in the ways people think about and relate to the everyday physical environment."
Population: College and adults.
Publication Dates: 1971–74.
Acronym: ERI.
Scores, 9: Pastoralism, Urbanism, Environmental Adaptation, Stimulus Seeking, Environmental Trust, Antiquarianism, Need Privacy, Mechanical Orientation, Communality.

Administration: Group.
Price Data, 1990: $11 per 25 test booklets; $27 per 50 answer sheets with profiles; $28 per 100 answer sheets; $44 per set of scoring stencils; $25 per 100 profile sheets; $9 per manual ('74, 29 pages); $10 per specimen set.
Time: (25–40) minutes.
Author: George E. McKechnie.
Publisher: Consulting Psychologists Press, Inc.
Cross References: See T3:837 (3 references); for reviews by James M. Richards, Jr. and Lawrence J. Stricker, see 8:550 (1 reference).

[920]

Eosys Word Processing Aptitude Battery.
Purpose: For use in selection, allocation, and development of word processor operators.
Population: Job candidates for work processor operator positions.
Publication Date: 1983.
Acronym: WPAB.
Scores, 5: Verbal Skills (WP1), Checking Skills (WP2), Written Instructions (WP3), Coded Information (WP4), Numerical Computation (WP5).
Administration: Group.
Price Data, 1988: £424 per complete kit; £110 per 10 test booklets including all 5 tests and command card for WP4 (reusable); £53 per set of scoring keys; £42 per 10 sets of answer sheets and profile; £3 per 10 group score sheets; £39.50 per set of administration cards; £66 per manual/user's guide (59 pages).
Time: (10) minutes per WP1, WP2, WP5; (12) minutes per WP3; (15) minutes per WP4.
Authors: Gill Nyfield, Susan Bawtree, Michael Pearn (test), David Hawkey (test), and Emma Bird (manual).
Publisher: Saville & Holdsworth Ltd. [England].

[921]

EPS Sentence Completion Technique.
Purpose: "A semi-projective instrument specifically designed for use with individuals in the mildly mentally retarded and borderline intelligence ranges."
Population: Mildly mentally handicapped ages 14 and over.
Publication Date: 1989–91.
Scores: Interpretation on 4 levels: Individual Items, Problem Areas (Interpersonal Relationships, Psychological Functioning, Work/School, Independence, Sexuality, Family, Residential Living and Adjustment, Behavior, Health), Thematic Interpretation, Specific Questions/Clinical Hypotheses.
Administration: Individual.
Editions, 2: School, nonschool.
Price Data, 1994: $18 per complete kit including user's guide ('91, 4 pages) and 50 test booklets.
Time: (10–15) minutes.
Authors: Douglas C. Strohmer and H. Thompson Prout.
Publisher: Psychological Assessment Resources, Inc.

[922]

EQ Questionnaire.
Purpose: "To measure entrepreneurial and executive effectiveness to be used as a personal and organizational development tool."
Population: Adults.
Publication Date: 1993.
Acronym: EQ Questionnaire.
Scores: 13 dimensions: Management Support Variables (Venture Adaptibility Factor, Risk Threshold Factor, Leadership Ability Factor, Self-Discipline Factor, Time Management Factor), Managerial Typing Preferences (Creative vs. Traditional, Strategic vs. Functional, Planning vs. Reacting, Goal-oriented vs. Activity-oriented), Psychological Type Preferences (Extroverted vs. Introverted, Sensing vs. Intuitive, Thinking vs. Feeling, Perceptive vs. Judging).
Administration: Group.
Price Data, 1993: $37.50 per test (includes scoring service).
Time: (35-45) minutes.
Comments: Test booklet title is EQ Questionnaire; computer scoring only by publisher.
Authors: Wonderlic Personnel Test, Inc.
Publisher: Wonderlic Personnel Test, Inc.

[923]

ERB Comprehensive Testing Program III.
Purpose: "Designed to measure attainment of major educational objectives regardless of particular curriculum programs and methods."
Population: Grades 1-2, 2-3, 3-4, 4-6, 6-8, 8-12.
Publication Dates: 1974-92.
Acronym: CTPIII.
Administration: Group.
Forms, 2: 1, 2.
Price Data: Available from publisher.
Comments: "All quantitative ability and mathematics tests are written to the NCTM standards; where applicable, items intended to tap higher-order thinking skills are included and are identified on reports."
Author: Educational Records Bureau.
Publisher: Educational Testing Service.
   a) ACHIEVEMENT TESTS, LEVEL A.
   Population: Grades 1-2.
   Scores, 4: Auditory Comprehension, Reading Comprehension, Word Analysis, Mathematics.
   Time: (155-235) minutes in several sessions.
   b) ACHIEVEMENT TESTS, LEVEL B.
   Population: Grades 2-3.
   Scores, 5: Auditory Comprehension, Reading Comprehension, Word Analysis, Writing Mechanics, Mathematics.
   Time: (190-290) minutes in several sessions.
   c) ABILITY/ACHIEVEMENT TEST, LEVEL C.
   Population: Grades 3-4.
   Scores, 7: Ability (Verbal, Quantitative), Auditory Comprehension, Reading Comprehension,

Writing Mechanics, Writing Process, Mathematics.
   Time: 310(330) minutes in several sessions.
   d) ABILITY/ACHIEVEMENT TEST, LEVEL D.
   Population: Grades 4-6.
   Scores, 7: Ability (Verbal, Quantitative), Vocabulary, Reading Comprehension, Writing Mechanics, Writing Process, Mathematics.
   Time: (290) minutes in several sessions.
   e) ABILITY/ACHIEVEMENT TEST, LEVEL E.
   Population: Grades 6-8.
   Scores, 8: Ability (Verbal, Quantitative), Vocabulary, Reading Comprehension, Writing Mechanics, Writing Process, Mathematics, Algebra I [optional end-of-course test].
   f) ABILITY/ACHIEVEMENT TEST, LEVEL F.
   Population: Grades 8-12.
   Scores, 10: Ability (Verbal, Quantitative), Vocabulary, Reading Comprehension, Writing Mechanics, Writing Process, Mathematics (Algebra I, Algebra II, Geometry [optional end-of-course tests]).
Cross References: For a review by Kathleen Barrows Chesterfield of an earlier edition, see 9:397.

[924]

ERB Writing Assessment.
Purpose: "Provides a direct measure of writing ability."
Population: Grades 4-6, 7-9, 10-12.
Publication Dates: 1989.
Scores, 7: Topic Development, Organization, Support, Sentence Structure, Word Choice, Mechanics, Total.
Administration: Group.
Price Data, 1993: $5.50 per student for test materials in packages of 5, 10, and 20 plus shipping; $27 per computer disk (IBM only); $50 per data tape; $4.50 per additional set of anchor papers; $1 per additional analytic scoring guide; $6.30 per perusal set (per level); $140 per written analysis of overall results by class or grade.
Comments: Writing samples scored by Measurement Incorporated.
Author: Educational Records Bureau.
Publisher: Educational Records Bureau, Inc.
   a) LEVEL I.
   Purpose: To assess student's descriptive writing.
   Population: Grades 4-6.
   Time: (35-40) minutes (2 sessions).
   b) LEVEL II.
   Purpose: To assess student's expository writing.
   Population: Grades 7-9.
   Time: (45-50) minutes (2 sessions).
   c) LEVEL III.
   Purpose: To assess student's persuasive writing.
   Population: Grades 10-12.
   Time: (45-50) minutes (2 sessions).

[925]
Erhardt Developmental Prehension Assessment.
Purpose: Designed "for charting the prehensile development . . . of the child who is delayed or abnormal or both."
Population: Children with cerebral palsy (spastic, athetoid, or mixed) from birth to adolescence.
Publication Dates: 1982–89.
Acronym: EDPA.
Scores: 3 areas: Involuntary Hand-Arm Patterns (Positional-Reflexive), Voluntary Movements (Cognitively Directed), Pre-Writing Skills.
Administration: Individual.
Price Data, 1993: $10 per 5 Erhardt Developmental Prehension Assessment booklets ('89, 20 pages); $35 per Developmental Hand Dysfunction manual ('89, 151 pages).
Time: Administration time not reported.
Comments: Research base and reliability information included in text entitled *Developmental Hand Dysfunction, Theory, Assessment, and Treatment.*
Author: Rhoda P. Erhardt.
Publisher: Therapy Skill Builders.

[926]
Erhardt Developmental Vision Assessment.
Purpose: Designed to assess visual-motor development.
Population: All ages.
Publication Dates: 1982–90.
Acronym: EDVA.
Scores: Item scores only.
Administration: Individual.
Price Data, 1993: $10 per 5 assessment booklets; $39 per Developmental Visual Dysfunction book ('90, 222 pages).
Time: Administration time not reported.
Comments: Administered with the help of an assistant; ratings by therapist; short screening form for visual assessment also available.
Author: Rhoda P. Erhardt.
Publisher: Therapy Skill Builders.

[927]
Erotometer: A Technique for the Measurement of Heterosexual Love.
Purpose: Designed to measure attitudes toward heterosexual love.
Population: Adults.
Publication Date: 1971.
Scores: Total score only.
Administration: Group.
Price Data: Instrument is available without charge from the author.
Time: [10] minutes.
Comments: The manual is a reprint of a journal article by the author.
Author: Panos D. Bardis.
Publisher: Panos D. Bardis.

Cross References: For additional information, see 8:337 (1 reference).

[928]
ESL/Adult Literacy Scale.
Purpose: Developed to identify "the appropriate starting level for ESL and literacy instruction."
Population: Adults.
Publication Date: 1989.
Scores, 6: Listening, Grammar, Life Skills, Reading, Composition, Total.
Administration: Individual.
Manual: No manual.
Price Data, 1991: $14 per 25 test booklets; $3 per scoring overlay; $3 per instruction sheet.
Time: [15–20] minutes.
Author: Michael Roddy.
Publisher: Academic Therapy Publications.
Cross References: For reviews by Anne L. Harvey and Dianna L. Newman and Kathleen T. Toms, see 11:138.

[929]
ETS Tests of Applied Literacy Skills.
Purpose: To measure adult literacy.
Population: Adults.
Publication Date: 1991.
Scores, 3: Total score for each of 3 subtests: Quantitative Literacy, Document Literacy, Prose Literacy.
Administration: Group.
Forms, 2: Forms A and B for each test.
Price Data: Available from publisher.
Time: 6(20) minutes for the battery; 2(20) minutes of any one subtest.
Authors: Educational Testing Service, Irwin J. Kirsch (manual), Anne Jungeblut (manual), and Anne Campbell (manual), with contributions from Norman E. Freeberg, Robert J. Mislevy, Donald A. Rock, and Kentaro Yamamoto.
Publisher: Simon & Schuster, Higher Education Group.

[930]
ETSA Tests.
Purpose: To measure "aspects of intelligence, specific abilities or aptitudes, and certain personality characteristics . . . to supplement the other factors upon which hiring, placing, training and promotion decisions are based."
Population: Employees and job applicants.
Publication Dates: 1959–85.
Scores: 8 tests: General Mental Ability Test, Office Arithmetic Test, General Clerical Ability Test, Stenographic Skills Test, Mechanical Familiarity Test, Mechanical Knowledge Test, Sales Aptitude Test, Personal Adjustment Index.
Administration: Individual and group.
Price Data: Available from publisher.
Comments: Publisher recommends use of General

Mental Ability Test (1A) and one or more others depending on nature of job.
Authors: Manual by Charles K. Stouffer and Susan Anne Stouffer; technical handbook by S. Trevor Hadley and George A. W. Stouffer.
Publisher: Educators'/Employers' Tests & Services Associates.

a) GENERAL MENTAL ABILITY TEST (1A).
Time: 45(50) minutes.
b) OFFICE ARITHMETIC TEST (2A).
Time: 60(65) minutes.
c) GENERAL CLERICAL ABILITY TEST (3A).
Time: 30(35) minutes.
d) STENOGRAPHIC SKILLS TEST (4A).
Subtests, 2: Typing Test, Shorthand Test.
Time: 45(50) minutes.
e) MECHANICAL FAMILIARITY TEST (5A).
Time: 60(65) minutes.
f) MECHANICAL KNOWLEDGE TEST (6A).
Time: 90(95) minutes.
g) SALES APTITUDE TEST (7A).
Time: 60(65) minutes.
h) PERSONAL ADJUSTMENT INDEX (8A).
Time: 45(50) minutes.
Cross References: For reviews by Roland H. Good, III and Hilda Wing, see 11:139; for additional information, see 9:399 and T3:846; for reviews by Marvin D. Dunnette and Raymond A. Katzell of an earlier edition, see 6:1025.

[931]
Evaluating Courses for Inclusion of New Scholarship on Women.
Purpose: A student evaluation questionnaire designed to evaluate course content in terms of information presented about women.
Population: Post-secondary students.
Publication Date: 1988.
Scores: 4 ratings: Evaluation of Course Readings, Evaluation of the Syllabus, Evaluation of the Class, Overall Course Evaluation.
Administration: Group.
Manual: No manual.
Price Data, 1988: $2 or less per questionnaire.
Time: Administration time not reported.
Author: Women's Studies Program, Duke University.
Publisher: Association of American Colleges.

[932]
Evaluating Educational Programs for Intellectually Gifted Students.
Purpose: "Designed to guide the evaluation of educational programming relative to the special educational needs of intellectually gifted students, grades K–12, that have been demonstrated to influence socioemotional and cognitive development."
Population: Learning environments for grades K–12.
Publication Date: 1984.
Acronym: EEPIGS.

Scores: Overall rating of educational programs for intellectually gifted students.
Administration: Individual or group.
Forms, 4: Form A: Socioemotional Needs; Form B: Cognitive Development and Intellectual Needs; Form C: Identified Program Strengths; Form D: Identified Program Weakness.
Price Data, 1994: $25 per 50 copies of Forms A and B, 25 copies of Forms C and D, and administrative manual (14 pages); $8 per manual; $8 per 50 Form A or Form B; $8 per 25 Form C and Form D.
Time: Administration time not reported.
Comments: Ratings by educators.
Authors: Joanne Rand Whitmore.
Publisher: D.O.K. Publishers, Inc.
Cross References: For reviews by Linda E. Brody and Nicholas Colangelo, see 10:111.

[933]
Evaluating Movement and Posture Disorganization in Dyspraxic Children.
Purpose: Designed to determine and analyze the normal and disorganized components of movement and posture.
Population: Learning disabled children ages 5 and above.
Publication Date: 1989.
Scores, 2: Quality Performance List, Problem Performance List.
Subtests, 10: Supine to Stand, Supine to Flexion Hold, Prone Reach, Alternating Prone Reach, Kneel-Walk Forward and Back, Alternating One Foot Kneel, Alternating Half Kneel-Stand, One-Foot Balance, Squat Pick-up, Unilateral/Bilateral Toss.
Administration: Individual.
Price Data, 1993: $89 per 5 manuals (52 pages) and analysis of movement and posture disorganization (VHS videotape); $16.95 per 5 manuals.
Time: (45) minutes for subtests; (30) minutes for videotape.
Comments: "Criteria-referenced" test; full-color videotape shows examples of normal and disorganized movement responses for each subtest.
Author: W. Michael Magrun.
Publisher: Therapy Skill Builders.

[934]
Evaluating the Participant's Employability Skills.
Purpose: "To evaluate the participant's overall understanding of the employment process."
Population: Individuals seeking employment.
Publication Dates: 1984–89.
Administration: Group.
Manual: No manual.
Price Data, 1992: $89.99 per Apple or IBM diskette including both pre- and post-tests; $105 per Windows version.
Time: [45–60] minutes.
Author: Education Associates, Inc..
Publisher: Education Associates, Inc.

a) PRE-EVALUATING THE PARTICIPANT'S EMPLOY-ABILITY SKILLS.
Scores: Total score only.
Price Data: $.79 per pre-test.
b) POST-EVALUATING THE PARTICIPANT'S EMPLOY-ABILITY SKILLS.
Scores: Total score only.
Price Data: $.79 per post-test.

[935]
Evaluation Aptitude Test.
Purpose: Constructed to assess deductive reasoning.
Population: Candidates for college and graduate school entrance.
Publication Dates: 1951–52.
Acronym: EAT.
Scores, 5: Neutral Syllogisms, Emotionally Toned Syllogisms, Total, Emotial Bias, Indecision.
Administration: Group.
Price Data: Available from publisher.
Time: 50(55) minutes.
Author: DeWitt E. Sell.
Publisher: Psychometric Affiliates.
Cross References: For reviews by J. Thomas Hastings and Walker H. Hill, see 5:691.

[936]
Evaluation Disposition Toward the Environment.
Purpose: Evaluates "value orientation used to approach environmental experiences and responsibilities."
Population: High school and college.
Publication Date: 1976.
Acronym: EDEN.
Scores, 7: Aesthetic, Experiential, Knowledge Seeking, Prudent, Active, Responsible, Practical.
Administration: Group.
Price Data: Not available.
Time: (45) minutes.
Comments: Scoring must be done by publisher.
Author: Norman J. Milchus.
Publisher: Person-O-Metrics, Inc. [No reply from publisher; status unknown].

[937]
Evaluation Modality Test.
Purpose: Developed to analyze the characteristics of "the mode in which an individual valuates."
Population: Adults.
Publication Date: 1956.
Acronym: EMT.
Scores, 4: Realism, Moralism, Individualism, Total.
Administration: Individual or group.
Price Data: Available from publisher.
Time: (25–35) minutes.
Author: Hugo O. Engelmann.
Publisher: Psychometric Affiliates.
Cross References: For a review by Wilson H. Guertin, see 5:51.

[938]
Evanston Early Identification Scale, Field Research Edition.
Purpose: For identifying children who can be expected to have difficulty in school.
Population: Ages 5-0 to 6-3.
Publication Date: 1967.
Acronym: EEIS.
Price Data: Not available.
Authors: Myril Landsman and Harry Dillard.
Publisher: Myril Landsman and Harry Dillard [No reply from publisher; status unknown].
Cross References: For reviews by James J. McCarthy and Jerome Rosner, see 7:747 (1 reference).

TEST REFERENCES
1. Goldstein, P. K., O'Brien, J. D., & Katz, G. M. (1981). A learning disability screening program in a public school: Pediatrics, screening, learning disability. *The American Journal of Occupational Therapy, 35,* 451-455.

[939]
Examination for the Certificate of Proficiency in English.
Purpose: Represents "the ability to speak fluently in English, to understand conversational usage, to recognize correct grammatical forms, to read various types of prose with ease, and to write fluently, clearly, and with a minimum of error."
Population: Nonnative speakers of English.
Publication Dates: 1953–89.
Acronym: ECPE.
Scores, 4: Written Composition, Listening Comprehension, Multiple-Choice Cloze Reading Test, 100-Item Objective Test of Grammar-Vocabulary-Reading Comprehension.
Administration: Group.
Restricted Distribution: Distribution restricted to ECPE examiners.
Price Data, 1983: Examination fee includes scoring service, $20 per candidate.
Time: 130(140) minutes.
Comments: "For students of English outside of the United States"; administration once a year at 75 sites in 40 countries; candidates who do not pass free preliminary screening test and oral interview are discouraged from paying the $20 examination fee for this main battery of 4 tests.
Authors: The English Language Institute of the University of Michigan, Testing and Certification Division.
Publisher: The English Language Institute of the University of Michigan, Testing and Certification Division.

[940]
Examining for Aphasia, Third Edition.
Purpose: "For evaluating possible aphasic language impairments and other acquired impairments that are often closely related to language functions."
Population: Adolescents and adults.
Publication Dates: 1946–94.

Acronym: EFA.

Scores, 41: Agnosias (Common Objects, Pictures, Colors, Geometric Forms, Numerals, Letters, Printed Words, Almost Alike Pictures, Printed Sentences, Nonverbal Noises, Object Identification, Total); Aphasias (Word Identification, Comprehension of Sentences, Comprehension of Multiple Choice, Oral Paragraphs, Silent Reading Sentences, Silent Reading Paragraphs, Total); Apraxias (Body Parts, Simple Skills, Pretend Action, Numerals, Words, Sentences, Total), Aphasios (Automatic Speech, Writing Numerals, Writing Letters, Spelling, Writing from Dictation, Naming Body Parts, Word Finding, Arithmetic Computations, Arithmetic Problems, Total); Composites (Receptive, Expressive, Subaphasic, Aphasia, Total).

Administration: Individual.

Price Data, 1994: $114 per complete kit including 25 examiner record books, 25 Profile/Response forms, picture book, examiner's manual ('94, 35 pages), and object kit; $34 per 25 examiner record booklets; $18 per 25 Profile/Response forms; $29 per picture book; $27 per examiner's manual; $11 per object kit.

Time: (30–120) minutes.

Comments: Shortened version of test may be administered for screening purposes.

Author: Jon Eisenson.

Publisher: PRO-ED, Inc.

Cross References: See T2:2071 (3 references) and P:76 (2 references); for excerpted reviews by Louis M. DiCarlo and Laurance F. Shaffer, see 5:52 (3 references); for a review by D. Russell Davis and excerpted reviews by Nolan D. C. Lewis and one other, see 4:42; for a review by C. R. Strother and an excerpted review, see 3:39.

TEST REFERENCES

1. Skenes, L. L., & McCauley, R. J. (1985). Psychometric review of nine aphasia tests. *Journal of Communication Disorders, 18,* 461-474.
2. Nicholas, L. E., MacLennan, D. L., & Brookshire, R. H. (1986). Validity of multiple-sentence reading comprehension tests for aphasic adults. *Journal of Speech and Hearing Disorders, 51,* 82-87.

[941]

[Executive, Industrial, and Sales Personnel Forms].

Purpose: To improve selection of executive, industrial, office, and sales employees through a structured assessment system.

Population: Applicants for executive, industrial, office, and sales positions.

Administration: Individual.

Price Data: Not available.

Author: Robert N. McMurry.

Publisher: Dartnell [No reply from publisher; status unknown].

a) [EXECUTIVE PERSONNEL FORMS].
1) *Application for Executive Position.*
Publication Dates: 1949–64.
2) *Patterned Interview Form—Executive Position.*
Publication Dates: 1949–65.

3) *Patterned Interview Form.*
Population: Applicants for positions of supervisor, foreman, engineer.
Publication Dates: 1955–68.
4) *Telephone Check on Executive Applicant.*
Publication Dates: 1950–64.
5) *Selection and Evaluation Summary.*
Publication Dates: 1950–64.
6) *Position Analysis.*
Publication Dates: 1956–58.
7) *Physical Record.*
Publication Date: 1958.

b) [INDUSTRIAL PERSONNEL FORMS].
1) *Application for Position.*
Publication Dates: 1950–64.
2) *Application for Employment.*
Publication Dates: 1950–59.
3) *Application for Office Position.*
Publication Dates: 1953–64.
4) *Patterned Interview (Short Form).*
Publication Dates: 1949–64.
5) *Patterned Interview Form.*
Population: Applicants for positions of supervisor, foreman, engineer.
Publication Dates: 1955–68.
6) *Telephone Check [With Previous Employers].*
Publication Dates: 1949–59.
7) *Telephone Check With Schools.*
Publication Dates: 1949–57.
8) *Selection and Evaluation Summary.*
Publication Dates: 1950–64.
9) *Position Analysis.*
Publication Dates: 1956–58.
10) *Physical Record.*
Publication Date: 1958.

c) [SALES PERSONNEL FORMS].
1) *Application for Sales Position.*
Publication Dates: 1950–67.
2) *Patterned Interview—Sales Position.*
Publication Dates: 1950–64.
3) *Telephone Check on Sales Applicant.*
Publication Dates: 1949–64.
4) *Sales Application Verification.*
Publication Dates: 1953–59.
5) *Home Interview Report Form.*
Publication Dates: 1954–59.
6) *Selection and Evaluation Summary.*
Publication Dates: 1950–64.
7) *Sales Position Analysis.*
Publication Dates: 1962–65.
8) *Physical Record.*
Publication Date: 1958.
9) *Salesman Performance Inventory.*
Publication Date: 1965.
Scores, 20: General Appraisal, Physical and Personal Factors, External Influences, Job Knowledge, Motivational Factors, Identification with the Company, Company Policies, Planning and Organization, Administrative Duties, Personal Relationships, Prospecting, Sales Approaches, Analyzing Prospect Needs, Product

Presentation, Handling Objections, Closing Skills, Follow-ups and Call-Backs, Customer Relations, Special Situations, Related Duties. 10) *Man Specification Sheet—Sales.*
Publication Date: 1968.
Cross References: For additional information and a review by John P. Foley, Jr., see 6:1119 (1 reference); for a review by Floyd L. Ruch, see 4:773.

[942]

Executive Profile Survey.
Purpose: Constructed to assess "self-attitudes, self-beliefs, and value patterns" needed for executive-level jobs.
Population: Prospective executives.
Publication Dates: 1947–83.
Scores: 11 dimensions: Ambitious, Assertive, Enthusiastic, Creative, Spontaneous, Self-Focused, Considerate, Open-Minded, Relaxed, Practical, Systematic.
Administration: Group or individual.
Price Data, 1994: $25 per 25 reusable test booklets; $18 per manual ('83, 82 pages); $36.75 per introductory kit.
Time: (60) minutes.
Comments: Self-administered; manual title is Perspectives on the Executive Personality.
Authors: Virgil R. Lang and Samuel E. Krug (manual).
Publisher: Institute for Personality and Ability Testing, Inc.
Cross References: For a review by William I. Sauser, Jr., see 9:401.

[943]

The Experiencing Scale.
Purpose: Assess the degree to which a patient communicates and employs a personal, phenomenological perspective in a therapy session.
Population: Counselors and counselor trainees.
Publication Date: 1969.
Acronym: EXP.
Scores, 2: Mode, Peak; based on a 7-point rating scale.
Administration: Individual.
Price Data, 1993: $26 per Volumes I and II; $42 per Volume III.
Time: Administration time not reported.
Comments: "Evaluating the quality of patient self-involvement in psychotherapy directly from tape recordings or typescripts of the therapy session"; tape or transcript of session required.
Authors: M. H. Klein, P. L. Mathieu, E. T. Gendlin, and D. J. Kiesler.
Publisher: Bureau of Audio-Visual Instruction, University of Wisconsin-Extension.

TEST REFERENCES

1. Rennie, D. L., Brewster, L. J., & Toukmanian, S. G. (1985). The counsellor trainee as client: Client process as a predictor of counselling skill acquisition. *Canadian Journal of Behavioural Science, 17,* 16-28.

[944]

Explore the World of Work.
Purpose: Designed to stimulate job awareness and exploration for jobs requiring up to 2 years of training.
Population: Elementary and special education.
Publication Dates: 1989–91.
Acronym: E-WOW.
Scores, 6: Business/Office/Sales, Industry/Mechanics/Transportation/Construction, Art/Communications/Design, Health/Education/Social Service, Forestry/Agriculture/Natural Resources, Scientific/Technical/Health.
Administration: Group.
Price Data, 1990: $.50 per folder/questionnaire; $89.95 per E-WOW computer software (Apple only).
Time: (40–70) minutes.
Comments: Children's Occupational Outlook Handbook suggested to complete follow-up activities on the questionnaire; self-scored.
Authors: Lori Constantino, Bob Kauk, and CFKR Career Materials, Inc. (manuals).
Publisher: CFKR Career Materials, Inc.

[945]

Expressional Growth Through Handwriting Evaluation Scale.
Purpose: Measure legibility in handwriting.
Population: Grades 1–7, 8–9, high school.
Publication Dates: 1958–68.
Scores: Total score only.
Administration: Individual or group.
Manual: No manual.
Price Data, 1988: $1.25 per 3 tests (specify grade); $7.50 per supervisor's special evaluation scales 1–8.
Time: Administration time not reported.
Comments: Formerly called Evaluation Scales for Guiding Growth in Handwriting; 1968 scales identical with 1958 scales except for grading instructions.
Authors: Frank N. Freeman (original edition) and Zaner-Bloser Co. staff.
Publisher: Zaner-Bloser Co.
Cross References: For a review by Theodore L. Harris, see 6:713 (2 references).

[946]

Expressive One-Word Picture Vocabulary Test, Revised.
Purpose: To obtain an estimate of a child's verbal intelligence.
Population: Ages 2–12, 12–16.
Publication Dates: 1979–90.
Acronym: EOWPVT.
Scores: Total score only.
Levels, 2: [Lower Level], Upper-Extension.
Price Data, 1994: $10 per 25 remedial checklists.
Time: (10–15) minutes per level.
Comments: Spanish form available.
Author: Morrison F. Gardner.
Publisher: Academic Therapy Publications.

a) [LOWER LEVEL].
Population: Ages 2–12.
Publication Date: 1979–90.
Administration: Individual.
Price Data: $75 per test kit including test plates, 25 English record forms, and manual ('90, 88 pages); $20 per 25 English record forms; $10 per 25 Spanish record forms; $35 per test plates; $17 per manual; $17 per specimen set including manual and sample form.

b) UPPER-EXTENSION.
Population: Ages 12–16.
Publication Date: 1983.
Administration: Individual and group.
Price Data: $68 per test kit including test plates, 50 English record forms, and manual (39 pages); $20 per 50 English record forms; $10 per 25 Spanish record forms; $10 per 50 group administration forms; $30 per test plates; $15 per manual; $15 per specimen set including manual and sample form.

Cross References: For reviews by Jack A. Cummings and Gilbert M. Spivack of the Lower Level, see 9:403 (2 references).

TEST REFERENCES

1. Aram, D. M., Ekelman, B. L., Rose, D. F., & Whitaker, H. A. (1985). Verbal and cognitive sequelae following unilateral lesions acquired in early childhood. *Journal of Clinical and Experimental Neuropsychology, 7*, 55-78.
2. Teuber, J. F., & Furlong, M. J. (1985). The concurrent validity of the Expressive One-Word Picture Vocabulary Test for Mexican-American children. *Psychology in the Schools, 22*, 269-273.
3. Berninger, V. W. (1986). Normal variation in reading acquisition. *Perceptual and Motor Skills, 62*, 691-716.
4. Goldstein, D. J., Smith, K. B., & Waldrep, E. E. (1986). Factor analytic study of the Kaufman Assessment Battery for Children. *Journal of Clinical Psychology, 42*, 890-894.
5. Berninger, V. W., Proctor, A., Bruyn, I. D., & Smith, R. (1988). Relationship between levels of oral and written language in beginning readers. *Journal of School Psychology, 26*, 341-357.
6. Fisher, W., Burd, L., & Kerbeshian, J. (1988). Markers for improvement in children with pervasive developmental disorders. *Journal of Mental Deficiency Research, 32*, 357-369.
7. Caulfield, M. B., Fischel, J. E., DeBaryshe, B. D., & Whitehurst, G. J. (1989). Behavioral correlates of developmental expressive language disorder. *Journal of Abnormal Child Psychology, 17*, 187-201.
8. Sussman, J. E., & Carney, A. E. (1989). Effects of transition length on the perception of stop consonants by children and adults. *Journal of Speech and Hearing Research, 32*, 151-160.
9. Vance, B., West, R., & Kutsick, K. (1989). Prediction of Wechsler Preschool and Primary Scale of Intelligence IQ scores for preschool children using the Peabody Picture Vocabulary Test—R and the Expressive One Word Picture Vocabulary Test. *Journal of Clinical Psychology, 45*, 642-644.
10. Campbell, T. F., & Dollaghan, C. A. (1990). Expressive language recovery in severely brain-injured children and adolescents. *Journal of Speech and Hearing Disorders, 55*, 567-581.
11. Johnston, J. R., & Bowman, S. (1990). Gardner Picture Vocabulary Tests: Relationship between performance in expression and reception. *International Journal of Clinical Neuropsychology, 12*, 103-106.
12. Kleppe, S. A., Katayama, K. M., Shipley, K. G., & Foushee, D. R. (1990). The speech and language characteristics of children with Prader-Willi syndrome. *Journal of Speech and Hearing Disorders, 55*, 300-309.
13. Nakamura, M., Plante, E., & Swisher, L. (1990). Predictors of novel inflection learning by preschool-aged boys. *Journal of Speech and Hearing Research, 33*, 747-754.
14. Dale, P. S. (1991). The validity of a parent report measure of vocabulary and syntax at 24 months. *Journal of Speech and Hearing Research, 34*, 565-571.
15. Ezell, H. K., & Goldstein, H. (1991). Observational learning of comprehension monitoring skills in children who exhibit mental retardation. *Journal of Speech and Hearing Research, 34*, 141-154.
16. Hunt, P., Alwell, M., & Goetz, L. (1991). Establishing conversational exchanges with family and friends: Moving from training to meaningful communication. *The Journal of Special Education, 25*(3), 305-319.
17. Menyunk, P., Chesnick, M., Liebergott, J. W., Korngold, B., D'Agostino, R., & Belanger, A. (1991). Predicting reading problems in at-risk children. *Journal of Speech and Hearing Research, 34*, 893-903.
18. Roseberry, C. A., & Cornell, P. J. (1991). The use of an invented language rule in the differentiation of normal and language-impaired Spanish-speaking children. *Journal of Speech and Hearing Research, 34*, 596-603.
19. Sussman, J. E. (1991). Stimulus ratio effects on speech discrimination by children and adults. *Journal of Speech and Hearing Research, 34*, 671-678.
20. Whitehurst, G. J., Smith, M., Fischel, J. E., Arnold, D. S., & Lonigan, C. J. (1991). The continuity of babble and speech in children with specific expressive language delay. *Journal of Speech and Hearing Research, 34*, 1121-1129.
21. Fein, D., Lucci, D., Braverman, M., & Waterhouse, L. (1992). Comprehension of affect in context in children with pervasive developmental disorders. *Journal of Child Psychology and Psychiatry, 33*, 1157-1167.
22. Peña, E., Quinn, R., & Iglesias, A. (1992). The application of dynamic methods to language assessment: A nonbiased procedure. *The Journal of Special Education, 26*, 269-280.
23. Valdez-Menchaca, M. C., & Whitehurst, G. J. (1992). Accelerating language development through picture book reading: A systematic extension to Mexican day care. *Developmental Psychology, 28*, 1106-1114.

[947]

The Extended Merrill-Palmer Scale.

Purpose: Assesses the content, semantic or figural, and process, production or evaluation, of thinking in young children.
Population: Ages 3–5.
Publication Date: 1978.
Scores: 4 Dimensions: Semantic Production, Figural Production, Semantic Evaluation, Figural Evaluation.
Administration: Individual.
Price Data, 1994: $500 per complete kit; $25 per 50 scoring forms (ages 36–47 mo., 48–59 mo., or 60–71 mo.); $45 per manual (142 pages); $75 per 50 task record forms.
Time: (45) minutes.
Comments: The Extended Merrill-Palmer Scale may be used either independently of, or in conjunction with the original Merrill-Palmer Scale (1614).
Authors: Rachael Stutsman Ball, Philip Merrifield, and Leland H. Stott.
Publisher: Stoelting Co.

[948]

Eyberg Child Behavior Inventory.

Purpose: "To provide a comprehensive, narrow-band measure of conduct problem behaviors."
Population: Ages 2–16.
Publication Dates: 1978–80.
Acronym: ECBI.
Scores: Ratings on 2 scales: Problem, Intensity.
Administration: Individual.
Price Data, 1994: No charge for one copy; may be photocopied for research or clinical use.
Time: (5–10) minutes.
Comments: Ratings by parents.
Author: Sheila M. Eyberg.
Publisher: Sheila M. Eyberg, Ph.D.
Cross References: For a review by Michael L. Reed, see 9:404 (6 references); see also T3:858 (2 references).

TEST REFERENCES

1. Kniskern, J. R., Robinson, E. A., & Mitchell, S. K. (1983). Mother-child interaction in home and laboratory settings. *Child Study Journal, 13,* 23-39.

2. Dembo, M. H., Sweitzer, M., & Lauritzen, P. (1984). An evaluation of group parent education: Behavioral, PET, and Adlerian programs. *Review of Educational Research, 55,* 155-200.

3. Webster-Stratton, C. (1984). Randomized trial of two parent-training programs for families with conduct disordered children. *Journal of Consulting and Clinical Psychology, 52,* 666-678.

4. Koverola, C., Manion, I., & Wolfe, D. (1985). A microanalysis of factors associated with child-abusive families: Identifying individual treatment priorities. *Behaviour Research and Therapy, 23,* 499-506.

5. Webster-Stratton, C. (1985). Comparisons of behavior transactions between conduct-disordered children and their mothers in the clinic and at home. *Journal of Abnormal Child Psychology, 13,* 169-183.

6. Webster-Stratton, C. (1985). Mother perceptions and mother-child interactions: Comparison of a clinic-referred and a nonclinic group. *Journal of Clinical Child Psychology, 14,* 334-339.

7. Webster-Stratton, C. (1985). The effects of father involvement in parent training for conduct problem children. *The Journal of Child Psychology and Psychiatry and Allied Disciplines, 26,* 801-810.

8. Dumas, J. E. (1986). Parental perception and treatment outcome in families of aggressive children: A causal model. *Behavior Therapy, 17,* 420-432.

9. Dumas, J. E., & Albin, J. B. (1986). Parent training outcome: Does active parental involvement matter? *Behaviour Research and Therapy, 24,* 227-230.

10. Frentz, C., & Kelley, M. L. (1986). Parents' acceptance of reductive treatment methods: The influence of problem severity and perception of child behavior. *Behavior Therapy, 17,* 75-81.

11. Bathurst, K., & Gottfried, A. W. (1987). Untestable subjects in child development research: Developmental implications. *Child Development, 58,* 1135-1144.

12. MacQuiddy, S. L., Maise, S. J., & Hamilton, S. B. (1987). Empathy and affective perspective-taking skills in parent- identified conduct-disordered boys. *Journal of Clinical Child Psychology, 16,* 260-268.

13. Mouton, P. Y., & Tuma, J. M. (1988). Stress, locus of control, and role satisfaction in clinic and control mothers. *Journal of Clinical Child Psychology, 17,* 217-224.

14. Webster-Stratton, C. (1988). Mothers' and fathers' perceptions of child deviance: Roles of parent and child behaviors and parent adjustment. *Journal of Consulting and Clinical Psychology, 56,* 909-915.

15. Webster-Stratton, C., Kolpacoff, M., & Hollinsworth, T. (1988). Self-administered videotape therapy for families with conduct-problem children: Comparison with two cost-effective treatments and a control group. *Journal of Consulting and Clinical Psychology, 56,* 558-566.

16. Caulfield, M. B., Fischel, J. E., DeBarsyhe, B. D., & Whitehurst, G. J. (1989). Behavioral correlates of developmental expressive language disorder. *Journal of Abnormal Child Psychology, 17,* 187-201.

17. Boggs, S. R., Eyberg, S., & Reynolds, L. A. (1990). Construct validity of the Eyberg Child Behavior Inventory. *Journal of Clinical Child Psychology, 19,* 75-78.

18. Burns, G. L., & Patterson, D. R. (1990). Conduct problem behaviors in a stratified random sample of children and adolescents: New standardization data on the Eyberg Child Behavior Inventory. *Psychological Assessment, 2,* 391-397.

19. Quittner, A. L., Glueckauf, R. L., & Jackson, D. N. (1990). Chronic parenting stress: Moderating versus mediating effects of social support. *Journal of Personality and Social Psychology, 59,* 1266-1278.

20. Burns, G. L., & Patterson, D. R. (1991). Factor structure of the Eyberg Child Behavior Inventory: Unidimensional or multidimensional measure of disruptive behavior? *Journal of Clinical Child Psychology, 20,* 439-444.

21. McNeil, C. B., Eyberg, S., Eisenstadt, T. H., Newcomb, K., & Funderburk, B. (1991). Parent-child interaction therapy with behavior problem children: Generalization of treatment effects to the school setting. *Journal of Clinical Child Psychology, 20,* 140-151.

22. Simonian, S. J., Tarnowski, K. J., Stancin, T., Friman, P. C., & Atkins, M. S. (1991). Disadvantaged children and families in pediatric primary care settings: II. Screening for behavior disturbance. *Journal of Clinical Child Psychology, 20,* 360-371.

23. Spitzer, A., Webster-Stratton, C., & Hollinsworth, T. (1991). Coping with conduct-problem children: Parents gaining knowledge and control. *Journal of Clinical Child Psychology, 20,* 413-427.

24. Larsen, R. J. (1992). Neuroticism and selective encoding and recall of symptoms: Evidence from a combined concurrent-retrospective study. *Journal of Personality and Social Psychology, 62,* 480-488.

25. Spaccarelli, S., Cotler, S., & Penman, D. (1992). Problem-solving skills training as a supplement to behavioral parent training. *Cognitive Therapy and Research, 16,* 1-18.

26. Webster-Stratton, C. (1992). Individually administered videotape parent training: "Who benefits?" *Cognitive Therapy and Research, 16,* 31-53.

[949]

Eysenck Personality Inventory.

Purpose: Measures two independent dimensions of personality: Extraversion-Introversion and Neuroticism-Stability.

Population: Adults.

Publication Dates: 1963–69.

Acronym: EPI.

Scores, 3: Extraversion, Neuroticism, Lie.

Administration: Group.

Time: (10–15) minutes.

Comments: Revision of Maudsley Personality Inventory; for revised edition of EPI, see Eysenck Personality Questionnaire—Revised (950); no reliability data for Lie scores; authors recommend use of both forms to obtain adequate reliability for individual measurements; U.S. and British Editions are identical except for three words and directions.

Authors: H. J. Eysenck and Sybil B. G. Eysenck.

a) UNITED STATES EDITION.

Population: Grades 9–16 and adults.

Publication Dates: 1963–69.

Forms, 2: A, B.

Price Data, 1986: $7 per 25 inventories (specify Form A, Form B, or Industrial); $6.60 per hand-scoring key; $2.75 per manual ('68, 27 pages); $5.75 per specimen set; $1.10 per test for scoring service.

Foreign Language Edition: Spanish edition ('72) available.

Comments: A printing with the title Eysenck Personality Inventory is available for industrial use.

Publisher: EdITS/Educational and Industrial Testing Service.

b) BRITISH EDITION.

Population: Adults.

Publication Dates: 1963–64.

Forms, 2: A, B.

Price Data, 1994: £6.99 per 20 inventories (Form A or Form B); £5.50 per scoring key; £5.99 per manual ('64, 24 pages); £6.50 per specimen set.

Publisher: Hodder & Stoughton Educational [England].

Cross References: See 9:405 (91 references); see also T3:859 (245 references); for a review by Auke Tellegen, see 8:553 (405 references); see also T2:1174 (140 references); for reviews by Richard I. Lanyon and excerpted reviews by A. W. Heim and James Linder, see 7:776 (121 references); see also P:77 (52 references); for a review by James C. Lingoes, see 6:93 (1 reference).

TEST REFERENCES

1. Gilbert, D. G. (1980). Introversion and self-reported reason for and times of urge for smoking. *Addictive Behaviors, 5,* 97-99.

2. Gilbert, D. G., & Hagen, R. L. (1980). The effects of nicotine and extraversion of self-report, skin conductance, electromyographic, and heart responses to emotional stimuli. *Addictive Behaviors, 5,* 247-257.

3. Kilpatrick, D. G., McAlhany, D. A., McCurdy, R. L., Shaw,

D. L., & Roitzsch, J. C. (1982). Aging, alcoholism, anxiety, and sensation seeking: An exploratory investigation. *Addictive Behaviors, 7,* 97-100.

4. Amies, P. L., Gelder, M. G., & Shaw, P. M. (1983). Social phobia: A comparative clinical study. *British Journal of Psychiatry, 142,* 174-179.

5. Lester, D., Hvezda, J., Sullivan, S., & Plourde, R. (1983). Maslow's hierarchy of needs and psychological health. *Journal of General Psychology, 109,* 83-85.

6. Standage, K. F. (1983). Observations on the handedness preferences of patients with personality disorders. *British Journal of Psychiatry, 142,* 575-578.

7. Webb, N. M., & Cullian, L. K. (1983). Group interaction and achievement in small groups: Stability over time. *American Educational Research Journal, 20,* 411-423.

8. Winter, D. A. (1983). Logical inconsistency in construct relationships: Conflict or complexity? *British Journal of Medical Psychology, 56,* 79-87.

9. Anderson, D. J., Noyes, R., Jr., & Crowe, R. R. (1984). A comparison of panic disorder and generalized anxiety disorder. *American Journal of Psychiatry, 141,* 572-575.

10. Bartram, D., & Bayliss, R. (1984). Automated testing: Past, present and future. *Journal of Occupational Psychology, 57,* 221-237.

11. Bouras, N., Bartlett, J. R., Neil-Dwyer, G., & Bridges, P. K. (1984). Psychological aspects of patients having multiple operations for low back pain. *British Journal of Medical Psychology, 57,* 147-151.

12. Campbell, J. B., & Reynolds, J. H. (1984). A comparison of the Guilford and Eysenck factors of personality. *Journal of Research in Personality, 18,* 305-320.

13. DeLeo, D., Vallerini, A., & Magni, G. (1984). Eysenck Personality Inventory and choice of psychiatry as a career. *Psychological Reports, 54,* 718.

14. Delmonte, M. M. (1984). Factors influencing the regularity of meditation practice in a clinical population. *British Journal of Medical Psychology, 57,* 275-278.

15. Diener, E., & Emmons, R. A. (1984). The independence of positive and negative affects. *Journal of Personality and Social Psychology, 47,* 1105-1117.

16. Diener, E., Larsen, R. J., & Emmons, R. A. (1984). Person x situation interactions: Choice of situations and congruence response models. *Journal of Personality and Social Psychology, 47,* 580-592.

17. Dor-Shav, N. K., & Horowitz, Z. (1984). Intelligence and personality variables of parents of autistic children. *The Journal of Genetic Psychology, 144,* 39-50.

18. Emmons, R. A. (1984). Factor analysis and construct validity of the Narcissistic Personality Inventory. *Journal of Personality Assessment, 48,* 291-300.

19. Evans, P. D., Phillips, K. C., & Fearn, J. M. (1984). On choosing to make aversive events predictable or unpredictable: Some behavioural and psychophysiological findings. *British Journal of Psychology, 75,* 377-391.

20. Fairburn, C. G., & Cooper, P. J. (1984). The clinical features of bulimia nervosa. *British Journal of Psychiatry, 144,* 238-246.

21. Farmer, E. W., Hunter, J., & Belyavin, A. J. (1984). Performance under time constraint: The role of personality. *Perceptual and Motor Skills, 59,* 875-884.

22. Gupta, U. (1984). Phenobarbitone and the relationship between extraversion and reinforcement in verbal operant conditioning. *British Journal of Psychology, 75,* 499-506.

23. Hanson, C. L., Henggeler, S. W., Haefele, W. F., & Rodick, J. D. (1984). Demographic, individual, and family relationship correlates of serious and repeated crime among adolescents and their siblings. *Journal of Consulting and Clinical Psychology, 52,* 528-538.

24. Hersen, M., Bellack, A. S., Himmelhoch, J. M., & Thase, M. E. (1984). Effects of social skill training, amitriptyline, and psychotherapy in unipolar depressed women. *Behavior Therapy, 15,* 21-40.

25. Mathew, R. J., Weinman, M. L., & Barr, D. L. (1984). Personality and regional cerebral blood flow. *British Journal of Psychiatry, 144,* 529-532.

26. McGee, R., Silva, P. A., & Williams, S. (1984). Perinatal, neurological, environmental and developmental characteristics of seven-year-old children with stable behaviour problems. *The Journal of Child Psychology and Psychiatry and Allied Disciplines, 25,* 573-586.

27. Montgomery, W. A., & Jones, G. E. (1984). Laterality, emotionality, and heartbeat perception. *Psychophysiology, 21,* 459-465.

28. Peterson, C. A. (1984). "Hedonism" is no fun. Notes on Burgess's "Hedonism" construct. *British Journal of Criminology, 24,* 296-300.

29. Ruback, R. B., Dabbs, J. M., Jr., & Hopper, C. H. (1984). The process of brainstorming: An analysis with individual and group vocal parameters. *Journal of Personality and Social Psychology, 47,* 558-567.

30. Schramski, T. G., Beutler, L. E., Lauver, P. J., Arizmendi,

T. A., & Shanfield, S. B. (1984). Factors that contribute to posttherapy persistence of therapeutic change. *Journal of Clinical Psychology, 40,* 78-85.

31. Shadish, W. R. (1984). Intimate behavior and the assessment of benefits in clinical groups. *Small Group Behavior, 15,* 204-221.

32. Skinner, N. F., & Peters, P. L. (1984). National personality characteristics: Comparison of Canadian, American and British samples. *Psychological Reports, 54,* 121-122.

33. Smith, T. W., Follick, M. J., & Korr, K. S. (1984). Anger, neuroticism, Type A behaviour and the experience of angina. *British Journal of Medical Psychology, 57,* 249-252.

34. Spotts, J. V., & Shontz, F. C. (1984). Correlates of sensation seeking by heavy, chronic drug users. *Perceptual and Motor Skills, 58,* 427-435.

35. Templer, D. I., King, F. L., Brooner, R. F., & Corgiat, M. (1984). Assessment of body elimination attitude. *Journal of Clinical Psychology, 40,* 754-759.

36. Tucker, L. A. (1984). Physical attractiveness, somatotype, and the male personality: A dynamic interactional perspective. *Journal of Clinical Psychology, 40,* 1226-1234.

37. Willmott, M., & Brierley, H. (1984). Cognitive characteristics and homosexuality. *Archives of Sexual Behavior, 13,* 311-319.

38. Ahmed, S. M. S., Valliant, P. M., & Swindle, D. (1985). Psychometric properties of Coopersmith Self-Esteem Inventory. *Perceptual and Motor Skills, 61,* 1235-1241.

39. Andrykowski, M. A., Redd, W. H., & Hatfield, A. K. (1985). Development of anticipatory nausea: A prospective analysis. *Journal of Consulting and Clinical Psychology, 53,* 447-454.

40. Arnetz, B. B. (1985). Gerontic occupational therapy—Psychological and social predictors of participation and therapeutic benefits. *The American Journal of Occupational Therapy, 39,* 460-465.

41. Beutler, L. E., Storm, A., Kirkish, P., Scogin, F., & Gaines, J. A. (1985). Parameters in the prediction of police officer performance. *Professional Psychology: Research and Practice, 16,* 324-335.

42. Boyce, P., & Parker, G. (1985). Neuroticism as a predictor of outcome in depression. *The Journal of Nervous and Mental Disease, 173,* 685-688.

43. Branthwaite, A., & Garcia, S. (1985). Depression in the young unemployed and those on Youth Opportunities Schemes. *British Journal of Medical Psychology, 58,* 67-74.

44. Clark, D. M., & Teasdale, J. D. (1985). Constraints on the effects of mood on memory. *Journal of Personality and Social Psychology, 48,* 1595-1608.

45. Colley, A., Roberts, N., & Chipps, A. (1985). Sex role identity, personality and participation in team and individual sports by males and females. *International Journal of Sport Psychology, 16,* 103-112.

46. Daino, A. (1985). Personality traits of adolescent tennis players. *International Journal of Sport Psychology, 16,* 120-125.

47. Daruna, J. H., Karrer, R., & Rosen, A. J. (1985). Introversion, attention, and the late positive component of event-related potentials. *Biological Psychology, 20,* 249-259.

48. Davidson, J., Miller, R., & Strickland, R. (1985). Neuroticism and personality disorder in depression. *Journal of Affective Disorders, 8,* 177-182.

49. Duckitt, A., Brown, D., Edwards, G., Oppenheimer, E., Sheehan, M., & Taylor, C. (1985). Alcoholism and the nature of outcome. *British Journal of Addiction, 80,* 153-162.

50. Eastwood, R. M., Whitton, J. L., Kramer, P. M., & Peter, A. M. (1985). Infradian rhythms. *Archives of General Psychiatry, 42,* 295-299.

51. Emmons, R. A., & Diener, E. (1985). Personality correlates of subjective well-being. *Personality and Social Psychology Bulletin, 11,* 89-97.

52. Gold, D., & Andres, D. (1985). Personality test reliability: Correlates for older subjects. *Journal of Personality Assessment, 49,* 530-532.

53. Goodchild, M. E., & Duncan-Jones, P. (1985). Chronicity and the General Health Questionnaire. *British Journal of Psychiatry, 146,* 55-61.

54. Graziano, W. G., Feldesman, A. B., & Rahe, D. F. (1985). Extraversion, social cognition, and the salience of aversiveness in social encounters. *Journal of Personality and Social Psychology, 48,* 971-980.

55. Henggeler, S. W., Hanson, C. L., Borduin, C. M., Watson, S. M., & Brunk, M. A. (1985). Mother-son relationships of juvenile felons. *Journal of Consulting and Clinical Psychology, 53,* 942-943.

56. Huber, V. L. (1985). Effects of task difficulty, goal setting, and strategy on performance of a heuristic task. *Journal of Applied Psychology, 70,* 492-504.

57. Hughes, M., & McLellan, D. L. (1985). Increased co-activation of the upper limb muscles in writer's cramp. *Journal of Neurology, Neurosurgery, and Psychiatry, 48,* 782-787.

58. Last, C. G., Thase, M. E., Hersen, M., Bellack, A. S., & Himmelhoch, J. M. (1985). Patterns of attrition for psychosocial and phar-

macologic treatments of depression. *Journal of Clinical Psychiatry, 46,* 361-365.

59. Lorr, M., & Wunderlich, R. A. (1985). A measure of impulsiveness and its relations to extraversion. *Educational and Psychological Measurement, 45,* 251-257.

60. Mavissakalian, M. (1985). Male and female agoraphobia: Are they different? *Behaviour Research and Therapy, 23,* 469-471.

61. Mintz, J., Boyd, G., Rose, J. E., Charuvastra, V. C., & Jarvik, M. E. (1985). Alcohol increases cigarette smoking: A laboratory demonstration. *Addictive Behaviors, 10,* 203-207.

62. Mwamwenda, T. S., Dionne, J., & Mwamwenda, B. B. (1985). Theoretical and empirical link between psychological differentiation and extraversion. *Psychological Reports, 56,* 147-154.

63. Paden-Levy, D. (1985). Relationship of extraversion, neuroticism, alienation, and divorce incidence with pet-ownership. *Psychological Reports, 57,* 868-870.

64. Parker, G., & Blignault, I. (1985). Psychosocial predictors of outcome in subjects with untreated depressive disorder. *Journal of Affective Disorders, 8,* 73-81.

65. Parker, G., Tennant, C., & Blignault, I. (1985). Predicting improvement in patients with non-endogenous depression. *British Journal of Psychiatry, 146,* 132-139.

66. Revell, A. D., Warburton, D. M., & Wesnes, K. (1985). Smoking as a coping strategy. *Addictive Behaviors, 10,* 209-224.

67. Sandin, B., & Chorot, P. (1985). Changes in skin, salivary, and urinary PH as indicators of anxiety level in humans. *Psychophysiology, 22,* 226-230.

68. Schmitz, P. G. (1985). Sociocultural and personality differences in the dimension of the open and closed mind. *High School Journal, 68,* 348-364.

69. Shadish, W. R., Jr. (1985). Transitory emotional states and encounter group training. *Small Group Behavior, 16,* 477-486.

70. Stanford, R. G., Angelini, R. F., & Raphael, A. J. (1985). Cognition and mood during ganzfeld: Effects of extraversion and noise versus silence. *Journal of Parapsychology, 49,* 165-191.

71. Tennant, C. C., & Langeluddecke, P. M. (1985). Psychological correlates of coronary heart disease. *Psychological Medicine, 15,* 581-588.

72. vonKnorring, L., & Oreland, L. (1985). Personality traits and platelet monoamine oxidase in tobacco smokers. *Psychological Medicine, 15,* 327-334.

73. Wilson-Barnett, J., & Trimble, M. R. (1985). An investigation of hysteria using the Illness Behaviour Questionnaire. *British Journal of Psychiatry, 146,* 601-608.

74. Zeldow, P. B., Clark, D., & Daugherty, S. R. (1985). Masculinity, femininity, Type A behavior, and psychosocial adjustment in medical students. *Journal of Personality and Social Psychology, 48,* 481-492.

75. Alagaratnam, T. T., & Kung, N. Y. T. (1986). Psychosocial effects of mastectomy: Is it due to mastectomy or to the diagnosis of malignancy? *British Journal of Psychiatry, 149,* 296-299.

76. Bancroft, J., Dickerson, M., Fairburn, C. G., Gray, J., Greenwood, J., Stevenson, N., & Warner, P. (1986). Sex therapy outcome research: A reappraisal of methodology: 1. A treatment study of male sexual dysfunction. *Psychological Medicine, 16,* 851-863.

77. Blaszczynski, A. P., Wilson, A. C., & McConaghy, N. (1986). Sensation seeking and pathological gambling. *British Journal of Addiction, 81,* 113-117.

78. Brown, R. J., & Donderi, D. C. (1986). Dream content and self-reported well-being among recurrent dreamers, past-recurrent dreamers, and noncurrent dreamers. *Journal of Personality and Social Psychology, 50,* 612-623.

79. Burns, L. E., Thorpe, G. L., & Cavallaro, L. A. (1986). Agoraphobia 8 years after behavioral treatment: A follow-up study with interview, self-report, and behavioral data. *Behavior Therapy, 17,* 580-591.

80. Cann, D. R., & Donderi, D. C. (1986). Jungian personality typology and the recall of everyday and archetypal dreams. *Journal of Personality and Social Psychology, 50,* 1021-1030.

81. Daoussis, L., & McKelvie, S. J. (1986). Musical preferences and effects of music on a reading comprehension test for extraverts and introverts. *Perceptual and Motor Skills, 62,* 283- 289.

82. Emmons, R. A., & Diener, E. (1986). Influence of impulsivity and sociability on subjective well-being. *Journal of Personality and Social Psychology, 50,* 1211-1215.

83. Flannery, R. B., Jr. (1986). Negative affectivity, daily hassles, and somatic illness: Preliminary inquiry concerning hassles measurement. *Educational and Psychological Measurement, 46,* 1001-1004.

84. Gardner, D. G. (1986). Activation theory and task design: An empirical test of several new predictions. *Journal of Applied Psychology, 71,* 411-418.

85. Goldsmith, R. E., & Matherly, T. A. (1986). The Kirton Adaptation Innovation Inventory, faking, and social desirability: A replication and extension. *Psychological Reports, 58,* 269-270.

86. Graff, R. W., Whitehead, G. I., III, & LeCompte, M. (1986). Group treatment with divorced women using cognitive-behavioral and supportive-insight methods. *Journal of Counseling Psychology, 33,* 276-281.

87. Henggeler, S. W., Rodick, J. D., Borduin, C. M., Hanson, C. L., Watson, S. M., & Urey, J. R. (1986). Multisystematic treatment of juvenile offenders: Effects on adolescent behavior and family interaction. *Developmental Psychology, 22,* 132-141.

88. Howarth, E. (1986). What does Eysenck's psychoticism scale really measure? *British Journal of Psychology, 77,* 223-227.

89. Levin, I., & Stokes, J. P. (1986). An examination of the relation of individual difference variables to loneliness. *Journal of Personality, 54,* 717-733.

90. Livesay, J. R. (1986). Clinical utility of Wechsler's deterioration index in screening for behavioral impairment. *Perceptual and Motor Skills, 63,* 619-626.

91. McClure, R. F., & Mears, F. G. (1986). Videogame playing and psychopathology. *Psychological Reports, 59,* 59-62.

92. Miller, I. W., Norman, W. H., & Dow, M. G. (1986). Psychosocial characteristics of 'double depression.' *American Journal of Psychiatry, 143,* 1042-1044.

93. Paulhus, D. L., & Martin, C. L. (1986). Predicting adult temperament from minor physical anomalies. *Journal of Personality and Social Psychology, 50,* 1235-1239.

94. Pitman, R. K., & Orr, S. P. (1986). Testing of the conditioning model of neurosis: Differential aversive conditioning of angry and neutral facial expressions in anxiety disorder patients. *Journal of Abnormal Psychology, 95,* 208-213.

95. Rabins, P. V., Brooks, B. R., O'Donnell, P., Pearlson, G. D., Moberg, P., Jubelt, B., Coyle, P., Dalos, N., & Folstein, M. F. (1986). Structural brain correlates of emotional disorder in multiple sclerosis. *Brain, 109,* 585-597.

96. Riggio, R. E., & Friedman, H. S. (1986). Impression formation: The role of expressive behavior. *Journal of Personality and Social Psychology, 50,* 421-427.

97. Shadish, W. R., Jr. (1986). The validity of a measure of intimate behavior. *Small Group Behavior, 17,* 113-120.

98. Suominen-Troyer, S., Davis, K. J., Ismail, A. H., & Salvendy, G. (1986). Impact of physical fitness on strategy development in decision-making tasks. *Perceptual and Motor Skills, 62,* 71-77.

99. Taylor, C., Brown, D., Duckitt, A., Edwards, G., Oppenheimer, E., & Sheehan, M. (1986). Alcoholism and the patterning of outcome: A multivariate analysis. *British Journal of Addiction, 81,* 815-823.

100. Werner, P. D., & Pervin, L. A. (1986). The content of personality inventory items. *Journal of Personality and Social Psychology, 51,* 622-628.

101. Andrykowski, M. A., & Redd, W. H. (1987). Longitudinal analysis of the development of anticipatory nausea. *Journal of Consulting and Clinical Psychology, 55,* 36-41.

102. Buigues, J., & Vallejo, J. (1987). Therapeutic response to phenelzine in patients with panic disorder and agoraphobia with panic attacks. *The Journal of Clinical Psychiatry, 48,* 55-59.

103. Cowles, M., & Davis, C. (1987). The subject matter of psychology: Volunteers. *British Journal of Social Psychology, 26,* 97-102.

104. deMan, A. F., Balkou, S., & Iglesias, R. I. (1987). A French-Canadian adaptation of the Scale for Suicide Ideation. *Canadian Journal of Behavioural Science, 19,* 50-55.

105. Fairburn, C. G., Kirk, J., O'Conner, M., Anastasiades, P., & Cooper, P. J. (1987). Prognostic factors in bulimia nervosa. *British Journal of Clinical Psychology, 26,* 223-224.

106. Fergusson, D. M., & Horwood, L. J. (1987). Vulnerability to life events exposure. *Psychological Medicine, 17,* 739-749.

107. Fichter, M. M., & Daser, C. (1987). Symptomatology, psychosexual development and gender identity in 42 anorexic males. *Psychological Medicine, 17,* 409-418.

108. Frazier, S. E. (1987). Introversion-extraversion measures in elite and nonelite distance runners. *Perceptual and Motor Skills, 64,* 867-872.

109. Gabrys, J. B., Schumph, D., & Utendale, K. A. (1987). Short-term memory for two meaningful stories and self-report on the adult Eysenck Personality Questionnaire. *Psychological Reports, 61,* 51-59.

110. Gath, D., Osborn, M., Bungay, G., Iles, S., Day, A., Bond, A., & Passingham, C. (1987). Psychiatric disorder and gynaecological symptoms in middle aged women: A community survey. *British Medical Journal, 294,* 213-218.

111. Grove, W. M., Andreasen, N. C., Young, M., Endicott, J., Keller, M. B., Hirschfeld, R. M. A., & Reich, T. (1987). Isolation and characterization of a nuclear depressive syndrome. *Psychological Medicine, 17,* 471-484.

112. Henggeler, S. W., Edwards, J., & Borduin, C. M. (1987). The family relations of female juvenile adelinquents. *Journal of Abnormal Child Psychology, 15,* 199-209.

113. Hirschowitz, R. (1987). Behavioral and personality correlates of

a need for power in a group of English-speaking South African women. *The Journal of Psychology, 121,* 575-590.

114. Lester, D. (1987). An exploratory study of the validity of administering the Hand Test in a group format. *Perceptual and Motor Skills, 65,* 430.

115. Mogg, K., Mathews, A., & Weinman, J. (1987). Memory bias in clinical anxiety. *Journal of Abnormal Psychology, 96,* 94-98.

116. Noller, P., Law, H., & Comrey, A. L. (1987). Cattell, Comrey, and Eysenck personality factors compared: More evidence for the five robust factors? *Journal of Personality and Social Psychology, 53,* 775-782.

117. Pennington, D. C. (1987). Confirmatory hypothesis testing in face-to-face interaction: An empirical refutation. *British Journal of Social Psychology, 26,* 225-235.

118. Pittman, R. K., Green, R. C., Jenike, M. A., & Mersulam, M. M. (1987). Clinical comparison of Tourette's disorder and obsessive-compulsive disorder. *American Journal of Psychiatry, 144,* 1166-1171.

119. Revelle, W. (1987). Personality and motivation: Sources of inefficiency in cognitive performance. *Journal of Research in Personality, 21,* 436-452.

120. Saper, Z., & Forest, J. (1987). Personality variables and interest in self-help books. *Psychological Reports, 60,* 563-566.

121. Sipps, G. J., & Alexander, R. A. (1987). The multifactorial nature of extraversion-introversion in the Myers-Briggs Type Indicator and Eysenck Personality Inventory. *Educational and Psychological Measurement, 47*(3), 543-552.

122. Steller, M., Haenert, P., & Eiselt, W. (1987). Extraversion and the detection of information. *Journal of Research in Personality, 21,* 334-342.

123. Steptoe, A., & Fidler, H. (1987). Stage fright in orchestral musicians: A study of cognitive and behavioural strategies in performance anxiety. *British Journal of Psychology, 78,* 241-249.

124. Zeldow, P. B., Daugherty, S. R., & Clark, D. C. (1987). Masculinity, femininity, and psychosocial adjustment in medical students: A 2-year follow-up. *Journal of Personality Assessment, 51,* 3-14.

125. Öhrström, E., Björkman, M., & Rylander, R. (1988). Noise annoyance with regard to neurophysiological sensitivity, subjective noise sensitivity and personality variables. *Psychological Medicine, 18,* 605-613.

126. Alder, E., & Bancroft, J. (1988). The relationship between breast feeding persistence, sexuality and mood in postpartum women. *Psychological Medicine, 18,* 389-396.

127. Beach, D. A. (1988). Health Care Providers Inventory: A method for evaluating nursing aides. *The Journal of Psychology, 122,* 89-94.

128. Bergeman, C. S., Plomin, R., McClearn, G. E., Pedersen, N. L., & Friberg, L. T. (1988). Genotype-environment interaction in personality development: Identical twins reared apart. *Psychology and Aging, 3,* 399-406.

129. Bergin, A. E., Stinchfield, R. D., Gaskin, T. A., Masters, K. S., & Sullivan, C. E. (1988). Religious life-styles and mental health: An exploratory study. *Journal of Counseling Psychology, 35,* 91-98.

130. Bond, M. J., & Feather, N. T. (1988). Some correlates of structure and purpose in the use of time. *Journal of Personality and Social Psychology, 55,* 321-329.

131. Briggs, S. R. (1988). Shyness: Introversion or neuroticism? *Journal of Research in Personality, 22,* 290-307.

132. Briggs, S. R., & Cheek, J. M. (1988). On the nature of self-monitoring: Problems with assessment, problems with validity. *Journal of Personality and Social Psychology, 54,* 663-678.

133. Calvert, S. H., Beutler, L. E., & Crago, M. (1988). Psychotherapy outcome as a function of therapist-patient matching on selected variables. *Journal of Social and Clinical Psychology, 6,* 104-117.

134. Carr, A. J., & Wilde, G. J. S. (1988). Effects of actual and potential stressor control on physiological and self-reported stress responses. *Journal of Social and Clinical Psychology, 6,* 371-387.

135. Cartwright, D., & DeBruin, J. (1988). Imagery measures of ego, id, superego, and identity: Validity studies. *Multivariate Behavioral Research, 23,* 505-515.

136. Comrey, A. L., Noller, P., & Law, H. (1988). Eysenck Personality Inventory item factor structure. *Multivariate Behavioral Research, 23,* 159-170.

137. Davidson, J., Glover, V., Clow, A., Kudler, H., Meador, K., & Sandler, M. (1988). Tribulin in post-traumatic stress disorder. *Psychological Medicine, 18,* 833-836.

138. Davis, C., & Cowles, M. (1988). A laboratory study of temperament and arousal: A test of Gale's hypothesis. *Journal of Research in Personality, 22*(1), 101-116.

139. Dodwell, D. (1988). Comparison of self-ratings with informant-ratings of pre-morbid personality on two personality rating scales. *Psychological Medicine, 18,* 495-501.

140. Huppert, F. A., Gore, M., & Elliott, B. J. (1988). The value of an improved scoring system (CGHQ) for the General Health Ques-

tionnaire in a representative community sample. *Psychological Medicine, 18,* 1001-1006.

141. Levenson, M. R., Aldwin, C. M., Bossé, R., & Spiro, A., III. (1988). Emotionality and mental health: Longitudinal findings from the normative aging study. *Journal of Abnormal Psychology, 97,* 94-96.

142. Lobel, T. E. (1988). Personality correlates of Type A coronary-prone behavior. *Journal of Personality Assessment, 52,* 434-440.

143. Meyers, L. S., & Wong, D. T. (1988). Validation of a new test of locus of control: The Internal Control Index. *Educational and Psychological Measurement, 48,* 753- 761.

144. Parker, G., & Barnett, B. (1988). Perceptions of parenting in childhood and social support in adulthood. *American Journal of Psychiatry, 145,* 479-482.

145. Pedersen, N. L., Plomin, R., McClearn, G. E., & Friberg, L. (1988). Neuroticism, extraversion, and related traits in adult twins reared apart and reared together. *Journal of Personality and Social Psychology, 55,* 950-957.

146. Robertson, M. M., Trimble, M. R., & Lees, A. J. (1988). The psychopathology of Gilles de la Tourette syndrome. *British Journal of Psychiatry, 152,* 383-390.

147. Rose, R. J., Koskenvuo, M., Kaprio, J., Sarna, S., & Langinvainio, H. (1988). Shared genes, shared experiences, and similarity of personality: Data from 14,288 adult Finnish co-twins. *Journal of Personality and Social Psychology, 54,* 161-171.

148. Semin, G. R., & Fiedler, K. (1988). The cognitive functions of linguistic categories in describing persons: Social cognition and language. *Journal of Personality and Social Psychology, 54,* 558-568.

149. Tremblay, R. E., LeBlanc, M., & Schwartzman, A. E. (1988). The predictive power of first-grade peer and teacher ratings of behavior: Sex differences in antisocial behavior and personality at adolescence. *Journal of Abnormal Child Psychology, 16,* 571-583.

150. Wolfe, R. N., & Kasmer, J. A. (1988). Type versus trait: Extraversion, impulsivity, sociability, and preferences for cooperative and competitive activities. *Journal of Personality and Social Psychology, 54,* 864-871.

151. Aldwin, C. M., Levenson, M. R., Spiro, A., III, & Bossé, R. (1989). Does emotionality predict stress? Findings from the normative aging study. *Journal of Personality and Social Psychology, 56,* 618-624.

152. Andrews, G., Pollock, C., & Stewart, G. (1989). The determination of defense style by questionnaire. *Archives of General Psychiatry, 46,* 455-460.

153. Damrad-Frye, R., & Laird, J. D. (1989). The experience of boredom: The role of the self-perception of attention. *Journal of Personality and Social Psychology, 57,* 315-320.

154. Davis, C., & Cowles, M. (1989). Automated psychological testing: Method of administration, need for approval, and measures of anxiety. *Educational and Psychological Measurement, 49,* 311-320.

155. Headey, B., & Wearing, A. (1989). Personality, life events, and subjective well-being: Toward a dynamic equilibrium model. *Journal of Personality and Social Psychology, 57,* 731-739.

156. Hoehn-Saric, R., McLeod, D. R., & Zimerli, W. D. (1989). Somatic manifestation in women with generalized anxiety disorder. *Archives of General Psychiatry, 46,* 1113-1119.

157. Hotard, S. R., McFatter, R. M., McWhirter, R. M., & Stegall, M. E. (1989). Interactive effects of extraversion, neuroticism, and social relationships on subjective well- being. *Journal of Personality and Social Psychology, 57,* 321-331.

158. Jorm, A. F., Duncan-Jones, P., & Scott, R. (1989). An analysis of the re-test artefact in longitudinal studies of psychiatric symptoms and personality. *Psychological Medicine, 19,* 487-493.

159. Kentle, R. L. (1989). Headache symptomology and neuroticism in a college sample. *Psychological Reports, 65,* 976-978.

160. MacKinnon, A. J., Henderson, A. S., Scott, R., & Duncan-Jones, P. (1989). The Parental Bonding Instrument (PBI): An epidemiological study in a general population sample. *Psychological Medicine, 19,* 1023-1034.

161. Matthews, G., Jones, D. M., & Chamberlain, A. G. (1989). Interactive effects of extraversion and arousal on attentional task performance: Multiple resources or encoding processes? *Journal of Personality and Social Psychology, 56,* 629-639.

162. Robertson, M. M., Trimble, M. R., & Lees, A. J. (1989). Self-injurious behaviour and the Gilles de la Tourette syndrome: A clinical study and review of the literature. *Psychological Medicine, 19,* 611-625.

163. Schweizer, E., Case, W. G., & Rickels, K. (1989). Benzodiazepine dependence and withdrawal in elderly patients. *American Journal of Psychiatry, 146,* 529-531.

164. Shields, S. A., Mallory, M. E., & Simon, A. (1989). The Body Awareness Questionnaire: Reliability and validity. *Journal of Personality Assessment, 53,* 802-815.

165. Suis, J., & Wan, C. K. (1989). The relation between Type A

behavior and chronic emotional distress: A meta-analysis. *Journal of Personality and Social Psychology, 57,* 503-512.

166. Tashakkori, A., Barefoot, J., & Mehryar, A. H. (1989). What does the Beck Depression Inventory measure in college students?: Evidence from a non-western culture. *Journal of Clinical Psychology, 45,* 595-602.

167. Wilhelm, K., & Parker, G. (1989). Is sex necessarily a risk factor to depression? *Psychological Medicine, 19,* 401-413.

168. Windle, M. (1989). Temperament and personality: An exploratory interinventory study of the DOTS-R, EASI-II, and EPI. *Journal of Personality Assessment, 53,* 487-501.

169. Zinbarg, R., & Revelle, W. (1989). Personality and conditioning: A test of four models. *Journal of Personality and Social Psychology, 57,* 301-314.

170. Ahmed, S. M. S. (1990). Psychometric properties of the boredom proneness scale. *Perceptual and Motor Skills, 71,* 963-966.

171. Bolger, N. (1990). Coping as a personality process: A prospective study. *Journal of Personality and Social Psychology, 59,* 525-537.

172. Boyce, P., Parker, G., Hickie, I., Wilhelm, K., Brodaty, H., & Mitchell, P. (1990). Personality differences between patients with remitted melancholic and nonmelancholic depression. *American Journal of Psychiatry, 147,* 1476-1483.

173. Craig, A. (1990). An investigation into the relationship between anxiety and stuttering. *Journal of Speech and Hearing Disorders, 55,* 290-294.

174. Dickman, S. J. (1990). Functional and dysfunctional impulsivity: Personality and cognitive correlates. *Journal of Personality and Social Psychology, 58,* 95-102.

175. Krause, N., Liang, J., & Keith, V. (1990). Personality, social support, and psychological distress in later life. *Psychology and Aging, 5,* 315-326.

176. Larsen, R. J., & Kasimatis, M. (1990). Individual differences in entrainment of mood to the weekly calendar. *Journal of Personality and Social Psychology, 58,* 164-171.

177. Malloy, P. F., & Levis, D. J. (1990). A human laboratory test of Eysenck's theory of incubation: A search for the revolution of the neurotic paradox. *Journal of Psychopathology and Behavioral Assessment, 12,* 309-327.

178. Matthews, G., Coyle, K., & Craig, A. (1990). Multiple factors of cognitive failure, and their relationships with stress vulnerability. *Journal of Psychopathology and Behavioral Assessment, 12,* 49-64.

179. Raviv, S., Geron, E., & Low, M. (1990). Factor analysis of the relationships between personality and motor characteristics of men and women. *Perceptual and Motor Skills, 71,* 487-497.

180. Sanitioso, R., Kunda, Z., & Fong, G. T. (1990). Motivated recruitment of autobiographical memories. *Journal of Personality and Social Psychology, 59,* 229-241.

181. Shaughnessy, M. F., Neely, R., Manx, A., & Nystal, M. (1990). Effects of birth order, sex, and astrological sign on personality. *Psychological Reports, 66,* 272-274.

182. Skaggs, L. P., Rocklin, T. R., Dansereau, D. F., Hall, R. H., O'Donnell, A. M., Lambiotte, J. G., & Young, M. D. (1990). Dyadic learning of technical material: Individual differences, social interaction, and recall. *Contemporary Educational Psychology, 15,* 47-63.

183. Stanton, W. R., Feehan, M., McGee, R., & Silva, P. A. (1990). The relative value of reading ability and IQ as predictors of teacher-reported behavior problems. *Journal of Learning Disabilities, 23,* 514-517.

184. Webster-Stratton, C. (1990). Long-term follow-up of families with young conduct problem children: From preschool to grade school. *Journal of Clinical Child Psychology, 19,* 144-149.

185. Bagenholm, A., & Gillberg, C. (1991). Psychosocial effects on siblings of children with autism and mental retardation: A population-based study. *Journal of Mental Deficiency Research, 35,* 291-307.

186. Beaulieu, R. P. (1991). Peak activation time, extraversion, and students' achievement. *Perceptual and Motor Skills, 73,* 1217-1218.

187. Bolger, N., & Eckenrode, J. (1991). Social relationships, personality, and anxiety during a major stressful event. *Journal of Personality and Social Psychology, 61,* 440-449.

188. Boyce, P., Parker, G., Barnett, B., Cooney, M., & Smith, F. (1991). Personality as a vulnerability factor to depression. *British Journal of Psychiatry, 159,* 106-114.

189. Dritschel, B. H., & Teasdale, J. D. (1991). Individual differences in affect-related cognitive operations elicited by experimental stimuli. *British Journal of Clinical Psychology, 30,* 151-160.

190. Duggan, C. F., Sham, P., Lee, A. S., & Murray, R. M. (1991). Does recurrent depression lead to a change in neuroticism? *Psychological Medicine, 21,* 985-990.

191. Elliott, B. J., & Huppert, F. A. (1991). In sickness and in health: Associations between physical and mental well-being, employment and parental status in a British nationwide sample of married women. *Psychological Medicine, 21,* 515-524.

192. Feehan, M., McGee, R., Stanton, W. R., & Silva, P. A. (1991). Strict and inconsistent discipline in childhood: Consequences for adolescent mental health. *British Journal of Clinical Psychology, 30,* 325-331.

193. Ganster, D. C., Sime, W. E., Schaubroeck, J., & Mayes, B. T. (1991). The nomological validity of the Type A personality among employed adults. *Journal of Applied Psychology, 76(1),* 143-168.

194. Green, D. E., & Walkey, F. H. (1991). A fourth-order analysis of the Eysenck Personality Inventory: Some predictable results from an unusual analysis. *Social Behavior and Personality, 19,* 157-164.

195. Hickie, I., Parker, G., Wilhelm, K., & Tennant, C. (1991). Perceived interpersonal risk factors of non-endogenous depression. *Psychological Medicine, 21,* 399-412.

196. King, R., Curtis, D., & Knoblich, G. (1991). Complexity preference in substance abusers and controls: Relationships to diagnosis and personality variables. *Perceptual and Motor Skills, 72,* 35-39.

197. Kotzé, H. F., & Möller, A. T. (1991). Subliminal stimulation, choice behavior and some personality correlates of subliminal sensitivity. *Perceptual and Motor Skills, 72,* 315-322.

198. O'Keane, V., & Dinan, T. G. (1991). Prolactin and cortisol responses to d-fenfluramine in major depression: Evidence for diminished responsivity of central serotonergic function. *American Journal of Psychiatry, 148,* 1009-1015.

199. Pearson, G. L., & Freeman, F. G. (1991). Effects of extraversion and mental arithmetic on heart-rate reactivity. *Perceptual and Motor Skills, 72,* 1239-1248.

200. Porrata, J. L. (1991). Comparison of special education and regular students in Puerto Rico on the Eysenck Personality Questionnaire. *Psychological Reports, 69,* 108-110.

201. Turner, S., Sloper, P., Knussen, C., & Cunningham, C. (1991). Factors relating to self-sufficiency in children with Down's syndrome. *Journal of Mental Deficiency Research, 35,* 13-24.

202. Webb, N. M. (1991). Task-related verbal interaction and mathematics learning in small groups. *Journal for Research in Mathematics Education, 22,* 366-389.

203. Williams, K. J., Suls, J., Alliger, G. M., Learner, S. M., & Wan, C. K. (1991). Multiple role juggling and daily mood states in working mothers: An experience sampling study. *Journal of Applied Psychology, 76(5),* 664-674.

204. Wilson, P. H., Henry, J., Bowen, M., & Haralambous, G. (1991). Tinnitus reaction questionnaire: Psychometric properties of a measure of distress associated with tinnitus. *Journal of Speech and Hearing Research, 34,* 197-201.

205. Arbuckle, T. Y., Gold, D. P., Andres, D., Schwartzman, A., & Chaikelson, J. (1992). The role of psychosocial context, age, and intelligence in memory performance of older men. *Psychology and Aging, 7,* 25-36.

206. Berger, B. G., & Owen, D. R. (1992). Mood alteration with yoga and swimming: Aerobic exercise may not be necessary. *Perceptual and Motor Skills, 75,* 1331-1343.

207. Berquier, A., & Ashton, R. (1992). Characteristics of the frequent nightmare sufferer. *Journal of Abnormal Psychology, 101,* 246-250.

208. Engle-Friedman, M., Bootzin, R. R., Hazlewood, L., & Tsao, C. (1992). An evaluation of behavioral treatments for insomnia in the older adult. *Journal of Clinical Psychology, 48,* 77-90.

209. Feingold, A. (1992). Good-looking people are not what we think. *Psychological Bulletin, 111,* 304-341.

210. Finch, J. F., & Zautra, A. J. (1992). Testing latent longitudinal models of social ties and depression among the elderly: A comparison of distribution-free and maximum likelihood estimates with nonnormal data. *Psychology and Aging, 7,* 107-118.

211. Greenberg, J., Simon, L., Pyszczynski, T., Solomon, S., & Chatel, D. (1992). Terror management and tolerance: Does mortality salience always intensify negative reactions to others who threaten one's worldview? *Journal of Personality and Social Psychology, 63,* 212-220.

212. Hale, W. D., Fiedler, L. R., & Cochran, C. D. (1992). The Revised Generalized Expectancy for Success Scale: A validity and reliability study. *Journal of Clinical Psychology, 48,* 517-521.

213. Hunt, H. T., Gervais, A., Shearing-Johns, S., & Travis, F. (1992). Transpersonal experiences in childhood: An exploratory empirical study of selected adult groups. *Perceptual and Motor Skills, 75,* 1135-1153.

214. Keitner, G. I., Ryan, C. E., Miller, L. W., & Norman, W. H. (1992). Recovery and major depression: Factors associated with twelve-month outcome. *American Journal of Psychiatry, 149,* 93-99.

215. McFarlane, A. C. (1992). Avoidance and intrusion in posttraumatic stress disorder. *Journal of Nervous and Mental Disease, 180,* 439-445.

216. Parker, G., Hadzi-Pavlovic, D., Brodaty, H., Boyce, P., Mitchell, P., Wilhelm, K., & Hickie, I. (1992). Predicting the course of melancholic and nonmelancholic depression: A naturalistic comparison study. *Journal of Nervous and Mental Disease, 180,* 693-702.

217. Stein, C. H. (1992). Ties that bind: Three studies of obligation in adult relationships with family. *Journal of Social and Personal Relationships, 9*(4), 525-547.

218. Szabo, A. (1992). Habitual participation in exercise and personality. *Perceptual and Motor Skills, 74,* 978.

219. Bullock, W. A., & Gilliland, K. (1993). Eysenck's arousal theory of introversion-extraversion: A converging measures investigation. *Journal of Personality and Social Psychology, 64,* 113-123.

220. Hanson, R. K., Steffy, R. A., & Gauthier, R. (1993). Long-term recidivism of child molesters. *Journal of Consulting and Clinical Psychology, 61,* 646-652.

221. Marco, C., & Suls, J. (1993). Daily stress and the trajectory of mood: Spillover, response assimilation, contrast, and chronic negative affectivity. *Journal of Personality and Social Psychology, 64,* 1053-1063.

222. Mayer, J. D., Gaschke, Y. N., Braverman, D. L., & Evans, T. W. (1992). Mood-congruent judgement is a general effect. *Journal of Personality and Social Psychology, 63,* 119-132.

223. Regestein, Q. R., Dambrosia, J., Hallet, M., Murawski, B., & Paine, M. (1993). Daytime alertness in patients with primary insomnia. *American Journal of Psychiatry, 150,* 1529-1534.

224. Sloper, P., & Turner, S. (1993). Risk and resistance factors in the adaptation of parents of children with severe physical disability. *Journal of Child Psychology and Psychiatry, 34,* 167-188.

225. Stanley, M. A., Prather, R. C., Beck, J. G., Brown, T. C., Wagner, A. L., & Davis, M. L. (1993). Psychometric analyses of the Leyton Obsessional Inventory in patients with obsessive-compulsive and other anxiety disorders. *Psychological Assessment, 5,* 187-192.

226. Zebb, B. J., & Meyers, L. S. (1993). Reliability and validity of the revised California Psychological Inventory Vector 1 Scale. *Educational and Psychological Measurement, 53,* 271-280.

[950]

Eysenck Personality Questionnaire [Revised].

Publication Dates: 1975–93.

Acronym: EPQ-R.

Scores, 5: Psychotcism or Tough-Mindedness, Extraversion, Neuroticism or Emotionality, Lie, Addiction.

Administration: Group.

Time: (10–15) minutes.

Comments: Revision of the still-in-print Eysenck Personality Inventory (949).

Authors: H. J. Eysenck and Sybil B. G. Eysenck.

a) UNITED STATES EDITION.

Purpose: Designed to measure four dimensions of personality in adults.

Population: College and general adults including those with lower education levels.

Publication Dates: 1975–93.

Price Data, 1993: $12 per 25 tests [$45.75 per 100, $170.75 per 500]; $5.75 per 25 profile sheets [$19 per 100, $55 per 500]; $30 per hand-scoring keys; $25 per specimen set including manual and one copy of each form.

Publisher: EdITS/Educational and Industrial Testing Service.

b) BRITISH EDITION.

Purpose: Measures three main personality factors: Psychoticism, Extraversion, and Neuroticism.

Population: Ages 7–15, 16 and over.

Publication Dates: 1975–91.

Price Data, 1994: £29.99 per specimen set; £7.99 per 20 questionnaires; £13.99 per scoring keys; £16.99 per manual.

Publisher: Hodder & Stoughton Educational [England].

Cross References: See 9:406 (32 references); see also T3:860 (72 references); for reviews by Jack Block, Paul Kline, Lawrence J. Stricker, and Auke Tellegen, see 8:554 (84 references).

TEST REFERENCES

1. Oei, T. P. S., & Jackson, P. (1980). Long-term effects of group and individual social skills training with alcoholics. *Addictive Behaviors, 5,* 129-136.

2. Gossop, M., Eiser, J. R., & Ward, E. (1982). The addict's perceptions of their own drug-taking: Implications for the treatment of drug dependence. *Addictive Behaviors, 7,* 189-194.

3. Abou-Saleh, M. T. (1983). Platelet MAO, personality and response to lithium prophylaxis. *Journal of Affective Disorders, 5,* 55-65.

4. Abou-Saleh, M. T., & Coppen, A. (1983). Classification of depressive illnesses: Clinico-psychological correlates. *Journal of Affective Disorders, 6,* 53-66.

5. Abou-Saleh, M. T., & Coppen, A. (1983). Subjective side-effects of amitriptyline and lithium in affective disorders. *British Journal of Psychiatry, 142,* 391-397.

6. Adcock, N. V., & Ross, M. W. (1983). Early memories, early experiences and personality. *Social Behavior and Personality, 11*(2), 95-100.

7. Calloway, P., Fonagy, P., & Wakeling, A. (1983). Autonomic arousal in eating disorders: Further evidence for the clinical subdivision of anorexia nervosa. *British Journal of Psychiatry, 142,* 38-42.

8. Gudjonsson, G. H. (1983). Suggestibility, intelligence, memory recall and personality: An experimental study. *British Journal of Psychiatry, 142,* 35-37.

9. Hall, S. M., Bachman, J., Henderson, J. B., Barstow, R., & Jones, R. T. (1983). Smoking cessation in patients with cardiopulmonary disease: An initial study. *Addictive Behaviors, 8,* 33-42.

10. Hoehn-Saric, R., & Barksdale, V. C. (1983). Impulsiveness in obsessive-compulsive patients. *British Journal of Psychiatry, 143,* 177-182.

11. Lloyd, G. G., & Cawley, R. H. (1983). Distress or illness? A study of psychological symptoms after myocardial infarction. *British Journal of Psychiatry, 142,* 120-125.

12. Loo, R., & Shiomi, K. (1983). Extreme samples on the Eysenck Personality Questionnaire Psychoticism scale. *Social Behavior and Personality, 11*(2), 29-32.

13. McConaghy, N., Armstrong, M. S., Blaszczynski, A., & Allcock, C. (1983). Controlled comparison of aversive therapy and imaginal desensitization in compulsive gambling. *British Journal of Psychiatry, 142,* 366-372.

14. McElroy, J. C., Morrow, P. C., & Ackerman, R. J. (1983). Personality and interior office design: Exploring the accuracy of visitor attributions. *Journal of Applied Psychology, 68,* 541-544.

15. Rust, J. D., & Kinnard, K. Q. (1983). Personality characteristics of the users of corporal punishment in the schools. *Journal of School Psychology, 21,* 91-105.

16. Skinner, N. F. (1983). Personality correlates of machiavellianism: V. Machiavellianism, extraversion and toughmindedness in business. *Social Behavior and Personality, 11*(1), 29-32.

17. Tyler, J. D., Clark, J. A., Olson, D., Klapp, D. A., & Cheloha, R. S. (1983). Measuring mental health values. *Counseling and Values, 28,* 20-30.

18. Wilhite, S. C. (1983). Prepassage questions: The influence of structural importance. *Journal of Educational Psychology, 75,* 234-244.

19. Bass, C. (1984). Psychosocial outcome after coronary artery bypass surgery. *British Journal of Psychiatry, 145,* 526-532.

20. Berman, T., & Paisey, T. (1984). Personality in assaultive and non-assaultive juvenile male offenders. *Psychological Reports, 54,* 527-530.

21. Boyd, G. M., & Maltzman, I. (1984). Effects of cigarette smoking on bilateral skin conductance. *Psychophysiology, 21,* 334-341.

22. Campbell, J. B., & Reynolds, J. H. (1984). A comparison of the Guilford and Eysenck factors of personality. *Journal of Research in Personality, 18,* 305-320.

23. Chambless, D. L., Caputo, G. C., Bright, P., & Gallagher, R. (1984). Assessment of fear in agoraphobics: The Body Sensations Questionnaire and the Agoraphobic Questionnaire. *Journal of Consulting and Clinical Psychology, 52,* 1090-1097.

24. Clayer, J. R., Ross, M. W., & Campbell, R. L. (1984). Child-rearing patterns and dimensions of personality. *Social Behavior and Personality, 12,* 153-156.

25. Clifford, C. A., Murray, R. M., & Fulker, D. W. (1984). Genetic and environmental influences on obsessional traits and symptoms. *Psychological Medicine, 14,* 791-800.

26. Dunbar, G. C., & Lishman, W. A. (1984). Depression, recognition-memory and hedonic tone: A signal detection analysis. *British Journal of Psychiatry, 144,* 376-382.

27. Fox, S. (1984). The sociability aspect of extraversion as a situation-specific dimension. *Social Behavior and Personality, 12*(1), 7-10.

28. Furnham, A. (1984). Personality, social skills, anomie and delinquency: A self-report study of a group of normal non-delinquent adolescents. *Journal of Child Psychology and Psychiatry, 25*, 409-420.

29. Hoelscher, T. J., Lichstein, K. L., & Rosenthal, T. L. (1984). Objective vs subjective assessment of relaxation compliance among anxious individuals. *Behaviour Research and Therapy, 22*, 187-193.

30. Hurlburt, G., Gade, E., & Fuqua, D. (1984). Personality differences between Alcoholics Anonymous members and nonmembers. *Journal of Studies on Alcohol, 45*, 170-171.

31. Katz, R. (1984). Unconfounded electrodermal measures in assessing the aversiveness of predictable and unpredictable shocks. *Psychophysiology, 21*, 452-458.

32. Kendell, R. E., Mackenzie, W. E., West, C., McGuire, R. J., & Cox, J. L. (1984). Day-to-day mood changes after childbirth: Further data. *British Journal of Psychiatry, 145*, 620-625.

33. Kumar, R., & Robson, K. M. (1984). A prospective study of emotional disorders in childbearing women. *British Journal of Psychiatry, 144*, 35-47.

34. Lennox, R. D., & Wolfe, R. N. (1984). Revision of the self-monitoring scale. *Journal of Personality and Social Psychology, 46*, 1349-1364.

35. Loo, R. (1984). Personality correlates of the fear of death and dying scale. *Journal of Clinical Psychology, 40*, 120-122.

36. O'gorman, J. G., & Mallise, L. R. (1984). Extraversion and the EEG: II. A test of Gale's hypothesis. *Biological Psychology, 19*, 113-127.

37. Oei, T. P. S., & Jackson, P. R. (1984). Some effective therapeutic factors in group cognitive-behavioral therapy with problem drinkers. *Journal of Studies on Alcohol, 45*, 119-123.

38. Parkes, K. R. (1984). Locus of control, cognitive appraisal, and coping in stressful episodes. *Journal of Personality and Social Psychology, 46*, 655-668.

39. Parkes, K. R. (1984). Smoking and the Eysenck personality dimensions. *Psychological Medicine, 14*, 825-834.

40. Perera, M., & Eysenck, S. B. G. (1984). A cross-cultural study of personality. *Journal of Cross-Cultural Psychology, 15*, 353-371.

41. Romney, D. M., & Syverson, K. L. (1984). An attempt to identify the personality dimensions of the violent offender. *Social Behavior and Personality, 12*(1), 55-60.

42. Yates, A. J., & Sambrailo, F. (1984). Bulimia nervosa: A descriptive and therapeutic study. *Behaviour Research and Therapy, 22*, 503-517.

43. Blaszczynski, A. P., Buhrich, N., & McConaghy, N. (1985). Pathological gamblers, heroin addicts and controls compared on the E.P.Q "addiction scale." *British Journal of Addiction, 80*, 315-319.

44. Chambless, D. L. (1985). The relationship of severity of agoraphobia to associated psychopathology. *Behaviour Research and Therapy, 23*, 305-310.

45. Chambless, D. L., Caputo, G. C., Jasin, S. E., Gracely, E. J., & Williams, C. (1985). The Mobility Inventory for Agoraphobia. *Behaviour Research and Therapy, 23*, 35-44.

46. Clark, D. A., & Hemsley, D. R. (1985). Individual differences in the experience of depressive and anxious, intrusive thoughts. *Behaviour Research and Therapy, 23*, 625-633.

47. Erdle, S., Murray, H. G., & Rushton, J.P. (1985). Personality, classroom behavior, and student ratings of college teaching effectiveness: A path analysis. *Journal of Educational Psychology, 77*, 394-407.

48. Eysenck, S. B., & Yani, O. (1985). A cross-cultural study of personality: Israel and England. *Psychological Research, 57*, 111-116.

49. Fourie, D. P. (1985). Geophysical variables and behavior: XXIV. Seasonal factors in extraversion. *Psychological Reports, 56*, 3-8.

50. Gentry, T. A., Wakefield, J. A., Jr., & Friedman, A. F. (1985). MMPI Scales for measuring Eysenck's personality factors. *Journal of Personality Assessment, 49*, 146-149.

51. Katz, R., & Wykes, T. (1985). The psychological difference between temporally predictable and unpredictable stressful events: Evidence for information control theories. *Journal of Personality and Social Psychology, 48*, 781-790.

52. Lang, R. A., Lloyd, C. A., & Fiqia, N. A. (1985). Goal attainment scaling with hospitalized sexual offenders. *The Journal of Nervous and Mental Disease, 173*, 527-537.

53. Lefkowitz, M. M., & Tesiny, E. P. (1985). Depression in children: Prevalence and correlates. *Journal of Consulting and Clinical Psychology, 53*, 647-656.

54. Malamuth, N. M., & Check, J. V. P. (1985). The effects of aggressive pornography on beliefs in rape myths: Individual differences. *Journal of Research in Personality, 19*, 299-320.

55. Okasha, A., Kamel, M., Lotaif, F., Khalil, A. H., & Bishry, Z. (1985). Academic difficulty among male Egyptian university students: II. Associations with demographic and psychological factors. *British Journal of Psychiatry, 146*, 144-150.

56. Roy, A., Sutton, M., & Pickar, D. (1985). Neuroendocrine and

personality variables in dysthymic disorder. *American Journal of Psychiatry, 142*, 94-97.

57. Seeman, K., Yesavage, J., & Widrow, L. A. (1985). Correlations of self-directed violence in acute schizophrenics with clinical ratings and personality measures. *The Journal of Nervous and Mental Disease, 173*, 298-302.

58. Shapurian, R., & Hojat, M. (1985). Psychometric characteristics of a Persian version of the Eysenck Personality Questionnaire. *Psychological Reports, 57*, 631-639.

59. Stelmack, R. M., & Michaud-Achorn, A. (1985). Extraversion, attention, and habituation of the auditory evoked response. *Journal of Research in Personality, 19*, 416-428.

60. Stokes, J. P. (1985). The relation of social network and individual difference variables to loneliness. *Journal of Personality and Social Psychology, 48*, 981-990.

61. Syverson, K. L., & Romney, D. M. (1985). A further attempt to differentiate violent from nonviolent offenders by means of a battery of psychological tests. *Canadian Journal of Behavioural Science, 17*, 87-91.

62. Wilhite, S. C. (1985). Differential effects of high-level and low-level postpassage questions. *American Journal of Psychology, 98*, 41-58.

63. Wrate, R. M., Rooney, A. C., Thomas, P. F., & Cox, J. L. (1985). Postnatal depression and child development: A three-year follow-up study. *British Journal of Psychiatry, 146*, 622-627.

64. Adam, K., Tomeny, M., & Oswald, I. (1986). Physiological and psychological differences between good and poor sleepers. *Journal of Psychiatric Research, 20*, 301-316.

65. Barrett, P., Eysenck, H. J., & Lucking, S. (1986). Reaction time and intelligence: A replicated study. *Intelligence, 10*, 9-40.

66. Bijnen, E. J., VanDerNet, T. Z. J., & Poortinga, Y. H. (1986). On cross-cultural comparative studies with the Eysenck Personality Questionnaire. *Journal of Cross-Cultural Psychology, 17*, 3-16.

67. Buss, D. M., & Barnes, M. (1986). Preferences in human mate selection. *Journal of Personality and Social Psychology, 50*, 559-570.

68. Chambless, D. L., & Mason, J. (1986). Sex, sex-role stereotyping and agoraphobia. *Behaviour Research and Therapy, 24*, 231-235.

69. Clark, D. A. (1986). Factors influencing the retrieval and control of negative cognitions. *Behaviour Research and Therapy, 24*, 151-159.

70. Donaldson, G., McCorkle, R., Georgiadou, F., & Benoliel, J. Q. (1986). Distress, dependency, and threat in newly diagnosed cancer and heart disease patients. *Multivariate Behavioral Research, 21*, 267-298.

71. Edman, G., Asberg, M., Levander, S., & Schalling, D. (1986). Skin conductance habituation and cerebrospinal fluid 5-hydroxyindoleacetic acid in suicidal patients. *Archives of General Psychiatry, 43*, 586-592.

72. Emmons, R. A., & Diener, E. (1986). An interactional approach to the study of personality and emotion. *Journal of Personality, 54*, 371-384.

73. Emmons, R. A., & Diener, E. (1986). Situation selection as a moderator of response consistency and stability. *Journal of Personality and Social Psychology, 51*, 1013-1019.

74. Emmons, R. A., Diener, E., & Larsen, R. J. (1986). Choice and avoidance of everyday situations and affect congruence: Two models of reciprocal interactionism. *Journal of Personality and Social Psychology, 51*, 815-826.

75. Eysenck, H. J. (1986). Cross-cultural comparisons. The validity of assessment by indices of factor comparison. *Journal of Cross-Cultural Psychology, 17*, 506-515.

76. Eysenck, S. B. G., & Long, F. Y. (1986). A cross-cultural comparison of personality in adults and children: Singapore and England. *Journal of Personality and Social Psychology, 50*, 124-130.

77. Grayson, D. A. (1986). Latent trait analysis of the Eysenck Personality Questionnaire. *Journal of Psychiatric Research, 20*, 217-235.

78. Gupta, S., & Cummings, L. L. (1986). Perceived speed of time and task affect. *Perceptual and Motor Skills, 63*, 971-980.

79. Herbert, J., Moore, G. F., de la Riva, C., & Watts, F. N. (1986). Endocrine responses and examination anxiety. *Biological Psychology, 22*, 215-226.

80. Hojat, M., Shapurian, R., & Mehryar, A. H. (1986). Psychometric properties of a Persian version of the short form of the Beck Depression Inventory for Iranian College Students. *Psychological Reports, 59*, 331-338.

81. Kelly, I. W., Dickson, D. H., & Saklofske, D. H. (1986). Personality and the acceptance of Barnum statements under a condition of ambiguous relevance. *Perceptual and Motor Skills, 63*, 795-800.

82. Kline, P., & Cooper, C. (1986). Psychoticism and creativity. *The Journal of Genetic Psychology, 147*, 183-188.

83. Kosson, D. S., & Newman, J. P. (1986). Psyopathy and the allocation of attentional capacity in a divided-attention situation. *Journal of Abnormal Psychology, 95*, 257-263.

84. MacCarthy, B., & Furnham, A. (1986). Patients' conceptions of psychological adjustment in the normal population. *British Journal of Clinical Psychology, 25*, 43-50.

85. Malamuth, N. M. (1986). Predictors of naturalistic sexual aggression. *Journal of Personality and Social Psychology, 50*, 953-962.

86. Master, D. R., Thompson, C., Dunn, G., & Lishman, W. A. (1986). Memory selectivity and unilateral cerebral dysfunction. *Psychological Medicine, 16*, 781-788.

87. Mullan, M. J., Gurling, H. M. D., Oppenheim, B. E., & Murray, R. M. (1986). The relationship between alcoholism and neurosis: Evidence from a twin study. *British Journal of Psychiatry, 148*, 435-441.

88. Newman, J. P., & Kosson, D. S. (1986). Passive avoidance learning in psychopathic and nonpsychopathic offenders. *Journal of Abnormal Psychology, 95*, 252-256.

89. Nichols, S. L., & Neuman, J. P. (1986). Effects of punishment on response latency in extraverts. *Journal of Personality and Social Psychology, 50*, 624-630.

90. Parkes, K. R. (1986). Coping in stressful episodes: The role of individual differences, environmental factors, and situational characteristics. *Journal of Personality and Social Psychology, 51*, 1277-1292.

91. Philips, H. C., & Jahanshahi, M. (1986). The components of pain behaviour report. *Behaviour Research and Therapy, 24*, 117-125.

92. Phillips, G. T., Gossop, M., & Bradley, B. (1986). The influence of psychological factors on the opiate withdrawal syndrome. *British Journal of Psychiatry, 149*, 235-238.

93. Sheehan, M., Oppenheimer, E., & Taylor, C. (1986). Why drug users sought help from one London drug clinic. *British Journal of Addiction, 81*, 765-775.

94. Tennant, C. C., Goulston, K. J., & Dent, O. F. (1986). The psychological effects of being a prisoner of war: Forty years after release. *American Journal of Psychiatry, 143*, 618-621.

95. Tennant, C., Goulston, K., & Dent, O. (1986). Clinical psychiatric illness in prisoners of war of the Japanese: Forty years after release. *Psychological Medicine, 16*, 833-839.

96. Tennant, C., Goulston, K., & Langeluddecke, P. (1986). Psychological correlates of gastric and duodenal ulcer disease. *Psychological Medicine, 16*, 365-371.

97. Bass, C., & Akhras, F. (1987). Physical and psychological correlates of severe heart disease in men. *Psychological Medicine, 17*, 695-703.

98. Beech, H., & Claridge, G. (1987). Individual differences in negative priming: Relations with schizotypal personality traits. *British Journal of Psychology, 78*, 349-356.

99. Buss, D. M., Gomes, M., Higgins, D. S., & Lauterbach, K. (1987). Tactics of manipulation. *Journal of Personality and Social Psychology, 52*, 1219-1229.

100. Caird, D. (1987). Religiosity and personality: Are mystics introverted, neurotic, or psychotic? *British Journal of Social Psychology, 26*, 345-346.

101. French, C. C., & Beaumont, J. G. (1987). The reaction of psychiatric patients to computerized assessment. *British Journal of Clinical Psychology, 26*, 267-278.

102. Gabrys, J. B., Schumph, D., & Utendale, K. A. (1987). Short-term memory for two meaningful stories and self-report on the adult Eysenck Personality Questionnaire. *Psychological Reports, 61*, 51-59.

103. Jakes, S., & Hemsley, D. R. (1987). Personality and reports of hallucination and imagery in a normal population. *Perceptual and Motor Skills, 64*, 765-766.

104. Katz, R., & McGuffin, P. (1987). Neuroticism in familial depression. *Psychological Medicine, 17*, 155-161.

105. Kline, P., Auld, F., & Cooper, C. (1987). Five new personality scales: Their location in the factor space of personality measures. *Journal of Clinical Psychology, 43*, 328-336.

106. Kline, P., Auld, K., & Cooper, C. (1987). Five new personality scales: Their location in the factor space of personality measures. *Journal of Clinical Psychology, 43*, 328-336.

107. Lobel, T. E., & Winch, G. L. (1987). Neuroticism, anxiety, and psychosocial development. *British Journal of Clinical Psychology, 26*, 63-64.

108. McCrae, R. R. (1987). Creativity, divergent thinking, and openness to experience. *Journal of Personality and Social Psychology, 52*, 1258-1265.

109. Patterson, C. M., Kosson, D. S., & Newman, J. P. (1987). Reaction to punishment, reflectivity, and passive avoidance learning in extraverts. *Journal of Personality and Social Psychology, 52*, 565-575.

110. Raine, A., & Jones, F. (1987). Attention, autonomic arousal, and personality in behaviorally disordered children. *Journal of Abnormal Child Psychology, 15*, 583-599.

111. Rawlings, D. (1987). Four experiments on the relation between Eysenck's psychoticism dimension and the Pavlovian concept of nervous system mobility. *Journal of Research in Personality, 21*, 114-126.

112. Revelle, W. (1987). Personality and motivation: Sources of inefficiency in cognitive performance. *Journal of Research in Personality, 21*, 436-452.

113. Shapurian, R., Hojat, M., & Nayerahmadi, H. (1987). Psycho-

metric characteristics and dimensionality of a Persian version of Rosenberg Self-esteem scale. *Perceptual and Motor Skills, 65*, 27-34.

114. Teasdale, J. D., & Dent, J. (1987). Cognitive vulnerability to depression: An investigation of two hypotheses. *British Journal of Clinical Psychology, 26*, 113-126.

115. Dent, J., & Teasdale, J. D. (1988). Negative cognition and the persistence of depression. *Journal of Abnormal Psychology, 97*, 29-34.

116. Jahanshahi, M., & Marsden, C. D. (1988). Personality in torticollis: A controlled study. *Psychological Medicine, 18*, 375-387.

117. Klion, R. E. (1988). Construct system organization and schizophrenia: The role of construct integration. *Journal of Social and Clinical Psychology, 6*, 439-447.

118. Malamuth, N. M. (1988). Predicting laboratory aggression against female and male targets: Implications for sexual aggression. *Journal of Research in Personality, 22*, 474-495.

119. Pearson, P. R. (1988). A comparison of the Psychoticism Scale of the EPQ and the EPQ-R. *The Journal of Psychology, 122*, 623-624.

120. Sanario, E. (1988). Obsessions and compulsions: The Padua Inventory. *Behaviour Research and Therapy, 26*, 169-177.

121. Skinner, N. F. (1988). Personality correlates of Machiavellianism: VI Machiavellianism and the psychopath. *Social Behavior and Personality, 16*, 33-37.

122. Williams, W. M., & Sternberg, R. J. (1988). Group intelligence: Why some groups are better than others. *Intelligence, 12*, 351-377.

123. Wolfe, R. N., & Kasmer, J. A. (1988). Type versus trait: Extraversion, impulsivity, sociability, and preferences for cooperative and competitive activities. *Journal of Personality and Social Psychology, 54*, 864-871.

124. Zuckerman, M., Kuhlman, D. M., & Camac, C. (1988). What lies beyond E and N? Factor analysis of scales believed to measure basic dimensions of personality. *Journal of Personality and Social Psychology, 54*, 96-107.

125. Bentrall, R. P., Claridge, G. S., & Slade, P. D. (1989). The multidimensional nature of schizotypal traits: A factor analytic study with normal subjects. *British Journal of Clinical Psychology, 28*, 363-375.

126. Botwin, M. D., & Buss, D. M. (1989). Structure of act- report data: Is the five-factor model of personality recaptured? *Journal of Personality and Social Psychology, 56*, 988-1001.

127. Helmes, E. (1989). Evaluating the internal structure of the Eysenck Personality Questionnaire: Objective criteria. *Multivariate Behavioral Research, 24*, 353-364.

128. Lefkowitz, M. M., Tesiny, E. P., & Solodow, W. (1989). A rating scale for assessing dysphoria in youth. *Journal of Abnormal Child Psychology, 17*, 337-347.

129. Lowenstein, L. F. (1989). The etiology, diagnosis, and treatment of the fire-setting behaviour of children. *Child Psychiatry and Human Development, 19*, 186-194.

130. Lubusko, A., & Forest, J. (1989). Memory for information in self-help psychology books. *Psychological Reports, 65*, 891-896.

131. Lynn, R., Hampson, S., & Agahi, E. (1989). Television violence and aggression: A genotype-environment, correlation and interaction theory. *Social Behavior and Personality, 17*, 143-164.

132. Meyer, G. J., & Shack, J. R. (1989). Structural convergence of mood and personality: Evidence for old and new directions. *Journal of Personality and Social Psychology, 57*, 691-706.

133. Norton, N. C. (1989). Three scales of alexithymia: Do they measure the same thing? *Journal of Personality Assessment, 53*, 621-637.

134. Raine, A., & Allbutt, J. (1989). Factors of schizoid personality. *British Journal of Clinical Psychology, 28*, 31-40.

135. Wilson, G. D., Barrett, P. T., & Gray, J. A. (1989). Human reactions to reward and punishment: A questionnaire examination of Gray's personality theory. *British Journal of Psychology, 80*, 509-515.

136. Bachorowski, J., & Newman, J. P. (1990). Impulsive motor behavior: Effects of personality and goal salience. *Journal of Personality and Social Psychology, 58*, 512-518.

137. Baker, L. A., & Daniels, D. (1990). Nonshared environmental influences and personality differences in adult twins. *Journal of Personality and Social Psychology, 58*, 103-110.

138. Brandt, J., Celentano, D., Stewart, W., Linet, M., & Folstein, M. F. (1990). Personality and emotional disorder in a community sample of migraine headache sufferers. *American Journal of Psychiatry, 147*, 303-308.

139. Endler, N. S., & Parker, J. D. A. (1990). Multidimensional assessment of coping: A critical evaluation. *Journal of Personality and Social Psychology, 58*, 844-854.

140. Heath, A. C., & Martin, N. G. (1990). Psychoticism as a dimension of personality: A multivariate genetic test of Eysenck and Eysenck's psychoticism construct. *Journal of Personality and Social Psychology, 58*, 111-121.

141. Hough, L. M., Eaton, N. K., Dunnette, M. D., Kamp, J. D., & McCloy, R. A. (1990). Criterion-related validities of personal-

ity constructs and the effect of response distortion on those validities. *Journal of Applied Psychology, 75*(5), 581-595.

142. King, L. A., & Emmons, R. A. (1990). Conflict over emotional expression: Psychological and physical correlates. *Journal of Personality and Social Psychology, 58*, 864-877.

143. Parks, K. R. (1990). Coping, negative affectivity, and the work environment: Additive and interactive predictors of mental health. *Journal of Applied Psychology, 75*(4), 399-409.

144. Ryckman, R. M., Hammer, M., Kaczor, L. M., & Gold, J. A. (1990). Construction of a hypercompetitive attitude scale. *Journal of Personality Assessment, 55*, 630-639.

145. Alexander, D. A., & Wells, A. (1991). Reactions of police officers to body-handling after a major disaster: A before-and-after comparison. *British Journal of Psychiatry, 159*, 547-555.

146. Buckalew, L. W., Buckalew, N. M., & Bowling, W. J. (1991). Attentional performance, gender and an index of excitability. *Social Behavior and Personality, 19*, 21-27.

147. Capel, S. A. (1991). A longitudinal study of burnout in teachers. *The British Journal of Educational Psychology, 61*, 36-45.

148. Cassidy, T., & Lynn, R. (1991). Achievement motivation, educational attainment, cycles of disadvantage and social competence: Some longitudinal data. *The British Journal of Educational Psychology, 61*, 1-12.

149. deBeurs, E., Lange, A., VanDyck, R., Blonk, R., & Koele, P. (1991). Behavioral assessment of avoidance in agoraphobia. *Journal of Psychopathology and Behavioral Assessment, 13, 13*, 285-300.

150. Forest, J. J. (1991). Effects of attitudes and interests on personality change induced by psychological self-help books. *Psychological Reports, 68*, 587-592.

151. Francis, L. J. (1991). Personality and attitude towards religion among adult churchgoers in England. *Psychological Reports, 69*, 791-794.

152. Francis, L. J., & Pearson, P. R. (1991). Personality characteristics of mid-career male Anglican clergy. *Social Behavior and Personality, 19*, 81-84.

153. Girodo, M. (1991). Drug corruption in undercover agents: Measuring the risk. *Behavioral Sciences and the Law, 9*, 361-370.

154. Katz, Y. J., & Francis, L. J. (1991). The dual nature of the EPQ Lie Scale? A study among university students in Israel. *Social Behavior and Personality, 19*, 217-222.

155. Kendler, K. S., MacLean, C., Neale, M., Kessler, R., Heath, A., & Eaves, L. (1991). The genetic epidemiology of bulimia nervosa. *American Journal of Psychiatry, 148*, 1627-1637.

156. Kirkcaldy, B. D., & Ciefen, G. (1991). Personality correlates of intelligence in a clinical group. *Psychological Reports, 69*, 947-952.

157. Larsen, R. J., & Ketelaar, T. (1991). Personality and susceptibility to positive and negative emotional states. *Journal of Personality and Social Psychology, 61*, 132-140.

158. McConaghy, N., Blaszczynski, A., & Frankova, A. (1991). Comparison of imaginal desensitization with other behavioural treatments of pathological gambling: A two- to nine-year follow-up. *British Journal of Psychiatry, 159*, 390-393.

159. Slade, P. D., Newton, T., Butler, N. M., & Murphy, P. (1991). An experimental analysis of perfectionism and dissatisfaction. *British Journal of Clinical Psychology, 30*, 169-176.

160. Young, R. M., Oei, T. P., & Crook, G. M. (1991). Development of a drinking self-efficacy questionnaire. *Journal of Psychopathology and Behavioral Assessment, 13*, 1-15.

161. Ball, S. A., & Zuckerman, M. (1992). Sensation seeking and selective attention: Focused and divided attention on a dichotic listening task. *Journal of Personality and Social Psychology, 63*, 825-831.

162. Barrett, P. T., & Eysenck, H. J. (1992). Brain evoked potentials and intelligence: The Hendrickson Paradigm. *Intelligence, 16*, 361-381.

163. Beyler, J., & Schmeck, R. R. (1992). Assessment of individual differences in preferences for holistic-analytic strategies: Evaluation of some commonly available instruments. *Educational and Psychological Measurement, 52*, 709-719.

164. Desrosiers, G., & Robinson, D. (1992). Memory and hedonic tone: "Personality" or "mood" congruence? *Psychological Medicine, 22*, 117-129.

165. Egan, V., & Deary, I. J. (1992). Are specific inspection time strategies prevented by concurrent tasks? *Intelligence, 16*, 151-167.

166. Francis, L. J., & Katz, Y. J. (1992). The comparability of the short form EPQ-R indices of extraversion, neuroticism, and the lie scale with the EPQ for a sample of 190 student teachers in Israel. *Educational and Psychological Measurement, 52*, 695-700.

167. Gangestad, S. W., Simpson, J. A., DiGeronimo, K., & Biek, M. (1992). Differential accuracy in person perception across traits: Examination of a functional hypothesis. *Journal of Personality and Social Psychology, 62*, 688-698.

168. Heath, A. C., Neale, M. C., Kessler, R. C., Eaves, L. J., & Kendler, K. S. (1992). Evidence for genetic influences on personality from self-reports and informant ratings. *Journal of Personality and Social Psychology, 63*, 85-96.

169. Holroyd, S., Rabins, P. V., Finkelstein, D., Nicholson, M. C., Chase, G. A., & Wisniewski, S. C. (1992). Visual hallucinations in patients with macular degeneration. *American Journal of Psychiatry, 149*, 1701-1706.

170. Jones, D. L., & Francis, L. J. (1992). Personality profile of Methodist ministers in England. *Psychological Reports, 70*, 538.

171. Kennedy, H. G., & Grubin, D. H. (1992). Patterns of denial in sex offenders. *Psychological Medicine, 22*, 191-196.

172. King, D. J., & Henry, G. (1992). The effect of neuroleptics on cognitive and psychomotor function. *British Journal of Psychiatry, 160*, 647-653.

173. Kollai, M., & Kollai, B. (1992). Cardiac vagal tone in generalised anxiety disorder. *British Journal of Psychiatry, 161*, 831-835.

174. Marks, M. N., Wieck, A., Seymour, A., Checkley, S. A., & Kumar, R. (1992). Women whose mental illnesses recur after childbirth and partners' levels of expressed emotion during late pregnancy. *British Journal of Psychiatry, 161*, 211-216.

175. Matthews, G., Jones, D. M., & Chamberlain, A. G. (1992). Predictors of individual differences in mail-coding skills and their variation with ability level. *Journal of Applied Psychology, 77*, 406-418.

176. Riccio, M., Thompson, C., Wilson, B., Morgan, D. J. R., & Lant, A. F. (1992). Neuropsychological and psychiatric abnormalities in myalgic encephalomyelitis: A preliminary report. *British Journal of Clinical Psychology, 31*, 111-120.

177. Schaubroek, J., Ganster, D. C., & Fox, M. L. (1992). Dispositional affect and work-related stress. *Journal of Applied Psychology, 77*, 322-335.

178. Scott, J., Eccleston, D., & Boys, R. (1992). Can we predict the persistence of depression? *British Journal of Psychiatry, 161*, 633-637.

179. Smith, A. P. (1992). Effects of time of day, introversion, and neuroticism on selectivity in memory and attention. *Perceptual and Motor Skills, 74*, 851-860.

180. Vallejo, J., Olivares, J., Marcos, T., Bulbena, A., & Menchon, J. M. (1992). Clomipramine versus phenelzine in obsessive-compulsive disorder. *British Journal of Psychiatry, 161*, 665-670.

181. Watson, D., Clark, L. A., McIntyre, C. W., & Hamaker, S. (1992). Affect, personality, and social activity. *Journal of Personality and Social Psychology, 63*, 1011-1025.

182. Breslau, N. B., Kilbey, M. M., & Andreski, P. (1993). Vulnerability to psychopathology in nicotine-dependent smokers: An epidemiologic study of young adults. *American Journal of Psychiatry, 150*, 941-946.

183. Davidson, J. R. T., Kudler, H. S., Saunders, W. B., Erickson, L., Smith, R. D., Stein, R. M., Lipper, S., Hammett, E. B., Mahorney, S. L., & Cavenar, J. O. (1993). Predicting response to amitriptyline in posttraumatic stress disorder. *American Journal of Psychiatry, 150*, 1024-1029.

184. Izard, C. E., Libero, D. Z., Putnam, P., & Haynes, O. M. (1993). Stability of emotion experiences and their relations to traits of personality. *Journal of Personality and Social Psychology, 64*, 847-860.

185. Janzen, B. L., Saklofske, D. H., & Kelly, I. W. (1993). Personality and bulimic symptomatology. *Journal of Clinical Psychology, 49*, 649-654.

186. Kendler, K. S., Kessler, R. C., Neale, M. C., Heath, A. C., & Eaves, L. J. (1993). The prediction of major depression in women: Toward an integrated etiologic model. *American Journal of Psychiatry, 150*, 1139-1148.

187. McGue, M., Bacon, S., & Lykken, D. T. (1993). Personality stability and changes in early adulthood: A behavioral genetic analysis. *Developmental Psychology, 29*, 96-109.

188. Stelmack, R. M., Houlihan, M., & McGarry-Roberts, P. A. (1993). Personality, reaction time, and event-related potentials. *Journal of Personality and Social Psychology, 65*, 399-409.

189. Zukerman, M., Kuhlman, D. M., Joireman, J., Teta, P., & Kraft, M. (1993). A comparison of three structural models for personality: The big three, the big five, and the alternative five. *Journal of Personality and Social Psychology, 65*, 757-768.

190. Karney, B. R., Bradbury, T. N., Finchman, F. D., & Sullivan, K. T. (1994). The role of negative affectivity in the association between attributions and marital satisfaction. *Journal of Personality and Social Psychology, 66*, 413-424.

[951]

FACES III.

Purpose: To determine the structure of the family, in terms of the Circumplex Model.

Population: Families.

Publication Date: 1985.

Acronym: FACES III.

Scores: 2 dimensions: Family Cohesion, Family Adaptability.

Administration: Group.

Price Data, 1987: $30 per set of inventory materials including FACES III scale, which may be copied for use after obtaining permission, and manual (49 pages).

Special Edition: Couple version available for couples without children.

Time: [15] minutes.

Comments: Also known as Family Adaptability & Cohesion Evaluation Scales; self-report instrument.

Authors: David H. Olson, Joyce Portner, and Yoav Lavee.

Publisher: Family Social Science.

Cross References: For additional information, see 11:140 (26 references).

TEST REFERENCES

1. Eigen, C. A., & Hartman, B. W. (1987). Replicating the factor structure of Family Adaptability and Cohesion Scales II. *Psychological Reports, 60,* 775-782.
2. Eigen, C. A., Hartman, B. W., & Hartman, P. T. (1987). Relations between family interaction patterns and career indecision. *Psychological Reports, 60,* 87-94.
3. Harter, S., Alexander, P. C., & Neimeyer, R. A. (1988). Long-term effects of incestuous child abuse in college women: Social adjustment, social cognition, and family characteristics. *Journal of Consulting and Clinical Psychology, 56,* 5-8.
4. Brooks, D. M., & Kennedy, G. E. (1989). British and American attitudes toward family relationships. *Psychological Reports, 64,* 815-818.
5. Henggeler, S. W., Watson, S. M., Whelan, J. P., & Malone, C. M. (1990). The adaptation of hearing parents of hearing-impaired youths. *American Annals of the Deaf, 135,* 211-216.
6. Horwitz, W. A., & Kazak, A. E. (1990). Family adaptation to childhood cancer: Sibling and family systems variables. *Journal of Clinical Child Psychology, 19,* 221-228.
7. Kawash, G., & Kozeluk, L. (1990). Self-esteem in early adolescence as a function of position within Olson's Circumplex Model of Marital and Family Systems. *Social Behavior and Personality, 18,* 189-196.
8. King, S. (1990). Comparing two causal models of career maturity for hearing-impaired adolescents. *American Annals of the Deaf, 135,* 43-49.
9. Rienzi, B. M. (1990). Influence and adaptability in families with deaf parents and hearing children. *American Annals of the Deaf, 135,* 402-408.
10. Barnett, J. K., Papini, D. R., & Gbur, E. (1991). Familial correlates of sexually active pregnant and nonpregnant adolescents. *Adolescence, 26,* 457-472.
11. Bomba, A. K., Moran, J. D., III., & Goble, C. B. (1991). Relationship between familial style and creative potential of preschool children. *Psychological Reports, 68,* 1323-1326.
12. Carson, D. K., Gertz, L. M., Donaldson, M. A., & Wonderlich, S. A. (1991). Intrafamilial sexual abuse: Family-of-origin and family-of-procreation characteristics of female adult victims. *The Journal of Psychology, 125,* 579-597.
13. Henggeler, S. W., Burr-Harris, A. W., Borduin, C. M., & McCallum, G. (1991). Use of the Family Adaptability and Cohesion Evaluation Scales in child clinical research. *Journal of Abnormal Child Psychology, 19,* 53-63.
14. Pike, K. M., & Rodin, J. (1991). Mothers, daughters, and disordered eating. *Journal of Abnormal Psychology, 100,* 198-204.
15. Smith, T. A. (1991). Family cohesion in remarried families. *Journal of Divorce & Remarriage, 17,* 49-66.
16. Hackle, L. S., & Ruble, D. N. (1992). Changes in the marital relationship after the first baby is born: Predicting the impact of expectancy confirmation. *Journal of Personality and Social Psychology, 62,* 944-957.
17. Hanson, C. L., Henggeler, S. W., Harris, M. A., Cigrang, J. A., Schinkel, A. M., Rodrigue, J. R., & Klesges, R. C. (1992). Contributions of sibling relations to the adaptation of youths with insulin-dependent diabetes mellitus. *Journal of Consulting and Clinical Psychology, 60,* 104-112.
18. Henggeler, S. W., Melton, G. B., & Smith, L. A. (1992). Family preservation using multisystemic therapy: An effective alternative to incarcerating serious juvenile offenders. *Journal of Consulting and Clinical Psychology, 60,* 953-961.
19. Jordan, B. K., Marmar, C. R., Fairbank, J. A., Schlenger, W. E., Kulka, R. A., Hough, R. L., & Weiss, D. S. (1992). Problems in families of male Vietnam veterans with posttraumatic stress disorder. *Journal of Consulting and Clinical Psychology, 60,* 916-926.
20. Mann, B. J. (1992). Family process and hypnotic susceptibility: A preliminary investigation. *Journal of Nervous and Mental Disease, 180,* 192-196.
21. Miller, K. E., King, C. A., Shain, B. N., & Naylor, M. W. (1992). Suicidal adolescents' perceptions of their family environment. *Suicide and Life-Threatening Behavior, 22,* 226-239.
22. Prange, M. E., Greenbaum, P. E., Silver, S. E., Friedman, R. M., Kutash, K., & Duchnowski, A. J. (1992). Family functioning and psychopathology among adolescents with severe emotional disturbances. *Journal of Abnormal Child Psychology, 20,* 83-102.
23. Weinberg, R. A., Scarr, S., & Waldman, I. D. (1992). The Minnesota Transracial Adoption Study: A follow-up of IQ test performance at adolescence. *Intelligence, 16,* 117-135.
24. DeLoye, G. J., Henggeler, S. W., & Daniels, C. M. (1993). Developmental and family correlates of children's knowledge and attitudes regarding AIDS. *Journal of Pediatric Psychology, 18,* 209-219.
25. Domenico, D., & Windle, M. (1993). Intrapersonal and interpersonal functioning among middle-aged female adult children of alcoholics. *Journal of Consulting and Clinical Psychology, 61,* 659-666.
26. Henggeler, S. W., Melton, G. B., Smith, L. A., Foster, S. L., Hanley, J. H., & Hutchinson, C. M. (1993). Assessing violent offending in serious juvenile offenders. *Journal of Abnormal Child Psychology, 21,* 233-243.
27. Holmbeck, G. N., & Wandrei, M. L. (1993). Individual and relational predictors of adjustment in first-year college students. *Journal of Counseling Psychology, 40,* 73-78.
28. Jackson-Wilson, A. G., & Borgers, S. B. (1993). Disaffiliation revisited: A comparison of homeless and nonhomeless women's perceptions of family of origin and social supports. *Sex Roles, 28,* 361-377.
29. Reis, S. D., & Heppner, P. P. (1993). Examination of coping resources and family adaptation in mothers and daughters of incestuous versus nonclinical families. *Journal of Counseling Psychology, 40,* 100-108.
30. Swartzman-Schatman, B., & Schinke, S. P. (1993). The effect of mid life divorce on late adolescent and young adult children. *Journal of Divorce & Remarriage, 19,* 209-218.
31. Worden, J. W., & Silverman, P. S. (1993). Grief and depression in newly widowed parents with school-age children. *Omega, 27,* 251-261.

[952]

Facial Action Coding System.

Purpose: Constructed to assess facial movements or expressions.

Population: Adults.

Publication Date: 1978.

Acronym: FACS.

Scores, 4: Upper Face, Lower Face, Head/Eye Position, Full Face.

Administration: Individual.

Price Data, 1992: $290 per complete kit including 500 scoring sheets, 146 illustrative facial photographs, VHS videocassette, manual (341 pages), and investigator's guide (111 pages); $16 per 100 scoring sheets; $64 per VHS videocassette; $12 per investigator's guide no. 1; $20 per investigator's guide no. 2; $275 per training film (16mm).

Time: Administration time not reported.

Authors: Paul Ekman and Wallace V. Friesen.

Publisher: Consulting Psychologists Press, Inc.

TEST REFERENCES

1. Matsumoto, D. (1987). The role of facial response in the experience of emotion: More methodological problems and a meta-analysis. *Journal of Personality and Social Psychology, 52,* 769-774.
2. Pizzamiglio, L., Caltagirone, C., Mammucari, A., Ekman, P., & Friesen, W. V. (1987). Imitation of facial movements in brain damaged patients. *Cortex, 23,* 207-221.
3. Cacioppo, J. T., Martzke, J. S., Petty, R. E., & Tassinary, L. G. (1988). Specific forms of facial EMG response index emotions during an interview: From Darwin to the continuous flow hypothesis of affect-laden

information processing. *Journal of Personality and Social Psychology, 54,* 592-604.

4. Ekman, P., Friesen, W. V., & O'Sullivan, M. (1988). Smiles when lying. *Journal of Personality and Social Psychology, 54,* 414-420.

5. Mammucari, A., Caltagirone, C., Ekman, P., Friesen, W., Gainotti, G., Pizzamiglio, L., & Zoccolotti, P. (1988). Spontaneous facial expression of emotions in brain-damaged patients. *Cortex, 24,* 521-533.

6. Davidson, R. J., Ekman, P., Saron, C. D., Senulis, J. A., & Friesen, W. V. (1990). Approach-withdrawal and cerebral asymmetry: Emotional expression and brain physiology I. *Journal of Personality and Social Psychology, 58,* 330-341.

7. Ekman, P., Davidson, R. J., & Friesen, W. V. (1990). The Duchenne smile: Emotional expression and brain physiology II. *Journal of Personality and Social Psychology, 58,* 343-353.

8. Dale, J. A., Hudak, M. A., & Wasikowski, P. (1991). Effects of dyadic participation and awareness of being monitored on facial action during exposure to humor. *Perceptual and Motor Skills, 73,* 984-986.

9. During, S. M., & McMahon, R. J. (1991). Recognition of emotional facial expressions by abusive mothers and their children. *Journal of Clinical Child Psychology, 20,* 132-139.

10. Berenbaum, H., & Oltmanns, T. F. (1992). Emotional experience and expression in schizophrenia and depression. *Journal of Abnormal Psychology, 101,* 37-44.

11. Frank, M. G., Ekman, P., & Friesen, W. (1993). Behavioral markers and recognizability of the smile of enjoyment. *Journal of Personality and Social Psychology, 64,* 83-93.

[953]
The Facial Interpersonal Perception Inventory.

Purpose: Designed to evaluate real versus ideal perceptions of self and others.
Population: Ages 5 and over.
Publication Date: 1980.
Acronym: FIPI.
Scores, 15: Total Positive Self-Perception, Pleasant-Unpleasant (PU), Accepting-Rejecting (AR), Sleep-Tension (ST), Inconsistency, Within Factor Inconsistency, Inconsistency F Ratio, Total Self-Ideal, Self-Perception Incongruence, PU Incongruence, AR Incongruence, ST Incongruence, Between Factor Incongruence, Within Factor Incongruence, Incongruence F Ratio.
Administration: Group or individual.
Price Data, 1993: $25 per 50 tests; $12 per specimen set; $2 per test scoring service ($50 minimum).
Time: Administration time not reported.
Authors: Joseph J. Luciani and Richard E. Carney.
Publisher: Timao Foundation for Research and Development.
Cross References: For reviews by Charles D. Claiborn and Fred Zimring, see 9:407.

[954]
Factor Tests of Social Intelligence.

Purpose: Designed to be measures of the ability to cognize or understand the thoughts, feelings, and intentions of other people.
Population: Grade 6 to adult.
Publication Date: 1976.
Scores, 5: Total score for each of 4 subtests (Expression Grouping, Missing Cartoons, Social Translations, Cartoon Predictions), Total.
Administration: Group.
Price Data, 1993: $12 per sampler set including manual (23 pages), and 4 test booklets; $15 per 25 answer sheets; $8 per scoring keys; $10 per manual.
Time: [50] minutes.

Authors: Maureen O'Sullivan and J. P. Guilford.
Publisher: Consulting Psychologists Press, Inc.

[955]
Faculty Morale Scale for Institutional Improvement.

Purpose: To assess levels of faculty morale.
Population: College faculty.
Publication Dates: 1954–63.
Scores: Total score only.
Administration: Group.
Price Data: Available from publisher.
Time: Administration time not reported.
Authors: A Local Chapter Committee, American Association of University Professors.
Publisher: Psychometric Affiliates.

[956]
Faculty Orientations Survey.

Purpose: Designed to assess faculty members' "attitudes about postsecondary educational purposes, processes, and power."
Population: College and university faculty.
Publication Date: 1975.
Acronym: FOS.
Scores: 7 scale Scores: Achievement, Assignment Learning, Assessment, Affiliation, Inquiry, Independent Study, Interaction.
Administration: Group.
Manual: No manual.
Price Data: Available from publisher.
Time: (20) minutes.
Comments: For research purposes only.
Author: Barry R. Morstain.
Publisher: Barry R. Morstain.

[957]
A Familism Scale.

Purpose: Measures attitudes related to family.
Population: Adolescents and adults.
Publication Date: 1959.
Scores, 3: Nuclear, Extended, Total.
Administration: Group.
Price Data: Instrument is available without charge from author.
Time: [8] minutes.
Comments: Manual is a reprint of 1959 journal article by author.
Author: Panos D. Bardis.
Publisher: Panos D. Bardis.

TEST REFERENCES

1. Fu, V. R., Hinkle, D. E., & Hanna, M. A. K. (1986). A three-generational study of the development of individual dependency and family interdependence. *Genetic, Social, and General Psychology Monographs, 112,* 155-171.

[958]
Family Adjustment Test.

Purpose: "Designed to measure feelings of intrafamily homeyness-homelessness."

Population: Ages 12 and over.
Publication Dates: 1952–54.
Acronym: FAT.
Scores, 11: Attitudes Toward Mother, Attitudes Toward Father, Father-Mother Attitude Quotient, Oedipal, Struggle for Independence, Parent-Child Friction-Harmony, Interparental Friction-Harmony, Family Inferiority-Superiority, Rejection of Child, Parental Qualities, Total.
Administration: Group.
Price Data, 1985: $8.50 per 25 test booklets; $5 per specimen set.
Time: (35–40) minutes.
Comments: Title on test is Elias Family Opinion Survey.
Author: Gabriel Elias.
Publisher: Psychometric Affiliates.
Cross References: See T2:1181 (12 references) and P:80 (1 reference); for a review by John Elderkin Bell, see 6:95; for a review by Albert Ellis, see 5:53 (6 references).

TEST REFERENCES

1. Garbarino, C., & Strange, C. (1993). College adjustment and family environments of students reporting parental alcohol problems. *Journal of College Student Development, 34,* 261-266.

[959]

Family Apperception Test.
Purpose: Designed to assess family system variables.
Population: Ages 6 and over.
Publication Dates: 1985–91.
Acronym: FAT.
Scores: 35 to 40: Obvious Conflict (Family Conflict*, Marital Conflict*, Other Conflict, Absence of Conflict), Conflict Resolution (Positive Resolution, Negative or No Resolution*), Limit Setting (Appropriate/Compliance, Appropriate/Noncompliance*, Inappropriate/Compliance*, Inappropriate/Noncompliance*), Quality of Relationships (Mother = Ally, Father = Ally, Sibling = Ally, Spouse = Ally, Other = Ally, Mother = Stressor*, Father = Stressor*, Sibling = Stressor*, Spouse = Stressor*, Other = Stressor), Boundaries (Enmeshment*, Disengagement*, Mother/Child Coalition*, Father/Child Coalition*, Other Adult/Child Coalition*, Open System, Closed System*), Dysfunctional Circularity*, Abusive Remarks (Physical Abuse*, Sexual Abuse*, Neglect/Abandonment*, Substance Abuse*), Unusual Responses*, Refusals, Total Dysfunctional Index (total of scores with *) plus 5 optional Emotional Tone Scores: Sadness/Depression, Anger/Hostility, Worry/Anxiety, Happiness/Satisfaction, Other.
Administration: Individual.
Price Data, 1993: $125 per complete kit including set of test pictures, 100 scoring sheets, and manual ('91, 36 pages); $62.50 per set of test pictures; $19.50 per 100 scoring sheets; $45 per manual.
Time: (30–35) minutes.
Comments: Projective test.

Authors: Alexander Julian III, Wayne M. Sotile, Susan E. Henry, and Mary O. Sotile.
Publisher: Western Psychological Services.

[960]

Family Day Care Rating Scale.
Purpose: Assesses the quality of family day care.
Population: Consumers of day care services, day care providers, agency supervisors, and researchers.
Publication Date: 1989.
Acronym: FDCRS.
Scores, 6: Space and Furnishings for Care and Learning, Basic Care, Language and Reasoning, Learning Activities, Social Development, Adult Needs.
Administration: Group.
Price Data, 1994: $8.95 per manual (48 pages); $7.95 per 30 scoring sheets.
Time: (2) hours.
Authors: Thelma Harms and Richard M. Clifford.
Publisher: Teachers College Press.
Cross References: For a review by Annette M. Iverson, see 11:141.

[961]

Family Environment Scale, Second Edition.
Purpose: Developed to "measure the social-environmental characteristics of all types of families."
Population: Family members.
Publication Dates: 1974–86.
Acronym: FES.
Scores, 10: Cohesion, Expressiveness, Conflict, Independence, Achievement Orientation, Intellectual-Cultural Orientation, Active-Recreational Orientation, Moral-Religious Emphasis, Organization, Control.
Administration: Group.
Editions, 3: Real (R), Ideal (I), Expectations (E).
Price Data, 1992: $15 per 25 Form R test booklets; $16 per 25 test booklets (select Form I or Form E); $10 per 50 answer sheets; $15 per 25 self-scorable answer sheets; $7 per set of scoring stencils; $8 per 50 profiles; $80 per prepaid narrative; $15 per 25 interpretive report forms; $13 per manual ('86, 68 pages); $19 per specimen set.
Time: [15–20] minutes.
Comments: A part of the Social Climate Scales (2495).
Authors: Rudolf H. Moos and Bernice S. Moos (manual).
Publisher: Consulting Psychologists Press, Inc.
Cross References: For reviews by Nancy A. Busch-Rossnagel and Nadine M. Lambert of an earlier edition, see 9:408 (18 references); see also T3:872 (14 references); for a review by Philip H. Dreyer, see 8:557 (4 references). For a review of the Social Climate Series, see 8:681.

TEST REFERENCES

1. Moos, R. H., & Billings, A. G. (1982). Children of alcoholics during the recovery process: Alcoholic and matched control families. *Addictive Behaviors, 7,* 155-163.

2. Billings, A. G. (1983). Social-environmental factors among light and heavy cigarette smokers: A controlled comparison with non-smokers. *Addictive Behaviors, 8,* 381-391.

3. Billings, A. G., & Moos, R. H. (1983). Psychosocial processes of recovery among alcoholics and their families: Implications for clinicians and program evaluators. *Addictive Behaviors, 8,* 205-218.

4. Boake, C., & Salmon, P. G. (1983). Demographic correlates and factor structure of the Family Environment Scale. *Journal of Clinical Psychology, 39,* 95-100.

5. Gilbert, J. (1983). Deliberate metallic paint inhalation and cultural marginality: Paint sniffing among acculturating central California youth. *Addictive Behaviors, 8,* 79-82.

6. Nihira, K., Meyers, C. E., & Mink, I. T. (1983). Reciprocal relationship between home environment and development of TMR adolescents. *American Journal of Mental Deficiency, 88,* 139-149.

7. Wilson, R. S., & Matheny, A. P., Jr. (1983). Mental development: Family environment and genetic influences. *Intelligence, 7,* 195-215.

8. Anderson, E. A., & Lynch, M. M. (1984). A family impact analysis: The deinstitutionalization of the mentally ill. *Family Relations, 33,* 41-46.

9. Billings, A. G., & Moos, R. H. (1984). Chronic and nonchronic unipolar depression: The differential role of environmental stressors and resources. *The Journal of Nervous and Mental Disease, 172,* 65-75.

10. Daniels, D., Plomin, R., & Greenhalgh, J. (1984). Correlates of difficult temperament in infancy. *Child Development, 55,* 1184-1194.

11. McGee, R., Silva, P. A., & Williams, S. (1984). Perinatal, neurological, environmental and developmental characteristics of seven-year-old children with stable behaviour problems. *The Journal of Child Psychology and Psychiatry and Allied Disciplines, 25,* 573-586.

12. Mink, I. T., Meyers, C. E., & Nihira, K. (1984). Taxonomy of family life styles: II. Homes with slow-learning children. *American Journal of Mental Deficiency, 89,* 111-123.

13. Mitchell, R. E., & Moos, R. H. (1984). Deficiencies in social support among depressed patients: Antecedents or consequences of stress? *Journal of Health and Social Behavior, 25,* 438-452.

14. Moos, R. H., & Moos, B. S. (1984). The process of recovery from alcoholism: III. Comparing functioning in families of alcoholics and matched control families. *Journal of Studies on Alcohol, 45,* 111-118.

15. Nihira, K., Mink, I. T., & Meyers, C. E. (1984). Salient dimensions of home environment relevant to child development. *International Review of Research in Mental Retardation, 12,* 149-175.

16. Novak, A. R. (1984). A systems theory approach to deinstitutionalization policies and research. *International Review of Research in Mental Retardation, 12,* 245-283.

17. Oliveri, M. E., & Reiss, D. (1984). Family concepts and their measurement: Things are seldom what they seem. *Family Process, 23,* 33-48.

18. Potasznik, H., & Nelson, G. (1984). Stress and social support: The burden experienced by the family of a mentally ill person. *American Journal of Community Psychology, 12,* 589-607.

19. Radetsky, D. S., Handelsman, M. M., & Browne, A. (1984). Individual and family environment patterns among Jews and non-Jews. *Psychological Reports, 55,* 787-793.

20. Roehl, J. E., & Okun, M. A. (1984). Depression symptoms among women reentering college: The role of negative life events and family social support. *Journal of College Student Personnel, 25,* 251-254.

21. Sines, J. O. (1984). Relations between the Family Environment Scale (FES) and the MMPI. *Journal of Personality Assessment, 48,* 6-10.

22. Woody, J. D., Colley, P. E., Schlegelmilch, J., Maginn, P., & Balsanek, J. (1984). Child adjustment to parental stress following divorce. *Social Casework: The Journal of Contemporary Social Work, 65,* 405-412.

23. Abbott, D. A., & Brody, G. H. (1985). The relation of child age, gender, and number of children to the marital adjustment of wives. *Journal of Marriage and the Family, 47,* 77-84.

24. Billings, A. G., & Moos, R. H. (1985). Life stressors and social resources affect posttreatment outcomes among depressed patients. *Journal of Abnormal Psychology, 94,* 140-153.

25. Billings, A. G., & Moos, R. H. (1985). Psychosocial processes of remission in unipolar depression: Comparing depressed patients with matched community controls. *Journal of Consulting and Clinical Psychology, 53,* 314-325.

26. Bloom, B. L. (1985). A factor analysis of self-report measures of family functioning. *Family Process, 24,* 225-239.

27. Daniels, D., & Plomin, R. (1985). Origins of individual differences in infant shyness. *Developmental Psychology, 21,* 118-121.

28. Deardorff, P. A., McIntosh, J. A., Adamek, C. A., Bier, M., & Saalfeld, S. (1985). Automatic Thoughts Questionnaire: A study of concurrent validity. *Psychological Reports, 57,* 831-834.

29. Ellis, D. G., & Hamilton, M. (1985). Syntactic and pragmatic code usage in interpersonal communication. *Communication Monographs, 52,* 264-279.

30. Enos, D. M., & Handal, P. J. (1985). Relation of sex and age to old and new Family Environment Scale standard scores of white adolescents: Preliminary norms. *Psychological Reports, 57,* 327-330.

31. Felner, R. D., Aber, M. S., Primavera, J., & Cauce, A. M. (1985). Adaptation and vulnerability in high-risk adolescents: An examination of environmental mediators. *American Journal of Community Psychology, 13,* 365-379.

32. Hannum, J. W., & Mayer, J. M. (1985). Validation of two family assessment approaches. *Journal of Marriage and the Family, 46,* 741-748.

33. Hauser, S. T., Jacobson, A. M., Wertlieb, D., Brink, S., & Wentworth, S. (1985). The contribution of family environment to perceived competence and illness adjustment in diabetic and acutely ill adolescents. *Family Relations, 34,* 99-108.

34. Hilliard, J. P., Fritz, G. K., & Lewiston, N. J. (1985). Levels of aspiration of parents for their asthmatic, diabetic, and healthy children. *Journal of Clinical Psychology, 41,* 587-597.

35. Hiltonsmith, R. W. (1985). Relationship between perception of family social climate and behavior in the home setting. *Psychological Reports, 56,* 979-983.

36. Hirsch, B. J. (1985). Adolescent coping and support across multiple social environments. *American Journal of Community Psychology, 13,* 381-392.

37. Hirsch, B. J., Moos, R. H., & Reischl, T. M. (1985). Psychosocial adjustment of adolescent children of a depressed, arthritic, or normal parent. *Journal of Abnormal Psychology, 94,* 154-164.

38. Holahan, C. J., & Moos, R. H. (1985). Life stress and health: Personality, coping, and family support in stress resistance. *Journal of Personality and Social Psychology, 49,* 739-747.

39. Janos, P. M., Fung, H. C., & Robinson, N. M. (1985). Self-concept, self-esteem, and peer relations among gifted children who feel "different". *Gifted Child Quarterly, 29,* 78-82.

40. Justice, R. (1985). Factors mediating child abuse as a response to stress. *Child Abuse & Neglect, 9,* 359-363.

41. Leon, G. R., Lucas, A. R., Colligan, R. C., Ferdinande, R. J., & Kamp, J. (1985). Sexual, body-image, and personality attitudes in anorexia nervosa. *Journal of Abnormal Child Psychology, 13,* 245-257.

42. McGee, R., Williams, S., & Silva, P. A. (1985). Factor structure and correlates of ratings of inattention, hyperactivity, and antisocial behavior in a large sample of 9-year old children from the general population. *Journal of Consulting and Clinical Psychology, 53,* 480-490.

43. Nihira, K., Mink, I. T., & Meyers, C. E. (1985). Home environment and development of slow-learning adolescents: Reciprocal relations. *Developmental Psychology, 21,* 784-794.

44. Ordman, A. M., & Kirschenbaum, D. S. (1985). Cognitive-behavioral therapy for bulimia: An initial outcome study. *Journal of Consulting and Clinical Psychology, 53,* 305-313.

45. Parnicky, J. J., Williams, S., & Silva, P. A. (1985). Family Environment Scale: A Dunedin (New Zealand) pilot study. *Australian Psychologist, 20,* 195-204.

46. Patterson, J. M. (1985). Critical factors affecting family compliance with home treatment for children with cystic fibrosis. *Family Relations, 34,* 79-89.

47. Pino, C. J. (1985). A content validity study of the children's version of the Family Environment Scale. *Child Study Journal, 15,* 311-316.

48. Plomin, R., Loehlin, J. C., & DeFries, J. C. (1985). Genetic and environmental components of "environmental" influences. *Developmental Psychology, 21,* 391-402.

49. Raviv, A., & Palgi, Y. (1985). The perception of social-environmental characteristics in kibbutz families with family-based and communal sleeping arrangements. *Journal of Personality and Social Psychology, 49,* 376-385.

50. Anderson, S. A. (1986). Cohesion, adaptability and communication: A test of an Olson Circumplex Model hypothesis. *Family Relations, 35,* 289-293.

51. Anderson-Kulman, R. E., & Paludi, M. A. (1986). Working mothers and the family context: Predicting positive coping. *Journal of Vocational Behavior, 28,* 241-253.

52. Billings, A. G., & Moos, R. H. (1986). Children of parents with unipolar depression: A controlled 1-year follow-up. *Journal of Abnormal Child Psychology, 14,* 149-166.

53. Coleman, S. B., Kaplan, J. D., & Downing, R. W. (1986). Life cycle and loss—The spiritual vacuum of heroin addiction. *Family Process, 25,* 5-23.

54. Enos, D. M., & Handal, P. J. (1986). The relation of parental marital status and perceived family conflict to adjustment in white adolescents. *Journal of Consulting and Clinical Psychology, 54,* 820-824.

55. Fitting, M., Rabins, P., Lucas, M. J., & Eastham, J. (1986).

Caregivers for dementia patients: A comparison of husbands and wives. *The Gerontologist, 26*, 248-252.

56. Hanson, S. M. H. (1986). Healthy single parent families. *Family Relations, 35*, 125-132.

57. Holahan, C. J., & Moos, R. H. (1986). Personality, coping, and family resources in stress resistance: A longitudinal analysis. *Journal of Personality and Social Psychology, 51*, 389-395.

58. Kazdin, A. E., & Kolko, D. J. (1986). Parent psychopathology and family functioning among childhood firesetters. *Journal of Abnormal Child Psychology, 14*, 315-329.

59. Margalit, M., & Heiman, T. (1986). Learning-disabled boys' anxiety, parental anxiety, and family climate. *Journal of Clinical Child Psychology, 15*, 248-253.

60. Schnur, D. B., Friedman, S., Dorman, M., Redford, H. R., & Kesselman, M. (1986). Assessing the family environment of schizophrenic patients with multiple hospital admissions. *Hospital and Community Psychiatry, 37*, 249-252.

61. Searight, H. R., & Openlander, P. (1986). Family environments of continuing and noncontinuing college students. *Psychological Reports, 59*, 299-302.

62. Shapiro, J., & Tittle, K. (1986). Psychosocial adjustment of poor Mexican mothers of disabled and nondisabled children. *American Journal of Orthopsychiatry, 56*, 289-302.

63. Spiegel, D., & Wissler, T. (1986). Family environment as a predictor of psychiatric rehospitalization. *American Journal of Psychiatry, 143*, 56-60.

64. Asarnow, J. R., Carlson, G. A., & Guthrie, D. (1987). Coping strategies, self-perceptions, hopelessness, and perceived family environments in depressed and suicidal children. *Journal of Consulting and Clinical Psychology, 55*, 361-366.

65. Bathurst, K., & Gottfried, A. W. (1987). Untestable subjects in child development research: Developmental implications. *Child Development, 58*, 1135-1144.

66. Brunk, M., Henggeler, S. W., & Whelan, J. P. (1987). Comparison of multisystemic therapy and parent training in the brief treatment of child abuse and neglect. *Journal of Consulting and Clinical Psychology, 55*, 171-178.

67. Burgess, A. W., Hartman, C. R., & McCormack, A. (1987). Abused to abuser: Antecedents of socially deviant behaviors. *American Journal of Psychiatry, 144*, 1431-1436.

68. Cantor, N., Norem, J. K., Niedenthal, P. M., Langston, C. A., & Brower, A. M. (1987). Life tasks, self-concept ideals, and cognitive strategies in a life transition. *Journal of Personality and Social Psychology, 53*, 1178-1191.

69. Daniels, D., Moos, R. H., Billings, A. G., & Miller, J. J., III. (1987). Psychosocial risk and resistance factors among children with chronic illness, healthy siblings, and healthy controls. *Journal of Abnormal Child Psychology, 15*, 295-308.

70. Faust, J. (1987). Correlates of the drive for thinness in young female adolescents. *Journal of Clinical Child Psychology, 16*, 313-319.

71. Holahan, C. J., & Moos, R. H. (1987). Personal and contextual determinants of coping strategies. *Journal of Personality and Social Psychology, 52*, 946-955.

72. Holahan, C. J., & Moos, R. H. (1987). Risk, resistance, and psychological distress: A longitudinal analysis with adults and children. *Journal of Abnormal Psychology, 96*, 3-13.

73. Krantz, S. E., & Moos, R. H. (1987). Functioning and life context among spouses of remitted and nonremitted depressed patients. *Journal of Consulting and Clinical Psychology, 55*, 353-360.

74. LaCoste, L. D., Ginter, E., & Whipple, G. (1987). Intrafamily communication and familial environment. *Psychological Reports, 61*, 115-118.

75. Mink, I. T., & Nihira, K. (1987). Direction of effects: Family life styles and behavior of TMR children. *American Journal of Mental Deficiency, 92*, 57-64.

76. Oliver, J. M., Handal, P. J., Finn, T., & Herdy, S. (1987). Depressed and nondepressed students and their siblings in frequent contact with their families: Depression and perceptions of the family. *Cognitive Therapy and Research, 11*, 501-515.

77. Pats, B. F. (1987). Variables affecting college seniors' expectations about returning home. *Journal of College Student Personnel, 28*, 246-252.

78. Rich, A. R., & Bonner, R. L. (1987). Interpersonal moderators of depression among college students. *Journal of College Student Personnel, 28*, 337-342.

79. Sarason, B. R., Shearin, E. N., Pierce, G. R., & Sarason, I. G. (1987). Interrelations of social support measures: Theoretical and practical implications. *Journal of Personality and Social Psychology, 52*, 813-832.

80. Searight, H. R., Searight, P. R., & Scott, E. (1987). Family environments of children with school behavior problems. *Psychological Reports, 60*, 1263-1266.

81. Tolan, P. H. (1987). Implications of age of onset for delinquency risk. *Journal of Abnormal Child Psychology, 15*, 47-65.

82. Albertson, L. M., & Kagan, D. M. (1988). Dispositional stress, family environment, and class climate among college teachers. *Journal of Research and Development in Education, 21*(2), 53-61.

83. Bergeman, C. S., Plomin, R., McClearn, G. E., Pedersen, N. L., & Friberg, L. T. (1988). Genotype-environment interaction in personality development: Identical twins reared apart. *Psychology and Aging, 3*, 399-406.

84. Kennedy, M. G., Filner, R. D., Cauce, A., & Primavera, J. (1988). Social problem solving and adjustment in adolescence: The influence of moral reasoning level, scoring alternatives, and family climate. *Journal of Clinical Child Psychology, 17*, 73-83.

85. Kent, J. S., & Clopton, J. R. (1988). Bulimia: A comparison of psychological adjustment and familial characteristics in a nonclinical sample. *Journal of Clinical Psychology, 44*, 964-971.

86. Kurdek, L. A., & Sinclair, R. J. (1988). Adjustment of young adolescents in two-parent nuclear, stepfather, and mother-custody families. *Journal of Consulting and Clinical Psychology, 56*, 91-96.

87. McGee, R., Williams, S., & Silva, P. A. (1988). Slow starters and long-term backward readers: A replication and extension. *British Journal of Educational Psychology, 58*, 330-337.

88. Mink, I. T., Blacher, J., & Nihira, K. (1988). Taxonomy of family life styles: III. Replication with families with severely mentally retarded children. *American Journal on Mental Retardation, 93*, 250-264.

89. Minnes, P. M. (1988). Family resources and stress associated with having a mentally retarded child. *American Journal on Mental Retardation, 93*, 184-192.

90. Oliver, J. M., Handal, P. J., Enos, D. M., & May, M. J. (1988). Factor structure of the Family Environment Scale: Factors based on items and subscales. *Educational and Psychological Measurement, 48*, 469-477.

91. Oliver, J. M., May, M. J., & Handal, P. J. (1988). The factor structure of the Family Environment Scale: Factors derived from subscales. *Journal of Clinical Psychology, 44*, 723-727.

92. Slater, E. J., & Calhoun, K. S. (1988). Familial conflict and marital dissolution: Effects on the social functioning of college students. *Journal of Social and Clinical Psychology, 6*, 118-126.

93. Dinning, W. D., & Berk, L. A. (1989). The Children of Alcoholics Screening Test: Relationship to sex, family environment, and social adjustment in adolescents. *Journal of Clinical Psychology, 45*, 335-339.

94. Dyson, L., Edgar, E., & Crnic, K. (1989). Psychological predictors of adjustment by siblings of developmentally disabled children. *American Journal on Mental Retardation, 94*, 292-302.

95. Hoge, R. D., Andrews, D. A., Faulkner, P., & Robinson, D. (1989). The Family Relationship Index: Validity data. *Journal of Clinical Psychology, 45*, 897-903.

96. Langston, C. A., & Cantor, N. (1989). Social anxiety and social constraint: When making friends is hard. *Journal of Personality and Social Psychology, 56*, 649-661.

97. Margalit, M., Leyser, Y., & Avraham, Y. (1989). Classification and validation of family climate subtypes in kibbutz fathers of disabled and nondisabled children. *Journal of Abnormal Child Psychology, 17*, 91-107.

98. Robinowitz, R., Roberts, W. R., Dolan, M. P., Patterson, E. T., Charles, H. L., Atkins, H. G., & Penk, W. E. (1989). Carcinogenicity and teratogenicity vs. psychogenicity: Psychological characteristics associated with self-reported Agent Orange exposure among Vietnam combat veterans who seek treatment for substance abuse. *Journal of Clinical Psychology, 45*, 718-728.

99. Scalf-McIver, L., & Thompson, K. (1989). Family correlates of bulimic characteristics in college females. *Journal of Clinical Psychology, 45*, 467-472.

100. Swanson, J. W., Holzer, C. E., III, Canavan, M. M., & Adams, P. L. (1989). Psychopathology and economic status in mother-only and mother-father families. *Child Psychiatry and Human Development, 20*, 15-24.

101. Swindle, R. W., Jr., Cronkite, R. C., & Moos, R. H. (1989). Life stressors, social resources, coping, and the 4-year course of unipolar depression. *Journal of Abnormal Psychology, 98*, 468-477.

102. de Man, A., Hall, V., & Stout, D. (1990). Family environment and multidimensional locus of control. *Social Behavior and Personality, 18*, 197-200.

103. Kolko, D. J., & Kazdin, A. E. (1990). Matchplay and firesetting in children: Relationship to parent, marital, and family dysfunction. *Journal of Clinical Child Psychology, 19*, 229-238.

104. Kronenberger, W. G., & Thompson, R., Jr. (1990). Dimensions of family functioning in families with chronically ill children: A higher order factor analysis of the family environment scale. *Journal of Clinical Child Psychology, 19*, 380-388.

105. Rodrigue, J. R., Morgan, S. B., & Geffken, G. (1990). Families of autistic children: Psychological functioning of mothers. *Journal of Clinical Child Psychology, 19*, 371-379.

106. Rosenthal, D. A., & Feldman, S. S. (1990). The acculturation of Chinese immigrants: Perceived effects on family functioning of length of residence in two cultural contexts. *The Journal of Genetic Psychology, 151,* 495-514.

107. Solomon, Z., Waysman, M., & Mikulincer, M. (1990). Family functioning, perceived societal support, and combat-related psychopathology: The moderating role of loneliness. *Journal of Social and Clinical Psychology, 9,* 456-472.

108. Zirkel, S., & Cantor, N. (1990). Personal construal of life tasks: Those who struggle for independence. *Journal of Personality and Social Psychology, 58,* 172-185.

109. Brinson, J. A. (1991). A comparison of the family environments of Black male and female adolescent alcohol users. *Adolescence, 26,* 877-884.

110. Bullock, J. R. (1991). Parental perceptions of the family and children's peer relations. *The Journal of Psychology, 125,* 419-426.

111. Carson, D. K., Gertz, L. M., Donaldson, M. A., & Wonderlich, S. A. (1991). Intrafamilial sexual abuse: Family-of-origin and family-of-procreation characteristics of female adult victims. *The Journal of Psychology, 125,* 579-597.

112. Dyson, L. L. (1991). Families of young children with handicaps: Parental stress and family functioning. *American Journal on Mental Retardation, 95,* 623-629.

113. Eisenberg, N., Fabes, R. A., Schaller, M., Miller, P., Carlo, G., Poulin, R., Shea, C., & Shell, R. (1991). Personality and socialization correlates of vicarious emotional responding. *Journal of Personality and Social Psychology, 61,* 459-470.

114. Hafner, R. J., & Miller, R. M. (1991). Predicting schizophrenia outcome with self-report measures of family interaction. *Journal of Clinical Psychology, 47,* 33-41.

115. Holahan, C. J., & Moos, R. H. (1991). Life stressors, personal and social resources, and depression: A 4-year structural model. *Journal of Abnormal Psychology, 100,* 31-38.

116. Horton, A. D., & Retzlaff, P. D. (1991). Family assessment: Toward DSM-III-R relevancy. *Journal of Clinical Psychology, 47,* 94-100.

117. Schill, T., Begler, J., Morales, J., & Ekstrom, B. (1991). Self-defeating personality and perceptions of family environment. *Psychological Reports, 69,* 744-746.

118. Turner, S., Sloper, P., Knussen, C., & Cunningham, C. (1991). Factors relating to self-sufficiency in children with Down's syndrome. *Journal of Mental Deficiency Research, 35,* 13-24.

119. Asarnow, J. R. (1992). Suicidal ideation and attempts during middle childhood: Associations with perceived family stress and depression among child psychiatric inpatients. *Journal of Clinical Child Psychology, 21,* 35-40.

120. Barrera, M., Jr., & Garrison-Jones, C. (1992). Family and peer social support as specific correlates of adolescent depressive symptoms. *Journal of Abnormal Child Psychology, 20,* 1-16.

121. Calloni, J. C., & Handal, P. J. (1992). Differential parental attachment: Empirical support for the self-in-relation model. *Perceptual and Motor Skills, 75,* 904-906.

122. Carver, M. R., & Jones, W. H. (1992). The Family Satisfaction Scale. *Social Behavior and Personality, 20,* 71-84.

123. Clair, D. J., & Genest, M. (1992). The Children of Alcoholics Screening Test: Reliability and relationship to family environment, adjustment, and alcohol-related stressors of adolescent offspring of alcoholics. *Journal of Clinical Psychology, 48,* 414-420.

124. Jarmas, A. L., & Kazak, A. E. (1992). Young adult children of alcoholic fathers: Depressive experiences, coping styles, and family systems. *Journal of Consulting and Clinical Psychology, 60,* 244-251.

125. Kent, J. S., & Clopton, J. R. (1992). Bulimic women's perceptions of their family relationships. *Journal of Clinical Psychology, 48,* 281-292.

126. Klesges, R. C., Haddok, C. K., Klesges, L. M., Eck, L. H., & Hanson, C. L. (1992). Relationship between psychosocial functioning and body fat in preschool children: A longitudinal investigation. *Journal of Consulting and Clinical Psychology, 60,* 793-796.

127. Kolko, D. J., & Kazdin, A. E. (1992). The emergence and recurrence of child firesetting: A one-year prospective study. *Journal of Abnormal Child Psychology, 20,* 17-37.

128. Mollerstrom, W. W., Patchner, M. A., & Milner, T. S. (1992). Family functioning and child abuse potential. *Journal of Clinical Psychology, 48,* 445-454.

129. Thompson, R. J., Jr., Zeman, J. L., Fanurik, D., & Sirotkin-Roses, M. (1992). The role of parent stress and coping and family functioning in parent and child adjustment to Duchenne Muscular Dystrophy. *Journal of Clinical Psychology, 48,* 11-19.

130. Chipuer, H. M., Plomin, R., Pedersen, N. L., McClearn, G. E., & Nesselroade, J. R. (1993). Genetic influence on family environment: The role of personality. *Developmental Psychology, 29,* 110-118.

131. Lopez, F. G., & Truman, C. W. (1993). High-trait and low-trait angry college students: A comparison of family environment. *Journal of Counseling and Development, 71,* 524-527.

132. Walker, L. S., Garber, J., & Greene, J. W. (1993). Psychosocial correlates of recurrent childhood pain: A comparison of pediatric patients with recurrent abdominal pain, organic illness, and psychiatric disorders. *Journal of Abnormal Psychology, 102,* 248-258.

133. Weist, M. D., Finney, J. W., Barnard, M. J., Davis, C. D., & Ollendick, T. H. (1993). Empirical selection of psychosocial treatment targets for children and adolescents with diabetes. *Journal of Pediatric Psychology, 18,* 11-28.

134. Woodall, K. L., & Matthews, K. A. (1993). Changes in and stability of hostile characteristics: Results from a 4-year longitudinal study of children. *Journal of Personality and Social Psychology, 64,* 491-499.

135. Cutrona, C. E., Cole, V., Colangelo, N., Assouline, S. G., & Russell, D. W. (1994). Perceived parental social support and academic achievement: An attachment theory perspective. *Journal of Personality and Social Psychology, 66,* 369-378.

136. May, K. M., & Sowa, C. J. (1994). Personality characteristics and family environments of short-term counseling clients. *Journal of College Student Development, 35,* 59-62.

[962]

Family Relations Test.

Purpose: "Designed to give concrete representation of the subject's childhood family."

Publication Dates: 1965–78.

Acronym: FRT.

Scores: Nobody, Self, Father, Mother, Siblings, and Others scores for 2 areas: Outgoing Feelings, Incoming Feelings.

Administration: Individual.

Time: (20–25) minutes.

Publisher: NFER-Nelson Publishing Co., Ltd. [England].

a) CHILDREN'S VERSION.

Price Data, 1989: £81.65 per complete set; $44.30 per set of figures; £10.10 per manual ('78, 56 pages).

Authors: Eva Bene and James Anthony.

1) *Younger Children.*

Population: Ages 7–12.

Price Data: £6.05 per 25 record/score sheets.

2) *Older Children.*

Population: Ages 13–17.

Price Data: £12.10 per 25 record/score sheets.

b) ADULT VERSION.

Population: Adults.

Price Data: £113.85 per complete set; £28.70 per 25 record/score sheets; £22.95 per manual ('65, 28 pages).

Author: Eva Bene.

c) MARRIED COUPLES VERSION.

Population: Married couples.

Price Data: Same as for *b* above.

Authors: Eva Bene and James Anthony (test).

Cross References: See 9:409 (3 references); see also T3:874 (33 references), 8:558 (18 references), and T2:1182 (4 references); for an excerpted review by B. Semeonoff of a and b, see 7:79 (7 references); see also P:81 (2 references); for reviews by John E. Bell, Dale B. Harris, and Arthur R. Jensen of a, see 5:132 (1 reference).

TEST REFERENCES

1. Anderson, J. Z., & White, G. D. (1986). An empirical investigation of interaction and relationship patterns in functional and dysfunctional nuclear families and stepfamilies. *Family Process, 25,* 407-422.

[963]

Family Relations Test: Children's Version.
Purpose: "To assess the relative importance that different family members have for children" and to explore the child's emotional relations with his family.
Population: Ages 3–7, 7–15.
Publication Dates: 1957–85.
Administration: Individual.
Levels, 2: Form for Young Children, Form for Older Children.
Price Data, 1988: £70.15 for complete set including manual ('85, 59 pages), test figures and item cards, scoring and record sheets for older children, and record/score sheets for young children.
Time: 25(40) minutes.
Authors: Eva Bene (test and revised manual) and James Anthony (test).
Publisher: NFER-Nelson Publishing Co., Ltd. [England].

a) FORM FOR YOUNG CHILDREN.
Population: Ages 3–7.
Scores, 8: Outgoing Feelings (Positive Total, Negative Total), Incoming Feelings (Positive Total, Negative Total), Dependency Feelings, Sum of Positive, Sum of Negative, Total Involvement.

b) FORM FOR OLDER CHILDREN.
Population: Ages 7–15.
Scores, 12: Sum of Outgoing Positive, Sum of Outgoing Negative, Sum of Incoming Positive, Sum of Incoming Negative, Total Involvement, Sum of Positive Mild, Sum of Positive Strong, Sum of Negative Mild, Sum of Negative Strong, Maternal Overprotection, Paternal Overindulgence, Maternal Overindulgence.

Cross References: For reviews by Cindy I. Carlson and Steven I. Pfeiffer, see 11:142; for information on the complete test, see 9:409 (3 references), T3:874 (33 references), 8:558 (18 references), and T2:1182 (4 references); for an excerpted review by B. Semeonoff of the Children's Version and the Adult Version, see 7:79 (7 references); see also P:81 (2 references); for reviews by John E. Bell, Dale B. Harris, and Arthur R. Jensen of the Children's Version, see 5:132 (1 reference).

[964]

Family Relationship Inventory.
Purpose: "Method of examining family relationships, designed to clarify individual feelings and interpersonal behavior."
Population: Young children, adolescents, and adults.
Publication Dates: 1972–84.
Acronym: FRI.
Scores, 2: Positive, Negative, for each family member.
Administration: Individual or family groups.
Price Data, 1994: $70 per complete kit including item cards, 25 scoring forms, 50 tabulating forms, 50 individual relationship wheel forms, 25 familygram forms, and test manual ('82, 36 pages); $30 per set of item cards; $16.50 per 100 scoring forms; $16.50 per 100 tabulating forms; $16.50 per 100 individual relationship wheels; $16.50 per 100 familygrams.
Time: Administration time not reported.
Comments: Based upon Family Relationship Scale.
Authors: Ruth B. Michaelson, Harry L. Bascom, Louise Nash, W. Lee Morrison, and Robert M. Taylor.
Publisher: Psychological Publications, Inc.
Cross References: For a review by Mary Henning-Stout, see 10:112.

TEST REFERENCES

1. Crapps, J. M., & Stoneman, Z. (1989). Friendship patterns and community integration of family care residents. *Research in Developmental Disabilities, 10*, 153-169.
2. Frey, K. S., Greenberg, M. T., & Fewell, R. R. (1989). Stress and coping among parents of handicapped children: A multidimensional approach. *American Journal on Mental Retardation, 94*, 240-249.

[965]

Family Risk Scales.
Purpose: Designed to be used as a standardized measure of a child's risk of entering foster care.
Population: Families.
Publication Date: 1987.
Scores: 28 scales: Habitability of Residence, Suitability of Living Conditions, Financial Problems, Adult Relationships, Family's Social Support, Parents' Physical Health, Parents' Mental Health, Knowledge of Child Care, Parents' Substance Abuse, Parents' Motivation, Attitude to Placement, Parental Cooperation, Child's Cooperation, Preparation for Parenthood (Adult), Preparation for Parenthood (Child), Supervision Under Age 10, Parenting Age 10 and Up, Physical Punishment, Verbal Discipline, Emotional Care Under Age 2, Emotional Care Age 2 and Up, Physical Needs of Child, Sexual Abuse, Child's Physical Health, Child's Mental Health, School Adjustment, Delinquent Behavior, Home-Related Behavior.
Administration: Individual.
Price Data: Available from publisher.
Time: (20–30) minutes.
Authors: Stephen Magura, Beth Silverman Moses, and Mary Ann Jones.
Publisher: Child Welfare League of America, Inc.

[966]

Family Satisfaction Scale.
Purpose: Designed to measure satisfaction on the dimensions of family cohesion and family adaptability.
Population: Families.
Publication Date: 1982.
Scores, 3: Family Cohesion, Family Adaptability, Total Family Satisfaction.
Administration: Group.
Price Data, 1990: $10 (plus postage) per manual (7 pages) and scale.
Time: Administration time not reported.
Authors: David H. Olson and Marc Wilson.
Publisher: Family Social Science.

TEST REFERENCES

1. Brooks, D. M., & Kennedy, G. E. (1989). British and American attitudes toward family relationships. *Psychological Reports, 64,* 815-818.
2. Carver, M. R., & Jones, W. H. (1992). The Family Satisfaction Scale. *Social Behavior and Personality, 20,* 71-84.
3. Weinberg, R. A., Scarr, S., & Waldman, I. D. (1992). The Minnesota Transracial Adoption Study: A follow-up of IQ test performance at adolescence. *Intelligence, 16,* 117-135.

[967]

A Family Violence Scale.

Purpose: To indicate the occurrence of family violence in one's childhood.
Population: Adolescents and adults.
Publication Date: 1973.
Scores: Total Family Violence Score.
Administration: Group.
Price Data: Available from publisher.
Time: Administration time not reported.
Author: Panos D. Bardis.
Publisher: Panos D. Bardis.
Cross References: See 8:340 (1 reference).

[968]

Famous Sayings.

Purpose: Designed to assess personality traits by measuring attitudes toward various famous sayings.
Population: Grades 9-16 and business and industry.
Publication Dates: 1957-58.
Scores, 4: Conventional Mores, Hostility, Fear of Failure, Social Acquiescence.
Administration: Group.
Price Data, 1989: $13 per complete kit including manual ('58, 19 pages, reprint of an article from *Psychological Reports*), 50 test blanks, and scoring stencil; $10 per 50 test blanks; $3 per manual.
Time: (15-30) minutes.
Author: Bernard M. Bass.
Publisher: Psychological Test Specialists.
Cross References: See T3:876 (1 reference), T2:1183 (8 references), and P:82 (4 references); for reviews by Wesley C. Becker and Robert L. Thorndike, see 6:96 (17 references).

[969]

The Farnsworth-Munsell 100-Hue Test for the Examination of Color Discrimination.

Purpose: A "method for testing color discrimination."
Population: Mental ages 12 and over.
Publication Dates: 1942-57.
Scores: Total score only.
Administration: Individual.
Price Data: Not available.
Time: (5-10) minutes.
Comments: Formerly called Farnsworth-Munsell 100-Hue Test for Anomalous Color Vision.
Author: Dean Farnsworth.
Publisher: Munsell Color [No reply from publisher; status unknown].
Cross References: See T3:878 (5 references); see also T2:1913 (23 references) and 5:775 (1 reference); for a review by Elsie Murray, see 4:657 (2 references).

TEST REFERENCES

1. Mendlewicz, J., Linkowski, P., & Wilmotte, J. (1980). Relationship between schizoaffective illness and affective disorders or schizophrenia: Morbidity risk and genetic transmission. *Journal of Affective Disorders, 2,* 289-302.
2. Fine, B. J. (1983). Field-dependence and color discrimination ability in females. *Perceptual and Motor Skills, 57,* 983-986.
3. Fine, B. J., & Kobrick, J. L. (1983). Individual differences in distance estimation: Comparison of judgments in the field with those from projected slides of the same scenes. *Perceptual and Motor Skills, 57,* 3-14.
4. Kim, V., & Solomons, N. W. (1983). Performance of genetically-colorblind individuals on a rapid dark adaptation test based on the Purkinje shift. *Perceptual and Motor Skills, 56,* 251-258.
5. Mair, R. G., Doty, R. L., Kelly, K. M., Wilson, C. S., Langlais, P. J., McEntee, W. J., & Vollmecke, T. A. (1986). Multimodal sensory discrimination deficits in Korsakoff's psychosis. *Neuropsychologia, 24,* 831-839.
6. Cameron, B. A., Brown, D. M., Carson, D. K., Meyer, S. S., & Bittner, M. T. (1993). Children's creative thinking and color discrimination. *Perceptual and Motor Skills, 76,* 595-598.

[970]

Farnum Music Test.

Purpose: Readiness test for instrumental music.
Population: Grades 4-9.
Publication Dates: 1969-70.
Scores, 5: Notation, Cadence, Patterns, Symbol, Total.
Administration: Group.
Price Data: Not available.
Time: (40-45) minutes.
Comments: Test administered by 12-inch monaural record; the music notation subtest was formerly published under title of The Farnum Music Notation Test (1953).
Authors: Stephen E. Farnum.
Publisher: Bond Publishing Co. [No reply from publisher; status unknown].
Cross References: For reviews by Roger P. Phelps and Walter L. Wehner, see 8:93.

[971]

The Farnum String Scale: A Performance Scale for All String Instruments.

Purpose: Measurement of ability to play a stringed instrument.
Population: Grades 7-12.
Publication Date: 1969.
Scores, 4: Total score only for each test (Violin, Viola, Cello, String Bass).
Administration: Individual.
Price Data, 1989: $6 per scale book ('69, 28 pages); $12.95 per scale pad.
Time: Administration time not reported.
Author: Stephen E. Farnum.
Publisher: Hal Leonard Music, Inc.
Cross References: For additional information and a review by Walter L. Wehner, see 8:94.

[972]

Fast Health Knowledge Test, 1986 Revision.

Purpose: "To measure discrimination and judgment in matters of health."

Population: High school and college.
Publication Date: 1986.
Scores, 11: Personal Health, Exercise-Relaxation-Sleep, Nutrition, Consumer Health, Contemporary Health Problems, Substance of Abuse, Safety and First Aid, Disease Control, Mental Health, Family Life and Sex Education, Total.
Administration: Group.
Price Data, 1986: $60 per 50 copies (administrative materials included with each order).
Time: 40(50) minutes.
Author: Charles G. Fast.
Publisher: Charles G. Fast.
Cross References: For a review by Linda K. Bunker, see 10:113.

[973]
F.A.T.S.A. Test (Flowers Auditory Test of Selective Attention).

Purpose: "Test of auditory attention span with emphases on the assessment of auditory 'vigilance' and/or auditory 'watch-keeping' skills."
Population: Grades 1–6.
Publication Date: 1972.
Acronym: FATSA.
Scores: Total score only.
Administration: Group.
Price Data, 1985: $79 per complete kit; $7.50 per 12 test booklets.
Time: (30) minutes.
Comments: Test administered by tape recording (5-inch reel) or tape cassette; experimental edition.
Author: Arthur Flowers.
Publisher: Perceptual Learning Systems.
Cross References: For reviews by Stephen B. Hood and Eugene C. Sheeley, see 8:935-6.

TEST REFERENCES

1. Barnett, D. L., Nichols, A. C., & Gould, D. G. (1982). The effects of open-space versus traditional, self-contained classrooms on the auditory selective attending skills of elementary school children. *Language, Speech and Hearing Services in Schools, 13*, 138-143.

[974]
Fear Survey Schedule.

Purpose: "Designed to identify and quantify patients' reactions to a variety of sources of maladaptive emotional reactions."
Population: College and adults.
Publication Dates: 1964–77.
Acronym: FSS.
Scores: Total score only.
Administration: Group.
Price Data, 1993: $10.25 per 25 response forms and manual ('77, 11 pages).
Time: (15) minutes.
Comments: Self-rating.
Authors: Joseph Wolpe and Peter J. Lang.
Publisher: EdITS/Educational and Industrial Testing Service.
Cross References: See 9:411 (23 references) and

T3:883 (53 references); for a review by Charles D. Spielberger, see 8:559 (32 references); see also T2:1185 (14 references); for a review by R. G. Demaree, see 7:80 (17 references).

TEST REFERENCES

1. Kilpatrick, D. G., McAlhany, D. A., McCurdy, R. L., Shaw, D. L., & Roitzsch, J. C. (1982). Aging, alcoholism, anxiety, and sensation seeking: An exploratory investigation. *Addictive Behaviors, 7*, 97-100.
2. Frank, E., & Stewart, B. D. (1984). Depressive symptoms in rape victims: A revisit. *Journal of Affective Behaviors, 7*, 77-85.
3. Arrindell, W. A., & van der Ende, J. (1985). An empirical test of the utility of the observations-to-variables ratio in factor and components analysis. *Applied Psychological Measurement, 9*, 165-178.
4. Thyer, B. A., Himle, J., Curtis, G. C., Cameron, O. G., & Nesse, R. M. (1985). A comparison of panic disorder and agoraphobia with panic attacks. *Comprehensive Psychiatry, 26*, 208-214.
5. Turner, S. M., McCann, B. S., Beidel, D. C., & Mezzich, J. E. (1986). DSM-III classification of the anxiety disorders: A psychometric study. *Journal of Abnormal Psychology, 95*, 168-172.
6. Turner, S. M., Williams, S. L., Beidel, D. C., & Mezzich, J. E. (1986). Panic disorder and agoraphobia with panic attacks: Covariation along the dimensions of panic and agoraphobic fear. *Journal of Abnormal Psychology, 95*, 384-388.
7. Arrindell, W. A., & Emmelkamp, P. M. G. (1987). Psychological states and traits in female agoraphobics: A controlled study. *Journal of Psychopathology and Behavioral Assessment, 9*, 237-253.
8. Cameron, O. G., Liepman, M. R., Curtis, G. C., & Thyer, B. A. (1987). Ethanol retards desensitisation of simple phobias in non-alcoholics. *The British Journal of Psychiatry, 150*, 845-849.
9. Goestch, V. L., Tishelman, A. C., & Adams, H. E. (1987). Specific fears as predictors of generalized anxiety. *Journal of Psychopathology and Behavioral Assessment, 9*, 383-387.
10. Stewart, B. D., Hughes, C., Frank, E., Anderson, B., Kendall, K., & West, D. (1987). The aftermath of rape: Profiles of immediate and delayed treatment seekers. *The Journal of Nervous and Mental Disease, 175*, 90-94.
11. Beidel, D. C., & Turner, S. M. (1988). Comorbidity of test anxiety and other anxiety disorders in children. *Journal of Abnormal Child Psychology, 16*, 275-287.
12. Sanario, E. (1988). Obsessions and compulsions: The Padua Inventory. *Behaviour Research and Therapy, 26*, 169-177.
13. Strauss, C. C., Last, C. G., Hersen, M., & Kazdin, A. E. (1988). Association between anxiety and depression in children and adolescents with anxiety disorders. *Journal of Abnormal Child Psychology, 16*, 57-68.
14. Strauss, C. C., Lease, C. A., Last, C. G., & Francis, G. (1988). Overanxious disorder: An examination of developmental differences. *Journal of Abnormal Child Psychology, 16*, 433-443.
15. Cotton, C. R., & Range, L. M. (1990). Children death concepts: Relationship to cognitive functioning, age, experience with death, fear of death, and hopelessness. *Journal of Clinical Child Psychology, 19*, 123-127.
16. Goetsch, V. L., & Adams, H. E. (1990). A multicomponent investigation of the interaction of generalized anxiety and phobia. *Journal of Psychopathology and Behavioral Assessment, 12*, 329-344.
17. Clark, D. B., & Agras, W. S. (1991). The assessment and treatment of performance anxiety in musicians. *American Journal of Psychiatry, 148*, 598-605.
18. Cook, E. W., III, Hawk, L. W., Jr., & Davis, T. L. (1991). Affective individual differences and startle reflex modulation. *Journal of Abnormal Psychology, 100*, 5-13.
19. deBeurs, E., Lange, A., VanDyck, R., Blonk, R., & Koele, P. (1991). Behavioral assessment of avoidance in agoraphobia. *Journal of Psychopathology and Behavioral Assessment, 13, 13*, 285-300.
20. Friedman, A. G., Campbell, T., & Okifuji, A. (1991). Specific fears as predictors of generalized anxiety in children. *Journal of Psychopathology and Behavioral Assessment, 13*, 45-52.
21. Belicki, K. (1992). Nightmare frequency versus nightmare distress: Relations to psychopathology and cognitive style. *Journal of Abnormal Psychology, 101*, 592-597.
22. Inderbitzen-Pisaruk, H., Shawchuck, C. R., & Hoiser, T. S. (1992). Behavioral characteristics of child victims of sexual abuse: A comparison study. *Journal of Clinical Child Psychology, 21*, 14-19.
23. Klieger, D. M. (1992). The non-standardization of the Fear Survey Schedule. *Journal of Behavior Therapy and Experimental Psychiatry, 23*, 81-88.
24. Leone, C., & Aronow, R. E. (1992). Thought, process constraints, and cognitive style: Individual differences in self-generated reduction of fear. *Journal of Social and Clinical Psychology, 11*, 365-376.

25. Öst, L. (1992). Blood and injection phobia: Background and cognitive, physiological, and behavioral variables. *Journal of Abnormal Psychology, 101*, 68-74.

26. Riskind, J. H., Kelley, K., Harman, W., Moore, R., & Gaines, H. S. (1992). The loomingness of danger: Does it discriminate focal phobia and general anxiety from depression. *Cognitive Therapy and Research, 16*, 603-622.

27. Gullone, E., & Neville, J. K. (1993). The fears of youth in the 1990's: Contemporary normative data. *Journal of Genetic Psychology, 154*, 137-153.

28. Kleiger, D. M., & Franklin, M. E. (1993). Validity of the Fear Survey Schedule in phobia research: A laboratory test. *Journal of Psychopathology and Behavioral Assessment, 15*, 207-217.

29. Klieger, D. M., & Gallagher, R. W. (1993). The measurement and mismeasurement of ophidiophobia in analogue research: A procedural review. *Journal of Clinical Psychology, 49*, 140-153.

30. Last, C. G., & Perrin, S. (1993). Anxiety disorders in African-American and White children. *Journal of Abnormal Child Psychology, 21*, 153-164.

[975]

Fels Parent Behavior Rating Scales.

Purpose: Designed to measure certain aspects of parent-child relationships.
Population: Parents.
Publication Dates: 1937–49.
Acronym: FPBRS.
Scores, 30: Adjustment of Home, Activeness of Home, Discord in Home, Sociability of Family, Coordination of Household, Child-Centeredness of Home, Duration of Contact with Mother, Intensity of Contact with Mother, Restrictiveness of Regulation, Readiness of Enforcement, Severity of Actual Penalties, Justification of Policy, Democracy of Policy, Clarity of Policy, Effectiveness of Policy, Disciplinary Friction, Quantity of Suggestion, Coerciveness of Suggestion, Accelerational Attempt, General Babying, General Protectiveness, Readiness of Criticism, Direction of Criticism, Readiness of Explanation, Solicitousness for Welfare, Acceptance of Child, Understanding, Emotionality Toward Child, Affectionateness Toward Child, Rapport with Child.
Administration: Individual.
Price Data: Free test provided by publisher.
Time: Administration time not reported.
Authors: Alfred L. Baldwin, Joan Kalhorn, Fay Huffman Breese, and Horace Champney.
Publisher: Virginia Crandall.
Cross References: See T2:1186 (6 references) and P:84 (8 references); for a review by Dale B. Harris, see 4:43 (15 references).

[976]

50 Grammar Quizzes for Practice and Review.

Purpose: Designed to "guide students to learn correct grammar, improve their writing skills, and write clearly and effectively."
Population: Students.
Publication Date: 1985.
Scores: No scores.
Administration: Group.
Parts, 6: Part I: Writing Clear, Complete Sentences (15 quizzes); Part II: Correcting Errors in Agreement: Pronouns and Antecedents, Subjects and Verbs (3 study guides and 9 quizzes); Part III: Correcting Pronoun and Verb Shifts (2 sets of instructions and 5 quizzes); Part IV: Correcting Errors in the Use of Modifiers (4 quizzes); Part V: Correcting Errors in the Use of Parallel Structure (study guide and 3 quizzes); Part VI: Writing Precise, Effective Sentences (3 study guides and 14 quizzes).
Price Data, 1993: $39.95 for complete set of display copy.
Time: Administration time not reported.
Comments: Reproduction rights limited to purchaser of masters and a single classroom teacher.
Author: Joan R. Markos.
Publisher: J. Weston Walch.

[977]

Figurative Language Interpretation Test.

Purpose: Designed to assess comprehension of figurative language (simile, metaphor, hyperbole, and personification), "which is integral to language development and reading comprehension."
Population: Grades 4–10.
Publication Date: 1991.
Acronym: FLIT.
Scores: Total score only.
Administration: Group or individual.
Forms, 2: A, B.
Price Data, 1991: $45 per test kit including manual (32 pages), 25 each of Forms A and B, 50 answer sheets, and scoring template; $15 per specimen set.
Time: Less than (60) minutes.
Author: Barbara C. Palmer.
Publisher: Academic Therapy Publications.

[978]

Figure Classification Test.

Purpose: Designed to "measure abstract reasoning ability."
Population: Applicants for industrial work with 7 to 9 years of schooling.
Publication Date: 1976.
Scores: Total score only.
Administration: Group.
Price Data: Price information available from publisher for test materials including manual (21 pages).
Foreign Language Edition: Manual written in both English and Afrikaans.
Time: 60(70) minutes.
Comments: Separate answer sheets must be used.
Author: T. R. Taylor.
Publisher: National Institute for Personnel Research of the Human Sciences Research Council [South Africa].

TEST REFERENCES

1. Federico, P. (1986). Crystallized and fluid intelligence in a "new" instructional situation. *Contemporary Educational Psychology, 11*, 33-53.

[979]

Fine Dexterity Test.

Purpose: To provide "a measure of manual dexterity using a fine test task."
Population: Applicants for jobs involving fine motor dexterity.

Publication Date: 1983.
Acronym: FDT.
Scores, 2: Finger Dexterity, Fine Tool Dexterity.
Administration: Group.
Price Data, 1984: £42 per complete kit; £3.10 per set of spare collars and washers; manual free on request (10 pages).
Time: 6(8) minutes.
Author: Educational & Industrial Test Services, Ltd.
Publisher: Educational & Industrial Test Services, Ltd. [England].

[980]

Fire Promotion Tests—Complete Service.
Purpose: Custom-made test to fit duties and responsibilities for promotion of firefighters.
Population: Firefighters.
Publication Dates: 1979–93.
Scores: 8 subtests: Knowledge of Fire Protection/Prevention Practices, Fire Investigation Knowledges, Fire Attack-Related Technical Knowledges, Extinguishment-Related Technical Knowledges, Emergency Medical Care Knowledges, Supervisory and Managerial Knowledges, Administrative Knowledges, Comprehension Ability, and Total.
Administration: Group.
Price Data: $700 for first 5 candidates; $16.50–$41 for each additional candidate ($700 minimum).
Time: (210) minutes.
Comments: Candidate Study Guide available; formerly called Deluxe Fire Promotion Tests.
Author: McCann Associates, Inc.
Publisher: McCann Associates, Inc.

[981]

Firefighter Selection Test.
Purpose: "To rank-order applicants according to their probability of success in training and success on the job" as a firefighter.
Population: Applicants for firefighter trainee positions.
Publication Date: 1983.
Acronym: FST.
Scores: Total score only.
Administration: Group.
Price Data, 1990: Leasing fee, $155 for package of 10 tests including administrator's guide, technical manual, and scoring key.
Time: 150(170) minutes.
Comments: Measures mechanical comprehension, reading comprehension, and report interpretation.
Author: Psychological Services, Inc.
Publisher: Psychological Services, Inc.
Cross References: For reviews by David O. Anderson and Cynthia Ann Druva-Roush, see 11:143.

[982]

The FIRO Awareness Scales.
Purpose: Developed to evaluate interpersonal relations.
Population: Grades 4–6; high school and over.

Publication Dates: 1957–78.
Administration: Group.
Time: (10–15) minutes.
Authors: Will Schutz and Marilyn Wood (FIRO-BC).
Publisher: Consulting Psychologists Press, Inc.

a) FUNDAMENTAL INTERPERSONAL RELATIONS ORIENTATION—BEHAVIOR.
Purpose: Constructed to measure "a person's characteristic behavior toward other people."
Population: High school and over.
Acronym: FIRO-B.
Scores, 6: 2 scores (Expressed, Wanted) for each of 3 dimensions (Inclusion, Control, Affection).
Price Data, 1990: $9 per 25 test booklets; $14 per 25 self-scorable test booklets; $5 per set of scoring stencils; $6.50 per specimen set.

b) FUNDAMENTAL INTERPERSONAL RELATIONS ORIENTATION—BEHAVIOR OF CHILDREN.
Purpose: Same as *a* above.
Population: Grades 4–6.
Acronym: FIRO-BC.
Scores, 6: Same as *a* above.
Price Data: $10 per 25 test booklets; $10.50 per set of scoring stencils; $10 per specimen set.

c) FUNDAMENTAL INTERPERSONAL RELATIONS ORIENTATION—FEELINGS.
Purpose: Designed to measure "a person's characteristic feelings toward others."
Population: High school and over.
Acronym: FIRO-F.
Scores, 6: Same as *a* above.
Price Data: $9 per 25 test booklets; $8 per set of scoring stencils; $8 per specimen set.

d) LIFE INTERPERSONAL HISTORY ENQUIRY.
Purpose: Developed "to measure the relations between parents and children from the point of view of the child after the child has become an adult."
Population: High school and over.
Acronym: LIPHE.
Scores, 12: (6 for each parent): Inclusion (Behavior, Feelings), Control (Behavior, Feelings), Affection, Parental Disapproval.
Price Data: $16 per 25 test booklets; $4.50 per set of scoring stencils; $4.50 per specimen set.

e) COPING OPERATIONS PREFERENCE ENQUIRY.
Purpose: Designed to assess "preference for using each of five coping mechanisms, or mechanisms of defense."
Population: High school and over.
Acronym: COPE.
Scores, 5: Denial, Isolation, Projection, Regression-Dependency, Turning-Against-Self.
Price Data: $17 per 25 test booklets (select Male or Female); $3 per specimen set.

f) MARITAL ATTITUDES EVALUATION.
Purpose: Constructed "to explore the relationship between two people who have close contact with each other."
Population: High school and over.
Acronym: MATE.

Scores, 5: Inclusion (Behavior, Feelings), Control (Behavior, Feelings), Affection.
Price Data: $15 per 25 test booklets; $4 per set of scoring stencils; $4 per specimen set.
g) EDUCATIONAL VALUES.
Purpose: Developed "to assess values regarding several aspects of education."
Population: High school and over.
Acronym: VAL-ED.
Scores, 12: Importance, Mind, Teacher-Student (Control, Affection), Teacher-Community (Inclusion, Control, Affection), Administrator-Teacher (Inclusion, Control, Affection), Administrator-Community (Control, Affection).
Price Data: $12 per 25 test booklets; $5 per set of scoring stencils; $5 per specimen set.
Cross References: For a review by Peter D. Lifton, see 9:416 (12 references); see also T3:890 (45 references), 8:555 (147 references), and T2:1176 (58 references); for a review by Bruce Bloxom, see 7:78 (70 references); see also P:79 (30 references) and 6:94 (15 references).

TEST REFERENCES

1. Burton, S. A., & Goggin, W. C. (1984). FIRO-BC normative and psychometric data on 9- through 13-year old children. *Journal of Clinical Psychology*, 40, 760-772.
2. Shadish, W. R. (1984). Intimate behavior and the assessment of benefits in clinical groups. *Small Group Behavior*, 15, 204-221.
3. Spencer, E. F. D. (1984). Does it matter who lives where? *NASPA Journal*, 22(2), 26-31.
4. Ware, M. E., Millard, R. J., & Matthews, J. R. (1984). Stategies for evaluating field-placement programs. *Psychological Reports*, 55, 571-578.
5. Beutler, L. E., Storm, A., Kirkish, P., Scogin, F., & Gaines, J. A. (1985). Parameters in the prediction of police officer performance. *Professional Psychology: Research and Practice*, 16, 324-335.
6. Burton, S. A., & Goggin, W. C. (1985). Age, gender, and interpersonal behavior development using the FIRO-BC. *Journal of Personality Assessment*, 49, 168-171.
7. Dhillon, A. M., & Davis, H., IV. (1985). Socialization, locus of control, and dogmatism as related to counsellors' office settings. *Psychological Reports*, 56, 328-330.
8. Horne, T., & Carron, A. V. (1985). Compatibility in coach-athlete relationships. *Journal of Sport Psychology*, 7, 137-149.
9. Reading, J., & Amatea, E. S. (1986). Role deviance or role diversification: Reassessing the psychological factors affecting the parenthood choice of career-oriented women. *Journal of Marriage and the Family*, 48, 255-260.
10. Burton, S. A., & Goggin, W. C. (1987). Factor structure and concurrent validity of the Fundamental Interpersonal Relations Orientation Behavior Scale for Children. *Journal of Clinical Child Psychology*, 16, 164-167.
11. Calsyn, D. A., Roszell, D. K., & Anderson, L. S. (1988). Interpersonal style differences among drug abusers. *Journal of Clinical Psychology*, 44, 821-830.
12. Hafner, R. J., & Spence, N. S. (1988). Marriage duration, marital adjustment and psychological symptoms: A cross-sectional study. *Journal of Clinical Psychology*, 44, 309-316.
13. Lowman, R. L., & Leeman, G. E. (1988). The dimensionality of social intelligence: Social abilities, interests, and needs. *The Journal of Psychology*, 122, 279-290.
14. Moore, R. H. (1988). The concurrent validity of the MacAndrew Alcoholism Scale among at-risk adolescent females. *Journal of Clinical Psychology*, 44, 1005-1008.
15. Brems, C., & Johnson, M. E. (1990). Reexamination of the Bem Sex-Role Inventory: The interpersonal BSRI. *Journal of Personality Assessment*, 55, 484-498.
16. McRae, L. S. E., & Young, J. D. (1990). Field independence and the FIRO-B. *Perceptual and Motor Skills*, 70, 493-494.
17. Salminen, S. (1991). Convergent and discriminant validity of FIRO-B questionnaire. *Psychological Reports*, 69, 787-790.
18. Hurley, J. R. (1992). Further evidence against the construct validity of the FIRO-B scales. *Psychological Reports*, 70, 639-640.

[983]

First Grade Readiness Checklist.
Purpose: To help parents determine a child's readiness for first grade.
Population: First grade entrants.
Publication Date: 1972.
Scores: Total score only.
Administration: Group.
Price Data: Not available.
Time: Administration time not reported.
Comments: Upward extension of the School Readiness Checklist (2364); handbook for both instruments entitled *Ready or Not?*; checklist to be used by parents.
Authors: John J. Austin and J. Clayton Lafferty.
Publisher: Research Concepts [No reply from publisher; status unknown].
Cross References: For reviews by Kathryn Clark Gerken and Maribeth Gettinger, see 10:114.

[984]

First Year Algebra Test: National Achievement Tests.
Purpose: Designed to measure the student's knowledge of first year algebra.
Population: One year high school.
Publication Dates: 1958–62.
Scores: Total score only.
Administration: Group.
Forms, 2: A, B.
Price Data: Available from publisher.
Time: (40–45) minutes.
Authors: Ray Webb and Julius H. Hlavaty.
Publisher: Psychometric Affiliates.
Cross References: For a review by Donald L. Meyer, see 6:600.

[985]

FirstSTEP: Screening Test for Evaluating Preschoolers.
Purpose: "Designed to identify preschool children who are at risk for developmental delays in the five areas mandated by IDEA (PL 99-457)."
Population: Ages 2-9 to 6-2.
Publication Dates: 1990–93.
Scores, 7: Cognitive, Language, Motor, Composite, Social-Emotional, Adaptive Behavior, Parent/Teacher.
Administration: Individual.
Levels, 3: Ages 1–2, Ages 3–4, Ages 5–7.
Price Data, 1994: $130 per complete kit including 5 record forms each for levels 1, 2, and 3, 25 Social-Emotional/Adaptive Behavior booklets, 25 Parent booklets, manipulatives, plastic case, and manual ('93, 166 pages).
Time: (15–20) minutes.
Author: Lucy J. Miller.
Publisher: The Psychological Corporation.

[986]

The Fisher-Logemann Test of Articulation Competence.
Purpose: "Designed to . . . facilitate . . . analysis and categorization of articulatory errors."

Population: Preschool to adult, grade 3 to adult.
Publication Date: 1971.
Acronym: FLTAC.
Scores: No scores.
Administration: Individual.
Price Data, 1990: $55.50 per test portfolio; $16.20 per 50 record forms (specify Picture Test or Sentence Test); $10.50 per manual (42 pages).
Time: (40–45) minutes.
Authors: Hilda B. Fisher and Jerilyn A. Logemann.
Publisher: The Riverside Publishing Co.

a) PICTURE TEST.
Population: Preschool to adult.
Comments: 3 areas are covered: Singleton Consonants, Consonant Blends, Vowel Phonemes and Diphthongs; a shortened screening form consisting of 11 of the Singleton Consonants may be administered.

b) SENTENCE ARTICULATION TEST.
Population: Grade 3 to adult.
Comments: 5 areas are covered: Consonant Pairs, Singleton Consonants, Nasals, Vowel Phonemes, Diphthongs.

Cross References: See T3:896 (9 references); for reviews by Marie C. Fontana and Lawrence J. Turton, see 8:961.

TEST REFERENCES

1. Albertini, J. A., Smith, J. M., & Metz, D. E. (1983). Small group versus individual speech therapy with hearing-impaired young adults. *The Volta Review, 85*, 83-89.
2. Davis, J. M., Elfenbein, J., Schum, R., & Bentler, R. A. (1986). Effects of mild and moderate hearing impairments on language, educational, and psychosocial behavior of children. *Journal of Speech and Hearing Disorders, 51*, 53-62.
3. Smith, M. A., Schloss, P. J., & Israelite, N. K. (1986). Evaluation of a simile recognition treatment program for hearing-impaired students. *Journal of Speech and Hearing Disorders, 51*, 134-139.
4. Lieberth, A. K., & Whitehead, R. L. (1987). Orosensory perception and articulatory proficiency in hearing-impaired adults. *Perceptual and Motor Skills, 64*, 611-617.
5. Abraham, S., Stoker, R., & Allen, W. (1988). Speech assessment of hearing-impaired children and youth: Patterns of test use. *Language, Speech, and Hearing Services in Schools, 19*, 17-27.
6. Ohde, R. N., & Sharf, D. J. (1988). Perceptual categorization and consistency of synthesized /r-w/ continua by adults, normal children and /r/-misarticulating children. *Journal of Speech and Hearing Research, 31*, 556-568.

[987]

The Five P's (Parent/Professional Preschool Performance Profile).

Purpose: Designed to "systematically collect information regarding the child's current level of functioning" and to "establish a data base for the IEP."
Population: Children with disabilities functioning between the ages of 6 and 60 months.
Publication Dates: 1982–87.
Scores: 13 scales in 6 areas of development: Classroom Adjustment, Self-Help Scales (Toileting and Hygiene, Mealtime Behaviors, Dressing), Language Development (Communicative Competence, Receptive Language, Expressive Language), Social Development (Emerging Self, Relationships to Adults, Relationships to Children), Motor Development (Gross Motor/Balance/Coordination Skills, Perceptual/Fine Motor Skills), Cognitive Developmental Skills.
Administration: Individual.
Price Data, 1993: $125 per materials for class of 10 children including 10 sets of Five P's educational assessment booklets, 11 Five P's instructional manuals, 10 graphic profiles, 1 bound copy of The Five P's annual goals and short-term instructional objectives; $12.50 per materials for each additional child; $45 per training video (25 minutes); $5 per Five P's instructional manual; $6 per set of research papers (2 papers—Validity and Reliability); $75 per sample packet including PDQ (Parent Data Questionnaire—3 forms), Five P's educational assessment packet (includes scale booklets, graphic profile, Five P's instructional manual, training video, research papers, Five P's annual goals and short-term instructional objectives; $125 per set of PDQs (10 each form for screening or evaluation: Form A for children 24–35 months, Form B for children 36–47 months, Form C for children 48–60 months).
Foreign Language Editions: Spanish edition available; Hebrew translation of older edition available.
Time: Administration time not reported.
Comments: Ratings by parents and teachers.
Authors: Judith Simon Bloch and John S. Hicks (technical manual).
Publisher: Variety Pre-Schooler's Workshop.
Cross References: For a review by Barbara Perry-Sheldon, see 10:116.

[988]

Flanagan Aptitude Classification Tests.

Purpose: Measurement of aptitudes for sixteen on-the-job skills.
Population: Grades 9–12 and adults.
Publication Dates: 1951–60.
Acronym: FACT.
Administration: Group.
Price Data, 1985: $31.50 per 20 test booklets (1A-16A); $10 per interpretive leaflet; $3 per student booklet; $5 per counselor's booklet; $10 per technical supplement; $25 per technical report; $10 each per FACT 15A Reasoning manual and 16A ingenuity manual; $10 per examiner's manual ('53, 27 pages).
Author: John C. Flanagan.
Publisher: Science Research Associates/London House.

a) FACT 1A, INSPECTION.
Publication Dates: 1953–56.
Time: 6(12) minutes.

b) FACT 2A AND 2B, CODING.
Publication Dates: 1953–56.
Forms, 2: A, B.
Time: 10(30) minutes.

c) FACT 3A AND 3B, MEMORY.
Publication Dates: 1953–56.
Forms, 2: A, B.
Time: 4(5) minutes.

d) FACT 4A, PRECISION.
Publication Dates: 1953–56.
Time: 8(15) minutes.
e) FACT 5A, ASSEMBLY.
Publication Dates: 1953–56.
Time: 12(18) minutes.
f) FACT 6A, SCALES.
Publication Dates: 1953–56.
Time: 16(28) minutes.
g) FACT 7A, COORDINATION.
Publication Dates: 1953–56.
Time: 2.6(8) minutes.
h) FACT 8A, JUDGEMENT AND COMPREHENSION.
Publication Dates: 1953–56.
Time: (35–40) minutes.
i) FACT 9A, ARITHMETIC.
Publication Dates: 1953–56.
Time: 10(20) minutes.
j) FACT 10A, PATTERNS.
Publication Dates: 1953–56.
Time: 20(28) minutes.
k) FACT 11A, COMPONENTS.
Publication Dates: 1953–56.
Time: 20(24) minutes.
l) FACT 12A, TABLES.
Publication Dates: 1953–56.
Time: 10(15) minutes.
m) FACT 13A AND 13B, MECHANICS.
Publication Dates: 1953–56.
Forms, 2: A, B.
Time: 20(25) minutes.
n) FACT 14A, EXPRESSION.
Publication Dates: 1953–56.
Time: (35–45) minutes.
o) FACT 15A, REASONING.
Publication Dates: 1957–60.
Time: 24(30) minutes.
p) FACT 16A, INGENUITY.
Publication Dates: 1957–60.
Time: 24(30) minutes.
Cross References: See T3:899 (2 references), and T2:1072 (1 reference); for an excerpted review by Harold D. Murphy (with John P. McQuary), see 7:675 (10 references); for reviews by Norman Frederiksen and William B. Michael, see 6:770 (7 references); for reviews by Harold P. Bechtoldt, Ralph F. Berdie, and John B. Carroll, see 5:608.

[989]

Flanagan Industrial Tests.
Purpose: For use with adults in personnel selection programs for a variety of jobs.
Population: Business and industry job applicants.
Publication Dates: 1960–75.
Acronym: FIT.
Scores: Total score only for each test.
Administration: Group.
Price Data, 1985: $24 per 19 test booklets for any one test; $10 per scoring stencil for any one test; $10 per examiner's manual ('75, 36 pages).

Comments: Adaptation for business use of the Flanagan Aptitude Classification Tests; tests (representing specific job elements) may be used in a variety of combinations.
Author: John C. Flanagan.
Publisher: Science Research Associates/London House.
a) ARITHMETIC.
Time: 5(7) minutes.
b) ASSEMBLY.
Time: 10(13) minutes.
c) COMPONENTS.
Time: 10(12) minutes.
d) COORDINATION.
Time: 5(7) minutes.
e) ELECTRONICS.
Time: 15(17) minutes.
f) EXPRESSION.
Time: 5(8) minutes.
g) INGENUITY.
Time: 15(18) minutes.
h) INSPECTION.
Time: 5(9) minutes.
i) JUDGMENT AND COMPREHENSION.
Time: 15(17) minutes.
j) MATHEMATICS AND REASONING.
Time: 15(18) minutes.
k) MECHANICS.
Time: 15(18) minutes.
l) MEMORY.
Time: 10(19) minutes.
m) PATTERNS.
Time: 5(7) minutes.
n) PLANNING.
Time: 15(18) minutes.
o) PRECISION.
Time: 5(8) minutes.
p) SCALES.
Time: 5(7) minutes.
q) TABLES.
Time: 5(8) minutes.
r) VOCABULARY.
Time: 15(17) minutes.
Cross References: For reviews by David O. Herman and Arthur C. MacKinney, see 8:981 (3 references); for reviews by C. J. Adcock and Robert C. Droege and an excerpted review by John L. Horn, see 7:977 (1 reference).

TEST REFERENCES

1. Hakstain, A. R., Woolsey, L. K., & Schroeder, M. L. (1987). Validity of a large-scale assessment battery in an industrial setting. *Educational and Psychological Measurement, 47*(1), 165–178.

[990]

Fleishman Job Analysis Survey.
Purpose: "A means for analyzing the knowledge, skills and abilities needed to perform jobs."
Population: Adults.
Publication Date: 1992.

Acronym: F-JAS.
Scores, 72: 52 Abilities Scales: Cognitive (Oral Comprehension, Written Comprehension, Oral Expression, Written Expression, Fluency of Ideas, Originality, Memorization, Problem Sensitivity, Mathematical Reasoning, Number Facility, Deductive Reasoning, Inductive Reasoning, Information Ordering, Category Flexibility, Speed of Closure, Flexibility of Closure, Spatial Orientation, Visualization, Perceptual Speed, Selective Attention, Time Sharing), Psychomotor (Control Precision, Multilimb Coordination, Response Orientation, Rate Control, Reaction Time, Arm-Hand Steadiness, Manual Dexterity, Finger Dexterity, Wrist-Finger Speed, Speed of Limb Movement), Physical (Static Strength, Explosive Strength, Dynamic Strength, Trunk Strength, Extent Flexibility, Dynamic Flexibility, Gross Body Coordination, Gross Body Equilibrium, Stamina), Sensory/ Perceptual (Near Vision, Far Vision, Visual Color Discrimination, Night Vision, Peripheral Vision, Depth Perception, Glare Sensitivity, Hearing Sensitivity, Auditory Attention, Sound Localization, Speech Recognition, Speech Clarity); 9 Interactive/Social Scales (Persuasion, Social Sensitivity, Oral Fact Finding, Oral Defense, Resistance to Premature Judgement, Persistence, Resilience, Behavior Flexibility, Sales Interest); 11 Knowledge/Skills Scales (Electrical/ Electronic Knowledge, Mechanical Knowledge, Knowledge of Tools and Uses, Map Reading, Drafting, Reading Plans, Driving, Typing, Shorthand, Spelling, Grammar).
Administration: Group.
Levels, 3: Job-Level Analysis, Job Dimension-Level Analysis, Task-Level Analysis.
Price Data, 1993: $35 per sampler set including test booklet, answer sheet, and administrator's guide (34 pages); $75 per 5 reusable test booklets; $25 per 25 self-scorable answer sheets; $10 per 20 tally sheets; $25 per administrator's guide; $45 per Handbook of Human Abilities (132 pages).
Time: (40) minutes.
Comments: Previously referred to as the Task Assessment Scales, Ability Requirement Scales, Manual for the Ability Requirement Scales (MARS); Handbook of Human Abilities contains ability definitions, tasks, jobs, and test descriptions.
Authors: Edwin A. Fleishman and Maureen E. Reilly.
Publisher: Consulting Psychologists Press, Inc.

[991]

Florida Cumulative Guidance Record, Revised.
Purpose: Cumulative guidance record.
Population: Grades 1–12.
Publication Dates: 1950–77.
Price Data: No current price information.
Author: Edward Drew Co.
Publisher: Edward Drew Co. [No reply from publisher; status unknown].

[992]

Flowers-Costello Tests of Central Auditory Abilities.
Purpose: Designed to identify children with auditory perceptual dysfunctions.
Population: Grades K–6.
Publication Date: 1970.
Scores, 3: Low Pass Filtered Speech, Competing Messages, Total.
Administration: Individual.
Price Data, 1990: $125 per complete kit including test tape, picture booklets, manual, and score sheets.
Time: (15) minutes.
Authors: Arthur Flowers, Mary Rose Costello, and Victor Small.
Publisher: Perceptual Learning Systems.
Cross References: See T3:905 (3 references) and T2:2035 (2 references).

[993]

Fluharty Preschool Speech and Language Screening Test.
Purpose: Designed to measure early speech and language performance, and identify children in need of further diagnostic evaluation.
Population: Ages 2–6.
Publication Date: 1978.
Scores, 4: Identification Total, Articulation Total, Comprehension Total, Repetition Total.
Administration: Individual.
Price Data, 1989: $45 per complete kit including 100 response forms, 10 picture cards, and manual (19 pages); $15 per 100 response forms.
Time: (6–10) minutes.
Author: Nancy Buono Fluharty.
Publisher: The Riverside Publishing Co.
Cross References: For reviews by Nicholas W. Bankson and Harold A. Peterson, see 9:422 (1 reference).

TEST REFERENCES

1. Allen, D. V., & Bliss, L. S. (1987). Concurrent validity of two language screening tests. *Journal of Communication Disorders, 20*, 305-317.
2. Walker, J. F., Archibald, L., Cherniak, S. R., & Fish, V. G. (1992). Articulation rate in 3- and 5-year-old children. *Journal of Speech and Hearing Research, 35*, 4-13.

[994]

Food Choice Inventory.
Purpose: Assesses food choice behaviors of junior and senior high school students and adults.
Population: Junior and senior high school students and adults.
Publication Date: 1985.
Scores, 9: Will Eat (HIGH Nutrient-Value Foods, LOW Nutrient-Value Foods, TOTAL Foods), Like But Try NOT to Eat (HIGH Nutrient-Value Foods, LOW Nutrient-Value Foods, TOTAL Foods), Will Not Eat (HIGH Nutrient-Value Foods, LOW Nutrient-Value Foods, TOTAL Foods).
Price Data: Price data for complete set including

inventory manual (11 pages), scoring overlay, and group record sheet available from local Dairy Council.
Time: (4–10) minutes.
Authors: National Dairy Council and University of Illinois at Chicago.
Publisher: National Dairy Council.
Cross References: For a review by C. Alan Titchenal, see 10:118.

[995]
Food Protection Certification Test.
Purpose: "To test persons who have ongoing on-site responsibility for protecting the consumer from food-borne illness in food preparation, serving, or dispensing establishments."
Population: Food industry personnel.
Publication Date: 1985–93.
Scores, 3: Purchasing/Receiving/Storing Food, Processing/Serving/Dispensing Food, Employees/Facilities/Equipment.
Administration: Group.
Price Data, 1991: $18 registration fee providing for administration and scoring of the test and mailing of results to examinee; $3 per practice test.
Time: (120) minutes.
Comments: Tests administered per request of certified site examiner.
Author: Center for Occupational and Professional Assessment.
Publisher: Educational Testing Service.

[996]
The Forer Structured Sentence Completion Test.
Purpose: Designed to measure personality variables and attitudes that may be of some value in treatment planning.
Population: Ages 10–18 and adults.
Publication Dates: 1957–67.
Acronym: FSSCT.
Scores: No scores; 100 items in 18 areas: Interpersonal Figures (Mother, Males, Females, Groups, Father, Authority), Wishes, Causes of Own (Aggression, Anxiety/Fear, Giving Up [Adolescents] or Depression [Adults], Failure, Guilt, Inferiority Feelings [Adolescents]), Reactions To (Aggression, Rejection, Failure, Responsibility, School [Adolescents], Sexual Stimuli [Adults], Love and Marriage [Adults]).
Administration: Group.
Editions, 4: Separate editions for boys, girls, men, and women.
Price Data, 1993: $75 per kit including 40 tests, 40 checklists, and manual ('57, 34 pages) for any of each level; $16.50 per 25 tests (specify edition); $16.50 per 25 checklists (specify level); $25 per manual.
Time: [30–45] minutes.
Author: Bertram R. Forer.
Publisher: Western Psychological Services.
Cross References: See T2:1461 (3 references) and

P:429 (4 references); for reviews by Charles N. Cofer and Percival M. Symonds, see 5:134 (5 references).

[997]
The Forer Vocational Survey.
Purpose: "Designed as a method for studying personality as it relates to vocational matters."
Population: Adolescents and adults.
Publication Date: 1957.
Acronym: FVS.
Scores: No scores; 80 items in 11 areas: Reactions to Authorities, Reactions to Co-Workers, Reactions to Criticism, Reactions to Challenge, Reactions to Orders, Reactions to Responsibility, Causes of Aggression, Causes of Anxiety, Causes of Failure, Causes of Job Turnover, Vocational Goals.
Administration: Group.
Forms, 2: M (Men), W (Women).
Price Data, 1993: $70 per 25 tests of each form, 50 record forms, and manual (7 pages plus test and record form); $16.50 per 25 tests of any form; $16.50 per 25 record forms; $21 per manual.
Time: [20–30] minutes.
Comments: Manual title is Forer Vocational Survey: Men-Women.
Author: Bertram R. Forer.
Publisher: Western Psychological Services.
Cross References: For reviews by Benjamin Balinsky and Charles N. Cofer and an excerpted review by Laurence Siegel, see 5:135.

[998]
Form Series Test (A) (Industrial Version).
Purpose: Nonverbal test of inductive reasoning ability.
Population: Individuals with less than 6 years of schooling.
Publication Dates: 1969–75.
Acronym: FST.
Scores: Item scores only.
Administration: Group.
Price Data: Available from publisher.
Time: (40–50) minutes.
Authors: G. V. Grant and K. F. Mauer.
Publisher: National Institute for Personnel Research of the Human Sciences Research Council [South Africa].

[999]
Formal Reading Inventory.
Purpose: To identify students experiencing difficulties, to identify particular strengths and weaknesses, to evaluate a student's progress, and to serve as a measurement device in research studies.
Population: Grades 1–12.
Publication Dates: 1985–86.
Acronym: FRI.
Scores, 2: Silent Reading Quotient, Oral Miscues.
Administration: Individual.
Forms, 4: A, B, C, D.
Price Data, 1994: $74 per complete kit including

50 student record forms, student book, and manual ('86, 108 pages); $19 per 50 student record forms; $31 per student book; $27 per manual.
Time: Administration time not reported.
Author: J. Lee Wiederholt.
Publisher: PRO-ED, Inc.
Cross References: For a review by Richard L. Allington, see 10:120.

TEST REFERENCES

1. O'Conner, P. D., Sofo, F., Kendall, L., & Olsen, G. (1990). Reading disabilities and the effects of colored filters. *Journal of Learning Disabilities, 23,* 597-603.

[1000]

Forms for Behavior Analysis with Children.
Purpose: A collection of assessment measures "designed to provide a comprehensive portrait of childhood problems with an eye to how the information can be used to design behavioral treatments."
Population: Children.
Publication Date: 1983.
Scores: 21 measures: Behavior Analysis History Questionnaire, Behavior Status Checklist, Reinforcement Survey Schedules, Assertive Behavior Survey Schedule, Bodily Cues for Tension and Anxiety, Fear Inventory, Medical History Inventory, Parental Reaction Survey Schedule, Physical Complaint Survey Schedule, School Behavior Status Checklist, Self-Evaluation Scale, Parents' and Children's Reinforcement Survey Schedule, Reinforcement Menu, Response Cost Survey Schedule, School Reinforcement Survey Schedule, Behavior Record Form, Home Visit Observation Form, Behavior Rating Card, Motivation Assessment of Parents and Children, Progress Chart, Session Report.
Administration: Group.
Forms, 5: C (child), A (adolescent), P (parent), S (school personnel), T (therapist).
Price Data, 1991: $39.95 per manual (208 pages) including reproducible forms.
Time: Administration time not reported.
Comments: Forms (C, A, P, S, T) refer to the person who is to complete the form; "Different assessment formats are encompassed, ranging from direct observations and interviews to informant ratings and self-report."
Authors: Joseph R. Cautela, Julie Cautela, and Sharon Esonis.
Publisher: Research Press.
Cross References: For reviews by Sarah J. Allen and Karen T. Carey, see 11:144.

[1001]

Four Picture Test, Third Revised Edition.
Purpose: A projective technique "of the Thematic Apperception type" requiring written, rather than verbal, responses.
Population: Ages 10 and over.
Publication Dates: 1948-83.
Acronym: FPT.
Scores: No scores.

Administration: Group.
Price Data: Price information available from publisher for materials including manual ('83, 26 pages).
Time: (30–45) minutes.
Comments: Projective analysis guidelines provided in manual.
Author: D. J. van Lennep.
Publisher: Swets Test Services [The Netherlands].
Cross References: See P:431 (3 references); for a review by S. G. Lee and Johann M. Schepers of an earlier edition, see 6:213 (3 references); for reviews by John E. Bell, E. G. Bradford, and Ephraim Rosen of the original edition, see 4:105 (3 references, 1 excerpt).

[1002]

Fox Critical Reasoning Test—Verbal.
Purpose: To measure verbal critical reasoning.
Population: Graduates and applicants for managerial positions.
Publication Date: 1992.
Acronym: FCRV.
Scores: Total score only.
Administration: Group.
Price Data: Available from publisher.
Time: 30(35) minutes.
Author: The Morrisby Organisation.
Publisher: The Morrisby Organisation [England].

[1003]

The Fred Test.
Purpose: Assesses the oral proficiency for English as a Second Language placement.
Population: Non-native speakers of English.
Publication Date: 1983.
Scores, 4: Comprehension, Connected Discourse, Asking Questions, Total.
Administration: Individual.
Price Data: Not available.
Time: (10) minutes.
Author: Language Innovations, Inc.
Publisher: Language Innovations, Inc. [No reply from publisher; status unknown].

[1004]

French Comprehension Test.
Purpose: "Designed to measure the French comprehension skills of children in the beginning grades of total French immersion programs."
Population: Grades K–2, 1–5.
Publication Dates: 1975–77.
Scores, 4: Words and Sentences, Questions, Stories, Total.
Administration: Group.
Price Data, 1990: $16 per cassette tape.
Time: (40) minutes.
Author: Henri C. Barik.
Publisher: Ontario Institute for Studies in Education [Canada].
a) PRIMER.
Population: Grades K–2.

Price Data: $23.25 per 35 tests; $6 per manual ('77, 19 pages).

b) LEVEL I.

Population: Grades 1–5.

Price Data: $25.85 per 35 tests; $6 per manual ('76, 24 pages).

Cross References: See T3:918 (1 reference); for additional information and an excerpted review by Alison D'Anglejan, see 8:120 (1 reference).

[1005]

French Reading Diagnostic Tests for Early French Immersion Primary Classes.

Purpose: "To provide information of strengths and weaknesses in silent reading performance in French for Early French Immersion (EFI) pupils in Canada to integrate this information into the reteaching process."

Population: Grades 1–3 English-speaking pupils whose main language of instruction is French.

Publication Date: 1982.

Administration: Group.

Parts, 4: Phonic and Visual Skills, Vocabulary, Sentence Comprehension, Story Comprehension.

Price Data, 1987: $23.25 per 30 tests (Grade 1); $28.95 per 30 tests (Grade 2 or 3); $12 per guide (56 pages).

Time: Administration time not reported.

Author: Margaret Tourond.

Publisher: The Ontario Institute for Studies in Education [Canada].

[1006]

Frenchay Aphasia Screening Test.

Purpose: "To screen for aphasia as an aid to appropriate diagnosis, referral, and treatment."

Population: Normals and aphasics.

Publication Date: 1987.

Acronym: FAST.

Scores, 5: Comprehension, Expression, Reading, Writing, Total.

Administration: Individual.

Price Data, 1988: £25 per complete set including 25 record forms, picture card, and manual (12 pages); £5 per 24 record forms.

Time: (3–10) minutes.

Authors: Pamela Enderby, Victorine Wood, and Derick Wade.

Publisher: NFER-Nelson Publishing Co., Ltd. [England].

Cross References: For a review by Roger L. Towne, see 11:145.

TEST REFERENCES

1. House, A., Dennis, M., Mogridge, L., Warlow, C., Hawton, K., & Jones, L. (1991). Mood disorders in the year after first stroke. *British Journal of Psychiatry, 158*, 83-92.

[1007]

Frenchay Dysarthria Assessment.

Purpose: Developed to diagnose dysarthria.

Population: Ages 12 and over.

Publication Date: 1983.

Scores, 11: Reflex, Respiration, Lips, Jaw, Palate, Laryngeal, Tongue, Intelligibility, Rate, Sensation, Associated Factors.

Administration: Individual.

Price Data, 1994: $34 per complete kit including examiner's manual (59 pages) and scoring form; $19 per 25 scoring forms.

Time: [20] minutes.

Comments: Tongue depressor, stop watch, tape recorder, glass of water, and word cards needed for administration.

Author: Pamela M. Enderby.

Publisher: PRO-ED, Inc.

TEST REFERENCES

1. Dening, T. R., & Berrios, G. E. (1989). Wilson's disease: A prospective study of psychopathology in 31 cases. *British Journal of Psychiatry, 155*, 206-213.

2. Wallace, G. L. (1991). Assessment of oral peripheral structure and function in normal aging individuals with the Frenchay. *Journal of Communication Disorders, 24*, 101-109.

[1008]

Frostig Movement Skills Test Battery, Experimental Edition.

Purpose: Designed to assess strengths and weaknesses in the sensory motor development of elementary school age children.

Population: Ages 6–12.

Publication Date: 1972.

Acronym: FMSTB.

Scores, 6: Hand-Eye Coordination, Strength, Balance, Visually Guided Movement, Flexibility, Total.

Administration: Individual.

Price Data, 1990: $115 per equipment kit including manual, 50 recording sheets, all special items needed (wooden blocks, block transfer kit, bean bags, floor targets, carpenter's rule, and brackets for walking board); $7 per manual ('72, 35 pages); $8 per 50 recording sheets.

Time: [20] minutes.

Author: Russel E. Orpet.

Publisher: Consulting Psychologists Press, Inc.

Cross References: See T3:922 (5 references); for reviews by Thomas Oakland and Carl L. Rosen, see 8:871 (4 references).

TEST REFERENCES

1. Gabert, T. E., Jee, A., & Collins, W. E. (1982). Influence of passive and active vestibular stimulation on balance of young children. *Perceptual and Motor Skills, 54*, 548-550.

[1009]

Fuld Object-Memory Evaluation.

Purpose: Designed to "evaluate memory and learning under conditions that virtually guarantee attention and minimize anxiety."

Population: Ages 70–90 regardless of language and sensory handicaps.

Publication Date: 1977.

Acronym: FOME.

Scores, 5: Total Recall, Storage, Consistency of

Retrieval, Ability to Benefit from Reminding, Ability to Say Words in Categories.
Administration: Individual.
Forms, 2: Record Form I, II.
Price Data, 1994: $65 per complete kit; $20 per 30 record forms; $20 per manual (24 pages).
Time: Administration time not reported.
Author: Paula Altman Fuld.
Publisher: Stoelting Co.
Cross References: For a review by Eric F. Gardner, see 9:427.

TEST REFERENCES

1. Muramoto, O. (1984). Selective reminding in normal and demented aged people: Auditory verbal versus visual spatial task. *Cortex, 20,* 461-478.
2. Fuld, P. A., Muramoto, O., Blau, A., Westbrook, L., & Katzman, R. (1988). Cross-cultural and multi-ethnic dementia evaluation by mental status and memory testing. *Cortex, 24,* 511-519.
3. Fitten, L. J., Perryman, K. M., Gross, P. L., Fine, H., Cummins, J., & Marshall, C. (1990). Treatment of Alzheimer's disease with short- and long-term oral THA and lecithin: A double-blind study. *American Journal of Psychiatry, 147,* 239-242.
4. Fuld, P. A., Masur, D. M., Blau, A. D., Crystal, H., & Aronson, M. K. (1990). Object-memory evaluation for prospective detection of dementia in normal functioning elderly: Predictive and normative data. *Journal of Clinical and Experimental Neuropsychology, 12,* 520-528.
5. Marcopulos, B. A., & Graves, R. E. (1990). Antidepressant effect on memory in depressed older persons. *Journal of Clinical and Experimental Neuropsychology, 12,* 655-663.
6. Kern, R. S., Van Gorp, W. G., Cummings, J. L., Brown, W. S., & Osatu, S. S. (1992). Confabulation in Alzheimer's disease. *Brain and Cognition, 19,* 172-182.

[1010]
Full-Range Picture Vocabulary Test.
Purpose: Designed as an "individual test of intelligence based on verbal comprehension."
Population: Ages 2 and over.
Publication Date: 1948.
Scores: Total score only.
Administration: Individual.
Forms, 2: A, B.
Manual: No manual.
Price Data, 1989: $15 per complete kit including instructions, norms, set of plates, and sample answer sheets; $2.50 per 25 answer sheets (specify Form A or B).
Time: (10–15) minutes.
Comments: No reading required of examinee.
Authors: Robert B. Ammons and Helen S. Ammons.
Publisher: Psychological Test Specialists.
Cross References: See T3:923 (4 references); for a review by Jerome M. Sattler, see 8:216 (6 references); see also T2:496 (33 references) and 6:521 (30 references); for reviews by William D. Altus and William M. Cruickshank, see 4:340 (10 references).

TEST REFERENCES

1. Hooper, F. H., Hooper, J. O., & Colbert, K. K. (1985). Personality and memory correlates of intellectual functioning in adulthood: Piagetian and psychometric assessments. *Human Development, 28,* 101-107.
2. Gabrys, J. B., Schumph, D., & Utendale, K. A. (1987). Short-term memory for two meaningful stories and self-report on the adult Eysenck Personality Questionnaire. *Psychological Reports, 61,* 51-59.
3. Reid, J. B., Kavanagh, K., & Baldwin, D. V. (1987). Abusive parents' perceptions of child problem behaviors: An example of parental bias. *Journal of Abnormal Child Psychology, 15,* 457-466.

[1011]
The Fullerton Language Test for Adolescents, Second Edition.
Purpose: Constructed to "distinguish normal from language-impaired adolescents."
Population: Ages 11–18.
Publication Dates: 1980–86.
Scores, 8: Auditory Synthesis, Morphology Competency, Oral Commands, Convergent Production, Divergent Production, Syllabication, Grammatic Competency, Idioms.
Administration: Individual.
Price Data, 1990: $33 per complete kit including stimulus items, 25 scoring forms and profiles, and manual ('86, 55 pages); $3 per set of stimulus items; $15 per 25 scoring forms and profiles; $17 per manual; $22 per specimen set.
Time: (45) minutes.
Author: Arden R. Thorum.
Publisher: Consulting Psychologists Press, Inc.
Cross References: For a review by Diane J. Sawyer, see 10:122; for a review of the experimental edition by Margaret C. Byrne, see 9:428.

TEST REFERENCES

1. Lieberman, R. J., Heffron, A. M. C., West, S. J., Hutchinson, E. C., & Swen, T. W. (1987). A comparison of four adolescent language tests. *Language, Speech, and Hearing Services in Schools, 18,* 250-265.
2. Brasseur, J., & Jimenez, B. C. (1989). Performance of university students on the Fullerton subtest of idioms. *Journal of Communication Disorders, 22,* 351-359.
3. Nippold, M. A., & Martin, S. T. (1989). Idiom interpretation in isolation versus context: A developmental study with adolescents. *Journal of Speech and Hearing Research, 32,* 59-66.

[1012]
Functional Communication Profile.
Purpose: Designed to measure functional language performance in aphasic patients.
Population: Aphasic adults.
Publication Dates: 1956–69.
Acronym: FCP.
Scores, 6: Movement, Speaking, Understanding, Reading, Other, Total.
Administration: Individual.
Price Data, 1990: $1 per 25 profiles and 2 conversion charts; $4 per manual ('69, 36 pages).
Time: (15–30) minutes for interview.
Comments: Ratings by experienced clinician following nonstructured interview.
Author: Martha Taylor Sarno.
Publisher: Institute of Rehabilitation Medicine, New York University Medical Center.
Cross References: See T3:925 (3 references); for additional information and reviews by Raphael M. Haller and Harvey Halpern, see 8:962 (11 references).

TEST REFERENCES

1. Behrmann, M., & Penn, C. (1984). Non-verbal communication of aphasic patients. *British Journal of Disorders of Communication, 19,* 155-168.
2. Lendrem, W., & Lincoln, N. B. (1985). Spontaneous recovery of language in patients with aphasia between 4 and 34 weeks after stroke. *Journal of Neurology, Neurosurgery, and Psychiatry, 48,* 743-748.

3. Skenes, L. L., & McCauley, R. J. (1985). Psychometric review of nine aphasia tests. *Journal of Communication Disorders, 18*, 461-474.

[1013]

Functional Fitness Assessment for Adults over 60 Years.

Purpose: Designed to "assess the functional fitness of adults over 60 years of age."
Population: Adults over age 60.
Publication Date: 1990.
Scores, 7: Body Composition (Body Weight, Standing Height Measurement), Flexibility, Agility/Dynamic Balance, Coordination, Strength, Endurance.
Administration: Group.
Price Data, 1993: $7.50 per manual (24 pages).
Time: Administration time not reported.
Authors: Wayne H. Osness, Marlene Adrian, Bruce Clark, Werner Hoeger, Diane Rabb, and Robert Wiswell.
Publisher: American Alliance for Health, Physical Education, Recreation and Dance.

[1014]

Functional Grammar Test.

Purpose: To assess student mastery of English grammar.
Population: High school and college.
Publication Date: 1970.
Acronym: FGT.
Scores: Total score only.
Administration: Group.
Forms, 2: A, B.
Price Data: Available from publisher.
Time: (15–20) minutes.
Author: Joyce E. Lackey.
Publisher: Psychometric Affiliates.

[1015]

Functional Needs Assessment.

Purpose: Designed to provide an integrated, systematic method for assessment, treatment planning, clinical program designing, and progress monitoring.
Population: Chronic psychiatric patients.
Publication Date: 1990.
Acronym: FNA.
Scores, 26: Physical Ability, Receptive Communication, Expressive Communication, Place Orientation, Time Orientation, Personal Knowledge, Numerical Concepts, Toileting Skills, Bathing Skills, Personal Hygiene, Dressing Skills, Dining Skills, Safety and Prevention, Care of Living Quarters, Kitchen Skills, Laundry Skills, Community Mobility, Food Preparation, Money Management, Shopping and Purchasing, Participation in Treatment, Task Skills, Prevocational Skills, Social Etiquette, Planning and Decision Making, Leisure Skills.
Administration: Individual.
Price Data, 1991: $49 per complete kit including 20 assessment forms and manual (95 pages); $24.95 per 10 assessment forms.

Time: (60) minutes.
Comments: Ratings by therapist using "criterion-referenced" assessment.
Author: Lynn Blewett Dombrowski.
Publisher: Therapy Skill Builders.

[1016]

Functional Performance Record.

Purpose: "For recording the observable actions and behaviours of people whose physical, social or psychological functioning is impaired."
Population: Individuals of all ages with disabilities.
Publication Date: 1989.
Acronym: FPR.
Scores: 27 topic areas: Activity Level, Aggression, Attention Span, Domestic/Survival Skills, Dressing Female/Male, Feeding, Fits and Faints, Hearing, Incontinence, Memory, Mobility, Motor Co-ordination and Loss of Balance, Movement of Limbs and Trunk, Number Skills, Personal Hygiene, Personal Safety, Reading Skills, Social Behaviour, Socially Unacceptable Behaviour, Speech and Language Reception, Speech and Language Production, Toileting, Touch, Temperature and Hypothermia, Transportation, Vision, Writing Skills.
Administration: Individual.
Price Data, 1992: £51.75 per administration manual (33 pages); £19 per 5 checklists; £155.25 per administration set diskette; £103.50 per client diskette; £747.50 per database software pack.
Time: Untimed.
Author: David J. Mulhall.
Publisher: NFER-Nelson Publishing Co., Ltd. [England].

[1017]

Functional Skills Screening Inventory.

Purpose: "To be used in natural settings to assess critical living and working skills in persons with moderate to severe handicapping conditions."
Population: Age 6 through adult.
Publication Dates: 1984–86.
Acronym: FSSI.
Scores, 9: Categorized into 3 priority levels: Basic Skills and Concepts, Communication, Personal Care, Homemaking, Work Skills and Concepts, Community Living, Social Awareness, Functional Skills Subtotal, Problem Behaviors.
Administration: Individual.
Price Data, 1987: $98 per master copy including assessment booklet for unlimited assessments, score sheets, and user's guide ('86, 117 pages); $14.50 per sample set including one completed assessment plus user's guide; $380 per FSSI interactive computer program for use with IBM PC (or $340 for use with Apple IIe) plus user's guide; $22.50 per demo disk with complete documentation.
Time: [60–120] minutes per assessment.
Comment: A domain-referenced behavioral checklist.
Authors: Heather Becker, Sally Schur, Michele Paoletti-Schelp, and Ed Hammer.

Publisher: Functional Assessment and Training Consultants.

Cross References: For reviews by Diane Browder and G. Michael Poteat, see 10:123 (3 references).

[1018]

Functional Time Estimation Questionnaire.

Purpose: To provide "an overview of children's abilities to estimate time correctly."
Population: Ages 7–11.
Publication Date: 1990.
Acronym: FTEQ.
Scores: Total score only.
Administration: Group or individual.
Price Data, 1991: $40 per complete kit including 25 tests and manual ('90, 47 pages); $20 per 25 tests; $17 per manual; $17 per specimen set including 1 test and manual.
Time: (30–35) minutes.
Comments: FTEQ is the seventh version of the Dodd Test of Time Estimation.
Authors: John M. Dodd, Larry Burd, and John R. Cook.
Publisher: Academic Therapy Publications.

TEST REFERENCES

1. Nelson, J. R., Smith, D. J., Dodd, J. M., & Smith, M. (1991). Comparative time estimation skills of Hispanic children. *Perceptual and Motor Skills, 73*, 915-918.

[1019]

GAP Reading Comprehension Test, Third Edition.

Purpose: Assesses reading comprehension and can indicate reading progress.
Population: Ages 7–12.
Publication Dates: 1965–85.
Acronym: GAP.
Scores: Total Errors.
Administration: Group.
Price Data: Not available.
Time: 15(20) minutes.
Comments: Cloze technique.
Author: John McLeod.
Publisher: Heinemann Publishers Australia Pty Ltd. [No reply from publisher; status unknown].
Cross References: For reviews by Alan S. Kaufman and Gloria E. Miller, see 10:124 (4 references); see also T3:928 (4 references) and T2:1550 (3 references); for reviews by Donald B. Black and Earl F. Rankin of an earlier edition, see 7:688.

TEST REFERENCES

1. Underwood, J., & Underwood, G. (1987). Data organisation and retrieval by children. *British Journal of Educational Psychology, 57*, 313-329.
2. O'Connor, N., & Hermelin, B. (1991). A specific linguistic ability. *American Journal on Mental Retardation, 95*, 673-680.

[1020]

GAPADOL.

Purpose: To identify retarded and superior reading ability.

Population: Ages 10–16.
Publication Date: 1972.
Scores: Total score only.
Administration: Group.
Price Data: Not available.
Time: (30) minutes.
Comments: Cloze technique; upward extension for "adolescent children" of GAP Reading Comprehension Test (1019).
Authors: J. McLeod and J. Anderson.
Publisher: Heinemann Publishers Australia Pty Ltd. [No reply from publisher; status unknown].
Cross References: See T3:929 (1 reference); for a review by Ira E. Aaron, see 8:726.

TEST REFERENCES

1. Hunt, D., & Randhawa, B. S. (1983). Cognitive processes and achievement. *The Alberta Journal of Educational Research, 29*, 206-215.
2. Klose, A. E., Schwartz, S., & Brown, J. W. M. (1983). The imageability effect in good and poor readers. *Bulletin of the Psychonomic Society, 21*, 446-448.
3. Schwartz, S., Griffin, T. M., & Brown, J. (1983). Power and speed components of individual differences in letter matching. *Intelligence, 7*, 369-378.

[1021]

Gates-MacGinitie Reading Tests, Canadian Edition.

Purpose: Constructed to assess reading achievement.
Publication Dates: 1978–92.
Administration: Group.
Forms, 2: 3, 4.
Price Data, 1994: $33.95 per 35 test booklets (select level); $4.45 per scoring key (select level); $6.45 per 10 class record sheets; $20.45 per manual (select level); $16.95 per out-of-level norms booklet; $29 per examination kit; scoring service available from publisher.
Comments: 1981 edition still available.
Authors: Walter H. MacGinitie and Ruth K. MacGinitie.
Publisher: Nelson Canada [Canada].
a) LEVEL PRE.
Population: Grades K.7–1.2.
Scores: Total score only.
Price Data: $40.95 per test booklets.
Time: (90) minutes
b) LEVEL R.
Population: Grades 1.0–1.9.
Scores: Total score only.
Time: (70) minutes.
c) LEVEL A.
Population: Grades 1.3–1.9.
Scores, 3: Vocabulary, Comprehension, Total.
Price Data: $3.50 per decoding skills analysis forms.
Time: 55 minutes.
d) LEVEL B.
Population: Grade 2.
Scores, 3: Same as for *c* above.
Price Data: Same as for *c* above.
Time: Same as for *c* above.

e) LEVEL C.
Population: Grade 3.
Scores, 3: Same as for *c* above.
Time: Same as for *c* above.
f) LEVEL D 4.
Population: Grade 4.
Scores, 3: Same as for *c* above.
Price Data: $16.45 per 35 hand-scorable answer sheets; $35.90 per 100 machine-scorable answer sheets; $255 per 250 NCS answer sheets; $9.45 per set of scoring stencils.
Time: Same as for *c* above.
g) LEVEL D 5/6.
Population: Grades 5–6.
Scores, 3: same as for *c* above.
Price Data: same as for *f* above.
h) LEVEL E.
Population: Grades 7–9.
Scores, 3: Same as for *c* above.
Price Data: Same as for *f* above.
Time: Same as for *c* above.
i) LEVEL F.
Population: Grades 10–12.
Scores, 3: Same as for *c* above.
Price Data: Same as for *f* above.
Time: Same as for *c* above.
Cross References: For reviews by Mariam Jean Dreher and Susanna W. Pflaum of an earlier edition, see 9:431.

TEST REFERENCES

1. Brailsford, A., Snart, F., & Das, J. P. (1984). Strategy training and reading comprehension. *Journal of Learning Disabilities, 17,* 287-290.
2. Braun, C., & Gordon, C. J. (1984). Writing instruction as a meta-textual aid to story schema applications. *National Reading Conference Yearbook, 33,* 61-65.
3. Carey, S. T., & Cummins, J. (1984). Communication skills in immersion programs. *The Alberta Journal of Educational Research, 30,* 270-283.
4. Gordon, C. J., & Braun, C. (1986). Mental processes in reading and writing: A critical look at self-reports as supportive data. *The Journal of Educational Research, 79,* 292-301.
5. Fagan, W. T. (1987). A comparison of the reading processes of adult illiterates and four groups of school age readers. *The Alberta Journal of Educational Research, 33,* 123-136.
6. Gallivan, J. (1988). Concept knowledge as a predictor of first- and fourth-grade reading achievement. *Perceptual and Motor Skills, 66*(2), 407-410.

[1022]
Gates-MacGinitie Reading Tests, Third Edition.
Purpose: Measures reading achievement.
Population: Grades K.6–12.
Publication Dates: 1926–89.
Administration: Group.
Levels: 9; 2 forms: K, L.
Price Data, 1990: $1.95 per scoring booklet for any one level; $9 per 35 class summary sheets; $9 per technical report ('89, 92 pages); $1.95 per administrator's summary; $66 per score conversion software package.
Authors: Walter H. MacGinitie and Ruth K. Mac-Ginitie.
Publisher: The Riverside Publishing Co.

a) LEVEL PRE.
Population: Grades K.6–1.2.
Scores, 5: Literacy Concepts, Reading Instruction Relational Concepts, Oral Language Concepts, Letters and Letter-Sound Correspondences, Total.
Price Data, 1990: $51 per 35 MRC machine-scorable test booklets (includes administration directions and machine-scoring materials); $60 per 35 NCS machine-scorable test booklets (includes administration directions); $39 per 35 hand-scored test booklets (includes administration directions, scoring key, class summary sheet); $4.95 per administration directions ('89, 75 pages); $6 per manual for scoring and interpretation ('89, 41 pages).
Time: (85–105) minutes.
b) LEVEL R.
Population: Grades 1.0–1.9.
Scores, 5: Initial Consonants, Final Consonants, Vowels, Use of Context, Total.
Price Data, 1990: $48 per 35 MRC machine-scorable test booklets (includes same materials as Level PRE above); $56.25 per 35 NCS machine-scorable test booklets (includes same materials as Level PRE above); $34.50 per 35 hand-scored test booklets (includes same materials as Level PRE above); $3.99 per directions for administration ('89, 58 pages); $6 per manual for scoring and interpretation ('89, 45 pages).
Time: (55–70) minutes.
c) LEVEL 1.
Population: Grades 1.3–1.9.
Scores, 3: Vocabulary, Comprehension, Total.
Price Data, 1990: $48 per 35 MRC machine-scorable test booklets (includes same materials as Level PRE above); $56.25 per 35 NCS machine-scorable test booklets (includes same materials as Level PRE above); $34.50 per 35 hand-scored test booklets (includes same materials as Level PRE above, plus a decoding skills analysis); $3.99 per directions for administration, Levels 1 and 2; $6 per manual for scoring and interpretation, Levels 1 and 2.
Time: 55(60) minutes.
d) LEVEL 2.
Population: Grade 2.
Scores, 3: Same as Level 1 above.
Price Data, 1990: Same as Level 1 above.
Time: Same as Level 1 above.
e) LEVEL 3.
Population: Grade 3.
Scores, 3: Same as Level 1 above.
Price Data, 1990: Same as Level R above.
Time: Same as Level 1 above.
f) LEVEL 4.
Population: Grade 4.
Scores, 3: Same as Level 1 above.
Price Data, 1990: $34.95 per 35 reusable test booklets; $33 per 100 MRC answer sheets; $21 per 35 self-scorable answer sheets; $117 per 250 self-scorable answer sheets; $99 per 250 NCS 7010

answer sheets; $9 per MRC scoring templates; $3.99 per directions for administration; $6 per manual for scoring and interpretation.

Time: Same as Level 1 above.

g) LEVEL 5/6.

Population: Grades 5–6.

Scores, 3: Same as Level 1 above.

Price Data, 1990: Same as Level 4 above.

Time: Same as Level 1 above.

h) LEVEL 7/9.

Population: Grades 7–9.

Scores, 3: Same as Level 1 above.

Price Data, 1990: Same as Level 4 above.

Time: Same as Level 1 above.

i) LEVEL 10/12.

Population: Grades 10–12.

Scores, 3: Same as Level 1 above.

Price Data, 1990: Same as Level 4 above.

Time: Same as Level 1 above.

Cross References: For a review by Mark E. Swerdlik, see 11:146 (78 references); for reviews by Robert Calfee and William H. Rupley of an earlier edition, see 9:430 (15 references); see also T3:932 (77 references) and 8:726A (34 references); for reviews by Carolyn L. Burke and Byron H. Van Roekel and an excerpted review by William R. Powell of an earlier edition, see 7:689.

TEST REFERENCES

1. Ledger, G. W. (1985). Pictograph reading; metacognition and deliberate strategic control. *National Reading Conference Yearbook, 34,* 219-226.
2. Kamhi, A. G., Catts, H. W., Mauer, D., Apel, K., & Gentry, B. (1988). Phonological and spatial processing abilities in language- and reading-impaired children. *Journal of Speech and Hearing Disorders, 53,* 316-327.
3. Searls, E. F., & Neville, D. D. (1988). An exploratory review of sentence-combining research related to reading. *Journal of Research and Development in Education, 21*(3) 1-15.
4. Hagerty, P. J., Hiebert, E. H., & Owens, M. K. (1989). Students' comprehension, writing, and perceptions in two approaches to literacy instruction. *Yearbook of the National Reading Conference, 38,* 453-459.
5. Hanson, V. L., & McGarr, N. S. (1989). Rhyme generation by deaf adults. *Journal of Speech and Hearing Research, 32,* 2-11.
6. Pikulski, J. J., & Webb-Tobin, A. (1989). Factors associated with long-term reading achievement of early readers. *Yearbook of the National Reading Conference, 38,* 123-133.
7. Barnhart, J. E. (1990). Differences in story retelling behaviors and their relation to reading comprehension in second graders. *Yearbook of the National Reading Conference, 39,* 257-266.
8. Glosser, G., & Friedman, R. B. (1990). The continuum of deep/phonological alexia. *Cortex, 26,* 343-359.
9. Kamhi, A. G., Catts, H. W., & Mauer, D. (1990). Explaining speech production deficits in poor readers. *Journal of Learning Disabilities, 23,* 633-636.
10. Hughes, J. R., Zagar, R., Sylvies, R. B., Arbit, J., Busch, K. G., & Bowers, N. D. (1991). Medical, family, and scholastic conditions in urban delinquents. *Journal of Clinical Psychology, 47,* 448-463.
11. Fuchs, L. S., & Fuchs, D. (1992). Identifying a measure for monitoring student reading progress. *School Psychology Review, 21*(1), 45-58.
12. Freeman, J. G. (1993). Two factors contributing to elementary school teachers' predictions of students' scores on the Gates-MacGinitie Reading Test, Level D. *Perceptual and Motor Skills, 76,* 536-538.
13. Raju, N. S., Drasgow, F., & Slinde, J. A. (1993). An empirical comparison of the area methods, Lord's chi-square test, Mantel-Haenszel technique for assessing differential item functioning. *Educational and Psychological Measurement, 53,* 301-314.

Gates-McKillop-Horowitz Reading Diagnostic Test, Second Edition.

Purpose: "Assess the strengths and weaknesses in reading and related areas of a particular child."

Population: Grades 1–6.

Publication Dates: 1962–81.

Scores, 23: Omissions, Additions, Repetitions, Mispronunciations (Directional Errors, Wrong Beginning, Wrong Middle, Wrong Ending, Wrong in Several Parts, Accent Errors, Total), Reading Sentences, Words-Flash, Words-Untimed, Word-Attack (Syllabication, Recognizing and Blending Common Word Parts, Reading Words, Giving Letter Sounds, Naming Capital Letters, Naming Lower-Case Letters), Vowels, Auditory (Blending, Discrimination), Spelling.

Administration: Individual.

Price Data, 1988: $2.50 per test materials; $7.50 per 30 pupil record booklets; $1 per manual of directions ('81, 16 pages); $3.50 per manual of directions kit (includes test materials, 1 pupil record booklet, manual of directions).

Time: Administration time not reported.

Comments: Revision of Gates-McKillop Reading Diagnostic Tests.

Authors: Arthur I. Gates, Anne S. McKillop, and Elizabeth Cliff Horowitz.

Publisher: Teachers College Press.

Cross References: For reviews by Priscilla A. Drum and P. David Pearson and Patricia Herman, see 9:432 (2 references); for a review by Harry Singer of an earlier edition, see 8:759 (8 references); see also T2:1629 (11 references); for reviews by N. Dale Bryant and Gabriel M. Della-Piana, see 6:824 (2 references); for a review by George D. Spache of the earlier edition, see 5:662; for a review by T. L. Torgerson, see 3:510 (3 references).

TEST REFERENCES

1. Hardman, P. K. (1984). The training of psycho-educational technicians (para-professionals) to administer a screening battery which delineates dyslexia and hyperkinesis. *Journal of Learning Disabilities, 17,* 453-456.
2. Ludlow, C. L., Rosenberg, J., Fair, C., Buck, D., Schesselman, S., & Salazar, A. (1986). Brain lesions associated with nonfluent aphasia fifteen years following penetrating head injury. *Brain, 109,* 55-79.
3. Lovett, M. W. (1987). A developmental approach to reading disability: Accuracy and speed criteria of normal and deficient reading skill. *Child Development, 58,* 234-260.

The Geist Picture Interest Inventory.

Purpose: Designed to "assess quantitatively eleven male and twelve female general interest areas and identify motivating forces behind occupational choice."

Population: Grades 8–16 and adults.

Publication Dates: 1959–71.

Acronym: GPII.

Scores: 18 (males) or 19 (females) scores: 11 or 12 Interest scores (Persuasive, Clerical, Mechanical, Musical, Scientific, Outdoor, Literary, Computa-

tional, Artistic, Social Service, Dramatic, Personal Service—females only), and 7 Motivation scores (Family, Prestige, Financial, Intrinsic and Personality, Environmental, Past Experience, Could Not Say).
Administration: Group or individual.
Forms, 2: M (male), F (female).
Price Data, 1993: $90 per kit including 10 tests of each form (male or female), manual ('71, 42 pages plus tests and motivation questionnaires), and 10 motivation questionnaires; $32.50 per 20 tests of male form; $30 per 20 tests of female form; $52 per manual; $13.50 per 20 motivation questionnaires of male form; $10.50 per 20 motivation questionnaires of female form.
Foreign Language Edition: Spanish edition available (male form only).
Time: (40–65) minutes.
Author: Harold Geist.
Publisher: Western Psychological Services.
Cross References: See T2:2180 (18 references); for reviews by Milton E. Hahn and Benjamin Shimberg, and an excerpted review by David V. Tiedeman, see 6:1054 (12 references).

[1025]

General Chemistry Test: National Achievement Tests.
Purpose: Designed to measure students' knowledge in three areas of general chemistry.
Population: Grades 10–16.
Publication Dates: 1958–59.
Scores, 4: Uses-Processes-Results, Formulae and Valence, Miscellaneous Facts, Total.
Administration: Group.
Manual: No manual.
Price Data: Available from publisher.
Time: 40(45) minutes.
Authors: Lester D. Crow and Roy S. Cook.
Publisher: Psychometric Affiliates.
Cross References: For a review by J. A. Campbell, see 6:918.

TEST REFERENCES

1. Costello, B. R. (1988). Examining the career interests of tenth grade students at Langwarrin post primary school, Australia. *College Student Journal, 22*, 185-191.

[1026]

General Clerical Ability Test: ETSA Test 3A.
Purpose: "Measure the general skills required of clerks in routine office work."
Population: Job applicants.
Publication Dates: 1960–84.
Scores: Total score only.
Administration: Group or individual.
Price Data, 1993: $15 per 10 tests and scoring key.
Time: 30(35) minutes.
Author: Psychological Services Bureau.
Publisher: Educators'/Employers' Tests and Services Associates.
Cross References: For additional information, see

9:399; for reviews of an earlier version of the ETSA Tests by Marvin D. Dunnette and Raymond A. Katzell, see 6:1025.

[1027]

General Clerical Test.
Purpose: Developed to assess clerical speed and accuracy, numerical skills, and language-related skills.
Population: Clerical applicants and workers.
Publication Dates: 1972–88.
Acronym: GCT.
Scores, 4: Clerical, Numerical, Verbal, Total.
Administration: Group.
Price Data, 1994: $96 per 25 Clerical/Numerical/Verbal test booklets; $62 per 25 Clerical/Numerical test booklets; $62 per 25 Verbal test booklets; $350 per 100 Clerical/Numerical/Verbal test booklets; $220 per 100 Clerical/Numerical test booklets; $220 per 100 Verbal only test booklets; $30 per set of handscoring keys; $30 per manual ('88, 68 pages); $32 per examination kit.
Time: 46(51) minutes.
Author: The Psychological Corporation.
Publisher: The Psychological Corporation.

[1028]

General Health Questionnaire.
Purpose: Designed to screen for nonpsychotic psychiatric disorders.
Population: Adolescents to adults.
Publication Dates: 1969–88.
Scores: Total scores only for GHQ-60 and GHQ-30; Total and scale scores for GHQ-28: Somatic Symptoms, Anxiety/Insomnia, Social Dysfunction, Severe Depression.
Administration: Group.
Forms, 3: GHQ-60, GHQ-30 (short form), GHQ-28 (research form).
Price Data, 1992: £7.50 per 25 GHQ-28 or GHQ-30 questionnaires (select form); £11.25 per 25 GHQ-60 questionnaires; £34.50 per user's guide.
Time: [3–8] minutes.
Comments: Self-administered.
Authors: David Goldberg and Paul Williams (user's guide).
Publisher: NFER-Nelson Publishing Co., Ltd. [England].
Cross References: For a review by John D. Black, see 9:434 (50 references); see also T3:941 (34 references) and 8:565 (15 references).

TEST REFERENCES

1. Brodaty, H., & Andrews, G. (1983). Brief psychotherapy in family practice: A controlled prospective intervention trial. *British Journal of Psychiatry, 143*, 11-19.
2. Cooper, P. J., & Fairburn, C. G. (1983). Binge-eating and self-induced vomiting in the community: A preliminary study. *British Journal of Psychiatry, 142*, 139-144.
3. Gordon, T., & Breakey, W. R. (1983). A comparison of the outcomes of short- and standard-stay patients at one-year follow-up. *Hospital and Community Psychiatry, 34*, 1054-1056.
4. Henderson, A. S., & Moran, P. A. P. (1983). Social relationships

during the onset and remission of neurotic symptoms: A prospective community study. *British Journal of Psychiatry, 143*, 467-472.

5. Hobbs, P., Ballinger, C. B., & Smith, A. H. W. (1983). Factor analysis and validation of the general health questionnaire in women: A general practice survey. *British Journal of Psychiatry, 142*, 257-264.

6. Hughes, J. E., Barraclough, B. M., Hamblin, L. G., & White, J. E. (1983). Psychiatric symptoms in dermatology patients. *British Journal of Psychiatry, 143*, 51-54.

7. Jackson, P. R., Stafford, E. M., Banks, M. H., & Warr, P. B. (1983). Unemployment and psychological distress in young people: The moderating role of employment commitment. *Journal of Applied Psychology, 525-535.*

8. Jackson, S. E. (1983). Participation in decision making as a strategy for reducing job-related strain. *Journal of Applied Psychology, 68*, 3-19.

9. Kemp, N. J., & Mercer, A. (1983). Unemployment, disability and rehabilitation centres (sic) and their effects on mental health. *Journal of Occupational Psychology, 56*, 37-48.

10. Kemp, N. J., Wall, T. D., Clegg, C. W., & Cordery, J. L. (1983). Autonomous work groups in a greenfield site: A comparative study. *Journal of Occupational Psychology, 56*, 271-288.

11. Kennedy, S., Thompson, R., Stancer, H. C., Roy, A., & Persad, E. (1983). Life events precipitating mania. *British Journal of Psychiatry, 142*, 398-403.

12. Tarrier, N., Maguire, P., & Kincey, J. (1983). Locus of control and cognitive behavior therapy with mastectomy patients: A pilot study. *British Journal of Medical Psychology, 56*, 265-270.

13. Byrne, D. G. (1984). Personal assessments of life-event stress and the near future onset of psychological symptoms. *British Journal of Medical Psychology, 57*, 241-248.

14. Byrne, P. (1984). Psychiatric morbidity in a gynaecology clinic: An epidemiological survey. *British Journal of Psychiatry, 144*, 28-34.

15. Cairns, E., & Wilson, R. (1984). The impact of political violence on mild psychiatric morbidity in Northern Ireland. *British Journal of Psychiatry, 145*, 631-635.

16. Carter, J. A., & Duncan, P. A. (1984). Binge-eating and vomiting: A survey of a high school population. *Psychology in the Schools, 21*, 198-203.

17. Catalan, J., Gath, D., Bond, A., & Martin, P. (1984). The effects of non-prescribing on anxiolytics in general practice: II. Factors associated with outcome. *British Journal of Psychiatry, 144*, 603-610.

18. Catalan, J., Gath, D., Edmonds, G., & Ennis, J. (1984). The effects of non-prescribing of anxiolytics in general practice: I. Controlled evaluation of psychiatric and social outcome. *British Journal of Psychiatry, 144*, 593-602.

19. D'Arcy, C., & Siddique, C. M. (1984). Psychological distress among Canadian adolescents. *Psychological Medicine, 14*, 615-628.

20. Gibbons, J. S., Horn, S. H., Powell, J. M., & Gibbons, J. L. (1984). Schizophrenic patients and their families: A survey in a psychiatric service based on a DGH unit. *British Journal of Psychiatry, 144*, 70-77.

21. Gilleard, C. J., Belford, H., Gilleard, E., Whittick, J. E., & Gledhill, K. (1984). Emotional distress amongst the supporters of the elderly mentally infirm. *British Journal of Psychiatry, 145*, 172-177.

22. Gilleard, C. J., Gilleard, E., & Whittick, J. E. (1984). Impact of psychogeriatric day hospital care on the patient's family. *British Journal of Psychiatry, 145*, 487-492.

23. Hobbs, P., Ballinger, C. B., Greenwood, C., Martin, B., & McClure, A. (1984). Factor analysis and validation of the General Health Questionnaire in men: A general practice survey. *British Journal of Psychiatry, 144*, 270-275.

24. Jackson, P. R., & Warr, P. B. (1984). Unemployment and psychological ill-health: The moderating role of duration and age. *Psychological Medicine, 14*, 605-614.

25. Kumar, R., & Robson, K. M. (1984). A prospective study of emotional disorders in childbearing women. *British Journal of Psychiatry, 144*, 35-47.

26. Livingston, M., & Livingston, H. (1984). Emotional distress in nurses at work. *British Journal of Medical Psychology, 57*, 291-294.

27. Tarrier, N., & Barrowclough, C. (1984). Psychophysiological assessment of expressed emotion in schizophrenia: A case example. *British Journal of Psychiatry, 145*, 197-203.

28. Tarrier, N., & Maguire, P. (1984). Treatment of psychological distress following mastectomy: An initial report. *Behaviour Research and Therapy, 22*, 81-84.

29. Waring, E. M., & Patton, D. (1984). Marital intimacy and depression. *British Journal of Psychiatry, 145*, 641-644.

30. Brugha, T. S., & Conroy, R. (1985). Categories of depression: Reported life events in a controlled design. *British Journal of Psychiatry, 147*, 641-646.

31. Chan, D. W. (1985). The Chineses version of the General Health Questionnaire: Does language make a difference? *Psychological Medicine, 15*, 147-155.

32. Cheng, T. (1985). A pilot study of mental disorders in Taiwan. *Psychological Medicine, 15*, 195-203.

33. Deighton, C. M., & Nicol, A. R. (1985). Abnormal illness behaviour in young women in a primary care setting: Is Briquet's syndrome a useful category? *Psychological Medicine, 15*, 515-520.

34. Ennis, J., Barnes, R. A., & Kennedy, S. (1985). The dexamethasone suppression test and suicidal patients. *British Journal of Psychiatry, 147*, 419-423.

35. Fitzpatrick, R., Ikkos, G., & Frost, D. (1985). The recognition of psychological disturbance in a sexually transmitted diseases clinic. *International Journal of Social Psychiatry, 31*, 306-312.

36. Goodchild, M. E., & Duncan-Jones, P. (1985). Chronicity and the General Health Questionnaire. *British Journal of Psychiatry, 146*, 55-61.

37. Kemery, E. R., Bedeian, A. G., Mossholder, K. W., & Touliatos, J. (1985). Outcomes of role stress: A multisample constructive replication. *Academy of Management Journal, 28*, 363-375.

38. Layton, C. (1985). The relationship between externality and general, nonpsychotic psychiatric morbidity in normal males. *Perceptual and Motor Skills, 61*, 746.

39. Livingston, M. G., Brooks, D. N., & Bond, M. R. (1985). Patient outcome in the year following severe head injury and relatives' psychiatric and social functioning. *Journal of Neurology, Neurosurgery, and Psychiatry, 48*, 876-881.

40. Livingston, M. G., Brooks, D. N., & Bond, M. R. (1985). Three months after severe head injury: Psychiatric and social impact on relatives. *Journal of Neurology, Neurosurgery, and Psychiatry, 48*, 870-875.

41. Mari, J. J., & Williams, P. (1985). A comparison of the validity of two psychiatric screening questionnaires (GHQ-12 and SRQ-20) in Brazil, using Relative Operating Characteristic (ROC) analysis. *Psychological Medicine, 15*, 651-659.

42. Melville, D. I., Hope, D., Bennison, D., & Barraclough, B. (1985). Depression among men made involuntarily redundant. *Psychological Medicine, 15*, 789-793.

43. MicKalide, A. D., & Andersen, A. E. (1985). Subgroups of anorexia nervosa and bulimia: Validity and utility. *Journal of Psychiatric Research, 19*, 121-128.

44. Power, K. G., Cooke, D. J., & Brooks, D. N. (1985). Life stress, medical lethality, and suicidal intent. *British Journal of Psychiatry, 147*, 655-659.

45. Siciliani, O., Bellantuono, C., Williams, P., & Tansella, M. (1985). Self-reported use of psychotropic drugs and alcohol abuse in South-Verona. *Psychological Medicine, 15*, 821-826.

46. Sireling, L. I., Paykel, E. S., Freeling, P., Rao, B. M., & Patel, S. P. (1985). Depression in general practice: Case thresholds and diagnosis. *British Journal of Psychiatry, 147*, 113-119.

47. Stanley, B., & Gibson, A. J. (1985). The prevalence of chronic psychiatric morbidity: A community sample. *British Journal of Psychiatry, 146*, 372-376.

48. Stansfeld, S. A., Clark, C. R., Jenkins, L. M., & Tarnpolsky, A. (1985). Sensitivity to noise in a community sample: I. Measurement of psychiatric disorder and personality. *Psychological Medicine, 15*, 243-254.

49. Ullah, P., Banks, M., & Warr, P. (1985). Social support, social pressures and psychological distress during unemployment. *Psychological Medicine, 15*, 283-295.

50. VanDenAkker, O., & Steptoe, A. (1985). The pattern and prevalence of symptoms during the menstrual cycle. *British Journal of Psychiatry, 147*, 164-169.

51. Warr, P., & Jackson, P. (1985). Factors influencing the psychological impact of prolonged unemployment and of re-employment. *Psychological Medicine, 15*, 795-807.

52. Vázquez-Barquero, J. L., Acero, J. A. P., & Martin, C. P. (1985). The psychiatric correlates of coronary pathology: Validity of the GHQ-60 as a screening instrument. *Psychological Medicine, 15*, 589-596.

53. Warr, P., Banks, M., & Ullah, P. (1985). The experience of unemployment among black and white urban teenagers. *British Journal of Psychology, 75*, 75-87.

54. Windholz, M. J., Marmar, C. R., & Horowitz, M. J. (1985). A review of the research on conjugal bereavement: Impact on health and efficacy of intervention. *Comprehensive Psychiatry, 26*, 433-447.

55. Wolfe, D. A., Jaffe, P., Wilson, S. K., & Zak, L. (1985). Children of battered women: The relation of child behavior to family violence and maternal stress. *Journal of Consulting and Clinical Psychology, 53*, 657-665.

56. Bridges, K. W., & Goldberg, D. P. (1986). The validation of the GHQ-28 and the use of the MMSE in neurological in-patients. *British Journal of Psychiatry, 148*, 548-553.

57. Cheng, T., & Williams, P. (1986). The design and development of a screening questionnaire (CHQ) for use in community studies of mental disorders in Taiwan. *Psychological Medicine, 16*, 415-422.

58. deJesus Mari, J., & Williams, P. (1986). A validity study of a

psychiatric screening questionnaire (SRQ-20) in primary care in the city of Sao Paulo. *British Journal of Psychiatry, 148,* 23-26.

59. Donovan, A., Oddy, M., Pardoe, R., & Ades, A. (1986). Employment status and psychological well-being: A longitudinal study of 16-year-old school leavers. *Journal of Child Psychology and Psychiatry and Allied Disciplines, 27,* 65-76.

60. Duncan-Jones, P., Grayson, D. A., & Moran, P. A. P. (1986). The utility of latent trait models in psychiatric epidemiology. *Psychological Medicine, 16,* 391-405.

61. Enos, D. M., & Handal, P. J. (1986). The relation of parental marital status and perceived family conflict to adjustment in white adolescents. *Journal of Consulting and Clinical Psychology, 54,* 820-824.

62. Fairley, M., Langeluddecke, P., & Tennant, C. (1986). Psychological and physical morbidity in the aftermath of a cyclone. *Psychological Medicine, 16,* 671-676.

63. Firth, J., & Shapiro, D. A. (1986). An evaluation of psychotherapy for job-related distress. *Journal of Occupational Psychology, 59,* 111-119.

64. Garralda, M. E., & Bailey, D. (1986). Children with psychiatric disorders in primary care. *Journal of Child Psychology and Psychiatry and Allied Disciplines, 27,* 611-624.

65. Jandorf, L., Deblinger, E., Neale, J. M., & Stone, A. A. (1986). Daily versus major life events as predictors of symptom frequency: A replication study. *The Journal of General Psychology, 113,* 205-218.

66. Jenkins, R. (1986). Sex differences in alcohol consumption and its associate mobidity in young civil servants. *British Journal of Addiction, 81,* 525-535.

67. Layton, C. (1986). Employment, unemployment, and response to the General Health Questionnaire. *Psychological Reports, 58,* 807-810.

68. Layton, C. (1986). Note on test-retest characteristics of the General Health Questionnaire. *Perceptual and Motor Skills, 62,* 221-222.

69. Layton, C., & Rust, J. (1986). The factor structure of the 60 item General Health Questionnaire. *Social Behavior and Personality, 14,* 123-131.

70. Leaf, R. C., Gross, P. H., Todres, A. K., Marcus, S., & Bradford, B. (1986). Placebo-like effects of education about Rational-Emotive Therapy. *Psychological Reports, 58,* 351-370.

71. Lloyd, G., Chick, J., Crombie, E., & Anderson, S. (1986). Problem drinkers in medical wards: Consumption patterns and disabilities in newly identified male cases. *British Journal of Addiction, 81,* 789-795.

72. Lobo, A., Pérez-Encheverría, M. J., & Artal, J. (1986). Validity of the scale version of the General Health Questionnaire (GHQ-28) in a Spanish population. *Psychological Medicine, 16,* 135-140.

73. Rabins, P. V., Brooks, B. R., O'Donnell, P., Pearlson, G. D., Moberg, P., Jubelt, B., Coyle, P., Dalos, N., & Folstein, M. F. (1986). Structural brain correlates of emotional disorder in multiple sclerosis. *Brain, 109,* 585-597.

74. Sanderman, R. (1986). Causal attributions, real life-events and personality characteristics: A preliminary study. *Psychological Reports, 59,* 795-801.

75. Strauss, M. E., & Brandt, J. (1986). Attempt at preclinical identification of Huntington's Disease using the WAIS. *Journal of Clinical and Experimental Neuropsychology, 8,* 210-218.

76. Wade, D. T., Hewer, R. L., David, R. M., & Enderby, P. M. (1986). Aphasia after stroke: Natural history and associated deficits. *Journal of Neurology, Neurosurgery, and Psychiatry, 49,* 11-16.

77. Wall, T. D., Kemp, N. J., Jackson, P. R., & Clegg, C. W. (1986). Outcomes of autonomous workgroups: A long-term field experiment. *Academy of Management Journal, 29,* 280-304.

78. Wolfe, D. A., Zak, L., Wilson, S., & Jaffe, P. (1986). Child witnesses to violence between parents: Critical issues in behavioral and social adjustment. *Journal of Abnormal Child Psychology, 14,* 95-104.

79. Archer, J., & Rhodes, V. (1987). Bereavement and reactions to job loss: A comparative review. *British Journal of Social Psychology, 26,* 211-224.

80. Bell, J., & Garthwaite, P. H. (1987). The psychological effects of service in British Antarctica: A study using the General Health Questionnaire. *The British Journal of Psyychiatry, 150,* 213-218.

81. Eagles, J. M., Beattie, J. A. G., Blackwood, G. W., Restall, D. B., & Ashcroft, G. W. (1987). The mental health of elderly couples: I. The effects of a cognitively impaired spouse. *The British Journal of Psychiatry, 150,* 299-303.

82. Eagles, J. M., Craig, A., Rawlinson, F., Restall, D. B., Beattie, J. A. G., & Besson, J. A. O. (1987). The psychological well-being of supporters of the demented elderly. *The British Journal of Psychiatry, 150,* 293-298.

83. Eagles, J. M., Walker, L. G., Blackwood, G. W., Beattie, J. A. G., & Restall, D. B. (1987). The mental health of elderly couples II. Concordance for psychiatric morbidity in spouses. *The British Journal of Psychiatry, 150,* 303-308.

84. Elsass, L., & Kinsella, G. (1987). Social interaction following severe closed head injury. *Psychological Medicine, 17,* 67-78.

85. Gath, D., Osborn, M., Bungay, G., Iles, S., Day, A., Bond, A., & Passingham, C. (1987). Psychiatric disorder and gynaecological symptoms in middle aged women: A community survey. *British Medical Journal, 294,* 213-218.

86. General health queries help to determine elderly's mental status. (1987). *Geriatrics, 42*(4), 32.

87. Gilleard, C. J. (1987). Influence of emotional distress among supporters on the outcome of psychogeriatric daycare. *The British Journal of Psychiatry, 150,* 219-223.

88. Goldberg, D. P., Bridges, K., Duncan-Jones, P., & Grayson, D. (1987). Dimensions of neuroses seen in primary-care settings. *Psychological Medicine, 17,* 461-470.

89. Hawton, K., McKeown, S., Day, A., Martin, P., O'Connor, M., & Yule, J. (1987). Evaluation of out-patient counselling compared with general practitioner care following overdoses. *Psychological Medicine, 17,* 751-761.

90. Hesketh, B., Shouksmith, G., & Kang, J. (1987). A case study and balance sheet approach to unemployment. *Journal of Counseling and Development, 66,* 175-179.

91. Hodiamont, P., Peer, N., & Syben, N. (1987). Epidemiological aspects of psychiatric disorder in a Dutch health area. *Psychological Medicine, 17,* 495-505.

92. Lindsay, W. R., Gamsu, C. V., McLaughlin, E., Hood, E. M., & Espie, C. A. (1987). A controlled trial of treatments for generalized anxiety. *British Journal of Clinical Psychology, 26,* 3-15.

93. McEwan, K. L., Costello, C. G., & Taylor, P. J. (1987). Adjustment to infertility. *Journal of Abnormal Psychology, 96,* 108-116.

94. Murphy, J. M., Berwick, D. M., Weinstein, M. C., Borus, J. F., Budman, S. H., & Klerman, G. L. (1987). Performance of screening and diagnostic tests: Application of receiver operating characteristic analysis. *Archives of General Psychiatry, 44,* 550-555.

95. Surtees, P. G. (1987). Psychiatric disorder in the community and the General Health Questionnaire. *The British Journal of Psychiatry, 150,* 828-835.

96. Vázquez-Barquero, J. L., Díez-Manrique, J. F., Peña, C., Aldama, J., Rodríguez, C. S., Arango, J. M., & Mirapeix, C. (1987). A community mental health survey in Cantabria: A general description of morbidity. *Psychological Medicine, 17,* 227-241.

97. VonKorff, M., Shapiro, S., Burke, J. D., Teitlebaum, M., Skinner, E. A., German, P., Turner, R. W., Klein, L., & Burns, B. (1987). Anxiety and depression in a primary care clinic: Comparisons of Diagnostic Interview Schedule, General Health Questionnaire, and practitioner assessments. *Archives of General Psychiatry, 44,* 152-156.

98. Wilkinson, G., Borsey, D. Q., Leslie, P., Newton, R. W., Lind, C., & Ballinger, C. B. (1987). Psychiatric disorder in patients with insulin-dependent diabetes mellitus attending a general hospital clinic: (i) two-stage screening and (ii) detection by physicians. *Psychological Medicine, 17,* 515-517.

99. Alder, E., & Bancroft, J. (1988). The relationship between breast feeding persistence, sexuality and mood in postpartum women. *Psychological Medicine, 18,* 389-396.

100. Bond, M. J., & Feather, N. T. (1988). Some correlates of structure and purpose in the use of time. *Journal of Personality and Social Psychology, 55,* 321-329.

101. Huppert, F. A., Gore, M., & Elliott, B. J. (1988). The value of an improved scoring system (CGHQ) for the General Health Questionnaire in a representative community sample. *Psychological Medicine, 18,* 1001-1006.

102. Johnson-Sabine, E., Wood, K., Patton, G., Mann, A., & Wakeling, A. (1988). Abnormal eating attitudes in London schoolgirls—a prospective epidemiological study: Factors associated with abnormal response on screening questionnaires. *Psychological Medicine, 18,* 615-622.

103. Kinsella, G., Moran, C., Ford, B., & Ponsford, J. (1988). Emotional disorder and its assessment within the severe head injured population. *Psychological Medicine, 18,* 57-63.

104. Lewis, S. N. C., & Cooper, C. L. (1988). The transition to parenthood in dual-earner couples. *Psychological Medicine, 18,* 477-486.

105. Logsdail, S. J., Callanan, M. M., & Ron, M. A. (1988). Psychiatric morbidity in patients with clinically isolated lesions of the type seen in multiple sclerosis: A clinical and MRI study. *Psychological Medicine, 18,* 355-364.

106. McFarlane, A. C. (1988). Relationship between psychiatric impairment and a natural disaster: The role of distress. *Psychological Medicine, 18,* 129-139.

107. Power, M. J. (1988). The "worst ever" version of the General Health Questionnaire. *Journal of Clinical Psychology, 44,* 215-216.

108. Romans-Clarkson, S. E., Walton, V. A., Herbison, G. P., & Mullen, P. E. (1988). Marriage, motherhood and psychiatric morbidity in New Zealand. *Psychological Medicine, 18,* 983-990.

109. Sharp, D. J. (1988). Validation of the 30-item General Health Questionnaire in early pregnancy. *Psychological Medicine, 18,* 503-507.

110. Sutcliffe, C., & Larner, S. (1988). Counseling carers of the elderly at home: A preliminary study. *British Journal of Clinical Psychology, 27,* 177-178.

111. Vazquez-Barquero, J. L., Williams, P., Díez-Manrique, J. F., Lequerica, J., & Arenal, A. (1988). The factor structure of the GHQ-60 in a community sample. *Psychological Medicine, 18,* 211-218.

112. Whittick, J. E. (1988). Dementia and mental handicap: Emotional distress in careers. *British Journal of Clinical Psychology, 27,* 167-172.

113. Williams, P., & Skuse, D. (1988). Depressive thoughts in general practice attenders. *Psychological Medicine, 18,* 469-475.

114. Andrich, D., & van Schoubroeck, L. (1989). The General Health Questionnaire: A psychometric analysis using latent trait theory. *Psychological Medicine, 19,* 469-485.

115. Cairns, E., Wilson, R., McClelland, R., & Gillespie, A. (1989). Improving the validity of the GHQ30 by rescoring for chronicity: A failure to replicate. *Journal of Clinical Psychology, 45,* 793-798.

116. Chan, D. W. (1989). Dimensionality and adjustment correlates of locus of control among Hong Kong Chinese. *Journal of Personality Assessment, 53,* 145-160.

117. Dening, T. R., & Berrios, G. E. (1989). Wilson's disease: A prospective study of psychopathology in 31 cases. *British Journal of Psychiatry, 155,* 206-213.

118. Huxley, P., Raval, H., Korer, J., & Jacob, C. (1989). Psychiatric morbidity in the clients of social workers: Clinical outcome. *Psychological Medicine, 19,* 189-197.

119. MacKinnon, A. J., Henderson, A. S., Scott, R., & Duncan-Jones, P. (1989). The Parental Bonding Instrument (PBI): An epidemiological study in a general population sample. *Psychological Medicine, 19,* 1023-1034.

120. Ormel, J., Koeler, M. W. J., van den Brink, W., & Giel, R. (1989). Concurrent validity of GHQ-28 and PSE as measures of change. *Psychological Medicine, 19,* 1007-1013.

121. Ron, M. A., & Logsdail, S. J. (1989). Psychiatric morbidity in multiple sclerosis: A clinical and MRI study. *Psychological Medicine, 19,* 887-895.

122. Shek, D. T. L. (1989). Validity of the Chinese version of the General Health Questionnaire. *Journal of Clinical Psychology, 45,* 890-897.

123. Ullah, P., & Brotherton, C. (1989). Sex, social class and ethnic differences in the expectations of unemployment and psychological well-being of secondary school pupils in England. *British Journal of Educational Psychology, 59,* 49-58.

124. Wilmink, F. W., & Snijders, T. A. B. (1989). Polytomous logistic regression analysis of the General Health Questionnaire and the Present State Examination. *Psychological Medicine, 19,* 755-764.

125. Baba, V. V. (1990). Methodological issues in modeling absence: A comparison of least squares and Tobit analyses. *Journal of Applied Psychology, 75(4),* 428-432.

126. Bluen, S. D., Barling, J., & Burns, W. (1990). Predicting sales performance, job satisfaction, and depression by using the achievement strivings and impatience-irritability dimensions of type A behavior. *Journal of Applied Psychology, 75(2),* 212-216.

127. Brandt, J., Celentano, D., Stewart, W., Linet, M., & Folstein, M. F. (1990). Personality and emotional disorder in a community sample of migraine headache sufferers. *American Journal of Psychiatry, 147,* 303-308.

128. Krause, N., Liang, J., & Keith, V. (1990). Personality, social support, and psychological distress in later life. *Psychology and Aging, 5,* 315-326.

129. Parks, K. R. (1990). Coping, negative affectivity, and the work environment: Additive and interactive predictors of mental health. *Journal of Applied Psychology, 75(4),* 399-409.

130. Shek, D. T. L. (1990). Reliability and factorial structure of the Chinese version of the Beck Depression Inventory. *Journal of Clinical Psychology, 46,* 35-43.

131. Wall, T. D., Corbett, J. M., Martin, R., Clegg, C. W., & Jackson, P. R. (1990). Advanced manufacturing technology work design, and performance: A change study. *Journal of Applied Psychology, 75(6),* 691-697.

132. Winefield, H. R., Goldney, R. D., Tiggemann, M., & Winefield, A. H. (1990). Parental rearing behaviors: Stability of reports over time and relation to adult interpersonal skills. *The Journal of Genetic Psychology, 151,* 211-219.

133. Abiodun, O. A., & Ogunremi, O. O. (1991). Psychotropic drug use in medical and surgical wards of a teaching hospital in northern Nigeria. *British Journal of Psychiatry, 159,* 570-572.

134. Bassett, S. S., & Folstein, M. F. (1991). Cognitive impairment and functional disability in the absence of psychiatric diagnosis. *Psychological Medicine, 21,* 77-84.

135. Bell, G., Reinstein, D. Z., Rajiyah, G., & Rosser, R. (1991). Psychiatric screening of admissions to an accident and emergency ward. *British Journal of Psychiatry, 158,* 554-557.

136. Blakely, A. A., Howard, R. C., Sosich, R. M., Murdoch, J. C., Menkes, D. B., & Spears, G. F. S. (1991). Psychiatric symptoms, personality and ways of coping in chronic fatigue syndrome. *Psychological Medicine, 21,* 347-362.

137. Bridges, K., Goldberg, D., Evans, B., & Sharpe, T. (1991). Determinants of somatization in primary care. *Psychological Medicine, 21,* 473-483.

138. Catalan, J., Gath, D. H., Anastasiades, P., Bond, S. A. K., Day, A., & Hall, L. (1991). Evaluation of a brief psychological treatment for emotional disorders in primary care. *Psychological Medicine, 21,* 1013-1018.

139. Christensen, H., & Henderson, A. S. (1991). Is age kinder to the initially more able? A study of eminent scientists and academics. *Psychological Medicine, 21,* 935-946.

140. Clairns, E., McWhirter, L., Barry, R., & Duffy, U. (1991). The development of psychological well-being in late adolescence. *Journal of Child Psychology and Psychiatry, 32,* 635-643.

141. Elliott, B. J., & Huppert, F. A. (1991). In sickness and in health: Associations between physical and mental well-being, employment and parental status in a British nationwide sample of married women. *Psychological Medicine, 21,* 515-524.

142. Feinstein, A., & Dolan, R. (1991). Predictors of post-traumatic stress disorder following physical trauma: An examination of the stressor criterion. *Psychological Medicine, 21,* 85-91.

143. Joseph, S., Brewin, C. R., Yule, W., & Williams, R. (1991). Causal attributions and psychiatric symptoms in survivors of the Herald of Free Enterprise disaster. *British Journal of Psychiatry, 159,* 542-546.

144. Katon, W., & Roy-Byrne, P. P. (1991). Mixed anxiety and depression. *Journal of Abnormal Psychology, 100,* 337-345.

145. Kelly, B., Dunne, M., Raphael, B., Buckham, C., Zournazi, A., Smith, S., & Statham, D. (1991). Relationships between mental adjustment to HIV diagnosis, psychological morbidity and sexual behavior. *British Journal of Clinical Psychology, 30,* 370-372.

146. Leaf, R. C., & Alington, D. E. (1991). Countering perfectionism in research on clinical practice. III: Implications for randomized designs of the presence of uncontrolled interactions and spontaneous changes. *The Journal of Psychology, 125,* 657-669.

147. Miller, P. McC., & Surtees, P. G. (1991). Psychological symptoms and their course in first-year medical students as assessed by the Interval General Health Questionnaire (I-GHQ). *British Journal of Psychiatry, 159,* 199-207.

148. Norman, R. M. G., & Malla, A. K. (1991). Dysphoric mood and symptomatology in schizophrenia. *Psychological Medicine, 21,* 897-903.

149. O'Brien, L. S., & Hughes, S. J. (1991). Symptoms of post-traumatic stress disorder in Falklands veterans five years after the conflict. *British Journal of Psychiatry, 159,* 135-141.

150. Ron, M. A., Callanan, M. M., & Warrington, E. K. (1991). Cognitive abnormalities in multiple sclerosis: A psychometric and MRI study. *Psychological Medicine, 21,* 59-68.

151. Stansfeld, S. A., Gallacher, J. E. J., Sharp, D. S., & Yarnell, J. W. G. (1991). Social factors and minor psychiatric disorder in middle-aged men: A validation study and a population survey. *Psychological Medicine, 21,* 157-167.

152. Stein, A., Gath, D. H., Bucher, J., Bond, A., Day, A., & Cooper, P. J. (1991). The relationship between post-natal depression and mother-child interaction. *British Journal of Psychiatry, 158,* 46-52.

153. Winefield, A. H., Winefield, H. R., Tiggemann, M., & Goldney, R. D. (1991). A longitudinal study of the psychological effects of unemployment and unsatisfactory employment on young adults. *Journal of Applied Psychology, 76(3),* 424-431.

154. Brooker, C., Tarrier, N., Barrowclough, C., Butterworth, A., & Goldberg, D. (1992). Training community psychiatric nurses for psychosocial intervention. *British Journal of Psychiatry, 160,* 836-844.

155. Cushway, D. (1992). Stress in clinical psychology trainees. *British Journal of Clinical Psychology, 31,* 169-179.

156. Joseph, S., Andrews, B., Williams, R., & Yule, W. (1992). Crisis support and psychiatric symptomatology in adult survivors of the Jupiter cruise ship disaster. *British Journal of Clinical Psychology, 31,* 63-73.

157. Kennedy, H. G., & Grubin, D. H. (1992). Patterns of denial in sex offenders. *Psychological Medicine, 22,* 191-196.

158. Lewis, G., Pelosi, A. J., Araya, R., & Dunn, G. (1992). Measuring psychiatric disorder in the community: A standardized assessment for use by lay interviewers. *Psychological Medicine, 22,* 465-486.

159. Martyns-Yellowe, I. S. (1992). The burden of schizophrenia on the family. *British Journal of Psychiatry, 161,* 779-782.

160. McFarlane, A. C., & Papay, P. (1992). Multiple diagnoses in posttraumatic stress disorder in the victims of a natural disaster. *Journal of Nervous and Mental Disease, 180,* 498-504.

161. Meakin, C. J. (1992). Screening for depression in the medically ill: The future of paper and pencil tests. *British Journal of Psychiatry, 160,* 212-216.

162. Moore, E., Ball, R. A., & Kuipers, L. (1992). Expressed emotion in staff working with the long-term adult mentally ill. *British Journal of Psychiatry, 161,* 802-808.

163. O'Driscoll, M. P., Ilgen, D. R., & Hildreth, K. (1992). Time devoted to job and off-job activities, interrole conflict and affective experiences. *Journal of Applied Psychology, 77,* 272-279.

164. Oldridge, M. L., & Hughes, I. C. T. (1992). Psychological well-being in families with a member suffering from schizophrenia. *British Journal of Psychiatry, 161,* 249-251.

165. Terry, D. J. (1992). Stress, coping and coping resources as correlates of adaptation in myocardial infarction patients. *British Journal of Clinical Psychology, 31,* 215-225.

166. The Scottish Schizophrenia Research Group. (1992). The Scottish first episode schizophrenia study: VIII. *British Journal of Psychiatry, 161,* 496-500.

167. Vázquez-Barguero, J. L., Diez-Maurique, J. F., Gaite, L., Garcia, C. I., Artal, J., Roberts, S. E., & Wilkinson, G. (1992). Why people with probable minor psychiatric morbidity consult a doctor. *Psychological Medicine, 22,* 495-502.

168. Williams, H. J., Wagner, H. L., & Calam, R. M. (1992). Eating attitudes in survivors of unwanted sexual experiences. *British Journal of Clinical Psychology, 31,* 203-206.

169. Aderibigbe, Y. A., Goreje, O., & Omigbodun, O. (1993). Postnatal emotional disorders in Nigerian women. *British Journal of Psychiatry, 163,* 645-650.

170. Brodaty, H., Harris, L., Peters, K., Wilhelm, K., Hickie, I., Boyce, P., Mitchell, P., Parker, G., & Eyers, K. (1993). Prognosis of depression in the elderly. *British Journal of Psychiatry, 163,* 589-596.

171. Cox, J. L., Murray, D., & Chapman, G. (1993). A controlled study of the onset, duration and prevalence of postnatal depression. *British Journal of Psychiatry, 163,* 27-31.

172. Craig, T. K. J., Boardman, A. P., Mills, K., Daly-Jones, O., & Drake, H. (1993). The south London somatisation study I: Longitudinal course and the influence of early life experiences. *British Journal of Psychiatry, 163,* 579-588.

173. Dua, J., & Price, I. (1993). Effectiveness of training in negative thought reduction and positive thought increment in reducing thought-produced distress. *Journal of Genetic Psychology, 154,* 97-109.

174. Hickie, I., Hickie, C., Lloyd, A., Silove, D., & Wakefield, D. (1993). Impaired invivo immune responses in patients with melancholia. *British Journal of Psychiatry, 162,* 651-657.

175. Leaf, R. C., DiGiuseppe, R., Mass, R., & Alington, D. E. (1993). Statistical methods for analyses of incomplete clinical service records: Concurrent use of longitudinal and cross-sectional data. *Journal of Consulting and Clinical Psychology, 61,* 495-505.

176. Lovestone, S., & Kumar, R. (1993). Postnatal psychiatric illness: The impact on partners. *British Journal of Psychiatry, 163,* 210-216.

177. Nathawat, S. S., & Mathur, A. (1993). Marital adjustment and subjective well-being in Indian-educated housewives and working women. *The Journal of Psychology, 127,* 353-358.

178. Robertson, M. M., Channon, S., Baker, J., & Flynn, D. (1993). The psychopathology of Gilles de la Tourette's Syndrome. *British Journal of Psychiatry, 162,* 114-117.

179. Shek, D. T. L. (1993). Factor structure of the Chinese version of the General Health Questionnaire (GHQ-30): A confirmatory factor analysis. *Journal of Clinical Psychology, 49,* 678-684.

180. Shek, D. T. L. (1993). The Chinese version of the State-Trait Anxiety Inventory: Its relationship to different measures of psychological well-being. *Journal of Clinical Psychology, 49,* 349-358.

181. Wohlfarth, T. D., VanDenBrink, W., Ormel, J., Koeter, M. W. J., & Oldehinkel, A. J. (1993). The relationship between social dysfunctioning and psychopathology among primary care attenders. *British Journal of Psychiatry, 163,* 37-44.

182. Hatcher, S. (1994). Debt and deliberate self-poisoning. *British Journal of Psychiatry, 164,* 111-114.

183. Mullen, P. E., & Martin, J. (1994). Jealousy: A community study. *British Journal of Psychiatry, 164,* 35-43.

[1029]

General Management In-Basket.

Purpose: "Designed to assess supervisory/managerial skills independent of any particular job classification; may be used for selection and/or career development."

Population: Supervisors and managers.

Publication Dates: 1986–94.

Acronym: GMIB.

Scores, 5: Leadership Style and Practices, Handling Priorities and Sensitive Situations, Managing Conflict, Organizational Practices/Management Control, Total.

Administration: Group.

Forms, 4: Private and public sector forms include Standard Version, Police Versions, Fire Versions, and Engineer Version.

Restricted Distribution: Clients must pay a one-time overhead/sign-up fee of $150–$300.

Price Data, 1993: $75 per candidate for rental/scoring and bar chart; $70 per optional GMIB Feedback Report.

Time: 165 (175) minutes.

Author: Richard C. Joines.

Publisher: Management & Personnel Systems, Inc.

[1030]

General Mental Ability Test: ETSA Test 1A.

Purpose: Measurement of "ability to learn."

Population: Job applicants.

Publication Dates: 1960–84.

Scores: Total score only.

Administration: Group and individual.

Price Data, 1993: $15 per 10 tests and scoring key.

Time: (45–50) minutes.

Author: Psychological Services Bureau, Inc.

Publisher: Educators'/Employers' Tests and Services Associates.

Cross References: See 9:435; see also T3:942 (1 reference); for reviews of an earlier version of the ETSA Tests by Marvin D. Dunnette and Raymond A. Katzell, see 6:1025.

[1031]

General Physics Test: National Achievement Tests.

Purpose: "Constructed to test the student's basic knowledge of Physics and his ability to apply that knowledge."

Population: Grades 10–16.

Publication Dates: 1958–62.

Scores, 3: Uses and Application of Principles, Miscellaneous Facts and Scientists, Total.

Administration: Group.

Manual: No manual.

Price Data: Available from publisher.

Time: 40(45) minutes.

Authors: Lester D. Crow and Roy S. Cook.

Publisher: Psychometric Affiliates.

Cross References: For a review by Theodore G. Phillips, see 6:930.

[1032]

General Science Test.

Purpose: "Designed to measure technical and scientific knowledge."

Population: Matriculants and higher.

Publication Dates: 1955–70.

Acronym: GST.

Scores, 2: Technical and Scientific Knowledge, Technical Reading Comprehension.

Administration: Group.

Price Data: Available from publisher.

Time: 55(65) minutes.
Comments: Revision of Test A/12: Technical and Scientific Knowledge Test and Test A/13: Technical Reading Comprehension.
Author: National Institute for Personnel Research of the Human Sciences Research Council.
Publisher: National Institute for Personnel Research of the Human Sciences Research Council [South Africa].
Cross References: See T2:1784 (1 reference).

[1033]

General Science Test: National Achievement Tests.
Purpose: Designed to measure students' knowledge of general science.
Population: Grades 7–9.
Publication Dates: 1936–50.
Scores, 7: General Concepts, Identifications, Men of Science, Definitions, Uses of Objects, Miscellaneous Facts, Total.
Administration: Group.
Manual: No manual.
Price Data: Available from publisher.
Time: (30–45) minutes.
Authors: Robert K. Speer, Lester D. Crow, and Samuel Smith.
Publisher: Psychometric Affiliates.
Cross References: For a review by Robert M. W. Travers, see 5:712; for reviews by Francis D. Curtis and G. W. Hunter, see 2:1602.

[1034]

The Gesell Child Developmental Age Scale.
Purpose: Designed to determine in which of the 10 Gesell early development periods a child is presently functioning.
Population: Ages 2–10.
Publication Date: 1990.
Acronym: GCDAS.
Scores, 11: Developmental Patterns (Bladder and Bowel Control, Parallel Play, Speech and Sentences, Analogies and Numbers, Sociability and Play, Monopolizes Situation, Ethical Sense, Competitive, Self Motivation and Reasonableness, Loyalty and Hero Worship), Total Developmental Age.
Administration: Individual.
Price Data, 1990: $11 per manual (16 pages); $25 per diskette with program.
Time: Administration time not reported.
Comments: GCDAS program uses a PCXT or AT like computer with 256K memory; separate ratings by mother, teacher, therapist.
Author: Russell N. Cassel.
Publisher: Psychologists and Educators, Inc.

[1035]

The Gesell Developmental Observation.
Purpose: Assesses a child's developmental age to aid in grade placement and development of instructional programs.

Population: Ages 4.5–9.
Publication Dates: 1964–80.
Administration: Individual.
Price Data, 1994: $30.95 per Gesell Assessment Kit including right and left assessments, Monroe Visual III, Monroe Visual I, copy form, cylinder and cube, cubes, and cube assessment direction booklet; $22.95 per School Readiness text: manual ('78, 238 pages); $21.50 per manual (Spanish Edition).
Foreign Language Edition: Also available in Spanish.
Comments: Manual title is School Readiness; test formerly called The Gesell School Readiness Test.
Authors: Frances L. Ilg, Louise Bates Ames, Jacqueline Haines, and Clyde Gillespie.
Publisher: Programs for Education, Inc.

a) KINDERGARTEN ASSESSMENT.
Population: Ages 4.5–6.
Subtests, 6: Interview, Cube Test, Paper and Pencil Test, Copy Forms, Incomplete Man, Animals and Interests Test.
Price Data: $99.50 per kindergarten start-up package; $38.75 per 50 kindergarten assessment recording sheets.
Time: (20) minutes.

b) SCHOOL-AGE ASSESSMENT.
Population: Ages 5–9 years.
Subtests, 9: Interview, Cube Test, Paper and Pencil Test, Copy Forms, Incomplete Man, Right and Left, Monroe Visual I Test, Animals and Interests Test, Monroe Visual III Test.
Price Data: $115 per school-age start-up package; $45 per 50 school-age assessment recording sheets.
Time: (40) minutes.
Cross References: For reviews by Robert H. Bradley and Everett Waters, see 9:438; see also T3:953 (6 references) and T2:1703 (4 references); for excerpted reviews by L. J. Borstelmann and Edith Meyer Taylor, see 7:750 (5 references).

TEST REFERENCES

1. Bagnato, S. J., & Neisworth, J. T. (1983). Monitoring developmental progress of young exceptional children: The Curricular Efficiency Index (CEI). *The Journal of Special Education, 17,* 189-193.
2. Larsen, J. M., Hite, S. J., & Hart, C. H. (1983). The effects of preschool on educationally advantaged children: First phases of a longitudinal study. *Intelligence, 7,* 345-352.
3. Lewis, D. O., Shanok, S. S., Grant, M., & Ritvo, E. (1983). Homicidally aggressive young children: Neuropsychiatric and experiential correlates. *The American Journal of Psychiatry, 140,* 148-153.
4. Call, J. D. (1984). Child abuse and neglect in infancy: Sources of hostility within the parent-infant dyad and disorders of attachment in infancy. *Child Abuse & Neglect, 8,* 185-202.
5. Jago, J. L., Jago, A. G., & Hart, M. (1984). An evaluation of the total communication approach for teaching language skills to developmentally delayed preschool children. *Education and Training of the Mentally Retarded, 19,* 175-182.
6. May, D. C., & Welch, E. (1984). Developmental placement: Does it prevent future learning problems? *Journal of Learning Disabilities, 17,* 338-341.
7. May, D. C., & Welch, E. L. (1984). The effects of developmental placement and early retention on children's later scores on standardized tests. *Psychology in the Schools, 21,* 381-385.
8. Smith, L., & Hagen, V. (1984). Relationship between the home environment and sensorimotor development of Down Syndrome and nonretarded infants. *American Journal of Mental Deficiency, 89,* 124-132.
9. Ungerer, J. A., & Sigman, M. (1984). The relation of play and

sensorimotor behavior to language in the second year. *Child Development, 55,* 1448-1455.

10. Vaughn, B. E., Kopp, C. B., & Krakow, J. B. (1984). The emergence and consolidation of self-control from eighteen to thirty months of age: Normative trends and individual differences. *Child Development, 55,* 990-1004.

11. Wood, C., Powell, S., & Knight, R. C. (1984). Predicting school readiness: The validity of developmental age. *Journal of Learning Disabilities, 17,* 8-11.

12. May, D. (1986). Relationships between the Gesell School Readiness Test and standardized achievement and intelligence measures. *Educational and Psychological Measurement, 46,* 1051-1059.

13. May, D. C., & Kundert, D. K. (1992). Kindergarten screenings in New York state: Tests, purposes, and recommendations. *Psychology in the Schools, 29*(1), 35-41.

[1036]
Gesell Preschool Test.

Purpose: "Designed to measure . . . relative maturity ratings in four basic fields of behavior."
Population: Ages 2.5–6.
Publication Date: 1980.
Scores: Ratings in 4 areas: Motor, Adaptive, Language, Personal-Social.
Administration: Group.
Price Data, 1994: $47 per 50 tests; $104.05 per kit (reusable materials only); $29 per formboard; $28 per picture vocabulary cards; $10 per color forms; $9 per letters and numbers; $5.50 per pellets and bottles; $12.50 per copy forms; $14.95 per manual (72 pages); $5 per 25 developmental schedules; $9.50 per 10 one-inch cubes; $13.75 per typical response cards for incomplete man test.
Time: (30–45) minutes.
Comments: Abbreviated adaptation of the Gesell Developmental Schedules (see 6:522) and the Gesell Developmental Tests (see 7:750).
Authors: Jacqueline Haines, Louise Bates Ames, and Clyde Gillespie.
Publisher: Programs for Education, Inc. Publishers.
Cross References: For reviews by Nadeen L. Kaufman and Jack A. Naglieri, see 9:437 (8 references).

[1037]
Gibson Spiral Maze, Second Edition.

Purpose: Measures "the speed, accuracy, and general style of people's muscular reactions in response to carefully controlled stimuli."
Population: Children and adults.
Publication Dates: 1961–65.
Scores, 2: Time score, Error score.
Administration: Individual.
Price Data, 1994: £7.99 per 20 test copies; £4.99 per manual ('65, 15 pages); £5.50 per specimen set.
Time: (2) minutes.
Comments: Forms part of the Clifton Assessment Procedures for the Elderly.
Authors: H.B. Gibson.
Publisher: Hodder and Stoughton [England].
Cross References: See T3:955 (1 reference); T2:1191 (3 references), 7:82 (3 references), and P:90 (2 references).

TEST REFERENCES

1. Gilleard, C. J. (1982). Effects of aging on Gibson Spiral Maze performance. *Perceptual and Motor Skills, 55,* 1098.

2. Ong, Y. L. (1983). Lithium levels in white blood cells and their relationship to observed side effects. *British Journal of Psychiatry, 143,* 36-39.

3. Zimmerman-Tansella, C. (1984). Psychological performance of anxious patients in tests used in anxiolytic drug trials. *Journal of Clinical Psychology, 40,* 1143-1150.

[1038]
Gifted and Talented Scale.

Purpose: "Designed to identify those children who should be admitted into school programs for the Gifted and Talented."
Population: Grades 4–6.
Publication Date: No date on test materials.
Scores, 6: Numerical Reasoning, Vocabulary, Synonyms/Antonyms, Similarities, Analogies, Total.
Administration: Group.
Price Data, 1993: $55 per complete kit including 25 record forms and manual (17 pages); $45 per 25 record forms; $5 per answer key; $7.50 per manual.
Time: Administration time not reported.
Author: Dallas Educational Services.
Publisher: Dallas Educational Services.
Cross References: For reviews by Linda E. Brody and Nicholas Colangelo, see 10:125.

[1039]
Gifted Evaluation Scale.

Purpose: A means to "document the five characteristics of giftedness in the federal definition: intellectual, creative, specific academic, leadership ability, or in the performing and visual arts."
Population: Ages 4.5–19.
Publication Dates: 1987–90.
Acronym: GES.
Scores, 7: 5 subscales (Intellectual, Creativity, Specific Academic Aptitude, Leadership Ability, Performing and Visual Arts), Quotient Score, Percentile Score.
Administration: Individual.
Price Data, 1993: $60 per complete kit including GES technical manual ('87, 40 pages); 50 GES rating forms, and Gifted Intervention Manual ('90, 107 pages); $28 per 50 rating forms.
Time: (15–20) minutes.
Comments: Ratings by teachers; manual title is Gifted Intervention Manual.
Authors: Stephen B. McCarney and Diana Henage (manual).
Publisher: Hawthorne Educational Services, Inc.

[1040]
The Gifted Program Evaluation Survey.

Purpose: Constructed to evaluate the effectiveness of a gifted program as perceived by parents, teachers, students, and administrators.
Population: Gifted and talented programs.
Publication Date: 1991.
Scores: Item scores only.
Administration: Individual.
Forms, 4: Parent, Teacher, Student, Administrator.

Price Data, 1991: $24.95 per evaluation kit consisting of manual/forms (42 pages).
Time: Administration time not reported.
Author: Richard Lahey.
Publisher: United/DOK Publishers.

[1041]
Gillingham-Childs Phonics Proficiency Scales.

Purpose: Mastery tests in reading and spelling designed to check knowledge of the sequential steps of Gillingham's reading approach.
Population: Grades 2–8.
Publication Dates: 1966–73.
Acronym: GCPPS.
Administration: Individual.
Levels, 2: Series 1 and Series 2.
Time: (10–15) minutes per scale.
Comments: "Criterion-referenced."
Publisher: Educators Publishing Service, Inc.

a) SERIES I: BASIC READING AND SPELLING.
Publication Dates: 1966–70.
Scores: 15 scales in 2 areas (Reading and Spelling): Letter-Sound Connections—Reading, 3-Letter Regular Words, 3-Letter Nonce Words, Consonant Digraphs and Blends—Regular Words, Consonant Digraphs and Blends—Nonce Words, Monosyllables Ending in F/L/S, Vowel-Consonant-E—Regular Words, Vowel-Consonant-E—Nonce Words, Syllable Division Between Two Consonants—Regular Words, Syllable Division Between Two Consonants—Nonce Words, Doubling Final Consonants in Monosyllables, Knowing the Alphabet, "RED WORDS" for Reading—First Level, Basic Plural Rule, Vowel-Consonant-E—Adding Suffixes.
Administration: Individual in part.
Price Data, 1987: $3.25 per reading record booklet; $4 per spelling record booklet; $6.50 per scales for student's oral reading and written spelling; $.50 per directions for use ('70, 8 pages).
Authors: Sally B. Childs, Anna Gillingham (test), and Bessie W. Stillman (test).

b) SERIES 2: ADVANCED READING.
Publication Dates: 1970–73.
Scores: 18 scales: Letter-Sound Connections, New Content—Vowel y Short, New Content: Hard and Soft c and g, New Content: Final e/o/y, New Content: Wild-Old Words, Review Lists Based on Scales 2–5 (Regular Words, Nonce Words), New Content: th, New Content: ay, New Content: oa, New Content: au, Review Lists Based on Scales 7–10 (Regular Words, Nonce Words), Prefixes and Suffixes, Words Irregular for Reading (Level 2, Level 3), Reading Pronunciations, Syllable Division—Rule 2.
Administration: Individual.
Price Data, 1987: $6.50 per test booklet; $2.50 per record booklet; $.50 per directions for use.
Authors: Sally B. Childs and Ralph de S. Childs.
Cross References: For reviews by Shirley C. Feldmann and Lawrence M. Kasdon, see 8:760.

[1042]
Gilmore Oral Reading Test.

Purpose: "Developed to provide . . . a means of analyzing the oral reading performance of pupils."
Population: Grades 1–8.
Publication Dates: 1951–68.
Acronym: GORT.
Scores, 3: Accuracy, Comprehension, Rate.
Administration: Individual.
Forms, 2: C, D.
Price Data, 1994: $17 per examination kit including manual ('68, 31 pages) and record blank; $28.50 per reading paragraphs (both forms); $48.50 per 35 record blanks (specify Form C or D); $15.50 per manual.
Time: (15–20) minutes.
Author: John V. Gilmore and Eunice C. Gilmore.
Publisher: The Psychological Corporation.
Cross References: See T3:958 (13 references); for an excerpted review by Jerry Stafford, see 8:785 (17 references); see also T2:1679 (5 references); for reviews by Albert J. Harris and Kenneth J. Smith, see 7:737 (17 references); for reviews by Lydia A. Duggins and Maynard C. Reynolds of the original edition, see 5:671.

TEST REFERENCES

1. Witkin, B. R., Butler, K. G., & Whalen, T. E. (1977). Auditory processing in children: Two studies of component factors. *Language, Speech, and Hearing Services in Schools, 8,* 140-154.
2. Murray, M. E. (1978). The relationship between personality adjustment and success in remedial programs in dyslexic children. *Contemporary Educational Psychology, 3,* 330-339.
3. Hollensworth, R., & White, R. B. (1981). Relationship between reading scores on the Wide Range Achievement Test and the Gilmore Oral Reading Test in young children. *Psychological Reports, 48,* 191-193.
4. Long, R. L., McIntyre, C. W., & Murray, M. E. (1982). Visual selective attention in learning disabled and normal boys. *Bulletin of the Psychonomic Society, 19,* 15-18.
5. Moore, M. J., Kagan, J., Sahl, M., & Grant, S. (1982). Cognitive profiles in reading disability. *Genetic Psychology Monographs, 105,* 41-93.
6. Epstein, M. H., & Cullinan, D. (1983). Academic performance of behaviorally disordered and learning-disabled pupils. *The Journal of Special Education, 17,* 303-307.
7. Harris-Stefanakis, E. (1983). Developing a learning disabilities program in an overseas community school: American Community School in Athens, Greece. *Journal of Learning Disabilities, 16,* 198-201.
8. Mazer, S. R., McIntyre, C. W., Murray, M. E., Till, R. E., & Blackwell, S. L. (1983). Visual persistence and information pick-up in learning disabled children. *Journal of Learning Disabilities, 16,* 221-225.
9. Colligan, R. C., & Bajuniemi, L. E. (1984). Multiple definitions of reading disability: Implications for preschool screening. *Perceptual and Motor Skills, 59,* 467-475.
10. Punnett, A. F., & Steinhauer, G. D. (1984). Relationship between reinforcement and eye movements during ocular motor training with learning disabled children. *Journal of Learning Disabilities, 17,* 16-19.
11. Rose, T. L. (1984). The effects of two practice procedures on oral reading. *Journal of Learning Disabilities, 17,* 544-548.
12. Weithorn, C. J., Kagen, E., & Marcus, M. (1984). The relationship of activity level ratings and cognitive inpulsivity to task performance and academic achievement. *The Journal of Child Psychology and Psychiatry and Allied Disciplines, 25,* 587-606.
13. Broman, M., Rudel, R. G., Helfgott, E., & Krieger, J. (1986). Inter- and intrahemispheric processing of letter stimuli by dyslexic children and normal readers. *Cortex, 22,* 447-459.
14. Risko, V. J., & Alvarez, M. C. (1986). An investigation of poor readers' use of thematic strategy to comprehend text. *Reading Research Quarterly, 21,* 298-316.
15. Lovett, M. W. (1987). A developmental approach to reading disability: Accuracy and speed criteria of normal and deficient reading skill. *Child Development, 58,* 234-260.

16. Abikoff, H., Ganeles, D., Reiter, G., Blum, C., Foley, C., & Klein, R. G. (1988). Cognitive training in academically deficient ADDH boys receiving stimulant medication. *Journal of Abnormal Child Psychology, 16*, 411-432.

17. Zentall, S. S., & Dwyer, A. M. (1989). Color effects on the impulsivity and activity of hyperactive children. *Journal of School Psychology, 27*, 165-173.

18. Weber, R. M. (1990). The construction of narratives by good and poor readers. *Yearbook of the National Reading Conference, 39*, 295-301.

19. O'Neill, M. E., & Douglas, V. I. (1991). Study strategies and story recall in attention deficit disorder and reading disability. *Journal of Abnormal Child Psychology, 19*, 671-692.

20. Biederman, J., Faraone, S. V., Spenser, T., Wilens, T., Norman, D., Lapey, K. A., Mick, E., Lehman, B. K., & Doyle, A. (1993). Patterns of psychiatric comorbidity, cognition, and psychosocial functioning in adults with attention deficit hyperactivity disorder. *American Journal of Psychiatry, 150*, 1792-1798.

21. Faraone, S. V., Biederman, J., Lehman, B. K., Keenan, K., Norman, D., Seidman, L. J., Kolodny, R., Krauss, I., Perrin, J., & Chen, W. J. (1993). Evidence for the independent familial transmission of attention deficit hyperactivity disorder and learning disabilities: Results from a family genetic study. *American Journal of Psychiatry, 150*, 891-895.

[1043]

Global Assessment Scale.

Purpose: "For evaluating the overall functioning of a subject during a specified time period on a continuum from psychological or psychiatric sickness to health."

Population: Psychiatric patients and possible psychiatric patients.

Publication Dates: 1976–85.

Acronym: GAS.

Scores: Mental Health-Illness rating of individual on a continuum of 1 to 100.

Administration: Individual.

Price Data, 1994: $.25 per scale; $2.50 per case vignettes and keys ('85, 17 pages); $.50 per instructions ('78, 8 pages).

Authors: Robert L. Spitzer, Miriam Gibbon, and Jean Endicott.

Publisher: Department of Research Assessment and Training, New York State Psychiatric Institute.

Cross References: For a review by Michael J. Subkoviak, see 11:147 (22 references).

TEST REFERENCES

1. Clark, A., & Friedman, M. J. (1983). Nine standardized scales for evaluating treatment outcome in a mental health clinic. *Journal of Clinical Psychology, 39*, 939-950.

2. Karzmark, P., Greenfield, T., & Cross, H. (1983). The relationship between level of adjustment and expectations for therapy. *Journal of Clinical Psychology, 39*, 930-932.

3. Carpenter, W. T., Jr., Heinrichs, D. W., & Hanlon, T. E. (1987). A comparative trial of pharmacologic strategies in schizophrenia. *American Journal of Psychiatry, 144*, 1466-1470.

4. Coryell, W., & Zimmerman, M. (1987). Progress in the classification of functional psychoses. *American Journal of Psychiatry, 144*, 1471-1474.

5. Kettering, R. L., Harrow, M., Grossman, L., & Meltzer, H. Y. (1987). The prognostic relevance of delusions in depression: A follow-up study. *American Journal of Psychiatry, 144*, 1154-1160.

6. Tucker, L., Bauer, S. F., Wagner, S., Harlam, D., & Sher, I. (1987). Long-term hospital treatment of borderline patients: A descriptive outcome study. *American Journal of Psychiatry, 144*, 1443-1448.

7. Beiser, M., Fleming, J. A. E., Iacono, W. G., & Lin, T. (1988). Refining the diagnosis of schizophreniform disorder. *American Journal of Psychiatry, 145*, 695-700.

8. Frank, E., Carpenter, L. L., & Kupfer, D. J. (1988). Sex differences in recurrent depression: Are there any that are significant? *American Journal of Psychiatry, 145*, 41-45.

9. Horowitz, L. M., Rosenberg, S. E., Baer, B. A., Ureño, G., & Villaseñor, V. S. (1988). Inventory of Interpersonal Problems: Psycho-

metric properties and clinical applications. *Journal of Consulting and Clinical Psychology, 56*, 885-892.

10. Janicak, P. G., Pandey, G. N., Davis, J. M., Boshes, R., Bresnahan, D., & Sharma, R. (1988). Response of psychotic and nonpsychotic depression to phenelzine. *American Journal of Psychiatry, 145*, 93-95.

11. Klein, D. N., Taylor, E. B., Harding, K., & Dickstein, S. (1988). Double depression and episodic major depression: Demographic, clinical, familial, personality, and socioenvironmental characteristics and short-term outcome. *American Journal of Psychiatry, 145*, 1226-1231.

12. Kocsis, J. H., Frances, A. J., Voss, C., Mason, B. J., Mann, J. J., & Sweeney, J. (1988). Imipramine and social-vocational adjustment in chronic depression. *American Journal of Psychiatry, 145*, 997-999.

13. Marmar, C. R., Horowitz, M. J., Weiss, D. S., Wilner, N. R., & Kaltreider, N. B. (1988). A controlled trial of brief psychotherapy and mutual-help group treatment of conjugal bereavement. *American Journal of Psychiatry, 145*, 203-209.

14. Seligman, M. E. P., Castellon, C., Cacciola, J., Schulman, P., Luborsky, L., Ollove, M., & Downing, R. (1988). Explanatory style change during cognitive therapy for unipolar depression. *Journal of Abnormal Psychology, 97*, 13-18.

15. Siris, S. G., Adan, F., Cohen, M., Mandeli, J., Aronson, A., & Casey, E. (1988). Postpsychotic depression and negative symptoms: An investigation of syndromal overlap. *American Journal of Psychiatry, 145*, 1532-1537.

16. Westermeyer, J. (1988). DSM-III psychiatric disorders among Hmong refugees in the United States: A point prevalence study. *American Journal of Psychiatry, 145*, 197-202.

17. Westermeyer, J., & Neider, J. (1988). Social networks and psychopathology among substance abusers. *American Journal of Psychiatry, 145*, 1265-1269.

18. Coryell, W. H., & Zimmerman, M. (1989). HPA axis hyperactivity and recovery from functional psychoses. *American Journal of Psychiatry, 146*, 473-477.

19. Dening, T. R., & Berrios, G. E. (1989). Wilson's disease: A prospective study of psychopathology in 31 cases. *British Journal of Psychiatry, 155*, 206-213.

20. Gartner, A. F., Marcus, R. N., Halmi, K., & Loranger, A. W. (1989). DSM-III-R personality disorders in patients with eating disorders. *American Journal of Psychiatry, 146*, 1585-1591.

21. Kopala, L., Clark, C., & Hurwitz, T. A. (1989). Sex differences in olfactory function in schizophrenia. *American Journal of Psychiatry, 146*, 1320-1322.

22. Lee, C. M., & Gotlib, I. H. (1989). Clinical status and emotional adjustment of children of depressed mothers. *American Journal of Psychiatry, 146*, 478-483.

23. Lezenwegar, M. F., & Loranger, A. W. (1989). Psychosis proneness and clinical psychopathology: Examination of the correlates of schizotypy. *Journal of Abnormal Psychology, 98*, 3-8.

24. Carpenter, W. T., Jr., Hanlon, T. E., Heinrichs, D. W., Summerfelt, A. T., Kirkpatrick, B., Levine, J., & Buchanan, R. W. (1990). Continuous versus targeted medication in schizophrenic outpatients: Outcome results. *American Journal of Psychiatry, 147*, 1138-1148.

25. Fritsch, R. C., & Holmstrom, R. W. (1990). Assessing object representations as a continuous variable: A modification of the concept of the object on the Rorschach scale. *Journal of Personality Assessment, 55*, 319-334.

26. Goff, D. C., Brotman, A. W., Waites, M., & McCormick, S. (1990). Trial of fluoxetine added to neuroleptics for treatment-resistance schizophrenic patients. *American Journal of Psychiatry, 147*, 492-494.

27. Greenwald, D. F. (1990). Child functioning predictors of outcome among boys at risk for psychological disorder. *The Journal of Genetic Psychology, 151*, 139-151.

28. Lewine, R. R. J. (1990). A discriminant validity study of negative symptoms with a special focus on depression and antipsychotic medication. *American Journal of Psychiatry, 147*, 1463-1466.

29. Rogers, R., Gillis, J. R., Turner, R. E., & Frise-Smith, T. (1990). The clinical presentation of command hallucinations in a forensic population. *American Journal of Psychiatry, 147*, 1304-1307.

30. Sharma, R. P., Janicak, P. G., Javaid, J. I., Pandey, G. N., Gierl, B., & Davis, J. M. (1990). Platelet MAO inhibition, urinary MHPG, and leukocyte B-adrenergic receptors in depressed patients treated with phenelzine. *American Journal of Psychiatry, 147*, 1318-1321.

31. Zimmerman, M., Coryell, W. H., & Black, D. W. (1990). Variability in the application of contemporary diagnostic criteria: Endogenous depression as an example. *American Journal of Psychiatry, 147*, 1173-1179.

32. Coryell, W., Endicott, J., & Keller, M. B. (1991). Predictors of relapse into major depressive disorder in a nonclinical population. *American Journal of Psychiatry, 148*, 1353-1358.

33. Dixon, L., Haas, G., Weiden, P. J., Sweeney, J., & Frances, A. J. (1991). Drug abuse in schizophrenic patients: Clinical correlates and reasons for use. *American Journal of Psychiatry, 148*, 224-230.

34. Katsanis, J., & Iacono, W. G. (1991). Clinical, neuropsychological, and brain structural correlates of smooth-pursuit eye tracking performance in chronic schizophrenia. *Journal of Abnormal Psychology, 100,* 526-534.

35. Keitner, G. I., Ryan, C. E., Miller, I. W., Kohn, R., & Epstein, N. B. (1991). 12-month outcome of patients with major depression and comorbid psychiatric or medical illness (compound depression). *American Journal of Psychiatry, 148,* 345-350.

36. Kochanska, G. (1991). Patterns of inhibition to the unfamiliar in children of normal and affectively ill mothers. *Child Development, 62,* 250-263.

37. Kuhlman, T., Bernstein, M., Kloss, J., Sincaban, V., & Harris, L. (1991). A team format for the Global Assessment Scale: Reliability and validity on an inpatient unit. *Journal of Personality Assessment, 56*(2), 335-347.

38. Massey, O. T., & Murphy, S. E. (1991). A study of the utility of The Child Behavior Checklist with residentially placed children. *Evaluation and Program Planning, 14,* 319-324.

39. Thase, M. E., Simons, A. D., Cahalane, J., McGeary, J., & Harden, T. (1991). Severity of depression and response to cognitive behavior therapy. *American Journal of Psychiatry, 148,* 784-789.

40. Allard, R., Marshall, M., & Plante, M. (1992). Intensive followup does not decrease the risk of repeat suicide attempts. *Suicide and Life-Threatening Behavior, 22,* 303-314.

41. Bornstein, R. F., & O'Neill, R. M. (1992). Parental perceptions and psychopathology. *Journal of Nervous and Mental Disease, 180,* 475-483.

42. Brekke, J. S. (1992). An examination of the relationships among three outcome scales in schizophrenia. *Journal of Nervous and Mental Disease, 180,* 162-167.

43. Freeman, T. W., Clothier, J. L., Pazzaglia, P., Lesem, M. D., & Swann, A. C. (1992). A double-blind comparison of valproate and lithium in the treatment of acute mania. *American Journal of Psychiatry, 149,* 108-111.

44. Goodman, S. H., & Emory, E. K. (1992). Perinatal complications in births to low socioeconomic status schizophrenic and depressed women. *Journal of Abnormal Psychology, 101,* 225-229.

45. Hogan, T. P., & Awad, A. G. (1992). Subjective response to neuroleptics and outcome in schizophrenia: A re-examination comparing two measures. *Psychological Medicine, 22,* 347-352.

46. Kelly, T. A., & Strupp, H. H. (1992). Patient and therapist values in psychotherapy: Perceived changes, assimilation, similarity, and outcome. *Journal of Consulting and Clinical Psychology, 60,* 34-40.

47. Lebovits, A. H., & Levin, S. (1992). Correlates of a residential pesticide contamination in a self-selected sample. *The Journal of Psychology, 126,* 189-205.

48. Levinson, D. F., Singh, H., & Simpson, G. M. (1992). Timing of acute clinical response to fluphenazine. *British Journal of Psychiatry, 160,* 365-371.

49. Luchins, D. L., Dyson, V., Hanrahan, P., Marks, R., & Blake, L. (1992). Failure of a binaural comprehension deficit to select responses to earplug use in schizophrenia. *British Journal of Psychiatry, 161,* 397-398.

50. Mowbray, C. T., Greenfield, A., & Freddolino, P. P. (1992). An analysis of treatment services provided in group homes for adults labeled mentally ill. *Journal of Nervous and Mental Disease, 180,* 551-559.

51. Simons, A. D., & Thase, M. E. (1992). Biological markers, treatment outcome, and 1-year follow-up in endogeneous depression: Electroencephalographic sleep studies and response to cognitive therapy. *Journal of Consulting and Clinical Psychology, 60,* 392-401.

52. Albus, M., & Scheibe, G. (1993). Outcome of panic disorder with or without concomitant depression: A 2-year prospective follow-up study. *American Journal of Psychiatry, 150,* 1878-1880.

53. Cornelius, J. R., Soloff, P. H., Perel, J. M., & Ulrich, R. F. (1993). Continuation pharmacotherapy of borderline personality disorder with haloperidol and phenelzine. *American Journal of Psychiatry, 150,* 1843-1848.

54. Gara, M. A., Woolfolk, R. L., Cohen, B. D., Goldston, R. B., Allen, L. A., & Novalany, J. (1993). Perception of self and others in major depression. *Journal of Abnormal Psychology, 102,* 93-100.

55. Gould, M. S., Bird, H., & Jaramillo, B. S. (1993). Correspondence between statistically derived behavior problem syndromes and child psychiatric diagnoses in a community sample. *Journal of Abnormal Child Psychology, 21,* 287-313.

56. Joseph, P. L., & Potter, M. (1993). Diversion from custody I: Psychiatric assessment at the magistrate's court. *British Journal of Psychiatry, 162,* 325-330.

57. Mayer, C., Kelterborn, G., & Naber, D. (1993). Age of onset in schizophrenia: Relations to psychopathology and gender. *British Journal of Psychiatry, 162,* 665-671.

58. Meltzer, H. Y., Cola, P., Way, L., Thompson, P. A., Bastani, B., Davies, M. A., & Snitz, B. (1993). Cost effectiveness of clozapine in neuroleptic-resistant schizophrenia. *American Journal of Psychiatry, 150,* 1630-1638.

59. Rund, B. R. (1993). Backward-masking performance in chronic and nonchronic schizophrenics, affectively disturbed patients, and normal control subjects. *Journal of Abnormal Psychology, 102,* 74-81.

60. Tsuang, D., & Coryell, W. (1993). An 8-year follow-up of patients with DSM-III-R psychotic depression, schizoaffective disorder, and schizophrenia. *American Journal of Psychiatry, 150,* 1182-1188.

61. Wade, S. L., Monroe, S. M., & Michelson, L. K. (1993). Chronic life stress and treatment outcome in agoraphobia with panic attacks. *American Journal of Psychiatry, 150,* 1491-1495.

62. Warshaw, M. G., Fierman, E., Pratt, L., Hunt, M., Yonkers, K. A., Massion, A. O., & Keller, M. B. (1993). Quality of life and dissociation in anxiety disorder patients with histories of trauma or PTSD. *American Journal of Psychiatry, 150,* 1512-1516.

[1044]

GOALS: A Performance-Based Measure of Achievement.

Purpose: A measure of student achievement using open-ended questions requiring reasoning skills.

Population: Grades 1–12.

Publication Date: 1992–93.

Administration: Group.

Forms, 2: A, B.

Levels, 12: 1–12.

Price Data, 1994: $12.50 per 25 test booklets including directions for administering; $6.50 per scoring guide; $4 per directions for administering; $15 per 1991 norms booklet; $2.50 per Option 1 computer scoring by publisher of one domain including scoring and two copies of the Student Performance Roster; $2 per each additional domain; $.13 per additional copy of Student Performance Roster); $450 set-up charge for Option 2 computer scoring by publisher including scoring and recording of scores in test booklets; $2 per domain scored; $1 per domain for Option 3 scoring (school district scores tests and records scores on a scannable scoring sheet; publisher processes score sheets and sends two copies of Student Performance Roster; $.30 per additional domain); $1.25 per domain for Option 4 scoring (school district records scores in tests booklets; publisher sends two copies of Student Performance Roster; $.50 per additional domain); $.35 per class profile ($25 per order each additional copy); $.30 per school profile ($20 per order each additional copy); $.25 per district profile ($15 per order each additional copy); $.45 per administrator's data summary-school ($20 per order each additional copy); $.40 per administrator's data summary-district ($15 per order each additional copy); $.60 per administrator's data summary-school and district ($25 per additional copy); $.50 per student profile ($.15 per additional copy); $.40 per student record label; $.40 per master list of test results ($.13 per additional copy); $.40 per student performance roster ($.13 per additional copy); $.25 per student data diskette; $70 per reel charge for student data tape ($.25 per student); $450 per set-up charge for customer data input (plus cost of additional reports ordered).

Time: (40–60) minutes.

Comments: Produces norm-referenced and holistic-analytic scores.

Author: The Psychological Corporation.
Publisher: The Psychological Corporation.

a) MATHEMATICS.
Scores, 8: Content (Problem Solving, Procedures), Process (Applying Mathematical Skills and Concepts to Solve Problems, Drawing Conclusions Using Mathematical Skills and Concepts, Integrating Mathematical Concepts and Skills to Solve Problems, Analyzing Problems Using Mathematical Skills and Concepts, Creating Solutions Through Synthesis of Mathematical Concepts and Skills, Evaluating Problems Using Mathematical Skills and Concepts).

b) LANGUAGE.
Scores, 5: Content (Narrative Writing, Expository Writing), Process (Skill in Composing, Understanding of Usage, Application in Mechanics).

c) READING.
Scores, 5: Content (Narrative Text, Information Text), Process (Global Understanding, Identification and Application of Strategies, Critical Analysis).

d) SCIENCE.
Scores, 5: Content (Live Science, Physical Science, Earth/Space Science), Process (Collecting and Recording Scientific Data, Applying Science Concepts and Drawing Conclusions).

e) SOCIAL SCIENCE.
Scores, 5: Content (Geographic/Economic/and Cultural Foundations of Society, Historical and Political Bases of Society), Process (Understanding of Basic Conceptual Social Science Frameworks, Creative Thinking and Problem-Solving Skills, Inquiry and Decision Making Using Social Science Tools).

TEST REFERENCES

1. Gierut, J. A., Elbert, M., & Dinnsen, D. A. (1987). A functional analysis of phonological knowledge and generalization learning in misarticulating children. *Journal of Speech and Hearing Research, 30,* 462-479.
2. Abraham, S., Stoker, R., & Allen, W. (1988). Speech assessment of hearing-impaired children and youth: Patterns of test use. *Language, Speech, and Hearing Services in Schools, 19,* 17-27.
3. Edmonds, P., & Haynes, W. O. (1988). Topic manipulation and conversational participation as a function of familiarity in school-age languaged-impaired and normal language peers. *Journal of Communication Disorders, 21,* 209-228.
4. Hoffman, P. R., & Norris, J. A. (1989). On the nature of phonological development: Evidence from normal children's spelling errors. *Journal of Speech and Hearing Research, 32,* 787-794.
5. Elbert, M., Dinnsen, D. A., Swartzlander, P., & Chin, S. B. (1990). Generalization to conversational speech. *Journal of Speech and Hearing Disorders, 55,* 694-699.
6. Kleppe, S. A., Katayama, K. M., Shipley, K. G., & Foushee, D. R. (1990). The speech and language characteristics of children with Prader-Willi syndrome. *Journal of Speech and Hearing Disorders, 55,* 300-309.
7. Tyler, A. A., Edwards, M. L., & Saxman, J. H. (1990). Acoustic validation of phonological knowledge and its relationship to treatments. *Journal of Speech and Hearing Disorders, 55,* 251-261.
8. Burchinal, M., & Appelbaum, M. I. (1991). Estimating individual developmental functions: Methods and their assumptions. *Child Development, 62,* 23-43.
9. Elbert, M., Powell, T. W., & Swartzlander, P. (1991). Toward a technology of generalization: How many exemplars are sufficient? *Journal of Speech and Hearing Research, 34,* 81-87.
10. Kamen, R. S., & Watson, B. C. (1991). Effects of long-term tracheostomy on spectral characteristics of vowel production. *Journal of Speech and Hearing Research, 34,* 1057-1065.
11. Rice, M. L., Sell, M. A., & Hadley, P. A. (1991). Social interactions of speech- and language-impaired children. *Journal of Speech and Hearing Research, 34,* 1299-1307.
12. Ruscello, D. M., St. Louis, K. O., & Mason, N. (1991). School-aged children with phonologic disorders: Coexistence with other speech/language disorders. *Journal of Speech and Hearing Research, 34,* 236-242.
13. Sussman, J. E. (1991). Stimulus ratio effects on speech discrimination by children and adults. *Journal of Speech and Hearing Research, 34,* 671-678.
14. Williams, A. L. (1991). Generalization patterns associated with training least phonological knowledge. *Journal of Speech and Hearing Research, 34,* 722-733.
15. Walker, J. F., Archibald, L., Cherniak, S. R., & Fish, V. G. (1992). Articulation rate in 3- and 5-year-old children. *Journal of Speech and Hearing Research, 35,* 4-13.

[1045]

Goldman-Fristoe Test of Articulation.
Purpose: Designed to provide "a systematic means of assessing an individual's articulation of the consonant sounds."
Population: Ages 2 and over.
Publication Dates: 1969–86.
Scores: 3 subtests: Sounds-in-Words, Sounds-in-Sentences, Stimulability.
Administration: Individual.
Price Data, 1993: $119.95 per complete kit including easel containing test plates, manual ('86, 33 pages), and 25 response forms; $15.95 per 25 response forms; $95.50 per set of test plates in easel; $21.50 per manual.
Time: [10–15] minutes.
Authors: Ronald Goldman and Macalyne Fristoe.
Publisher: American Guidance Service.
Cross References: For a review by Donald E. Mowrer, see 10:126 (7 references); see also T3:960 (21 references); for reviews by Margaret C. Byrne and Ralph L. Shelton, and an excerpted review by Dorothy Sherman, see 7:952 (4 references).

[1046]

Goldman-Fristoe-Woodcock Test of Auditory Discrimination.
Purpose: "Designed to provide measures of speech-sound discrimination ability."
Population: Ages 3-8 years and over.
Publication Date: 1970.
Acronym: GFW.
Scores, 2: Quiet, Background Noise.
Administration: Individual.
Price Data, 1993: $69.95 per kit including easel kit containing test plates, 50 response forms, test audiocassette, and manual (31 pages); $11.95 per 50 response forms; $15.95 per training plates; $6.45 per manual.
Time: (15–20) minutes.
Authors: Ronald Goldman, Macalyne Fristoe, and Richard W. Woodcock.
Publisher: American Guidance Service.
Cross References: See T3:962 (14 references); for an excerpted review by Alex Bannatyne, see 8:938 (18 references); see also T2:2037 (4 references); for reviews by Eugene C. Sheeley and Ralph L. Shelton

and an excerpted review by Barton B. Proger, see 7:938.

TEST REFERENCES

1. Marston, L. E., & Larkin, M. (1979). Auditory assessment of reading underachieving children. *Language, Speech, and Hearing in Schools, 10,* 212-220.
2. Hutton, J. B. (1983). Effect of middle ear pathology on selected psychoeducational measures following surgical treatment. *Perceptual and Motor Skills, 57,* 1095-1100.
3. Bountress, N. G. (1984). A second look at tests of speech-sound discrimination. *Journal of Communication Disorders, 17,* 349-359.
4. Gierut, J. A., Elbert, M., & Dinnsen, D. A. (1987). A functional analysis of phonological knowledge and generalization learning in misarticulating children. *Journal of Speech and Hearing Research, 30,* 462-479.
5. Powers, L. A., & Madison, C. L. (1987). Effects of presentation mode on discrimination skills of articulatory disordered children. *Perceptual and Motor Skills, 64,* 775-779.
6. Beitchman, J. H., Peterson, M., & Clegg, M. (1988). Speech and language impairment and psychiatric disorder: The relevance of family demographic variables. *Child Psychiatry and Human Development, 18,* 191-207.
7. Sanger, D. D., Keith, R. W., Deshayes, I. L., & Stevens, P. K. (1990). A comparison of the SSW and language test results. *Journal of Communication Disorders, 23,* 433-443.
8. Brown, J. R. (1992). Trial by fire: One perspective for guessing. *Psychology in the Schools, 29*(1), 71-77.

[1047]

The Golombok Rust Inventory of Marital State.

Purpose: Constructed to assess the overall quality of the relationship between married or cohabitating heterosexual couples.
Population: Married or unmarried heterosexual couples living together.
Publication Date: 1988.
Acronym: GRIMS.
Scores: Total score only.
Administration: Group.
Price Data, 1992: £46 per complete kit including 20 record forms and manual (31 pages); £28.75 per 20 record forms.
Time: [10–15] minutes.
Authors: John Rust, Ian Bennun, Michael Crowe, and Susan Golombok.
Publisher: NFER-Nelson Publishing Co., Ltd. [England].

TEST REFERENCES

1. Rust, J., Golombok, S., & Collier, J. (1988). Marital problems and sexual dysfunction: How are they related? *British Journal of Psychiatry, 152,* 629-631.

[1048]

The Golombok Rust Inventory of Sexual Satisfaction.

Purpose: Designed to provide "an objective assessment of the quality of a sexual relationship and of a person's function within it."
Population: Sex therapy clients.
Publication Date: 1986.
Acronym: GRISS.
Scores, 13: Impotence, Premature Ejaculation, Male Non-sensuality, Male Avoidance, Male Dissatisfaction, Infrequency, Non-communication, Female Dissatisfaction, Female Avoidance, Female Non-sensuality, Vaginismus, Anorgasmia, Total.

Forms, 2: Male, Female.
Administration: Group.
Price Data, 1989: £25.30 per complete set; £6.65 per 10 questionnaires of each form; £12.10 per manual (28 pages).
Time: [10] minutes.
Authors: John Rust and Susan Golombok.
Publisher: NFER-Nelson Publishing Co., Ltd. [England].
Cross References: For a review by Kevin E. O'Grady, see 10:127 (2 references).

TEST REFERENCES

1. Rust, J., Golombok, S., & Collier, J. (1988). Marital problems and sexual dysfunction: How are they related? *British Journal of Psychiatry, 152,* 629-631.

[1049]

Goodenough-Harris Drawing Test.

Purpose: Developed for use "as a measure of intellectual maturity."
Population: Ages 3–15.
Publication Dates: 1926–63.
Scores: Total score only.
Administration: Group.
Price Data, 1994: $39.50 per 35 test booklets; $38 per set of quality scale cards; $35 per manual ('63, 80 pages); $73.50 per examiner's kit.
Time: (10–15) minutes.
Comments: Revision and extension of the Goodenough Draw-a-Man Test.
Authors: Dale B. Harris and Florence L. Goodenough (test).
Publisher: The Psychological Corporation.
Cross References: See 9:441 (6 references); see also T3:964 (52 references), 8:187 (87 references), and T2:381 (93 references); for reviews by Anne Anastasi and James A. Dunn, and excerpted reviews by M. L. Kellmer Pringle, Marjorie P. Honzik, Carol Hunter, Adolph G. Woltmann, Marvin S. Kaplan, and Mary J. Rouse, see 7:352 (158 references); see also 6:460 (43 references) and 5:335 (34 references); for a review by Naomi Stewart of the original edition, see 4:292 (60 references).

TEST REFERENCES

1. Guidubaldi, J., & Perry, J. D. (1984). Concurrent and predictive validity of the Battelle Development Inventory at the first grade level. *Educational and Psychological Measurement, 44,* 977-985.
2. Halperin, J. M., Gittelman, R., Klein, D. F., & Rudel, R. B. (1984). Reading disabled hyperactive children: A distinct subgroup of Attention Deficit Disorder with hyperactivity? *Journal of Abnormal Child Psychology, 12,* 1-14.
3. Hardman, P. K. (1984). The training of psycho-educational technicians (para-professionals) to administer a screening battery which delineates dyslexia and hyperkinesis. *Journal of Learning Disabilities, 17,* 453-456.
4. Miljkovitch, M., & Landry, S. (1984). Longitudinal study of a series of 213 spontaneous drawings of a person by a child between the ages of 4.6 and 10 years. *Perceptual and Motor Skills, 59,* 387-393.
5. Saracho, O. N. (1984). The Goodenough-Harris Drawing Test as a measure of field-dependence/independence. *Perceptual and Motor Skills, 59,* 887-892.
6. Nwanze, H. O. (1985). Relations between spelling performance in Nigerian elementary school children. *The Journal of Social Psychology, 125,* 45-52.
7. Levy, A. J., & Barowsky, E. I. (1986). Comparison of computer-

administered Harris-Goodenough Draw-A-Man test with standard paper-and-pencil administration. *Perceptual and Motor Skills, 63,* 395-398.

8. Saracho, O. N. (1986). Validation of two cognitive measures to assess field-dependence/independence. *Perceptual and Motor Skills, 63,* 255-263.

9. Dudek, S. Z., Strobel, M., & Thomas, A. D. (1987). Chronic learning problems and maturation. *Perceptual and Motor Skills, 64,* 407-429.

10. Huesmann, L. R., Eron, L. D., & Yarmel, P. W. (1987). Intellectual functioning and aggression. *Journal of Personality and Social Psychology, 52,* 232-240.

11. McCullers, J. C., Fabes, R. A., & Moran, J. D., III. (1987). Does intrinsic motivation theory explain the adverse effects of rewards on immediate task performance? *Journal of Personality and Social Psychology, 52,* 1027-1033.

12. Mehryar, A. H., Tashakkori, A., & Yousefi, F. (1987). The application of the Goodenough-Harris Draw-A-Man Test to a group of Iranian children in the city of Shiraz. *British Journal of Educational Psychology, 57,* 401-406.

13. O'Connor, N., & Hermelin, B. (1987). Visual and graphic abilities of the idiot savant artist. *Psychological Medicine, 17,* 79-90.

14. Ward, R., & Eliot, J. (1987). A study of migrant children. *Psychological Reports, 60,* 120-122.

15. Babad, E., Bernieri, F., & Rosenthal, R. (1989). Nonverbal communication and leakage in the behavior of biased and unbiased teachers. *Journal of Personality and Social Psychology, 56,* 89-94.

16. van der Lely, H. K. J., & Harris, M. (1990). Comprehension of reversible sentences in specifically language-impaired children. *Journal of Speech and Hearing Disorders, 55,* 101-117.

17. Baroody, A. J., & Gatzke, M. R. (1991). The estimation of set size by potentially gifted kindergarten-age children. *Journal for Research in Mathematics Education, 22,* 59-68.

18. Atlas, J. A., & Miller, A. L. (1992). Human figure drawings as estimates of intelligence for adolescents in an inpatient psychiatric unit. *Perceptual and Motor Skills, 75,* 690.

19. May, D. C., & Kundert, D. K. (1992). Kindergarten screenings in New York state: Tests, purposes, and recommendations. *Psychology in the Schools, 29*(1), 35-41.

20. Dyer, F. T. (1993). Clinical presentation of the lead-poisoned child on mental ability tests. *Journal of Clinical Psychology, 49,* 94-101.

[1050]
The Goodman Lock Box.

Purpose: Designed to assess "mental organization and psychomotor competence."

Population: Children suspected of a developmental delay or specific learning disability or behavioral problem with chronological or mental ages 2.5–5.5.

Publication Date: 1981.

Scores: 5 scale scores: Competence (Total Adaptive, Total Nonadaptive, Number Unlocked), Organization, Aimless Actions.

Administration: Individual.

Price Data, 1994: $895 per complete kit including all testing materials, record forms, and manual (53 pages); $25 per 30 record forms; $25 per manual.

Time: 6.5(10) minutes.

Author: Joan F. Goodman.

Publisher: Stoelting Co.

Cross References: For reviews by Stephen N. Elliott and Kathleen D. Paget, see 9:442.

TEST REFERENCES

1. Berry, P., Gunn, P., & Andrews, R. J. (1984). The behaviour of Down's syndrome children using the "lock box": A research note. *Journal of Child Psychology and Psychiatry, 25,* 125-131.

2. Glutting, J. J., & Nester, A. (1986). Koppitz emotional indicators as predictors of kindergarten children's learning- related behavior. *Contemporary Educational Psychology, 11,* 117-126.

3. Glutting, J. J., & McDermott, P. A. (1988). Generality of test-session observations to kindergarteners' classroom behavior. *Journal of Abnormal Child Psychology, 16,* 527-537.

[1051]
The Gordon Diagnostic System.

Purpose: "An assessment device that aids in the diagnosis of attention deficits, especially Attention Deficit Hyperactivity Disorder (ADHD) and AIDS Dementia Complex . . . provides . . . information about an individual's ability to sustain attention and exert self-control."

Population: Children, adolescents, and adults.

Publication Dates: [1982–83].

Acronym: GDS.

Scores: 3 tests: Vigilance Task, Distractibility Test, Delay Task.

Administration: Individual.

Price Data, 1992: $1,595 per GDS III microprocessor-based, portable unit including all tasks, capacity for automatic output to a printer, instruction manual ('83,), interpretive guide, 4 issues of ADHD/Hyperactivity Newsletter, and 1-year warranty; $200 per 2-month trial rental; $299 per GDS compatible printer; $30 per 50 GDS record forms.

Time: (9) minutes per task.

Author: Michael Gordon.

Publisher: GSI, Inc.

TEST REFERENCES

1. Gordon, M., & Mettelman, B. B. (1988). The assessment of attention: I. Standardization and reliability of a behavior-based measure. *Journal of Clinical Psychology, 44,* 682-690.

2. Gordon, M., DiNiro, D., & Mettelman, B. B. (1988). Effect upon outcome of nuances in selection criteria for ADHD/hyperactivity. *Psychological Reports, 62,* 539-544.

3. Breen, M. J. (1989). Cognitive and behavioral differences in AdHD boys and girls. *Journal of Child Psychology and Psychiatry and Allied Disciplines, 30,* 711-716.

4. Bauermeister, J. J., Berríos, V., Jiménez, A. L., Acevedo, L., & Gordon, M. (1990). Some issues and instruments for the assessment of attention-deficit hyperactivity disorder in Puerto Rican children. *Journal of Clinical Child Psychology, 19,* 9-16.

5. Grant, M. L., Ilai, D., Nussbaum, N. L., & Bigler, E. D. (1990). The relationship between continuous performance tasks and neuropsychological tests in children with attention-deficit hyperactivity disorder. *Perceptual and Motor Skills, 70,* 435-445.

6. Robins, P. M. (1992). A comparison of behavioral and attentional functioning in children diagnosed as hyperactive or learning-disabled. *Journal of Abnormal Child Psychology, 20,* 65-82.

[1052]
Gordon Occupational Check List II.

Purpose: "Designed for persons seeking education and job training below the college level."

Population: Grades 8–12 and adults.

Publication Dates: 1961–81.

Acronym: GOCL.

Scores, 6 or 12: Business, Outdoor, Arts, Technology (Mechanical, Industrial), Service, and 6 optional summarization scores (preceding 6 areas).

Administration: Group or individual.

Price Data, 1994: $63 per 35 check lists including manual ('82, 19 pages) and 35 job title supplements; $17.50 per manual; $22 per examination kit including check list, manual, and job title supplement.

Time: (20–25) minutes.

Author: Leonard V. Gordon.

Publisher: The Psychological Corporation.

Cross References: For a review by Donald G.

Zytowski, see 9:443; for reviews by John N. McCall and Bert W. Westbrook of an earlier edition, see 7:1019; for reviews by John O. Crites and Kenneth B. Hoyt of an earlier edition, see 6:1056.

[1053]

Gordon Personal Profile—Inventory.
Purpose: Constructed to assess "eight important factors in the personality domain."
Population: Grades 9–12 and college and adults.
Publication Dates: 1951–93.
Acronym: GPP-I.
Administration: Group.
Price Data, 1994: $53 per 25 profile-inventory test booklets; $29 per 25 test booklets (select profile or inventory); $29 per 25 answer sheets (select profile or inventory); $9.50 per set of keys for hand scoring booklets (select profile or inventory); $9.50 per set of keys for hand scoring answer sheets (select profile or inventory); $37 per manual ('93, 104 pages); $42 per specimen set.
Time: (20–25) minutes.
Comments: Combination of Gordon Personal Profile and Gordon Personal Inventory; separate booklet editions still available.
Author: Leonard V. Gordon.
Publisher: The Psychological Corporation.
   a) GORDON PERSONAL PROFILE.
   Scores, 5: Ascendancy, Responsibility, Emotional Stability, Sociability, Self-Esteem (Total).
   b) GORDON PERSONAL INVENTORY.
   Scores, 4: Cautiousness, Original Thinking, Personal Relations, Vigor.
Cross References: For reviews by Douglas Fuchs and Alfred B. Heilbrun, Jr., see 10:128 (4 references); see also 9:444 (1 reference), T3:966 (6 references), 8:568 (34 references), 8:569 (52 references), T2:1194 (56 references), and P:93 (23 references); for reviews by Charles F. Dicken and Alfred B. Heilbrun, Jr., see 6:102 (13 references) and 6:103 (25 references); for reviews by Benno G. Fricke and John A. Radcliffe and excerpted reviews by Laurance F. Shaffer and Laurence Siegel, see 5:58 and 5:59 (16 references).

TEST REFERENCES

1. Hough, L. M., Eaton, N. K., Dunnette, M. D., Kamp, J. D., & McCloy, R. A. (1990). Criterion-related validities of personality constructs and the effect of response distortion on those validities. *Journal of Applied Psychology, 75*(5), 581-595.
2. Guastello, S. J., Rieke, M. L., Guastello, D. D., & Billings, S. W. (1992). A study of cynicism, personality, and work values. *The Journal of Psychology, 126*, 37-48.

[1054]

Gottschaldt Figures [NIPR].
Purpose: Designed as "a test of analytical ability."
Population: Job applicants with at least 10 years of education.
Publication Dates: 1943–56.
Scores: Total score only.
Administration: Group.
Manual: No manual.

Price Data: Available from publisher.
Foreign Language Edition: Available in English and Afrikaans.
Time: 20(25) minutes.
Comments: South African adaptation of U.S. Army Air Forces Test AC121.
Author: National Institute for Personnel Research of the Human Sciences Research Council.
Publisher: National Institute for Personnel Research of the Human Sciences Research Council [South Africa].
Cross References: See T3:968 (2 references).

TEST REFERENCES

1. Adi, H., & Pulos, S. (1980). Individual differences and formal operational performance of college students. *Journal for Research in Mathematics Education, 11*, 150-156.
2. Lawson, A. E., & Bealer, J. M. (1984). Cultural diversity and differences in formal reasoning ability. *Journal of Research in Science Teaching, 21*, 735-743.
3. Niaz, M., & Lawson, A. E. (1985). Balancing chemical equations: The role of developmental level and mental capacity. *Journal of Research in Science Teaching, 22*, 41-51.

[1055]

Graded Naming Test.
Purpose: Constructed to detect "minor degrees of naming difficulty . . . in patients with left hemisphere lesions."
Population: Ages 20 and over.
Publication Date: 1983.
Scores: Total score only.
Administration: Individual.
Price Data: Available from publisher.
Time: Administration time not reported.
Authors: Pat McKenna and Elizabeth K. Warrington.
Publisher: NFER-Nelson Publishing Co., Ltd. [England].

TEST REFERENCES

1. Maher, E., Smith, E. M., & Lees, A. J. (1985). Cognitive deficits in the Steele-Richardson-Olszewski syndrome (progressive supranuclear palsy). *Journal of Neurology, Neurosurgery, and Psychiatry, 48*, 1234-1239.
2. McCarthy, R., & Warrington, E. K. (1985). Category specificity in an agrammatic patient: The relative impairment of verb retrieval and comprehension. *Neuropsychologia, 23*, 709-727.
3. Cockburn, J., Wilson, B., Baddeley, A., & Hiorns, R. (1990). Assessing everyday memory in patients with dysphasia. *British Journal of Clinical Psychology, 29*, 353-360.
4. Boyd, J. L., Cruickshank, C. A., Kenn, C. W., Madeley, P., Mindham, R. H. S., Oswald, A. G., Smith, R. J., & Spokes, E. G. S. (1991). Cognitive impairment and dementia in Parkinson's disease: A controlled study. *Psychological Medicine, 21*, 911-921.
5. Cormier, P., Margison, J. A., & Fisk, J. D. (1991). Contribution of perceptual and lexical-semantic errors to the naming impairments in Alzheimer's disease. *Perceptual and Motor Skills, 73*, 175-183.
6. Ron, M. A., Callanan, M. M., & Warrington, E. K. (1991). Cognitive abnormalities in multiple sclerosis: A psychometric and MRI study. *Psychological Medicine, 21*, 59-68.
7. Shallice, T., & Kartsounis, L. D. (1993). Selective impairment of retrieving pepple's names: A category specific disorder? *Cortex, 29*, 281-291.

[1056]

Graded Word Spelling Test.
Purpose: Designed to measure spelling achievement.
Population: Ages 6-0 to adult.
Publication Date: 1977.

Scores: Total words correct.
Administration: Group.
Price Data, 1994: £5.25 per test booklet/manual (15 pages).
Time: (20–30) minutes.
Author: P. E. Vernon.
Publisher: Hodder & Stoughton Educational [England].

TEST REFERENCES

1. Bishop, D. V. M., & Robson, J. (1989). Accurate non-word spelling despite congenital inability to speak: Phoneme-grapheme conversation does not require subvocal articulation. *British Journal of Psychology, 80,* 1-13.
2. Phillips, C. J. (1989). Children's learning skills: A cautionary note on ethnic differences. *British Journal of Educational Psychology, 59,* 108-112.

[1057]

Graduate and Managerial Assessment.

Purpose: Constructed to assess numerical skills needed in finance-related occupations.
Population: Undergraduate and graduate students.
Publication Date: 1985.
Acronym: GMA.
Scores: 3 tests: Numerical, Abstract, Verbal.
Administration: Group.
Forms, 2: A, B.
Price Data, 1989: £56.95 per reference set; £43.10 per 10 Numerical test booklets; £49.45 per 10 Verbal test booklets; £60.95 per 10 Abstract test booklets; £28.75 per 25 self-scoring answer sheets; £8.05 per 10 administrator's test records; £13.25 per set of instruction cards; £26.45 per manual (59 pages).
Time: 30(35) minutes per test.
Authors: Psychometric Research Unit, The Hatfield Polytechnic.
Publisher: NFER-Nelson Publishing Co., Ltd. [England].
Cross References: For reviews by Philip G. Benson and Rhonda L. Gutenberg, see 10:129.

[1058]

Graduate Management Admission Test.

Purpose: Designed to measure "general verbal and mathmatical skills important in the study of management at the graduate level."
Population: Applicants to study in graduate management education.
Publication Dates: 1954–94.
Acronym: GMAT.
Scores, 3: Verbal, Quantitative, Total.
Administration: Group.
Price Data, 1993: $52 per student (fee includes reporting of scores to 5 schools).
Time: 180(210) minutes; 210(235) minutes including Writing Assessment.
Comments: Test administered 4 times annually (January, March, June, October) at centers established by publisher; Analytical Writing Assessment added October 1994.
Author: Graduate Management Admission Council.

Publisher: Educational Testing Service.
Cross References: For reviews by Lawrence A. Crosby and James Ledvinka, see 9:447 (1 reference); see also T3:973 (6 references), 8:1074 (11 references), and T2:2325 (5 references); for reviews by Jerome E. Doppelt and Gary R. Hanson of earlier forms, see 7:1080 (10 references).

TEST REFERENCES

1. Angoff, W. H., & Schrader, W. B. (1984). A study of hypotheses basic to the use of rights and formula scores. *Journal of Educational Measurement, 21,* 1-17.
2. Remus, W., & Wong, C. (1984). The impact of grade inflation on five admission criteria. *College Student Journal, 18,* 359-363.
3. Gatignon, H., & Reibstein, D. J. (1986). Pooling Logit Models. *Journal of Marketing Research, 23,* 281-285.
4. Graham, L. D. (1991). Predicting academic success of students in a master of business administration program. *Educational and Psychological Measurement, 51,* 721-727.
5. Brockner, J., Wiesenfeld, B. M., Reed, T., Grover, S., & Martin, C. (1993). Interactive effect of job content and context on the reactions of layoff survivors. *Journal of Personality and Social Psychology, 64,* 187-197.
6. Zwick, R. (1993). The validity of the GMAT for the prediction of grades in doctoral study in business and management: An empirical Bayes approach. *Journal of Educational Statistics, 18,* 91-107.

[1059]

The Graduate Record Examinations Biochemistry, Cell and Molecular Biology.

Purpose: Designed to assess the qualifications of graduate school applicants for advanced study and for fellowships in biochemistry, cell biology, and molecular biology, along with related programs in microbiology and genetics.
Population: Graduate school candidates.
Publication Dates: 1990–94.
Acronym: GRE.
Scores, 4: Biochemistry, Cell Biology, Molecular Biology and Genetics, Total.
Administration: Group.
Price Data: Available from publisher.
Time: (170) minutes.
Comments: Beginning in the fall of 1994, test administered 3 times annually (April, October, December) at centers established by publisher.
Author: Educational Testing Service.
Publisher: Educational Testing Service.
Cross References: For reviews of the GRE program, see 7:667 (1 review) and 5:601 (1 review).

[1060]

The Graduate Record Examinations Chemistry Test.

Purpose: Designed to assess the qualifications of graduate school applicants for advanced study and for fellowships in chemistry.
Population: Graduate school candidates.
Publication Dates: 1939–94.
Acronym: GRE.
Scores: Total score only.
Administration: Group.
Price Data: Available from publisher.
Time: (170) minutes.
Comments: Beginning in the fall of 1994, test

administered 3 times annually (April, October, December) at centers established by publisher.
Author: Educational Testing Service.
Publisher: Educational Testing Service.
Cross References: See 8:852 (1 reference) and 7:848 (1 reference); for a review by Max D. Engelhart of an earlier form, see 6:919. For reviews of the GRE program, see 7:667 (1 review) and 5:601 (1 review).

TEST REFERENCES

1. Humphreys, L. G. (1988). Trends in levels of academic achievement of blacks and other minorities. *Intelligence, 12*, 231-260.

[1061]

The Graduate Record Examinations Computer Science Test.

Purpose: Designed to assess the qualifications of graduate school applicants for advanced study and for fellowships in computer science.
Population: Graduate school candidates.
Publication Date: 1976-94.
Acronym: GRE.
Scores: Total score only.
Administration: Group.
Price Data: Available from publisher.
Time: (170) minutes.
Comments: Test administered 3 times annually (April, October, December) at centers established by publisher.
Author: Educational Testing Service.
Publisher: Educational Testing Service.

[1062]

The Graduate Record Examinations Economics Test.

Purpose: Designed to assess the qualifications of graduate school applicants for advanced study and for fellowships in economics.
Population: Graduate school candidates.
Publication Dates: 1939-94.
Acronym: GRE.
Scores: Total score only.
Administration: Group.
Price Data: Available from publisher.
Time: (170) minutes.
Comments: Beginning in the fall of 1994, test administered 3 times annually (April, October, December) at centers established by publisher.
Author: Educational Testing Service.
Publisher: Educational Testing Service.
Cross References: For a review by Irving Morrissett, see 8:897; see also 6:987 (1 reference). For reviews of the GRE program, see 7:667 (1 review) and 5:601 (1 review).

[1063]

The Graduate Record Examinations Education Test.

Purpose: Designed to assess the qualifications of graduate school applicants for advanced study and for fellowships in education.

Population: Graduate school candidates.
Publication Dates: 1946-94.
Acronym: GRE.
Scores: Total score only.
Administration: Group.
Price Data: Available from publisher.
Time: (170) minutes.
Comments: Beginning in the fall of 1994, test administered 3 times annually (April, October, December) at centers established by publisher.
Author: Educational Testing Service.
Publisher: Educational Testing Service.
Cross References: See 8:372 (3 references) and 7:578 (9 references); for a review by D. Welty Lefeter of an earlier form, see 6:698 (7 references); for a review by Harry N. Rivlin, see 5:537. For reviews of the GRE program, see 7:667 (1 review) and 5:601 (1 review).

TEST REFERENCES

1. Humphreys, L. G. (1988). Trends in levels of academic achievement of blacks and other minorities. *Intelligence, 12*, 231-260.

[1064]

The Graduate Record Examinations Engineering Test.

Purpose: Designed to assess the qualifications of graduate school applicants for advanced study and for fellowships in engineering.
Population: Graduate school candidates.
Publication Dates: 1939-94.
Acronym: GRE.
Scores, 3: Engineering, Mathematics Usage, Total.
Administration: Group.
Price Data: Available from publisher.
Time: (170) minutes.
Comments: Beginning in the fall of 1994, test administered 3 times annually (April, October, December) at centers established by publisher.
Author: Educational Testing Service.
Publisher: Educational Testing Service.
Cross References: For reviews of the GRE program, see 7:667 (1 review) and 5:601 (1 review).

TEST REFERENCES

1. Humphreys, L. G. (1988). Trends in levels of academic achievement of blacks and other minorities. *Intelligence, 12*, 231-260.

[1065]

The Graduate Record Examinations Biology Test.

Purpose: Designed to assess the qualifications of graduate school applicants for advanced study and for fellowships in cellular and molecular biology, organismal biology, and ecology and evolution biology.
Population: Graduate school candidates.
Publication Dates: 1939-94.
Acronym: GRE.
Scores, 4: Cellular and Molecular Biology, Organismal Biology, Ecology and Evolution, Total.
Administration: Group.

Price Data: Available from publisher.

Time: (170) minutes.

Comments: Beginning in the fall of 1994, test administered 3 times annually (April, October, December) at centers established by publisher.

Author: Educational Testing Service.

Publisher: Educational Testing Service.

Cross References: For a review by Clark W. Horton of an earlier form, see 5:727. For reviews of the GRE program, see 7:667 (1 review) and 5:601 (1 review).

[1066]

The Graduate Record Examinations Geology Test.

Purpose: Designed to assess the qualifications of graduate school applicants for advanced study and for fellowships in geology.

Population: Graduate school candidates.

Publication Dates: 1939–94.

Acronym: GRE.

Scores, 4: Stratigraphy/Sedimentology/Paleontology/ Geomorphology and Hydrology, Structural Geology and Geophysics, Mineralogy/Petrology and Geochemistry, Total.

Administration: Group.

Price Data: Available from publisher.

Time: (170) minutes.

Comments: Beginning in the fall of 1994, test administered 3 times annually (April, October, December) at centers established by publisher.

Author: Educational Testing Service.

Publisher: Educational Testing Service.

Cross References: See 7:852 (1 reference). For reviews of the GRE program, see 7:667 (1 review) and 5:601 (1 review).

[1067]

The Graduate Record Examinations History Test.

Purpose: Designed to assess the qualifications of graduate school applicants for advanced study and for fellowships in history.

Population: Graduate school candidates.

Publication Dates: 1939–94.

Acronym: GRE.

Scores, 3: European History, United States History, Total.

Administration: Group.

Price Data: Available from publisher.

Time: (170) minutes.

Comments: Beginning in the fall of 1994, test administered 3 times annually (April, October, December) at centers established by publisher.

Author: Educational Testing Service.

Publisher: Educational Testing Service.

Cross References: See 7:919 (1 reference); for a review by Robert H. Ferrell of an earlier version, see 5:818. For reviews of the GRE program, see 7:667 (1 review) and 5:601 (1 review).

[1068]

The Graduate Record Examinations Literature in English Test.

Purpose: Designed to assess the qualifications of graduate school applicants for advanced study and for fellowships in literature in English literature.

Population: Graduate school candidates.

Publication Dates: 1939–94.

Acronym: GRE.

Scores: Total score only.

Administration: Group.

Price Data: Available from publisher.

Time: (170) minutes.

Comments: Beginning in the fall of 1994, test administered 3 times annually (April, October, December) at centers established by publisher.

Author: Educational Testing Service.

Publisher: Educational Testing Service.

Cross References: For a review by Edward M. White, see 8:69; see also 7:219 (1 reference); for a review by Robert C. Pooley of an earlier form, see 5:215. For reviews of the GRE program, see 7:667 (1 review) and 5:601 (1 review).

[1069]

The Graduate Record Examinations Mathematics Test.

Purpose: Designed to assess the qualifications of graduate school applicants for advanced study and for fellowships in mathematics.

Population: Graduate school candidates.

Publication Dates: 1939–94.

Acronym: GRE.

Scores: Total score only.

Administration: Group.

Price Data: Available from publisher.

Time: (170) minutes.

Comments: Beginning in the fall of 1994, test administered 3 times annually (April, October, December) at centers established by publisher.

Author: Educational Testing Service.

Publisher: Educational Testing Service.

Cross References: See 8:272 (1 reference); for a review by Paul C. Rosenbloom of an earlier form, see 6:578; for a review by Eric F. Gardner, see 5:427 (1 reference); for reviews of the GRE program, see 7:667 (1 review) and 5:601 (1 review).

TEST REFERENCES

1. Humphreys, L. G. (1988). Trends in levels of academic achievement of blacks and other minorities. *Intelligence, 12,* 231-260.

[1070]

The Graduate Record Examinations Music Test.

Purpose: Designed to assess the qualifications of graduate school applicants for advanced study and for fellowships in music.

Population: Graduate school candidates.

Publication Dates: 1990–94.

Acronym: GRE.

Scores, 3: History and Theory, Listening and Literature, Aural Skills, Total.
Administration: Group.
Price Data: Available from publisher.
Time: (190) minutes.
Comments: Test revised in 1990 to include a listening component and free-response questions that require the test taker to write responses in music notation; test administered 2 times annually (October, December) at centers established by publisher.
Author: Educational Testing Service.
Publisher: Educational Testing Service.
Cross References: For a review of the GRE program, see 7:667.

[1071]
The Graduate Record Examinations Physics Test.
Purpose: Designed to assess the qualifications of graduate school applicants for advanced study and for fellowships in physics.
Population: Graduate school candidates.
Publication Dates: 1939–94.
Acronym: GRE.
Scores: Total score only.
Administration: Group.
Price Data: Available from publisher.
Time: (170) minutes.
Comments: Beginning in the fall of 1994, test administered 3 times annually (April, October, December) at centers established by publisher.
Author: Educational Testing Service.
Publisher: Educational Testing Service.
Cross References: See 8:866 (1 reference); for a review by Theodore G. Phillips, see 6:931; for a review by Leo Nedelsky, see 5:754. For reviews of the GRE program, see 7:667 (1 review) and 5:601 (1 review).

[1072]
The Graduate Record Examinations Political Science Test.
Purpose: Designed to assess the qualifications of graduate school applicants for advanced study and for fellowships in political science.
Population: Graduate school candidates.
Publication Dates: 1939–94.
Acronym: GRE.
Scores: Total score only.
Administration: Group.
Price Data: Available from publisher.
Time: (170) minutes.
Comments: Beginning in the fall of 1994, test administered 3 times annually (April, October, December) at centers established by publisher.
Author: Educational Testing Service.
Publisher: Educational Testing Service.
Cross References: For a review by Christine McGuire of an earlier form, see 5:835. For reviews

of the GRE program, see 7:667 (1 review) and 5:601 (1 review).

TEST REFERENCES
1. Humphreys, L. G. (1988). Trends in levels of academic achievement of blacks and other minorities. *Intelligence, 12,* 231-260.

[1073]
The Graduate Record Examinations Psychology Test.
Purpose: Designed to assess the qualifications of graduate school applicants for advanced study and for fellowships in psychology.
Population: Graduate school candidates.
Publication Dates: 1939–94.
Acronym: GRE.
Scores, 3: Experimental Psychology, Social Psychology, Total.
Administration: Group.
Price Data: Available from publisher.
Time: (170) minutes.
Comments: Beginning in the fall of 1994, test administered 3 times annually (April, October, December) at centers established by publisher.
Author: Educational Testing Service.
Publisher: Educational Testing Service.
Cross References: See 8:461 (3 references), T2:1005 (2 references), and 7:644 (9 references); for a review by Harold Seashore of an earlier form, see 5:583. For reviews of the GRE program, see 7:667 (1 review) and 5:601 (1 review).

TEST REFERENCES
1. Ware, M. E. (1984). Helping students to evaluate areas of graduate study in psychology. *College Student Journal, 18,* 2-11.
2. Daehnert, C., & Carter, J. D. (1987). The prediction of success in a clinical psychology graduate program. *Educational and Psychological Measurement, 47*(4), 1113-1125.
3. Humphreys, L. G. (1988). Trends in levels of academic achievement of blacks and other minorities. *Intelligence, 12,* 231-260.

[1074]
The Graduate Record Examinations Sociology Test.
Purpose: Designed to assess the qualifications of graduate school applicants for advanced study and for fellowships in sociology.
Population: Graduate school candidates.
Publication Dates: 1939–94.
Acronym: GRE.
Scores: Total score only.
Administration: Group.
Price Data: Available from publisher.
Time: (170) minutes.
Comments: Beginning in the fall of 1994, test administered 3 times annually (April, October, December) at centers established by publisher.
Author: Educational Testing Service.
Publisher: Educational Testing Service.
Cross References: For a review by J. Richard Wilmeth, see 6:1021. For reviews of the GRE program, see 7:667 (1 review) and 5:601 (1 review).

[1075]

Graduate Record Examinations: Subject Tests.

Purpose: Designed to assess the qualifications of graduate school applicants in specific fields of study.
Population: Graduate school candidates.
Publication Dates: 1939–94.
Acronym: GRE.
Scores: 17 subtests: Biochemistry, Cell and Molecular Biology, Biology, Chemistry, Computer Science, Economics, Education, Engineering, Geology, History, Literature in English, Mathematics, Music, Physics, Political Science, Psychology, Sociology.
Administration: Group.
Price Data: Available from publisher.
Time: (170–180) minutes.
Comments: Beginning in the fall of 1994, all tests except for the Music Test administered 3 times annually (April, October, December) at centers established by publisher; the Music Test is administered 2 times annually (October, December) at centers established by publisher.
Author: Educational Testing Service.
Publisher: Educational Testing Service.
Cross References: See T3:994 (5 references) and 8:476 (6 references); for a review by Leona E. Tyler of an earlier program, see 7:667 (10 references); see also 6:762 (1 reference; for a review by Harold Seashore, see 5:601 (12 references); see also 4:527 (24 references).

TEST REFERENCES

1. Specht, H., Britt, D., & Frost, C. (1984). Undergraduate education and professional achievement of MSWs. *Social Work, 29,* 219-224.
2. Oltman, P. K., & Hartnett, R. T. (1985). The role of the Graduate Record Examinations in graduate admissions. *Journal of Higher Education, 56,* 523-537.

[1076]

The Graduate Record Examinations—General Test.

Purpose: "Designed to assess the Verbal, Quantitative and Analytical reasoning abilities of graduate school applicants."
Population: Graduate school candidates.
Publication Dates: 1949–94.
Acronym: GRE.
Scores, 3: Verbal Reasoning, Quantitative Reasoning, Analytical Reasoning.
Administration: Group or individual.
Price Data: Available from publisher.
Time: (210) minutes for paper-and-pencil administration; (270) minutes for computer-based test.
Comments: Test administered 4 times annually (April, June, October, December) at centers established by publisher; available in paper-and-pencil form or computer-based and computer-adaptive testing; large scale paper-and-pencil administrations are being reduced; computer-administered tests are being delivered daily by appointment.
Author: Educational Testing Service.
Publisher: Educational Testing Service.
Cross References: For reviews by Sanford J. Cohn and Richard M. Jaeger, see 9:448 (9 references); see also T3:995 (26 references), 8:188 (45 references), T2:382 (15 references), and 7:353 (43 references); for reviews by Robert L. French and Warren W. Willingham of an earlier edition, see 6:461 (17 references); for a review by John T. Dailey, see 5:336 (7 references); for reviews by J. P. Guilford and Carl I. Hovland, see 4:293 (2 references); for reviews of the GRE program, see 7:667 (1 reference) and 5:601 (1 reference).

TEST REFERENCES

1. Swinton, S. S., & Powers, D. E. (1983). A study of the effects of special preparation on GRE analytical scores and item types. *Journal of Educational Psychology, 75,* 104-115.
2. Hosford, R. E., Johnson, M. E., & Atkinson, D. R. (1984). Academic criteria, experiential background and personal interviews as predictors of success in a counselor education program. *Counselor Education and Supervision, 23,* 268-275.
3. Milner, M., McNeil, J. S., & King, S. W. (1984). The GRE: A question of validity in predicting performance in professional schools of social work. *Educational and Psychological Measurement, 44,* 945-950.
4. Stricker, L. J. (1984). The stability of a partial correlation index for identifying items that perform differentially in subgroups. *Educational and Psychological Measurement, 44,* 831-837.
5. Ware, M. E. (1984). Helping students to evaluate areas of graduate study in psychology. *College Student Journal, 18,* 2-11.
6. Henk, W. A., Helfeldt, J. D., & Rinehart, S. D. (1985). A meta-cognitive approach to estimating intersentential integration in cloze tests. *National Reading Conference Yearbook, 34,* 213-218.
7. Oltman, P. K., & Hartnett, R. T. (1985). The role of the Graduate Record Examinations in graduate admissions. *Journal of Higher Education, 56,* 523-537.
8. Osigweh, C. A. B. (1985). Measuring performance in a business school. *Delta Pi Epsilon Journal, 27,* 130-141.
9. Powers, D. E. (1985). Effect of coaching on GRE aptitude test scores. *Journal of Educational Measurement, 22,* 121-136.
10. Powers, D. E. (1985). Effects of test preparation on the validity of a graduate admissions test. *Applied Psychological Measurement, 9,* 179-190.
11. Scott, S. R., & Shaw, M. E. (1985). Black and white performance in graduate school and policy implications of the use of Graduate Record Examination scores in admissions. *Journal of Negro Education, 54,* 14-23.
12. Thornell, J. G., & McCoy, A. (1985). The predictive validity of the Graduate Record Examinations for subgroups of students in different academic disciplines. *Educational and Psychological Measurement, 45,* 415-419.
13. Angoff, W. H., & Cowell, W. R. (1986). An examination of the assumption that the equating of parallel forms is population-independent. *Journal of Educational Measurement, 23,* 327-345.
14. Dorans, N. J., & Kingston, N. M. (1986). The effects of violations of unidimensionality on the estimation of item and ability parameters and on item response theory equating of the GRE Verbal scale. *Journal of Educational Measurement, 22,* 249-262.
15. Kaiser, J. (1986). The validity of the GRE Aptitude Test for foreign students. *The College Student Journal, 20,* 403-410.
16. Daehnert, C., & Carter, J. D. (1987). The prediction of success in a clinical psychology graduate program. *Educational and Psychological Measurement, 47*(4), 1113-1125.
17. Ford, H. T., Jr., Puckett, J. R., & Tucker, L. A. (1987). Predictors of grades assigned by graduate teaching assistants in physical education. *Psychological Reports, 60,* 735-739.
18. House, J. D., Johnson, J. J., & Tolone, W. L. (1987). Predictive validity of the Graduate Record Examination for performance in selected graduate psychology courses. *Psychological Reports, 60,* 107-110.
19. Kunkel, M. A., & Meara, N. M. (1987). Selected characteristics of counseling psychology applicants, training programs, and host departments as a function of administrative housing. *Journal of Counseling Psychology, 34,* 333-336.
20. Humphreys, L. G. (1988). Trends in levels of academic achievement of blacks and other minorities. *Intelligence, 12,* 231-260.
21. Payne, D. A. (1988). Brain dominance cognitive style and the Graduate Record Examination Aptitude Test. *Educational and Psychological Measurement, 48,* 175-179.

22. Dollinger, S. J. (1989). Predictive validity of the Graduate Record Examination in a clinical psychology program. *Professional Psychology: Research and Practice, 20,* 56-58.

23. Bennett, R. E., Sebrechts, M. M., & Rock, D. A. (1991). Expert-system scores for complex constructed-response quantitative items: A study of convergent validity. *Applied Psychological Measurement, 15,* 227-239.

24. Larson, L. M., Suzuki, L. A., Gillespie, K. N., Potenza, M. T., Bechtel, M. A., & Toulouse, A. L. (1992). Development and validation of the Counseling Self-Estimate Inventory. *Journal of Counseling Psychology, 39,* 105-120.

25. Matthews, T. A., & Martin, D. J. (1992). Reciprocal suppression and interaction effects of age with undergraduate grades and GRE on graduate performance in a college of education. *Educational and Psychological Measurement, 52,* 453-456.

26. Popham, J. W. (1992). Appropriate expectations for content judgments regarding teacher licensure tests. *Applied Measurement in Education, 5,* 285-301.

27. Ayers, J. B., & Quattlebaum, R. F. (1993). TOEFL performance and success in a masters program in engineering. *Educational and Psychological Measurement, 52,* 973-975.

28. Carson, C. C., Huelskamp, R. M., & Woodall, T. D. (1993). Perspectives on education in America: An annotated briefing, April 1992. *Journal of Educational Research, 86,* 267-278.

29. Goldberg, E. L., & Alliges, G. M. (1993). Assessing the validity of the GRE for students in psychology: A validity generalization approach. *Educational and Psychological Measurement, 52,* 1019-1028.

30. House, J. D., & Johnson, J. J. (1993). Graduate Record Examination scores and academic background variables as predictors of graduate degree completion. *Educational and Psychological Measurement, 53,* 551-556.

31. Kirchner, G. L. (1993). Gender as a moderator variable in predicting success in a master of arts in teaching program. *Educational and Psychological Measurement, 53,* 155-157.

[1077]

Grammar Test Packet.

Purpose: Provides tests over all phases of grammar, punctuation, and capitalization, plus general review.

Population: High school students.

Publication Date: No date.

Scores, 16: Nouns, Pronouns, Verbs, Adjectives and Adverbs, Prepositions/Conjunctions/Interjections, Correct Usage, Variety in Sentence Arrangement, Final Examination, Diagnostic and Achievement scores for each of the following: Parts of Speech, Parts of Sentence, Joining Parts of the Sentence, Capitalization and Punctuation.

Administration: Group.

Price Data, 1989: $3.95 per complete packet including answer keys.

Time: Administration time not reported.

Authors: Kenneth Stratton and George Christian.

Publisher: Stratton-Christian Press, Inc.

[1078]

Grammatical Analysis of Elicited Language— Pre-Sentence Level.

Purpose: Designed to provide in-depth grammatical analysis of children's expressive language.

Population: Hearing-impaired children ages 3–6.

Publication Date: 1983.

Acronym: GAEL-P.

Scores: 3 sections (Readiness Skills, Single Words, Word Combinations) yielding 3 scores: Comprehension, Prompted Production, Imitated Production.

Administration: Individual.

Price Data, 1987: $320 per complete kit including manual (81 pages), scoring forms, and videotape; $25

per videotape; $16 per manual; $6 per 25 record forms.

Time: Administration time not reported.

Comments: Simple Sentence Level (GAEL-S; 1079) and Complex Sentence Level (GAEL-C) also available.

Authors: Jean S. Moog, Victoria J. Kozak, and Ann E. Geers.

Publisher: Central Institute for the Deaf.

TEST REFERENCES

1. Abraham, S., & Stoker, R. (1988). Language assessment of hearing-impaired children and youth: Patterns of test use. *Language, Speech, and Hearing Services in Schools, 19,* 160-174.

[1079]

Grammatical Analysis of Elicited Language— Simple Sentence Level, Second Edition.

Purpose: "To assess the deaf child's facility in producing the structures of English" using expressive skills at the simple sentence level.

Population: Hearing-impaired ages 5–9.

Publication Dates: 1978–85.

Acronym: GAEL-S.

Scores: 2 overall scores (Prompted Productions, Imitated Productions) plus Mastery Points in 11 categories (Articles, Noun Modifiers, Pronouns, Subject Nouns, Object Nouns, WH-Questions, Verbs, Verb Inflections, Copulas, Prepositions, Conjunctions/Negatives).

Administration: Individual.

Price Data, 1988: $320 per complete kit including scoring forms, profile sheets, toys, manual ('85, 157 pages), and videotape; $17 per 25 transcription sheets and record forms; $6 per 50 summary and profile sheets; $25 per ½-inch videotape demonstrating administration of the test to a hearing-impaired child (if not purchased with the kit); $22 per manual.

Time: (60) minutes.

Comments: Pre-Sentence Level (GAEL-P) and Complex Sentence Level (GAEL-C) also available; Mastery Points are "criterion-referenced" and overall scores are norm-referenced.

Authors: Jean S. Moog and Ann E. Geers.

Publisher: Central Institute for the Deaf.

Cross References: For a review by June Ellen Shepherd, see 11:148 (2 references).

[1080]

Grandparents Strengths and Needs Inventory.

Purpose: "To help grandparents recognize their favorable qualities and identify aspects of their family relationships in which further growth is needed."

Population: Grandparents of children 6 and over.

Publication Date: 1993.

Acronym: GSNI.

Scores, 6: Satisfaction, Success, Teaching, Difficulty, Frustration, Information Needs.

Administration: Group.

Price Data, 1993: $65 per complete kit including 20 identification forms and 20 inventory booklets each:

grandparent, parent, and grandchild versions, 20 profiles, and manual (20 pages).
Foreign Language Edition: Spanish version available.
Time: Administration time not reported.
Comments: Parent and grandchild inventories included for comparison purposes.
Authors: Robert D. Strom and Shirley K. Strom.
Publisher: Scholastic Testing Service, Inc.

[1081]
Grassi Basic Cognitive Evaluation.
Purpose: Identify developmental deficits.
Population: Ages 3–9.
Publication Date: 1973.
Scores, 29: Discriminations (5 scores), Conceptualization (5 scores), Identifications (3 scores), Orientation (3 scores), Visualization, Number Concepts (3 scores), Kinesthesia (2 scores), Auditory Perception, Sequencing (2 scores), Recall (2 scores), Total, Basic Learning Quotient (ratio of a GBCE score to mental age on the Stanford-Binet Intelligence Scale).
Administration: Individual.
Price Data: Available from publisher.
Time: [20] minutes.
Author: Joseph R. Grassi.
Publisher: Joseph R. Grassi, Inc.
Cross References: See T3:1004 (1 reference); for additional information and reviews by J. Jeffrey Grill and Lester Mann, see 8:430.

[1082]
The Grassi Block Substitution Test: For Measuring Organic Brain Pathology.
Purpose: Intended for measurement of organic brain pathology.
Population: Mental patients.
Publication Dates: 1947–66.
Scores: Total score only.
Administration: Individual.
Price Data: Available from publisher.
Time: Administration time not reported.
Comments: Manual out of print.
Author: Joseph R. Grassi.
Publisher: Joseph R. Grassi, Inc.
Cross References: See T3:1005 (1 reference), T2:1196 (7 references), and P:94 (13 references); for excerpted reviews by J. G. McMurray and one other, see 5:60 (5 references).

[1083]
Gravidometer.
Purpose: Measures knowledge about human pregnancy.
Population: Adolescents and adults.
Publication Date: 1974.
Scores: Total score only.
Administration: Group.
Manual: No manual.
Price Data: Instrument is available without charge from author.

Time: [10] minutes.
Author: Panos D. Bardis.
Publisher: Panos D. Bardis.

[1084]
Gray Oral Reading Tests, Third Edition.
Purpose: Designed to be "an objective measure of growth in oral reading and an aid in the diagnosis of reading difficulties."
Population: Ages 7-0 to 18-11.
Publication Dates: 1967–92.
Acronym: GORT-3.
Scores, 3: Passage, Comprehension, Oral Reading Quotient.
Administration: Group.
Price Data, 1994: $114 per complete kit including 25 Form A Profile/Examiner record forms and 25 Form B Profile/Examiner record forms; $29 per student book; $29 per 25 Profile/Examiner record forms; $31 per examiner's manual ('92, 71 pages); $79 per Apple or IBM Software Scoring and Report System.
Time: (15–30) minutes.
Authors: J. Lee Wiederholt and Brian R. Bryant.
Publisher: PRO-ED, Inc.
Cross References: For reviews by Julia A. Hickman and Robert J. Tierney, see 10:131 (15 references).

TEST REFERENCES

1. Hoy, E., Weiss, G., Minde, K., & Cohen, N. (1978). The hyperactive child at adolescence: Cognitive, emotional, and social functioning. *Journal of Abnormal Child Psychology, 6,* 311-324.
2. Gregory, J. F. (1986). Phrasing in the speech and reading of the hearing impaired. *Journal of Communication Disorders, 19,* 289-297.
3. Goodman, N. C. (1987). Girls with learning disabilities and their sisters: How are they faring in adulthood? *Journal of Clinical Child Psychology, 16,* 290-300.
4. Webster, R. E. (1988). Variability in reading achievement test scores as related to reading curriculum. *Educational and Psychological Measurement, 48,* 815-825.
5. Glosser, G., & Friedman, R. B. (1990). The continuum of deep/phonological alexia. *Cortex, 26,* 343-359.
6. Watson, M., Stewart, M., & Krause, K. (1990). Identification of time-compressed sentential stimuli by good vs. poor readers. *Perceptual and Motor Skills, 71,* 107-114.
7. Wolff, P. H., Michel, G. F., & Ovrut, M. (1990). The timing of syllable repetitions in developmental dyslexia. *Journal of Speech and Hearing Research, 33,* 281-289.
8. Steffens, M. L., Eilers, R. E., Gross-Glenn, K., & Jallad, B. (1992). Speech perception in adult subjects with familial dyslexia. *Journal of Speech and Hearing Research, 35,* 192-200.
9. Pennington, B. F., Groisser, D., & Welsh, M. C. (1993). Contrasting cognitive deficits in attention deficit hyperactivity disorder versus reading disability. *Developmental Psychology, 29,* 511-523.

[1085]
Gray Oral Reading Tests—Diagnostic.
Purpose: Developed to assess oral reading proficiency in students having difficulties in reading continuous print.
Population: Ages 5-6 to 12-11.
Publication Date: 1991.
Acronym: GORT-D.
Scores, 4: Total Reading, Meaning Cues, Graphic/Phonemic Cues, Function Cues.
Administration: Individual.
Forms, 2: A, B.
Price Data, 1994: $114 per complete kit including

student book, 25 each Form A and B record forms, and examiner's manual (78 pages); $21 per student book; $34 per 25 record forms; $29 per manual; $79 per computer scoring system (Apple or IBM).
Time: (50–90) minutes.
Comments: Expanded edition of the Gray Oral Reading Tests—Third Edition (1084).
Authors: Brian R. Bryant and J. Lee Wiederholt.
Publisher: PRO-ED, Inc.
Cross References: For reviews by William R. Merz, Sr. and Steven A. Stahl, see 11:149 (1 reference).

[1086]
Gregorc Style Delineator.
Purpose: "Designed to aid an individual to recognize and identify the channels through which he/she receives and expresses information."
Population: Adults.
Publication Dates: 1982–90.
Scores, 4: Concrete Sequential score, Abstract Sequential score, Abstract Random score, Concrete Random score.
Administration: Group.
Price Data, 1993: $42.95 per sample set including *An Adult's Guide to Style* ('82, 74 pages), *Inside Styles: Beyond the Basics* ('85, 285 pages), the Gregorc Style Delineator, and a one-page synopsis of the manual; $15.95 per technical manual ('82, 46 pages); $42.50 per 25 instrument packets or $24.95 per 10 instrument packets including guidelines for group administration; $9.95 per audiocassette on careful use; $14.95 per *An Adult's Guide to Style*; $29.95 per *Inside Style: Beyond the Basics*.
Time: 3(5) minutes.
Comments: Self-assessment instrument.
Author: Anthony F. Gregorc.
Publisher: Gregorc Associates, Inc.

TEST REFERENCES

1. Joniak, A. J., & Isaksen, S. G. (1988). The Gregorc Style Delineator: Internal consistency and its relationship to Kirton's adaptive-innovative distinction. *Educational and Psychological Measurement, 48*, 1043-1049.
2. O'Brien, T. P. (1990). Construct validation of the Gregorc Style Delineator: An application of LISREL 7. *Educational and Psychological Measurement, 50*, 631-636.

[1087]
Grid Test of Schizophrenic Thought Disorder.
Purpose: "Developed to detect the presence of schizophrenic thought disorder."
Population: Adults.
Publication Date: 1967.
Acronym: GTSTD.
Scores, 2: Intensity, Consistency.
Administration: Individual.
Price Data, 1987: £7 per complete kit; £1 per 25 record sheets; £1 per 25 analysis sheets; £3 per manual (21 pages); £4 per specimen set.
Time: (15–25) minutes.
Comments: 1 form (set of 8 photographs).
Authors: D. Bannister and Fay Fransella.

Publisher: Psychological Test Publications [England].
Cross References: See T3:1009 (3 references); for a review by Robert W. Payne, see 8:571 (30 references); see also T2:1198 (8 references); for a review by David Jones, see 7:84 (7 references); see also P:96 (8 references).

TEST REFERENCES

1. Allon, R., Stewart, M. F., Lancee, W. J., & Brawley, P. (1981). Conditional probabilities and the Grid Test of Schizophrenic Thought Disorder. *British Journal of Clinical Psychology, 20*, 57-66.
2. Stefan, C., & Malloy, P. (1982). An investigation of the construct validity of the Bannister-Fransella Grid Test of Schizophrenic Thought Disorder. *British Journal of Clinical Psychology, 21*, 199-204.
3. Cyr, J. J. (1983). Measuring consistency with the Grid Test. *The British Journal of Clinical Psychology, 22*, 219-220.
4. Kirk, J. W. (1984). Psychological construing and meaningfulness in schizophrenia. *British Journal of Medical Psychology, 57*, 153-158.

[1088]
Griffiths Mental Development Scales.
Purpose: To measure trends of development that are significant for intelligence, or indicative of mental growth.
Publication Dates: 1951–78.
Administration: Individual.
Restricted Distribution: Restricted to persons who qualify by attending an approved course; details may be obtained from distributor.
Price Data, 1993: £180 per Scale 1; £220 per Scale 2; £1.50 per record book (Scale 2); £.75 per record form (Scale 1); £19.50 per *The Abilities of Babies* ('76, 239 pages); £19.50 per *The Abilities of Young Children* ('70, 187 pages).
Author: Ruth Griffiths.
Publisher: Association for Research in Infant and Child Development; distributed by The Test Agency Ltd. [England].
a) SCALE 1.
Population: Ages 0–2.
Scores, 6: Locomotor, Personal-Social, Hearing and Speech, Eye and Hand, Performance, Total.
Time: [20–40] minutes.
b) SCALE 2.
Population: Ages 2–8.
Scores, 7: Same as Scale 1 plus Practical Reasoning.
Time: Administration time not reported.
Cross References: See 9:450 (1 reference); for a review by C. B. Hindley of Scale 1, see 6:523 (4 references); for a review by Nancy Bayley of Scale 1, see 5:404 (3 references).

TEST REFERENCES

1. Mansell, J., Jenkins, J., Felce, D., & Kock, U. D. (1984). Measuring the activity of severely and profoundly mentally-handicapped adults in ordinary housing. *Behaviour Research and Therapy, 22*, 23-29.
2. Cochran, M. M., & Gunnarsson, L. (1985). A follow-up study of group day care and family-based childrearing patterns. *Journal of Marriage and the Family, 47*, 297-309.
3. Felce, D., Thomas, M., Kock, U. D., & Saxby, H. (1985). An ecological comparison of small community-based houses and traditional institutions—II. Physical setting and the use of opportunities. *Behaviour Research and Therapy, 23*, 337-348.
4. Shaner, J. M., Peterson, K. L., & Roscoe, B. (1985). Older ado-

lescent females' knowledge of child development norms. *Adolescence, 20,* 53-59.

5. Chambers, C. M., & Grantham-McGregor, S. M. (1986). Research note: Patterns of mental development among young, middle-class Jamaican children. *Journal of Child Psychology and Psychiatry and Allied Disciplines, 27,* 117-123.

6. Parks, P. L., & Smeriglio, V. L. (1986). Relationships among parenting knowledge, quality of stimulation in the home and infant development. *Family Relations, 35,* 411-416.

7. Holdgrafer, G. (1987). A child learns a word: Effects of the principle of informativeness. *Perceptual and Motor Skills, 65,* 195-200.

8. Tannock, R. (1988). Mothers' directiveness in their interactions with their children with and without Down Syndrome. *American Journal on Mental Retardation, 93,* 154-165.

9. Davis, H., & Rushton, R. (1991). Counselling and supporting parents of children with developmental delay: A research evaluation. *Journal of Mental Deficiency Research, 35,* 89-112.

10. Webb, T., & Thake, A. (1991). Moderate and mild mental retardation in the Martin-Bell syndrome. *Journal of Mental Deficiency Research, 35,* 521-528.

[1089]
Grooved Pegboard Test.
Purpose: To assess manipulative dexterity.
Population: Ages 5 to 8-12, 9 to 14-12, 15 to adult.
Publication Date: 1989.
Scores, 3: Total Time, Number of "Drops," Total Pegs Correctly Placed.
Administration: Individual.
Price Data, 1991: $80 per Grooved Pegboard; $26.50 per 30 replacement pegs.
Time: Trial discontinued after 5 minutes.
Comments: Ages 5 to 8-12 only complete first two rows of the Pegboard.
Author: Ronald Trites (manual).
Publisher: Lafayette Instrument.

TEST REFERENCES

1. Feehan, M., Stanton, W. R., McGee, R., Silva, P. A., & Moffitt, T. E. (1990). Is there an association between lateral preference and delinquent behavior. *Journal of Abnormal Psychology, 99,* 198-201.

2. Rausch, R., Boone, K., & Ary, C. M. (1991). Right-hemisphere dominance in temporal lobe epilepsy: Clinical and neuropsychological correlates. *Journal of Clinical and Experimental Neuropsychology, 13,* 217-231.

[1090]
Group Achievement Identification Measure.
Purpose: "To determine the degree to which children exhibit the characteristics of underachievers so that preventative or curative efforts may be administered."
Population: Grades 5-12.
Publication Date: 1986.
Acronym: GAIM.
Scores, 6: Competition, Responsibility, Achievement Communication, Independence/Dependence, Respect/Dominance, Total.
Administration: Group.
Price Data, 1993: $12 per individual inventory including prepaid computer scoring by publisher; $95 per class set of 30 inventories including prepaid computer scoring by publisher; manual for administration and interpretation (12 pages) included with test orders.
Time: (30) minutes.
Comments: Self-report inventory.
Author: Sylvia B. Rimm.
Publisher: Educational Assessment Service, Inc.

Cross References: For reviews by Robert K. Gable and Jeffrey Jenkins, see 11:151.

[1091]
Group Cohesiveness: A Study of Group Morale.
Purpose: Designed to assess group cohesiveness.
Population: Adults.
Publication Dates: 1957-58.
Acronym: GC.
Scores, 5: Satisfaction of Individual Motives, Satisfaction of Interpersonal Relations, Homogeneity of Attitude, Satisfaction With Leadership, Total.
Administration: Group.
Price Data: Available from publisher.
Time: (10-15) minutes.
Comments: Self-administered.
Author: Bernard Goldman.
Publisher: Psychometric Affiliates.
Cross References: See T2:1199 (1 reference) and P:97; for reviews by Eric F. Gardner and Cecil A. Gibb, see 6:104 (1 reference).

[1092]
Group Diagnostic Reading Aptitude and Achievement Tests.
Purpose: Diagnose whether children need remedial work in reading.
Population: Grades 3-9.
Publication Date: 1939.
Scores, 15: Reading (Paragraph Understanding, Speed), Word Discrimination (Vowels, Consonants, Reversals, Additions and Omissions), Arithmetic, Spelling, Visual Ability (Letter Memory, Form Memory), Auditory Ability (Letter Memory, Discrimination and Orientation), Motor Ability (Copying Text, Crossing Out Letters), Vocabulary.
Administration: Group.
Manual: No manual.
Price Data: Available from publisher.
Time: (60-70) minutes.
Authors: Marion Monroe and Eva Edith Sherman.
Publisher: C. H. Nevins Printing Co.
Cross References: For additional information, see 6:825.

TEST REFERENCES

1. Berninger, V. W. (1987). Global component, and serial processing of printed words in beginning reading. *Journal of Experimental Child Psychology, 43,* 387-418.

[1093]
Group Diagnostic Reading Aptitude and Achievement Tests, Intermediate Form.
Purpose: Designed to assess reading achievement and to diagnose reading problems.
Population: Grades 3-9.
Publication Date: [Orig. 1937].
Scores, 13: Achievement [Reading (Paragraph Understanding, Speed, Word Discrimination), Arithmetic, Spelling], Diagnostic [Word Discrimination Errors, Visual (Letter Memory, Form Memory),

Auditory (Letter Memory, Discrimination and Orientation), Motor (Copying Text, Cross Out Letters), Language-Vocabulary].
Administration: Group.
Price Data, 1992: $.27 per book; $5.50 per set of visual test cards; $2.20 per set of norms.
Time: (40) minutes (includes both timed and untimed tests).
Authors: Marion Monroe and Eva Edith Sherman.
Publisher: C. H. Nevins Printing Co.

[1094]
Group Embedded Figures Test.
Purpose: Developed to evaluate field-dependence.
Population: College.
Publication Date: 1971.
Acronym: GEFT.
Scores: Total score only.
Administration: Group.
Price Data, 1990: $19 per 25 test booklets; $1.75 per set of scoring stencils; $7.50 per manual (32 pages); $2.50 per specimen set.
Time: 12(15) minutes.
Comments: Adaptation of the individually administered Embedded Figures Test; manual is a combined manual for this test, the Embedded Figures Test, and the Children's Embedded Figures Test.
Authors: Philip K. Oltman, Evelyn Raskin, Herman A. Witkin, and Stephen A. Karp (manual).
Publisher: Consulting Psychologists Press, Inc.
Cross References: See 9:452 (41 references) and T3:1013 (88 references); for reviews by Leonard D. Goodstein and Alfred E. Hall, see 8:572 (47 references); see also T2:1201 (3 references); for references to reviews of the individual test, see 8:548.

TEST REFERENCES

1. Renninger, K. A., & Snyder, S. S. (1983). Effects of cognitive style on perceived satisfaction and performance among students and teachers. *Journal of Educational Psychology, 75,* 668-676.
2. Sewell, T. E., Farley, F. H., & Sewell, F. B. (1983). Anxiety, cognitive style, and mathematics achievement. *Journal of General Psychology, 109,* 59-66.
3. Sims, M. T., Graves, R. J., & Simpson, G. C. (1983). Mineworkers' scores on the Group Embedded Figures Test. *Journal of Occupational Psychology, 56,* 335-337.
4. Copeland, B. D. (1984). The relationship of cognitive style to the evaluation of university art instructors. *Studies in Art Education: A Journal of Issues and Research, 25,* 109-114.
5. Davey, B., & LaSasso, C. (1984). The interaction of reader and task factors in the assessment of reading comprehension. *The Journal of Experimental Education, 52,* 199-206.
6. DiNuovo, S. (1984). Administration times for Witkin's Group Embedded Figures Test. *Perceptual and Motor Skills, 58,* 134.
7. DiNuovo, S. (1984). Influence of instructions and cognitive articulation on reducing the Muller-Lyer illusion with a repeated trial. *Perceptual and Motor Skills, 59,* 791-796.
8. Edge, O. P., & Friedberg, S. H. (1984). Factors affecting achievementin the first course in calculus. *The Journal of Experimental Education, 52,* 136-140.
9. Hansen, L. (1984). Field dependence-independence and language testing: Evidence from six Pacific island cultures. *TESOL Quarterly, 18,* 311-324.
10. Hill, D. M., & Redden, M. G. (1984). Spatial puzzles and the assessment of children's problem-solving performance. *School Science and Mathematics, 84,* 475-483.
11. Jedrczak, A., Clements, G. (1984). The TM-SIDHI Programme and field independence. *Perceptual and Motor Skills, 59,* 999-1000.
12. Jolly, P. E., & Strawitz, B. M. (1984). Teacher-student cognitive style and achievement in biology. *Science Education, 68,* 487-492.
13. Kepner, M. D., & Neimark, E. D. (1984). Test-retest reliability and differentiated patterns of score change on the Group Embedded Figures Test. *Journal of Personality and Social Psychology, 46,* 1405-1413.
14. McDonald, E. R. (1984). The relationship of student and faculty field dependence/independence congruence to student academic achievement. *Educational and Psychological Measurement, 44,* 725-731.
15. Myer, K. A., & Hensley, J. H. (1984). Cognitive style, gender, and self-report of principle as predictors of adult performance on Piaget's water level task. *The Journal of Genetic Psychology, 144,* 179-183.
16. Park, O. (1984). Example comparison strategy versus attribute identification strategy in concept learning. *American Educational Research Journal, 21,* 145-162.
17. Pine, C. J. (1984). Field-dependence factors in American Indian and Caucasian obesity. *Journal of Clinical Psychology, 40,* 205-209.
18. Roberge, J. J., & Flexer, B. K. (1984). Cognitive style, operativity, and reading achievement. *American Educational Research Journal, 21,* 227-236.
19. Roberts, F. C., & Park, O. (1984). Feedback strategies and cognitive style in computer-based instruction. *Journal of Instructional Psychology, 11,* 63-74.
20. Strawitz, B. M. (1984). Cognitive style and the acquisition and transfer of the ability to control variables. *Journal of Research in Science Teaching, 21,* 133-141.
21. Strawitz, B. M. (1984). Cognitive style and the effects of two instructional treatments on the acquisition and transfer of the ability to control variables: A longitudinal study. *Journal of Research in Science Research, 21,* 833-841.
22. Swinnen, S. (1984). Some evidence for the hemispheric asymmetry model of lateral eye movements. *Perceptual and Motor Skills, 58,* 79-88.
23. Abraham, R. G. (1985). Field independence-dependence and the teaching of grammar. *TESOL Quarterly, 19,* 689-702.
24. Davey, B., & Kapinus, B. A. (1985). Prior knowledge and recall of unfamiliar information: Reader and text factors. *Journal of Educational Research, 78,* 147-151.
25. Davey, B., & LaSasso, C. (1985). Relations of cognitive style to assessment components of reading comprehension for hearing-impaired adolescents. *Volta Review, 87,* 17-27.
26. DeBerry, S. (1985). Correlation of field independence with ability to reduce muscle tension and anxiety. *Perceptual and Motor Skills, 61,* 1221-1222.
27. Donovan, D. M., Kivlahan, D. R., Walker, R. D., & Umlauf, R. (1985). Derivation and validation of neuropsychological clusters among men alcoholics. *Journal of Studies on Alcohol, 46,* 205-211.
28. Durso, F. T., Reardon, R., Jolly, E. J. (1985). Self-nonself-segregation and reality monitoring. *Journal of Personality and Social Psychology, 48,* 447-455.
29. Edwards, R. V., & Lee, A. M. (1985). The relationship of cognitive style and instructional strategy to learning and transffer of motor skills. *Research Quarterly for Exercise and Sport, 56,* 286-290.
30. Falcone, D. J. (1985). Laterality and field dependence. *Perceptual and Motor Skills, 61,* 651-657.
31. Fallik, B., & Eliot, J. (1985). Intuition, cognitive style, and hemispheric processing. *Perceptual and Motor Skills, 60,* 683-697.
32. Firth, R. S., & Fitzgerald, D. (1985). Group Embedded Figures Test: Normative data for male automotive mechanical apprentice tradesmen. *Perceptual and Motor Skills, 60,* 803-806.
33. Friedrich, W. N., Tyler, J. D., & Clark, J. A. (1985). Personality and psychophysiological variables in abusive, neglectful, and low-income control mothers. *The Journal of Nervous and Mental Disease, 173,* 449-460.
34. Gonzales, R. R., & Roll, S. (1985). Relationship between acculturation, cognitive style, and intelligence. *Journal of Cross-Cultural Psychology, 16,* 190-205.
35. Guthrie, K. H. (1985). Locus of control and field independence-dependence as factors in the development of moral judgment. *The Journal of Genetic Psychology, 146,* 13-18.
36. Jolly, E. J., & Reardon, R. (1985). Cognitive differentiation, automaticity and interruptions of automatized behaviors. *Personality and Social Psychology Bulletin, 11,* 301-314.
37. Larson, C. O., Dansereau, D. F., O'Donnell, A. M., Hythecker, V. I., Lambiotte, J. G., & Rocklin, T. R. (1985). Effects of metacognitive and elaborative activity on cooperative learning and transfer. *Contemporary Educational Psychology, 10,* 342-348.
38. Leahy, M. D., & Zalatimo, S. D. (1985). Group Embedded Figures Test: Psychometric data for a sample of high school students. *Perceptual and Motor Skills, 61,* 1243-1248.
39. Manning-Melean, L., & Fernández-Ballesteros, R. (1985). Tactile perceptual task and field dependence-independence. *Perceptual and Motor Skills, 61,* 503-506.
40. McDonald, B. A., Larson, C. O., Dansereau, D. F., & Spurlin, J. E. (1985). Cooperative dyads: Impact on text learning and transfer. *Contemporary Educational Psychology, 10,* 369-377.

41. Mwamwenda, T. S., Dionne, J., & Mwamwenda, B. B. (1985). Theoretical and empirical link between psychological differentiation and extraversion. *Psychological Reports, 56*, 147-154.

42. O'Donnell, A. M., Dansereau, D. F., Rocklin, T. R., Hythecker, V. I., Lambiotte, J. G., Larson, C. O., & Young, M. D. (1985). Effects of elaboration frequency on cooperative learning. *Journal of Educational Psychology, 77*, 572-580.

43. Pincus, K. V. (1985). Group Embedded Figures Test: Psychometric data for a sample of accountants compared with student norms. *Perceptual and Motor Skills, 60*, 707-712.

44. Stone, E. F., & Gueutal, H. G. (1985). An empirical derivation of the dimensions along which characteristics of jobs are perceived. *Academy of Management Journal, 28*, 376-396.

45. Trout, J. S., & Crawley, F. E. (1985). The effects of matching instructional strategy with selected student characteristics on ninth grade physical science students' attitudes and achievement. *Journal of Research in Science Teaching, 22*, 407-419.

46. Abraham, M. R., & Renner, J. W. (1986). The sequence of learning cycle activities in high school chemistry. *Journal of Research in Science Teaching, 23*, 121-143.

47. Arnoult, M. D., Gillfillan, L. G., & Voorhees, J. W. (1986). Annoyingness of aircraft noise in relation to cognitive activity. *Perceptual and Motor Skills, 63*, 599-616.

48. Burton, L. (1986). Relationship between musical accompaniment and learning style in problem solving. *Perceptual and Motor Skills, 62*, 48-50.

49. Collins-Eiland, K., Dansereau, D. F., Brooks, L. W., & Holley, C. D. (1986). Effects of conversational noise, locus of control, and field dependence/independence on the performance of academic tasks. *Contemporary Educational Psychology, 11*, 139-149.

50. Cooper, C., & Kline, P. (1986). An evaluation of the Defence Mechanism Test. *British Journal of Psychology, 77*, 19-32.

51. Crow, L. W., & Piper, M. K. (1986). A study of field independent biased mental ability tests in community college science classes. *Journal of Research in Science Teaching, 23*, 817-822.

52. DeBiasio, A. R. (1986). Problem solving in triads composed of varying numbers of field-dependent and field-independent subjects. *Journal of Personality and Social Psychology, 51*, 749-754.

53. Dillbeck, M. C., Assimakis, P. D., Raimondi, D., Orme-Johnson, D. W., & Rowe, R. (1986). Longitudinal effects of the Transcendental Meditation and TM-Sidhi program on cognitive ability and cognitive style. *Perceptual and Motor Skills, 62*, 731-738.

54. Drouin, D., Talbot, S., & Goulet, C. (1986). Cognitive styles of French Canadian athletes. *Perceptual and Motor Skills, 63*, 1139-1142.

55. Fallik, B., & Eliot, J. (1986). An examination of possible age differences in interrelationships between intuition, cognitive style, and hemispheric preference variables. *Perceptual and Motor Skills, 63*, 1251-1257.

56. Fallik, B., & Eliot, J. (1986). Relation between intuition and college majors. *Perceptual and Motor Skills, 63*, 328.

57. Halpin, G., & Peterson, H. (1986). Accommodating instruction to learners' field independence/dependence: A study of effects on achievement and attitudes. *Perceptual and Motor Skills, 62*, 967-974.

58. Hauptman, A., & Eliot, J. (1986). Contribution of figural proportion, figural memory, figure-ground perception and severity of hearing loss to performance on spatial tests. *Perceptual and Motor Skills, 63*, 187-190.

59. Manning, L. (1986). Interhemispheric asymmetry in facial expression recognition: Relationship to field-dependence. *Cortex, 22*, 601-610.

60. Newsome, G. L., III. (1986). The effects of reader perspective and cognitive style on remembering important information from texts. *Journal of Reading Behavior, 18*, 117-133.

61. O'Donnell, A. M., Dansereau, D. F., Hythecker, V. I., Larson, C. O., Rocklin, T. R., Lambiotte, J. G., & Young, M. D. (1986). The effects of monitoring on cooperative learning. *Journal of Experimental Education, 54*, 169-173.

62. Rossel, C. L. (1986). Relationship of field dependence-independence to documentation of nursing-process components by registered nurses in a clinical setting. *Perceptual and Motor Skills, 63*, 315-318.

63. Swinnen, S., Vandenberghe, J., & VanAssche, E. (1986). Role of cognitive style constructs field dependence-independence and reflection-impulsivity in skill acquisition. *Journal of Sport Psychology, 8*, 51-69.

64. Ward, T. B., Foley, C. M., & Cole, J. (1986). Classifying multidimensional stimuli: Stimulus, task, and observer factors. *Journal of Experimental Psychology: Human Perception and Performance, 12*, 211-225.

65. Weiner, N. C., & Robinson, S. E. (1986). Cognitive abilities, personality and gender differences in math achievement of gifted adolescents. *Gifted Child Quarterly, 30*, 83-87.

66. Williams, R. A., Lusk, S. L., & Kline, N. W. (1986). Knowledge of aging and cognitive styles in baccalaureate nursing students. *The Gerontologist, 26*, 545-550.

67. York, D. C., & Tinsley, H. E. A. (1986). The relationship between cognitive styles and Holland's personality types. *Journal of College Student Personnel, 27*, 535-541.

68. Highhouse, S., & Doverspike, D. (1987). The validity of the Learning Style Inventory 1985 as a predictor of cognitive style and occupational preference. *Educational and Psychological Measurement, 47*(3), 749-754.

69. Jones, E. B., O'Gorman, J. G., & Byrne, B. (1987). Forgetting of word associates as a function of recall interval. *British Journal of Psychology, 78*, 79-89.

70. Kinnear, P. R., & Wood, M. (1987). Memory for topographic contour maps. *British Journal of Psychology, 78*, 395-402.

71. Lambiotte, J. G., Dansereau, D. F., Rocklin, T. R., Fletcher, B., Hythecker, V. I., Larson, C. O., & O'Donnell, A. M. (1987). Cooperative learning and test taking: Transfer of skills. *Contemporary Educational Psychology, 12*, 52-61.

72. Marx, R. W., Howard, D. C., & Winne, P. H. (1987). Student's perception of instruction, cognitive style, and achievement. *Perceptual and Motor Skills, 65*, 123-134.

73. McDonald, R. A., & Eliot, J. (1987). Variables contributing to successful aerial photographic interpretation. *Perceptual and Motor Skills, 64*, 551-557.

74. Patti, P., Kose, G., & Duncan, J. (1987). Effects of discrimination training on reading improvement among adults. *Perceptual and Motor Skills, 65*, 723-728.

75. Robertson, E. D., Fournet, G. P., Zelhart, P. F., & Estes, R. E. (1987). Relationship of field dependence/independence to adaptation-innovation in alcoholics. *Perceptual and Motor Skills, 65*, 771-776.

76. Thompson, B., & Melancon, J. G. (1987). Validity of a measure of critical thinking skills. *Psychological Reports, 60*, 1223-1230.

77. Thompson, B., & Melanion, J. G. (1987). Measurement characteristics of the Group Embedded Figures Test. *Educational and Psychological Measurement, 47*(3), 765-772.

78. Corman, L. S., & Platt, R. G. (1988). Correlations among the Group Embedded Figures Test, the Myers-Briggs Type Indicator and demographic characteristics: A business school study. *Perceptual and Motor Skills, 66*(2), 507-511.

79. Wise, P. S., & Cramer, S. H. (1988). Correlates of empathy and cognitive style in early adolescence. *Psychological Reports, 63*, 179-192.

80. Cummings, A. L., Murray, H. G., & Martin, J. (1989). Protocol analysis of the social problem solving of teachers. *American Educational Research Journal, 26*, 25-43.

81. Arthur, W., Barrett, G. V., & Doverspike, D. (1990). Validation of an information-processing-based test battery for the prediction of handling accidents among petroleum-product transport drivers. *Journal of Applied Psychology, 75*(6), 621-628.

82. Kitamura, F., & Matsunaga, K. (1990). Field dependence and body balance. *Perceptual and Motor Skills, 71*, 723-734.

83. McRae, L. S. E., & Young, J. D. (1990). Field independence and the FIRO-B. *Perceptual and Motor Skills, 70*, 493-494.

84. Skaggs, L. P., Rocklin, T. R., Dansereau, D. F., Hall, R. H., O'Donnell, A. M., Lambiotte, J. G., & Young, M. D. (1990). Dyadic learning of technical material: Individual differences, social interaction, and recall. *Contemporary Educational Psychology, 15*, 47-63.

85. Terelak, J. (1990). Field dependence/independence and eye-hands-legs coordination. *Perceptual and Motor Skills, 71*, 947-950.

86. Arthur, W., Jr., & Day, D. V. (1991). Examination of the construct validity of alternative measures of field dependence/independence. *Perceptual and Motor Skills, 72*, 851-859.

87. Bostic, J. Q., & Tallent-Runnels, M. K. (1991). Cognitive styles: A factor analysis of six dimensions with implications for consolidation. *Perceptual and Motor Skills, 72*, 1299-1306.

88. Dwyer, F. M., & Moore, D. M. (1991). Effect of color coding on visually oriented tests with students of different cognitive styles. *The Journal of Psychology, 125*, 677-680.

89. Meng, K., & Patty, D. (1991). Field dependence and contextual organizers. *Journal of Educational Research, 84*, 183-189.

90. Pennings, A. H. (1991). Altering the strategies in embedded-figure and water-level tasks via instruction: A neo-Piagetian learning study. *Perceptual and Motor Skills, 72*, 639-660.

91. Schwartz, N. H., & Phillippe, A. E. (1991). Individual differences in the retention of maps. *Contemporary Educational Psychology, 16*, 171-182.

92. Wilkinson, W. K., & Schwartz, N. H. (1991). A factor-analytic study of epistemological orientation and related variables. *The Journal of Psychology, 125*, 91-100.

93. Davies, M. F. (1992). Field dependence and hindsight bias: Cognitive restructuring and the generation of reasons. *Journal of Research in Personality, 26*, 58-74.

94. Wiegmann, D. A., Dansereau, D. F., McCagg, E. C., Rewey, K. L., & Pitre, V. (1992). Effects of knowledge map characteristics on information processing. *Contemporary Educational Psychology, 17*, 136-155.

95. Härtel, C. E. (1993). Rating format research revisited: Format effectiveness and acceptability depend on rater characteristics. *Journal of Applied Psychology, 78*, 212-217.

[1095]

Group Environment Scale, Second Edition.

Purpose: Designed to "measure the social-environmental characteristics of task-oriented, social, and psychotherapy and mutual support groups."
Population: Group members and leaders.
Publication Dates: 1974–86.
Acronym: GES.
Scores, 10: Cohesion, Leader Support, Expressiveness, Independence, Task Orientation, Self-Discovery, Anger and Aggression, Order and Organization, Leader Control, Innovation.
Administration: Group.
Forms, 3: Real (R), Ideal (I), Expectation (E).
Price Data, 1990: $10 per 25 test booklets; $7 per 50 answer sheets; $3 per set of scoring stencils; $5 per 50 profiles; $13 per manual ('86, 30 pages); $18 per specimen set.
Time: (15–20) minutes.
Comments: A part of the Social Climate Scales (2495).
Author: Rudolf H. Moos.
Publisher: Consulting Psychologists Press, Inc.
Cross References: For a review by Arthur M. Nezu, see 10:132 (6 references); for reviews by Michael J. Curtis and Robert J. Illback, see 9:453 (4 references); for reviews by David P. Campbell and Robyn M. Dawes, see 8:573; see also T3:1015 (1 reference); for a review of the Social Climate Scales, see 8:681.

TEST REFERENCES

1. Sanders, J., Jr., Jones, E., & Sanders, R. C. (1987). Human relations laboratory groups for enhancing personal growth and self-discovery among graduate students. *College Student Journal, 21*, 249-253.
2. Toro, P. A., Zimmerman, M. A., Seidman, E., Reischl, T. M., Rappaport, J., Luke, D. A., & Roberts, L. J. (1988). Professionals in mutual help groups: Impact on social climate and members' behavior. *Journal of Consulting and Clinical Psychology, 56*, 631-632.
3. Williams, J. M., & Widmeyer, W. N. (1991). The cohesion-performance outcome relationship in a coaching sport. *Journal of Sport & Exercise Psychology, 13*, 364-371.
4. Davis, J. M., & Hartsough, C. S. (1992). Assessing psychological environment in mental health consultation groups. *Psychology in the Schools, 29*, 224-229.
5. Robison, F. F., & Hardt, D. A. (1992). Effects of cognitive and behavioral structure and discussion of corrective feedback outcomes on counseling group development. *Journal of Counseling Psychology, 39*, 473-481.

[1096]

Group Inventory for Finding Creative Talent.

Purpose: "Identify students with attitudes and values usually associated with creativity."
Population: Grades K–2, 3–4, 5–6.
Publication Dates: 1976–80.
Acronym: GIFT.
Scores, 4: Imagination, Independence, Many Interests, Total.
Administration: Group or individual.
Levels, 3: Primary, Elementary, Upper Elementary.

Price Data, 1993: $55 per 30 test booklets and scoring service (scoring must be done by publisher); $12 per specimen set.
Foreign Language Edition: Spanish, French, Hebrew, and German editions available.
Time: (20–45) minutes.
Author: Sylvia B. Rimm.
Publisher: Educational Assessment Service, Inc.
Cross References: For reviews by Patricia L. Dwinell and Dan Wright, see 9:454 (1 reference); see also T3:1016 (1 reference).

TEST REFERENCES

1. Johnson, S. T., Starnes, W. T., Gregory, D. & Blaylock, A. (1985). Program of assessment, diagnosis, and instruction (PADI): Identifying and nurturing potentially gifted and talented minority students. *Journal of Negro Education, 54*, 416-430.
2. Moore, M. T. (1985). The relationship between the originality of essays and variables in the problem-discovery process: A study of creative and noncreative middle school students. *Research in the Teaching of English, 19*, 84-95.
3. Wakefield, J. F. (1985). Towards creativity: Problem finding in a divergent-thinking exercise. *Child Study Journal, 15*, 265-270.

[1097]

Group Inventory For Finding Interests.

Purpose: "Identify students with attitudes and interests usually associated with creativity."
Population: Grades 6–12.
Publication Dates: 1979–80.
Acronym: GIFFI.
Scores: 5 dimensional scores: Creative Arts and Writing, Challenge-Inventiveness, Confidence, Imagination, Many Interests.
Administration: Group or individual.
Levels, 2: Level 1: Grades 6–9; Level 2: Grades 9–12.
Price Data, 1993: $70 per 30 test booklets and scoring service (scoring must be done by publisher); $12 per specimen set.
Foreign Language Editions: Spanish and Hebrew editions available.
Time: (20–40) minutes.
Authors: Sylvia B. Rimm and Gary A. Davis.
Publisher: Educational Assessment Service, Inc.
Cross References: For a review by M. O'Neal Weeks, see 9:455 (1 reference).

[1098]

Group Literacy Assessment.

Purpose: To sample children's overall skills level with written material.
Population: End of junior school and beginning of secondary school.
Publication Date: 1981.
Acronym: GLA.
Scores, 3: Proof-Reading, Fill the Gaps, Total.
Administration: Group.
Price Data, 1994: £3.99 per 20 tests; £5.25 per manual (16 pages); £5.50 per specimen set.
Time: 16(30) minutes.
Author: Frank A. Spooncer.
Publisher: Hodder & Stoughton Educational [England].

Cross References: For a review by Gail E. Tompkins, see 9:456.

[1099]

Group Mathematics Test, Second Edition.
Purpose: General assessment of mathematical understanding.
Population: Ages 6.5–8.10 and older underachieving students.
Publication Dates: 1970–80.
Acronym: GMT.
Scores, 3: Oral, Computation, Total.
Administration: Group.
Forms, 2: A, B.
Price Data, 1994: £3.75 per 20 tests (Form A or B); £4.50 per manual ('80, 25 pages); £4.75 per specimen set.
Time: (40–50) minutes.
Author: D. Young.
Publisher: Hodder & Stoughton Educational [England].
Cross References: For reviews by Mary Kay Corbitt and Douglas H. Crawford, see 9:457; for a review by John Cook of an earlier edition, see 8:273.

TEST REFERENCES

1. Blatchford, P., Burke, J., Farquhar, C., Plewis, I., & Tizard, B. (1989). Teacher expectations in infant school: Associations with attainment and progress, curriculum coverage and classroom interaction. *British Journal of Educational Psychology, 59*, 19-30.

[1100]

The Group Personality Projective Test.
Purpose: Designed as "a test of . . . personality . . . concerned with assessing personal, social, and emotional need projections."
Population: Ages 12 and over.
Publication Dates: 1956–61.
Scores, 7: Tension Reduction Quotient, Nurturance, Withdrawal, Neuroticism, Affiliation, Succorance, Total.
Administration: Group.
Price Data, 1989: $27 per complete kit including manual ('61, 20 pages, reprint of article by Cassel & Kahn from *Psychological Reports*), 7 scoring keys, 12 test booklets, and 100 answer and profile sheets; $25 per 25 test booklets; $4 per 7 scoring keys; $13 per 100 answer and profile sheets; $4 per manual.
Time: (40–45) minutes.
Comments: Formerly called Kahn Stick Figure Personality Test.
Authors: Russell N. Cassel and Theodore C. Kahn.
Publisher: Psychological Test Specialists.
Cross References: See T3:1020 (3 references) and T2:1466 (5 references); for reviews by Edwin I. Megargee, Stuart Oskamp, and Marvin Reznikoff, see 7:167 (5 references); see also P:434 (2 references) and 6:214 (7 references).

[1101]

Group Process Questionnaire.
Purpose: "Designed to help groups assess how effective they are."
Population: Adults.
Publication Date: 1988
Scores, 29 to 145: My Rating, Group Rating, and How I Did scores for Behavior Scale (Task Behavior, Maintenance Behavior), for Total Scale, and for 12 optional categories (Initiating, Seeking Information or Opinions, Giving Information or Opinions, Clarifying and Elaborating, Summarizing, Consensus-Testing, Listening, Harmonizing, Gatekeeping, Encouraging, Compromising, Standard Setting/Testing), and My Rating and Group Rating scores for 5 additional optional categories (Leadership, Time Utilization, Results, Acceptance, Inclusion).
Administration: Group.
Price Data: Available from publisher.
Time: (60) minutes.
Comments: Scale for ratings by group members and for self-ratings.
Authors: Richard Hill, D. Joseph Fisher, Tom Webber, and Kathleen A. Fisher.
Publisher: Aviat.

[1102]

Group Reading Test, Third Edition.
Purpose: Measures early and intermediate reading skills.
Population: Ages 6-4 to 11-11 and 8-0 to 11-11 below average.
Publication Dates: 1968–91.
Acronym: GRT.
Scores: Total score only.
Administration: Group.
Price Data, 1994: £3.75 per 20 Form A; £3.75 per 20 Form B; £5.50 per manual; £3.25 per template A or template B; £5.99 per specimen set.
Time: (13) minutes.
Author: Dennis Young.
Publisher: Hodder & Stoughton Educational [England].
Cross References: For reviews by Patrick Groff and Douglas A. Pidgeon of the Second Edition, see 9:458 (1 reference); for a review by Ralph D. Dutch of the original edition, see 8:729.

TEST REFERENCES

1. Hannon, P. (1987). A study of the effects of parental involvement in the teaching of reading on children's reading test performance. *British Journal of Educational Psychology, 57*, 56-72.
2. Sugden, D., & Wann, C. (1987). The assessment of motor impairment in children with moderate learning difficulties. *British Journal of Educational Psychology, 57*, 225- 236.
3. Blatchford, P., Burke, J., Farquhar, C., Plewis, I., & Tizard, B. (1989). Teacher expectations in infant school: Associations with attainment and progress, curriculum coverage and classroom interaction. *British Journal of Educational Psychology, 59*, 19-30.
4. Banks, J., Gray, C., & Fyfe, R. (1990). The written recall of printed stories by severely deaf children. *The British Journal of Educational Psychology, 60*, 192-206.

[1103]

Group Shorr Imagery Test.
Purpose: Designed as a projective measure of personality conflict.
Population: Adults.
Publication Date: 1977.

Acronym: GSIT.
Scores, 6: Item scores in 5 areas (Human, Animal, Inanimate, Botanical, Others) plus Total score for Conflict.
Administration: Group.
Price Data, 1990: $37.50 per kit including manual (no date, 4 pages), monograph, 25 record forms, and 25 score sheets; $5 per 25 record forms and 25 score sheets; $.50 per record form and score sheet.
Time: Administration time not reported.
Comments: Tape cassette used for administration; group form of the Shorr Imagery Test (2454).
Author: Joseph E. Shorr.
Publisher: Institute for Psycho-Imagination Therapy.

[1104]

Group Styles Inventory.
Purpose: Designed to "assess the particular style or styles of your work group following a simulated or real problem-solving session or meeting."
Population: Group members.
Publication Date: 1990.
Acronym: GSI.
Scores: 12 styles in 3 general clusters: Constructive (Achievement, Self-Actualizing, Humanistic-Encouraging, Affiliative), Passive/Defensive (Approval, Conventional, Dependent, Avoidance), Aggressive/Defensive (Oppositional, Power, Competitive, Perfectionistic).
Administration: Group.
Price Data: Price information for test materials including Participant Guide (50 pages) and Leader's Guide (72 pages) available from publisher.
Time: [10–15] minutes.
Authors: Robert A. Cooke and Clayton J. Lafferty.
Publisher: Human Synergistics, Inc.

[1105]

Group Test 82.
Purpose: Designed to assess spatial perception.
Population: Ages 15 and over.
Publication Dates: 1959–74.
Scores: Total score only.
Administration: Group.
Manual: No manual.
Price Data, 1989: £14.95 per 10 test booklets; £4.60 per 10 answer sheets; £2.90 per marking key; £2.90 per instruction card.
Time: 24 minutes.
Comments: Subtest of N.I.I.P. Engineering Apprentice Selection Test Battery.
Author: National Institute of Industrial Psychology.
Publisher: NFER-Nelson Publishing Co., Ltd. [England].

[1106]

Group Test for Indian South Africans.
Purpose: Measurement of intellectual potential.
Population: Standards 4–6, 7–8, 9–10 in South African schools.

Publication Dates: 1967–71.
Acronym: GTISA.
Scores, 3: Verbal, Nonverbal, Total.
Administration: Group.
Levels: 3.
Price Data: Available from publisher.
Time: 68(103) minutes.
Comments: Adaptation for Indian pupils of the New South African Group Test.
Author: Human Sciences Research Council.
Publisher: Human Sciences Research Council [South Africa].
a) JUNIOR.
Population: Standards 4–6.
Publication Dates: 1968–71.
Comments: Indian standardization by F. W. O. Heinichen, R. J. Prinsloo, and S. Oosthuizen.
b) INTERMEDIATE.
Population: Standards 7–8.
Publication Dates: 1967–69.
c) SENIOR.
Population: Standards 9–10.
Publication Dates: 1968–69.

[1107]

Group Tests 70 and 70B.
Purpose: To assess reasoning ability or nonverbal intelligence.
Population: Ages 15 and over.
Publication Dates: 1939–70.
Acronyms: GT 70 and GT 70B.
Scores: Total score only.
Administration: Group.
Forms, 2: 70, 70B.
Price Data: Available from publisher.
Time: 18(35) minutes.
Author: National Institute of Industrial Psychology.
Publisher: NFER-Nelson Publishing Co., Ltd. [England].
Cross References: See T2:388 (9 references) and 7:355 (5 references); for a review by George Westby of form 70, see 4:297 (5 references).

[1108]

Group Tests 90A and 90B.
Purpose: Designed as "tests of intelligence and verbal aptitude."
Population: Ages 15 and over.
Publication Dates: 1950–70.
Scores: Total score only.
Administration: Group.
Price Data: Available from publisher.
Time: 20(30) minutes.
Comments: Subtest of N.I.I.P. Engineering Apprenticeship Selection Test Battery.
Author: National Institute of Industrial Psychology.
Publisher: NFER-Nelson Publishing Co., Ltd. [England].
Cross References: See T3:1038 (1 reference), T2:390 (2 references), and 7:357 (1 reference); for a review by John Liggett of Form 90A, see 5:340.

[1109]

Group Tests of Musical Abilities.
Purpose: Developed to measure an individual's musical ability level.
Population: Ages 7–14.
Publication Date: 1988.
Scores, 2: Pitch, Pulse.
Administration: Group.
Price Data, 1992: £28.75 per starter pack including cassette tape, 25 answer sheets, and manual (25 pages); £10.95 per cassette tape; £7.50 per 25 answer sheets; £10.35 per manual.
Time: [15–20] minutes.
Comments: A good quality audiocassette player needed to administer test.
Author: Janet Mills.
Publisher: NFER-Nelson Publishing Co., Ltd. [England].

[1110]

GROW—The Marriage Enrichment Program.
Purpose: "An integrated program of assessment, learning activities, and personal development designed to support professional marital and relationship counseling."
Population: Couples.
Publication Dates: 1982–84.
Acronym: GROW.
Scores, 16: Caring, Warm, Sensitive, Trusting, Sociable, Optimistic, Adventurous, Participating, Assertive, Controlling, Confident, Self-Reliant, Flexible, Creative, Innovative, Calm.
Administration: Group or individual.
Price Data, 1994: $25 per introductory kit; $18.40–$22 per feedback reports (per couple); $10.50 per program manual ('84, 18 pages); $60 per GROW license.
Time: (25–35) minutes.
Comments: Incorporates a short version of the Adult Personality Inventory as an assessment tool to personalize the marriage enrichment program.
Authors: Thomas J. Henry, Virginia M. Henry, and Samuel E. Krug.
Publisher: MetriTech, Inc.
Cross References: For reviews by James R. Clopton and Joseph P. Stokes, see 10:133.

[1111]

Guidance Test Battery for Secondary Pupils (Standard 8).
Purpose: To determine the level of achievement in the official languages, arithmetic, and reasoning ability, for guidance and selection purposes.
Population: Junior secondary Bantu pupils in Form III of South African schools.
Publication Dates: 1969–71.
Acronym: GBS.
Scores, 7: English Vocabulary, English Sentences, Series Completion, Arithmetic, Afrikaans Vocabulary, Afrikaans Sentences, Verbal Reasoning.
Administration: Group.

Forms, 2: A, B.
Price Data: Available from publisher.
Time: [3] hours.
Comments: All test materials (except language subtests) in both English and Afrikaans.
Authors: J. D. Van Staden, G. J. Ligthelm, J. P. du Toit, A. P. J. Pottas, and G. Engelbrecht (revision).
Publisher: Human Sciences Research Council [South Africa].

[1112]

Guide to the Assessment of Test Session Behavior for the WISC-III and the WIAT.
Purpose: Assesses "whether a child's behavior during WISC-III and/or WIAT testing differs substantially from the behavior of other children of the same age."
Population: Ages 6–16-11.
Publication Date: 1992–93.
Acronym: GATSB.
Scores: 3 scales: Avoidance, Inattentiveness, Uncooperative Mood.
Administration: Individual.
Price Data, 1994: $59 per complete kit including 25 ready-score answer forms and manual (88 pages); $24 per 25 ready-score answer documents; $29 per manual.
Time: (5–10) minutes.
Authors: Joseph J. Glutting and Tom Oakland.
Publisher: The Psychological Corporation.

[1113]

The Guilford-Zimmerman Aptitude Survey.
Purpose: Measurement of verbal and abstract intelligence, numerical facility, and perception.
Population: Grades 9–16 and adults.
Publication Dates: 1947–56.
Acronym: GZAS.
Administration: Group.
Price Data, 1989: $130 per complete kit; $9.50 per 50 answer sheets (needed only for parts 1, 2, 5, & 6); $10 per 50 profiles; $12 per manual ('56, 7 pages); $16 per specimen set.
Authors: J. P. Guilford and Wayne S. Zimmerman.
Publisher: Consulting Psychologists Press, Inc.
a) PART 1, VERBAL COMPREHENSION.
Price Data: $13 per 25 tests; $6.50 per scoring key.
Time: 25(30) minutes.
b) PART 2, GENERAL REASONING.
Price Data: $13 per 25 tests; $6.50 per scoring key.
Time: 35(40) minutes.
c) PART 3, NUMERICAL OPERATIONS.
Price Data: $19 per 25 tests; $13 per scoring key.
Time: 8(13) minutes.
d) PART 4, PERCEPTUAL SPEED.
Price Data: $15 per 25 tests; $13 per scoring key.
Time: 5(10) minutes.
e) PART 5, SPATIAL ORIENTATION.
Price Data: $19 per 25 tests; $6.50 per scoring key.

Time: 10(20) minutes.

f) PART 6, SPATIAL VISUALIZATION.

Price Data: $19 per 25 tests; $6.50 per scoring key.

Time: 10(15) minutes.

Cross References: See T3:1044 (4 references); for a review by M. Y. Quereshi, see 8:486 (9 references); see also T2:1074 (19 references) and 6:772 (17 references); for reviews by Anne Anastasi, Harold Bechtoldt, John B. Carroll, and P. E. Vernon, see 4:715 (15 references).

TEST REFERENCES

1. Burnett, S. A., Lane, D. M., & Dratt, L. M. (1982). Spatial ability and handedness. *Intelligence, 6*, 57-68.
2. Johnson, E. S. (1984). Sex differences in problem solving. *Journal of Educational Psychology, 76*, 1359-1371.
3. Hunt, E., Pellegrino, J. W., Frick, R. W., Farr, S. A., & Alderton, D. (1988). The ability to reason about movement in the visual field. *Intelligence, 12*, 77-100.

[1114]

The Guilford-Zimmerman Interest Inventory.

Purpose: A vocational interest measure.

Population: College and adults.

Publication Dates: 1962–89.

Acronym: GZII.

Scores, 10: Natural, Mechanical, Scientific, Creative, Literary, Artistic, Service, Enterprising, Leadership, Clerical.

Administration: Group.

Price Data, 1992: $16 per 25 test booklets; $28 per 25 self-scorable answer sheets; $22 per 25 report forms; $29 per manual ('89, 15 pages); $30 per specimen set.

Time: (20–30) minutes.

Comments: Self-report and self-scorable.

Authors: Joan S. Guilford and Wayne S. Zimmerman.

Publisher: Consulting Psychologists Press, Inc.

Cross References: For information regarding a previous edition, see T3:1045. See also T2:2185 (7 references); for a review by Kenneth B. Hoyt, see 6:1057.

[1115]

The Guilford-Zimmerman Temperament Survey.

Purpose: To assess multiple facets of personality.

Population: Ages 16 through adult.

Publication Dates: 1949–78.

Acronym: GZTS.

Scores, 10: General Activity, Restraint, Ascendance, Sociability, Emotional Stability, Objectivity, Friendliness, Thoughtfulness, Personal Relations, Masculinity.

Administration: Individual or group.

Price Data, 1994: $36.75 per 25 test booklets; $18.90 per set of scoring keys; $11.55 per 25 nonprepaid answer sheets; $52.50 per 25 prepaid answer sheets; $10.50 per 25 profiles; $25.20 per GZTS handbook; $10.50 per 25 interpretation worksheets

(specify male or female); $11.55 per manual ('78, 19 pages).

Time: (45) minutes.

Comments: Revision and condensation of 3 tests: Inventory of Factors, Guilford-Martin Personnel Inventory, and Inventory of Factors STDCR.

Authors: J. P. Guilford and Wayne S. Zimmerman.

Publisher: Consulting Psychologists Press, Inc.

Cross References: For a review by John B. Gormly, see 9:460 (4 references); see also T3:1046 (24 references), 8:574 (72 references), T2:1207 (188 references), P:104 (132 references), and 6:110 (120 references); for a review by David R. Saunders, see 5:65 (48 references); for reviews by William Stephenson and Neil Van Steenberg and an excerpted review by Lawrence F. Shaffer, see 4:49 (5 references).

TEST REFERENCES

1. Campbell, J. B., & Reynolds, J. H. (1984). A comparison of the Guilford and Eysenck factors of personality. *Journal of Research in Personality, 18*, 305-320.
2. Hirschfeld, R. M. A., Klerman, G. L., Clayton, P. J., Keller, M. B., & Andreasen, N. C. (1984). Personality and gender-related differences in depression. *Journal of Affective Disorders, 7*, 211-221.
3. Lester, D., & Levitt, A. (1984). Using the Personal Orientation Device to predict Guilford-Zimmerman Temperament Survey scores. *Perceptual and Motor Skills, 58*, 50.
4. Hentschel, U., & Kiessling, M. (1985). Season of birth and personality: Another instance of noncorrespondence. *The Journal of Social Psychology, 125*, 577-585.
5. Osborne, S. (1985). Effects of teacher experience and selected temperament variables on coping strategies used with distractible children. *American Educational Research Journal, 22*, 79-86.
6. Rucker, M. H., & King, D. C. (1985). Reactions to leadership style as a function of locus of control and ascendancy of subordinates. *Social Behavior and Personality, 13*(1), 91-107.
7. Hirschfeld, R. M. A., Klerman, G. L., Andreasen, N. C., Clayton, P. J., & Keller, M. B. (1986). Psycho-social predictors of chronicity in depressed patients. *British Journal of Psychiatry, 148*, 648-654.
8. Reich, J., Noyes, R., Jr., Coryell, W., & O'Gorman, T. W. (1986). The effect of state anxiety on personality measurement. *American Journal of Psychiatry, 143*, 760-763.
9. Gerbing, D. W., Ahadi, S. A., & Pattar, J. H. (1987). Toward a conceptualization of impulsivity: Components across the behavioral and self-report domains. *Multivariate Behavioral Research, 22*, 357-379.
10. Grove, W. M., Andreasen, N. C., Young, M., Endicott, J., Keller, M. B., Hirschfeld, R. M. A., & Reich, T. (1987). Isolation and characterization of a nuclear depressive syndrome. *Psychological Medicine, 17*, 471-484.
11. Noller, P., Law, H., & Comrey, A. L. (1987). Cattell, Comrey, and Eysenck personality factors compared: More evidence for the five robust factors? *Journal of Personality and Social Psychology, 53*, 775-782.
12. Reich, J., & Chaudry, D. (1987). Personality of panic disorder alcohol abusers. *The Journal of Nervous and Mental Disease, 175*, 224-228.
13. Reich, J., Noyes, R., Jr., Hirschfeld, R., Coryell, W., & O'Gorman, T. (1987). State and personality in depressed and panic patients. *American Journal of Psychiatry, 144*, 181-187.
14. Lanning, K. (1988). Individual differences in scalability: An alternative conception of consistency for personality theory and measurement. *Journal of Personality and Social Psychology, 55*, 142-148.
15. Hirschfeld, R. M. A., Klerman, G. L., Lavori, P., Keller, M. B., Griffith, P., & Loryell, W. (1989). Premorbid personality assessments of first onset of major depression. *Archives of General Psychiatry, 46*, 345-350.
16. Schuerger, J. M., Zarrella, K. L., & Hotz, A. S. (1989). Factors that influence the temporal stability of personality by questionnaire. *Journal of Personality and Social Psychology, 56*, 777-783.
17. Dickman, S. J. (1990). Functional and dysfunctional impulsivity: Personality and cognitive correlates. *Journal of Personality and Social Psychology, 58*, 95-102.
18. Hough, L. M., Eaton, N. K., Dunnette, M. D., Kamp, J. D., & McCloy, R. A. (1990). Criterion-related validities of personality constructs and the effect of response distortion on those validities. *Journal of Applied Psychology, 75*(5), 581-595.

[1116]
Hahnemann Elementary School Behavior Rating Scale.

Purpose: Designed "to provide a standard system for identifying and measuring classroom behaviors of elementary school students in both regular and open classrooms."
Population: Elementary school students in both regular and open classrooms.
Publication Date: 1975.
Acronym: HESB.
Scores, 14: Originality, Independent Learning, Involvement, Productive with Peers, Intellectual Dependency with Peers, Failure Anxiety, Unreflectiveness, Irrelevant Talk, Disruptive Social Environment, Negative Feelings, Holding Back/Withdrawn, Critical-Competitive, Blaming, Approach to Teacher, plus 2 added items: Inattention, Academic Achievement.
Administration: Individual.
Price Data, 1982: $11 per 50 scale forms; $4 per manual (52 pages); $8.50 per 25 scale forms and manual.
Time: [10] minutes.
Comments: Ratings by teachers.
Authors: George Spivack and Marshall Swift.
Publisher: Hahnemann Medical College and Hospital, Department of Mental Health Sciences.

TEST REFERENCES

1. Brodzinsky, D. M., Schechter, D. E., Braff, A. M., & Singer, L. M. (1984). Psychological and academic adjustment in adopted children. *Journal of Consulting and Clinical Psychology, 52*, 582-590.
2. Gullo, D. F., & Clements, D. H. (1984). The effects of kindergarten schedule on achievement, classroom behavior, and attendance. *Journal of Educational Research, 78*, 51-56.
3. Guidubaldi, J., & Cleminshaw, H. (1985). Divorce, family health, and child adjustment. *Family Relations, 34*, 35-41.
4. Guidubaldi, J., Cleminshaw, H. K., Perry, J. D., Nastasi, B. K., & Lightel, J. (1986). The role of selected family environment factors in children's post-divorce adjustment. *Family Relations, 35*, 141-151.
5. Day, J. D., & Cordón, L. A. (1993). Static and dynamic measures of ability: An experimental comparison. *Journal of Educational Psychology, 85*, 75-82.

[1117]
Hahnemann High School Behavior Rating Scale.

Purpose: Designed to "identify and measure classroom behaviors of junior and senior high school students."
Population: Grades 7-12.
Publication Dates: 1971-72.
Acronym: HHSB.
Scores, 13: Reasoning Ability, Originality, Verbal Interaction, Rapport with Teacher, Anxious Producer, General Anxiety, Quiet-Withdrawn, Poor Work Habits, Lack Intellectual Independence, Dogmatic-Inflexible, Verbal Negativism, Disturbance-Restless, Expressed Inability.
Administration: Individual.
Price Data, 1985: $.25 per scale form; $10 per manual ('72, 48 pages) and 25 scale forms; $4 per manual.

Time: Administration time not reported.
Comments: Ratings by teachers.
Authors: George Spivack and Marshall Swift.
Publisher: Hahnemann Medical College & Hospital, Department of Mental Health Sciences.
Cross References: For a review by Bert O. Richmond, see 9:462 (2 references); see T3:1050 (2 references).

TEST REFERENCES

1. Janes, C. L., Weeks, D. G., & Worland, J. (1983). School behavior in adolescent children of parents with mental disorder. *The Journal of Nervous and Mental Disease, 171*, 234-240.
2. Harpin, P., & Sandler, I. (1985). Relevance of social climate: An improved approach to assessing person x environment interactions in the classroom. *American Journal of Community Psychology, 13*, 339-352.
3. Brodzinsky, D. M., Radice, C., Huffman, L., & Merkler, K. (1987). Prevalence of clinically significant symptomatology in a nonclinical sample of adopted and nonadopted children. *Journal of Clinical Child Psychology, 16*, 350-356.

[1118]
Hall Occupational Orientation Inventory.

Purpose: Designed to help individuals understand their values, needs, interests, and preferred life-styles, and how these relate to career goals and future educational plans.
Population: Grades 3-7, 8-16 and adults, low-literate adults, junior high students—adults.
Publication Dates: 1968-89.
Administration: Group or individual.
Price Data, 1993: $28.30 per 20 inventory booklets; $20.60 per 20 interpretive folders; $20.60 per 20 response sheets; $15.50 per Hall Career Education Reader; $15.50 per counselor's manual ('76, 54 pages); $25 per specimen set (specify Intermediate, Young Adult/College, or Adult Basic form; $21.50 without manual); $92.50 per 20 Form II self-interpretive folders; $15.50 per Form II professional manual; $32 per Form II specimen set ($25 without manual).
Time: (30-60) minutes.
Authors: L. G. Hall, R. B. Tarrier (manual), and D. L. Shappel (manual).
Publisher: Scholastic Testing Service, Inc.
a) INTERMEDIATE FORM.
Population: Grades 3-7.
Publication Dates: 1968-76.
Scores, 22: Free Choice, Chance Game, Effort to Learn, Belonging, Being Safe, Goals, Being Important, Being Yourself, Being Proud, Order, Working Alone, Working with Your Hands, Working with People, Places, Ready to Learn, Rewards, Physical Fitness, The World Around You, Others, Skills, Use of Time, Being on Guard.
b) YOUNG ADULT/COLLEGE FORM.
Population: Grades 8-16 and adults.
Publication Dates: 1968-88.
Scores, 22: Creativity-Independence, Risk, Information-Knowledge, Belongingness, Security, Aspiration, Esteem, Self-Actualization, Personal Satisfaction, Routine-Dependence, Data Orienta-

tion, Things Orientation, People Orientation, Location Concern, Aptitude Concern, Monetary Concern, Physical Abilities Concern, Environment Concern, Co-worker Concern, Qualifications Concern, Time Concern, Deciding-Influencing.

c) ADULT BASIC FORM.
Population: Low-literate adults.
Publication Dates: 1968–76.
Scores, 22: Same as for *b* above.

d) FORM II.
Population: Junior high students–adults.
Scores, 15: Creativity-Independence, Information-Knowledge, Belongingness, Security, Aspiration, Esteem, Self-Actualization, Personal Satisfaction, Routine-Dependence, People-Social-Accommodating, Data-Information, Things-Physical, People-Business-Influencing, Ideas-Scientific, Aesthetics-Arts.

Cross References: See T3:1051 (4 references); for reviews by Robert H. Dolliver and Austin C. Frank, see 8:1003 (5 references); see also T2:2187 (3 references); for a review by Donald G. Zytowski of the original edition, see 7:104 (4 references).

[1119]

Halstead-Reitan Neuropsychological Test Battery.

Purpose: "Developed to evaluate the brain-behavior functioning of individuals."
Population: Ages 5–8, 9–14, 15 and over.
Publication Dates: 1979–93.
Scores: 1 combined score for each battery and for areas of function, plus scores for individual tests.
Price Data: Available from publisher.
Comments: Consists of three neuropsychological test batteries, one for each age level; each battery includes a Neuropsychological Deficit Scale, which provides normative ranges for each test, for areas of function, and for the entire battery in addition to cut-off scores (brain impairment versus normal brain status) for each variable, area, and summary score.
Author: Ralph M. Reitan.
Publisher: Reitan Neuropsychology Laboratory.

a) REITAN-INDIANA NEUROPSYCHOLOGICAL TEST BATTERY FOR CHILDREN.
Population: Ages 5–8.
1) *Category.*
Comments: Projection box with slide projector and slides necessary for administration.
2) *Tactual Performance.*
Scores, 3: Total Time, Memory, Localization.
Comments: 6-figure board.
3) *Finger Tapping.*
Comments: Electronic finger tapper necessary for administration.
4) *Matching Pictures.*
5) *Individual Performance.*
Subtests, 4: Matching Figures, Star, Matching V's, Concentric Squares.
6) *Marching.*
7) *Progressive Figures.*

8) *Color Form.*
Scores, 2: Total Time, Errors.
9) *Lateral Dominance Examination.*
10) *Target.*
11) *Aphasia Screening.*
12) *Sensory Perceptual.*
Subtests, 6: Imperception (Tactile, Auditory, Visual), Tactile Finger Recognition, Finger-Tip Symbol Writing and Recognition, Tactile Form Recognition.
13) *Grip Strength.*
Scores, 2: Preferred Grip, Nonpreferred Grip.
Comments: Hand dynamometer necessary for administration.
14) *Lateral Dominance.*
15) *Name Writing.*

b) HALSTEAD-REITAN NEUROPSYCHOLOGICAL TEST BATTERY FOR CHILDREN.
Population: Ages 9–14.
1) *Category.*
Comments: Similar to *a* above.
2) *Tactual Performance.*
Comments: Same as *a* above.
3) *Seashore Rhythm Test.*
4) *Speech-Sounds Perception.*
5) *Trail Making.*
6) *Finger Tapping.*
Comments: Manual finger tapping apparatus necessary for administration.
7) *Aphasia Screening.*
8) *Sensory-Perceptual.*
Subtests, 5: Sensory Imperception (Tactile, Auditory, Visual), Finger Agnosia, Finger-Tip Number Writing.
9) *Tactile Form Recognition.*
10) *Grip Strength.*
Scores, 2: Preferred Grip, Nonpreferred Grip.
Comments: Hand dynamometer necessary for administration.
11) *Lateral Dominance.*
12) *Name Writing.*

c) HALSTEAD-REITAN NEUROPSYCHOLOGICAL TEST BATTERY FOR ADULTS.
Population: Ages 15 and over.
Comments: Battery has 11 tests same as *b* above with a number of changes in equipment, administration, and scoring forms for this level.

Cross References: For reviews by Raymond S. Dean and Manfred J. Meier, see 9:463 (79 references); see also T3:1052 (4 references).

TEST REFERENCES

1. Goldstein, G., & Shelly, C. (1982). A multivariate neuropsychological approach to brain lesion localization in alcoholism. *Addictive Behaviors, 7,* 165-175.
2. Berg, R. A., Ch'ien, L. T., Bownan, W. P., Ochs, J., Lancaster, W., Goff, J. R., & Anderson, H. R., Jr. (1983). The neuropsychological effects of acute lymphocytic leukemia and its treatment—a three year report: Intellectual functioning and academic achievement. *Clinical Neuropsychology, 5,* 9-13.
3. Bolter, J. F., Stanczak, D. E., & Long, C. J. (1983). Neuropsychological consequences of acute, high-level gasoline inhalation. *Clinical Neuropsychology, 5,* 4-7.
4. Bornstein, R. A. (1983). Relationship of age and education to neu-

ropsychological performance in patients with symptomatic carotid artery disease. *Journal of Clinical Psychology, 39,* 470-478.

5. Dean, R. S. (1983). Neuropsychological correlates of total seizures with major motor epileptic children. *Clinical Neuropsychology, 5,* 1-3.

6. Goebel, R. A. (1983). Detection of faking on the Halstead-Reitan Neuropsychological Test Battery. *Journal of Clinical Psychology, 39,* 731-742.

7. Klesges, R. C. (1983). The relationship between neuropsychological, cognitive, and behavioral assessments of brain functioning in children. *Clinical Neuropsychology, 5,* 28-32.

8. Query, W. T., Carlson, K., & Dryer, S. (1983). Neuropsychological test performance and hypnotic susceptibility. *Journal of Clinical Psychology, 39,* 804-806.

9. Tarter, R. E., Goldstein, G., Alterman, A., Petrarulo, E. W., & Elmore, S. (1983). Alcoholic seizures: Intellectual and neuropsychological sequelae. *The Journal of Nervous and Mental Disease, 171,* 123-125.

10. Teeter, P. A. (1983). The relationship between measures of cognitive-intellectual and neuropsychological abilities for young children. *Clinical Neuropsychology, 5,* 151-158.

11. Tramontana, M. G., Sherrets, S. D., & Wolf, B. A. (1983). Comparability of the Luria-Nebraska and Halstead-Reitan Neuropsychological Batteries for older children. *Clinical Neuropsychology, 5,* 186-190.

12. Wedding, D. (1983). Comparison of statistical and actuarial models for predicting lateralization of brain damage. *Clinical Neuropsychology, 5,* 15-20.

13. Barth, J. T., Macciocchi, S. N., Ranseen, J., Boyd, T., & Mills, G. (1984). The effects of prefontal leucotomy: Neuropsychological findings in long term chronic psychiatric patients. *Clinical Neuropsychology, 6,* 120-123.

14. Berg, R. A., Bolter, J. F., Ch'ien, L. T., & Cummins, J. (1984). A standardized assessment of emotionality in children suffering from epilepsy. *Clinical Neuropsychology, 6,* 247-248.

15. Berg, R. A., Bolter, J. F., Ch'ien, L. T., Williams, S. J., Lancaster, W., & Cummins, J. (1984). Comparative diagnostic accuracy of the Halstead-Reitan and Luria-Nebraska Neuropsychological Adult and Children's Batteries. *Clinical Neuropsychology, 6,* 200-204.

16. Carr, E. G., & Wedding, D. (1984). Neuropsychological assessment of cerebral ventricular size in chronic schizophrenics. *Clinical Neuropsychology, 6,* 106-111.

17. Cullum, C. M., Steinman, D. R., & Bigler, E. D. (1984). Relationship between fluid and crystallized cognitive functions using Category Test and WAIS scores. *Clinical Neuropsychology, 6,* 172-174.

18. Cushman, L., Brinkman, S. D., Ganji, S., & Jacobs, L. A. (1984). Neuropsychological impairment after carotid endarterectomy correlates with intraoperative ischemia. *Cortex, 20,* 403-412.

19. Dodrill, C. B., & Clemmons, D. (1984). Use of neuropsychological tests to identify high school students with epilepsy who later demonstrate inadequate performances in life. *Journal of Consulting and Clinical Psychology, 52,* 520-527.

20. Drudge, O. W., Williams, J. M., Kessler, M., & Gomes, F. B. (1984). Recovery from severe closed head injuries: Repeat testings with the Halstead-Reitan Neuropsychological Battery. *Journal of Clinical Psychology, 40,* 259-265.

21. Klesges, R. C., Fisher, L., Pheley, A., Boschee, P., & Vasey, M. (1984). A major validational study of the Halstead-Reitan in the prediction of CAT-scan assessed brain damage in adults. *Clinical Neuropsychology, 6,* 29-34.

22. Miran, M., & Miran, E. (1984). Cerebral asymmetries: Neuropsychological measurement and theoretical issues. *Biological Psychology, 19,* 295-304.

23. Novack, T. A., Daniel, M. S., & Long, C. J. (1984). Factors related to emotional adjustment following head injury. *Clinical Neuropsychology, 6,* 139-142.

24. Parker, J. B., Chelune, G. J., Hamblin, D. K., & Kitchens, E. M. (1984). Verbal impairment in alcoholics. *Addictive Behaviors, 9,* 287-290.

25. Pettinati, H. M., & Bonner, K. M. (1984). Cognitive functioning in depressed geriatric patients with a history of ECT. *American Journal of Psychiatry, 141,* 49-52.

26. Rubinow, D. R., Post, R. M., Savard, R., Gold, P. W. (1984). Cortisol hypersecretion and cognitive impairment in depression. *Archives of General Psychiatry, 41,* 279-283.

27. Russell, E. W. (1984). Psychometric parameters of the average impairment scale. *Journal of Consulting and Clinical Psychology, 52,* 717-718.

28. Seidenberg, M., Gamache, M. P., Beck, N. C., Smith, M., Giordani, B., Berent, S., Sackellares, J. C., & Boll, T. J. (1984). Subject variables and performance on the Halstead Neuropsychological Test Battery: A multivariate analysis. *Journal of Consulting and Clinical Psychology, 52,* 658-662.

29. Skenazy, J. A., & Bigler, E. D. (1984). Neuropsychological findings in diabetes mellitus. *Journal of Clinical Psychology, 40,* 246-258.

30. Stanton, B. A., Jenkins, C. D., Savageau, J. A., Zyzanski, S. J., & Aucoin, R. (1984). Age and educational differences on the Trail Making Test and Wechsler Memory Scales. *Perceptual and Motor Skills, 58,* 311-318.

31. Steinmeyer, C. H. (1984). Are the rhythm tests of the Halstead-Reitan and Luria-Nebraska batteries differentially sensitive to right temporal lobe lesions? *Journal of Clinical Psychology, 40,* 1464-1466.

32. Taylor, M. A., & Abrams, R. (1984). Cognitive impairment in schizophrenia. *American Journal of Psychiatry, 141,* 196-201.

33. Tramontana, M. G., Klee, S. H., & Boyd, T. A. (1984). WISC-R interrelationships with the Halstead-Reitan and Children's Luria Neuropsychological Batteries. *Clinical Neuropsychology, 6,* 1-8.

34. Webster, J. S., Jones, S., Blanton, P., Gross, R., Beissel, G. F., & Wofford, J. D. (1984). Visual scanning training with stroke patients. *Behavior Therapy, 15,* 129-143.

35. Woodward, J. A., Bisbee, C. T., & Bennett, J. E. (1984). MMPI correlates of relatively localized brain damage. *Journal of Clinical Psychology, 40,* 961-969.

36. Bawden, H. N., Knights, R. M., & Winogron, H. W. (1985). Speeded performance following head injury in children. *Journal of Clinical and Experimental Neuropsychology, 7,* 39-54.

37. Bornstein, R. A. (1985). Normative data on selected neuropsychological measures from a nonclinical sample. *Journal of Clinical Psychology, 41,* 651-659.

38. Bornstein, R. A., Watson, G. D., & Kaplan, M. J. (1985). Effects of flurazepam and triazolam on neuropsychological performance. *Perceptual and Motor Skills, 60,* 47-52.

39. Daniel, M., Haban, G. F., Hutcherson, W. L., Bolter, J., & Long, C. (1985). Neuropsychological and emotional consequences of accidental, high-voltage electrical shock. *Clinical Neuropsychology, 7,* 102-106.

40. Dodrill, C. B. (1985). Incidence and doubtful significance of nonstandard orientations in reproduction of the key from the Aphasia Screening Test. *Perceptual and Motor Skills, 60,* 411-415.

41. Donovan, D. M., Kivlahan, D. R., Walker, R. D., & Umlauf, R. (1985). Derivation and validation of neuropsychological clusters among men alcoholics. *Journal of Studies on Alcohol, 46,* 205-211.

42. Dorman, C., Laatsch, L. K., & Hurley, A. D. (1985). The applicability of neuropsychological test batteries for assessment of the congenitally brain disordered. *Clinical Neuropsychology, 7,* 111-117.

43. Goldman, M. S., Klisz, D. K., & Williams, D. L. (1985). Experience-dependent recovery of cognitive functioning in young alcoholics. *Addictive Behaviors, 10,* 169-176.

44. Goldstein, G., Shelly, C., Mascia, G. V., & Tarter, R. E. (1985). Relationships between neuropsychological and psychopathological dimensions in male alcoholics. *Addictive Behaviors, 10,* 365-372.

45. Greenlief, C. L., Margolis, R. B., & Erker, G. J. (1985). Application of the Trail Making Test in differentiating neuropsychological impairment of elderly persons. *Perceptual and Motor Skills, 61,* 1283-1289.

46. Heaton, R. K., Nelson, L. M., Thompson, D. S., Burks, J. S., & Franklin, G. M. (1985). Neuropsychological findings in relapsing-remitting and chronic-progressive multiple sclerosis. *Journal of Consulting and Clinical Psychology, 53,* 103-110.

47. Hesselbrock, M. N., Weidenman, M. A., & Reed, H. B. C. (1985). Effect of age, sex, drinking history and antisocial personality on neuropsychology of alcoholics. *Journal of Studies on Alcohol, 46,* 313-320.

48. Karzmark, P., Heaton, R. K., Lehman, R. A. W., & Crouch, J. (1985). Utility of the Seashore Tonal Memory Test in neuropsychological assessment. *Journal of Clinical and Experimental Neuropsychology, 7,* 367-374.

49. Kupke, T., & Lewis, R. (1985). WAIS and neuropsychological tests: Common and unique variance within an epileptic population. *Journal of Clinical and Experimental Neuropsychology, 7,* 353-366.

50. Kupke, T., & O'Brien, W. (1985). Neuropsychological impairment and behavioral limitations exhibited within an alcohol treatment program. *Journal of Clinical and Experimental Neuropsychology, 7,* 292-304.

51. Lueger, R. J., Albott, W. L., Hilgendorf, W. A., & Gill, K. J. (1985). Neuropsychological and academic achievement correlates of abnormal WISC-R Verbal-Performance discrepancies. *Journal of Clinical Psychology, 41,* 801-805.

52. McNamara, K. M., Wechsler, F. S., & Larson, P. (1985). Neuropsychological investigation in cerebral Whipple's disease: A case study. *Clinical Neuropsychology, 7,* 131-137.

53. McSweeny, A. J., Grant, I., Heaton, R. K., Prigatano, G. P., & Adams, K. M. (1985). Relationship of neuropsychological status to everyday functioning in healthy and chronically ill persons. *Journal of Clinical and Experimental Neuropsychology, 7,* 281-291.

54. Moses, J. A., Jr. (1985). The relative contributions of Halstead-Reitan Neuropsychological Battery and WAIS subtest variables to cognitive performance level. *Clinical Neuropsychology, 7,* 117-122.

55. Moses, J. A., Jr. (1985). The relative contributions of WAIS and

Halstead-Reitan Neuropsychological Battery variables to cognitive performance level: A second response to Chelune. *Clinical Neuropsychology, 7,* 77-80.

56. O'Donnell, J. P. (1985). Language and visuospatial abilities in learning-disabled, brain-damaged, and nondisabled young adults. *Perceptual and Motor Skills, 60,* 807-814.

57. Ownby, R. L., & Matthews, C. G. (1985). On the meaning of the WISC-R third factor: Relations to selected neuropsychological measures. *Journal of Consulting and Clinical Psychology, 53,* 531-534.

58. Pendleton, M. G., Heaton, R. K., Lehman, R. A. W., Hulihan, D., & Anthony, W. Z. (1985). Word Finding Test performance: Effects of localization of cerebral damage, level of neuropsychological impairment, age, and education. *Journal of Clinical Psychology, 41,* 82-85.

59. Pennington, B. F., Heaton, R. K., Karzmark, P., Pendleton, M. G., Lehman, R., & Shucard, D. W. (1985). The neuropsychological phenotype in Turner syndrome. *Cortex, 21,* 391-404.

60. Reinvang, I., & Sundet, K. (1985). The validity of functional assessment with neuropsychological tests in aphasic stroke patients. *Scandinavian Journal of Psychology, 26,* 208-218.

61. Seidenberg, M., Parker, J. C., Nichols, W. K., Davenport, J., & Hewett, J. E. (1985). Carotid stenosis and atherosclerotic heart disease: Interactive effects on cognitive status. *Clinical Neuropsychology, 7,* 45-48.

62. Sherrill, R. E., Jr. (1985). Comparison of three short forms of the Category test. *Journal of Clinical and Experimental Neuropsychology, 7,* 231-238.

63. Skenazy, J. A., & Bigler, E. D. (1985). Psychological adjustment and neuropsychological performance in diabetic patients. *Journal of Clinical Psychology, 41,* 391-396.

64. Taylor, M. A., & Abrams, R. (1985). Short-term cognitive effects of unilateral and bilateral ECT. *British Journal of Psychiatry, 146,* 308-311.

65. Townes, B. D., Martin, D. C., Nelson, D., Prosser, R., Pepping, M., Maxwell, J., Peel, J., & Preston, M. (1985). Neurobehavioral approach to classification of psychiatric patients using a competency model. *Journal of Consulting and Clinical Psychology, 53,* 33-42.

66. Atteberry-Bennett, J., Barth, J. T., Loyd, B. H., & Lawrence, E. C. (1986). The relationship between behavioral and cognitive deficits, demographics and depression in patients with minor head injuries. *Clinical Neuropsychology, 8,* 114-117.

67. Bornstein, R. A. (1986). Classification rates obtained with "standard" cut-off scores on selected neuropsychological measures. *Journal of Clinical and Experimental Neuropsychology, 8,* 413-420.

68. Boucher, M. L., Dewan, M. J., Donnelly, M. P., Pandurangi, A. K., Bartell, K., Diamond, T., & Major, L. F. (1986). Relative utility of three indices of neuropsychological impairment in a young, chronic schizophrenic population. *The Journal of Nervous and Mental Disease, 174,* 44-46.

69. Brandon, A. D., Chavez, E. L., & Bennett, T. L. (1986). A comparative evaluation of two neurological finger tapping instruments: Hastead Reitan and Western Psychological Services. *Clinical Neuropsychology, 8,* 64-65.

70. Cullum, C. M., & Bigler, E. D. (1986). Ventricle size, cortical atrophy and the relationship with neuropsychological status in closed head injury: A quantitative analysis. *Journal of Clinical and Experimental Neuropsychology, 8,* 437-452.

71. Curry, J. F., Logue, P. E., & Butler, B. (1986). Child and adolescent norms for Russell's revision of the Wechsler Memory Scale. *Journal of Clinical Child Psychology, 15,* 214-220.

72. Drew, R. H., Templer, D. I., Schuyler, B. A., Newell, T. G., & Cannon, W. G. (1986). Neuropsychological deficits in active licensed professional boxers. *Journal of Clinical Psychology, 42,* 520-525.

73. Elias, M. F., Robbins, M. A., Schultz, N. R., Jr., & Streeten, D. H. P. (1986). A longitudinal study of neuropsychological test performance for hypertensive and normotensive adults: Initial findings. *Journal of Gerontology, 41,* 503-505.

74. Finlayson, M. A. J., Sullivan, J. F., & Alfano, D. P. (1986). Halstead's Category test: Withstanding the test of time. *Journal of Clinical and Experimental Neuropsychology, 8,* 706-709.

75. Hillbom, M., & Holm, L. (1986). Contribution of traumatic head injury to neuropsychological deficits in alcoholics. *Journal of Neurology, Neurosurgery, and Psychiatry, 49,* 1348-1353.

76. Hinshaw, S. P., Carte, E. T., & Morrison, D. C. (1986). Concurrent prediction of academic achievement in reading disabled children: The role of neuropsychological and intellectual measures at different ages. *Clinical Neuropsychology, 8,* 3-8.

77. Josiassen, R. C., Curry, L. M., Mancall, E. L., Shagass, C., & Roemer, R. A. (1986). Relationship between evoked potential and neuropsychological findings in persons "at risk" for Huntington's Disease. *Journal of Clinical and Experimental Neuropsychology, 8,* 21-36.

78. Livesay, J. R. (1986). Clinical utility of Wechsler's deterioration index in screening for behavioral impairment. *Perceptual and Motor Skills, 63,* 619-626.

79. Lorig, T. S., Gehring, W. J., & Hyrn, D. L. (1986). Period analysis of the EEG during performance of the Trail Making Test. *Clinical Neuropsychology, 8,* 97-99.

80. Magner, J. R., Kirzinger, S. S., & Spector, J. (1986). Viral encephalitis: Neuropsychological assessment in differential diagnosis and evaluation of sequelae. *Clinical Neuropsychology, 8,* 127-132.

81. McCue, P. M., Shelly, C., & Goldstein, G. (1986). Intellectual, academic and neuropsychological performance levels in learning disabled adults. *Journal of Learning Disabilities, 19,* 233-236.

82. Moses, J. A., Jr. (1986). The relative efficiency of WAIS IQ and subtest variables as predictors of Halstead-Reitan Neuropsychological Battery performance level. *Clinical Neuropsychology, 8,* 49-52.

83. Nici, J., & Reitan, R. M. (1986). Patterns of neuropsychological ability in brain-disordered versus normal children. *Journal of Consulting and Clinical Psychology, 54,* 542-545.

84. Nussbaum, N. L., & Bigler, E. D. (1986). Neuropsychological and behavioral profiles of empirically derived subgroups of learning disabled children. *Clinical Neuropsychology, 8,* 82-89.

85. Nussbaum, N. L., Bigler, E. D., & Koch, W. (1986). Neuropsychologically derived subgroups of learning disabled children: Personality/ behavioral dimensions. *Journal of Learning Disabilities, 19,* 57-67.

86. Ober, B. A., Dronkers, N. F., Koss, E., Delis, D. C., & Friedland, R. P. (1986). Retrieval from semantic memory in Alzheimer-type dementia. *Journal of Clinical and Experimental Neuropsychology, 8,* 75-92.

87. Parker, J. C., Smarr, K. L., Granberg, B. W., Nichols, W. K., & Hewett, J. E. (1986). Neuropsychological parameters of carotid endarterectomy: A two-year prospective analysis. *Journal of Consulting and Clinical Psychology, 54,* 676-681.

88. Pugh, M., & Bigler, E. D. (1986). Schizophrenia and prior history of "MBD": Neuropsychological findings. *Clinical Neuropsychology, 8,* 22-26.

89. Rothke, S. (1986). The role of set shifting cues on the Wisconsin Card Sorting Test and Halstead Category Test. *Clinical Neuropsychology, 8,* 11-14.

90. Steinman, D. R., & Bigler, E. D. (1986). Neuropsychological sequelae of ruptured anterior communicating artery aneurysm. *Clinical Neuropsychology, 8,* 135-140.

91. Svanum, S., & Schladenhauffen, J. (1986). Lifetime and recent alcohol consumption among male alcoholics. Neuropsychological implications. *The Journal of Nervous and Mental Disease, 174,* 214-220.

92. Taylor, A. E., Saint-Cyr, J. A., & Lang, A. E. (1986). Frontal lobe dysfunction in Parkinson's disease: The cortical focus of neostriatal outflow. *Brain, 109,* 845-883.

93. Tramontana, M. G., & Boyd, T. A. (1986). Psychometric screening of neuropsychological abnormality in older children. *Clinical Neuropsychology, 8,* 53-59.

94. Williams, J. M., & Shane, B. (1986). The Reitan-Indiana Aphasia Screening Test: Scoring and factor analysis. *Journal of Clinical Psychology, 42,* 156-160.

95. Bornstein, R. A., Baker, G. B., & Douglass, A. B. (1987). Short-term retest reliability of the Halstead-Reitan Battery in a normal sample. *The Journal of Nervous and Mental Disease, 175,* 229-232.

96. Corrigan, J. D., & Hinkeldey, N. S. (1987). Comparison of intelligence and memory in patients with diffuse and focal injury. *Psychological Reports, 60,* 899-906.

97. Corrigan, J. D., Agresti, A. A., & Hinkeldey, N. S. (1987). Psychometric characteristics of the Category Test: Replication and extension. *Journal of Clinical Psychology, 43,* 368-376.

98. Goldstein, G., & Shelly, C. (1987). The classification of neuropsychological deficit. *Journal of Psychopathology and Behavioral Assessment, 9,* 183-202.

99. Gur, R. E., Resnick, S. M., Alavi, A., Gur, R. G., Caroff, S., Dann, R., Silver, F. L., Saykin, A. J., Chawluk, J. B., Kushner, M., & Reivich, M. (1987). Regional brain function in schizophrenia: A position emission tomography study. *Archives of General Psychiatry, 44,* 119-125.

100. Huesmann, L. R., Eron, L. D., & Yarmel, P. W. (1987). Intellectual functioning and aggression. *Journal of Personality and Social Psychology, 52,* 232-240.

101. Klonoff, H., Fleetham, J., Taylor, D. R., & Clark, C. (1987). Treatment outcome of obstructive sleep apnea: Physiological and neuropsychological concomitants. *The Journal of Nervous and Mental Disease, 175,* 208-212.

102. Naugle, R. I., Cullum, C. M., Bigler, E. D., & Massman, P. J. (1987). Handedness and dementia. *Perceptual and Motor Skills, 65,* 207-210.

103. Rounsaville, B. J., Dolinsky, Z. S., Babor, T. F., & Meyer, R. E. (1987). Psychopathology as a predictor of treatment outcome in alcoholics. *Archives of General Psychiatry, 44,* 505-513.

104. Schofield, N. J., & Ashman, A. F. (1987). The cognitive processing of gifted, high average, and low average ability students. *British Journal of Educational Psychology, 57,* 9-20.

105. Seidman, L. J., Sokolove, R. L., McElroy, C., Knapp, P. H., & Sabin, T. (1987). Lateral ventricular size and social network differentiation in young, nonchronic schizophrenic patients. *American Journal of Psychiatry, 144,* 512-514.

106. Telzrow, C. F., & Harr, G. A. (1987). Common variance among three measures of nonverbal cognitive ability: WISC-R performance scale, WJPB-TCA reasoning cluster, and Halstead Category Test. *Journal of School Psychology, 25,* 93-95.

107. Yeudall, L. T., Reddon, J. R., Gill, D. M., & Stefanyk, W. O. (1987). Normative data for the Halstead-Reitan neuropsychological tests stratified by age and sex. *Journal of Clinical Psychology, 43,* 346-367.

108. Brodsky, P. (1988). Follow-up on the youngest REHABIT client: Importance of caution. *Perceptual and Motor Skills, 66*(2), 383-386.

109. D'Amato, R. C., Gray, J. W., & Dean, R. S. (1988). A comparison between intelligence and neuropsychological functioning. *Journal of School Psychology, 26,* 283- 292.

110. D'Amato, R. C., Gray, J. W., & Dean, R. S. (1988). Construct validity of the PPVT with neuropsychological, intellectual, and achievement measures. *Journal of Clinical Psychology, 44,* 934-939.

111. Fowler, P. C., Zillmer, E., & Newman, A. C. (1988). A multifactor model of the Halstead-Reitan Neuropsychological Test Battery and its relationship to cognitive status and psychiatric diagnosis. *Journal of Clinical Psychology, 44,* 898-906.

112. Lewis, D. O., Pincus, J. H., Bard, B., Richardson, E., Princhep, L. S., Feldman, M., & Yeager, C. (1988). Neuropsychiatric, psychoeducational, and family characteristics of 14 juveniles condemned to death in the United States. *American Journal of Psychiatry, 145,* 584-589.

113. Pauker, J. D. (1988). Constructing overlapping cell tables to maximize the clinical usefulness of normative test data: Rationale and an example from neuropsychology. *Journal of Clinical Psychology, 44,* 930-934.

114. Petiet, C. A., Townes, B. D., Brooks, R. J., & Kramer, J. H. (1988). Neurobehavioral and psychosocial functioning of women exposed to high altitude in mountaineering. *Perceptual and Motor Skills, 67,* 443-452.

115. Tucker, D. M., Roeltgen, D. P., Tully, R., Hartmann, J., & Boxell, C. (1988). Memory dysfunction following unilateral transection of the fornix: A hippocampal disconnection syndrome. *Cortex, 24,* 465-472.

116. Zarantonello, M. M. (1988). Comparability of the WAIS and the WAIS-R: A consideration of level of neuropsychological impairment. *Journal of Consulting and Clinical Psychology, 56,* 295-297.

117. Boone, K. B., & Rausch, R. (1989). Seashore Rhythm Test performance in patients with unilatral temporal lobe damage. *Journal of Clinical Psychology, 45,* 614-618.

118. Davis, R. D., Adams, R. E., Gates, D. O., & Cheramie, G. M. (1989). Screening for learning disabilities: A neuropsychological approach. *Journal of Clinical Psychology, 45,* 423-429.

119. Foxcroft, C. D. (1989). Factor analysis of the Reitan-Indiana Neuropsychological Test Battery. *Perceptual and Motor Skills, 69,* 1303-1313.

120. Hill, R. D. (1989). Residual effects of cigarette smoking on cognitive performance in normal aging. *Psychology and Aging, 4,* 251-254.

121. Leckliter, I. N., & Matarazzo, J. D. (1989). The influence of age, education, IQ, gender, and alcohol abuse on Halstead-Reitan Neuropsychological Test Battery performance. *Journal of Clinical Psychology, 45,* 484-512.

122. Bates, M. E., & Tracy, J. I. (1990). Cognitive functioning in young "social drinkers": Is there impairment to detect? *Journal of Abnormal Psychology, 99,* 242-249.

123. Brooks, D. A., Dean, R. S., & Gray, J. W. (1990). Simultaneous and successive processing dimensions of the Halstead-Reitan Neuropsychological Battery. *International Journal of Clinical Neuropsychology, 12,* 98-102.

124. Dikmen, S., Machamer, J., Temkin, N., & McLean, A. (1990). Neuropsychological recovery in patients with moderate to severe head injury: 2 year follow-up. *Journal of Clinical and Experimental Neuropsychology, 12,* 507-519.

125. Fischer, W. E., & Dean, R. S. (1990). Factor structure of the Halstead Category Test by age and gender. *International Journal of Clinical Neuropsychology, 12,* 180-183.

126. Grant, M. L., Ilai, D., Nussbaum, N. L., & Bigler, E. D. (1990). The relationship between continuous performance tasks and neuropsychological tests in children with Attention-deficit Hyperactivity Disorder. *Perceptual and Motor Skills, 70,* 435-445.

127. Hirt, M., & Pithers, W. (1990). Arousal and maintenance of schizophrenic attention. *Journal of Clinical Psychology, 46,* 15-21.

128. Hom, J., & Reitan, R. M. (1990). Generalized cognitive function after stroke. *Journal of Clinical and Experimental Neuropsychology, 12,* 644-654.

129. Moehle, K. A., Rasmussen, J. L., & Fitzhugh-Bell, K. B. (1990). Factor analysis of neuropsychological tests in an adult sample. *International Journal of Clinical Neuropsychology, 12,* 107-115.

130. O'Donnell, J. P., & Leicht, D. J. (1990). WAIS VIQ-PIQ differences: Validation and theoretical implications for young adults with learning disabilities. *International Journal of Clinical Neuropsychology, 12,* 140-146.

131. O'Donnell, J. P., Randazzo, C. E., & Ramanaiah, N. V. (1990). Abbreviating the Speech-Sounds Perception Test: Results for non-disabled and head-injured young adults. *International Journal of Clinical Neuropsychology, 12,* 184-187.

132. Bornstein, R. A., & Yang, V. (1991). Neuropsychological performance in medicated and unmedicated patients with Tourette's disorder. *American Journal of Psychiatry, 148,* 468-471.

133. Braggio, J. T., Pishkin, V., & Lovallo, W. R. (1991). Psychological activity and neuropsychological test performance in alcoholics. *Journal of Clinical Psychology, 47,* 823-839.

134. Brooker, A. E., Dougherty, D. S., Love, K. F., & Kelly, W. M. (1991). Neuropsychological, neurological, and MRI correlates of dementia in advanced Huntington's disease: A single case study. *Perceptual and Motor Skills, 72,* 1363-1374.

135. Brown, F. H., Jr., Dodrill, C. B., Clark, T., & Zych, K. (1991). An investigation of the relationship between self-report of memory functioning and memory test performance. *Journal of Clinical Psychology, 47,* 772-777.

136. Cosgrove, J., & Newell, T. G. (1991). Recovery of neuropsychological functions during reduction in use of phencyclidine. *Journal of Clinical Psychology, 47,* 159-169.

137. Gass, C. S. (1991). Emotional variables and neuropsychological test performance. *Journal of Clinical Psychology, 47,* 100-104.

138. Hirt, M., & Pithers, W. (1991). Selective attention and levels of coding in schizophrenia. *British Journal of Clinical Psychology, 30,* 139-149.

139. Kundert, D. K., McIntosh, D. E., Shine, A. E., & Dean, R. S. (1991). A study of neuropsychological impairment among shool-identified learning-disabled students. *Journal of School Psychology, 29,* 353-360.

140. Lewinsohn, P. M., Rohde, P., Seeley, J. R., & Fischer, S. A. (1991). Age and depression: Unique and shared effects. *Psychology and Aging, 6,* 247-260.

141. Maj, M., Janssen, R., Satz, P., Zavdig, M., Starace, F., Boor, D., Sughondhabirom, B., Bing, E., Luabeya, M. K., Ndetei, D., Riedel, R., Schulte, G., & Sartorius, N. (1991). The World Health Organization's cross-cultural study on neuropsychiatric aspects of infection with the human immunodeficiency virus 1 (HIV-1): Preparation and pilot phase. *British Journal of Psychiatry, 159,* 351-356.

142. Mitrushina, M., & Satz, P. (1991). Effect of repeated administration of a neuropsychological battery in the elderly. *Journal of Clinical Psychology, 47,* 790-801.

143. Sherer, M., Parsons, D. A., Nixon, S. J., & Adams, R. L. (1991). Clinical validity of the Speech-Sounds Perception Test and the Seashore Rhythm Test. *Journal of Clinical and Experimental Neuropsychology, 13,* 741-751.

144. Smith, D. E., & McCrady, B. S. (1991). Cognitive impairment among alcoholics: Impact on drink refusal skill acquisition and treatment outcome. *Addictive Behaviors, 16,* 265-274.

145. Tamkin, A. S., & Dolenz, J. J. (1991). Some correlates of the Weigl Color-Form Sorting Test in alcoholics. *Journal of Clinical Psychology, 47,* 170-174.

146. Fals-Stewart, W. (1992). An interrater reliability study of the Trail Making Test (parts A and B). *Perceptual and Motor Skills, 74,* 39-42.

147. Fals-Stewart, W. (1992). Using subtests of the brain age quotient to screen for cognitive deficits among substance abusers. *Perceptual and Motor Skills, 75,* 244-246.

148. Minshew, N. J., Goldstein, G., Muenz, L. R., & Payton, J. B. (1992). Neuropsychological functioning in nonmentally retarded autistic individuals. *Journal of Clinical and Experimental Neuropsychology, 14,* 749-761.

149. Persinger, M. A. (1992). Neuropsychological profiles of adults who report "sudden remembering" of early childhood memories: Implications for claims of sex abuse and alien visitation/abduction experiences. *Perceptual and Motor Skills, 75,* 259-266.

150. Putnam, S. H., Adams, K. M., & Schneider, A. M. (1992). One-day test-retest reliability of neuropsychological tests in a personal injury case. *Psychological Assessment, 4,* 312-316.

151. Reitan, R. M., & Wolfson, D. (1992). Conventional intelligence measurements and neuropsychological concepts of adaptive abilities. *Journal of Clinical Psychology, 48,* 521-529.

152. Reitan, R. M., Wolfson, D., & Hom, J. (1992). Left cerebral

dominance for bilateral simultaneous sensory stimulation? *Journal of Clinical Psychology, 48,* 760-766.

153. Richards, P., & Persinger, M. A. (1992). Toe graphaesthesia as a discriminator of brain impairment: The outstanding feet for neuropsychology. *Perceptual and Motor Skills, 74,* 1027-1030.

154. Robins, P. M. (1992). A comparison of behavioral and attentional functioning in children diagnosed as hyperactive or learning-disabled. *Journal of Abnormal Child Psychology, 20,* 65-82.

155. Waldmann, B. W., Dickson, A. L., Monahan, M. C., & Kazelskis, R. (1992). The relationship between intellectual ability and adult performance on the Trail Making Test and the Symbol Digit Modalities Test. *Journal of Clinical Psychology, 48,* 360-363.

156. Bryson, G. J., Silverstein, M. L., Nathan, A., & Stephen, L. (1993). Differential rate of neuropsychological dysfunction in psychiatric disorders: Comparison between the Halstead-Reitan and Luria-Nebraska batteries. *Perceptual and Motor Skills, 76,* 305-306.

157. Horton, A. M., Jr. (1993). Posttraumatic stress disorder and mild head trauma: Follow-up of a case study. *Perceptual and Motor Skills, 76,* 243-246.

158. O'Donnell, W. E., DeSoto, C. B., & DeSoto, J. L. (1993). Validity and reliability of the revised Neuropsychological Impairment Scale (NIS). *Journal of Clinical Psychology, 49,* 372-382.

159. Robinette, R. L., Sherer, M., & Adams, R. L. (1993). The development of verbal and nonverbal factorially derived memory measures. *Journal of Clinical Psychology, 49,* 89-94.

[1120]

Halstead Russell Neuropsychological Evaluation System.

Purpose: Provides "comprehensive measures of the functions relevant to neuropsychological assessment."

Population: Neuropsychological patients.

Publication Date: 1993.

Acronym: HRNES.

Scores, 3: Percent Impaired Score, Average Index Score, Lateralization Key.

Administration: Individual.

Price Data, 1993: $450 per complete kit including manual (99 pages), 10 recording booklets, and 3.5-inch IBM unlimited use microcomputer disk; $49.50 per 10 recording booklets; $52 per manual; $395 per unlimited use microcomputer disk.

Time: Administration time not reported.

Comments: HRNES computer program compiles raw scores from up to 22 tests, corrects them for age and education, and converts them to scaled scores; includes unlimited use disk.

Authors: Elbert W. Russell and Regina I. Starkey.

Publisher: Western Psychological Services.

[1121]

The Hand Test, Revised 1983.

Purpose: "A diagnostic technique that uses pictures of hands as [a] projective medium . . . the examinee 'projects' by telling what the hand is doing."

Population: Ages 5 and over.

Publication Dates: 1959–91.

Scores, 41: 24 quantitative scores: Interpersonal (Affection, Dependence, Communication, Exhibition, Direction, Aggression, Total), Environmental (Acquisition, Active, Passive, Total), Maladjustive (Tension, Crippled, Fear, Total), Withdrawal (Description, Bizarre, Failure, Total), Experience Ratio, Acting Out Ratio, Pathological, Average Initial Response Time, High Minus Low Score; plus 17 qualitative scores: Ambivalent, Automatic Phrase, Cylindrical, Denial, Emotion, Gross, Hiding, Immature, Impotent, Inanimate, Movement, Oral, Perplexity, Sensual, Sexual, Original, Repetition.

Administration: Individual.

Price Data, 1993: $130 per kit of 25 scoring booklets, picture cards, manual ('83, 90 pages plus scoring booklet) and manual supplement on interpreting child and adolescent responses ('91); $16.50 per 25 scoring booklets; $27.50 per picture cards; $48 per per manual.

Time: (10) minutes.

Author: Edwin E. Wagner.

Publisher: Western Psychological Services.

Cross References: For a review by Marcia B. Shaffer of an earlier edition, see 10:134 (5 references); see 9:464 (16 references), T3:1053 (21 references), 8:575 (29 references), T2:1470 (15 references), and P:438 (12 references); for a review by Goldine C. Gleser and an excerpted review by Irving R. Stone of an earlier edition, see 6:216 (6 references).

TEST REFERENCES

1. Hayslib, B., Jr., & Panek, P. Z. (1983). Physical self-maintenance, mental status, and personality in institutionalized elderly adults. *Journal of Clinical Psychology, 39,* 479-485.

2. McGiboney, G. W., Carter, C., & Jones, W. (1984). Hand Test and the High School Personality Questionnaire: Structural analysis. *Perceptual and Motor Skills, 58,* 287-290.

3. Panek, P. E., & Wagner, E. E. (1986). Hand Test personality variables related to automotive moving violations in female drivers. *Journal of Personality Assessment, 50,* 208- 211.

4. Greene, R. S., & Dawson, J. E. (1987). Hand Test, WAIS-R and Luria-Nebraska intercorrelations. *Perceptual and Motor Skills, 64,* 906.

5. Lester, D. (1987). An exploratory study of the validity of administering the Hand Test in a group format. *Perceptual and Motor Skills, 65,* 430.

6. Castle, S. R., & Stoner, S. B. (1989). Age and sex differences in the responses of adolescents to The Hand Test. *Psychological Reports, 65,* 939-944.

7. Panek, P. E., & Wagner, E. E. (1989). Validation of two Hand Test indices of aggressive behavior in an institutional setting. *Journal of Personality Assessment, 53,* 169- 172.

8. Rasch, M. A., & Wagner, E. E. (1989). Initial psychological effects of sexual abuse on female children as reflected in the Hand Test. *Journal of Personality Assessment, 53,* 761-769.

9. Hayslip, B., Jr., Panek, P. E., & Stoner, S. B. (1990). Cohort differences in Hand Test performance: A time lagged analysis. *Journal of Personality Assessment, 54,* 704-710.

10. Hilsenroth, M. J., & Sivec, H. J. (1990). Relationships between Hand Test variables and maladjustment in school children. *Journal of Personality Assessment, 55,* 344-349.

11. Lenihan, G. O., & Kirk, W. G. (1990). Personality characteristics of eating-disordered outpatients as measured by The Hand Test. *Journal of Personality Assessment, 55,* 350-361.

12. Maloney, P., & Wagner, E. E. (1990). Predicting normal age-related changes with intelligence, projective, and perceptual-motor test variables. *Perceptual and Motor Skills, 71,* 1225-1226.

13. Wagner, E. E., Rasch, M. A., & Marsico, D. S. (1990). Hand Test characteristics of severely behavior handicapped children. *Journal of Personality Assessment, 54,* 802-806.

14. Carter, D. E., & Moran, J. J. (1991). Interscorer reliability for the Hand Test administered to children. *Perceptual and Motor Skills, 72,* 759-765.

15. Cates, J. A., & Lapham, R. F. (1991). Personality assessment of the prelingual, profoundly deaf child or adolescent. *Journal of Personality Assessment, 56,* 118-129.

16. Moran, J. J., & Carter, D. (1991). Comparisons among children's responses to the Hand Test by grade, race, sex, and social class. *Journal of Clinical Psychology, 47,* 647-664.

17. Panek, P. E., & Wagner, E. E. (1993). Hand Test characteristics of dual diagnosed mentally retarded older adults. *Journal of Personality Assessment, 61,* 324-328.

[1122]
Hand-Tool Dexterity Test.
Purpose: Intended to "provide a measure of proficiency in using ordinary mechanic's tools."
Population: Adolescents and adults.
Publication Dates: 1946–81.
Acronym: HTDT.
Scores: Total score only.
Administration: Individual.
Price Data, 1994: $430 per complete set including all necessary equipment and manual ('81, 19 pages); $30.50 per manual.
Time: (5–10) minutes.
Comments: Examinee's score based on time it takes to finish test.
Author: George K. Bennett.
Publisher: The Psychological Corporation.
Cross References: See T3:1054 (1 reference) and 7:1044 (4 references); for reviews by C. H. Lawshe, Jr. and Neil D. Warren, see 3:649 (2 references).

[1123]
Hannah-Gardner Test of Verbal and Nonverbal Language Functioning.
Purpose: Designed as a screening device for identifying English- and Spanish-speaking preschool children with language deficits.
Population: Ages 3.5–5.5.
Publication Date: 1978.
Scores, 7: Visual Perception, Conceptual Development, Auditory Perception, Linguistic Development, Total, Nonverbal, Verbal.
Administration: Individual.
Price Data: Available from publisher.
Foreign Language Edition: Spanish version available.
Time: (25–30) minutes.
Authors: Elaine P. Hannah and Julie O. Gardner.
Publisher: SenCom Associates.

[1124]
Happiness Measures.
Purpose: Assesses a respondent's perception of amount of happiness or unhappiness and estimate of time experienced as happy or unhappy.
Population: Ages 16 and over.
Publication Dates: 1980–87.
Acronym: HM.
Scores, 5: Scale, Happy Percentage Estimate, Unhappy Percentage Estimate, Neutral Percentage Estimate, Combination.
Administration: Group.
Manual: No manual.
Price Data: Available from publisher.
Time: (1–5) minutes.
Comments: Test booklet title is Emotions Questionnaire.
Author: Michael W. Fordyce.
Publisher: Cypress Lake Media.

Cross References: For a review by William A. Stock, see 11:154.

[1125]
Harding Skyscraper.
Purpose: Intended as a measure of high level intellectual functioning.
Population: Ages 17 and over with intelligence level in top 1% of population.
Publication Dates: 1973–75.
Scores: Overall performance score.
Administration: Group.
Manual: No manual.
Price Data: Available from publisher.
Time: (90–120) minutes.
Comments: Tests are rented.
Author: C. Chris Harding.
Publisher: C. Chris Harding [Australia].
Cross References: For a review by Donald J. Treffinger, see 9:466; see also 8:189 (2 references).

[1126]
Harding Stress-Fair Compatibility Test.
Purpose: Intended to measure compatibility between people.
Population: Adults.
Publication Date: 1980.
Acronym: HSFCT.
Scores, 11: Intellectual, Extraversion, Sensitivity, Idealism, Motivation, Awareness, Independence, Reasonability, Objectivity, Dominance, Compatibility.
Administration: Group.
Price Data: Available from publisher.
Time: Administration time not reported.
Author: C. Chris Harding.
Publisher: C. Chris Harding [Australia].
Cross References: For reviews by Charles D. Claiborn and Douglas S. Payne, see 9:467.

[1127]
The Hare Psychopathy Checklist—Revised.
Purpose: "Designed to assess psychopathic (antisocial) personality disorders in forensic populations."
Population: Prison inmates.
Publication Dates: 1990–91.
Acronym: PCL-R.
Scores, 3: Factor 1, Factor 2, Total.
Administration: Individual.
Price Data, 1993: $250 per complete kit including manual ('91, 77 pages), 1 rating booklet, 25 Quik-Score™ forms, and 25 interview guides; $100 per manual; $40 per rating booklet; $50 per 25 Quik-Score™ forms; $100 per 25 interview guides.
Time: (90–180) minutes.
Comments: Time includes interview and review of available collateral information; Factor 1 description: Selfish, callous, and remorseless use of others; Factor 2 description: Chronically unstable and antisocial lifestyle, social deviance.

Author: Robert D. Hare.
Publisher: Multi-Health Systems, Inc.

TEST REFERENCES

1. Hart, S. D., Kropp, P. R., & Hare, R. D. (1988). Performance of male psychopaths following conditional release from prison. *Journal of Consulting and Clinical Psychology, 56,* 227-232.
2. Serin, R. C. (1992). The clinical application of the Psychopathy Checklist—Revised (PCL-R) in a prison population. *Journal of Clinical Psychology, 48,* 637-642.
3. Harris, G. T., Rice, M. E., & Quinsey, V. L. (1994). Psychopathy as a taxon: Evidence that psychopaths are a discrete class. *Journal of Consulting and Clinical Psychology, 62,* 387-397.

[1128]

The Harrington-O'Shea Career Decision-Making System Revised.

Purpose: An interest inventory that provides an assessment of career interests, job choices, school subjects, future plans, values, and abilities.
Population: Grade 7 and over.
Publication Dates: 1976–93.
Acronym: CDM-R.
Administration: Group or individual.
Price Data: Available from publisher.
Foreign Language Edition: Hand-scored versions of original CDM also available in Spanish.
Authors: Thomas F. Harrington and Arthur J. O'Shea.
Publisher: American Guidance Service, Inc.
 a) LEVEL 1.
 Publication Date: 1992.
 Scores: 6 scores: Crafts, Scientific, The Arts, Social, Business, Office Operations, used to identify occupational areas from among 18 career clusters: Manual, Skilled Crafts, Technical, Math-Science, Medical-Dental, Literary, Art, Music, Entertainment, Customer Service, Personal Service, Social Service, Education, Sales, Management, Legal, Clerical, Data Analysis.
 Time: (20–25) minutes.
 Comments: Hand-scored.
 b) LEVEL 2.
 Publication Dates: 1976–92.
 Scores: Same as *a* above and questions in 5 areas: Job Choices, School Subjects, Future Plans, Values, Abilities.
 Time: (30–35) minutes.
 Comments: Hand-scored edition and machine-scored edition (group summary reports available for machine-scored edition); computer option available through Guidance Information System® (Houghton-Mifflin).
Cross References: For a review by Caroline Manuele-Adkins of an earlier edition, see 10:136 (1 reference); see also T3:1054 (3 references); for a review by Carl G. Willis of an earlier edition, see 8:1004.

TEST REFERENCES

1. Kapes, J. T., & Vansickle, T. R. (1992). Comparing paper-pencil and computer-based versions of the Harrington-O'Shea Career Decision-Making System. *Measurement and Evaluation in Counseling and Development, 25,* 5-13.

[1129]

The Harrison-Stroud Reading Readiness Profiles.

Purpose: Designed as "tests of specific abilities and skills that children use in beginning to learn to read."
Population: Grades K–1.
Publication Dates: 1949–56.
Scores, 7: Using Symbols, Making Visual Discriminations (2 parts), Using the Context, Making Auditory Discriminations, Using Context and Auditory Clues, Giving the Names of Letters.
Administration: Individual in part.
Price Data, 1990: $9 per examination kit; $49.50 per package of 35 test booklets including manual ('56, 24 pages), class record sheet, Letter Card, and Mask; $1.95 per Letter Card; $2.10 per Letter Card Mask; $1.50 per class record sheet; $4.80 per manual.
Time: (80–90) minutes in 3 sessions.
Authors: M. Lucile Harrison and James B. Stroud.
Publisher: The Riverside Publishing Co.
Cross References: See T2:1705 (17 references); for a review by S. S. Dunn, see 5:677 (2 references); for a review by William S. Gray, see 4:568.

[1130]

The Hartman Value Profile.

Purpose: Assesses the development of the capacity to make certain evaluative judgments.
Population: Age 12 and older.
Publication Dates: 1965–72.
Acronym: HVP.
Scores: 4 parts: The Development of the Capacities to Make Valuations in the Outside World, The Development of the Capacities to Make Valuations of One's Own Self, The Development of the Balance Between the Capacities to Value the Outside World and to Value One's Own Self, The Development of Certain Selected Value Capacities.
Administration: Group.
Price Data: Not available.
Time: Administration time not reported.
Authors: Robert S. Hartman and Mario Cardenas Trigos.
Publisher: Research Concepts [No reply from publisher; status unknown].
Cross References: See T2:1211 (2 references) and P:106 (2 references).

TEST REFERENCES

1. Simmons, D. D. (1980). Purpose-in-Life and the three aspects of valuing. *Journal of Clinical Psychology, 36,* 921-922.

[1131]

Harvard Group Scale of Hypnotic Susceptibility.

Purpose: Constructed to assess susceptibility to hypnosis.
Population: College.
Publication Dates: 1959–62.
Scores: Total score only.
Administration: Group.

Price Data, 1990: $30 per 25 response booklets; $7.50 per manual ('62, 21 pages); $8 per specimen set.

Time: (50–70) minutes.

Comments: Adaptation for group administration of Form A of the Stanford Hypnotic Susceptibility Scale.

Authors: Ronald E. Shor and Emily Carota Orne.

Publisher: Consulting Psychologists Press, Inc.

Cross References: See 9:469 (6 references), T3:1063 (57 references), 8:576 (46 references), T2:1212 (19 references), and P:107 (12 references); for a review by Seymore Fisher, see 6:112 (4 references).

TEST REFERENCES

1. Reid, G., Steggles, S., & Fehr, R. (1982). State, emotionality, belief, and absorption in ESP scoring. *Journal of the Association for the Study of Perception, 17,* 28-38.
2. Crawford, H. J., & Allen, S. N. (1983). Enhanced visual memory during hypnosis as mediated by hypnotic responsiveness and cognitive strategies. *Journal of Experimental Psychology: General, 112,* 662-685.
3. Sanders, G. S., & Simmons, W. L. (1983). Use of hypnosis to enhance eyewitness accuracy: Does it work? *Journal of Applied Psychology, 68,* 70-77.
4. Schubert, D. K. (1983). Comparison of hypnotherapy with systematic relaxation in the treatment of cigarette habituation. *Journal of Clinical Psychology, 39,* 198-202.
5. Sheehan, P. W., & Tilden, J. (1984). Real and simulated occurrences of memory distortion in hypnosis. *Journal of Abnormal Psychology, 93,* 47-57.
6. Bower, G. H., & Mayer, J. D. (1985). Failure to replicate mood-dependent retrieval. *Bulletin of the Psychonomic Society, 23,* 39-42.
7. Bridges, C. F., Critelli, J. W., & Loos, V. E. (1985). Hypnotic susceptibility, inhibitory control, and orgasmic consistency. *Archives of Sexual Behavior, 14,* 373-376.
8. Manganello, J. L., Carlson, T. K., Zarrillo, D. L., & Teevan, R. C. (1985). Relationship between hypnotic susceptibility, fear of failure and need for achievement. *Psychological Reports, 56,* 239-242.
9. Pettinati, H. M., Horne, R. L., & Staats, J. M. (1985). Hypnotizability in patients with anorexia nervosa and bulimia. *Archives of General Psychiatry, 42,* 1014-1016.
10. Wallace, B., & Priebe, F. A. (1985). Hypnotic susceptibility, interference, and alternation frequency to the Necker cube illusion. *Journal of General Psychology, 112,* 271-277.
11. Belicki, K., & Belicki, D. (1986). Predisposition for nightmares: A study of hypnotic ability, vividness of imagery, and absorption. *Journal of Clinical Psychology, 42,* 714-718.
12. De Pascalis, V., & Palumbo, G. (1986). EEG alpha assymetry: Task difficulty and hypnotizability. *Perceptual and Motor Skills, 62,* 139-150.
13. Nash, M. R., Drake, S. D., Wiley, S., Khalsa, S., & Lynn, S. J. (1986). Accuracy of recall by hypnotically age-regressed subjects. *Journal of Abnormal Psychology, 95,* 298-300.
14. Shields, I. W., & Knox, V. J. (1986). Level of processing as a determinant of hypnotic hypermnesia. *Journal of Abnormal Psychology, 95,* 358-364.
15. Stanley, S. M., Lynn, S. J., & Nash, M. R. (1986). Trance logic, susceptibility screening, and the transparency response. *Journal of Personality and Social Psychology, 50,* 447-454.
16. Wallace, B. (1986). Latency and frequency reports to the Necker cube illusion: Effects of hypnotic susceptibility and mental arithmetic. *The Journal of General Psychology, 113,* 187-194.
17. Wilson, L., & Kihlstrom, J. F. (1986). Subjective and categorical organization of recall during posthypnotic amnesia. *Journal of Abnormal Psychology, 95,* 264-273.
18. Gfeller, J. D., Lynn, S. J., & Pribble, W. E. (1987). Enhancing hypnotic susceptibility: Interpersonal and rapport factors. *Journal of Personality and Social Psychology, 52,* 586-595.
19. Lynn, S. J., Neufeld, V., & Matyi, C. L. (1987). Inductions versus suggestions: Effects of direct and indirect wording on hypnotic responding and experience. *Journal of Abnormal Psychology, 96,* 76-79.
20. Lynn, S. J., Snodgrass, M., Rhue, J. W., & Hardaway, R. (1987). Goal-directed fantasy, hypnotic susceptibility, and expectancies. *Journal of Personality and Social Psychology, 53,* 933-938.
21. Nadon, R., Laurence, J., & Perry, C. (1987). Multiple predictors of hypnotic susceptibility. *Journal of Personality and Social Psychology, 53,* 948-960.

22. Rhue, J. W., & Lynn, S. J. (1987). Fantasy proneness and psychopathology. *Journal of Personality and Social Psychology, 53,* 327-336.
23. Spanos, N. P., Robertson, L. A., Menary, E. P., Brett, P. J., & Smith J. (1987). Effects of repeated baseline testing on cognitive-skill-training-induced increments in hypnotic susceptibility. *Journal of Personality and Social Psychology, 52,* 1230-1235.
24. Wagner, M. W., & Ratzeburg, F. H. (1987). Hypnotic suggestibility and paranormal belief. *Psychological Reports, 60,* 1069-1070.
25. Bates, B. L., Miller, R. J., Cross, H. J., & Brigham, T. A. (1988). Modifying hypnotic suggestibility with the Carleton Skills Training Program. *Journal of Personality and Social Psychology, 55,* 120-127.
26. Lynn, S. J., Weekes, J. R., Matyi, C. L., & Neufeld, V. (1988). Direct versus indirect suggestions, archaic involvement, and hypnotic experience. *Journal of Abnormal Psychology, 97,* 296-301.
27. McCann, T., & Sheehan, P. W. (1988). Hypnotically induced pseudomemories—Sampling their conditions among hypnotizable subjects. *Journal of Personality and Social Psychology, 54,* 339-346.
28. McConkey, K. M., & Kinoshita, S. (1988). The influence of hypnosis on memory after one day and one week. *Journal of Abnormal Psychology, 97,* 48-53.
29. Radtke, H. L., Bertrand, L. D., & Spanos, N. P. (1988). Hypnotic amnesia and temporal organization: Effects of learning set, stimulus type, number of presentations, and hypnotic susceptibility. *Canadian Journal of Behavioural Science, 20,* 201-220.
30. Stava, L. J., & Jaffa, M. (1988). Some operationalizations of the neodissociation concept and their relationship to hypnotic susceptibility. *Journal of Personality and Social Psychology, 54,* 989-996.
31. Whitehouse, W. G., Dinges, D. F., Orne, E. C., & Orne, M. T. (1988). Hypnotic hypermnesia: Enhanced memory accessibility or report bias? *Journal of Abnormal Psychology, 97,* 289-295.
32. Bryant, R. A., & McConkey, K. M. (1989). Hypnotic blindness, awareness, and attribution. *Journal of Abnormal Psychology, 98,* 443-447.
33. Bryant, R. A., & McConkey, K. M. (1989). Hypnotic blindness: A behavioral and experiential analysis. *Journal of Abnormal Psychology, 98,* 71-77.
34. Coe, W. C., & Sluis, A. S. E. (1989). Increasing contextual pressures to breach posthypnotic amnesia. *Journal of Personality and Social Psychology, 57,* 885-894.
35. Coe, W. C., Basden, B. H., Basden, D., Fikes, T., Gargano, G. J., & Webb, M. (1989). Directed forgetting and posthypnotic amnesia: Information processing and social contexts. *Journal of Personality and Social Psychology, 56,* 189-198.
36. Kirsch, I., Silva, C. E., Carone, J. E., Johnston, J. D., & Simon, B. (1989). The surreptitious observation design: An experimental paradigm for distinguishing artifact from essence in hypnosis. *Journal of Abnormal Psychology, 98,* 132-136.
37. Lynn, S. J., Weekes, J. R., & Milano, M. J. (1989). Reality versus suggestion: Pseudomemory in hypnotizable and simulating subjects. *Journal of Abnormal Psychology, 98,* 137-144.
38. Moss, B. F., & Magaro, P. A. (1989). Personality types and hetero- versus auto-hypnosis. *Journal of Personality and Social Psychology, 57,* 532-538.
39. Sheehan, P. W., & Statham, D. (1989). Hypnosis, the timing of its introduction, and acceptance of misleading information. *Journal of Abnormal Psychology, 98,* 170-176.
40. Bryant, R. A., & McConkey, K. M. (1990). Hypnotic blindness and the relevance of cognitive style. *Journal of Personality and Social Psychology, 59,* 756-761.
41. Dixon, M., Brunet, A., & Laurence, J.-R. (1990). Hypnotizability and automaticity: Toward a parallel distributed processing model of hypnotic responding. *Journal of Abnormal Psychology, 99,* 336-343.
42. Green, J. P., Lynn, S. J., Weekes, J. R., Carlson, B. W., Brentar, J., Latham, L., & Kurzhals, R. (1990). Literalism as a marker of hypnotic "trance": Disconfirming evidence. *Journal of Abnormal Psychology, 99,* 16-21.
43. Labelle, L., Laurence, J. R., Nadon, R., & Perry, C. (1990). Hypnotizability, preference for an imagic cognitive style, and memory creation in hypnosis. *Journal of Abnormal Psychology, 99,* 222-228.
44. Wallace, B. (1990). Imagery vividness, hypnotic susceptibility, and the perception of fragmented stimuli. *Journal of Personality and Social Psychology, 58,* 354-359.
45. Davidson, T. M., & Bowers, K. S. (1991). Selective hypnotic amnesia: Is it a successful attempt to forget or an unsuccessful attempt to remember? *Journal of Abnormal Psychology, 100,* 133-143.
46. Glisky, M. L., Tataryn, D. J., Tobias, B. A., Kihlstrom, J. F., & McConkey, K. M. (1991). Absorption, openness to experience, and hypnotizability. *Journal of Personality and Social Psychology, 60,* 263-272.
47. Levitt, E. E., & Waldo, T. G. (1991). Hypnotically induced auditory hallucinations and the mouth-opening maneuver: A failure to duplicate findings. *American Journal of Psychiatry, 148,* 658-660.
48. Lynn, S. J., Milano, M., & Weekes, J. R. (1991). Hypnosis

and pseudomemories: The effects of prehypnotic expectancies. *Journal of Personality and Social Psychology, 60,* 318-326.

49. Lynn, S. J., Weekes, J. R., Neufeld, V., Zivney, O., Brentar, J., & Weiss, F. (1991). Interpersonal climate and hypnotizability level: Effects on hypnotic performance, rapport, and archaic involvement. *Journal of Personality and Social Psychology, 60,* 739-743.

50. McConkey, K. M., Bryant, R. A., Bibb, B. C., & Kihlstrom, J. F. (1991). Trance logic in hypnosis and imagination. *Journal of Abnormal Psychology, 100,* 464-472.

51. Miller, M. F., Barabasz, A. F., & Barabasz, M. (1991). Effects of active alert and relaxation hypnotic inductions on cold pressor pain. *Journal of Abnormal Psychology, 100,* 223-226.

52. Nadon, R., Hoyt, I. P., Register, P. A., & Kihlstrom, J. F. (1991). Absorption and hypnotizability: Context effects reexamined. *Journal of Personality and Social Psychology, 60,* 144-153.

53. Sheehan, P. W., Statham, D., & Jamieson, G. A. (1991). Pseudomemory effects and their relationship to level of susceptibility to hypnosis and state instruction. *Journal of Personality and Social Psychology, 60,* 130-137.

54. Dixon, M., & Laurence, J. (1992). Hypnotic susceptibility and verbal automaticity: Automatic and strategic processing differences in the Stroop color-naming task. *Journal of Abnormal Psychology, 101,* 344-347.

55. Mann, B. J. (1992). Family process and hypnotic susceptibility: A preliminary investigation. *Journal of Nervous and Mental Disease, 180,* 192-196.

56. Murrey, G. J., Cross, H. J., & Whipple, J. (1992). Hypnotically created pseudomemories: Further investigation into the "memory distortion or response bias" question. *Journal of Abnormal Psychology, 101,* 75-77.

57. Sheehan, P. W., Green, V., & Truesdale, P. (1992). Influence of rapport on hypnotically induced pseudomemory. *Journal of Abnormal Psychology, 101,* 690-700.

58. Wallace, B. (1993). Day persons, night persons, and variability in hypnotic susceptibility. *Journal of Personality and Social Psychology, 64,* 827-833.

[1132]

Hassles and Uplifts Scales, Research Edition.

Purpose: To identify sources of stress and positive aspects of daily living that help counteract the damaging effects of stress.

Population: Adults.

Publication Date: 1989.

Administration: Group.

Price Data, 1990: $13.50 per 25 test booklets (specify Hassles or Uplifts Scale); $16 per 25 Combined Scales test booklets; $19.50 per manual (43 pages); $20 per specimen set (includes manual and 1 of each test booklet).

Time: (10–15) minutes per test.

Comments: Self-administered; tests available as separates.

Authors: Richard S. Lazarus and Susan Folkman.

Publisher: Consulting Psychologists Press, Inc.

a) THE DAILY HASSLES SCALE.

Scores, 2: Frequency, Severity.

b) THE UPLIFTS SCALE.

Scores, 2: Frequency, Intensity.

c) THE COMBINED HASSLES AND UPLIFTS SCALES.

Scores, 2: Hassles, Uplifts.

Cross References: For reviews by Karen S. Budd and Nancy Heilman and by Barbara A. Reilly, see 11:155 (6 references).

TEST REFERENCES

1. Wolf, T. M., Kissling, G. E., & Burgess, L. A. (1987). Hassles and uplifts during the freshman year of medical school. *Psychological Reports, 60,* 85-86.

2. Johnson, J. G., & Bornstein, R. F. (1991). Does daily stress independently predict psychopathology? *Journal of Social and Clinical Psychology, 10,* 58-74.

[1133]

Hausa Speaking Test.

Purpose: To evaluate the level of oral proficiency in Hausa attained by non-native speakers.

Population: Adults.

Publication Date: 1989.

Acronym: HaST.

Scores: Total score only.

Administration: Individual or group.

Price Data: Available from publisher.

Time: (40) minutes.

Comments: Examinee responses recorded on test tape scored by publisher.

Author: Staff of the Division of Foreign Language Education.

Publisher: Center for Applied Linguistics.

[1134]

Hay Aptitude Test Battery.

Purpose: "Helps select applicants with the ability to deal accurately with numerical and alphabetical detail and the ability to work with numbers."

Population: Applicants for clerical and plant positions.

Publication Dates: 1947–88.

Scores, 3: Number Perception, Name Finding, Number Series Completion.

Administration: Group.

Price Data, 1991: $100 per 25 complete batteries; $30 per 25 warm-up tests; $40 per 25 of any other test.

Time: 13(30) minutes.

Comments: Cassette tape available for administration.

Author: Edward N. Hay.

Publisher: E. F. Wonderlic Personnel Test, Inc.

a) THE WARM-UP TEST 1.

Time: 1(3) minutes.

b) NUMBER PERCEPTION TEST.

Forms, 2: A, B.

Time: 4(9) minutes.

c) NAME FINDING TEST.

Time: 4(9) minutes.

d) NUMBER SERIES COMPLETION TEST.

Time: 4(9) minutes.

Cross References: For a review by Robert P. Vecchio of an earlier edition, see 9:470; see also T2:2132 (2 references) and 5:849 (2 references); for reviews by Reign H. Bittner and Edward E. Cureton, see 4:725 (8 references).

[1135]

Health and Daily Living.

Purpose: "To examine the influence of extratreatment factors on treatment outcome as well as to explore the social resources and coping processes people use to prevent and adapt to stressful life circumstances."

Publication Dates: 1984–90.

Acronym: HDL.

Administration: Group.

Forms, 2: Youth Form, Adult Form B.

Price Data, 1993: $12 per test.

Time: (30–45) minutes.

Comments: May be administered as an interview or as a questionnaire.

Authors: Rudolf H. Moos, Ruth C. Cronkite, Andrew G. Billings, and John W. Finney.

Publisher: Social Ecology Laboratory.

a) YOUTH FORM.

Population: Students ages 12–18.

Scores: 9 indices: Health-Related (Self-Confidence, Positive Mood, Distressed Mood, Physical Symptoms, Medical Conditions, Health-Risk Behaviors), Social Functioning (Family Activities, Activities with Friends, Social Integration in School).

b) ADULT FORM B.

Population: Adults.

Scores: 47 indices: Health-Related Functioning (Self-Confidence, Physical Symptoms, Medical Conditions, Global Depression, Depressive Mood and Ideation, Endogenous Depression, Depressive Features, Depressed Mood/Past 12 Months, Alcohol Consumption—Quantity, Alcohol Consumption—Quantity/Frequency, Drinking Problems, Smoking Symptoms, Medication Use), Social Functioning and Resources (Social Activities with Friends, Network Contacts, Number of Close Relationships, Quality of Significant Relationship), Family Functioning and Home Environment (Family Social Activities, Family Task Sharing, Tasks Performed by Self, Tasks Performed by Partner, Family Arguments, Negative Home Environment), Children's Health and Functioning (Children's Physical Health Problems, Children's Psychological Health Problems, Children's Total Health Problems, Children's Behavioral Problems, Children's Health-Risk Behaviors), Life Change Events (Negative Life Change Events, Exit Events, Positive Life Change Events), Coping Responses (Active Cognitive Coping, Active Behavioral Coping, Avoidance Coping, Logical Analysis, Information Seeking, Problem Solving, Affective Regulation, Emotional Discharge, Help-Seeking/Mental Health Professional, Help-Seeking/Non-Mental Health Professional), Family Level Composite (Quality of Conjugal Relationship, Family Social Activites, Family Agreement on Task Sharing, Family Agreement on Household Tasks, Family Arguments, Negative Home Environment).

Cross References: For reviews by Arthur M. Nezu and Steven P. Schinke, see 10:137 (8 references).

TEST REFERENCES

1. Foster, J. M., & Gallagher, D. (1986). An exploratory study comparing depressed and nondepressed elders' coping strategies. *Journal of Gerontology, 41*, 91-93.

2. Holahan, C. J., & Moos, R. H. (1986). Personality, coping, and family resources in stress resistance: A longitudinal analysis. *Journal of Personality and Social Psychology, 51*, 389-395.

3. Daniels, D., Moos, R. H., Billings, A. G., & Miller, J. J., III. (1987). Psychosocial risk and resistance factors among children with chronic illness, healthy siblings, and healthy controls. *Journal of Abnormal Child Psychology, 15*, 295-308.

4. Holahan, C. J., & Moos, R. H. (1987). Risk, resistance, and
psychological distress: A longitudinal analysis with adults and children. *Journal of Abnormal Psychology, 96*, 3-13.

5. Krantz, S. E., & Moos, R. H. (1987). Functioning and life context among spouses of remitted and nonremitted depressed patients. *Journal of Consulting and Clinical Psychology, 55*, 353-360.

6. Thompson, L. W., Gallagher, D., & Breckenridge, J. S. (1987). Comparative effectiveness of psychotherapies for depressed elders. *Journal of Consulting and Clinical Psychology, 55*, 385-390.

7. Cooper, M. L., Russell, M., & George, W. H. (1988). Coping, expectancies, and alcohol abuse: A test of social learning formulations. *Journal of Abnormal Psychology, 97*, 218-230.

8. Frenzel, M. P., McCaul, K. D., Glasgow, R. E., & Schafer, L. C. (1988). The relationship of stress and coping to regimen adherence and glycemic control of diabetes. *Journal of Social and Clinical Psychology, 6*, 77-87.

9. Krantz, S. E., & Moos, R. H. (1988). Risk factors at intake predict nonremission among depressed patients. *Journal of Consulting and Clinical Psychology, 56*, 863-869.

10. Gotlib, I. H., & Lee, C. M. (1989). The social functioning of depressed patients: A longitudinal assessment. *Journal of Social and Clinical Psychology, 8*, 223-237.

11. Swindle, R. W., Jr., Cronkite, R. C., & Moos, R. H. (1989). Life stressors, social resources, coping, and the 4-year course of unipolar depression. *Journal of Abnormal Psychology, 98*, 468-477.

12. Schlosser, B. (1990). The assessment of subjective well-being and its relationship to the stress process. *Journal of Personality Assessment, 54*, 128-140.

13. Windle, M., & Miller, B. A. (1990). Problem drinking and depression among DWI offenders: A three-wave longitudinal study. *Journal of Consulting and Clinical Psychology, 58*, 166-174.

14. Cahir, N., & Morris, R. D. (1991). The Psychology Student Stress Questionnaire. *Journal of Clinical Psychology, 47*, 414-417.

15. Hinrichsen, G. A. (1991). Adjustment of caregivers to depressed older adults. *Psychology and Aging, 6*, 631-639.

16. Cushway, D. (1992). Stress in clinical psychology trainees. *British Journal of Clinical Psychology, 31*, 169-179.

17. Margalit, M., Raviv, A., & Ankonina, D. B. (1992). Coping and coherence among parents with disabled children. *Journal of Clinical Child Psychology, 21*, 202-209.

18. Timko, C., Stovel, K. W., Moos, R. H., & Miller, J. J., III. (1992). A longitudinal study of risk and resistance factors among children with juvenile rheumatic disease. *Journal of Clinical Child Psychology, 21*, 132-142.

19. Catanzaro, S. J., & Greenwood, G. (1994). Expectancies for negative mood regulation, coping, and dysphoria among college students. *Journal of Counseling Psychology, 41*, 34-44.

[1136]

Health and Safety Education Test: National Achievement Tests.

Purpose: Designed to measure students' knowledge of health and safety.

Population: Grades 3–6.

Publication Dates: 1947–60.

Scores, 5: Good Habits, Cause and Effect, Facts, Application of Rules, Total.

Administration: Group.

Manual: No manual.

Price Data: Available from publisher.

Time: 40(45) minutes.

Authors: Lester D. Crow and Loretta C. Ryan.

Publisher: Psychometric Affiliates.

Cross References: For a review by Clarence H. Nelson, see 5:555.

[1137]

Health Attribution Test.

Purpose: Constructed to measure "beliefs about the causes and cures of illness."

Population: High school and college and adult patients.

Publication Date: 1990.

Acronym: HAT.

Scores, 3: Internal Scale, Powerful Others Scale, Chance Scale.
Administration: Group.
Price Data, 1994: $18.50 per complete kit including 10 test booklets and manual (24 pages); $23 per 25 combined test booklet, answer sheet, and scoring key; $14 per manual.
Time: (10) minutes.
Authors: Jeanne Achterberg and G. Frank Lawlis.
Publisher: Institute for Personality and Ability Testing, Inc.
Cross References: For reviews by Dianna L. Newman and Stephen Olejnik, see 11:156.

[1138]

Health Education Test: Knowledge and Application: Acorn National Achievement Tests, Revised Edition.
Purpose: Constructed to measure the student's knowledge and application of health information.
Population: Grades 7–13.
Publication Dates: 1946–56.
Scores, 3: Knowledge, Application, Total.
Administration: Group.
Manual: No manual.
Price Data: Available from publisher.
Time: 40(45) minutes.
Authors: John H. Shaw and Maurice E. Troyer.
Publisher: Psychometric Affiliates.
Cross References: See T2:928 (1 reference) and 5:557 (1 reference); for reviews by H. H. Remmers and Mabel E. Rugen, see 3:421.

[1139]

Health Knowledge Test for College Freshmen: National Achievement Tests.
Purpose: Designed to measure the health knowledge of college freshmen.
Population: College freshmen.
Publication Date: 1956.
Scores: Total score only.
Administration: Group.
Price Data: Available from publisher.
Time: 40(45) minutes.
Author: A. Frank Bridges.
Publisher: Psychometric Affiliates.
Cross References: For a review by James E. Bryan, see 5:558 (3 references).

[1140]

Health Problems Checklist.
Purpose: To facilitate "the rapid assessment of the health status and potential health problems of clients typically seen in psychotherapy settings."
Population: Adults.
Publication Dates: 1984–89.
Scores: Items in 13 areas: General Health, Cardiovascular/Pulmonary, Endocrine/Hematology, Gastrointestinal, Dermatological, Visual, Auditory/Olfactory, Mouth/Throat/Nose, Orthopedic, Neurological, Genitourinary, Habits, History; no formal scoring procedure.
Administration: Group.
Manual: No manual.
Price Data, 1994: $26 per 50 checklists.
Time: (10–20) minutes.
Author: John A. Schinka.
Publisher: Psychological Assessment Resources, Inc.
Cross References: For a review by Robert M. Kaplan and Michelle T. Toshima of an earlier version, see 10:138.

[1141]

Health Test: National Achievement Tests.
Purpose: To assess students' information, judgment, and evaluation of health knowledge and habits.
Population: Grades 3–8.
Publication Dates: 1937–57.
Scores, 5: Recognizing Best Habits, Health Comparisons, Causes and Effects, Health Facts, Total.
Administration: Group.
Forms, 2: A, B.
Manual: No manual.
Price Data: Available from publisher.
Time: (40) minutes.
Authors: Robert K. Speer and Samuel Smith.
Publisher: Psychometric Affiliates.
Cross References: For a review by Benno G. Fricke, see 5:560; for a review by Jacob S. Orleans, see 4:485.

[1142]

Healy Pictorial Completion Test.
Purpose: Designed to provide a "measure of mental ability and intelligence based on the subject's apperceptive ability."
Population: Ages 5 and over.
Publication Dates: [1914–21].
Scores, 2: Total Errors, Illogical Errors.
Administration: Individual.
Price Data, 1994: $200 per complete kit (Test I); $200 per complete kit (Test II).
Time: Administration time not reported.
Author: William Healy.
Publisher: Stoelting Co.
a) TEST I.
Publication Date: 1914.
Comments: Modification appears in Arthur Point Scale of Performance Tests.
b) TEST II.
Publication Date: [1917–21].
Comments: Subtest of Arthur Point Scale of Performance Tests.
Cross References: See T2:558 (37 references).

[1143]

Hearing Measurement Scale.
Purpose: Measurement of the hearing handicap of persons with sensorineural hearing loss.
Population: Adults.
Publication Date: 1979.

Acronym: HMS.

Scores, 8: Speech Hearing, Hearing for Nonspeech Sounds, Spatial Localization, Emotional Response to Hearing Impairment, Speech Distortion, Tinnitus, Personal Opinion of Hearing, Total.

Administration: Group or individual.

Price Data: Available from publisher.

Time: (20–40) minutes.

Comments: Self-administered questionnaire for the assessment of hearing handicap; norms for men only.

Author: William G. Noble.

Publisher: University of New England [Australia].

Cross References: For a review by Judy R. Dubno, see 9:472.

[1144]
Hebrew Speaking Test.

Purpose: "Designed to evaluate the level of oral proficiency attained by English speaking learners of Hebrew."

Population: Adults.

Publication Date: 1989.

Acronym: HST.

Scores, 7: Personal Conversation, Giving Directions, Detailed Description, Picture Sequence Narration, Topical Discourse, Situational Discourse, Total.

Administration: Group.

Price Data: Available from publisher.

Time: (45–50) minutes.

Comments: Mail-in scoring.

Author: Center for Applied Linguistics.

Publisher: Center for Applied Linguistics.

[1145]
HELP CHECKLIST (Hawaii Early Learning Profile).

Purpose: Assesses developmental skills/behaviors.

Population: Ages birth–3.

Publication Dates: 1984–88.

Acronym: HELP Checklist.

Scores: Item scores only; 6 developmental areas: Cognitive, Language, Gross Motor, Fine Motor, Social, Self-Help.

Administration: Individual.

Price Data, 1990: $2.95 per checklist.

Time: Administration time not reported.

Comments: Ratings by professionals.

Authors: Setsu Furuno, Katherine A. O'Reilly, Carol M. Hosaka, Takayo T. Inatsuka, Barbara Zeisloft-Falbey, and Toney Allman.

Publisher: VORT Corporation.

Cross References: For reviews by William Steven Lang and Koressa Kutsick Malcolm, see 11:157.

[1146]
Help Desk Support Staff Selector.

Purpose: To evaluate essential skills for the Help Desk position.

Population: Candidates for Help Desk positions.

Publication Date: 1993.

Acronym: HLPDSK.

Scores: Total score only.

Administration: Group.

Price Data, 1994: $299 per candidate.

Time: (180) minutes.

Comments: Detailed evaluation report provided on each candidate.

Author: Bruce A. Winrow.

Publisher: Walden Personnel Testing & Training, Inc. [Canada].

[1147]
**Help for Special Preschoolers
ASSESSMENT CHECKLIST: Ages 3–6.**

Purpose: Comprehensive screening and assessment of developmentally delayed children.

Population: Ages 2-6 to 6-0.

Publication Date: 1987.

Scores: Ratings in 5 developmental areas: Self Help, Motor Development, Communication, Social Skills, Learning/Cognitive; 28 goals areas: Self-Help (Eating and Drinking, Toileting, Grooming, Dressing, Undressing, Oral and Nasal Hygiene, Self-Identification), Motor Development (Sensory Perception, Fine Motor, Gross Motor, Wheelchair, Swimming), Communication (Auditory Perception, Language Comprehension, Language, Sign Language, Speechreading), Social Skills (Adaptive Behaviors, Responsible Behaviors, Interpersonal Relationships, Personal Welfare, Social Manners), Learning/Cognitive (Attention Span, Basic Reading, Math, Writing Skills, Reasoning Skills, Music/Rhythm).

Administration: Individual.

Price Data, 1990: $2.95 per test booklet (20 pages).

Time: Administration time not reported.

Comments: Adaptation of Behavioral Characteristics Progression (BCP); upward extension of Hawaii Early Learning Profile (1145); "criterion-referenced."

Author: The Santa Cruz County Office of Education.

Publisher: VORT Corporation.

Cross References: For reviews by Harlan J. Stientjes and Gerald Tindal, see 11:158.

[1148]
Henderson-Moriarty ESL/Literacy Placement Test.

Purpose: "A placement instrument, a means of identifying literacy learners and assigning them to appropriate classes."

Population: Adult learners of English as a Second Language who have minimal or no oral English skills and minimal or no reading and writing skills in any language using the Roman alphabet.

Publication Date: 1982.

Acronym: HELP.

Scores, 2: Oral (and reading), Written (and reading).

Administration: Individual.

Price Data, 1990: $18.95 per examiner's guide (97 pages) including test booklet, test materials, and answer sheets.

Time: [15–20] minutes.
Comments: Some test materials must be furnished by the examiner.
Authors: Cindy Henderson, Pia Moriarty, and Mary Kay Mitchell (illustrations).
Publisher: The Alemany Press.
Cross References: For a review by Charles W. Stansfield, see 10:139.

[1149]

Henmon-Nelson Ability Test, Canadian Edition.

Purpose: "Designed to measure those aspects of cognitive ability which are important for success in academic work and in similar endeavors outside the classroom."
Population: Grades 3–6, 6–9, 9–12.
Publication Dates: 1957–1990.
Scores: Total score only.
Administration: Group.
Price Data, 1994: $49.45 per 35 reusable or consumable test booklets (specify level); $37.45 per 100 answer sheets (hand/machine scorable); $10.45 per scoring mask (all levels); $10 per examiner's manual ('90, 44 pages); $8.95 per 10 class record sheets; $12.45 per examination kit.
Time: (30) minutes.
Comments: Adapted from the 1973 U.S. edition of the test (The Henmon-Nelson Tests of Mental Ability, 1150).
Authors: Tom A. Lamke, M. J. Nelson, and Joseph L. French.
Publisher: Nelson Canada [Canada].
Cross References: See T3:1073 (13 references); for a review by Eric F. Gardner, see 8:190 (14 references); see also T2:391 (52 references); for a review by Norman E. Wallen and an excerpted review by John O. Crites of an earlier edition, see 6:462 (11 references); for reviews by D. Welty Lefever and Leona E. Tyler and an excerpted review by Laurance F. Shaffer, see 5:342 (14 references); for a review by H. M. Fowler, see 4:299 (25 references); for reviews by Anne Anastasi, August Dvorak, Howard Easley, and J. P. Guilford and an excerpted review by Francis N. Maxfield, see 2:1398.

[1150]

The Henmon-Nelson Tests of Mental Ability.

Purpose: "Designed to measure those aspects of mental ability which are important for success in academic work and in similar endeavors outside the classroom."
Population: Grades K–2, 3–6, 6–9, 9–12.
Publication Dates: 1931–74.
Scores: Total score only.
Administration: Group.
Levels, 4: Grades K–2 (Primary Battery), 3–6, 6–9, 9–12.
Price Data, 1990: $7.80 per examination kit including test booklets for K–12, MRC answer card, class record sheet, K–2 examiner's manual ('74, 40 pages), and 3–12 examiner's manual ('73, 47 pages);

$47.55 per 35 consumable test booklets (K–2); $35.55 per 35 consumable test booklets (specify 3–6, 6–9, or 9–12); $35.55 per 35 reusable test booklets (specify 3–6, 6–9, or 9–12); $24.60 per MRC answer cards (3–12); $12 per 35 class record sheets (K–12); $4.80 per examiner's manual (K–2); $4.80 per examiner's manual (3–12); $.86 per student basic scoring service.
Time: 25(30) minutes for K–2; 30(35) minutes for 3–12.
Comments: Primary Battery is orally administered.
Authors: Tom A. Lamke, Martin J. Nelson, and Joseph L. French.
Publisher: The Riverside Publishing Co.
Cross References: See T3:1073 (13 references); for a review by Eric F. Gardner, see 8:190 (14 references); see also T2:391 (52 references); for a review by Norman E. Wallen and an excerpted review by John O. Crites of an earlier edition, see 6:462 (11 references); for reviews by D. Welty Lefever and Leona E. Tyler and an excerpted review by Laurance F. Shaffer, see 5:342 (14 references); for a review by H. M. Fowler, see 4:299 (25 references); for reviews by Anne Anastasi, August Dvorak, Howard Easley, and J. P. Guilford and an excerpted review by Francis N. Maxfield, see 2:1398.

TEST REFERENCES

1. Watson, C. G., Klett, W. G., Kucala, T., Nixon, C., Schaefer, A., & Gasser, B. (1981). Prediction of the WAIS scores from the 1973 Henmon-Nelson revision. *Journal of Clinical Psychology, 37*, 840-842.
2. Aaron, P. G., Baker, C., & Hickox, G. L. (1982). In search of the third dyslexia. *Neuropsychologia, 20*, 203-208.
3. Jensen, A. R. (1983). Critical flicker frequency and intelligence. *Intelligence, 7*, 217-225.
4. Watson, C. G., & Vassar, P. (1983). The MMPI's of left- and right-handed subjects. *Perceptual and Motor Skills, 57*, 487-490.
5. Allen, W. H., & VanSickle, R. (1984). Learning teams and low achievers. *Social Education, 48*, 60-64.
6. Kepner, M. D., & Neimark, E. D. (1984). Test-retest reliability and differentiated patterns of score change on the Group Embedded Figures Test. *Journal of Personality and Social Psychology, 46*, 1405-1413.
7. Klett, W. G., Watson, C. G., & Hoffman, P. T. (1986). The Henmon-Nelson and Slosson tests as predictors of WAIS-R IQ. *Journal of Clinical Psychology, 42*, 343-347.
8. Watson, C. G., Wold, J., Vassar, P., Manifold, V., & Kucala, T. (1987). Performance asymptotes in schizophrenia: A further test of the Broen-Storms theory. *Journal of Clinical Psychology, 43*, 303-309.
9. Kuhne, A., Baraga, E., & Czekala, J. (1988). Completeness and internal consistency of DSM-III criteria for post-traumatic stress disorder. *Journal of Clinical Psychology, 44*, 717-722.
10. Williams, W. M., & Sternberg, R. J. (1988). Group intelligence: Why some groups are better than others. *Intelligence, 12*, 351-377.
11. Retherford, R. D., & Sewell, W. H. (1989). How intelligence affects fertility. *Intelligence, 13*, 169-185.
12. Watson, C. G., Plemel, D., Schaefer, A., Raden, M., Alfano, A. M., Anderson, P. E. D., Thomas, D., & Anderson, D. (1992). The comparative concurrent validities of the Shipley Institute of Living Scale and the Henmon-Nelson Tests of Mental Ability. *Journal of Clinical Psychology, 48*, 233-239.
13. Kuhne, A., Orr, S., & Baraga, E. (1993). Psychometric evaluation of post-traumatic stress disorder: The Multidimensional Personality Questionnaire as an adjunct to the MMPI. *Journal of Clinical Psychology, 49*, 218-225.

[1151]

Herrmann Brain Dominance Instrument.

Purpose: Designed to measure "human mental preferences" and thinking styles.
Population: Adults.

Publication Dates: 1981–1990.
Acronym: HBDI.
Scores, 12: Left Mode Dominance, Right Mode Dominance, Quadrant (Upper Left, Lower Left, Lower Right, Upper Right), Adjective Pairs (subset of 4 Quadrant Scores), Cerebral Mode Dominance, Limbic Mode Dominance.
Administration: Individual or group.
Manual: No manual.
Price Data: Prices and validation studies available from publisher.
Time: (15–20) minutes.
Comments: Survey booklet title is Participant Survey Form of the Herrmann Brain Dominance Instrument; self-administered; must be scored by publisher or certified practitioner.
Author: Ned Herrmann.
Publisher: Applied Creative Services, Ltd. dba The Ned Herrmann Group.
Cross References: For a review by Rik Carl D'Amato, see 11:159.

[1152]

Heterosocial Adequacy Test.
Purpose: A behavioral role-playing test for the assessment of heterosocial skills.
Population: Male college students.
Publication Dates: 1978–79.
Acronym: HAT.
Administration: Group.
Price Data: Not available.
Time: Administration time not reported.
Author: Michael G. Perri, C. Steven Richards, and Jerry D. Goodrich.
Publisher: Michael G. Perri, C. Steven Richards, and Jerry D. Goodrich [No reply from publisher; status unknown].

[1153]

High Level Battery: Test A/75.
Purpose: To provide "measures of general intelligence, arithmetical ability and certain language abilities."
Population: Adults with at least 12 years of education.
Publication Dates: 1960–72.
Scores: Total scores only for 4 tests in a single booklet: Mental Alertness, Arithmetical Problems, Reading Comprehension (English, Afrikaans), Vocabulary (English, Afrikaans).
Administration: Group.
Price Data: Available from publisher.
Time: 197 (215) minutes.
Comments: Formerly listed as National Institute for Personnel Research High Level Battery.
Author: D. P. M. Beukes (manual).
Publisher: National Institute for Personnel Research of the Human Sciences Research Council [South Africa].
Cross References: See 6:778 (1 reference).

[1154]

High Level Estimation Test.
Purpose: Measures ability to perform quick approximate calculations of arithmetic expressions through the use of rounding strategies.
Population: Individuals with 10 or more years of formal education.
Publication Date: 1985.
Acronym: ET-HL.
Scores: Item scores only.
Administration: Group.
Price Data: Available from publisher.
Time: 20(25) minutes.
Comments: English and Afrikaans included in same manual and materials.
Authors: T. R. Taylor and M. E. Halstead.
Publisher: National Institute for Personnel Research of the Human Sciences Research Council [South Africa].

[1155]

High Level Figure Classification Test.
Purpose: Designed to assess intellectual ability.
Population: Grades 10–12.
Publication Date: 1983.
Acronym: HL FCT.
Scores: Total score only.
Administration: Group.
Price Data: Available from publisher.
Foreign Language Edition: Test printed in both English and Afrikaans.
Time: 30(40) minutes.
Authors: M. Werbeloff and T. R. Taylor.
Publisher: National Institute for Personnel Research of the Human Sciences Research Council [South Africa].

[1156]

High School Career-Course Planner.
Purpose: Designed "to develop a high school course plan that is consistent with self-assessed career goals."
Population: Grades 8 and 9.
Publication Dates: 1983–90.
Acronym: HSCCP.
Scores: Total score only.
Administration: Group.
Price Data, 1992: $.50 per HSCCP folder and User's Guide ('90, 4 pages); $2 per Job-O dictionary; $16.50 per Occupational Outlook Handbook; $89.95 per HSCCP computer program.
Time: (50) minutes; (5–8) minutes for computer version.
Comments: Computer version also available.
Author: CFKR Career Materials, Inc.
Publisher: CFKR Career Materials, Inc.

[1157]

High School Characteristics Index.
Purpose: "Designed to measure the psychological characteristics" of a school environment.
Population: Grades 9–13, 4–13.

Publication Dates: 1960–73.
Scores, 40: 30 press scores (Abasement-Assurance, Achievement, Adaptability-Defensiveness, Affiliation, Aggression-Blame Avoidance, Change-Sameness, Conjunctivity-Disjunctivity, Counteraction, Deference-Restiveness, Dominance-Tolerance, Ego Achievement, Emotionality-Placidity, Energy-Passivity, Exhibitionism-Inferiority Avoidance, Fantasied Achievement, Harm Avoidance-Risk Taking, Humanities and Social Science, Impulsiveness-Deliberation, Narcissism, Nurturance, Objectivity-Projectivity, Order-Disorder, Play-Work, Practicalness-Impracticalness, Reflectiveness, Science, Sensuality-Puritanism, Sexuality-Prudishness, Supplication-Autonomy, Understanding), 7 factor scores (Intellectual Climate, Expressiveness, Group Social Life, Personal Dignity/Supportiveness, Achievement Standards, Orderliness/Control, Peer Group Dominance) based on combinations of the press scores, 3 second-order factor scores (Development Press, Orderliness/Control, Peer Group Dominance).
Administration: Group.
Forms, 2: High School Characteristics Index, Elementary and Secondary School Index.
Price Data: Not available.
Comments: Previously listed under Stern Environment Indexes; self-administered.
Author: George G. Stern.
Publisher: FAAX Corporation [No reply from publisher; status unknown].
a) HIGH SCHOOL CHARACTERISTICS INDEX.
Population: Grades 9–13.
Acronym: HSCI.
Time: (40–45) minutes.
b) ELEMENTARY AND SECONDARY SCHOOL ENVIRONMENT INDEX.
Population: Grades 4–13.
Acronym: ESI.
Time: (15–20) minutes.
Comments: Short version of HSCI.
Cross References: See T3:1080 (1 reference) and T2:1395 (38 references); for reviews by Wilbur L. Layton and Rodney W. Skager, see 7:143 (159 references); see also P:256 (65 references) and 6:92 (19 references).

TEST REFERENCES

1. Gem, J. M. (1984). Research into the climates of Australian schools, colleges, and universities: Contributions and potential of need-press theory. *The Australian Journal of Education, 28,* 227-248.

[1158]
High School Interest Questionnaire.
Purpose: Measurement of occupational interest.
Population: Standards 7–10 in South African schools.
Publication Dates: 1973–74.
Scores, 8: Language, Performing Arts, Fine Arts, Social, Science, Technical, Business, Office Work.
Administration: Group.
Price Data: Available from publisher.

Time: (45–60) minutes.
Author: J. B. Wolfaardt.
Publisher: Human Sciences Research Council [South Africa].

[1159]
High School Personality Questionnaire.
Purpose: Measures primary personality characteristics in adolescents.
Population: Ages 12–18.
Publication Dates: 1953–84.
Acronym: HSPQ.
Scores, 18: 14 primary factor scores (Warmth, Intelligence, Emotional Stability, Excitability, Dominance, Enthusiasm, Conformity, Boldness, Sensitivity, Withdrawal, Apprehension, Self-Sufficiency, Self-Discipline, Tension), 4 second-order factor scores (Extraversion, Anxiety, Tough Poise, Independence).
Administration: Group.
Forms, 4: A, B, C, D (authors recommend administration of 2 or more forms).
Price Data, 1994: $18 per 25 reusable test booklets (specify Form A, B, C, or D); $13.50 per scoring keys for all forms; $10.75 per 25 machine-scorable answer sheets; $10.75 per 50 hand-scoring answer sheets; $15 per 50 hand-scoring answer-profile sheets; $10.75 per 50 profile sheets; $10.75 per 50 second-order worksheets; $13 per manual ('84, 101 pages); $22.25 per introductory kit; computer scoring and interpretive services available from publisher at $25 or less per individual report depending upon quantity requested.
Time: (45–60) minutes per form.
Comments: Previously listed as Jr.-Sr. High School Personality Questionaire.
Authors: Raymond B. Cattell, Mary D. Cattell, and Edgar Johns (manual and norms).
Publisher: Institute for Personality and Ability Testing, Inc.
Foreign Adaptation: British adaptation; ages 13–15; 1973; supplement by Peter Saville and Laura Finlayson; NFER-Nelson Publishing Co., Ltd. [England].
Cross References: For reviews by Richard I. Lanyon and Steven V. Owen, see 11:188 (17 references); see also 9:559 (8 references), T3:1233 (22 references), 8:597 (68 references), and T2:1253 (37 references); for reviews by Robert Hogan and Douglas N. Jackson, see 7:97 (53 references); see also P:136 (29 references); for reviews by C. J. Adcock and Philip E. Vernon of an earlier edition, see 6:131 (17 references); see also 5:72 (4 references).

TEST REFERENCES

1. Gallucci, N. T., & Ambler, J. E. (1987). Differentiating under- and overcontrolled behavior of adolescent outpatients with the High School Personality Questionnaire. *Psychological Reports, 60,* 335-338.
2. Kawash, G. F., & Clewes, J. L. (1988). A factor analysis of a short form of the CRPBI: Are children's perceptions of control and discipline multidimensional? *The Journal of Psychology, 122,* 57-67.
3. Schuerger, J. M., Zarrella, K. L., & Hotz, A. S. (1989). Factors that influence the temporal stability of personality by questionnaire. *Journal of Personality and Social Psychology, 56,* 777-783.

4. Clark, M. L., & Ayers, M. (1992). Friendship similarity during early adolescence: Gender and racial patterns. *The Journal of Psychology, 126*, 393-405.

[1160]
High School Reading Test: National Achievement Tests.

Purpose: Designed to measure the student's mastery and application of factual material in English, reading, literature, and vocabulary.

Population: Grades 7–12.

Publication Dates: 1939–52.

Scores, 6: Vocabulary, Word Discrimination, Sentence Meaning, Noting Details, Interpreting Paragraphs, Total.

Administration: Group.

Forms, 2: A, B.

Price Data: Available from publisher.

Time: (40) minutes.

Authors: Robert K. Speer and Samuel Smith.

Publisher: Psychometric Affiliates.

Cross References: For a review by Victor H. Noll, see 5:634; for a review by Holland Roberts, see 4:536; for a review by Robert L. McCaul, see 3:488.

[1161]
High-School Subject Tests.

Purpose: Developed to assess student achievement in English, mathematics, social studies, and science.

Population: Grades 9–12.

Publication Dates: 1980–88.

Administration: Group.

Price Data, 1993: $41.50 per 35 test booklets with administration directions (select test); $15.75 per 35 machine-scorable answer sheets; $4.50 per directions for administration; $22.50 per Teacher's Manual and Technical Information ('90, 110 pages); $15 per specimen set (specify English, mathematics, social studies, or science); $35 per all-subjects specimen set; scoring service available from publisher.

Time: (40) minutes per test.

Authors: Louis A. Gatta, John W. Wick, Robert B. Adams, Larry M. Faulkner, Karen J. Kuehner, Vincent F. Malek, and John W. McConnell.

Publisher: American College Testing.

a) LITERATURE AND VOCABULARY.

Scores, 5: Literal Comprehension, Inferential Comprehension, Vocabulary, Literary Terms, Total.

b) LANGUAGE.

Scores, 4: Spelling, Punctuation/Capitalization, Correctness of Expression, Total.

c) WRITING AND MECHANICS.

Scores, 4: Paragraph Development, Grammar/Word Choice/Usage, Paragraph Structure, Total.

d) GENERAL MATHEMATICS.

Scores, 6: Computation (Recall, Comprehension), Geometry and Measurement, Tables/Graphs/Charts, Calculators and Decision-Making, Total.

e) PRE-ALGEBRA.

Scores, 6: Numbers and Operations, Equations and Inequalities, Geometry, Expressions, Applications, Total.

Forms, 2: B-1, B-2.

f) ALGEBRA.

Scores, 8: Polynomials, Exponents and Rational Expressions, Definitions and Theory, Linear Equations and Inequalities, Systems and Coordinates, Radicals and Quadratics, Word Problems, Total.

g) ADVANCED ALGEBRA.

Scores, 7: Linear Sentences and Applications, Algebraic Expressions, Exponents and Logarithms, Polynomial and Radical Equations, Analysis of Graphs, Systems, Total.

Forms, 2: B-1, B-2.

h) GEOMETRY.

Scores, 6: Angles, Segments/Lines/Rays, Similarity and Congruence, Perimeter and Area, Circles, Total.

i) COMPUTER LITERACY.

Scores, 6: Information Processing-Input/Output, Computer Hardware-Processors and Storage Devices, Computer Software and Applications, Networking and Telecommunications, Computer Issues and Problems, Total.

j) PHYSICAL SCIENCE.

Scores, 9: Measurement/Mass/Volume/Density, Particle Nature of Matter, Heat Energy, Structure of the Atom and Chemical Formulas, Solutions and Behavior of Matter, Energy and Motion, Electricity, Light and Sound, Total.

k) BIOLOGY.

Scores, 10: Cell Structure and Function, Cellular Chemistry, Viruses/Monerans/Protists/Fungi, Plants, Animals, Human Body Systems and Physiology, Genetics, Ecology, Biological Analysis and Experimentation, Total.

l) CHEMISTRY.

Scores, 8: Chemical Symbols/Equations/Moles, Solutions, The Gaseous Phase, Atomic/Molecular Structure and Bonding, Energy/Reaction Rates/Equilibrium, Acids and Bases, Oxidation/Reduction, Total.

Forms, 2: B-1, B-2.

m) PHYSICS.

Scores, 10: Linear Motion, Analyzing Graphs and Using Vectors, Dynamics and Momentum, Motion in Two Dimensions, Energy and Work, Gravitation, Kinetic Theory/Heat/Nuclear Reactions, Light and Optics, Electricity and Magnetism, Total.

n) WORLD HISTORY.

Scores, 8: Anthropology and Archeaology, Economic History, Biography, Philosophy and Religion, Interpretation of Information, Governmental History, General Knowledge, Total.

o) AMERICAN HISTORY.

Scores, 9: Chronology, Government, Ideology, Foreign Policy, Geography, Politics, Economic History, Social History, Total.

p) AMERICAN GOVERNMENT.

Scores, 10: Principles of Government, Guarantees

of Liberty, American Symbols and Political Traditions, Governmental Powers, Law Making and the Amendment Process, Duties and Qualifications of Federal Officials, Branches of Government-Duties and Checks, Presidential Succession and Appointment, Elections and Voting Procedure, Total.

q) CONSUMER ECONOMICS.

Scores, 9: Insurance, Credit, Banking and Investment, Economics, Consumer in the Marketplace, Money Management, Housing, Taxes, Total.

Cross References: For reviews by Jim C. Fortune and John M. Williams and by Robert A. Reineke, see 11:160; for reviews by Robert K. Gable and Francis X. Archambault and by Gary W. Phillips, see 9:476.

[1162]

Hill Interaction Matrix.

Purpose: "To study group development, group composition, and therapist style."

Population: Prospective members, members, and leaders of psychotherapy groups.

Publication Dates: 1954–94.

Acronym: HIM.

Scores: Matrix of 4 columns (Topics, Groups, Personal, Relationship) and 4 rows (Conventional, Assertive, Speculative, Confrontive) produces 16 scores, 8 marginal Total scores, Grand Total, and other derivative scores.

Administration: Group or individual.

Price Data: Available from publisher.

Time: (20) minutes.

Author: Wm. Fawcett Hill.

Publisher: Howdah Press.

a) HIM A AND B.

Population: Prospective members and members of psychotherapy groups.

Publication Dates: 1954–68.

Editions, 2: HIM-A, HIM-B.

b) HIM-G.

Population: Observers and leaders of psychotherapy groups.

Publication Dates: 1967–68.

Manual: No manual.

Cross References: See T3:1099 (9 references), 8:577 (35 references), and T2:1214 (29 references).

TEST REFERENCES

1. Banet, A. G., Jr. (1977). The HIM as a group energy map. *Small Group Behavior, 8,* 396-397.
2. Conyne, R. K., & Rapin, L. S. (1977). A HIM-G interaction process analysis study of facilitator- and self-directed groups. *Small Group Behavior, 8,* 333-340.
3. Conyne, R. K., & Rapin, L. S. (1977). Facilitator- and self-directed groups. *Small Group Behavior, 8,* 341-350.
4. Conyne, R. K., & Rapin, L. S. (1977). Programmed groups: A process analysis of facilitator- and self-directed treatments. *Small Group Behavior, 8,* 403-413.
5. Hill, W. F. (1977). Hill Interaction Matrix (HIM): The conceptual framework, derived rating scales, and an updated bibliography. *Small Group Behavior, 8,* 251-268.
6. Lambert, M. J., & DeJulio, S. S. (1977). Toward a validation of diverse measures of human interaction and counseling process. *Small Group Behavior, 8,* 393-395.
7. Magyar, C. W., & Apostal, R. A. (1977). Interpersonal growth contracts and leader experience: Their effects in encounter groups. *Small Group Behavior, 8,* 381-392.
8. McIntire, W. G., Drummond, R. J., & Carter, C. E. (1977). The HIM-B as a family interaction assessment technique. *Small Group Behavior, 8,* 361-368.
9. Pattinson, P. R., Rardin, M. W., & Lindberg, F. H. (1977). Effects of immediate feedback on the therapeutic content of group leader's statements. *Small Group Behavior, 8,* 303-311.
10. Powell, E. R. (1977). HIM correlational study. *Small Group Behavior, 8,* 369-380.
11. Silbergeld, S., Manderscheid, R. W., & Koenig, G. R. (1977). Evaluation of brief intervention models by the Hill Interaction Matrix. *Small Group Behavior, 8,* 281-302.
12. Sisson, C. J., Sisson, P. J., & Gazda, G. M. (1977). Extended group counseling with psychiatry residents: HIM and the Bonney scale compared. *Small Group Behavior, 8,* 351-360.
13. Uhlemann, M. R., & Weigel, R. G. (1977). Behavior change outcomes of marathon group treatment. *Small Group Behavior, 8,* 269-280.
14. DeJulio, S., Bentley, J., & Cockayne, T. (1979). Pregroup norm setting: Effects on encounter group interaction. *Small Group Behavior, 10,* 368-388.
15. Melnick, J., & Rose, G. S. (1979). Expectancy and risk taking propensity: Predictors of group performance. *Small Group Behavior, 10,* 389-401.
16. Silbergeld, S., Thune, E. S., & Manderscheid, R. W. (1979). The group therapist leadership role: Assessment in adolescent coping courses. *Small Group Behavior, 10,* 176-199.
17. Stava, L. J., & Bednar, R. L. (1979). Process and outcome in encounter groups: The effects of group composition. *Small Group Behavior, 10,* 200-213.
18. Tindall, J. (1979). Time-limited and time-extended encounter groups: Descriptive stage development. *Small Group Behavior, 10,* 402-413.
19. Guyer, C. G., II, & Matthews, C. O., II. (1981). Nonverbal warm-up exercises with adolescents: Effects on group counseling. *Small Group Behavior, 12,* 55-67.
20. Thune, E. S., Manderscheid, R. W., & Silbergeld, S. (1981). Sex, status, and cotherapy. *Small Group Behavior, 12,* 415-442.
21. Burlingame, G., Fuhriman, A., & Drescher, S. (1984). Scientific inquiry into small group process: A multidimensional approach. *Small Group Behavior, 15,* 441-470.
22. Etringer, B. D., Gregory, V. R., & Lando, H. A. (1984). Influence of group cohesion on the behavioral treatment of smoking. *Journal of Consulting and Clinical Psychology, 52,* 1080-1086.
23. Gruner, L. (1984). Membership composition of open and closed therapeutic groups: A research note. *Small Group Behavior, 15,* 222-232.
24. Kanas, N., Barr, M. A., & Dossick, S. (1985). The homogeneous schizophrenic inpatient group: An evaluation using the Hill Interaction Matrix. *Small Group Behavior, 16,* 397-409.
25. Kivlighan, D. M., Jr. (1990). Career group therapy. *The Counseling Psychologist, 18,* 64-79.

[1163]

Hill Performance Test of Selected Positional Concepts.

Purpose: "Designed to assess specific positional concepts with visually impaired children."

Population: Visually impaired children ages 6–10.

Publication Date: 1981.

Scores, 5: Ability to Identify Positional Relationships of Body Parts, Ability to Move Various Body Parts in Relationship to Each Other, Ability to Move Body in Relationship to Objects, Ability to Form Object to Object Relationships, Total.

Administration: Individual.

Price Data, 1994: $33 per complete kit; $15 per 20 record forms; $20 per manual (40 pages).

Time: Administration time not reported.

Comments: Revision of Concepts Involved in Body Position and Space.

Author: Everett W. Hill.

Publisher: Stoelting Co.

Cross References: For a review by Homer B. C. Reed, Jr., see 9:477.

[1164]

Hilson Adolescent Profile.
Purpose: "Designed as a screening tool to assess the presence and extent of adolescent behavior patterns and problems."
Population: Ages 10 to 19.
Publication Dates: 1984–87.
Acronym: HAP.
Scores, 16: Guarded Responses, Alcohol Use, Drug Use, Educational Adjustment Difficulties, Law Violations, Frustration Tolerance, Antisocial/Risk-Taking, Rigidity/Obsessiveness, Interpersonal/Assertiveness Difficulties, Homelife Conflicts, Social/Sexual Adjustment, Health Concerns, Anxiety/Phobic Avoidance, Depression/Suicide Potential, Suspicious Temperament, Unusual Responses.
Administration: Group.
Price Data, 1994: $60 per starter kit including manual ('87, 82 pages); scoring service offered by publisher.
Special Edition: Audiotape edition available.
Time: (45–55) minutes.
Comments: Self-administered; computer-scored.
Authors: Robin E. Inwald.
Publisher: Hilson Research, Inc.
Cross References: For a review by Allen K. Hess, see 11:161.

[1165]

Hilson Adolescent Profile—Version S.
Purpose: "Designed as a screening tool to identify adolescent emotional difficulties, depression and/or suicidal tendencies, homelife conflicts, and other behavior patterns."
Population: Ages 10–19.
Publication Date: 1993.
Acronym: HAP-S.
Scores, 7: Guarded Responses, Educational Adjustment Difficulties, Frustration Tolerance, Homelife Conflicts, Social/Sexual Adjustment, Depression/Suicide Potential, Unusual Responses.
Administration: Group.
Price Data, 1993: $60 per starter kit including manual ('93, 37 pages); $2 per test booklet; $2.50 per 10 Scantron/standard answer sheets; $3 per 10 Sentry answer sheets; $15 per manual; scoring services offered by publisher at $5–$8 (volume discounts available).
Time: (15–25) minutes.
Comments: Short version of the Hilson Adolescent Profile (1164).
Author: Robin Inwald.
Publisher: Hilson Research, Inc.

[1166]

Hilson Career Satisfaction Index.
Purpose: To aid in employee "fitness-for-duty" evaluations, promotion, and special assignment decisions.
Population: Public safety/security officers.
Publication Date: 1989.
Acronym: HCSI.

Scores, 13: Stress Patterns, Stress Symptoms, Drug/Alcohol Abuse, Interpersonal Support, Anger/Hostility Patterns, Disciplinary History, Excusing Attitudes, Aggression/Hostility, Dissatisfaction with Career, Dissatisfaction with Supervisor, Relationship with Co-Workers, Dissatisfaction with Job, Defensiveness.
Administration: Group.
Price Data, 1993: $60 per complete starter kit including test booklet, 3 computer-scorable answer sheets, and manual ('89, 40 pages); $2 per test booklet; $2.50 per 10 Scantron/standard answer sheets; $3 per 10 Sentry answer sheets; $15 per manual; scoring services offered by publisher at $10–$12.75 per test (volume discounts available).
Time: (25–35) minutes.
Author: Robin Inwald.
Publisher: Hilson Research, Inc.

TEST REFERENCES

1. Girodo, M. (1991). Drug corruption in undercover agents: Measuring the risk. *Behavioral Sciences and the Law, 9*, 361-370.

[1167]

Hilson Personnel Profile/Success Quotient.
Purpose: To identify individual "strengths," behavior patterns, and personality characteristics "leading to success in a variety of work settings."
Population: High school through adult.
Publication Date: 1988.
Acronym: HPP/SQ.
Scores, 13: Candor, Achievement History, Social Ability (Extroversion, Popularity/"Charisma," Sensitivity to Approval), "Winner's" Image (Competitive Spirit, Self-Worth, Family Achievement Expectations), Initiative (Drive, Preparation Style, Goal Orientation, Anxiety About Organization), Success Quotient.
Administration: Group.
Price Data, 1994: $60 per complete starter kit including 3 scorings; $2 per test booklet; $2.50 per 10 answer sheets; $15 per manual (83 pages); $10–$12.75 per test (according to volume) for computer scoring.
Time: (20–30) minutes.
Author: Robin E. Inwald.
Publisher: Hilson Research, Inc.
Cross References: For a review by Joseph G. Law, Jr., see 11:162.

[1168]

The Hoffer-Osmond Diagnostic Test.
Purpose: "Designed to survey and assess the range of an individual's sensory perceptions and mood changes" as "a tool for diagnosing the degree of mental illness."
Population: Mental patients age 13 and over.
Publication Dates: 1961–81.
Acronym: The HOD Test.
Scores, 6: Total, Perceptual, Paranoid, Depression, Ratio, Short Form.
Administration: Group.
Price Data: Not available.

Time: (15–20) minutes.
Authors: Abram Hoffer, Humphry Osmond, and Harold Kelm.
Publisher: PACE Learning Systems, Inc. [No reply from publisher; status unknown].
Cross References: See T2:1215 (6 references) and P:110 (22 references); for reviews by Maurice Lorr and William Schofield, see 6:114 (6 references).

[1169]

Hogan Personality Inventory [Revised].
Purpose: Measure of normal personality designed for use in personnel selection, individualized assessment, and career-related decision making.
Population: College students and adults.
Publication Date: 1985–92.
Acronym: HPI.
Scores: 7 primary scale scores (Intellectance, Adjustment, Ambition, Sociability, Likeability, Prudence, School Success), 6 occupational scale scores (Service Orientation, Stress Tolerance, Reliability, Clerical Potential, Sales Potential, Managerial Potential), and Validity scale score.
Administration: Group.
Price Data, 1993: $5 per 5 reusable test booklets; $6.25 per 25 answer sheets; $30 per technical manual ('92, 126 pages); $30 per specimen set including manual, sample report, reusable test booklet, and answer sheet; scoring services producing interpretive and/or graphic reports available from publisher ($25 per interpretive Personality Report, $10 per graphic, $5 per data file, $.50 per faculty research; $5 per interpretive for Occupational Scale and/or Clerical Scales, or Managerial Scales, $2 per graphic); $5 per nonscanable answer sheet for data entry.
Time: (10–15) minutes.
Authors: Robert Hogan and Joyce Hogan (manual).
Publisher: Hogan Assessment Systems.
Cross References: For reviews of an earlier edition by James J. Hennessy and Rolf A. Peterson, see 10:140.

TEST REFERENCES

1. Briggs, S. R., & Cheek, J. M. (1988). On the nature of self-monitoring: Problems with assessment, problems with validity. *Journal of Personality and Social Psychology, 54,* 663-678.
2. Johnson, J. A., Germer, C. K., Efran, J. S., & Overton, W. F. (1988). Personality as the basis for theoretical predilections. *Journal of Personality and Social Psychology, 55,* 824-835.
3. Hogan, J. (1989). Personality correlates of physical fitness. *Journal of Personality and Social Psychology, 56,* 284-288.
4. Trapnell, P. D., & Wiggins, J. S. (1990). Extension of the Interpersonal Adjective Scales to include the Big Five dimensions of personality. *Journal of Personality and Social Psychology, 59,* 781-790.
5. Goldberg, L. R. (1992). The development of markers for the big-five factor structure. *Psychological Assessment, 4,* 26-42.
6. Kugler, K., & Jones, W. H. (1992). On conceptualizing and assessing guilt. *Journal of Personality and Social Psychology, 62,* 318-327.
7. Nolan, Y., Johnson, J. A., & Pincus, A. L. (1994). Personality and drunk driving: Identification of DUI types using the Hogan Personality Inventory. *Psychological Assessment, 6,* 33-40.

[1170]

Holtzman Inkblot Technique.
Purpose: Designed as a projective personality test.

Population: Ages 5 and over.
Publication Dates: 1958–72.
Acronym: HIT.
Scores, 20–22: Reaction Time (*a* only), Rejection, Location, Space, Form Definiteness, Form Appropriateness, Color, Shading, Movement, Pathognomic Verbalization, Integration, Content (Human, Animal, Anatomy, Sex, Abstract), Anxiety, Hostility, Barrier, Penetration, Balance (*a* only), Popular.
Administration: Group or individual.
Price Data, 1994: $7.50 per 25 Hill clinical summary forms; $6 per norms for computer-scored inkblots; $23 per Workbook for the Holtzman Inkblot Technique; $20.50 per administration and scoring guide.
Authors: Wayne H. Holtzman, Joseph S. Thorpe (book), Jon D. Swartz (book), and E. Wayne Herron (book).
Publisher: The Psychological Corporation.
a) INDIVIDUAL TEST.
Publication Dates: 1958–72.
Forms, 2: A, B.
Price Data: $415 per complete set for Forms A and B combined including 45 inkblots, 25 record forms with summary sheets, and scoring guide; $223 per complete set (specify Form A or B); $198 per set of 47 inkblots (specify Form A or B); $13 per 25 record forms (specify A or B).
b) GROUP TEST.
Publication Dates: 1958–70.
Manual: No manual.
Price Data: $12 per 50 Gorham-Holtzman group record forms; $6 per normative item statistics.
Comments: Administration slides for either form must be constructed locally.
Author: Donald R. Gorham (record form).
Cross References: For reviews by Bert P. Cundick and David M. Dush, see 9:480 (17 references); see also T3:1106 (25 references); for a review by Rolf A. Peterson, see 8:578 (96 references); see also T2:1471 (42 references); for excerpted reviews by Raymond J. McCall and David G. Martin, see 7:169 (106 references); see also P:439 (90 references); for reviews by Richard N. Coan, H. J. Eysenck, Bertram R. Forer, and William N. Thetford, see 6:217 (22 references).

TEST REFERENCES

1. Ewing, J. H., Scott, D. G., Mendez, A. A., & McBride, T. J. (1984). Effects of aerobic exercise upon affect and cognition. *Perceptual and Motor Skills, 59,* 407-414.
2. Lanyon, R. I. (1984). Personality assessment. *Annual Review of Psychology, 35,* 667-701.
3. Mittenberg, W., & Petersen, J. D. (1984). Validation of the Holtzman Anxiety Scale by Vasomotor biofeedback. *Journal of Personality Assessment, 48,* 360-364.
4. Fabes, R. A., McCullers, J. C., & Moran, J. D., III. (1985). Effects of material rewards on inkblot perception and organization. *American Journal of Psychology, 98,* 399-407.
5. Vilkki, J. (1985). Amnesic syndromes after surgery of anterior communicating artery aneurysms. *Cortex, 21,* 431-444.
6. Vincent, K. R., & Duthie, B. (1986). The Rorschach as an alternate form of the Holtzman Inkblot Technique. *Social Behavior and Personality, 14*(2), 193-195.
7. Holtzman, W. H. (1988). Beyond the Rorschach. *Journal of Personality Assessment, 52,* 578-609.
8. Guarnaccia, V., & Curry, K. (1990). Contingent reinforcement

effects on movement responses of prison inmates to the Holtzman Inkblot Technique. *Journal of Personality Assessment, 55,* 263-269.

9. Francis, J. R., & Hayslip, B., Jr. (1991). The viability of an abbreviated version of the Holtzman Inkblot Technique with older adults. *The Journal of Psychology, 125,* 543-548.

10. Hayslip, B., Jr., & Francis, J. R. (1991). Toward the equivalence of the HIT and HIT25 in community-residing older adults. *Journal of Personality Assessment, 56*(3), 388-394.

11. Richaud de Minzi, M. C., & Sacchi, C. (1991). Popular response: Different ways of perceiving the world. *Perceptual and Motor Skills, 72,* 67-72.

12. Jensen, C. F. (1993). Control issues and body image in panic disorder. *Perceptual and Motor Skills, 76,* 432-435.

[1171]

Home Environment Questionnaire, HEQ-2R and HEQ-1R.

Purpose: Measures "dimensions of the child's psychological environment that exert specific types of pressure on the child."

Population: Grades 4–6.

Publication Date: 1983.

Acronym: HEQ.

Scores, 10: P(ress) Achievement, P Aggression-External, P Aggression-Home, P Aggression-Total, P Supervision, P Change, P Affiliation, P Separation, P Sociability, P Socioeconomic Status.

Administration: Individual or Group.

Forms, 2: HEQ-2R for use with two-parent families and HEQ-1R for use with single-parent families.

Price Data, 1986: $5 per 25 booklets (specify HEQ-1R or HEQ-2R); $7 per 9 scoring keys (specify HEQ-1R or HEQ-2R); $7 per manual (22 pages); $30 per specimen set including 25 each HEQ-2R and HEQ-1R, scoring keys, manual, and norms.

Time: Administration time not reported.

Comments: Ratings by child's mother.

Author: Jacob O. Sines.

Publisher: Psychological Assessment and Services, Inc.

Cross References: For a review by Steven I. Pfeiffer and Julia Pettiette-Doolin, see 10:141 (1 reference).

TEST REFERENCES

1. Kolko, D. J., & Kazdin, A. E. (1990). Matchplay and firesetting in children: Relationship to parent, marital, and family dysfunction. *Journal of Clinical Child Psychology, 19,* 229-238.

[1172]

Home Observation for Measurement of the Environment.

Purpose: Screen for sources of potential environmental retardation or environmental risk.

Population: Birth to age 3, early childhood, middle childhood.

Publication Dates: 1978–84.

Acronym: HOME.

Administration: Individual.

Price Data, 1993: $9 per administration manual; $.10 per scoring sheet (specify level).

Time: (60) minutes.

Authors: Bettye M. Caldwell and Robert H. Bradley.

Publisher: Bettye M. Caldwell and Robert H. Bradley.

a) INFANT/TODDLER HOME INVENTORY.

Population: Birth–3 years.

Scores, 7: Responsivity, Acceptance, Organization, Learning Materials, Involvement, Variety, Total.

b) EARLY CHILDHOOD HOME INVENTORY.

Population: 3–6 years.

Scores, 9: Learning Materials, Language Stimulation, Physical Environment, Responsivity, Academic Stimulation, Modeling, Variety, Acceptance, Total.

c) MIDDLE CHILDHOOD HOME INVENTORY.

Population: 6–10 years.

Scores, 8: Responsivity, Encouragement of Maturity, Acceptance, Learning Materials, Enrichment, Family Companionship, Paternal Involvement, Total.

Cross References: See 9:481 (13 references); see also T3:1108 (14 references).

TEST REFERENCES

1. Nihira, K., Meyers, C. E., & Mink, I. T. (1983). Reciprocal relationship between home environment and development of TMR adolescents. *American Journal of Mental Deficiency, 88,* 139-149.

2. Smeriglio, V. L., & Parks, P. (1983). Measuring mothers' perceptions about the influences of infant caregiving practices. *Child Psychiatry and Human Development, 13,* 189-200.

3. Wilson, R. S., & Matheny, A. P., Jr. (1983). Mental development: Family environment and genetic influences. *Intelligence, 7,* 195-215.

4. Adams, J. L., Campbell, F. A., & Ramey, C. T. (1984). Infants' home environments: A study of screening efficiency. *American Journal of Mental Deficiency, 89,* 133-139.

5. Belsky, J., Garduque, L., & Hrncir, E. (1984). Assessing performance, competence, and executive capacity in infant play: Relations to home environment and security of attachment. *Developmental Psychology, 20,* 406-417.

6. Booth, C. L., Lyons, N. B., & Barnard, K. E. (1984). Synchrony in mother-infant interaction: A comparison of measurement methods. *Child Study Journal, 14,* 95-114.

7. Bradley, R. H., & Caldwell, B. M. (1984). The HOME Inventory and family demographics. *Developmental Psychology, 20,* 315-320.

8. Bradley, R. H., Casey, P. M., & Wortham, B. (1984). Home environments of low SES non-organic failure-to-thrive infants. *Merrill-Palmer Quarterly, 30,* 393-402.

9. McGowan, R. J., & Johnson, D. J. (1984). The mother-child relationship and other antecedents of academic performance: A causal analysis. *Hispanic Journal of Behavioral Sciences, 6,* 205-224.

10. Nihira, K., Mink, I. T., & Meyers, C. E. (1984). Salient dimensions of home environment relevant to child development. *International Review of Research in Mental Retardation, 12,* 149-175.

11. Olson, S. L., Bates, J. E., & Bayles, K. (1984). Mother-infant interaction and the development of individual differences in children's cognitive competence. *Developmental Psychology, 20,* 166-179.

12. Ramey, C. T., Yeates, K. O., & Short, E. J. (1984). The plasticity of intellectual development: Insights from preventive intervention. *Child Development, 55,* 1913-1925.

13. Stevens, J. H., Jr. (1984). Black grandmothers' and black adolescent mothers' knowledge about parenting. *Developmental Psychology, 20,* 1017-1025.

14. Stevens, J. H., Jr. (1984). Child development knowledge and parenting skills. *Family Relations, 33,* 237-244.

15. Daniels, D., & Plomin, R. (1985). Origins of individual differences in infant shyness. *Developmental Psychology, 21,* 118-121.

16. Feldman, M. A., Case, L., Towns, F., & Betel, J. (1985). Parent education project I: Development and nurturance of children of mentally retarded parents. *American Journal of Mental Deficiency, 90,* 253-258.

17. Haskins, R. (1985). Public school aggression among children with varying day-care experience. *Child Development, 56,* 689-703.

18. Plomin, R., Loehlin, J. C., & DeFries, J. C. (1985). Genetic and environmental components of "environmental" influences. *Developmental Psychology, 21,* 391-402.

19. Schilmoeller, G. L., & Baranowski, M. D. (1985). Childrearing of firstborns by adolescent and older mothers. *Adolescence, 20,* 805-822.

study of the HOME scale for infants. *Developmental Psychology, 21,* 1196-1203.

21. Adamakos, H., Ryan, K., Ullman, D. G., Pascoe, J., Diaz, R., & Chessare, J. (1986). Maternal social support as a predictor of mother-child stress and stimulation. *Child Abuse and Neglect, 10,* 463-470.

22. Breitmayer, B. J., & Ramey, C. T. (1986). Biological nonoptimality and quality of postnatal environment as codeterminants of intellectual development. *Child Development, 57,* 1151-1165.

23. Cotterell, J. L. (1986). Work and community influences on the quality of child rearing. *Child Development, 57,* 362-374.

24. Durrett, M. E., Richards, P., Otaki, M., Pennebaker, J. W., & Nyquist, L. (1986). Mother's involvement with infant and her perception of spousal support, Japan and America. *Journal of Marriage and the Family, 48,* 187-194.

25. Karr, S. K., & Easley, B. (1986). Exploration of effects of divorce on the Preschool Home Inventory. *Psychological Reports, 59,* 659-662.

26. Parks, P. L., & Smeriglio, V. L. (1986). Relationships among parenting knowledge, quality of stimulation in the home and infant development. *Family Relations, 35,* 411-416.

27. Reis, J., Barbera-Stein, L., & Bennett, S. (1986). Ecological determinants of parenting. *Family Relations, 35,* 547-554.

28. Bathurst, K., & Gottfried, A. W. (1987). Untestable subjects in child development research: Developmental implications. *Child Development, 58,* 1135-1144.

29. Garcia-Coll, C. T., Hoffman, J., & Oh, W. (1987). The social ecology and early parenting of Caucasian adolescent mothers. *Child Development, 58,* 955-963.

30. Ernhart, C. B., Marler, M. R., & Morrow-Tlucak, M. (1987). Size and cognitive development in the early preschool years. *Psychological Reports, 61,* 103-106.

31. Mink, I. T., & Nihira, K. (1987). Direction of effects: Family life styles and behavior of TMR children. *American Journal of Mental Deficiency, 92,* 57-64.

32. Bradley, R. H., Caldwell, B. M., Rock, S. L., Hamrick, H. M., & Harris, P. (1988). Home Observation for Measurement of the Environment: Development of a home inventory for use with families having children 6 to 10 years old. *Contemporary Educational Psychology, 13,* 58-71.

33. Mink, I. T., Blacher, J., & Nihira, K. (1988). Taxonomy of family life styles: III. Replication with families with severely mentally retarded children. *American Journal on Mental Retardation, 93,* 250-264.

34. Rice, T., Fulker, D. W., DeFries, J. C., & Plomin, R. (1988). Path analysis of IQ during infancy and early childhood and an index of the home environment in the Colorado Adoption Project. *Intelligence, 12,* 27-45.

35. Sagi, A., Jaffe, M., Tirosh, E., Findler, L., & Harel, J. (1988). Maternal risk status and outcome measures: A three-stage study in Israel. *Child Psychiatry and Human Development, 19,* 145-157.

36. Wolfe, D. A., Edwards, B., Manion, I., & Koverola, C. (1988). Early intervention for parents at risk of child abuse and neglect: A preliminary investigation. *Journal of Consulting and Clinical Psychology, 56,* 40-47.

37. Bradley, R. H., Rock, S. L., Caldwell, B. M., & Brisby, J. A. (1989). Uses of the HOME inventory for families with handicapped children. *American Journal on Mental Retardation, 94,* 313-330.

38. Jacobson, S. W., & Frye, K. F. (1991). Effect of maternal social support on attachment: Experimental evidence. *Child Development, 62,* 572-582.

39. Mann, J., Ten Have, T., Plunkett, J. W., & Meisels, S. J. (1991). Time sampling: A methodological critique. *Child Development, 62,* 227-241.

40. Bradley, R. H., Whiteside, L., Caldwell, B. M., Casey, P. H., Kelleher, K., Pope, S., Swanson, M., Barrett, K., & Cross, D. (1993). Maternal IQ, the home environment, and child IQ in low birthweight, premature children. *International Journal of Behavioral Development, 16,* 61-74.

41. Johnson, D. L., Swank, P., Howie, V. M., Baldwin, C. D., Owen, M., & Luttman, D. (1993). Does HOME add to the prediction of child intelligence over and above SES? *Journal of Genetic Psychology, 154,* 33-40.

42. Spieker, S. J., & Bensley, L. (1994). Roles of living arrangements and grandmother social support in adolescent mothering and infant attachment. *Developmental Psychology, 30,* 102-111.

[1173]

Home Screening Questionnaire.

Purpose: Constructed to screen the home environment for factors related to the child's growth and development.

Population: Birth to age 3, ages 3-6.

Publication Date: 1981.

Acronym: HSQ.

Scores, 3: Questions, Toy Checklist, Total.

Administration: Individual.

Price Data, 1994: $7.75 per 25 questionnaires; $7.75 per reference manual (32 pages).

Time: (15-20) minutes.

Comments: Ratings by parents; abbreviated adaptation of the Home Observation for Measurement of the Environment.

Authors: Cecilia E. Coons, Elizabeth C. Gay, Alma W. Fandal, Cynthia Ker, and William K. Frankenburg.

Publisher: Denver Developmental Materials, Inc.

[1174]

The Hooper Visual Organization Test.

Purpose: Measures an individual's ability to organize visual stimuli.

Population: Ages 13 and over.

Publication Dates: 1957-83.

Acronym: VOT.

Scores: Total score only.

Administration: Group or individual.

Price Data, 1993: $180 per complete kit; $16.50 per 25 test booklets; $30 per reusable test pictures booklet; $12.50 per scoring key; $19.50 per 100 answer sheets; $35 per manual ('83, 39 pages).

Time: (10-15) minutes.

Author: H. Elston Hooper.

Publisher: Western Psychological Services.

Cross References: See T3:1109 (6 references), T2:1216 (5 references), and P:111 (7 references); for reviews by Ralph M. Reitan and Otfried Spreen of an earlier edition, see 6:116 (4 references).

TEST REFERENCES

1. Schaeffer, J., Andrysiak, T., & Ungerleider, J. T. (1981). Cognition and long-term use of ganja (cannabis). *Science, 213,* 465-466.

2. Boyd, J. L. (1982). Reply to Rathbun and Smith: Who made the Hooper blooper? *Journal of Consulting and Clinical Psychology, 50,* 284-285.

3. Boyd, J. L. (1982). Reply to Woodward. *Journal of Consulting and Clinical Psychology, 50,* 289-290.

4. Farver, P. F., & Farver, T. B. (1982). Performance of normal older adults on tests designed to measure parietal lobe functions. *The American Journal of Occupational Therapy, 36,* 444-449.

5. Rathbun, J., & Smith, A. (1982). Comment on the validity of Boyd's validation study of the Hooper Visual Organization Test. *Journal of Consulting and Clinical Psychology, 50,* 281-283.

6. Woodward, C. A. (1982). The Hooper Visual Organization Test: A case against its use in neuropsychological assessment. *Journal of Consulting and Clinical Psychology, 50,* 286-288.

7. Speedie, L. J., & Heilman, K. M. (1983). Anterograde memory deficits for visuospatial material after infarction of the right thalamus. *Archives of Neurology, 40,* 183-186.

8. Weintraub, S., & Mesulam, M. (1983). Developmental learning disabilities of the right hemisphere: Emotional, interpersonal, and cognitive components. *Archives of Neurology, 40,* 463-468.

9. Alfano, A. M., Thurstin, A. N., Bancroft, W., Jr., Haygood, J. M., & Sherer, T. M. (1984). Development and validation of an automatic treatment referral system. *Journal of Clinical Psychology, 40,* 842-850.

10. Boller, F., Passafiume, D., Keefe, N. C., Rogers, K., Morrow, L., & Kim, Y. (1984). Visuospatial impairment in Parkinson's Disease: Role of perceptual and motor factors. *Archives of Neurology, 41,* 485-490.

11. Ryan, C., Vega, A., Longstreet, C., & Drash, A. (1984). Neuropsychological changes in adolescents with insulin-dependent diabetes. *Journal of Consulting and Clinical Psychology, 52,* 335-342.

12. Tamkin, A. S., & Jacobsen, R. (1984). Age-related norms for the Hooper Visual Organization Test. *Journal of Clinical Psychology, 40,* 1459-1463.

13. Tamkin, A. S., Kunce, J. T., Blount, J. B., Jr., & Magharious, W. (1984). The effectiveness of the Weigl Color-Form Sorting Test in screening for brain dysfunction. *Journal of Clinical Psychology, 40,* 1454-1459.

14. Hilgert, L. D., & Treloar, J. H. (1985). The relationship of the Hooper Visual Organization Test to sex, age, and intelligence of elementary school children. *Measurement and Evaluation in Counseling and Development, 17,* 203-206.

15. Berry, D. T. R., Webb, W. B., Block, A. J., Bauer, R. M., & Switzer, D. A. (1986). Nocturnal hypoxia and neuropsychological variables. *Journal of Clinical and Experimental Neuropsychology, 8,* 229-238.

16. Cerella, J., DiCara, R., Williams, D., & Bowles, N. (1986). Relations between information processing and intelligence in elderly adults. *Intelligence, 10,* 75-91.

17. Hyer, L., Harkey, B., & Harrison, W. R. (1986). MMPI scales and subscales: Patterns of older, middle-aged, and younger inpatients. *Journal of Clinical Psychology, 42,* 596-601.

18. Tamkin, A. S., Hyer, L. A., & Carson, M. F. (1986). Comparison among four measures of depression in younger and older alcoholics. *Psychological Reports, 59,* 287-293.

19. Thurstin, A. H., Alfano, A. M., & Sherer, M. (1986). Pretreatment MMPI profiles of A.A. members and nonmembers. *Journal of Studies on Alcohol, 47,* 468-471.

20. Stuss, D. T., Kates, M. H., Poirier, C. A., Hylton, D., Humphreys, P., Keene, D., & Laflèche G. (1987). Evaluation of information-processing speed and neuropsychological functioning in patients with myotonic dystrophy. *Journal of Clinical and Experimental Neuropsychology, 9,* 131-146.

21. Tucker, D. M., Roeltgen, D. P., Tully, R., Hartmann, J., & Boxell, C. (1988). Memory dysfunction following unilateral transection of the fornix: A hippocampal disconnection syndrome. *Cortex, 24,* 465-472.

22. Bolla-Wilson, K., Robinson, R. G., Starkstein, S. E., Boston, J., & Price, T. R. (1989). Lateralization of dementia of depression in stroke patients. *American Journal of Psychiatry, 146,* 627-634.

23. Minden, S. L., Moes, E. J., Orav, J., Kaplan, E., & Reich, P. (1990). Memory impairment in multiple sclerosis. *Journal of Clinical and Experimental Neuropsychology, 12,* 566-586.

24. Kramer, J. H., Kaplan, E., Blusewicz, M. J., & Preston, K. A. (1991). Visual hierarchical analysis of block design configural errors. *Journal of Clinical and Experimental Neuropsychology, 13,* 455-465.

25. Shay, K. A., & Roth, D. L. (1992). Association between aerobic fitness and visuospatial performance in healthy older adults. *Psychology and Aging, 7,* 15-24.

26. Swirsky-Sacchetti, T., Field, H. L., Mitchell, D. R., Seward, J., Lublin, F. D., Knobler, R. L., & Gonzalez, C. F. (1992). The sensitivity of the Mini-Mental State Exam in the white matter dementia of multiple sclerosis. *Journal of Clinical Psychology, 48,* 779-786.

27. Taylor, R. (1992). Art training and the Rey figure. *Perceptual and Motor Skills, 74,* 1105-1106.

28. Swirsky-Sacchetti, T., Gorton, G., Samuel, S., Sobel, R., Genetta-Wadley, A., & Burleigh, B. (1993). Neuropsychological function in borderline personality disorder. *Journal of Clinical Psychology, 49,* 385-396.

[1175]

How A Child Learns.

Purpose: Designed to identify strengths and weaknesses in a child's learning styles.

Population: Classroom teachers.

Publication Dates: 1970-71.

Scores: 4 areas: Auditory, Visual, Verbal, Manual.

Administration: Individual.

Price Data: Not available.

Time: Administration time not reported.

Comments: Manual title is Classroom Analysis of Learning Skills and Disabilities: An Observational Approach.

Authors: Thomas Gnagey and Patricia Gnagey (manual).

Publisher: Facilitation House [No reply from publisher; status unknown].

Cross References: For a review by Glenn Moe, see 9:484.

[1176]

How Am I Doing? A Self-Assessment for Child Caregivers.

Purpose: Designed to identify areas of strength and skill development needs of caregivers of children with disabilities.

Population: Caregivers of children with disabilities.

Publication Date: 1993.

Scores: 8 sections: Arrival and Departure, Free Choice Play, Structured Group Activities, Outside Play, Meal Time, Toileting, Nap Time, Throughout the Day.

Administration: Group.

Price Data: Price data available from publisher.

Time: Administration time not reported.

Author: Irene Carney.

Publisher: Child Development Resources.

[1177]

How Supervise?

Purpose: Designed to assess the knowledge of practices affecting worker efficiency.

Population: Supervisors.

Publication Dates: 1943-71.

Scores: Total score only.

Administration: Group.

Forms, 3: A, B, M.

Price Data, 1994: $54 per 25 test booklets (specify form); $17 per manual ('71, 17 pages); $17 per examination kit including test booklets for all three forms and manual.

Time: [40] minutes.

Authors: Quentin W. File and H. H. Remmers.

Publisher: The Psychological Corporation.

Cross References: See T2:2448 (11 references); for a review by Joel T. Campbell, see 6:1189 (9 references); see also 5:926 (18 references); for a review by Milton M. Mandell, see 4:774 (8 references); for reviews by D. Welty Lefever, Charles I. Moiser, and C. H. Ruedisili, see 3:687 (5 references).

TEST REFERENCES

1. Schippmann, J. S., & Prien, E. P. (1985). The Ghiselli Self-description Inventory: A psychometric appraisal. *Psychological Reports, 57,* 1171-1177.

2. Schippmann, J. S., & Prien, E. P. (1986). Individual difference correlates of two leadership styles. *Psychological Reports, 59,* 817-818.

[1178]

How Well Do You Know Your Interests?

Purpose: Designed to identify "an individual's attitudes of liking, disliking, or apathy toward . . . work activities."

Population: Grades 9-12, college, adults.

Publication Dates: 1957-75.

Scores, 54: Numerical, Clerical, Retail Selling, Outside Selling, Selling Real Estate, One-Order Selling, Sales Complaints, Selling Intangibles, Buyer, Labor Management, Production Supervision, Busi-

ness Management, Machine Operation, Repair & Construction, Machine Design, Farm or Ranch, Gardening, Hunting, Adventure, Social Service, Teaching Service, Medical Service, Nursing Service, Applied Chemistry, Basic Chemical Problems, Basic Biological Problems, Basic Physical Problems, Basic Psychological Problems, Philosophical, Visual Art (Appreciative, Productive, Decorative), Amusement (Appreciative, Productive, Managerial), Literary (Appreciative, Productive), Musical (Appreciative, Performing, Composing), Sports (Appreciative, Participative), Domestic Service, Unskilled Labor, Disciplinary, Power Seeking, Propaganda, Self-Aggrandizing, Supervisory Initiative, Bargaining, Arbitrative, Persuasive, Disputatious, Masculinity (for males only) or Femininity (for females only).
Administration: Group.
Levels, 3: Secondary School, College, Personnel.
Price Data, 1991: $11 per complete kit including 3 test booklets of each edition, scoring keys, and manual ('74, 24 pages); $20 per 25 test booklets (select level); $6.75 per set of scoring keys; $6.75 per manual; $6.75 per handbook on interpretation ('75, 19 pages).
Time: (15–20) minutes.
Authors: Thomas N. Jenkins (test booklets, manual), John H. Coleman (manual, handbook), and Harold T. Fagin (manual).
Publisher: Psychologists and Educators, Inc.
Cross References: See 7:1022 (2 references); for a review by John R. Hills and an excerpted review by Gordon V. Anderson, see 6:1059 (1 reference); for reviews by Jerome E. Doppelt and Henry S. Dyer, see 5:859.

[1179]
How Well Do You Know Yourself?
Purpose: Developed to assess personality characteristics.
Population: Grades 9–12, college, office and factory workers.
Publication Dates: 1959–76.
Scores, 19: Irritability, Practicality, Punctuality, Novelty-Loving, Vocational Assurance, Cooperativeness, Ambitiousness, Hypercriticalness, Dejection, General Morale, Persistence, Nervousness, Seriousness, Submissiveness, Impulsiveness, Dynamism, Emotional Control, Consistency, Test Objectivity.
Administration: Group.
Levels, 3: Secondary School, College, Personnel.
Price Data, 1991: $11 per complete kit including test booklets (3 of each level) and manual ('74, 30 pages); $20 per 25 test booklets (select level); $6.75 per set of scoring keys; $6.75 per manual.
Time: Administration time not reported.
Authors: Thomas N. Jenkins, John H. Coleman (manual), and Harold T. Fagin (manual).
Publisher: Psychologists and Educators, Inc.
Cross References: See 11:166 (1 reference) and T2:1220 (2 references); for reviews by Lee J. Cronbach and Harrison G. Gough and excerpted reviews

by Edward S. Bordin and Laurence Siegel, see 6:118 (2 references).

[1180]
Howarth Mood Adjective Checklist.
Purpose: To measure personality and affect dimensions.
Population: College and adults.
Publication Dates: 1979–80.
Acronym: HMACL.
Scores, 10: Aggression, Skepticism, Egotism, Outgoingness, Control, Anxiety, Co-operative, Fatigue, Concentration, Sadness.
Administration: Group or individual.
Price Data: Not available.
Time: (25–35) minutes.
Author: Edgar Howarth.
Publisher: Edgar Howarth [No reply from publisher; status unknown].
Cross References: For a review by Robert R. Hutzell, see 9:485 (1 reference).

[1181]
Howarth Personality Questionnaire.
Purpose: To measure personality dimensions.
Population: College and adults.
Publication Dates: 1971–80.
Acronym: HPQ.
Scores, 10: Sociability, Anxiety, Dominance, Conscience, Hypochondriac-Medical, Impulsive, Co-operative-Considerateness, Inferiority, Persistence, Suspicion vs. Trust.
Administration: Group.
Price Data: Not available.
Time: (25–35) minutes.
Author: Edgar Howarth.
Publisher: Edgar Howarth [No reply from publisher; status unknown].
Cross References: For reviews by Anthony J. Devito and Stephen L. Franzoi, see 9:486.

TEST REFERENCES

1. Comrey, A. L. (1984). Comparison of two methods to identify major personality factors. *Applied Psychological Measurement, 8*, 397-408.
2. Howarth, E. (1986). What does Eysenck's psychoticism scale really measure? *British Journal of Psychology, 77*, 223-227.

[1182]
Howell Prekindergarten Screening Test.
Purpose: Provides for early identification of children "who may need special assistance to ensure their successful entry into formal education; . . . whose skills seem appropriate for typical kindergarten work; . . . [or those] students with unusually well developed skills which can be most fully enhanced by specially designed educational experiences."
Population: Prekindergarten students.
Publication Date: 1984.
Scores, 23: Shapes, Listening Comprehension, Auditory Memory, Colors, Color Words, Vocabulary, Classification, Letter Identification, Rhyming, Letter

Writing, Directionality & Spatial Relationships, Consonant Sounds, Visual Motor, Visual Discrimination, Name, Math (Number Identification, Number Writing, Counting Sets, Math Concepts, Addition & Subtraction, Total), Copying, Total.
Administration: Group.
Price Data, 1994: $1.95 per student test booklet; $15.95 per user's guide and technical manual; $24.95 per specimen set.
Time: (60) minutes.
Authors: Howell Township Public Schools, Joseph P. Ryan (manual), and Ronald J. Mead (manual).
Publisher: Book-Lab.
Cross References: For reviews by Carl J. Dunst and Candice Feiring, see 10:142.

[1183]

H-T-P: House-Tree-Person Projective Technique.

Purpose: "To provide psychologists and psychiatrists . . . with an examining procedure with which to acquire diagnostically and prognostically significant data concerning a subject's total personality."
Population: Ages 3 and over.
Publication Dates: 1946–93.
Scores: Total score only.
Administration: Individual.
Price Data, 1993: $180 per complete kit; $10.50 per 25 drawing forms; $16.50 per 25 scoring folders; $37.50 per interpretive catalogue; $37.50 per diagnostic handbook; $24.50 per research manual; $65 per revised manual ('93).
Time: (60–90) minutes.
Authors: John N. Buck, W. L. Warren (revision), William H. Urban (interpretive catalog), Isaac Jolles (children's interrogation folder), L. Stanley Wench (diagnostic handbook), and Emmanuel F. Hammer (clinical research manual).
Publisher: Western Psychological Services.
Cross References: See T2:1469 (61 references) and P:437 (24 references); for a review by Mary R. Haworth of an earlier edition, see 6:215 (32 references); for a review by Philip L. Harriman, see 5:139 (61 references); for reviews by Albert Ellis and Ephraim Rosen and an excerpted review, see 4:107 (14 references); for reviews by Morris Krugman and Katherine N. Wilcox, see 3:47 (5 references).

TEST REFERENCES

1. Hampson, S. E., & Kline, P. (1977). Personality dimensions differentiating certain groups of abnormal offenders from non-offenders. *British Journal of Criminology, 17,* 310-331.
2. Bieliauskas, V. J., & Farragher, J. (1983). The effect of change on the size of the drawing sheet on the H-T-P IQ scores. *Journal of Clinical Psychology, 39,* 1033-1034.
3. Perkins, C. F., & Wagemaker, H. (1983). The HTP as a measure of change in dialyzed schizophrenic patients. *Journal of Clinical Psychology, 39,* 448-453.
4. DiClementi, J. D., & Handelsman, M. M. (1987). Effects of perceived sophistication and test validity on acceptance of generalized feedback. *Journal of Clinical Psychology, 43,* 341-345.
5. Kline, P. (1987). The experimental study of the psychoanalytic unconscious. *Personality and Social Psychology Bulletin, 13,* 363-378.
6. Lewis, D. O., Pincus, J. H., Bard, B., Richardson, E., Princhep, L. S., Feldman, M., & Yeager, C. (1988). Neuropsychiatric, psycho-

educational, and family characteristics of 14 juveniles condemned to death in the United States. *American Journal of Psychiatry, 145,* 584-589.

[1184]

Hudson Education Skills Inventory.

Purpose: Assesses "the academic performance level of students with dysfunctional learning patterns."
Population: Grades K–12.
Publication Date: 1989.
Acronym: HESI.
Scores: Item scores only.
Subtests, 3: Mathematics, Reading, Writing; available as separates.
Administration: Individual.
Price Data, 1994: $219 per complete battery including 1 each of complete Mathematics, Reading, and Writing kits; $79 per complete Mathematics, Reading, or Writing kit; $25 per student book; $28 per instructional planning form; $29 per examiner's manual (Mathematics, 119 pages; Reading, 86 pages; Writing, 177 pages); $79 per software report system (Apple and IBM versions available).
Time: Administration time not reported.
Comments: "Criterion-referenced."
Publisher: PRO-ED, Inc.
  a) MATHEMATICS.
Acronym: HESI-M.
Scores: 14 skill areas: Numeration, Addition of Whole Numbers, Subtraction of Whole Numbers, Multiplication of Whole Numbers, Division of Whole Numbers, Fractions, Decimals, Percentages, Time, Money, Measurement, Statistics/Graphs/Tables, Geometry, Word Problems.
Authors: Floyd G. Hudson and Steven E. Colson.
  b) READING.
Acronym: HESI-R.
Scores: 5 skill areas: Readiness, Vocabulary, Phonic Analysis, Structural Analysis, Comprehension.
Authors: Floyd G. Hudson, Steven E. Colson, and Doris L. Hudson Welch.
  c) WRITING.
Acronym: HESI-W.
Scores: 3 parts, 14 skill areas: Composition (Capitalization, Punctuation, Grammar, Vocabulary, Sentences, Paragraphs), Spelling (Readiness, Consonants, Vowels, Structural Changes, Selected Word Groups), Handwriting (Readiness, Manuscript, Cursive).
Authors: Floyd G. Hudson, Steven E. Colson, Alison K. Banikowski, and Teresa A. Mehring.
Cross References: For reviews by Ronald K. Hambleton and Ernest W. Kimmel, see 11:167.

[1185]

Hughes Basic Gross Motor Assessment.

Purpose: Designed to detect disorders in motor performance.
Population: Ages 6–12 believed to have minor motor dysfunctions.
Publication Date: 1979.

Acronym: BGMA.
Scores: 8 subtests: Static Balance, Stride Jump, Tandem Walking, Hopping, Skipping, Target, Yo-Yo, Ball Handling Skills.
Administration: Individual.
Price Data: Available from publisher.
Time: Administration time not reported.
Author: Jeanne E. Hughes.
Publisher: Nancy Hughes.
Cross References: See 9:487 (1 reference).

[1186]

Human Information Processing Survey.
Purpose: "Assesses processing preference—left, right, integrated, or mixed [brain functioning]."
Population: Adults.
Publication Date: 1984.
Acronym: HIP Survey.
Scores, 3: Right, Left, Integrated.
Administration: Group.
Editions, 2: Research Edition, Professional Edition.
Price Data, 1993: $56 per professional edition starter set including administrator's manual (44 pages), 10 survey forms, and 10 strategy and tactics profiles booklets; $45 per 10 survey forms and strategy and tactics profiles; $22.50 per manual (professional and research editions); $70 per research edition starter set including administrator's manual, 20 reusable survey forms, 20 profile forms, and 20 response sheets; $24.50 per 20 profile forms and response sheets (research edition); $25.50 per specimen set for each edition.
Time: Administration time not reported.
Authors: E. Paul Torrance, William Taggart (manual), and Barbara Taggart.
Publisher: Scholastic Testing Service, Inc.
Cross References: For a review by J. P. Das, see 10:144 (1 reference).

TEST REFERENCES

1. Taggart, W. M., Kroeck, K. G., & Escoffier, M. R. (1991). Validity evidence for the Myers-Briggs Type Indicator as a measure of hemisphere dominance: Another view. *Educational and Psychological Measurement, 51*, 775-783.

[1187]

Human Loyalty Expressionaire.
Purpose: "Measures human loyalty and global awareness" for use in peace and global studies courses.
Population: College and university students.
Publication Date: No date on test materials.
Scores: Total score only.
Administration: Group.
Price Data: Available from publisher.
Time: Administration time not reported.
Author: Theodore J. Lentz.
Publisher: Lentz Peace Research Laboratory.

[1188]

Human Relations Inventory.
Purpose: Designed to measure social conformity.
Population: Grades 9–16 and adults.

Publication Dates: 1954–59.
Acronym: HRI.
Scores: Total score only.
Administration: Group.
Price Data: Available from publisher.
Time: (20) minutes.
Author: Raymond E. Bernberg.
Publisher: Psychometric Affiliates.
Cross References: See T2:1221 (4 references), P:114 (1 reference), and 6:119 (6 references); for reviews by Raymond C. Norris and John A. Radcliffe, see 5:68.

[1189]

Human Resource Development Report.
Purpose: Assesses an individual's management style, "provides insights into the individual's personality, describes personal strengths, and identifies areas for potential growth and development."
Population: Managerial candidates.
Publication Dates: 1982–87.
Acronym: HRDR.
Scores: 5 dimensions: Leadership, Interaction with Others, Decision-Making Abilities, Initiative, Personal Adjustment.
Administration: Group.
Price Data, 1994: $34.50 per introductory kit including 16 PF test booklet, answer sheet, prepaid processing form to receive Human Resource Development Report, and user's guide ('87, 47 pages); $24 per 25 16PF reusable test booklets; $10.75 per 25 16PF machine-scorable answer sheets; $16 per user's guide; $25 or less per Human Resource Development Report available from publisher scoring service.
Time: 45(60) minutes.
Comments: Based on the Sixteen Personality Factor Questionnaire (2470); must be scored by publisher.
Author: IPAT staff.
Publisher: Institute for Personality and Ability Testing, Inc.
Cross References: For reviews by S. Alvin Leung and Mary A. Lewis, see 11:169.

[1190]

Humanics National Child Assessment Form.
Purpose: To serve as developmental checklists of skills that occur during the first 6 years of life.
Population: Ages 0–3, 3–6.
Publication Dates: 1981–83.
Administration: Group.
Levels, 2: Birth to age 3, ages 3 to 6.
Price Data, 1987: $1 per checklist (specify level).
Time: Administration time varies.
Comments: Behavior checklists to be completed by parents or teachers.
Publisher: Humanics Limited.
a) BIRTH TO THREE.
  Scores: Item scores in 5 areas: Social-Emotional, Language, Cognitive, Gross Motor, Fine Motor.
  Price Data: $14.95 per user's guide entitled

Humanics National Infant-Toddler Assessment Handbook ('81, 167 pages).
Authors: Marsha Kaufman (checklist), T. Thomas McMurrain (checklist), Jane A. Caballero (handbook), and Derek Whordley (handbook).
b) AGES THREE TO SIX.
Scores: Item scores in 5 areas: Social-Emotional, Language, Cognitive, Motor Skills, Hygiene/Self-Help.
Price Data: $.25 per individualized educational program form; $16.95 per user's guide entitled *Humanics National Preschool Assessment Handbook* ('83, 235 pages).
Authors: Derek Whordley (handbook) and Rebecca J. Doster (handbook).
Cross References: For reviews by Arthur S. Ellen and David MacPhee, see 11:170.

[1191]

The Hundred Pictures Naming Test.
Purpose: "A confrontation naming test designed to evaluate rapid naming ability."
Population: Ages 4-6 to 11-11.
Publication Date: 1992.
Acronym: HPNT.
Scores, 3: Error, Accuracy, Time.
Administration: Individual.
Price Data, 1992: $195 per complete kit including manual (84 pages), test book, and 25 response forms; $10 per 25 response forms.
Time: (6) minutes.
Authors: John P. Fisher and Jennifer M. Glenister.
Publisher: Australian Council for Educational Research Ltd. [Australia].

[1192]

Hunter-Grundin Literacy Profiles.
Purpose: Designed to monitor the written and spoken language skills of children.
Population: Ages 6.5–8, 7.10–9.3, 9–10, 9.10–11.5, 10.10–12.7.
Publication Dates: 1979–89.
Scores: 6 tests: Attitude to Reading (Levels 1 and 2 only), Reading for Meaning, Spelling, Free Writing, Spoken Language, Profile of Personal Interests (Levels 4 and 5 only).
Administration: Individual and group.
Levels: 5 overlapping levels.
Manual: Separate manual for each level.
Price Data: Available from publisher.
Time: (3–10) minutes per test at any one level.
Comments: Ratings by teacher in part.
Authors: Elizabeth Hunter-Grundin and Hans U. Grundin.
Publisher: The Test Agency Ltd. [England].
a) LEVEL 1.
Population: Ages 6.5–8.
b) LEVEL 2.
Population: Ages 7.10–9.3.
c) LEVEL 3.
Population: Ages 9–10.

d) LEVEL 4.
Population: Ages 9.10–11.5.
e) LEVEL 5.
Population: Ages 10.10–12.7.
Cross References: For reviews of a previous edition by Martha C. Beech and Patricia H. Kennedy, see 9:491.

[1193]

Hutchins Behavior Inventory.
Purpose: Designed to assess "the interaction of thoughts, feelings, and actions."
Population: High school and over.
Publication Date: 1992.
Acronym: HBI.
Scores, 9: Thinking, Feeling, Acting, Comparison (Thinking-Feeling, Feeling-Acting, Acting-Thinking), Characteristic (Thinking, Feeling, Acting).
Administration: Group.
Price Data, 1992: $45 per 25 tests/answer sheets; $18 per manual (44 pages); $19 per sampler set.
Time: (10–15) minutes.
Authors: David E. Hutchins and Ralph O. Mueller.
Publisher: Consulting Psychologists Press, Inc.

TEST REFERENCES

1. Mueller, R. O., Hutchins, D. E., & Vogler, D. E. (1990). Validity and reliability of the Hutchins Behavior Inventory: A confirmatory maximum likelihood analysis. *Measurement and Evaluation in Counseling and Development, 22,* 203-214.

[1194]

ICES: Instructor and Course Evaluation System.
Purpose: Developed to measure instructional performance.
Population: College students.
Publication Dates: 1976–78.
Acronym: ICES.
Administration: Group.
Manual: No manual.
Price Data: Not available.
Time: Administration time not reported.
Comments: Instructors choose items from a pool of over 450 covering student perceptions of teaching styles, student outcomes, and course characteristics.
Author: Measurement & Research Division, University of Illinois at Urbana-Champaign.
Publisher: Measurement & Research Division, University of Illinois at Urbana-Champaign [No reply from publisher; status unknown].
Cross References: For a review by E. A. Nelsen, see 9:492.

[1195]

IDEA.
Purpose: Provides student ratings of college-level teaching.
Population: College faculty.
Publication Dates: 1975–93.
Scores, 3 or 8 parts to report: Evaluation (progress ratings), Course Description (standard form

only), Students' Self Ratings, Methods (standard form only), Additional Questions (standard form only), Diagnostic Summary (standard form only), Summary Profile.

Administration: Group.

Price Data: Available from publisher.

Time: (10–20) minutes.

Authors: Donald P. Hoyt, Richard E. Owens, William E. Cashin (technical reports), Glenn R. Sixbury (technical reports No. 7 and 8).

Publisher: Center for Faculty Evaluation and Development.

Cross References: For a review by John C. Ory, see 9:493 (2 references).

TEST REFERENCES

1. Fourgurean, J. M. (1987). A K-ABC and WISC-R comparison for Latino learning-disabled children of limited English proficiency. *Journal of School Psychology, 25,* 15-21.

[1196]

IDEA Oral Language Proficiency Test.

Purpose: To "assist in the initial identification designation and redesignation of a student as being NES, LES, or FES (Non-Limited-Fluent English Speaking)."

Population: Preschool–grade 12.

Publication Dates: 1983–90.

Acronym: IPT.

Scores, 4: Vocabulary, Comprehension, Syntax, Verbal Expression.

Administration: Individual.

Price Data: Available from publisher.

Foreign Language Edition: English and Spanish versions available for each level.

Publisher: Ballard & Tighe, Inc.

a) PRE-IPT.

Population: Ages 3–5.

Publication Date: 1988

Time: (8–13) minutes.

Authors: Constance O. Williams, Wanda S. Ballard, and Phyllis L. Tighe.

b) IPT-I.

Population: Grades K–6.

Publication Dates: 1990.

Time: (14–19) minutes.

Authors: Wanda S. Ballard, Phyllis L. Tighe, and Enrique F. Dalton.

c) IPT-II.

Population: Grades 7–12.

Publication Date: 1983. Time (15–20) minutes.

Authors: Enrique F. Dalton and Beverly A. Amori.

[1197]

IDEA Reading and Writing Proficiency Test.

Purpose: To provide "comprehensive assessment for the initial identification and redesignation of Limited English Proficient (LEP) students."

Population: Grades 2–12.

Publication Dates: 1992–93.

Acronym: IPT R & W.

Scores, 8: Reading (Vocabulary, Vocabulary in Context, Reading for Understanding, Reading for Life Skills, Language Usage), Writing (Conventions, Write a Story, Write Your Own Story).

Administration: Group.

Levels, 3: Grades 2–3, Grades 4–6, Grades 7–12.

Price Data: Available from publisher.

Time: (70–115) minutes.

Comments: Used in conjunction with the IDEA Oral Language Proficiency Test (1196).

Authors: Beverly A. Amori, Enrique F. Dalton, and Phyllis L. Tighe.

Publisher: Ballard & Tighe.

[1198]

IDEAS: Interest Determination, Exploration and Assessment System.

Purpose: "To be used as an introduction to career exploration for students and adults."

Population: Grades 7–12 and adults.

Publication Dates: 1977–94.

Acronym: IDEAS.

Scores, 16: Mechanical/Fixing, Protective Services, Nature/Outdoors, Mathematics, Science, Medical, Creative Arts, Writing, Community Service, Educating, Child Care, Public Speaking, Business, Sales, Office Practices, Food Service.

Administration: Group or individual.

Price Data, 1994: $51 per 50 booklets; $8.95 per manual ('90, 80 pages); $15 per preview package.

Time: (40–45) minutes.

Comments: Self-administered, self-scored.

Author: Charles B. Johansson.

Publisher: NCS Assessments.

Cross References: For a review by Robert J. Miller, see 11:172; for a review by M. O'Neal Weeks of an earlier edition, see 9:516.

[1199]

The Identi-Form System for Gifted Programs.

Purpose: "An aid to both the identification of gifted students, and the individualization of programming for these students following selection."

Population: Grades K–12.

Publication Date: 1982.

Scores: Ratings in 4 areas: Intellectual Abilities, Creative Abilities, Personal Characteristics, Artistic Performing Abilities.

Price Data, 1994: $25 per complete kit including reproducible rating form and manual (216 pages).

Time: Administration time not reported.

Comments: "Incorporates test, performance and anecdotal data in a total assessment of the child."

Authors: Patricia Weber and Catherine Battaglia.

Publisher: United/DOK Publishers.

Cross References: For a review by James O. Rust, see 10:364.

[1200]

The IES Test.
Purpose: "Constructed within the framework of the psychoanalytic theory of personality development" with the goal of increased "understanding of individual dynamics and . . . knowledge of personality functioning."
Population: Ages 10 and over and latency period girls.
Publication Dates: 1956–58.
Administration: Individual.
Price Data, 1989: $43.50 per complete kit including Picture Title cards, Picture Story Completion cards, Photo-Analysis cards, 25 Arrow-Dot test forms, 25 record forms, instruction cards, manual ('58, 44 pages), and heavy storage boxes; $10 per 100 record forms; $9 per 25 Arrow-Dot test forms; $6 per manual.
Time: (30) minutes.
Authors: Lawrence A. Dombrose and Morton S. Slobin.
Publisher: Psychological Test Specialists.
a) ARROW-DOT TEST.
Purpose: Reaction to goal barriers.
Publication Dates: 1957–58.
Scores, 3: Impulses, Ego, Superego.
b) PICTURE STORY COMPLETION TEST.
Purpose: Conception of outside world.
Publication Dates: 1956–58.
Scores, 3: Same as *a* above.
c) PHOTO-ANALYSIS TEST.
Purpose: Desired self-gratification.
Publication Dates: 1956–58.
Scores, 3: Same as *a* above.
d) PICTURE TITLE TEST.
Purpose: Recognition and acceptance of ego pressures.
Publication Dates: 1956–58.
Scores, 5: Impulses, Ego, Superego, Defense, Superego plus Defense.
Cross References: See T3:1123 (3 references), T2:1475 (16 references), and P:443 (26 references); for reviews by Douglas P. Crowne and Walter Katkovsky and an excerpted review by John O. Crites, see 6:220 (15 references).

TEST REFERENCES

1. Goldberg, L. S. (1982). Psychological barriers to achievement in women. *Perceptual and Motor Skills, 54,* 153-154.
2. Gudjonsson, G. H. (1984). Interrogative suggestibility and perceptual motor performance. *Perceptual and Motor Skills, 58,* 671-672.
3. Omololu, C. B., & Ohwovoriole, A. E. (1984). IES Arrow-Dot performance of Nigerian professionals, medical students, and psychiatric in-patients. *Perceptual and Motor Skills, 58,* 566.
4. Omololu, C. B. (1985). IES arrow-dot performance of Nigerian juvenile delinquents and secondary school students. *Perceptual and Motor Skills, 60,* 18.

[1201]

Illinois Course Evaluation Questionnaire.
Purpose: Measures college course effectiveness.
Population: College.

Publication Dates: 1965–74.
Acronym: CEQ.
Scores, 30: General Course Attitude (4 item scores, total), Method of Instruction (4 item scores, total), Course Content (4 item scores, total), Interest and Attention (4 item scores, total), Instructor—General (2 item scores, total), Instructor—Specific (5 item scores, total), Total.
Administration: Group.
Price Data: Not available.
Time: Administration time not specified.
Comments: Ratings by students.
Authors: Richard E. Spencer (Forms 66 and 32), Lawrence M. Aleamoni, and Dale C. Brandenburg.
Publisher: Measurement & Research Division, University of Illinois at Urbana-Champaign [No reply from publisher; status unknown].
Cross References: See T3:1125; for a review by Robert J. Menges, see 8:373 (10 references); see also T2:864 (1 reference) and 7:579 (2 references).

[1202]

Illinois Test of Psycholinguistic Abilities, Revised Edition.
Purpose: Designed for assessing psycholinguistic abilities in children.
Population: Ages 2–10.
Publication Dates: 1961–68.
Acronym: ITPA.
Scores, 13: Auditory Reception, Visual Reception, Visual Sequential Memory, Auditory Association, Auditory Sequential Memory, Visual Association, Visual Closure, Verbal Expression, Grammatic Closure, Manual Expression, Auditory Closure (Optional), Sound Blending (Optional), Total.
Administration: Individual.
Price Data, 1990: $110 per complete kit including 2 picture books, objects needed to administer various subtests, audio demonstration cassette, 25 record forms, examiner's manual ('68, 134 pages), technical manual, guidebook, and supplementary articles, all in a carrying case; $15.75 per 25 record forms and Visual Closure picture strips; $12.50 per examiner's manual; $10 per technical manual.
Time: (40–60) minutes.
Authors: Samuel A. Kirk, James J. McCarthy, Winifred D. Kirk, and John N. Paraskevopoulos (technical manual).
Publisher: University of Illinois Press.
Cross References: See 9:496 (37 references) and T3:1126 (145 references); for reviews by James Lumsden and J. Lee Wiederholt, and an excerpted review by R. P. Waugh, see 8:431 (269 references); see also T2:981 (113 references); for reviews by John B. Carroll and Clinton I. Chase, see 7:442 (239 references); see also 6:549 (22 references).

TEST REFERENCES

1. Weed, K., & Ryan, E. B. (1983). Alphabetical seriation as a reading readiness indicator. *Journal of General Psychology, 109,* 201-210.

2. Albery, L., & Enderby, P. (1984). Intensive speech therapy for cleft palate children. *British Journal of Disorders of Communication, 19,* 115-124.

3. Cermak, S. A., & Ayres, A. J. (1984). Crossing the body midline in learning-disabled and normal children. *The American Journal of Occupational Therapy, 38,* 35-39.

4. Champion, L., Doughtie, E. B., Johnson, P. J., & McCreary, J. H. (1984). Preliminary investigation into the Rorschach response patterns of children with documented learning disabilities. *Journal of Clinical Psychology, 40,* 329-333.

5. Chapman, J. W., Silva, P. A., & Williams, S. M. (1984). Academic self-concept: Some developmental and emotional correlates in nine-year-old children. *American Journal of Educational Psychology, 54,* 284-292.

6. Crispin, L., Hamilton, W., & Trickey, G. (1984). The relevance of visual sequential memory to reading. *British Journal of Educational Psychology, 54,* 24-30.

7. Halperin, J. M., Gittelman, R., Klein, D. F., & Rudel, R. B. (1984). Reading disabled hyperactive children: A distinct subgroup of Attention Deficit Disorder with hyperactivity? *Journal of Abnormal Child Psychology, 12,* 1-14.

8. Leong, C. K. (1984). Cognitive processing, language awareness and reading in grade 2 and grade 4 children. *Contemporary Educational Psychology, 9,* 369-383.

9. Mather, P. L., & Black, K. N. (1984). Heredity and environmental influences on preschool twins' language skills. *Developmental Psychology, 20,* 303-308.

10. McGee, R., Silva, P. A., & Williams, S. (1984). Perinatal, neurological, environmental and developmental characteristics of seven-year-old children with stable behaviour problems. *The Journal of Child Psychology and Psychiatry and Allied Disciplines, 25,* 573-586.

11. Miran, M., & Miran, E. (1984). Cerebral asymmetries: Neuropsychological measurement and theoretical issues. *Biological Psychology, 19,* 295-304.

12. Perlmutter, B. F., & Bryan, J. H. (1984). First impressions, ingratiation, and the learning disabled child. *Journal of Learning Disabilities, 17,* 157-161.

13. Seifert, M. (1984). IRA award-winning research. *The Reading Teacher, 38,* 322-328.

14. Silva, P. A., Justin, C., McGee, R., & Williams, S. M. (1984). Some developmental and behavioural characteristics of seven-year-old children with delayed speech development. *British Journal of Disorders of Communication, 19,* 147-154.

15. Tobey, E. A., & Cullen, J. K., Jr. (1984). Temporal integration of tone glides by children with auditory-memory and reading problems. *Journal of Speech and Hearing Research, 27,* 527-533.

16. Woo, E. Y. C., & Hoosain, R. (1984). Visual and auditory functions of Chinese dyslexics. *Psychologia, 27,* 164-170.

17. Alderton, D. L., Goldman, S. R., & Pellegrino, J. W. (1985). Individual differences in process outcomes for verbal analogy and classification solution. *Intelligence, 9,* 69-85.

18. Butler, S. R., Marsh, H. W., Sheppard, M. J., & Sheppard, J. L. (1985). Seven-year longitudinal study of the early prediction of reading achievement. *Journal of Educational Psychology, 77,* 349-361.

19. Connelly, J. B. (1985). Published tests—which ones do special education teachers perceive as useful? *Journal of Special Education, 19,* 149-155.

20. Jordan, T. E. (1985). Prospective longitudinal study of superior cognitive readiness for school, from 1 year to 7 years. *Contemporary Educational Psychology, 10,* 203-219.

21. Kirchner, D. M., & Klatzky, R. L. (1985). Verbal rehearsal and memory in language-disordered children. *Journal of Speech and Hearing Research, 28,* 556-565.

22. Leong, C. K., Cheng, S. C., & Das, J. P. (1985). Simultaneous-successive synthesis and planning in Chinese readers. *International Journal of Psychology, 20,* 19-31.

23. Mayberry, W., & Gilligan, M. B. (1985). Ocular pursuit in mentally retarded, cerebral-palsied, and learning-disabled children. *The American Journal of Occupational Therapy, 39,* 589-595.

24. Moog, J., & Geers, A. (1985). EPIC: A program to accelerate academic progress in profoundly hearing-impaired children. *Volta Review, 87,* 259-277.

25. Pickering, D. M., & Bowey, J. A. (1985). Psycholinguistic performance of children varying in socioeconomic status and home-language background. *Perceptual and Motor Skills, 61,* 1143-1146.

26. Strawser, S., & Weller, C. (1985). Use of adaptive behavior and discrepancy criteria to determine learning disabilities severity subtypes. *Journal of Learning Disabilities, 18,* 205-211.

27. Tallal, P., Stark, R. E., & Mellits, D. (1985). The relationship between auditory temporal analysis and receptive language development: Evidence from studies of developmental language disorder. *Neuropsychologia, 23,* 527-534.

28. Weismer, S. E. (1985). Constructive comprehension abilities exhibited by language-disordered children. *Journal of Speech and Hearing Research, 28,* 175-184.

29. Crittenden, M. R., & Holaday, B. (1986). Psychosocial factors associated with physical growth and behavior adaptations of children with renal dysfunction. *Perceptual and Motor Skills, 62,* 437-438.

30. Hinshaw, S. P., Carte, E. T., & Morrison, D. C. (1986). Concurrent prediction of academic achievement in reading disabled children: The role of neuropsychological and intellectual measures at different ages. *Clinical Neuropsychology, 8,* 3-8.

31. Rantakallio, P., & von Wendt, L. (1986). Mental retardation and subnormality in a birth cohort of 12,000 children in Northern Finland. *American Journal of Mental Deficiency, 90,* 380-387.

32. Shinn-Strieker, T. (1986). Patterns of cognitive style in normal and handicapped children. *Journal of Learning Disabilities, 19,* 572-576.

33. Twomey, A. T., & DeLacey, P. (1986). Correlates of a culture-of-poverty measure. A study of Australian aboriginal and white populations. *Journal of Cross-Cultural Psychology, 17,* 67-82.

34. Kalliopuska, M., & Karila, I. (1987). Association of motor performance and cognitive, linguistic, and socioemotional factors. *Perceptual and Motor Skills, 65,* 399-405.

35. Liles, B. Z. (1987). Episode organization and cohesive conjunctives in narratives of children with and without language disorder. *Journal of Speech and Hearing Research, 30,* 185-196.

36. Lovett, M. W. (1987). A developmental approach to reading disability: Accuracy and speed criteria of normal and deficient reading skill. *Child Development, 58,* 234-260.

37. Abraham, S., & Stoker, R. (1988). Language assessment of hearing-impaired children and youth: Patterns of test use. *Language, Speech, and Hearing Services in Schools, 19,* 160-174.

38. Kunsinen, J., & Leskinen, E. (1988). Latent structure analysis of longitudinal data on relations between intellectual abilities and school achievement. *Multivariate Behavioral Research, 23,* 103-118.

39. McGee, R., Williams, S., & Silva, P. A. (1988). Slow starters and long-term backward readers: A replication and extension. *British Journal of Educational Psychology, 58,* 330-337.

40. Altepeter, T. S. (1989). The PPVT-R as a measure of psycholinguistic functioning: A caution. *Journal of Clinical Psychology, 45,* 935-941.

41. Haxby, J. V. (1989). Neuropsychological evaluation of adults with Down's syndrome: Patterns of selective impairment in non-demented old adults. *Journal of Mental Deficiency Research, 33,* 193-210.

42. Sininger, Y. S., Klatzky, R. L., & Kirchner, D. M. (1989). Memory scanning speed in language-disordered children. *Journal of Speech and Hearing Research, 32,* 289-297.

43. Becker, M., Warr-Leeper, G. A., & Leeper, H. A., Jr. (1990). Fetal alcohol syndrome: A description of oral motor, articulatory, short-term memory, grammatical, and semantic abilities. *Journal of Communication Disorders, 23,* 97-124.

44. Bell, T. K. (1990). Rapid sequential processing in dyslexic and ordinary readers. *Perceptual and Motor Skills, 71,* 1155-1159.

45. Condino, R., Im-Humber, K., & Stark, R. E. (1990). Cognitive processing in specifically language-impaired children. *The Journal of Psychology, 124,* 465-479.

46. Nakamura, M., Plante, E., & Swisher, L. (1990). Predictors of novel inflection learning by preschool-aged boys. *Journal of Speech and Hearing Research, 33,* 747-754.

47. van der Lely, H. K. J., & Harris, M. (1990). Comprehension of reversible sentences in specifically language-impaired children. *Journal of Speech and Hearing Disorders, 55,* 101-117.

48. Menyuk, P., Chesnick, M., Liebergott, J. W., Korngold, B., D'Agostino, R., & Belanger, A. (1991). Predicting reading problems in at-risk children. *Journal of Speech and Hearing Research, 34,* 893-903.

49. Russell, R. L., Greenwald, S., & Shirk, S. R. (1991). Language change in child psychotherapy: A meta-analytic review. *Journal of Consulting and Clinical Psychology, 59,* 916-919.

50. Whitehurst, G. J., Arnold, D. S., Smith, M., Fischel, J. E., Lonigan, C. J., & Valdez-Menchaca, M. C. (1991). Family history in developmental expressive language delay. *Journal of Speech and Hearing Research, 34,* 1150-1157.

51. Whitehurst, G. J., Smith, M., Fischel, J. E., Arnold, D. S., & Lonigan, C. J. (1991). The continuity of babble and speech in children with specific expressive language delay. *Journal of Speech and Hearing Research, 34,* 1121-1129.

52. Highnam, C., & Sheppard, J. (1992). Spontaneous verbal rehearsal effects upon recognition among first-graders. *Perceptual and Motor Skills, 75,* 970.

53. Rose, S. A., Feldman, J. F., & Wallace, I. F. (1992). Infant information processing in relation to six-year cognitive outcomes. *Child Development, 63,* 1126-1141.

[1203]

Illness Behaviour Questionnaire, Second Edition.

Purpose: "To record aspects of illness behaviour, particularly those attitudes that suggest inappropriate or maladaptive modes of responding to one's state of health."

Population: Pain clinic, psychiatric, and general practice patients.

Publication Date: 1983.

Acronym: IBQ.

Scores, 8: 7 factors (General Hypochondriasis, Disease Conviction, Psychological vs. Somatic Perception of Illness, Affective Inhibition, Affective Disturbance, Denial, Irritability) and Whitely Index of Hypochondriasis.

Administration: Individual or group.

Price Data: Available from publisher.

Time: (10) minutes.

Comments: Self-report instrument.

Authors: I. Pilowsky and N. D. Spence.

Publisher: I. Pilowsky [South Australia].

TEST REFERENCES

1. Stein, N., Fruchter, H. J., & Trief, P. (1983). Experiences of depression and illness behavior in patients with intractable chronic pain. *Journal of Clinical Psychology, 39,* 31-33.
2. Colgan, S., Creed, F., & Klass, H. (1988). Symptom complaints, psychiatric disorder and abnormal illness behaviour in patients with upper abdominal pain. *Psychological Medicine, 18,* 887-892.
3. Simon, G. E., Katon, W. J., & Sparks, P. J. (1990). Allergic to life: Psychological factors in environmental illness. *American Journal of Psychiatry, 147,* 901-906.
4. Bridges, K., Goldberg, D., Evans, B., & Sharpe, T. (1991). Determinants of somatization in primary care. *Psychological Medicine, 21,* 473-483.
5. Dworkin, R. H., Hartstein, G., Rosner, H. L., Walther, R. R., Sweeney, E. W., & Brand, L. (1992). A high-risk method for studying psychosocial antecedents of chronic pain: The prospective investigation of Herpes Zoster. *Journal of Abnormal Psychology, 101,* 200-205.
6. Riccio, M., Thompson, C., Wilson, B., Morgan, D. J. R., & Lant, A. F. (1992). Neuropsychological and psychiatric abnormalities in myalgic encephalomyelitis: A preliminary report. *British Journal of Clinical Psychology, 31,* 111-120.

[1204]

Imagery and Disease.

Purpose: Constructed to evaluate the process of disease using a combination of guided imagery, relaxation, patient drawings, and structured interview.

Publication Dates: 1978–84.

Administration: Individual.

Price Data, 1994: $20.50 per handbook ('84, 261 pages).

Time: Administration time not reported.

Comments: Previous edition entitled Imagery of Cancer (9:499).

Authors: Jeanne Achterberg and G. Frank Lawlis.

Publisher: Institute for Personality and Ability Testing, Inc.

a) IMAGE-CA.

Population: Cancer patients.

Scores, 14: Disease Dimensions (Vividness of Cancer Cells, Activity of the Cancer Cells, Strength of Cancer Cells), The Body's Defenses (Vividness of White Blood Cells, Activity of White Blood Cells, Numerosity of White Blood Cells, Size of White Blood Cells, Strength of White Blood Cells), Treatment (Vividness of Treatment, Effectiveness of Treatment), General Characteristics of the Imagery (Symbolism, Overall Strength of Imagery, Estimated Regularity of Imagery, Clinical Judgment).

b) IMAGE-SP.

Population: Spinal pain patients.

Scores, 2: Affective, Prediction of Treatment Response.

c) IMAGE-DB.

Population: Diabetic patients.

Scores, 16: Vividness of the Pancreas, Activity of the Pancreas, Strength of the Pancreas, Size of the Pancreas, Vividness of the Beta Cells, Activity of the Beta Cells, Numerosity of the Beta Cells, Size of Beta Cells, Strength of the Beta Cells, Vividness of the Insulin, Quantity of Insulin, Effectiveness of the Insulin, Symbolization Versus Realism, Overall Strength of Imagery, Overall Regularity of the Positive Image, Clinical Impressions.

[1205]

Impact Message Inventory, Research Edition.

Purpose: "Designed to measure . . . interpersonal style."

Population: College.

Publication Dates: 1975–87.

Acronym: IMI.

Scores, 15: Dominant, Competitive, Hostile, Mistrustful, Detached, Inhibited, Submissive, Succorant, Abasive, Deferent, Agreeable, Nurturant, Affiliative, Sociable, Exhibitionistic.

Administration: Group.

Forms, 2: Male Targets, Female Targets.

Price Data, 1992: $17 per 25 test booklets (select Male or Female); $14 per 50 answer sheets; $15 per manual ('87, 60 pages); $16 per specimen set.

Time: [15] minutes.

Comments: Self-report inventory.

Author: Donald J. Kiesler.

Publisher: Consulting Psychologists Press, Inc.

Cross References: For reviews by Fred H. Borgen and Stanley R. Strong of an earlier edition, see 9:500 (1 reference); see also T3:1130 (1 reference).

TEST REFERENCES

1. Kivlighan, D. M., McGovern, T. V., & Corazzini, J. G. (1984). Effects of content and timing of structuring interventions on group therapy process and outcome. *Journal of Counseling Psychology, 31,* 363-370.
2. Lowenstein, D. A., & Hokanson, J. E. (1986). The processing of social information by mildly and moderately dysphoric college students. *Cognitive Therapy and Research, 10,* 447-460.
3. Stephens, R. S., Hokanson, J. E., & Welker, R. (1987). Responses to depressed interpersonal behavior: Mixed reactions in a helping role. *Journal of Personality and Social Psychology, 52,* 1274-1282.
4. Kiesler, D. J., & Goldston, C. S. (1988). Client-therapist complimentarity: An analysis of the Gloria films. *Journal of Counseling Psychology, 35,* 127-133.
5. Strong, S. R., Hills, H. I., Kilmartin, C. T., DeVries, H., Lanier, K., Nelson, B. N., Strickland, D., & Meyer, C. W., III. (1988). The dynamic relations among interpersonal behaviors: A test of

complementarity and anticomplementarity. *Journal of Personality and Social Psychology, 54,* 798-810.

6. Dobson, K. S. (1989). Real and perceived interpersonal responses to subclinically anxious and depressed targets. *Cognitive Therapy and Research, 13,* 37-47.

7. Gotlib, I. H., & Whiffen, V. E. (1989). Depression and marital functioning: An examination of specificity and gender differences. *Journal of Abnormal Psychology, 98,* 23-30.

8. Bluhm, C., & Widiger, T. A. (1990). Interpersonal complementarity and individual differences. *Journal of Personality and Social Psychology, 58,* 464-471.

9. Shean, G., & Uchenwa, U. (1990). Interpersonal style and anxiety. *The Journal of Psychology, 124,* 403-408.

10. Swaney, K. B., & Stone, G. L. (1990). Therapist awareness of covert reactions to client interpersonal behavior. *Journal of Social and Clinical Psychology, 9,* 375-389.

11. Segrin, C., & Dillard, J. P. (1992). The interactional theory of depression: A meta-analysis of the research literature. *Journal of Social and Clinical Psychology, 11,* 43-70.

12. Simon, L., Graul, R., Friedlander, M. L., & Heatherington, L. (1992). Client gender and sex role: Predictors of counselors' impressions and expectations. *Journal of Counseling and Development, 71,* 48-52.

13. Van Denburg, T. F., Schmidt, J. A., & Kiesler, D. J. (1992). Interpersonal assessment in counseling and psychotherapy. *Journal of Counseling and Development, 71,* 84-90.

[1206]

Independent Living Behavior Checklist.

Purpose: Identify and define independent living skills.

Population: Behaviorally impaired adults.

Publication Date: 1979.

Acronym: ILBC.

Scores: 6 areas: Mobility Skills, Self-Care Skills, Home Maintenance and Safety Skills, Good Skills, Social and Communication Skills, Functional Academic Skills.

Administration: Individual.

Price Data, 1988: $8 per text with skill summary charts.

Time: Administration time varies according to objective.

Comments: "Criterion-referenced."

Authors: Richard T. Walls, Thomas Zane, and John E. Thvedt.

Publisher: West Virginia Research and Training Center.

Cross References: For reviews by Jean Dirks and Louis J. Finkle, see 9:503.

[1207]

Independent Mastery Testing System for Math Skills.

Purpose: "To monitor the student's mastery of basic mathematics skills, to diagnose specific student weaknesses, to recommend a program of further study, and to provide the teacher with a comprehensive record of student progress."

Population: Adult students.

Publication Date: 1984.

Acronym: IMTS.

Scores: 13 tests: Adding and Subtracting Whole Numbers, Multiplying and Dividing Whole Numbers, Adding and Subtracting Fractions, Multiplying and Dividing Fractions, Adding and Subtracting Decimals, Multiplying and Dividing Decimals, Percents Skills, Charts and Graphs Skills, Measurement Skills, The Language of Algebra, The Uses of Algebra, Geometry—Angles, Geometry—Plane and Solid Figures.

Administration: Individual.

Forms: 3 parallel forms of each test.

Price Data: Not available.

Time: Administration time not reported.

Comments: Computer-administered instructional management system; Apple II, Apple II +, Apple IIe, or Apple IIc computer necessary for administration.

Authors: Cambridge, The Adult Education Company in association with Moravian College, Bethlehem, PA.

Publisher: Simon & Schuster Higher Education Group [No reply from publisher; status unknown].

Cross References: For a review by Richard M. Jaeger, see 10:147.

[1208]

Independent Mastery Testing System for Writing Skills.

Purpose: "To monitor the student's mastery of basic grammar and writing skills, to diagnose specific student weaknesses, to recommend a program of further study, and to provide the teacher with a comprehensive record of student progress."

Population: Adult students.

Publication Date: 1984.

Acronym: IMTS.

Scores: 15 tests: Recognizing Sentences, Verb Tenses, Subject-Verb Agreement—Part A, Subject-Verb Agreement—Part B, Pronouns—Part A, Pronouns—Part B, Plurals and Possessives, Adjectives and Adverbs—Part A, Adjectives and Adverbs—Part B, Sentence Structure, Prepositions and Conjunctions, Logic and Organization, Capitalization, Punctuation, Spelling.

Administration: Individual.

Forms: 3 parallel forms (1, 2, 3) of each test.

Price Data: Not available.

Time: Administration time not reported.

Comments: Computer-administered instructional management system; Apple II, Apple II +, Apple IIe, or Apple IIc computer necessary for administration.

Author: Cambridge, The Adult Education Company, in association with Moravian College, Bethlehem, PA.

Publisher: Simon & Schuster Higher Education Group [No reply from publisher; status unknown].

Cross References: For a review by Pamela A. Moss, see 11:173.

[1209]

Independent School Entrance Examination.

Purpose: Developed to assess verbal ability, quantitative ability, reading comprehension, and mathematics achievement for use in admissions into independent schools and to provide independent schools with a candidate's writing sample given under standard conditions.

Population: Grades 5–7, 8–11, or candidates for grades 6–8 and 9–12.

Publication Date: 1989.
Acronym: ISEE.
Scores, 4: Verbal Ability, Quantitative Ability, Reading Comprehension, Mathematics Achievement.
Administration: Group.
Levels, 2: Middle, Upper.
Forms, 2: A, B.
Price Data: Price data including technical manual ('89, 104 pages) available from publisher.
Time: 130 minutes; 30 minutes for essay component.
Comments: Test book name is ISEE; essay component is not scored but is sent to schools.
Author: Educational Records Bureau, Inc.
Publisher: Educational Records Bureau, Inc.
Cross References: For reviews by Mary Anne Bunda and Joyce R. McLarty, see 11:174.

[1210]

Index of Personality Characteristics.
Purpose: "To screen the personal and social adjustment of school-aged children and adolescents."
Population: Ages 8-0 to 17-11.
Publication Date: 1988.
Acronym: IPC.
Scores, 9: Personality Quotient, Academic Scale, Nonacademic Scale, Perception of Self Scale, Perception of Others Scale, Acting In Scale, Acting Out Scale, Internal Locus of Control Scale, External Locus of Control Scale.
Administration: Group.
Price Data, 1994: $69 per complete kit; $28 per 50 student response booklets; $19 per 50 profile and record forms; $25 per manual (69 pages).
Time: (30–45) minutes.
Comments: Self-ratings scale; may be orally administered.
Authors: Linda Brown and Margaret C. Coleman.
Publisher: PRO-ED, Inc.
Cross References: For reviews by Patricia A. Bachelor and Jayne E. Stake, see 11:175.

[1211]

Indiana Physical Fitness Test.
Purpose: For identifying the physical fitness status of students.
Population: Grades 4–12.
Publication Date: 1964.
Scores, 4: Straddle Chins, Squat Thrusts, Push Ups, Vertical Jump.
Administration: Individual.
Price Data: Not available.
Time: (50) minutes.
Authors: Karl W. Bookwalter and Harold J. Walter (norms).
Publisher: Indiana Public Health Foundation, Inc. [No reply from publisher; status unknown].

[1212]

Indiana-Oregon Music Discrimination Test.
Purpose: Designed to be a measure of music appreciation.

Population: Grades 5 through graduate school.
Publication Dates: 1967–75 (no dates on test materials).
Scores: Total score only.
Administration: Group.
Price Data, 1987: $12.50 per complete kit including 3 answer sheets, 12-inch record, 2 scoring keys, and manual (17 pages).
Time: [30–40] minutes.
Comments: Revision of Oregon Music Discrimination Test ('34) by Kate Hevner; first 30 items (Test E) primarily for grades 5–9, first 37 items (Test J) primarily for grades 7–9, all 43 items (Test S) primarily for grades 9 and over; answer sheets must be reproduced locally.
Authors: Newell H. Long.
Publisher: Midwest Music Tests.
Cross References: See T3:1135 (1 reference); for reviews by Richard Colwell and Paul R. Lehman, see 8:96 (16 references).

[1213]

Individual Scale for Indian South Africans.
Purpose: "To measure certain aspects of developmental intelligence."
Population: Ages 8–17.
Publication Date: 1971.
Acronym: ISISA.
Scores, 13: Verbal (Vocabulary, Comprehension, Similarities, Problems, Memory, Total), Nonverbal (Pattern Completion, Blocks, Absurdities, Form Board, Mazes, Total), Total.
Administration: Individual.
Price Data: Available from publisher.
Time: Administration time not reported.
Comments: Scale may only be administered by testers who are proficient in psychological testing techniques and who have been properly trained to administer this test; adaptation for Indian pupils of the New South African Individual Scale.
Authors: R. J. Prinsloo and F. W. O. Heinichen in collaboration with D. J. Swart.
Publisher: Human Sciences Research Council [South Africa].

[1214]

Individual Service Strategy Portfolio.
Purpose: Designed to help human service organizations gather information about clients' vocational plans and to assist in creating such plans.
Population: Human service clients.
Publication Date: 1993.
Acronym: ISSP.
Scores: Total Assets and Barriers for 7 categories: Personal Considerations, Health, Work Orientation, Career Planning Skills, Job Seeking Skills, Job Adaptation Skills, Education and Training.
Administration: Individual.
Price Data: Available from publisher.
Time: Administration time not reported.
Authors: LaVerne L. Ludden (manual and portfo-

lio), Bonnie R. Maitlen (manual and portfolio), and J. Michael Farr (portfolio).

Publisher: JIST Works, Inc.

[1215]

Individual Style Survey.

Purpose: "Intended to be an educational tool for self and interpersonal development."

Publication Dates: 1989–90.

Administration: Group.

Price Data: Available from publisher.

Time: (60–90) minutes.

Comments: Self-administered, self-scored survey.

Author: Norman Amundson.

Publisher: Psychometrics Canada Ltd. [Canada].

a) INDIVIDUAL STYLE SURVEY.

Population: Adults.

Publication Date: 1989.

Acronym: ISS.

Scores, 14: 8 categories of behavior (Forceful, Assertive, Outgoing, Spontaneous, Empathetic, Patient, Reserved, Analytical) yielding 4 styles (Dominant, Influencing, Harmonious, Cautious) that combine to form 2 summary scores (People/Task Orientation, Introspective/Interactive Stance).

b) MY PERSONAL STYLE.

Population: Ages 10–18.

Publication Date: 1990.

Acronym: MPS.

Scores, 14: 8 categories (Carefree, Outgoing, Straight Forward, Forceful, Precise, Reserved, Patient, Sensitive) yielding 4 styles (Influencing, Strong Willed, Cautious, Peaceful) that combine to form 2 summary scores (People/Task Orientation, Expressive/Thoughtful Stance).

Comments: Simplified version of the Individual Style Survey for use with young people.

[1216]

Individualised Classroom Environment Questionnaire.

Purpose: "An instrument for measuring perceptions of the classroom environment among secondary school students or their teachers."

Population: Junior and senior high school students and teachers.

Publication Date: 1990.

Acronym: ICEQ.

Scores, 5: Personalisation, Participation, Independence, Investigation, Differentiation.

Administration: Group.

Forms, 4: Actual Classroom-Long Form, Actual Classroom-Short Form, Preferred Classroom-Long Form, Preferred Classroom-Short Form.

Price Data, 1991: A$49.95 per complete materials including manual (39 pages).

Time: (10–15) minutes for short form; (15–30) minutes for long form.

Comments: Test forms contained in manual may be photocopied by purchaser.

Author: Barry J. Fraser.

Publisher: Australian Council for Educational Research Ltd. [Australia].

Cross References: For a review by Lawrence M. Aleamoni, see 11:176.

[1217]

Individualized Criterion Referenced Testing.

Purpose: "Designed to measure student achievement against a specific set of math and reading objectives."

Publication Dates: 1973–90.

Acronym: ICRT.

Administration: Individual or group.

Price Data: Price information available from publisher for test material including technical manual ('90, 81 pages), teacher's guide for Reading ('90, 87 pages), and teacher's guide for Math ('90, 79 pages).

Time: Administration time not reported.

Comments: Designed to be taken at the student's functional level rather than grade level; each student takes 5 booklets measuring 40 objectives; each test booklet contains 16 items measuring 8 objectives; computer scoring with 10-day turnaround available from publisher; administration time varies with individual students.

Authors: Wanda M. Richardson, Deanna Thompson, Jo Riffe, and Anna Mae Callaway.

Publisher: Educational Development Corporation.

a) ICRT MATH.

Population: Grades 1, 2, 3, 4, 5, 6, 7, 8, 9.

Acronym: ICRTM.

Scores: Total score only.

Comments: Skills are tested in six strands: Whole Number Operations, Measurement, Decimal-Percent, Fractions, Geometry, Special Topics; criterion and norm-referenced scores.

b) ICRT READING.

Population: Grades 1, 2, 3, 4, 5, 6, 7, 8.

Acronym: ICRTR.

Scores: Total score only.

Comments: Skills are tested in four strands: Phonetic Analysis, Structural Analysis, Word Function, Comprehension; criterion and norm-referenced scores.

Cross References: For a review of ICRTM by Jane Dass, see 8:275; for reviews of ICRTR by Ruth N. Hartley and Martin Kling, see 8:764.

[1218]

Indonesian Speaking Test.

Purpose: "Designed to evaluate the level of oral proficiency attained by English speaking learners of Indonesian."

Population: Adults.

Publication Date: 1989.

Acronym: IST.

Scores, 6: Personal Conversation, Giving Directions, Picture Sequence Narration, Topical Discourse, Situational Discourse, Total.

Administration: Group.

Price Data: Available from publisher.

Time: (40–45) minutes.

Comments: Mail-in scoring.
Author: Center for Applied Linguistics.
Publisher: Center for Applied Linguistics.

[1219]

Industrial Reading Test.
Purpose: "Measures an individual's ability to comprehend written technical materials."
Population: Grade 9 and over vocational students and applicants or trainees in technical or vocational training programs.
Publication Dates: 1976–78.
Acronym: IRT.
Scores: Total score only.
Forms, 2: A, B.
Administration: Group.
Restricted Distribution: Distribution of Form A restricted to business firms.
Price Data, 1994: $56 per 25 test booklets (specify form); $39 per IBM 805/OpScan Answer Documents; $16 per keys for hand scoring IBM 805/OpScan Answer Documents (specify form); $21 per manual ('78, 30 pages).
Time: 40(45) minutes.
Comments: Separate IBM 805/OpScan answer sheets must be used with reusable booklets for Form A or B.
Author: Psychological Measurement Division.
Publisher: The Psychological Corporation.
Cross References: For a review by Darrell L. Sabers, see 9:504.

[1220]

The Industrial Sentence Completion Form.
Purpose: Designed for use "in industrial selection and evaluation situations."
Population: Industrial applicants.
Publication Date: 1963.
Scores: No scores.
Administration: Group.
Manual: No manual.
Price Data: Available from publisher.
Time: (20–30) minutes.
Comments: Experimental form.
Author: Martin M. Bruce.
Publisher: Martin M. Bruce, Ph.D., Publishers.

[1221]

Industrial Test Battery.
Purpose: Intended to assess an individual's conceptual reasoning and spatial abilities.
Population: Individuals with less than 7 years of formal schooling.
Publication Date: 1986.
Acronym: ITB.
Scores: Total score only for each test.
Subtests, 3: Anomalous Concept Test (ACT), Anomalous Figure Test (AFT), Series Induction Test (SIT).
Administration: Group.
Price Data: Available from publisher.

Foreign Language Edition: Tests printed in both English and Afrikaans.
Time: 20(30) minutes for ACT; 25(35) minutes for AFT; 30(40) minutes for SIT.
Author: T. R. Taylor.
Publisher: National Institute for Personnel Research of the Human Sciences Research Council [South Africa].

[1222]

The Infanib.
Purpose: Designed to provide a systematic scorable method to assess the neurological status of infants, especially infants who are premature or have special conditions.
Population: Infants from birth to 18 months corrected gestational age.
Publication Date: 1994.
Scores, 20: Hands Open, Hands Closed, Scarf Sign, Heel-To-Ear, Popliteal Angle, Leg Abduction, Dorsiflexion of the Foot, The Foot Grasp, Tonic Labyrinthine Supine, Asymmetric Tonic Neck Reflex, Pull-To-Sitting, Body Denotative, Body Rotative, All-Fours, Tonic Labyrinthine Prone, Sitting, Sideways Parachute, Backwards Parachute, Standing-Positive Support Reaction, Forward Parachute.
Administration: Individual.
Price Data: Available from publisher.
Time: Untimed.
Comments: "Criterion-referenced" test with ratings determined by therapist.
Author: Patricia H. Ellison.
Publisher: Therapy Skill Builders.

[1223]

Infant Mullen Scales of Early Learning.
Purpose: Assesses a child's cognitive abilities and gross motor base for learning.
Population: Infants (birth to 39 months).
Publication Date: 1984–89.
Acronym: Infant MSEL.
Scores: 5 scales: Gross Motor Base, Visual Receptive Organization, Visual Expressive Organization, Language Receptive Organization, Language Expressive Organization.
Administration: Individual.
Price Data: Available from publisher.
Time: (15–45) minutes.
Authors: Eileen M. Mullen.
Publisher: American Guidance Service, Inc.
Cross References: For a review by Verna Hart, see 11:177.

[1224]

The Infant Reading Tests.
Population: Ages 4-7 to 7.
Publication Date: 1979.
Administration: Group.
Price Data, 1989: $19.25 per complete set for pre-reading including 25 of each test and manual (12 pages); $14.25 per complete set for reading including

25 of each test and manual; $7.10 per pre-reading group set including 8 of each test; $5.55 per reading group set including 8 of each test; $1.25 per manual.
Time: (20) minutes.
Authors: Alan Brimer and Bridie Raban.
Publisher: Educational Evaluation Enterprises [England].

a) PRE-READING TESTS.
Purpose: Developed to assess "linguistic competence; the ability to use printed symbols; the recognition of speech sounds; and the discrimination of printed shapes varying in orientation."
1) *Test 1.*
Scores: Total score only.
2) *Test 2.*
Scores, 3: Beginning Sounds, Middle Sounds, End Sounds.
3) *Test 3.*
Scores: Total score only.

b) READING TESTS.
Purpose: Constructed to assess "contributory skills of word recognition, sentence completion and reading comprehension."
Scores: Total score only.
Levels, 3: Test 1, Test 2, Test 3.
Cross References: For a review by Carl J. Dunst, see 9:505.

[1225]

Infant Screening.
Purpose: Constructed to identify children at risk for "educational, social and emotional difficulties."
Population: Ages 5–6.
Publication Date: 1981.
Scores: 6 areas: Visual Reception, Auditory Reception, Association Skill, Sequential Skill, Expression, Reading Difficulties.
Administration: Group.
Price Data, 1988: £3.25 per 10 test booklets; £2.75 per 20 checklists; £4.25 per 25 pupil profiles; £9.50 per teacher's book (73 pages) and 8 diagnostic test cards.
Time: Administration time not reported.
Author: Humberside Education Authority.
Publisher: Macmillan Education Ltd. [England].
Cross References: For reviews by Cathy F. Telzrow and Stanley F. Vasa, see 10:148.

[1226]

Infant/Toddler Environment Rating Scale.
Purpose: Developed to assess "the quality of center-based child care for children up to 30 months of age."
Population: Infant/toddler day care centers.
Publication Date: 1990.
Acronym: ITERS.
Scores, 8: Furnishings and Display for Children, Listening and Talking, Personal Care Routines, Learning Activities, Interaction, Program Structure, Adult Needs, Total.
Administration: Individual.

Price Data, 1993: $8.95 per rating scale; $7.95 per 30 scoring sheets.
Time: (120) minutes to observe and rate.
Comments: Adaptation of the Early Childhood Environment Rating Scales (9:365) and the Family Day Care Rating Scale (960).
Authors: Thelma Harms, Debby Cryer, and Richard M. Clifford.
Publisher: Teachers College Press.

[1227]

Inferred Self-Concept Scale.
Purpose: Designed to determine children's self-concept based on behavior ratings in the school setting.
Population: Grades 1–6.
Publication Dates: 1969–73.
Acronym: ISCS.
Scores: Total score only.
Administration: Individual.
Price Data, 1993: $45 per complete kit; $19.50 per 100 scales; $26.50 per manual ('73, 13 pages including test).
Time: [3–5] minutes.
Comments: Ratings by teachers and counselors.
Author: E. L. McDaniel.
Publisher: Western Psychological Services.
Cross References: For a review by Norman D. Sundberg, see 8:584; see also T2:1231 (1 reference).

TEST REFERENCES
1. Chiu, L. H. (1988). Measures of self-esteem for school-age children. *Journal of Counseling and Development, 66,* 298-301.

[1228]

Influence Strategies Exercise.
Purpose: Designed to identify various influence strategies used by individuals.
Population: Managers and employees.
Publication Date: 1990.
Acronym: ISE.
Scores, 9: Empowerment, Interpersonal Awareness, Bargaining, Relationship Building, Organizational Awareness, Common Vision, Impact Management, Logical Persuasion, Coercion.
Administration: Group.
Parts, 2: Participant Version, Employee Version (optional).
Price Data, 1993: $60 per complete kit including 10 exercises and 10 profiles and interpretive notes (19 pages); $25 per 10 employee version exercises.
Time: (20–25) minutes.
Comments: Self-administered questionnaire.
Author: McBer & Company.
Publisher: McBer & Company.

[1229]

Informal Reading Comprehension Placement Test [Revised].
Purpose: "Assesses the instructional and independent comprehension levels of students from pre-readiness (grade 1) through level twelve plus (grade 12)."

Population: Grades 1–8 for typical learners and grades 8–12 remedially; adult education students.
Publication Dates: 1983–93.
Scores, 3: Word Comprehension, Passage Comprehension, Total Comprehension.
Administration: Individual.
Price Data, 1994: $49.95 per test.
Time: (35–50) minutes for the battery; (15–20) minutes for Part 1; (20–30) minutes for Part 2.
Comments: Automatically administered, scored, and managed; for use with adults, the placements are correlated with Tests of Adult Basic Education (2812); test administered in two parts; Apple II or IBM microcomputer necessary for administration.
Authors: Ann Edson and Eunice Insel.
Publisher: Educational Activities, Inc.
Cross References: For reviews by Gloria A. Galvin and Claudia R. Wright, see 11:178.

[1230]
Information System Skills.
Purpose: Constructed to predict "a person's success in operating terminal based information systems."
Population: Information processing job applicants.
Publication Date: 1983.
Acronym: ISS.
Scores, 4: Reasoning, Form Recognition, Document Checking, Speed.
Administration: Group.
Price Data: Available from publisher.
Time: 36 minutes and 30 seconds (45 minutes).
Author: Malcolm Morrisby.
Publisher: Educational & Industrial Test Services Ltd.

[1231]
Information Test on Drugs and Drug Abuse.
Purpose: To discover what subjects know about drugs and drug abuse.
Population: Grades 9–16 and adults.
Publication Dates: 1957–68.
Scores: Total score only.
Administration: Group.
Manual: No manual.
Price Data: Available from publisher.
Time: Administration time not reported.
Comments: For research purposes only.
Author: H. Frederick Kilander and Glenn C. Leach.
Publisher: Glenn C. Leach, Publisher.

[1232]
Information Test on Human Reproduction.
Purpose: To discover what subjects know about human reproduction.
Population: Grades 9–16 and adults.
Publication Dates: 1950–67.
Scores: Total score only.
Administration: Group.
Manual: No manual.
Price Data: Available from publisher.
Time: Administration time not reported.
Comments: For research purposes only.

Author: H. Frederick Kilander.
Publisher: Glenn C. Leach, Publisher.
Cross References: See T2:934 (1 reference).

[1233]
Information Test on Smoking and Health.
Purpose: To discover what subjects know about issues related to smoking and health.
Population: Grades 9–16 and adults.
Publication Date: 1984.
Scores: Total score only.
Administration: Group.
Manual: No manual.
Price Data: Available from publisher.
Time: Administration time not reported.
Comments: For educational or research purposes only.
Author: H. Frederick Kilander.
Publisher: Glenn C. Leach, Publisher.

[1234]
Informeter: An International Technique for the Measurement of Political Information.
Purpose: Designed to measure political information.
Population: Adults.
Publication Date: 1972.
Scores, 5: Local, National, International, Miscellaneous, Total.
Administration: Group.
Manual: No manual.
Price Data: Available without charge from author.
Time: [15] minutes.
Author: Panos D. Bardis.
Publisher: Panos D. Bardis.

[1235]
Initial Placement Inventory.
Purpose: "Designed to aid the classroom teacher in determining the appropriate placement of the student for instruction in SERIES r, Macmillan Reading."
Population: Grades 1–8.
Publication Date: 1980.
Scores: 3 areas: Silent Reading (Number of Correct Answers, Reading Level, Placement Level), Word Recognition (Total score only), Oral Reading (Number of Decoding Errors, Reading Level, Number of Correct Comprehensive Questions, Reading Level).
Administration: Individual.
Levels: Selected levels for grades 1–8 in 3 areas.
Price Data: Not available.
Time: Administration time not reported.
Comments: Criterion-referenced.
Author: Madeline A. Weinstein.
Publisher: MacMillan Publishing Co., Inc. [No reply from publisher; status unknown].

[1236]
Inquiry Mode Questionnaire: A Measure of How You Think and Make Decisions.
Purpose: Developed to measure "individual preferences in the way people think."
Population: Business and industry.

Publication Dates: 1977–89.
Acronym: INQ.
Scores, 5: Synthesist, Idealist, Pragmatist, Analyst, Realist.
Administration: Group or individual.
Price Data: Not available.
Time: (20) minutes.
Comments: Manual title is *INQ Styles of Thinking.*
Authors: Allen F. Harrison and Robert M. Bramson.
Publisher: INQ Educational Materials Inc. [No reply from publisher; status unknown.]

[1237]

INSIGHT Inventory.
Purpose: To help "participants improve their communication with others, thereby enhancing teamwork and interpersonal relationships."
Population: High school students or employees.
Publication Dates: 1988–90.
Scores, 16: 8 profile scores for each area Work Style and Personal Style: Getting Your Way (Direct, Indirect), Responding to People (Reserved, Outgoing), Pacing Activity (Urgent, Steady), Dealing with Details (Unstructured, Precise).
Administration: Group.
Forms, 2: A, B.
Price Data, 1993: $25 preview package including interviewing with INSIGHT, Forms A and B, and style feedback set; $195 per INSIGHT training manual including training guide, skill building exercises, technical manual ('89, 65 pages), and overhead transparency masters; $12 per style feedback set; $295 per video program; $395 per trainer's package including training manual and video program; $12 per Form A; $6 per Form B.
Time: (15–30) minutes.
Comments: Self-report behavior profile.
Author: Patrick Handley.
Publisher: Human Resource Development Press.

[1238]

Institutional Goals Inventory.
Purpose: Developed "as a tool that a college may use in identifying basic campus goals and in determining priorities among diverse goals."
Population: College faculty and students and other subgroups.
Publication Dates: 1972–77.
Acronym: IGI.
Scores: 3 scores (Goal Is, Goal Should Be, Discrepancy) for total group and each subgroup for each of 90 goal statements and each of 20 goal summary areas (based on 80 of the goal statements): Academic Development, Intellectual Orientation, Individual Personal Development, Humanism/Altruism, Cultural/Aesthetic Awareness, Traditional Religiousness, Vocational Preparation, Advanced Training, Research, Meeting Local Needs, Public Service, Social Egalitarianism, Social Criticism/Activism, Freedom, Democratic Governance, Community, Intellectual/Aesthetic

Environment, Innovation, Off-Campus Learning, Accountability/Efficiency.
Administration: Group.
Price Data, 1994: $15 per specimen set including copies of the instrument, a prospectus, manual ('77, 102 pages), and other supporting publications.
Foreign Language Editions: French Canadian and English Canadian editions available.
Time: (45) minutes.
Authors: Richard E. Peterson and Norman P. Uhl.
Publisher: Educational Testing Service.
Cross References: For additional information and reviews by Clifford E. Lunneborg and M. Y. Quereshi, see 8:375 (31 references); see also T2:1235 (2 references).

[1239]

The Instructional Environment System-II: A System to Identify a Student's Instructional Needs (Second Edition).
Purpose: "Designed to assist education professionals in a systematic analysis of a target student's instructional environment, which includes both school and home contexts."
Population: Grades K–12.
Publication Dates: 1987–93.
Acronym: TIES-II.
Scores: 12 Instructional Environment Components (Instructional Match, Teacher Expectations, Classroom Environment, Instructional Presentation, Cognitive Emphasis, Motivational Strategies, Relevant Practice, Informed Feedback, Academic Engaged Time, Adaptive Instruction, Progress Evaluation, Student Understanding), 5 Home Support for Learning Components (Expectations and Attributions, Discipline Orientation, Home Affective Environment, Parent Participation, Structure for Learning).
Administration: Individual.
Forms, 4: Instructional Needs Checklist, Parent Interview Record, Home Support for Learning Form, Instructional Environment Form.
Price Data, 1994: $47.50 per TIES-II Program Kit including 15 copies of each of the 4 forms and manual ('93, 199 pages); $19.50 per replacement forms set including 15 copies of each of the 4 forms.
Time: Administration time not reported.
Comments: Observational and interview data from teachers, parents, and students is gathered by an education professional; can be used in regular classrooms, homes, special education, and in different content areas.
Authors: James Ysseldyke and Sandra Christenson.
Publisher: Sopris West, Inc.
Cross References: For reviews by Kenneth W. Howell and by William T. McKee and Joseph C. Witt of an earlier form, see 10:149.

[1240]

Instructional Leadership Evaluation and Development Program (*ILEAD*).
Population: School climates and leadership.

Publication Dates: 1985–88.
Acronym: *ILEAD*.
Administration: Individual or group.
Price Data: Available from publisher.
Time: Administration time varies with form.
Authors: Larry A. Braskamp (School Climate Inventories, School Administrator Assessment Survey), Martin L. Maehr (same material as above), and MetriTech, Inc. (manual and Instructional Leadership Inventory).
Publisher: MetriTech, Inc.

a) SCHOOL CLIMATE INVENTORY (FORM T).
Purpose: "Designed to assess instructional leadership behavior, job satisfaction and commitment, and school culture or climate from the teachers' perspective."
Scores, 12: Instructional Leadership (Defines Mission, Manages Curriculum, Supervises Teaching, Monitors Student Progress, Promotes Instructional Climate), Climate (Satisfaction, Commitment, Strength, Accomplishment, Recognition, Power, Affiliation).
Comments: Ratings by teachers.

b) SCHOOL CLIMATE INVENTORY (FORM S).
Purpose: "Designed to assess school climate from the student perspective."
Scores, 5: Strength of Climate, Accomplishment, Recognition, Power, Affiliation.
Comments: Ratings by students in grades 3–12.

c) SCHOOL ADMINISTRATOR ASSESSMENT SURVEY.
Purpose: "Designed to simultaneously assess the person, the job, and the culture or climate of the setting in which the person works."
Scores, 19: Personal Incentive (Accomplishment, Recognition, Power, Affiliation), Self-Concept (Self-Reliance, Self-Esteem, Goal-Directedness), Job Opportunity (Accomplishment, Recognition, Power, Affiliation, Advancement), Organizational Culture (Accomplishment, Recognition, Power, Affiliation, Satisfaction, Strength of Culture, Commitment).
Comments: Adaptation of SPECTRUM; self-ratings by principals.

d) INSTRUCTIONAL LEADERSHIP INVENTORY.
Purpose: "Designed to assess instructional leadership behavior."
Scores, 8: Instructional Leadership (Defines Mission, Manages Curriculum, Supervises Teaching, Monitors Student Progress, Promotes Instructional Climate), Contextual (Staff, School, Community).
Comments: Self-ratings by principals.

TEST REFERENCES

1. Smith, J. A., Martin, L. M., & Midgley, C. (1992). Relationship between personal and contextual characteristics and principals' administrative behaviors. *Journal of Educational Research*, 86, 111-118.

[1241]
Instrument for Disability Screening [Developmental Edition].
Purpose: To screen for learning disabilities.
Population: Primary grade children.
Publication Date: 1980.
Acronym: IDS.
Scores, 9: Hyperactive/Aggression, Visual, Speech/Auditory, Reading, Drawing/Writing, Inactivity, Concepts, Psychomotor Development, Total.
Administration: Individual.
Manual: No manual.
Price Data: Not available.
Time: (5-15) minutes.
Author: James R. Beatty.
Publisher: James R. Beatty [No reply from publisher; status unknown].
Cross References: See T3:1161 (3 references); for reviews by Norman A. Buktenica and Stephen J. Pfeifer, see 9:515.

[1242]
Instrument Technician.
Purpose: Developed to measure knowledge and skills required for instrument technician jobs.
Population: Applicants and incumbents for jobs requiring technical knowledge of instrumentation.
Publication Dates: 1989–90.
Scores, 12: Mathematics, Digital Electronics, Analog Electronics, Schematics and Electrical Print Reading, Process Control, Power Supplies, Basic AC/DC Theory, Test Instruments, Mechanical, Computer and PLC, Chemical Processes, Total.
Administration: Group.
Price Data, 1993: $498 per complete kit including 10 reusable test booklets, 100 answer sheets, manual ('90, 13 pages), and answer key.
Time: Administration time not reported.
Author: Roland T. Ramsay.
Publisher: Ramsay Corporation.

[1243]
Instrument Timbre Preference Test.
Purpose: "To act as an objective aid to the teacher and the parent in helping a student choose an appropriate woodwind or brass instrument to learn to play in beginning instrumental music and band."
Population: Grades 4–12.
Publication Dates: 1984–85.
Acronym: ITPT.
Scores, 7: Flute, Clarinet, Saxophone and French Horn, Oboe/English Horn/Bassoon, Trumpet and Cornet, Trombone/Baritone/French Horn, Tuba and Sousaphone.
Administration: Group.
Price Data, 1987: $39 per complete kit including 100 test sheets, scoring masks, cassette tape, and manual ('84, 53 pages); $13.50 per 100 test sheets; scoring service available from publisher.
Time: (30) minutes.
Author: Edwin E. Gordon.
Publisher: G.I.A. Publications, Inc.
Cross References: For reviews by Richard Colwell and Paul R. Lehman, see 10:150.

[1244]
Integrated Assessment System.

Purpose: "A series of performance tasks that can be used independently or in combination with a norm-referenced achievement test to offer a comprehensive view of student achievement."

Population: Grades 1–9.
Publication Dates: 1990–92.
Acronym: IAS.
Subtests: 3.
Administration: Group.
Authors: Roger Farr and Beverly Farr (Language Arts and Spanish only).
Publisher: The Psychological Corporation.

a) IAS-LANGUAGE ARTS.
Population: Grades 1–8.
Scores, 3: Response to Reading, Management of Content, Command of Language.
Price Data, 1994: $104 per complete grade 1 package including 25 each of three student booklets and directions for administering; $182 per complete grades 2–8 package including three sets of guided-writing-activity black line masters, directions for administering, three packages of 25 response forms, and response form directions; $18 per grade 1 examination kit including student booklet, directions for administering, and one passage specific scoring rubric; $22.50 per grades 2–8 examination kit including reading passage, guided-writing-activity black line master, response form, response form directions, directions for administering, and one passage-specific scoring rubric; $26 per grade 1 activity package including 25 of one student booklet and directions for administering; $65 per grades 2–8 activity package and directions for administering; $65 per grades 2–8 activity package including 25 of one reading passage and directions for administering; $5.50 per grades 2–8 response form package; $7 per grades 1–8 directions for administering; $15.50 per grades 1–8 scoring guides; $24 per grade 1 reading passage only; $59 per grades 2–8 reading passage only; $12.50 per grades 2–8 guided-writing-activity black line masters; $35.50 per technical report ('91, 53 pages); $210.50 per scoring workshop kit including videotape, trainer's manual, 25 overhead transparencies, and masters of model papers and training papers; $130 per portfolio starter kit including classroom storage box, 25 student portfolios, and teacher's manual; $42 per student portfolio folders; $42 per teacher's manual; $63.50 per introductory videotape and viewer's guide; $4.16 per basic scoring service; $6.24 per 25 student demographic sheets.
Time: (120–240) minutes.

1) *IAS-Language Arts, Spanish Edition*.
Scores: Same as *a* above.
Price Data, 1994: $17.50 per grade 1 examination kit including student booklet, directions for administering, and a passage specific scoring rubric; $21.50 per grades 2–8 examination kit including reading passage, guided-writing-activity black line master, one response form, response form directions, directions for administering, and passage specific scoring rubric; $25 per grade 1 activity package including 25 copies of one student booklet and one directions for administering; $62.50 per grades 2–8 activity package including 25 copies of one reading passage, one directions for administering, and one guided-writing-activity black line master; $5.50 per grades 2–8 response form package including 25 response forms and response form directions; $1 per response form directions; $7 per grades 1–8 directions for administering; $15 per grades 1–8 scoring guides; $23 per 25 grade 1 reading passage; $57 per 25 grades 2–8 reading passage; $12 per grades 2–8 guided-writing-activity black line masters; $4.16 per basic scoring service; $6.24 per student demographic sheet.

b) IAS-MATHEMATICS.
Population: Grades 1–9.
Scores, 4: Reasoning, Conceptual Knowledge, Communication Procedures.
Price Data, 1994: $17.50 per examination kit including student booklet, directions for administering, and scoring rubric; $27 per activity package including 25 student booklets and directions for administering; $7.50 per directions for administering; $16 per scoring guides; $120 per scoring training kit including binder and overhead transparencies; $9.31 per basic scoring holistic and analytic; $6.24 per 25 student demographic sheet.
Time: (80–90) minutes.

c) IAS-SCIENCE.
Population: Grades 1–8.
Scores, 4: Experimenting, Collecting Data, Drawing Conclusions, Communicating.
Price Data, 1994: $17.50 per examination kit including student booklet, directions for administering, and scoring rubric; $25 per activity package including 25 student booklets and one directions for administering; $7 per directions for administering; $16 per scoring guides; $30 per manipulative materials; $120 per scoring workshop kit including trainer's manual; $5.15 per basic scoring service; $6.25 per 25 student demographic sheet.
Time: (80–90) minutes.

[1245]
Integrated Literature and Language Arts Portfolio Program.

Purpose: "To assess students' reading and language arts proficiency."
Population: Grades 2–8.
Publication Date: 1991.
Scores, 7 to 9: Prior Knowledge/Predicting Content, Reading Strategies, Vocabulary, Constructing Meaning (Literal, Analytical, Extended), Feature Scores (Responsiveness to Task, Development and Organization, Language Use) or 1 Holistic Score.
Administration: Group.

Levels: 2 forms for each of 8 levels.
Price Data, 1992: $39 per 25 Student Activity Booklets including Directions for Administration and 1 Class Record Form (specify form and level); $5.40 per Student Activity Booklet Scoring Guide (specify form and level); $9 per Local Scoring Leader's Handbook (23 pages); $27.90 per 25 Student Portfolio Folders; $9 per 25 Individual Observation Check Lists; $4.20 per Teacher's Directions (specify form and level); $12 per 25 Class Record Forms levels 2–8; $15 per Technical manual (64 pages).
Time: Three 45-minute sessions.
Author: Nambury Raju.
Publisher: Riverside Publishing Co.

[1246]
INteraction CHecklist for Augmentative Communication, Revised Edition.
Purpose: Designed to assess features of interaction between augmentative system users and their partners.
Population: Augmentative system users.
Publication Dates: 1984–91.
Acronym: INCH.
Scores, 13: Strategies (Initiation, Facilitation, Regulation, Termination); Modes (Linguistic, Paralinguistic, Kinesic, Proxemic, Chronemic); Contexts (Familiar-Trained, Familiar-Untrained, Unfamiliar-Trained, Unfamiliar-Untrained).
Administration: Individual.
Price Data, 1993: $31 per complete kit including manual ('91, 74 pages) and 15 checklists; $8 per 15 checklists.
Time: Administration time not reported.
Comments: Behavior checklist.
Authors: Susan Oakander Bolton and Sallie E. Dashiell.
Publisher: Imaginart Communication Products.

[1247]
Interaction Index.
Purpose: "To identify the cause(s) of poor on-the-job relationships and prescribe steps for improvement."
Population: Adults.
Publication Date: 1989.
Scores, 8: Give Positive Strokes, Give Negative Strokes, Accept Positive Strokes, Accept Negative Strokes, Ask for Positive Strokes, Ask for Negative Strokes, Refuse to Give Positive Strokes, Refuse to Give Negative Strokes.
Administration: Group.
Price Data, 1989: $4 per one test booklet and one scoring and interpretation booklet (8 pages); $15 per Leader's Guide.
Time: (10–15) minutes.
Authors: Michalak Training Associates, Inc.
Publisher: Michalak Training Associates, Inc.

[1248]
Interest Questionnaire for Indian South Africans.
Purpose: Measurement of vocational interests of Indian South Africans.

Population: Standards 6–10 in South African schools.
Publication Dates: 1969–71.
Acronym: IQISA.
Scores, 7: Language, Arts, Social Service, Science, Mechanics, Business, Office Work.
Administration: Group.
Price Data: Available from publisher.
Time: (90–120) minutes.
Author: S. Oosthuizen.
Publisher: Human Sciences Research Council [South Africa].

[1249]
Intermediate Measures of Music Audiation.
Purpose: "To identify children with exceptionally high music aptitude . . . who can profit from the opportunity to participate in additional group study and special private instruction . . . to evaluate the comparative tonal and rhythm aptitudes of each child with exceptionally high music aptitude."
Population: Grades 1–4.
Publication Dates: 1978–82.
Acronym: IMMA.
Scores, 3: Tonal, Rhythm, Composite.
Administration: Group.
Price Data, 1986: $62 per complete kit containing 1 tonal tape and 1 rhythm tape, 100 tonal answer sheets, 100 rhythm answer sheets, 2 sets of scoring masks, 100 profile cards, 4 class record sheets, and test manual ('82, 44 pages); $13 per tonal tape; $13 per rhythm tape; $8 per 100 tonal answer sheets; $8 per 100 rhythm answer sheets; $1 per set of tonal or rhythm scoring masks; $13 per 100 profile cards; $1.75 per 10 class record sheets; $12.95 per manual.
Time: (20) minutes per Tonal test; (20) minutes per Rhythm test.
Comments: Advanced version of the Primary Measures of Music Audiation (9:988); tests administered by 7 ½ ips tape recordings.
Author: Edwin E. Gordon.
Publisher: G.I.A. Publications, Inc.

[1250]
Intermediate Personality Questionnaire for Indian Pupils (Standards 6 to 8).
Purpose: "For determining the structural aspects of personality."
Population: Standards 6–8 in South African schools.
Publication Date: 1974.
Acronym: IPQI.
Scores, 10: Social Extraversion, Verbal Intelligence, Emotional Stability, Adventuresomeness, Creativity, Dominance, Perseverance, Relaxedness, Spirit of Enterprise, Environmental Relatedness.
Administration: Group.
Price Data: Available from publisher.
Time: (30–45) minutes.
Comments: Technical report available only in Afrikaans.
Author: S. Oosthuizen.

Publisher: Human Sciences Research Council [South Africa].

[1251]

Interpersonal Behavior Survey.

Purpose: "Developed to distinguish assertive behaviors from aggressive behaviors."

Population: Grades 9–16 and adults.

Publication Date: 1980.

Acronym: IBS.

Scores, 21: Denial, Infrequency, Impression Management, General Aggressiveness—Rational, Hostile Stance, Expression of Anger, Disregard for Rights, Verbal Aggressiveness, Physical Aggressiveness, Passive Aggressiveness, General Assertiveness—Rational, Self-Confidence, Initiating Assertiveness, Defending Assertiveness, Frankness, Praise, Requesting Help, Refusing Demands, Conflict Avoidance, Dependency, Shyness, plus additional scores (General Aggressiveness—Empirical, General Assertiveness—Empirical) and 10 short-form scores.

Administration: Group.

Price Data, 1993: $100 per complete kit; $21 per 10 administration booklets; $29.50 per set of scoring keys; $19.50 per 100 answer sheets; $19.50 per 100 profiles; $45 per manual (78 pages including test, answer sheet, and profile).

Time: (40–50) minutes.

Authors: Paul A. Mauger, David R. Adkinson, Suzanne K. Zoss (test), Gregory Firestone (test), and J. David Hook (test).

Publisher: Western Psychological Services.

Cross References: For reviews by Stephen L. Franzoi and Robert R. Hutzell, see 9:518.

TEST REFERENCES

1. Margalit, B. A., & Mauger, P. A. (1984). Cross-cultural demonstration of orthogonality of assertiveness and aggressiveness: Comparison between Israel and the United States. *Journal of Personality and Social Psychology, 46,* 1414-1421.
2. Margalit, B. A., & Mauger, P. A. (1985). Aggressiveness and assertiveness. *Journal of Cross-Cultural Psychology, 16,* 497-511.
3. Heiby, E. M. (1986). Social versus self-control skills deficits in four cases of depression. *Behavior Therapy, 17,* 158-169.
4. Lynn, R., Hampson, S., & Agahi, E. (1989). Television violence and aggression: A genotype-environment, correlation and interaction theory. *Social Behavior and Personality, 17,* 143-164.
5. Matheny, K. B., Aycock, D. W., Curlette, W. L., & Junker, G. N. (1993). The Coping Resources Inventory for stress: A measure of perceived resourcefulness. *Journal of Clinical Psychology, 49,* 815-830.

[1252]

Interpersonal Check List.

Purpose: "To obtain self-descriptions or descriptions by others with respect to an interpersonal domain of personality."

Population: Adults.

Publication Dates: 1955.

Acronym: ICL.

Scores, 24: 16 interpersonal scores, 4 intensity scores, plus 4 summary scores: Number of Items Checked, Average Intensity, Dominance, Love.

Administration: Group.

Price Data, 1994: Single reproducible copy now available without charge.

Time: (15–20) minutes.

Comments: Descriptions by others; descriptions of self and others, ideal self; for research use only.

Authors: Rolfe LaForge, Timothy Leary (test); Robert Suczek (test), and Mervin Freedman (test).

Publisher: Rolfe LaForge.

Cross References: See T3:1170 (16 references); see also T2:1240 (115 references) and P:127 (70 references); for a review by P. M. Bentler, see 6:127 (39 references).

TEST REFERENCES

1. Hokanson, J. E., Rubert, M. P., Welker, R. A., Hollander, G. R., & Hedeen, C. (1989). Interpersonal concomitants and antecedents of depression among college students. *Journal of Abnormal Psychology, 98,* 209-217.
2. Hatfield, F. C. (1978). Effects of interpersonal attraction and tolerance-intolerance of ambiguity on athletic team productivity. *International Journal of Sport Psychology, 9,* 214-226.
3. Stava, L. J., & Bednar, R. L. (1979). Process and outcome in encounter groups: The effects of group composition. *Small Group Behavior, 10,* 200-213.
4. Clark, T. L., & Taulbee, E. S. (1981). A comprehensive and indexed bibliography of the Interpersonal Check List. *Journal of Personality Assessment, 45,* 505-525.
5. Boals, G. F., Peterson, D. R., Farmer, L., Mann, D. F., & Robinson, D. L. (1982). The reliability, validity, and utility of three data modes in assessing marital relationships. *Journal of Personality Assessment, 46,* 85-95.
6. Doerr, H. O., & Carr, J. E. (1982). Videotape 'self-confrontation effect' as function of person viewed and task performed. *Perceptual and Motor Skills, 54,* 419-433.
7. Paddock, J. R., Woodruff, D. L., & Pate, C. (1984). Examining nonspecific relationship factors in the behavioral treatment of seriously emotionally disturbed (SED) adolescents: An interpersonal communications approach. *Journal of Clinical Child Psychology, 13,* 74-80.
8. York, M. W., Sherrie, A. B., & Colindres, C. (1984). Categories of implicit interpersonal communication. *Perceptual and Motor Skills, 59,* 855-862.
9. Emmons, R. A., & Diener, E. (1985). Personality correlates of subjective well-being. *Personality and Social Psychology Bulletin, 11,* 89-97.
10. McLeod, M., & Nowicki, S., Jr. (1985). Cooperative behavior as a function of interpersonal style in preschoolers. *Journal of Personality, 53,* 36-45.
11. Perlmutter, K. B., Paddock, J. R., & Duke, M. P. (1985). The role of verbal, vocal, and nonverbal cues in the communication of evoking message styles. *Journal of Research in Personality, 19,* 31-43.
12. Hurley, J. R., & Cosgro, M. A. (1986). An interpersonal-Jungian interface: Links of divergent personality measures. *Journal of Clinical Psychology, 42,* 469-474.
13. Paddock, J. R., & Nowicki, S., Jr. (1986). The circumplexity of Leary's interpersonal circle: A multidimensional scaling perspective. *Journal of Personality Assessment, 50,* 279-289.
14. Scribner, C. M., & Handler, L. (1987). The interpreter's personality in Draw-A-Person interpretation: A study of interpersonal style. *Journal of Personality Assessment, 51,* 112-122.
15. Raskin, R., & Terry, H. (1988). A principal-components analysis of the narcissistic personality inventory and further evidence of its construct validity. *Journal of Personality and Social Psychology, 54,* 890-902.
16. York, M. W., Wilderman, S. K., & Hardy, S. T. (1988). Categories of implicit interpersonal communication: Cross cultural responses. *Perceptual and Motor Skills, 67,* 735-741.
17. Hokanson, J. E., Hummer, J. T., & Butler, A. C. (1991). Interpersonal perceptions by depressed college students. *Cognitive Therapy and Research, 15,* 443-457.
18. Van Denburg, T. F., Schmidt, J. A., & Kiesler, D. J. (1992). Interpersonal assessment in counseling and psychotherapy. *Journal of Counseling and Development, 71,* 84-90.

[1253]

Interpersonal Communication Inventory.

Purpose: To assess "a client's interpersonal communication as it provides clues to communication difficulties outside of the family relationship."

Population: Grade 9 to adult.

Publication Dates: 1969–76.
Acronym: ICI.
Scores, 12: Self-Disclosure, Awareness, Evaluation and Acceptance of Feedback, Self-Expression, Attention, Coping with Feelings, Clarity, Avoidance, Dominance, Handling Differences, Perceived Acceptance, Total.
Administration: Group.
Price Data, 1993: $.75 per inventory; $3.50 per guide ('76, 15 pages).
Time: (20) minutes.
Author: Millard J. Bienvenu.
Publisher: Millard J. Bienvenu.
Cross References: See T3:1171 (2 references); see also 8:589 (3 references) and T2:1241 (1 reference).

TEST REFERENCES

1. Hansford, B. C., & Neidhart, H. M. (1980). A view of fifteen-year-old girls in Australian schools. *Adolescence, 15,* 633-641.
2. Helfenstein, D. A., & Wechsler, F. S. (1982). The use of Interpersonal Process Recall (IPR) in the remediation of interpersonal and communication skills deficits in the newly brain-injured. *Clinical Neuropsychology, 4,* 139-143.
3. Neiman, G. S., & Rubin, R. B. (1991). Changes in communication apprehension, satisfaction, and competence in foreign dialect and stuttering clients. *Journal of Communication Disorders, 24,* 353-366.

[1254]

Interpersonal Conflict Scale.
Purpose: "Designed for the reporting of perceived feelings to statements about spouse behavior."
Population: Adults.
Publication Date: 1981.
Scores, 8: Agreement in Thinking, Communication, Disagreement in Behavior, Perception of the Other's Feelings, Companionship and Sharing, Emotional Satisfaction, Security, Recognition.
Administration: Group.
Price Data: Not available.
Time: (10–15) minutes.
Comments: Separate forms for males and females.
Authors: Carol Hoskins and Philip Merrifield.
Publisher: Family Life Publications, Inc. [No reply from publisher; status unknown].
Cross References: For a review by Stanley R. Strong, see 9:519.

[1255]

Interpersonal Relations Questionnaire.
Purpose: "To identify specific problems in connection with interpersonal relations and identity formation."
Population: "White pupils" in Standards 5–7 in South African schools.
Publication Date: 1981–88.
Acronym: IRQ.
Scores, 13: Self-Confidence, Self-Esteem, Self-Control, Nervousness, Health, Family Influences, Personal Freedom, Sociability A, Sociability T, Sociability D, Moral Sense, Formal Relations, Lie Scale.
Administration: Group.
Price Data: Available from publisher.
Time: (105–120) minutes.

Comments: Supplementary manual in English and Afrikaans.
Authors: Marianne Joubert and Dawn Schlebusch (supplementary manual).
Publisher: Human Sciences Research Council [South Africa].

[1256]

Interpersonal Style Inventory.
Purpose: To measure "an individual's characteristic ways of relating to other people . . . also evaluates style of impulse control and characteristic modes of dealing with work and play."
Population: Ages 14 and over.
Publication Dates: 1977–86.
Acronym: ISI.
Scores: 15 in 5 areas: Interpersonal Involvement (Sociable, Help Seeking, Nurturant, Sensitive), Socialization (Conscientious, Trusting, Tolerant), Autonomy (Directive, Independent, Rule Free), Self-Control (Deliberate, Orderly, Persistent), Stability (Stable, Approval Seeking).
Administration: Group.
Price Data, 1993: $100 per complete kit; $21.50 per 10 administration booklets; $42.50 per manual ('86, 69 pages); $12.50 or less per answer sheet scoring service; $210 for IBM microcomputer disk.
Time: (40–45) minutes.
Authors: Maurice Lorr, Richard P. Youniss, and G. J. Huba (computerized interpretation program and related chapters in manual).
Publisher: Western Psychological Services.
Cross References: For reviews by Randy W. Kamphaus and Gerald L. Stone, see 10:151 (4 references); for reviews by John Duckitt and Stuart A. Karabenick of an earlier edition, see 9:521; see also T3:1173 (1 reference).

TEST REFERENCES

1. Lorr, M., & Wunderlich, R. A. (1985). A measure of impulsiveness and its relations to extraversion. *Educational and Psychological Measurement, 45,* 251-257.
2. Myhill, J. E., & Lorr, M. (1988). The place of self-esteem in interpersonal behavior. *Journal of Clinical Psychology, 44,* 206-209.
3. Lorr, M., & Suziedelis, A. (1990). Distinctive personality profiles of the Interpersonal Style Inventory. *Journal of Personality Assessment, 54,* 491-500.
4. Lorr, M., Youniss, R. P., & Kluth, C. (1992). The Interpersonal Style Inventory and the five-factor model. *Journal of Clinical Psychology, 48,* 202-206.
5. Nory, D. M. (1992). Psychometric properties of the Interpersonal Style Inventory. *Journal of Clinical Psychology, 48,* 308-314.
6. Strack, S. (1992). Profile clusters for men and women on the Personality Adjective Check List. *Journal of Personality Assessment, 59,* 204-217.

[1257]

Intra- and Interpersonal Relations Scale.
Purpose: Identify children's attitudes toward themselves and their relationships with their parents.
Population: Bantu pupils in Forms IV and V in South African schools.
Publication Dates: 1973–75.
Acronym: IIPS.
Scores, 4: Self-Image, Mother-Child Relationship, Father-Child Relationship, Ideal Self.

Administration: Group.
Price Data: Available from publisher.
Time: (40–60) minutes.
Comments: Test materials in both English and Afrikaans.
Author: G. G. Minnaar.
Publisher: Human Sciences Research Council [South Africa].

[1258]

Intrex Questionnaires.
Purpose: Designed to measure the patient's perceptions of self and others, based on trait x state x situational philosophy and Structural Analysis of Social Behavior (SASB).
Population: Psychiatric patients and normals.
Publication Dates: 1980–88.
Scores: Pattern Coefficient scores in each of 3 areas (2 equivalent forms): Interpersonal Transitive-Focus on Other, Interpersonal Intransitive-Focus on Self, Intrapsychic Introjection; 7 subtests: Introject (Best, Worst), He/I Present Tense (Best/Worst), She/I Present Tense (Best/Worst), He/I Past Tense (Best/Worst), She/I Past Tense (Best/Worst), Mother with Father/Father with Mother Present Tense (Best/Worst), Mother with Father/Father with Mother Past Tense (Best/Worst).
Administration: Group or individual.
Restricted Distribution: Clinical users must meet degree requirements and attend workshop on clinical uses of SASB conducted by various sponsors.
Price Data, 1991: $1 per clinical patient for short form or long form; no charge for research use of long form; $.10 for research use of short form; $20 per short form manual ('88, 106 pages); $20 per patient for profile processing by publisher; $50 per set of 5 IBM software programs for research use.
Time: (60) minutes for complete battery, short form.
Author: Lorna Smith Benjamin.
Publisher: Intrex Interpersonal Institute, Inc.

TEST REFERENCES

1. Alpher, V. S. (1992). Introject and identify: Structural-interpersonal analysis and psychological assessment of multiple personality disorder. *Journal of Personality Assessment, 58*(2), 347-367.
2. Van Denburg, T. F., Schmidt, J. A., & Kiesler, D. J. (1992). Interpersonal assessment in counseling and psychotherapy. *Journal of Counseling and Development, 71*(1), 84-90.

[1259]

Intuitive Mechanics (Weights & Pulleys).
Purpose: "To measure the ability to understand mechanical relationships, to visualize internal movement in a mechanical system."
Population: Engineering students and industrial workers.
Publication Dates: 1956–59.
Scores: Total score only.
Administration: Group.
Price Data, 1992: $30 per 25 booklets; $5 per score key; $10 per interpretation and research manual ('59, 9 pages).

Time: (3) minutes.
Authors: L. L. Thurstone and T. E. Jeffrey.
Publisher: SRA/London House.
Cross References: For a review by William A. Owens, see 9:523.

[1260]

Inventory for Client and Agency Planning.
Purpose: Developed "to assess the status, adaptive functioning, and service needs of clients."
Population: Ages 3 months to adult.
Publication Date: 1986.
Acronym: ICAP.
Scores, 10: Maladaptive Behavior Indexes (Internalized, Asocial, Externalized, General), Adaptive Behavior (Motor Skills, Social and Communication Skills, Personal Living Skills, Community Living Skills, Total), Service Level Index.
Administration: Individual.
Price Data, 1989: $75 per complete kit; $30 per 25 response booklets; $50 per manual (155 pages).
Time: (20–30) minutes.
Comments: Statistically related to the Scales of Independent Behavior and the Woodcock-Johnson Psycho-Educational Battery; to be completed by "a respondent who has known a client for at least 3 months and who sees him or her on a day-to-day basis."
Authors: Robert H. Bruininks, Bradley K. Hill, Richard F. Weatherman, and Richard W. Woodcock.
Publisher: The Riverside Publishing Co.
Cross References: For reviews by Ronn Johnson and Richard L. Wikoff, see 10:152.

TEST REFERENCES

1. Heller, T., & Factor, A. (1991). Permanency planning for adults with mental retardation living with family caregivers. *American Journal on Mental Retardation, 96,* 163-176.
2. McGrew, K. S., Ittenbach, R. F., Bruininks, R. H., & Hill, B. K. (1991). Factor structure of maladaptive behavior across the lifespan of persons with mental retardation. *Research in Developmental Disabilities, 12,* 181-199.
3. McGrew, K. S., Bruininks, R. H., Thurlow, M. I., & Lewis, D. R. (1992). Empirical analysis of multidimensional measures of community adjustment for young adults with mental retardation. *American Journal on Mental Retardation, 96,* 475-487.

[1261]

Inventory for Counseling & Development.
Purpose: To assess the personal, social, and academic functioning of college students.
Population: College students.
Publication Dates: 1981–94.
Scores, 23: Agreement, Favorable Impression, Infrequent, Insecurity, Alienation, Exam Tension, Ambition, Persistence, Practicality, Sociability, Teacher-Student Interaction, Intellectuality, Originality, Adaptability, Orderliness, Liberal-Conservative, Socio-Political Interest, Sexual Beliefs, Sex Role Differences, Academic Performance, Academic Excellence, Academic Capacity, Academic Motivation.
Administration: Group or individual.
Price Data, 1994: $13 per 10 reusable test booklets; $85 per handscoring kit; $35 per 25 handscoring

answer keys; $4.60–$5.25 per mail-in scoring answer sheet (includes cost of scoring and profile report); $5.25–$6.60 per Arion teleprocessing; $12 per 25 Arion answer sheets; $12 per 25 Microtest answer sheets; $3.60–$4.25 per Microtest profile report (for on-site scoring); $11.75 per manual ('88, 106 pages); $42.85 per preview package for the mail-in or Microtest system including 3 interpretive reports, manual, and user's guide; $15 per interpretive report user's guide.
Time: (60–120) minutes.
Authors: Norman S. Giddan, F. Reid Creech, and Victor R. Lovell.
Publisher: NCS Assessments.
Cross References: For reviews by Nambury S. Raju and Eleanor E. Sanford, see 11:182.

[1262]
Inventory No. II.
Purpose: Intended as a "mental ability test" measuring "the ability of the individual to solve problems involving word meanings and verbally constructed conceptual relations, as well as those which require the manipulations of number relationships."
Population: Ages 16 and over.
Publication Date: 1956.
Scores: Total score only.
Administration: Group.
Price Data: Available from publisher.
Time: 15 minutes.
Author: Stevens, Thurow & Associates, Inc.
Publisher: Stevens, Thurow & Associates, Inc.

[1263]
Inventory of Anger Communication.
Purpose: "To identify the subjective and interactional aspects of anger in assessing how one communicates around anger."
Population: High school and adults.
Publication Dates: 1974–76.
Acronym: IAC.
Scores: Total score only.
Administration: Group.
Price Data, 1993: $.75 per inventory; $2 per manual ('76, 10 pages).
Time: [15–20] minutes.
Author: Millard J. Bienvenu.
Publisher: Millard J. Bienvenu.
Cross References: For additional information, see 8:591 (1 reference).

[1264]
An Inventory of Certain Feelings.
Purpose: To identify preoccupation with anxieties.
Population: Applicants for employment.
Publication Date: 1952.
Scores: Total score only.
Administration: Group.
Price Data: Available from publisher.
Time: Administration time not reported.

Author: Maurice H. Krout.
Publisher: Johanna Krout Tabin.

[1265]
Inventory of Drinking Situations.
Purpose: "Designed to assess situations in which a client drank heavily over the past year."
Population: Ages 18 to 75.
Publication Date: 1987.
Acronym: IDS.
Scores, 8: Personal Status (Unpleasant Emotions, Physical Discomfort, Pleasant Emotions, Testing Personal Control, Urges and Temptations), Situations Involving Other People (Conflict with Others, Social Pressure to Drink, Pleasant Times with Others).
Administration: Group.
Forms, 2: IDS-100, IDS-42 (Brief Version).
Price Data, 1993: $25 per specimen set including user's guide (53 pages), 25 questionnaires, 25 answer sheets, 25 profiles; $13.50 per user's guide; $12.75 per 25 IDS-42 (Brief Version) questionnaires, 25 answer sheets, and 25 profile sheets; $14.75 per 25 IDS-100 questionnaires, 25 answer sheets, and 25 profile sheets; $140 per computer software program (50 uses); $450 per computer software program (200 uses).
Foreign Language Edition: Both forms available in French.
Time: (20–25) minutes.
Comments: IDS-42 (Brief Version) is for research use only.
Authors: Helen M. Annis, J. Martin Graham, and Christine S. Davis.
Publisher: Addiction Research Foundation [Canada].

TEST REFERENCES

1. Cannon, D. S., Leeka, J. K., Patterson, E. T., & Baker, T. B. (1990). Principal components analysis of the Inventory of Drinking Situations: Empirical categories of drinking by alcoholics. *Addictive Behaviors, 15,* 265-269.
2. Allen, J. P., & Litten, R. Z. (1993). Psychometric and laboratory measures to assist in the treatment of alcoholism. *Clinical Psychology Review, 13,* 223-239.

[1266]
Inventory of Interests.
Purpose: Identifies the level of expressed interest for "over 136 occupations and 56 subjects."
Population: Adolescents and adults.
Publication Date: 1971.
Scores: Ratings in 2 areas: Occupations, Subjects of Interest.
Administration: Group.
Price Data: Not available.
Foreign Language Editions: Spanish manual and tests also available.
Time: Administration time not reported.
Author: Guidance Testing Associates.
Publisher: Guidance Testing Associates [No reply from publisher; status unknown].
Cross References: For a review by James D. Wiggins, see 9:525.

[1267]
Inventory of Language Abilities.
Purpose: "A screening device for use by the classroom teacher in identifying children with possible language learning disabilities."
Population: Grades K–2 and handicapped children in special classes.
Publication Date: 1972.
Acronym: ILA.
Scores: Behavior checklists in 11 areas: Auditory Reception, Visual Reception, Auditory Association, Visual Association, Verbal Expression, Manual Expression, Auditory Memory, Visual Memory, Grammatic Closure, Visual Closure, Auditory Closure and Sound Blending.
Administration: Individual.
Price Data: Not available.
Time: Administration time not reported.
Comments: A component of the MWM Program for Developing Language Abilities.
Authors: Esther H. Minskoff, Douglas E. Wiseman, and J. Gerald Minskoff.
Publisher: Educational Performance Associates, Inc. [No reply from publisher; status unknown].
Cross References: For a review by Rita Sloan Berndt, see 9:526.

[1268]
Inventory of Language Abilities, Level II.
Purpose: "For use by the classroom teacher in identifying children with possible language learning disabilities."
Population: Grades 3–5 and older language disabled students.
Publication Date: 1981.
Scores: Behavior checklists in 11 areas: Auditory Reception, Visual Reception, Auditory Association, Visual Association, Verbal Expression, Manual Expression, Auditory Memory, Visual Memory, Grammatic Closure, Visual Closure, Auditory Closure and Sound Blending.
Administration: Individual.
Price Data: Not available.
Time: Administration time not reported.
Comments: A component of the MWM Program for Developing Language Abilities, and an upward extension of the Inventory of Language Abilities (1267); ratings by each teacher involved with child.
Authors: Esther H. Minskoff, Douglas E. Wiseman, and J. Gerald Minskoff.
Publisher: Educational Performance Associates, Inc. [No reply from publisher; status unknown].
Cross References: For a review by Lynn S. Bliss, see 10:153.

[1269]
Inventory of Learning Processes—R.
Purpose: To measure learning styles of college and university students.
Population: College and university students.
Publication Dates: 1977–92.

Acronym: ILP-R.
Scores, 14: Academic Subject (Intrinsic Motivation, Self-efficacy, Non-reiterative Processing, Self-esteem, Total), Reflective Processing (Deep Processing, Elaborative Processing, Self-expression, Total), Agentic Processing (Conventional, Serial Processing, Fact Retention, Total), Methodical Study.
Administration: Group.
Price Data, 1993: $3 per test booklet (includes answer sheets).
Time: Administration time not reported.
Authors: Ronald R. Schmeck and Elke Geisler-Bernstein.
Publisher: Ronald R. Schmeck (the author).

[1270]
Inventory of Perceptual Skills.
Purpose: "Assesses visual and auditory perceptual skills."
Population: Ages 5–10.
Publication Date: 1983.
Acronym: IPS.
Scores, 11: Visual Perception Skills (Visual Discrimination, Visual Memory, Object Recognition, Visual-Motor Coordination, Total), Auditory Perception Skills (Auditory Discrimination, Auditory Memory, Auditory Sequencing, Auditory Blending, Total), Total.
Administration: Individual.
Price Data, 1994: $45 per complete kit including manual (16 pages), stimulus cards, student workbook, and record books; $20 per 10 student record books; $15 per manual; $15 per stimulus cards; $6 per student workbook.
Time: (15) minutes.
Author: Donald R. O'Dell.
Publisher: Stoelting Co.

[1271]
The Inventory of Positive Thinking Traits.
Purpose: "Designed to assess the attitudes of individuals in terms of their positivity and negativity."
Population: Adults and adolescents.
Publication Date: 1992.
Scores: Total score only.
Administration: Individual and group.
Price Data: Available from publisher.
Time: (10) minutes.
Author: Millard J. Bienvenu.
Publisher: Millard J. Bienvenu, Northwest Publications.

[1272]
An Inventory of Religious Activities and Interests.
Purpose: "Measures interest in activities performed by persons employed in a variety of church-related occupations."
Population: High school and college.
Publication Dates: 1967–70.
Acronym: IRAI.

Scores: 11 scales: Counselor, Administrator, Teacher, Scholar, Evangelist, Spiritual Guide, Preacher, Reformer, Priest, Musician, Check Scale.
Administration: Group.
Price Data: Available from publisher.
Time: (40–45) minutes for both forms.
Comments: For research use only.
Author: Sam C. Webb.
Publisher: Ministry Inventories.
Cross References: See T2:1025A (2 references); for a review by Donald G. Zytowski, see 7:1023.

[1273]

Inventory of Suicide Orientation-30.
Purpose: "To assess and help identify adolescents who are at risk for suicide orientation by measuring the strength of their suicide orientation."
Population: Adolescents.
Publication Dates: 1988–94.
Acronym: ISO-30.
Scores, 2: Final Raw Score, Final Critical Item Score.
Administration: Group.
Price Data, 1994: $75 per 10 handscoring answer sheets (reorder); $12 per 25 computer scoring answer sheets; $2.50 per computer scoring report; other price data available from publisher.
Foreign Language Edition: Also available in Spanish.
Time: (5–15) minutes.
Authors: John D. King and Brian Kowalchuk.
Publisher: NCS Assessments.

[1274]

Inventory of Vocational Interests: Acorn National Aptitude Tests.
Purpose: Designed to provide evidence of vocationally significant interests.
Population: Grades 7–16 and adults.
Publication Dates: 1943–60.
Scores, 5: Mechanical, Academic, Artistic, Business and Economic, Farm-Agricultural.
Administration: Group.
Price Data: Available from publisher.
Time: (35) minutes.
Authors: Andrew Kobal, J. Wayne Wrightstone, and Karl R. Kunze.
Publisher: Psychometric Affiliates.
Cross References: For a review by John W. French, see 6:1060; for reviews by Marion A. Bills, Edward S. Bordin, Harold D. Carter, and Patrick Slater, see 3:638.

[1275]

Inwald Personality Inventory [Revised].
Purpose: "To aid public safety/law enforcement and security agencies in selecting new officers."
Population: Public safety, security, and law enforcement applicants (post-conditional job offer only).
Publication Dates: 1980–92.

Acronym: IPI.
Scores, 26: Guardedness, Externalized Behavior Measures (Actions [Alcohol, Drugs, Driving Violations, Job Difficulties, Trouble with the Law and Society, Absence Abuse], Attitudes [Substance Abuse, Antisocial Attitudes, Hyperactivity, Rigid Type, Type A]), Internalized Conflict Measures (Illness Concerns, Treatment Programs, Anxiety, Phobic Personality, Obsessive Personality, Depression, Loner, Unusual Experiences/Thoughts), Interpersonal Conflict Measures (Lack of Assertiveness, Interpersonal Difficulties, Undue Suspiciousness, Family Conflicts, Sexual Concerns, Spouse/Mate Conflicts.
Administration: Group.
Price Data, 1993: $60 per complete starter kit including test booklet, 3 computer-scorable answer sheets, and manual ('92, 78 pages); $2 per test booklet; $2.50 per 10 Scantron/standard answer sheets; $3 per 10 Sentry answer sheets; $15 per manual; scoring service offered by publisher at $10–$12.75 per test; (all prices may be adjusted for volume discounts).
Time: (30–45) minutes.
Author: Robin Inwald.
Publisher: Hilson Research, Inc.
Cross References: For reviews of an earlier edition by Samuel Juni and Niels G. Waller, see 11:183 (2 references); for reviews of an earlier edition by Brian Bolton and Jon D. Swartz, see 9:530.

TEST REFERENCES

1. Inwald, R. E., & Brockwell, A. L. (1991). Predicting the performance of government security personnel with the IPI and MMPI. *Journal of Personality Assessment, 56,* 522-535.

[1276]

Inwald Survey 5.
Purpose: "To aid in employee selection."
Population: All occupations including public safety/security, clerical, managerial, sales, and entry-level.
Publication Dates: 1992–93.
Acronym: IS5.
Scores, 11: Lack of Insight/Candor, Frustration/Anger Patterns, Distrust of Others, Work Adjustment Difficulties, Attitudes (Antisocial Behaviors), Behavior Patterns (Integrity Concerns), Lack of Competitive Motivation, Work Effort Concerns, Lack of Sensitivity, Leadership Avoidance, Introverted Personality Style.
Administration: Group.
Price Data, 1993: $60 per complete starter kit including test booklet, 3 computer-scorable answer sheets, and manual ('92, 25 pages); $2 per test booklet; $2.50 per 10 Scantron/standard answer sheets; $3 per 10 Sentry answer sheets; $15 per manual; scoring services offered by the publisher at $9.50–$12 (volume discounts available).
Time: (25–30) minutes.
Comments: "Appropriate under ADA and can be administered pre-employment."
Author: Robin Inwald.
Publisher: Hilson Research, Inc.

[1277]

Iowa Algebra Aptitude Test, Fourth Edition.
Purpose: "To assess student readiness for Algebra I."
Population: Grades 7–8.
Publication Dates: 1931–93.
Acronym: IAAT.
Scores, 5: Interpreting Mathematical Information, Translating to Symbols, Finding Relationships, Using Symbols, Total.
Administration: Group.
Price Data, 1993: $48 per 25 test booklets Form 1 or 2; $4.50 per Directions for Administration ('93, 13 pages); $24 per 25 self-scoring answer sheets; $66 per 100 computer-scored answer sheets; $18 per 25 class record sheets; $15 per Manual for Test Use and Interpretation ('93, 26 pages); $18 per 25 report to parents and students; $1,200 per scanning and scoring system; $18 per examination kit.
Time: (50) minutes.
Authors: Harold L. Schoen, Timothy N. Ansley, H. D. Hoover, Beverly S. Rich, Sheila I. Barron, and Robert A. Bye. (Earlier edition by Harry A. Greene and Darrell Sabers).
Publisher: The Riverside Publishing Co.
Cross References: See T2:681 (7 references); for reviews by W. L. Bashaw and Cyril J. Hoyt, and an excerpted review by Russell A. Chadbourn of an earlier edition, see 7:505 (8 references); for reviews by Harold Gulliken and Emma Spaney of an earlier edition, see 4:393; for a review by David Segel, see 3:327 (2 references); for reviews by Richard M. Drake and M. W. Richardson, see 2:1441 (1 reference).

[1278]

Iowa Parent Behavior Inventory.
Purpose: Designed "to measure parental behavior in relation to a child."
Population: Parents.
Publication Dates: 1976–79.
Acronym: ITBI.
Administration: Group.
Price Data, 1984: $.10 per test; $3 per manual ('79, 41 pages including both forms and score sheet).
Time: Administration time not reported.
Authors: Sedahlia Jasper Crase, Samuel G. Clark, and Damaris Pease.
Publisher: Iowa State University Research Foundation, Inc.
a) MOTHER FORM.
Publication Date: 1977.
Scores, 6: Parental Involvement, Limit Setting, Responsiveness, Reasoning Guidance, Free Expression, Intimacy.
b) FATHER FORM.
Publication Date: 1977.
Scores, 5: Parental Involvement, Limit Setting, Responsiveness, Reasoning Guidance, Intimacy.
Cross References: For reviews by Verna Hart and Richard L. Wikoff, see 9:531 (1 reference).

TEST REFERENCES

1. Abraham, K. G., Kuehl, R. O., & Christopherson, V. A. (1983). Age-specific influence of parental behaviors on the development of empathy in preschool children. *Child Study Journal, 13,* 175-185.
2. Mullis, R. L., Smith, D. W., & Vollmers, K. E. (1983). Prosocial behaviors in young children and parental guidance. *Child Study Journal, 13,* 13-21.
3. Poresky, R. H., & Whitsitt, T. M. (1985). Young girls' intelligence and motivation: Links with maternal employment and education but not systems theory. *The Journal of Psychology, 119,* 475-480.

[1279]

Iowa Social Competency Scales.
Purpose: To provide an "easily administered and objectively scored individual rating instrument for parents relative to the social behavior (competencies) of normal children."
Population: Ages 3–12.
Publication Dates: 1976–82.
Acronym: ISCS.
Administration: Group.
Price Data: Available from publisher.
Time: Administration time not reported.
Comments: Ratings by parents.
Authors: Damaris Pease, Samuel G. Clark, and Sedahlia Jasper Crase.
Publisher: Iowa State University Research Foundation, Inc.
a) PRESCHOOL.
Population: Ages 3–6.
1) *Mother.*
Scores, 5: Social Activator, Hypersensitivity, Reassurance, Uncooperativeness, Cooperativeness.
2) *Father.*
Scores, 5: Social Activator, Hypersensitivity, Reassurance, Social Ineptness, Attentiveness.
3) *Combined.*
Scores, 3: Social Activator, Hypersensitivity, Reassurance.
b) SCHOOL-AGE.
Population: Ages 6–12.
Comments: Adaptation of Devereux Elementary School Behavior Rating Scale.
1) *Mother.*
Scores, 6: Task Oriented, Disruptive, Leader, Physically Active, Affectionate Toward Parent, Apprehensive.
2) *Father.*
Scores, 5: Capable, Defiant, Leader, Active with Peers, Affectionate Toward Parent.
Cross References: For a review by Gloria E. Miller, see 10:154; see also 9:532 (2 references).

[1280]

Iowa Tests of Basic Skills, Form J.
Purpose: Constructed to "provide for comprehensive measurement of growth in the fundamental skills: Listening, word analysis, vocabulary, reading, the mechanics of writing, methods of study, and mathematics."
Publication Dates: 1955–90.
Acronym: ITBS.

Administration: Group.

Price Data, 1991: $3 per scoring key booklet; $9 per 35 pupil profile charts; $9 per 35 profile charts for averages; $9 per 35 class record folders (select Levels 5–8 or 9–14); $7.95 per 35 reports to parents (select English or Spanish); $8.40 per teacher's guide (select Level 5–6, 7–8, or 9–14); $2.10 per teacher's guide for practice tests (select Level 5–6, 7–8, 9–14); $21 per school administrator's manual; $6 per school administrator's supplement ('90, 53 pages); $1.98 per administrator's summary ('90, 30 pages); $8.10 per skills objectives booklet ('90, 129 pages); $8.10 per norms booklet (select large city, Catholic, high socioeconomic, or low socioeconomic); $21 per examination kit.

Comments: Forms G and H, parallel forms, available from publisher; Form G Listening Supplement and Writing Supplement may be used with Form J; earlier Forms 7 and 8 still available from publisher.

Authors: A. N. Hieronymus, H. D. Hoover, K. R. Oberley (everything except school administrator's supplement), N. K. Cantor (everything except school administrator's supplement), D. A. Frisbie (everything except teacher's guides for practice tests), S. B. Dunbar (everything except teacher's guides for practice tests), J. C. Lewis (everything except teacher's guides for practice tests and school administrator's supplement), and E. F. Lindquist (teacher's guide for practice tests, Levels 9–14).

Publisher: The Riverside Publishing Co.

a) EARLY PRIMARY BATTERY.

Price Data, 1991: $7.35 per 35 practice tests including teacher's guide; $4.20 per administrator's directions (select Level).

1) *Level 5.*

Population: Grades K.1–1.5.

Scores, 6: Listening, Word Analysis, Vocabulary, Language, Mathematics, Basic Composite.

Price Data: $63 per 35 MRC machine-scorable test booklets including teacher's guide and materials needed for machine scoring; $72.15 per 35 NCS test booklets including administration directions; $27 per set of scoring stencils.

Time: (125–150) minutes, including 10-minute practice test.

2) *Level 6.*

Population: Grades K.8–1.9.

Scores, 8: Listening, Word Analysis, Vocabulary, Language, Mathematics, Basic Composite, Reading, Complete Composite.

Price Data, $86.25 per 35 MRC machine-scorable test booklets including teacher's guide and materials needed for machine scoring; $100.35 per 35 NCS test booklets including administration directions; $36.75 per set of scoring stencils.

Time: (125–205) minutes, including 10-minute practice test.

b) PRIMARY BATTERY.

Scores: Basic Battery, 12 scores: Word Analysis, Vocabulary, Reading Comprehension (Pictures, Sentences, Stories, Total), Spelling, Mathematics (Concepts, Problem Solving, Computation, Total), Basic Composite; Complete Battery, 22 scores: Listening, Word Analysis, Vocabulary, Reading Comprehension (Pictures, Sentences, Stories, Total), Language (Spelling, Capitalization, Punctuation, Usage and Expression, Total), Work-Study (Visual Materials, Reference Materials, Total), Mathematics (Concepts, Problem Solving, Computation, Total), Complete Composite, Social Studies (optional), Science (optional).

Forms, 3: Basic, Complete, Complete Plus Social Studies and Science.

Price Data: $72 per 35 MRC machine-scorable basic battery tests including teacher's guide and materials needed for machine scoring (select Level); $86.25 per 35 MRC machine-scorable complete battery tests including teacher's guide and materials needed for machine scoring (select Level); $90.75 per 35 MRC machine-scorable complete battery plus social studies and science tests including teacher's guide and materials needed for machine scoring (select Level); $83.10 per 35 NCS basic battery tests including administration directions (select Level); $100.35 per 35 NCS complete battery tests including administration directions (select Level); $12.30 per 35 practice tests; $51.45 per set of scoring stencils (select Level); $4.20 per administrator's directions (select Level).

Time: (134–180) minutes for Basic Battery; (227–285) minutes for Complete Battery; (267–335) minutes for Complete Battery Plus Social Studies and Science.

1) *Level 7.*

Population: Grades 1.7–2.6.

2) *Level 8.*

Population: Grades 2.5–3.5.

c) MULTILEVEL BATTERY.

Scores: Basic Battery, 8 scores: Vocabulary, Reading Comprehension, Spelling, Mathematics (Concepts, Problem Solving, Computation, Total), Basic Composite; Complete Battery, 17 scores: Vocabulary, Reading Comprehension, Language (Spelling, Capitalization, Punctuation, Usage and Expression, Total), Work-Study (Visual Materials, Reference Materials, Total), Mathematics (Concepts, Problem Solving, Computation, Total), Complete Composite, Social Studies (optional), Science (optional).

Forms, 3: Basic, Complete, Complete Plus Social Studies and Science.

Price Data: $90.75 per 35 Level 9 machine-scorable booklets (Complete Plus Social Studies and Science) including administration directions and materials needed for machine scoring; $4.95 per complete battery multilevel test booklet containing Levels 9–14; $3.90 per basic battery multilevel test booklet containing Levels 9–14; $68.75 per 35 complete battery plus social studies and science test booklets including administration directions (select Level); $36 per 35 multilevel social studies/science test booklets including administration directions; $51 per 100 practice tests including 3 teacher's guides; $21.30 per 35 MRC answer sheets including teacher's guide, 35 pupil report folders, and class record folder (select Level); $129 per 250 NCS answer folders (select Level); $18 per 100 practice test answer sheets; $16.35 per set of scoring stencils (select Level); $4.05 per administrator's directions; $3.15 per social studies/science directions for administration.

Time: (135–167) minutes for Basic Battery; (256–305) minutes for Complete Battery; (326–385) minutes for Complete Battery Plus Social Studies and Science.

1) *Level 9.*
Population: Grade 3.
2) *Level 10.*
Population: Grade 4.
3) *Level 11.*
Population: Grade 5.
4) *Level 12.*
Population: Grade 6.
5) *Level 13.*
Population: Grade 7.
6) *Level 14.*
Population: Grades 8–9.

Cross References: For reviews by Suzanne Lane and Nambury S. Raju, see 11:184 (24 references); for reviews by Robert L. Linn and Victor L. Willson of Forms G and H, see 10:155 (45 references); for reviews by Peter W. Airasian and Anthony J. Nitko of Forms 7 and 8, see 9:533 (29 references); see also T3:1192 (97 references); for reviews by Larry A. Harris and Fred Pyrczak of Forms 5–6, see 8:19 (58 references); see T2:19 (87 references) and 6:13 (17 references); for reviews by Virgil E. Herrick, G. A. V. Morgan, and H. H. Remmers, and an excerpted review by Laurence Siegel of Forms 1–2, see 5:16. For reviews of the modern mathematics supplement, see 7:481 (2 reviews).

TEST REFERENCES

1. Hunnicutt, R. C., & Larkins, A. G. (1985). An experimental comparison of three methods of using examples and nonexamples to teach social studies concepts. *Journal of Instructional Psychology, 12,* 144-151.
2. Taylor, B. (1985). Toward an understanding of factors contributing to children's difficulty summarizing text book material. *National Reading Conference Yearbook, 34,* 125-131.
3. Colangelo, N., Kelly, K. R., & Schrepfer, R. M. (1987). A comparison of gifted, general, and special learning needs students on academic and social self-concept. *Journal of Counseling and Development, 66,* 73-77.
4. Kastler, L. A., Roser, N. L., & Hoffman, J. V. (1987). Understandings of the forms and functions of written language: Insights from children and parents. *Yearbook of the National Reading Conference, 36,* 85-92.
5. Mosenthal, J. H. (1987). Learning from discussion: Requirements and constraints on classroom instruction in reading comprehension strategies. *Yearbook of the National Reading Conference, 36,* 169-176.
6. Carpenter, T. P., Fennema, E., Peterson, P. L., Chiang, C., & Loef, M. (1989). Using knowledge of children's mathematics thinking in classroom teaching: An experimental study. *American Educational Research Journal, 26,* 499-531.
7. Knight, S. L. (1989). The effects of cognitive strategy instruction on elementary students' reading outcomes. *Yearbook of the National Reading Conference, 38,* 241-251.
8. Way, D., Forsyth, R. A., & Ansley, T. N. (1989). IRT ability estimates from customised achievement tests without representative content sampling. *Applied Measurement in Education, 2,* 15-35.
9. Ansley, T. N., & Forsyth, R. A. (1990). An investigation of the nature of the interaction of reading and computational abilities in solving mathematics word problems. *Applied Measurement in Education, 3*(4), 319-329.
10. Cox, B. E. (1990). The effects of structural factors of expository texts on teachers' judgements of writing quality. *Yearbook of the National Reading Conference, 39,* 137-143.
11. Habenicht, D. J., Byoune, H. O., & Futcher, W. G. A. (1990). Hemisphericity and reading achievement for black and caucasian elementary students. *Perceptual and Motor Skills, 71,* 923-931.
12. Heuvelman, L. R., & Graybill, D. (1990). Assessment of children's fantasies with the Make A Picture Story: Validity and norms. *Journal of Personality Assessment, 55,* 578-592.
13. Kamil, M. L., & Rauscher, W. C. (1990). Effects of grouping and difficulty of materials on reading achievement. *Yearbook of the National Reading Conference, 39,* 121-127.
14. Mosenthal, J. H. (1990). Developing low-performing, fourth-grade, inner-city students' ability to comprehend narrative. *Yearbook of the National Reading Conference, 39,* 275-286.
15. Haddad, F. A., & Juliano, J. M. (1991). Relations among scores on Matrix Analogies Test, Draw-A-Person, and the Iowa Tests of Basic Skills for low socioeconomic children. *Psychological Reports, 69,* 299-302.
16. Reynolds, A. J. (1991). Early schooling of children at risk. *American Educational Research Journal, 28,* 392-422.
17. Rosenbach, J. H., & Rusch, R. R. (1991). IQ and achievement: 1930s to 1980s. *Psychology in the Schools, 28,* 304-309.
18. Smith, M. L. (1991). Meanings of test preparation. *American Educational Research Journal, 28,* 521-542.
19. Sprinthall, R. C., & Nolan, T. E. (1991). Efficacy of representing quantities with different pictures in solving arithmetic word problems. *Perceptual and Motor Skills, 72,* 274.
20. Duax, T. (1992). Attrition at a nonselective magnet school: A case study of a Milwaukee public school. *Journal of Research and Development in Education, 25,* 172-181.
21. Eckenrode, J., Laird, M., & Doris, J. (1992). School performance and disciplinary problems among abused and neglected children. *Developmental Psychology, 29,* 53-62.
22. Forsyth, R. A., Ansley, T. N., & Twing, J. S. (1992). The validity of normative data provided for customized tests: Two perspectives. *Applied Measurement in Education, 5*(1), 49-62.
23. Kruger, L. J., & Wandle, C. (1992). A preliminary investigation of special needs students' global and mathematics self-concepts. *Psychology in the Schools, 29,* 281-289.
24. Meyer, M. J., Day, S. L., & Lee, Y. B. (1992). Symmetry in building block design for learning disabled and nonlearning disabled boys. *Perceptual and Motor Skills, 74,* 1031-1039.
25. Qualls-Payne, A. L. (1992). A comparison of score level estimates of the standard error of measurement. *Journal of Educational Measurement, 29,* 213-225.
26. Walczyk, J. J., & Raska, L. J. (1992). The relation between low- and high-level reading skills in children. *Contemporary Educational Psychology, 17,* 38-46.
27. Wilson, M. S., Schendel, J. M., & Ulman, J. E. (1992). Curriculum-based measures, teachers' ratings, and group achievement scores: Alternative screening measures. *Journal of School Psychology, 30*(1), 59-76.
28. Brown, S. M., & Walberg, H. J. (1993). Motivational effects on test scores of elementary students. *Journal of Educational Research, 86,* 133-136.
29. Farley, M. J., & Elmore, P. B. (1993). The relationship of reading comprehension to critical thinking skills, cognitive ability, and vocabulary for a sample of underachieving college freshmen. *Educational and Psychological Measurement, 52,* 921-931.
30. Lehrer, R., & Littlefield, J. (1993). Relationships among cognitive components in Logo learning and transfer. *Journal of Educational Psychology, 85,* 317-330.
31. Mavrogenes, N. A., & Bezruczko, N. (1993). Influences on writing development. *Journal of Educational Research, 86,* 237-245.
32. Reis, S. M., & Purcell, J. H. (1993). An analysis of content elimination and strategies used by elementary classroom teachers in the curriculum compacting process. *Journal for the Education of the Gifted, 16,* 147-170.
33. Reyes, O., & Jason, L. A. (1993). Pilot study examining factors associated with academic success for Hispanic high school students. *Journal of Youth and Adolescence, 22,* 57-71.

[1281]

Iowa Tests of Educational Development, [Eighth Edition].

Purpose: Designed "to assess intellectual skills that are important in adult life and provide the basis for continued learning."

Population: Grades 9–10, 11–12.
Publication Dates: 1942–88.
Acronym: ITED.
Scores, 9: Correctness and Appropriateness of Expression (Test E), Ability to Do Quantitative Thinking (Test Q), Analysis of Social Studies Materials (Test SS), Analysis of Natural Science Materials (Test NS), Ability to Interpret Literary Materials (Test L), Vocabulary (Test V), Use of Sources of Information (Test SI), Composite, Reading Total.
Forms, 2: X-8, Y-8.
Administration: Group.
Levels, 2: Level I (Grades 9–10), Level II (Grades 11–12) in each form.
Price Data, 1990: $49.80 per 25 test booklets with 1 Directions for Administration (specify Form X-8 or Form Y-8 and test level); $17.70 per 50 MRC answer sheets to be scored by publisher including materials needed for machine scoring (specify Level I or Level II); $9 per 50 parent communications brochures entitled "ITED Scores and What They Mean"; $1.50 per Directions for Administration ('88, 13 pages); $5.40 per Teacher, Administrator, and Counselor Manual ('88, 87 pages); $6.60 per Norms Booklet; $4.65 per Teacher's Guide to Interpreting ITED Results; $1.98 per Administrator's Summary; $13.50 per Examination Kit.
Time: 250(280) minutes.
Authors: Prepared under direction of Leonard S. Feldt, Robert A. Forsyth, and Stephanie D. Alnot with assistance of Timothy N. Ansley and Gayle B. Bray.
Publisher: The Riverside Publishing Co.
Cross References: For a review by S. E. Phillips, see 10:156 (3 references); for reviews by Edward Kifer and James L. Wardrop of an earlier form, see 9:534 (5 references); see also T3:1193 (14 references); see T2:20 (85 references); for reviews by Ellis Batton Page and Alexander G. Wesman of earlier forms, see 6:14 (23 references); for reviews by J. Murray Lee and Stephen Wiseman, see 5:17 (9 references); for a review by Eric Gardner, see 4:17 (3 references); for reviews by Henry Chauncey, Gustav J. Froelich, and Lavone A. Hanna, see 3:12.

TEST REFERENCES

1. Healy, C. C., & Mourton, D. L. (1987). The relationship of career exploration, college jobs, and grade point average. *Journal of College Student Personnel, 28*, 28-34.
2. Ansley, T. N., Spratt, K. F., & Forsyth, R. A. (1989). The effects of using calculators to reduce the computational burden on a standardized test of mathematics problem solving. *Educational and Psychological Measurement, 49*, 277-286.
3. McNamara, T. P., Sternberg, R. J., & Hardy, J. K. (1991). Processing verbal relations. *Intelligence, 15*, 193-221.
4. Becker, D. F., & Forsyth, R. A. (1992). An empirical investigation of Thurstone and IRT methods of scaling achievement tests. *Journal of Educational Measurement, 29*, 341-354.

[1282]

Iowa Tests of Music Literacy, Revised.
Purpose: Assesses "a student's comparative strengths and weaknesses in six dimensions of tonal and rhythm audiation and notational audiation" and compares these scores to the student's "music aptitude."
Population: Grades 4–12.
Publication Dates: 1970–91.
Scores, 9: Tonal Concepts (Audiation/Listening, Audiation/Reading, Audiation/Writing, Total), Rhythm Concepts (Audiation/Listening, Audiation/Reading, Audiation/Writing, Total), Total.
Administration: Group.
Price Data, 1993: $295 per complete kit for all six levels including manual, six cassette tapes, 50 answer sheets, six record folders, and scoring masks; $75 per complete kit for one level (specify level) including manual, one cassette tape, scoring masks, 50 answer sheets, and 6 record folders; $8 per 50 tonal answer sheets; $8 per 50 rhythm answer sheets; $15 per 50 cumulative record folders; $3 per 6 class record sheets; $15 per manual; $15 per cassette tape (specify level).
Time: 36(45) minutes for tonal concepts; 36(45) minutes for rhythm concepts.
Author: Edwin E. Gordon.
Publisher: G.I.A. Publications, Inc.
Cross References: For a review by Paul R. Lehman of an earlier edition, see 8:97 (16 references); see also T2:199 (5 references) and 7:245 (2 references).

[1283]

The IOX Basic Skills Word List.
Purpose: Designed for reading teachers as "a resource for reading instruction and readability determination."
Population: Grades 1–12.
Publication Date: 1980.
Scores: Total score only.
Administration: Group.
Price Data: Available from publisher.
Time: Administration time not reported.
Author: Instructional Objective Exchange.
Publisher: IOX Assessment Associates.
Cross References: For reviews by Mariam Jean Dreher and Susanna W. Pflaum, see 9:536.

[1284]

IPAT Anxiety Scale.
Purpose: Intended as a means of getting clinical information concerning anxiety.
Population: Ages 14 and over.
Publication Dates: 1957–76.
Acronym: ASQ.
Scores: Total, plus 7 optional (recommended for experimental use only) scores: Covert Anxiety, Overt Anxiety, 5 component scores (Apprehension, Tension, Low Self-Control, Emotional Instability, Suspicion).
Administration: Group.
Price Data, 1994: $10.50 per 25 test booklets; $4 per scoring key; $10.75 per handbook ('76, 112 pages); $15 per testing kit including handbook, test booklet, scoring key.
Time: (5–10) minutes.
Authors: Raymond B. Cattell, Samuel E. Krug (manual), and Ivan H. Scheier (manual).

Publisher: Institute for Personality and Ability Testing, Inc.

Foreign Adaptations: South African Adaptation. Ages 15 and over; 1968; adaptation by Elizabeth M. Madge; Human Sciences Research Council [South Africa].

Cross References: See 9:537 (14 references); see also T3:1197 (48 references); for reviews by Richard I. Lanyon and Paul McReynolds, see 8:582 (85 references); see also T2:1225 (120 references) and P:116 (45 references); for a review by Jacob Cohen of an earlier edition, see 6:121 (23 references); for reviews by J. P. Guilford and E. Lowell Kelly and an excerpted review by Laurance F. Shaffer, see 5:70.

TEST REFERENCES

1. Brand, H. J., & Hanekom, F. W. (1984). Adjustment problems of a group of committed children. *Psychological Reports, 54*, 515-518.
2. Egeland, B., & Farber, E. A. (1984). Infant-mother attachment: Factors related to its development and changes over time. *Child Development, 55*, 753-771.
3. Kermis, W. J. (1984). TCIQ: An identification by intensity and frequency of 'potent' testing cues in science. *Journal of Research in Science Teaching, 21*, 609-621.
4. Trueman, D. (1984). Anxiety and depersonalization and derealization experiences. *Psychological Reports, 54*, 91-96.
5. Yates, A. J., & Sambrailo, F. (1984). Bulimia nervosa: A descriptive and therapeutic study. *Behaviour Research and Therapy, 22*, 503-517.
6. Bass, B. A., & Levkulic, P. G. (1985). Effects of verbal reinforcements upon WAIS scores of examinees high and low in anxiety. *Psychological Reports, 56*, 261-262.
7. Dobson, K. S. (1985). An analysis of anxiety and depression scales. *Journal of Personality Assessment, 49*, 522-527.
8. Grace, P. S., Jacobson, R. S., & Fullager, C. J. (1985). A pilot comparison of purging and non-purging bulimics. *Journal of Clinical Psychology, 41*, 173-180.
9. Healy, C. C., & Mourton, D. L. (1985). Congruence and vocational identity: Outcomes of career counseling with persuasive power. *Journal of Counseling Psychology, 32*, 441-444.
10. Silva, J. M., III, Schultz, B. B., Haslam, R. W., Martin, T. P., & Murray, D. F. (1985). Discriminating characteristics of contestants at the United States Olympic Wrestling Trials. *International Journal of Sport Psychology, 16*, 79-102.
11. Sirignano, S. W., & Lachman, M. E. (1985). Personality change during the transition to parenthood: The role of perceived infant temperament. *Developmental Psychology, 21*, 558-567.
12. Fernandez, E., Brechtel, M., & Mercer, A. (1986). Personal and simulated computer-aided counseling: Perceived versus measured counseling outcomes for college students. *Journal of College Student Personnel, 27*, 224-228.
13. Solyom, L., Ledwidge, B., & Solyom, C. (1986). Delineating social phobia. *British Journal of Psychiatry, 149*, 464-470.
14. Healy, C. C., & Mourton, D. L. (1987). The relationship of career exploration, college jobs, and grade point average. *Journal of College Student Personnel, 28*, 28-34.
15. Zurawski, R. M., & Smith, T. W. (1987). Assessing irrational beliefs and emotional distress: Evidence and implications of limited discriminant validity. *Journal of Counseling Psychology, 34*, 224-227.
16. Kotzé, H. F., & Möller, A. T. (1991). Subliminal stimulation, choice behavior and some personality correlates of subliminal sensitivity. *Perceptual and Motor Skills, 72*, 315-322.
17. Quintana, S. M., & Kerr, J. (1993). Relational needs in late adolescent separation-individuation. *Journal of Counseling and Development, 71*, 349-354.

[1285]

IPAT Depression Scale.

Purpose: Designed to estimate depression level.
Population: Adults.
Publication Date: 1976.
Scores: Total score only.
Administration: Individual.
Price Data, 1994: $10.50 per 25 expendable test booklets (4 pages); $4 per scoring key; $11.75 per manual (62 pages); $16 per testing kit including manual, expendable test booklet, and scoring key.
Time: (10–20) minutes.
Comments: Test booklet title is Personal Assessment Inventory; all items are from the Clinical Analysis Questionnaire (519).
Authors: Samuel E. Krug and James E. Laughlin.
Publisher: Institute for Personality and Ability Testing, Inc.
Cross References: See T3:1198 (1 reference); for reviews by Allan L. LaVoie and David T. Lykken, see 8:583.

TEST REFERENCES

1. Skinner, N. F. (1982). Personality characteristics of volunteers for painful experiments. *Bulletin of the Psychonomic Society, 20*, 299-300.
2. Skinner, N. F. (1982). Personality correlates of Machiavellianism: IV. Machiavellianism and psycholopathology. *Social Behavior and Personality, 10*, 201-203.
3. Sirignano, S. W., & Lachman, M. E. (1985). Personality change during the transition to parenthood: The role of perceived infant temperament. *Developmental Psychology, 21*, 558-567.
4. Friedemann, M. L. (1986). Family economic stress and unemployment: Child's peer behavior and parents' depression. *Child Study Journal, 16*, 125-142.
5. Quintana, S. M., & Kerr, J. (1993). Relational needs in late adolescent separation-individuation. *Journal of Counseling and Development, 71*, 349-354.

[1286]

IPI Job-Tests Program.

Purpose: "Screening, selection, and promotion of job applicants and employees."
Population: Job applicants and employees in industry.
Publication Dates: 1948–87.
Administration: Group or individual.
Price Data, 1994: $155 per Test Examination Kit including 1 specimen set of each of 18 tests; $399 per Job-Field Examination Kit which includes all test forms, hiring summary worksheets, aptitude profile sheets, and scoring keys for all job fields; $16 per instruction kit including 1 copy of each recommended test in the job field battery, instructions for administration, scoring, and interpreting tests, and scoring keys; $10 per test package for each job field.
Foreign Language Editions: French and Spanish editions available.
Comments: Program is composed of 18 tests "used in different combinations to form specific batteries for each of the job-test fields"; job fields include Computer Programmer, Contact Clerk, Customer Service Representative, Dental Office Assistant, Dental Technician, Designer, Engineer, Factory Machine Operator, Factory Supervisor, General Clerk, Inspector, Instructor, Junior Clerk, Numbers Clerk, Office Machine Operator, Office Technical, Office Supervisor, Optometric Assistant, Sales Clerk, Sales Engineer, Salesperson, Sales Supervisor, Scientist, Secretary, Semi-Skilled Worker, Senior Clerk, Skilled Worker, Unskilled Worker, Vehicle Operator, and Writer.
Author: Industrial Psychology International, Ltd.
Publisher: Industrial Psychology International, Ltd.

a) OFFICE TERMS.
Price Data: $21 per 20 test booklets; $6 per manual ('81, 5 pages); $9 per specimen set including 3 test booklets, administration directions, scoring key, and interpretation and technical manual.
Time: (6) minutes.
b) NUMBERS.
Price Data: $21 per 20 test booklets; $6 per manual ('81, 7 pages); $9 per specimen set (including manual).
Time: (6) minutes.
c) PERCEPTION.
Price Data: Same as *a* above.
Time: Same as *a* above.
d) JUDGMENT.
Price Data: Same as *a* above.
Time: Same as *a* above.
e) FLUENCY.
Price Data: $21 per 20 test booklets; $6 per manual ('81, 5 pages); $9 per specimen set.
Time: Same as *a* above.
f) PARTS.
Price Data: $21 per 20 test booklets; $6 per manual ('81, 6 pages); $9 per specimen set.
Time: Same as *a* above.
g) MEMORY.
Price Data: $35 per 20 test booklets; $6 per manual ('81, 5 pages); $14 per specimen set.
Time: Same as *a* above.
h) BLOCKS.
Price Data: $21 per 20 test booklets; $6 per manual (for use with Blocks, Dexterity, Dimension, Precision, Tools, and Motor, '87, 7 pages); $9 per specimen set.
Time: Same as *a* above.
i) DEXTERITY.
Price Data: Same as *h* above.
Time: Same as *a* above.
j) DIMENSION.
Price Data: Same as *h* above.
Time: Same as *a* above.
k) PRECISION.
Price Data: Same as *h* above.
Time: Same as *a* above.
l) TOOLS.
Price Data: Same as *h* above.
Time: Same as *a* above.
m) MOTOR.
Price Data: Same as *h* above.
Time: Same as *a* above.
n) SALES TERMS.
Price Data: $21 per 20 test booklets; $6 per manual; $9 per specimen set.
Time: (6) minutes.
o) FACTORY TERMS.
Price Data: Same as *n* above.
Time: (6) minutes.
p) CPF SECOND EDITION.
Acronym: CPF.
Price Data: $21 per 20 test booklets; $14 per specimen set; $10 per manual.

Time: (5–10) minutes.
Authors: Samuel E. Krug.
q) NPF SECOND EDITION.
Acronym: NPF.
Price Data: Same as *p* above.
Time: Same as *p* above.
Authors: Same as *p* above.
r) 16 PERSONALITY FACTOR TEST: INDUSTRIAL EDITION A.
Acronym: 16PF.
Price Data: $35 per 20 test booklets; $14 per specimen set.
Time: (60–70) minutes.
Author: R. B. Cattell.
Cross References: For reviews by Laura L. B. Barnes and Mary A. Lewis, see 11:185; see also T2:1078 (12 references); for reviews by William H. Helme and Stanley I. Rubin, see 6:774; for a review by Harold P. Bechtoldt of the Factored Aptitude Series, see 5:602; for a review by D. Welty Lefever and an excerpted review by Laurance F. Shaffer of an earlier edition of this series, see 4:712 (1 reference).

[1287]

IPMA Correctional Officer Test.
Purpose: To assess skills and abilities needed in an entry-level correctional officer position.
Population: Prospective correctional personnel.
Publication Date: 1991.
Administration: Group.
Parts: 1 test: Entry-Level Correctional Officer.
Restricted Distribution: Restricted to public personnel agencies who have completed a Test Security Agreement and returned it to the publisher.
Price Data, 1994: $40 basic rental fee; $10 per test booklet (agency member); $11.50 per test booklet (non-agency member); $15 per manual; $30 per set scoring fee plus $.25 per answer sheet.
Time: (120) minutes.
Author: International Personnel Management Association.
Publisher: International Personnel Management Association.

[1288]

IPMA Fire Service Tests.
Purpose: To assess skills and abilities needed in fire service positions.
Population: Prospective Fire Service personnel.
Publication Dates: 1973–94.
Scores: Varies by test.
Administration: Group.
Parts: 10 tests: Entry-Level Firefighter (4 exams); Study Guides (for 2 entry-level exams); Fire Supervisor (Sergeant/Lieutenant); Fire Administrator (Captain); Fire Administrator (Battalion Chief); Fire Administrator (Deputy Chief); Fire Administrator (Chief); Fire Engineer.
Restricted Distribution: Restricted to public personnel agencies who have completed a Test Security Agreement and returned it to the publisher.

Price Data, 1994: $40 basic rental fee; $10 per test booklet (agency member); $11.50 per test booklet (non-agency member); $15 per manual; $30 per set scoring fee plus $.25 per answer sheet.
Time: (120–195) minutes; varies by test.
Authors: International Personnel Management Association.
Publisher: International Personnel Management Association.
Cross References: For a review by Lawrence Allen, see 9:538.

[1289]

IPMA Police Service Tests.
Purpose: To assess skills and abilities needed in police service positions
Population: Prospective police service personnel.
Publication Dates: 1983–92.
Administration: Group.
Parts: 15 tests: Entry-Level Police Officer Background Data Questionnaire; Entry-Level Police Officer (5 exams); Study Guides (for 2 entry-level exams); Police Radio Dispatcher; Police Supervisor (Corporal/Sergeant) (4 exams); Police Administrator (Lieutenent); Police Administrator (Captain); Police Administrator (Assistant Chief); Police Administrator (Chief).
Restricted Distribution: Restricted to public personnel agencies who have completed a Test Security Agreement and returned it to the publisher.
Price Data, 1994: $40 basic rental fee; $10 per test booklet (agency member); $11.50 per test booklet (non-agency member); $15 per manual; $30 per set scoring fee plus $.25 per answer sheet.
Time: (60–210) minutes depending on test.
Author: International Personnel Management Association.
Publisher: International Personnel Management Association.

[1290]

Irenometer.
Purpose: Measures attitudes toward peace.
Population: Adults.
Publication Date: 1984.
Scores: Total score only.
Administration: Group.
Manual: No manual.
Price Data: Instrument is available without charge from author.
Time: [12] minutes.
Author: Panos D. Bardis.
Publisher: Panos D. Bardis.

[1291]

IS Manager/Consultant Skills Evaluation.
Purpose: To assess essential skills needed for the position of IS Manager or IS Consultant.
Population: Candidates for IS Manager or IS Consultant positions.
Publication Date: 1992.
Acronym: ISMGR.

Scores: Total score only.
Administration: Group.
Price Data, 1994: $299 per person.
Time: (180) minutes.
Comments: Detailed report provided on each candidate.
Author: Bruce A. Winrow.
Publisher: Walden Personnel Testing & Training, Inc. [Canada].

[1292]

I-SPEAK Your Language℠: A Survey of Personal Styles.
Purpose: Designed to teach employees how to identify and modify their communication style to work best with others in a variety of situations.
Population: Employees.
Publication Dates: 1972–93.
Scores, 8: Favorable Conditions (Intuitor, Thinker, Feeler, Senser), Stress Conditions (Intuitor, Thinker, Feeler, Senser).
Administration: Group or individual.
Price Data, 1993: $45 per 10 questionnaires; $12.95 per Self-Development Exercises manual ('92, 59 pages); $12.95 per manual ('93, 46 pages); $25 per specimen set including questionnaire, manual, and Self-Development Exercises manual.
Time: (20) minutes.
Comments: Also available in Spanish (except Self-Development Exercises manual).
Author: Drake Beam Morin, Inc.
Publisher: DBM Publishing.

[1293]

IS Project Leader Skills Evaluation.
Purpose: To assess essential skills needed for the position of IS Project Leader.
Population: Candidates for Project Leader position.
Publication Date: 1993.
Acronym: ISPROJ.
Scores: Total score only.
Administration: Group.
Price Data, 1994: $299 per candidate.
Time: (180) minutes.
Comments: Detailed report provided on each candidate.
Author: Bruce A. Winrow.
Publisher: Walden Personnel Testing & Training, Inc. [Canada].

[1294]

Is This Autism?
Purpose: Designed to indicate the presence of autistic features in each area in order to develop educational and therapeutic programs.
Population: Ages 2–8.
Publication Date: 1987.
Scores: Item scores only in 8 areas: General Observations, Attention Control, Sensory Function, Non-Verbal Symbolic Function, Concept Formation, Sequencing and Rhythmic Abilities, Speech and Language, Educational Attainments and Intelligence.

Administration: Individual.

Price Data, 1992: £32.20 per complete kit including handbook (31 pages); £18.70 per 10 checklists.

Time: Untimed.

Comments: Other test materials (e.g., Playdo, cubes) must be supplied by examiner.

Authors: Maureen Aarons and Tessa Gittens.

Publisher: NFER-Nelson Publishing Co., Ltd. [England].

[1295]

It Scale for Children.

Purpose: Developed to assess sex-role preference.

Population: Ages 5–6.

Publication Date: 1956.

Acronym: ITSC.

Scores: Total score only.

Administration: Individual.

Manual: No manual.

Price Data: Available from publisher.

Comments: For research use only.

Time: Administration time not reported.

Author: D. G. Brown.

Publisher: Psychological Test Specialists.

Cross References: See T3:1201 (5 references); see also 8:592 (23 references), T2:1247 (25 references), and P:131 (7 references); for reviews by Philip L. Harriman and Boyd R. McCandless, see 6:129 (18 references).

TEST REFERENCES

1. Rekers, G. A., & Mead, S. (1979). Early intervention for female sexual identity disturbance: Self-monitoring of play behavior. *Journal of Abnormal Child Psychology, 7,* 405-423.
2. Paludi, M. A. (1981). Sex role discrimination among girls: Effect on IT Scale for Children scores. *Developmental Psychology, 17,* 851-852.
3. Paludi, M. A., Geschke, D., Smith, M., & Strayer, L. A. (1984). The development of a measure of preschoolers' knowledge of sex-determined role standards. *Child Study Journal, 14,* 171-183.
4. Stingle, S. F., & Cook, H. (1985). Age and sex differences in the cooperative and noncooperative behavior of pairs of American children. *The Journal of Psychology, 119,* 335-345.
5. Rekers, G. A., Rosen, A. C., & Morey, S. M. (1990). Projective test findings for boys with gender disturbance: Draw-A-Person test, It Scale, and Make-A-Picture Story test. *Perceptual and Motor Skills, 71,* 771-779.

[1296]

Jackson Personality Inventory.

Purpose: "To provide . . . a set of measures of personality reflecting a variety of interpersonal, cognitive, and value orientations."

Population: Grades 10–16 and adults.

Publication Date: 1976.

Acronym: JPI.

Scores, 16: Anxiety, Breadth of Interest, Complexity, Conformity, Energy Level, Innovation, Interpersonal Affect, Organization, Responsibility, Risk Taking, Self Esteem, Social Adroitness, Social Participation, Tolerance, Value Orthodoxy, Infrequency.

Administration: Group.

Price Data, 1990: $28.50 per examination kit including 10 reusable booklets, scoring template, 25 answer sheets, 25 profiles, and manual (38 pages); $19 per 25 reusable test booklets; $6 per scoring template;

$4.75 per 25 answer sheets; $4.75 per 25 profiles; $10.50 per manual; $3.50 per Basic Report (machine-scorable answer sheet and 2-page report).

Foreign Language Edition: Available in French (booklets only).

Time: (40–50) minutes.

Comments: Statistical data free on request from author.

Author: Douglas N. Jackson.

Publisher: Sigma Assessment Systems, Inc., Research Psychologists Press Division.

Cross References: See T3:1203 (6 references); for reviews by Lewis R. Goldberg and David T. Lykken, see 8:593 (6 references).

TEST REFERENCES

1. Mulcahy, G. A., & Schachter, J. G. (1982). Cognitive self-modeling, conventional group counselling, and change in interpersonal skills. *Genetic Psychology Monographs, 106,* 117-175.
2. Martin, J. D., MaKinster, J. G., & Pfaadt, N. K. (1983). Intercorrelations among white space responses on Rorschach, Ego Strength, Conformity and Self-Esteem. *Perceptual and Motor Skills, 57,* 743-748.
3. Alleman, E., Cochran, J., Doverspike, J., & Newman, I. (1984). Enriching mentoring relationships. *The Personnel and Guidance Journal, 62,* 329-332.
4. Goldsmith, R. E. (1984). Personality characteristics associated with adaption-innovation. *The Journal of Psychology, 117,* 159-165.
5. Lalonde, R. N., & Gardner, R. C. (1984). Investigating a causal model of second language acquisition: Where does personality fit? *Canadian Journal of Behavioural Science, 16,* 224-237.
6. Pekarik, G., Blodgett, C., Evans, R. G., & Wierzbicki, M. (1984). Variables related to continuance in a behavioral weight loss program. *Addictive Behaviors, 9,* 413-416.
7. Riggs, J. M., & Cantor, N. (1984). Getting acquainted: The role of the self-concept and preconceptions. *Personality and Social Psychology Bulletin, 10,* 432-445.
8. Scarpello, V., & Whitten, B. J. (1984). Multitrait-multimethod validation of personality traits possessed by industrial personnel in research and development. *Educational and Psychological Measurement, 44,* 395-404.
9. Tunnell, G. (1984). The discrepancy between private and public selves: Public self-consciousness and its correlates. *Journal of Personality Assessment, 48,* 549-555.
10. Burisch, M. (1985). I wish it were true: Confessions of a secret deductivist. *Journal of Research in Personality, 19,* 343-347.
11. DiClemente, C. C., Prochaska, J. O., & Gibertini, M. (1985). Self-efficacy and the stages of self-change of smoking. *Cognitive Therapy and Research, 9,* 181-200.
12. Paunonen, S. V., & Jackson, D. N. (1985). On ad hoc personality scales: A reply to Burisch. *Journal of Research in Personality, 19,* 348-353.
13. Goldsmith, R. E. (1986). Convergent validity of four innovativeness scales. *Educational and Psychological Measurement, 46,* 81-87.
14. Kohn, P. M., Annis, H. M., & Chan, D. W. (1986). Maturational changes in Canadian adolescents' cognitive attitudinal structure concerning marijuana. *The Journal of Genetic Psychology, 147,* 321-331.
15. Nobo, J., & Evans, R. G. (1986). The WAIS-R Picture Arrangement and Comprehension Subtests as measures of social behavior characteristics. *Journal of Personality Assessment, 50,* 90-92.
16. Trulson, M. E. (1986). Martial arts training: A novel "cure" for juvenile delinquency. *Human Relations, 39,* 1131-1140.
17. Goldsmith, R. E. (1987). Creative level and creative style. *British Journal of Social Psychology, 26,* 317-323.
18. Paunonen, S. V. (1987). Test construction and targeted factor solutions derived by multiple group and procrustes methods. *Multivariate Behavioral Research, 22,* 437- 455.
19. Epstein, S., & Fast, G. J. (1988). Relation between self- and other-acceptance and its moderation by identification. *Journal of Personality and Social Psychology, 54,* 309-315.
20. Zuckerman, M., Kuhlman, D. M., & Camac, C. (1988). What lies beyond E and N? Factor analysis of scales believed to measure basic dimensions of personality. *Journal of Personality and Social Psychology, 54,* 96-107.
21. Harris, V. S., & McHale, S. M. (1989). Family life problems, daily caregiving activities and the psychological well-being of mothers of mentally retarded children. *American Journal on Mental Retardation, 94,* 231-239.
22. Jackson, J. M., Procidano, M. E., & Cohen, C. J. (1989). Sub-

ject pool sign-up procedures: A threat to external validity. *Social Behavior and Personality*, *17*, 29-43.

23. Reddon, J. R., & Jackson, D. N. (1989). Readability of three adult personality tests: Basic Personality Inventory, Jackson Personality Inventory, and Personality Research Form-E. *Journal of Personality Assessment*, *53*, 180-183.

24. Hough, L. M., Eaton, N. K., Dunnette, M. D., Kamp, J. D., & McCloy, R. A. (1990). Criterion-related validities of personality constructs and the effect of response distortion on those validities. *Journal of Applied Psychology*, *75*(5), 581-595.

25. Langan-Fox, J. (1991). "Operant" and "Respondent" measures of dispositions: Sex differences in the degree of independence between needs, values, and traits. *Journal of Research in Personality*, *25*, 372-385.

26. Usala, P. D., & Hertzog, C. (1991). Evidence of differential stability of state and trait anxiety in adults. *Journal of Personality and Social Psychology*, *60*, 471-479.

27. Ireland, S. R., Warren, Y. M., & Herringer, L. G. (1992). Anxiety and color saturation preference. *Perceptual and Motor Skills*, *75*, 545-546.

28. Redmond, M. R., Mumford, M. D., & Teach, R. (1993). Putting creativity to work: Effects of leader behavior on subordinate creativity. *Organizational Behavior and Human Decision Processes*, *55*, 120-151.

[1297]
Jackson Vocational Interest Survey.

Purpose: "To assist high school and college students and adults with educational and career planning."
Population: High school and over.
Publication Dates: 1976–85.
Acronym: JVIS.
Scores: 34 Basic Interest scale scores: Creative Arts, Performing Arts, Mathematics, Physical Science, Engineering, Life Science, Social Science, Adventure, Nature-Agriculture, Skilled Trades, Personal Service, Family Activity, Medical Service, Dominant Leadership, Job Security, Stamina, Accountability, Teaching, Social Service, Elementary Education, Finance, Business, Office Work, Sales, Supervision, Human Relations Management, Law, Professional Advising, Author Journalism, Academic Achievement, Technical Writing, Independence, Planfulness, Interpersonal Confidence.
Administration: Group.
Price Data, 1990: $17.50 per examination kit including reusable test booklet, machine-scorable answer sheet for Extended Report, hand-scorable answer sheet, profiles, and manual ('77, 107 pages); $19 per 25 reusable test booklets; $4.75 per 25 hand-scorable answer sheets; $4.75 per 25 profiles; $10.50 per manual; $3.50 per Basic Report (machine-scorable answer sheet and 4-page report); $7 per Extended Report (machine-scorable answer sheet and 12-page report).
Foreign Language Editions: Available in French (booklets and Extended Reports) and Spanish (booklets only).
Time: (45–60) minutes.
Author: Douglas N. Jackson.
Publisher: Sigma Assessment Systems, Inc., Research Psychologists Press Division.
Cross References: For reviews by Douglas T. Brown and John W. Shepard, see 10:158 (1 reference); for reviews by Charles Davidshofer and Ruth G. Thomas, see 9:542; see also T3:1204 (1 reference).

TEST REFERENCES

1. Zarrella, K. L., & Schuerger, J. M. (1990). Temporal stability of occupational interest inventories. *Psychological Reports*, *66*, 1067-1074.

[1298]
Jacobsen-Kellogg Self Description Inventory-II.

Purpose: Measures four aspects of social desirability.
Population: College students and adults.
Publication Date: 1983 (no date on test materials).
Acronym: SDI-II.
Scores, 5: Attribution of Positive Traits, Attribution of Negative Traits, Denial of Positive Traits, Denial of Negative Traits, Total.
Administration: Group.
Manual: No manual.
Price Data: Not available.
Time: Administration time not repored.
Authors: Leonard I. Jacobsen and Richard W. Kellogg.
Publisher: Leonard I. Jacobsen [No reply from publisher; status unknown].

[1299]
Jansky Diagnostic Battery.

Purpose: To provide a profile of reading weaknesses and strengths.
Population: Kindergarten.
Publication Date: No date on test materials.
Scores: Ratings in 4 areas: Oral Language, Pattern Matching, Pattern Memory, Visuo Motor Organization.
Administration: Individual.
Manual: No manual.
Price Data: Available from publisher.
Time: Administration time not reported.
Author: Jeannette Jansky.
Publisher: Jeannette Jansky.

[1300]
Jansky Screening Index.

Purpose: Designed to identify children who are at risk of failing in reading.
Population: Kindergarten.
Publication Date: 1972.
Acronym: JSI.
Scores, 5: Letter Naming, Picture Naming, Gates Matching, Bender, Sentence Memory.
Administration: Individual.
Price Data: Available from publisher.
Time: (15–20) minutes.
Comments: Appendix E (pp. 150–159) of *Preventing Reading Failure* ('72) can be used as a manual.
Authors: Jeannette Jansky and Katrina de Hirsch.
Publisher: Jeannette Jansky.
Cross References: See T3:1205 (1 reference) and 8:800 (14 references).

[1301]
Jenkins Activity Survey.

Purpose: "Constructed to measure Type A behavior."
Population: Employed adults ages 25–65.
Publication Dates: 1965–79.

Acronym: JAS.
Scores, 4: Type A, Speed and Impatience, Job Involvement, Hard Driving and Competitive.
Administration: Group.
Price Data, 1994: $195 per 10 questionnaires with prepaid scoring certificate; $41 per 25 questionnaires; $23 per manual ('79, 31 pages); $24 per examination kit; $18.82 per test for scoring service.
Time: (15–20) minutes.
Authors: C. David Jenkins, Stephen J. Zyzanski, and Ray H. Rosenman.
Publisher: The Psychological Corporation.
Cross References: For a review by James A. Blumenthal, see 9:545 (41 references); see also T3:1206 (1 reference).

TEST REFERENCES

1. Prior, D. W., Goodyear, R. K., & Holen, M. C. (1983). EMG biofeedback training of Type A and Type B behavior pattern subjects. *Journal of Counseling Psychology, 30,* 316-322.
2. Benfari, R. C., & Eaker, E. (1984). Cigarette smoking outcomes at four years of follow-up, psychosocial factors, and reactions to group intervention. *Journal of Clinical Psychology, 40,* 1089-1097.
3. Boyd, D. P. (1984). Type A behavior, financial performance and organizational growth in small business firms. *Journal of Occupational Psychology, 57,* 137-140.
4. Boyd, G. M., & Maltzman, I. (1984). Effects of cigarette smoking on bilateral skin conductance. *Psychophysiology, 21,* 334-341.
5. Burke, R. J. (1984). Beliefs and fears underlying Type A behaviour. *Psychological Reports, 54,* 655-662.
6. Contrada, R. J., Wright, R. A., & Glass, D. C. (1984). Task difficulty, Type A behavior pattern, and cardiovascular response. *Psychophysiology, 21,* 638-646.
7. Grimm, L. G., & Yarnold, P. R. (1984). Performance standards and the Type A behavior pattern. *Cognitive Therapy and Research, 8,* 59-66.
8. Holmes, D. S., McGilley, B. M., & Houston, B. K. (1984). Task-related arousal of Type A and Type B persons: Level of challenge and response specificity. *Journal of Personality and Social Psychology, 46,* 1322-1327.
9. Hull, E. M., Young, S. H., Ziegler, M. G. (1984). Aerobic fitness affects cardiovascular and catecholamine responses to stressors. *Psychophysiology, 21,* 353-360.
10. Lane, J. D., White, A. D., & Williams, R. B., Jr. (1984). Cardiovascular effects of mental arithmetic in Type A and Type B females. *Psychophysiology, 21,* 39-46.
11. Leak, G. K., & McCarthy, K. (1984). Relationship between Type A behavior subscales and measures of positive mental health. *Journal of Clinical Psychology, 40,* 1406-1408.
12. Levine, R. V., & Bartlett, K. (1984). Pace of life, punctuality, and coronary heart disease in six countries. *Journal of Cross-Cultural Psychology, 15,* 233-235.
13. MacDougall, J. M., & Dembroski, T. M. (1984). The type A behavior pattern and attributions for success or failure. *Personality and Social Psychology Bulletin, 10,* 544-553.
14. Muskatel, N., Woolfolk, R. L., Carrington, P., Lehrer, P. M., & McCann, B. S. (1984). Effect of meditation training on aspects of coronary-prone behavior. *Perceptual and Motor Skills, 58,* 515-518.
15. O'Neill, R. M. (1984). Anality and Type A coronary-prone behavior pattern. *Journal of Personality Assessment, 48,* 627-628.
16. Ortega, D. F., & Pipal, J. E. (1984). Challenge seeking and the Type A coronary-prone behavior pattern. *Journal of Personality and Social Psychology, 46,* 1328-1334.
17. Perkins, K. A. (1984). Heart rate change in Type A and Type B males as a function of response cost and task difficulty. *Psychophysiology, 21,* 14-21.
18. Ray, J. J. (1984). Confusions in defining "A-B" personality type: A rejoinder to Jenkins & Zyanski. *British Journal of Medical Psychology, 57,* 385.
19. Rhodewalt, F. (1984). Self-involvement, self-attribution, and the Type A coronary-prone behavior pattern. *Journal of Personality and Social Psychology, 47,* 662-670.
20. Rhodewalt, F., Hays, R. B., Cheners, M. M., & Wysocki, J. (1984). Type A behavior, perceived stress, and illness: A person-situation analysis. *Personality and Social Psychology Bulletin, 10,* 149-159.
21. Rose, R. L., & Veiga, J. F. (1984). Assessing the sustained effects of a stress management intervention on anxiety and locus of control. *Academy of Management Journal, 27,* 190-198.
22. Ruback, R. B., Dabbs, J. M., Jr., & Hopper, C. H. (1984). The process of brainstorming: An analysis with individual and group vocal parameters. *Journal of Personality and Social Psychology, 47,* 558-567.
23. Smith, T. W., Follick, M. J., & Korr, K. S. (1984). Anger, neuroticism, Type A behaviour and the experience of angina. *British Journal of Medical Psychology, 57,* 249-252.
24. Smith, T. W., Houston, B. K., & Stucky, R. J. (1984). Type A behavior, irritability, and cardiovascular response. *Motivation and Emotion, 8,* 221-230.
25. Stevens, M. J., Pfost, K. S., & Ackerman, M. D. (1984). The relationship between sex-role orientation and the Type A behavior pattern: A test of the main effect hypothesis. *Journal of Clinical Psychology, 40,* 1338-1341.
26. Strube, M. J., & Lott, C. L. (1984). Time urgency and the Type A behavior pattern: Implications for time investment and psychological entrapment. *Journal of Research in Personality, 18,* 395-409.
27. Strube, M. J., Turner, C. W., Cerro, D., Stevens, J., & Hinchey, F. (1984). Interpersonal aggression and the Type A coronary-prone behavior pattern: A theoretical distinction and practical implications. *Journal of Personality and Social Psychology, 47,* 839-847.
28. van Schijndel, M., DeMay, H., & Näring, G. (1984). Effects of behavioral control and Type A behavior on cardiovascular responses. *Psychophysiology, 21,* 501-509.
29. Vingerhoets, A. J. J. M., & Flohr, P. J. M. (1984). Type A behaviour and self-reports of coping preferences. *British Journal of Medical Psychology, 57,* 15-21.
30. Yarnold, P. R., & Mueser, K. T. (1984). Time urgency of type A individuals: Two replications. *Perceptual and Motor Skills, 59,* 334.
31. Auten, P. D., Hull, D. B., & Hull, J. H. (1985). Sex role orientation and Type A behavior pattern. *Psychology of Women Quarterly, 9,* 288-290.
32. Baron, R. A., Russell, G. W., & Arms, R. L. (1985). Negative ions and behavior: Impact on mood, memory, and aggression among Type A and Type B persons. *Journal of Personality and Social Psychology, 48,* 746-754.
33. Barton, S., & Hicks, R. A. (1985). Type A-B behavior and incidence of infectious mononucleosis in college students. *Psychological Reports, 56,* 545-546.
34. Begley, T. M., & Boyd, D. P. (1985). The relationship of the Jenkins Activity Survey to Type A behavior among business executives. *Journal of Vocational Behavior, 27,* 316-328.
35. Contrada, R. J., Wright, R. A., & Glass, D. C. (1985). Psychophysiologic correlates of Type A behavior: Comments on Houston (1983) and Holmes (1983). *Journal of Research in Personality, 19,* 12-30.
36. Damos, D. L., & Bloem, K. A. (1985). Type A behavior pattern, multiple-task performance, and subjective estimation of mental workload. *Bulletin of the Psychonomic Society, 23,* 53-56.
37. Diethrich, E. B., & Krus, D. J. (1985). Further validation of the Arizona Heart Institute Cardiovascular Risk Factor Questionnaire. *Educational and Psychological Measurement, 45,* 915-923.
38. Fekken, G. C., Jackson, D. N., & Holden, R. R. (1985). The Jenkins Activity Survey (Form T): Is a two-factor solution appropriate? *Canadian Journal of Behavioural Science, 17,* 74-78.
39. Finnegan, D. L., & Suler, J. R. (1985). Psychological factors associated with maintenance of improved health behaviors in postcoronary patients. *The Journal of Psychology, 119,* 87-94.
40. Friedman, H. S., Hall, J. A., & Harris, M. J. (1985). Type A behavior, nonverbal expressive style, and health. *Journal of Personality and Social Psychology, 48,* 1299-1315.
41. Froyd, J., & Perry, N. (1985). Relationships among locus of control, coronary-prone behavior, and suicidal ideation. *Psychological Reports, 57,* 1155-1158.
42. Harbin, T. J., & Blumenthal, J. A. (1985). Relationships among age, sex, the Type A behavior pattern, and cardiovascular reactivity. *Journal of Gerontology, 40,* 714-720.
43. Hicks, R. A., Cheers, Y., & Juarez, M. (1985). Stomach disorders and Type A-B behavior. *Psychological Reports, 57,* 1254.
44. Jones, K. V. (1985). Type A and academic performance: A negative relationship. *Psychological Reports, 56,* 260.
45. Kelly, K. E., & Houston, B. K. (1985). Type A behavior in employed women: Relation to work, marital, and leisure variables, social support, stress, tension, and health. *Journal of Personality and Social Psychology, 48,* 1067-1079.
46. Leak, G. K., Millard, R. J., Perry, N. W., & Williams, D. E. (1985). An investigation of the nomological network of social interest. *Journal of Research in Personality, 19,* 197-207.
47. Miller, S. M., Lack, E. R., & Asroff, S. (1985). Preference for control and the coronary-prone behavior pattern: "I'd rather do it myself." *Journal of Personality and Social Psychology, 49,* 492-499.

48. Nagy, S. (1985). Burnout and selected variables as components of occupational stress. *Psychological Reports, 56*, 195-200.

49. Nagy, S., & Davis, L. G. (1985). Burnout: A comparative analysis of personality and environmental variables. *Psychological Reports, 57*, 1319-1326.

50. O'Looney, B. A., Harding, C. M., & Eiser, J. R. (1985). Is there a substitute for structured interview assessments of Type A behaviour? *British Journal of Medical Psychology, 58*, 343-350.

51. Potts, M. K., Katz, B. P., & Brandt, K. D. (1985). Prevalence and correlates of the Type A behavior pattern in patients with rheumatoid arthritis. *Psychological Reports, 57*, 699-706.

52. Rainey, D. W. (1985). The JAS-T and Type A students: A replication note. *Journal of Personality Assessment, 49*, 528-529.

53. Smith, T. W., & O'Keefe, J. L. (1985). The inequivalence of self-reports of Type A behavior: Differential relationships of the Jenkins Activity Survey and the Framingham Scale with affect, stress, and control. *Motivation and Emotion, 9*, 299-311.

54. Strube, M. J. (1985). Attributional style and the Type A coronary-prone behavior pattern. *Journal of Personality and Social Psychology, 49*, 500-509.

55. Strube, M. J., & Lott, C. L. (1985). Type A behavior pattern and the judgment of noncontingency: Mediating roles of mood and perspective. *Journal of Personality and Social Psychology, 49*, 510-519.

56. Strube, M. J., & Werner, C. (1985). Relinquishment of control and the Type A behavior pattern. *Journal of Personality and Social Psychology, 48*, 688-701.

57. Strube, M. J., Berry, J. M., & Moergen, S. (1985). Relinquishment of control and the Type A behavior pattern: The role of performance evaluation. *Journal of Personality and Social Psychology, 49*, 831-842.

58. Tardy, C. H., Childs, R. J., & Hampton, M. M. (1985). Communication and Type A coronary-prone behavior: Preliminary studies of expressive and instrumental communication. *Perceptual and Motor Skills, 61*, 603-614.

59. Tennant, C. C., & Langeluddecke, P. M. (1985). Psychological correlates of coronary heart disease. *Psychological Medicine, 15*, 581-588.

60. Thurman, C. W. (1985). Effectiveness of cognitive-behavioral treatments in reducing Type A behavior among university faculty—one year later. *Journal of Counseling Psychology, 32*, 445-448.

61. Thurman, C. W. (1985). Effectiveness of cognitive-behavioral treatments in reducing Type A behavior among university faculty. *Journal of Counseling Psychology, 32*, 74-83.

62. Yarnold, P. R., Mueser, K. T., & Grimm, L. G. (1985). Interpersonal dominance of Type As in group discussions. *Journal of Abnormal Psychology, 94*, 233-236.

63. Zeldow, P. B., Clark, D., & Daugherty, S. R. (1985). Masculinity, femininity, Type A behavior, and psychosocial adjustment in medical students. *Journal of Personality and Social Psychology, 48*, 481-492.

64. Bruch, M. A., Pearl, L., & Giordano, S. (1986). Differences in the cognitive processes of academically successful and unsuccessful test-anxious students. *Journal of Counseling Psychology, 33*, 217-219.

65. Caracciolo, S., & Molinari, S. (1986). Convergent validity of self-reported Type A behavior pattern of patients with coronary artery disease. *Psychological Reports, 58*, 831-838.

66. Chen, W., & Coorough, R. (1986). Effect of EMG-biofeedback training in reduction of muscle tension for individuals displaying Type A behavior patterns. *Perceptual and Motor Skills, 62*, 841-842.

67. Crews, D. J., Shirreffs, J. H., Thomas, G., Krahenbuhl, G. S., & Helfrich, H. M. (1986). Psychological and physiological attributes associated with performance of selected players of the Ladies Professional Golf Association tour. *Perceptual and Motor Skills, 63*, 235-238.

68. Davis, S. F., Grover, C. A., Sadowski, C. J., Tramill, J. L., & Kleinhammer-Tramill, P. J. (1986). The relationship between the Type A behavior pattern and process versus impact achievement motivation. *Bulletin of the Psychonomic Society, 24*, 441-443.

69. Ditto, B. (1986). Parental history of essential hypertension, active coping, and cardiovascular reactivity. *Psychophysiology, 23*, 62-70.

70. Frantz, M. E. (1986). An exploratory study of the relationship between Type A and sensation-seeking behavior. *Perceptual and Motor Skills, 63*, 531-536.

71. Hamberger, L. K., & Hastings, J. E. (1986). Irrational beliefs underlying Type A behavior: Evidence for a cautious approach. *Psychological Reports, 59*, 19-25.

72. Heilbrun, A. B., Jr., & Renert, D. (1986). Type A behavior, cognitive defense, and stress. *Psychological Reports, 58*, 447-456.

73. Heilbrun, A. B., Jr., Palchanis, N., & Friedberg, E. (1986). Self-report measurement of Type A behavior: Toward refinement and improved prediction. *Journal of Personality Assessment, 50*, 525-539.

74. Hicks, R. A., Olsen, C., & Smith-Robison, D. (1986). Type A-B behavior and the premenstrual syndrome. *Psychological Reports, 59*, 353-354.

75. Jamieson, J. L., & Kaszor, N. D. (1986). Social comparison and recovery from stress. *Canadian Journal of Behavioural Science, 18*, 140-145.

76. Janisse, M. P., Edguer, N., & Dyck, D. G. (1986). Type A behavior, anger expression, and reactions to anger imagery. *Motivation and Emotion, 10*, 371-386.

77. Lawler, K. A., & Schmied, L. A. (1986). Cardiovascular responsivity, Type A behavior, and parental history of heart disease in young women. *Psychophysiology, 23*, 28-32.

78. McCranie, E. W., & Simpson, M. E. (1986). Parental child-rearing antecedents of Type A behavior. *Personality and Social Psychology Bulletin, 12*, 493-501.

79. Paulhus, D. L., & Martin, C. L. (1986). Predicting adult temperament from minor physical anomalies. *Journal of Personality and Social Psychology, 50*, 1235-1239.

80. Perry, A. R. (1986). Type A behavior pattern and motor vehicle driver's behavior. *Perceptual and Motor Skills, 63*, 875-878.

81. Schmied, L. A., & Lawler, K. A. (1986). Hardiness, Type A behavior, and the stress-illness relation in working women. *Journal of Personality and Social Psychology, 51*, 1218-1223.

82. Shipper, F., Kreitner, R., Reif, W. E., & Lewis, K. E. (1986). A study of four psychometric properties of the Jenkins Activity Survey Type A Scale with suggested modifications and validation. *Educational and Psychological Measurement, 46*, 551-564.

83. Siegel, J. M. (1986). The Multidimensional Anger Inventory. *Journal of Personality and Social Psychology, 51*, 191-200.

84. Strube, M. J., & Boland, S. M. (1986). Postperformance attributions and task persistence among Type A and Type B individuals: A clarification. *Journal of Personality and Social Psychology, 50*, 413-420.

85. Strube, M. J., Berry, J. M., Lott, C. L., Fogelman, R., Steinhart, G., Moergen, S., & Davison, L. (1986). Self-schematic representation of the Type A and B behavior pattern. *Journal of Personality and Social Psychology, 51*, 170-180.

86. Strube, M. J., Lott, C. L., Heilizer, R., & Gregg, B. (1986). Type A behavior pattern and the judgment of control. *Journal of Personality and Social Psychology, 50*, 403-412.

87. Tennant, C., Goulston, K., & Langeluddecke, P. (1986). Psychological correlates of gastric and duodenal ulcer disease. *Psychological Medicine, 16*, 365-371.

88. Valliant, P. M., & Leith, B. (1986). Impact of relaxation training and cognitive therapy on coronary patients post surgery. *Psychological Reports, 59*, 1271-1278.

89. Yarnold, P. R., Grimm, L. G., & Mueser, K. T. (1986). Social conformity and the Type A behavior pattern. *Perceptual and Motor Skills, 62*, 99-104.

90. Drennen, W. T., Ford, H. H., & Rutledge, L. L. (1987). Biofeedback, competitive set, and Type A/Type B interactions with female college students. *Psychological Reports, 60*, 983-989.

91. Dyck, D. G., Moser, C. G., & Janisse, M. P. (1987). Type A behavior and situation-specific perceptions of control. *Psychological Reports, 60*, 991-999.

92. Fontana, A. F., Rosenberg, R. L., Marcus, J. L., & Kerns, R. D. (1987). Type A behavior pattern, inhibited power motivation, and activity inhibition. *Journal of Personality and Social Psychology, 52*, 177-183.

93. Friedman, H. S., & Booth-Kewley, S. (1987). Personality, Type A behavior, and coronary heart disease: The role of emotional expression. *Journal of Personality and Social Psychology, 53*, 783-792.

94. Heilbrun, A. B., Jr., & Friedberg, E. B. (1987). Type A behavior and stress in college males. *Journal of Personality Assessment, 51*, 555-564.

95. Heppner, P. P., Kampa, M., & Brunning, L. (1987). The relationship between problem-solving self-appraisal and indices of physical and psychological health. *Cognitive Therapy and Research, 11*(2), 155-168.

96. Hooker, K., Blumenthal, J. A., & Siegler, I. (1987). Relationships between motivation and hostility among Type A and Type B middle-aged men. *Journal of Research in Personality, 21*, 103-113.

97. Kelly, K. R., & Stone, G. L. (1987). Effects of three psychological treatments and self-monitoring on the reduction of Type A behavior. *Journal of Counseling Psychology, 34*, 46-54.

98. Keltikangas-Jarvinen, L. (1987). Agreement among different measurements of type A behavior in adolescents and young adults. *Psychological Reports, 61*, 13-14.

99. Lee, D. J., King, D. W., & King, L. A. (1987). Measurement of the Type A behavior pattern by self-report questionnaires: Several perspectives on validity. *Educational and Psychological Measurement, 47*(2), 409-423.

100. Lobel, T. E., & Gilat, I. (1987). Type A behavior pattern, ego identity, and gender. *Journal of Research in Personality, 21*, 389-394.

101. McCann, B. S., Woolfolk, R. L., Lehrer, P. M., & Schwarcz, Louis. (1987). Gender differences in the relationship between hostility

and the Type A behavior pattern. *Journal of Personality Assessment, 51,* 355-366.

102. Ward, C. H., & Eisler, R. M. (1987). Type A achievement striving and failure to achieve personal goals. *Cognitive Therapy and Research, 11,* 463-471.

103. Yarnold, P. R., & Bryant, F. B. (1987). Dimensions of social insecurity and their relation to coronary-prone behaviour in college under-graduates. *Psychological Medicine, 17,* 715-725.

104. Yarnold, P. R., Grimm, L. G., & Lyons, J. S. (1987). The Wiggins interpersonal behavior circle and Type A behavior pattern. *Journal of Research in Personality, 21,* 185-196.

105. Becker, M. A., & Byrne, D. (1988). Type A behavior, distraction, and sexual arousal. *Journal of Social and Clinical Psychology, 6,* 472-481.

106. Feather, N. T., & Volkmer, R. E. (1988). Preference for situations involving effort, time pressure, and feedback in relation to Type A behavior, locus of control, and test anxiety. *Journal of Personality and Social Psychology, 55,* 266-271.

107. Heilbrun, A. B., Jr., & Friedberg, E. B. (1988). Type A personality, self-control, and vulnerability to stress. *Journal of Personality Assessment, 52,* 420-433.

108. Kirmeyer, S. L., & Biggers, K. (1988). Environmental demand and demand engendering behavior: An observational analysis of the Type A pattern. *Journal of Personality and Social Psychology, 54,* 997-1005.

109. Lobel, T. E. (1988). Personality correlates of Type A coronary-prone behavior. *Journal of Personality Assessment, 52,* 434-440.

110. MacEvoy, B., Lambert, W. W., Karlberg, P., Karlberg, J., Klackenberg-Larsson, I., & Klackenberg, G. (1988). Early affective antecedents of adult Type A behavior. *Journal of Personality and Social Psychology, 54,* 108-116.

111. Milgram, N. A., Sroloff, B., & Rosenbaum, M. (1988). The procrastination of everyday life. *Journal of Research in Personality, 22,* 197-212.

112. O'Keeffe, J. L., & Smith, T. W. (1988). Self-regulation and Type A behavior. *Journal of Research in Personality, 22,* 232-251.

113. Ortega, D. F., & Weinstein, K. (1988). Cognitive simplicity in the Type A "coronary-prone" pattern. *Cognitive Therapy and Research, 12,* 81-87.

114. Prkachin, K. M., & Harvey, J. (1988). Perception of contingency and the Type A behavior pattern: A signal-detection analysis. *Journal of Research in Personality, 22,* 75-88.

115. Rappaport, N. B., McAnulty, D. P., & Brantley, P. J. (1988). Exploration of the Type A behavior pattern in chronic headache sufferers. *Journal of Consulting and Clinical Psychology, 56,* 621-623.

116. Ray, J. J. (1988). A-B personality type and dominance: A comment on Yarnold and Grimm. *Journal of Research in Personality, 22,* 252-253.

117. Rhodewalt, F., Strube, M. J., Hill, C. A., & Sansone, C. (1988). Strategic self-attribution and Type A behavior. *Journal of Research in Personality, 22,* 60-74.

118. Yarnold, P. R., & Grimm, L. G. (1988). Interpersonal dominance and coronary-prone behavior: Reply to Ray. *Journal of Research in Personality, 22,* 254-258.

119. Yarnold, P. R., Mueser, K. T., & Lyons, J. S. (1988). Type A behavior, accountability, and work rate in small groups. *Journal of Research in Personality, 22,* 353-360.

120. Bishop, E. G., Hailey, B. J., & O'Rourke, D. F. (1989). Reliability of the Jenkins Activity Survey-Form T: Temporal stability and internal consistency. *Journal of Personality Assessment, 53,* 60-65.

121. Bryant, F. B., & Yarnold, P. R. (1989). A measurement model for the short form of the student Jenkins Activity Survey. *Journal of Personality Assessment, 53,* 188-191.

122. Contrada, R. J. (1989). Type A behavior, personality hardiness, and cardiovascular responses to stress. *Journal of Personality and Social Psychology, 57,* 895-903.

123. Strube, M. J. (1989). Evidence for the *type* in Type A behavior: A taxometric analysis. *Journal of Personality and Social Psychology, 56,* 972-987.

124. Suis, J., & Wan, C. K. (1989). The relation between Type A behavior and chronic emotional distress: A meta-analysis. *Journal of Personality and Social Psychology, 57,* 503-512.

125. Watkins, P. L., Fisher, E. B., Jr., Southard, D. R., Ward, C. H., & Schechtman, K. B. (1989). Assessing the relationship of Type A beliefs to cardiovascular disease risk and psychosocial distress. *Journal of Psychopathology and Behavioral Assessment, 11,* 113-125.

126. Bluen, S. D., Barling, J., & Burns, W. (1990). Predicting sales performance, job satisfaction, and depression by using the achievement strivings and impatience-irritability dimensions of type A behavior. *Journal of Applied Psychology, 75(2),* 212-216.

127. Decker, J. J., & Lesler, D. (1990). Type A personality and poor driving habits. *Perceptual and Motor Skills, 71,* 1352.

128. Edwards, J. R., Baglioni, A. J., & Cooper, C. L. (1990).

Examining the relationships among self-report measure of the Type A behavior pattern: The effects of dimensionality, measurement error, and differences in underlying constructs. *Journal of Applied Psychology, 75(4),* 440-454.

129. Furnham, A. (1990). The Protestant work ethic and Type A behaviour: A pilot study. *Psychological Reports, 66,* 323-328.

130. Perry, A. R., Kane, K. M., Bernesser, K. J., & Spiker, P. T. (1990). Type A behavior, competitive achievement-striving, and cheating among college students. *Psychological Reports, 66,* 459-465.

131. Bruch, M. A., McCann, M., & Harvey, C. (1991). Type A behavior and processing of social conflict information. *Journal of Research in Personality, 25,* 434-444.

132. Bryant, F. B., Yarnold, P. R., & Morgan, L. (1991). Type A behavior and reminiscence in college undergraduates. *Journal of Research in Personality, 25,* 418-433.

133. Edwards, J. R., & Baglioni, A. J. (1991). Relationship between Type A behavior pattern and mental and physical symptoms: A comparison of global and component measures. *Journal of Applied Psychology, 76(2),* 276-290.

134. Greenglass, E. R., & Julkunen, J. (1991). Cook-Medley hostility, anger, and the Type A behavior pattern in Finland. *Psychological Reports, 68,* 1059-1066.

135. Kunen, S., & Stamps, L. (1991). A discriminant function analysis of Type A behavior using the 16PF Personality questionnaire. *Educational and Psychological Measurement, 51,* 923-929.

136. Landy, F. J., Rastegary, H., Thayer, J., & Colvin, C. (1991). Time urgency: The construct and its measurement. *Journal of Applied Psychology, 76(5),* 644-657.

137. Mizes, J. S. (1991). Construct validity and factor stability of the Anorectic Cognitions Questionnaire. *Addictive Behaviors, 16,* 89-93.

138. Welsh, M. C., Labké, E. E., & Delaney, D. (1991). Cognitive strategies and personality variables in adherence to exercise. *Psychological Reports, 68,* 1327-1335.

139. Wright, L., May, K., & Jackson, K. (1991). Exaggerated social control and its relationship to the Type A behavior pattern as measured by the structured interview. *Journal of Research in Personality, 25,* 135-136.

140. Malatesta-Magai, C., Jonas, R., Shepard, B., & Culver, L. C. (1992). Type A behavior pattern and emotion expression in younger and older adults. *Psychology and Aging, 7,* 551-561.

141. McKelvie, S. J. (1992). Sleep duration and self-reported Type A behavior: A replication. *The Journal of Psychology, 126,* 285-289.

142. Öhman, A., Burell, G., Ramund, B., & Fleischman, N. (1992). Decomposing coronary-prone behavior: Dimensions of Type A behavior in the videotaped structured interview. *Journal of Psychopathology and Behavioral Assessment,* 21-54.

143. Rohmer, S. C., & Meadows, M. E. (1992). Relation of eye color and gender to Type A scores and vocational preference. *Perceptual and Motor Skills, 75,* 1283-1288.

144. Williams, M., Davison, G. C., Nezami, Z., & DeGuattro, V. L. (1992). Articulated thoughts of Type A and B individuals in response to social criticism. *Cognitive Therapy and Research, 16,* 19-30.

145. Wright, L. (1992). Are the physical and TABP risk factors for heart disease unique to CHD? *Journal of Clinical Psychology, 48,* 705-710.

146. Kopper, B. A. (1993). Role of gender, sex role identity, and Type A behavior in anger expression and mental health functioning. *Journal of Counseling Psychology, 40,* 232-237.

[1302]

Jenkins Non-Verbal Test, 1986 Revision.

Purpose: Designed to measure general reasoning ability based on nonverbal material.

Population: Australian years 3-8.

Publication Dates: 1986-89.

Scores: Total score only.

Administration: Group.

Price Data, 1994: A$5 per reusable test booklet; $4.50 per 10 answer sheets; $4.10 per scoring key; $16.70 per manual ('89, 30 pages); $26 per specimen set.

Time: 25(40) minutes.

Comments: Adaptation of the Scale of Non-Verbal Ability; intended to be used in conjunction with verbal general ability measures.

Author: M. de Lemos.

Publisher: Australian Council for Educational Research Ltd. [Australia].

[1303]

Jesness Behavior Checklist.
Purpose: "Designed to provide a systematic way of recording data about social behavior."
Population: Delinquents ages 13–21.
Publication Dates: 1970–71.
Scores, 14: Unobtrusiveness/Obtrusiveness, Friendliness/Hostility, Responsibility/Irresponsibility, Considerateness/Inconsiderateness, Independence/Dependence, Rapport/Alienation, Enthusiasm/Depression, Sociability/Poor Peer Relations, Conformity/Non-Conformity, Calmness/Anxiousness, Effective Communications/Inarticulateness, Insight/Unawareness and Indecisiveness, Social Control/Attention-Seeking, Anger Control/Hypersensitivity.
Administration: Individual.
Editions, 2: Observer, Self-Appraisal.
Price Data, 1990: $10 per 25 rating forms (select Observer or Self-Appraisal); $29 per set of scoring stencils; $5 per 25 profiles; $12 per manual ('71, 32 pages); $12.50 per specimen set.
Time: (10–20) minutes.
Author: Carl F. Jesness.
Publisher: Consulting Psychologists Press, Inc.
Cross References: See T3:1208 (1 reference); for reviews by Dorcas Susan Butt and Edwin I. Megargee, see 8:594 (3 references).

TEST REFERENCES

1. Carbonell, J. L. (1983). Inmate classification systems: A cross-tabulation of two methods. *Criminal Justice and Behavior, 10*, 285-292.
2. Jesness, C. F., & Wedge, R. F. (1984). Validity of a revised Jesness Inventory I-level classification with delinquents. *Journal of Consulting and Clinical Psychology, 52*, 997-1010.
3. Jesness, C. F. (1986). Validity of Jesness Inventory classification with nondelinquents. *Educational and Psychological Measurement, 46*, 947-961.
4. Lytton, H., Maunula, S. R., & Watts, D. (1987). Moral judgements and reported moral acts: A tenuous relationship. *The Alberta Journal of Educational Research, 33*, 150-162.
5. Massey, O. T., & Murphy, S. E. (1991). A study of the utility of The Child Behavior Checklist with residentially placed children. *Evaluation and Program Planning, 14*, 319-324.
6. Wiederanders, M. R., & Choate, P. A. (1994). Beyond recidivism: Measuring community adjustments of conditionally released insanity acquittees. *Psychological Assessment, 6*, 61-66.

[1304]

JEVS Work Sample Evaluation System.
Purpose: To measure job skills.
Population: High school and adults.
Publication Dates: 1969–76.
Scores: 28 tests: Nut-Bolt-Washer Assembly, Rubber Stamping, Washer Threading, Budgette Assembly, Sign Making, Tile Sorting, Nut Packing, Collating Leather Samples, Grommet Assembly, Union Assembly, Belt Assembly, Ladder Assembly, Metal Square Fabrication, Hardware Assembly, Telephone Assembly, Lock Assembly, Filing by Numbers, Proofreading, Filing by Letters, Nail and Screw Sorting, Adding Machine, Payroll Computation, Computing Postage, Register Reading, Pipe Assembly, Blouse Making, Vest Making, Condensing Principle.
Administration: Individual.
Price Data: Not available.

Time: (19–194) minutes per test.
Comments: Also called Philadelphia J.E.V.S. Work Sample Battery.
Author: Jewish Employment and Vocational Service.
Publisher: Jewish Employment and Vocational Service [No reply from publisher; status unknown].
Cross References: See 8:982 (3 references).

TEST REFERENCES

1. Berven, N. L., & Maki, D. R. (1979). Performance on Philadelphia JEVS work samples and subsequent employment status. *Journal of Applied Rehabilitation Counseling, 10*, 214-218.

[1305]

JIIG-CAL Occupational Interests Guide.
Purpose: To assist in careers education and guidance.
Publication Dates: 1980–92.
Scores: Self-ratings on 2 of six sections chosen by the student (Unskilled, Semi-Skilled, Skilled Craft, Skilled Technician, Semi-Professional, Graduate Professional) yielding six preference scores: Interest in Practical Work/Using Your Hands/Science and Engineering, Working with Living Things, Clerical/Secretarial/Saleswork Including Business and Some Aspects of Law, Work Involving Neatness and an Eye for Colour and Shape, Interest in Working with People in Need, Interest in Working Where You Meet People Including Acting and Writing.
Administration: Group.
Foreign Language Editions: Australian Edition available.
Price Data, 1994: £39.50 per Occupational Interests Guide specimen set; £6.55 per 20 OIG instruction booklets; £10.25 per 20 guide booklets; £17.99 per 100 response sheet IG; £3.99 per 20 answer sheet P3; £4.50 per 20 subject answer sheet SP; £10.50 per scoring templates PI/IG; £3.30 per Illustration Booklet; £27.50 per Reference Manual to the JIIG-CAL system.
Time: (120–180) minutes.
Comments: JIIG—Job Ideas and Information Generator/CAL—Computer Assisted Learning; revision of the APU Occupational Interests Guide; distribution restricted to persons who have completed a training course; one component of a program including a job file and computer programs.
Authors: S. J. Closs (classroom guide, manual, and test materials), P. R. MacLean and M. V. Walker (classroom guide).
Publisher: Hodder & Stoughton Educational [England].
a) JIIG-CAL FOR ADULTS.
Population: Age 18 and over.
1) *Stepping Stones.*
Purpose: Provides careers guidance.
Price Data: £23.99 per adviser's pack; £6.50 per 20 Skills Review; £3.99 per 20 response sheet JA.
b) JIIG-CAL FOR YOUNG PEOPLE.
1) *Subject Choice.*
Purpose: "For helping individuals to choose which school subjects they might like to study."

Population: Year 9/S2 in British/Scottish school systems.
Price Data: £8.50 per 20 questionaires; £9.75 per Teacher's Notes; £11 per Supplement to Teacher's Notes.
2) Job Ideas and Career Plans.
Purpose: "A careers education and guidance programme."
Population: Years 10–11/S3–S4 in British/Scottish school systems.
Price Data: £35 per resource pack; £17.99 per 100 response sheet JY; £12.99 per handbook.
3) HEadlight.
Purpose: Designed for making higher education choices.
Population: Students in or entering higher education.
Price Data: £12.99 per student planner.
Cross References: For reviews by Jo-Ida C. Hansen and David O. Herman, see 9:546.

[1306]

Job Activity Preference Questionnaire.
Purpose: To obtain a measure of job interests or preferences.
Population: Adults.
Publication Dates: 1972–81.
Acronym: JAPQ.
Scores, 16: Making Decisions/Communicating and Having Responsibility, Operating Vehicles, Using Machines-Tools-Instruments, Performing Physical Activities, Operating Keyboard and Office Equipment, Monitoring and/or Controlling Equipment and/or Processes, Working Under Uncomfortable Conditions, Working with Art-Decor/Entertainment, Performing Supervisory Duties, Performing Estimating Activities, Processing Written Information, Working With Buyers-Customers-Salespersons, Working Under Hazardous Conditions, Peforming Paced and/or Repetitive Activities, Working with Aerial and Aquatic Equipment, Catering/Serving/Smelling/Tasting.
Administration: Group.
Price Data: Available from publisher.
Time: Administration time not reported.
Comments: Restructured and simplified version of Position Analysis Questionnaire (2054).
Authors: Robert C. Mecham, Alma F. Harris (test), Ernest J. McCormick (test), and P. R. Jeanneret (test).
Publisher: PAQ Services, Inc.
Cross References: For reviews by Norman G. Peterson and Paul R. Sackett, see 9:547.

[1307]

[Job Application Forms].
Purpose: System for interpreting information gathered on job application forms.
Population: Job applicants and employees.
Publication Dates: 1957–71.
Administration: Group.

Price Data: Not available.
Time: Administration time not reported.
Author: Hilton Shepherd Co., Inc.
Publisher: Hilton Shepherd Co., Inc. [No reply from publisher; status unknown].
a) JOB APPLICATION FORM.
Population: Job applicants.
Publication Date: [1960].
b) PERSONNEL INVENTORY FORM.
Population: Employees being considered for transfer or promotion.
Publication Date: [1960].
c) EMPLOYMENT APPLICATION FORM.
Population: Job applicants.
Publication Date: 1960–66.
d) PERSONNEL RECORD FORM.
Publication Date: 1960–68.
e) CONTENT CONTROL SHEET.
Publication Date: 1960–68.
f) MEDICAL EMPLOYMENT FORM.
Population: Administrators, nurses, and technologists.
Publication Date: 1960–67.
g) EMPLOYMENT APPLICATION.
Population: Nonmedical personnel.
Publication Date: 1960–67.
h) BANK EMPLOYMENT FORM.
Population: Applicants for positions in banks and financial institutions.
Publication Date: 1971.

[1308]

Job Attitude Analysis.
Purpose: Devised to "reveal a person's underlying attitudes pertinent for success and satisfaction in his work."
Population: Production and clerical workers.
Publication Dates: 1961–70.
Acronym: JAA.
Scores: Total score only.
Administration: Group.
Price Data: Available from publisher.
Time: Administration time not reported.
Comments: An inventory for employment interviewing and vocational counseling.
Author: P. L. Mellenbruch.
Publisher: Psychometric Affiliates.
Cross References: For additional information, see 7:980 (1 reference).

[1309]

Job Attitude Scale.
Purpose: Designed to assess intrinsic and extrinsic job orientations.
Population: Adults.
Publication Dates: 1971–88.
Acronym: JAS.
Scores, 17: Praise and Recognition, Growth in Skill, Creative Work, Responsibility, Advancement, Achievement, Salary, Security, Personnel Policies, Competent Supervision, Relations-Peers, Relations-

Subordinates, Relations-Supervisor, Working Conditions, Status, Family Needs-Salary, Total Intrinsic.
Administration: Group.
Forms, 2: Full, Abbreviated.
Price Data: Available from publisher.
Time: (15–20) minutes.
Author: Shoukry D. Saleh.
Publisher: Shoukry D. Saleh [Canada].
Cross References: For a review by Gregory J. Boyle, see 11:186; see also 8:1049 (9 references).

[1310]

Job Awareness Inventory.
Purpose: Designed to be "useful as a pre-test . . . in pre-vocational and career education skills."
Population: Average and special needs students in Grades 10–12.
Publication Dates: 1980–81.
Acronym: JAI.
Scores, 5: Occupations, Do You Know How To, General Information, Interview Actions, Total.
Administration: Group.
Forms, 2: A (pretest), B (posttest).
Price Data: Available from publisher.
Time: Administration time not reported.
Comments: "Criterion-referenced"; no suggested standards of mastery.
Author: Teen Makowski.
Publisher: Media Materials, Inc.
Cross References: For a review by Charles Davidshofer, see 9:548.

[1311]

A Job Choice Decision-Making Exercise.
Purpose: Serves as a behavioral decision theory measurement approach to need for affiliation, need for power, and need for achievement.
Population: High school and college and adults.
Publication Dates: 1981–86.
Acronym: JCE.
Scores, 3: Affiliation, Power, Achievement.
Administration: Group.
Price Data, 1988: $4 per exercise booklet; $150 per scoring software program including scoring manual ('85, 28 pages); $35 per *Managerial and Technical Motivation* book ('86, 178 pages, available from Praeger Publishers, in lieu of manual).
Time: [15–20] minutes.
Comments: IBM or compatible computer required for scoring program.
Authors: Michael J. Stahl and Anil Gulati (scoring software and scoring manual).
Publisher: Assessment Enterprises.
Cross References: For a review by Nicholas A. Vacc and J. Scott Hinkle, see 11:187.

[1312]

Job Descriptive Index and Retirement Descriptive Index.
Administration: Group or individual.
Price Data, 1993: $25 (plus $5 shipping and han-

dling) per bound photocopy of out-of-print book *The Measurement of Satisfaction in Work and Retirement* ('75, 193 pages).
Time: [10–15] minutes per Index.
Authors: Patricia C. Smith, Lorne M. Kendall, and Charles L. Hulin.
Publisher: Bowling Green State University.
a) JOB DESCRIPTIVE INDEX [REVISED 1987].
Purpose: Designed to measure satisfaction with facets of the job and global job satisfaction (i.e., Job in General [JIG] Scale).
Population: Employees.
Publication Dates: 1969–90.
Acronym: JDI.
Scores, 6: Work on Present Job, Present Pay, Opportunities for Promotion, Supervision, People on Your Present Job (Co-Workers), Job in General.
Price Data: $42 (plus $5 shipping and handling) per 100 Revised JDI test booklets; $5 per set of hand-scoring keys; $25 (plus $5 shipping and handling) per User's Manual ('90, 147 pages) for the Job Descriptive Index and Job in General Scales (including hand-scoring key).
b) RETIREMENT DESCRIPTIVE INDEX [REVISED 1993].
Purpose: Designed to measure satisfaction with facets of retirement and global retirement satisfaction (i.e., Retirement in General [RIG] Scale).
Population: Retirees.
Publication Dates: 1969–93.
Acronym: RDI.
Scores, 5: Present Work and Activities, Financial Situation, Present Health, People You Associate With, Retirement in General.
Price Data: $34 (plus $5 shipping and handling) per 100 Revised RDI test booklets; $5 per set of hand-scoring keys.
Cross References: For reviews of an earlier edition by John O. Crites and Barbara A. Kerr of the Job Descriptive Index, see 9:550 (49 references).

TEST REFERENCES

1. Ayman, R., & Chemers, M. M. (1983). Relationship of supervisory behavior ratings to work group effectiveness and subordinate satisfaction among Iranian managers. *Journal of Applied Psychology, 68,* 338-341.
2. Bateman, T. S., & Strasser, S. (1983). A cross-lagged regression test of the relationships between job tension and employee satisfaction. *Journal of Applied Psychology, 68,* 439-445.
3. Garland, H. (1983). Influence of ability, assigned goals, and normative information on personal goals and performance: A challenge to the goal attainability assumption. *Journal of Applied Psychology, 68,* 20-30.
4. Sterns, L., Alexander, R. A., Barrett, G. V., & Dambrot, F. H. (1983). The relationship of extraversion and neuroticism with job preferences and job satisfaction for clerical employees. *Journal of Occupational Psychology, 56,* 145-153.
5. Bateman, T. S., & Strasser, S. (1984). A longitudinal analysis of the antecedents of organizational commitment. *Academy of Management Journal, 27,* 95-112.
6. Johnson, A. L., Luthans, F., & Hennessey, H. W. (1984). The role of locus of control in leader influence behavior. *Personnel Psychology, 37,* 61-75.
7. Joyce, W. F., & Slocum, J. W., Jr. (1984). Collective climate: Agreement as a basis for defining aggregate climates in organizations. *Academy of Management Journal, 27,* 721-742.
8. Maillet, L. J. (1984). Influence of perceived job enrichment and goal characteristics on employees' satisfaction, motivation, and performance. *Psychological Reports, 54,* 131-137.

9. Mangelsdorff, A. D. (1984). Issues affecting Army psychologists' decision to remain in the service: A follow-up study. *Professional Psychology: Research and Practice, 15*(4), 544-552.

10. Norris, D. R., & Niebuhr, R. E. (1984). Attributional influences on the job performance-job satisfaction relationship. *Academy of Management Journal, 27,* 424-431.

11. O'Connor, E. J., Peters, L. H., Pooyan, A., Weekley, J., Frank, B., & Erenkrantz, B. (1984). Situational constraint effects on performance, affective reactions, and turnover: A field replication and extension. *Journal of Applied Psychology, 69,* 663-672.

12. Parasuraman, S., & Alutto, J. A. (1984). Sources and outcomes of stress in organizational settings: Toward the development of a structural model. *Academy of Management Journal, 27,* 330-350.

13. Scandura, T. A., & Graen, G. B. (1984). Moderating effects of initial leader-member exchange status on the effects of a leadership intervention. *Journal of Applied Psychology, 69,* 428-436.

14. Silver, E. J., Lubin, R. A., & Silverman, W. P. (1984). Serving profoundly mentally retarded persons: Staff attitudes and job satisfaction. *American Journal of Mental Deficiency, 89,* 297-301.

15. Stumpf, S. A., & Hartman, K. (1984). Individual exploration to organizational commitment or withdrawal. *Academy of Management Journal, 27,* 308-329.

16. Adler, S., Skov, R. B., & Salvemini, N. J. (1985). Job characteristics and job satisfaction: When cause becomes consequence. *Organizational Behavior and Human Decision Processes, 35,* 266-278.

17. Bhagat, R. S., McQuaid, S. J., Lindholm, H., & Segovis, J. (1985). Total life stress: A multimethod validation of the construct and its effects on organizationally valued outcomes and withdrawal behaviors. *Journal of Applied Psychology, 70,* 202-214.

18. Blau, G. J. (1985). Relationship of extrinsic, intrinsic, and demographic predictors to various types of withdrawal behaviors. *Journal of Applied Psychology, 70,* 442-450.

19. Cellar, D. F., Kernan, M. C., & Barrett, G. V. (1985). Conventional wisdom and ratings of job characteristics: Can observers be objective? *Journal of Management, 11,* 131-138.

20. Drasgow, F., & Kanfer, R. (1985). Equivalence of psychological measurement in heterogeneous populations. *Journal of Applied Psychology, 70,* 662-680.

21. Falck, V. T., & Kilcoyne, M. E., Jr. (1985). Occupational stress in special education: A challenge for school health professionals. *Journal of School Health, 55,* 258-261.

22. Ferris, G. R. (1985). Role of leadership in the employee withdrawal process: A constructive replication. *Journal of Applied Psychology, 70,* 777-781.

23. Frank, S., Cosey, D., Angevine, J., & Cardone, L. (1985). Decision making and job satisfaction among youth workers in community-based agencies. *American Journal of Community Psychology, 13,* 269-287.

24. Hatfield, J. D., Robinson, R. B., & Huseman, R. C. (1985). An empirical evaluation of a test for assessing job satisfaction. *Psychological Reports, 56,* 39-45.

25. Heneman, H. G., III, & Schwab, D. P. (1985). Pay satisfaction: Its multidimensional nature and measurement. *International Journal of Psychology, 20,* 129-141.

26. O'Brien, G. E., & Pere, T. K. (1985). The effects of ability, self-esteem and task difficulty on performance and task satisfaction. *Australian Journal of Psychology, 37,* 309-323.

27. Parsons, C. K., Herold, D. M., & Leatherwood, M. L. (1985). Turnover during initial employment: A longitudinal study of the role of causal attributions. *Journal of Applied Psychology, 70,* 337-341.

28. Pettersen, N. (1985). Specific versus generalized locus of control scales related to job satisfaction. *Psychological Reports, 56,* 60-62.

29. Rosse, J. G., & Hulin, C. L. (1985). Adaptation to work: An analysis of employee health, withdrawal, and change. *Organizational Behavior and Human Decision Processes, 36,* 324-347.

30. Roznowski, M., & Hulin, C. L. (1985). Influences of functional specialty and job technology on employees' perceptual and affective responses to their jobs. *Organizational Behavior and Human Decision Processes, 36,* 186-208.

31. Schell, B. H., & Zinger, J. T. (1985). An investigation of self-actualization, job satisfaction, and job commitment for Ontario funeral directors. *Psychological Reports, 57,* 455-464.

32. Scott, K. D., & Taylor, G. S. (1985). An examination of conflicting findings on the relationship between job satisfaction and absenteeism: A meta-analysis. *Academy of Management Journal, 28,* 599-612.

33. Vecchio, R. P. (1985). Predicting employee turnover from leader-member exchange: A failure to replicate. *Academy of Management Journal, 28,* 478-485.

34. Watson, C. J., Watson, K. D., & Stowe, J. D. (1985). Univariate and multivariate distributions of the Job Descriptive Index's measure of job satisfaction. *Organizational Behavior and Human Decision Processes, 35,* 241-251.

35. Birnbaum, P. H., Farh, J., & Wong, G. Y. Y. (1986). The job

characteristics model in Hong Kong. *Journal of Applied Psychology, 71,* 598-605.

36. Cron, W. L., & Slocum, J. W., Jr. (1986). The influence of career stages on salespeople's job attitudes, work perceptions, and performance. *Journal of Marketing Research, 23,* 119-129.

37. Dalessio, A., Silverman, W. H., & Schuck, J. R. (1986). Paths to turnover: A re-analysis and review of existing data on the Mobley, Horner, and Hollingsworth turnover model. *Human Relations, 39,* 245-263.

38. Fry, L. W., Kerr, S., & Lee, C. (1986). Effects of different leader behaviors under different levels of task interdependence. *Human Relations, 39,* 1067-1081.

39. Hollenbeck, J. R., & Williams, C. R. (1986). Turnover functionality versus turnover frequency: A note on work attitudes and organizational effectiveness. *Journal of Applied Psychology, 71,* 606-611.

40. Howard, J. H., Cunningham, D. A., & Rechnitzer, P. A. (1986). Role ambiguity, Type A behavior, and job satisfaction: Moderating effects on cardiovascular and biochemical responses associated with coronary risk. *Journal of Applied Psychology, 71,* 95-101.

41. Hulin, C. L., & Mayer, L. J. (1986). Psychometric equivalence of a translation of the Job Descriptive Index into Hebrew. *Journal of Applied Psychology, 71,* 83-94.

42. Humphrys, P., & O'Brien, G. E. (1986). The relationship between skill utilization, professional orientation and job satisfaction for pharmacists. *Journal of Occupational Psychology, 59,* 315-326.

43. Jordan, P. C. (1986). Effect of an extrinsic reward on intrinsic motivation: A field experiment. *Academy of Management Journal, 29,* 405-412.

44. Jung, K. G., Dalessio, A., & Johnson, S. M. (1986). Stability of the factor structure of The Job Descriptive Index. *Academy of Management Journal, 29,* 609-616.

45. McShane, S. L. (1986). The multidimensionality of union participation. *Journal of Occupational Psychology, 59,* 177-187.

46. Snyder, R. A., Verderber, K. S., & Morris, J. H. (1986). Voluntary union membership of women and men: Differences in personal characteristics, perceptions and attitudes. *Journal of Occupational Psychology, 59,* 205-216.

47. Spector, P. E. (1986). Perceived control by employees: A meta-analysis of studies concerning autonomy and participation at work. *Human Relations, 39,* 1005-1016.

48. Barone, D. F., Caddy, G. R., Katell, A. D., Roselione, F. B., & Hamilton, R. A. (1988). The Work Stress Inventory: Organizational stress and job risk. *Educational and Psychological Measurement, 48,* 141-154.

49. Rasmussen, J. L. (1989). Score distributions of the Job Descriptive Index: An evaluation of the effects of transformation. *Educational and Psychological Measurement, 49,* 89-98.

50. Netemeyer, R. G., Johnston, M. W., & Burton, S. (1990). Analysis of role conflict and role ambiguity in a structural equations framework. *Journal of Applied Psychology, 75*(2), 148-157.

51. Stone, E. F., Stone, D. L., & Gueutal, H. G. (1990). Influence of cognitive ability on responses to questionnaire measures: Measurement precision and missing response problems. *Journal of Applied Psychology, 75*(4), 418-427.

52. Konovsky, M. A., & Cropanzano, R. (1991). Perceived fairness of employee drug testing as a predictor of employee attitudes and job performance. *Journal of Applied Psychology, 76*(5), 698-707.

53. Buckley, M. R., Carraher, S. M., & Cote, J. A. (1992). Measurement issues concerning the use of inventories of job satisfaction. *Educational and Psychological Measurement, 52,* 529-543.

54. Obermesik, J. W., & Jones, M. E. (1992). Effects of worker classification and employment relatedness on student employee job satisfaction. *Journal of College Student Development, 33,* 34-38.

55. Rentsch, J. R., & Steel, R. P. (1992). Construct and concurrent validation of the Andrews and Withey Job Satisfaction Questionnaire. *Educational and Psychological Measurement, 52,* 357-367.

56. Sawyer, J. E. (1992). Goal and process clarity: Specification of multiple constructs of role ambiguity and a structural equation model of their antecedent and consequences. *Journal of Applied Psychology, 77,* 130-142.

57. Wanous, J. P., Poland, T. D., Premack, S. L., & Davis, K. S. (1992). The effects of met expectations on newcomer attitudes and behaviors: A review and meta-analysis. *Journal of Applied Psychology, 77,* 288-297.

58. Barling, J., MacEwen, K. E., & Nolte, M. (1993). Homemaker role experiences affect toddler behaviors via maternal well-being and parenting behavior. *Journal of Abnormal Child Psychology, 21,* 213-229.

59. Harrison, D. A., & McLaughlin, M. E. (1993). Cognitive processes in self-report responses: Tests of item context effects in work attitude measures. *Journal of Applied Psychology, 78,* 129-140.

60. Judge, T. A. (1993). Does affective disposition moderate the rela-

tionship between job satisfaction and voluntary turnover? *Journal of Applied Psychology, 78,* 395-401.

61. Judge, T. A., & Locke, E. A. (1993). Effect of dysfunctional thought processes on subjective well-being and job satisfaction. *Journal of Applied Psychology, 78,* 475-490.

62. Norvell, N., & Belles, D. (1993). Psychological and physical benefits of circuit weight training in law enforcement personnel. *Journal of Consulting and Clinical Psychology, 61,* 520-527.

63. Vecchio, R. P. (1993). The impact of differences in subordinate and supervisor age on attitudes and performance. *Psychology and Aging, 8,* 112-119.

[1313]

JOB-O.
Purpose: "To facilitate self-awareness, career-awareness, and career exploration."
Publication Dates: 1981–92.
Administration: Group.
Price Data, 1992: $1.65 per test booklet; $.30 per answer folder; $4.95 per administration (Professional) manual ('85, 20 pages).
Comments: Also known as Judgement of Occupational Behavior-Orientation.
Authors: Arthur Cutler, Francis Ferry, Robert Kauk, and Robert Robinett.
Publisher: CFKR Career Materials, Inc.

a) JOB-O E (ELEMENTARY).
Population: Grades 4–7.
Scores: 6 ratings: Mechanical/Construction/Agriculture, Scientific/Technical, Creative/Artistic, Social/Legal/Educational, Managers/Sales, Administrative Support.
Time: Administration time not reported.

b) JOB-O.
Population: Junior high school through adult.
Scores, 9: Education, Interest, Inclusion, Control, Affection, Physical Activity, Hands/Tools/Machinery, Problem-Solving, Creative-Ideas.
Foreign Language Editions: Spanish and Vietnamese test booklets and answer sheets available.
Price Data: $89.95 per Apple or IBM software.
Time: (60–65) minutes.

c) JOB-O A (ADVANCED).
Population: Grades 10–12 and adult.
Scores, 16: Occupational Interest, Training Time, Reasoning Skills, Mathematical Skills, Language Skills, Working with Data, Working with People, Working with Things, Working Conditions, Physical Demands, Leadership, Helping People, Problem-Solving, Initiative, Team Work, Public Contact.
Price Data: $99.95 per IBM software.
Time: [50–55] minutes.
Comments: May be self-administered.
Cross References: For a review by James W. Pinkney of an earlier edition, see 10:160; for a review by Bruce J. Eberhardt of an earlier edition, see 9:560.

[1314]

Job Search Inventory.
Purpose: "To help the job applicant choose realistic occupations for a job search based on a consideration of background and interests."
Population: Job applicants.

Publication Date: 1985.
Acronym: JSI.
Scores, 5: 4 ratings (Interest, Leisure, Training, Work) and Total for each work activity.
Administration: Group.
Price Data: Available from publisher.
Time: (20–60) minutes.
Comments: "For use with the occupational classification structure of the Guide for Occupational Exploration."
Author: New York State Employment Service.
Publisher: U.S. Department of Labor.

[1315]

Job Seeking Skills Assessment.
Purpose: "For assessing clients' ability to complete a job application form and participate in the employment interview, and to serve as a guide for integrating the results into program planning."
Population: Vocational rehabilitation clients.
Publication Date: 1988.
Acronym: JSSA.
Scores, 2: Job Application, Employment Interview.
Administration: Group.
Price Data, 1994: $10 per manual (96 pages).
Time: Administration time not reported.
Comments: Designed as a component of the Diagnostic Employability Profile (DEP).
Authors: Suki Hinman, Bob Means, Sandra Parkerson, and Betty Odendahl.
Publisher: Arkansas Research & Training Center in Vocational Rehabilitation.

[1316]

Job Skills Tests.
Purpose: "Evaluate the ability of industrial workers to perform (various) operations."
Population: Job applicants and industrial workers.
Publication Dates: 1981–91.
Administration: Group or individual.
Price Data: Available from publisher.
Author: Roland T. Ramsay.
Publisher: Ramsay Corporation.

a) READING.
Purpose: "Ability to read a passage and answer questions about the passage."
Publication Date: 1983–91.
Time: 30(35) minutes.

b) ORAL DIRECTIONS.
Purpose: "Ability to follow directions."
Publication Date: 1983.
Time: (20) minutes.

c) MEASUREMENT.
Purpose: "Ability to measure."
Publication Dates: 1981–83.
Time: Administration time not reported.

d) ARITHMETIC.
Purpose: "Arithmetic skills."
Publication Date: 1983–91.
Time: 20(25) minutes.

[1317]

Job Style Indicator.

Purpose: Analyzes how employers and their staff perceive a job.
Population: Adults.
Publication Date: 1988.
Acronym: JSI.
Scores, 4: Behavioral, Cognitive, Interpersonal, Affective.
Administration: Group.
Price Data, 1993: $6 per test booklet; $35 per leader's manual (80 pages); $15 per audiotape (Living and Working With Style).
Time: (30–60) minutes.
Comments: May be used in conjunction with Personal Style Indicator (1992).
Authors: Terry D. Anderson and Everett T. Robinson (JSI and PSI/JSI Leader's Manual), Jonathon Clark and Susan Clark (audiotape).
Publisher: Consulting Resource Group International, Inc.

[1318]

Job Training Assessment Program.

Purpose: Providing a program that assesses a training applicant's likelihood of success in locally available training programs using a machine-scorable paper and pencil test.
Population: Job applicants.
Publication Dates: 1984–85.
Acronym: JOBTAP.
Scores, 8: Basic Work Skills (Speed, Useful Productivity), Inspection/Visualization, Understanding Training and Work Manuals, Applying Training and Work Manual Information, Performing Simple Calculations, Solving Numerical Problems, Following Complex Procedures.
Administration: Group.
Price Data, 1988: $750 per basic package including test booklets and answer sheets, test administrator's manual ('84, 13 pages), technical manual ('84, 62 pages), score interpretation guide, software to score all answer sheets on an IBM PC-XT or compatible to produce reports; price data available from publisher for practice workbook for participants, resume booklet, portfolio, implementation plan, and technical report.
Time: 140(150) minutes.
Comments: Provides a 3-phase process of placement: assessment, planning, and implementation.
Authors: Raymond G. Wasdyke, Norman E. Freeberg, and Donald A. Rock.
Publisher: Educational Testing Service.
Cross References: For reviews by James B. Rounds and Paul W. Thayer, see 10:159.

[1319]

Jobmatch.

Purpose: Developed "to identify jobs or work areas towards which individuals should be well-disposed."
Population: Pupils geared toward nonacademic occupations.
Publication Date: 1982.
Scores: 40 profile scores compared to dispositional profiles of particular occupations.
Administration: Individual.
Price Data: Available from publisher.
Time: (15–20) minutes.
Comments: Self-administered, self-scored.
Author: Industrial Training Research Unit.
Publisher: Macmillan Education Ltd. [England].
Cross References: For a review by George Domino, see 9:553.

[1320]

The John Test.

Purpose: Assesses "oral proficiency for English as a Second Language placement."
Population: Non-native speakers of English.
Publication Date: No date on test materials.
Scores, 4: Comprehension, Connected Discourse, Asking Questions, Total.
Administration: Individual.
Price Data: Not available.
Time: (10) minutes.
Author: Language Innovations, Inc.
Publisher: Language Innovations, Inc. [No reply from publisher; status unknown].

[1321]

Johnson-Kenney Screening Test.

Purpose: "Designed to identify children who may have perceptual motor problems that would interfere with adequate development in reading."
Population: Ages 5.5–6.5.
Publication Dates: 1970–73.
Acronym: JKST.
Scores, 12: Number Concepts (Counting and Recognition, Writing Numerals), Visual Motor Coordination, Discrimination of Form, Symbol Recognition, Spatial Relations, Position in Space, Perceiving Relationships, Auditory Discrimination, Color Recognition, Total, Draw a Person.
Administration: Group.
Price Data: Available from publisher.
Time: [110–120] minutes.
Authors: Rosalie C. Johnson and Rose K. Kenney (test).
Publisher: J-K Screening Test.
Cross References: For a review by Frank R. Vellutino, see 8:433 (2 references).

[1322]

Johnston Informal Reading Inventory.

Purpose: "To assess the reading comprehension of junior and senior high school students."
Population: Grades 7–12.
Publication Date: 1982.
Acronym: JIRI.
Scores, 2: Vocabulary Screening, Reading Comprehension.

Administration: Group or individual.
Price Data, 1992: $9.95 per complete set including manual (106 pages) and Forms C, B, and L.
Time: (20) minutes.
Comments: Forms B and C are approximately parallel and Form L is longer; "high-interest materials utilized."
Author: Michael C. Johnston.
Publisher: Educational Publications.

[1323]
Joliet 3-Minute Preschool Speech and Language Screen.
Purpose: "Differentiates individuals with intact skills from those with suspected problems in phonology, semantics, and grammar."
Population: 2.5–3 years, 3–4.5 years.
Publication Date: 1992.
Scores: 3 areas: Grammar, Semantics, Phonology.
Administration: Individual.
Price Data, 1994: $55 per complete kit including 12 vocabulary plates, 2 reproducible scoring sheets, recordkeeping manual, manual (57 pages), and Apple II recordkeeping disk.
Time: (3) minutes.
Author: Mary C. Kinzler.
Publisher: Communication Skills Builders.

[1324]
Joliet 3-Minute Speech and Language Screen (Revised).
Purpose: To "identify children with age-appropriate phonological, grammatical, and semantic structures."
Population: Grades K, 2, 5.
Publication Dates: 1983–92.
Scores, 5: Receptive Vocabulary, Grammar (Evoked Sentences), Phonology, Voice, Fluency.
Administration: Individual.
Levels, 3: Grades K, 2, 5.
Price Data, 1994: $55 per complete kit including manual ('92, 39 pages), vocabulary plates, recordkeeping manual (15 pages), 2 scoring forms, and record-keeping disk in binder.
Time: (2-5) minutes.
Authors: Mary C. Kinzler and Constance Cowing Johnson.
Publisher: Communication Skill Builders.
Cross References: For a review of the original edition by Robert E. Owens, Jr., see 9:555 (1 reference).

[1325]
The Jones-Mohr Listening Test.
Purpose: "To provide feedback on listening efficiency and to measure the effect of skill building in this area."
Population: Persons in educational and training programs.
Publication Date: 1976.
Scores: Total score only.
Administration: Group.

Forms, 2: A, B.
Price Data, 1989: $49.95 per kit including 50 test forms, audiocassette, and facilitator's guide (26 pages); $4.95 per 25 test forms (specify form).
Time: (25–30) minutes.
Authors: John E. Jones and Lawrence Mohr.
Publisher: Pfeiffer & Company International Publishers.
Cross References: For reviews by Lear Ashmore and John F. Schmitt, see 9:556 (1 reference).

[1326]
Jordan Left-Right Reversal Test (1990 Edition).
Purpose: Constructed "to measure letter and number reversals in the area of visual receptive functioning."
Population: Ages 5–12.
Publication Dates: 1973–90.
Scores: Total score only.
Administration: Individual or group.
Levels: 2 overlapping levels (ages 5–12, 9–12) in a single booklet.
Price Data, 1994: $60 per complete kit including 50 test forms, 50 laterality checklists, 50 remedial checklists, and manual ('90, 64 pages); $20 per 50 test forms; $10 per 50 laterality checklists; $10 per 50 remedial checklists; $17 per manual; $17 per specimen set.
Time: (20) minutes.
Comments: "Norm-referenced."
Author: Brian T. Jordan.
Publisher: Academic Therapy Publications.
Cross References: For reviews by Mary S. Poplin and Joseph Torgesen, see 9:557; see also T3:1224 (2 references); for reviews by Barbara K. Keogh and Richard J. Reisboard, and excerpted reviews by Alex Bannatyne and Alan Krichev, see 8:434 (5 references).

TEST REFERENCES

1. Heydorn, B. L. (1984). Symbol reversals, reading achievement, and handedness of first grade students. *Perceptual and Motor Skills, 58,* 589-590.
2. Heydorn, B. L. (1984). Treatment versus non-treatment in reduction of symbol reversals by first grade children. *Perceptual and Motor Skills, 59,* 36-38.
3. Heydorn, B. L. (1985). Effect of practice of correct symbol reversals on reading achievement by first-grade children. *Perceptual and Motor Skills, 60,* 509-510.
4. Boone, H. C. (1986). Relationship of left-right reversals to academic achievement. *Perceptual and Motor Skills, 62,* 27-33.

[1327]
Joseph Pre-School and Primary Self-Concept Screening Test.
Purpose: Constructed as an early screen for learning problems.
Population: Ages 3-6 to 9-11.
Publication Date: 1979.
Scores: Global Self Concept.
Administration: Individual.
Price Data, 1994: $150 per complete kit including manual (66 pages), 56 stimulus cards, 100 identity reference drawings, and 100 record forms; $35 per

100 record forms; $80 per set of stimulus cards; $30 per set of identity drawings; $25 per manual.
Time: (5–7) minutes.
Comments: May be used with non-verbal children.
Author: Jack Joseph.
Publisher: Stoelting Co.
Cross References: For reviews by Kathryn Clark Gerken and Cathy Fultz Telzrow, see 9:558.

[1328]
Journalism Test.
Purpose: To evaluate students' knowledge of journalism.
Population: High school.
Publication Date: 1957.
Scores, 16: News Values, Arrangement of Facts, Paragraphing, Sentence Variety, News Source, Sports, Feature Values, Speech-Interview, Editorials, News Style, Columns, Advertising, Makeup, Headlines, Terminology, Copyreading.
Administration: Group.
Manual: No manual.
Price Data, 1989: $.43 per test, minimum order of 10; scoring key included.
Time: [60] minutes.
Authors: Frances Miller and Kenneth Stratton.
Publisher: Stratton-Christian Press, Inc.

[1329]
Jung Personality Questionnaire.
Purpose: "To assist pupils in choosing a career."
Population: Standards 7 and 8 and 10 in South African school system.
Publication Date: 1983.
Acronym: JPQ.
Scores, 4: Extraversion vs. Introversion, Thinking vs. Feeling, Sensation vs. Intuition, Judgement vs. Perception.
Administration: Group.
Price Data: Available from publisher.
Foreign Language Edition: Afrikaans edition available.
Time: (25–35) minutes.
Comments: "Criterion-referenced."
Author: L. B. H. duToit.
Publisher: Human Sciences Research Council [South Africa].

[1330]
Junior Aptitude Tests for Indian South Africans.
Purpose: Aptitude measurement of Indian pupils in Standards 6 to 8 for vocational guidance.
Population: Standards 6–8 in South African schools.
Publication Date: 1971.
Acronym: JATISA.
Scores, 10: Verbal Reasoning, Series Completion, Social Insight, Language Usage, Numerical Reasoning, Spatial Perception (2-D, 3-D), Visual Arts, Clerical Speed and Accuracy, Mechanical Insight.
Administration: Group.

Price Data: Available from publisher.
Time: 207(237) minutes.
Author: S. Oosthuizen.
Publisher: Human Sciences Research Council [South Africa].

TEST REFERENCES
1. Lynn, R., & Holmshaw, M. (1990). Black-White differences in reaction times and intelligence. *Social Behavior and Personality, 18,* 299-308.

[1331]
Junior Eysenck Personality Inventory.
Purpose: "Designed to measure . . . neuroticism or emotionality, and extraversion-introversion in children."
Population: Ages 7–16.
Publication Dates: 1963–70.
Acronym: JEPI.
Scores, 3: Extraversion, Neuroticism, Lie.
Administration: Group.
Price Data, 1993: $9 per 25 inventories [$31.25 per 100, $117 per 500]; $7 per scoring key; $2.90 per manual ('63, 11 pages); $5.75 per specimen set including manual and 1 copy of all forms.
Foreign Language Edition: Spanish edition available.
Time: [15–20] minutes.
Author: Sybil B. G. Eysenck.
Publisher: EdITS/Educational and Industrial Testing Service.
Cross References: See 9:561 (10 references), T3:1229 (24 references), 8:596 (36 references), and T2:1252 (14 references); for reviews by Maurice Chazan and Robert D. Wirt and excerpted reviews by Gertrude H. Keir and B. Semeonoff, see 7:96 (19 references); see also P:135 (7 references).

TEST REFERENCES
1. Blagg, N. R., & Yule, W. (1984). The behavioural treatment of school refusal—A comparative study. *Behaviour Research and Therapy, 22,* 119-127.
2. Eysenck, S. B. G., & Dimitriou, E. C. (1984). Cross-cultural comparison of personality: Greek children and English children. *Social Behavior and Personality, 12*(1), 45-54.
3. Place, M., Kolvin, I., MacMillan, A., & Nicol, R. (1985). The relevance of the multiple criterion screen to an adolescent population. *Psychological Medicine, 15,* 661-670.
4. Poole, M. E., & Low, B. C. (1985). Career and marriage: Orientations of adolescent girls. *The Australian Journal of Education, 29,* 36-46.
5. Aplin, D. Y., & Rowson, V. J. (1986). Personality and functional hearing loss in children. *British Journal of Clinical Psychology, 25,* 313-314.
6. Kotsopoulos, S., & Mellor, C. (1986). Extralinguistic speech characteristics of children with conduct and anxiety disorders. *Journal of Child Psychology and Psychiatry and Allied Disciplines, 27,* 99-108.
7. Riding, R. J., & Banner, G. E. (1986). Sex and personality differences in second language performance in secondary school pupils. *British Journal of Educational Psychology, 56,* 366-370.
8. Riding, R. J., & Cowley, J. (1986). Extraversion and sex differences in reading performance in eight-year-old children. *British Journal of Educational Psychology, 56,* 88-94.
9. Francis, L. J., Pearson, P. R., & Kay, W. K. (1988). Religiosity and lie scores: A question of interpretation. *Social Behavior and Personality, 16,* 91-95.
10. Lefkowitz, M. M., Tesiny, E. P., & Solodow, W. (1989). A rating scale for assessing dysphoria in youth. *Journal of Abnormal Child Psychology, 17,* 337-347.
11. Lynn, R., Hampson, S., & Agahi, E. (1989). Genetic and environmental mechanisms determining intelligence, neuroticism, extraver-

sion and psychoticism: An analysis of Irish siblings. *British Journal of Psychology, 80,* 499-507.

12. Cassidy, T., & Lynn, R. (1991). Achievement motivation, educational attainment, cycles of disadvantage and social competence: Some longitudianal data. *The British Journal of Educational Psychology, 61,* 1-12.

13. Weinberg, R. A., Scarr, S., & Waldman, I. D. (1992). The Minnesota Transracial Adoption Study: A follow-up of IQ test performance at adolescence. *Intelligence, 16,* 117-135.

[1332]

Junior High School Mathematics Test: Acorn Achievement Tests.

Purpose: Designed to test the pupil's knowledge of junior high level mathematics concepts, skills, and insights.

Population: Grades 7–9.

Publication Dates: 1942–52.

Scores, 4: Concepts, Problem Analysis, Problems, Total.

Administration: Group.

Price Data: Available from publisher.

Time: 52(57) minutes.

Author: Harry Eisner.

Publisher: Psychometric Affiliates.

Cross References: For a review by Myron F. Rosskopf, see 5:429; for a review by William Betz, see 3:310.

[1333]

Junior Rating Scale.

Purpose: Designed to provide teachers with a framework to record and display visually ratings of pupils' strengths and needs.

Population: Ages 8–11.

Publication Date: 1990.

Acronym: JRS.

Scores: 5 subscale scores: Language/Education, Motor Skills, Behaviour, Social Integration, General Development.

Administration: Individual.

Price Data: Available from publisher.

Time: Untimed.

Comments: Developed from Infant Rating Scale (9:505).

Authors: J. A. Abraham and G. A. Lindsay.

Publisher: NFER-Nelson Publishing Co., Ltd. [England].

[1334]

Junior Scholastic Proficiency Battery.

Purpose: Measures "proficiency in certain broad scholastic fields of study . . . [for use] as an aid in the guidance of pupils."

Population: Standards 5–8 in South African school system.

Publication Dates: 1975–88.

Acronym: JSPB.

Scores, 6: First Language (Afrikaans or English), Mathematics, Natural Sciences, Geography, History, Second Language (English or Afrikaans).

Administration: Group.

Price Data: Available from publisher.

Time: 94(114) minutes.

Comments: Test materials in both Afrikaans and English.

Authors: J. J. Wolmarans, V. H. Paul (manual), and F. A. Verwey (test).

Publisher: Human Sciences Research Council [South Africa].

[1335]

Junior South African Individual Scales.

Purpose: Measures general intellectual level.

Population: South African children ages 3.0–7.11.

Publication Dates: 1981–88.

Acronym: JSAIS.

Scores, 27: Verbal (Vocabulary, Reading Knowledge, Story Memory, Picture Riddles, Word Association, Social Reasoning, Picture Analogies, Word Fluency), Numerical (Number and Quantity A, Number and Quantity B, Number and Quantity A & B, Memory for Digits A, Memory for Digits B, Memory for Digits A & B), Visual-Spatial (Form Board, Block Designs, Absurdities A, Absurdities B, Form Discrimination A & B, Grouping, Gestalt Completion, Picture Series, Picture Puzzles, Visual Memory A, Visual Memory B, Visual Memory A & B, Copying).

Administration: Individual.

Price Data: Available from publisher.

Foreign Language Edition: Afrikaans edition available.

Time: (60–90) minutes.

Authors: Elizabeth M. Madge (manuals, Parts 1-3), A. R. vandenBerg (manual, Part 3), Maryna Robinson (manual, Part 3), and J. Landman (appendix to manuals).

Publisher: Human Sciences Research Council [South Africa].

TEST REFERENCES

1. Brand, H. J. (1991). Correlation for scores on Revised Test of Visual-Motor Integration and Copying Test for a South African sample. *Perceptual and Motor Skills, 73,* 225-226.

[1336]

Juvenile Justice Policy Inventory.

Purpose: "Designed to assess both individual attitudes toward juvenile justice policies and characteristic methods of dealing with juvenile offenders."

Population: Juvenile justice professionals.

Publication Date: 1973.

Scores, 4: Reintegration, Rehabilitation, Reform, Restraint.

Administration: Group.

Price Data: Available from publisher.

Time: Administration time not reported.

Author: Vincent O'Leary.

Publisher: National Council on Crime and Delinquency.

[1337]

Kagan Affective Sensitivity Scale.

Purpose: "Designed to measure sensitivity to emotions in interpersonal interactions."

Population: Persons in the helping professions.
Publication Dates: 1980–93.
Acronym: KASS.
Scores, 22: Between, Within, Adult, Child, Male, Female, Black, White, Total, Affection, Anger, Confusion, Distrust, Fear/Anxiety, Guilt/Shame, Happiness, Helplessness, Sadness, Counseling/Psychotherapy, School, Medical, Informal.
Administration: Group.
Form, 1: H.
Price Data, 1994: $500 per 80-minute videotape, examiner's manual ('80, 31 pages), and test.
Time: (80) minutes.
Comments: Consists of a series of filmed encounters between 2 or more persons; previously listed as Affective Sensitivity Scale.
Author: Norman Kagan.
Publisher: Mason Media, Inc.
Cross References: For a review by Donald A. Leton of the earlier edition, see 9:60.

TEST REFERENCES

1. Carlozzi, A. F., Gaa, J. P., & Liberman, D. B. (1983). Empathy and ego development. *Journal of Counseling Psychology, 30,* 113-116.

[1338]

Kahn Intelligence Tests: Experimental Form.
Purpose: Designed to measure intelligence in special populations.
Population: Ages 1 month and over (particularly the verbally or culturally handicapped).
Publication Date: 1960.
Acronym: KIT:EXP.
Scores, 7: Main Scale plus 6 optional scales: Brief Scale, Concept Formation, Recall, Motor Coordination, Scale for Use With the Deaf, Scale for Use With the Blind.
Administration: Individual.
Price Data, 1989: $52 per complete kit including plastic objects, felt strip, storage box, manual (34 pages, reprint of article from *Percept & Motor Skills*), and 50 record sheets; $16 per 50 record sheets; $5 per manual; $3 per replacement plastic object.
Time: Administration time not reported.
Comments: Uses same test objects as Kahn Test of Symbol Arrangement (1339).
Author: Theodore C. Kahn.
Publisher: Psychological Test Specialists.
Cross References: See T3:1236 (2 references) and T2:502 (1 reference); for a review by Marjorie P. Honzik, see 7:411 (6 references); see also 6:524 (2 references).

TEST REFERENCES

1. Raggio, D. J. (1993). Correlations of the Kahn Intelligence Test and the WAIS-R IQs among mentally retarded adults. *Perceptual and Motor Skills, 76,* 252-254.

[1339]

Kahn Test of Symbol Arrangement.
Purpose: Designed to identify "the nature of the testee's cultural-symbolic thinking."

Population: Ages 6 and over.
Publication Dates: 1949–60.
Acronym: KTSA.
Scores: Total score only.
Administration: Individual.
Price Data, 1989: $50 per complete kit including plastic objects, felt strip, 10 individual record sheets, general manual ('56, 37 pages), and clinical manual ('57, 75 pages); $15 per 50 record sheets; $4 per general manual; $6 per clinical manual; $3 per replacement plastic object.
Time: (15–30) minutes.
Author: Theodore C. Kahn.
Publisher: Psychological Test Specialists.
Cross References: See T3:1237 (4 references), T2:1478 (27 references), P:447 (36 references), and 6:224 (10 references); for reviews by Cherry Ann Clark and Richard Jessor and an excerpted review by Laurance F. Shaffer, see 5:145 (16 references); for a review by Edward Joseph Shoben, Jr., see 4:110 (2 references).

TEST REFERENCES

1. Reeves, W. H. (1978). Perception and conceptual thinking in language disabled children. *Journal of the Association for the Study of Perception, 13*(1), 24-29.

[1340]

Katz Adjustment Scale.
Purpose: Assesses aspects of a patient's functioning in the community using the patient and a close relative as respondents.
Population: Normal and mentally disordered adults.
Publication Dates: 1961–76.
Acronym: KAS.
Administration: Group.
Price Data: Available from publisher.
Time: Administration time not reported.
Comments: For research use only; test booklet title is KAS Behavior Inventories.
Authors: Martin M. Katz, Samuel B. Lyerly (manual), and Henri A. Lowery (supplement).
Publisher: Martin M. Katz [No reply from publisher; status unknown].
a) SCALES DESIGNED FOR RELATIVE'S RATINGS (R SCALES).
Forms, 5: R1 (Relatives Ratings of Patient's Symptoms and Social Behavior), R2 (Level of Performance of Socially Expected Activities), R3 (Level of Expectations for Performance of Social Activities), RS4 (Level of Free Time Activities), R5 (Level of Satisfaction with Free Time Activities).
b) SCALES DESIGNED FOR PATIENT'S SELF-RATINGS (S SCALES).
Forms, 5: S1 (Symptom Discomfort), S2, S3, RS4, S5.
Cross References: See T3:1240 (18 references), 8:599 (3 references), T2:1255 (12 references), and P:138 (10 references).

TEST REFERENCES

1. Glick, I. D., Hargreaves, W. A., Drues, J., Showstack, J. A., & Katzow, J. J. (1977). Short vs. long hospitalization: A prospective controlled study. *Archives of General Psychiatry, 34,* 314-317.

2. Engelhardt, D. M., Rudorfer, L., & Rosen, B. (1978). Haloperidol and thiothixene in the long-term treatment of chronic schizophrenic outpatients in an urban community: Social and vocational adjustment. *The Journal of Clinical Psychiatry, 39,* 834-840.

3. Quitkin, F., Rifkin, A., Kane, J., Ramos-Lorenzi, J. R., & Klein, D. F. (1978). Long-acting oral vs. injectable antipsychotic drugs in schizophrenics: A one-year double-blind comparison in multiple episode schizophrenics. *Archives of General Psychiatry, 35,* 889-892.

4. Goldstein, S. E., & Birnbom, F. (1979). Nylidrin HCl in the treatment of symptoms of the aged: A double-blind placebo controlled study. *The Journal of Clinical Psychiatry, 40,* 520-524.

5. Hogarty, G. E., Schooler, N. R., Ulrich, R., Mussare, F., Ferro, P., & Herron, E. (1979). Fluphenazine and social therapy in the aftercare of schizophrenic patients. *Archives of General Psychiatry, 36,* 1283-1294.

6. Prusoff, B. A., Williams, D. H., Weissman, M. M., & Astrachan, B. M. (1979). Treatment of secondary depression in schizophrenia: A double-blind, placebo-controlled trial of amitriptyline added to perphenazine. *Archives of General Psychiatry, 36,* 569-575.

7. Nevid, J. S., Capurso, R., & Morrison, J. K. (1980). Patient's adjustment to family-care as related to their perceptions of real-ideal differences in treatment environments. *American Journal of Community Psychology, 8,* 117-120.

8. Young, M. A., & Meltzer, H. Y. (1980). The relationship of demographic, clinical, and outcome variables to neuroleptic treatment requirements. *Schizophrenia Bulletin, 6,* 88-101.

9. Summers, F. (1981). The post-acute functioning of the schizophrenic. *Journal of Clinical Psychology, 37,* 705-714.

10. Mitchell, R. E. (1982). Social networks and psychiatric clients: The personal and environmental context. *American Journal of Community Psychology, 10,* 387-401.

11. Harrow, M., Silverstein, M., & Marengo, J. (1983). Disordered thinking: Does it identify nuclear schizophrenia? *Archives of General Psychiatry, 40,* 765-771.

12. Merikangas, K. R., Bromet, E.J., & Spiker, D. G. (1983). Assortative mating, social adjustment, and course of illness in primary affective disorder. *Archives of General Psychiatry, 40,* 795-800.

13. Summers, F., & Hersh, S. (1983). Psychiatric chronicity and diagnosis. *Schizophrenia Bulletin, 9,* 122-133.

14. Summers, F., Harrow, M., & Westermeyer, J. (1983). Neurotic symptoms in the postacute phase of schizophrenia. *The Journal of Nervous and Mental Disease, 171,* 216-221.

15. Chu, C. R. L., Lubin, B., & Sue, S. (1984). Reliability and validity of the Chinese Depression Adjective Check Lists. *Journal of Clinical Psychology, 40,* 1409-1413.

16. Harder, D. W., Greenwald, D. F., & Wechsler, S. (1984). The Urist Rorschach Mutuality of Autonomy Scale as an indicator of psychopathology. *Journal of Clinical Psychology, 40,* 1078-1083.

17. Stanton, A. H., Gunderson, J. G., Knapp, P. H., Frank, A. F., Vannicelli, M. L., Schnitzer, R., & Rosenthal, R. (1984). Effects of psychotherapy in schizophrenia: I. Design and implementation of a controlled study. *Schizophrenia Bulletin, 10,* 520-563.

18. Lorimor, R. J., Kaplan, H. B., & Pokorny, A. D. (1985). Self-derogation and adjustment in the community: A longitudinal study of psychiatric patients. *American Journal of Psychiatry, 142,* 1442-1446.

19. McSweeny, A. J., Grant, I., Heaton, R. K., Prigatano, G. P., & Adams, K. M. (1985). Relationship of neuropsychological status to everyday functioning in healthy and chronically ill persons. *Journal of Clinical and Experimental Neuropsychology, 7,* 281-291.

20. Newton, A., & Johnson, D. A. (1985). Social adjustment and interaction after severe head injury. *British Journal of Clinical Psychology, 24,* 225-234.

21. Klonoff, P. S., Costa, L. D., & Snow, W. G. (1986). Predictors and indicators of quality of life in patients with closed-head injury. *Journal of Clinical and Experimental Neuropsychology, 8,* 469-485.

22. Rabiner, C. J., Wegner, J. T., & Kane, J. M. (1986). Outcome study of first-episode psychosis, I: Relapse rates after 1 year. *American Journal of Psychiatry, 143,* 1155-1158.

23. Sartorius, N., Jablensky, A., Korten, A., Ernberg, G., Anker, M., Cooper, J. E., & Day, R. (1986). Preliminary communication: Early manifestations and first-contact incidence of schizophrenia in different cultures: A preliminary report on the initial evaluation phase of the WHO collaborative study on determinants of outcome of severe mental disorders. *Psychological Medicine, 16,* 909-928.

24. Wallace, C. J. (1986). Functional assessment in rehabilitation. *Schizophrenia Bulletin: National Institute of Mental Health, 12,* 604-630.

25. Johnson, D. A., & Newton, A. (1987). Social adjustment and interaction after severe head injury: II. Rationale and bases for intervention. *British Journal of Clinical Psychology, 26,* 289-298.

26. Kettering, R. L., Harrow, M., Grossman, L., & Meltzer, H. Y. (1987). The prognostic relevance of delusions in depression: A follow-up study. *American Journal of Psychiatry, 144,* 1154-1160.

27. Marengo, J. T., Harrow, M., & Westermeyer, J. F. (1991). Early longitudinal course of acute-chronic and paranoid-undifferentiated schizophrenia subtypes and schizophrenia disorder. *Journal of Abnormal Psychology, 100,* 600-603.

28. Fenton, G., McClelland, R., Montgomery, A., MacFlynn, G., & Rutherford, W. (1993). The postconcussional syndrome: Social antecedents and psychological sequelae. *British Journal of Psychiatry, 162,* 493-497.

29. Keiller, S. W., & Graham, J. R. (1993). The meaning of low scores on MMPI-2 clinical scales of normal subjects. *Journal of Personality Assessment, 61,* 211-223.

30. DeSouza, E. R., Lubin, B., & Zanelli, J. (1994). Norms, reliability, and concurrent validity measures of the Portuguese version of the Depression Adjective Check Lists. *Journal of Clinical Psychology, 50,* 208-215.

[1341]

Katz-Zalk Opinion Questionnaire.

Purpose: Measures "racial attitudes in children."

Population: Grades 1-6.

Publication Dates: 1973-75.

Scores, 3: Negative, Positive, Total.

Administration: Group.

Price Data: Not available.

Time: [30-45] minutes.

Comments: Prepublication form called Projective Prejudice Test.

Authors: Phyllis A. Katz and Sue R. Zalk.

Publisher: Sue R. Zalk [No reply from publisher; status unknown].

Cross References: For additional information, see 8:600 (3 references).

[1342]

Kaufman Adolescent and Adult Intelligence Test.

Purpose: Designed as a "measure of general intelligence."

Population: Ages 11 to 85 + .

Publication Date: 1993.

Acronym: KAIT.

Scores, 9 to 14: Crystalized Scale (Definitions, Auditory Comprehension, Double Meanings, Famous Faces [alternate subtest], Total), Fluid Scale (Rebus Learning, Logical Steps, Mystery Codes, Memory for Block Designs [alternate subtest], Total), Measures of Delayed Recall [optional] (Rebus Delayed Recall, Auditory Delayed Recall), Mental Status [supplementary subtest], Total.

Administration: Individual.

Price Data, 1994: $495 per complete kit; $40 per record set including 25 each, record booklets and mystery code booklets; $40 per manual (161 pages); $135 per KAIT Assist (IBM); $79 per KAIT training video.

Time: (58-73) minutes for Core Battery; (83-102) minutes for Expanded Battery.

Authors: Alan S. Kaufman and Nadeen L. Kaufman.

Publisher: American Guidance Service, Inc.

TEST REFERENCES

1. Ittenbach, R. F., & Harrison, P. Y. (1990). Predicting ego-strength from problem-solving ability of college students. *Measurement and Evaluation in Counseling and Development, 23,* 128-136.

[1343]

Kaufman Assessment Battery for Children.

Purpose: Designed as a clinical instrument for assessing cognitive development.

Population: Ages 2.5 to 12.5.

Publication Date: 1983.

Acronym: K-ABC.

Scores: 16 subtests with a maximum of 13 administered to any particular child: 10 mental processing subtests: Magic Window (Ages 2.5–5.0), Face Recognition (Ages 2.5–5.0), Hand Movements (Ages 2.5–12.5), Gestalt Closure (Ages 2.5–12.5), Number Recall (Ages 2.5–12.5), Triangles (Ages 4.0–12.5), Word Order (Ages 4.0–12.5), Matrix Analogies (Ages 5.0–12.5), Spatial Memory (Ages 5.0–12.5), Photo Series (Ages 6.0–12.5) plus 6 achievement subtests: Expressive Vocabulary (Ages 2.5–5.0), Faces and Places (Ages 2.5–12.5), Arithmetic (Ages 3.0–12.5), Riddles (Ages 3.0–12.5), Reading/Decoding (Ages 5.0–12.5), Reading/Understanding (Ages 7.0–12.5).

Administration: Individual.

Price Data, 1993: $299.95 per complete kit including all test materials, 25 individual test records, administrative and scoring manual (272 pages), and interpretive manual (352 pages); $359.95 per complete kit with briefcase; $29.95 per 25 individual test records; $19.95 per administration and scoring manual; $21.75 per interpretive manual; $40.75 per 2-manual set. Special Edition: Nonverbal scale available for hearing impaired, speech- and language-disordered, and non-English speaking children ages 4.0–12.5.

Time: (35) minutes for age 2.5; (40–45) minutes for age 3; (45–55) minutes for age 4; (50–60) minutes for age 5; (60–70) minutes for age 6; (75–85) minutes for ages 7.0–12.5.

Authors: Alan S. Kaufman and Nadeen L. Kaufman.

Publisher: American Guidance Service.

Cross References: For reviews by Anne Anastasi and William E. Coffman, see 9:562 (3 references).

TEST REFERENCES

1. Anastasi, A. (1984). The K-ABC in historical and contemporary perspective. *The Journal of Special Education, 18,* 357-366.
2. Chatman, S. P., Reynolds, C. R., & Willson, V. L. (1984). Multiple indexes of test scatter on the Kaufman Assessment Battery for Children. *Journal of Learning Disabilities, 17,* 523-531.
3. Das, J. P. (1984). Simultaneous and successive processes and K-ABC. *The Journal of Special Education, 18,* 229-238.
4. Dean, R. S. (1984). Functional lateralization of the brain. *The Journal of Special Education, 18,* 239-256.
5. Goetz, E. T., & Hall, R. J. (1984). Evaluation of the Kaufman Assessment Battery for Children from an information processing perspective. *The Journal of Special Education, 18,* 281-296.
6. Gunnison, J. A. (1984). Developing educational intervention from assessments involving the K-ABC. *The Journal of Special Education, 18,* 325-343.
7. Hopkins, K. D., & Hodge, S. E. (1984). Review of the Kaufman Assessment Battery (K-ABC) for Children. *Journal of Counseling and Development, 63,* 105-107.
8. Jensen, A. R. (1984). The Black-White difference on the K-ABC: Implications for future tests. *The Journal of Special Education, 18,* 377-408.
9. Kamphaus, R. W., & Reynolds, C. R. (1984). Development and structure of the Kaufman Assessment Battery for Children. *The Journal of Special Education, 18,* 213-228.
10. Kaufman, A. S. (1984). K-ABC and controversy. *The Journal of Special Education, 18,* 409-444.
11. Kaufman, A. S., & Kamphaus, R. W. (1984). Factor analysis of the Kaufman Assessment Battery for Children (K-ABC) for ages 2 ½ through 12 ½ years. *Journal of Educational Psychology, 76,* 623-637.
12. Keith, T. Z., & Dunbar, S. B. (1984). Hierarchical factor analysis of the K-ABC: Testing alternative models. *The Journal of Special Education, 18,* 367-375.
13. Majovski, L. V. (1984). The K-ABC: Theory and applications for child neuropsychological assessment and research. *The Journal of Special Education, 18,* 257-268.
14. McLoughlin, C. S., & Ellison, C. L. (1984). Comparison of scores for normal preschool children on the Peabody Picture Vocabulary Test—Revised and the achievement scales of the Kaufman Assessment Battery for Children. *Psychological Reports, 55,* 107-114.
15. Mehrens, W. A. (1984). A critical analysis of the psychometric properties of the K-ABC. *The Journal of Special Education, 18,* 297-310.
16. Naglieri, J. A. (1984). Concurrent and predictive validity of the Kaufman Assessment Battery for Children with a Navajo sample. *Journal of School Psychology, 22,* 373-380.
17. Narrett, C. M. (1984). Kaufman Assessment Battery for Children (K-ABC). *The Reading Teacher, 37,* 626-631.
18. Obrzut, A., Obrzut, J. E., & Shaw, D. (1984). Construct validity of the Kaufman Assessment Battery for Children with learning disabled and mentally retarded. *Psychology in the Schools, 21,* 417-424.
19. Reynolds, C. R., Willson, V. L., & Chatman, S. (1984). Relationships between age and raw score increases on the Kaufman-Assessment Battery for Children. *Psychology in the Schools, 21,* 19-24.
20. Salvia, J., & Hritcko, T. (1984). The K-ABC and ability training. *The Journal of Special Education, 18,* 345-356.
21. Sternberg, R. J. (1984). The Kaufman Assessment Battery for Children: An information-processing analysis and critique. *The Journal of Special Education, 18,* 269-279.
22. Telzrow, C. F. (1984). Practical applications of the K-ABC in the identification of handicapped preschoolers. *The Journal of Special Education, 18,* 311-324.
23. Valencia, R. R. (1984). Concurrent validity of the Kaufman Assessment Battery for Children in a sample of Mexican-American children. *Educational and Psychological Measurement, 44,* 365-372.
24. Zins, J. E., & Barnett, D. W. (1984). A validity study of the K-ABC, the WISC-R, and the Stanford-Binet with nonreferred children. *Journal of School Psychology, 22,* 369-371.
25. Bing, S. B., & Bing, J. R. (1985). Comparison of the K-ABC and PPVT-R with Head Start children. *Psychology in the Schools, 22,* 245-249.
26. Childers, J. S., Durham, T. W., Bolen, L. M., & Taylor, L. H. (1985). A predictive validity study of the Kaufman Assessment Battery for Children with the California Achievement Test. *Psychology in the Schools, 22,* 29-33.
27. Cooley, E. J., & Ayres, R. (1985). Convergent and discriminant validity of the mental processing scales of the Kaufman Assessment Battery for Children. *Psychology in the Schools, 22,* 373-377.
28. Harrington, R. G., McVey, D., & Follett, G. (1985). The reliability of the Spatial Memory subtest on the K-ABC. *Psychology in the Schools, 22,* 250-253.
29. Hooper, S. R., & Hynd, G. W. (1985). Differential diagnosis of subtypes of developmental dyslexia with the Kaufman Assessment Battery for Children (K-ABC). *Journal of Clinical Child Psychology, 14,* 145-152.
30. Kamphaus, R. W. (1985). Test scoring and interpretive software review K-ABC Assist (1984). *Clinical Neuropsychology, 7,* 169-170.
31. Klanderman, J. W., Perney, J., & Kroeschell, Z. B. (1985). Comparisons of the K-ABC and WISC-R for LD children. *Journal of Learning Disabilities, 18,* 524-527.
32. Klanderman, J., Devine, J., & Mollner, C. (1985). The K-ABC: A construct validity study with the WISC-R and Stanford-Binet. *Journal of Clinical Psychology, 41,* 273-281.
33. Levenson, R. L., Jr. (1985). Kaufman Assessment Battery for Children: Alternate solutions to Triangles, Item 17. *Perceptual and Motor Skills, 61,* 73-74.
34. McCallum, R. S., Karnes, F. A., & Oehler-Stinnett, J. (1985). Construct validity of the K-ABC for gifted children. *Psychology in the Schools, 22,* 254-259.
35. Naglieri, J. A. (1985). Assessment of mentally retarded children

with the Kaufman Assessment Battery for Children. *American Journal of Mental Deficiency, 89*, 367-371.

36. Naglieri, J. A. (1985). Use of the WISC-R and K-ABC with learning disabled, borderline mentally retarded, and normal children. *Psychology in the Schools, 22*, 133-141.

37. Reynolds, C. R., Willson, V. L., & Chatman, S. P. (1985). Regression analyses of bias on the Kaufman Assessment Battery for Children. *Journal of School Psychology, 23*, 195-204.

38. Valencia, R. R. (1985). Stability of the Kaufman Assessment Battery for Children for a sample of Mexican-American children. *Journal of School Psychology, 23*, 189-193.

39. Willson, V. L., Reynolds, C. R., Chatman, S. P., & Kaufman, A. S. (1985). Confirmatory analysis of simultaneous, sequential, and achievement factors on the K-ABC at 11 age levels ranging from 2 ½ to 12 ½ years. *Journal of School Psychology, 23*, 261-269.

40. Chelune, G. J., Ferguson, W., Koon, R., & Dickey, T. O. (1986). Frontal lobe disinhibition in attention deficit disorder. *Child Psychiatry and Human Development, 16*, 221-234.

41. Conboy, T. J., McFarland, C. E., & Boll, T. J. (1986). Simultaneous-successive factor structure of the WISC-R: A validation study. *Perceptual and Motor Skills, 63*, 963-969.

42. Goldstein, D. J., Smith, K. B., & Waldrep, E. E. (1986). Factor analytic study of the Kaufman Assessment Battery for Children. *Journal of Clinical Psychology, 42*, 890-894.

43. Hooper, S. R., & Hynd, G. W. (1986). Performance of normal and dyslexic readers on the Kaufman Assessment Battery for Children (K-ABC): A discriminant analysis. *Journal of Learning Disabilities, 19*, 206-210.

44. Inglis, J., & Lawson, J. S. (1986). A principal components analysis of the Kaufman Assessment Battery for Children (K-ABC): Implications for the test results of children with learning disabilities. *Journal of Learning Disabilities, 19*, 80-85.

45. Kamphaus, R. W., & Kaufman, A. S. (1986). Factor analysis of the Kaufman Assessment Battery for Children (K-ABC) for separate groups of boys and girls. *Journal of Clinical Child Psychology, 15*, 210-213.

46. Kaufman, A. S., & McLean, J. E. (1986). K-ABC/WISC-R factor analysis for a learning disabled population. *Journal of Learning Disabilities, 19*, 145-153.

47. McRae, S. G. (1986). Sequential-simultaneous processing and reading skills in primary grade children. *Journal of Learning Disabilities, 19*, 509-511.

48. Mulhern, R. K., Williams, J. M., LeSure, S. S., & Kun, L. E. (1986). Neuropsychological performance of children surviving cerebellar tumors: Six case studies. *Clinical Neuropsychology, 8*, 72-76.

49. Naglieri, J. A. (1986). WISC-R and K-ABC comparison for matched samples of black and white children. *Journal of School Psychology, 24*, 81-88.

50. Naglieri, J. A., & Hill, D. S. (1986). Comparison of WISC-R and K-ABC regression lines for academic prediction with black and white children. *Journal of Clinical Child Psychology, 15*, 352-355.

51. Tharinger, D. J., Laurent, J., & Best, L. R. (1986). Classification of children referred for emotional and behavioral problems: A comparison of PL 94-142 SED criteria, DSM III, and the CBCL system. *Journal of School Psychology, 24*, 111-121.

52. Valencia, R. R., & Rankin, R. J. (1986). Factor analysis of the K-ABC for groups of Anglo and Mexican American children. *Journal of Educational Measurement, 23*, 209-219.

53. Bathurst, K., & Gottfried, A. W. (1987). Untestable subjects in child development research: Developmental implications. *Child Development, 58*, 1135-1144.

54. Fourgurean, J. M. (1987). A K-ABC and WISC-R comparison for Latino learning-disabled children of limited English proficiency. *Journal of School Psychology, 25*, 15-21.

55. Hinshaw, S. P., Morrison, D. C., Carte, E. T., & Cornsweet, C. (1987). Factorial dimensions of the Revised Behavior Problem Checklist: Replication and validation within a kindergarten sample. *Journal of Abnormal Child Psychology, 15*, 309-327.

56. Karras, D., Newlin, D. B., Franzen, M. D., Golden, C. J., Wilhening, G. N., Rothermel, R. D., & Tramontana, M. J. (1987). Development of factor scales for the Luria-Nebraska Neuropsychological Battery—Children's Revision. *Journal of Clinical Child Psychology, 16*, 19-28.

57. Kaufman, A. S., & McLean, J. E. (1987). Joint factor analysis of the K-ABC and WISC-R with normal children. *Journal of School Psychology, 25*, 105-118.

58. Keith, T. Z., Fehrmann, P. G., Harrison, P. L., & Pottebaum, S. M. (1987). The relation between adaptive behavior and intelligence: Testing alternative explanations. *Journal of School Psychology, 25*, 31-43.

59. Moon, S., Ishikuma, T., & Kaufman, A. S. (1987). Joint factor analysis of the K-ABC and McCarthy scales. *Perceptual and Motor Skills, 65*, 699-704.

60. Naglieri, J. A., & Jensen, A. R. (1987). Comparison of black-white differences on the WISC-R and the K-ABC: Spearman's hypothesis. *Intelligence, 11*, 21-43.

61. Obrzut, A., Nelson, R. B., & Obrzut, J. E. (1987). Construct validity of the Kaufman Assessment Battery for Children with mildly mentally retarded students. *American Journal of Mental Deficiency, 92*, 74-77.

62. Pueschel, S. M., Gallagher, P. L., Zartler, A. S., & Pezzullo, J. C. (1987). Cognitive and learning processes in children with Down syndrome. *Research in Developmental Disabilities, 8*, 21-37.

63. Whitworth, R. H., & Chrisman, S. M. (1987). Validation of the Kaufman Assessment Battery for Children comparing Anglo and Mexican-American preschoolers. *Educational and Psychological Measurement, 47*(3), 695-702.

64. Ayres, R. R., Cooley, E. J., & Severson, H. H. (1988). Educational translation of the Kaufman Assessment Battery for Children: A construct validity study. *School Psychology Review, 17*, 113-124.

65. Bennett, D. E., & Clarizio, H. F. (1988). A comparison of methods for calculating a severe discrepancy. *Journal of School Psychology, 26*, 359-369.

66. Bloom, A. S., Allard, A. M., Zelko, F. A. J., Brill, W. J., Topinka, C. W., & Pfohl, W. (1988). Differential validity of the K-ABC for lower functioning preschool children versus those of higher ability. *American Journal on Mental Retardation, 93*, 273-277.

67. Burns, C. W., & Reynolds, C. R. (1988). Patterns of sex differences in children's information processing with and without independence from g. *Journal of School Psychology, 26*, 233-242.

68. Camarata, S. M., Hughes, C. A., & Ruhl, K. L. (1988). Mild/moderate behaviorally disordered students: A population at risk for language disorders. *Language, Speech, and Hearing Services in Schools, 19*, 191-200.

69. Ishikuma, T., Moon, S. B., & Kaufman, A. S. (1988). Sequential-simultaneous analysis of Japanese children's performance on the Japanese McCarthy Scales. *Perceptual and Motor Skills, 66*(2), 355-362.

70. Kaufman, A. S., & Applegate, B. (1988). Short forms of the K-ABC Mental Processing and Achievement Scales at Ages 4 to 12 ½ Years for clinical and screening purposes. *Journal of Clinical Child Psychology, 17*, 359-369.

71. Kaufman, A. S., & O'Neal, M. R. (1988). Analysis of the cognitive, achievement, and general factors underlying the Woodcock-Johnson Psycho-Educational Battery. *Journal of Clinical Child Psychology, 17*, 143-151.

72. Lyon, M. A., Smith, D. K., & Klass, P. D. (1988). Comparison of K-ABC performance between at-risk and normal preschool children. *Perceptual and Motor Skills, 66*(2), 619-626.

73. McCallum, R. S., Merritt, F. M., Dickson, A. L., Oehler-Stinnett, J., & Spencer, T. R. (1988). Planning ability across ranges of intellectual ability: An examination of the Luria-Das information-processing model. *Journal of School Psychology, 26*, 405-411.

74. Stroebel, S. S., & Evans, J. R. (1988). Neuropsychological and environmental characteristics of early readers. *Journal of School Psychology, 26*, 243-252.

75. Strommen, E. (1988). Confirmatory factor analysis of the Kaufman Assessment Battery for Children: A reevaluation. *Journal of School Psychology, 26*, 13-23.

76. Bracken, B. A., & Howell, K. K. (1989). K-ABC subtest specificity recalculated. *Journal of School Psychology, 27*, 335-345.

77. Braden, J. P. (1989). Fact or artifact? An empirical test of Spearman's Hypothesis. *Intelligence, 13*, 149-155.

78. Forness, S. R., & Kavale, K. A. (1989). Identification and diagnostic issues in special education: A status report for child psychiatrists. *Child Psychiatry and Human Development, 19*, 279-301.

79. Glutting, J. J. (1989). Introduction to the structure and application of the Stanford-Binet Intelligence Scale—Fourth Edition. *Journal of School Psychology, 27*, 69-80.

80. Krohn, E. J., & Lamp, R. E. (1989). Concurrent validity of the Stanford-Binet Fourth Edition and K-ABC for Head Start Children. *Journal of School Psychology, 27*, 59-67.

81. Mantzicopoulous, P., Morrison, D. C., Hinshaw, S. P., & Carte, E. T. (1989). Nonpromotion in kindergarten: The role of cognitive, perceptual, visual-motor, behavioral, achievement, socioeconomic, and demographic characteristics. *American Educational Research Journal, 26*, 107-121.

82. Nolan, R. F., Watlington, D. K., & Willson, V. L. (1989). Gifted and nongifted race and gender effects on the item functioning on the Kaufman Assessment Battery for Children. *Journal of Clinical Psychology, 45*, 645-650.

83. Posey, W., Sapp, G. L., & Gladding, S. T. (1989). Validating the Kaufman Test of Educational Achievement, Brief Form with educable mentally retarded students. *Psychological Reports, 65*, 1225-1226.

84. Rushton, J. P. (1989). Japanese inbreeding depression scores: Pre-

dictors of cognitive differences between blacks and whites. *Intelligence, 13*, 43-51.

85. Willson, V. L., Nolan, R. F., Reynolds, C. R., & Kamphaus, R. W. (1989). Race and gender effects on item functioning on the Kaufman Assessment Battery for Children. *Journal of School Psychology, 27*, 289-296.

86. Das, J. P., Mensink, D., & Janzen, H. (1990). The K-ABC, coding, and planning: An investigation of cognitive processes. *Journal of School Psychology, 28*, 1-11.

87. Grant, M. L., Ilai, D., Nussbaum, N. L., & Bigler, E. D. (1990). The relationship between continuous performance tasks and neuropsychological tests in children with Attention-deficit Hyperactivity Disorder. *Perceptual and Motor Skills, 70*, 435-445.

88. Gridley, B. E., Miller, G., Barke, C., Fischer, W., & Smith, D. (1990). Construct validity of the K-ABC with an at-risk preschool population. *Journal of School Psychology, 28*, 39-49.

89. Hendershott, J. L., Searight, H. R., Hatfield, J. L., & Rogers, B. J. (1990). Correlations between the Stanford-Binet, Fourth Edition and the Kaufman Assessment Battery for Children for a preschool sample. *Perceptual and Motor Skills, 71*, 819-825.

90. Rice, M. L., Buhr, J. C., & Nemeth, M. (1990). Fast mapping word-learning abilities of language-delayed preschoolers. *Journal of Speech and Hearing Disorders, 55*, 33-42.

91. Bracken, B. A., Howell, K. K., Harrison, T. E., Stanford, L. D., & Zahn, B. H. (1991). Ipsative subtest pattern stability of the Bracken Basic Concept Scale and the Kaufman Assessment Battery for Children in a preschool sample. *School Psychology Review, 20*, 315-330.

92. Cormier, P., Margison, J. A., & Fisk, J. D. (1991). Contribution of perceptual and lexical-semantic errors to the naming impairments in Alzheimer's disease. *Perceptual and Motor Skills, 73*, 175-183.

93. Donders, J., Rourke, B. P., & Canady, A. I. (1991). Neuropsychological functioning of hydrocephalic children. *Journal of Clinical and Experimental Neuropsychology, 13*, 607-613.

94. Hadley, P. A., & Rice, M. L. (1991). Conversational responsiveness of speech- and language-impaired preschoolers. *Journal of Speech and Hearing Research, 34*, 1308-1317.

95. John, K. R., & Rattan, G. (1991). A comparison of short-term memory tests as predictors of reading achievement for learning-disabled and educable mentally retarded students. *Journal of School Psychology, 29*, 309-318.

96. Powell, T. W., Elbert, M., & Dinnsen, D. A. (1991). Stimulability as a factor in the phonological generalization of misarticulating preschool children. *Journal of Speech and Hearing Research, 34*, 1318-1328.

97. Rothlisberg, B. A., & McIntosh, D. E. (1991). Performance of a referred sample on the Stanford-Binet IV and the K-ABC. *Journal of School Psychology, 29*, 367-370.

98. Short, E. J., Schatschneider, C., Cuddy, C. L., Evans, S. W., Dellick, D. M., & Basili, L. A. (1991). The effect of thinking aloud on the problem-solving performance of bright, average, learning disabled, and developmentally handicapped students. *Contemporary Educational Psychology, 16*, 139-153.

99. Vincent, K. R. (1991). Black/White IQ differences: Does age make the difference? *Journal of Clinical Psychology, 47*, 266-276.

100. Watkins, R. V., & Rice, M. L. (1991). Verb particle and preposition acquisition in language-impaired preschoolers. *Journal of Speech and Hearing Research, 34*, 1130-1141.

101. Yoder, P. J., Kaiser, A. P., & Alpert, C. L. (1991). An exploratory study of the interaction between language teaching methods and child characteristics. *Journal of Speech and Hearing Research, 34*, 155-167.

102. Allen, L., Cipielewski, J., & Stanovich, K. E. (1992). Multiple indicators of children's reading habits and attitudes: Construct validity and cognitive correlates. *Journal of Educational Psychology, 84*, 489-503.

103. Donders, J. (1992). Validity of the Kaufman Assessment Battery for Children when employed with children with traumatic brain injury. *Journal of Clinical Psychology, 48*, 225-230.

104. Ganschow, L., Sparks, R., & Helmick, M. (1992). Speech/language referral practices by school psychologists. *School Psychology Review, 21*(2), 313-326.

105. Glutting, J. J., McGrath, E. A., Kamphaus, R. W., & McDermott, P. A. (1992). Taxonomy and validity of subtest profiles on the Kaufman Assessment Battery for Children. *The Journal of Special Education, 26*, 85-115.

106. Kline, R. B., Snyder, J., Guilmette, S., & Castellanos, M. (1992). Relative usefulness of evaluation, variability, and shape information for WISC-R, K-ABC, and Fourth Edition Stanford-Binet profiles in predicting achievement. *Psychological Assessment, 4*, 426-432.

107. Laurent, J., Swerdlik, M., & Ryburn, M. (1992). Review of validity research on the Stanford-Binet Intelligence Scale: Fourth Edition. *Psychological Assessment, 4*, 102-112.

108. Marlowe, W. B. (1992). The impact of a right prefrontal lesion on the developing brain. *Brain and Cognition, 20*, 205-213.

109. Schort, E. J. (1992). Cognitive, metacognitive, motivational, and affective differences among normally achieving, learning-disabled, and developmentally handicapped students: How much do they affect school achievement? *Journal of Clinical Child Psychology, 21*, 229-239.

110. Stavrou, E., & French, J. L. (1992). The K-ABC and cognitive processing styles in autistic children. *Journal of School Psychology, 30*, 259-267.

111. Wright-Strawderman, C., & Watson, B. L. (1992). The prevalence of depressive symptoms in children with learning disabilities. *Journal of Learning Disabilities, 25*, 258-264.

112. Good, R. H., III., Vollmer, M., Creek, R. J., Katz, L., & Chowdhri, S. (1993). Treatment utility of the Kaufman Assessment Battery for Children: Effects of matching instruction and student processing strength. *School Psychology Review, 22*, 8-26.

113. Jorgenson, C. B., Jorgenson, D. E., Gillis, M. K., & McCall, C. M. (1993). Validation of a screening instrument for young children with teacher assessment of school performance. *School Psychology Quarterly, 8*, 125-139.

114. Patel, P., Goldberg, D., & Moss, S. (1993). Psychiatric morbidity in older people with moderate and severe learning disability: II. *British Journal of Psychiatry, 163*, 481-491.

[1344]

Kaufman Brief Intelligence Test.

Purpose: Intended as a brief measure of verbal and nonverbal intelligence.

Population: Ages 4–90.

Publication Date: 1990.

Acronym: K-BIT.

Scores, 3: Vocabulary, Matrices, IQ Composite.

Subtests, 2: Vocabulary (including Part A, Expressive Vocabulary and Part B, Definitions) and Matrices.

Administration: Individual.

Price Data, 1993: $99.95 per complete kit including easel, manual (123 pages), and 25 individual test records; $24.95 per 25 individual test records; $26.95 per manual.

Time: (15–30) minutes.

Comments: Definitions task not administered to children ages 4–7 years; examiners are encouraged to teach individuals, using teaching items, how to solve the kinds of items included in both subtests.

Authors: Alan S. Kaufman and Nadeen L. Kaufman.

Publisher: American Guidance Service.

TEST REFERENCES

1. Prewett, P. N. (1992). The relationship between the Kaufman Brief Intelligence Test (K-BIT) and the WISC-R with referred students. *Psychology in the Schools, 29*(1), 25-27.

2. Klinge, V., & Dorsey, J. (1993). Correlates of the Woodcock-Johnson Reading Comprehension and Kaufman Brief Intelligence Test in a forensic psychiatric population. *Journal of Clinical Psychology, 49*, 593-598.

3. Naugle, R. I., Chelune, G. J., & Tucker, G. D. (1993). Validity of the Kaufman Brief Intelligence Test. *Psychological Assessment, 5*, 182-186.

4. Prewett, P. N. (1993). The relationship between the Kaufman Brief Intelligence Test (K-BIT) and the WISC-R with incarcerated juvenile delinquents. *Educational and Psychological Measurement, 52*, 977-982.

[1345]

Kaufman Developmental Scale.

Purpose: Designed to assess the "level of development . . . and an overall level of functioning."

Population: Birth to age 9 and mentally retarded of all ages.

Publication Dates: 1972–75.

Acronym: KDS.

Scores, 7: Gross Motor, Fine Motor, Receptive,

Expressive, Personal Behavior, Inter-Personal Behavior, Total.
Administration: Individual.
Price Data, 1994: $350 per complete kit including test materials, manual ('74, 83 pages), 25 record forms, and carrying case; $50 per 25 evaluation booklets; $25 per 25 record forms; $50 per manual.
Time: Administration time not reported.
Author: H. Kaufman.
Publisher: Stoelting Co.
Cross References: For a review by Dorothy H. Eichorn, see 8:218.

[1346]
Kaufman Infant and Preschool Scale.
Purpose: Designed to measure "early, high-level cognitive thinking, and indicates possible need for intervention."
Population: Ages 1 month–48 months and mentally retarded individuals whose preacademic functioning age does not exceed 48 months.
Publication Date: 1979.
Acronym: KIPS.
Scores: Tasks in 3 areas: General Reasoning, Storage, Verbal Communication.
Administration: Individual.
Price Data, 1994: $300 per complete kit including all manipulatives, stimulus cards, and 10 evaluation booklets; $30 per 10 evaluation booklets; $20 per set of stimulus cards; $25 per manual (40 pages).
Time: (20–30) minutes.
Author: H. Kaufman.
Publisher: Stoelting Co.
Cross References: For reviews by Roy A. Kress and Phyllis Anne Teeter, see 9:563.

[1347]
Kaufman Survey of Early Academic and Language Skills.
Purpose: A measure of children's language, preacademic skills, and articulation.
Population: 3-0 to 6-11.
Publication Date: 1993.
Acronym: K-SEALS.
Scores, 8: Vocabulary, Numbers/Letters and Words, Articulation Survey, Early Academic and Language Skills Composite, Language Scales (Expressive Skills, Receptive Skills), Early Academic Scales (Number Skills, Letter and Word Skills).
Subtests, 3: Vocabulary, Numbers/Letters and Words, Articulation Survey.
Administration: Individual.
Price Data, 1993: $140 per complete kit including manual (109 pages), presentation easel, and 25 record booklets; $18 per 25 record booklets.
Time: (15–25) minutes.
Comments: The Early Academic Scales can be interpreted only for ages 5-0 to 6-11.
Authors: Alan S. Kaufman and Nadeen L. Kaufman.
Publisher: American Guidance Service, Inc.

[1348]
Kaufman Test of Educational Achievement.
Population: Grades 1 through 12.
Publication Date: 1985.
Acronym: K-TEA.
Administration: Individual.
Price Data, 1993: $225.95 per special edition complete kit including test plates of easily cleaned plastic, 2 sets of record books, 2 samples reports to parents, 2 shelf storage boxes, and manuals; $199.95 per regular edition complete kit.
Authors: Alan S. Kaufman and Nadeen L. Kaufman.
Publisher: American Guidance Service.
a) BRIEF FORM.
Purpose: "Screening of students on global achievement skills to determine the need for follow-up testing and evaluation."
Scores, 4: Reading, Mathematics, Spelling, Battery Composite.
Price Data: $98.95 per special edition brief form kit including 77 test plates in easel, package of 25 record booklets, sample reports to parents, shelf storage boxes, and manual (306 pages); $81.95 per regular edition brief form kit; $24.95 per 25 record booklets; $18.75 per 25 reports to parents; $28 per manual.
Time: (30) minutes.
b) COMPREHENSIVE FORM.
Purpose: "Provides an analysis of a child's educational strengths and weaknesses in reading, mathematics, and spelling, to identify possible skill areas (e.g., reading comprehension, mathematics computation) needing remediation or enrichment."
Scores, 8: Reading Decoding, Reading Comprehension, Reading Composite, Mathematics Applications, Mathematics Computation, Mathematics Composite, Spelling, Battery Composite.
Price Data: $164.95 per special edition comprehensive form kit including 133 test plates in easel, 25 record booklets (including error analyses), sample report to parents, shelf storage box, and manual (654 pages); $142.95 per regular edition comprehensive form kit; $32.95 per 25 record booklets; $19.75 per 25 reports to parents; $45.50 per manual.
Time: (60–75) minutes.
Cross References: For reviews by Elizabeth J. Doll and Jerome M. Sattler, see 10:161.

TEST REFERENCES

1. Prewett, P. N., Bardos, A., & Fowler, D. B. (1991). Relationship between the KTEA brief and comprehensive forms and the WRAT-R level 1 with referred elementary school students. *Educational and Psychological Measurement, 51,* 729-734.
2. Bell, P. F., Lentz, F. E., Jr., & Graden, J. L. (1992). Effect of curriculum-test overlap on standardized achievement test scores: Identifying systematic confounds in educational decision making. *School Psychology Review, 21,* 644-655.
3. Ganschow, L., Sparks, R., & Helmick, M. (1992). Speech/language referral practices by school psychologists. *School Psychology Review, 21*(2), 313-326.
4. Minshew, N. J., Goldstein, G., Muenz, L. R., & Payton, J. B. (1992). Neuropsychological functioning in nonmentally retarded autistic

individuals. *Journal of Clinical and Experimental Neuropsychology, 14*, 749-761.

5. Williams, D., & Mateer, C. A. (1992). Developmental impact of frontal lobe injury in middle childhood. *Brain and Cognition, 20*, 196-204.

[1349]

Keegan Type Indicator.

Purpose: Measures perception, judgment, and attitude (extraversion/introversion) based on C. G. Jung's theory of psychological types.
Population: Adults.
Publication Dates: 1980–82.
Acronym: KTI.
Scores, 3: Extraversion vs. Introversion, Sensation vs. Intuition, Thinking vs. Feeling.
Administration: Group.
Price Data: Price data, including user's manual ('80, 12 pages) and instructor's manual ('80, 21 pages), available from publisher.
Time: [20] minutes.
Author: Warren J. Keegan.
Publisher: Warren Keegan Associates Press.
Cross References: For a review by Arlene C. Rosenthal, see 10:162.

[1350]

Keele Pre-School Assessment Guide.

Purpose: Developed to plot the progress of individual children and to be a curriculum guide for preschoolers.
Population: Children in nursery school.
Publication Date: 1980.
Acronym: KPAG.
Scores: Ratings by teachers or counselors in 5 areas: Social Behavior, Cognition, Physical Skills, Socialization, Language.
Administration: Individual.
Price Data, 1989: £7.20 per 25 record forms; £4.05 per manual (36 pages).
Time: Administration time not reported.
Comments: Experimental form; criterion-referenced.
Author: Stephen Tyler.
Publisher: NFER-Nelson Publishing Co., Ltd. [England].
Cross References: For reviews by Cathy W. Hall and Robert F. McMorris, see 9:565.

[1351]

Kelvin Measurement of Ability in Infant Classes.

Purpose: Provides information on young children's abilities.
Population: Ages 8–12.
Publication Dates: 1935–56.
Scores: Total score only.
Administration: Group.
Price Data: Not available.
Time: Administration time not reported.
Author: C. M. Fleming.
Publisher: Gibson (Robert) & Sons, Glasgow, Ltd.

[Scotland] [No reply from publisher; status unknown].
Cross References: See T2:395 (1 reference).

[1352]

Kendrick Cognitive Tests for the Elderly.

Purpose: To detect early dementia and depressive psychosis by assessment of short-term memory and speed of responding.
Population: Ages 55 and over.
Publication Dates: 1979–85.
Subtests, 2: Object Learning Test, Digit Copying Test.
Administration: Individual.
Price Data, 1989: £39.70 per complete set (contains 1 of each item); £16.10 per Object Learning Test; £4.05 per Digit Copying Test; £8.05 per 25 record forms; £11.50 per manual ('85, 32 pages).
Time: (15–20) minutes.
Comments: Formerly known as Kendrick Battery for the Detection of Dementia in the Elderly; battery should be repeated 6 weeks after initial testing.
Author: Don C. Kendrick.
Publisher: NFER-Nelson Publishing Co., Ltd. [England].
a) OBJECT LEARNING TEST.
Acronym: KOLT.
Scores: Total score only.
Forms, 2: A, B (4 cards).
Comments: Test of recall of everyday objects.
b) DIGIT COPYING TEST.
Acronym: KDCT.
Scores: Total score only.
Forms: 1 form (2 pages).
Comments: Test of speed performance.
Cross References: See 11:189 (2 references); for reviews by Joseph D. Matarazzo and K. Warner Schaie of the earlier form, see 9:566 (2 references).

TEST REFERENCES

1. O'Brien, J. T., Sahakian, B. J., & Checkley, S. A. (1993). Cognitive impairments in patients with seasonal affective disorder. *British Journal of Psychiatry, 163*, 338-343.

[1353]

The Kent Infant Development Scale, Second Edition.

Purpose: Designed to assess "the developmental status of infants and young children with disabilities."
Population: Infants and young children with disabilities chronologically or developmentally under 1 year.
Publication Dates: 1978–90.
Acronym: KID Scale.
Scores, 6: Cognitive, Motor, Language, Self-Help, Social, Full Scale.
Administration: Individual.
Price Data, 1993: $5 per sample tests; $15 per manual ('85, 39 pages) and Addendum ('90, 30 pages); $1.50 per test booklet; $9 per 25 answer sheets; $25 per plastic templates and 10 profile sheets; scoring service available from publisher at $7 per answer sheet processed; $125 per Apple II or IBM

compatible scoring disk (unlimited scorings) with User's Guide, test manual, test booklets, and answer sheets.

Foreign Language Editions: German, Dutch, Spanish normed versions available; Russian, Hungarian, and Vietnamese translations available.

Time: (45) minutes.

Comments: Ratings by parent or caregiver.

Authors: Jeanette Reuter, with Lewis Katoff (original test), with Virginia Dunn (1st edition of the test manual), with Laura Bickett (2nd edition of the test manual), and with Louis Reuter (the 1990 Addendum).

Publisher: Kent Developmental Metrics; Swets Test Services: Dutch Distributor.

Cross References: For reviews by Candice Feiring and Edward S. Shapiro, see 10:163 (2 references); for a review by Candice Feiring of an earlier edition, see 9:567; see also T3:1246 (1 reference).

[1354]

Keyboard Skills Test.

Purpose: Designed to measure typing skills both in terms of speed and accuracy.

Population: High school and college and adults.

Publication Date: 1988.

Acronym: KST.

Scores, 3: Gross Words Per Minute and Number of Errors, Net Words Per Minute, Error Rate.

Administration: Group.

Forms: 4 equivalent forms: A, B, C, D.

Price Data, 1994: $13.45 per 10 test form booklets; $11.45 per 35 typing worksheets; $7.95 per 10 practice exercise booklets; $16.95 per Administration and Scoring Manual (41 pages); $22.45 per Technical Manual (51 pages).

Time: 13(45) minutes.

Authors: J. A. Gordon Booth and Carol DeCoff.

Publisher: Nelson Canada [Canada].

Cross References: For a review by Robert Fitzpatrick, see 11:190.

[1355]

KeyMath Revised: A Diagnostic Inventory of Essential Mathematics.

Purpose: Designed to assess understanding and applications of mathematics concepts and skills.

Population: Grades K–9.

Publication Dates: 1971–88.

Acronym: KeyMath-R.

Scores, 17: Basic Concepts (Numeration, Rational Numbers, Geometry, Total), Operations (Addition, Subtraction, Multiplication, Division, Mental Computation, Total), Applications (Measurement, Time and Money, Estimation, Interpreting Data, Problem Solving, Total), Total.

Administration: Individual.

Forms, 2: A, B.

Price Data, 1993: $334.95 per complete kit including Form A and B test easels, 25 each Form A and B test records, sample report to parents and manual ('88, 349 pages); $179.95 per single form (A or B) kit including test easels, 25 test records, sample report to parents, and manual; $36.95 per 25 test records (select A or B); $18.95 per 25 report to parents; $36.95 per manual.

Time: (35–50) minutes.

Comments: Revision of KeyMath Diagnostic Arithmetic Test.

Author: Austin J. Connolly.

Publisher: American Guidance Service.

Cross References: For reviews by Michael D. Beck and Carmen J. Finley, see 11:191 (26 references); see also T3:1250 (12 references); for an excerpted review by Alex Bannatyne, see 8:305 (10 references).

TEST REFERENCES

1. Fleener, F. T. (1987). Learning disabilities and other attributes as factors in diligent activities among adolescents in a nonurban area. *Psychological Reports, 60,* 327-334.
2. Waldron, K. A., & Saphire, D. G. (1990). An analysis of WISC-R factors for gifted students with learning disabilities. *Journal of Learning Disabilities, 23,* 491-498.
3. Burns, C. W. (1992). Psychoeducational decision making, test scores, and descriptive data: Selected methodological issues. *Journal of School Psychology, 30*(1), 1-16.
4. Forness, S. R., Swanson, J. M., Cantwell, D. P., Youpa, D., & Hanna, G. L. (1992). Stimulant medication and reading performance: Follow-up on sustained does in ADHD boys with and without conduct disorders. *Journal of Learning Disabilities, 25,* 115-123.
5. Coon, H., Carey, G., Fulker, D. W., & DeFries, J. C. (1993). Influences of school environment on the academic achievement scores of adopted and nonadopted children. *Intelligence, 17,* 79-104.

[1356]

Khan-Lewis Phonological Analysis.

Purpose: "Diagnosis and description of articulation or phonological disorders in children of preschool age."

Population: Ages 2-0 to 5-11.

Publication Date: 1986.

Acronym: KLPA.

Scores, 16: Developmental Phonological Processes (Deletion of Final Consonants, Initial Voicing, Syllable Reduction, Palatal Fronting, Deaffrication, Velar Fronting, Consonant Harmony, Stridency Deletion, Stopping of Fricatives and Affricates, Cluster Simplification, Final Devoicing, Liquid Simplification), Nondevelopmental Phonological Processes (Deletion of Initial Consonants, Glottal Replacement, Backing to Velars), Composite.

Administration: Group.

Price Data, 1993: $59.95 per complete kit including 25 analysis forms, folder, and manual (112 pages); $39.95 per 25 analysis forms; $11 per folder; $21.25 per manual.

Time: (5–10) minutes.

Comments: Supplements the Goldman-Fristoe Test of Articulation.

Authors: Linda M. L. Khan and Nancy P. Lewis.

Publisher: American Guidance Service.

Cross References: For a review by Donald E. Mowrer, see 10:164.

TEST REFERENCES

1. Kamen, R. S., & Watson, B. C. (1991). Effects of long-term tracheostomy on spectral characteristics of vowel production. *Journal of Speech and Hearing Research, 34,* 1057-1065.

[1357]

Kilander-Leach Health Knowledge Test.

Purpose: "Designed to measure a college student's knowledge and understanding of matters pertaining to health."
Population: Grades 12–16.
Publication Dates: 1936–72.
Acronym: KLHKT.
Scores: Total score only.
Administration: Group.
Manual: No manual.
Price Data: Available from publisher.
Time: (45–50) minutes.
Comments: Formerly called Kilander Health Knowledge Test.
Authors: H. Frederick Kilander; revised by Glenn C. Leach.
Publisher: Glenn C. Leach, Publisher.
Cross References: See T2:935 (5 references); for a review by James E. Bryan, see 7:609 (2 references); see also 5:562 (3 references); for excerpted reviews by Lois M. Shoemaker and one other of an earlier form, see 2:1503.

[1358]

Kilmann-Saxton Culture-Gap Survey [Revised].

Purpose: Assesses "actual versus desired cultural norms."
Population: Work team members, employees.
Publication Dates: 1983–91.
Acronym: CGS.
Scores, 4: Task Support, Social Relationships, Task Innovation, Personal Freedom.
Administration: Group.
Price Data, 1994: $6.25 per survey.
Time: (30) minutes.
Authors: Ralph H. Kilmann and Mary J. Saxton.
Publisher: XICOM, Inc.
Cross References: For reviews of an earlier edition by Andres Barona and Gargi Roysircar Sodowsky, see 11:192.

[1359]

Kindergarten Language Screening Test.

Purpose: Designed to compare kindergarten children's present language abilities to a normative group.
Population: Kindergarten.
Publication Dates: 1978–83.
Acronym: KLST.
Scores: Total score only.
Administration: Group.
Price Data, 1994: $44 per complete kit including manual ('83, 16 pages); $19 per 50 forms; $9 per picture cards; $19 per manual.
Time: (10) minutes.
Authors: Sharon V. Gauthier and Charles L. Madison.
Publisher: PRO-ED, Inc.

TEST REFERENCES
1. Madison, C. L., Roach, M. E., Santema, S. J., Akmal, E. S., & Guenzel, C. A. (1989). The effect of pictured visual cues on elicited sentence imitation. *Journal of Communication Disorders, 22,* 81-91.
2. Stone, B. J., & Gridley, B. E. (1991). Test bias of a kindergarten screening battery: Predicting achievement for White and Native American elementary students. *School Psychology Review, 20,* 132-139.

[1360]

Kindergarten Readiness Test.

Purpose: Determines the readiness of children to begin kindergarten.
Population: Ages 4–6.
Publication Date: 1988.
Acronym: KRT.
Scores: Total score only.
Administration: Individual.
Price Data, 1992: $69 per complete kit; $16 per manual (39 pages); $35 per 25 test booklets; $6 per 25 performance grid sheets; $6 per 25 letter to parent; $6 per 25 scoring interpretation; $14 per stimulus items.
Time: (15) minutes.
Authors: Sue L. Larson and Gary J. Vitali.
Publisher: Slosson Educational Publications, Inc.

[1361]

Kindergarten Screening Inventory.

Purpose: To help teachers identify educationally relevant differences among entering kindergarten children.
Population: Entering kindergarten children.
Publication Date: 1980.
Acronym: KSI.
Scores: 16 subtests: Naming and Matching (Familiar Objects, Money, Basic Colors, Shapes, Sets, Numerals, Letters), Spatial Relationship Words, Sequence Words and Ordinal Numbers, Sequencing, Counting, Child Writes Own Name, Tracing Basic Strokes, Copying Basic Strokes, Tracing Letters and Numerals, Copying Letters and Numerals.
Administration: Individual.
Price Data, 1988: $9.95 per complete kit including test cards, 32 record forms, and manual (8 pages).
Time: Administration time not reported.
Authors: Michael N. Milone, Jr. and Virginia H. Lucas.
Publisher: Zaner-Bloser, Co.
Cross References: For reviews by Dennis C. Harper and Sue White, see 10:165.

[1362]

Kinetic Drawing System for Family and School: A Handbook.

Purpose: Designed "as a projective technique which assesses a child's perceptions of relationships among the child, peers, family, school, and significant others."
Population: Ages 5–20.
Publication Date: 1985.
Acronym: KDS.
Scores: 5 diagnostic categories: Actions of and

Between Figures, Figure Characteristics, Position/Distance/Barriers, Style, Symbols.
Administration: Individual.
Price Data, 1993: $55 per complete kit; $24.50 per 25 scoring booklets; $32.50 per handbook (82 pages including scoring booklet).
Time: (20–40) minutes.
Comments: A combination of the Kinetic Family Drawing and Kinetic School Drawing.
Authors: Howard M. Knoff and H. Thompson Prout (handbook).
Publisher: Western Psychological Services.
Cross References: For reviews by Bert P. Cundick and Richard A. Weinberg, see 10:166 (4 references).

TEST REFERENCES

1. Tharinger, D. J., & Stark, K. (1990). A qualitative versus quantitative approach to evaluating The Draw-A-Person and Kinetic Family Drawing: A study of mood- and anxiety-disorder children. *Psychological Assessment, 2,* 365-375.
2. Goldman, R. K., & Gilbert, D. C. (1992). Prediction of risk in kindergarten children. *Perceptual and Motor Skills, 75,* 1033-1034.

[1363]

Kipnis-Schmidt Profiles of Organizational Influence Strategies.

Purpose: To "measure how people use influence in their organizations."
Population: Organizational members.
Publication Date: 1982.
Acronym: POIS.
Scores, 12 or 14: Friendliness, Bargaining, Reason, Assertiveness, Sanctions (Form S only), Higher Authority, Coalition scores for each of 2 areas (First Attempt to Influence, Attempts to Overcome Resistance to Influence).
Administration: Group.
Forms, 3: M (Influencing Your Manager), C (Influencing Your Co-Workers), S (Influencing Your Subordinates).
Price Data, 1989: $49.50 per set of 10 forms (specify Form M, C, S, or respondent's guides); $62.50 per trainer's package including 1 copy of each instrument, respondent's guide, and manual (16 pages).
Time: (20–30) minutes.
Authors: David Kipnis and Stuart M. Schmidt.
Publisher: Pfeiffer & Company International Publishers.

TEST REFERENCES

1. Deluga, R. J. (1990). The effects of transformational, transactional, and laissezfaire leadership characteristics on subordinate influencing behavior. *Basic and Applied Social Psychology, 11*(2), 191-203.
2. Fagenson, E. A. (1990). Perceived masculine and feminine attributes examined as a function of individuals' sex and level in the organizational power hierarchy: A test of four theoretical perspectives. *Journal of Applied Psychology, 72*(2), 204-211.

[1364]

Kirton Adaption-Innovation Inventory.

Purpose: A measure . . . of a person's preference for, or style of, creativity, problem solving and decision making.

Population: British and U.S. adults and teenagers over age 14.
Publication Dates: 1976–87.
Acronym: KAI.
Scores, 4: Sufficiency v. Proliferation of Originality, Efficiency, Rule/Group Conformity, Total.
Administration: Individual or group.
Price Data: Available from publisher.
Time: (5–10) minutes.
Comments: Translations available for Italian, Slovak, French, and Dutch adults and teenagers.
Author: Michael Kirton.
Publisher: Occupational Research Centre [England].
Cross References: For reviews by Gregory J. Boyle and Gerald E. DeMauro, see 11:193 (8 references).

TEST REFERENCES

1. Holland, P. A. (1987). Adaptors and innovators: Application of the Kirton Adaption-Innovation Inventory to bank employees. *Psychological Reports, 60,* 263-270.
2. Beene, J. M., & Zelhart, P. F. (1988). Factor analysis of the Kirton Adaption-Innovation Inventory. *Perceptual and Motor Skills, 66*(2), 667-671.
3. Elder, R. L., & Johnson, D. C. (1989). Varying relationships between Adaption-Innovation and social desirability. *Psychological Reports, 65,* 1151-1154.
4. Foxall, G. R. (1990). An empirical analysis of mid-career manager's adaptive-innovative cognitive styles and task orientations in three countries. *Psychological Reports, 66,* 1115-1124.
5. Foxall, G. R., & Bhate, S. (1991). Psychology of computer use: xix. Extent of computer use: Relationships with adaptive-innovative cognitive style and personal involvement in computing. *Perceptual and Motor Skills, 72,* 195-202.
6. Holland, P. A., & Bailey, B. A. (1991). Adaptors and innovators: Selection versus induction. *Psychological Reports, 68,* 1283-1290.
7. Kirton, M., Bailey, A., & Glendinning, W. (1991). Adaptors and innovators: Preference for educational procedures. *The Journal of Psychology, 125,* 445-455.
8. Foxall, G. R. (1992). Gender differences in cognitive styles of MBA students in three countries. *Psychological Reports, 70,* 169-170.
9. Foxall, G. R., & Bhate, S. (1993). Cognitive styles and personal involvement of market initiators for "healthy" food brands: Implications for adoption theory. *Journal of Economic Psychology, 14,* 33-56.

[1365]

Kit of Factor Referenced Cognitive Tests.

Purpose: "To provide research workers with a means of identifying certain aptitude factors in factor-analytic studies."
Population: Various grades 6–college level.
Publication Dates: 1954–78.
Administration: Group.
Price Data, 1993: $30 per complete set (tests and manual, '76, 230 pages); $10 per manual; a license agreement is required for the use of the tests ($.10 a copy with a minimum of $35 for graduate students, $.20 a copy with a minimum of $50 for other researchers).
Time: Administration time not reported.
Comments: Formerly called the Kit of Reference Tests for Cognitive Factors.
Authors: Tests and manual written by Ruth B. Ekstrom, John W. French, Harry H. Harman, and Diran Dermen.
Publisher: Educational Testing Service.
  a) FACTOR CF: FLEXIBILITY OF CLOSURE.
    1) *Hidden Figures Test.*

2) *Hidden Patterns Test.*
3) *Copying Test.*

b) FACTOR CS: SPEED OF CLOSURE.
1) *Gestalt Completion Test.*
2) *Concealed Words Test.*
3) *Snowy Pictures.*

c) FACTOR CV: VERBAL CLOSURE.
1) *Scrambled Words.*
2) *Hidden Words.*
3) *Incomplete Words.*

d) FACTOR FA: ASSOCIATIONAL FLUENCY.
1) *Controlled Associations Test.*
2) *Opposites Test.*
3) *Figures of Speech.*

e) FACTOR FE: EXPRESSIONAL FLUENCY.
1) *Making Sentences.*
2) *Arranging Words.*
3) *Rewriting.*

f) FACTOR FF: FIGURAL FLUENCY.
1) *Ornamentation Test.*
2) *Elaboration Test.*
3) *Symbols Test.*

g) FACTOR FI: IDEATIONAL FLUENCY.
1) *Topics Test.*
2) *Theme Test.*
3) *Thing Categories Test.*

h) FACTOR FW: WORD FLUENCY.
1) *Word Endings Test.*
2) *Word Beginnings Test.*
3) *Word Beginnings and Endings Test.*

i) FACTOR I: INDUCTION.
1) *Letter Sets Test.*
2) *Locations Test.*
3) *Figure Classifications.*

j) FACTOR IP: INTEGRATIVE PROCESSES.
1) *Calendar Test.*
2) *Following Directions.*

k) FACTOR MA: ASSOCIATIVE MEMORY.
1) *Picture-Number Test.*
2) *Object-Number Test.*
3) *First and Last Names Test.*

l) FACTOR MS: MEMORY SPAN.
1) *Auditory Number Span Test.*
2) *Visual Number Span Test.*
3) *Auditory Letter Span Test.*

m) FACTOR MV: VISUAL MEMORY.
1) *Shape Memory Test.*
2) *Building Memory.*
3) *Map Memory.*

n) FACTOR N: NUMBER.
1) *Addition Test.*
2) *Division Test.*
3) *Subtraction and Multiplication Test.*
4) *Addition and Subtraction Correction.*

o) FACTOR P: PERCEPTUAL SPEED.
1) *Finding A's Test.*
2) *Number Comparison Test.*
3) *Identical Pictures Test.*

p) FACTOR RG: GENERAL REASONING.
1) *Arithmetic Aptitude Test.*
2) *Mathematics Aptitude Test.*

3) *Necessary Arithmetic Operations Test.*

q) FACTOR RL: LOGICAL REASONING.
1) *Nonsense Syllogisms Test.*
2) *Diagramming Relationships.*
3) *Inference Test.*
4) *Deciphering Languages.*

r) FACTOR S: SPATIAL ORIENTATION.
1) *Card Rotations Test.*
2) *Cube Comparisons Test.*

s) FACTOR SS: SPATIAL SCANNING.
1) *Maze Tracing Speed Test.*
2) *Choosing a Path.*
3) *Map Planning Test.*

t) FACTOR V: VERBAL COMPREHENSION.
1) *Vocabulary Test I.*
2) *Vocabulary Test II.*
3) *Extended Range Vocabulary Test.*
4) *Advanced Vocabulary Test I.*
5) *Advanced Vocabulary Test II.*

u) FACTOR VZ: VISUALIZATION.
1) *Form Board Test.*
2) *Paper Folding Test.*
3) *Surface Development Test.*

v) FACTOR XF: FIGURAL FLEXIBILITY.
1) *Toothpicks Test.*
2) *Planning Patterns.*
3) Storage Test.

w) FACTOR XU: FLEXIBILITY OF USE.
1) *Combining Objects.*
2) *Substitute Uses.*
3) *Making Groups.*
4) *Different Uses.*

Cross References: See 9:572 (27 references), T3:1257 (78 references), and T2:561 (103 references).

TEST REFERENCES

1. Schaie, K. W., Dutta, R., & Willis, S. L. (1991). Relationship between rigidity-flexibility and cognitive abilities in adulthood. *Psychology and Aging, 6*, 371-383.
2. Anderson, R. C., Pichert, J. W., & Shirey, L. L. (1983). Effects of the reader's schema at different points in time. *Journal of Educational Psychology, 75*, 271-279.
3. Cornelius, S. W., Willis, S. L., Nesselroade, J. R., & Baltes, P. B. (1983). Convergence between attention variables and factors of psychometric intelligence in older adults. *Intelligence, 7*, 253-269.
4. Hunt, D., & Randhawa, B. S. (1983). Cognitive processes and achievement. *The Alberta Journal of Educational Research, 29*, 206-215.
5. Nathan, B. R., & Lord, R. G. (1983). Cognitive categorization and dimensional schemata: A process approach to the study of halo in performance ratings. *Journal of Applied Psychology, 68*, 102-114.
6. Reynolds, R. E., & Schwartz, R. M. (1983). Relation to metaphoric processing to comprehension and memory. *Journal of Educational Psychology, 75*, 450-459.
7. Stankov, L. (1988). Aging, attention, and intelligence. *Psychology and Aging, 3*, 59-74.
8. Sternberg, R. J., & Gardner, M. K. (1983). Unities in inductive reasoning. *Journal of Experimental Psychology: General, 112*, 80-116.
9. Wilhite, S. C. (1983). Prepassage questions: The influence of structural importance. *Journal of Educational Psychology, 75*, 234-244.
10. Bartram, D., & Bayliss, R. (1984). Automated testing: Past, present and future. *Journal of Occupational Psychology, 57*, 221-237.
11. Bassett, G., & Hamilton, J. (1984). The relation of stress coping capability to level of job difficulty/complexity for educational administrators and business managers. *College Student Journal, 18*, 180-185.
12. Bethell-Fox, C. E., Lohman, D. F., & Snow, R. E. (1984). Adaptive reasoning: Componential and eye movement analysis of geometric analogy performance. *Intelligence, 8*, 205-238.
13. Cardy, R. L., & Kehoe, J. F. (1984). Rater selective attention

ability and appraisal effectiveness: The effect of a cognitive style on the accuracy of differentiation among ratees. *Journal of Applied Psychology, 69,* 589-594.

14. Damos, D. L. (1984). Individual differences in multiple-task performance and subjective estimates of workload. *Perceptual and Motor Skills, 59,* 567-580.

15. Decker, S. N., & Corley, R. P. (1984). Bannatyne's "genetic dyslexic" subtype: A validation study. *Psychology in the Schools, 21,* 300-304.

16. Derry, S. J. (1984). Effects of an organizer on memory for prose. *Journal of Educational Psychology, 76,* 98-107.

17. Frank, B. M. (1984). Effect of field independence-dependence and study technique on learning from a lecture. *American Educational Research Journal, 21,* 669-678.

18. Gerver, D., Longley, P., Long, J., & Lambert, S. (1984). Selecting trainee conference interpreters: A preliminary study. *Journal of Occupational Psychology, 57,* 17-31.

19. Gibson, S., & Dembo, M. H. (1984). Teacher efficacy: A construct validation. *Journal of Educational Psychology, 76,* 569-582.

20. Holliday, W. G., Whittaker, H. G., & Loose, K. D. (1984). Differential effects of verbal aptitude and study questions on comprehension of science concepts. *Journal of Research in Science Teaching, 21,* 143-150.

21. Hultsch, D. F., Hertzog, C., & Dixon, R. A. (1984). Text recall in adulthood: The role of intellectual abilities. *Developmental Psychology, 20,* 1193-1209.

22. Jedrczak, A., Clements, G. (1984). The TM-SIDHI Programme and field independence. *Perceptual and Motor Skills, 59,* 999-1000.

23. Johnson, E. S. (1984). Sex differences in problem solving. *Journal of Educational Psychology, 76,* 1359-1371.

24. Kyllonen, P. C., & Lohman, D. F. (1984). Componential modeling of alternative strategies for performing spatial tasks. *Journal of Educational Psychology, 76,* 1325-1345.

25. Kyllonen, P. C., Lohman, D. F., & Snow, R. E. (1984). Effects of aptitudes, strategy training, and task facets on spatial task performance. *Journal of Educational Psychology, 76,* 130-145.

26. Lachman, M. E., & Jelalian, E. (1984). Self-efficacy and attributions for intellectual performance in young and elderly adults. *Journal of Gerontology, 39,* 577-582.

27. Lehman, J. R., Koran, J. J., & Koran, M. L. (1984). Interaction of learner characteristics with learning from three models of the periodic table. *Journal of Research in Science Teaching, 21,* 885-893.

28. McGue, M., Bouchard, T. J., Jr., Lykken, D. T., & Feuer, D. (1984). Information processing abilitites in twins reared apart. *Intelligence, 8,* 239-258.

29. Pallrand, G. J., & Seeber, F. (1984). Spatial ability and achievement in introductory physics. *Journal of Research in Science Teaching, 21,* 507-516.

30. Pattison, P., & Grieve, N. (1984). Do spatial skills contribute to sex differences in different types of mathematical problems? *Journal of Educational Psychology, 76,* 678-689.

31. Sternberg, R. J., & Soriano, L. J. (1984). Styles of conflict resolution. *Journal of Personality and Social Psychology, 47,* 115-126.

32. Swinnen, S. (1984). Some evidence for the hemispheric asymmetry model of lateral eye movements. *Perceptual and Motor Skills, 58,* 79-88.

33. Webb, N. M. (1984). Microcomputer learning in small groups: Cognitive requirements and group processes. *Journal of Educational Psychology, 76,* 1076-1088.

34. Wilhite, S. C. (1984). Hierarchical importance of pre-passage questions: Effects on cued recall. *Journal of Reading Behavior, 16,* 41-59.

35. Wittig, M. A., Sasse, S. H., & Giacomi, J. (1984). Predictive validity of five cognitive skills tests among women receiving engineering training. *Journal of Research in Science Teaching, 21,* 537-546.

36. Baker, D. R. (1985). Predictive value of attitude, cognitive ability, and personality to science achievement in the middle school. *Journal of Research in Science Teaching, 27,* 103-113.

37. Englund, C. E., Ryman, D. H., Naitoh, P., & Hodgdon, J. A. (1985). Cognitive performance during successive sustained physical work episodes. *Behavior Research Methods, Instruments, & Computers, 17,* 75-85.

38. Kausler, D. H., Lichty, W., & Davis, R. T. (1985). Temporal memory for performed activities: Intentionality and adult age differences. *Developmental Psychology, 21,* 1132-1138.

39. Kausler, D. H., Lichty, W., & Freund, J. S. (1985). Adult age differences in recognition memory and frequency judgments for planned versus performed activities. *Developmental Psychology, 21,* 647-654.

40. Keating, D. P., List, J. A., & Merriman, W. E. (1985). Cognitive processing and cognitive ability: A multivariate validity investigation. *Intelligence, 9,* 149-170.

41. Laux, L. F., & Lane, D. M. (1985). Information processing components of substitution test performance. *Intelligence, 9,* 111-136.

42. List, J. A., Keating, D. P., & Merriman, W. E. (1985). Differ-

ences in memory retrieval: A construct validity investigation. *Child Development, 56,* 138-151.

43. Lord, T. R. (1985). Enhancing the visuo-spatial aptitude of students. *Journal of Research in Science Teaching, 22,* 395-405.

44. Merriman, W. E., Keating, D. P., & List, J. A. (1985). Mental rotation of facial profiles: Age-, sex-, and ability related differences. *Developmental Psychology, 21,* 888-900.

45. Noppe, L. D. (1985). The relationship of formal thought and cognitive styles to creativity. *The Journal of Creative Behavior, 19,* 88-96.

46. Noppe, L. D. (1985). The relationship of formal thought and cognitive styles to creativity. *The Journal of Creative Behavior, 19,* 88-96.

47. O'Brien, G. E., & Pere, T. K. (1985). The effects of ability, self-esteem and task difficulty on performance and task satisfaction. *Australian Journal of Psychology, 37,* 309-323.

48. Roach, D. A. (1985). Effects of cognitive style, intelligence, and sex on reading achievement. *Perceptual and Motor Skills, 61,* 1139-1142.

49. Ackerman, P. L. (1986). Individual differences in information processing: An investigation of intellectual abilities and task performance during practice. *Intelligence, 10,* 101-139.

50. Bryden, M. P. (1986). Dichotic listening performance, cognitive ability, and cerebral organization. *Canadian Journal of Psychology, 40,* 445-456.

51. Elmore, P. B., & Vasu, E. S. (1986). A model of statistics achievement using spatial ability, feminist attitudes and mathematics-related variables as predictors. *Educational and Psychological Measurement, 46,* 215-222.

52. Federico, P. (1986). Crystallized and fluid intelligence in a "new" instructional situation. *Contemporary Educational Psychology, 11,* 33-53.

53. Hauptman, A., & Eliot, J. (1986). Contribution of figural proportion, figural memory, figure-ground perception and severity of hearing loss to performance on spatial tasks. *Perceptual and Motor Skills, 63,* 187-190.

54. Kiewra, K. A., & Frank, B. M. (1986). Cognitive style: Effects of structure at acquisition and testing. *Contemporary Educational Psychology, 11,* 253-263.

55. Stallings, S. L., & Derry, S. J. (1986). Can an advance organizer technique compensate for poor reading conditions? *Journal of Experimental Education, 54,* 217-222.

56. Swinnen, S., Vandenberghe, J., & VanAssche, E. (1986). Role of cognitive style constructs field dependence-independence and reflection-impulsivity in skill acquisition. *Journal of Sport Psychology, 8,* 51-69.

57. Thomas, C. R. (1986). Field independence and technology students' achievement. *Perceptual and Motor Skills, 62,* 859-862.

58. van de Vijver, F. J. R., Daal, M., & van Zonneveld, R. (1986). The trainability of formal thinking: A cross-cultural comparison. *International Journal of Psychology, 21,* 589-615.

59. Watkins, D., Hattie, J., & Astilla, E. (1986). Approaches to studying by Filipino students: A longitudinal investigation. *British Journal of Educational Psychology, 56,* 357-362.

60. Cochran, K. F., & Davis, J. K. (1987). Individual differences in inference processes. *Journal of Research in Personality, 21,* 197-210.

61. Fogarty, G. (1987). Timesharing in relation to broad ability domains. *Intelligence, 11,* 207-231.

62. Goodenough, D. R., Oltman, P. K., & Cox, P. W. (1987). The nature of individual differences in field dependence. *Journal of Research in Personality, 21,* 81-99.

63. Kent, J., & Plomin, R. (1987). Testing specific cognitive abilities by telephone and mail. *Intelligence, 11,* 391-400.

64. May, J., & Kline, P. (1987). Measuring the effects upon cognitive abilities of sleep loss during continuous operations. *British Journal of Psychology, 78,* 443-455.

65. Sternberg, R. J., & Dobson, D. M. (1987). Resolving interpersonal conflicts: An analysis of stylistic consistency. *Journal of Personality and Social Psychology, 52,* 794-812.

66. Hunt, E., Pellegrino, J. W., Frick, R. W., Farr, S. A., & Alderton, D. (1988). The ability to reason about movement in the visual field. *Intelligence, 12,* 77-100.

67. Kagan, D. M. (1988). Measurements of divergent and complex thinking. *Educational and Psychological Measurement, 48,* 873-884.

68. Kirby, J. R., Moore, P. J., & Schofield, N. J. (1988). Verbal and visual learning styles. *Contemporary Educational Psychology, 13,* 169-184.

69. Salthouse, T. A., Kausler, D., & Saults, J. S. (1988). Investigations of student status, background variables, and feasibility of standard tasks in a cognitive aging research. *Psychology and Aging, 3,* 29-37.

70. Sholl, M. J. (1988). The relation between sense of direction and mental geographic updating. *Intelligence, 12,* 299-314.

71. Vernon, P. A., & Strudensky, S. (1988). Relationships between problem-solving and intelligence. *Intelligence, 12,* 435-453.

72. Hayslip, B., Jr. (1989). Alternative mechanisms for improvements in fluid ability performance among older adults. *Psychology and Aging, 4,* 122-124.

73. Lachman, M. E., & Leff, R. (1989). Perceived control and intellectual functioning in the elderly: A 5-year longitudinal study. *Developmental Psychology*, 25, 722-728.
74. Larson, G. E., & Saccuzzo, D. P. (1989). Cognitive correlates of general intelligence: Toward a process theory of g. *Intelligence*, 13, 5-31.
75. Schaie, K. W. (1989). Perceptual speed in adulthood: Cross-sectional and longitudinal studies. *Psychology and Aging*, 4, 443-453.
76. Sternberg, R. J., & Gastel, J. (1989). Coping with novelty in human intelligence: An empirical investigation. *Intelligence*, 13, 187-197.
77. Brookings, J. B. (1990). A confirmatory factor analytic study of time-sharing performance and cognitive abilities. *Intelligence*, 14, 43-59.
78. Hertzog, C., Dixon, R. A., & Hultsch, D. F. (1990). Relationships between metamemory, memory predictions, and memory task performance in adults. *Psychology and Aging*, 5, 215-227.
79. Hultsch, D. F., Hertzog, C., & Dixon, R. A. (1990). Ability correlates of memory performance in adulthood and aging. *Psychology and Aging*, 5, 356-368.
80. Adams, C. (1991). Qualitative age differences in memory for text: A life-span developmental perspective. *Psychology and Aging*, 6, 323-336.
81. Christensen, H., & Henderson, A. S. (1991). Is age kinder to the initially more able? A study of eminent scientists and academics. *Psychological Medicine*, 21, 935-946.
82. Connelly, S. L., Hasher, L., & Zacks, R. T. (1991). Age and reading: The impact of distraction. *Psychology and Aging*, 6, 533-541.
83. Gould, O. N., Trevithick, L., & Dixon, R. A. (1991). Adult age differences in elaborations produced during prose recall. *Psychology and Aging*, 6, 93-99.
84. Salthouse, T. A. (1991). Age and experience effects on the interpretation of orthographic drawings of three-dimensional objects. *Psychology and Aging*, 6, 426-433.
85. Schmidt, C. P., & Stephans, R. (1991). Locus of control and field dependence as factors in students' evaluations of applied music instruction. *Perceptual and Motor Skills*, 73, 131-136.
86. Hultsch, D., Hertzog, C., Small, B. J., McDonald-Miszczak, L., & Dixon, R. A. (1992). Short-term longitudinal change in cognitive performance in later life. *Psychology and Aging*, 7, 571-584.
87. Lindenberger, U., Kliegl, R., & Baltes, P. B. (1992). Professional expertise does not eliminate age differences in imagery-based memory performance during adulthood. *Psychology and Aging*, 7, 585-593.
88. Miller, L. T., & Vernon, P. A. (1992). The general factor in short-term memory, intelligence, and reaction time. *Intelligence*, 16, 5-29.
89. Simon, S. L., Walsh, D. A., Regnier, V. A., & Krauss, I. K. (1992). Spatial cognition and neighborhood use: The relationship in older adults. *Psychology and Aging*, 7, 389-394.
90. Lindenberger, U., Mayr, U., & Kliegal, R. (1993). Speed and intelligence in old age. *Psychology and Aging*, 8, 207-220.
91. Kane, M. J., Hashner, L., Stoltzfus, E. R., Zacks, R. T., & Connelly, S. L. (1994). Inhibitory attentional mechanisms and aging. *Psychology and Aging*, 9, 103-112.
92. Spencer, W. D., & Raz, N. (1994). Memory for facts, source, and context: Can frontal lobe dysfunction explain age-related differences? *Psychology and Aging*, 9, 149-159.

[1366]

Knowledge of Occupations Test.

Purpose: "To measure the extent to which high school students have knowledge of occupations."
Population: High school.
Publication Date: 1974.
Acronym: KOT.
Scores, 9: Earnings, Licensing and Certification, Job Descriptions, Employment Trends, Training, Terminology, Graphs, Tools, Total.
Administration: Group.
Price Data, 1987: $20 per 25 tests; $2.75 per answer key; $8.25 per 25 answer sheets; $8.25 per 25 profiles; $6.75 per manual (8 pages); $9 per specimen set including manual and forms (keys not included).
Time: 40(45) minutes.
Author: Leroy G. Baruth.
Publisher: Psychologists and Educators, Inc.
Cross References: For reviews by David O. Herman and Dean H. Nafziger, see 8:1008 (1 reference).

[1367]

Knox's Cube Test.

Purpose: A nonverbal mental test designed to measure "the attention span and short-term memory of children and adults."
Population: Ages 3–8, 9 and over.
Publication Date: 1980.
Acronym: KCT.
Scores: Total score only.
Administration: Individual.
Levels, 2: Junior Test Form, Senior Test Form.
Price Data, 1994: $95 per complete kit (specify level); $15 per 15 tests and report forms (specify level); $75 per set of blocks; $25 per manual (53 pages).
Time: Administration time not reported.
Authors: Mark H. Stone and Benjamin D. Wright.
Publisher: Stoelting Co.
Cross References: For reviews by Raymond S. Dean and Jerome M. Sattler, see 9:574 (2 references).

TEST REFERENCES

1. Bornstein, R. A. (1983). Relationship of age and education to neuropsychological performance in patients with symptomatic carotid artery disease. *Journal of Clinical Psychology*, 39, 470-478.
2. Aguirre, M., Broughton, R., & Stuss, D. (1985). Does memory impairment exist in narcolepsy-cataplexy? *Journal of Clinical and Experimental Neuropsychology*, 7, 14-24.
3. Bornstein, R. A., Watson, G. D., & Kaplan, M. J. (1985). Effects of flurazepam and triazolam on neuropsychological performance. *Perceptual and Motor Skills*, 60, 47-52.
4. McGlone, J. (1985). Can spatial deficits in Turner's Syndrome be explained by focal CNS dysfunction or atypical speech lateralization? *Journal of Clinical and Experimental Neuropsychology*, 7, 375-394.
5. Munroe, R. H., Munroe, R. L., & Brasher, A. (1985). Precursors of spatial ability: A longitudinal study among the Logoli of Kenya. *The Journal of Social Psychology*, 125, 23-33.
6. Ownby, R. L., & Matthews, C. G. (1985). On the meaning of the WISC-R third factor: Relations to selected neuropsychological measures. *Journal of Consulting and Clinical Psychology*, 53, 531-534.
7. Mendez, M. F., & Ashla-Mendez, M. (1991). Differences between multi-infarct dementia and Alzheimer's disease on unstructured neuropsychological tasks. *Journal of Clinical and Experimental Neuropsychology*, 13, 923-932.

[1368]

Kohlberg's Moral Judgment Interview.

Purpose: To identify stages of moral development.
Population: Ages 10 and over.
Publication Date: 1983.
Scores: Moral Development Stages.
Price Data: Not available.
Time: Administration time not reported.
Authors: Anne Colby and Lawrence Kohlberg.
Publisher: Cambridge University Press [No reply from publisher; status unknown].
Cross References: See T3:1262 (2 references).

TEST REFERENCES

1. Gibbs, J. C., Arnold, K. D., Morgan, R. L., Schwartz, E. S., Gavaghan, M. P., & Tappan, M. B. (1984). Construction and validation of a multiple-choice measure of moral reasoning. *Child Development*, 55, 527-536.
2. Hauser, S. T., Powers, S. I., Noan, G. G., & Jacobson, A. M. (1984). Familial contexts of adolescent ego development. *Child Development*, 55, 195-213.
3. Pratt, M. W., Golding, G., & Hunter, W. J. (1984). Does morality have a gender? Sex, sex role, and moral judgment relationships across the adult lifespan. *Merrill-Palmer Quarterly*, 30, 321-340.

4. Walker, L. J. (1984). Sex differences in the development of moral reasoning: A critical review. *Child Development, 55,* 677-691.

5. Sigman, M., & Erdynast, A. (1988). Interpersonal understanding and moral judgement in adolescents with emotional and cognitive disorders. *Child Psychiatry and Human Development, 19,* 36-44.

6. Gibson, D. R. (1990). Relation of socioeconomic status to logical and sociomoral judgement of middle-aged men. *Psychology and Aging, 5,* 510-513.

7. Mwamwenda, T. S. (1991). Graduate students' moral reasoning. *Psychological Reports, 68,* 1368-1370.

8. Walker, L. J., & Taylor, J. H. (1991). Family interactions and the development of moral reasoning. *Child Development, 62,* 264-283.

9. Bush, A. J., Krebs, D. L., Carpendale, J. I. (1993). The structural consistency of moral judgement about AIDS. *Journal of Genetic Psychology, 154,* 167-175.

[1369]

Kohn Problem Checklist/Kohn Social Competence Scale.

Purpose: "Designed to assess the social and emotional functioning of preschool and kindergarten children through the systematic observation of classroom behavior."

Population: Ages 3–6.

Publication Dates: 1979–88.

Acronym: KPC/KSC.

Scores, 2: Apathy–Withdrawal, Anger–Defiance.

Administration: Individual.

Price Data, 1994: $75 per complete KPC/KSC combined kit including 25 ready-score answer sheets from each test, and manual ('88, 47 pages); $77.50 per 100 KPS ready-score answer sheets; $31 per manual for both KPC and KSC.

Time: Administration time not reported.

Author: Martin Kohn.

Publisher: The Psychological Corporation.

Cross References: For reviews of the Kohn Problem Checklist by James L. Carroll and Bert O. Richmond, see 9:575 (2 references); for reviews of the Kohn Social Competence Checklist by James L. Carroll and Ronald S. Drabman, see 9:575 (5 references).

TEST REFERENCES

1. Connolly, J. A., & Doyle, A. (1984). Relation of social fantasy play to social competence in preschoolers. *Developmental Psychology, 20,* 797-806.

2. Guidubaldi, J., & Perry, J. D. (1984). Concurrent and predictive validity of the Battelle Development Inventory at the first grade level. *Educational and Psychological Measurement, 44,* 977-985.

3. Kashani, J. H., Holcomb, W. R., & Orvaschel, H. (1986). Depression and depressive symptoms in preschool children from the general population. *American Journal of Psychiatry, 143,* 1138-1143.

4. Smith, D. E., & Moran, J. D., III. (1990). Socioemotional functioning of creative preschoolers. *Perceptual and Motor Skills, 71,* 267-273.

5. Jacobsen, T., Edelstein, W., & Hofmann, V. (1994). A longitudinal study of the relation between representations of attachment in childhood and cognitive functioning in childhood and adolescence. *Developmental Psychology, 30,* 112-124.

[1370]

The Kohs Block-Design Test.

Purpose: Designed as "performance tests that have been standardized to measure intelligence."

Population: Mental ages 5–20.

Publication Date: [1919].

Scores: Total score only.

Administration: Individual.

Price Data, 1994: $135 per complete kit including cubes, cards, manual (20 pages), and 50 record blanks; $20 per 50 record blanks; $20 per set of design cards; $85 per set of blocks; $50 per manual.

Time: (30–40) minutes.

Comments: Formerly called The Block-Design Test; modifications appear in Arthur Point Scale of Performance Tests, New Guinea Performance Scales, Ohwaki-Kohs Tactile Block Design Intelligence Test for the Blind, and Pacific Design Construction Test.

Author: S. C. Kohs.

Publisher: Stoelting Co.

Cross References: See T3:1265 (4 references) and T2:545 (74 references).

TEST REFERENCES

1. Binnie-Dawson, J. L. M. (1984). Bio-social and endocrine bases of spatial ability. *Psychologia, 27,* 129-151.

2. Muramoto, O. (1984). Selective reminding in normal and demented aged people: Auditory verbal versus visual spatial task. *Cortex, 20,* 461-478.

3. Swinnen, S. (1984). Some evidence for the hemispheric asymmetry model of lateral eye movements. *Perceptual and Motor Skills, 58,* 79-88.

4. Lonner, W. J., Thorndike, R. M., Forbes, N. E., & Ashworth, C. (1985). The influence of television on measured cognitive abilities. *Journal of Cross-Cultural Psychology, 16,* 355-380.

5. Tirosh, E., Taub, Y., Scher, A., Jaffe, M., & Hochberg, Z. (1989). Short-term efficacy of thyroid hormone supplementation for patients with Down Syndrome and low-borderline thyroid function. *American Journal on Mental Retardation, 93,* 652-656.

[1371]

Kolbe Conative Index.

Purpose: Constructed to measure "instinctive talent."

Population: Adults.

Publication Dates: 1987–91.

Acronym: KCI.

Scores: Degree of Intensity in 4 Action Modes (Fact Finder, Follow Thru, Quick Start, Implementor).

Administration: Group or individual.

Restricted Distribution: Available only to Certified Kolbe Consultants who must attend a 3-day seminar and complete an extended training program.

Price Data: Available from publisher.

Time: (25) minutes.

Comments: Untimed and self-administered.

Author: Kathy Kolbe.

Publisher: KolbeConcepts, Inc.

[1372]

Kolbe Conative Index, Forms B and C.

Purpose: Designed to help "identify the characteristics necessary to succeed on a specific job."

Population: Employees.

Publication Dates: 1989–94.

Acronym: KCI-B; KCI-C.

Scores, 4: Fact Finder, Follow Thru, Quick Start, Implementor.

Administration: Group or individual.

Price Data: Available from publisher.

Time: (15–20) minutes.

Author: Kathy Kolbe.

Publisher: KolbeConcepts, Inc.

[1373]
Krantz Health Opinion Survey.

Purpose: "To measure attitudes toward different treatment approches."
Population: College, healthy adults, and chronic disease populations.
Publication Date: 1980.
Acronym: KHOS.
Scores, 3: Information, Behavioral Involvement, Total.
Administration: Group.
Manual: No manual.
Price Data: Test materials available free of charge from author.
Time: (10–15) minutes.
Authors: David S. Krantz, Andrew Baum, and Margaret V. Wideman.
Publisher: David S. Krantz.
Cross References: For a review by James A. Blumenthal, see 9:578 (1 reference); see also T3:1267 (1 reference).

TEST REFERENCES

1. Martelli, M. F., Auerbach, S. M., Alexander, J., & Mercuri, L. G. (1987). Stress management in the health care setting: Matching interventions with patient coping styles. *Journal of Consulting and Clinical Psychology, 55*, 201-207.

[1374]
Kuder General Interest Survey, Form E.

Purpose: Constructed to assess "broad interest areas" related to occupational choices.
Population: Grades 6–12.
Publication Dates: 1963–91.
Scores, 11: Outdoor, Mechanical, Computational, Scientific, Persuasive, Artistic, Literary, Musical, Social Service, Clerical, Verification.
Administration: Group.
Price Data, 1994: $49.35 per complete hand-scored kit including 25 consumable booklets, 25 interpretive leaflets, and instructions for administration; $44.85 per complete locally machine-scored kit including same materials above; $79.30 per CTB machine-scored kit including materials above plus 2 answer sheet return envelopes, 2 scoring control cards, and complete scoring; $15.25 per 25 punch pins and backboards; $22 per 100 punch pins; $40 per 100 backboards; $11.95 per Job and College Major Charts; $5.60 per manual ('88, 48 pages); $8.40 per specimen set; information regarding microcomputer administration and scoring available from publisher.
Time: [45–60] minutes.
Comments: Extension of the Kuder vocational interest inventories series.
Author: G. Frederic Kuder.
Publisher: CTB Macmillan/McGraw-Hill.
Cross References: See T3:1269 (4 references); see also 8:1009 (16 references); for reviews of an earlier edition by Barbara A. Kirk, Paul R. Lohnes, and John N. McCall, and excerpted reviews by T. R. Husek and Robert F. Stahmann, see 7:1024 (8 references).

TEST REFERENCES

1. Best, S., & Knap-Lee, L. (1982). Relationship of interest measurement derived from the COPSystem Interest Inventory and the Kuder General Interest Survey: Construct validation of two measures of occupational activity preferences. *Educational and Psychological Measurement, 42*, 1289-1293.
2. Donovan, E. P., Fronk, R. H., & Horton, P. B. (1985). A new science and engineering career interest survey for middle school students. *Journal of Research in Science Teaching, 22*, 19-30.
3. Lampe, R. E. (1985). Self-scoring accuracy of the Kuder General Interest Survey. *The School Counselor, 32*, 319-324.
4. Zytowski, D. G. (1992). Three generations: The continuing evaluation of Frederic Kuder's interest inventories. *Journal of Counseling and Development, 71*, 245-248.

[1375]
Kuder Occupational Interest Survey, Revised (Form DD), 1985.

Purpose: Measures individual interests in order to "suggest promising occupations and college majors in rank order, based on examinee's interest pattern."
Population: Grade 10 through adult.
Publication Dates: 1956–85.
Acronym: KOIS.
Scores, 4: Dependability, Vocational Interest Estimates (10 areas), Occupational Scales (approximately 100), College Major Scales (approximately 40).
Administration: Group.
Price Data, 1987: $73.50 per set of materials and scoring for 20 students; $16.75 per Kuder Interpretive Audiocassette; manual ('79, 70 pages) and manual supplement available free on request; $7 per specimen set including survey booklet, interpretive leaflet, general manual, and scoring for one individual.
Time: (30–45) minutes.
Comments: Includes Vocational Interest Estimate scales identical in content to those of the Kuder Preference Record, Form C and the Kuder General Interest Survey, Form E.
Authors: Frederic Kuder, Esther E. Diamond, and Donald G. Zytowski (manual supplement).
Publisher: Science Research Associates, Inc.
Cross References: For reviews by Edwin L. Herr and Mary L. Tenopyr, see 10:167 (3 references); see also T3:1270 (12 references), 8:1010 (41 references), and T2: 2194 (13 references); for reviews by Robert H. Dolliver and W. Bruce Walsh, and excerpted reviews by Frederick G. Brown and Robert F. Stahmann, see 7:1025 (19 references).

TEST REFERENCES

1. Zytowski, D. G. (1992). Three generations: The continuing evaluation of Frederic Kuder's interest inventories. *Journal of Counseling and Development, 71*, 245-248.

[1376]
Kuder Preference Record—Vocational.

Purpose: Designed to measure interests of high school students and adults.
Population: Grades 9–16 and adults.
Publication Dates: 1934–70.
Acronym: KPR-V.
Scores, 11: Outdoor, Mechanical, Computation, Scientific, Persuasive, Artistic, Literary, Musical, Social Service, Clerical, Verification.

Administration: Group.
Price Data, 1987: $38.75 per 25 tests, Form CP (includes answer pad, 2 profiles, 1 memorandum of instructions); $12.10 per 25 pins and 25 blackboards; manual ('60, 27 pages) available free on request; $7.25 per specimen set.
Time: (30–50) minutes.
Comments: Also called Kuder C; for a revision and downward extension, see Kuder General Interest Survey (Kuder E).
Author: Frederic Kuder.
Publisher: Science Research Associates, Inc.
Cross References: See T3:1271 (4 references); for a review by Lenore W. Harmon, see 8:1011 (36 references); see also T2:2195 (302 references); for a review by Martin Katz, see 6:1063 (148 references); for reviews by Clifford P. Froehlich and John Pierce-Jones, see 5:863 (211 references); for reviews by Edward S. Bordin, Harold D. Carter, and H. M. Fowler, see 4:742 (144 references); for reviews by Ralph F. Berdie, E. G. Chambers, and Donald E. Super and an excerpted review by Arthur H. Brayfield of an earlier edition, see 3:640 (60 references); for reviews by A. B. Crawford and Arthur E. Traxler, see 2:1671 (2 references).

TEST REFERENCES

1. Glass, C. R., & Knight, L. A. (1988). Cognitive factors in computer anxiety. *Cognitive Therapy and Research, 12*, 351-366.

[1377]

Kuhlmann-Anderson Tests, Eighth Edition.
Purpose: "Designed to provide a measure of an individual's academic potential through assessing cognitive skills related to the learning process."
Population: Grades K, 1, 2–3, 3–4, 5–6, 7–9, 9–12.
Publication Dates: 1927–82.
Acronym: KA.
Scores, 6: 3 raw scores (Verbal, Non-verbal, Full) and 3 derived scores.
Administration: Group.
Levels, 7: K, A, BC, CD, EF, G, and H.
Manual: Separate manual of directions for each level.
Price Data: Available from publisher.
Authors: F. Kuhlmann (fourth and earlier editions) and Rose G. Anderson.
Publisher: Scholastic Testing Service, Inc.
a) LEVEL K.
Population: Kindergarten.
Time: 28(60–75) minutes in 2 days.
b) LEVEL A.
Population: Grade 1.
Time: 28(60–75) minutes in 2 days.
c) LEVEL BC.
Population: Grades 2, 3.
Time: 28(60–75) minutes in 2 days.
d) LEVEL CD.
Population: Grades 3, 4.
Time: 35(60–75) minutes.

e) LEVEL EF.
Population: Grades 5, 6.
Time: 40(60–75) minutes.
f) LEVEL G.
Population: Grades 7–9.
Time: 40(60–75) minutes.
g) LEVEL H.
Population: Grades 9–12.
Time: 40(60–75) minutes.
Cross References: For reviews by Michael D. Hiscox and Ronald C. Rodgers, see 9:579 (2 references); see T3:1272 (13 references) and T2:398 (53 references); for reviews by William B. Michael and Douglas A. Pidgeon, and an excerpted review by Frederick B. Davis of the seventh edition, see 6:466 (11 references); see also 5:348 (15 references); for reviews by Henry E. Garrett and David Segel of an earlier edition, see 5:302 (10 references); for reviews by W. G. Emmett and Stanley S. Maryolf, see 3:236 (25 references); for a review by Henry E. Garrett, see 2:1404 (15 references); for reviews by Psyche Cattell, S. A. Courtis, and Austin H. Turney, see 1:1049.

TEST REFERENCES

1. McDermott, P. A. (1984). Comparative functions of preschool learning style and IQ in predicting future academic performance. *Contemporary Educational Psychology, 9*, 38-47.
2. Wagner, D. A., & Spratt, J. E. (1987). Cognitive consequences of contrasting pedagogies: The effects of Quranic preschooling in Morocco. *Child Development, 58*, 1207-1219.

[1378]

Kundu Introversion Extraversion Inventory.
Purpose: Designed to obtain a measure of the introversion-extraversion dimension of adult behavior to be used for diagnosis, selection, or career guidance.
Population: Adults.
Publication Date: 1976.
Scores: Total score only.
Administration: Group.
Price Data: Available from publisher.
Time: (20–40) minutes.
Author: Ramanath Kundu.
Publisher: Ramanath Kundu [India].

[1379]

Kundu Neurotic Personality Inventory.
Purpose: Designed to measure neurotic tendencies.
Population: Adults.
Publication Dates: 1965–87.
Acronym: KNPI.
Scores: Item scores only.
Administration: Individual or group.
Price Data: Available from publisher.
Foreign Language Edition: Bengali edition available.
Time: (20–30) minutes.
Author: Ramanath Kundu.
Publisher: Ramanath Kundu [India].
Cross References: See T2:1257 (2 references) and P:140 (5 references).

[1380]

Kwalwasser Music Talent Test.
Purpose: Assesses an individual's "musical talent" by means of pitch, time, loudness, and rhythm.
Population: Grades 4–6, 7–16, and adults.
Publication Date: 1953.
Scores: Total score only.
Administration: Group.
Price Data: Not available.
Time: Administration time not reported.
Author: Jacob Kwalwasser.
Publisher: Belwin-Mills Publishing Corporation [No reply from publisher; status unknown].
Cross References: See T2:203 (4 references); for reviews by Paul R. Farnsworth and Kate Heriner Mueller, see 5:248.

[1381]

La Monica Empathy Profile.
Purpose: "To measure and improve a person's ability to care, manage, and provide the empathy needed for optimum performance in fields where personal interaction is intense and frequent."
Population: Managers/helpers/teachers in industry, education, and health care.
Publication Dates: 1980–86.
Acronym: LEP.
Scores, 5: Nonverbal Behavior, Perceiving Feelings and Listening, Responding Verbally, Respect of Self and Others, Openness/Honesty and Flexibility.
Administration: Group or individual.
Price Data, 1993: $5.25 or less per instrument ('86, 21 pages includes profile, instructions, and scoring information).
Time: [15] minutes.
Comments: Self-administered; self-scored.
Authors: Elaine L. La Monica.
Publisher: XICOM, Inc.
Cross References: For reviews by Susan McCammon and LeAdelle Phelps, see 10:168.

[1382]

La Prueba de Realización, Segunda Edición.
Purpose: Constructed to assess achievement in the areas of reading/language, writing, mathematics, social studies, and science of students whose primary language is Spanish.
Publication Dates: 1984–91.
Administration: Group.
Price Data, 1992: $12.47 per 35 parent letters; $15 per teacher's guide and technical summary; $27 per specimen set.
Comments: Form A still available.
Authors: Nancy S. Cole, E. Roger Trent, and Dena C. Wadell.
Publisher: The Riverside Publishing Co.
a) LEVEL 6.
Population: Kindergarten.
Scores, 2: Reading/Language, Mathematics.
Price Data: $81 per 35 machine-scorable test booklets; $12.60 per 35 practice tests; $4.20 per directions for administration; $2.25 per practice test directions for administration.
Time: (50–70) minutes in 2 sessions.
b) LEVEL 7.
Population: Grade 1.
Scores, 2: Same as *a* above.
Price Data: Same as *a* above.
Time: (53-73) minutes in 2 sessions.
c) LEVEL 8.
Population: Grades 2–3.
Scores, 4: Reading/Language, Mathematics, Social Studies, Science.
Price Data: $90 per 35 machine-scorable test booklets; $12.60 per 35 practice tests; $4.20 per directions for administration; $2.25 per practice test directions for administration.
Time: (110–140) minutes in 4 sessions.
d) LEVEL 9.
Population: Grades 3–4.
Scores, 5: Reading, Writing, Mathematics, Social Studies, Science.
Price Data: $93 per 35 machine-scorable test booklets; $12.60 per 35 practice tests; $4.20 per directions for administration; $2.25 per practice test directions for administration.
Time: (115–165) minutes in 3 sessions.
e) LEVEL 10.
Population: Grades 4–5.
Scores, 5: Same as *d* above.
Price Data: $75 per 35 reusable test booklets; $12.60 per 35 practice tests; $18 per 35 answer sheets; $4.20 per directions for administration; $2.25 per practice test directions for administration.
Time: Same as *d* above.
f) LEVEL 11.
Population: Grades 5–6.
Scores, 5: Same as *d* above.
Price Data: Same as *e* above.
Time: Same as *d* above.
g) LEVEL 12.
Population: Grades 6–7.
Scores, 5: Same as *d* above.
Price Data: Same as *e* above.
Time: Same as *d* above.
h) LEVEL 13.
Population: Grade 7–8.
Scores, 5: Same as *d* above.
Price Data: Same as *e* above.
Time: Same as *d* above.
i) LEVEL 14.
Population: Grades 8–12.
Scores, 5: Same as *d* above.
Price Data: Same as *e* above.
Time: Same as *d* above.

[1383]

The Lake St. Clair Incident.
Purpose: To examine group and individual decision-making processes, help individuals and groups per-

ceive and evaluate their interactions and styles of communicating, and utilize the instrument to simply have fun or create an environment.
Population: Adults.
Publication Dates: 1977–78.
Acronym: LSC.
Scores, 3: Autocratic, Consultative, Consensual.
Administration: Individual in part.
Price Data, 1993: $32.50 per 25 test booklets; $24.50 per manual ('77, 22 pages); $55 per kit including 25 test booklets and manual.
Time: (65–80) minutes.
Authors: Albert A. Canfield.
Publisher: Western Psychological Services.
Cross References: For a review by Jack L. Bodden, see 9:582.

[1384]
Language Arts Assessment Portfolio.

Purpose: To "analyze and evaluate student achievement in all areas of the language arts: reading, writing, listening, and speaking."
Population: Grades 1–6.
Publication Date: 1992.
Acronym: LAAP.
Administration: Individual.
Levels: 3 levels.
Price Data, 1993: $99.95 per complete LAAP kit Level 1, 2 or 3; $23.95 per 30 portfolio folders; $23.95 per 30 evaluation booklets; $79 per LAAP training video.
Time: Administration time not reported.
Comments: Assessment done with students' own language arts materials.
Author: Bjorn Karlsen.
Publisher: American Guidance Service, Inc.
a) LEVEL I.
Population: Grade 1.
Scores: 15–24 language arts skill areas: Reading Analysis (Reading Comprehension, Oral Reading, Decoding), Optional Reading Analysis (Silent Reading Problems, Oral Reading Problems), Writing Analysis [Process (Story Creation), Product (Sentence Structure, Story Content, Spelling, Mechanics)], Optional Writing Analysis (Spelling, Mechanics), Listening Analysis [Listening in Interaction (Attentiveness, Understanding), Listening to Teaching (Memory, Interpretation)], Optional Listening Analysis (Auditory Decoding, Rhymes and Rhythms, Phonetic Elements, Structural Elements), Speaking Analysis [Oral Interaction, Oral Presentation (Delivery)], Optional Speaking Analysis (Language Development).
b) LEVEL II.
Population: Grades 2–3.
Scores: 16–25 language arts skill areas: Reading Analysis (Silent Reading Comprehension, Oral Reading, Decoding), Optional Reading Analysis (Silent Reading Problems, Oral Reading Problems), Writing Analysis [Process (Story Creation, Process Awareness), Product (Story Content, Orga-

nization, Spelling, Mechanics)], Optional Writing Analysis [Spelling Error Analysis, Mechanics (Punctuation, Capitalization)], Listening Analysis [Listening in Interaction (Attentiveness, Understanding), Listening to Teaching (Memory, Interpretation)], Optional Listening Analysis (Auditory Decoding, Phonetic Elements, Structural Elements), Speaking Analysis [Oral Interaction, Oral Presentation (Delivery)], Optional Speaking Analysis (Language Development).
c) LEVEL III.
Population: Grades 4–6.
Scores: Same as *b* above except that Attentiveness is not included for Listening Analysis.

TEST REFERENCES

1. Farr, R., & Jungsma, E. (1993). The convergent/discriminant validity of integrated reading/writing assessment. *Journal of Research and Development, 26*, 83-91.

[1385]
Language Assessment Battery.

Purpose: "Designed to assess reading, writing, listening comprehension and speaking in English and Spanish."
Population: Grades K–12.
Publication Date: 1976.
Acronym: LAB.
Editions, 2: English, Spanish.
Price Data, 1989: $15 per 35 digitek answer sheets; $3.60 per scoring stencil; $9 per technical manual (48 pages); $18 per specimen set.
Authors: Board of Education of the City of New York.
Publisher: The Riverside Publishing Co.
a) LEVEL I.
Population: Grades K–2.
Scores, 3: Listening and Speaking, Reading, Writing.
Administration: Individual.
Price Data: $18 per 35 test booklets; $3.90 per picture stimulus booklet; $4.50 per examiner's directions (18 pages).
Time: (5–10) minutes.
b) LEVEL II.
Population: Grades 3–6.
Scores, 4: Listening, Reading, Writing, Speaking.
Administration: Group.
Price Data: $33 per 35 test booklets; $1.50 per picture stimulus card; $3.90 per examiner's directions (14 pages).
Time: (40–50) minutes.
d) LEVEL III.
Population: Grades 7–12.
Scores, 4: Same as *b* above.
Administration: Group.
Price Data: Same as *b* above.
Time: (40–50) minutes.
Cross References: For a review by Kathleen Barrows Chesterfield, see 9:583.

TEST REFERENCES

1. Figueroa, R. A., Sandoval, J., & Merino, B. (1984). School psychology and limited-English-proficient (LEP) children: New competencies. *Journal of School Psychology, 22,* 131-143.

2. O'Brien, M. L. (1989). Psychometric issues relevant to selecting items and assembling parallel forms of language proficiency instruments. *Educational and Psychological Measurement, 49,* 347-353.

3. Musselman, C., & Churchill, A. (1991). Conversational control in mother-child dyads. *American Annals of the Deaf, 136,* 5-16.

[1386]

Language Assessment Scales, Reading and Writing.

Purpose: Designed to measure "English language skills in reading and writing necessary for functioning in a mainstream academic environment."
Population: Language-minority students in grades 2–3, 4–6, 7–11.
Publication Date: 1988.
Acronym: LAW R/W.
Scores, 3: Reading, Writing, Total.
Administration: Group.
Levels, 3: 1, 2, 3.
Forms, 2: A, B.
Price Data, 1992: $83.30 per 35 Level 1 test booklets and examiner's manual (67 pages); $35.70 per 35 Level 2 or Level 3 Reading test booklets and Reading/Writing examiner's manual (Level 2, 79 pages; Level 3, 73 pages); $27.30 per 35 Level 2 or Level 3 Writing test booklets; $21.50 per 50 CompuScan answer sheets (select Level 2 or 3); $74.50 per 9 Level 1 scoring stencils; $10.35 per set of scoring stencils (select Level 2 or 3); $7.95 per examiner's manual (select level); $11.20 per technical report (98 pages); $54 per training kit.
Time: (50–75) minutes for Level 1; (49–87) minutes for Level 2; (53–86) minutes for Level 3.
Comments: May be used in conjunction with Language Assessment Scales—Oral (1387).
Authors: Sharon E. Duncan and Edward A. DeAvila.
Publisher: CTB Macmillan/McGraw-Hill.

TEST REFERENCES

1. Booth, J. (1984). A comparison of SLEP scores with SRA and LAS scores. *TESOL Quarterly, 18,* 738-740.

2. Gallegos, R., & Franco, J. N. (1985). Effects of a bilingual education program on language and academic achievement. *Perceptual and Motor Skills, 60,* 438.

3. Powers, S., Johnson, D. M., Slaughter, H. B., Crowder, C., & Jones, P. B. (1985). Reliability and validity of the Language Proficiency Measure. *Educational and Psychological Measurement, 45,* 959-963.

4. Reyes, E. I., Duran, G. Z., & Bos, C. S. (1989). Language as a resource for mediating comprehension. *Yearbook of the National Reading Conference, 38,* 253-260.

5. Ainsa, P. A. (1990). Modeling effects of college students on kindergarten children at-risk. *College Student Journal, 24,* 111-116.

[1387]

Language Assessment Scales—Oral.

Purpose: Designed to "measure those English and language skills necessary for functioning in a mainstream academic environment."
Population: Grades 1–6, 7–12.
Publication Dates: 1987–91.
Acronym: LAS-O.

Scores, 6: Vocabulary, Listening Comprehension, Story Retelling, Minimal Sound Pairs, Phonemes, Total.
Administration: Individual.
Forms, 2: C, D.
Parts, 2: Oral Language (for Level 1 & 2), Pronunciation (for grades 2–12).
Price Data, 1992: $34.55 per test review kits including administration manual ('90, 20 pages; specify level), scoring and interpretation manual ('90, 35 pages; specify level), student test booklet or multicopy scoresheet, and cue picture booklet along with a test reviewer's guide (specify level and form); $21 per 50 scoresheets; $23.75 per reusable cue picture booklet; $13.50 per audiocassette (specify level and form); $16.50 per administration manual (specify level); $18.35 per scoring and interpretation manual (specify level); $8.95 per technical manual ('91, 144 pages).
Foreign Language Edition: Spanish edition ('90) available.
Time: [15] minutes.
Authors: Edward A. DeAvila and Sharon E. Duncan.
Publisher: CTB Macmillan/McGraw-Hill.
Comments: Language Proficiency Score also incorporates Language Assessment Scales, Reading and Writing (1386).
Cross References: For a review of the Language Assessment Scales by Lyn Haber, see 9:584 (1 reference).

[1388]

Language Facility Test.

Purpose: Measures language and grammar skills in both English or Spanish.
Population: Ages 3 and over.
Publication Dates: 1965–80.
Acronym: LFT.
Scores: 2 scoring systems: (9 point qualitative scale for evaluating communication in primary language, error analysis for standard English) for verbal responses to 12 pictures.
Administration: Individual.
Price Data: Not available.
Time: (10–15) minutes.
Author: John T. Dailey.
Publisher: The Allington Corporation [No reply from publisher; status unknown].
Cross References: For a review by Charles Stansfield, see 9:585; see also T3:1282 (1 reference); for a review by Nicholas Anastasiow of an earlier form, see 7:955 (1 reference).

[1389]

Language Imitation Test.

Purpose: "Developed for use as a language assessment technique, specifically for the severely educational subnormal."
Population: Educationally subnormal children.
Publication Date: No date on test materials.
Acronym: LIT.

Scores: 6 subtest scores: Sound Imitation, Word Imitation, Syntactic Control 1, Syntactic Control 2, Word Organization Control, Sentence Completion.
Administration: Individual.
Price Data, 1986: £6.25 per specimen set; £4.55 per 25 record forms; £5.95 per manual (no date, 41 pages).
Time: Administration time not reported.
Authors: Paul Berry and Peter Mittler.
Publisher: NFER-Nelson Publishing Co., Ltd. [England].
Cross References: For a review by Rita Sloan Berndt, see 9:586 (1 reference).

[1390]
Language Processing Test.
Purpose: Designed to identify "students' language processing strengths and weaknesses in a hierarchical framework."
Population: Ages 5-0 to 11-11.
Publication Date: 1985.
Acronym: LPT.
Scores, 8: Labeling, Stating Functions, Associations, Categorization, Similarities, Differences, Multiple Meanings, Attributes.
Administration: Individual.
Price Data, 1988: $44.90 per complete test kit including 20 test forms and examiner's manual (91 pages); $14.95 per 20 test forms; $29.95 per examiner's manual.
Time: (30) minutes.
Authors: Gail J. Richard and Mary Anne Hanner.
Publisher: LinguiSystems, Inc.
Cross References: For reviews by Thomas W. Guyette and Lyn Haber, see 10:169.

[1391]
Language Proficiency Test.
Purpose: Developed to "assess oral/aural, reading, and writing skills."
Population: Grades 9 and over.
Publication Date: 1981.
Acronym: LPT.
Scores, 6–9: Aural/Oral (Commands, Short Answers [optional], Comprehension [optional]), Reading (Vocabulary, Comprehension), Writing (Grammar, Sentence Response, Paragraph Response, Translation [optional]).
Administration: Individual in part.
Price Data, 1989: $28 per complete kit including 10 test booklets and manual (29 pages).
Time: (80–100) minutes.
Authors: Joan Gerard and Gloria Weinstock.
Publisher: Academic Therapy Publications.
Cross References: For a review by John M. Keene, Jr., see 9:588.

[1392]
Language Proficiency Tests.
Purpose: "To assess a testee's proficiency in English . . . and to be of some diagnostic value and thus to be of assistance to teachers in planning the content of their teaching."
Population: Bantu pupils in Standards 9 and 10 of South African school system.
Publication Dates: 1974–75.
Acronym: LPTE.
Scores, 4: Language Usage, Vocabulary, Reading Comprehension, Total.
Administration: Group.
Levels, 2: Forms IV and V (Standards 9 and 10).
Price Data: Available from publisher.
Foreign Language Edition: Afrikaans edition available.
Time: 102(156) minutes.
Comments: Tests for Forms IV and V are identical with English subtests of Form A and B, respectively, of General Tests of Language and Arithmetic for Students ('72).
Author: J. C. Chamberlain.
Publisher: Human Sciences Research Council [South Africa].

[1393]
Language, Sampling, Analysis, and Training, Revised Edition.
Purpose: Designed to analyze utterances of an individual according to a specific grammatical system in order to plan an intervention program.
Population: Children with language delay.
Publication Dates: 1974–77.
Administration: Individual.
Price Data, 1990: $13 per handbook and 3 complete sets of worksheets; $9 per handbook ('77, 60 pages); $30 per 25 worksheets; $15 per 50 transcription sheets; $13 per Word/Morpheme Tally and Summary; $15 per Sequence of Language Acquisition; $9 per baseline and goal analysis; $9 per training worksheet; $13 per score sheet.
Comments: Visual and verbal stimuli for eliciting language sample determined by examiner; tape recommended to record responses; no reading by examinees.
Authors: Dorothy Tyack and Robert Gottsleben.
Publisher: Consulting Psychologists Press, Inc.
a) TRANSCRIPTION SHEETS.
Time: (30–90) minutes.
b) WORD/MORPHEME TALLY AND SUMMARY.
Scores, 6: 3 Totals (Sentences, Words, Morphemes) and 3 means (Word/Sentence, Morphemes/Sentence, Wordmorpheme Index).
Time: (10) minutes.
c) SEQUENCE OF LANGUAGE ACQUISITION.
Scores, 6: Assessment of 6 areas: Noun Phrase Constituents, Verb Phrase Constituents, Constructions, Complex Sentences, Negation, Questions.
Time: (30) minutes.
d) BASELINE AND GOAL DATA.
Time: (20) minutes.
e) TRAINING WORKSHEET.
Time: (10) minutes.
f) SCORE SHEET.
Comments: Used during training session.

Cross References: For a review by Margaret C. Byrne, see 9:590.

[1394]
Language Sampling and Analysis.
Purpose: Helps pinpoint language problems and measures an individual child's language change or development.
Population: Ages 1.5–14.5.
Publication Date: 1978.
Acronym: LSA.
Scores: Overall Performance score.
Administration: Individual.
Forms, 2: Form B: Language sample data sheet; Form C: Summary and Analysis sheet.
Price Data: Not available.
Time: (30) minutes.
Comments: Supplement to Utah Test of Language Development (2872).
Authors: Merlin J. Mecham and J. Dean Jones.
Publisher: Communication Research Associates, Inc. [No reply from publisher; status unknown].

[1395]
Language-Structured Auditory Retention Span Test.
Purpose: Designed to assess the ability to maintain short-term memory for linguistically significant information.
Population: Ages 3.7–adult.
Publication Dates: 1973–89.
Acronym: LARS.
Scores, 2: Mental Age (MA), "Quotient" (MA/CA).
Administration: Individual.
Forms, 2: A, B.
Price Data, 1991: $40 per complete kit including manual ('89, 64 pages), 50 recording Form A, and 50 remedial checklists; $12 per manual; $18 per 50 recording Form A; $18 per recording Form B; $7 per pad of 50 remedial checklists; $12 per specimen set (manual and sample forms).
Time: (12–15) minutes.
Comments: Immediate recall of words and sentences presented orally; new edition includes remedial activities; "norm-referenced."
Author: Luis Carlson.
Publisher: Academic Therapy Publications.
Cross References: For a review by Rodney W. Roth, see 11:195; for a review of old edition by James B. Lingwall, and an excerpted review by Alan Krichev, see 8:941 (1 reference).

[1396]
Laurita-Trembley Diagnostic Word Processing Test.
Purpose: "Designed to diagnose the extent of an individual's readiness, or ability, to categorize words for encoding and decoding."
Population: Grades 1.9–4.9, 5.0–college.
Publication Date: 1979.

Scores, 4: Raw Score, Word Count, Vertical Word Processing, Horizontal Word Processing.
Administration: Group.
Levels, 2: Grades 1.9–4.9, 5.0–college.
Price Data, 1985: $24.95 per complete kit including manual (73 pages); $5 per 20 answer sheets; $5 per 10 progress charts.
Time: Administration time not reported.
Authors: Raymond E. Laurita and Phillip W. Trembley.
Publisher: Leonardo Press.
Cross References: For reviews by Linnea C. Ehri and Gerald S. Hanna, see 9:592.

[1397]
Law Enforcement Assessment and Development Report.
Purpose: Intended to identify individuals who can become successful law enforcement officers.
Population: Applicants for law enforcement positions.
Publication Dates: 1981–87.
Acronym: LEADR.
Scores, 5: 4 profile dimensions (Emotional Adjustment, Integrity/Control, Intellectual Efficiency, Interpersonal Relations), Performance Indicators.
Administration: Group.
Price Data, 1994: $34.25 per 25 reusable test booklets; $10.75 per 25 answer sheets; $16 per manual ('87, 51 pages); $38.75 per introductory kit including manual, test booklet, answer sheet, and prepaid processing form; $25 or less per individual score report.
Time: (90) minutes.
Comments: Test represents a computer-based analysis from two of Cattell's personality questionnaires, Form A of the 16 Personality Factor Questionnaire (2470) and Part II of the Clinical Analysis Questionnaire (519); questionnaires must be scored by publisher.
Author: IPAT staff.
Publisher: Institute for Personality and Ability Testing, Inc.
Cross References: For a review by David S. Hargrove, see 10:170; for a review by Lawrence Allen of the earlier edition, see 9:593.

[1398]
Law Enforcement Candidate Record.
Purpose: "To predict law enforcement officer success despite any manifest organizational differences."
Population: Candidates for law enforcement positions.
Publication Dates: 1986–94.
Acronym: LECR.
Scores: 5 tests: Vocabulary, Arithmetic Reasoning, Spatial Analysis/Reasoning, Number Scanning, Memory/Recall, plus an autobiographical questionnaire.
Administration: Group.
Price Data: Available from publisher.

Time: 63(73) minutes for tests; none stated for the autobiographical questionnaire.
Author: Richardson, Bellows, Henry, & Co., Inc.
Publisher: Richardson, Bellows, Henry, & Co., Inc.

[1399]
Law Enforcement Perception Questionnaire.
Purpose: Developed to "assess attitudes toward law enforcement and law enforcement personnel."
Population: Law enforcement personnel.
Publication Date: 1970.
Acronym: LEPQ.
Scores: Total score only.
Administration: Group.
Price Data: Available from publisher.
Time: Administration time not reported.
Author: Frank Lee.
Publisher: Psychometric Affiliates.

[1400]
Law School Admission Test.
Purpose: "To measure skills that are considered essential for success in law school."
Population: Law school entrants.
Publication Dates: 1948–91.
Acronym: LSAT.
Scores: Total score plus unscored writing sample.
Administration: Group.
Price Data, 1993: $74 per LSAT; $44 per late registration; $22 per test center change; $22 per test date change; $164 per nonpublished test center (U.S.A., Canada, Puerto Rico); $219 per nonpublished test center (all other countries); $27 per hand scoring; $30 per reporting renewal; $27 per former registrants score report; $75 per LSDAS subscription (12 months plus one law school report); $7 per law school report ordered at time of subscription; $9 per law school report ordered after initial subscription; $44 per LSDAS subscription renewal.
Time: 175(200) minutes per LSAT; 30(40) minutes per writing sample.
Comments: Test administered 4 times annually (June, October, December, February) at centers established by the publisher.
Authors: Law School Admission Council, administered by Law School Admission Service.
Publisher: Law School Admission Council/Law School Admission Service.
Cross References: For a review by Gary B. Melton, see 9:594 (2 references); see also T3:1292 (6 references), 8:1093 (7 references), and T2:2349 (7 references); for a review by Leo A. Munday of earlier forms, see 7:1098 (23 references); see also 5:928 (7 references); for a review by Alexander G. Wesman, see 4:815 (6 references).

TEST REFERENCES
1. Braun, H. I., & Szatrowski, T. H. (1984). The scale-linkage algorithm: Construction of a universal criterion scale for families of institutions. *Journal of Educational Statistics, 9*, 311-330.
2. Braun, H. I., & Szatrowski, T. H. (1984). Validity studies based on a universal criterion scale. *Journal of Educational Statistics, 9*, 331-344.
3. Linn, R. L., & Hastings, C. N. (1984). A meta analysis of the validity of predictors of performance in law school. *Journal of Educational Measurement, 21*, 245-259.
4. Dachowski, M., & Rodriguez, J. (1985). A coaching seminar for the LSAT. *Journal of College Student Personnel, 26*, 89.

[1401]
The Lawrence Psychological Forensic Examination.
Purpose: "A guide for comprehensive psychological assessments and report writing with clients in the criminal, juvenile and civil justice systems."
Population: Juvenile, criminal, and civil justice clients.
Publication Dates: 1978–83.
Acronym: LAW-PSI.
Scores: No scores as such; ratings and judgments.
Administration: Individual.
Price Data: Available from publisher.
Comments: Ratings by mental health professional; handbook contains descriptive legal information for report writing, and 3 tests.
Author: Stephen B. Lawrence.
Publisher: Lawrence Psychological Center.
  a) LAWRENCE PSYCHOLOGICAL FORENSIC EXAMINATION.
  Comments: Guided forensic interview to determine precise mental states of mind, life history, or prediction of future client behavior.
  b) LAWRENCE MENTAL COMPETENCY TEST.
  Acronym: LAW-COMP.
  Comments: To aid clinicians in making judgments needed to determine a client's present legal mental competency to stand trial.
  c) LAWRENCE PSYCHOLOGICAL FORENSIC EXAMINATION REPORT EVALUATION.
  Acronym: LAW-PSI/EVAL.
  Comments: A rating instrument for evaluating written forensic reports.
Cross References: For a review by Samuel Roll, see 10:171.

[1402]
Leader Behavior Analysis II.
Purpose: Developed to assess leadership style.
Population: Middle and upper level managers.
Publication Date: 1991.
Acronym: LBAII.
Scores, 6: Style Flexibility, Style Effectiveness, Directing Style, Coaching Style, Supporting Style, Delegating Style.
Administration: Group.
Editions, 2: Self, Other.
Price Data, 1990: $29.50 per complete kit including 1 LBAII-Self instrument, 8 LBAII-Other instruments, data summary sheet, and scoring instructions; $2.95 per instrument (select Self or Other).
Time: [15–20] minutes.
Comments: Ratings by employees and self-ratings.
Authors: Drea Zigarmi, Douglas Forsyth, Kenneth Blanchard, and Ronald Hambleton (tests).

Publisher: Blanchard Training & Development, Inc.

TEST REFERENCES

1. Stone, R. (1993). A SPSS/PC+ program listing for scoring the Leader Behavior Analysis II—Self Scale. *Educational and Psychological Measurement, 53,* 111-117.

[1403]
Leader Behavior Description Questionnaire, Form 12.

Purpose: Developed to obtain supervisees' descriptions of a supervisor.

Population: Supervisors.

Publication Dates: 1957–63.

Acronym: LBDQ-12.

Scores, 12: Representation, Demand Reconciliation, Tolerance of Uncertainty, Persuasiveness, Initiation of Structure, Tolerance of Freedom, Role Assumptions, Consideration, Production Emphasis, Predictive Accuracy, Integration, Superior Orientation.

Administration: Group.

Price Data: Available from publisher.

Time: (20) minutes.

Comments: Revision of Leader Behavior Description Questionnaire with 10 additional scores; for research use only; employee ratings of a supervisor; scores based upon responses of 4 to 10 raters.

Authors: John K. Hemphill and Alvin E. Coons (original edition); Ralph M. Stogdill (manual); Bureau of Business Research (current edition), Ohio State University.

Publisher: Business Research Support Services, Ohio State University.

Cross References: See 9:596 (22 references) and T3:1296 (16 references); for a review by Robert L. Dipboye, see 8:1175 (101 references); see also T2:2452 (19 references) and 7:1147 (48 references).

TEST REFERENCES

1. Ayman, R., & Chemers, M. M. (1983). Relationship of supervisory behavior ratings to work group effectiveness and subordinate satisfaction among Iranian managers. *Journal of Applied Psychology, 68,* 338-341.
2. Kemp, N. J., Wall, T. D., Clegg, C. W., & Cordery, J. L. (1983). Autonomous work groups in a greenfield site: A comparative study. *Journal of Occupational Psychology, 56,* 271-288.
3. Spector, P. E., & Michaels, C. E. (1983). A note on item order as an artifact in organizational surveys. *Journal of Occupational Psychology, 56,* 35-36.
4. Arcy, T. (1984). Self perceptions of leader behavior of secondary and post secondary career oriented and vocational administrators. *College Student Journal, 18,* 169-176.
5. Gutkin, T. B., & Bossard, M. D. (1984). The impact of consultant, consultee, and organizational variables on teacher attitudes toward consultation services. *Journal of School Psychology, 22,* 251-258.
6. Johnson, A. L., Luthans, F., & Hennessey, H. W. (1984). The role of locus of control in leader influence behavior. *Personnel Psychology, 37,* 61-75.
7. Niebuhr, R. E., & Davis, K. R., Jr. (1984). Self-esteem: Relationship with leader behavior perceptions as moderated by the duration of the superior-subordinate dyad association. *Personality and Social Psychology Bulletin, 10,* 51-59.
8. Stout, J. K. (1984). Supervisors' structuring and consideration behaviors and workers' job satisfaction, stress, and health problems. *Rehabilitation Counseling Bulletin, 28,* 133-138.
9. Brollier, C. (1985). Occupational therapy management and job performance of staff. *The American Journal of Occupational Therapy, 39,* 649-654.
10. Levanoni, E., & Knoop, R. (1985). Does task structure moderate the relationship of leaders' behavior and employees' satisfaction. *Psychological Reports, 57,* 611-623.
11. Millard, R. J., & Smith, K. H. (1985). Moderating effects of leader sex on the relation between leadership style and perceived behavior patterns. *Genetic, Social, and General Psychology Monographs, 111,* 305-316.
12. Penley, L. E., & Hawkins, B. (1985). Studying interpersonal communication in organizations: A leadership application. *Academy of Management Journal, 28,* 309-326.
13. Spector, P. E. (1985). Measurement of human service staff satisfaction: Development of the job satisfaction survey. *American Journal of Community Psychology, 13,* 693-713.
14. Fry, L. W., Kerr, S., & Lee, C. (1986). Effects of different leader behaviors under different levels of task interdependence. *Human Relations, 39,* 1067-1081.
15. Knoop, R. (1986). Causes of alienation among university professors. *Perceptual and Motor Skills, 63,* 677-678.
16. Oldham, G. R., Kulik, C. T., Ambrose, M. L., Stepina, L. P., & Brand, J. F. (1986). Relations between job facet comparisons and employee reactions. *Organizational Behavior and Human Decision Process, 38,* 28-47.
17. Oldham, G. R., Kulik, C. T., Stepina, L. P., & Ambrose, M. L. (1986). Relations between situational factors and the comparative referents used by employees. *Academy of Management Journal, 29,* 599-608.
18. Bernardin, H. J. (1987). Effect of reciprocal leniency on the relation between consideration scores from the Leader Behavior Description Questionnaire and performance ratings. *Psychological Reports, 60,* 479-487.
19. Lane, T. (1987). Consideration and initiating structure: Are they basic dimensions of leader behavior? *Social Behavior and Personality, 15,* 21-33.
20. Fraser, S. L., & Lord, R. G. (1988). Stimulus prototypicality and general leadership impressions: Their role in leadership and behavioral ratings. *The Journal of Psychology, 122,* 291-303.
21. Willett, L. H., & Licata, J. W. (1990). Student brinkmanship, residence hall leadership, and social climate. *College Student Journal, 23,* 343-345.
22. Punnett, B. J. (1991). Language, cultural values and preferred leadership style: A comparison of anglophones and francophones in Ottawa. *Canadian Journal of Behavioural Science, 23,* 241-244.
23. Zaccaro, S. J., Foti, R. J., & Kenny, D. A. (1991). Self-monitoring and trait-based variance in leadership: An investigation of leader flexibility across multiple group situations. *Journal of Applied Psychology, 76(2),* 308-315.
24. Fried, Y., Tiegs, R. B., & Bellamy, A. R. (1992). Personal and interpersonal predictors of supervisors' avoidance of evaluating subordinates. *Journal of Applied Psychology, 77,* 462-468.
25. Okeafor, K. R., & Frere, R. M. (1992). Administrators' confidence in teachers, leader consideration and coupling in schools. *Journal of Research and Development in Education, 25,* 204-212.
26. Vecchio, R. P. (1993). The impact of differences in subordinate and supervisor age on attitudes and performance. *Psychology and Aging, 8,* 112-119.

[1404]
The Leadership Ability Evaluation.

Purpose: Designed to assess "the decision making pattern or social climate created by a person when he functions as a leader in influencing other persons or groups."

Population: Grades 9–16 and adults.

Publication Date: 1961.

Scores, 5: Laissez Faire, Democratic-Cooperative, Autocratic-Submissive, Autocratic-Aggressive, Decision Pattern.

Administration: Group.

Price Data, 1993: $50 per complete kit; $25 per 25 tests; $26 per manual (18 pages).

Time: [30] minutes.

Author: Russell N. Cassel and Edward J. Stancik (test).

Publisher: Western Psychological Services.

Cross References: See T2:1259 (3 references) and P:142; for reviews by John D. Black and Cecil A. Gibb, see 6:133 (4 references).

[1405]

Leadership and Self-Development Scale.
Purpose: Measurement of the effectiveness of a leadership workshop for college women.
Population: College.
Publication Dates: 1976–79.
Scores, 9: Assertiveness, Risk Taking, Self-Concept, Setting Goals, Decision Making, Obtaining a Followership, Conflict Resolution, Group Roles, Evaluation.
Administration: Group.
Manual: No manual; mimeographed research report ('76, 20 pages).
Price Data: Free upon request from publisher.
Time: Administration time not reported.
Authors: Virginia Hoffman and Patricia B. Elmore.
Publisher: Patricia B. Elmore.
Cross References: For a review by Robert R. McCrae, see 9:597; see also T3:1298 (2 references).

[1406]

Leadership Appraisal Survey.
Purpose: "An assessment of leadership practices and attitudes as viewed through the eyes of others."
Population: Adults.
Publication Dates: 1971–79.
Scores, 5: Philosophy, Planning, Implementation, Evaluation, Total.
Administration: Group.
Manual: No manual.
Price Data, 1992: $49.95 per 10-pack of test instruments.
Time: Administration time not reported.
Comments: Self-administered survey.
Author: Jay Hall.
Publisher: Teleometrics International.
Cross References: See T3:2351 (1 reference); for a review by Abraham K. Korman of the Styles of Leadership and Management, see 8:1185 (8 references).

[1407]

Leadership Competency Inventory.
Purpose: Measures an individual's use of four competencies related to leadership.
Population: Adults.
Publication Date: 1993.
Acronym: LCI.
Scores, 4: Information Seeking, Conceptual Thinking, Strategic Orientation, Service Orientation.
Administration: Group.
Price Data, 1993: $60 per complete kit including 10 profiles and interpretive notes (25 pages), and 10 questionnaires; $25 per 10 (employee version) questionnaires.
Time: Administration time not reported.
Comments: Self-scored questionnaire.
Author: Stephen P. Kelner.
Publisher: McBer & Company.

[1408]

Leadership Effectiveness Analysis.
Purpose: Developed to identify leadership skills.

Population: Managers and supervisors.
Publication Dates: 1981–90.
Acronym: LEA.
Scores, 23: Conservative, Innovative, Technical, Self, Strategic, Persuasive, Outgoing, Excitement, Restraint, Structuring, Tactical, Communication, Delegation, Control, Feedback, Management Focus, Dominant, Production, Cooperation, Consensual, Authority, Empathy, Exaggeration.
Administration: Group.
Price Data: Not available.
Time: (45) minutes.
Authors: James T. Mahoney, Thomas M. Rand (manual), and F. Carl Mahoney (manual).
Publisher: Management Research Group [No reply from publisher; status unknown].

[1409]

Leadership Opinion Questionnaire.
Purpose: To measure supervisory leadership dimensions.
Population: Supervisors and prospective supervisors.
Publication Dates: 1960–75.
Acronym: LOQ.
Scores, 2: Structure, Consideration.
Administration: Individual or group.
Price Data, 1985: $26 per 20 tests; $10 per revised manual ('69, 15 pages).
Time: (10–15) minutes.
Comments: Self-administering; tape cassette ('75) available for administration.
Author: Edwin A. Fleishman.
Publisher: Science Research Associates/London House.
Cross References: For additional information, see T3:1300 (10 references), 8:1177 (52 references), and T2:2454 (15 references); for a review by Cecil A. Gibb, see 7:1149 (41 references); for reviews by Jerome E. Doppelt and Wayne K. Kirchner, see 6:1190 (6 references).

TEST REFERENCES

1. Nystrom, P. C. (1978). Managers and the hi-hi leader myth. *Academy of Management Journal, 21,* 325-331.
2. DeJulio, S. S., Larson, K., Dever, E. L., & Paulman, R. (1981). The measurement of leadership potential in college students. *Journal of College Student Personnel, 22,* 207-213.
3. Tucker, J. H. (1983). Leadership orientation as a function of interpersonal need structure: A replication with negative results. *Small Group Behavior, 14,* 107-114.
4. Dapra, R. A., Zarrillo, D. L., Carlson, T. K., & Teevan, R. C. (1985). Fear of failure and indices of leadership utilized in the training of ROTC cadets. *Psychological Reports, 56,* 27-30.
5. Thomas, V. G., & Littig, L. W. (1985). A typology of leadership style: Examining gender and race effects. *Bulletin of the Psychonomic Society, 23,* 132-134.
6. Schippmann, J. S., & Prien, E. P. (1986). Individual difference correlates of two leadership styles. *Psychological Reports, 59,* 817-818.
7. Hakstain, A. R., Woolsey, L. K., & Schroeder, M. L. (1987). Validity of a large-scale assessment battery in an industrial setting. *Educational and Psychological Measurement, 47*(1), 165-178.

[1410]

Leadership Practices Inventory [Management Research Associates].
Purpose: Designed to examine ideal and actual styles of management.

Population: Supervisors.
Publication Dates: 1955–67.
Scores: 2 scores (Ideal, Actual) for each of 4 leadership styles, 5 management areas, and 2 derived totals.
Administration: Group.
Price Data: Price data for test materials including manual ('67, 14 pages) available from publisher.
Time: (30–45) minutes.
Author: Charles W. Nelson.
Publisher: Management Research Associates.

TEST REFERENCES

1. Posner, B. Z., & Kouzes, J. M. (1988). Development and validation of the Leadership Practices Inventory. *Educational and Psychological Measurement, 48,* 483- 496.

[1411]

Leadership Practices Inventory [Pfeiffer & Company International Publishers].
Purpose: Designed to provide ratings of five leadership behaviors.
Population: Managers.
Publication Date: 1990–92.
Acronym: LPI.
Scores, 5: Challenging the Process, Inspiring a Shared Vision, Enabling Others to Act, Modeling the Way, Encouraging the Heart.
Administration: Group.
Editions, 2: Self, Other.
Price Data, 1991: $29.95 per trainer's package including LPI: Self-Assessment booklet and inventory, LPI: Other inventory, technical manual ('92, 31 pages) and trainer's manual ('90, 39 pages); $8.95 per LPI: Self-Assessment booklet and inventory; $3.95 per LPI: Other inventory; $195 per IBM-PC (or compatible) scoring software.
Time: Administration time not reported.
Comments: Scale for ratings by employees and for self-ratings.
Authors: James M. Kouzes and Barry Z. Posner.
Publisher: Pfeiffer & Company International Publishers.

TEST REFERENCES

1. Posner, B. Z., & Brodsky, B. (1992). A leadership development instrument for college students. *Journal of College Student Development, 33,* 231-237.
2. Posner, B. Z., & Kouzes, J. M. (1993). Psychometric properties of the Leadership Practices Inventory—updated. *Educational and Psychological Measurement, 53,* 191-199.

[1412]

The Leadership Q-Sort Test (A Test of Leadership Values).
Purpose: Designed to "assess an individual's values with respect to the leadership role."
Population: Adults.
Publication Date: 1958.
Acronym: LQST.
Scores, 7: Personal Integrity, Consideration of Others, Mental Health, Technical Information, Decision Making, Teaching and Communication, Total.
Administration: Individual or group.

Price Data: Available from publisher.
Time: (40–45) minutes.
Author: Russell N. Cassel.
Publisher: Psychometric Affiliates.
Cross References: For reviews by Joel T. Campbell, Cecil A. Gibb, and William Stephenson, see 6:134 (6 references).

[1413]

Leadership Skills Inventory.
Purpose: "Assess strengths and weaknesses in the area of leadership."
Population: Grades 4–12.
Publication Date: 1985.
Acronym: LSI.
Scores, 9: Fundamentals of Leadership, Written Communication Skills, Speech Communication Skills, Values Clarification, Decision Making Skills, Group Dynamics Skills, Problem Solving Skills, Personal Development Skills, Planning Skills.
Administration: Individual or Group.
Price Data, 1994: $59 per complete kit; $29 per 25 inventory booklets; $17 per activities manual (52 pages); $17 per administration manual (19 pages).
Time: (45) minutes.
Comments: Self-administered and self-scored.
Authors: Frances A. Karnes and Jane C. Chauvin.
Publisher: PRO-ED, Inc.
Cross References: For reviews by Barbara A. Kerr and Steven W. Lee, see 10:172 (2 references).

[1414]

Leadership Skills Inventory [Consulting Resource Group].
Purpose: Helps individuals develop the ability to handle the "people" side of enterprise.
Population: Adults.
Publication Date: 1992.
Acronym: LSI.
Scores, 7: Transforming Leadership Principles, Awareness and Self-Management Skills, Interpersonal Communication Skills, Counseling and Problem Management Skills, Consulting Skills for Developing Groups and Organizations, Style/Role and Skill Shifting for Developing Versatility, Grand Total.
Administration: Group.
Editions, 2: Self Assessment, Other.
Price Data, 1993: $10 per test booklet (Other); $12 per test booklet (Self Assessment).
Time: (40–50) minutes.
Comments: Self-administered and self-scored; book entitled *Transforming Leadership: New Skills for Extraordinary Future* serves as manual.
Author: Terry D. Anderson.
Publisher: Consulting Resource Group International, Inc.

[1415]

Learned Behaviors Profile—Self/Other.
Purpose: "Designed to help people explore their patterns of behavior."

Population: Adults.
Publication Date: 1990.
Acronym: LBP.
Scores, 6: Caretaker, People-Pleaser, Workaholic, Martyr, Perfectionist, Tap Dancer.
Administration: Group.
Editions, 2: Self, Other.
Price Data, 1990: $7.95 per LBP: Self inventory (31 pages); $2.95 per LBP: Other inventory (6 pages); each includes administrator's guide (no date, 2 pages).
Time: Administration time not reported.
Comments: Self-administered, self-scored.
Authors: J. William Pfeiffer and Judith A. Pfeiffer.
Publisher: Pfeiffer & Company International Publishers.
Cross References: For reviews by Diane Billings Findley and John R. Graham, see 11:197.

[1416]
Learning Ability Profile.
Purpose: Designed to provide "a quantifiable index of the subject's inductive and deductive reasoning, cognitive and problem solving skills."
Population: Grades 5–16 and adults.
Publication Dates: 1975–78.
Acronym: LAP.
Scores, 5: Total and 4 derived scores (Certainty, Problem Solving, Flexibility, Frustration).
Administration: Group.
Price Data, 1993: $60 per person.
Time: Untimed.
Author: Margherita M. Henning.
Publisher: Walden Personnel Testing & Training Systems, Inc.
Cross References: For reviews by Philip M. Clark and Robert J. Illback, see 9:599 (1 reference).

[1417]
Learning and Study Strategies Inventory.
Purpose: "To measure students' use of learning and study strategies and methods."
Population: College students.
Publication Date: 1987.
Acronym: LASSI.
Scores, 10: Attitude, Motivation, Time Management, Anxiety, Concentration, Information Processing, Selecting Main Ideas, Study Aids, Self Testing, Test Strategies.
Administration: Group or individual.
Price Data, 1990: $3 per packet including test booklet, manual (15 pages), and score interpretation information, $2 per computer administration; information on volume discounts available from publisher.
Time: (30) minutes.
Comments: Manual title is LASSI User's Manual; Apple II and IBM PC microcomputer versions available.
Authors: Claire E. Weinstein.
Publisher: H and H Publishing Co.
Cross References: For reviews by Martha W.

Blackwell and Steven C. Hayes, see 11:198 (3 references).

TEST REFERENCES
1. Schommer, M., Crouse, A., & Rhodes, N. (1992). Epistemological beliefs and mathematical text comprehension: Believing it is simple does not make it so. *Journal of Educational Psychology, 84,* 435-443.

[1418]
Learning and Study Strategies Inventory— High School Version.
Purpose: Designed to assist high school students "in determining their study skills strategies, problems and attitudes, and learning practices."
Population: Grades 9–12.
Publication Date: 1990.
Acronym: LASSI-HS.
Scores, 10: Attitude, Motivation, Time Management, Anxiety, Concentration, Information Processing, Selecting Main Ideas, Study Aids, Self Testing, Test Strategies.
Administration: Group.
Price Data, 1994: $2.25 per self-scored form; $2.50 per computer scored form.
Time: (25–30) minutes.
Authors: Claire E. Weinstein and David R. Palmer.
Publisher: H & H Publishing Company.

[1419]
Learning Behaviors Scale, Research Edition.
Purpose: Identifies dysfunctional learning behaviors for an early assessment of how a child will perform academically.
Population: Kindergarten.
Publication Date: 1981–88.
Acronym: LBS.
Comments: Manual title is Learning Behaviors Scale and Study of Children's Learning Behaviors; ratings by teachers; manual also used with the Study of Children's Learning Behaviors (SCLB; 11:388).
Scores, 4: Impulsive-Distractible, Apprehensive-Avoidant, Moody-Uncooperative, Total.
Administration: Individual.
Price Data, 1994: $50.50 per complete kit including 5 LBS and 5 SCLB Ready-Score™ questionnaires and manual ('88, 113 pages); $40 per 25 Ready-Score™ questionnaires; $33.50 per manual.
Time: (1–2) minutes per child.
Authors: Denis H. Stott, Paul A. McDermott, Leonard F. Green, and Jean M. Francis.
Publisher: The Psychological Corporation.
Cross References: For reviews by Lizanne DeStefano and Brian K. Martens, see 11:199 (1 reference).

TEST REFERENCES
1. Glutting, J. J., & McDermott, P. A. (1990). Childhood learning potential as an alternative to traditional ability measure. *Psychological Assessment, 2,* 398-403.

[1420]
The Learning Channel Preference Checklist.
Purpose: Intended as an "indicator of learning style preference."

Population: Grades 5–13.
Publication Date: 1990.
Acronym: LCPC.
Scores, 3: Visual, Auditory, Haptic.
Administration: Group.
Price Data, 1993: $24.95 per complete kit including manual (8 pages) and 25 checklists.
Time: [15–20] minutes.
Author: Lynn O'Brien.
Publisher: Research for Better Schools.
Cross References: For a review by William L. Deaton, see 11:200.

[1421]

Learning Disability Evaluation Scale.
Purpose: Designed as a measure of learning disabilities.
Population: Ages 4.5–19.
Publication Dates: 1983–91.
Acronym: LDES.
Scores, 8: Listening, Thinking, Speaking, Reading, Writing, Spelling, Mathematical Calculations, Learning Quotient.
Administration: Individual.
Price Data, 1993: $129 per complete kit including pre-referral learning problem checklist form, pre-referral intervention strategies documentation, technical manual ('83, 52 pages), rating form, Parent's Guide to Learning Disabilities ('91, 200 pages), and learning disability intervention manual ('89, 217 pages); $25 per 50 pre-referral learning problem checklist forms; $25 per 50 pre-referral intervention strategies documentation; $12 per manual; $30 per 50 rating forms; $22 per learning disability intervention manual; $15 per Parent's Guide to Learning Disabilities; $12 per computerized quick score (Apple II); $149 per computerized version of learning disability intervention manual (Apple II).
Time: (20) minutes.
Comments: Ratings by teacher.
Author: Stephen B. McCarney and Angela Marie Bauer (intervention manuals).
Publisher: Hawthorne Educational Services.

[1422]

Learning Disability Rating Procedure.
Purpose: "A method by which an elementary or secondary student is systematically rated on each of ten indicators selected for their association with learning disabilities."
Population: Grades K–12.
Publication Date: 1981.
Acronym: LDRP.
Scores, 11: IQ, Reading Decoding, Listening Comprehension, Comprehension Variance, Socially Inappropriate Behavior, Expressive Verbal Language Development, Learning Motivation, Expressive Writing Development, Independent Work Level/Distractibility, Severe Discrepancy Level, Total.
Administration: Individual.
Price Data, 1994: $35 per complete kit including

manual (42 pages), 50 rating forms, and vinyl folder; $18 per 50 rating forms; $14 per manual; $14 per specimen set including manual and sample form.
Time: Administration time not reported.
Authors: Gerald J. Spadafore and Sharon J. Spadafore.
Publisher: Academic Therapy Publications.
Cross References: For a review by Robert J. Illback, see 9:600.

[1423]

Learning Efficiency Test-II (1992 Revision).
Purpose: "Yields information about a person's preferred modality for learning and provides insights about the impact of interference on memory storage and retrieval, and the kinds of metacognitive strategies used during learning."
Population: Ages 5–75.
Publication Dates: 1981–92.
Acronym: LET-II.
Scores, 15: Visual Ordered Recall (Immediate Recall, Short Term Recall, Long Term Recall) Visual Unordered Recall (Immediate Recall, Short Term Recall, Long Term Recall), Auditory Ordered Recall (Immediate Recall, Short Term Recall, Long Term Recall), Auditory Unordered Recall (Immediate Recall, Short Term Recall, Long Term Recall), Total Visual Memory, Total Auditory Memory, Global Memory.
Administration: Individual.
Price Data, 1994: $63 per test kit including manual ('92, 159 pages), stimulus cards, and 50 record forms; $25 per specimen set including manual and sample forms; $13 per stimulus cards; $22 per 50 record forms; $25 per manual.
Time: (10–15) minutes.
Author: Raymond E. Webster.
Publisher: Academic Therapy Publications.
Cross References: For a review by Robert G. Harrington of an earlier form, see 9:601.

TEST REFERENCES

1. Kataria, S., Hall, C. W., Wong, M. M., & Keys, G. F. (1992). Learning styles of LD and NLD ADHD children. *Journal of Clinical Psychology, 48*, 371–378.

[1424]

Learning Environment Inventory.
Purpose: "Measures student perceptions of 15 dimensions of the social climate of high school classrooms."
Population: Grades 7–12.
Publication Date: 1982.
Acronym: LEI.
Scores, 15: Cohesiveness, Diversity, Formality, Speed, Material Environment, Friction, Goal Direction, Favoritism, Difficulty, Apathy, Democracy, Cliqueness, Satisfaction, Disorganization, Competitiveness.
Administration: Group.
Price Data: Not available.
Time: (20–50) minutes.

Comments: Combined manual (57 pages) for this and My Class Inventory (1700).
Authors: Barry J. Fraser, Gary J. Anderson, and Herbert J. Walberg.
Publisher: Western Australian Institute of Technology [No reply from publisher; status unknown].
Cross References: For reviews by J. R. Barclay and J. C. Reed, see 9:602 (1 reference).

TEST REFERENCES

1. Chávez, R. C. (1984). The use of high-inference measures to study classroom climates: A review. *Review of Educational Research, 54,* 237-261.
2. Hofstein, A., & Lazarowitz, R. (1986). A comparison of the actual and preferred classroom learning environment in biology and chemistry as perceived by high school students. *Journal of Research in Science Teaching, 23,* 189-199.
3. Randhawa, B. S. (1990). Structure of learning environment variables under two instructional conditions. *Psychological Reports, 66,* 531-538.

[1425]

Learning Inventory of Kindergarten Experiences.

Purpose: Developed to screen for kindergarten readiness.
Population: Beginning kindergarten.
Publication Date: 1988.
Acronym: LIKE.
Scores: Item scores only in 4 areas: Motor, Language, Preacademic, Prereading.
Administration: Individual.
Price Data, 1990: $175 per complete kit including paper supplies (50 record sheets, 50 summary sheets, 5 grid summary sheets, pads of 50 circles, squares, and geometric shapes, strips and squares of colored paper, 10 letter cards, 6 numeral cards, 18 picture cards), test manual (42 pages), and instruction manual (14 pages); $50 per set of paper supplies; $25 per 50 record sheets; $20 per set of manuals.
Time: Administration time not reported.
Authors: Nathaniel O. Owings, Paulette E. Mills, and Cynthia Best O'Dell.
Publisher: University of Washington Press.

[1426]

Learning Methods Test.

Purpose: Determine "the student's ability to learn new words under different teaching procedures."
Population: Grades Kgn, 1, 2, 3.
Publication Dates: 1954-55.
Acronym: LMT.
Scores: Comparative Effectiveness of Four Methods of Teaching New Words: Visual, Phonic, Kinesthetic, Combination.
Administration: Individual.
Price Data: Not available.
Time: (85-100) minutes in 5 sessions for pretest, training, and post-test.
Author: Robert E. Mills.
Publisher: The Mills Center [No reply from publisher; status unknown].
Cross References: See T2:1666 (3 references); for

reviews by Thomas E. Culliton, Jr. and William Eller, see 6:836 (1 reference).

[1427]

Learning Preference Inventory.

Purpose: "To assist teachers in the task of identifying individual student learning preferences or styles."
Population: Elementary through adult students.
Publication Dates: 1978-80.
Acronym: LPI.
Scores: 6 preference scores: Sensing-Feeling, Sensing-Thinking, Intuitive-Thinking, Intuitive-Feeling, Introversion, Extraversion.
Administration: Group.
Price Data, 1988: $175 per complete kit including 35 inventories, 35 Student Diagnostic Behavior Checklist folders, 35 individual computer printouts, 1 class profile printout, 1 copy each of Learning Style Inventory and Teaching Style Inventory (for teacher self-assessment), Learning Styles and Strategies Manual, and user's manual ('80, 60 pages); $142 per complete kit without computer scoring; $3 per inventory with prepaid computer scoring; $2 per inventory without computer scoring.
Time: [30] minutes.
Comments: Identifies learning styles based on Jungian typology.
Authors: Harvey F. Silver and J. Robert Hanson.
Publisher: Hanson Silver Strong & Associates, Inc.
Cross References: For reviews by Bruce H. Biskin and Jeffrey Jenkins, see 11:201 (2 references).

[1428]

Learning Preference Scales.

Purpose: "Provides a measure of the preference for cooperative, competitive and individualised learning."
Publication Date: 1992.
Acronym: LPS.
Scores, 5: Cooperation, Competition, Individualism, Combined Involvement, Cooperative Involvement.
Administration: Group.
Price Data, 1993: $59.95 per complete kit including manual (54 pages) and one copy of each scale.
Time: (10-45) minutes.
Authors: Lee Owens and Jennifer Barnes.
Publisher: Australian Council for Educational Research, Ltd. [Australia].
a) LEARNING PREFERENCE SCALES—STUDENTS.
Population: Grades 4-12.
Acronym: LPSS.
b) LEARNING PREFERENCE SCALES—TEACHERS.
Population: Elementary and secondary teachers.
Acronym: LPST.
c) LEARNING PREFERENCE SCALES—PARENTS.
Population: Parents of school students.
Acronym: LPSP.

[1429]

Learning Process Questionnaire.

Purpose: "To assess the extent to which a secondary school student endorses different approaches to learning and the more important motives and strategies comprising those approaches."

Population: Secondary students.
Publication Dates: 1985–87.
Acronym: LPQ.
Scores, 9: Surface Motive, Surface Strategy, Deep Motive, Deep Strategy, Achieving Motive, Achieving Strategy, Surface Approach, Deep Approach, Achieving Approach.
Administration: Individual or group.
Price Data, 1994: A$5.70 per 10 questionnaires; $4.20 per 10 answer sheets; $4.10 per score key; $29.95 per monograph entitled *Student Approaches to Learning and Studying* ('87, 151 pages); $15.50 per manual ('87, 36 pages).
Time: 20(40) minutes.
Comments: Tertiary counterpart of the Study Process Questionnaire (2608).
Author: John Biggs.
Publisher: Australian Council for Educational Research Ltd. [Australia].
Cross References: For reviews by Robert D. Brown and Cathy W. Hall, see 11:202 (1 reference); for a review by Cathy W. Hall of the Study Process Questionnaire, see 11:389.

[1430]

Learning Skills Profile.
Purpose: To assess the gap between personal aptitudes and critical skills required by a job.
Population: Junior high to adults.
Publication Date: 1993.
Acronym: LSP.
Scores, 36: 3 scores: Personal Learning Skill, Job Skill Demand, and Learning Gap in each of 12 skill areas: Interpersonal Skills (Leadership Skill, Relationship Skill, Help Skill), Analytical Skills (Theory Skill, Quantitative Skill, Technology Skill), Information Skills (Sense-Making Skill, Information-Gathering Skill, Information Analysis Skill), Behavioral Skills (Goal Setting Skill, Action Skill, Initiative Skill).
Administration: Group.
Price Data, 1993: $85 per complete kit including 5 workbooks and profiles, and 1 set of reusable LSP cards and instructions; $65 per 5 workbooks and profiles; $32 per reusable LSP cards and instructions.
Time: Administration time not reported.
Comments: Self-scored profile.
Authors: Richard E. Boyatzis and David A. Kolb.
Publisher: McBer & Company.

[1431]

Learning Style Identification Scale.
Purpose: "For educators to make tentative identifications of the learning styles their students use."
Population: Grades 1–8.
Publication Date: 1981.
Acronym: LSIS.
Scores, 4: Scores obtained by rating 4 areas (Intra-

personal Information, Extrapersonal Information, Cognitive Development, Self-Concept).
Administration: Group.
Price Data, 1989: $30 per 30 tests and manual (65 pages); $11 per additional 30 tests.
Time: [15–20] minutes.
Comments: Ratings by teachers.
Authors: Paul J. Malcom, William C. Lutz, Mary A. Gerken, and Gary M. Hoeltke.
Publisher: Publishers Test Service.
Cross References: For reviews by Michael W. Pratt and K. Ann Renninger, see 9:606.

[1432]

Learning Style Inventory [Price Systems, Inc.].
Purpose: Identifies "the conditions under which an individual is most likely to learn, remember, and achieve."
Population: Grades 3–12.
Publication Dates: 1976–94.
Acronym: LSI.
Scores: 22 areas: Noise Level, Light, Temperature, Design, Motivation, Persistent, Responsible, Structure, Learning Alone/Peer Oriented, Authority Figures Present, Learn in Several Ways, Auditory, Visual, Tactile, Kinesthetic, Requires Intake, Evening/Morning, Late Morning, Afternoon, Needs Mobility, Parent Figure Motivated, Teacher Motivated, plus a Consistency score.
Administration: Group.
Price Data, 1993: $2.50 per 10 answer sheets for grades 3 and 4 or for grades 5 and above; $.40 per individual interpretative booklet; $9.50 per manual ('89, 95 pages); $3.25 per research report; $295 per computerized self-administered inventory program with 100 administrations ($60 per 100 additional administrations) (specify IBM or Apple); $395 per Scan and Score programs; $.60 per answer form to use with Scan and Score; $4 or less per individual profile available from publisher's scoring service; $7.50 or less per group and subscale summaries; summaries available from publisher only in addition to individual profiles.
Time: (20–30) minutes.
Comments: Apple, IBM, or IBM-compatible computer required for (optional) computerized administration; 3000, 3051 NCS, OPScan 5, Scrantron 8000, 8200, 8400, or Scanning System 380 scanner required for (optional) Scan and Score System.
Authors: Rita Dunn, Kenneth Dunn, and Gary E. Price.
Publisher: Price Systems, Inc.
Cross References: For reviews by Jan N. Hughes and Alida S. Westman, see 11:203 (6 references).

TEST REFERENCES

1. Nganwa-Bagumah, M., & Mwamwenda, T. S. (1991). Effects on reading comprehension tests of matching and mismatching students' design preferences. *Perceptual and Motor Skills, 72,* 947-951.
2. Wratcher, M. A. (1991). Helping freshmen to maximize their learning potential. *Journal of College Student Development, 32,* 380-381.

3. Young, F. L., & McIntyre, J. D. (1992). A comparative study of the learning style preferences of students with learning disabilities and students who are gifted. *Journal of Learning Disabilities, 25*, 124-132.

[1433]

Learning Style Profile.
Purpose: Designed to evaluate student learning style as the basis for student advisement and placement, instructional strategy, and the evaluation of learning."
Population: Grades 6–12.
Publication Dates: 1986–90.
Acronym: LSP.
Scores, 23: Cognitive Skills (Analytic, Spatial, Discrimination, Categorizing, Sequential Processing, Memory), Perceptual Responses (Visual, Auditory, Emotive), Persistence Orientation, Verbal Risk Orientation, Study and Instructional Preferences (Verbal-Spatial, Manipulative, Study Time [Early Morning, Late Morning, Afternoon, Evening], Grouping, Posture, Mobility, Sound, Lighting, Temperature).
Administration: Group.
Price Data: Price information available from publisher for materials including Technical Manual ('88, 105 pages).
Time: (50–60) minutes.
Authors: James W. Keefe (test, Handbook II), John S. Monk (test), Charles A. Letteri (test, Handbook I), Marlin Languis (test), Rita Dunn (test), John M. Jenkins (Handbook I), and Patricia Rosenlund (Handbook I).
Publisher: National Association of Secondary School Principals.

TEST REFERENCES

1. Frey, D., & Simonson, M. (1993). Assessment of cognitive style to examine students' use of hypermedia within historic costume. *Home Economics Research Journal, 21*, 403-421.

[1434]

Learning Styles and Strategies.
Purpose: "Assists teachers and administrators in better understanding their own learning and teaching styles."
Population: Teachers.
Publication Date: 1980.
Scores, 4: Sensing/Feeling, Sensing/Thinking, Intuitive/Thinking, Intuitive/Feeling.
Administration: Group.
Price Data, 1988: $25 per manual (130 pages) including Learning Style Inventory and Teaching Style Inventory.
Time: Administration times not reported.
Comments: Self-administered, self-scored; tests available as separates.
Authors: Harvey F. Silver and J. Robert Hanson.
Publisher: Hanson Silver Strong & Associates, Inc.
a) LEARNING STYLE INVENTORY.
Purpose: "A self-diagnostic tool for adults to assess learning styles preferences."
Price Data: $2 per inventory including scoring key and information.

b) TEACHING STYLE INVENTORY.
Purpose: "A self-diagnostic tool to identify one's preferred teaching style."
Price Data: $2 per inventory including scoring key and information.
Cross References: For reviews by Bert A. Goldman and Dan Wright, see 11:204.

[1435]

Learning Styles Inventory [Creative Learning Press, Inc.].
Purpose: "Designed to measure student attitudes toward nine general modes of instruction."
Population: Grades 4–12 and teachers.
Publication Date: 1978.
Acronym: LSI.
Scores: 9 factor scores: Projects, Drill and Recitation, Peer Teaching, Discussion, Teaching Games, Independent Study, Programmed Instruction, Lecture, Simulation.
Administration: Group.
Forms, 2: Student, Teacher.
Price Data, 1987: $20.95 per class set including 30 student forms, 1 teacher form, and computer scoring; $7.95 per manual (44 pages); $8.50 per specimen set.
Time: (30) minutes.
Comments: "A measure of student preference for instructional techniques."
Authors: Joseph S. Renzulli and Linda H. Smith.
Publisher: Creative Learning Press, Inc.
Cross References: For a review by Benson P. Low, see 9:608.

TEST REFERENCES

1. Smith, L. H., & Renzulli, J. S. (1984). Learning style preferences: A practical approach for classroom teachers. *Theory Into Practice, 23*, 44-50.

[1436]

Learning Styles Inventory [Piney Mountain Press, Inc.].
Purpose: Designed to identify learning needs of students.
Population: Students and adults.
Publication Date: 1988.
Scores: 9 subtopics in 2 areas: Learning (Auditory Language, Visual Language, Auditory Numerical, Visual Numerical, Auditory-Visual-Kinesthetic), Working (Group Learner, Individual Learner, Oral Expressive, Written Expressive).
Administration: Individual or group.
Price Data, 1990: $395 per complete kit including instructor guide, software, video, and 100 response sheets; $1,095 per Learning Styles Inventory Media Kit with Chatsworth Card Reader.
Time: [11] minutes.
Author: Piney Mountain Press, Inc.
Publisher: Piney Mountain Press, Inc.

[1437]

Learning through Listening.
Purpose: Designed to assess listening comprehension.

Population: Ages 10–11, 13–14, 17–18.
Publication Date: 1976.
Scores, 6: Content, Contextual Constraints, Phonology, Register, Relationship, Total.
Administration: Group.
Levels, 3: A, B, C.
Price Data: Available from publisher.
Time: (28–37) minutes for Part I, (29–41) minutes for Part II with a 15–30 minute break between parts.
Authors: Andrew Wilkinson, Leslie Stratta, and Peter Dudley.
Publisher: Macmillan Education Ltd. [England].
Cross References: For a review by Allen Berger, see 9:610.

[1438]

Learning-Style Inventory [McBer and Company].
Purpose: Designed to help individuals assess their modes of learning and learning styles.
Population: Grade 6 through adults.
Publication Dates: 1976–85.
Acronym: LSI.
Scores, 8: Concrete Experience, Reflective Observation, Abstract Conceptualization, Active Experimentation, Accomodator, Diverger, Converger, Assimilator.
Administration: Group.
Price Data, 1993: $65 per 10 inventories; $29 per LSI flipcharts; $38 per 11 transparencies; $50 per user's guide; Bibliography of Research and Technical Specifications available free with order.
Foreign Language Editions: Available in French and Spanish.
Time: 15 minutes.
Comments: Self-administered.
Author: David A. Kolb.
Publisher: McBer and Company.
Cross References: For a review by Noel Gregg, see 10:173 (17 references); see also 9:607 (7 references).

TEST REFERENCES

1. Johnson, J. A., Germer, C. K., Efran, J. S., & Overton, W. F. (1988). Personality as the basis for theoretical predilections. *Journal of Personality and Social Psychology, 55,* 824-835.
2. Green, D., & Parker, R. M. (1989). Vocational and academic attributes of students with different learning styles. *Journal of College Student Development, 30,* 395-400.
3. Magolda, M. B. B. (1989). Gender differences in cognitive development: An analysis of cognitive complexity and learning styles. *Journal of College Student Development, 30,* 213-220.
4. Shapiro, S. B., & Fitzgerald, L. F. (1989). The development of an objective scale to measure a transpersonal orientation to learning. *Educational and Psychological Measurement, 49,* 375-384.
5. Sims, R. S., Veres, J. G., III, & Shake, L. G. (1989). An exploratory examination of the convergence between the Learning Styles Questionnaire and the Learning Style Inventory II. *Educational and Psychological Measurement, 49,* 227-233.
6. Titus, T. G., Bergandi, T. A., & Shryock, M. (1989). Adolescent learning styles. *Journal of Research and Development in Education, 23,* 163-171.
7. Atkinson, G., Jr., Murrell, P. H., & Winters, M. R. (1990). The Self Directed Search: A Guide to Educational and Vocational Planning. *Psychological Reports, 66,* 160-162.
8. Geiger, M. A., & Pinto, J. K. (1991). Changes in learning style preference during a three-year longitudinal study. *Psychological Reports, 69,* 755-762.
9. Sein, M. K., & Robey, D. (1991). Learning style and the efficacy of computer training methods. *Perceptual and Motor Skills, 72,* 243-248.
10. Geiger, M. A., Boyle, E. J., & Pinto, J. (1992). A factor analysis of Kolb's revised Learning Style Inventory. *Educational and Psychological Measurement, 52,* 753-759.
11. Goldstein, M. B., & Bokoros, M. A. (1992). Tilting at windmills: Comparing the Learning Style Inventory and the learning style Questionnaire. *Educational and Psychological Measurement, 52,* 701-708.
12. Winston, R. B., Jr., Vahala, M. E., Nichols, E. C., Gillis, M. E., Wintrow, M., & Rome, K. D. (1994). A measure of college classroom climate: The college classroom environment scales. *Journal of College Student Development, 35,* 11-18.

[1439]

Leatherman Leadership Questionnaire [Revised].
Purpose: "To aid in selecting leaders, providing specific feedback to participants on their leadership knowledge for career counseling, conducting accurate needs analysis, and screening for assessment centers or giving pre/post assessment feedback."
Population: Managers, supervisors, team leaders, and potential leaders.
Publication Dates: 1987–92.
Acronym: LLQ.
Scores, 28: Assigning Work, Career Counseling, Coaching Employees, Oral Communication, Managing Change, Handling Employee Complaints, Dealing with Employee Conflicts, Counseling Employees, Helping an Employee Make Decisions, Delegating, Taking Disciplinary Action, Handling Emotional Situations, Setting Goals/Planning with Employees, Handling Employee Grievances, Conducting Employee Meetings, Giving Positive Feedback, Negotiating, Conducting Performance Appraisals, Establishing Performance Standards, Persuading/Influencing Employees, Making Presentations to Employees, Problem Solving with Employees, Conducting Selection Interviews, Team Building, Conducting Termination Interviews, Helping an Employee Manage Time, One-on-One Training, Total.
Subtests: 2: May be administered in separate parts.
Administration: Group.
Price Data, 1992: $1,500 per administrator's kit including administrator's manual ('92, 52 pages), overhead transparencies, 10 sets of reusable questionnaire booklets, and 10 sets of answer sheets with scoring service; $65 per additional answer sheets and scoring service including development manual ('92, 347 pages); $55 per additional answer sheets and scoring service; $20 per additional sets of questionnaire booklets; $1 each for "confidential service" (participant's scoring sheet sealed in an envelope), $100 per extra administrator's kit.
Time: (300–325) minutes for battery; (150–165) minutes per part.
Comments: Complete test administered in 2 parts; machine scored by publisher.
Author: Richard W. Leatherman.
Publisher: International Training Consultants, Inc.
Cross References: For reviews by Walter Katkovsky and William D. Porterfield of an earlier edition, see 11:205.

[1440]
Leeds Scales for the Self-Assessment of Anxiety and Depression.

Purpose: Self-assessment measure of the severity of symptoms of clinical anxiety and depression.
Population: Psychiatric patients.
Publication Date: 1976.
Scores, 4: Depression (General, Specific), Anxiety (General, Specific).
Administration: Group or individual.
Price Data, 1987: £1.75 per 25 questionnaires; £1 per 2 scoring stencils; £4.25 per complete set; £3 per specimen set; £2 per manual (26 pages).
Time: Administration time not reported.
Comments: Self-rating scale.
Authors: R. P. Smith, G. W. K. Bridge, and Max Hamilton.
Publisher: Psychological Test Publications [England].
Cross References: For reviews by John Duckitt and H. J. Eysenck, see 9:611 (4 references).

TEST REFERENCES

1. Saleem, P. T. (1984). Dexamethasone suppression test in depressive illness: Its relation to anxiety symptoms. *British Journal of Psychiatry, 144,* 181-184.
2. Imlah, N. W. (1985). An evaluation of alprazolam in the treatment of reactive or neurotic (secondary) depression. *British Journal of Psychiatry, 146,* 515-519.
3. Eagles, J. M., Beattie, J. A. G., Blackwood, G. W., Restall, D. B., & Ashcroft, G. W. (1987). The mental health of elderly couples: I. The effects of a cognitively impaired spouse. *The British Journal of Psychiatry, 150,* 299-303.
4. Eagles, J. M., Walker, L. G., Blackwood, G. W., Beattie, J. A. G., & Restall, D. B. (1987). The mental health of elderly couples II. Concordance for psychiatric morbidity in spouses. *The British Journal of Psychiatry, 150,* 303-308.
5. Oatley, K., & Hodgson, D. (1987). Influence of husbands on the outcome of their agoraphobic wives' therapy. *The British Journal of Psychiatry, 150,* 380-386.
6. Kinsella, G., Moran, C., Ford, B., & Ponsford, J. (1988). Emotional disorder and its assessment within the severe head injured population. *Psychological Medicine, 18,* 57-63.
7. Shek, D. T. L. (1990). Reliability and factorial structure of the Chinese version of the Beck Depression Inventory. *Journal of Clinical Psychology, 46,* 35-43.
8. Mehrabian, A., & Bernath, M. S. (1991). Factorial composition of commonly used self-report depression inventories: Relationships with basic dimensions of temperament. *Journal of Research in Personality, 25,* 262-275.
9. Shek, D. T. L. (1991). What does the Chinese version of the Beck Depression Inventory measure in Chinese students—General psychopathology or depression? *Journal of Clinical Psychology, 47,* 381-390.
10. Davies, R. H., Harris, B., Thomas, D. R., Cook, N., Read, G., & Riad-Fahmy, D. (1992). Salivary testosterone levels and major depressive illness in men. *British Journal of Psychiatry, 161,* 629-632.
11. Shek, D. T. L. (1993). The Chinese version of the State-Trait Anxiety Inventory: Its relationship to different measures of psychological well-being. *Journal of Clinical Psychology, 49,* 349-358.

[1441]
Leisure Activities Blank.

Purpose: Designed to identify past leisure activities and future involvement in such activities.
Population: Ages 20 and over.
Publication Dates: 1974–75.
Acronym: LAB.
Scores, 16: Past Participation (Mechanics, Crafts, Intellectual, Slow Living, Sports, Glamour Sports), Future Participation (Adventure, Mechanics, Crafts, Easy Living, Intellectual, Ego Recognition, Slow Living, Clean Living), Validity Scales (Frequent Past, Frequent Future).
Administration: Group.
Price Data, 1990: $5 per 25 test booklets; $13 per 50 profile sheets; $31 per set of scoring stencils; $9.50 per manual ('75, 43 pages); $9 per specimen set.
Time: 15–30 minutes.
Author: George E. McKechnie.
Publisher: Consulting Psychologists Press, Inc.
Cross References: For reviews by David P. Campbell and Leonard S. Feldt, see 8:602 (3 references).

TEST REFERENCES

1. Rule, W. R., & Traver, M. D. (1982). Early recollections and expected leisure activities. *Psychological Reports, 51,* 295-301.
2. Ragheb, M. G., & McKinney, J. (1993). Campus recreation and perceived academic stress. *Journal of College Student Development, 34,* 5-10.

[1442]
The Leisure Diagnostic Battery.

Purpose: Developed to assess leisure functioning.
Population: Ages 9–18, adult.
Publication Date: 1987.
Administration: Group.
Levels, 2: Version A, Version B.
Price Data, 1991: $19.95 per manual ('87, 102 pages).
Time: (30–60) minutes.
Authors: Peter A. Witt and Gary D. Ellis.
Publisher: American Alliance for Health, Physical Education, Recreation, and Dance.
a) SHORT FORM.
Scores, 6: Perceived Leisure (Competence, Control), Leisure Needs, Depth of Involvement in Leisure Experiences, Playfulness, Total.
b) LONG FORM.
Scores, 6 to 9: Same as for *a* above plus 3 optional scores: Barriers to Leisure Involvement Scale, Leisure Preference Inventory, Knowledge of Leisure Opportunities Test.

[1443]
Leisure Interest Inventory.

Purpose: Designed to assess "preferred leisure activities."
Population: College students.
Publication Date: 1969.
Acronym: LII.
Scores, 5: Sociability, Games, Art, Mobility, Immobility.
Administration: Group.
Price Data: Available from publisher.
Time: (20–25) minutes.
Author: Edwina E. Hubert.
Publisher: Edwina E. Hubert, Ph.D.

[1444]
Leisure Search Inventory.

Purpose: To identify employment opportunities related to leisure interests.

Population: Adults.
Publication Date: 1994.
Acronym: LSI.
Scores: 12 areas: Artistic, Scientific, Plants and Animals, Protective, Mechanical, Industrial, Business Detail, Selling, Accommodating, Humanitarian, Leading-Influencing, Physical Performing.
Administration: Group.
Manual: No manual.
Price Data: Available from publisher.
Time: Administration time not reported.
Comments: Self-administered and self-scored.
Author: John J. Liptak.
Publisher: JIST Works, Inc.

[1445]

The Leiter Adult Intelligence Scale.
Purpose: Designed to measure adult general intelligence.
Population: Adults.
Publication Dates: 1949–72.
Acronym: LAIS.
Scores, 3: Verbal, Performance (Non-Verbal), Total.
Administration: Individual.
Price Data, 1994: $225 per complete kit including all test materials, manual ('72, 57 pages), and 100 record blanks; $30 per 100 record blanks; $30 per manual.
Time: (40–60) minutes.
Comments: Revision of Leiter-Partington Adult Performance Scale; includes The FR-CR Test, Partington's Pathways Test, The Leiter Adaptation of Arthur's Stencil Design Test, and The Leiter Adaptation of the Painted Cube Test.
Author: Russell Graydon Leiter.
Publisher: Stoelting Co.
Cross References: See T2:504 (12 references); for reviews by Paul C. Davis and Frank B. Jex, and an excerpted review by Laurance F. Shaffer, see 6:525 (15 references); for reviews by Harold A. Delp and Herschel Manuel and an excerpted review by Laurance E. Shaffer of the original edition, see 4:350 (4 references). For a review of The FR-CR Test, see 4:339; for an excerpted review of The Leiter Adaptation of Arthur's Stencil Design Test, see 4:347; for an excerpted review of The Leiter Adaptation of the Painted Cube Test, see 4:348; for reviews of Partington's Pathways Test, see 4:355 (1 review, 1 excerpt).

[1446]

Leiter International Performance Scale.
Purpose: Devised for "mental measurement entirely non-language in nature."
Population: Ages 2–18, 3–8.
Publication Dates: 1936–55.
Acronym: LIPS.
Scores: Total score only.
Administration: Individual.
Price Data, 1994: $750 per set of testing materials; $250 per Tray 1 (covers years 2 through 7); $275 per

Tray 2 (covers years 8 through 12); $250 per Tray 3 (covers years 14 through 18); $70 per carrying case for 3 trays; $25 per 25 record booklets; $35 per wooden frame; $45 per wooden frame, modified for use with cerebral palsied and other severely, physically disabled; $70 per handbook.
Authors: Russell Graydon Leiter and Grace Arthur (*b*).
Publisher: Stoelting Co.
a) 1948 REVISION.
Population: Ages 2–18.
Publication Dates: 1936–52.
Time: (30–60) minutes.
b) ARTHUR ADAPTATION.
Population: Ages 3–8.
Publication Dates: 1952–55.
Time: (30–60) minutes.
Comments: Author recommends use with Arthur Point Scale of Performance Tests; administered by pantomime.
Cross References: See T3:1319 (16 references) and T2:505 (18 references); for a review by Emmy E. Werner, see 6:526 (10 references); see also 5:408 (17 references); for a review by Gwen F. Arnold and an excerpted review by Laurance F. Shaffer of *a*, see 4:349 (25 references).

TEST REFERENCES

1. Norton, G. R., & Lester, C. J. (1979). The effects of modeling and verbal cues on concept acquisition of moderate retardates. *Cognitive Therapy and Research, 3,* 87-90.
2. McLeavey, B. C., Toomey, J. F., & Dempsey, P. J. R. (1982). Nonretarded and mentally retarded children's control over syntactic structures. *American Journal of Mental Deficiency, 86,* 485-494.
3. Fey, M. E., & Leonard, L. B. (1984). Partner age as a variable in the conversational performance of specifically language-impaired and normal-language children. *Journal of Speech and Hearing Research, 27,* 413-423.
4. Greenberg, M. T., Calderon, R., & Kusche, C. (1984). Early intervention using simultaneous communication with deaf infants: The effect on communication development. *Child Development, 55,* 607-616.
5. Johnston, J. R., & Kamhi, A. G. (1984). Syntactic and semantic aspects of the utterances of language-impaired children: The same can be less. *Merrill-Palmer Quarterly, 30,* 65-85.
6. Lederberg, A. R. (1984). Interaction between deaf preschoolers and unfamiliar hearing adults. *Child Development, 55,* 598-606.
7. Mask, N., & Bowen, C. E. (1984). Comparison of the WISC-R and the Leiter International Performance Scale with average and above-average students. *Journal of Clinical Psychology, 40,* 303-305.
8. Telzrow, C. F. (1984). Practical applications of the K-ABC in the identification of handicapped preschoolers. *The Journal of Special Education, 18,* 311-324.
9. Cunningham, C. E., Siegel, L. S., van der Spuy, H. I. J., Clark, M. L., & Bow, S. J. (1985). The behavioral and linguistic interactions of specifically language-delayed and normal boys with their mothers. *Child Development, 56,* 1389-1403.
10. Kashani, J. H., Carlson, G. A., Horwitz, E., & Reid, J. C. (1985). Dysphoric mood in young children referred to a child development unit. *Child Psychiatry and Human Development, 15,* 234-242.
11. Dollaghan, C., & Kaston, N. (1986). A comprehension monitoring program for language impaired children. *Journal of Speech and Hearing Disorders, 51,* 264-271.
12. Kashani, J. H., Horwitz, E., Ray, J. S., & Reid, J. C. (1986). DSM-III diagnostic classification of 100 preschoolers in a child development unit. *Child Psychiatry and Human Development, 16,* 137-147.
13. Konstantareas, M. M., Hauser, P., Lennox, C., & Homatidis, S. (1986). Season of birth in infantile autism. *Child Psychiatry and Human Development, 17,* 53-65.
14. Leonard, L. B. (1986). Conversational replies of children with specific language impairment. *Journal of Speech and Hearing Research, 29,* 114-119.
15. Rantakallio, P., & von Wendt, L. (1986). Mental retardation and

subnormality in a birth cohort of 12,000 children in Northern Finland. *American Journal of Mental Deficiency, 90,* 380-387.

16. Lachiewicz, A. M., Gullion, C. M., Spiridigliozzi, G. A., & Aylsworth, A. S. (1987). Declining IQs of young males with the fragile x syndrome. *American Journal on Mental Retardation, 92,* 272-278.

17. Lovaas, O. I. (1987). Behavioral treatment and normal educational and intellectual functioning in young autistic children. *Journal of Consulting and Clinical Psychology, 55,* 3-9.

18. Fisher, W., Burd, L., & Kerbeshian, J. (1988). Markers for improvement in children with pervasive developmental disorders. *Journal of Mental Deficiency Research, 32,* 357-369.

19. Loveland, K. A., & Kelley, M. L. (1988). Development of adaptive behavior in adolescents and young adults with autism and Down Syndrome. *American Journal on Mental Retardation, 93,* 84-92.

20. Abbeduto, L., Furman, L., & Davies, B. (1989). Relation between the receptive language and mental age of persons with mental retardation. *American Journal on Mental Retardation, 93,* 535-543.

21. Caulfield, M. B., Fischel, J. E., DeBaryshe, B. D., & Whitehurst, G. J. (1989). Behavioral correlates of developmental expressive language disorder. *Journal of Abnormal Child Psychology, 17,* 187-201.

22. Mead, R. A., & Lapidus, L. B. (1989). Psychological differentiation, arousal, and lipreading efficiency in hearing-impaired and normal children. *Journal of Clinical Psychology, 45,* 851-859.

23. Skarakis-Doyle, E., & Mullin, K. (1990). Comprehension monitoring in language-disordered children: A preliminary investigation of cognitive and linguistic factors. *Journal of Speech and Hearing Disorders, 55,* 700-705.

24. Skarakis-Doyle, E., MacLellan, N., & Mullin, K. (1990). Nonverbal indicants of comprehension monitoring in language-disordered children. *Journal of Speech and Hearing Disorders, 55,* 461-467.

25. Ziegler, M., Tallal, P., & Curtiss, S. (1990). Selecting language-impaired children for research studies: Insights from the San Diego longitudinal study. *Perceptual and Motor Skills, 71,* 1079-1089.

26. Abbeduto, L., Davies, B., Solesby, S., & Furman, L. (1991). Identifying the referents of spoken messages: Use of context and clarification requests by children with and without mental retardation. *American Journal on Mental Retardation, 95,* 551-562.

27. Fishler, K., & Koch, R. (1991). Mental development in Down syndrome mosaicism. *American Journal on Mental Retardation, 96,* 345-351.

28. Loveland, K. A., & Kelley, M. L. (1991). Development of adaptive behavior in preschoolers with autism or Down syndrome. *American Journal on Mental Retardation, 96,* 13-20.

29. Atkinson, L., Bevc, I., Dickens, S., & Blackwell, J. (1992). Concurrent validites of the Stanford-Binet (Fourth Edition), Leiter, and Vineland with developmentally delayed children. *Journal of School Psychology, 30*(2), 165-173.

30. Burt, D. B., Loveland, K. A., & Lewis, K. R. (1992). Depression and the onset of dementia in adults with mental retardation. *American Journal on Mental Retardation, 96,* 502-511.

31. Webster, P. E., & Plante, A. S. (1992). Phonologically impaired preschoolers: Rhyme with an eye toward reading. *Perceptual and Motor Skills, 75,* 1195-1204.

32. Wright-Strawderman, C., & Watson, B. L. (1992). The prevalence of depressive symptoms in children with learning disabilities. *Journal of Learning Disabilities, 25,* 258-264.

33. Bloom, A. S., & Zelko, F. A. (1994). Variability in adaptive behavior in children with developmental delay. *Journal of Clinical Psychology, 50,* 261-265.

[1447]

Let's Talk Inventory for Children.

Purpose: "To identify children who have inadequate or delayed social-verbal communication skills; provides a uniform and standardized method of eliciting and probing selected speech acts, representing the ritualizing, informing, controlling, and feeling functions of verbal communication."

Population: Ages 4–8.

Publication Date: 1987.

Acronym: LTI-C.

Scores, 2: Formulation, Association.

Administration: Individual.

Price Data, 1994: $103 per complete kit including 25 record forms, stimulus manual, and examiner's

manual (82 pages); $21.50 per 25 record forms; $45 per stimulus manual; $37.50 per examiner's manual.

Time: 30(40) minutes.

Comments: Downward extension of Let's Talk Inventory for Adolescents (9:613).

Authors: Candice M. Bray and Elisabeth H. Wiig.

Publisher: The Psychological Corporation.

Cross References: For reviews by Merith Cosden and Janet Norris, see 11:206.

[1448]

Levine-Pilowsky [Depression] Questionnaire.

Purpose: A questionnaire technique for classifying depression.

Population: Adults.

Publication Date: 1979.

Acronym: LPD.

Scores: 8 subscales: Insomnia (Initial), Sleep (General), Paranoia, Appetite, Insomnia (Late), Crying, Diurnal Variation, Hopelessness.

Administration: Individual or group.

Manual: No manual.

Price Data: Available from publisher.

Time: (10) minutes.

Author: I. Pilowsky.

Publisher: I. Pilowsky [Australia].

TEST REFERENCES

1. Watts, F. N., MacLeod, A. K., & Morris, L. (1988). A remedial strategy for memory and concentration problems in depressed patients. *Cognitive Therapy and Research, 12,* 185-193.

2. Watts, F. N., & Cooper, Z. (1989). The effects of depression on structural aspects of the recall of prose. *Journal of Abnormal Psychology, 98,* 150-153.

3. Fergusson, D. M., Lynskey, M. T., & Horwood, L. J. (1993). The effect of maternal depression on maternal ratings of child behavior. *Journal of Abnormal Child Psychology, 21,* 245-269.

[1449]

Lewis Counselling Inventory.

Purpose: Designed as an "instrument for identifying those pupils most in need of guidance and counselling."

Population: Adolescents in school.

Publication Date: 1978.

Scores, 8: Relationship With Teachers, Relationship With Family, Irritability, Social Confidence, Relationship With Peers, Health, Total, Lie Scale.

Administration: Group.

Parts, 2: 1, 2 (optional supplementary questionnaire).

Price Data, 1989: £6.90 per 25 inventories (Part 1); £4.05 per 25 questionnaires (Part 2); £13.55 per 6 keys; £12.10 per manual (29 pages); £12.65 per specimen set; automated version available, £51.75 per disk pack (40 track or 80 track).

Time: (10–15) minutes for each part.

Authors: D. G. Lewis and P. D. Pumfrey.

Publisher: NFER-Nelson Publishing Co., Ltd. [England].

Cross References: For reviews by Deborah N. Bauserman and Gerald L. Stone, see 9:614.

[1450]

Lexington Developmental Scales.
Purpose: To "provide an individual graph or profile which depicts the child's developmental age level."
Population: Ages birth–6 years.
Publication Dates: 1973–77.
Acronym: LDS.
Scores: Contains behavioral and experimental items rated by examiner in 4 areas: Motor, Language, Cognitive, Personal and Social.
Administration: Individual administration to ages birth–2 years.
Price Data: Not available.
Time: (60) minutes in children birth–2 years; time varies for older children.
Comments: Long and Short Forms; may be used by parents and volunteers; "particularly helpful in pre- and post-testing"; additional testing materials must be supplied by the examiner.
Authors: United Cerebral Palsy of the Bluegrass, John V. Irwin, Margaret Norris Ward, Ann B. Greis, Carol C. Deen, Valerie C. Cooley, Alice A. Auvenshine, Rhea A. Taylor, C. A. Coleman.
Publisher: Child Development Centers of the Bluegrass, Inc. [No reply from publisher; status unknown].
Cross References: For reviews by Michael J. Roznowski and Zona R. Weeks, see 9:615 (1 reference); see also T3:1322 (1 reference).

TEST REFERENCES

1. Leonard, L. B. (1986). Conversational replies of children with specific language impairment. *Journal of Speech and Hearing Research, 29,* 114-119.

[1451]

Library Skills.
Purpose: Designed to assess knowledge of library organization.
Population: High school.
Publication Date: No date.
Scores: 7 areas: Dewey Decimal System, Card Catalog, Parts of a Book, Reader's Guide, Magazines, Reference Books, Bibliography.
Administration: Group.
Manual: No manual.
Price Data, 1990: $8.95 per complete kit including 25 test booklets and answer key; $.36 per test booklet.
Time: Administration time not reported.
Author: Clarice Schmeiser.
Publisher: Stratton-Christian Press, Inc.

[1452]

The Life Adjustment Inventory.
Purpose: Developed to survey "the extent to which a secondary school curriculum meets the needs of all its pupils."
Population: Grades 9–12.
Publication Date: 1951.
Scores, 14: General Feeling of Adjustment to the Curriculum, Reading and Study Skills, Communica-

tion and Listening Skills, General Social Skills and Etiquette, Boy-Girl Relationships, Religion/Morals/ Ethics, Functional Citizenship, Vocational Orientation and Preparation, Education for Physical and Mental Health, Education for Family Living, Orientation to Science, Consumer Education, Development of Appreciation for and Creativity in the Arts, Education for Wise Use of Leisure Time.
Administration: Group.
Price Data: Available from publisher.
Time: (20–25) minutes.
Authors: Ronald C. Doll and J. Wayne Wrightstone.
Publisher: Psychometric Affiliates.
Cross References: See P:145 (1 reference); for reviews by John W. M. Rothney and Helen Schacter, see 4:67.

[1453]

Life Event Scales for Children and Adolescents.
Purpose: "To quantify the environmental stress the child or adolescent has had to cope with in the recent past."
Population: Ages 6–11, 12 and over.
Publication Date: 1981.
Acronym: LES-C, LES-A.
Scores, 4: 3, 6, 9, 12 months.
Administration: Group.
Levels, 2: Children, adolescent.
Manual: No manual.
Price Data: Not available.
Time: (5) minutes.
Author: R. Dean Coddington.
Publisher: Stress Research Company [No reply from publisher; status unknown].

TEST REFERENCES

1. Lorimor, R. J., Kaplan, H. B., & Pokorny, A. D. (1985). Self-derogation and adjustment in the community: A longitudinal study of psychiatric patients. *American Journal of Psychiatry, 142,* 1442-1446.
2. Wertlieb, D., Weigel, C., & Feldstein, M. (1987). Stress, social support, and behavior symptoms in middle childhood. *Journal of Clinical Child Psychology, 16,* 204-211.
3. Warren-Sohlberg, L., & Jason, L. A. (1992). How the reason for a school move relates to school adjustment. *Psychology in the Schools, 29*(1), 78-84.

[1454]

Life Experiences Checklist.
Purpose: Designed to assess a client's quality of life.
Population: Adults.
Publication Date: 1990.
Acronym: LEC.
Scores, 6: Home, Leisure, Relationships, Freedom, Opportunities, Total.
Administration: Individual.
Price Data, 1990: £28.75 per complete set; £17.25 per 25 checklists.
Time: (10) minutes.
Author: Alastair Ager.
Publisher: NFER-Nelson Publishing Co., Ltd. [England].

[1455]

Life Roles Inventory.
Purpose: "Designed to assess the importance of life-career values and the relative importance of five major life roles."
Population: Junior high students–adults.
Publication Date: 1985.
Acronym: LRI.
Subtests: 2 subtests.
Administration: Group.
Price Data: Available from publisher.
Foreign Language Edition: French edition ('85) available.
Authors: George W. Fitzsimmons, Donald Macnab, and Catherine Casserly.
Publisher: Psychometrics Canada Ltd. [Canada].

a) VALUES SCALE.
Scores, 20: Ability Utilization, Achievement, Advancement, Aesthetics, Altruism, Authority, Autonomy, Creativity, Economics, Life Style, Personal Development, Physical Activity, Prestige, Risk, Social Interaction, Social Relations, Variety, Working Conditions, Cultural Identity, Physical Prowess.
Time: (20–25) minutes.

b) SALIENCE INVENTORY.
Scores, 15: 5 scores (Studying, Working, Community Service, Home and Family, Leisure) in each of 3 areas (Participation, Commitment, Role Values).
Time: (25–30) minutes.

[1456]

Life Skills, Forms 1 and 2.
Purpose: Designed to assess students' functional competencies in reading and math.
Population: Grades 9–12 and adults.
Publication Dates: 1979–80.
Scores, 3: Reading, Mathematics, Total.
Administration: Group.
Forms, 2: 1, 2.
Price Data, 1989: $69 per 35 tests (specify Form 1 or 2); $43.50 per 100 MRC answer sheets; $88.50 per self-mark answer sheets; $52.50 per 100 NCS answer sheets; $21 per technical supplement; $6 per examination kit; $5.25 per examiner's manual ('80, 32 pages).
Time: (80–100) minutes.
Comments: Separate answer sheets (MRC, NCS, 7010, carbon-backed, self-mark) must be used.
Authors: Kenneth Majer and Dena Wadell.
Publisher: The Riverside Publishing Co.
Cross References: For reviews by Gwyneth M. Boodoo and Philip L. Smith, see 9:618.

[1457]

Life Space Analysis Profile.
Purpose: Evaluates factors that contribute to life space, including self image, home, family and work/career.
Population: Adults.

Publication Date: 1991.
Acronym: LSAP.
Scores: 18 scores in 3 major areas: Self Space (Activity, Interpersonal Relationships, Being Alone, Emotional, Body, Psychological), Home/Family Space (Financial, Leisure, Physical Environment, Origins, Mate, Offspring), Work Space (Career, Compensation, Relationships, Skills, Climate, Goals).
Administration: Individual.
Price Data, 1993: $40 for IBM software (specify 5.25-inch or 3.5-inch).
Time: (30) minutes.
Comments: PC-based; confidential.
Author: John W. Baker, II.
Publisher: XICOM, Inc.

[1458]

Life Style Questionnaire.
Purpose: To provide information regarding vocational interests and attitudes.
Population: Ages 14 and over.
Publication Date: No date on test materials.
Acronym: LSQ.
Scores: 13 scales: Expressive/Imaginative, Logical/Analytical, Managerial/Enterprising, Precise/Administrative, Active/Concrete, Supportive/Social, Risk Taking/Uncertainty, Perseverance/Determination, Self Evaluation, Sensitivity/Other Awareness, Affiliation, Degree to Which a Vocation is Associated with Self Fulfilment, Degree of Certainty.
Administration: Group or individual.
Price Data, 1993: £35 per specimen set; £3.50 per answer sheet and graph; £6.50 per questionnaire booklet; £25 per manual (26 pages); £300 per computer software version.
Time: Administration time not reported.
Author: James S. Barrett.
Publisher: The Test Agency Ltd. [England].
Cross Reference: For a review by Robert B. Slaney, see 9:169.

[1459]

Life Styles Inventory.
Purpose: Designed to assess an individual's thinking and behavioral styles.
Population: Adults.
Publication Dates: 1973–90.
Acronym: LSI.
Administration: Individual.
Price Data: Price data for test materials including Leader's Guide ('89, 211 pages), Self-Development Guide ('89, 75 pages), and Description by Others Self-Development Guide ('90, 123 pages) available from publisher.
Time: (20–25) minutes.
Author: J. Clayton Lafferty.
Publisher: Human Synergistics, Inc.

a) LSI1: LIFE STYLES INVENTORY (SELF DESCRIPTION).
Scores, 12: Constructive Styles (Achievement, Self-Actualizing, Humanistic-Encouraging, Affili-

ative), Passive/Defensive Styles (Approval, Conventional, Dependent, Avoidance), Aggressive/Defensive Styles (Oppositional, Power, Competitive, Perfectionistic).

b) LSI2: LIFE STYLES INVENTORY (DESCRIPTION BY OTHERS).

Scores, 12: Same as for *a* above.

Comments: Administered to manager and 4 or 5 others.

Cross References: For reviews by Henry M. Cherrick and Linda M. DuBois, see 9:620 (1 reference).

TEST REFERENCES

1. Cooke, R. A., & Rousseau, D. M. (1983). Relationship of life events and personal orientations to symptoms of strain. *Journal of Applied Psychology, 68,* 446-458.
2. Leak, G. K., Millard, R. J., Perry, N. W., & Williams, D. E. (1985). An investigation of the nomological network of social interest. *Journal of Research in Personality, 19,* 197-207.
3. Cooke, R. A., Rousseau, D. M., & Lafferty, J. C. (1987). Thinking and behavioral styles: Consistency between self-descriptions and descriptions by others. *Educational and Psychological Measurement, 47*(3), 815-823.
4. Ware, M. E., & Perry, N. W. (1987). Facilitating growth in a personal development course. *Psychological Reports, 60,* 491-500.
5. Leak, G. K. (1991). An examination of the construct validity of the social anhedonia scale. *Journal of Personality Assessment, 56,* 84-95.
6. Levin, J. (1991). The circumplex pattern of the Life Styles Inventory: A reanalysis. *Educational and Psychological Measurement, 51,* 567-572.

[1460]

Life Themes Inventory.

Purpose: Describes "each person's view of his own developmental status, taken along a life-span perspective."

Population: Ages 14 and over.

Publication Dates: 1981-82.

Acronym: LTI.

Scores: 14 primary outcome scales: 10 primary life themes (Self-Integration, Self-Sustenance, Self-Perception, Self-Gratification, Self-Mobilization, Self-Regard, Self-Discipline, Self-Discovery, Self-Idealism, Self-Purification) plus 4 grouped themes (Intrapersonal, Interactional, Transpersonal, Cumulative).

Administration: Group.

Versions, 2: Diagnostic, Screening.

Price Data: Not available.

Time: (180) minutes for diagnostic version; (45) minutes for screening version.

Authors: Kelly R. Bennett, William H. Seauer, and Gina Caeglio.

Publisher: Life Themes, Inc. [No reply from publisher; status unknown].

[1461]

Lifestyle Assessment Questionnaire.

Purpose: Provides individuals with a measurement of their lifestyle status in various wellness categories, offers a health risk appraisal component that lists the individual's top ten risks of death, projects an achievable health age, makes suggestions for lifestyle improvement, and offers a stimulus for positive lifestyle change by providing a guide to successful implementation of that change.

Population: Adults with a minimum of 10th grade education.

Publication Dates: 1978-91.

Scores, 16: Physical (Exercise, Nutrition, Self-Care, Vehicle Safety, Drug Usage), Social/Environmental, Emotional (Emotional Awareness and Acceptance, Emotional Management), Intellectual, Occupational, Spiritual, Actual Age, Appraised Health Age, Achievable Health Age, Top 10 Risks of Death, Lifestyle Improvement Suggestions.

Administration: Group.

Price Data, 1993: $3 per literature set including questionnaire, results folder, Behavior Change Guide, and scannable answer sheet; $.25 per scannable answer sheet; $10 per individual National Wellness Processing Center scoring; $1,995 per software program and license.

Time: (45–60) minutes.

Comments: Computer scoring or scoring by National Wellness Institute available; information on up to six wellness areas included in scoring report; individual and group reports available.

Authors: Dennis Elsenrath, Bill Hettler, and Fred Leafgren.

Publisher: National Wellness Institute.

TEST REFERENCES

1. DeStefano, T. J., & Harger, B. (1990). Promoting the wellness life-style on a college campus. *Journal of College Student Development, 31,* 461-462.
2. DeStefano, T. J., & Richardson, P. (1992). The relationship of paper-and-pencil wellness measures to objective physiological indexes. *Journal of Counseling and Development, 71*(2), 226-230.
3. Palombi, B. J. (1992). Psychometric properties of wellness instruments. *Journal of Counseling and Development, 71*(2), 221-225.

[1462]

Light's Retention Scale [Revised Edition 1991].

Purpose: Aids the school professional in determining whether the student would benefit from grade retention.

Population: Grades K–12.

Publication Dates: 1981-91.

Acronym: LRS.

Scores, 20: Sex of Student, Student's Age, Knowledge of English Language, Physical Size, Present Grade Placement, Previous Grade Retentions, Siblings, Parents' School Participation, Experiential Background, Transiency, School Attendance, Estimate of Intelligence, History of Learning Disabilities, Present Level of Academic Achievement, Student's Attitude About Possible Retention, Motivation to Complete School Tasks, Immature Behavior, Emotional Problems, History of Delinquency, Total.

Administration: Individual.

Price Data, 1994: $63 per complete test kit including manual ('91, 78 pages), 50 recording forms, and 50 parent guides; $20 per manual; $22 per 50 recording forms; $18 per 50 parent guides; $14 per 25 parent consent forms; $20 per specimen set.

Time: (10–15) minutes.

Comments: Ratings by teachers and parents; a non-psychometric instrument used as a counseling tool with a specific retention candidate.

Author: H. Wayne Light.

Publisher: Academic Therapy Publications.

Cross References: For reviews by Bruce K. Alcorn and Frederic J. Medway, see 11:208 (2 references); for reviews by Michael J. Hannafin and Patti L. Harrison of an earlier edition, see 9:622; see also T3:1328 (1 reference).

[1463]

Ligondè Equivalence Test.

Purpose: Measurement of "gains and deterioration of school knowledge."

Population: Adults who left elementary or secondary school 15 to 20 years ago.

Publication Date: 1967.

Acronym: LET.

Scores: Total score only.

Administration: Group.

Price Data, 1993: Can$20 per 25 tests; $15 per specimen set (must be purchased to obtain manual [11 pages]).

Time: 15(20) minutes.

Comments: Also called School Equivalence Test.

Authors: Paultre Ligondè.

Publisher: Institute of Psychological Research, Inc. [Canada].

Cross References: For a review by J. Douglas Ayers, see 8:21.

[1464]

The Lincoln-Oseretsky Motor Development Scale.

Purpose: "Designed to test the motor ability of children."

Population: Ages 6–14.

Publication Dates: 1948–56.

Scores: Total score only.

Administration: Individual.

Price Data, 1994: $235 per complete kit including 50 record blanks and manual ('48, 79 pages); $20 per 50 record blanks; $20 per 50 mazes; $20 per 50 concentric circles; $25 per manual.

Time: Administration time not reported.

Comments: Revision of Oseretsky Tests of Motor Proficiency.

Author: William Sloan.

Publisher: Stoelting Co.

Cross References: See T3:1331 (5 references) and T2:1895 (27 references); for a review by Anna Espenschade, see 5:767 (10 references).

TEST REFERENCES

1. Hoy, E., Weiss, G., Minde, K., & Cohen, N. (1978). The hyperactive child at adolescence: Cognitive, emotional, and social functioning. *Journal of Abnormal Child Psychology, 6,* 311-324.
2. Winsberg, B. G., Bialer, I., Kupietz, S., Botti, E., & Balka, E. B. (1980). Home vs hospital care of children with behavior disorders: A controlled investigation. *Archives of General Psychiatry, 37,* 413-418.
3. Wender, P. H., Reimherr, F. W., & Wood, D. R. (1981). Attention deficit disorder ("minimal brain dysfunction") in adults: A replication study of diagnosis and drug treatment. *Archives of General Psychiatry, 38,* 449-456.
4. Lovrich, D., & Stamm, J. S. (1983). Event-related potential and behavioral correlates of attention in reading retardation. *Journal of Clinical Neuropsychology, 5,* 13-37.
5. Dudek, S. Z., Strobel, M., & Thomas, A. D. (1987). Chronic learning problems and maturation. *Perceptual and Motor Skills, 64,* 407-429.

[1465]

Lindamood Auditory Conceptualization Test, Revised Edition.

Purpose: To measure "speech sound discrimination and perception of number, order and sameness or difference of speech sounds in sequences."

Population: Preschool children and over.

Publication Dates: 1971–79.

Acronym: LACT.

Scores, 3: Isolated Sounds in Sequence, Sounds Within a Syllable Pattern, Total.

Administration: Individual.

Forms, 2: A, B.

Price Data, 1987: $42 per complete kit including 50 each of tests A and B, 2 examiner's cue sheets (English and Spanish), 24 wooden blocks, cassette, and manual ('79, 80 pages); $10 per 50 each of tests A and B.

Time: (10–35) minutes.

Comments: No reading by examinees.

Authors: Charles H. Lindamood and Patricia C. Lindamood.

Publisher: The Riverside Publishing Co.

Cross References: For reviews by Nicholas G. Bountress and James R. Cox, see 9:623 (1 reference).

TEST REFERENCES

1. Leong, C. K. (1984). Cognitive processing, language awareness and reading in grade 2 and grade 4 children. *Contemporary Educational Psychology, 9,* 369-383.
2. Torgesen, J. K., & Wagner, R. K. (1992). Toward development of a kindergarten group test for phonological awareness. *Journal of Research and Development in Education, 25,* 111-120.

[1466]

Linguistic Awareness in Reading Readiness.

Purpose: Designed for determining individual strengths and weaknesses "with regard to their understanding of the linguistic concepts that they need for reasoning about the tasks of reading instruction."

Population: Grades K–1.

Publication Date: 1983.

Acronym: LARR.

Scores: Total scores only.

Administration: Group.

Forms, 2: A, B.

Parts, 3: Recognizing Literacy Behaviour, Understanding Literacy Functions, Technical Language of Literacy.

Price Data, 1989: £10.10 per 10 booklets and 1 class record form for Part 1, Form A or B; £8.65 per 10 booklets and 1 class record form for Parts 2 or 3, Form A or B; £1.75 per class record forms for Parts 1, 2, and 3; £12.65 per manual (36 pages); £19.55 per specimen set (1 each of the 3 Form A booklets, the 3 Form B booklets, the 3 record forms, and 1 manual).

Time: (20–25) minutes for each part.
Authors: John Downing, Douglas Ayers, and Brian Schaefer.
Publisher: NFER-Nelson Publishing Co., Ltd. [England].

TEST REFERENCES

1. Downing, J. (1984). A source of cognitive confusion for beginning readers: Learning in a second language. *The Reading Teacher, 37*, 366-370.
2. Ledger, G. W. (1985). Pictograph reading: metacognition and deliberate strategic control. *National Reading Conference Yearbook, 34*, 219-226.
3. Ryan, E. B., Ledger, G. W., & Weed, K. A. (1987). Acquisition and transfer of an integrative imagery strategy by young children. *Child Development, 58*, 443-452.

[1467]

Listening Comprehension.

Purpose: Assessment of listening comprehension via the examinee's ability to carry out specific directions.
Population: Grades 1–3.
Publication Date: 1976.
Scores, 7: Following Directions, Sequencing, Using Content in Listening, Finding Main Ideas, Forming Sensory Images from Oral Description, Sensing Emotion and Moods Through Word Usage and Manner of Delivery, Making Inferences and Drawing Conclusions.
Administration: Group.
Price Data, 1988: $6 per Informal Inventories booklet including 11 spirit duplicating masters, teacher's key, and manual (26 pages); $6 per Games and Activities booklet (43 pages).
Time: Administration time not reported.
Authors: Susan Hohl and B. Cheney Edwards.
Publisher: Educators Publishing Service, Inc.
Cross References: For a review by William A. Mehrens, see 9:625.

[1468]

Listening Comprehension Test.

Purpose: To estimate a student's ability to comprehend orally presented basic English structures.
Population: Nonnative speakers of English who wish to pursue academic work at universities where English is the medium of instruction.
Publication Date: 1986.
Acronym: LCT.
Scores: Total score only.
Administration: Group.
Forms, 3: 4, 5, 6 (equivalent forms).
Price Data, 1993: $46 per complete kit including 20 test booklets, 3 scoring stencils, 100 answer sheets, cassette tape, and manual (17 pages); $5 per 20 test booklets; $6 per scoring stencils; $5 per 100 answer sheets; $12 per cassette; $6 per manual; no charge for specimen set.
Time: 15(20) minutes.
Comments: Created for use as one of the component tests of the Michigan English Language Assessment Battery.

Authors: H. Koba, M. Spaan, and L. Strowe.
Publisher: English Language Institute, The University of Michigan.

[1469]

Listening Comprehension Test in English.

Purpose: To provide an estimate of oral ability in English.
Population: South African "Black" pupils in Standard 5 and Standard 8.
Publication Date: 1979.
Scores: Total score only.
Administration: Group.
Levels, 2: 2 forms: A, B.
Price Data: Available from publisher.
Time: [50–55] minutes.
Comments: Cassette player necessary for administration.
Author: Ester van der Schyff.
Publisher: Human Sciences Research Council [South Africa].
a) STANDARD 5.
Population: South African "Black" pupils in Standard 5.
b) STANDARD 8.
Population: South African "Black" pupils in Standard 8.

[1470]

The Listening for Meaning Test.

Purpose: Constructed as a measure of receptive language through the recognition of pictures.
Population: Ages 3-0 to 18–11.
Publication Dates: 1981–82.
Acronym: LFMT.
Scores: Total score only.
Administration: Individual.
Price Data, 1989: £13.80 per complete kit including book of plates, 50 record sheets, and manual ('82, 12 pages); £9.50 per book of plates; £3.45 per 50 record sheets; £1.45 per manual.
Time: Administration time not reported.
Author: M. A. Brimer.
Publisher: Educational Evaluation Enterprises [England].

[1471]

Literature Tests/Objective and Essay.

Purpose: To assess students' literal and interpretive comprehension of over 200 works of contemporary and classical literature.
Population: Middle school and high school.
Publication Dates: 1929–90.
Scores: Total score only.
Administration: Group.
Manual: No manual.
Price Data, 1994: $2.50 per 50-question test; $3.50 per 100-question test; $3.50 per essay test.
Time: Administration time not reported.
Comments: Over 700 tests on specific literary works;

formerly called Book Review Tests and Objective Tests in English.
Author: Perfection Learning Corp.
Publisher: Perfection Learning Corp.

[1472]
Living in the Reader's World: Locator Test.
Purpose: Diagnose nonproficient reader's appropriate starting point in a 4-book adult education reading program.
Population: Adults at reading grade levels 2.0–6.0.
Publication Date: 1983.
Administration: Group.
Price Data: Not available.
Time: Administration time not reported.
Comments: Upward extension of the Maryland/Baltimore County Design for Adult Basic Education.
Author: Cambridge, The Adult Education Co.
Publisher: Simon & Schuster Higher Education Group [No reply from publisher; status unknown].

[1473]
Living Language.
Purpose: "Remedial teaching programme, concentrating on spoken language, for use with all children who are failing to develop adequate language skills"; includes assessment of prelanguage/language skills for placement in this program.
Population: Language-impaired children.
Publication Date: 1985.
Scores: No scores.
Administration: Individual.
Levels, 3: Pre-Language, Starter, Main Programme.
Manual: No manual.
Price Data, 1989: £55.20 per complete kit including general manual (57 pages), subtest manuals (Before Words [31 pages], First Words [16 pages], Putting Words Together [67 pages], set of 10 record booklets (Pre-Language [8 pages], Starter Programme [8 pages], Main Programme [12 pages]), and assessment pictures (50 pages); £4.45 per 10 Pre-Language or Starter Programme record booklets; £5.45 per 10 Main Programme record booklets; £10.10 per general handbook; £5.75 per Before Words manual; £12.10 per First Words or Putting Words Together manual; £48.30 per Introductory Video.
Time: Administration time variable.
Comments: General manual title is Teaching Spoken Language; subtest manual titles are Before Words, First Words, and Putting Words Together; test booklet titles are Pre-Language Record Booklet, Starter Programme Record Booklet, and Main Programme (Level I) Record Booklet; subtests available as separates.
Author: Ann Locke.
Publisher: NFER-Nelson Publishing Co., Ltd. [England].

[1474]
LOCO (Learning Opportunities Coordination): A Scale for the Assessment of Coordinated Learning Opportunities in Living Units for People with a Handicap.
Purpose: Designed "for indicating to what extent a Living Unit for people with handicaps is able to contribute significantly to their social and personal development and to maintain a level of reasonable independence."
Population: Residents of any type of living units where people with a handicap live with the assistance of care givers.
Publication Date: 1987.
Acronym: LOCO.
Scores, 4: Basic Training Conditions, Essential Items, Additional Items, Total.
Administration: Group.
Price Data, 1993: $20 (U.S.) per complete test.
Time: Administration time not reported.
Comments: Can be used in conjunction with P-A-C (Progress Assessment Chart) (2134).
Authors: H. C. Gunzburg and A. L. Gunzburg.
Publisher: SEFA (Publications) Ltd. [England].

[1475]
Loewenstein Occupational Therapy Cognitive Assessment.
Purpose: "A cognitive battery of tests for both primary assessments and ongoing evaluation in the occupational therapy treatment of brain-injured patients."
Population: Ages 6 to 12 and brain-injured adults.
Publication Date: 1990.
Acronym: LOTCA.
Scores: 21 tests in 4 areas: Orientation (Orientation for Place, Orientation for Time), Visual and Spatial Perception (Object Identification, Shapes Identification, Overlapping Figures, Object Constancy, Spatial Perception, Praxis), Visual Motor Organization (Copying Geometric Forms, Reproduction of a Two-Dimensional Model, Pegboard Construction, Colored Block Design, Plain Block Design, Reproduction of a Puzzle, Drawing a Clock), Thinking Operations (Categorization, ROC Unstructured, ROC Structured, Pictorial Sequence A, Pictorial Sequence B, Geometric Sequence).
Administration: Individual.
Price Data, 1993: $198 per complete kit including manual (56 pages), test booklet, and other materials packed in a plastic carrying case.
Time: (30–45) minutes.
Authors: Loewenstein Rehabilitation Hospital;, Malka Itzkovich (manual), Betty Elazar (manual), Sarah Averbuch (manual), Naomi Katz (principal researcher), and Levy Rahmani (advisor).
Publisher: Maddak Inc.

[1476]
Logical Reasoning.
Purpose: Designed to measure sensitivity to logical

necessity, consistency and inconsistency, and relationships.

Population: Grades 9–16 and adults.
Publication Date: 1955.
Scores: Total score only.
Administration: Group.
Parts, 2: 1, 2.
Price Data, 1989: $17.25 per 25 test booklets; $4.50 per scoring key; $10 per 50 answer sheets; $1.50 per manual (4 pages); $2.50 per specimen set.
Time: 20(25) minutes.
Comments: Two parallel parts may be administered separately or together.
Authors: Alfred F. Hertzka and J. P. Guilford.
Publisher: Consulting Psychologists Press, Inc.
Cross References: See T2:1761 (10 references); for reviews by Duncan Howie and Charles R. Langmuir, see 5:694 (1 reference).

TEST REFERENCES

1. Bright, G. W., Harvey, J. G., & Wheeler, M. M. (1983). Use of a game to instruct on logical reasoning. *School Science and Mathematics, 83*, 396-405.
2. Stefanich, G. P., Unruh, R. D., Perry, B., & Phillips, G. (1983). Convergent validity of group tests of cognitive development. *Journal of Research in Science Teaching, 20*, 557-563.
3. Isaacson, D. K., & Williams, J. D. (1984). The relationship of conceptual systems theory and Piagetian theory. *The Journal of Psychology, 117*, 3-6.

[1477]

The Lollipop Test: A Diagnostic Screening Test of School Readiness—Revised.
Purpose: "A screening test to identify the child's deficits (and strengths) in readiness skills."
Population: First grade entrants.
Publication Dates: 1981–89.
Scores, 5: Identification of Colors and Shapes and Copying Shapes, Picture Description and Position and Spatial Recognition, Identification of Numbers and Counting, Identification of Letters and Writing, Total.
Administration: Individual.
Price Data, 1990: $29.95 per complete kit including 5 test booklets, stimulus cards, and manual ('89, 35 pages); $24.95 per 25 test booklets; $10.95 per set of stimulus cards; $14.95 per manual.
Foreign Language Edition: Available in Spanish.
Time: (15–20) minutes.
Author: Alex L. Chew.
Publisher: Humanics Publishing Group.
Cross References: For reviews by Sylvia T. Johnson and Albert C. Oosterhof, see 11:210 (5 references); for reviews by Isabel L. Beck and Janet A. Norris of an earlier edition, see 9:629.

TEST REFERENCES

1. Eno, L., & Woehlke, P. (1987). Comparison of achievement in half-day, every-day and all-day, alternate-day early childhood programs for handicapped children. *Psychological Reports, 60*, 923-927.
2. Chew, A. L., & Lang, W. S. (1993). Concurrent validation and regression line comparisons on the Spanish edition of The Lollipop Test (La Prueba Lollipop) on a bilingual population. *Educational and Psychological Measurement, 53*, 173-182.

[1478]

London House Personnel Selection Inventory.
Purpose: "Helps identify individuals who are likely to be honest and have positive attitudes toward work, safety and customer service."
Population: Job applicants.
Publication Dates: 1975–80.
Acronym: PSI.
Scores: 14 scales: Honesty, Supervision Attitudes, Tenure, Employee/Customer Relations, Drug Avoidance, Work Values, Safety, Math, Emotional Stability, Nonviolence, Productivity, Responsibility, Applicant Employability Index, Detailed Personal and Behavioral History.
Administration: Group.
Forms: 19 versions available including non-integrity test versions.
Price Data: Available from publisher.
Time: Administration time not reported.
Author: SRA/London House.
Publisher: SRA/London House.
Cross References: For a review by William I. Sauser, see 9:631; see also T3:1339 (2 references).

TEST REFERENCES

1. Werner, S. H., & Ash, P. (1988). Reading grade level of the London House Personnel Selection Inventory series (PSI). *Educational and Psychological Measurement, 48*, 1105- 1110.

[1479]

London Reading Test.
Purpose: Constructed to assess "reading attainment."
Population: Ages 10-7 to 12-4.
Publication Dates: 1978–80.
Acronym: LRT.
Scores: Total score only.
Administration: Group.
Forms, 2: A, B.
Price Data: Available from publisher.
Time: (60) minutes.
Authors: Margaret Biscoe, Ced Bradshaw, Sheila Clarke, Miles Halliwell, David Morgan, Theresa Nunn, Helen Quigley, and Irene Zelickman.
Publisher: NFER-Nelson Publishing Co., Ltd. [England].
Cross References: For reviews by Amos L. Hahn and David M. Memory, see 9:632.

TEST REFERENCES

1. Hewison, J. (1988). The long term effectiveness of parental involvement in reading: A follow-up to the Haringey Reading Project. *British Journal of Educational Psychology, 58*, 184-190.

[1480]

Longitudinal Interval Follow-up Evaluation, 2nd Edition.
Purpose: "To provide a longitudinal picture of the subject's psychiatric course and psychosocial functioning over a six month period."
Population: Individuals who have received treatment for depression.

Publication Dates: 1979–83.
Acronym: LIFE II.
Scores: 5 areas: Course of Psychopathology, Treatment for Psychiatric Condition, Medical Illness and Treatment, Psychosocial Functioning, Monthly Global Assessment of Symptoms and Functioning.
Administration: Individual structured interview.
Price Data: Not available.
Time: Administration time not reported.
Authors: Martin B. Keller, Robert W. Shapiro, et al.
Publisher: Boston Massachusetts General Hospital [No reply from publisher; status unknown].
Cross References: See 9:633 (2 references).

TEST REFERENCES

1. Coryell, W., Lavori, P., Endicott, J., Keller, M., & VanEerdewegh, M. (1984). Outcome in schizoaffective, psychotic, and nonpsychotic depression: Course during a six-to 24 month follow-up. *Archives of General Psychiatry, 41,* 787-791.
2. Hirschfeld, R. M. A., Klerman, G. L., Clayton, P. J., Keller, M. B., & Andreasen, N. C. (1984). Personality and gender-related differences in depression. *Journal of Affective Disorders, 7,* 211-221.
3. Gonzales, L. R., Lewinsohn, P. M., & Clarke, G. N. (1985). Longitudinal follow-up of unipolar depressives: An investigation of predictors of relapse. *Journal of Consulting and Clinical Psychology, 53,* 461-469.
4. Coryell, W., & Zimmerman, M. (1987). Progress in the classification of functional psychoses. *American Journal of Psychiatry, 144,* 1471-1474.
5. Grove, W. M., Andreasen, N. C., Young, M., Endicott, J., Keller, M. B., Hirschfeld, R. M. A., & Reich, T. (1987). Isolation and characterization of a nuclear depressive syndrome. *Psychological Medicine, 17,* 471-484.
6. Keller, M. B., Lavori, P. W., Friedman, B., Nielsen, E., Endicott, J., McDonald-Scott, P., & Andreasen, N. C. (1987). The Longitudinal Interval Follow-Up Evaluation: A comprehensive method for assessing outcome in prospective longitudinal studies. *Archives of General Psychiatry, 44,* 540-548.
7. Reich, J., Noyes, R., Jr., Hirschfeld, R., Coryell, W., & O'Gorman, T. (1987). State and personality in depressed and panic patients. *American Journal of Psychiatry, 144,* 181-187.
8. Coryell, W., Endicott, J., Andreasen, N. C., Keller, M. B., Clayton, P. J., Hirschfeld, R. M. A., Scheftner, W. A., & Winokur, G. (1988). Depression and panic attacks: The significance of overlap as reflected in follow-up and family study data. *American Journal of Psychiatry, 145,* 293-300.
9. Clark, D. C., Gibbons, R. D., Fawcett, J., & Scheftner, W. A. (1989). What is the mechanism by which suicide attempts predispose to later suicide attempts? A mathematical model. *Journal of Abnormal Psychology, 98,* 42-49.
10. Coryell, W., Keller, M., Endicott, J., Andreasen, N., Clayton, P., & Hirschfeld, R. (1989). Bipolar II illness: Course and outcome over a five-year period. *Psychological Medicine, 19,* 129-141.
11. Hasin, D. S., Endicott, J., & Keller, M. B. (1989). RDC alcoholism in patients with major affective syndromes: Two-year course. *American Journal of Psychiatry, 146,* 318-323.
12. Coryell, W., Endicott, J., & Keller, M. (1990). Outcome of patients with chronic affective disorder: A five-year follow-up. *American Journal of Psychiatry, 147,* 1627-1633.
13. Rohde, P., Lewinsohn, P. M., & Seeley, J. R. (1990). Are people changed by the experience of having an episode of depression? A further test of the scar hypothesis. *Journal of Abnormal Psychology, 99,* 264-271.
14. O'Connell, R. A., Mayo, J. A., Flatow, L., Cuthbertson, B., & O'Brien, B. E. (1991). Outcome of bipolar disorder on long-term treatment with lithium. *British Journal of Psychiatry, 159,* 123-129.
15. Coryell, W., Endicott, J., & Winokur, G. (1992). Anxiety syndromes as epiphenomena of primary major depression: Outcome and familial psychopathology. *American Journal of Psychiatry, 149,* 100-107.
16. Goering, P. N., Lancee, W. J., & Freeman, S. J. J. (1992). Marital support and recovery from depression. *British Journal of Psychiatry, 160,* 76-82.
17. Scott, J., Eccleston, D., & Boys, R. (1992). Can we predict the persistence of depression? *British Journal of Psychiatry, 161,* 633-637.

Looking at MySELF.

Purpose: Designed to help students "build self-esteem."
Population: Grades 3–6, Grades 7–12.
Publication Date: 1991–93.
Scores: Total score only.
Administration: Group.
Forms, 2: Form I, Form II.
Price Data, 1993: $42.50 per 25 reusable booklets and 25 consumable activity folders; $9.25 per 25 additional consumable activity folders; $32 per 100 consumable activity folders; $4.95 per audio cassette tape; $24.50 per 5 self-esteem posters; $69.95 per software packages (IBM, Apple, or Macintosh).
Time: (120–180) minutes or in steps in a weekly program.
Author: CFKR Career Materials, Inc.
Publisher: CFKR Career Materials, Inc.

Lorimer Braille Recognition Test: A Test of Ability in Reading Braille Contractions.

Purpose: Designed to test blind children's performance in reading Braille contractions.
Population: Students (ages 7–13) in grade 2 Braille.
Publication Date: 1962.
Scores: Total score only.
Administration: Group.
Price Data: Price data, including manual (27 pages) (available in printed form or Braille), available from publisher.
Time: Administration time not reported.
Author: John Lorimer.
Publisher: Association for the Education and Welfare of the Visually Handicapped [England].
Cross References: See 6:854 (1 reference).

LOTE Reading and Listening Tests.

Purpose: Designed to assess achievement in a foreign language.
Population: Secondary school students in their second year of learning another language.
Publication Dates: 1990–91.
Scores, 2: Listening, Reading.
Administration: Group.
Editions, 3: French, Japanese, Modern Greek.
Price Data, 1990: A$25 per test pack including 10 test booklets, 10 magazines, photocopy master for answer/profile sheet, and score key (select French, Japanese, or Modern Greek); A$12 per cassette (select French, Japanese, or Modern Greek); A$25 per manual ('91, 23 pages); A$30 per specimen set (select French, Japanese, or Modern Greek).
Time: 42(50) minutes.
Comments: Cassette recorder necessary for administration.
Author: Susan A. Zammit.

Publisher: Australian Council for Educational Research Ltd. [Australia].

[1484]
Louisville Behavior Checklist.
Purpose: "Designed to help parents conceptualize and communicate concerns about their children."
Population: Ages 4–6, 7–12, 13–17.
Publication Dates: 1977–84.
Acronym: LBC.
Administration: Group.
Price Data, 1993: $200 per complete kit including materials for all 3 forms; $99.50 per complete kit of any 1 form; $12.50 per 25 questionnaires (specify Form E1, E2, or E3); $29.50 per scoring keys (specify Form E1, E2, or E3); $19.50 per 100 answer-profile sheets; $45 per manual ('84, 124 pages); $195 per microcomputer edition for IBM or Apple; $11 or less per questionnaire scoring service.
Time: Administration time not reported.
Author: Lovick C. Miller.
Publisher: Western Psychological Services.

a) FORM E1.
Population: Ages 4–6.
Scores: 20 scales: Infantile Aggression, Hyperactivity, Antisocial Behavior, Aggression, Social Withdrawal, Sensitivity, Fear, Inhibition, Intellectual Deficit, Immaturity, Cognitive Disability, Normal Irritability, Prosocial Deficit, Rare Deviance, Neurotic Behavior, Psychotic Behavior, Somatic Behavior, Sexual Behavior, School Disturbance Predictor, Severity Level.

b) FORM E2.
Population: Ages 7–12.
Scores: 19 scales: Infantile Aggression, Hyperactivity, Antisocial Behavior, Aggression, Social Withdrawal, Sensitivity, Fear, Inhibition, Academic Disability, Immaturity, Learning Disability, Normal Irritability, Prosocial Deficit, Rare Deviance, Neurotic Behavior, Psychotic Behavior, Somatic Behavior, Sexual Behavior, Severity Level.

c) FORM E3.
Population: Ages 13–17.
Scores: 13 scales: Egocentric-Exploitive, Destructive-Assaultive, Social Delinquency, Adolescent Turmoil, Apathetic Isolation, Neuroticism, Dependent-Inhibited, Academic Disability, Neurological or Psychotic Abnormality, General Pathology, Longitudinal, Severity Level, Total Pathology.
Cross References: For a review by Francis E. Lentz, Jr., see 10:176 (6 references); for a review by Betty N. Gordon, see 9:635 (5 references); see also T3:1343 (1 reference).

TEST REFERENCES

1. Miller, L. C., & Roid, G. H. (1988). Factor-analytically derived scales for the Louisville Behavior Checklist. *Journal of Consulting and Clinical Psychology, 56*, 302-304.
2. Kelly, E. J., & Vactor, J. C. V. (1991). Distinguishing between conduct problem and emotionally disturbed students in secondary school: A five-instrument discriminant analysis. *Psychological Reports, 69*, 303-311.

[1485]
A Love Attitudes Inventory.
Purpose: "Designed to measure attitudes toward love."
Population: Grades 12 and college.
Publication Date: 1971.
Acronym: LAI.
Scores: Total score only.
Administration: Group.
Price Data: Not available.
Time: Administration time not reported.
Author: David Knox.
Publisher: Family Life Publications, Inc. [No reply from publisher; status unknown].
Cross References: For a review by Philip H. Dreyer, see 9:636 (2 references); see also T2:821 (1 reference).

[1486]
Lucas Grason-Stadler Audiometers.
Purpose: Designed to provide basic audiometric screening and diagnosis.
Population: Ages 6 and over.
Publication Dates: 1950–83.
Administration: Individual.
Price Data: Available from publisher.
Author: Lucas Grason-Stadler Co., Inc.
Publisher: Lucas Grason-Stadler Co., Inc.

a) GSI 10 MICROPROCESSOR-BASED AUDIOMETER.
b) GSI 16 AUDIOMETER.
c) GSI 17 AUDIOMETER.
d) GSI 40 INDUSTRIAL HEALTH MONITOR.
Cross References: See T2:2038 (11 references) and 6:946 (6 references).

[1487]
Luria-Nebraska Neuropsychological Battery: Children's Revision.
Purpose: "To diagnose general and specific cognitive deficits, including lateralization and localization of focal brain impairments, and to aid in the planning and evaluation of rehabilitation programs."
Population: Ages 8–12.
Publication Date: 1987.
Acronym: LNNB-C.
Scores, 16: Clinical scales (Motor Functions, Rhythm, Tactile Functions, Visual Functions, Receptive Speech, Expressive Speech, Writing, Reading, Arithmetic, Memory, Intellectual Processes), Optional scales (Spelling, Motor Writing), Summary scales (Pathognomonic, Left Sensorimotor, Right Sensorimotor).
Administration: Individual.
Price Data, 1993: $385 per complete kit including manual (266 pages) and all required materials in a carrying case; $22.50 per 10 patient response booklets; $52.50 per 10 administration and scoring booklets; $200 per Adult Form I cards plus 3 additional cards and audiotape; $53 per supplementary test materials including the 4 additional cards and audiotape; $85 per manual; $19.50 per prepaid WPS Test Report

answer sheet; $275 per 25-use IBM microcomputer disk (specify 5.25-inch or 3.5-inch); $245 per 25-use Apple microcomputer disk; $19.50 each per FAX scoring service.

Time: (90–120) minutes.

Comments: Uses the same stimulus materials, with the addition of 3 extra cards and an audiotape, as Form I of the adult version of the Luria-Nebraska Neuropsychological Battery; other test materials (e.g., tape recorder, stopwatch, eraser, door key) must be supplied by examiner.

Author: Charles J. Golden.

Publisher: Western Psychological Services.

Cross References: For a review by Stephen R. Hooper, see 11:211 (3 references).

TEST REFERENCES

1. Morgan, S. B., & Brown, T. L. (1988). Luria-Nebraska Neuropsychological Battery—Children's Revision: Concurrent validity with three learning disability subtypes. *Journal of Consulting and Clinical Psychology, 56,* 463-466.
2. Faustman, W. O., Bono, M. A., Moses, J. A., & Csernansky, J. G. (1992). Season of birth and neuropsychological impairment in schizophrenia. *Journal of Nervous and Mental Disease, 180,* 644-648.

[1488]

Luria-Nebraska Neuropsychological Battery: Forms I and II.

Purpose: Designed "to diagnose general and specific cognitive deficits, including lateralization and localization of focal brain impairments, and to aid in the planning and evaluation of rehabilitation programs."

Population: Ages 15 and over.

Publication Dates: 1980–85.

Acronym: LNNB.

Scores, 27: Clinical and Summary scales (Motor Functions, Rhythm, Tactile Functions, Visual Functions, Receptive Speech, Expressive Speech, Writing, Reading, Arithmetic, Memory, Intellectual Processes, Intermediate Memory [Form II only], Pathognomonic, Left Hemisphere, Right Hemisphere, Profile Elevation, Impairment), Localization scales (Left Frontal, Left Sensorimotor, Left Parietal-Occipital, Left Temporal, Right Frontal, Right Sensorimotor, Right Parietal-Occipital, Right Temporal), Optional scales (Spelling, Motor Writing), plus 28 Factor scales.

Administration: Individual.

Forms, 2: I, II.

Price Data, 1993: $425 per Form I set including manual ('85, 423 pages), test materials, 10 administration and scoring booklets, 10 patient response booklets, and 2 computer-scored answer sheets; $390 per Form II set; $210 per Form I test materials; $175 per Form II test materials; $52.50 per 10 administration and scoring booklets (Form I); $47.50 per 10 administration and scoring booklets (Form II); $16.50 per 10 patient response booklets (Forms I and II); $125 per manual; $17.25–$19.50 per computer-scored answer sheet; $275 per IBM microdisk for LNNB, Forms I, II, and Children's Revision; $245 per Apple disk (provides scoring only, no interpretation).

Time: (90–150) minutes.

Comments: Uses cards adapted from Luria's Neuropsychological Investigation by Anne-Lise Christensen (Form II includes improved, spiral-bound stimulus cards); tape provided for rhythm subtest; Form I can be scored by hand or computer; Form II is computer scored only.

Authors: Charles J. Golden, Arnold D. Purisch, and Thomas A. Hammeke.

Publisher: Western Psychological Services.

Cross References: For reviews by Jeffrey H. Snow and Wilfred G. van Gorp, see 11:212 (105 references); for a review by Russell L. Adams, see 9:637 (41 references); see also T3:1346 (8 references).

TEST REFERENCES

1. Goldstein, G., & Shelly, C. (1987). The classification of neuropsychological deficit. *Journal of Psychopathology and Behavioral Assessment, 9,* 183-202.
2. Silverstein, M. L., McDonald, C., & Meltzer, H. Y. (1988). Differential patterns of neuropsychological deficit in psychiatric disorders. *Journal of Clinical Psychology, 44,* 412-415.
3. Horton, A. M., Jr., Vaeth, J., & Anilane, J. (1990). Computerized interpretation of the Luria-Nebraska Neuropsychological Battery: A pilot study. *Perceptual and Motor Skills, 71,* 83-86.
4. MacInnes, W. D., Rysavy, J. A., McGill, J. E., Mahoney, P. D., Wilmot, M. D., Frick, M. P., & Elyaderani, M. K. (1990). The usefulness and limitations of CT scans in the diagnosis of Alzheimer's Disease. *International Journal of Clinical Neuropsychology, 12,* 127-130.
5. Moses, J. A., Jr. (1990). Comparative factor structure of the Luria-Nebraska Neuropsychological Battery C3 and C4 scales for neurologic and psychiatric samples. *International Journal of Clinical Neuropsychology, 12,* 116-126.
6. Moses, J. A., Jr. (1990). Comparative factor structure of the Luria-Nebraska Neuropsychological Battery C5 and C6 scales for neurologic and psychiatric samples. *International Journal of Clinical Neuropsychology, 12,* 147-165.
7. Wong, J. L., Schefft, B. K., & Moses, J. A., Jr. (1990). A normative study of the Luria-Nebraska Neuropsychological Battery Form II. *International Journal of Clinical Neuropsychology, 12,* 175-179.
8. Middleton, D. K., Lambert, M. J., & Seggar, L. B. (1991). Neuropsychological rehabilitation: Microcomputer-assisted treatment of brain-injured adults. *Perceptual and Motor Skills, 72,* 527-530.
9. Kern, R. S., Van Gorp, W. G., Cummings, J. L., Brown, W. S., & Osatu, S. S. (1992). Confabulation in Alzheimer's disease. *Brain and Cognition, 19,* 172-182.
10. Raskin, S. A., Borod, J. C., & Tweedy, J. R. (1992). Set-shifting and spatial orientation in patients with Parkinson's disease. *Journal of Clinical and Experimental Neuropsychology, 14,* 801-821.
11. Tsushima, W. T., & Wong, J. M. (1992). Comparison of legal and medical referrals to neuropsychological examination following head injury. *Forensic Reports, 5,* 359-366.
12. Wong, J. L., Schefft, B. K., & Moses, J. A., Jr. (1992). Comparison of empirically derived and predicted standard scores for Form II of the Luria-Nebraska Neuropsychological Battery. *Perceptual and Motor Skills, 75,* 731-736.
13. Bryson, G. J., Silverstein, M. L., Nathan, A., & Stephen, L. (1993). Differential rate of neuropsychological dysfunction in psychiatric disorders: Comparison between the Halstead-Reitan and Luria-Nebraska batteries. *Perceptual and Motor Skills, 76,* 305-306.
14. Swirsky-Sacchetti, T., Gorton, G., Samuel, S., Sobel, R., Genetta-Wadley, A., & Burleigh, B. (1993). Neuropsychological function in borderline personality disorder. *Journal of Clinical Psychology, 49,* 385-396.
15. Wong, J. L., & Gilpin, A. R. (1993). Verbal vs. visual categories on the Weschler Memory Scale—Revised: How meaningful a distinction? *Journal of Clinical Psychology, 49,* 847-852.
16. Zarantonello, M. M., Munley, P. H., & Milanovich, J. (1993). Predicting Wechsler Adult Intelligence Scale—Revised (WAIS-R) IQ scores from the Luria-Nebraska Neuropsychological Battery (Form I). *Journal of Clinical Psychology, 49,* 225-233.

[1489]

M-Scale: An Inventory of Attitudes Toward Black/White Relations in the United States.

Purpose: To "measure attitudes toward black-white relations in the United States."

Population: College and adults.
Publication Dates: 1968–69.
Acronym: MS.
Scores: Total score only.
Administration: Group.
Price Data: Available from publisher.
Time: (15–20) minutes.
Comments: "Reliability coefficient appears to be too low (*r* = .27) to use the Scale as a predictive instrument"; no data on validity; norms for managers only; for experimental and research use.
Author: James H. Morrison.
Publisher: James H. Morrison.
Cross References: For a review by Marvin E. Shaw, see 8:605 (1 reference); see also T2:1266 (1 reference).

[1490]

MAC Checklist for Evaluating, Preparing, and/or Improving Standardized Tests for Limited English Speaking Students.

Purpose: Aids in the review, critique, or preparation of ESL assessment instruments.
Population: ESL test developers, reviewers, and users.
Publication Date: 1981.
Scores: 5 criterion categories: Evidence of Validity, Evidence of Examinee Appropriateness, Evidence of Proper Item Construction, Evidence of Technical Merit, Evidence of Administrative Excellence.
Administration: Group.
Price Data: Available from publisher.
Time: Administration time not reported.
Author: Jean D'Arcy Maculaitis.
Publisher: Jean D'Arcy Maculaitis.
Cross References: For reviews by Eugene E. Garcia and Charles W. Stansfield, see 10:177.

[1491]

MacArthur Communicative Development Inventories.

Purpose: "Evaluates young children's communication skills with norm-referenced parent checklists."
Population: 8–30 months.
Publication Date: 1993.
Acronym: CDI.
Scores, 16: Words and Gestures [Early Words (First Signs of Understanding, Phrases, Starting to Talk, Vocabulary Checklist), Actions and Gestures (First Communicative Gestures, Games and Routines, Actions with Objects, Pretend To Be a Parent, Imitating Other Adult Actions, Pretend Gestures)], Words and Sentences [Words Children Use (Vocabulary Checklist, How Children Use Words), Sentences and Grammar (Word Endings/Part I, Word Forms, Word Endings/Part II, Examples of the Child's Three Longest Sentences)].
Administration: Individual.
Price Data, 1994: $56.05 per complete kit including User's Guide and Technical Manual (114 pages), 20 Words and Gestures forms, and 20 Words and Sentences forms; $35.70 per User's Guide and Technical Manual; $20.35 per 20 Words and Gestures; $20.35 per 20 Words and Sentences.
Time: (20–30) minutes.
Authors: Larry Fenson, Philip S. Dale, J. Steven Reznick, Donna Thal, Elizabeth Bates, Jeffery P. Hartung, Steve Pethick, and Judy S. Reilly.
Publisher: The Psychological Corporation.

[1492]

The Macmillan Diagnostic Reading Pack.

Purpose: Developed for "use in teaching reading and diagnosing reading problems."
Population: Reading ages 5–6, 6–7, 7–8, 8–9.
Publication Date: 1980.
Administration: Individual.
Price Data: Available from publisher.
Time: Administration time not reported.
Comments: Manual and checklist title is Teach Yourself to Diagnose Reading Problems.
Author: Ted Ames.
Publisher: Macmillan Education Ltd. [England].
a) STAGE 1.
Scores: Item scores in 11 subareas: Visual Skills (32 Key Words, Letter-Matching, Upper and Lower Case Matching, Visual Memory/Recognition, Visual Memory/Reproduction), Auditory Skills (Transcribing Sounds, Sound Value of Letters, Auditory Discrimination, Short-Term Auditory Memory), Phonic Blending (Blending 2/3 Letter Words, Auditory Blending).
b) STAGE 2.
Scores: Item scores in 10 subareas: Key Words (68 Key Words, 32 Key Words), Phonic Recognition (Final Consonant Blends/Consonant Digraphs/Initial Consonant Blends, Consonant and Vowel Sounds), Phonic Blending (Consonant Blends and Digraphs, Blending 2/3 Letter Words), Phonic Spelling (Spelling of 2/3 Letter Words, Transcribing Sounds), Oral Reading (Accuracy, Comprehension).
c) STAGE 3.
Scores: Item scores in 10 subareas: Key Words (68 Key Words, 32 Key Words), Phonic Recognition (Long Vowels and Vowel Digraphs, Final Consonant Blends/Consonant Digraphs/Initial Consonant Blends), Phonic Blending (Vowel Digraphs, Consonant Blends and Digraphs), Phonic Spelling (Spelling of Short Vowel Words Containing Consonant Blends and Digraphs, Spelling of 2/3 Letter Words), Oral Reading (Accuracy, Comprehension).
d) STAGE 4.
Scores: Item scores in 8 subareas: Phonic Recognition (Long Vowels and Vowel Digraphs, Final Consonant Blends), Phonic Blending (Vowel Digraphs, Consonant Blends and Digraphs), Phonic Spelling (Spelling of Regular Single Syllable Words, Spelling of Short Vowel Words Containing Consonant Blends and Digraphs), Oral Reading (Accuracy, Comprehension).

Cross References: For reviews by Jane Hansen and James V. Hoffman, see 9:638.

[1493]

Macmillan Graded Word Reading Test.
Purpose: Developed to assess the standards and processes of reading.
Population: Ages 6-3 to 13-3.
Publication Date: 1985.
Acronym: GWRT.
Scores: Total score only.
Administration: Individual.
Forms, 2: 1, 2.
Price Data, 1988: £14.95 per 25 record sheets, teacher's manual (24 pages), and word card.
Time: (5–10) minutes.
Authors: Macmillan Test Unit and Bridie Raban.
Publisher: Macmillan Education Ltd. [England].
Cross References: For reviews by Bruce A. Bracken and Deborah B. Erickson, see 10:178.

[1494]

Macmillan Group Reading Test.
Purpose: Developed as "a means of monitoring standards of reading and investigating the range of reading attainment in a school or a class."
Population: Ages 6-3 to 13-3.
Publication Date: 1985.
Scores: Total score only.
Administration: Group.
Forms, 2: A, B.
Price Data, 1988: £4.50 per 25 tests; £4.50 per teacher's manual (23 pages).
Time: (30) minutes.
Author: Macmillan Test Unit.
Publisher: Macmillan Education Ltd. [England].
Cross References: For reviews by Koressa Kutsick and Gail E. Tompkins, see 10:179.

[1495]

Macmillan Reader Placement Test.
Purpose: Designed to place children at the level most appropriate for reading instruction.
Population: Grades 1 and over.
Publication Date: 1967–72.
Scores: 2 tests: Word Pronunciation, Oral Reading.
Administration: Individual.
Price Data: Not available.
Time: 20(25) minutes.
Comments: Part of Macmillan Reading Program; can be used as supplement.
Authors: Edward R. Sipay, Albert J. Harris, and Mae Knight Clark.
Publisher: Macmillan Publishing Co. [No reply from publisher; status unknown].

[1496]

MacQuarrie Test for Mechanical Ability.
Purpose: Designed to assess mechanical ability.
Population: Grades 7 and over.
Publication Dates: 1925–43.

Scores, 8: Tracing, Tapping, Dotting, Copying, Location, Blocks, Pursuit, Total.
Administration: Group.
Price Data: Available from publisher.
Time: Administration time not reported.
Author: T. W. MacQuarrie.
Publisher: CTB Macmillan/McGraw-Hill.
Cross References: See T3:1356 (2 references), T2:2251 (38 references), and 4:749 (15 references); for reviews by John R. Kinzer, C. H. Lawshe, Jr., and Alec Rodger, see 3:661 (43 references).

[1497]

Maculaitis Assessment Program, Commercial Edition.
Purpose: "Designed for the purposes of: 1) selection, 2) placement, 3) diagnosis, 4) proficiency and 5) achievement" of nonnative speakers of English in grades K–12.
Population: ESL students in grades K–3, K–1, 2–3, 4–5, 6–8, 9–12.
Publication Date: 1982.
Acronym: MAC.
Administration: Individual.
Price Data, 1990: $225.80 per MAC: K–12 sampler set including technical manual (296 pages), examiner's manual (142 pages), and 1 each of all other test materials; $34.50 per technical manual; $19.75 per examiner's manual.
Author: Jean D'Arcy Maculaitis.
Publisher: Berrent Publishing Company.
a) BASIC CONCEPTS TEST.
Population: ESL students in grades K–3.
Scores, 8: Color Identification, Shape Identification, Number Identification (Counting, Spoken), Letter Identification (Alphabet, Spoken), Identification of Relationships, Total.
Price Data: $20.10 per examiner's kit.
Time: (15–20) minutes.
b) MAC K—1.
Population: ESL students in grades K–1.
Scores, 7: Oral Expression (Asking Questions, Connected Discourse), Listening Comprehension (Commands, Situations, Minimal Pairs), Vocabulary Recognition, Total.
Price Data: $21.85 per examiner's kit.
Time: (25–30) minutes.
c) MAC 2—3.
Population: ESL students in grades 2–3.
Scores, 16: Oral Expression (Answering Questions, Connected Discourse), Vocabulary Knowledge (Identification, Noun Definition), Listening Comprehension (Identifying Words, Counting Words, Answering Questions, Comprehending Statements), Word Recognition Skills (Alphabetizing, Recognizing Vowels and Consonants, Recognizing Long and Short Vowels, Using Word Families, Determining Singular and Plural Forms, Recognizing Silent Letters), Reading Comprehension, Total.

Price Data: $33.70 per examiner's kit.
Time: (79–89) minutes.
d) MAC 4—5.
Population: ESL students in grades 4–5.
Scores, 15: Oral Expression (Asking Questions, Connected Discourse, Vocabulary Knowledge), Listening Comprehension (Positional Auditory Discrimination, Answering Questions, Comprehending Statements, Comprehending Dialogues), Reading Comprehension (Recognizing Homonyms, Recognizing Antonyms, Recognizing Abbreviations, Reading Outcomes), Writing Ability (Grammatical Structure, Pictorial, Paragraph Construction), Total.
Price Data: $26 per examiner's kit.
Time: (119–134) minutes.
e) MAC 6—8.
Population: ESL students in grades 6–8.
Scores, 11: Oral Expression (Answering Questions, Asking Questions, Connected Discourse), Listening Comprehension (Answering Questions, Comprehending Statements, Comprehending Dialogues), Reading Comprehension (Vocabulary, Reading Outcomes), Writing Ability (Grammatical Structure, Application Forms), Total.
Price Data: $26 per examiner's kit.
Time: (108–123) minutes.
f) MAC 9—12.
Population: ESL students in grades 9–12.
Scores, 11: Same as MAC 6–8.
Price Data: $43.90 per examiner's kit including listening tapes.
Time: (108–123) minutes.
Cross References: For reviews by J. Manuel Casas, David Strand, and Eugene E. Garcia, see 10:180.

[1498]
Maferr Inventory of Feminine Values.
Purpose: To distinguish between family, home, other oriented women, and self-oriented women.
Publication Dates: 1955–79.
Acronym: MIFV.
Administration: Group or individual.
Price Data: Not available.
Foreign Language Edition: Finnish, French, German, Greek, Japanese, Portuguese, and Spanish editions available for Adult Inventory.
Time: (10–15) minutes per test.
Comments: For research use only; perception of sex roles; 5 tests labeled forms (consisting of the same 34 items with differing directions and scrambled order); manual and score sheets are for adult level, but authors claim they may be used for developmental level also.
Authors: Anne G. Steinmann, David J. Fox, with Mary Toro.
Publisher: Maferr Foundation, Inc. [No reply from publisher; status unknown].
a) MAFERR DEVELOPMENTAL INVENTORY OF FEMININE VALUES.
Population: Junior and senior high school.
Publication Date: 1966.

Scores: 5 tests: Female Self Perception, Female Perception of Ideal Woman, Female Perception of Man's Ideal Woman, Female Perception of Mother's Ideal, Female Perception of Father's Ideal.
Forms, 5: A, B, C, M, P.
b) ADULT INVENTORY.
Population: College and adults.
Publication Dates: 1955–79.
Scores: 5 tests: Women's Self-Perception, Woman's Ideal Woman, Woman's Perception of Man's Ideal Woman, Man's Ideal Woman, Man's Perception of Woman's Ideal Woman.
Forms, 5: A, B, C, BB, G.
Cross References: For a review by Carol Adams, see 9:641 (2 references); for reviews by Goldine C. Gleser and Lenore W. Harmon, see 8:607 (28 references); see also T2:1267 (11 references).

TEST REFERENCES

1. Dabrowski, I. (1985). Liberating the "deviant" feminist image through education. *Social Behavior and Personality, 13*(1), 73-81.

[1499]
Maferr Inventory of Masculine Values.
Purpose: To distinguish between family home-oriented men and self-oriented men.
Publication Dates: 1966–79.
Acronym: MIMV.
Administration: Group or individual.
Price Data: Not available.
Foreign Language Edition: Finnish, French, German, Greek, Japanese, Portuguese, and Spanish editions available for adult inventory.
Time: (10–15) minutes per test.
Comments: For research use only; perception of sex roles; 5 tests labeled forms (consisting of the same 34 items with differing directions and scrambled order).
Authors: Anne G. Steinmann, David J. Fox, with Mary Toro.
Publisher: Maferr Foundation, Inc. [No reply from publisher; status unknown].
a) MAFERR DEVELOPMENTAL INVENTORY OF MASCULINE VALUES.
Population: Junior and senior high school.
Publication Date: 1966.
Scores: 5 tests: Male Self Perception, Male Perception of Ideal Man, Male Perception of Woman's Ideal Man, Male Perception of Mother's Ideal, Male Perception of Father's Ideal.
Forms, 5: H, D, E, M, P.
b) ADULT INVENTORY.
Population: College and adults.
Publication Dates: 1966–79.
Scores: 5 tests: Man's Self Perception, Men's Ideal Man, Man's Perception of Woman's Ideal Man, Woman's Ideal Man, Woman's Perception of Man's Ideal Man.
Forms, 5: H, D, E, DD, F.
Cross References: For reviews by Stuart A. Karabenick and Frank D. Payne, see 9:642 (1 reference);

for a review by Leonard D. Goodstein, see 8:608 (4 references); see also T2:1268 (1 reference).

[1500]

Maintest.
Purpose: "Developed to measure the mechanical and electrical knowledge and skills required for maintenance jobs."
Population: Applicants and incumbents for jobs requiring practical mechanical and electrical knowledge.
Publication Date: 1991.
Scores, 22: Hydraulics, Pneumatics, Welding, Power Transmission, Lubrication, Pumps, Piping, Rigging, Mechanical Maintenance, Shop Machines/Tools/Equipment, Combustion, Motors, Digital Electronics, Schematics and Print Reading, Control Circuits, Power Supplies, Basic AC and DC Theory, Power Distribution, Test Instruments, Computers and PLC, Electrical Maintenance, Total.
Administration: Group.
Price Data, 1993: $500 per 10 instruments including manual (17 pages).
Time: (150–160) minutes.
Comments: Tests scored by publisher; percentile ranks given for local and national norms.
Author: Roland T. Ramsay.
Publisher: Ramsay Corporation.

[1501]

The Major-Minor-Finder, 1986–1996 Edition.
Purpose: Designed to assist students in selecting a college major.
Population: High school and college.
Publication Dates: 1978–87.
Acronym: MMF.
Scores: No scores; decisions based on number of matches for each major.
Administration: Group.
Price Data, 1992: $38.75 per 25 test booklets; $7.50 per 25 answer folders; $4.50 per manual ('86, 20 pages); $9.95 per supplemental College Major Handbook ('87, 72 pages); $89.95 per microcomputer version (select Apple or IBM).
Time: (40) minutes per printed version; (10) minutes per microcomputer version.
Authors: Arthur Cutler, Francis Ferry, Robert Kauk, and Robert Robinett.
Publisher: CFKR Career Materials, Inc.
Cross References: For a review by James W. Pinkney, see 10:181; for reviews by Rodney L. Lowman and Daryl Sander of an earlier edition, see 9:643.

[1502]

Making a Terrific Career Happen.
Purpose: For use in guiding examinees in self-evaluation and exploration of careers.
Population: High school graduates, college students, and adults.
Publication Date: 1992.

Acronym: MATCH.
Scores: Interest scores in 14 COPSystem Career Clusters: Business-Professional, Business-Skilled, Science-Professional, Science-Skilled, Technology-Professional, Technology-Skilled, Consumer Economics, Outdoor, Clerical, Communication, Arts-Professional, Arts-Skilled, Service-Professional, Service-Skilled.
Administration: Group.
Price Data, 1993: $9.50 per MATCH self-scoring form (includes COPSystem booklets and Narrative Report) [$85.50 per 10].
Time: Administration time varies.
Comments: Self-administered and interpreted.
Author: Lisa Knapp-Lee.
Publisher: EdITS/Educational and Industrial Testing Service.

[1503]

Management and Graduate Item Bank.
Purpose: "For use in the selection, development or guidance of personnel at graduate level or in management positions."
Population: Graduate level and senior management applicants for the following areas: finance, computing, engineering, corporate planning, purchasing, personnel, and marketing.
Publication Dates: 1985–87.
Acronym: MGIB.
Scores, 2: Verbal Critical Reasoning, Numerical Critical Reasoning.
Administration: Group.
Price Data, 1986: £55 per administration set including manual ('87, 39 pages), supplementary norms manual ('87, 39 pages), test log, test booklets, answer sheets, administration instructions, and scoring stencils; £45 per 10 Verbal test booklets ('85, 16 pages); £65 per 10 Numerical test booklets ('85, 15 pages); £35 per 50 Verbal or Numerical answer sheets; £7 per Verbal or Numerical scoring stencil; £7 per Verbal (3 pages) or Numerical (3 pages) administration instructions; £22 per manual.
Time: 60(65) minutes.
Comments: Abbreviated adaptation of the Advanced Test Battery (129); subtests available as separates.
Authors: Saville & Holdsworth Ltd. and Linda Espey (supplementary norms manual).
Publisher: Saville & Holdsworth Ltd. [England].
Cross References: For reviews by James T. Austin and H. John Bernardin and by R. W. Faunce, see 11:213.

[1504]

Management Appraisal Survey.
Purpose: "An assessment of managerial practices and attitudes as viewed through the eyes of employees."
Population: Employees.
Publication Dates: 1967–80.
Scores, 5: Overall Leadership Style, Philosophy, Planning, Implementation, Evaluation.
Administration: No manual.

Price Data, 1992: $49.95 per 10-pack test instruments.
Time: Administration time not reported.
Comments: Self-administered survey.
Authors: Jay Hall, Jerry B. Harvey, and Martha S. Williams.
Publisher: Teleometrics International.
Cross References: See T3:2351 (1 reference); for a review by Abraham K. Korman of the Styles of Leadership and Management, see 8:1185 (8 references).

[1505]
Management Change Inventory.
Purpose: Measures knowledge of sound methods of introducing change.
Population: Managers and prospective managers.
Publication Dates: 1970–81.
Scores: Total score only.
Administration: Group.
Price Data, 1990: $40 per complete kit of 10 test booklets, fact sheet, and user's guide.
Time: (20–25) minutes.
Comments: Self-administered.
Authors: W. J. Reddin and E. Keith Stewart.
Publisher: Organizational Tests Ltd. [Canada].
Cross References: For reviews by Frederick Bessai and Ralph F. Darr, Jr., see 11:214.

[1506]
Management Coaching Relations.
Purpose: Measures "knowledge of sound methods of coaching subordinates who may be supervisors or managers."
Population: Managers and potential managers.
Publication Dates: 1970–81.
Acronym: MCR.
Scores: Total score only.
Administration: Group.
Manual: No manual; fact sheet available.
Price Data, 1990: $40 per complete kit including 10 test booklets, fact sheet, and user's guide.
Time: (15–20) minutes.
Comments: Self-administered; may be self-scored.
Authors: W. J. Reddin and E. Keith Stewart.
Publisher: Organizational Tests Ltd. [Canada].

[1507]
Management Development Profile.
Purpose: Provides field managers with feedback on their managerial skills and suggestions on how to improve those skills.
Population: Managers.
Publication Dates: 1988–91.
Scores, 18: Tasks (Staffing, Training, Counseling, Appraisal, Sales Support, Sales Motivation, Management Development, Business Management), Skills (Interpersonal Relations, Communication, Adaptability, Problem Solving, Planning, Delegation and Time Management), Attributes (Integrity and Loyalty, Stress Tolerance, Achievement Motivation, Self-Improvement).

Administration: Group.
Price Data, 1993: $40 per Administrator's Manual ('89, 40 pages); $110 per profile; $275 per enhanced version including extended feedback report and results for each of the 92 items in the questionnaire.
Time: Administration time not reported.
Comments: Profiles scored by publisher.
Authors: James O. Mitchel (administrator's guide) and LIMRA International.
Publisher: LIMRA International.

[1508]
Management Effectiveness Analysis.
Purpose: Constructed to assess management skills.
Population: Managers.
Publication Dates: 1981–90.
Acronym: MEA.
Scores, 22: Conservative, Innovative, Technical, Directive, Democratic, Strategic, Tactical, Structuring, Delegation, Communication, Team, Individualist, Management Focus, Production, People, Excitement, Restraint, Control, Feedback, Persuasive, Cooperation, Exaggeration.
Administration: Group.
Price Data: Not available.
Time: (45) minutes.
Authors: James T. Mahoney, Thomas M. Rand (manual), and F. Carl Mahoney (manual).
Publisher: Management Research Group [No reply from publisher; status unknown].

[1509]
Management Effectiveness Profile System.
Purpose: "Identifies managers' current strengths and weaknesses and provides direction for individual development."
Population: Managers and coworkers.
Publication Date: 1983.
Acronym: MEPS.
Scores: 2 scores (Self, Other) in 15 management skill areas: Setting Goals and Objectives, Identifying and Solving Problems, Planning Effectively, Organizing, Making Decisions, Delegating, Building Teams, Evaluating Performance, Developing Subordinates, Managing Conflict, Using Time Effectively, Handling and Preventing Stress, Demonstrating Commitment, Increasing Trust, Being Results Oriented.
Administration: Group.
Forms, 2: Self Description, Description by Others.
Price Data, 1990: $75 per Self-Description Inventory, Self-Description Response Sheet, 5 Description by Others Inventories, 5 Description by Others Response Sheets, Management Skills Profile, Item-By-Item Feedback Booklet, Self-Development Guide, and Scorer's Worksheets; $15 per leader's guide (69 pages); $75 per MEPS Follow-up.
Comments: Originally called Management Practices Audit; administered to manager and 4 or 5 coworkers.
Author: Human Synergistics.
Publisher: Human Synergistics.

[1510]

Management Interest Inventory.
Purpose: "To assist both organizations and individuals in making decisions relating to selection, placement, and career development at management level."
Population: Managers.
Publication Dates: 1983–86.
Scores, 54: Management Functions Preference Scores and Experience Scores (Production Operations, Technical Services, Research and Development, Distribution, Purchasing, Sales, Marketing Support, Personnel and Training, Data Processing, Finance, Legal and Secretarial, Administration, Total, Spread Across Functions); Management Skills Preference Scores and Experience Scores (Information Collecting, Information Processing, Problem-Solving, Decision-Making, Modelling, Communicating Orally, Communicating in Writing, Organising Things, Organising People, Persuading, Developing, Representing, Total).
Administration: Group.
Price Data, 1987: £45 per administration set; £20 per 10 nonreusable booklets; £26.50 per scoring keys; £20 per manual and user's guide ('86, 51 pages).
Time: (20–40) minutes.
Authors: Roger Holdsworth (test), Ruth Holdsworth (test), Lisa Cramp (test), and Miranda Blum (manual).
Publisher: Saville & Holdsworth Ltd. [England].
Cross References: For a review by David M. Saunders, see 11:216.

[1511]

Management Inventory on Leadership, Motivation and Decision-Making.
Purpose: Designed for use in the training and selection of managers.
Population: Managers and manager trainees.
Publication Date: 1991.
Acronym: MILMD.
Scores: Total score only.
Administration: Group.
Price Data, 1991: $30 per 20 test and answer booklets; $2 per Instructor Manual ('91, 8 pages); $5 per Review Set including one test, one answer booklet, and Instructor Manual.
Time: (15–20) minutes.
Author: Donald L. Kirkpatrick.
Publisher: Donald L. Kirkpatrick.

[1512]

Management Inventory on Managing Change.
Purpose: To assess managers' attitudes, knowledge, and opinions regarding principles and approaches for facilitating change.
Population: Managers.
Publication Dates: 1978–83.
Acronym: MIMC.
Scores: Total score only.

Administration: Group or individual.
Price Data, 1994: $30 per 20 tests and answer booklets; $2 per instructor's manual ('83, 8 pages); $5 per review set (includes test, answer booklet, and manual).
Time: (15–25) minutes.
Author: Donald L. Kirkpatrick.
Publisher: Donald L. Kirkpatrick.

[1513]

Management Inventory on Modern Management.
Purpose: "Developed to cover eight different topics of importance to managers."
Population: Managers.
Publication Date: 1984.
Acronym: MIMM.
Scores: 8 areas: Leadership Styles, Selecting and Training, Communicating, Motivating, Managing Change, Delegating, Decision Making, Managing Time; Total score is sum of the 8 areas.
Administration: Group or individual.
Price Data, 1994: $30 per 20 tests and answer booklets; $2 per manual (12 pages); $5 per specimen set.
Time: (20) minutes.
Comments: Self-scored training tool.
Author: Donald L. Kirkpatrick.
Publisher: Donald L. Kirkpatrick (the Author).
Cross References: For a review by Lenore W. Harmon, see 10:183.

[1514]

Management Inventory on Performance Appraisal and Coaching.
Purpose: "To determine the need for training in 'performance appraisal and coaching.' "
Population: Managers.
Publication Date: 1990.
Acronym: MIPAC.
Scores: Total score only.
Administration: Group.
Price Data, 1990: $27 per 20 tests and answer booklets; $7.50 per optional audiocassette; $1.50 per manual (7 pages); $3 per specimen set.
Time: (20–25) minutes.
Comments: Self-administered, self-scored.
Author: Donald L. Kirkpatrick.
Publisher: Donald L. Kirkpatrick.

[1515]

Management Inventory on Time Management.
Purpose: Tests time management ability of managerial personnel.
Population: Managers.
Publication Date: 1980.
Acronym: MITM.
Scores: Total score only.
Administration: Group or individual.

Price Data, 1994: $30 per 20 tests and answer booklets; $2 per instructor's manual (8 pages); $5 per review set (includes test, answer booklet, and manual).
Time: (15–25) minutes.
Author: Donald L. Kirkpatrick.
Publisher: Donald L. Kirkpatrick.

[1516]

Management Practices Update.
Purpose: To provide individuals with information about managerial behavior in areas of interpersonal relationships, the management of motivation, and personal "style" of management.
Population: Individuals involved in the management of others.
Publication Date: 1987.
Acronym: MPU.
Scores, 12: Section I (Exposure, Feedback), Section II (Basic, Safety, Belonging, Ego Status, Actualization), Section III (Team Management, Middle-of-the-Road Management, Task Management, Country Club Management, Impoverished Management).
Administration: Group.
Levels: 3 parts: I (Interpersonal Relationships), II (Management of Motivation), III (Analysis of Management Style).
Price Data, 1990: $10 per manual (25 pages).
Time: Administration time not reported.
Comments: Represents a shortened version of Personnel Relations Survey (2006), Management of Motives Index, and Styles of Management Inventory (2620).
Author: Jay Hall.
Publisher: Teleometrics International.

[1517]

Management Relations Survey.
Purpose: To assess employees' perceptions of their practices toward their managers.
Population: Subordinates to managers.
Publication Dates: 1970–87.
Acronym: MRS.
Scores, 2: Exposure, Feedback.
Administration: Group.
Price Data, 1990: $6.95 per manual ('87, 14 pages).
Time: Administration time not reported.
Comments: Companion instrument to Personnel Relations Survey (2006); based on the Johari Window Model of interpersonal relations.
Author: Jay Hall.
Publisher: Teleometrics International.
Cross Reference: For a review by Walter C. Borman, see 8:1178 (1 reference).

[1518]

Management Style Diagnosis Test, Third Edition.
Purpose: Developed to measure a manager's perception of his or her managerial style.

Population: Managers.
Publication Dates: 1965–75.
Acronym: MSDT.
Scores, 12: Dimension Scores (Task Orientation, Relationships Orientation, Effectiveness), Managerial Style Scores (Deserter, Missionary, Autocrat, Compromiser, Bureaucrat, Developer, Benevolent Autocrat, Executive), Managerial Style Synthesis.
Administration: Group.
Price Data, 1989: $45 per complete kit.
Time: (40–60) minutes.
Comments: Self-administered, self-scored; second edition still available.
Author: W. J. Reddin.
Publisher: Organizational Tests Ltd. [Canada].
Cross References: For a review by Abraham K. Korman of an earlier edition, see 8:1179 (5 references).

[1519]

Management Style Inventory [Hanson Silver Strong & Associates].
Purpose: To assess management style.
Population: Administrators and leaders.
Publication Date: 1981.
Acronym: MSI.
Scores: 4 Management Styles: Sensing Feeling, Sensing Thinking, Intuitive Thinking, Intuitive Feeling.
Administration: Group.
Price Data, 1990: $3 per inventory.
Time: Administration time not reported.
Comments: Previously included under title Hanson Silver Management Style Inventory (10:135).
Authors: J. Robert Hanson and Harvey F. Silver.
Publisher: Hanson Silver Strong & Associates, Inc.

[1520]

Management Style Inventory [Training House, Inc.].
Purpose: "This exercise is designed to give you some insights into your management style and how it affects others."
Population: Industry.
Publication Dates: 1986–87.
Scores, 5: Team Builder, Soft, Hard, Middle of Road, Ineffective.
Administration: Group or individual.
Price Data, 1993: $60 per 20 complete sets including test, answer sheet, and interpretation sheet.
Time: (20) minutes.
Comments: Self-administered, self-scored.
Author: Training House, Inc.
Publisher: Training House, Inc.
Cross References: For reviews by Ernest J. Kozma and Charles K. Parsons, see 11:220.

[1521]

Management Styles Inventory.
Purpose: Assesses individual management style under a variety of conditions.

Population: Adults.
Publication Dates: 1964–90.
Scores, 5: Philosophy, Planning and Goal Setting, Implementation, Performance Evaluation, Total.
Administration: Group.
Price Data, 1993: $6.95 per inventory.
Time: Untimed.
Comments: Self-administered survey.
Authors: Jay Hall, Jerry B. Harvey, and Martha S. Williams.
Publisher: Teleometrics International.

[1522]

Management Styles Questionnaire.
Purpose: To understand the concept of situational management, recognize the advantages and disadvantages of various styles of management, recognize which style(s) of management are appropriate for a particular work situation, identify one's on-the-job management style, and develop a plan for modifying one's management style.
Population: Managers and employees.
Publication Dates: 1974–83.
Acronym: MSQ.
Scores: Management Style.
Administration: Group.
Price Data, 1987: $6 per set including 1 participant form, 2 companion forms, and scoring and interpretation guide ('83, 15 pages); $15 per leader's guide (no date, 12 pages).
Time: 145(175) minutes.
Comments: Participant and companion forms.
Author: Don Michalak.
Publisher: Michalak Training Associates, Inc.
Cross References: For reviews by Seymour Adler and William I. Sauser, Jr., see 10:184.

[1523]

Management Transactions Audit.
Purpose: Assesses "ones interpersonal transactions and their implications for managerial effectiveness."
Population: Managers.
Publication Date: 1973.
Acronym: MTA.
Scores, 9: Transaction Scores (Parent Subsystem, Adult Subsystem, Child Subsystem); Tension Index Scores (Subordinates [Disruptive, Constructive], Colleagues [Disruptive, Constructive], Superiors [Disruptive, Constructive]).
Administration: Group.
Manual: No manual.
Price Data, 1992: $49.95 per 10-pack of test instruments.
Time: [15–30] minutes.
Comments: Self-administered survey.
Authors: Jay Hall and C. Leo Griffith.
Publisher: Teleometrics International.
Cross References: For reviews by Stephan J. Motowidlo and Ronald N. Taylor, see 8:1180.

[1524]

Manager Profile Record.
Purpose: "To identify candidates with a high potential for success in managerial and professional classifications."
Population: Prospective managers.
Publication Date: 1985.
Acronym: MPR.
Scores, 11: Background Record (Achievements: Academic Years, Present Self Concept, Present Social Orientation, Present Work Orientation, Total), Judgment Record (Staff Communication/Participation, Employee Selection-Development, Employee Motivation-Labor Relations, Management Style/Decision-Making, Total), Total Record.
Administration: Group.
Price Data: Available from publisher.
Time: (180) minutes.
Author: Richardson, Bellows, Henry & Co., Inc.
Publisher: Richardson, Bellows, Henry & Co., Inc.
Cross References: For a review by William I. Sauser, Jr., see 11:221.

[1525]

Manager Style Appraisal.
Purpose: A measure of managerial style.
Population: Adults.
Publication Dates: 1967–90.
Scores, 5: Philosophy, Planning and Goal Setting, Implementation, Performance Evaluation, Total.
Administration: Group.
Price Data, 1993: $6.95 per copy.
Time: Untimed.
Comments: Self-administered survey.
Authors: Jay Hall, Jerry B. Harvey, and Martha S. Williams.
Publisher: Teleometrics International.

[1526]

Manager/Supervisor Staff Selector.
Purpose: "Measures important intellectual and personality characteristics needed for the successful manager/supervisor."
Population: Candidates for managerial and supervisory positions.
Publication Dates: 1976–84.
Scores: 8 tests: Problem Solving Ability, Numerical Skills, Fluency, Business, Judgment, Supervisory Practices, CPF (interest in working with people), NPF (emotional stability).
Administration: Group.
Price Data, 1993: $299 per person.
Foreign Language Edition: French edition available.
Time: (120) minutes.
Comments: Information on scoring service available from publisher/distributor; detailed report provided for each candidate.
Authors: Tests from various publishers compiled, distributed, and scored by Walden Personnel Testing.

Publisher: Walden Personnel Testing & Training, Inc.
Cross References: For a review by Eric F. Gardner, see 10:186.

[1527]
Managerial and Professional Job Functions Inventory.
Purpose: "For defining the basic dimensions of jobs and assessing their relative importance for the job" and "assessing one's ability to perform them."
Population: Middle and upper level managers and non-management professionals.
Publication Dates: 1978–86.
Acronym: MP-JFI.
Scores, 16: Setting Organizational Objectives, Financial Planning and Review, Improving Work Procedures and Practices, Interdepartmental Coordination, Developing and Implementing Technical Ideas, Judgment and Decision Making, Developing Group Cooperation and Teamwork, Coping with Difficulties and Emergencies, Promoting Safety Attitudes and Practices, Communications, Developing Employee Potential, Supervisory Practices, Self-Development and Improvement, Personnel Practices, Promoting Community-Organization Relations, Handling Outside Contacts.
Administration: Group.
Forms, 2: Ability Rating, Importance Rating.
Price Data, 1988: $13.75 per 25 Ability or Importance test booklets; $2.50 per 25 scoring sheets; $5 per interpretation and research manual ('86, 28 pages); $10 per specimen set; scoring service available from publisher.
Time: (30–60) minutes.
Comments: Hand or machine scored.
Authors: Melany E. Baehr, Wallace G. Lonergan, and Bruce A. Hunt.
Publisher: London House, Inc.
Cross References: For reviews by L. Alan Witt and Sheldon Zedeck, see 11:222.

[1528]
Managerial Assessment of Proficiency MAP℠.
Purpose: "Shows a participant's strengths and weaknesses in twelve areas of managerial competency and two dimensions of management style."
Population: Managers.
Publication Dates: 1985–88.
Acronym: MAP.
Scores, 19: Administrative Competencies (Time Management and Prioritizing, Setting Goals and Standards, Planning and Scheduling Work, Administrative Composite), Communication Competencies (Listening and Organizing, Giving Clear Information, Getting Unbiased Information, Communication Composite), Supervisory Competencies (Training/Coaching/Delegating, Appraising People and Performance, Disciplining and Counseling, Supervisory Composite), Cognitive Competencies (Identifying and Solving Problems, Making Decisions/Weighing Risk, Thinking Clearly and Analytically, Cognitive Composite), Proficiency Composite, Theory X Style (Parent-Child), and Theory Y Style (Adult-Adult).
Administration: Group.
Price Data, 1991: $15,000 initial investment for purchase with licensing agreement (for high-volume users) including set of 4 videocassettes, 50 sets of participant materials including workbook ('88, 60 pages) and booklet entitled Interpreting Your Scores ('88, 24 pages), personal computer floppy disk for in-house scoring, scoring by publisher of first 25 participants, 1½-day training and pilot cycle by senior instructor from publisher; $40 per person for additional participant materials; $30 per person for additional (optional) scoring by publisher; $300 per person (minimum 12 persons) for contracting for in-house program including materials, scoring, and instructor/consultant time; $200–$250 per person for registration at public workshop held in Princeton, NJ by publishers.
Time: (360–420) minutes.
Comments: May be purchased with licensing agreement, contracted for in-house administration, or used by attending a public workshop provided by publisher; administered in part by videocassette.
Author: Scott B. Parry.
Publisher: Training House, Inc.
Cross References: For a review by Jerard F. Kehoe, see 11:223.

[1529]
Managerial Competence Index.
Purpose: "To assess the probable competence of one's approach to management."
Population: Individuals who manage or are being assessed for their potential to manage others.
Publication Date: 1980–89.
Acronym: MCI.
Scores, 5: Team Management, Middle-of-the-Road Management, Task Management, Country Club Management, Impoverished Management.
Administration: Group.
Price Data, 1990: $6.95 per manual ('89, 21 pages).
Time: Administration time not reported.
Authors: Jay Hall.
Publisher: Teleometrics International.
Cross References: For a review by Kurt F. Geisinger, see 11:224.

[1530]
Managerial Competence Review.
Purpose: To identify a manager's preferred managerial style and assess the relative competence of his/her approach to management.
Population: Subordinates to managers.
Publication Date: 1980–89.
Acronym: MCR.

Scores, 5: Relative measures of concern for people and concern for production ("9/9," "1/9," "5/5," "9/1," "1/1").
Administration: Group.
Price Data, 1990: $6.95 per manual ('89, 17 pages).
Time: Administration time not reported.
Comments: Companion instrument for Managerial Competence Index (1529).
Authors: Jay Hall.
Publisher: Teleometrics International.

[1531]
Managerial Philosophies Scale.
Purpose: Surveys the "manager's assumptions and working theories about the nature of those whose activities he or she coordinates."
Population: Managers.
Publication Date: 1975.
Acronym: MPS.
Scores, 2: Theory X (Reductive Management Beliefs), Theory Y (Developmental Management Beliefs).
Administration: Group.
Manual: No manual.
Price Data, 1992: $49.95 per 10-pack of test instruments.
Time: [15–30] minutes.
Comments: Self-administered survey.
Author: Jacob Jacoby and James R. Terborg.
Publisher: Teleometrics International.
Cross References: See T3:1366 (1 reference).

[1532]
Managerial Style Questionnaire.
Purpose: Measures individuals' perception of how they manage based on the assessment of six managerial styles.
Population: Persons in managerial situations.
Publication Dates: 1974–80.
Acronym: MSQ.
Scores, 6: Coercive, Authoritative, Affiliative, Democratic, Pacesetting, Coaching.
Administration: Group.
Forms, 2: Participant, Employee.
Price Data, 1993: $60 per 10 Participant version questionnaires, profiles, and interpretive notes; $25 per 10 Employee version questionnaires; $27 per MSQ flipcharts; $28 per 6 transparencies; $15 per trainer's guide ('80, 34 pages).
Foreign Language Edition: Available in Spanish.
Time: (10–20) minutes.
Comments: Self-scored instrument.
Author: McBer and Company.
Publisher: McBer and Company.
Cross References: For a review by H. John Bernardin and Joan E. Pynes, see 10:185; for a review by Frank L. Schmidt of an earlier edition, see 8:1182 (1 reference).

[1533]
The Manson Evaluation, Revised Edition.
Purpose: Identifies alcoholics and potential alcoholics.
Population: Adults.
Publication Dates: 1948–87.
Scores, 8: Anxiety, Depressive Fluctuations, Emotional Sensitivity, Resentfulness, Incompleteness, Aloneness, Interpersonal Relations, Total.
Administration: Individual or group.
Editions, 2: Paper-and-pencil, microcomputer.
Price Data, 1993: $55 per complete kit; $29.50 per 25 test booklets/profiles ('87); $27.50 per manual ('87, 28 pages); $125 per IBM computer package including diskette (tests up to 25) and user's guide.
Time: (10–20) minutes.
Comments: Self-administered.
Authors: Morse P. Manson and George J. Huba.
Publisher: Western Psychological Services.
Cross References: For reviews by Tony Toneatto and Jalie A. Tucker, see 11:226; see also T2:1271 (2 references) and P:152 (1 reference); for a review by Dugal Campbell, see 6:137 (5 references); for reviews by Charles H. Honzik and Albert L. Hunsicker, see 4:68 (4 references).

[1534]
Manual Dexterity Test.
Purpose: Designed to provide "a measure of manual speed and skill."
Population: Ages 16 and over.
Publication Date: No date.
Acronym: MDT.
Scores, 4: Speed, Speed and Skill, Manual Speed (average scale score of Speed, Speed and Skill), Manual Skill (difference between Speed, Speed and Skill scale scores).
Administration: Group.
Price Data, 1984: £2.70 per 25 booklets; manual free on request (15 pages); £.75 per specimen set.
Time: 2 minutes and 15 seconds (8 minutes).
Author: Educational & Industrial Test Services Ltd.
Publisher: Educational & Industrial Test Services Ltd. [England].

[1535]
Marital Check-Up Kit.
Purpose: "Designed to help couples examine their relationship and to determine ways in which it can be enriched or strengthened."
Population: Married couples.
Publication Date: 1980.
Acronym: MCK.
Scores: No scores.
Administration: Group.
Price Data: Available from publisher.
Time: Administration time not reported.
Comments: Can be administered to individuals, couples, or groups.
Author: Millard J. Bienvenu.
Publisher: Millard J. Bienvenu, Northwest Publications.

[1536]
A Marital Communication Inventory.

Purpose: Designed to assess the communications dimension of a marital relationship for purposes of counseling and marriage enrichment.
Population: Married couples.
Publication Dates: 1968–79.
Acronym: MCI.
Scores: Total score only.
Administration: Group.
Price Data, 1993: $1.50 per inventory; $2 per manual ('78, 8 pages).
Time: (20) minutes.
Author: Millard J. Bienvenu.
Publisher: Millard J. Bienvenu.
Cross References: For a review by Joseph P. Stokes, see 9:651 (1 reference).

TEST REFERENCES

1. Cline, V. B., Mejia, J., Coles, J., Klein, N., & Cline, R. A. (1984). The relationship between therapist behaviors and outcome for middle- and lower-class couples in marital therapy. *Journal of Clinical Psychology, 40,* 691-704.
2. Larson, J. H. (1984). The effect of husband's unemployment on marital and family relations in blue-collar families. *Family Relations, 33,* 503-511.
3. Arrindell, W. A., & Schaap, C. (1985). The Maudsley Marital Questionnaire (MMQ): An extension of its construct validity. *British Journal of Psychiatry, 147,* 295-299.
4. Holdt, P. A., & Stone, G. L. (1988). Needs, coping strategies, and coping outcomes associated with long-distance relationships. *Journal of College Student Development, 29,* 136-141.

[1537]
Marital Evaluation Checklist.

Purpose: "Provides a brief yet comprehensive survey of the most common characteristics and problem areas in a marital relationship."
Population: Married couples in counseling.
Publication Date: 1984.
Acronym: MEC.
Scores: 3 areas: Reasons for Marrying, Problems of the Current Relationship, Motivation for Counseling.
Administration: Group.
Price Data, 1994: $26 per 50 checklists, including fact sheet (no date, 1 page).
Time: (30–40) minutes.
Comments: Self-administered checklist.
Author: Leslie Navran.
Publisher: Psychological Assessment Resources, Inc.
Cross References: For a review by Richard B. Stuart, see 10:187.

[1538]
Marital Satisfaction Inventory.

Purpose: Designed to "provide a multidimensional self-report measure of marital interaction for use in both research and clinical settings."
Population: Married couples beginning counseling.
Publication Dates: 1979–81.
Acronym: MSI.
Scores, 11: Conventionalization, Global Distress, Affective Communication, Problem-Solving Communication, Time Together, Disagreement About Finances, Sexual Dissatisfaction, Role Orientation, Family History of Distress, Dissatisfaction With Children, Conflict Over Childrearing.
Administration: Group.
Price Data, 1993: $145 per kit including 2 reusable administration booklets, 50 hand-scored answer sheets, 50 profile forms, hand-scoring keys, manual ('81, 65 pages), and 2 test report: answer sheets; $49.50 per 5 reusable administration booklets; $19.50 per 100 profile forms; $19.50 per hand-scoring keys; $45 per manual; $13.50–$15 per test report: answer sheet; $210 per 26-use IBM microcomputer disk (specify 5.25-inch or 3.5-inch); $15 per FAX scoring service.
Time: Administration time not reported.
Comments: Separate answer sheets must be used.
Author: Douglas K. Snyder.
Publisher: Western Psychological Services.
Cross References: For reviews by David N. Dixon and E. M. Waring, see 9:652 (2 references).

TEST REFERENCES

1. Cochrane, G., & Friesen, J. (1986). Hypnotherapy in weight loss treatment. *Journal of Consulting and Clinical Psychology, 54,* 489-492.
2. Boen, D. L. (1988). A practitioner looks at assessment in marital counseling. *Journal of Counseling and Development,* 66, 484-486.
3. Jones, M. E., & Stanton, A. L. (1988). Dysfunctional beliefs, belief similarity, and marital distress: A comparison of models. *Journal of Social and Clinical Psychology, 7,* 1-14.
4. Snyder, D. K., Klein, M. A., Gdowski, C. L., Faulstich, C., & LaCombe, J. (1988). Generalized dysfunction in clinic and nonclinic families: A comparative analysis. *Journal of Abnormal Child Psychology, 16,* 97-109.
5. Wilson, G. L., Bornstein, P. H., & Wilson, L. J. (1988). Treatment of relationship dysfunction: An empirical evaluation of group and conjoint behavioral marital therapy. *Journal of Consulting and Clinical Psychology, 56,* 929-931.
6. Frank, B., Dixon, D. N., & Grosz, H. J. (1993). Conjoint monitoring of symptoms of premenstrual syndrome: Impact on marital satisfaction. *Journal of Counseling Psychology, 40,* 109-114.
7. Snyder, D. K., Mangrum, L. F., & Wills, R. M. (1993). Predicting couples' response to marital therapy: A comparison of short- and long-term predictors. *Journal of Consulting and Clinical Psychology, 61,* 61-69.

[1539]
A Marriage Adjustment Form.

Purpose: Assesses marital adjustment.
Population: Adults.
Publication Dates: 1939–61.
Acronym: MAF.
Scores: Total score only.
Administration: Group.
Price Data: Not available.
Time: Administration time not reported.
Comments: Problem checklist.
Author: Ernest W. Burgess.
Publisher: Family Life Publications, Inc. [No reply from publisher; status unknown].
Cross References: See T2:826 (3 references) and P:154 (1 reference); for a review by Lester Dearborn, see 6:681.

[1540]
A Marriage Analysis, Experimental Edition.

Purpose: Identifies "some of the problem or conflict areas in marriage."

Population: Married couples in counseling.
Publication Date: 1966.
Scores, 8: Role Concepts, Self-Image, Feelings Toward Spouse, Emotional Openness, Knowledge of Spouse, Sexual Adjustment and Security, Common Traits, Meaning of Marriage.
Administration: Group.
Price Data: Not available.
Time: Administration time not reported.
Authors: Daniel C. Blazier and Edgar T. Goosman.
Publisher: Family Life Publications, Inc. [No reply from publisher; status unknown].
Cross References: For reviews by Robert C. Challman and Robert A. Harper, see 7:566.

[1541]
The Marriage and Family Attitude Survey.
Purpose: "A diagnostic and educational instrument for understanding relationship attitudes" in marriage and family life.
Population: Adolescents and adults.
Publication Date: No date.
Scores: 10 areas: Cohabitation and Premarital Sexual Relations, Marriage and Divorce, Childhood and Child Rearing, Division of Household Labor and Professional Employment, Marital and Extramarital Sexual Relations, Privacy Rights and Social Needs, Religious Needs, Communication Expectations, Parental Relationships, Professional Counseling Services.
Administration: Group.
Price Data, 1988: $15 per 25 test forms; $4.50 per examiner's manual (no date, 8 pages); $5 per specimen set.
Time: (4–10) minutes.
Authors: Donald V. Martin and Maggie Martin.
Publisher: Psychologists and Educators, Inc.
Cross References: For reviews by Mark W. Roberts and by Donald U. Robertson and Virginia L. Brown, see 11:227.

[1542]
A Marriage Evaluation.
Purpose: "Designed to provide a rapid assessment of the strengths and weaknesses in a troubled marriage."
Population: Marital counselees.
Publication Date: 1977.
Scores, 6: Readiness Before Marriage, Decision Making, Communication, Values, Personal Growth in Marriage, Commitment and Expectations.
Administration: Group.
Price Data: Not available.
Time: (15–20) minutes.
Author: Henry C. Blount, Jr.
Publisher: Family Life Publications, Inc. [No reply from publisher; status unknown].
Cross References: For reviews by Howard J. Markman and Richard B. Stuart, see 9:653.

[1543]
The Marriage Expectation Inventories.
Purpose: Identifies areas of concern for engaged and married couples.

Population: Engaged and married couples.
Publication Dates: 1972–79.
Acronym: MEI.
Scores: Form 1: 9 areas: Love, Communication, Freedom, Sex, Money, Selfishness, Religious Expectations, Relatives, Expectations Related to Children; Form 2: 8 areas: Love, Communication, Freedom, Sex, Money, Selfishness, Religious Expectations, Relatives.
Administration: Group.
Forms, 2: 1 (engaged couples), 2 (married couples).
Price Data: Not available.
Time: (120) minutes.
Authors: Patrick J. McDonald, Ellen B. Pirro (inventories), Charles Cleveland (inventories), and Claudette McDonald (inventories).
Publisher: Family Life Publications, Inc. [No reply from publisher; status unknown].
Cross References: For reviews by David N. Dixon and E. M. Waring, see 9:654; for a review by James Leslie McCary of an earlier edition, see 8:345.

[1544]
Marriage Inventory.
Purpose: Evaluates the marital relationship by means of open-ended questions.
Population: Married couples in counseling.
Publication Date: 1971.
Scores: No scores.
Administration: Group.
Price Data: Not available.
Time: Administration time not reported.
Author: David Knox.
Publisher: Family Life Publications, Inc. [No reply from publisher; status unknown].
Cross References: For a review by Donald L. Mosher, see 8:346.

[1545]
A Marriage Prediction Schedule.
Purpose: Evaluates the relationship in terms of factors believed to contribute to marital success.
Population: Adults.
Publication Dates: 1939–61.
Acronym: MPS.
Scores: Total score only.
Administration: Group.
Price Data: Not available.
Time: Administration time not reported.
Author: Ernest W. Burgess.
Publisher: Family Life Publications, Inc. [No reply from publisher; status unknown].
Cross References: For a review by Lester W. Dearborn, see 6:684; see also 5:84 (8 references).

[1546]
A Marriage Role Expectation Inventory.
Purpose: Measures traditional and companionship expectations of marital relationships.
Population: Adolescents and adults.

Publication Dates: 1960–79.
Acronym: MREI.
Scores, 9: Authority, Homemaking, Children, Personality, Social Participation, Sexual Relations, Education, Employment and Support, Total.
Administration: Group.
Forms, 2: M (for males); F (for females).
Price Data: Not available.
Time: Administration time not reported.
Authors: Marie S. Dunn in collaboration with J. N. DeBonis.
Publisher: Family Life Publications, Inc. [No reply from publisher; status unknown].
Cross References: For a review by Howard J. Markman, see 9:655 (1 reference); for a review by Robert C. Challman of an earlier edition, see 6:685 (6 references).

TEST REFERENCES

1. Larson, J. H. (1984). The effect of husband's unemployment on marital and family relations in blue-collar families. *Family Relations, 33,* 503-511.

[1547]

Marriage Scale (For Measuring Compatibility of Interests).
Purpose: To identify attitudes toward a variety of relationship issues.
Population: Premarital and marital counselees.
Publication Dates: 1970–73.
Scores: Item scores only.
Administration: Group.
Price Data, 1987: $15 per 25 rating folders; $5 per specimen set with instructions.
Time: (10–15) minutes.
Comments: Self-administered.
Author: J. Gustav White.
Publisher: Psychologists and Educators, Inc.

[1548]

Martin S-D Inventory.
Purpose: Constructed to assess depression and suicide-proneness.
Population: Clients and patients.
Publication Dates: 1970–71.
Scores: Total score only.
Administration: Group.
Price Data, 1987: $8.25 per 25 test forms; $2.75 per set of score templates; $4.50 per pamphlet on suicide and depression ('71, 12 pages); $9 per specimen set.
Time: [15] minutes.
Comments: Self-ratings.
Author: William T. Martin.
Publisher: Psychologists and Educators, Inc.

TEST REFERENCES

1. Mehrabian, A., & Bernath, M. S. (1991). Factorial composition of commonly used self-report depression inventories: Relationships with basic dimensions of temperament. *Journal of Research in Personality, 25,* 262-275.

[1549]

Martinek-Zaichkowsky Self-Concept Scale for Children.
Purpose: "Designed to measure the global self-concept of children."
Population: Grades 1–8.
Publication Date: 1977.
Acronym: MZSCS.
Scores: Total score only.
Administration: Group or individual.
Price Data, 1987: $35 per 25 tests; $6.75 per manual (25 pages); $10 per specimen set.
Time: (10–15) minutes.
Comments: "A non-verbal, culture-free instrument."
Authors: Thomas J. Martinek and Leonard D. Zaichkowsky.
Publisher: Psychologists and Educators, Inc.
Cross References: For reviews by George M. Guthrie and David R. Wilson, see 9:656 (4 references); see also T3:1386 (3 references).

TEST REFERENCES

1. DeFranceso, J. J., & Taylor, J. (1985). Dimensions of self-concept in primary and middle school learning disabled and nondisabled students. *Child Study Journal, 15,* 99-105.
2. Hatfield, B. D., Vaccaro, P., & Benedict, G. J. (1985). Self-concept responses of children to participation in an eight-week precision jump-rope program. *Perceptual and Motor Skills, 61,* 1275-1279.
3. Smith, T. L. (1986). Self-concepts of youth sport participants and nonparticipants in grades 3 and 6. *Perceptual and Motor Skills, 62,* 863-866.
4. Blackbourn, J. M., & Wilson, J. (1988). Teacher validation of the Martinek-Zaichkowsky Self-Concept Scale for Children with mildly mentally retarded children. *Educational and Psychological Measurement, 48,* 439-443.
5. Folsom-Meek, S. L. (1991). Relationships among attributes, physical fitness, and self-concept development of elementary school children. *Perceptual and Motor Skills, 73,* 379-383.
6. Petrakis, E., & Bahls, V. (1991). Relation of physical education to self-concept. *Perceptual and Motor Skills, 73,* 1027-1031.

[1550]

Maryland/Baltimore County Design for Adult Basic Education.
Purpose: "Diagnoses a student's strengths, weaknesses, and deficiencies in skill areas that are prerequisite to literacy."
Population: Adult nonreaders.
Publication Date: 1982.
Scores: 21 subtest scores in 5 areas: Background Knowledge, Alphabet Recognition and Reproduction, Auditory Perception and Discrimination, Visual Perception and Discrimination, Sight Vocabulary.
Administration: Group and individual.
Price Data: Not available.
Time: (120–180) minutes.
Comments: Commonly called the "BCD Test."
Author: Baltimore County Public Schools Office of Adult Education.
Publisher: Simon & Schuster Higher Education Group [No reply from publisher; status unknown].
Cross References: For reviews by Mary M. Dupuis and Sharon L. Smith, see 9:658.

[1551]
Maryland Parent Attitude Survey.

Purpose: Designed to measure child-rearing attitudes.

Population: Parents.

Publication Dates: [1957–66].

Acronym: MPAS.

Scores, 4: Disciplinarian, Indulgent, Protective, Rejecting.

Administration: Group.

Price Data, 1993: $5 per test.

Time: [20–60] minutes.

Comments: For research use only; tests may be reproduced locally.

Author: Donald K. Pumroy.

Publisher: Donald K. Pumroy.

TEST REFERENCES

1. Turner, P. H., & Harris, M. B. (1984). Parental attitudes and preschool children's social competence. *The Journal of Genetic Psychology, 144*, 105-113.

[1552]
Maslach Burnout Inventory.

Purpose: Constructed to measure three aspects of burnout.

Population: Members of the helping professions, including educators.

Publication Date: 1981.

Acronym: MBI.

Scores, 6: 2 scores (Frequency, Intensity) for each of 3 subscales: Emotional Exhaustion, Depersonalization, Personal Accomplishment.

Administration: Group.

Forms, 2: Human Services, Educators.

Price Data, 1990: $6 per 25 Human Services surveys; $6.50 per 25 Educators surveys; $5.50 per 25 demographic data sheets (select Human Services or Educators); $1.75 per set of scoring stencils; $12 per manual (22 pages); $14 per specimen set.

Time: (20–30) minutes.

Comments: Test titles are Human Services Survey and Educators Survey; self-administered.

Authors: Christina Maslach and Susan E. Jackson.

Publisher: Consulting Psychologists Press, Inc.

Cross References: For reviews by David S. Hargrove and Jonathan Sandoval, see 10:189 (34 references).

TEST REFERENCES

1. Capel, S. A. (1987). The incidence of and influences on stress and burnout in secondary school teachers. *British Journal of Educational Psychology, 57*, 279-288.
2. Caton, D. J., Grossnickle, W. F., Cope, J. G., Long, T. E., & Mitchell, L. L. (1988). Burnout and stress among employees at a state institution for mentally retarded persons. *American Journal on Mental Retardation, 93*, 300-304.
3. Green, D. E., & Walkey, F. H. (1988). A confirmation of the three-factor structure of the Maslach Burnout Inventory. *Educational and Psychological Measurement, 48*, 579- 585.
4. Benedict, J. O., & Mondloch, G. J. (1989). Factors affecting burnout in paraprofessional residence hall staff members. *Journal of College Student Development, 30*, 293-297.

5. Hetherington, C., Oliver, M. K., & Phelps, C. E. (1989). Resident assistant burnout: Factors of job and gender. *Journal of College Student Development, 30*, 266-269.
6. Pierce, C. M. B., & Molloy, G. N. (1989). The construct validity of the Maslach Burnout Inventory: Some data from down under. *Psychological Reports, 65*, 1340-1342.
7. Raquepaw, J. M., & Miller, R. S. (1989). Psychotherapist burnout: A componential analysis. *Professional Psychology: Research and Practice, 20*, 32-36.
8. Snibbe, J. R., Radcliffe, T., Weisberger, C., Richards, M., & Kelly, J. (1989). Burnout among primary care physicians and mental health professionals in a managed health care setting. *Psychological Reports, 65*, 775-780.
9. St-Yves, A., Freeston, M. H., Godbout, F., Poulin, L., St-Amand, C., & Verret, M. (1989). Externality and burnout among dentists. *Psychological Reports, 65*, 755-758.
10. Arthur, N. M. (1990). The assessment of burnout: A review of three inventories useful for research and counseling. *Journal of Counseling and Development, 69*, 186-189.
11. Lee, R. T., & Ashforth, B. E. (1990). On the meaning of Maslach's three dimensions of burnout. *Journal of Applied Psychology, 75(6)*, 743-747.
12. Stone, G. L., & Archer, J., Jr. (1990). College and university counseling centers in the 1990s: Challenges and limits. *The Counseling Psychologist, 18*, 539-607.
13. Wolpin, J., Burke, R. J., & Greenglass, E. R. (1990). Golembiewski's phase model of psychological burnout: Some issues. *Psychological Reports, 66*, 451-457.
14. Capel, S. A. (1991). A longitudinal study of burnout in teachers. *The British Journal of Educational Psychology, 61*, 36-45.
15. Fimian, M. J., Lieberman, R. J., & Fastenau, P. S. (1991). Development and validation of an instrument to measure occupational stress in speech-language pathologists. *Journal of Speech and Hearing Research, 34*, 439-446.
16. Gold, Y., Roth, R. A., & Wright, C. R. (1991). The relationship of scores on the Educators Survey, a modified version of the Maslach Burnout Inventory, to three teaching-related variables for a sample of 132 beginning teachers. *Educational and Psychological Measurement, 51*, 429-438.
17. Harris, S. L., Handleman, J. S., Gill, M. J., & Fong, P. L. (1991). Does punishment hurt? The impact of aversives on the clinician. *Research in Developmental Disabilities, 12*, 17-24.
18. Mallett, K., Price, J. H., Jurs, S. G., & Slenker, S. (1991). Relationship among burnout, death anxiety, and social support in hospice and critical care nurses. *Psychological Reports, 68*, 1347-1359.
19. Abu-Hilal, M. M., & Salameh, K. M. (1992). Validity and reliability of the Maslach Burnout Inventory for a sample of non-western teachers. *Educational and Psychological Measurement, 52*, 161-169.
20. Berwick, K. R. (1992). Stress among student affairs administrators: The relationship of personal characteristics and organizational variables to work-related stress. *Journal of College Student Development, 33*, 11-19.
21. Chwalisz, K., Altmaier, E. M., & Russell, D. W. (1992). Causal attributions, self-efficacy cognitions, and coping with stress. *Journal of Social and Clinical Psychology, 11*, 377-400.
22. Friedman, I. A., & Farber, B. A. (1992). Professional self-concept as a predictor of teacher burnout. *Journal of Educational Research, 86*, 28-35.
23. Gryskiewicz, N., & Buttner, E. H. (1992). Testing the robustness of the progressive phase burnout model for a sample of entrepreneurs. *Educational and Psychological Measurement, 52*, 747-751.
24. Huebner, S. E. (1992). Burnout among school psychologists: An exploratory investigation into its nature, extent, and correlates. *School Psychology Quarterly, 7(2)*, 129-136.
25. Sherwin, E. D., Elliot, T. R., Rybarczyk, B. D., Frank, R. G., Hanson, S., & Hoffman, J. (1992). Negotiating the reality of caregiving: Hope, burnout and nursing. *Journal of Social and Clinical Psychology, 11*, 129-139.
26. Thornton, P. I. (1992). The relation of coping, appraisal, and burnout in mental health workers. *The Journal of Psychology, 126*, 261-271.
27. Walkey, F. H., & Green, D. E. (1992). An exhaustive examination of the replicable factor structure of the Maslach Burnout Inventory. *Educational and Psychological Measurement, 52*, 309-323.
28. Glass, D. C., McKnight, J. D., & Valdimarsdottir, H. (1993). Depression, burnout, and perceptions of control in hospital nurses. *Journal of Consulting and Clinical Psychology, 61*, 147-155.
29. Kelley, B. C., & Gill, D. L. (1993). An examination of personal/situational variables, stress appraisal, and burnout in collegiate teacher-coaches. *Research Quarterly for Exercise and Sport, 64*, 94-102.
30. Piedmont, R. L. (1993). A longitudinal analysis of burnout in the

health care setting: The role of personal dispositions. *Journal of Personality Assessment, 61*, 457-473.

[1553]

Matching Familiar Figures Test.

Purpose: Measurement of constructs of reflection and impulsivity.

Population: Ages 5–12, 13 and over.

Publication Date: 1965.

Acronym: MFF.

Scores: Total score only.

Administration: Individual.

Levels, 2: Elementary, Adolescent/Adult.

Manual: No manual.

Price Data: Available from publisher.

Time: Administration time not reported.

Authors: Jerome Kagan (test) and Neil J. Salkind (norms booklet).

Publisher: Jerome Kagan.

Cross References: See 9:662 (71 references).

TEST REFERENCES

1. Bowman, P. C., & Auerbach, S. M. (1982). Impulsive youthful offenders. *Criminal Justice and Behavior, 9*, 432-454.
2. Lin, A., Blackman, L. S., Clark, H. T., & Gordon, R. (1983). Far generalization of visual analogies strategies by impulsive and reflective EMR students. *American Journal of Mental Deficiency, 88*, 297-306.
3. Pratt, M. W., & Wickens, G. (1983). Checking it out: Cognitive style, context, and problem type in children's monitoring of text comprehension. *Journal of Educational Psychology, 75*, 716-726.
4. Thompson, R. W., Teare, J. F., & Elliott, S. N. (1983). Impulsivity: From theoretical constructs to applied interventions. *The Journal of Special Education, 17*, 158-169.
5. Brown, C. M., Meyers, A. W., & Cohen, R. (1984). Self-instruction training with preschoolers: Generalization to proximal and distal problem-solving tasks. *Cognitive Therapy and Research*, 427-438.
6. Brown, R. T., & Wynne, M. E. (1984). An analysis of attentional components in hyperactive and normal boys. *Journal of Learning Disabilities, 17*, 162-166.
7. Brown, R. T., Wynne, M. E., & Slimmer, L. W. (1984). Attention deficit disorder and the effect of methylphenidate on attention, behavioral, and cardiovascular functioning. *Journal of Clinical Psychiatry, 45*, 473-476.
8. Cameron, R. (1984). Problem-solving inefficiency and conceptual tempo: A task analysis of underlying factors. *Child Development, 55*, 2031-2041.
9. Christie, D., DeWitt, R. A., Kaltenbach, P., & Reed, D. (1984). Hyperactivity in children: Evidence for differences between parents' and teachers' perceptions of predominant features. *Psychological Reports, 54*, 771-774.
10. Clements, D. H., & Gullo, D. F. (1984). Effects of computer programming on young children's cognition. *Journal of Educational Psychology, 76*, 1051-1058.
11. Copeland, A. P., Reiner, E. M., & Jirkovsky, A. M. (1984). Examining a premise underlying self-instructional techniques. *Cognitive Therapy and Research, 8*, 619-629.
12. Davidson, W. B. (1984). Personality correlates of the Matching Familiar Figures Test in adults. *Journal of Personality Assessment, 48*, 478-482.
13. deHaas, P. A., & Young, R. D. (1984). Attention styles of hyperactive and normal girls. *Journal of Abnormal Child Psychology, 12*, 531-546.
14. Graybill, D., Jamison, M., & Swerdlik, M. E. (1984). Remediation of impulsivity in learning disabled children by special education resource teachers using verbal self-instruction. *Psychology in the Schools, 21*, 252-254.
15. Halperin, J. M., Gittelman, R., Klein, D. F., & Rudel, R. B. (1984). Reading disabled hyperactive children: A distinct subgroup of Attention Deficit Disorder with hyperactivity? *Journal of Abnormal Child Psychology, 12*, 1-14.
16. Halpern, H. G. (1984). An investigation of reading and conceptual tempo measures. *Reading World, 24*(1), 90-96.
17. Kagan, J., Reznick, J. S., Clarke, C., Snidman, N., & Garcia-Coll, C. (1984). Behavioral inhibition to the unfamiliar. *Child Development, 55*, 2212-2225.

18. Learner, K. M., & Richman, C. L. (1984). The effect of modifying the cognitive tempo of reading disabled children on reading comprehension. *Contemporary Educational Psychology, 9*, 122-134.
19. Lesnik-Oberstein, M., & Cohen, L. (1984). Cognitive style, sensation seeking, and assortative mating. *Journal of Personality and Social Psychology, 46*, 112-117.
20. Marriott, S. A., & Iwata, M. (1984). Group anger control training for junior high school delinquents. *Cognitive Therapy and Research, 8*, 299-311.
21. McClure, F. D., & Gordon, M. (1984). Performance of disturbed hyperactive and nonhyperactive children on an objective measure of hyperactivity. *Journal of Abnormal Child Psychology, 12*, 561-572.
22. Oas, P. (1984). Validity of the Draw-A-Person and Bender Gestalt Tests as measures of impulsivity with adolescents. *Journal of Consulting and Clinical Psychology, 52*, 1011-1019.
23. Platt, J. E., Campbell, M., Green, W. H., & Grega, D. M. (1984). Cognitive effects of lithium carbonate and haloperidol in treatment-resistant aggressive children. *Archives of General Psychiatry, 41*, 657-662.
24. Rosenbaum, M., & Baker, E. (1984). Self-control behavior in hyperactive and nonhyperactive children. *Journal of Abnormal Child Psychology, 12*, 303-318.
25. Schleser, R., Cohen, R., Meyers, A. W., & Rodick, J. D. (1984). The effects of cognitive level and training procedures on the generalization of self-instruction. *Cognitive Therapy and Research, 8*, 187-200.
26. Weithorn, C. J., & Kagen, E. (1984). Verbal mediation in highactive and cognitively impulsive second graders. *Journal of Learning Disabilities, 17*, 483-490.
27. Weithorn, C. J., Kagen, E., & Marcus, M. (1984). The relationship of activity level ratings and cognitive inpulsivity to task performance and academic achievement. *The Journal of Child Psychology and Psychiatry and Allied Disciplines, 25*, 587-606.
28. Zakay, D., Bar-El, Z., & Kreitler, S. (1984). Cognitive orientation and changing the impulsivity of children. *British Journal of Educational Psychology, 54*, 40-50.
29. Bjorklund, D. F., & Weiss, S. C. (1985). Influence of socioeconomic status on children's classification and free recall. *Journal of Educational Psychology, 77*, 119-128.
30. Brown, H. J., Singer, R. N., Cauraugh, J. H., & Lucariello, G. (1985). Cognitive style and learner strategy interaction in the performance of primary and related maze tasks. *Research Quarterly for Exercise and Sport, 56*, 10-14.
31. Brown, R. T., & Alford, N. (1984). Ameliorating attentional deficits and concommitant academic deficiencies in learning disabled children through cognitive training. *Journal of Learning Disabilities, 17*, 20-26.
32. Brown, R. T., Wynne, M. E., & Medenis, R. (1985). Methylphenidate and cognitive therapy: A comparison of treatment approaches with hyperactive boys. *Journal of Abnormal Child Psychology, 13*, 69-87.
33. Duncan, K. D. (1985). Representation of fault-finding problems and development of fault-finding strategies. *Programmed Learning & Educational Technology, 22*, 125-131.
34. Erickson, L. G., Stahl, S. A., & Rinehart, S. D. (1985). Metacognitive abilities of above and below average readers: Effects of conceptual tempo, passage level, and error type on error detection. *Journal of Reading Behavior, 17*, 235-252.
35. Friesen, W. J., & Wright, P. G. (1985). The validity of the Carlson Psychological Survey with adolescents. *Journal of Personality Assessment, 49*, 422-426.
36. Goldman, A. P., & Everett, F. (1985). Delay of gratification and time concept in reflective and impulsive children. *Child Study Journal, 15*, 167-180.
37. Harbin, T. J., & Blumenthal, J. A. (1985). Relationships among age, sex, the Type A behavior pattern, and cardiovascular reactivity. *Journal of Gerontology, 40*, 714-720.
38. Kappes, B. M., & Thompson, D. L. (1985). Biofeedback vs. video games: Effects on impulsivity, locus of control and self-concept with incarcerated juveniles. *Journal of Clinical Psychology, 41*, 698-706.
39. Li, A. K. F. (1985). Correlates and effects of training in make-believe play in preschool children. *The Alberta Journal of Educational Research, 31*, 70-79.
40. Locher, P. J. (1985). Use of haptic training to modify impulse and attention control deficits of learning disabled children. *Journal of Learning Disabilities, 18*, 89-93.
41. Miller, A. (1985). A developmental study of the cognitive basis of performance impairment after failure. *Journal of Personality and Social Psychology, 49*, 529-538.
42. Morrison, D. L. (1985). The effect of cognitive style and training on fault diagnosis performance. *Programmed Learning & Educational Technology, 22*, 132-139.

43. Nicholls, J. G., & Miller, A. T. (1985). Differentiation of the concepts of luck and skill. *Developmental Psychology, 21*, 76-82.

44. Oas, P. (1985). Impulsivity and delinquent behavior among incarcerated adolescents. *Journal of Clinical Psychology, 41*, 422-424.

45. Overton, W., Byrnes, J. P., & O'Brien, D. P. (1985). Developmental and individual differences in conditional reasoning: The role of contradiction training and cognitive style. *Developmental Psychology, 21*, 692-701.

46. Resendiz, P. S., & Fox, R. A. (1985). Reflection-impulsivity in Mexican children: Cross-cultural relationships. *Journal of General Psychology, 112*, 285-290.

47. Schmeidler, G. R. (1985). Field and stream: Background stimuli and the flow of ESP responses. *Journal of the American Society for Psychical Research, 79*, 13-26.

48. Shapiro, E. S., Lentz, F. E., & Sofman, R. (1985). Validity of rating scales in assessing aggressive behavior in classroom settings. *Journal of School Psychology, 23*, 69-79.

49. Yap, J. N. K., & Peters, R. D. (1985). An evaluation of two hypotheses concerning the dynamics of cognitive impulsivity: Anxiety-over-errors or anxiety-over-competence? *Developmental Psychology, 21*, 1055-1064.

50. Zieffle, T. H., & Romney, D. M. (1985). Comparison of self-instruction and relaxation training in reducing impulsive and inattentive behavior of learning disabled children on cognitive tasks. *Psychological Reports, 15*, 271-274.

51. Bernfeld, G. A., & Peters, R. D. (1986). Social reasoning and social behavior in reflective and impulsive children. *Journal of Clinical Child Psychology, 15*, 221-227.

52. Bjorklund, D. F., & Bernholtz, J. E. (1986). The role of knowledge base in the memory performance of good and poor readers. *Journal of Experimental Child Psychology, 41*, 367-393.

53. Block, J., Gjerde, P. F., & Block, J. H. (1986). More misgivings about the Matching Familiar Figures Test as a measure of reflection-impulsivity: Absence of construct validity in preadolescence. *Developmental Psychology, 22*, 820-831.

54. Brown, R. T., Borden, K. A., Wynne, M. E., Schleser, R., & Clingerman, S. R. (1986). Methylphenidate and cognitive therapy with ADD children: A methodological reconsideration. *Journal of Abnormal Child Psychology, 14*, 481-497.

55. Campbell, S. B., Ewing, L. J., Breaux, A. M., & Szumowski, E. K. (1986). Parent-referred problem three-year-olds: Follow-up at school entry. *Journal of Child Psychology and Psychiatry and Allied Disciplines, 27*, 473-488.

56. Conte, R., Kinsbourne, M., Swanson, J., Zirk, H., & Samuels, M. (1986). Presentation rate effects on paired associate learning by attention deficit disordered children. *Child Development, 57*, 681-687.

57. Copeland, A. P. (1985). Self-control ratings and mother-child interaction. *Journal of Clinical Child Psychology, 14*, 124-131.

58. deHaas, P. A. (1986). Attention styles and peer relationships of hyperactive and normal boys and girls. *Journal of Abnormal Child Psychology, 14*, 457-467.

59. DiPietro, J. A. (1986). Effect of physical stimulation on motor inhibition in children. *Perceptual and Motor Skills, 63*, 207-214.

60. Feindler, E. L., Ecton, R. B., Kingsley, D., & Dubey, D. R. (1986). Group anger-control training for institutionalized psychiatric male adolescents. *Behavior Therapy, 17*, 109-123.

61. Fuhrman, M. J., & Kendall, P. C. (1986). Cognitive tempo and behavioral adjustment in children. *Cognitive Therapy and Research, 10*, 45-50.

62. Goldstein, F. G., Rollins, H. A., Jr., & Miller, S. H. (1986). Temperament and cognitive style in school-age children. *Merrill-Palmer Quarterly, 32*, 263-273.

63. Hartley, R. (1986). 'Imagine you're clever.' *Journal of Child Psychology and Psychiatry and Allied Disciplines, 27*, 383-398.

64. Kotsopoulos, S., & Mellor, C. (1986). Extralinguistic speech characteristics of children with conduct and anxiety disorders. *Journal of Child Psychology and Psychiatry and Allied Disciplines, 27*, 99-108.

65. Rapport, M. D., Tucker, S. B., DuPaul, G. J., Merlo, M., & Stoner, G. (1986). Hyperactivity and frustration: The influence of control over and size of rewards in delaying gratification. *Journal of Abnormal Child Psychology, 14*, 191-204.

66. Reynolds, W. M., & Stark, K. D. (1986). Self-control in children: A multimethod examination of treatment outcome measures. *Journal of Abnormal Child Psychology, 14*, 13-23.

67. Rohrbeck, C. A., & Twentyman, C. T. (1986). Multimodal assessment of impulsiveness in abusing, neglecting, and nonmaltreating mothers and their preschool children. *Journal of Consulting and Clinical Psychology, 54*, 231-236.

68. Shinn-Strieker, T. (1986). Patterns of cognitive style in normal and handicapped children. *Journal of Learning Disabilities, 19*, 572-576.

69. Stahl, S. A., Erickson, L. G., & Rayman, M. C. (1986). Detec-

tion of inconsistencies by reflective and impulsive seventh-grade readers. *National Reading Conference Yearbook, 35*, 233-238.

70. Stahl, S. A., Rinehart, S. D., & Erickson, L. G. (1986). Detection of inconsistencies by above and below average reflective and impulsive sixth graders. *Journal of Educational Research, 79*, 185-189.

71. Swanson, H., & Schumacher, G. (1986). Reflection-impulsivity and script-action recall. *Bulletin of the Psychonomic Society, 24*, 28-30.

72. Swinnen, S., Vandenberghe, J., & VanAssche, E. (1986). Role of cognitive style constructs field dependence-independence and reflection-impulsivity in skill acquisition. *Journal of Sport Psychology, 8*, 51-69.

73. Walker, N. W. (1986). What ever happened to the norms for the Matching Familiar Figures Test? *Perceptual and Motor Skills, 63*, 1235-1242.

74. Wapner, J. G., & Connor, K. (1986). The role of defensiveness in cognitive impulsivity. *Child Development, 57*, 1370-1374.

75. Gerbing, D. W., Ahadi, S. A., & Pattar, J. H. (1987). Toward a conceptualization of impulsivity: Components across the behavioral and self-report domains. *Multivariate Behavioral Research, 22*, 357-379.

76. Haynes, V. F., & Miller, P. H. (1987). The relationship between cognitive style, memory and attention in preschoolers. *Child Study Journal, 17*, 21-33.

77. Horn, W. F., Ialongo, N., Popovich, S., & Peradotto, D. (1987). Behavioral parent training and cognitive-behavioral self-control therapy with ADD-H children: Comparative and combined effects. *Journal of Clinical Child Psychology, 16*, 57-68.

78. Kuehne, C., Kehle, T. J., & McMahon, W. (1987). Differences between children with attention deficit disorder, children with specific learning disabilities, and normal children. *Journal of School Psychology, 25*, 161-166.

79. Kurtz, B. E., & Borkowski, J. G. (1987). Development of strategic skills in impulsive and reflective children: A longitudinal study of metacognition. *Journal of Experimental Child Psychology, 43*, 129-148.

80. Rapport, M. D., Jones, J. T., DuPaul, G. T., Kelly, K. L., Gardner, M. J., Tucker, S. B., & Shea, M. S. (1987). Attention deficit disorder and methylphenidate: Group and single-subject analyses of dose effects on attention in clinic and classroom settings. *Journal of Clinical Child Psychology, 16*, 329-338.

81. Solís-Cámara, R. P., & Solís-Cámara, V. P. (1987). Is the Matching Familiar Figures Test a measure of cognitive style?: A warning for users. *Perceptual and Motor Skills, 64*(1), 59-74.

82. Stoner, S. B., & Glynn, M. A. (1987). Cognitive styles of school-age children showing attention deficit disorders with hyperactivity. *Psychological Reports, 61*, 119-125.

83. Toner, B. B., Garfinkel, P. E., & Garner, D. M. (1987). Cognitive style of patients with bulimic and diet-restricting anorexia nervosa. *American Journal of Psychiatry, 144*, 510-512.

84. Van den Brock, M. D., Bradshaw, C. M., & Szabadi, E. (1987). Performance of normal adults on the Matching Familiar Figures Test. *British Journal of Clinical Psychology, 26*, 71-72.

85. Werry, J. S., Elkind, G. S., & Reeves, J. C. (1987). Attention deficit, conduct, oppositional, and anxiety disorders in children: III. Laboratory differences. *Journal of Abnormal Child Psychology, 15*, 409-428.

86. Abikoff, H., Ganeles, D., Reiter, G., Blum, C., Foley, C., & Klein, R. G. (1988). Cognitive training in academically deficient ADDH boys receiving stimulant medication. *Journal of Abnormal Child Psychology, 16*, 411-432.

87. Davidson, W. B. (1988). Emotionality as a moderator of cognitive style on the Matching Familiar Figures Test in adults. *Journal of Personality Assessment, 52*, 506- 511.

88. Fischler, G. L., & Kendall, P. C. (1988). Social cognitive problem solving and childhood adjustment: Qualitative and topological analyses. *Cognitive Therapy and Research, 12*, 133-153.

89. McConaughy, S. H., Achenbach, T. M., & Gent, C. L. (1988). Multiaxial empirically based assessment: Parent, teacher, observational, cognitive, and personality correlates of child behavior profile types for 6- to 11-year-old boys. *Journal of Abnormal Child Psychology, 16*, 485-509.

90. van Merriënboer, J. J. G., & Jelsma, O. (1988). The Matching Familiar Figures Test: Computer or experimenter controlled administration? *Educational and Psychological Measurement, 48*(1), 161-164.

91. Borden, K. A., & Brown, R. T. (1989). Attributional outcomes: The subtle messages of treatments for attention deficit disorder. *Cognitive Therapy and Research, 13*, 147-160.

92. Heckel, R. V., Allen, S. S., Andrews, L., Roeder, G., Ryba, P., & Zook, W. (1989). Normative data on the Kagan Matching Familiar Figures Test for adult male incarcerates. *Journal of Clinical Psychology, 45*, 155-160.

93. Horn, W. F., Wagner, A. E., & Ialongo, N. (1989). Sex differences in school-aged children with pervasive attention deficit hyperactivity disorder. *Journal of Abnormal Child Psychology, 17*, 109-125.

94. Zentall, S. S., & Dwyer, A. M. (1989). Color effects on the impulsivity and activity of hyperactive children. *Journal of School Psychology, 27*, 165-173.

95. Condino, R., Im-Humber, K., & Stark, R. E. (1990). Cognitive processing in specifically language-impaired children. *The Journal of Psychology, 124,* 465-479.
96. Fisher, M., Barkley, R. A., Edelbrock, C. S., & Smallish, L. (1990). The adolescent outcome of hyperactive children diagnosed by research criteria: II. Academic, attentional, and neuropsychological status. *Journal of Consulting and Clinical Psychology, 58,* 580-588.
97. Kendall, P. C., Reber, M., McLeer, S., Epps, J., & Ronan, K. R. (1990). Cognitive-behavioral treatment of conduct-disordered children. *Cognitive Therapy and Research, 14,* 279-297.
98. Russell, R. L., Greenwald, S., & Shirk, S. R. (1991). Language change in child psychotherapy: A meta-analytic review. *Journal of Consulting and Clinical Psychology, 59,* 916-919.
99. Baer, R. A., & Nietzel, M. T. (1991). Cognitive and behavioral treatment of impulsivity in children: A meta-analysis review of the outcome literature. *Journal of Clinical Child Psychology, 20,* 400-412.
100. Bostic, J. Q., & Tallent-Runnels, M. K. (1991). Cognitive styles: A factor analysis of six dimensions with implications for consolidation. *Perceptual and Motor Skills, 72,* 1299-1306.
101. Roth, N., Beyreiss, J., Schlenzka, K., & Beyer, H. (1991). Coincidence of attention deficit disorder and atopic disorders in children: Empirical findings and hypothetical background. *Journal of Abnormal Child Psychology, 19,* 1-13.
102. DuPaul, G. J., Anastopoulos, A. D., Shelton, T. L., Guevremount, D. C., & Metevia, L. (1992). Multimethod assessment of attention-deficit hyperactivity disorder: The diagnostic utility of clinic-based tests. *Journal of Clinical Child Psychology, 21,* 394-402.
103. Kolko, D. J., & Kazdin, A. E. (1992). The emergence and recurrence of child firesetting: A one-year prospective study. *Journal of Abnormal Child Psychology, 20,* 17-37.
104. Robins, P. M. (1992). A comparison of behavioral and attentional functioning in children diagnosed as hyperactive or learning-disabled. *Journal of Abnormal Child Psychology, 20,* 65-82.
105. Day, J. D., & Cordón, L. A. (1993). Static and dynamic measures of ability: An experimental comparison. *Journal of Educational Psychology, 85,* 75-82.
106. Healey, J. M., Newcorn, J. H., Halperin, J. M., Wolf, J. E., Pascualvaca, D. M., Schmeidler, J., & O'Brien, J. D. (1993). The factor structure of ADHD items in DSM-III-R: Internal consistency and external validation. *Journal of Abnormal Child Psychology, 21,* 441-453.

[1554]
MATE [Marital ATtitude Evaluation].
Purpose: "Designed to explore the relation between two people who have close contact with each other."
Population: Couples.
Publication Date: 1989.
Acronym: MATE.
Scores: 5 scales: Inclusion Behavior, Inclusion Feelings, Control Behavior, Control Feelings, Affection.
Administration: Group.
Manual: Information included in manual of FIRO Awareness Scales (982).
Price Data, 1993: $11 per sampler set including test booklet/answer sheet and scoring key; $23 per 25 test booklet/answer sheets (non-reusable); $10 per scoring key; $15 per FIRO manual.
Time: Administration time not reported.
Comments: Based on FIRO Awareness Scales (982).
Author: Will Schutz.
Publisher: Consulting Psychologists Press, Inc.

[1555]
Mathematical Olympiads.
Purpose: Constructed "to discover and challenge secondary school students with outstanding mathematical talent."
Population: Secondary school.
Publication Dates: 1972–89.
Scores: Total score only.
Administration: Group.

Price Data: Available from publisher.
Author: Committee on the American Mathematic Competitions.
Publisher: Mathematical Association of America; American Mathematical Society.
a) USA MATHEMATICAL OLYMPIAD.
Acronym: USAMO.
Time: 210(220) minutes.
Comments: Test administered annually in April; "selection to participate . . . is based on both the AHSME and AIME scores."
b) INTERNATIONAL MATHEMATICAL OLYMPIAD.
Acronym: IMO.
Time: 540(550) minutes over 2 sessions.
Comments: Test administered annually in July; selection to participate is based on USAMO scores and other scores obtained during the training session.
Cross References: For reviews by Phillip L. Ackerman and William R. Koch, see 11:228.

[1556]
Mathematics 7.
Purpose: "Assess the mathematics attainment of children near the end of the school year in which they reach their seventh birthday."
Population: Ages 6-10 to 7-9.
Publication Date: 1987.
Scores: 1 individual total score, 4 item analysis categories: Understanding, Computational Skill, Application, Factual Recall.
Administration: Group.
Price Data, 1989: £6.25 per specimen set including Teacher's Guide (24 pages), test booklet, and group record sheet; £5.75 per Teacher's Guide; £10.30 per test booklets.
Time: (30–50) minutes.
Comments: Downward extension of Mathematics 8–12 Series; no norms for categories; orally administered.
Authors: Test Development Unit of the Foundation for Educational Research in England and Wales.
Publisher: NFER-Nelson Publishing Co., Ltd. [England].
Cross References: For reviews by Camilla Persson Benbow and Kevin Menefee, see 11:230.

[1557]
Mathematics 8–12.
Purpose: Designed "to assess the extent to which children have acquired the mathematical skills and concepts covered by each year's curriculum."
Population: Ages 8–12.
Publication Dates: 1983–85.
Scores, 5: Understanding, Computation, Application, Factual Recall, Total.
Administration: Group.
Levels, 5: Mathematics 8, Mathematics 9, Mathematics 10, Mathematics 11, Mathematics 12.
Price Data, 1989: £10.30 per 25 test booklets (specify Mathematics 8, 9, 10, 11, or 12); £6.05 per

Teacher's Guide; £8.40 per specimen set including 1 each of 8–12 test booklets, teacher's guide, and group record sheet.
Time: (60–80) minutes for each level.
Authors: Alan Brighouse, David Godber, and Peter Patilla.
Publisher: NFER-Nelson Publishing Co., Ltd. [England].

[1558]
Mathematics Attainment Test C1.
Purpose: Designed to concentrate on children's mathematical understanding.
Population: Ages 9–12.
Publication Dates: 1965–69.
Scores: Total score only.
Administration: Group.
Price Data, 1993: £8.05 per 10 booklets; £4.90 per manual.
Time: (50) minutes.
Author: National Foundation for Educational Research.
Publisher: NFER-Nelson Publishing Co., Ltd.
Cross References: For a review by John Cook, see 7:470.

[1559]
Mathematics Attainment Test DE2.
Purpose: Designed to assess "children's mathematical understanding rather than their skill at computation."
Population: Ages 10–12.
Publication Dates: 1967–70.
Scores: Total score only.
Administration: Group.
Price Data, 1989: £5.15 per 10 booklets; £3.20 per manual ('70, 8 pages).
Time: (50–60) minutes.
Comments: Formerly called Intermediate Mathematics Test I; Mathematics Attainment Test DE1 is no longer available.
Author: National Foundation for Educational Research in England and Wales.
Publisher: NFER-Nelson Publishing Co., Ltd. [England].

[1560]
Mathematics Attainment Test EF.
Purpose: Used to identify pupils who have learning difficulties in the area of mathematical understanding.
Population: Ages 11-0 to 13-6.
Publication Date: 1972.
Scores: Total score only.
Administration: Group.
Price Data, 1993: £12.10 per 10 reusable test booklets; £5.20 per 10 answer sheets; £4.35 per marking stencil; £4.90 per manual.
Time: (50) minutes.
Author: NFER-Nelson Publishing Co., Ltd.
Publisher: NFER-Nelson Publishing Co., Ltd. [England].

[1561]
Mathematics Attitude Inventory.
Purpose: "To measure the attitudes toward mathematics of secondary school students."
Population: Grades 7–12.
Publication Date: 1979.
Acronym: MAI.
Scores, 6: Perception of the Mathematics Teacher, Anxiety Toward Mathematics, Value of Mathematics in Society, Self-Concept in Mathematics, Enjoyment of Mathematics, Motivation in Mathematics.
Administration: Group.
Price Data, 1994: $50 per 50 tests; $5 per scoring key; $25 per manual (26 pages).
Time: (20–30) minutes.
Comments: Tests may be reproduced locally.
Author: Richard S. Sandman.
Publisher: Psychological Foundations of Education.
Cross References: For reviews by Harvey Resnick and Richard F. Schmid, see 9:664 (3 references); see also T3:1410 (1 reference).

[1562]
A Mathematics Test for Grades Four, Five and Six.
Purpose: Designed to measure "achievement in modern mathematics."
Population: Grades 4–6.
Publication Date: 1969.
Scores, 13: Understanding Numeration Systems, Set Terminology, Mathematical Structure, Addition and Subtraction of Whole Numbers, Multiplication of Whole Numbers, Division of Whole Numbers, Common Fractions, Decimal Fractions and Per Cent, Measurements, Geometry, Solving Problems with the Use of Number Sentences, Graphs and Scale Drawings, Total.
Administration: Group.
Price Data: Available from publisher.
Time: (120–180) minutes in 2 sessions.
Author: Stanley J. LeJeune.
Publisher: Psychometric Affiliates.
Cross References: For a review by William H. Nibbelink, see 8:280; for a review by Arthur Mittman, see 7:476.

[1563]
Mathematics Test for Seniors.
Purpose: To measure mathematical knowledge.
Population: Standards 9–10 in South African school system.
Publication Dates: 1971–73.
Scores: Total score only.
Administration: Group.
Levels: 2 overlapping levels (Standards 9, 10) in a single booklet.
Price Data: Available from publisher.
Time: 90(100) minutes.
Authors: J. F. Vorster (test) and S. J. P. Kruger (manual).

Publisher: Human Sciences Research Council [South Africa].

[1564]

Mathematics Test: McGraw-Hill Basic Skills System.

Purpose: Measures the student's general level of competence in mathematics needed for college level courses.
Population: Grades 11–14.
Publication Date: 1970.
Scores, 4: Arithmetic, Elementary Algebra, Intermediate Algebra, Total.
Administration: Group.
Price Data: Not available.
Time: 42 minutes.
Comments: Also called MHBSS Mathematics Tests; although designed for use with the MHBSS instructional program, the test may be used independently.
Author: Webster Division, McGraw-Hill Book Co., Inc.
Publisher: Webster Division McGraw-Hill Book Co., Inc. [No reply from publisher; status unknown].
Cross References: For reviews by J. Braswell & C. J. Huberty, see 7:477.

[1565]

Mathematics Topic Pre-Tests.

Purpose: "Designed as coarse screening device to help teachers find the gaps in their students' prior knowledge of particular mathematics."
Population: Form 3 (junior secondary) students in New Zealand school system.
Publication Date: 1990.
Scores: 2 tests: Percentages, Integers.
Administration: Group.
Price Data, 1990: NZ$4 per 20 resuable pretests (specify Percentages or Integers); $4 per 20 answer sheets; $3.50 per worksheet masters; $3.50 per teacher's manual (specify Percentages [12 pages] or Integers [12 pages]).
Time: (30) minutes per test.
Authors: New Zealand Council for Educational Research, Ministry of Education, and Hamilton Region Mathematics Writing Group.
Publisher: New Zealand Council for Educational Research [New Zealand].

[1566]

Matrix Analogies Test.

Purpose: Developed to "measure nonverbal reasoning ability."
Population: Ages 5-0 to 17-11.
Publication Date: 1985.
Author: Jack A. Naglieri.
Publisher: The Psychological Corporation.
a) SHORT FORM.
Acronym: MAT-SF.
Administration: Group.
Scores: Total score only.
Price Data, 1994: $50.50 per 15 test booklets;

$27.50 per 25 answer sheets; $21 per manual ('85, 45 pages); $25 per examination kit.
Time: 25(30) minutes.
b) EXPANDED FORM.
Acronym: MAT-EF.
Administration: Individual.
Scores, 5: Pattern Completion, Reasoning by Analogy, Serial Reasoning, Spatial Visualization, Total.
Price Data: $115.50 per complete kit including stimulus book, 50 answer sheets, and manual ('85, 82 pages); $50.50 per stimulus manual; $29.50 per 50 answer sheets; $37.50 per manual.
Time: (48) minutes.
Cross References: For a review by Robert F. McMorris, David L. Rule, and Wendy J. Steinberg, see 10:191 (1 reference).

TEST REFERENCES

1. Naglieri, J. A., & Das, J. P. (1988). Planning-arousal-simultaneous-successive (PASS): A model for assessment. *Journal of School Psychology, 26,* 35-48.
2. Naglieri, J. A., Prewett, P. N., & Bardos, A. N. (1989). An exploratory study of planning, attention, simultaneous, and successive cognitive processes. *Journal of School Psychology, 27,* 347-364.
3. Haddad, F. A., & Juliano, J. M. (1991). Relations among scores on Matrix Analogies Test, Draw-A-Person, and the Iowa Tests of Basic Skills for low socioeconomic children. *Psychological Reports, 69,* 299-302.
4. Saneda, R. M., & Serafica, F. C. (1991). Plans and the control of behavior in boys with and without learning disabilities. *Journal of Clinical Child Psychology, 20,* 386-391.
5. Bardos, A. N., Naglieri, J. A., & Prewett, P. N. (1992). Gender differences on planning, attention, simultaneous, and successive cognitive processing tasks. *Journal of School Psychology, 30,* 293-305.
6. Hurt, J., & Naglieri, J. A. (1992). Performance of delinquent and nondelinquent males on planning, attention, simultaneous, and successive cognitive processing tasks. *Journal of Clinical Psychology, 48,* 120-128.
7. Reardon, S. M., & Naglieri, J. A. (1992). PASS cognitive processing characteristics of normal and ADHD males. *Journal of School Psychology, 30*(2), 151-163.
8. McNeish, T. J., & Naglieri, J. A. (1993). Identification of individuals with serious emotional disturbance using the Draw a Person: Screening procedure for emotional disturbance. *The Journal of Special Education, 27,* 115-121.

[1567]

Maudsley Personality Inventory.

Purpose: Designed to measure two dimensions of personality such as extraversion-introversion and neuroticism-stability.
Population: College and adults.
Publication Dates: 1959–62.
Acronym: MPI.
Scores, 2: Extraversion, Neuroticism.
Administration: Group.
Comments: For revised edition, see Eysenck Personality Inventory (949).
Authors: H. J. Eysenck and Robert R. Knapp (manual for American edition).
a) BRITISH EDITION.
Publication Date: 1959.
Price Data, 1985: £1.50 per 20 tests; £1 per manual.
Time: Administration time not reported.
Publisher: Hodder & Stoughton [England].
b) AMERICAN EDITION.
Publication Dates: 1959–62.

Price Data, 1993: $7.75 per 25 tests [$29.25 per 100, $117 per 500]; $4.75 per hand-scoring keys; $2.90 per manual ('62, 21 pages); $6.25 per specimen set.

Time: (10–15) minutes.

Publisher: EdITS/Educational & Industrial Testing Service.

Cross References: See 9:668 (15 references), T3:1419 (39 references), 8:611 (129 reference); T2:1275 (273 references), and P:161 (149 references); for reviews by Arthur R. Jensen, James C. Lingoes, William Stephenson, and Phillip E. Vernon, and excerpted reviews by Edward S. Bordin, A. Bursil, and G. A. Foulds, see 6:138 (120 references).

TEST REFERENCES

1. Lomranz, J. (1983). Time estimation as a function of stimulus complexity and personality. *Social Behavior and Personality, 11*(2), 77-81.
2. Smith, C. A., Organ, D. W., & Near, J. P. (1983). Organizational citizenship behavior: Its nature and antecedents. *Journal of Aplied Psychology, 68*, 653-663.
3. Anderson, L. P., & Rehm, L. P. (1984). The relationship between strategies of coping and perception of pain in three chronic pain groups. *Journal of Clinical Psychology, 40*, 1170-1177.
4. Cherry, N. (1984). Nervous strain, anxiety and symptoms amongst 32-year-old men at work in Britain. *Journal of Occupational Psychology, 57*, 95-105.
5. Hirschfeld, R. M. A., Klerman, G. L., Clayton, P. J., Keller, M. B., & Andreasen, N. C. (1984). Personality and gender-related differences in depression. *Journal of Affective Disorders, 7*, 211-221.
6. Prola, M. (1984). A scale to measure optimism about college life. *Psychological Reports, 54*, 555-557.
7. Woodruffe, C. (1984). The consistency of presented personality: Additional evidence from aggregation. *Journal of Personality, 52*, 307-317.
8. Woody, G. E., McLellan, T., Luborsky, L., O'Brien, C. P., Blaine, J., Fox, S., Herman, I., & Beck, A. T. (1984). Severity of psychiatric symptoms as a predictor of benefits from psychotherapy: The Veterans Administration-Penn study. *American Journal of Psychiatry, 141*, 1172-1177.
9. Zimmerman-Tansella, C. (1984). Psychological performance of anxious patients in tests used in anxiolytic drug trials. *Journal of Clinical Psychology, 40*, 1143-1150.
10. Clark, D. C., Fawcett, J., Salazar-Grueso, E., & Fawcett, E. (1984). Seven-month clinical outcome of anhedonic and normally hedonic depressed inpatients. *American Journal of Psychiatry, 141*, 1216-1220.
11. Osuji, O. N. (1985). Personality factors in acceptance of loss among the physically disabled. *The Psychological Record, 35*, 23-28.
12. Rounsaville, B. J., & Kleber, H. D. (1985). Untreated opiate addicts: How do they differ from those seeking treatment? *Archives of General Psychiatry, 42*, 1072-1077.
13. Woody, G. E., McLellan, A. T., & Luborsky, L., & O'Brien, C. P. (1985). Sociopathy and psychotherapy outcome. *Archives of General Psychiatry, 42*, 1081-1086.
14. Crandell, C. J., & Chambless, D. L. (1986). The validation of an inventory for measuring depressive thoughts: The Crandell cognitions inventory. *Behaviour Research and Therapy, 24*, 403-411.
15. Faravelli, C., Ambonetti, A., Pallanti, S., & Pazzagli, A. (1986). Depressive relapses and incomplete recovery from index episode. *American Journal of Psychiatry, 143*, 888-891.
16. Hirschfeld, R. M. A., Klerman, G. L., Andreasen, N. C., Clayton, P. J., & Keller, M. B. (1986). Psycho-social predictors of chronicity in depressed patients. *British Journal of Psychiatry, 148*, 648-654.
17. Schenk, J., & Pfrang, H. (1986). Extraversion, neuroticism, and sexual behavior: Interrelationships in a sample of young men. *Archives of Sexual Behavior, 15*, 449-455.
18. Solyom, L., Ledwidge, B., & Solyom, C. (1986). Delineating social phobia. *British Journal of Psychiatry, 149*, 464-470.
19. Werner, P. D., & Pervin, L. A. (1986). The content of personality inventory items. *Journal of Personality and Social Psychology, 51*, 622-628.
20. Harrigan, J. A., Kues, J. R., Steffen, J. J., & Rosenthal, R. (1987). Self-touching and impressions of others. *Personality and Social Psychology Bulletin, 13*, 497-512.
21. Woody, G. E., McLellan, A. T., Luborsky, L., & O'Brien, C. P. (1987). Twelve-month follow-up of psychotherapy for opiate dependence. *American Journal of Psychiatry, 144*, 590-596.
22. Carmody, T. P., Crossen, J. R., & Wiens, A. N. (1989). Hostility as a health risk factor: Relationships with neuroticism, type A behavior, attentional focus, and interpersonal style. *Journal of Clinical Psychology, 45*, 754-762.
23. Hirschfeld, R. M. A., Klerman, G. L., Lavori, P., Keller, M. B., Griffith, P., & Loryell, W. (1989). Premorbid personality assessments of first onset of major depression. *Archives of General Psychiatry, 46*, 345-350.
24. Fukuda, K., Inamatsu, N., Kuroiwa, M., & Miyasita, A. (1991). Personality of healthy young adults with sleep paralysis. *Perceptual and Motor Skills, 73*, 955-962.
25. Goff, D. C., Olin, J. A., Jenike, M. A., Baer, L., & Buttolph, M. L. (1992). Disassociative symptoms in patients with obsessive-compulsive disorder. *Journal of Nervous and Mental Disease, 180*, 332-337.
26. Iizuka, Y. (1992). Extraversion, introversion, and visual interaction. *Perceptual and Motor Skills, 74*, 43-50.

[1568]

McCall-Crabbs Standard Test Lessons in Reading.

Purpose: Measurement of reading progress.

Population: Reading level grades 3–8.

Publication Dates: 1926–79.

Scores: Item and grade equivalent scores.

Administration: Group.

Levels, 6: Overlapping levels labeled A, B, C, D, E, F.

Price Data, 1994: $2.95 per test booklet (any level); $5.95 per 30 answer sheets; $1.50 per manual/answer key ('79, 16 pages).

Time: 3 minutes for any one test; 180 minutes for each booklet (60 tests per booklet).

Comments: Fourth edition.

Authors: William A. McCall and Lelah Crabbs Schroeder; revision by Robert P. Starr.

Publisher: Teachers College Press.

Cross References: For a review by Brendan John Bartlett, see 9:669.

TEST REFERENCES

1. Jacobowitz, T., & Haupt, E. J. (1984). Retrieval speed in reading comprehension: Failure to generalize. *National Reading Conference Yearbook, 33*, 241-246.

[1569]

McCarron-Dial System.

Purpose: A battery of neurometric and behavioral measures to be used for vocational, educational, and neuropsychological assessment particularly in meeting the programming needs of handicapped persons.

Population: Normal and handicapped individuals ages 3 to adult.

Publication Dates: 1973–86.

Acronym: MDS.

Scores: 5 factors: Verbal-Spatial-Cognitive, Sensory, Motor, Emotional, Integration-Coping.

Administration: Individual.

Parts: 3 components (Auxiliary Component, Haptic Visual Discrimination Test [HVDT], McCarron Assessment of Neuromuscular Development [MAND]).

Price Data, 1994: $2,325 per complete System including Auxiliary, HVDT, and MAND Components; price data for software for computer-assisted programs supporting the MDS available from publisher; price information for workshops and training available from publisher.

Comments: "A commitment to receive training is required for all purchasers of the McCarron-Dial System"; components available as separates.

Authors: Lawrence McCarron and Jack G. Dial.

Publisher: McCarron-Dial Systems.

a) AUXILIARY COMPONENT.

Publication Dates: 1973–86.

Price Data: $400 per set of materials in carrying case; $21.25 per 25 forms for Peabody Form L; $16.75 per 50 IEP forms; $26.50 per 25 IPP forms; $75 per manual ('86, 259 pages).

Comments: Manual title is Revised McCarron-Dial Evaluation System Manual; kit includes Peabody Picture Vocabulary Test—Revised (1945), Bender Visual Motor Gestalt Test, and Koppitz Scoring Manual for The Bender Gestalt Test for Young Children, the McCarron-Dial System Individual Evaluation Profile (IEP), the McCarron-Dial Individual Program Plan (IPP), the Observational Emotional Inventory, the Emotional Behavioral Checklist, and the Dial Behavior Rating Scale.

1) *Dial Behavior Rating Scale.*

Purpose: To provide an abbreviated assessment of essential personal, social, and work adjustment behaviors that relate to vocational placement, adjustment to work, and personal-social adjustment.

Publication Dates: 1973–86.

Acronym: BRS.

Price Data: $16.75 per 25 forms.

Author: Jack G. Dial.

2) *Observational Emotional Inventory.*

Publication Date: 1986.

Acronym: OEI.

Price Data: $11.50 per 25 forms.

Time: 120 minutes on each of 5 days.

Comments: Behavior checklist.

3) *Emotional Behavioral Checklist.*

Purpose: To assess an individual's overt emotional behavior.

Publication Date: 1986.

Acronym: EBC.

Price Data: $16.75 per 25 forms.

Comments: Behavior Checklist (alternate to OEI).

b) HAPTIC VISUAL DISCRIMINATION TEST.

Purpose: To measure an individual's haptic-visual integration skills.

Publication Dates: 1976–79.

Acronym: HVDT.

Scores, 4: Shape, Size, Texture, Configuration.

Price Data: $875 per complete kit including score forms, photographic plates, folding screen, sets of shapes, sizes, textures, and configurations, manual ('79, 261 forms) in a carrying case; $19 per 50 score forms; $40 per manual.

Time: (10–15) minutes per hand.

Comments: Manual title is Sensory Integration: The Haptic Visual Processes.

c) MCCARRON ASSESSMENT OF NEUROMUSCULAR DEVELOPMENT.

Purpose: "A standardized and quantitative procedure for assessing fine and gross motor abilities."

Population: Ages 3.5 to young adult.

Publication Dates: 1976–86.

Acronym: MAND.

Scores, 3: Fine Motor, Gross Motor, Total.

Price Data: $1,050 per complete kit including score forms, a dynamometer, stopwatch-timer, components for fine and gross motor testing, and manual ('82, 221 pages) in carrying case; $24.75 per 25 score forms; $50 per manual.

Time: (15) minutes.

Comments: Manual title is Revised McCarron Assessment of Neuromuscular Development Manual.

Author: Lawrence T. McCarron.

Cross References: For reviews by Calvin P. Garbin and David C. Solly, see 11:231 (1 reference).

[1570]
McCarthy Individualized Diagnostic Reading Inventory, Revised Edition.

Purpose: Measurement of reading proficiency for use in placement and planning in classrooms.

Population: Grades K–12.

Publication Dates: 1971–76.

Scores: 3 levels of qualitative ratings of reading (Independent, Instructional, Frustration) and item scores classified above or below 90% mastery criterion.

Administration: Individual.

Parts, 4: Part 1 (Placement for Instruction in Reading, Fluency, Comprehension, and Thinking Skills); Part 2 (Phonics, Work Recognition and Study Skills); Part 3 (Questionnaire Concerning a Student's Reading Interests and Habits); Part 4 (Outline for Planning Individualized Remediations).

Price Data, 1988: $1.60 per pupil test booklet; $7.50 per 12 individual record forms; $6.50 per teacher administration booklet; $2.40 per information booklet.

Time: (35–60) minutes for Part 1; 35(40) minutes for Part 2; administration time not reported for Part 3.

Author: William G. McCarthy.

Publisher: Educators Publishing Service, Inc.

Cross References: For reviews by Joyce Hood and Robert M. Wilson, see 9:670.

[1571]
McCarthy Scales of Children's Abilities.

Purpose: Developed to "determine . . . general intellectual level as well as . . . strengths and weaknesses in important abilities."

Population: Ages 2-4 to 8-7.

Publication Dates: 1970–72.

Acronym: MSCA.

Scores, 6: Verbal, Perceptual-Performance, Quantitative, Composite (General Cognitive), Memory, Motor.

Administration: Individual.

Price Data, 1994: $442 per complete set including all necessary equipment, 25 drawing booklets, 25 record forms, and manual ('72, 217 pages); $38.50 per 25 drawing booklets; $28.50 per 25 record forms; $49.50 per manual.

Time: (45–60) minutes.

Author: Dorothea McCarthy.

Publisher: The Psychological Corporation.

Cross References: For reviews by Kathleen D. Paget and David L. Wodrich, see 9:671 (29 references); see also T3:1424 (60 references); for reviews by Jane V. Hunt, Jerome M. Sattler, and Arthur B. Silverstein, and excerpted reviews by Everett E. Davis, Linda Hufano and Ralph Hoepfner, R. B. Ammons and C. H. Ammons, and Alan Krichev, see 8:219 (29 references).

TEST REFERENCES

1. Earls, F., & Cook, S. (1983). Play observations of three-year old children and their relationship to parental reports of behavior problems and temperament characteristics. *Child Psychiatry and Human Development, 13,* 225-232.
2. Meltzer, L. J., Levine, M. D., Hanson, M. A., Wasserman, R., Schneider, D., & Sullivan, M. (1983). Developmental attainment in preschool children: Analysis of concordance between parents and professionals. *The Journal of Special Education, 17,* 203-213.
3. Teeter, P. A. (1983). The relationship between measures of cognitive-intellectual and neuropsychological abilities for young children. *Clinical Neuropsychology, 5,* 151-158.
4. Teglasi, H., & Freeman, R. W. (1983). Rapport pitfalls of beginning testers. *Journal of School Psychology, 21,* 229-240.
5. Wilson, R. S., & Matheny, A. P., Jr. (1983). Mental development: Family environment and genetic influences. *Intelligence, 7,* 195-215.
6. Bickett, L., Reuter, J., & Stancin, T. (1984). The use of the McCarthy Scales of Children's Abilities to assess moderately mentally retarded children. *Psychology in the Schools, 21,* 305-312.
7. Blachman, B. A. (1984). Relationship of rapid naming ability and language analysis skills to kindergarten and first-grade reading achievement. *Journal of Educational Psychology, 76,* 610-622.
8. Bondy, A. S., Constantino, R., Norcross, J. C., & Sheslow, D. (1984). Comparison of Slosson and McCarthy scales for exceptional preschool children. *Perceptual and Motor Skills, 59,* 657-658.
9. Chang, S. T., & Bashaw, W. L. (1984). The reliability of the McCarthy Screening Test from the criterion-referenced testing perspective. *Journal of Clinical Psychology, 40,* 791- 800.
10. Collaborative Group on Antenatal Steroid Therapy. (1984). Effects on antenatal dexamethasone administration in the infant: Long-term follow-up. *The Journal of Pediatrics, 104,* 259-267.
11. Giblin, P. T., Starr, R. H., Jr., & Agronow, S. J. (1984). Affective behavior of abused and control children: Comparisons of parent-child interactions and the influence of home environment variables. *The Journal of Genetic Psychology, 144,* 69-82.
12. Gottfried, A. W. (1984). Measures of socioeconomic status in child development research: Data and recommendations. *Merrill-Palmer Quarterly, 31,* 85-92.
13. Horn, W. F., & O'Donnell, J. P. (1984). Early identification of learning disabilities: A comparison of two methods. *Journal of Educational Psychology, 76,* 1106-1118.
14. Hulse, J. A. (1984). Outcome for congenital hypothyroidism. *Archives of Disease in Childhood, 59,* 23-30.
15. Jacob, S., Benedict, H. E., Roach, J., & Blackledge, G. L. (1984). Cognitive, perceptual, and personal-social development of prematurely born preschoolers. *Perceptual and Motor Skills, 58,* 551-562.
16. Kaufman, A. S. (1984). K-ABC and controversy. *The Journal of Special Education, 18,* 409-444.
17. Laosa, L. M. (1984). Ethnic, socioeconomic, and home language influences upon early performance on measures of abilities. *Journal of Educational Psychology, 76,* 1178-1198.
18. Murray, A. M., & Mishra, S. P. (1984). Interactive effects of item content and ethnic group membership on performance on the

19. Piersel, W. C., & Kinsey, J. H. (1984). Predictive validity of the First Grade Screening Test. *Educational and Psychological Measurement, 44,* 921-924.
20. Purvis, M. A., & Bolen, L. M. (1984). Factor structure of the McCarthy Scales for males and females. *Journal of Clinical Psychology, 40,* 108-114.
21. Ramey, C. T., & Campbell, F. A. (1984). Preventive education for high-risk children: Cognitive consequences of the Carolina Abecedarian Project. *American Journal of Mental Deficiency, 88,* 515-523.
22. Sattler, J. M., & Altes, L. M. (1984). Performance of bilingual and monolingual Hispanic children on the Peabody Picture Vocabulary Test—Revised and the McCarthy Perceptual Performance Scale. *Psychology in the Schools, 21,* 313-316.
23. Spencer, M. B., & Wagner, M. (1984). Differential effects of expressive and receptive language use on the inference task performance of middle- and lower-income children. *The Journal of Black Psychology, 10,* 43-62.
24. Teeter, P. A. (1984). Cross-validation of the factor structure of the McCarthy Scales for kindergarten children. *Psychology in the Schools, 21,* 158-164.
25. Telzrow, C. F. (1984). Practical applications of the K-ABC in the identification of handicapped preschoolers. *The Journal of Special Education, 18,* 311-324.
26. Thomas, B. (1984). Early toy preferences of four-year-old readers and nonreaders. *Child Development, 55,* 424-430.
27. Tierney, I., Smith, L., Axworthy, D., & Ratcliffe, S. G. (1984). The McCarthy Scales of Children's Abilities—sex and handedness effects in 128 Scottish five-year-olds. *British Journal of Educational Psychology, 54,* 101-105.
28. Valencia, R. R. (1984). The McCarthy Scales and Kaufman's McCarthy Short Form correlations with the Comprehensive Test of Basic Skills. *Psychology in the Schools, 21,* 141-147.
29. Valencia, R. R., & Rothwell, J. G. (1984). Concurrent validity of the WPPSI with Mexican-American preschool children. *Educational and Psychological Measurement, 44,* 955-961.
30. Aram, D. M., Ekelman, B. L., Rose, D. F., & Whitaker, H. A. (1985). Verbal and cognitive sequelae following unilateral lesions acquired in early childhood. *Journal of Clinical and Experimental Neuropsychology, 7,* 55-78.
31. Branthwaite, A., & Trueman, M. (1985). Ambiguities in Watkins and Wiebe's regression analysis of the McCarthy Scales of Children's Abilities. *Educational and Psychological Measurement, 45,* 425-428.
32. Ernhart, C. B., Landa, B., & Wolf, A. W. (1985). Subclinical lead level and developmental deficit: Re-analyses of data. *Journal of Learning Disabilities, 18,* 475-479.
33. Massoth, N. A. (1985). The McCarthy Scales of Children's Abilities as a predictor of achievement: A five-year follow-up. *Psychology in the Schools, 22,* 10-13.
34. Reilly, T. P., Drudge, O. W., Rosen, J. C., Loew, D. E., & Fischer, M. (1985). Concurrent and predictive validity of the WISC-R, McCarthy Scales, Woodcock-Johnson, and academic achievement. *Psychology in the Schools, 22,* 380-382.
35. Reynolds, C. R. (1985). Standard score tables for the McCarthy Drawing Tests. *Psychology in the Schools, 22,* 117-121.
36. Tan, L. E. (1985). Laterality and motor skills in four-year-olds. *Child Development, 56,* 119-124.
37. Teeter, P. A. (1985). Neurodevelopmental investigation of academic achievement: A report of years 1 and 2 of a longitudinal study. *Journal of Consulting and Clinical Psychology, 53,* 709-717.
38. Valencia, R. R. (1985). Erratum to "stability of the McCarthy Scales of Children's Abilities over a one-year period for Mexican-American children." *Psychology in the Schools, 22,* 231.
39. Valencia, R. R., & Rankin, R. J. (1985). Evidence of content bias on the McCarthy scales with Mexican American children: Implications for test translation and nonbiased assessment. *Journal of Educational Psychology, 77,* 197-207.
40. Valencia, R. R., Henderson, R. W., & Rankin, R. J. (1985). Family status, family constellation, and home environmental variables as predictors of cognitive performance of Mexican American children. *Journal of Educational Psychology, 77,* 323-331.
41. Breitmayer, B. J., & Ramey, C. T. (1986). Biological nonoptimality and quality of postnatal environment as codeterminants of intellectual development. *Child Development, 57,* 1151-1165.
42. Byrne, J. M., Backman, J. E., Gates, R. D., & Clark-Touesnard, M. (1986). Interpretation of the Personality Inventory for Children—Revised (PIC-R): Influence of cognitive impairment. *Journal of Abnormal Child Psychology, 14,* 287-296.
43. Funk, S. G., Sturner, R. A., & Green, J. A. (1986). Preschool prediction of early school performance: Relationship of McCarthy Scales of Children's Abilities prior to school entry to achievement in kindergarten, first, and second grades. *Journal of School Psychology, 24,* 181-194.
44. Harrington, R. G., & Jennings, V. (1986). A comparison of three

short forms of the McCarthy Scales of Children's Abilities. *Contemporary Educational Psychology, 11,* 109-116.

45. Harris, K. R. (1986). The effects of cognitive behavior modification on private speech and task performance during problem solving among learning-disabled and normally achieving children. *Journal of Abnormal Child Psychology, 14,* 63-76.

46. Henderson, R. W., & Rankin, R. J. (1986). Preschoolers viewing of instructional television. *Journal of Educational Psychology, 78,* 44-51.

47. Kashani, J. H., Holcomb, W. R., & Orvaschel, H. (1986). Depression and depressive symptoms in preschool children from the general population. *American Journal of Psychiatry, 143,* 1138-1143.

48. Lidz, C. S., & Ballester, L. E. (1986). Diagnostic implications of McCarthy Scale General Cognitive Index/Binet IQ discrepancies for low-socioeconomic-status preschool children. *Journal of School Psychology, 24,* 381-385.

49. Lynn, R., & Hampson, S. (1986). Intellectual abilities of Japanese children: An assessment of $2^{1}/_{2}$–$8^{1}/_{2}$-year olds derived from the McCarthy Scales of Children's Abilities. *Intelligence, 10,* 41-58.

50. Madison, L. S., George, C., & Moeschler, J. B. (1986). Cognitive functioning in the fragile-x syndrome: A study of intellectual, memory and communication skills. *Journal of Mental Deficiency Research, 30,* 129-148.

51. Messer, D. J., McCarthy, M. E., McQuiston, S., MacTurk, R. H., Yarrow, L. J., & Vietze, P. M. (1986). Relation between mastery behavior in infancy and competence in early childhood. *Developmental Psychology, 22,* 366-372.

52. Rice, T., Corley, R., Fulker, D. W., & Plomin, R. (1986). The development and validation of a test battery measuring specific cognitive abilities in four-year-old children. *Educational and Psychological Measurement, 46,* 699-708.

53. Sawyer, D. J., & Lipa, S. E. (1986). Acquiring reading: An investigation of parsimony in the perceptual-cognitive learning system. *National Reading Conference Yearbook, 35,* 266-270.

54. Singer, L. (1986). Long-term hospitalization of failure-to-thrive infants: Developmental outcome at three years. *Child Abuse and Neglect, 10,* 479-486.

55. Achenbach, T. M., Edelbrock, C., & Howell, C. T. (1987). Empirically based assessment of the behavioral/emotional problems of 2- and 3-year-old children. *Journal of Abnormal Child Psychology, 15,* 629-650.

56. Bathurst, K., & Gottfried, A. W. (1987). Untestable subjects in child development research: Developmental implications. *Child Development, 58,* 1135-1144.

57. Byrne, J. M., Smith, D. J., & Backman, J. E. (1987). Cognitive impairment in preschoolers: Identification using the Personality Inventory for Children—Revised. *Journal of Abnormal Child Psychology, 15,* 239-246.

58. Eno, L., & Woehlke, P. (1987). Comparison of achievement in half-day, every-day and all-day, alternate-day early childhood programs for handicapped children. *Psychological Reports, 60,* 923-927.

59. Jennings, K. D., Fitch, D., & Suwalsky, J. T. D. (1987). Social cognition and social interaction in three-year-olds: Is social cognition truly social? *Child Study Journal, 17,* 1-14.

60. Karras, D., Newlin, D. B., Franzen, M. D., Golden, C. J., Wilhening, G. N., Rothermel, R. D., & Tramontana, M. J. (1987). Development of factor scales for the Luria-Nebraska Neuropsychological Battery—Children's Revision. *Journal of Clinical Child Psychology, 16,* 19-28.

61. Kee, D. W., Gottfried, A. W., Bathurst, K., & Brown, K. (1987). Left-hemisphere language specialization: Consistency in hand preference and sex differences. *Child Development, 58,* 718-724.

62. Moon, S., Ishikuma, T., & Kaufman, A. S. (1987). Joint factor analysis of the K-ABC and McCarthy scales. *Perceptual and Motor Skills, 65,* 699-704.

63. Russell, R. L., Stokes, J. M., & Snyder, D. K. (1987). Predicting sensitivity to nonverbal communication from the Personality Inventory for Children. *Journal of Consulting and Clinical Psychology, 55,* 439-440.

64. Soyster, H. D., & Ehly, S. W. (1987). Relation between parent-rated adaptive behavior and school ratings of students referred for evaluation as educable mentally retarded. *Psychological Reports, 60,* 271-277.

65. Vihman, M. M., & Greenlee, M. (1987). Individual differences in phonological development: Ages one and three years. *Journal of Speech and Hearing Research, 30,* 503-521.

66. Bernheimer, L. P., & Keogh, B. K. (1988). Stability of cognitive performance of children with developmental delays. *American Journal on Mental Retardation, 92,* 539-542.

67. Crittenden, P. M., & DiLalla, D. L. (1988). Compulsive compliance: The development of an inhibitory coping strategy in infancy. *Journal of Abnormal Child Psychology, 16,* 585-599.

68. Humphreys, L. G., & Davey, T. C. (1988). Continuity in intellectual growth from 12 months to 9 years. *Intelligence, 12,* 183-197.

69. Ishikuma, T., Moon, S. B., & Kaufman, A. S. (1988). Sequential-simultaneous analysis of Japanese children's performance on the Japanese McCarthy Scales. *Perceptual and Motor Skills, 66*(2), 355-362.

70. Keenan, P. A., & Lachar, D. (1988). Screening preschoolers with special problems: Use of the Personality Inventory for Children (PIC). *Journal of School Psychology, 26,* 1-11.

71. Loveland, K. A., & Kelley, M. L. (1988). Development of adaptive behavior in adolescents and young adults with autism and Down Syndrome. *American Journal on Mental Retardation, 93,* 84-92.

72. Martin, R. P., Drew, K. D., Gaddis, L. R., & Moseley, M. (1988). Prediction of elementary school achievement from preschool temperament: Three studies. *School Psychology Review, 17,* 125-137.

73. Pilkington, C. L., Piersel, W. C., & Ponterotto, J. G. (1988). Home language as a predictor of first-grade achievement for anglo- and Mexican-American children. *Contemporary Educational Psychology, 13,* 1-14.

74. Stroebel, S. S., & Evans, J. R. (1988). Neuropsychological and environmental characteristics of early readers. *Journal of School Psychology, 26,* 243-252.

75. Glutting, J. J., & McDermott, P. A. (1989). Using "teaching items" on ability tests: A nice idea, but does it work? *Educational and Psychological Measurement, 49,* 257-268.

76. Glutting, J. J., & McDermott, P. A. (1990). Childhood learning potential as an alternative to traditional ability measure. *Psychological Assessment, 2,* 398-403.

77. Hill, B. P., & Singer, L. T. (1990). Speech and language development after infant tracheostomy. *Journal of Speech and Hearing Disorders, 55,* 15-20.

78. Johnson, H. L., Glassman, M. B., Fiks, K. B., & Rosen, T. S. (1990). Resilient children: Individual differences in developmental outcome of children born to drug abusers. *The Journal of Genetic Psychology, 151,* 523-539.

79. Karr, S. K., Carvajal, H., & Palmer, B. L. (1992). Comparison of Kaufman's short form of the McCarthy Scales of Children's Abilities and the Stanford-Binet Intelligence Scales—Fourth Edition. *Perceptual and Motor Skills, 74,* 1120-1122.

80. Donders, J., Rourke, B. P., & Canady, A. I. (1991). Neuropsychological functioning of hydrocephalic children. *Journal of Clinical and Experimental Neuropsychology, 13,* 607-613.

81. Grover, J. R., & Fried, P. A. (1991). Developmental items on children's human figure drawings: A replication and extension of Koppitz to younger children. *Journal of Clinical Psychology, 47,* 140-148.

82. Loveland, K. A., & Kelley, M. L. (1991). Development of adaptive behavior in preschoolers with autism or Down syndrome. *American Journal on Mental Retardation, 96,* 13-20.

83. Powell, T. W., Elbert, M., & Dinnsen, D. A. (1991). Stimulability as a factor in the phonological generalization of misarticulating preschool children. *Journal of Speech and Hearing Research, 34,* 1318-1328.

84. Stone, B. J., & Gridley, B. E. (1991). Test bias of a kindergarten screening battery: Predicting achievement for White and Native American elementary students. *School Psychology Review, 20,* 132-139.

85. Thompson, N. M., Fletcher, J. M., Chapieski, L., Landry, S. H., Miner, M. E., & Bixby, J. (1991). Cognitive and motor abilities in preschool hydrocephalics. *Journal of Clinical and Experimental Neuropsychology, 13,* 245-258.

86. Turner, S., Sloper, P., Knussen, C., & Cunningham, C. (1991). Factors relating to self-sufficiency in children with Down's syndrome. *Journal of Mental Deficiency Research, 35,* 13-24.

87. Burt, D. B., Loveland, K. A., & Lewis, K. R. (1992). Depression and the onset of dementia in adults with mental retardation. *American Journal on Mental Retardation, 96,* 502-511.

88. Fein, D., Lucci, D., Braverman, M., & Waterhouse, L. (1992). Comprehension of affect in context in children with pervasive developmental disorders. *Journal of Child Psychology and Psychiatry, 33,* 1157-1167.

89. Finegan, J. K., Niccols, G. A., & Sitarenios, G. (1992). Relations between prenatal testosterone levels and cognitive abilities at 4 years. *Developmental Psychology, 28,* 1075-1089.

90. Fletcher, J. M., Francis, D. J., Thompson, N. M., Brookshire, B. L., Bohan, T. P., Landry, S. H., Davidson, K. C., & Miner, M. E. (1992). Verbal and nonverbal skill discrepancies in hydrocephalic children. *Journal of Clinical and Experimental Neuropsychology, 14,* 593-609.

91. Karr, S. K., Carvajal, H., & Palmer, B. L. (1992). Comparison of Kaufman's short form of the McCarthy Scales of Children's Abilities and the Stanford-Binet Intelligence Scales—Fourth edition. *Perceptual and Motor Skills, 74,* 1120-1122.

92. Morgan, R. L., Dawson, B., & Kerby, D. (1992). The performance of preschoolers with speech/language disorders on the McCarthy Scales of Children's Abilities. *Psychology in the Schools, 29*(1), 11-17.

93. Spitz, H. H. (1992). Does the Carolina Abecedarian Early Intervention Project prevent sociocultural mental retardation? *Intelligence, 16,* 225-237.
94. Ginsburg, H. J., Mendez, R., Padilla, E., Arocena, M., Adams, E. V., & Davis, P. (1993). Perceptual development and early childhood injuries: A prospective pilot study. *Perceptual and Motor Skills, 76,* 125-126.
95. Landry, S. H., Fletcher, J. M., Denson, S. E., & Chapieski, M. L. (1993). Longitudinal outcome for low birth weight infants: Effects of intraventricular hemorrhage and bronchopulmonary dysplasia. *Journal of Clinical and Experimental Neuropsychology, 15,* 205-218.
96. Russell, R. L., Stokes, J., Jones, M. E., Czogalik, D., & Rohleder, L. (1993). The role of nonverbal sensitivity in childhood psychopathology. *Journal of Nonverbal Behavior, 17*(1), 69-83.
97. Landry, S. H., Garner, P. W., Pirie, D., & Swank, P. R. (1994). Effects of social context and mothers' requesting strategies on Down's syndrome children's social responsiveness. *Developmental Psychology, 30,* 292-302.

[1572]

McCarthy Screening Test.

Purpose: Designed to "identify children who are likely to encounter difficulty in coping with schoolwork."
Population: Ages 4–6.5.
Publication Dates: 1970–78.
Acronym: MST.
Scores, 6: Right-Left Orientation, Verbal Memory, Draw-A-Design, Numerical Memory, Conceptual Grouping, Leg Coordination.
Administration: Individual.
Price Data, 1994: $173 per complete set including all necessary equipment, manual ('78, 71 pages), 25 record forms, 25 drawing booklets, and carrying case: $40 per 25 drawing booklets; $27.50 per 25 record forms; $9 per "Roger" card (Right-Left Orientation); $4.50 per tape; $5 per white card; $39.50 per manual; $62.50 per Conceptual Grouping blocks in box; $20 per carrying case.
Time: (20–30) minutes.
Comments: Adaptation of the McCarthy Scales of Children's Abilities (1571); criterion-referenced; percentile cut-off scores provided for classification as "at risk" for learning problems.
Authors: The Psychological Corporation.
Publisher: The Psychological Corporation.
Cross References: For reviews by Nadeen L. Kaufman and Jack A. Naglieri, see 9:672 (3 references); see also T3:1425 (2 references).

TEST REFERENCES

1. Clements, D. H., & Gullo, D. F. (1984). Effects of computer programming on young children's cognition. *Journal of Educational Psychology, 76,* 1051-1058.
2. Gullo, D. F., & Clements, D. H. (1984). Differences in achievement patterns for boys and girls in kindergarten and first grade: A longitudinal study. *Psychological Reports, 54,* 23-27.
3. Gullo, D. F., & Clements, D. H. (1984). The effects of kindergarten schedule on achievement, classroom behavior, and attendance. *Journal of Educational Research, 78,* 51-56.
4. Gullo, D. F., Clements, D. H., & Robertson, L. (1984). Prediction of academic achievement with the McCarthy Screening Test and Metropolitan Readiness Test. *Psychology in the Schools, 21,* 264-269.
5. Trueman, M., Lynch, A., & Branthwaite, A. (1984). A factor analytic study of the McCarthy Scales of Children's Abilities. *British Journal of Educational Psychology, 54,* 331-335.
6. Vance, B., & Bing, S. (1984). Relationship between the WISC-R and McCarthy Screening Test. *Journal of Clinical Psychology, 40,* 1044-1048.
7. Harrington, R. G., & Jennings, V. (1986). A comparison of three short forms of the McCarthy Scales of Children's Abilities. *Contemporary Educational Psychology, 11,* 109-116.
8. Vance, H. R., Hankins, N., & Brown, W. (1986). Predictive validity of the McCarthy Screening Test based on Wide Range Achievement Test. *Psychological Reports, 59,* 1060-1062.
9. Sloper, P., Knussen, C., Turner, S., & Cunningham, C. (1991). *Journal of Child Psychology and Psychiatry, 32,* 655-676.

[1573]

McCormick Job Performance Measurement "Rates—Scales."

Purpose: "Provides a method of rating employee job performance."
Population: Employees.
Publication Date: 1971.
Scores: 5 ratings by supervisors: Responsibility, Attitude, Time in Grade, Efficiency, Total.
Administration: Group.
Price Data: Not available.
Time: Administration time not reported.
Author: Ronald R. McCormick.
Publisher: Trademark Design Products, Inc. [No reply from publisher; status unknown].
Cross References: For a review by Alan R. Boss, see 8:1060 (1 reference).

[1574]

The McGuire-Bumpus Diagnostic Comprehension Test.

Purpose: Identifies specific areas related to reading skills.
Population: Grades 1.5–2.5, 2.5–3.5, 4–6.
Publication Dates: 1971–79.
Acronym: MBDCT.
Scores: 4 tests with 12 scores: LITERAL READING: 4 scores: Selecting Details, Translating Details, Identifying Signal Words, Selecting the Main Idea; INTERPRETIVE READING: 3 scores: Determining Implied Details, Identifying Organizational Patterns, Inferring the Main Idea; ANALYTIC READING: 3 scores: Identifying the Problem, Developing Hypotheses, Determining Relevant Details; CRITICAL READING: 2 scores: Selecting Criteria for Judgement, Making a Judgement.
Administration: Group.
Price Data: Not available.
Time: (30–40) minutes.
Comments: Criterion-referenced test.
Authors: Marion L. McGuire and Marguerite J. Bumpus.
Publisher: Croft, Inc. [No reply from publisher; status unknown].

[1575]

The *m*Circle™ Instrument.

Purpose: "Tests for and explores appropriate uses for five strategies routinely used by individuals to solve problems and reach resolution in human interaction."
Population: Business and industry.
Publication Date: 1986.
Scores, 5: Get Out, Give In, Take Over, Trade Off, Breakthrough.
Administration: Group.